From Gutenberg to the Internet

Pres Eckert (center left) and John Mauchly (center right) working with the ENIAC, the first large-scale general-purpose electronic digital computer, from which all later electronic digital computers descend. Also visible in the photograph (left to right) are Pfc. Homer Spence, Elizabeth Jennings, Herman H. Goldstine and Ruth Lichterman. First operational in May 1945, the ENIAC was announced to the public in February 1946. From 1945 to 1948 it was the only operating electronic digital computer in the world. It weighed 30 tons, contained 18,000 vacuum tubes, 70,000 resistors, 10,000 capacitors, 6000 switches, and 1500 relays, and required 174 kilowatts to run. (Photograph used by permission of the University of Pennsylvania's School of Engineering and Applied Science.)

From Gutenberg to the Internet

A Sourcebook on the History of Information Technology

Edited, with an Introductory Essay
and an Annotated Timeline

by

Jeremy M. Norman

Novato, California: historyofscience.com, 2005

Published by historyofscience.com
P.O. Box 867
Novato, California 94947–0867
orders@jnorman.com
www.historyofscience.com

Library of Congress Cataloging-in-Publication Data

Norman, Jeremy M.
    From Gutenberg to the Internet : a sourcebook on the history of information technology ; with an introductory essay comparing and contrasting the impact of Gutenberg's introduction of printing with the impact of the internet and an annotated timeline on the history of information technology / by Jeremy M. Norman.
       p. cm.
ISBN 0–930405–87–0 (alk. paper)
1. Information technology—History. I. Title.
58.5.N55 2005
004—dc22

                                      2004027426

The book is printed on acid-free paper, and its binding materials have been chosen for strength and durability.

Manufactured in the United States of America.

For Alexandra and Max,
who never knew the world
before the Internet.

v

TABLE OF CONTENTS

LIST OF ILLUSTRATIONS IN THE INTRODUCTION AND THE INTRODUCTORY NOTES

ACKNOWLEDGEMENTS

This book could not have been realized without the contributions of my long-time associate and co-author of *Origins of Cyberspace*, Diana H. Hook. Diana acted as editor, production manager, and general sounding board. Diana also scanned the original texts in the anthology, and put the mathematical formulae into the data files. In spite of advances in processing speed and OCR technology, the OCR program could not read the most of the mathematics, and typesetting the formulae remained a Herculean task for which I am especially grateful.

Paul Benkman of Tiki Bob Publishing & Design of San Francisco was responsible for the design and production of this book, including complex aspects of the typesetting and the redrawing of certain technical diagrams that were not reproducible in their original form.

Vinton Cerf and Robert Kahn permitted the reprinting of their paper on TCP.

Leonard Kleinrock, supportive of this project from its beginning, assisted in the selections from his writings and in their introductory notes.

John McCarthy permitted the reprinting of the Proposal for the Dartmouth Summer Research Program on Artificial Intelligence and his paper "Programs with Common Sense."

Gordon Moore permitted the reprinting of his paper on "Moore's Law."

Lawrence Roberts permitted the reprinting of his paper concerning the design of the ARPANET.

Bernard M. Rosenthal, a colleague of mine from the rare book business, put me in the right direction in my research concerning medieval manuscript book production.

Alain Rossmann read and commented usefully upon drafts of my introduction.

Ivan Sutherland permitted reprinting of portions of his thesis on *Sketchpad*.

The Alan Turing copyrights generously allowed reprinting portions of *On Computable Numbers* and *Computing Machinery and Intelligence*.

Michael Wilcox, designer book binder *extraordinaire*, generously allowed his cartoon for a unique hand-tooled binding to be modified electronically, but not quite beyond recognition, for the cover of this book.

Maurice Wilkes, who was supportive of my *Origins of Cyberspace* project, generously allowed the reprinting of two of his works on programming and microprogramming.

To Michael R. Williams, our consultant for *Origins of Cyberspace*, I owe special thanks. His advice and writing on technical matters for that bibliography enabled me to make better selections for this anthology.

Inevitably there will be questions as to why some papers were included and others left out. For all selections I was responsible.

Jeremy M. Norman

December 2004

1
Introduction

From Gutenberg's Press to the Foundations of the Internet

Only six electronic digital computers would be required to satisfy the computing needs of the entire United States.

—Howard H. Aiken (1947)

In 1834 the British mathematician, economist and engineer Charles Babbage conceived of the first general purpose programmable computer, the Analytical Engine. It was a mechanical device designed to be constructed out of thousands of precisely machined metal parts. Because it would have been enormously costly to build, and there was no urgent need for such a computer in Babbage's day, the Analytical Engine was never completed. Only small portions of it were built from Babbage's engineering drawings after his death. It is known primarily from an account of its design and programming originally published in French in a Swiss periodical by the Italian mathematician Luigi Menabrea, and translated into English with annotations by Babbage's friend Augusta Ada, Countess of Lovelace, the daughter of Lord Byron. In 1837, three years after Babbage planned the general purpose programmable computer, the American painter and inventor Samuel F. B. Morse invented a practical electromagnetic telegraph using an early version of his "Morse code." In contrast to Babbage's experience with the Analytical Engine, Morse and the other pioneers in electric telegraphy found ready acceptance of their inventions. On May 24, 1844, Morse transmitted the first message on an experimental telegraph line from Washington to Baltimore using the Morse code. The message, taken from the Bible, was "What hath God wrought?"

One year later, in 1845, a visionary proposed attempting to link the United States and Europe by an Atlantic telegraph cable. At that time it took about a week to communicate a message between Europe and America— the time that it took for the fastest steamship to cross the Atlantic. This was nine years before the entrepeneur Cyrus Field organized the New York, Newfoundland, and London Electric Telegraph Company with the intention of laying an Atlantic cable. In 1858, well before the cable was operational, the *Scientific American* called the Atlantic Telegraph "that instantaneous highway of thought between the Old and New Worlds." By July 27, 1866, after two failed attempts, and two years after Babbage had described in his autobiography (1864) his unsuccessful efforts to build his Analytical Engine, Cyrus Field's Atlantic telegraph connected Europe with the United States. The first message sent was "A treaty of peace has been signed between Austria and Prussia." The Atlantic cable opened for business almost immediately but only the rich could afford it—the initial rates were one dollar per letter, payable in gold. At this time the monthly wage for a laborer might have been twenty dollars. Within 20 years there were 107,000 miles of undersea cables linking all parts of the world.

Ten years after the successful completion of the Atlantic Cable, Alexander Graham Bell invented the telephone. Speaking to his assistant in the next room, Bell's first message over the telephone was, "Mr. Watson—come here— I want to see you." Telephone technology, including communication theory, would evolve along with electric telegraphy at Bell's company, American Telephone and Telegraph (A T & T), especially at Bell Telephone Laboratories (Bell Labs). Though the final "T" in A T and T is now of only historical interest, the two technologies operated side by side for many years, and the electric telegraph enjoyed a period of usefulness of more than one hundred years. In 1945 the number of telegraph messages sent in the United States finally peaked with the transmission of 236,169,000,000 messages.

Roughly one hundred years after Babbage and Morse, Howard H. Aiken and his team at Harvard were the first to realize Babbage's dream of building a general purpose programmable computer. With the support of the U. S. Navy and IBM to meet the urgent computational demands of World War II, Aiken's electromechanical Automatic Sequence Controlled Calculator, also known as the Harvard Mark I, became operational in 1944. Constructed out of switches, electromechanical relays, rotating shafts, and clutches, it was built using more than 750,000 components, and around 500 miles of wire. It measured about fifty feet in length and eight feet in height, with a total weight of about five tons. During operation it sounded like "a long room full of old ladies knitting away with steel needles." It performed mathematical calculations one hundred times the speed of man.

The following year, just months before the end of World War II, the ENIAC became operational. It was developed with the support of the U. S. Army by Pres Eckert and John Mauchly and their team at the University of Pennsylvania. Using 18,000 vacuum tubes as switches instead of the relays used in the Harvard Mark I, and weighing 30 tons, the ENIAC was the world's first large-scale general purpose electronic digital computer. Its design and construction required 200,000 man-hours of work. It was 1000 times faster than the Harvard Mark I, or 100,000 times the speed of a human doing mathematical calculations. The ENIAC consumed 174 kilowatts of electricity. For the next three to four years the ENIAC was the only operational electronic digital computer in the world. Pioneers in the nascent field of electronic computing knew that because of their enormously increased speed, electronic computers would eventually supersede mechanical or electromechanical calculators. Yet the earliest electronic digital machines were so large, so difficult to build, so expensive, so unreliable, and so hard to use that some of the earliest pioneers could not foresee their commercialization or widespread application. Howard H. Aiken, developer of one of the first general purpose programmable computers, may remain best known for his famous miscalculation, spoken in 1947 when the ENIAC was the only electronic digital computer on earth, that the computing needs of the entire United States could be satisfied by no more than six electronic digital computers.

Within fifteen years after the ENIAC was operational there were about 6,000 mainframes operational in the United States and about 10,000 worldwide. The fantastic extent to which computation increased between 1945 and 1960 may be difficult to imagine, even though during this time computers were typically inaccessible to the public, sequestered in special air-conditioned rooms staffed by professional data processing personnel, and used for scientific research or big business or government work. As an illustration of how much work could be done by only one electronic computer, it was estimated that during the operational life of the ENIAC from 1945 to 1955 this huge, comparatively primitive, and relatively slow electronic machine, operating at only 100,000 times the speed of man, performed more arithmetic calculations by itself than all of mankind had performed during the millennia up until its invention.

Between 1961 and 1964, Leonard Kleinrock at MIT developed a mathematical theory of data communication, including the theory of packet-switching. In October 1965 Lawrence Roberts put Kleinrock's theory to the test with the first actual network experiment, tying MIT's Lincoln Labs' TX-2 to SDC's Q32. This was the first time that two computers talked to each other, and the first time that packets were used to communicate between computers. October 29, 1969, under Kleinrock's supervision, the first host-to-host message was sent over the ARPANET from UCLA to Stanford Research Institute. Because the Stanford machine crashed during the effort to transmit the first word, "Login," the historic initial message was simply "Lo." When this happened, virtually no one but the participants in the experiment paid any attention. Networking computers was a concept too remote for anyone except computer professionals to imagine at that time. Though the ARPANET was funded by the

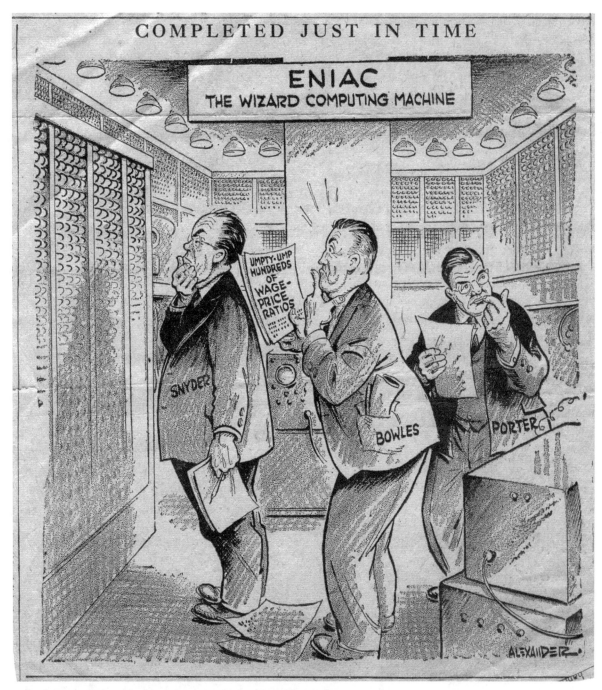

ENIAC The Wizard Computing Machine. The first cartoon to depict
the ENIAC. It is most probably the first cartoon to depict an electronic
digital computer. The cartoon was published in the *Philadelphia Bulletin*
on March 12, 1946, within a month after the public dedication of the
ENIAC. It depicts U.S. Treasury secretary John W. Snyder and two
other men identified as "Bowles" and "Porter" standing with perhaps
appropriately bewildered expressions in front of the unprecedented
new machine. From *Origins of Cyberspace* (2002), no. 1115.

Department of Defense, its purpose was to provide a means for the sharing of computer resources. In March, 1970 the ARPANET spanned the U.S. when a node was established at Bolt Beranek and Newman in Cambridge. Initially few computer centers cared to link up to the ARPANET since the value of computer resource sharing was unclear. Most early nodes on the ARPANET were connected because Lawrence Roberts, the architect of the ARPANET, and other early administrators at ARPA IPTO refused to fund the computers unless they were connected.

Three years later, in March 1973, the first ARPANET international connections were established with University College, London and NORSAR (Norway). The same year Vinton Cerf of Stanford and Robert Kahn of DARPA developed the Transmission Control Protocol (TCP) that provided all network transport and forwarding services. In 1972, while working at Bolt Baranek and Newman, Kahn had introduced the idea of open-architecture networking. He further developed his ideas when he moved to DARPA later that year. In 1978 TCP would be split into TCP/IP, in which IP provided only addressing and forwarding of individual packets and TCP was concerned with flow control and recovery from lost packets. Because of the general-purpose service provided by these protocols, and its open network architecture, the ARPANET would grow into today's Internet.

In 1984, after the development and acceptance of the personal computer, and after the ARPANET already linked several thousand hosts, the novelist William Gibson anticipated the new electronic world of the Internet, calling it cyberspace. In 1990 John Perry Barlow would first apply William Gibson's science fiction term, cyberspace, to the global electronic-social space of the Internet.

By December 2003 two-thirds of Americans had used the Internet, and it was estimated that sixty-six million were going online in a given day. In 2004 it was estimated that 800,000,000 people around the world were online. As a result of the Internet, it has been observed that the world operates increasingly as a global electronic information network, or, perhaps more accurately, as a global network of networks, comprised of an untold number of information networks and online communities. Nevertheless, we still read, exchange, and preserve or destroy an enormous number of documents handwritten or printed on paper. This anthology will take you back to a time not that long ago when the technology now so pervasive was in its early developmental stages, when a relatively small number of people laid the foundations for computing, telecommunications, and the Internet—a world before the personal computer and the seemingly unlimited reaches of cyberspace.

TRACING TECHNOLOGIES THAT EVENTUALLY CONVERGED IN THE INTERNET

Over the past ten years or so most of us have become accustomed to spending increasing amounts of time on our computers in the figurative electronic-social medium we call cyberspace. During this relatively brief period the Internet has had such a powerful impact on the way we live and on the way we create and use information that it is hard to believe that Tim Berners-Lee only released the specifications for the World Wide Web in 1992. Did the Internet have a history before it became such an important part of our lives? On what technologies was the Internet built? How and when did those technologies develop? To help answer these and other questions, *From Gutenberg to the Internet* presents original readings in the history of computing, data networking, and telecommunications arranged thematically by chapters, with introductory notes to each reading. Most of the readings record basic discoveries from the 1830s through the 1960s that laid the foundation of the world of digital information in which we live. Many were written by the people who made the discoveries. Others show what people thought about these subjects in the early years, or what people thought that these inventions would eventually be able to do.

The readings do not go all the way back to Gutenberg. Nor do they extend all the way to the Internet. These readings trace historic steps from the early nineteenth century development of telegraph systems—the first data networks—through the development of the earliest general purpose programmable computers to the foundation in 1969 of the ARPANET, the first national computer network, which would later grow into the Internet. They will allow you to review early developments and ideas that eventually led to the convergence of computing, data networking, and telecommunications in the Internet.

In tracing technology that eventually converged in the Internet, this anthology documents the development of information technology (IT). As we study the technologies involved with information, we should remember that information concerns the communication of knowledge as much as its creation and preservation. The word information has various meanings that include (1) the action of informing as in training, instruction, teaching or communicating knowledge or news (2) knowledge communicated concerning some particular fact, subject or event. Thus discussion of technology used to create, store or process information should also concern the way that information is communicated. Just like radio and television, books and computers connected to the Internet are, above all, communications media.

Information technology (IT) does not usually include books and other printed matter such as magazines and newspapers, which were for more than five hundred years a primary means for communicating relatively large amounts of recorded information, and the primary means, apart from writing, for the storage of information. IT chiefly concerns computers and other electronic modalities used to acquire, process, communicate and store information in digital form. On the other hand, information science, as opposed to IT, concerns the collection, organization, and management of recorded information in all its forms. This includes the organization of books, archives and libraries—the purview of librarianship—and aspects of IT. Many schools of librarianship are schools of both librarianship and information science. Informatics, a newer word that combines aspects of information science and information technology, has been defined as the "the art, science and human dimensions of IT" or the "study, application, and social consequences of IT." It deals with the application of IT in problem solving and thus typically is identified with the field in which it is applied, such as bioinformatics, chemical informatics, human-computer interaction design, new media, and health care informatics. While librarianship typically includes the management of printed as well as electronic information, informatics approaches information more strictly from the standpoint of computing and human-computer interaction, mainly to the exclusion of printed matter. As users of books and libraries as well as computers connected to the Internet, we frequently relate information that we read in books and other printed matter to electronic information that we find on the web, or we combine information from both printed and electronic sources. Thus, when we consider the history of recorded information, we should consider the relationship of printed information to electronic information creation, organization, storage, communication and exchange.

From Gutenberg to the Internet attempts to address these topics in three different ways:

(1) The sixty-three readings that make up most of this anthology reproduce landmarks in the history of the science and technology of computing, networking, and telecommunications that laid the foundation of the present world of digital information. With respect to their influence upon society, these landmarks, especially when viewed together, are similar in their significance to Gutenberg's invention of the printing press and printing by moveable type.

Even though this anthology was organized with the purpose of tracing the scientific and technological origins of IT and the Internet, the chapters or individual readings, may, of course, be used for a wide variety of other purposes, such as studying the history of early computing, early software, or the foundations of data communications. To a certain extent these readings are a "cookbook" from which readers should cook up their own historical approach.

(2) This introduction first discusses differences between printed and digital information and then briefly compares the transition from manuscript to print that took place more than five hundred years ago with the transition that began about 1830 from a world in which information was primarily distributed and preserved in print

to the present world in which print exists in association with various electronic media. The introduction also explains the organization of the anthology and makes general comments about each chapter.

(3) The annotated timeline includes a wide-ranging selection of events in the history of information. Threads or topics that the timeline follows with varying degrees of thoroughness include computing, networking, telegraph, telephone, radio, television, book history, printing, papermaking, publishing, information theory, cryptography, molecular biology and related fields in IT and informatics. Such a timeline cannot ever pretend to be complete or totally accurate, and I intend to keep expanding it and improving it on the web. You will find the expanded online interactive version of the timeline at www.historyofscience.com.

COMPARING WEB-BASED INFORMATION WITH PRINTED INFORMATION

Apart from issues such as language, or writing conventions, or legibility of type fonts, books printed 500 years ago still function effectively as information retrieval devices. While their content may go out of date, the way that books work does not become obsolete like computer hardware and software. Of course compared to manuscripts and printed books, electronic computing is a very new technology. Though the world's first full-scale general purpose electronic digital computer, the ENIAC, was first unveiled to the public in February 1946, this announcement had little impact on the public at large. A major reason why the public knew very little about electronic computers for several years after their invention was that there were so few of them, and they were not being used commercially until 1954 when the UNIVAC 1, serial number 8 was delivered to General Electric. This was the first time that an electronic computer was actually delivered to a private customer in the United States. Even the UNIVAC 1 serial 1 sold to the U.S. Census Bureau was not delivered until 1953.

Electronic computing probably first came to the attention of the general public in the United States on November 4, 1952 when the UNIVAC I serial 5 computer successfully predicted the election of President Dwight D. Eisenhower on the CBS television network ahead of the other television networks that were not using computers. That event was actually staged with the placement of a dummy UNIVAC console in CBS television's New York studio. The computer that actually made the prediction was located in Remington Rand UNIVAC's Philadelphia office, and information went back and forth between New York and Philadelphia by teletype. Though I was only seven years old at the time, I still remember the sensation this made on national television. For the first time we had a sense of the capability of an "electronic brain" to solve a practical problem faster than people. A result was that the other television networks also used electronic computers beginning with the next presidential election in 1956. Around this time the issue of electronic computers replacing people in various lines of work, including research, gradually became a more widely felt topic of concern.

Prior to the development of online information services, when electronic computers were being applied at corporations primarily for accounting purposes, the concept of using an electronic computer as an electronic library that would replace books was satirized in the 1957 film *Desk Set*. This was a romantic comedy starring Spencer Tracy, who portrayed an "efficiency expert," and Katharine Hepburn, who portrayed an extremely bookish librarian with unusual memory skills. Based on a Broadway play, *The Desk Set*, by William Marchant, the film featured a computer designed by Tracy's character, called the EMERAC, a name that resembled Remington Rand's UNIVAC. Probably inspired by the UNIVAC on CBS TV, the play and film were set at an imaginery television network. However, the technical consultation for the film was provided by IBM. Needless to say, Tracy's attempt to substitute electronic information for printed information failed hilariously in the film, confirming that at this time intelligent people using books were better at research than people trying to use a computer.

In the real world libraries were among the first institutions to attempt to automate information storage and retrieval functions as opposed to standard data processing, such as mathematical problem solving, accounting or statistical tabulation. Even though for most of us the opportunity and challenges of working with both printed and online information occurred mainly since the development of the World Wide Web in the 1990s, many large libraries have been working with both printed and electronic information since the late 1960s. The need to provide both printed and electronic information to their users presented challenges to institutional libraries because of the requirements of different media, especially in the early days of online information services when the user interface of software written for mainframes was relatively unfriendly and often required special expertise. Partly because of the special skills needed to deal with early electronic information, and the high cost of electronic information services, a cultural divide sometimes evolved at libraries between advocates of books and advocates of IT. With the recent proliferation of IT into many aspects of life as a result of our personal computers connected to the Internet, and the increasingly user-friendly software interfaces, most of us are turning to both printed and electronic media for information. As a result, the historic cultural gap between advocates of printed and electronic information may no longer be as large, if it still exists. For this reason one would hope that eventually the cultural divide between students of the history of electronic and printed information may also be reduced.

Probably the first library to apply IT was the National Library of Medicine in Bethesda. As compiler of the standard abstracts of medical literature, the series of printed volumes of *Index Medicus*, the NLM was overwhelmed by the explosive growth of medical information during the late 1950s and was forced to seek ways to automate the production of *Index Medicus,* founded in 1879. They also had a mandate to make up to date medical bibliographical information available online to other libraries and research institutions. NLM issued the request for proposal for MEDLARS (Medical Literature Analysis and Retrieval System) in February 1961. This later evolved into MEDLINE that currently contains citations and abstracts to 11,000,000 papers in the bio-medical sciences. Thus probably the earliest developments in informatics had to do with medicine. Related to this project, among the earliest efforts at online information retrieval and services seem to have taken place at Stanford Research Institute (SRI) in 1963. These chiefly concerned bibliographic searching, including retrieval of records based on bibliographical citation elements or abstracts, and full-text records.[1]

From the 1960s onward, paralleling the development of computer timesharing and the ARPANET, an increasing amount of information began to be stored in the databases of online information services such as Dialog, which was founded in 1966 by Roger K. Summit at Lockheed Missiles and Space Company, or LexisNexis which was founded about the same time as Data Corporation, a contractor to the U. S. Air Force. These were accessible to researchers who had online access at universities, especially at university libraries, and at research centers, large law firms, and large corporations. Some of the databases contained the texts of complete documents, but they were all specialized in their scope. Even though the online information services continued to expand both within and outside institutional libraries, books and other printed matter remained the primary sources for most information, and there was the perception that publication of and preservation of information required that it be printed and distributed on paper. For certain classes of documents this remains true in even the era of the Internet and the web.

During the mainframe era, and for roughly ten years after the adoption of personal computers, until about 1992, there was still an intellectual divide in the popular conception, if not at major academic libraries, between the growing applications for computers, and the immense store of knowledge preserved and distributed in books and other printed matter. Introduction and explosive growth of the web during the past dozen years presented the first challenge to the invaluable role played by printed books during the previous 550 years. But because of the huge success of books, a vast amount of information continues to be recorded, distributed, and sold in books and other printed matter even though the amount of information available on the web is increasing at exponential rates.

---

1   Charles P. Bourne and Trudi Bellardo Hahn, *A History of Online Information Services, 1963–1976* (Cambridge: MIT Press, 2003), 14–17.

It would be easy to suggest that the personal computer is the engine driving the current information revolution just as Gutenberg's press drove the information revolution of the fifteenth century, but that would be an oversimplification. While the computer is the most obvious manifestation, a physical symbol not unlike the printing press, it was computers connected to the Internet and the web that made the personal computer a communication device, and provided a radically new means for the distribution of information. This was the first method of distributing information in a graphic form similar to print but at lower cost and at incomparably higher speed throughout the connected world. These factors, plus the interactive multi-media capabilities and searchability of electronic data, made electronic publication on the Internet with its hyperlinks the first truly advantageous alternative to printing. Because of the complex interrelationship of electronic technologies involved with the Internet, the history of IT should be traced through each of these technologies, taking into account the social factors involved. This approach may be analogous to following the historical development of book production from the standpoints of manuscript copying, typecasting, typesetting, printing, paper, binding, and distribution.

As one might expect with radically new technology, the web also enabled entirely new publication modalities very different from print, such as blogs and huge cooperative encyclopedic publications like the *Wikipedia* (www.en.wikipedia.org) edited by people all over the world. But the use of search engines to search down to single words or names in billions of web pages, in less than a second, is one of the most dramatic aspects of the Internet.

Search engines make the Internet perform as if it were a single worldwide library—a library that is growing exponentially in size. To try to put the quantity of searchable web-based information that has been created in the past decade in perspective we might use the following example: the Library of Congress, the world's largest library of books and manuscripts, currently estimates its holdings at 29,000,000 books and 57,000,000 manuscripts out of a total of 125,000,000 physical objects. If we estimate that the average book contains 500 pages, the total number of pages for all the books in the Library of Congress would be 14,500,000,000. It took the Library of Congress roughly two hundred years to collect this many books with this many estimated pages. By contrast, Google.com, founded in 1998, stated in October 2004 that they were indexing over 4,000,000,000 web pages. Google no longer publishes the number of daily searches through all this data, but it is reasonable to assume that Google may handle over 100,000,000 searches each day with each search taking less than one second. Because the web did not exist before 1992 all 4,000,000,000 of these web page addresses or URLs (Uniform Resource Locators) had to be posted to the web during the past twelve years. Reflecting the exponential growth of the web, Google announced on November 10, 2004 that it had doubled the amount of information that it was indexing to about 8,000,000,000 URLs.

As we try to compare web information with printed information we might imagine trying to make a single physical search through all the billions of actual printed pages in the Library of Congress. How many lifetimes would that take? Of course if we searched through the Library of Congress we would not actually open and search through all book pages since long before electronic computing, the Library of Congress had developed elaborate knowledge classification and catalogue card indexing schemes that would have enabled us to narrow down our search to comparatively small segments of the library. There were also abstracting and indexing services that published indexes which could provide additional assistance. After the development of computer time-sharing, the Library of Congress catalogue was computerized. During the late 1960s Henriette Avram at LC organized the creation of the MARC format that enabled machine readable bibliographic records.[2] The LC online catalogue would enable us to sort LC holdings on different topics very rapidly in order to narrow down our search. Networked

---

2   Arlene G. Taylor, *The Organization of Information.* Second edition (Westport, CT: Libraries Unlimited, 2004), 65

databases of library holdings, such as OCLC (founded in 1967), and RLIN (founded in 1977), and other online indexing and abstracting databases would also be available, if necessary.

Before the web and the Internet, indexing individual pages of printed documents in online databases, or entering the texts of documents into databases, was an expensive, involved process focused on the development of proprietary databases on specialized topics. A major reason for this was that the cost of processing and sharing the information on mainframe computers was thousands of times higher than the current costs of accessing the information on the Internet with personal computers. High costs limited the production of databases to subjects in which sufficient research money was available to create the database and to pay for user fees. Partly because they are based upon this earlier mainframe financial model, but also because these databases remain expensive to maintain and update, the costs of searching proprietary databases remain significant in comparison to free information that might be found on the Internet by using search engines. Many proprietary databases containing unique stores of information have no competition. But for proprietary databases that now must compete with free information on the Internet, there are pressures to lower information costs.[3] When I wrote this introduction the National Federation of Abstracting and Information Services (NFAIS), founded in 1958, indicated that it represented approximately sixty of the world's leading producers of proprietary databases and information services in the sciences, engineering, social sciences, business, and the arts and humanities. Some of these databases were also accessible through Internet search engines.

Proprietary databases that may not be accessible through search engines like Google have been called the Deep Web, and it has been estimated that the Deep Web is many times larger than data on the Internet currently indexed by search engines. For example, Dialog currently contains more than fifteen terabytes of information and consists of over nine hundred databases, containing approximately 1.4 billion records. According to the company website, Dialog handles 700,000 searches and delivers 17,000,000 page views per month. Just one proprietary database available at Dialog since 1989 is the Beilstein organic chemistry collection. With research dating back to 1771, the Beilstein collection is the world's oldest authority for research and analysis in the field of organic chemistry. Beilstein Facts (File 390), with research back to 1771, provides chemical structures and comprehensive details on the properties of organic chemicals, including melting points, density, spectral data and more. Beilstein Reactions (File 391) contains data for more than 9 million chemical reactions and preparations. Beilstein Abstracts (File 393) includes citations from literature and patents published from 1771 through 1979, along with citations with abstracts of articles published since 1980 and drawn from approximately 175 key journals. The Beilstein collection dates to pioneering research and publishing by Friedrich Beilstein, a nineteenth-century German chemist who compiled his first handbook of organic chemistry in 1881. The first edition contained research on some 1,500 compounds. By 1998, when the last edition of the handbook was published in printed form, the research had grown to cover more than 7 million compounds. With millions of records, the project had obviously grown unmanageable and unwieldy in printed form, and in retrospect it seems remarkable that supplements continued to be printed as late as 1998. Ultimately the cost of the annual subscription to the printed edition, roughly $40,000 per year, became unaffordable to all but a very few academic libraries. This finally forced the end of the subscription model for the support of what had become the Beilstein database. Today, under the ongoing management of Frankfurt-based non-profit Beilstein Insitut zur Förderung der Chemischen Wissenschaft (Beilstein Institute for the Advancement of Chemical Sciences), the Beilstein collection covers more than 9 million chemical substances and 9.5 million chemical reactions extracted and indexed from 1.9 million references.

---

3   John J. Regazzi, The Battle for Mindshare: A battle beyond access and retrieval. 2004 Miles Conrad Memorial Lecture. 46th NFAIS Annual Conference, February 23, 2004. http://www.nfais.org/publications/ mc_lecture_2004.htm

Returning to our thought experiment about searching a selection of books in the Library of Congress, regardless of how we determined which hypothetical books that we wanted to see, if we had take physical books off the shelves, open them up and scan each page with our eyes for key words, assuming that the person who does the scanning reads the language in which the book is printed, it is hard to believe that we, as people, could scan more than one book page per second. Typically it might take a human considerably longer than this, but we will use this number for the sake of simplicity. As a practical example, we might reflect upon how long it would take a human to search through the hundreds of volumes of abstruse information in the printed edition of Beilstein, even using the numerous printed index volumes, versus the time it would take to query the online database. A manual search would probably take far longer than one page per second since the speed of a human searching would have something to do with the searcher's comprehension of the contents and the technical nature of information being searched. By comparison, when searching through electronic data, what is most important relative to the result is the structure of the query since the actual search time by computer has little or nothing to do with the content of the information being searched.

Searching at one page per second, is, of course, about eight billion times longer than it takes Google to search its indices. But at these numbers an exact speed comparison is impossible and probably meaningless anyway. Writing about this speed difference is almost like comparing a snail's pace with the speed of light.

If we searched at the rate of one printed book page per second without interruption we could theoretically scan 84,600 book pages in 24 hours (60 × 60 × 24). At this rate it would take us about 94,562 days, or more than 259 years to scan 8,000,000,000 pages! Obviously these numbers are inexact and unrealistic, but they give us a way to think about the enormous advantages of using computers over people for any large-scale information processing task. This is especially true when the data being searched—web pages—are designed and optimized for computers. While these numbers of book pages in the billions are immense to us relative to what we can view or touch, to computers they are totally inconsequential. As mentioned earlier in this introduction, even the ENIAC, the world's first general-purpose electronic digital computer, processed information in 1945 at 100,000 times the speed of man. Today, one criterion for measuring performance of the microprocessor in your personal computer is millions of instructions per second (MIPS). Pentium 4s benchmark in the thousands of MIPS. One of the fastest supercomputers currently available, NASA's *Project Columbia* supercomputer with 10,240 Intel Itanium 2 processors, operates at 42.7 trillion floating point calculations per second or 42.7 Teraflops. A trillion is one million million.[4]

Trying to compare the speed of a supercomputer or even any modern personal computer to a human may be absurd because the orders of magnitude are nearly impossible to imagine. It makes more sense to try to compare people to people and computers to computers. Yet since the earliest years of electronic computers, and prior to that, in days of mechanical and electric calculators when the lower speed differential was easier to comprehend, people wanted to make these speed comparisons. For example, the press release for *Project Columbia* stated that "If you could do one calculation per second by hand, it would take you a million years to do what this machine does in a single second." Since there are 31,536,000 seconds in a year (86,400 × 365), and Project Columbia can do in one second what we might do in a million years, the new supercomputer may be thought of as possibly 31,536,000,000,000 times the speed of man. This is also roughly 31,536,000 times the speed of the ENIAC that was first operational just sixty years ago.

As computing horsepower increases, the universe of electronic data generated by hundreds of millions of computers connected to the Internet is also expanding, though, of course, only a portion of the information generated is posted to the web. Nevertheless, we might pause for a moment to wonder whether or not the amount of digital

---

4   http://www.top500.org/news/articles/article_51.php

information generated by our computers on the Internet will ever create numbers too large for the search engines to crunch. Of course, we have no way of answering this question, and considering the growing power of computers, raising it may seem a little bit like worrying when the sun will burn out. However, just as astronomers have computed the theoretical time billions of years from now when our sun will theoretically burn out, as immense numbers in digital information approach infinity there could be a theoretical point when computers of any power could bog down, or be overwhelmed. Certainly the founders of Google contemplated working with very big numbers when they named their search engine after a wordplay on the mathematical term Googol—an enormous number equaling ten to the hundredth power (one followed by one hundred zeros). It has been estimated that the number of seconds that have elapsed since the beginning of the universe is ten to the seventeenth power, and the number of atoms in the universe have been estimated at ten to the seventy-ninth power.

In addition to incomparable speed there are numerous other advantages in searching databases to find information rather than searching through books. One is automatic translation. Search engines currently provide rough and spotty electronic translations in almost no time. Presumably these translations will improve. Another significant advantage of Internet searching is that you don't have to move any actual physical objects around. When you are done with your search you can simply delete it or save it, and if you are not satisfied you can refine your parameters and start over without having to return numerous actual books to the shelves.

Of course no sane person would actually consider scanning thousands of books with an average length of 500 pages in a search for information. But continuing with this thought experiment, let's say that we searched through the Library of Congress catalogue online and narrowed our search down to just 2000 books out of the LC collection of 29,000,000. These books would contain 1,000,000 pages. If we had to scan these with our eyes at the rate of 84,600 pages per 24 hours that scanning process would still take us more than eleven days. But, you might say, this experiment is flawed: it really would not be necessary to scan each of these million pages to find what we want, since we could use the indexes printed in the back of each book. Working that way, we might be able to search through 2000 indexes for our research topic in perhaps five days. That is true. But there are other flaws in the experiment. We have not taken into consideration the time that it would take for members of the library staff to page the physical volumes out of the 530 miles of bookshelves in the Library of Congress. Those of us who have used large institutional libraries know that this might add quite a long time, possibly weeks, to the process.

What a reasonable person might conclude from this exercise is what every experienced scholar knows: that it is usually impractical to search in detail through more than a few dozen books from an institutional library at any given time. Rather than actually searching through thousands of physical volumes we would have to use cataloguing and indexing tools to narrow down our search to a very specific group of books before we actually consulted the physical volumes. Undoubtedly this might cause us to miss information that we might accidentally find if we had access to a library's stacks, and we could search through more physical volumes. But unless we just happen to enjoy spending many hours looking through books as I do, we would have to weigh the serendipitous nature of the potential returns relative to our investment of time.

LIBRARIES OF BOOKS VERSUS A GLOBAL LIBRARY OF DATA

Apart from the obvious difference between the tangible and intangible, there are many differences between libraries of books and libraries of electronic data. When we click on a URL selected from the list provided by the search engine, and download the particular information that we want from sources anywhere on earth without having to leave our computer, the enhanced convenience of consulting the Internet over using any physical library, except perhaps the library on the bookshelves of our home or office, is very clear. Of course when we can't find what we happen to be looking for on the web we might not be so enthusiastic. Another difference between books and data is the exponential rate at which libraries of electronic data may expand. Recognizing the phenomenal growth of electronic information that is occurring on the Internet, we might ask how long it will take for the number of searchable pages on the Internet to exceed the number of printed pages in the Library of Congress. Even though this might at first sound like a reasonable, if not terribly useful question, it is not really a fair question since even the world's largest library cannot possibly attempt to collect all printed matter being produced in the world. Even if there was a mandate to do so, no human institution would have the resources to gather all the physical information, classify it scientifically, and then find the physical space to store the information in a scientific way. Too much information is being printed, too fast, and in too many places to make collecting it all physically possible.

Even if any hypothetical physical library was able to get its printed information sent to it for free, new electronic information would be generated on the Internet faster than a physical library could attempt to accession, catalogue, and organize printed information on shelves. In contrast, the Internet is, simply by the nature of its existence, acting as a kind of cumulative collection of a high percentage of the knowledge electronically generated all over the world. If we define the Internet as a global network of networks we may also view it as a vast global library of libraries of data—a so-called library without walls. It is a library that does not need to accession, catalogue, or organize information. That is continually updated by the search engines.

One of the most phenomenal accomplishments of the search engines is that they treat all the information on the Internet as if it is one gigantic worldwide library with a single cohesive library catalogue. That does not mean that when a search engine responds to a query that its answer is technically complete for all the information on the Internet; that may not technically be possible. It is not the practical goal of the search engine to provide a complete listing of every source that is relevant to all questions. For most questions the number of information sources listed by the search engine is far greater than we can use. What the search engine is attempting to do is to index as much of the information on the Internet as possible, and most importantly to rank the information it finds in order of relevance to our query so that we can use the most relevant results to answer our question in the way that is best for us. Because of the volume of information that the web search engines have to deal with, ranking the information by relevance is more important than completeness of the coverage of Internet resources.

But if we view the Internet as a vast library of data, questions remain, of course, as to how to store most of this information on the Internet for long periods of time, or even how much of it should be preserved. What happens when people want to turn off their web servers? Will the information then disappear? With respect to this problem, libraries, which have been the traditional long-term repositories of books, may find a new role as long-term repositories of data. Data acquisition librarians may find themselves selecting data both for current use and for long-term preservation.

Physical libraries of books, no matter how large, differ from libraries of electronic data in basic ways that have to do with the different roots of information science and information technology. Information science developed as a way of classifying and organizing information recorded in manuscript or print. This was necessary for the development of library cataloguing systems and for planning the arrangement of physical volumes on library shelves. The Library of Congress cataloguing scheme is based on a very elaborate system for information classification. The classification system was necessary as a way to understand the enormous variety of information and its interrelationships. It was also necessary as a method of physically arranging books on library shelves in a manner that would be rational to both users who would want to be able to see books on one subject in one place, and for librarians who would have to locate books on the shelves and re-shelve the books returned by users. In any large physical collection of books the organizational scheme of the library is central to its design and operation. It generally follows standard rules. For this reason users of one library following a standard classification system should be able to understand the arrangement of a different library, even a library on a different subject, if both libraries follow the same overall information classification scheme. Thus all departmental libraries at a university would, or should, fall under the same overall cataloguing scheme. The Internet made increasing standardization of library cataloguing more efficient with thousands of libraries increasingly linked to global library databases such as OCLC. But no matter how well catalogued library books are, or how standardized and integrated library catalogue systems have become, inevitably all libraries have uncatalogued material, or material that is not completely catalogued, or not catalogued online. This is one of many, many reasons why actual visits to study research collections at libraries are often necessary and highly worthwhile even in the era of the Internet. To facilitate this the OCLC database began making a limited number of its entries available through yahoo.com in late 2004.

For hundreds of years libraries could be organized by the scientific classification of information because the collections of institutional or public libraries were all consciously planned and built, with each volume in book collections deliberately selected, catalogued, and classified according to the overall scheme of the library. Depending upon the history and age of a library, aspects of these classification and shelving schemes may have evolved over time as the physical facility of a library changed, and/or collections on various subjects may have expanded or contracted according to administrative decisions or other factors. However, without the organization and classification scheme that enabled rational cataloguing and shelving, information in the library would be inaccessible both to librarians and users. In addition to the selection criteria used in professional selection processes by acquisitions librarians, books are added to libraries based upon acquisition budgets or gifts, and there is also the constraint of limited physical space for book storage in any library building, no matter how large the capacity seemed when the physical library was planned.

In contrast, libraries of data have few or none of these restraints. The data is stored by programs without having to be professionally selected or physically arranged, and as the cost of electronic memory declines, and data compression increases, more and more electronic data may be stored for the same or lower cost, within the same relatively tiny physical space compared to the space required to shelve books. Unlike arranging physical volumes on shelves, as long as the data is arranged in the storage medium in ways that computers can process, there is no need for any pre-arrangement of the data into scientific information classification schemes. The indexing of data on the Internet is done by search engine programs that prowl the web like spiders, but at incomparably higher speeds, and index the data independent of the data itself. The way that computers search the indexes is not unlike the way that we might use an automated cataloguing system for a library of books. The differences are that computers can compile database indexes and update them continuously with virtually no human intervention beyond highly sophisticated programming. For most efficient retrieval of information from a search engine what is required is the best structured query relevant to the research question, given the query technology of a particular search engine. The links to information supplied by the search engine do not depend upon the physical location of the search engine, or the location of the data, or the language in which it is written, unless these are specified in the search query: for example, we can request only information in English or only information produced in a certain country. The ability of the search engines to transcend all physical boundaries, cataloguing systems, or organizational or physical shelving schemes, is one of the most basic differences between the classification and storage of physical books in physical libraries, and the storage and use of electronic data processed by computers on the Internet.

Because electronic data on the Internet is stored on web servers all over the world, unconfined by the four walls of a physical library space, electronic data on the Internet can potentially reach nearly incalculable levels without the need for central administration. This is allowing data on the Internet to grow exponentially—thousands of times faster than any physical library could add volumes to its scientifically arranged scheme for classifying and shelving information. It is also allowing search engines to treat the Internet as essentially one enormous, rapidly growing library without walls.

To compare the growth of pages on the Internet with the accumulated page count of the Library of Congress, we might follow the growth of Google's search engine. Between 2001 and 2004, Google added approximately 1,000,000,000 new web pages to its indexes each year, reflective presumably of the expansion of the web itself. At this rate the content of the web will have exceeded the total page count of the books in the Library of Congress within ten or eleven years. This will be true even if the Library adds about 100,000 new books or roughly 50,000,000 new book pages each year. After Google suddenly doubled the number of pages that they search—an event that clearly reflects the rapid growth of information on the web—the point at which we might expect the volume of web information to surpass that of printed information in the Library of Congress may occur far sooner than we might have imagined.

In December 2004, just as I was finishing this book, Google announced its ambitious program, Google Print, to digitize over the next decade or so millions of books from the New York Public Library and the libraries of Stanford, Harvard, the University of Michigan, and Oxford University. They will make available on the Internet the complete text of books out of copyright, and the partial text of books still in copyright. This was certainly not a development that I imagined when I was writing this introduction, though Amazon.com had previously made available portions of some books within their website. Google Print will put Google in the business of supplying immense amounts of information for the web in addition to providing a search engine for organizing links to information provided by others.

Google stated that they expect the availability of the searchable texts of millions of digitized books on the Internet to increase the use of printed books and libraries, rather than to make libraries obsolete. Related to that assertion, the American Library Association announced around the same time that library usage in the United States had increased significantly in the ten years since the introduction of the web. In contrast to other electronic media, the web aspect of the Internet may be a significant stimulus to reading, since so much of the web is in written form, even though the Internet in its wider sense is a pipeline for the communication of digital information in all its forms. From the exponential growth of the web, and the parallel, but more modest increase in library usage, we may tentatively conclude that the more readily information can be made available, the more it may be used, whether it is on paper or in electronic form.

Google's partnership with major academic institutional libraries and publishers represents, in my opinion, a kind of merger between the worlds of print and the Internet, and perhaps the most significant development since creation of the search engine in the building of a figurative worldwide library without walls. Prior to this development most of the library catalogues of the world's major academic libraries and many local public libraries were available on the web, allowing readers far from actual physical libraries to check library holdings. On a more global basis library holdings could be accessed through the cooperative online databases of OCLC.

It was very recently announced that OCLC would begin to make its records available to the general public through Yahoo. This will further increase users' convenient access to libraries. All of these developments, of which Google Print is the newest and most dramatic, may reflect the end of the cultural divide between print and electronic information that began with the development of online information services in the 1960s when, as previously mentioned, electronic databases and their users developed a culture separate from the traditional book culture of libraries, as libraries were then defined as collections of books organized on shelves in a physical library space. It reflects the understanding that the Internet is indeed having an effect on information similar to the effect that the invention of printing had in the fifteenth century, except that rather than stimulating the growth of physical libraries that were built up over the centuries since the invention of printing, the Internet is stimulating the growth of a worldwide virtual library without walls. It also reflects the willingness of institutional libraries, including some of the oldest and most distinguished, to make their information available in the form that is most convenient to readers. Reflective of their traditional and culturally invaluable role as preservers as well as organizers and suppliers of information, the libraries involved in the Google Print project stated that they would only allow the scanning of printed material that would not be damaged in the scanning process.

Google's ambitious plan may eventually make the individual pages of texts of millions of books searchable in the ways in which web pages are currently searchable. Thus we may be able to do key word or phrase searches through entire libraries of millions of books published over hundreds of years, not just through individual books or web pages created during the past ten or twelve years. The implications of having this search technology available through millions of volumes of printed literature are profound. As the Google Print project advances it will blur the distinction between printed and electronic information. Electronic and print versions of books may also complement one another. Some of us may use both the print and electronic versions of the same books. I can foresee instances of reading a physical volume, and, if for some reason I cannot locate what I want in the physical book, turning to the online version in order to use computer search technology to locate what I want in the printed text. Or if am reading a printed book I might go to the online version in order to pull a quotation without having to retype it into something that I am writing on a computer. The prospect of being able to select from and search online through millions of books, and to read whatever I want from the convenience of my computer, is very exciting.

Is it possible that within the next ten years more information will be generated electronically and stored on the web than was printed in the 550 years since Gutenberg? Such a question would have seemed absurd just twenty years ago. Now it is worth thinking about even though there may be no definitive answer. Certainly the Google Print project alone will contribute substantially to the increase of digital information on the Internet. Ten years from now we may be able to quantify the amount of information available on the Internet with some level of accuracy since computers do quantification better than anything; however, we will never be able to estimate accurately the amount of information that was cumulatively printed from the mid-fifteenth century to the present. One reason is that so much printed information was destroyed over the centuries through war or natural disasters, or was never preserved in libraries in the first place.

Certainly if present trends continue it is inevitable that there will be more information generated electronically than anything printed in the past. One reason is that there are more educated people generating information than in the past. Rather than attempting to ask overly broad historical questions regarding the quantity of printed versus electronic information, more meaningful questions, for which we can find answers, would concern how these comparatively recent radical changes in the creation, storage, and transmission of information came about. If we step back just a few decades to the origins of the Internet in the early 1960s, and then step back further, perhaps another one hundred fifty years to around 1830, the foundations of the technologies underlying the Internet may be seen in the development of computing, networking and telecommunications. Tracing the foundations of these technologies that converged in the late 1960s to form the foundations of the Internet is what this anthology is about.

WILL THE INTERNET REPLACE BOOKS?

An early reaction to the explosive growth of the web was the prediction that the Internet would someday replace printed books. This concern was partly based on the observation that television news was credited for causing a major decline in newspaper readership. So far books have been replaced by web information only to a very limited extent. While the Internet has substituted online databases or new cooperative publications such as the previously mentioned *Wikipedia* for certain classes of expensive but frequently updated books like encyclopedias,[5] and an increasing number of books and other publications are now available on the Internet in digital form, the Internet, rather than replacing most books with electronic publications, has proven to be a wonderful way to find, buy and sell millions of printed books. Many periodicals have found the Internet an ideal way to archive their back issues, offering this as a value-added service to print subscribers, or a fee-based service to non-subscribers. A lot of books, including the one that you are now reading, use the web to offer special websites with online updates

---

5 Concerning changes to the editing and publication of encyclopedias brought about by the Internet, see Alex Soojung-Kim Pang, "The Work of the Encyclopedia in the Age of Electronic Reproduction," in E. Tribble and A. Trubek, eds., *Writing Material* (New York: Longman, 2003), 343–351.

and supplementary material.[6] Conversely, the Internet has offered newspapers and magazines, confronted with a decline of their sales on paper, the opportunity to develop continuously updated online editions with interactive and multi-media features.[7] One of the advantages that these online publications have for both readers and publishers is that the articles in these electronic publications are continuously indexed in the search engines on the Internet. As a result, users of the Internet may find and read articles concerning their specific interests in online newspapers and magazines published anywhere in the world, or they may read entire online newspapers whenever they want, mostly at no cost.

Faced with consolidation for decades, newspaper publishing remains in a state of change. In my lifetime the number of different newspapers published has been significantly reduced. For example, fifty years ago San Francisco, a city of about 750,000 people, had four daily newspapers. Now the city has only one morning paper and one afternoon paper. Marin County, California, an area of 250,000 people in which I live, is served by only one newspaper, and this is true of many communities. This trend of consolidation was probably just a normal and predictable consequence of capitalism in which media owners consolidated an industry in order to reduce competition and increase profitability. Decline in newspaper readership attributed to television may have been a convenient justification for this consolidation since some newspaper owners saw the potential impact of television and purchased television stations, further concentrating the communications media in their communities. These steps had the effect of making most surviving newspapers more profitable. But while television reduced readership of newspapers and thus reduced what they could charge for advertising, it did not directly impact a key source of newspaper revenue—classified advertising. Unlike other electronic media, the Internet has impacted newspapers' classified advertising revenues through online auctions, such as ebay.com, or online classified advertising sites such as craigslist.org that provide interactive alternatives to traditional classified advertising, covering a wider market in a format that may be more exciting and more effective for buyers and sellers.

Another aspect of the Internet that is also impacting newspaper publishing and other "broadcast media" including book publishers that supply identical copies of information to large numbers of people is the success of the Internet as an interactive one-on-one or person-to-person medium. In its most effective sense online journalism converts the traditional author to reader relationship that exists in print into a conversation between author and reader, or a seminar between the author and various readers. Because of this online publications also have the opportunity to build online communities. It has been observed that some of the best web businesses engage their customers in a kind of interactive "conversation." As I was putting the finishing touches on this introduction, I encountered an excellent example of this interactive conversation between authors and readers. Invited with my children to an early showing of a new computer-animated movie, *The Polar Express*, I happened to read the online review in *The New York Times* that had been posted the previous day. The review panned the film. By the time I saw the review online the newspaper had also posted the responses of twelve different readers who saw the film. Notably all of these readers felt that the professional reviewer had missed the many excellent qualities of the film. By posting both the professional review and the readers' responses *The New York Times* presents a far more balanced and useful interactive account of the film than just the review alone.

With the development of wireless web technology for portable computers, personal digital assistants (PDAs) and cell phones, another appealing aspect of electronic versus printed information is the convenient accessibility of data wherever we might happen to be. For example, a successful interactive website since its introduction in 1999 has been the restaurant and travel reviewing service, www.zagats.com. This originated in 1979 as a series of pocket-sized paperback guides to restaurants that published ratings averaged from ratings supplied by numerous

---

6   Please visit our website, www.historyofscience.com, to view periodic updates to *From Gutenberg to the Internet*.

7   http://www.ojr.org/ojr/business/1078349998.php

restaurant patrons rather than individual professional reviewers. The paperback guides still enjoy wide sales, but for a reasonable annual fee, subscribers to the website can access the information in the guides for different cities on their computers or wireless devices wherever they happen to be. They can also send in votes from their PDAs, and presumably eventually their cell phones, concerning their opinion of a restaurant where they are eating. This is an aspect of the "conversation" element of successful web businesses which I previously mentioned. There is, however, an etiquette to using cell phones in restaurants since Zagat's finds that a primary complaint of restaurant patrons is the annoying use of cell phones by other patrons.

A category of books that might seem to be a logical candidate for early replacement by electronic information, considering the amount of information available online, are books on how to use computers and software, and how to design and build websites. However, from the huge selection of new books published on these topics, it is clear that millions of people prefer to learn about aspects of computing from the printed page rather than online.[8] One measure of the success of printed books on topics relating to computing is the sales of the *For Dummies* series of paperbacks. This series, which began in 1991 with *DOS for Dummies*, had sold 125,000,000 books by 2004.[9] On the other hand, O'Reilly Media, another large publisher of computer-related books on paper, also offers a variety of online publications. It is fair to say that in spite of the increasing availability of electronic information in different formats and media, the number of books being currently printed and sold on the widest range of topics is enormous.

Rather than causing an overall reduction in printing, personal computers with printers are somewhat like printing presses, and the hundreds of millions of computers connected to the Internet generate a printed output that may be impossible to quantify. Will the Internet ever cause the majority of printed books to be replaced by electronic data without printing? If the past is any guide to the future, comparing the current transition in media with the transition that took place in Gutenberg's time should provide some clues.

The impact on the distribution of information caused by the introduction of printing by moveable type in Europe in the mid-fifteenth century has traditionally been described as revolutionary, reflective of relatively sudden, disruptive change, just as we commonly recognize that the effect of the Internet is revolutionizing the distribution of information in our time. Certainly it is true that both developments had wide impacts in the technological and socio-economic sense. The transition from one-at-a-time manuscript copying to printing in the relatively slow-moving fifteenth century probably had just as profound an effect as the Internet is having in our time. However, if we may draw one central generalization from a comparison of these two somewhat parallel developments separated by more than five centuries, it is that even though they had enormous consequences and effects, both developments may be characterized more accurately as transitions in which the new and old technologies co-existed and overlapped, rather than as developments in which the new replaced the old in sudden disruptive revolutions. Just as the book that you are reading now co-exists with the electronic media of the Internet, early printed books co-existed with manuscript copying for 150 years or longer.

COMPARING REVOLUTIONARY TRANSITIONS IN MEDIA SEPARATED BY FIVE HUNDRED YEARS

The transition from hand-copying of manuscripts to printing associated with Gutenberg in the fifteenth century, with all of its socio-economic consequences, was less technologically complex than the development of electronic digital media in the print-centric world of the twentieth century. The late twentieth century witnessed the transi-

---

8 Searching Amazon.com books under "website" in September, 2004 resulted in 36,657 hits.

9 http://www.dummies.com/WileyCDA/Section/id-100052.html. Of course, this series has since branched out from computing to cover things like *Wine-Tasting for Dummies* and *Cross-Training for Dummies*.

A medieval scribe depicted at his writing desk in a scriptorium. Fulfilling a commission from a customer outside the monastery or for use within the monastery itself, one scribe would produce a single copy of a manuscript at a time. Surrounding the scribe are other manuscripts in their heavy bindings of leather over oak boards with clasps and catches. The leather straps to which the clasps are attached seem exaggerated in length in this drawing.

tion, begun in the mid-nineteenth century, from the single mechanized medium of printing to a complex convergence of printing with computing, data networking and telecommunications leading eventually to hundreds of millions of computers connected to the Internet. Many thousands of people were involved in the scientific and technological developments underpinning this more recent very complex transition that occurred over 150 years in different countries. As the inventions became more and more complex, their development tended to involve more people, most of whom have been inevitably forgotten. History usually focuses only on the few primary inventors, and this anthology, even more selective by necessity, includes works by only a few dozen people. By comparison, in the fifteenth century the transition from hand-copying to printing took one manual process—hand-copying—that was gradually converted to a mechanized process, but one still powered by hand. This transition, associated with Johann Gutenberg, originally involved a small group of early printers and artisans in the German city of Mainz, and then gradually spread throughout Europe and around the world. As with any history, inevitably the record is incomplete, but printing preserved in libraries has left us a more extensive record than we have for other technologies. Many early printers are known at least by their names and by their work, but some printers, and most of the artisans, typesetters, and pressmen who played key roles in book production are unknown.

INFORMATION DISTRIBUTION BY MANUSCRIPT COPYING

Though the earlier transition from manuscript to print was much less complex technologically than the later transition from print as the primary information source to print in co-existence with electronic media, the earlier transition may have been comparable from the standpoint of social change. It was also revolutionary in its re-arrangement of the economic aspects of information distribution. Before the arrival of printing in the fifteenth century, distribution of information by manuscript copying was notably slow, and often limited to specific social or cultural groups within narrow geographical ranges:

> At the end of the Middle Ages an author often wrote with his own hand the presentation copy of a work he offered to a protector, and copyists, usually working on commission, grouped together in small, special-ized workshops to reproduce texts for university professors, humanists, or pious laymen. The majority of the manuscripts in circulation, however, were collections of notes or copies that students, churchmen, or men of letters made for their own use, which subsequently passed from hand to hand. There was no "mar-ket" strictly speaking, for a new book, and each social group exploited the stock of works that the passing generations had accumulated in any given place. People usually were generous about lending the books they owned. New works circulated—slowly—among the author's protectors, friends, and correspondents. The result was a variety of self-contained groups and cultural models that differed greatly from one epoch, one milieu, or one place to another.[10]

During this period book production was centered around universities. No longer were monastic scriptoria the main producers of copies of manuscripts. At this time both the high cost of manuscripts and the extended time required for their copying restricted the availability of texts, with the result that medieval libraries, including those at universities, were notably small:

> With the enormous increase in study, the period during which most texts were reproduced in monasteries came to an end. Henceforth texts were recopied and sold by booksellers and stationers under rules set by the university authorities. The latter made sure that "just" prices were charged; more important, they made sure that the texts were not corrupted. In order to facilitate the work of both the copyists and stu-dents, *exemplaria*—carefully corrected manuscripts—were rented out one quire at a time. This system may seem to us primitive, but for centuries it proved totally satisfactory, so much so that the stock of avail-able school texts grew in succeeding generations. Nonetheless, the manuscript remained a rare and expen-sive commodity because, until the appearance of paper, parchment was costly enough to dampen the zeal of most students. This meant that when a friar from one of the mendicant orders arrived at the university with four works on long-term loan from his order . . . he was considered affluent. According to university

---

10 Henri-Jean Martin, *The History and Power of Writing*, translated by Lydia G. Cochrane (Chicago: University of Chicago Press, 1994), 186.

regulations, students were supposed to have one course-book for every three students, but one might well wonder how they could possibly have procured them. Fortunately the "required texts" remained very few. In the fourteenth century, only some two hundred *exemplaria* circulated in Paris. In 1338 the library of the Sorbonne, the richest library in Christendom, had only 338 books for consultation chained to its reading desks and 1,728 works for loan in its registers, 300 of which were listed as lost. The collections of the other colleges of the period included no more than three hundred works, among them the great basic texts.[11]

Nevertheless, manuscript production also continued to a lesser extent at the monasteries:

Monasteries in the Secular Period continued to copy the manuscripts they needed for their own use, just as they had done in the "monastic" period. The rules of the monastic orders prescribed a certain number of hours each day for intellectual work, and copying as an important part of this. Organised on traditional lines, the scriptoria produced works of learning and service books, and went doing so until printing finally relegated the manuscript to the past—and indeed beyond, for, as much from tradition as necessity, monasteries still continued to copy missals, antiphonaries and breviaries until well into the 16th century. The pre-dominant feature of the new period which began at the beginning of the 13th century was that the monasteries were no longer the sole producers of books of all kinds and thenceforth scarcely produced more than were needed for their own use.

Intellectual life was now centered outside the monasteries, and it was in the universities that scholars, teachers and students, working cooperation with artisans and craftsmen, organized an active book trade.

Occasionally, and up until a later date in England than in France, a monastery where the art of calligraphy or illumination was particularly well preserved would still be approached by a monarch or nobleman with a request for a deluxe manuscript. The sale of these was a source of income to the abbeys, but the practice grew rarer and rarer . . . .[12]

Even though the production of manuscripts tended to be concentrated in intellectual centers such as Paris or London, by the early fifteenth century it had an international flavor, sometimes involving artisans with special skills imported from other countries and regions. For example, in England:

The more opulent productions usually came from London workshops. What proportion of the scribes and illuminators employed in the workshops were English-, Welsh- or Scottish-born is not easy to determine; certainly Frenchmen and Netherlanders were denizened in England from the 1430s onwards. A Dutchman who could write a good upright humanist hand was brought to Oxford via Italy in 1449, and died in England in 1478; another was employed there from 1503 to the time of his death in 1540. Italian professional copyists were already active in 1447. Greek visitors, long- and short-stay, wrote manuscripts in England in the second half of the fifteenth century.[13]

---

11 Martin, *op. cit.,* 153.

12 Lucien Febvre and Henri-Jean Martin, *The Coming of the Book. The Impact of Printing 1450-1800,* translated by David Gerard (London: NLB, 1976), 18-19. For information about medieval manuscripts and illumination see Christopher de Hamel, *Medieval Craftsmen: Scribes and Illuminators* (London: British Museum Press, 1992). For a more humorous study see Marc Grogin, *Anathema! Medieval Scribes and the History of Book Curses* (New York: Allanheld & Schram, 1983).

One would not want to provide the false impression that the late medieval system of manuscript copying, no matter how it was structured and organized, provided sufficient copies of texts for learning from books to have taken place in the manner with which we are accustomed. To the contrary, because manuscripts were exceedingly scarce and expensive, as they had been for centuries, the late medieval system of learning and teaching adapted itself to the very limited supply:

> In 1400 the university student (as distinct from the master or doctor) had relatively little use for books, or rather, for substantial texts. University and college statues required him to hear, to repeat and, on a limited scale, to dispute. His essential booklessness is well illustrated by the fact that, unlike the schools of the senior faculties, the arts school in Oxford was furnished not with desks but with benches only. Here the student sat to hear his Regent Masters read and expound the prescribed texts, sentence by sentence. The manuscripts which he begged, borrowed, stole, or transcribed to assist him in his studies might, indeed, include a small number of short texts, very probably annotated by a generation or more of previous users, but he had more use for compilations of *quaestiones* and of *tabulae*, synopses of the received wisdom of his teaching masters. He probably begged, borrowed, stole or bought the majority of them from his peers or from students barely senior to himself, either as individual items or as collections of booklets more or less roughly bound together. As he increased in seniority, the scholar's requirement for written texts grew: the bachelor still relied to a greater or lesser extent on compilations of *quaestiones* but the need for the basic texts themselves, as of Aristotle's natural philosophy, increased.

> Similarly the Regent Master did not, perhaps scorn to employ the lecture notes of his predecessors, but he could scarely have proceeded satisfactorily with his studies without access to substantial texts. . . . As he progressed up the academic ladder the student's dependence upon texts increased.[14]

GUTENBERG'S PRESS AND ITS IMPACT

This was the environment into which Gutenberg introduced printing by moveable type—an organized and international system of manuscript copying, centuries old, that tended to be concentrated in various centers to supply local markets, but also possibly to supply export markets, with expensive, slowly produced copies of texts: scholarly utilitarian works, or more expensive illuminated manuscripts. For example, Latin bibles, service books and books of devotion were more frequently written and decorated in France and in the Low Countries than in Britain, and some of these found their way into British libraries. How expensive hand-copied manuscripts were in the Middle Ages is difficult to determine; however, it has been suggested that some manuscripts might have been worth as much as a farm—an especially valuable commodity in an agricultural economy. Very wealthy households might have owned only three or four manuscript books, to which the owners would refer over and over again throughout the course of their lives. Because of the high value of these manuscripts, both as precious stores of information and as material objects, medieval manuscripts preserved in libraries were often chained to the bookcases at which readers were required to study them. Sometimes these chains attached to the bindings were locked to the bookcases with several locks. Of course, the limited supply and high cost of manuscripts restricted their circulation, and this general scarcity of reading copies of most texts, long or short, old and new, inevitably constrained the development and flow of ideas, both within local groups and in wider geographical areas. Nevertheless ideas—especially powerful ideas—have never been fully restrained by geographical or other physical lim-

---

13 Lotte Hellinga and J. B. Trapp , editors, "Introduction," in *The Cambridge History of the Book in Britain. Volume III, 1400-1557* (Cambridge: Cambridge University Press, 1999), 1–30. The quotation is from page 13.

14 Elisabeth Leedham-Green, "University Libraries and Book-sellers," in Hellinga and Trapp, *op. cit.,* 331–34.

The earliest illustration of a printing office. In contrast to the hand-copying of manuscripts, the printing process systematized the production of books, dividing the process up into various roles filled by different people. Productivity increased enormously as hundreds of copies of a book could be printed in substantially less time than it took a scribe to produce one copy by hand. On the left we see the Master of the Press, and the Printer's Devil holding an ink ball. Note how the artist shows the press being braced to the ceiling, an essential element that an artist unfamiliar with the printing process might have ignored. To the left of the press is the compositor setting type. On the far right may be an illustration of a bookseller in a bookshop. This was published as a woodcut illustration in the tradition of the dance of death in *La Grant Danse Macabre,* Lyons, 1499. This tradition of illustrations, repeated by countless artists and in many publications, taught that death comes to men in all walks of life.

its, and the circulation of manuscripts containing these ideas over borders or seas, while slow and costly, did occur as a result of international manuscript trade, and as a result of travel, diplomacy, and commerce. In spite of these constraints, and also because there were no higher expectations, the medieval system of information distribution functioned satisfactorily, within the limitations of supply and demand, for several hundred years. Still, the restricted accessibility and shortage of these scarce and expensive manuscripts, in the face of gradually increasing needs for information, left open for many years, if not centuries, the opportunity eventually seized by Gutenberg

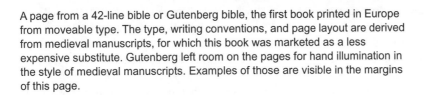

A page from a 42-line bible or Gutenberg bible, the first book printed in Europe from moveable type. The type, writing conventions, and page layout are derived from medieval manuscripts, for which this book was marketed as a less expensive substitute. Gutenberg left room on the pages for hand illumination in the style of medieval manuscripts. Examples of those are visible in the margins of this page.

for the introduction of new technology that would enable more rapid reproduction of texts, and thus allow faster and wider distribution of an increasingly diverse body of information at lower cost.

Gutenberg's press was an invention developed through many years of experimentation during the 1430s to early 1450s, first in Strasbourg and then in Mainz. The high developmental costs involved caused Gutenberg to borrow significant sums of money during the 1430s. Between 1450 and 1452 Gutenberg also borrowed 2,026 gulden from Johann Fust, a goldsmith and a lawyer, who became his partner in the printing project. Because Gutenberg was unable to pay these debts secured with his printing equipment, Fust filed a lawsuit on November 6, 1455 to gain possession of Gutenberg's press. It was Fust and his son-in-law Peter Schöffer, a scribe who had been employed by Gutenberg presumably as a typesetter and proofreader, who were the first to make a financial success out of Gutenberg's inventions.

What I loosely call Gutenberg's press was actually three separate but interrelated contributions. The timing of his first and perhaps most important contribution was dependent upon the development of the metal industry in southern Germany in the early fifteenth century. This was the invention of separate pieces of metal type. It was necessary to produce sets of characters strictly identical in size on shafts of exactly the same height. By trade Johann Gutenberg of Mainz had been a goldsmith, engraver and gem-cutter. It has been shown relatively recently by the bibliographer Paul Needham and physicist Blaise Agüera y Arcas that Gutenberg used types with subtle but individually identifiable characteristics, indicating that he may have cast his letters in molds of sand—molds that could not be reused because they would have had to be broken in order to get the letters out. Thus Gutenberg would have had to make his molds over and over again, causing each letter to be slightly different.[15]

By about 1468, the year of Gutenberg's death, printers or typesetters cut individual character punches in steel, the hardest available metal, which were then stamped into matrices made of lead or copper. The matrix served as a reusable mold for casting numerous identical examples of each metal type out of a mixture of lead, tin and antimony. Having a larger supply of type greatly increased the speed of printed book production since more pages could be set in type at one time without the need to redistribute the type. For centuries historians had assumed that Gutenberg had invented the system of cutting punches into matrices for the casting of type. If he did not, we may conclude that the early development of printing technology was more incremental than had been previously understood.

Gutenberg's second contribution was his printing press, which combined features of presses used in winemaking, bookbinding and paper-making together with the means of setting the type and locking it in place in frames or "chases." Combinations of these typeset pages would be arranged in "forms" to allow printing of pages on one side of a sheet. Gutenberg's third contribution was an oil-based printer's ink. This was very different from the water-based inks used in manuscript copying. If not his invention, it was a recent development, related to the oil paint used by Flemish painters. The ink-manufacturing process began by heating linseed oil until it became stringy, and then adding resin and soap; the result was combined with lampblack. The soap was necessary for helping the ink adhere to the type and allowing the ink to leave the type clean after each impression.

After printing a few short pieces such as Indulgences, Gutenberg issued his first book in 1455–45, in association with Fust and Schöffer. His 42-line bible, often called the "Gutenberg" bible, was a superb example of letterpress printing. From a letter written by Enea Silvio Piccolomini, later Pope Pius II, and dated March 12, 1455 we

---

15 http://www.bl.uk/treasures/gutenberg/type.htm. See also: http://www.nytimes.com/2001/01/27/arts/27PRIN.htm?ex=1095998400&en=8d15711ce38f9d71&ei=5070. These footnotes cite both web documents like this and references to printed publications. Will you be able to find these specific web references when you read this book? Who knows? The ephemeral nature of web documents, and they way that their addresses often change on the web, are factors that distinguish them from printed documents. Still, when you can find the references electronically they are far easier and faster to access than printed publications that you don't have at your elbow.

know that parts of the bible were on display at Frankfurt one year earlier, and that all copies were already sold in advance. Piccolomini commented that the book had such neat and large lettering—Gutenberg's black-letter type—that it could be read without spectacles.[16] The size of the edition was estimated at about 180 copies. Of this large book only forty-six copies remain extant, of which twelve are printed on vellum and thirty-four are on paper. Of these only four copies on vellum and seventeen copies on paper are complete.

Roughly two years later, on August 14, 1457, Fust and Schöffer issued an even more splendid book, the great Psalter of Mainz. This magnificently printed Psalter is the first printed book to give both the name of the printer and the date of printing. It has initial letters printed in red, light purple, and blue. In its colophon the printers boast about their new technology that produced this book without the scribe's traditional penmanship. Its colophon reads in translation, "The present copy of the Psalms, adorned with beauty of capital letters, and sufficiently marked out with rubrics, has been thus fashioned by an ingenious invention of printing and stamping without any driving of the pen. . . ." Only ten copies are known, all printed on vellum, suggestive of an edition substantially smaller than the 42-line bible since this book may have been intended for a local rather than an international market.

But no matter how well early books were printed, these products of new technology were initially marketed as less-expensive substitutes for manuscripts that had been handwritten to order, one at a time, either on vellum or on the less-expensive commodity of paper. The writing conventions or graphemes, typography, and page design of the earliest printed books closely followed the traditional appearance and complex writing conventions of manuscripts to which purchasers of books were accustomed.[17] Gutenberg's type derived directly from the black-letter style of manuscript lettering at the time, as did his layout in two columns.[18] Manuscript copies of some texts continued to circulate along with the early printed versions. It has also been shown that in the later part of the fifteenth century, scribes produced a large number of manuscript copies of printed books, presumably for patrons who preferred the traditional over the new technology, or possibly to substitute for a printed book if the printed edition was unavailable. Certain deluxe copies of early printed books were printed on vellum and sometimes illuminated in the style of deluxe manuscripts. A few special paper copies of early printed books were also painstakingly illuminated by hand. In numerous early editions printers left blank spaces around initial letters of paragraphs to allow for the addition of hand-painted historiated letters in the style of manuscripts. This work may have been done in printers' shops, or purchasers may have chosen their own rubricators or illuminators to customize their books. As the century progressed, or by the early sixteenth century, printers substituted woodcut historiated initials for work that had previously been done by hand. However, even as the use of printing expanded, and printed woodcut illustrations or engravings, either black and white or hand-colored, could substitute for the illustrations in illuminated manuscripts, the business of manuscript copying and illumination continued for at least one hundred years after the invention of printing. The production of deluxe illuminated manuscript Books of Hours written and hand-painted on vellum, which were far more luxurious and expensive than printed editions, continued in such countries as France, Italy, and the Netherlands well into the sixteenth century, and to some extent into the seventeenth century.

---

16 http://www.bl.uk/treasures/gutenberg/basics.htm. Another excellent website for Gutenberg information is http://www.gutenbergdigital.de/gudi/eframes/index.htm

17 L. Hellinga, "Printing," in Hellinga and Trapp, op. cit., 70–71.

18 Adrian Wilson, The Design of Books (New York: Reinhold Publishing Corporation, 1967), 12: "So strong was the black letter tradition that it survived for much printing in Germany until 1941 when the Hitler regime decreed that 'the so-called gothic type' was a Jewish invention and had to be abolished. The roman, or Antiqua, as it is called in Germany, was instituted as the official type of the nation, and so it continues today."

4.   IMPRESSIO LIBRORVM.   Ioan.Stradanus invent.   Phls Galle excud.

Poteſt vt vna vox capi aure plurima: Linunt ita vna ſcripta mille paginas.

Engraving of a printing shop c. 1580, by Jan Galle after the Flemish artist Jan van der Straet. On the right we see two presses. To the left the compositor sets type while the corrector standing behind him reads proofs, wearing an early form of spectacles. In the foreground an apprentice gathers the sheets. Freshly printed dampened sheets are hung to dry like laundry above the press. This engraving is number 4 in a series entitled *Nova Reperta* or *New Discoveries* that were deemed important at the time. The caption to the print, translated from the Latin, reads, "Printing Books. Just as one voice can be heard by a multitude of ears, so single writings cover a thousand sheets."

    While the manuscript copying trade continued, printing caught on relatively quickly. Partly because the production and distribution of manuscript books had been international in scope before the advent of printing, it did not take long for the new technology to spread from the city of Mainz throughout Germany, and over the rest of Europe. The earliest printers were Germans who had some connection with Gutenberg or with Fust and Schöffer. In 1464 the German printers Conrad Sweynheym and Arnold Pannartz established the first press in Italy at the monastery of Subiaco in 1464. By 1470 German printers had established a press at the Sorbonne in Paris, and by 1480 printing had spread throughout the continent of Europe and England.

    Printing greatly increased the speed of book production and lowered its unit cost. In order to lower the unit cost it was necessary to risk a large initial investment in expensive printing equipment, the cost of which needed to be amortized into the costs of the various books that would be issued from the press. This was a revolutionary economic change in the production and distribution of information that previously had been produced on demand only, one copy at a time, with only the expenses of the cost of paper and vellum, quill pens and ink, renting the individual quires of the standard *pecia* text, and the cost of the scribe's labor. Binding a manusript would have been a separate cost also paid for by the purchaser.

From the economic point of view, what Gutenberg achieved by mechanizing the copying of information was a unit cost-savings by the ability to divide labor and equipment amortization costs by the number of copies in an edition. The costs of paper or vellum involved in a printed book versus a manuscript may have been comparable or even higher than manuscript copying because of the inevitable wasting of paper or vellum through the correction of misprints and adjustments to the press during the printing process. Furthermore, the printer or bookseller, if a bookseller was acting as publisher, had to order a large quantity of paper or vellum in advance of printing the edition, and presumably had to pay for this before he sold all the books. Finally new costs involved in the sales and marketing of the edition had to be added into the equation. Early books were sold unbound, or the printer or bookseller would charge extra for a binding. The bindings of early printed books also closely resembled the bindings of manuscripts.

In the 1470s an Italian bishop explained that three printers working for three months could produce 300 copies of a book. He estimated that it would have taken three scribes a lifetime each to complete the same number.[19] Clearly this is only one man's estimate, and by necessity it is inexact since no two scribes would have worked at precisely the same pace, and the speed of production of a manuscript would have been greatly influenced by its length and other numerous factors that were unique to each project. However, assuming a working life of perhaps forty years in that era, this rough calculation reflects an increase in productivity of roughly 160 times or 16,000 percent—a very dramatic productivity gain. Nevertheless the market for printed books during the first two decades of printing was frequently smaller than 300 copies. Though such numbers may seem extremely small to us, they were relatively large for the earliest period of printing considering that before printing books had been produced only one copy at a time.

I did not find reliable information on the original sale prices of the earliest printed books, but Lucien Febvre and Henri-Jean Martin cite various early editions printed in runs of between 100 and 300 copies, with the exceptional book issued in as many as 1000 copies. We might assume that typically the smaller the printing the higher the price of a book may have been, though factors such as paper costs due to the format size or length of text would also be contributing factors. Printing a large volume in folio would, of course, have been more expensive than printing the same text in smaller type in small format since the folio would generally require more paper. After 1480, when the market for printed books became better organized, it is known that the overall price of books dropped to a fraction of what it had previously been, and the average run of a book, according to Haebler, was 400 to 500 copies, and higher print runs became increasingly common.[20]

The ability to distribute printed texts to more people at lower cost and at greater speed presented advantages to religious, educational, and governmental institutions as well as to authors, printers and book buyers. Though some professional scribes may have opposed the new technology that would inevitably impact their livelihood, it was estimated that perhaps 4–6% of scribes actually adopted the new technology and became printers. The first to do so was Peter Schöffer, a scribe who had worked as a manuscript copyist in Paris before apprenticing to Guten-

---

19 http://www.bl.uk/treasures/gutenberg/type.htm

20 Febvre and Martin, *op. cit.,* 218. By the close of the fifteenth century some of the largest publishers, such as Anton Koberger in Nuremberg, had achieved sales as high as 1500 copies. Research has suggested an average run between 1000 to 1500 copies for the early sixteenth century with occasional figures below that. Similar figures are given for average printings in the seventeenth century, with the average increasing to perhaps 2000 copies in the eighteenth century.

berg in Mainz. When Johann Fust took possession of Gutenberg's printing equipment he entrusted its operation to Schöffer.[21]

Church authorities and monasteries that operated scriptoria were often supportive of this new and improved means for spreading the word and the faith. The first printing press in Italy was established at the monastery of Subiaco, and in 1476 William Caxton set up the first printing press in England on the premises of Westminister Abbey, where a scriptorium was also located. This association of printing with religion persisted in the tradition, described by Joseph Moxon in the seventeenth century, of calling a printing-house a "chappel." Of course, other terminology in printing had a less sacrosanct flavor, such as the designation of printing as the "black art," and the custom of calling an apprentice in a printing shop the "printer's devil" because he would become black from contact with ink:

> Every *Printing-house* is by the Custom of Time out of mind, called *Chappel*; and all the Workmen that belong to it are *Members of the Chappel*; and the Oldest Freeman is *Father of the Chappel*. I suppose the stile [sic] was originally conferred upon it by the courtesie[sic] of some great Churchman, or men, (doubtless when *Chappels* were in more veneration than of late years they have been here in England) who for the Books of Divinity that proceeded from a Printing-house, gave it the Reverend Title of *Chappel*.[22]

The social response to the new technology introduced by Gutenberg was multifaceted. On the one hand information could be distributed to a far wider audience, far faster and at lower cost than before the invention of printing, and wider portions of literate society could afford printed books, enabling more people to follow debates and to take part in discussions on matters that concerned them. This had the effect of opening up or broadening the medieval "self-contained groups and cultural models" mentioned earlier in this introduction. On the other hand the increased availability and wider diversity of information led to more stringent attempts at censorship. In the world before printing, controversial ideas traveled slowly and were relatively easy to control, since religious authorities, through their administration of the universities, controlled the teaching curriculum. In any case, because the hand-copying of manuscripts was such a slow and relatively costly process, the process itself, as we have seen, tended to restrict the distribution and flow of new ideas. But once books or pamphlets could be published in editions of hundreds of copies at a time, and republished rapidly to meet demand by entrepeneurial printers and booksellers located all over Europe, new ideas would inevitably circulate.

In response to this perceived threat, in 1487 the dreaded Holy Inquisition, or the Congregation of the Holy Office, in charge of censorship for the Catholic Church, instituted prepublication censorship. Of course, while it clamped down on the free flow of information, the Inquisition also saw fit to use the press for propanda purposes to promote its own aims. The Inquisition's censorship campaigns expanded, especially during the Counter-Reformation in Italy in the sixteenth century; in 1559 it began publication of the *Index Librorum Prohibitorum*, the

---

21 See http://apm.brookes.ac.uk/publishing/contexts/impact/hindman.htm, a website on the history of publishing with an emphasis on the history of publishing in England. The home page is: http://apm.brookes.ac.uk/publishing/contexts/main/mainmenu.htm

22 Joseph Moxon, *Mechanick Exercises on the Whole Art of Printing (1683–4)*, edited by Herbert Davis and Harry Carter. Second edition (London: Oxford University Press, 1962), 323. By the eighteenth century the meaning of "Chapel" within the context of a printing house had evolved from the designation of a printing shop and its workmen into an organization of journeymen printers working there. The Chapel functioned both in a disciplinary capacity and as benevolent and social body with complex, arcane and imaginative rules. The Chapel also gave a corporate voice to grievances, and was instrumental in securing early wage agreements. In the nineteenth century, as labor began to organize, some of the functions of the Chapel were transferred to the early printing trade unions.

Index of Prohibited Books. On the other hand, easing of censorship restrictions could stimulate publishing. For example, after the lapse of the Printing Act in England in 1695 ended pre-publication censorship in that country, newspapers developed around England. The owners of these newspapers were often book publishers who found their newspapers excellent media in which to advertise their new books either direct from the publishers or from news agents who sold the papers in provincial areas. Eventually some of these news agents opened bookshops in the provincial areas that they serviced. The development of newspapers in England was thus one of the most significant forces in creating a national market for books, leading to larger print runs, lower production costs and a wider variety of publications.[23]

Like the press, the computer, as an information machine, became, especially after the development of the personal computer and the Internet, a tool as much for the expression of ideas as for the solution of mathematical problems. In free societies computers would foster freedom; under repressive regimes computers could become instruments of control. This was especially true before the 1990s when hundreds of millions of computers connected to the Internet made tight control of information extremely difficult for any regime. More than fifty years earlier, when electro-mechanical and electronic computers were being secretly developed in the United States during World War II, enemies of the United States in Nazi Germany used the most sophisticated electric punched-card tabulating machines as powerful tools to promote their goals of world domination and the Holocaust.[24] After the war, in 1949, George Orwell portrayed in his novel *1984* an imaginary regime that used computers for totalitarian purposes. Virtually all repressive totalitarian regimes would censor and burn books.

While the printing press became a powerful force supporting creativity and change, it was frequently met with equal force by agencies of power that sought to regulate the press to maintain their power. The Holy Inquisition frequently used intimidation and torture to prevent the propagation of ideas they considered dangerous, and through censorship practices they inevitably slowed progress or reduced innovation and creativity. As a sign of how much time changed, the archives of the Congregation of the Holy Office in Rome were recently opened for scholarly research purposes, allowing scholars in a free society to analyze the extent to which a repressive regime could stifle innovation.[25] Similarly, the archives of the Soviet KGB were opened to scholars in recent years.

But whether or not printed texts were subject to censorship restrictions that attempted to control the content of publications, the printing process did not necessarily result in more accurate texts than manuscript copying because typesetting introduced errors—sometimes far more errors than the old system of manuscript copying. This observation is contrary to the traditional historical view that printing was not only a faster means of information distribution but a more accurate one because it did not introduce all the different errors into texts that individual scribes might inevitably have introduced. Until the eighteenth century, when printers more typically had large supplies of type and could afford to keep type in forms which sending out proofs to authors for correction, authors did not often have the opportunity to correct typesetting errors unless they read proofs in the printer's shop while the book was being printed. This was especially hard to do in days when travel was arduous if the printer was not located close to the author. Assuming that the author was not present during the printing process, errors could be extensive, depending upon the extent to which the typesetter, or compositor, and the corrector, who was responsible for reading over the typeset text for errors, could understand the text. Authors typically had to correct errors in their books after they were printed, resulting in the addition of extensive sheets of errata bound in to the back of the book, which would, they hoped, be corrected in the next edition. Typesetting errors

23 Bob Clarke, The Time Machine, *Rare Book Review* 31 (October 2004): 32–34.

24 Edwin Black, *IBM and the Holocaust. The Strategic Alliance Between Nazi Germany and America's Most Powerful Corporation* (New York: Crown Publishers, 2001).

25 Gighola Fragnito (editor), *Church, Censorship, and Culture in Early Modern Italy,* translated by Adrian Belton (Cambridge: Cambridge University Press, 2001).

were especially typical in technical works that required scientific knowledge for comprehension. The English physician William Harvey made the decision to bypass numerous printers in England, having the first edition of his *De motu cordis* (1628), the book announcing his discovery of the circulation of the blood, printed by William Fitzer in Frankfurt. Harvey wrote his book in the international language of Latin and decided that his book would get greater distribution on the continent of Europe if it was published in the international publishing center of Frankfurt. However, Fitzer's compositors and correctors had difficulty reading Harvey's manuscript, and the book was printed with an unusually large number of typographical errors, resulting in several pages of errata for a relatively short book. Of course, even when authors did read proofs, errors could creep into typesetting, or remain uncorrected. This helps to explain the pages of errata at the end of so many books, including those published in the nineteenth and twentieth centuries. Treatises on mathematics with their complex formulae, including certain works in the present anthology, present exceptional challenges to typesetters.[26]

By the year 1480 most of the standard texts traditionally used for religious and educational purposes were available as printed books. As printing continued to gain in popularity, texts of new works began to be issued in print only without the circulation of manuscript copies, but the trade in manuscript books continued, and there is evidence that early readers made little or no distinction between printed and manuscript books, sometimes having both handwritten and printed texts bound together in single volumes, according to subject arrangements that made sense to them. While printing enabled both an increasing diverse and available supply of information, and provided tools to promote wider literacy, it co-existed to some extent with traditional manuscript copying for 150 years or more, reflecting an overlap of the old and new technologies, and a gradual transition from the old to the new media rather than a sudden disruptive revolution.[27] The steadily increasing selection of printed books also contributed to the growth of private libraries among widening strata of society. Library inventories preserved in Paris show how private library ownership spread first from churchmen and university teachers in the fifteenth century to an increasing number of lawyers and a fairly wide range of tradesmen and physicians and pharmacists in the sixteenth century.[28]

We may also consider Paris as an example of how printing gradually transformed the distribution of information in a major manuscript production center. From 1200 to 1500 this city provided the largest local market for manuscript books because it was the seat of a royal court and of a wealthy bishropic, the home of a growing governmental bureaucracy, and also the home of the Sorbonne, the foremost European university in its day. The first printing press arrived in Paris about 1470:

> Printed books had been known and used in Paris for several years. Fust and Schoeffer sold some of their stock there and Fust, who had in his youth been part of the German contingent at the university, had

---

26 See Hellinga, "Printing," in Hellinga and Trapp, *op. cit.,* 88-89 , and David McKitterick, *Print, Manuscript and the Search for Order 1450-1830* (Cambridge: Cambridge University Press, 2003).

27 In his introduction, McKitterick also points out that librarians and booksellers did not truly begin to distinguish between printed and manuscript books until the seventeenth century, and when they began to do so, the process of categorizing manuscripts separately from printed books created a false distinction: "In amalgamating manuscripts of all kinds, old codices and contemporary papers, the librarians (and, be it added, booksellers) of the seventeenth century confirmed assumptions that had only ever been partially true; that printing displaced manuscripts, and that the two media were definable most appropriately by their means of production. Differences were more important than similarities. Such widespread and ever more deeply rooted assumptions have coloured understanding of the history of authorship, books and communication generally ever since. They have defined how our libraries are organized; and therefore how readers are encouraged to pursue their goals, and therefore how to think. In the interests of connoisseurship, itself defined according to headings based on this distinction, the bibliophile and art market reflects genres and media, rather than historical fact" (p. 17).

28 Febvre and Martin, *op. cit.,* 262–63.

already made numerous business trips to Paris. He even had a permanent agent there, Hermann of Stat-boen. It was quite natural, then, that another German, Johann Heynlin von Stein, who was prior of the Sorbonne, should, in 1470, have had the idea of getting printers to come from Germany and of installing them in the buildings of the Sorbonne. This was how the first Paris press started. It was run by Ulrich Gering of Constance, Michael Friburger of Colmar, . . . and their assistant, Martin Kranz, a journeyman printer from Heynlin's home town.[29]

Printing had a gradual, but inexorable impact on the manuscript book trade in Paris:

Some aspects of the booktrade underwent a comparatively rapid transition. In Paris less than thirty years separated the pervasive desire to make printed books resemble manuscripts from the attempt to make manuscripts imitate printed books, a symbolic tipping of the scales. Antoine Vérard, for example, in the early 1490s was still producing for his royal patron printed books consciously meant to look like manu-scripts—works printed on vellum, with highlights and titles added in red by hand, with hand-painted miniatures and major initials added, even with meaningless ruling of the printed lines. By 1515–19 at the latest, early in the reign of Francis I (1515–1547), handwritten pages of the king's manuscripts were often deliberately modelled after pages of roman type, written with a regularity and sterility that could never be mistaken for a living script form.

Their routine commercial production of ordinary manuscript books began to decline in the last quarter of the fifteenth century in Paris, imperceptible at first, but inexorable and surprisingly swift, the transforma-tion of the world we have chronicled here was accomplished within a lifetime. . . . Those who produced manuscript books were not instantly thrown out of work by the printing press, far from it, though the effects differed from one book-craft to another. The parchmenters had seen their proportion of the book-trade seriously diminished by the development of plentiful supplies of good quality paper in Northern Europe, but this was a change that pre-dated the press; and the production of printed books on vellum, even though it comprised a small fraction of the total, was sufficient to forestall or at least disguise any change in the parchmenters' future prospects attributable to the printing press. A study of individual illu-minators across Western Europe found new employment in the illumination of printed books, especially the painting of elaborate frontispieces. Illuminators also provided designs for the engraved illustrations in printed books. . . .More to the point, manuscripts continued to be written and illuminated long after the press arrived in Paris in 1470, and so the same illuminator might work in both printed and manuscript books. Manuscript illuminators—including many of the finest—continued to paint until the end of the sixteenth century. . . . The changes wrought upon scribes by the arrival of the printing press were both more and less significant than its impact on the illuminators. The best of the scribes continued to work on Books of Hours and on the various sorts of special manuscripts; but, unlike the illuminators, scribes gained very little employment from the production of printed books, save for the addition of rubrics, and even that was primarily in the earliest books. . . . .Certainly by the year 1500 the number of copyists regu-larly employed in producing manuscript books was declining with each passing day.[30]

---

29 Febvre and Martin, *op. cit.*, 174.

30 Rouse and Rouse, *Manuscripts and their Makers: Commercial Book Producers in Medieval Paris 1200–1500* (Lon-don: Harvey Miller Publishers, 2000). The quotations are from vol. 1, 328–29. One observation that comes from this study is that various scribes, parchmenters, or bookbinders were also booksellers.

Within twenty years after Gutenberg's invention, printers had produced thousands of different documents in untold numbers of copies, enabling these documents of all kinds to be read by all levels of literate society, and drastically expanding the growth, diversity and general availability of information. This was especially true in comparison to the world before printing, when, as mentioned earlier in this introduction, a large university library would have been limited to around 300 manuscripts. It has been argued that early printers and booksellers were notably conservative in their choices of texts to publish, preferring to issue the old standbys that would have predictable sales. Because of this it has been repeatedly claimed that in the first generation after printing a far wider variety of people or a larger segment of the population had the opportunity to read traditional medieval thought than people in the earlier Middle Ages. Of course, to a large extent this was true, since, especially in a world in which innovation was unusual or even frowned upon, standard texts were much in demand, and they were printed over and over again, just as classics continue to be reissued today. However, the numbers of books and pamphlets published by the later part of the fifteenth century and increasingly during the sixteenth century also included new texts both long and short on a wide variety of subjects, and new editions of old texts that gradually incorporated more and more new scholarship and new ideas. An increasing number of books were also printed in the languages spoken by their readers rather than in Latin, the language of religion and scholarship. One result was the inevitable complaint that, compared to the traditional medieval environment in which the growth and development of information had been severely restrained, too much new work was being printed indiscriminately, for profit alone, without scholarly concern for selection and correctness.

We must also remember that the invention and spread of printing coincided with the rediscovery of classical authors by humanists during the Renaissance. Previously, during the Middle Ages, the educational system had been guided and controlled by the church. Educated people had concerned themselves primarily with actions in life that would lead to rewards in the hereafter. It was more important to memorize the limited number of writings of the accepted authorities than to ask new questions or seek new sources of information. Throughout the Middle Ages the classical writings of ancient, pagan Greece and Rome were mostly ignored. To study the classics in the Renaissance, humanists learned to read Greek and ancient Latin rather than just ecclesiastical Latin, and they sought out manuscripts that had collected dust in obscure libraries for about 1,000 years. The humanists and certain scholar printers rediscovered writings on science, medicine, government, rhetoric, philosophy, and art which they edited for publication both in manuscript and in print. The effect of making more widely available the unbelievably rich source of classical ideas through publication of classical works was incalculably influential on the development of western thought and has been very widely studied.

Like other topics touched upon in this introduction, the relationship between humanists and the Catholic Church during the Renaissance is involved and multi-faceted, the subject of countless books, and hardly possible to summarize in a few paragraphs. While the Holy Inquisition arm of the church was suppressing ideas that it found heretical, the church in Rome, the traditional patron of knowledge during the Middle Ages, remained the most significant patron of humanism during the Renaissance, acquiring for the Vatican Library the greatest collection of early Western manuscripts and early printed books in the world. How the church maintained its balance between supporting the revival of classical learning and innovative thought, while at the same time suppressing ideas deemed heretical, is an enormous research subject in itself. The most famous incident among many in this topic is the trial of Galileo Galilei.[31]

Just as today, innovative works were not always humane. For example, a new and sensational book first pub-

---

31 Anthony Grafton, editor, *Rome Reborn. The Vatican Library and Renaissance Culture.* Washington: Library of Congress, New Haven: Yale University Press, and Vatican City: Biblioteca Apostolica Vaticana, 1993. Among its outstanding features, this gorgeous book reproduces numerous elegantly written and illuminated manuscript books prepared both before and after the invention of printing.

lished circa 1486–87, was *Malleus maleficarum* or *The Hammer of Witches*. Written by the German Inquisitors Jakob Sprenger (1436–1495) and Heinrich Krämer (ca.1430–1505), this best-selling treatise sponsored by the Holy Inquisition was a manual on how to identify witches and how to force their confession. *Malleus maleficarum* underwent numerous editions throughout the fifteenth through seventeenth centuries. It was characterized as "without question the most important and most sinister work on demonology ever written. It crystallized into a fiercely stringent code previous folklore about black magic with church dogma on heresy, and, if any one work could, opened the floodgates of the inquisitorial hysteria."[32]

Before 1500 it was estimated that "printers brought out some 27,000 titles, in what must have been millions of copies."[33] Whatever the number of printed books and documents that were actually issued in the fifteenth century, it is evident that both the number of different documents in all categories of printing and the number of copies of these documents increased exponentially after the invention and spread of printing in a way that is certainly analogous to the further exponential growth of information that we are witnessing on the web.

Probably the first significant improvement to Gutenberg's press was the addition in the 1470s to 1480s of a moveable carriage that enabled the printer to place a larger "form" on the press corresponding to a whole sheet of the standard sizes of paper or vellum, and to print this in two pulls of the press. This improvement greatly speeded up the process of printing. As the use of printing continued to expand, the technology that Gutenberg invented, or which has been attributed to him, did not change, except for such incremental improvements, over perhaps two centuries or longer. Remarkably, the first manual on printing in any language was not published until 1683–84, when Joseph Moxon issued his *Mechanick Exercises on the Whole Art of Printing* as part of his survey of the chief trades of his day.[34] What the relatively late date of Moxon's publication confirms, of course, is not that the technology of printing remained unchanged between Gutenberg and Moxon, since there were incremental improvements, but that the technology of printing had remained a trade secret passed down through apprenticeship, without published guides, for over 200 years. In any case, just reading Moxon's comprehensive technical manual would not have allowed anyone to open a printing shop. The cost of the equipment was high, and the technical skills required to set type and operate the press were very difficult and time-consuming to learn. Apprenticeship remained the means of entry. Still, Moxon wrote from authority, having been a master printer for several years. He had also cut steel punches for letters, and made molds and matrices, and cast and sold type.

As the technology of book production, printing, and paper evolved over time the organization of books also evolved. The first printed books had no title pages or indexes. Initially footnotes did not appear in books.[35] Nevertheless, how we look at a printed book and read it has not changed. As a result, early printed books remain, apart from issues such as language or writing conventions or legibility of type fonts, just as effective information-retrieval devices today as they did when they were originally issued.

EARLY AMBIVALENCE ABOUT NEW TECHNOLOGY

Inevitably some of those who were associated with the old technology were ambivalent about the new even if they were also associated with the new. As late as 1492, the Benedictine monk Johannes Trithemius (1462–1516),

---

32 Rossel Hope Robbins, *The Encyclopedia of Witchcraft and Demonology* (New York: Crown Publishers, 1959), 337.

33 Anthony Grafton, "Living through Media Revolutions: Some Help from History," *Gazette of The Grolier Club*, n.s., no. 52 (2001): 5–30. The quotation is from page 13. Slightly different figures appear in Febvre and Martin, *op. cit.*, 262: 30,000–35,000 different editions before 1500, estimating a total printed output from this period of between 15 and 20 million copies.

34 Moxon, *op. cit.*

35 Anthony Grafton, *The Footnote. A Curious History* (Cambridge: Harvard University Press, 1997).

expressed technical concerns regarding the new technology. Trithemius believed that manuscripts written on vellum were a more permanent method of preserving information than books printed on paper. However, as a collector, he took advantage of the tremendously increased diversity of information resulting from printing to build up the library of his Abbey at Sponheim from only 40 works in when he became Abbot in 1482 to 2000 volumes of printed books and manuscripts when he left in 1505. This was an exceptionally large library for the time, especially in comparison to the previously mentioned estimate that university libraries, prior to the invention of printing, typically comprised about 300 manuscripts.[36] Trithemius also addressed the developing problem of organizing the wealth of new information that resulted from printing by writing and having printed the first specialized bibliography, *Liber de scriptoribus ecclesiasticis* (*Book on Ecclesiastical Writings*), published in 1494. This book lists about 1000 theological writers and their works. Overseeing a monastery that maintained a scriptorium, Trithemius exhorted his monks to continue copying in the face of the new technology in his treatise, *De laude scriptorum (In Praise of Scribes):*

> Brothers, nobody should say or think: "What is the sense of bothering with copying by hand when the art of printing has brought to light so many important books; a huge library can be acquired inexpensively." I tell you, the man who says this only tries to conceal his own laziness.

> All of you know the difference between a manuscript and a printed book. The word written on parchment will last a thousand years. The printed word is on paper. How long will it last? The most you can expect a book of paper to survive is two hundred years. Yet, there are many who think they can entrust their works to paper. Only time will tell.

> Yes, many books are now available in print but no matter how many books will be printed, there will always be some left unprinted and worth copying. No one will ever be able to locate and buy all printed books. . . .[37]

In a remarkable way Trithemius' concerns about the permanence of printing on paper relative to the permanence of manuscripts written on the more expensive parchment or vellum parallel widely held present concerns about the long-term preservation and usefulness of electronic data versus the known permanence and usability of information printed on paper. It is, of course, one thing to compare unproven methods of long-term data storage with printing on acid-free or 100% rag paper that may have a life of 300 years or more. It is another thing to compare data storage with printing on low quality paper that may deteriorate very rapidly. Converting information printed on deteriorating paper to electronic data will undoubtedly increase its longevity provided that there is adequate technology to preserve the data. Copying the same information onto acid-free paper will accomplish the same task. Until the problems of long-term storage of electronic data are solved, printing out electronic data on acid-free paper, providing there is the physical space to store it, will also remain an effective method of assuring the survival of data simply because we have sufficient documented evidence of the survival of information on acid-free paper. In the fifteenth century most paper was made entirely from linen rags, without the introduction of any acid or bleaching agent that would eventually cause chemical deterioration. This has allowed fifteenth century paper to retain its high quality to the present day. However, paper had only existed in Europe for roughly 200 years when Trithemius wrote, so its permanence was relatively unproven compared to parchment or vellum, which had been used in monasteries for much longer.

---

36 http://www.newadvent.org/cathen/15062a.htm

37 Translated in Evelyn B. Tribble and Ann Trubek (eds.), *Writing Material: Readings from Plato to the Digital Age* (New York: Longman, 2003).

Other concerns that Trithemius raised reflect the difficulty of obtaining books, another problem that we continue to face, though specialized search engines on the Internet have alleviated this problem somewhat. In our enthusiasm for the new technology of our time, we might be tempted to presume that once the new technology of printing had spread throughout Europe in the fifteenth century it would have rapidly become the preferred method for disseminating information. To a large degree this was true.[38] Nevertheless, just as printed books like the one that you are reading now co-exist with electronic media in our time, printing of books co-existed to a certain extent with hand-copying of manuscripts for a long time after the invention and spread of printing. This caused the impact of printing to be both revolutionary in the socio-economic and technological sense with respect to the extent and rate of change, but also transitional because the old and new technologies co-existed and overlapped for at least 150 years. Throughout the fifteenth and sixteenth centuries, and also the seventeenth and eighteenth centuries, if demand was perceived to be very small—perhaps a dozen copies or less—as might be the case for an esoteric scientific or medical work, or a very expensive special edition, the publishing method of choice might have been manuscript copying rather than printing, since printing was uneconomical for such small editions. Sometimes texts circulated in manuscript not just for economic reasons, but in order to avoid censorship. It was also not unusual during the Enlightenment period in France for anonymous or pseudonymous underground publications to circulate as manuscript copies among a small number of supportive readers or colleagues of the author before they were printed. Thus, for various reasons far too diverse to summarize, books continued to circulate as manuscript copies for hundreds of years after printing became the dominant technology:

> In practice, each new technology does not replace the previous one. Rather, it augments it, and offers alternatives. What we may loosely call the mechanical or electronic achievement is defined not only in its own terms, but also by its applications and purpose—in this case the conventions of letter forms and their use. Print sits beside manuscript, just as computerised IT sits beside print and manuscript. The significance of these relationships—not so much of different generations, as of related cousins, since in practice each lives alongside the next—is, apparently, easily missed.[39]

EARLY TELEGRAPH SYSTEMS

However long it took the new technology of printing to overlap, supersede, and eventually replace the old system of manuscript copying, once printing became the overall method of choice it remained the primary means of information distribution for several centuries, advancing in technology to meet the rising demand for books and the widest range of printed matter, from encyclopedias to soft drink cans, and facilitating the availability and diversity of information and the rise of literacy around the world. Yet in spite of the enormous success of print, it was never satisfactory for the speedy transmission of short messages—especially urgent military or political messages. Since ancient times the speed of sending a message from one point to another had been limited by the time it took a rider to carry the message on horseback. Wartime or government demands for more rapid communication challenged the ingenuity of inventors for centuries.

The first medium for the rapid transmission of information, which worked only for communication of comparatively short messages, was the telegraph, introduced at the very end of the eighteenth century. The earliest practical telegraph systems were optical, but in the 1840s, after the science of electricity had advanced sufficiently, these optical systems were superseded by electric telegraphs. The telegraph wires of the electromagnetic telegraph

---

38 For example, see Elizabeth Eisenstein, *The Printing Press as an Agent of Change. Communications and Cultural Transformations in Early-Modern Europe* (Cambridge: Cambridge University Press, 1979).

39 McKitterick, *op. cit.,* 20.

tended to follow railroad lines, which were actually the first networks to link the world. Railroads carried people, freight, and printed information far faster than ever before. It took more than fifty years to build the railroad lines that tied the world together, but they led to an economic boom and speculation in railroad stock not unlike the speculation in Internet stocks at the end of the twentieth century.[40] Just as we perceive the expansion of the Internet as explosive, the growth of railroads was seen as explosive, and the growth of telegraph networks, which to some extent paralleled the growth of railroads, was seen as explosive. And like the Internet, the electric telegraph caused revolutionary change in the speed of information transfer and in the way business was transacted.

As in the early optical telegraph systems, messages sent over the electric telegraph would be sent from point A to point B. From point B they would be re-transmitted to point C and so on until they eventually reached their final destination, the chief difference being that messages could be sent by wire much faster and over far longer distances between re-transmission points, without regard to time of day or weather. These messages required exclusive use of a circuit during the time in which the message was transmitted. This principle of circuit switching remained consistent in telegraph and analog telephone networks. It began to change only in the 1960s with the development of data networking, which incorporated resource sharing and packet switching first used in the ARPANET, then on the Internet, and in digital telephony.

Widespread demand throughout society for rapid communication drove the development of early electric messaging systems. The volume of telegraph traffic was monumental: in the year 1870, 9,158,000,000 telegraph messages were sent in the United States alone. In that year the United States population was 39,818,000. Data transmission developed over about 150 years, in co-existence with print, through telegraph and telephone networks, facsimile over telegraph and telephone lines, wireless telegraphy (radio), and television. Electric telegraph systems enjoyed a working life of more than 100 years, from the 1840s through the 1970s, with telegraph service reaching a peak in 1945. In that year 236,169,000,000 telegraph messages were sent in the United States. From that time onward telephone systems and facsimile over telephone lines gradually replaced the traditional use of telegraphy, making the final "T" in "A T and T" (American Telephone and Telegraph) increasingly a matter of purely historical interest.

In spite of their enormously wide use, none of the earlier electric or electronic media—telegraph, telephone, radio or television—ever directly competed with books. However, this has changed with the distribution of information to computers over the Internet through data networking and the World Wide Web, which was the first technology to substitute data-processed or digital information for what had previously been printed, in a graphic form similar to print, at a lower cost and at previously unimagined speed, throughout the connected world. As mentioned earlier, these factors, plus the interactive multi-media capabilities and searchability of electronic data, made electronic publication on the Internet with its hyperlinks the first truly advantageous alternative to printing. Rather than the broadcast aspects of the Internet that are analogous to publishing on paper, the ability of the Internet to function as a one-on-one interactive communications medium provided the opportunities for businesses to exploit these capabilities to develop services like online auctions that replaced traditionally profitable print services like classified advertising. The gradual replacement of traditional revenue streams for print publications such as newspapers by innovative online services would be a significant factor driving the transition from old to new media.

---

40 Peter F. Drucker, "Beyond the Information Revolution," *The Atlantic Monthly* 284, no. 4 (1999): 47–57. "The steam engine was to the first Industrial Revolution what the computer has been to the Information Revolution—its trigger, but above all its symbol. . . . E-commerce is to the Information Revolution what the railroad was to the Industrial Revolution—a totally new, totally unprecedented, totally unexpected development" (pp. 47–50).

THE FIRST FIFTY YEARS OF ELECTRONIC COMPUTING

As with the gradual transition from manuscript to print in the fifteenth century—but for a different and more complex series of technologic and socio-economic reasons—electronic computing required about fifty years of development, in much more rapidly changing times, before it evolved sufficiently as an interactive communications device (in conjunction with developments that led to the Internet) to impact society as a whole. Living as we do today in a world in which the evolution of technology is increasingly rapid, one conclusion that we may draw from readings in this historical anthology is that the development of these technologies was more gradual than we might have expected. In that respect, among others, the development of these technologies paralleled the gradual transition from manuscript to print more than 500 years before.

Using telephone relays, George Stibitz at Bell Telephone Laboratories developed some of the earliest electro-mechanical computers, starting with his exceeding primitive model "K" (for "kitchen table") machine in 1937. This was the same year that Claude Shannon showed in his master's thesis (Reading 12.1) that it was theoretically possible to design electro-mechanical or electronic calculating machines. On September 11, 1940, Stibitz's Complex Number Calculator, another electromechanical machine located in New York, was demonstrated via a remote teletype terminal at the American Mathematical Association Meeting in Dartmouth, New Hampshire. This was the first demonstration of remote computing. Both Norbert Wiener and John Mauchly (see Readings 8.2 and 8.10) spent a lot of time experimenting with the system. Less than two weeks later, on September 23, Wiener, inspired by the remote demonstration, sent to Vannevar Bush (see Reading 13.1) a letter to enclosing a *Memorandum on the Mechanical Solution of Partial Differential Equations* (Reading 7.3). This outlined a machine that had all the features of an electronic digital computer except for a stored program. Bush filed away the memo without acting upon it. Just two months later, in December of 1940, John Mauchly met John Atanasoff at the Philadelphia meeting of the American Association for the Advancement of Science in Philadelphia. Shortly thereafter Mauchly traveled to Iowa to meet with Atanasoff and to read Atanasoff's detailed memorandum on his early small scale electronic computer, the Atanasoff-Berry Computer or ABC machine. Two or three years later Mauchly incorporated some of Atanasoff's ideas, without credit to Atanasoff, into the design of the ENIAC during its development at the University of Pennsylvania.

In this book you will find the words "electric," "electromechanical," and "electronic" used to describe three interrelated but different types of computing machines. "Electric" means mechanical machines operated by electric motors. Tabulators of punched cards were electric. An analog machine like a differential analyzer could be operated by electric motors. "Electromechanical" describes a machine that used relays as switches. "Electronic" describes a machine that used vacuum tubes or transistors, or later electronic technology, as switches for computation. In early years electromechanical and electronic technology were sometimes combined. The ENIAC incorporated relays in input and output devices, but used 18,000 vacuum tubes for computation, thus making it the first large-scale, general-purpose electronic digital computer. In this book I use the words electronic and digital interchangeably when referring to digital information processed by computers.

The first electronic digital computers incorporating vacuum tubes as switches were very costly technological monsters of huge weight and size, using excessive amounts of energy and requiring nearly continuous maintenance. They were one thousand times faster than their equally oversized electromechanical predecessors, yet it took them days to solve problems that personal computers in 2004 could solve in seconds or fractions of seconds. Though the first electronic digital computer, the ENIAC (operational in 1945), showed great promise, it took three to four years before the next three electronic digital machines—the Manchester Mark I (initially the Manchester "Baby" prototype), the EDSAC at Cambridge, and the CSIRAC in Sydney, Australia—were operational, after which development progressed relatively rapidly, especially in the United States and England. In the United States the BINAC was operational for a short period around the same time. The ENIAC was also converted to a limited stored-program machine in 1947. Thus, whether we count three or five operational stored-program machines in late 1948 or 1949 is open to discussion. Because of expertise acquired in World War II cryptanalysis at Bletchley Park and in the development of radar technology, England was competitive with the United States in the development of electronic digital computers until about 1960. Conversely, Germany and Japan, having lost the war, were delayed in the development of this industry. France, a leader in the mechanical calculating machine industry before World War II, fell behind in electronic digital computing technology because of an initial failure to build stored-program computers.

The readings in this anthology focus on the theory, design, and operation of the first electronic computers. Except for the conceptual origins of computing and networking that occurred in the nineteenth century, the readings are limited to developments that occurred chiefly during the 1930s through the early 1950s, with some papers on the origins of the Internet dating up to 1969. Until the development of the personal computer that occurred from 1975 to 1981, high cost and complexity of programming and operation restricted electronic computers to government, large educational or scientific research institutions, and big business use. Nevertheless, Edmund C. Berkeley, one of the first writers on electronic computers for a popular audience, envisioned the personal computer as early as 1950 when he wrote:

> Some day we may even have small computers in our homes, drawing their energy from electric-power lines like refrigerators or radios. . . . They may recall facts for us that we would have trouble remembering. They may calculate accounts and income taxes. Schoolboys with homework may seek their help. They may even run through and list combinations of possibilities that we need to consider in making important decisions. We may find the future full of mechanical brains working about us.[41]

With the invention of the personal computer in the late 1970s, the impact of electronic computing began to be felt throughout society as a whole. No longer was computing limited to large installations staffed by professionals; now it was available to anyone with a personal computer and the will to learn. The impact of computing widened with the spread of personal computing and the growth of data networks. It was stimulated by improvements in hardware, by software advances that made the human-machine interface more functional and user-friendly, and by continuing cost reductions, offering more computer power for less money, as exemplified by "Moore's Law" (Reading 8.10). It was augmented by increases in bandwidth, by the eventual development of wireless handheld information processors, and the connection, starting in the late 1990s, of hundreds of millions of these wired and wireless devices to the Internet for the interactive exchange of electronic data. Because the readings in this anthology stop in the 1960s, the anthology does not cover the invention of the personal computer. However, it does deal with the origins of the Internet, which began with telegraph and telephone networks and communication theory.

Communication theory is often thought to have originated with Claude Shannon, who worked at Bell Laboratories and MIT, and published his *Mathematical Theory of Communication* in 1948 (Reading 12.2). However, like virtually all scientists, Shannon built on a body of previous work, in particular that of Norbert Wiener, Harry Nyquist, and Ralph Hartley. Shannon's work applied to telephone and telegraph messages and networks but did not apply to data communications, which have different characteristics. The idea of networking computers originated during the early 1960s at MIT with the work of J. C. R. Licklider,[42] Leonard Kleinrock, and Lawrence G. Roberts. Before them, scientists such as Turing who saw beyond the basic computational uses of the machines

---

41 Edmund C. Berkeley, "Simple Simon," *Scientific American* 183 (1950): 42.

42 W. Mitchell Waldrop, *The Dream Machine. J. C. R. Licklider and the Revolution that Made Computing Personal* (New York: Viking, 2001).

were more interested in developing computers to emulate human thought processes—the route toward artificial intelligence. Papers from the origins of that approach are in Chapter 11 of this anthology.

In February 1958, responding to the Soviet Union's launching of Sputnik (the first artificial earth satellite) in October 1957, President Dwight D. Eisenhower created the Advanced Research Planning Agency (ARPA). On October 1, 1962, J. C. R. Licklider was appointed the first director of the Pentagon's Information Processing Techniques Office (IPTO), a division of ARPA; Licklider would use his influence and cold war budget to promote the combination of electronic computing and networking for the goal of enhancing human activity. At MIT Licklider had been inspired by Norbert Wiener's Saturday evening soirées, where issues concerning computing and the relationship between men and machines were discussed. He believed that computers would eventually become personal communication devices—intimate symbiotic partners in human activity. When Licklider began promoting this concept, computers were mainframes, batch-processing was the rule, and time-sharing was the up and coming method of using mainframes. Networking mainframes was an idea in its early stages of formulation. At a meeting with Lawrence Roberts in November 1964, Licklider would inspire Roberts concerning the advantages of a national network of computers, and initiate the sequence of events leading to the ARPANET, the basis for today's Internet (see Readings 10.5, 10.6, and 13.6). After conducting the first actual computer network experiment in October 1965, Roberts would become ARPA IPTO Chief Scientist in December 1966, and chief architect of the ARPANET (see Reading 13.5.).

Leonard Kleinrock and Lawrence Roberts were both students of Claude Shannon at MIT. Along with Ivan Sutherland, the inventor of Sketchpad (the first graphical user interface), Kleinrock and Roberts used the MIT Lincoln Laboratories TX-2 computer for their research. On the same day in 1962 the three men each defended their Ph.D. dissertations, using the TX-2 for demonstrations before a Ph.D. committee that included Shannon and Marvin Minsky. Kleinrock's thesis proposal and the first part of his thesis are Readings 13.2 and 13.3 in this anthology. In 1961 Kleinrock began developing the theory of computer networking, including what later came to be known as packet switching. The introduction to Sutherland's thesis on *Sketchpad* is reproduced as Reading 10.7. Through the network design, initial network experiments, and early implementation of the ARPANET, Roberts and others would make computer networking a reality. Though this network was funded by the Department of Defense its original purposes were strictly computer resource sharing, order to spare the Department of Defense the cost of duplicating hardware and software at every research center. University computer centers initially had little enthusiasm for the concept of networking computers for collaboration in scientific research, but were forced into it by Roberts and other administrators who required connection to the ARPANET as a condition of funding their acquisitions of electronic computers. The value of the ARPANET for supporting scientific research as it related to national defense was a secondary but significant consideration.

The theoreticians and practical engineers who founded the ARPANET in the 1960s and 1970s could not possibly envisage its pervasive growth. At this time the relatively high cost of computing and the esoteric, relatively unfriendly nature of the software, limited its applications to big business, government and research centers. Nevertheless user friendly aspects of computing were conceptualized and developed at this time, especially at Stanford Research Institute when on December 8, 1968 Douglas Engelbart demonstrated an "oNLine System" (NLS), the features of which included hypertext, text editing, screen windowing and Electronic computing developed in parallel with communication theory and data communications. It took about fifty years after the invention of the ENIAC, in conjunction with a very complex series of developments, some of which are documented in the readings, and many more of which are cited on the timeline in this book, before the universal machine evolved into a personal communication device through the convergence on the Internet of computing, data networking and telecommunications.

FROM THE PRINTED PAGE TO UNLIMITED SEACHABILITY

This introduction attempted in a few pages to draw parallels between two transitions from old to new media, separated by over 500 years. Such an attempt may never be precise or complete. Among distinctions to be made between the two transitions, we may observe that the electronic computer, rather than replacing the press, is widening accessibility to printing, extending printing's usefulness and economic viability. Unlike Gutenberg's press, which was designed for the single purpose of printing, electronic computers are, to use Turing's words,[43] universal machines, programmable for virtually any purpose that dreamers may imagine and engineers can make happen. How these machines came into existence, and how this technology evolved and eventually converged with data communications and telecommunications may be explored in the readings in this anthology. Not only did these universal machines eventually transform the creation and distribution of information, but they also transformed how we perceive information, and how we interact with it. Their transformation of the media through their convergence with other technologies, was, as we have seen, in certain respects analogous to Gutenberg's discovery of printing, but, as universal machines, their effects were more diverse and multi-dimensional: computers allowed the creation of new forms of expression such as digital drawings, digital music, digital photography, digital films, and electronic games, which we may create or enjoy on the Internet. They provided alternative sources of reading material, and, through hyperlinks, searchable text, and search engines, they even changed the way we read and do research. They transformed the process of writing through advances in word-processing. Through desktop publishing, they turned computers into typesetters and computer printers into printing presses. By making this technology easy to use and relatively inexpensive, they allowed almost anyone to become a publisher either on paper or in electronic form. By enabling e-commerce, they provided new means for the sale of printed books, online music, and other goods and services. By enabling the creation of digital presses, they eventually transformed the technology of industrial printing itself. Beyond all the innovation, one of the most significant aspects of this more recent diversification of media was ultimately the democratization of publishing technology brought about by the personal computer connected to the Internet. This took previously arcane and hard-to-learn skills, and large, expensive, and difficult-to-use equipment, out of the hands of specialists, putting publishing skills and tools into the hands of almost anyone with a computer and a printer or an Internet connection. In a general sense it gave everyone access to the press.[44]

Ironically, the functioning of the Internet as a one-on-one medium rather than a broadcast medium in some circumstances lowered publication costs by revisiting aspects of the cost structure of publishing that existed during the medieval era of manuscript copying. As we have seen, during that era manuscripts were produced on demand, one at a time, very slowly and at high unit cost, but with little or no capital investment on the part of the scribe. Costs of manuscript production, if not paid directly by the patron, were paid by a bookseller who advanced the cost of vellum or paper, paid for the scribe's labor, and for an illuminator if required; the bookseller eventually recovered his costs and earned a profit from his client. One result of the system of medieval manuscript copying was a relatively static, limited flow of information that tended to circulate slowly within various narrow cultural groups. There were a few traveling manuscript booksellers who sold over wider geographical areas, but their sales of unique items were inevitably limited.

In the invention of printing Gutenberg and his successors introduced higher capital investment, achieving lower unit costs through initial expensive investments in capital and equipment that would be amortized over the life of the equipment. Labor and material costs added to the amortization costs would be divided by the number of copies of an edition in order to calculate the unit cost. This unit cost would typically be lower than manuscript copying. To achieve these unit cost savings it was necessary to risk capital in both equipment and the inventory of books unless all the books were pre-sold. These economic factors, in addition to the technological innovations,

---

43 See Reading 7.1.

and the new added costs of sales and marketing the editions, were parts of the revolution associated with Gutenberg. Initially the editions of printed books were very small, and limited to the printing of traditional and safe texts that printers and booksellers, some of whom began to act as publishers, could issue at low financial risk. But unit costs even of these very small editions typically remained lower than manuscript copies, and production of the edition was much faster. With sales of multiple copies rather than individual manuscripts the geographical range of customers for printed books rapidly widened. Early printers soon found that the market for books printed in Latin, the international language of their time, had no geographical limits providing that they set up their press in a location favorable to transportation and long distance communication, such as a city or town in a seaport or on a major river. From the earliest years of printing there were agents acting for printers or booksellers in multiple or distant locations, such as Hermann of Stratboen, previously mentioned, who was Paris agent for Fust and Schöffer, printers in Mainz. Schöffer also worked with agents in Venice, Basel and Strasbourg. Basel, located strategically on the Rhine, Paris, on the Seine, and Venice, a major international seaport, rapidly became some of the most important publishing centers. As the market for books became better organized, and books were more readily available, more people could examine books for sale and buy books, leading to lower production costs and lower selling prices. This gave more people the incentive to buy books on a wider range of subjects, resulting gradually in higher sales, greater production speed, and an increasingly more accessible, more diverse body of information. Of course, unlike the production to order of single copies of manuscripts, publishing editions of books inevitably involved substantial risk; recuperation of investment was rarely assured. These factors remain valid, with many variations, to the present day.

In comparison to books, electronic publications increase the speed of information delivery to an exponential degree, making a wider selection of information and other goods available at lower prices. Electronic publications downloaded off the Internet further reduce publication cost by transferring the cost of paper and printing from the publisher to the end user who pays for print-outs, if desired, from his/her personal computer and printer.

---

44 Over the past 40 years or more I witnessed changes in printing technology that seemed as disruptive as those in the data processing field. These included the closure of the last large commercial letterpresses in the United States, the retirement of the virtually all Linotype and Monotype machines that set characters in type cast from molten lead, the closure of metal type foundries except for those used by hobbyists or book arts productions, the transition from metal or "hot" type to computerized photo-typesetting using expensive special-purpose computers, with manual paste-up on boards for photo-offset printing, and the most recent transition brought about by software written for the personal computer to scalable digitized type fonts, digital imaging, and electronic page-layout programs that eliminated manual paste-up.

Inevitably there was resistance to new typesetting and printing technology from elements of the printing trades, many of whom had taken years to learn very difficult, arcane typesetting and printing skills that were now obsolete. For example, operating a Monotype machine required visualizing much of a printed page in the operator's head as the page was being set, since there was no visual display. This esoteric skill required a several year apprenticeship, along with high motivation, and in addition to the long learning curve, there were risks associated with working with molten lead. Traditional typesetting and printing were so labor intensive that many publishers and printers were eager to adopt new technology that promised significant cost savings. For example, type cast and set in metal, as it was universally done (whether by hand or machine) before the invention of computerized photo-typesetting, generally required that corrections had to be made by hand, a painstakingly slow process compared to the ease of revising a word-processed document. The substantial weight of the pages typeset in lead in their forms, required that metal typesetting be done in close proximity to the press.

As a rare book and manuscript dealer specializing in the history of science and technology, and also a book publisher, and the author, co-author or editor of various bibliographies, including *Origins of Cyberspace*, my background originated in the world of books and printing. With the introduction of the personal computer I gradually became more and more interested in the history of computing and related technologies. *From Gutenberg to the Internet* reflects a synthesis of my interests in these technologies with my background and experience in the world of books.

This dramatically lowers unit costs and also reduces financial risk to the publishers. More significantly, electronic publishers, including publishers of software, can distribute unlimited copies at electron speed without the costs of paper, printing, binding and postage. The same economics work for spam emailed to tens of millions of addresses in seconds at essentially no cost. This has, as we all know, resulted in an unprecedented explosion of spam. A good measure of the magnitude of this explosion was the announcement from Microsoft in November 2004 that Bill Gates was personally receiving 4,000,000 spams per day.

Other forms of electronic publication like blogs (weblogs) lower publishing costs even more by elimination of editorial and formatting costs. The first blog was actually at the first website, http://info.cern.ch./, built by Tim Berners-Lee at CERN in 1992. From this site Berners-Lee pointed with hyperlinks to all new sites as they came online in those early days of the Web.[45] When I wrote this book there were about 2,500,000 blogs online and growing in the worldwide online community called the blogosphere. Because the publication of a blog requires little more than a computer and an Internet connection, a blog can be published very rapidly by one person in response to a breaking news story or political development. For this reason blogs may thwart censorship, putting out on the Internet the blogger's version of events more rapidly than any government, no matter how fundamentalist or totalitarian, may impose control. As the work of an unknown person, whose motivations may also be unknown, it may be difficult for readers to judge the veracity of a blog, but as electronic publications distributed rapidly, sometimes in real time, blogs may be the purest expressions of individual freedom of the press.

Using a wireless Internet connection, a blogger may post information to the web while the blogger is listening to a speech in progress. Other people in the same audience may use wireless connections to read the blog while the speech is being delivered, and may possibly be influenced by the blogger's commentary while they are sharing the experience with the blogger. By using hyperlinks, blogs may also point directly to databases containing the primary source information behind a story. As publications that are continuously updated and revised, blogs bear little relationship to printed documents. Nevertheless, as still another example of the co-existence of printing with evolving new media, some blogs will inevitably be issued as printed books.

Another class of web publication too large and too interactive for publication in printed form are online encyclopedias like the previously-mentioned *Wikipedia, the Free Encyclopedia, www.en.wikipedia.org*. It describes itself as a multilingual "copyleft" encyclopedia that is editable by anyone. It is collaboratively edited and maintained by thousands of users via wiki software, and is hosted and supported by the non-profit Wikimedia Foundation. In addition to typical encyclopedia entries that have all the web advantages of searchability and hyperlinks, *Wikipedia* includes information more often associated with almanacs, gazetteers, and specialist magazines; and coverage of current events. When I wrote this introduction, three years after the founding of *Wikipedia* in 2001, there were over 375,000 articles in *Wikipedia's* English-language version. This compares to 120,000 articles in the latest version of the venerable *Encyclopaedia Britannica*, first published in 1771, the latest print version of which appears in thirty-two volumes. Online editions of *Wikipedia* are available in numerous other languages.

While allowing the creation of entirely new classes of publications, including cooperative publications like the *Wikipedia,* the web also provides new methods for selling printed books, such as online stores like Amazon.com, which maintain inventories incomparably larger and more diverse than any previous bookstores, or abebooks.com, which in 2004 provided a marketplace for 12,500 independent booksellers all over the world to list more than 60,000,000 books for sale at one website. One of the reasons for the success of these new companies is the behavior of the Internet as a one-on-one medium analogous to telegraph and telephone rather than a broadcast medium like radio, television, or publishing by printing on paper. Because web businesses frequently give

---

45 http://newhome.weblogs.com/historyOfWeblogs. TBL's original blog is archived at Cern as: http://www.w3.org/ History/19921103-hypertext/hypertext/WWW/News/9201.html. Tim Berners-Lee, *Weaving the Web: the Original Design and Ultimate Destiny of the World Wide Web by Its Inventor* (San Francisco: Harper, 1999).

information away for free, the success of some online companies may depend primarily on how well they are able to respond to their customer's needs and wants. Interactive computing allows companies to respond to unique individual requests in a way that is, ironically, analogous to the one-on-one manner in which medieval patrons commissioned hand-written copies of manuscripts for their libraries. For example, search engines like Google.com respond each day to hundreds of millions of specific different individual queries. Similarly Amazon.com customizes its website to the specific interests of each of its customers rather than presenting the same electronic "face" to all of its clients. Through highly advanced programming, these companies have found a new way to communicate with their clients on a level that is more personal and individualized, attempting to meet the very specific individual needs of a vast number of customers in ways that were never possible for very large companies in the past. What all these new web businesses have in common is that they were unrealizable before the World Wide Web.

We have seen in this brief summary how the arrival of printing from moveable type in the fifteenth century gradually transformed the medieval book trade from a pen-driven culture of on-demand, one at a time, manuscript copying to a culture in which manuscript copying was gradually dominated and eventually replaced by products of the press. A result of this transformation was a vast increase in the diversity and availability of information. To achieve these increases the printing press became the first artificial broadcast medium. The early printing shops became the focal points of information distribution in their regions. The success of printing gradually transformed interrelated groups of scribes, parchmenters, papermakers, bookbinders, and booksellers in medieval information distribution centers, of which Paris was the largest. For centuries these individual manuscript book producers had contracted to produce expensive single copies of manuscripts for individual patrons. With the advent of printing the production and distribution of information became increasingly focused around the press into concentrations of workers collaborating on producing printed books for wider audiences. Gradually these small print shops, the earliest mechanized information distribution centers, spread throughout the cities and towns of Europe and later the world. Through the editorial, typesetting and printing processes, printers and their associates such as booksellers and publishers transformed the distribution of written information beyond one-on-one hand-copying of individual manuscripts to the entrepreneurial distribution and sale of multiple printed copies of the same work. A major effect of this process was an explosion in quantity and diversity of information.

We have also seen how centuries later computing, data networking, and telecommunications converged in the Internet, carrying with them, in addition to digital versions of documents in a form similar to print, digital forms of radio, telephone, television, music, and film. We have also seen how web documents may be published in forms like traditional printed documents, such as .pdf files (Adobe Acrobat documents) or in completely new forms such as blogs or continuously updated cooperative encyclopedic works that could not exist without the Internet and the World Wide Web. We have also observed that as the volume of searchable information on the web increases, the power of search engines continues to improve its accessibility, making the rapidly expanding universe of electronic information more and more accessible, in ways that may be tailored to meet the specific needs of a virtually unlimited number of different people, automatically, and at amazing speed. As the Internet increases our access to information in so many forms it also reduces the cost of publishing and distributing information, in certain cases reducing electronic publishing costs to near zero. Underlying these factors is the function of the Internet as an interactive one-on-one communications medium, and a social space for building online communities or communications between individuals, though the Internet also functions as a broadcast medium.

If the past is any guide to the future, we may anticipate a continuing period of transition in which printed books, enhanced in their design and production by computing technology, may coexist, and even flourish along with the digital media of the Internet before an increasing percentage of printing is replaced with electronic information, including new media like electronic paper. Electronic paper may eventually combine the very high resolution, hand-held convenience, and ease of use of printing with searchability, hyperlinks and interactivity. If so, it will have considerable technical advantages over the printed page. Presumably it will also be reusable like a computer monitor, but will be comfortable to hold in our hands or on our lap like a book. By reducing the demand for paper made from cellulose, electronic paper could save hundreds of millions of trees each year. Certainly books read on electronic paper will never approach the physicality, or in some cases the sensuality, of printed books as objects to collect, to write in, to cherish, to organize, or just pile on the floor. However, use of electronic paper and other electronic substitutes for books may help stabilize the consumption of a valuable resource in the face of future economic growth. (Although considering the huge paper consumption by people using computer printers, and the economic development occurring in rapidly developing countries like China, the belief that electronic paper as a substitute for books may result in a dramatic reduction in paper consumption may be more of a utopian wish than a realistic expectation.)

Digital information, unlimited in its scope and diversity, will inevitably take forms that we cannot imagine today; but whatever those forms may be, it is very likely that printing of some sort will be involved. Because of the central role that printing continues to play with respect to so many different forms of information it is difficult to imagine that books or printing will ever disappear. Instead, just like digital information, new purposes and applications of printing will continue to be invented. Earlier in this essay I asked if the Internet, or more specifically the web, would ever replace a significant percentage of printed books. We have already seen how the web has replaced certain classes of printed books with new forms of online interactive publications, but for a wide variety of reasons, economic demand and new printing applications may substitute new uses of paper for those classes of books that have been replaced. Thus in a categorical sense we cannot answer the question with certainly. I have attempted to place the question in historical perspective by comparing the transitions from old to new media in our time with what happened more than five hundred years ago. Though I was unable to develop this comparison in sufficient length in this introduction, the further I research this complicated historical problem the more complex and fascinating the problem becomes, and the less certain the answer may be. Ultimately what may be most significant is the recognition that the Internet and the web have advanced to such an extent that the question was worth asking in the first place. This and other questions about the future of books may remain meaningful as long as people continue to read and create books and diverse electronic media.

THE BACKGROUND OF THIS BOOK

From Gutenberg to the Internet evolved from of an annotated descriptive bibliography of primary printed sources on the history of computing, networking and telecommunications that I co-authored with Diana H. Hook, entitled *Origins of Cyberspace: A Library on the History of Computing, Networking, and Telecommunications*. That book was published in 2002 in a deluxe edition limited to only 500 copies. *From Gutenberg to the Internet* is intended to make readings and illustrations from a few of the original documents described in *Origins of Cyberspace*, as well as other landmark texts, available to a wider audience.

In collecting the *Origins of Cyberspace* library, I became acquainted with the texts of pioneering documents describing technological innovations that changed the world. In the process of writing *Origins of Cyberspace* I also became acquainted with some of the pioneers themselves, including Herman Goldstine, Leonard Kleinrock, and Maurice V. Wilkes. All were generous in supplying information. As I continued to study in and around the topics involved I felt that selections from the early texts should be made available to a wider audience. The earliest documents in the history of the stored-program electronic computer come from a world about sixty years ago, in which only a few hundred people were concerned about inventing and building high speed computing machines. For centuries prior to these developments, computing had been done by human computers, first completely by hand, and later with the assistance of mechanical, electric, and electromechanical calculators. Others readings in this anthology are landmarks in the development of telecommunications or data communications. Some of these readings are visionary and theoretical—attempts to plan yet unbuilt inventions. Some are full of scientific formulae and mathematical proofs—efforts by mathematicians and engineers to show that these inventions could, or would, actually work. Others are attempts to understand the implications of these inventions. All of these readings have a common element—they trace aspects of our present world of the Internet back to their early roots, mostly in their developers' own words.

In each chapter of this anthology I included texts that may be read by generalists like me. Some chapters also include texts with more technical content that may appeal to readers with specialist scientific background. Whatever the background you bring to this book, I hope that it succeeds in offering you a flavor of times past in which innovators first formulated ideas and inventions that now pervade our world.

Another reason for writing and publishing this book is to help bridge the gap between those who approach the history of information from the standpoint of books and manuscripts and those who approach the same topics from the standpoint of electronic technology. A great deal has been and continues to be published on many aspects of the history of books and printing, and on the history of printing technology and publishing as they relate to the history of information and scholarship. Though some of those works make general references to developments in computing, few deal in any significant way with the technological developments that led to the Internet. Conversely, the numerous histories of computing generally avoid dealing with the history of books or printing. However, because virtually all of us now use both books and computers connected to the Internet as information sources, it may be time to bridge the traditional divide between book history and the history of electronic media.

Of course, one conclusion that may be drawn from the readings in this anthology is that the technologies underlying electronic media are very different from printing and its related technologies. Undoubtedly that is true, but the scholarly methods for approaching the history of the different topics are not necessarily as different as the technologies. Furthermore, the more we become involved with the operations of our computers on a daily basis, the more we may inquire as to how IT came about, just as we might explore the history of printing of books that we read on a daily basis.

Another reason that I would propose for the divide between scholarship on the history of "the book" and scholarship on the history of IT is that most libraries are full of source material for the history of books and printing while very few libraries have adequate coverage of primary source material on the history of computing and telecommunications. Thus it may be far more difficult to see some original source material on the history of IT than the more readily available source material for the history of books and printing.

A result of this cultural divide in scholarship on the history of technology relating to information is that on issues concerning the history of books and publishing there is a large scholarly literature and there are various anthologies available, some of which I cite in the *For Further Reading* section of this anthology. There is also an international database called *Book History Online* operated by the Koninglijke Bibliotheek, the National Library of the Netherands, in cooperation with national committees from all over the world. The database currently contains nearly 29,000 records.[46] On the other hand, when I wrote and published *From Gutenberg to the Internet* I was unaware of any other book or database that approached these topics from precisely this point of view. By organizing and making available in a convenient way some key documents in the history of IT, and by raising some of the issues that I have discussed in this introduction, I hope to help bridge this cultural divide, or help stimulate further scholarly discussion about issues concerning the historical relationship of printed and electronic information.

---

46 http://www0.kb.nl/bho/

PRIOR ANTHOLOGIES ON RELATED THEMES

Before compiling this work I reviewed prior anthologies on related themes. Surprisingly, there were few. All of these anthologies focused on computing. Because they were all written before the impact of personal computers connected to the Internet, none of them included material related to the convergence of computing with data networking and telecommunications that occurred through the Internet. Prior anthologies that came to my attention are the following:

John Diebold, editor, *The World of the Computer* (New York: Random House, 1973). Diebold, a pioneer in automation, prepared this collection of non-technical essays and papers during the mainframe era. It was intended to give readers, most of whom had never seen a computer close up, an appreciation for various issues in computing. Chapters include "The Computer Past and Present," "Computers in Use," "The Computer's Impact on Society," and "Computers and the Intelligence Argument." The editor provided a non-technical introduction to the book, and equally non-technical brief introductory comments to each chapter.

Phillip Laplante, editor, *Great Papers in Computer Science* (Minneapolis-St. Paul: West Publishing Co., IEEE Press, 1996). Laplante's well-chosen selections are scientifically oriented, and emphasize the post-1960 period rather than prior material. The book was intended for first year computer science students. Selection of the papers was done by surveying 1000 professors of computer science. Unfortunately the editing and typography leave something to be desired. The book is divided into the following chapters: "Algorithms and Data Structures," "Programming Languages," "Architecture," "Numerical and Scientific Computing," "Operating Systems," "Software Methodology and Engineering," "Databases," "Artificial Intelligence and Robotics," "Human-Computer Communications," "History." The introductory notes to each paper include first-person comments by authors of the papers reproduced. The last section on "History" reproduces secondary source material.

Zenon W. Pylyshyn, editor, *Perspectives on the Computer Revolution* (Englewood Cliffs, N. J.: Prentice-Hall, 1970). More comprehensive than Diebold's anthology, and intended to be read by people both inside and outside the professional computer community, Pylyshyn's collection is divided into the following chapters: "Some Landmarks in the History of Computers," "Theoretical Ideas: Algorithms, Automata, and Cybernetics," "Man-Machine Confrontation," "Machine Intelligence," "Man-Machine Partnership," "The Impact of the Computer Information Revolution," "Automation, Technology, and Social Issues," "Ethical and Moral Issues." The editor provided a brief introduction, and introductory comments to each chapter. He also included a useful annotated bibliography that included suggestions for further reading.

Brian Randell, editor, *The Origins of Digital Computers. Selected Papers,* third edition (New York: Springer-Verlag, 1982). Randell's anthology is scientifically rather than socially oriented, and intended for students of computer science or professionals in the computer industry. It included the first truly useful annotated bibliography of historical computing literature. Randell's introduction includes commentary on the texts, but the texts themselves are presented without any editorial comment. Chapters include: "Introduction," "Analytical Engines," "Tabulating Machines," "Zuse and Schreyer," "Aiken and IBM," "Bell Telephone Laboratories," "The Advent of Electronic Computers," "Stored Program Electronic Computers," "Bibliography." The first edition of this work was published in 1973.

THE ARRANGEMENT OF THIS ANTHOLOGY

The Table of Contents of *From Gutenberg to the Internet* may be viewed as an outline of this book. There you will see the thematic arrangement by chapters, and a listing of all the original readings that appear in each chapter. Prefacing most of the original readings are introductory notes that discuss the historical readings and their interrelationships. Here are some general comments on the scope of each chapter:

II. Timeline

The *From Gutenberg to the Internet* Timeline is an annotated chronology of wide-ranging scientific, social, and commercial developments in the history of Information technology from the years 100 to 2004, including computing, networking, telegraph, telephone, radio, television, printing, papermaking, publishing, molecular biology, cryptography information theory and related fields. It contains cross-references to most of the readings reprinted in this volume. The timeline covers a much wider range of information and technology than the rest of this book. It is also a work in progress. Visit the online interactive version of the timeline at www.historyof-science.com.

III. Human Computers

For centuries before the introduction in 1943–45 of programmed calculating machines, the term "computer," without the qualifier "human," generally applied to humans rather than machines. During this pre-1945 period the machines were more typically called "calculators," and the word "computer" was more generally applied to people. In the early nineteenth century Charles Babbage called his machines "calculating engines" (Difference Engine or Analytical Engine). In the first decade or so of electronic computing the word "calculator" was also sometimes used for electronic computers. The "C" in EDSAC, a first generation of stored-program electronic computer developed at Cambridge University, stood for calculator. In the UNIVAC, the first stored-program electronic digital computer sold commercially in the United States, the "C" stood for computer. In the United States the word "computer" first became closely associated in the public mind with the UNIVAC after the computer predicted the election of Dwight D. Eisenhower on television on November 4, 1952—so much so that IBM called their initial commercial offerings of electronic digital computers (IBM 701 and 702) "data processing machines" rather than "computers" to distinguish them from the UNIVAC. Only after electronic digital computers became relatively widespread in the late 1950s or early 1960s did the word "computer" begin to apply exclusively to machines rather than people. Exactly when that transition took place is not clear. In the second edition of the first textbook on software, by Wilkes, Wheeler, and Gill (1957)[47], the authors compare (on page 1) communicating a problem to a digital computer with communicating the same problem to a "human computer," thus indicating that the usage of the word "computer" to describe humans was still alive at this date. This may, however, be one of the later usages of "human computer" in a computing book other than a history of computing.

The readings in this chapter concern the special calculating ability that certain human computers apart from idiot savants developed in the pre-electronic computing era. During the nineteenth century and prior some human computers could perform complex mathematical calculations in their heads faster than any mechanical calculating machine. A few performed on stage professionally. In thinking about the history of computing we should remember that prior to World War II the term "computer" designated humans rather than machines.

Today remarkable achievements of mental calculation continue to occur, though mental prodigies in mathematics are no longer called human computers. It is also unlikely that they could beat an electronic computer in processing time, but they can beat humans who have to program the same problem into an electronic computer or calculator. For example, Gert Mittring, who has degrees in computer science, education, and psychology, holds the world's record for memorizing 22 random digits in just four seconds, and he calculated the thirteenth root of a 100-digit number in his head in just 11.8 seconds. Mittring extracted the 137th root out of a one thousand-digit number in his head within 13.3 seconds. Like the prodigies from the nineteenth century, Mittring sometimes demonstrates his special mental calculating abilities at public events or on television.[48]

---

47 Maurice V. Wilkes, David Wheeler, and Stanley Gill, *Programs for an Electronic Digital Computer.* Second edition (Reading, MA: Addison-Wesley, 1957).

IV. Mechanizing the Production of Mathematical Tables

Before and during Charles Babbage's time, and for more than one hundred years afterward, mathematical tables were the main work product of human computers. These included famous scientists such as Johannes Kepler, who prepared mathematical tables, or John Napier, inventor of logarithms and "Napier's bones," an early calculating device. A very few other human computers, including those mentioned in Chapter III, performed on stage, but most worked anonymously or published tables that were long ago forgotten. To prepare a mathematical table involved studying and correcting mistakes in previously published tables on the same topic. Only when adequate tables for specific topics did not exist was a table necessarily calculated from scratch, but even correcting existing tables involved a great deal of computation. The author of mathematical tables, revised or new, had to be familiar with the tables previously published in his field over centuries.[49] The 265 mathematical tables in Babbage's library catalogue confirm his serious interest in this subject.[50] Babbage published his own tables of logarithms after proofreading them against many other sets of tables he had collected to insure that they were correct.

Mechanizing the production of mathematical tables to improve their accuracy and speed their production was a major force driving advances in mechanical, electromechanical, and eventually electronic computing. Today it may be difficult to appreciate the central place that mathematical tables played in the history of computing. Surrounded by electronic computers and inexpensive handheld electronic calculators that made mathematical tables obsolete, we may have difficulty imagining the situation in which printed books of mathematical tables were essential computing aids for many specialized fields, including astronomy and navigation. The readings reproduced in this chapter describe Babbage's pioneering but only partly successful efforts to develop a difference engine to mechanize the production of mathematical tables in order to improve their accuracy. A few other pioneers were more successful in these efforts than Babbage.[51] Once the basic mechanization process was accomplished toward the end of the nineteenth century, the challenge was to increase the speed of the calculating process. In 1889 Herman Hollerith invented the electric punched card tabulator for use in the 1890 eleventh census of the United States. Using the Hollerith system, the census bureau reduced information processing time by 80% over manual methods.

---

48 http://130.94.161.3/Intertel/mittring-gert.html

49 James W. L. Glaisher, astronomer, table-maker and bibliographer of tables, provided a definition of the usefulness of tables in his exhaustive survey article on "table, mathematical" in *Encyclopaedia Britannica*, eleventh edition, XXVI (1911), 325: "The intrinsic value of a table may be estimated by the actual amount of time saved by consulting it; for example, a table of square roots to ten decimals is more valuable than a table of squares, as the extraction of the root would occupy more time than the multiplication of the number by itself. The value of a table does not depend upon the difficulty of calculating it; for, once made, it is made for ever, and as far as the user is concerned the amount of labor devoted to its original construction is immaterial. In some tables the labour required in the construction is the same as if all the tabular results had been calculated separately; but in the majority of instances a table can be formed by expeditious methods which are inapplicable to the calculation of an individual result. This is the case with tables of a continuous quantity, which may frequently be constructed by differences. . . .By having recourse to tables not only does the computer save time and labour, but he also obtains the certainty of accuracy."

50 Michael R. Williams, "The Scientific Library of Charles Babbage," *Annals of the History of Computing* 3 (1981): 235–40. Among other things, Williams points out that Babbage owned Rheticus's copy of the second edition of Copernicus's *De revolutionibus* (1566). Babbage also collected early calculating machines, including an original Morland calculator, and two machines constructed by Earl Stanhope (1753–1816).

51 Michael R. Williams, "Difference engines: From Müller to Comrie," in M. Campbell-Kelly, M., Croaken, R. Flood, and E. Robson, editors, *The History of Mathematical Tables: From Sumer to Spreadsheets* (Oxford: University Press, 2003).

Though the importance of Hollerith's invention may have been largely forgotten, electric punched card tabulating was the key technology underlying information processing until it was finally replaced by electronic computing in the early 1960s. Hollerith's company eventually became IBM, and until well after World War II the key profit center for IBM was the leasing of electric punched card tabulators and the sale of their proprietary punched cards. Other information processing companies such as Remington Rand had similar commitments to punched card tabulating. IBM gradually introduced limited programming capabilities into its punched card tabulators especially during World War II. The success of the punched card tabulating business was one reason for the relatively slow spread of electronic computing after the war. As an example of how big the electric punched card tabuling business was, in 1936 Vannevar Bush wrote that four billion punched cards were being used annually. This amounted to ten thousand tons of punched cards.

In the early 1930s Leslie John Comrie, working in England, figured out how to program human computers to operate electric punched card tabulators like difference engines. This significantly increased the speed of mathematical table production, and was a key development in the history of information processing before general purpose programmable computers were developed. Eventually the pressing need to calculate firing tables for a wide variety of different artillery pieces during World War II culminated in the development of the electronic digital computer. This is covered in Chapters VI, VII, and VIII and IX.

V. The Earliest Data Networks

The international data network of cyberspace had a remarkable historical antecedent in the first electronic data networks built for the electromagnetic telegraph around 1850. The electromagnetic telegraph had its own antecedents in the optical telegraphs invented by the Chappe family in France at the end of the eighteenth century. The Chappe optical telegraph could transmit one character in about thirty seconds. Because the transmission speed of optical telegraphy was affected by visibility, transmission in rain or snow was significantly slower than transmission on a clear day. Nevertheless, this method was several times faster than a horseback rider carrying a message. It was said that under optimal conditions a message could be transmitted from Paris to Milan in about thirty minutes.

Until the invention of the optical telegraph, the speed of message delivery by horseback had remained constant since ancient times. Innovators and entrepreneurs, such as Samuel F. B. Morse, continued to search for greater communication speed than optical telegraphy could provide. By 1837, only six years after Michael Faraday discovered electromagnetic induction, Morse had invented a practical form of electromagnetic telegraph using an early version of his "Morse code." In 1858 the yet unrealized Atlantic Cable, that would in 1866 allow telegraph messages to be transmitted between America and England, was called "that instantaneous highway of thought between the old and new worlds."[52] Does this not seem strikingly similar to the designation of the Internet as the "information superhighway" that was popular only a few years ago?

During the second half of the nineteenth century the telegraph remained the predominant method of transmitting electronic messages, and during this period other electronic messaging modalities tended to be described in telegraphic terms. Ternant, in his *History of Telegraphy*,[53] described the telephone in his chapter on acoustic telegraphy, and described the Morse system in his chapter on the electric telegraphy. In 1901 Guglielmo Marconi transmitted messages across the Atlantic Ocean by what he called wireless telegraphy—what we call radio.

---

52 Tom Standage, *The Victorian Internet* (New York: Walker, 1998), 74. Standage quotes from *Scientific American*, 1858.

53 A. L. Ternant, *The Story of the Telegraph*, translated by R. Routledge (London: G. Routledge & Son, 1895).

The Morse code, made up of dots and dashes, may be viewed as the first widely adopted data code. Transmission of images began with early systems of fascimile transmission over telegraph lines during the 1870s. The 1880s also witnessed the invention of the first television systems.

VI. Origins of the General Purpose Programmable Computer—Babbage's Analytical Engine

Apart from such telecommunications luminaries as Samuel F. B. Morse of the "Morse Code" and Alexander Graham Bell of the telephone, Charles Babbage may be the one computer pioneer that most readers will have heard of before opening the covers of *From Gutenberg to the Internet*. Yet Babbage differed from Morse and Bell in one essential way—his ideas were so far ahead of his time that there was little practical use for his calculating engines when he invented them. As a result, Babbage's Difference Engines were not completed in his lifetime and his Analytical Engine was never built, except for very small portions long after his death. Babbage's dream of the programmable computer, first expressed in his designs for his Analytical Engine about 1836, was not realized until 1943–45 with Howard Aiken's Harvard Mark I, Stibitz's Relay Interpolator, and Eckert and Mauchly's ENIAC . In contrast, both Morse and Bell lived to see their inventions proliferate and prosper.

> The features Babbage invested in the [Analytical] Engine are astonishing. It could be programmed by the use of punched cards.[54] It had a separate "memory" and "central processor". It was capable of "looping" or "iteration" (the ability to repeat a sequence of operations a programmable number of times) as well as conditional branching (the ability to take one course of action or another, depending on the outcome of a calculation—IF . . .THEN statements). It incorporated "microprogramming" as well as "pipelining" (the preparation of a result in advance of its need) and catered for the use of multiple processors to speed computation by splitting the task—the basis of modern parallel computing. It also featured a range of input and output devices, including graph plotters, printers, and card readers and punches. In short, Babbage had designed what we would now call a general purpose digital computing engine. . . . [55]

This chapter reproduces the famous original description of the design and programming of Babbage's Analytical Engine written by Luigi Menabrea and translated, with substantial additions, by Ada, Countess of Lovelace, daughter of Lord Byron. This paper has been frequently called the most important paper on the general purpose digital computer written in the nineteenth century. We also reproduce Babbage's own account of the machine from his autobiography. The chapter concludes with Percy Ludgate's account of a mechanical general purpose programmable computer that he designed very early in the twentieth century, which was never built.

VII. The Theory of the Universal Machine

The theoretical foundation for programmed electromechanical and electronic digital computing was discovered in mathematical logic in the nineteenth century,[56] and in the twentieth century during the years prior to World War II, though most of the theoreticians making the discoveries did not envisage the application of their ideas to computing. Of the theoreticians in mathematical logic, only Alan Turing envisaged the applications of his logical work in cryptography and in the development of actual computing machines.[57] Turing's paper "On Computable

---

54 Though he was unable to build the actual Analytical Engine, Babbage did experiment with how the punched cards would work. Samples of Babbage's original punched cards containing mathematical instructions are preserved in the Science Museum, London. One is reproduced in Williams, *A History of Computing Technology* (1985), p. 188.

55 Doron Swade, *The Cogwheel Brain: Charles Babbage and the Quest to Build the First Computer,* (London: Little, Brown, 2000). This was published in the United States under the title *The Difference Engine: Charles Babbage and the Quest to Build the First Computer* (New York, Penguin Putnam, 2001). The quotation is from pp. 114–15.

Numbers" (1936) included the first theoretical description of what he called a "universal machine." Excerpts from this paper are included in the anthology. Turing's universal machine was first called a "Turing machine" by Alonzo Church in his review of Turing's paper also reproduced in this anthology. One year after Turing published his paper, Claude Shannon showed in his master's thesis that it was possible to design electro-mechanical or electronic circuits that would act as calculating or computing machines (see Reading 12.1.).

Throughout his career Turing maintained parallel interests both in the theory of computing and in the application of these theories in the design, building, and programming of actual computers. At Bletchley Park in England during World War II, Turing and his team applied mathematical logic in the design and construction of the electromechanical and electronic cryptanalysis machines that successfully deciphered the German Enigma code.[58] This special-purpose work was kept an absolute secret until 1974,[59] and thus did not directly influence the history of computing in the standard way, but the experience was undoubtedly useful in the years immediately after World War II when Turing and other veterans of Bletchley Park were involved in the design of the first general-purpose stored-program computers built in England, including the Automatic Computing Engine (ACE). Speaking in February 1947, Turing stated that "digital computing machines such as the ACE . . . are in fact practical versions of the universal machine."[60] In the United States John von Neumann, stimulated by the ENIAC project and aware of Turing's ideas, especially in their adaptation to theories of brain function by McCulloch and Pitts, set out the theory of the stored-program electronic digital computer in his privately circulated *First Draft of a Report on the EDVAC* (1945). Portions of that founding document are reproduced in Chapter 8. Excerpts from the seminal paper by McCulloch and Pitts appear in Chapter 7.

VIII. Logical Design and Production of the First Electronic Digital Computers

This chapter collects, for the first time in one place, selections from key documents that concern the invention, design and operation of the earliest working electronic digital computers. These were first developed to meet the requirements for calculation during World War II that created a virtually insurmountable problem for human computers. The urgent need to produce accurate firing tables for a huge variety of new artillery in World War II created a demand for the production of mathematical tables in quantities the like of which no one had ever seen. Yet these tables still had to be produced by armies of human computers with the assistance of desktop calculators, and it took a very long time to produce each table:

> Each gunner would need a ballistic table containing the solutions to about 3,000 different trajectories and,
> if the table were for a very long range gun, it would have to consider extra factors such as air pressure,
> humidity, and wind speed to obtain the trajectory with any accuracy. The calculations for a single trajec-

56 In *The Universal Computer. The Road from Leibnitz to Turing* (New York: W. W. Norton, 2000), Martin Davis traces key ideas back to Leibnitz in the seventeenth century. Because most of Leibnitz's writings on logic were not published until the early twentieth century, his ideas had to be rediscovered, or developed in a different way, in the nineteenth century.

57 Just as I was finishing this book, a superb compendium of Turing's work was published: *The Essential Turing: Seminal Writings in Computing, Logic, Philosophy, Artificial Intelligence, and Artificial Life plus The Secrets of Enigma*, ed. B. Jack Copeland (Oxford: Clarendon Press, 2004).

58 Jack Gray and Keith Thrower, *How the Turing Bombe Smashed the Enigma Code* (Reading, England: Speedwell, 2001). A more comprehensive work is Michael Smith and Ralph Erskine, editors, *Action this Day. Bletchley Park from the Breaking of the Enigma Code to the Birth of the Modern Computer* (New York: Bantam, 2001).

59 The first book to end the secrecy was F. W. Winterbotham, *The Ultra Secret* (London: Weidenfeld & Nicholson, 1974).

60 Davis, *op. cit.,* 189.

tory would take a skilled person, working with an electrically driven desk calculator, about 20 hours to produce the results. [Thus calculations for ballistics tables for one type of artillery could take 60,000 hours, or 7500 8-hour days.] If the calculations for the trajectories were done on a machine such as the differential analyzer constructed at the Moore School, it would only take about 20 minutes of actual machine time per trajectory [1000 hours, or 125 8-hour days] but that was only after the differential analyzer was properly adjusted and set for the specific problem. The differential analyzer required constant attention and careful adjustment because, like any mechanical analog device, it suffered from accuracy limitations due to slippage and backlash problems in the gearing.

At the start of the Second World War the need for more and better trajectory tables became acute. The Ballistic Research Laboratory was using their copy of the differential analyzer full time and, in 1940, took over the one at the Moore School in order to increase their ability to cope with the problem. The Moore School also took over the task of training groups of women to help out by doing some of the calculations on desk calculators. These women, several hundred of whom were eventually trained, were given a three-month intensive course in the required areas of mathematics and operational skills. This calculational help was still not sufficient, and the production of adequate ballistic tables fell further and further behind.[61]

Among the documents reproduced in this chapter is the complete first report on the design, operation, and programming of the ENIAC, the first large-scale general purpose electronic digital computer, originally issued in 1945 by Eckert, Mauchly, Goldstine, and Brainerd. Months after this confidential report was issued, at the public dedication of the ENIAC in February 1946, the machine computed an artillery shell trajectory in twenty seconds. This was roughly twice as fast as the flight of the shell, and at least 1000 times the speed of the methods that it replaced. Of course, by this time there was little need for the computation of trajectory tables since the war was over. Instead the power of the world's first "supercomputer" was directed toward the solution of problems related to nuclear weapons.

The ENIAC was not a stored-program machine, though it was eventually converted into one, and it was only fast compared to the electromechanical monsters of its time. The ENIAC required patch cords to be plugged in from buses to panels for the solution of each program, and this greatly reduced its efficiency. Nevertheless, built into the design of the ENIAC were a surprising number of fundamental discoveries both in the hardware and software of electronic digital computers. Eckert, Mauchly, and others building the ENIAC at the Moore School recognized the machine's obvious limitations before the ENIAC was completed, and began developing ideas about the stored-program concept. The United States Army began funding design and planning of the first stored-program machine, the EDVAC, at the Moore School as early as October of 1944. The mathematician John von Neumann incorporated his own ideas about the stored-program concept, and those of the Moore School team, in his *First Draft of a Report on the EDVAC*, distributed privately in the spring and summer of 1945 prior to the publication of Eckert and Mauchly's ENIAC report.

The stored-program electronic digital computer was truly one of the inventions that changed the world. But what precisely did the stored-program concept involve? Perhaps the best definition was prepared by Maurice V. Wilkes. It consists of three parts:

Serial execution of instructions: instructions were to be executed one at a time, those concerned with the organization of the flow of control taking their turn with those calling for arithmetic operations.

---

61 Michael R. Williams (1997), *op. cit.*, 268.

Single memory: the memory would contain addressable words each composed of the same number of binary digits; addresses would consist of integers running consecutively through the memory. If a word were sent to the control unit it would be interpreted as an instruction, and if sent to the arithmetic unit it would be interpreted as an item of data.

Modification and construction of instructions: the programmer would be able to modify addresses, or indeed whole instructions, by performing arithmetical or logical operations on them in the arithmetic unit. Similarly, he would have the power to construct new instructions and plant them in a program.

The last three items constitute the stored program principle which, when used as a term of art, means something more than that the program is stored in a memory.[62]

We also include in this chapter readings relating to Eckert and Mauchly's successful attempt to obtain a general patent on the stored-program electronic computer, for which they applied in 1947. Portions of the patent (which was finally granted in 1964) are reproduced, as well as excerpts from the historic court ruling in 1974 rendering the ENIAC patent invalid. Selections of works by John von Neumann having to do with the theory, design, and programming of the stored-program electronic digital computer are also reproduced here, including selections from his earliest draft report on the EDVAC that played a key role in the invalidation of the ENIAC patent. We also include information on the Princeton Institute for Advanced Study computer for which von Neumann was responsible, as well as on the first IBM stored-program computer, which was based on the design of the Princeton IAS machine.

To give you an idea of the actual speed at which the earliest electro-mechanical and electronic computers operated, we include information on benchmarking from the first popular book on electronic computers, Edmund Berkeley's *Giant Brains, or Machines that Think* (1949). The chapter also includes a reproduction of an early brochure concerning the Whirlwind I computer, the first to include core memory and a primitive graphic display. This is one of the earliest detailed brochures ever issued on an electronic computer. We also include the original paper by Maurice V. Wilkes describing his invention of microprogramming, and the original paper by Gordon Moore describing "Moore's Law," relating to the rapidly increasing power of microprocessors that is one of the most significant forces behind the continuing increase in computing power for lower cost.

IX. The Origins of Computer Programming

This chapter concerns the design of the earliest programs for electromechanical and stored-program electronic computers. It begins with reproduction of a discussion on programming from the Harvard Computation Laboratory's *Manual of Operation for the Automatic Sequence-Controlled Calculator* (1946), written primarily by Howard Aiken and Grace Hopper. Hopper was the leading first-generation programmer in the United States, and the coiner of the term "bug" to describe programming errors. The chapter continues with theoretical papers on programming by Goldstine and von Neumann for the proposed Princeton IAS machine, issued in April 1947 before the IAS machine or any other truly stored-program computer had become operational. This is followed by the first publication of an ephemeral in-house document circulated in mimeograph, also in April 1947, to very few people within Eckert and Mauchly's fledgeling Electronic Control Co., the world's first electronic computer company. The reading concerns the earliest software planning for a stored-program computer intended for commercial applications. It is the first programming intended to be sold. In this reading the yet to be named machine is called a "statistical EDVAC"; it would later be named UNIVAC. These readings are followed by the introductory

---

62 Maurice V. Wilkes, *Computer Perspectives* (San Francisco: Morgan Kaufmann Publishers, 1995), 18.

chapter to the first textbook on programming, written by Wilkes, Wheeler, and Gill. This section of the anthology concludes with two fundamental papers by Grace M. Hopper: her pioneering "The Education of a Computer" and her "Automatic Programming—Definitions" from the *Symposium on Automatic Programming for Digital Computers* (1954), the first symposium on programming of electronic computers.

X. Early Applications of Electronic Computers

This chapter begins with a visionary paper from 1949 by Warren Weaver, head of science funding for the Rockefeller Foundation, on the potential use of electronic computers for automatic language translation. This paper represents the beginning of computer translation, now a widely available technology, especially through online translation services such as those provided by Google or by Babel Fish at Altavista.com. Following are two papers from the second British computer conference, held in Manchester in 1951. The first, by B. V. Bowden, contains one of the earliest discussions of expected business applications for electronic computers. At this early date no electronic computer was available for sale or lease to any business, however. The second paper concerns the first application of an electronic computer to a problem in the bio-medical sciences—the beginning of bioinformatics. The authors, John Kendrew and J. C. Bennett, programmed the EDSAC at Cambridge to calculate structure factors in the x-ray crystallography of the protein myoglobin. Kendrew would eventually receive the Nobel Prize for his work in this area. Following these papers are long selections from the first detailed report on the applications of electronic computers to business, issued in June 1953 by Richard W. Appel and colleagues at Harvard Business School. This report was issued before any electronic computer was actually available to any business in the United States. The following year General Electric at Appliance Park in Louisville, Kentucky would take delivery of the first stored-program electronic computer sold to a corporation in the United States—UNIVAC I, serial number 8. Chapter X ends with J. C. R. Licklider's visionary paper from 1960 on the symbiotic relationship between men and computers, followed by Licklider's paper published shortly thereafter on the value of improved graphical interfaces for man-computer interaction, and Ivan Sutherland's paper describing the invention of the first graphical user interface, called "Sketchpad."

XI. Computing and Intelligence

Though computers and the Internet have become so pervasive that we take their presence for granted, and we increasingly interact with computational intelligence in the form of interactive software, voice-recognition software, and other applications, certain issues of computational intelligence remain controversial, including the replacement of traditional human occupations by computers. This chapter explores the beginning of the man-computer intelligence debate that began in earnest after the first electronic digital computers in the late 1940s demonstrated that machines could surpass man in certain aspects of information processing. It begins with a generally forgotten paper by Sir Geoffrey Jefferson, a British neurological surgeon at Manchester who published a critique of the notion of computational intelligence in 1949 in response to what he perceived as exaggerated expectations for the potential of electronic computers. This paper came to the attention of Alan Turing who was also at Manchester at the time. In response Turing wrote "Computing and Intelligence," in which he proposed what has been called the "Turing Test" as a basis for judging whether or not computers might possess intelligence comparable to that possessed by humans. The chapter continues with papers by Claude Shannon concerning the problems of programming computers to play chess, in which some of the earliest developments in computational intelligence occurred, and another paper by Shannon on computers and automata. This is followed by the McCarthy, Minsky, Rochester, and Shannon's prospectus for the 1956 Darmouth Summer Research Program on Artificial Intelligence (1955), which coined the term "artificial intelligence" and set out many of the discipline's original goals. After this we reprint a paper by John McCarthy on the difficulty of programming computers to make decisions with that most basic of human intelligence attributes—common sense. The chapter concludes with a paper on Paul Armer summarizing work in computational intelligence up to about 1960, including references to Russian research that have a distinctive "cold war" quality.

XII. Early Communications Theory

This chapter begins with the full text of what has been considered the most famous or possibly the most important master's thesis of the twentieth century—Claude Shannon's thesis, submitted in 1937 only one year after Turing published "Non-Computable Numbers." (I decided to place Shannon's thesis in this chapter so that it would be next to Shannon's equally famous *Mathematical Theory of Communication*, but it might have been just as interesting to place it after Turing's paper in Chapter VII on the theory of the universal machine.) In his thesis Shannon recognized that the true/false values in Boolean two-valued logic were analogous to the open and closed states of electric circuits. From this it followed that Boolean algebra could be used to describe or to design electrical circuits. Because Boolean algebra makes it possible to devise a procedure or build a device, the state of which can store specific information, once Shannon showed that electrical circuitry can perform logical and mathematical operations, and can also store the result of these operations, the inference could be drawn that it was possible to design calculating machines using electrical switches. When Shannon wrote his thesis he was thinking of electro-mechanical relays used as switches in telephone technology, rather than vacuum tubes. It may or may not have been coincidental that George Stibitz at Bell Labs began experimenting with computing devices using relays the same year that Shannon submitted his dissertation. Following this are excerpts from Shannon's paper placing communication theory on a mathematical foundation. A result of Shannon's work was the proof that messages could be coded so that they would be reliably transmitted and received over a medium in spite of a certain amount of noise interfering with transmission. This is followed by Hamming's paper that first describing error detecting and error correcting codes used in data transmission—the Hamming codes.

XIII. Origins of the Internet

This chapter begins with Vannevar Bush's paper from 1945 describing a hypothetical machine, the Memex, that would incorporate means to associate electronic links between files of information much the way that the human memory retains associative links between information that individuals consider related. Though Bush's Memex machine was not a computer, its foreshadowing of the hyperlinks to which we have become accustomed on the World Wide Web gives it particular interest for its early prediction of features of the Internet.

The chapter continues with the works of J. C. L. Licklider, Director of the Pentagon's Information Processing Techniques Office (IPTO), a division of ARPA (the Advanced Research Projects Agency), who initiated the sequence of events leading to the ARPANET, the first national network of mainframes. The remainder of this chapter concerns the work of four founders of data networking, whose work resulted in the ARPANET, first operational in 1969, and the foundation on which the Internet was eventually built. These are Lawrence Roberts, Leonard Kleinrock, Vinton Cerf and Robert Kahn. Roberts was the overall designer of the ARPANET for the Advanced Research Projects Agency of the Defense Department. Kleinrock was the theoretician of data networking using packet-switching, founder of UCLA's Network Measurement Center, and founder of the first node on the ARPANET at UCLA. In this anthology we are pleased to publish Kleinrock's original thesis proposal and the first chapter of his thesis for the first time in book form. In these documents he first published a technology and a mathematical theory of data communications. Cerf and Kahn developed the Transmission Communications Protocol (TCP) that later became TCP/IP.

XIV. For Further Reading

This is a listing of the reference books that I found most useful in selecting the readings, and for writing the introduction and introductory notes to the readings in this anthology. Just before this book went to press I found another book that contains the phrase, "From Gutenberg to the Internet" in its subtitle. This is Asa Briggs and Peter Burke's *A Social History of the Media: From Gutenberg to the Internet* (Cambridge, England: Polity Press, 2002.) This is a valuable book that would undoubtedly have been useful in my research. It provides a balanced presentation of the social history of print, telecommunications, television, film, and computing rather than emphasizing the IT approach.

Endnotes

If you made it all the way through this introduction and would care to comment please email me at jnorman@jnorman.com. You may also want to check our website, www.historyofscience.com for occasional updates to *From Gutenberg to the Internet,* such as additional readings, downloadable illustrations, and updates to the timeline. On our website you will find an interactive version of the *From Gutenberg to the Internet Timeline* with hyperlinks connecting entries to other sites on the web. Regarding additions and revisions to the book or the website I will appreciate your recommendations. Thanks for your attention.

Jeremy M. Norman

December 2004

2

From Gutenberg to the Internet Timeline

From Gutenberg to the Internet Timeline

An Annotated Chronology of Wide-Ranging Scientific, Social, and Commercial Developments in the History of Information Technology from the Years 100 to 2004.

TOPICS OR THREADS IN THIS TIMELINE INCLUDE:

Computing, Networking, Telegraph, Telephone, Radio, Television, Printing, Papermaking, Publishing, Molecular Biology, Cryptography and Related Fields.

This timeline is a work in progress. View the online interactive version at www.historyofscience.com.

1st Century A.D.	The form of the manuscript book generally shifts from the scroll to the codex.
105	Ts'ai Lun, an official of the Imperial Court, reports to the Emperor of China that paper has been invented. Twentieth century archaeological investigations indicate that paper was actually invented in China about 200 years earlier.
529	St. Benedict founds the monastery at Monte Casino in Compania, Italy, introducing monastic life to Europe. Until roughly the year 1200 monastic scriptoria and other ecclesiastic establishments will remain essentially the only customers for books, and they will have a virtual monopoly on manuscript book production. Paper will not be introduced into Europe until about 1255. Prior to this time all manuscripts will be written on vellum or parchment.
590	The first monastery in Gaul (France) is founded at Luxeuil. It is recorded that Irish monks bring to this monastery numerous manuscripts.
713	The first newspaper, "Mixed News," is published in China.
751	Chinese prisoners taken at the Battle of Talas, near Samarkand, convey papermaking techniques to the Arabs.
793	Papermaking is established in Baghdad. It had reached Damascus and Cairo in about 750.
806	Hien Tsung becomes the Emperor of China. During his reign a shortage of copper leads to the introduction of paper money.
Died circa 850	Abu Ja'far Muhammad ibn Musa Al-Khwarizmi, a Tashkent cleric, develops the concept of a written process to be followed to achieve some goal. He writes a book on the subject giving the name "algorithm" to this process. The information in this work will eventually reach Europe in books on *Algorithmus* by other authors that will be printed through the second half of the 15th century and later.
868	The Diamond Sutra is published in China on May 11, 868 by Wang Chieh. A scroll sixteen feet long by one foot wide, it is the earliest dated example of woodblock printing.

Circa 1041–48	The Chinese alchemist Pi Sheng invents moveable type made of an amalgam of clay and glue hardened by baking. He composes texts by placing the types side by side on an iron plate coated with a mixture of resin, wax, and paper ash. Because the Chinese alphabet is ideographic rather than alphabetic, moveable type does not advance in China at this time.
11th Century	Through the Arab conquest of North Africa and Southern Spain, papermaking first reaches the Moorish parts of Spain in the 11th century. A paper mill is recorded at Fez in Morocco in 1100, and the first mill on the Spanish mainland is recorded at Xativa in 1151.
Circa 1200	The abacus appears in China. It is called *suan-pan* in Chinese. On each rod this abacus has 2 beads on the upper deck and 5 on the lower deck; such an abacus is also referred to as a 2/5 abacus. The 2/5 style will survive unchanged until about 1850 at which time the 1/5 (one bead on the top deck and five beads on the bottom deck) abacus will appear. (The earliest known abacus dates from Babylonia, circa 300 B.C.)
13th Century	Beginning around the year 1200, monasteries no longer remain the exclusive purchasers of books, and manuscript book production starts moving from the exclusive domain of monastic scriptoria to the secular community. Intellectual life begins to be increasingly centered outside the monasteries at the universities. There scholars, teachers and students, in cooperation with artisans and craftsmen, will organize an active manuscript book trade.
13th Century	The European table abacus or reckoning table has become standardized to some extent. The pebbles previously used as counters have been replaced by specially minted coin-like objects that are cast, thrown, or pushed on the abacus table. They are called *jetons* from *jeter* (to throw) in France and *werpgeld* for "thrown money" in Holland.
1255	A paper mill is established at Genoa, Italy. Paper is cheaper to manufacture than vellum.
1309	Date of the first recorded use of paper in England.
1397	Date of the oldest surviving Korean text printed from moveable type.
1403	Printing from moveable type is practiced in Korea during the 15th century. In 1403 a set of 100,000 copper types are cast by command of the king. These are used for printing many books in Korea until 1544.
1423	The earliest dated xylographic or wood-block print is issued in Europe.
1430s	Johann Gutenberg begins experimentation on printing.
1450s	Printed newsletters begin circulating in Europe.
1454	Gutenberg, working in Mainz, Germany, prints Indulgences and other small texts using moveable type. These are the earliest dated documents printed by this method in Europe.
1454	Gutenberg has printed at least part of the 42-line bible.
1455 March 12	Enea Silvio Piccolomini, later Pope Pius II, reports that in Frankfurt, the year before, a marvelous man had been promoting the sale of a printed bible. Piccolomini states that he saw parts of it and it had such clear, large lettering that one could read it without glasses. He also notes that every copy had been sold.
1455 November 6	Johann Fust, a goldsmith and lawyer, files a lawsuit against Gutenberg to recover money that he had advanced to Gutenberg beginning in 1450. The total claim is 2026 gulden with interest. As a result of the lawsuit Fust gains possession of Gutenberg's press and equipment.
1455–56	Gutenberg, working with Fust and Peter Schöffer, completes printing the 42-line bible, the first book printed in Europe from moveable type.
1456	The "Bloodletting Calendar" for 1457 becomes the first known medical or scientific work to be printed. Popular during the Middle Ages, this form of calendar gives the lucky and unlucky days on which to perform the medical practice of "blood-letting."

1457 August 14	Fust and Schöffer publish the *Psalterium Latinum* at Mainz. This magnificent book printed on vellum is the first printed book to give both the name of the printer and the date of printing It has initial letters printed in red, light purple, and blue. Its colophon boasts of the new technology involved in its production, reading in translation, "The present copy of the Psalms, adorned with beauty of capital letters, and sufficiently marked out with rubrics, has been thus fashioned by an ingenious invention of printing and stamping without any driving of the pen. . . ."
1465	The first book printed in Italy, an edition of Cicero's *De Oratore,* is issued from the press of the German printers Conrad Sweynheym and Arnold Pannartz at the monastery of Subiaco. It is also the first book printed in Roman type. The edition is about 100 copies.
1472	Paolo Bagellardo (d. 1494) has his treatise on pediatrics, *De Infantium Aegritudinibus et Remediis,* printed in Padua. This is the first medical treatise, and probably also the first scientific treatise, to make its original appearance in printed form rather than having prior circulation in manuscript.
1473–74	William Caxton issues the first book printed in English at Bruges, Belgium. It is his translation of *The Recuyell of the Histories of Troy.*
1476 29 September	Caxton's name is entered on the account role for having paid a year's rent in advance for the premises in which he will set up his press at Westminster Abbey in London.
1478	The anonymous *Arte dell'Abbaco . . .* (Treviso, 1478), on the operation of the abacus, is the first dated book on arithmetic. It is possible that some undated pamphlets on *Algorithmus* may predate this work.
1480	Printing has spread throughout the continent of Europe and England. Up to this date a typical print run of a book is between 100 and 300 copies.
1483	The Alphonsine Tables, a compilation of astronomical data tabulating the positions and movements of the planets, are printed in Venice. They are a revision and improvement of the Ptolemaic tables, compiled at Toledo, Spain, about 1252 by about 50 astronomers assembled for the purpose by King Alfonso X of Castile. They are among the earliest printed mathematical tables.
1492	Johannes Trithemius, in his treatise *In Praise of Scribes*, questions the durability of media used in long term information storage when he compares the durability of information written on traditional vellum with that written or printed on the newer medium of paper.
1494	Responding to the challenges of organizing the rapidly growing body of information caused by the development of printing, Trithemius writes and has printed the earliest subject bibliography, *Liber de Scriptoribus Ecclesiasticis (A Book on Ecclesiastical Writings)*.
1500	By this date printing presses are established in more than 250 cities in Europe. The average print run of a book is between 400–500 copies, with as many as 1000 copies of some books being printed. By this date it is estimated that printers issued from 27,000 to 35,000 different printed works of all kinds, including pamphlets and broadsides as well as books, with a total printed output of somewhere around 15 to 20 million copies.
1516	Trithemius's *Polygraphiae*, a book on many forms of writing, is published in the year of his death. It is the first book on codes and cryptography.
1599	Galileo Galilei develops his geometric and military compass into a general-purpose mechanical analog calculator. It becomes known in English as the sector. He publishes *Le Operazioni del Compasso Geometrico et Militare* in 1606 in an edition of only sixty printed copies. During the seventeenth century the sector will become one of the most widely used mechanical calculators for scientific purposes.
Circa 1600	The Japanese adopt the Chinese 1/5 abacus via Korea. In Japanese the abacus is called *soroban*. The 1/4 abacus will appear in Japan about 1930.
1609	Johann Carolus publishes the first newspaper, *Avisa Relation oder Zeitung*, in Strasbourg.
1614	John Napier of Scotland publishes his *Mirifici logarithmorum canonis descriptio,* announcing his invention of logarithms, with the goal of increasing calculating speed and reducing drudgery.
1617	Napier publishes *Rabdologiae* describing two calculating devices: "Napier's bones," and "Multiplicationis promptuarium," or the lightning calculator.

1621	*The Corante* is published. It is the first private newspaper published in English.
1622	William Oughtred invents the circular form of the slide rule.
1623	Wilhelm Schickard invents the first true mechanical calculating machine, known only from drawings discovered in the twentieth century.
1624	Henry Briggs publishes *Arithmetica Logarithmica*, the first set of modern logarithms.
1624–25	Joannes Kepler publishes *Chilias Logarithmorum* (1624) and *Supplementum* (1625), creating his logarithmic tables by a new geometrical procedure, the form thus differing from both Napier and Briggs.
1627	Kepler publishes *Tabulae Rudolphinae*, his computation of which had been greatly advanced by his use of logarithms, which he had begun employing in calculations in 1618. The culmination of work undertaken by Kepler at the direction of the dying Tycho Brahe in 1601, and based on Tycho's great storehouse of observations, the tables play a dominant role in astronomy throughout the seventeenth century.
1628	Adrian Vlacq publishes the first complete set of modern logarithms.
1639	The first printing press in North America is established at Cambridge, Massachusetts.
1642	Blaise Pascal invents his adding machine, the Pascaline. He will publish a pamphlet on the machine in 1645.
Circa 1650	The sliding-stick form of the slide rule is developed.
1662	John Graunt, a draper in London, founds the sciences of demography and vital statistics, and publishes the first tables of life expectancy in his *Natural and Political Observations Mentioned in a Following Index, and Made upon the Bills of Mortality*.
1668	Gaspard Schott's posthumous *Organum Mathematicum* is published, in which he describes his "mathematical organ" and his calculating machine based on Napier's rods.
1671	Pierre Petit describes an arithmetic cylinder, which he says is more affordable and easier to use than Pascal's Pascaline.
1672	Samuel Morland publishes *The Description and Use of Two Arithmetic Instruments*, the first monograph on a calculating machine published in English. The book describes modifications to the Pascaline.
	Gottfried Wilhelm Leibnitz demonstrates a poorly working wooden model of his calculating machine to the Royal Society of London.
1673–74	Leibnitz makes a drawing of his calculating machine mechanism. Using a stepped drum, this calculator mechanizes multiplication as well as addition by performing repetitive additions. In 1674 Leibnitz hires a Parisian clockmaker to build one copy of his machine. This copy is eventually lost until 1879, when it is found in an attic at Göttingen University. However, because of descriptions published from 1710 onward, the machine is well-enough known to have great influence. The stepped-drum gear is the only workable solution to calculating machine problems until about 1875.
1679 March 15	A dated manuscript by Leibnitz, preserved in the Niedersachsischen Landesbibliotheke, Hannover, "includes a brief discussion of the possibility of designing a mechanical binary calculator which would use moving balls to represent binary digits."
1683–84	Joseph Moxon publishes his *Mechanick Exercises on the Whole Art of Printing* as part of his survey of the chief trades of his day. This is the first manual ever published on printing—a trade that had been passed down through apprenticeship since the mid-15th century.
1690	*Publick Occurrences* is issued in Boston, but suppressed after only one issue. It is the first newspaper published in North America.
1690	William Rittenhouse founds the first paper mill in the United States on the banks of the Monoshone Creek near Germantown, Pennsylvania, outside Philadelphia.
1699	There are 150 paper mills in England. Together they employ 2500 people.

1702	Elizabeth Mallet begins publishing the *Daily Courant*, England's first daily newspaper. It will survive for 30 years.
1705	The *Boston News Letter* begins publication. It is the first "successful" newspaper in the North American colonies.
1710	Leibnitz publishes the first description of his stepped-drum calculator. By then the unique example of the machine has been lost.
1750	Printing by hand on wooden printing presses remains a very laborious process that has not improved dramatically since the 15th century. A competent printer can expect to print about 100 sheets per hour.
1755	Thomas Simpson describes the "advantage of taking the mean of a number of observations," a landmark in statistical inference, and the earliest formal treatment of any data-processing.
1763	Thomas Bayes's paper enunciating Bayes's Theorem for calculating "inverse probabilities" is published two years after his death.
1764	James Hargreaves invents the spinning jenny, which spins eight threads simultaneously.
1766	The British Government sanctions Nevil Maskelyne, the astronomer royal, to produce each year a set of navigational tables, to be called the *Nautical Almanac*. This is the first permanent table-making project in the world. The tables will greatly improve accuracy of navigation. They become known as the "Seaman's bible." The product of human computers working by hand, the accuracy of these tables is dependent upon the accuracy of the people producing them. These tables will become notorious for their errors during the time of Charles Babbage.
1769	Richard Arkwright patents his hydraulic spinning machine. He builds a factory for this machine in 1781, creating disruptive economic and social changes characteristic of the Industrial Revolution.
	Wolfgang von Kempelen builds his chess-playing Turk, an automaton that purports to play chess. Although the machine displays an elaborate gear mechanism, its cabinet actually conceals a human controlling the moves of the machine. The Turk will become the most famous automaton in history.
1770	The first banker's clearing house, the earliest large-scale data-processing organization, is founded in London.
1772	Wilhelm Haas of Basel builds a new type of printing press in which all parts subject to stress during the printing process are made of iron, including both the bed and the platen. This improves the efficiency of the press.
1776	The American Revolutionary War begins.
1788	James Watt invents the centrifugal governor and creates interest in other feedback devices.
1789	The French Revolution begins.
1791	Claude Chappe demonstrates his optical telegraph system. The first line from Paris to Lille will be constructed in 1794. **(See Reading 5.1.)**
	Wolfgang von Kempelen publishes a monograph in which describes the first successful speech synthesizer. Unlike von Kempelen's fraudulent chess-playing Turk (1769), this speech synthesizer actually works.
1798–99	Louis-Nicolas Robert invents the first paper-making machine. It makes a continuous, unbroken sheet of paper that must later be cut.
1798	William Stanhope builds the first printing press entirely out of iron.
1798	Alois Senefelder invents lithography— the first radically new method of printing since Gutenberg's invention of printing by moveable type.
1800	All phases of cloth production are performed by machines.
	In this year 11,000 tons of paper are produced in the United Kingdom.

1801	Gaspard Riche de Prony completes two manuscript sets of massive logarithmic and trigonometric tables calculated by employing systematic division of mental labor, including the use of mathematically untrained hairdressers unemployed after the French Revolution. The method of production of the tables will inspire Charles Babbage in the design of his Difference Engine No. 1 in 1822. The tables will not be published until 1891.
1803	Joseph-Marie Jacquard receives a patent for inventing his automatic loom, which uses punched cards to store patterns and reduces strenuous manual labor. In 1806 the loom is declared public property and Jacquard receives a pension. He is forced to flee from Lyons because of the anger of the weavers, who fear they will lose their jobs. However, Jacquard perseveres and by the time of his death there will be thirty thousand Jacquard looms installed in Lyons alone.
1803	Senefelder adapts printing by lithography to incorporate metal plates instead of lithographic stones.
1804	Henry and Sealy Fourdrinier buy the patents for the papermaking machine invented five years earlier in France by Louis-Nicholas Robert. Bryan Donkin, the Fourdriniers' engineer, makes modifications to the Robert design. With these modifications the machine forms the basis for modern papermaking. The machines become known as Fourdrinier machines. By 1838, over 100 Fourdrinier machines will be in operation throughout the United Kingdom. It will be claimed that the machines were producing as much paper in minutes as had previously taken weeks to make by hand.
1810	There are 185 paper mills in the United States.
1811	Workers and craftsmen concerned about the loss of jobs due to automation found the Luddite movement. Among the examples of automation they destroy are Jacquard looms.
1812	After two failed attempts, Friedrich Koenig of Suhl builds a steam operated twin cylinder printing press. This is the first printing press not powered by hand.
1814	*The Times* newspaper in London purchases a Koenig power press. The output of the new machine is 1,100 sheets an hour, more than four times higher than that of the manually operated press previously used by the newspaper. The machine is secretly installed in Printing House Square and on November 29 the first issue from the steam-driven machine is printed.
1816	Francis Ronalds builds the first working electric telegraph.
	Koenig adds a perfector to The Times power press, allowing the press to print almost as many copies on both sides of the sheet on one pass through the press as had been previously printed on one side only.
1820	Charles Xavier Thomas de Colmar of Alsace invents the arithmometer, the first commercially produced adding machine. The machine sells at a rate of one or two per month. These machines, which use Leibnitz's stepped drum technology, remain in production through about the start of World War I, but annual production remains very small.
1822	Babbage starts on a model of the Difference Engine, a special-purpose machine that links adding and subtracting mechanisms to one another to calculate the values of more complex mathematical functions. His goal is to produce more accurate mathematical tables, the most widely-used calculating aids in his day. He announces his plan to build this machine in an open letter to Sir Humphry Davy, president of the Royal Society, and receives government funding. **(See Reading 4.1)**
1825	George Stephenson's "Locomotion No. 1," the first steam engine to carry passengers and freight on a regular basis, begins operation. The Stockton and Darlington Railway opens for business.
	In the first quarter of the nineteenth century roughly 600 new books per year are produced throughout the United Kingdom (Twyman, *Printing 1770–1970*, 10).
1827	Cowper & Applegarth in England complete the design of a four cylinder steam-powered printing press with capacity of 4,000–5,000 impressions per hour.
1829	Stephenson's Rocket wins the Liverpool and Manchester Railway competition. The first steam locomotive runs in the United States.

	Louis Braille, blind from the age of 5, publishes the Braille system of printing and reading for the blind that will eventually become the standard method. The title of his book, published in French, is translated as the *Method of Writing Words, Music and Plain Song by Means of Dots, for Use by the Blind and Arranged by Them*. In 1837 he will add symbols for mathematics and music to his system.
	William Austin Burt invents an early typewriter.
1830	Circulation of *The Times* of London is 11,000.
1831	Michael Faraday discovers electromagnetic induction, the basis for electricity generation.
1832	Babbage publishes his *On the Economy of Machinery and Manufactures*, the first work on operations research, partially based on data he accumulated in order to build his Difference Engine. Babbage orders construction of a small working portion of his Difference Engine no. 1, approximately one-ninth of the full machine. This will be the only portion of his "calculating engines" that he ever completes.
1834	Babbage conceives of the Analytical Engine, a general-purpose machine that embodies in its design most of the features of the programmed digital computer.
1837	Samuel F. B. Morse invents a practical form of electromagnetic telegraph using an early version of his "Morse code." **(See Reading 5.2.)**
1842	The British government abandons financial support for the construction of Babbage's Difference Engine no. 1.
	Luigi Federico Menabrea, later to be prime minister of Italy, publishes the first description of the functional organization and mathematical operation of Babbage's Analytical Engine, including the first published computer programs.
1843	Augusta Ada King, Countess of Lovelace, daughter of Lord Byron, translates Menabrea's paper, adding annotations that provide further insight into Babbage's proposed Analytical Engine, a machine that incorporates many of the concepts of the programmed digital computer. *Sketch of the Analytical Engine Invented by Charles Babbage. . . with Notes by the Translator*. **(See Reading 6.1.)**
	In Germany ground wood pulp begins to be used in papermaking instead of linen rags. This is a mechanical rather than a chemical process.
	The Scheutzes, inspired by Lardner's account of Babbage's Difference Engine, construct the first working difference engine.
1844 May 24	Samuel F. B. Morse transmits the first message on a United States telegraph line (Washington to Baltimore) using the "Morse code" that will become standard in the United States and Canada.
	The anonymous author of the sensational evolutionary treatise *Vestiges of the Natural History of Creation* includes a lengthy quote from Babbage's discussion of programming the Difference Engine from the *Ninth Bridgewater Treatise* to explain how evolutionary change might occur through time. This is one of the earliest references to computing within the context of biology.
1845	The Atlantic Cable is proposed.
	William Fothergill Cooke and Charles Wheatstone perfect a single-needle telegraph apparatus, soon adopted throughout England.
1846	Richard Hoe of New York patents the horizontal rotary printing press, dramatically increasing the speed of printing.
1847	George Boole publishes *The Mathematical Analysis of Logic*, leading to what eventually would be called Boolean algebra. Years later, in 1938, Claude Shannon in his master's thesis will recognize that the true/false values in Boole's two-valued logic are analogous to the open and closed states of electric circuits.
1848	The first WH Smith railway bookstall is opened. Railroad transportation provides a whole new market for printing, publishing, and bookselling. Inexpensive novels or Yellowbacks will be published to supply a wider range of society. It becomes a common practice to publish novels in weekly, fortnightly or monthly parts to spread the cost.

	The Associated Press (AP) is founded in the United States to reduce the high cost of telegraphic transmissions among six highly competitive newspapers.
1850	John and Jacob Brett lay the first telegraph cable between England and France. After a French fisherman cuts the cable, thinking it was a new kind of seaweed, they install an armored cable in 1851 that will last for many years.
	Circulation of *The Times* of London is 38,000.
1850s	The use of "flong" for stereotype printing plates provides an advantage for the publication of mathematical tables since stereotype plates represent "an immutable form of information capture that offered immunity from the inherent vulnerability of moveable type to derangement during printing or storage." Swade, "The 'unerring certainty of mechanical agency': Machines and table making in the nineteenth century," in Cambell-Kelly (ed.), *The History of Mathematical Tables* (2003), 148.
1851	Alfred Smee suggests the possibility of information storage and retrieval by a mechanical logical machine operating analogously to the human mind. The problem is that the machine might occupy a space larger than London.
	After setting up a carrier-pigeon service between Aachen and Brussels, terminal points of the German and French-Belgian telegraph lines, Paul Julius Reuter, formerly known as Israel Beer Josaphat, founds the Reuters news agency in London using telegraph lines.
1853	The Scheutz team produces their second difference engine, an improvement over the first.
	First use of wood pulp instead of linen rags for paper making occurs in England.
1854	Boole publishes *An Investigation of the Laws of Thought*. Boole invents the first practical system of logic in algebraic form.
	Paris and London are connected by telegraph.
	Cyrus Field organizes the New York, Newfoundland, and London Electric Telegraph Company with the intention of laying an Atlantic Cable.
1856	The Atlantic Telegraph Company is formed by Cyrus Field in the United States and Charles Bright, John Brett, and Jacob Brett in England.
	The Prudential is founded. It is the first of the great industrial life insurance companies that will handle the policies of millions of people.
	George Parker Bidder, an engineer and one of the most remarkable human computers of all time, publishes his paper on *Mental Calculation*. **(See Reading 3.1)**
1857	The first attempt to lay the Atlantic Cable using the American sailing ship Niagara and the British sailing ship *Agamemnon* fails.
1858 June 25	The second attempt to lay the first Atlantic Cable using the same two ships initially succeeds.
August 16	Communication is established on the Atlantic Cable but it fails within three weeks.
1859	The British government, long after refusing funding to complete Babbage's Difference Engine no. 1 or to construct his Analytical Engine, pays for the construction of the Scheutzes' third difference engine. William Farr first uses it to print a table for his paper, published in *Philosophical Transactions*, "On the Construction of Life-Tables, Illustrated by a New Life-Table of the Healthy Districts of England."
1860	In this year 100,000 tons of paper are produced in the United Kingdom, almost a tenfold increase since 1800. Only 4% is made by hand. Because of reduction in labor costs the average cost of paper falls 60% in the period from 1800–1860 (Twyman).
1861	Telegraph lines connect New York and San Francisco.

1864	Farr uses the third Scheutz difference engine in the calculation of his *English Life Table*—the first instance of a printing calculator used extensively to do original work. Because the machine is very troublesome the tables are completed by human computers. **(See Reading 4.2)**
	Babbage publishes his autobiography, *Passages from the Life of a Philosopher*, in which he presents his most detailed descriptions of his Difference and Analytical Engines. **(See Reading 6.2.)**
1865	James Clerk Maxwell publishes "A Dynamical Theory of the Electro-Magnetic Field" in the *Transactions of the Royal Society*. It provides a theoretical framework, based on experiment and a few general dynamical principles, for the propagation of electromagnetic waves through space.
July	Using the Great Eastern steamship, the attempt to lay the second Atlantic Cable takes place. The cable snaps after twelve hundred miles.
1866 July 27	The *Great Eastern* lays the third and successful Atlantic Cable, finally establishing communication by electric telegraph between Europe and America.
	Benjamin Tilghman of the United States develops the sulfite pulping process for the manufacture of paper. The first mill using this process will be built in Sweden in 1874.
1867	Edward A. Calahan of the American Telegraph Company invents the first stock telegraph printing instrument. The distinct sound of this telegraph printing instrument eventually earns it the name of "stock ticker."
1868	*The Times* of London installs a Walter press that prints on continuous paper, further increasing the speed of production.
	James Clerk Maxwell publishes "On Governors," a classic paper on feedback mechanisms.
1870	William Stanley Jevons constructs his "logical piano," the first logic machine to solve complicated problems with superhuman speed.
	There are over 6000 miles of railroad track in England.
	9,158,000,000 telegraph messages are sent in the United States.
	Circulation of *The Times* of London is 70,000.
	British telegraph systems are nationalized.
1870s	The first successful chemical processes for making paper out of wood pulp are introduced. Throughout the 19th century it has been increasingly necessary to find workable substitutes for scarce linen rags, the supply of which cannot possibly keep up with the growing demands for paper. However, the bleaching agents used in this new process to make paper from wood pulp will reduce the longevity of paper. The pulping, bleaching, and sizing processes generate hydrochloric and sulfuric acids, which over time result in brittleness and deterioration of paper and the possible loss of information.
1872	Babbage's library is sold at auction. Containing over two thousand items on topics that include mathematical tables, cryptography, and calculating machines, including many rare volumes, it can be considered the first catalogue of a library on computing and its history.
1874	Christopher Sholes, Samuel Soule and Carlos Glidden invent the first practical typewriter. It is is produced by Remington, a firm of gunsmiths. Called the "Sholes & Glidden Type Writer," it has a keyboard with letters and numbers arranged in a four-line pattern (known as QWERTY from the first six letters in the top row), a wooden spacer bar and a vulcanized india-rubber platen or roller. It only prints capital letters.
Circa 1875	Baldwin (United States) and Odhner (Russia) invent calculators using a true variable-toothed gear, the first real advance in mechanical calculating technology since Leibnitz (1673). This technology's greater ease of use, its general reliability, and the compact size of the equipment incorporating it cause an explosion of sales in the calculator industry.
1875	JGA Eickhoff builds a four-cylinder perfecting press, capable of printing two sides of the paper simultaneously.

1876	Thomas Alva Edison invents the phonograph.
	The earliest international exposition exclusively of scientific instruments is held at the South Kensington Museum, London. A small section is devoted to arithmetic and calculating instruments.
	Martin Wiberg uses his difference engine to produce *Tables de Logarithms Calculées et Imprimées au Moyen de la Machine à Calculer du M. Wiberg.* This set of tables of seven-place logarithms from 1 to 100,000 is the first logarithmic table produced by a calculating machine.
March 10	Alexander Graham Bell invents the telephone. **(See Reading 5.3.)**
1877	Construction of the first regular telephone line is completed. It runs from Boston to Somerville, Massachusetts.
	It takes three hundred clerks working at the Prudential six months to review its 2,500,000 policies with the assistance of twenty-four Thomas de Colmar arithmometers.
	The first telephone switchboard is set up in Boston.
1878	The first regular telephone exchange is set up in New Haven, Connecticut.
	The Remington Model 2 typewriter introduces a shift key, allowing the typing of both upper and lower case letters.
1879	James and John Ritty patent a cash register.
	Thomas Alva Edison produces the first incandescent light bulb capable of burning for a substantial period of time.
1880	George R. Carey proposes one of the earliest systems of television transmission. **(See Reading 5.5.)**
1884	John H. Patterson and his associates acquire the Ritty patents and establish the National Cash Register Company (NCR).
1885	Gottlieb Daimler invents the internal combustion engine and Karl Benz builds a single-cylinder engine for a motor car.
1886	Mergenthaler Linotype is used by the New York Tribune newspaper. In 1887 they publish *The Tribune Book of Open-Air Sports,* the first book typeset by machine.
1887	Tolbert Lanston demonstrates his prototype of the Monotype machine, which casts letters in the form of individual pieces of lead type. It reads punched paper tape like a player piano.
	Heinrich Hertz proves the existence of electromagnetic waves, the theoretical basis for wireless communication.
1889	Babbage's son Henry Prevost Babbage completes and publishes his father's unfinished edition of mostly previously published, but hard-to-find writings on the Difference Engine no. 1 and Analytical Engine, together with a listing of his father's unpublished plans and notebooks, under the title of *Babbage's Calculating Engines.*
1890	Herman Hollerith patents an electromechanical machine for tabulating information stored on punched cards. This is used in the 1890 United States census— the first major data-processing project to use electrical machinery. Data-processing time is reduced by 80 percent over manual methods. **(See Reading 4.3.)**
	William S. Burroughs begins commercial production of his dependable key-driven printing adding machine.
	Felt introduces the Comptometer, a nonprinting key-driven machine whose chief advantages are speed, versatility, and ease of use.
1891	The logarithmic and trigonometric tables of Gaspard Riche de Prony, compiled in 19 volumes of manuscript at the end of the eighteenth century, are finally published in an abbreviated form in one volume. They are the most monumental work of calculation ever carried out by human computers.

1892	Hertz publishes his collected papers on electromagnetic waves. In this form Marconi will learn about Hertz's work and begin work on the development of radio.
1893	Karl Benz invents a four-wheel automobile.
	The "Millionaire" mechanical calculator is introduced in Switzerland. It allows direct multiplication by any digit and is used by government agencies and scientists, especially astronomers, well into the twentieth century.
September	The recently established Deutsche Mathematiker-Vereinigung holds an exhibition in Munich of Mathematical and Mathematical-Physical Models, Apparatus, and Instruments. This is the first international exhibition limited to mathematical devices, including calculating instruments; it reflects the huge growth in the field since the London exposition of 1876. The exhibition had been planned for the previous year but was canceled because of an outbreak of cholera in northern Germany.
1894	Philibert Maurice d'Ocagne publishes *Le Calcul Simplifiée par Procèdes Mécaniques et Graphiques*. This contains the first systematic classification of calculating machines.
1895	Guglielmo Marconi invents wireless telegraphy (radio). **(See Reading 5.4.)**
	The first mainline railway is electrified.
	About 240,000 telephones are in use in the United States.
1896	Hollerith founds the Tabulating Machine Company, which will eventually become IBM.
	Lord Northcliffe founds the *Daily Mail*. It will soon achieve a daily circulation of 1,000,000.
	Marconi transmits a radio signal across the English channel.
1900	David Hilbert publishes in *Mathematische Probleme* a list of twenty-three problems that he predicts will be of central importance to the advance of mathematics in the twentieth century. In the second of these problems he calls for a mathematical proof of the consistency of the arithmetic axioms—a question that will influence both the development of mathematical logic and computing.
	In this year 652,000 tons of paper are produced in the United Kingdom, roughly a sixfold increase since 1860. By this time 99% of the paper is produced by machine.
December 23	Canadian-American physicist Reginald A. Fessenden is the first to transmit human speech over radio waves using a spark-gap transmitter. He says, "One, two, three, four, is it snowing where you are Mr. Thiessen? If it is, would you telegraph back to me?" Mr. Thiessen, one mile way, heard the transmission. Fessenden's voice is the first ever to be transmitted by radio waves and heard by another person.
	Hollerith introduces the automatic card feed into his tabulating machine to improve the data processing of the 1900 census.
	The telegraph now connects most of the civilized world.
1901 December 12	Marconi believes that he hears the letter "S" transmitted by Morse Code from Poldhu to Signal Hill, St. Johns Newfoundland. For many years this feat is considered the first transatlantic radio transmission but later researchers will conclude that the reception was not possible, and that Marconi may have heard static caused by lightning instead of transmitted information.
1902	Arthur Korn invents an effective system of telephotography.
1904	Ira Rubel develops the first commercial lithographic offset system for printing on paper.
1905	James Ambrose Fleming invents the two-element vacuum tube, or diode, an essential step in the development of radio and later electronic computing.
1906	Lee de Forest introduces a third electrode called the grid into the vacuum tube. The resulting *triode* can be used both as an amplifier and a switch.
1907 July 17	Newspaper publisher E.W. Scripps combines three regional news services into the United Press Associations, the forerunner of UPI.

1908	Percy Ludgate designs a new version of Babbage's mechanical analytical engine, of which he publishes a brief description in 1909, and creates engineering drawings. The machine is never constructed, and the drawings are lost. **(See Reading 6.3.)**
1910	8468 new books are published in the United Kingdom this year.
1911	Hollerith sells Tabulating Machine Company to Charles R. Flint.
	Flint, a noted trust organizer, merges the Tabulating Machine Company with the Computing Scale Company, the International Time Recording Company, and the Bundy Manufacturing Company to form the Computing-Tabulating-Recording Company (C-T-R), producing and selling Hollerith tabulating equipment, time clocks, and other business machinery.
	James Powers begins manufacturing a punched-card system that competes with Hollerith's, operating mechanically rather than electrically. His machines are eventually made and sold by Remington Rand.
	Leonardo Torres y Quevedo builds the first decision-making automaton—a chess-playing machine that pits the machine's rook and king against the king of a human opponent. It is fully automatic with electrical sensing of the pieces on the board and a mechanical arm to move its own pieces.
1912	Brunsviga boasts that they have sold twenty thousand calculators based on the variable-toothed gear technology.
1914	Torres y Quevedo publishes *Ensayos sobre Automática*, which shows that he "would have been capable of building a general-purpose electromechanical computer had the practical need, motivation and financing been available." (Lee)
	Thomas J. Watson becomes president of C-T-R, and focuses the company on electric card-tabulating equipment for businesses.
1914	Edward Kleinschmidt invents the teletype, which replaces Morse code clickers in delivering news to newspapers. The teletype is first used by United Press.
July 24–27	The Napier Tercentenary Celebration is held in Edinburgh, though the mathematical meeting scheduled to follow it is canceled because war is considered imminent. The conference results in two scholarly publications on logarithms, mathematical tables, and mechanical calculators. These summarize both historical and current information for the period up to World War I. **(See Readings 3.2 and 6.3.)**
August 1–3	Germany declares war on Russia (August 1) and on France (August 3). World War I begins.
1915	Alexander Graham Bell in New York and Thomas J. Watson in San Francisco participate in the first transcontinental telephone call.
	Leopold Löwenheim publishes *Über Möglichkeiten im Relativkalkül,* containing the first appearance of what is now known as the Löwenheim-Skolem theorem, the first theorem of modern logic, anticipating Gödel's completeness theorem of 1930.
1917	Lenin and the Bolsheviks seize power in Russia.
	Johann Radon demonstrates that the image of a three-dimensional object can be constructed from an infinite number of two-dimensional images of the object. About sixty-five years later this will be demonstrated with the invention of computed tomography.
1918 October 19	The American Engineering Standards Committee (AESC) is formed by the American Institute of Electrical Engineers (now IEEE), the American Society of Mechanical Engineers (ASME), American Society of Civil Engineers (ASCE), American Institute of Mining and Metallurgical Engineers (AIMME) and the American Society for Testing Materials (ASTM). Its purpose is to establishing a national body to coordinate standards development and to serve as a clearinghouse for the work of standards developing agencies. The U.S. Departments of War, Navy and Commerce are invited to join this organization. AESC will become the American National Standards Institute (ANSI) in 1969.
November 11	Germany signs the Armistice, ending World War I.
1919	Early versions of the Enigma cipher machine are built in Europe.

	Eight hundred thousand Burroughs calculating machines have been sold worldwide.
1920	Karel Èapek publishes *R. U. R. (Rossum's Universal Robots)* in Prague. This play, written in Czech except for the title, introduces the word "robot," and explores the issue of whether worker-machines will replace people.
	Albert Skolem proves the Löwenheim-Skolem theorem, a landmark in computational logic.
1922	Lewis Fry Richardson, an early advocate of the team approach to the solution of large-scale computing problems, publishes *Weather Forecasting by Numerical Process,* in which he describes a fantasy weather forecast "factory" of sixty-four thousand human computers working in "a large hall like a theatre," calculating the world's weather forecasts from meteorological data supplied by weather balloons spaced two hundred kilometers apart around the globe.
1923	Vladimir Zworykin, a Russian immigrant to the United States, patents the "iconoscope," the first electronic television camera.
1924	Watson, president of C-T-R, changes the name of the company to International Business Machines Corporation (IBM**).**
	In *Certain Factors Affecting Telegraph Speed,* Harry Nyquist analyzes factors affecting telegraph transmission speed. He also presents the first statement of a logarithmic law for communication, and the first examination of the theoretical bounds for ideal codes for the transmission of information.
1925	Walter Gifford, president of AT&T, creates Bell Telephone Laboratories.
	Bell Labs develops the first high-fidelity sound recording. It extends the reproducible sound range by more than an octave on the high and low end.
1926	David Baxandall compiles an annotated and well-illustrated catalogue of *Calculating Machines and Instruments* at the Science Museum, South Kensington. Machines on exhibition include those formerly owned by Babbage. This may be the earliest historical exhibition on computing.
1927 January 25	James Henry Rand, Jr., merges Rand-Kardex with Remington Typewriters and several other office supply companies to form Remington Rand.
April 9	Bell Labs and the U.S. Department of Commerce conduct the first long distance test of television between Washington D.C. and New York City, sending images of President Hoover over telephone lines.
1928	Returning to a question he had raised in 1900, Hilbert asks, "Is mathematics complete, is it consistent, and is it decidable?" Three years later, the first two of these questions will be answered in the negative by Kurt Godel. Working independently, Alonzo Church, Alan Turing, and Emil Post will publish answers to the third question in 1936**.**
	IBM adopts the eighty-column punched card, the standard for about the next fifty years.
	Philo T. Farnsworth introduces the first all-electronic television.
	Leslie J. Comrie discovers how to use a commercial accounting machine as a difference engine. With this technique he reforms the production of the Nautical Almanac.
	Comrie uses punched-card machines to calculate the motions of the moon. This project, in which twenty million holes are punched into five hundred thousand cards, continues into 1929. It is the first use of punched cards in a purely scientific application. **(See Reading 4.4.)**
	Ralph V. R. Hartley publishes *Transmission of Information*, in which he arrives at some of the fundamental ideas of the mathematical theory of communication.
	John von Neumann publishes the minimax theorem, inventing the theory of games. It will be used later in game-playing programs.
	Zworykin demonstrates an all-electronic television camera and receiver.
March	*Television. The World's First Television Journal*, begins publication in England. **(See Readings 5.5 and 5.6.)**

1929	Leo Szilard discovers a theoretical model that serves both as a heat engine and an information engine, establishing the connection between entropy and information. "Ueber die Entropieverminderung in einem thermodynamischen System bei Eingriffen intelligenter Wesen," *Zeits. f. Phys.* 53(1929): 840–56, translated as "On the Decrease of Entropy in a Thermodynamic System by the Intervention of Intelligent Beings."
1930	Vannevar Bush of MIT develops the differential analyzer, a large analog computer more accurate than previous devices of this type.
May 16	Texas Instruments is founded as Geophysical Service. Initially it is the first independent contractor specializing in the reflection seismograph method of exploration of oil fields in Texas.
1931	Gödel proves the incompleteness and inconsistency of arithmetic, and invents the theory of recursive functions.
1933	Edwin Howard Armstrong develops wide-band frequency modulation, later called FM radio.
January 30	Adolf Hitler seizes power in Germany.
1934	Konrad Zuse, a German mechanical engineer, realizes that an automatic calculator would need only a control, a memory, and an arithmetic unit.
1935	IBM manufactures the 601 multiplying punch.
	IBM markets the first commercially successful electric typewriter, the Electromatic. IBM will produce electric typewriters until 1990.
	The Social Security Act of 1935 requires the U. S. government to keep continuous records on the employment of 26 million individuals.
September	IBM's German subsidiary, Deutsche Hollerith Maschinen, introduces the Dehomag D11 tabulator, the first automatic sequence-controlled calculator. It has internal instructions programmed with a plug board.
1936	Bush begins the Rapid Arithmetical Machine Project at MIT. In a paper called "Instrumental Analysis," he suggests how an electromechanical machine might be built to accomplish Babbage's goals for the Analytical Engine. This is almost exactly one hundred years after Babbage began designing his Analytical Engine. In the same paper Bush writes that four billion punched cards are being used annually in electric tabulating machines. This amounts to ten thousand tons of cards.
	Church publishes his logical proof of the undecidability of arithmetic, using his lambda calculus. Turing publishes "On Computable Numbers," a mathematical description of what he calls "universal machine" that can, in principle, solve any mathematical problem that can be presented to it in symbolic form. Turing models the machine processes after the functional processes of a human carrying out mathematical computation. **(See Reading 7.1.)** Emil Post independently arrives at a similar idea. Church calls Turing's universal machine a "Turing Machine". **(See Reading 7.2.)**
	The BBC begins public television broadcasting in England. The transmissions reach only the 20,000 homes with television sets within a 35-mile range of Alexandria Palace. Each set costs £100—roughly the cost of a small car.
	Bell Labs produces the first electronic speech synthesizer, called the *Voder*. This machine will be demonstrated at the 1939 World Fair by experts that use a keyboard and foot pedals to play the machine and emit speech.
April 11	Zuse applies for a patent on his electromagnetic, program-controlled calculator, which he built in the living room of his parents' apartment in Berlin. It is the first freely programmable, binary-based calculating machine ever built, but it does not function reliably. The patent application is the only surviving documentation of his prewar work on computers.
1936–38	Turing spends more than a year at Princeton to study mathematical logic with Church, who is pursuing research in recursion theory.
1937	Turing and von Neumann have their first discussions about computing and what will later be called "artificial intelligence" (AI) at Princeton

	Believing that war with Germany is inevitable, Turing builds in a Princeton machine shop an experimental electromechanical cryptanalysis machine capable of binary multiplication.
	Comrie founds Scientific Computing Service, the first independent scientific computing service bureau in the world.**(See Reading 4.5.)**
	John Atanasoff at Iowa State University, Ames, Iowa, conceives of the Atanasoff-Berry Computer (ABC), a special-purpose electronic computer.
	George Stibitz, a research mathematician at Bell Telephone Labs in New York, builds a binary adder out of a few light bulbs, batteries, and relays on his kitchen table. His "Model K" (for "Kitchen") is the first electromechanical computer built in America.
	Howard Aiken drafts a proposal for an automatic calculating machine and joins with IBM to produce the Harvard Mark I, an electromechanical calculating machine that will eventually weigh five tons.
	Claude Shannon, in his master's thesis written in 1937 and published in 1938, shows that the two-valued algebra developed by Boole can be used as a basis for the design of electrical circuits. The thesis will be used as a basis for electro-mechanical and electronic computer circuit designs. **(See Reading 12.1.)**
1938	Zuse completes his Z-1 mechanical computer in his parents' Berlin apartment. Independently of Shannon, he develops a form of symbolic logic to assist in the design of the binary circuits. With Helmut Schreyer, he begins work on the Z-2.
	H. G. Wells publishes a book of essays and speeches entitled **World Brain** which includes an essay entitled "The Idea of a Permanent World Encyclopaedia." This essay first appeared in the new Encyclopédie Française, August, 1937. Another essay entitled "The Brain Organization of the Modern World" describes Wells' vision for "...a sort of mental clearing house for the mind, a depot where knowledge and ideas are received, sorted, summarized, digested, clarified and compared." (p. 49) Wells believes that technological advances such as microfilm could be utilized towards this end so that "any student, in any part of the world, will be able to sit with his projector in his own study at his or her convenience to examine *any* book, *any* document, in an exact replica." (p. 54)
	Chester F. Carlson invents xerography. It will not become a commercial success until the invention of the xerographic copier in 1959.
1939	Atanasoff begins work on his special-purpose ABC machine, the earliest electronic digital computer. It will never be properly operational.
	IBM starts construction on Aiken's Harvard Mark I.
	Zuse completes his Z2 machine, which has two hundred relays.
April	Stibitz and Samuel Williams of Bell Telephone Labs begin construction of the Complex Number Calculator (later known as the Bell Labs Model I). This machine will be called "the first electromechanical computer for routine use." It uses telephone relays and coded decimal numbers as groups of four binary digits (bits) each.
September 1	Germany invades Poland. World War II begins.
September 3	Britain and France declare war on Germany.
September 4	Turing reports to the Government Code and Cypher School, Bletchley Park, in the town of Bletchley.
October 15	Zuse's associate, Helmut Schreyer, writes a memorandum concerning the Z-2, *Rechnische Rechenmachine* (unpublished at the time), in which he also says it would be possible to build a computer with vacuum tubes that would process "10,000 operations per second."
1940	Shannon writes *Communication in the Presence of Noise*. Because of the war it will not be published until 1948.

	Actress Hedi Lamarr and composer George Antheil invent "frequency-hopping" transmission, now called spread-spectrum. In 1941 Lamarr patents this under her married name of H. K. Markey as "Secret Communication System." She assigns the patent to the U.S. Government. This early version of frequency hopping uses a piano-roll to change between 88 frequencies, and is intended to make radio-guided torpedoes harder for enemies to detect or to jam.
January 8	Bell Labs Complex Number Calculator is operational.
March 7	Bush writes a memorandum entitled "Arithmetical Machine." This shows that the Rapid Arithmetical Machine Project begun in 1936 is already well-advanced conceptually. Bush continues to focus most of his computational energy on building the Rockefeller Differential Analyzer II.
June 22	France signs an armistice with Germany, followed by an armistice with Italy, which entered the war on June 10. The Vichy government is established.
August	Atansoff writes a thirty-five-page memorandum describing the design and principles of the ABC machine. It remains unpublished until 1973.
September 11	Stibitz's Complex Number Calculator, an electromechanical relay machine located in New York, is demonstrated via a remote teletype terminal at the American Mathematical Association Meeting in Dartmouth, New Hampshire. Wiener and John Mauchly spend a lot of time experimenting with the system. This is the first demonstration of remote computing.
September 23	Inspired by the September 11 demonstration, Wiener sends a letter to Bush enclosing a "Memorandum on the Mechanical Solution of Partial Differential Equations." This outlines a machine that has all the features of an electronic digital computer except for a stored program. The memorandum is not published until it appears in Wiener's *Collected Works*. **(See Reading 7.3.)**
December	Mauchly meets Atanasoff at the Philadelphia meeting of the American Association of the Advancement of Science. After corresponding with him about electronic calculating, Mauchly visits Atanasoff in Iowa and reads the thirty-five-page memorandum on the ABC machine that Atanasoff had written in August.
Winter	Turing and Gordon Welchman at Bletchley Park design an improved Bombe cryptanalysis machine for deciphering Enigma messages.
1940–41	Max Newman and his team at Bletchley Park, including Turing, create the top-secret Heath Robinson cryptographic computer, named after the cartoonist-designer of fantastic machines. This special-purpose relay computer successfully decodes messages encrypted by Enigma, the Nazi's first-generation enciphering machine.
1941	Schreyer, Zuse's associate, receives his doctorate in telecommunications engineering with a dissertation on the use of vacuum-tube relays in switching circuits. He converts Zuse's logical designs into electronic circuits, building a simple prototype of an electronic computer, which achieves a switching frequency of 10,000 Hz.
	IBM announces the Electromatic Model 04 electric typewriter, featuring proportional spacing. By assigning varied rather than uniform spacing to different sized characters, the Type 4 recreates the appearance of a printed page, an effect that is enhanced by a typewriter ribbon innovation that produces clearer, sharper words on the page.
May 12	Zuse completes his Z3 machine—the world's first fully functional electromechanical digital computer—with twenty-four hundred relays. It runs programs punched into rolls of discarded movie film. In 1944 it will be destroyed in bombing raids.
Summer	Pres Eckert and Mauchly meet at the Moore School of Electrical Engineering, University of Pennsylvania, and begin discussions on electronic computing.
October 8	Edmund C. Berkeley, an actuary at the Prudential Insurance Company in Boston, writes a report on the possible application of Stibitz's Complex Number Calculator for insurance-company calculations.
December 7	Japan's attack on Pearl Harbor causes the United States to declare war on Japan. Within days Germany and Italy declare war on the United States.

1942	Atanasoff's special-purpose ABC machine is nearly operational when work on it is abandoned because of the war.
	Having collaborated with Julian Bigelow, an engineer, Wiener publishes, as a classified document, *The Extrapolation, Interpretation and Smoothing of Stationery Time Series*. This contains, according to Shannon, "the first clear-cut formulation of communication theory as a statistical problem, the study of operations on time series."
	Zuse starts work on the Z4 electromechanical computer.
	Bush completes the Rockefeller Differential Analyzer II, with increased accuracy and higher speed. It contains two thousand vacuum tubes and weighs about one hundred thousand pounds. For security reasons its existence is not publicized until October 1945.
August	Mauchly writes a privately circulated confidential memorandum on "The Use of High Speed Vacuum Tube Devices for Calculating."
1943	Turing consults with Shannon and Harry Nyquist at Bell Labs in New York concerning the encipherment of "speech signals" between Roosevelt and Churchill (Hodges).
	IBM develops the Vacuum Tube Multiplier. This experimental machine is the first complete machine ever to perform arithmetic electronically, substituting vacuum tubes for electric relays.
	Project Whirlwind starts as an analog flight simulator project at MIT.
	Warren McCulloch and Walter Pitts publish "A Logical Calculus of the Ideas Imminent in Nervous Activity," describing the "McCulloch-Pitts neuron," the first mathematical model of neural networks. Building on ideas in Turing's "On computable numbers," the paper provides a way to describe brain functions in abstract terms, and shows that simple elements connected in a network can have immense computational power. It receives little attention until its ideas are applied by von Neumann, Wiener, and others. **(See Reading 7.4.)**
	Pitts, an autodidact without a high school or college diploma, accepts a position at MIT to work with Norbert Wiener.
	Mathematical Tables and Other Aids to Computation (MTAC), the world's first computing journal, begins publication. At this time mathematical tables prepared by human computers are the primary calculating aid. The journal will report on the new electromechanical and electronic "aids to computation" as they are developed.
1943 January	Aiken's electromechanical Harvard Mark I operates at IBM Endicott Labs in New York under wartime security. This is one of the first two programmed computers built by Americans.
April 8	With the goal of speeding up the calculation of artillery firing tables, Eckert and Mauchly of the Moore School submit a proposal to the Ballistic Research Laboratory at Aberdeen Proving Ground. It is entitled *Report on an Electronic Difference Analyzer*. The name tries to make the distinction between the electromechanical analog differential analyzer that the United States Army is currently using and the new electronic digital machine that will be developed. The proposal is submitted to army ordnance in May. When the first contracts are signed between the United States Army and the Moore School, the name of the machine is changed to "Electronic Numerical Integrator." Because Mauchly stresses that the machine can be used for more general problems, the device is called an "Electronic Numerical Integrator and Computer (ENIAC)." Eckert is appointed laboratory supervisor and chief engineer on the project. Mauchly, along with Eckert, is put in charge of engineering and testing.
May 31	Construction of the ENIAC starts at the Moore School. The actual contract between the Moore School and the army does not go into effect until July 1. For security reasons, the understandable rumor that the project is a "white elephant" is promoted rather than denied.
September	The Bell Labs Relay Interpolator (later called the Model II) operates for the first time. Using programs from punched tape this is possibly the first computer to run programs in the United States.
November 11	Schreyer's small prototype of an electronic computer is damaged in an air raid on Germany. The machine will be lost soon thereafter.

1944	Erwin Schrödinger publishes *What is Life? The Physical Aspect of the Living Cell*, a popularization of ideas about the physical basis of biological phenomena developed by Max Delbrück and N. V. Timofeeff-Ressovsky in a paper published in 1935. The work influences the young James D. Watson and others. Sydney Brenner points out a fundamental mistake in Schrödinger's understanding of how genes would operate: "Anyway, the key point is that Schrödinger says that the chromosomes contain the information to specify the future organism and the means to execute it. I have come to call this 'Schrödinger's fundamental error.' In describing the structure of the chromosome fibre as a code script he states that. 'The chromosome structures are at the same time instrumental in bringing about the development they foreshadow. They are code law and executive power, or to use another simile, they are the architect's plan and the builder's craft in one.' [Schrödinger, p. 20,]. What Schrödinger is saying here is that the chromosomes not only contain a description of the future organism, but also the means to implement the description, or program, as we might call it. And that is wrong! The chromosomes contain the information to specify the future organism and a description of the means to implement this, but not the means themselves. This logical difference was made crystal clear to me when I read the von Neumann article [Hixon Symposium] because he very clearly distinguishes between the things that read the program and the program itself. In other words, the program has to build the machinery to execute itself." (Brenner, *My Life*, 33–34)
January 29	Eckert submits a report entitled *Disclosure of Magnetic Calculating Machine*, which briefly describes means for storing data on magnetic disks and also the storing of programs on disks.
February	The top-secret Colossus programmable cryptanalysis machine designed by Tommy Flowers and his team is completed at Bletchley Park to crack the higher level encryption of the Nazi Lorenz SZ40 machine. It employs vacuum tubes and is between one hundred and one thousand times faster than Heath Robinson. By the end of the war there will be ten Colossi operating. They enable the decryption of sixty-three million characters of high-grade German messages. Even though these machines incorporate special purpose features of special purpose electronic digital computers, and have incalculable influence on the outcome of WWII, they will have little influence, in the conventional sense, on the development of future computing technology because they will remain top secret until about 1970.
May	Aiken's Mark I moves from IBM Endicott Labs to Harvard University where it is officially operational. The machine solves addition problems in less than a second, multiplication in six seconds, and division in 12 seconds. Grace Hopper writes some of its first programs, which run on punched tape.
July	Eckert has two accumulators of the ENIAC operational.
September	Von Neumann visits the ENIAC two-accumulator system for the first time, and becomes deeply interested in the project.
September 27	Eckert and Mauchly state that their conception of the ENIAC is complete. Eckert writes a letter to other members of the project asking them to state written claims to inventions on the project. None is received.
October	The United States Army extends the ENIAC contract to cover research on the planned EDVAC stored-program computer.
December	IBM produces the Pluggable Sequence Relay Calculator (PSRC) for the United States Army at Aberdeen Proving Ground. This special-purpose punched-card calculator developed by IBM for the United States Army for calculating artillery firing trajectories, is capable of performing a sequence of up to fifty arithmetic steps. For the rest of the war these punched-card calculators, programmed with plug boards, remain the fastest digital calculators in the United States. "These are the fastest relay calculators in operation; they perform six multiplications a second together with a great deal of addition, subtraction, reading, writing and consulting tables. They are not as elaborate as the Sequence Calculator at Harvard in that they have less storage capacity and less sequencing facilities; however, they are about twenty times as fast. Consequently, for those problems which can be handled in this way, they will do in one day what the Sequence Calculator will do in twenty days." (W.J. Eckert, 1947) http://www.columbia.edu/acis/history/aberdeen.html
1945	Zuse completes the Z4 shortly before V-E Day. It is a large, electromechanical programmable machine, the construction of which began about 1943. The machine is dismantled and shipped from Berlin to a village in the Bavarian Alps. In 1950 it is refurbished, modified, and installed at ETH in Zurich. For several years it is the only working electronic digital computer in continental Europe.
	Use of telegraphy peaks in the United States with the transmission of 236,169,000,000 messages.

Spring	The ENIAC, the world's first large-scale, electronic, general-purpose, digital computing machine, is completed and tested at the Moore School. With eighteen thousand vacuum tubes and weighing thirty tons, it is about one thousand times faster than the Harvard Mark I. The ENIAC is programmed by time-consuming plugging of patch cords from buses to panels for each individual problem. The ENIAC remains the only operational electronic digital computer in the world until the short-lived Manchester "Baby" prototype becomes operational in 1948.
April 25	The collapse of the Third Reich occurs after the meeting of Western and Russian armies at Torgau in Saxony.
May	A preliminary version of *First Draft on a Report on the EDVAC* is circulated to von Neumann's collaborators on this informal document.
May 7–8	The unconditional surrender of Germany takes place.
Summer	Hopper, working on construction of Aiken's Harvard Mark II, finds that a large moth beaten to death by a relay has caused the relay to fail. She removes the bug and enters the dead insect into a log book with the note, "First actual case of bug being found." This is first use of the term "bug" and the concept of "debugging" within the context of computing.
June 30	Von Neumann's office privately circulates the *First Draft on a Report on the EDVAC* to twenty-four people connected with the EDVAC project. This document, written between February and June, provides the first theoretical description of the basic details of a stored-program computer. Specific hardware is not mentioned in order to avoid the government's security classification, and to avoid engineering problems that might detract from the logical considerations under discussion. Influenced by Turing and by McCulloch and Pitts, von Neumann patterns the machine to some degree after human thought processes. **(See Reading 8.1.)**
July	Bush publishes his article "As We May Think," describing the futuristic "memex system," a microfilm machine capable of making permanent associative links in information. This hypothetical machine foreshadows aspects of the personal computer and the hyperlinks on the World Wide Web. **(See Reading 13.1.)**
August 14	The surrender of Japan marks the end of World War II.
Fall	Turing arrives at the National Physical Laboratory, Teddington, England, to work on the Automatic Computing Engine (ACE).
After September	Aiken publishes *Tables of the Modified Hankel Functions of Order One-Third and of Their Derivatives*. These tables, calculated by the Harvard Mark I, are the first published mathematical tables calculated by a programmed automatic computer, finally fulfilling the dream of Charles Babbage first expressed in 1822. They require the equivalent of forty-five days of computer time. Prior to the Mark I they would have required years of human computation.
November 30	Eckert, Mauchly, Brainerd, and Herman Goldstine issue the first confidential published report on the completed ENIAC, discussing how it operates and the methods by which it is programmed. **(See Reading 8.2.)**
Late 1945	Project Whirlwind switches from analog to digital electronics.
1946	The Moore School lectures on "The theory and techniques for design of electronic digital computers" take place. This series of lectures, attended by twenty-eight highly qualified experts, leads to widespread adoption of the EDVAC-type design, including stored programs, for nearly all subsequent computer development. On July 15 Eckert lectures on "A preview of a digital computing machine." He proposes replacing the three different kinds of memory used in the ENIAC (flip-flops in accumulators, function tables [read-only memory] and interconnecting cables with switches) with a single erasable high-speed memory, the mercury delay-line memory that he invented for this purpose.
	Aiken and Hopper publish *A Manual of Operation for the Automatic Sequence Controlled Calculator*. The instruction sequences scattered throughout this volume are among the earliest examples of digital computer programs.**(See Reading 9.1.)**
	There are six television stations in the United States.

	Turing prepares a typed proposal, "Proposed electronic calculator," outlining the development of the ACE.
February 14	The ENIAC is publicly unveiled in Philadelphia.
March	Von Neumann attempts to set up an electronic stored-program computer project at the Institute for Advanced Study (IAS) at Princeton. He tries to hire Eckert, who refuses the job.
March 15	Eckert and Mauchly leave the Moore School, and establish their own firm, Electronic Control Company. This is the first electronic computer company in the world. Their business plan states that they expect to sell an electronic computer for between $5000 and $30,000.
June	Bigelow, who previously collaborated with Wiener, joins von Neumann and Goldstine at the IAS Electronic Computer Project.
June 28	Burks, von Neumann, and Goldstine issue their *Preliminary Discussion of the Logical Design of an Electronic Computing Instrument*, discussing ideas to be incorporated into the stored-program computer at the IAS. **(See Reading 8.3.)**
July	Max Newman founds the computer laboratory at Manchester University via a grant from the Royal Society.
1947	EDVAC information is declassified.
	Louis Couffignal and Louis Brillouin hold a small conference on "large computers" in Paris, at which Couffignal discusses French work and Brillouin summarizes American accomplishments in electronic digital computing. Couffignal decides against building a stored-program computer, thus helping France to fall behind England and America in this technology; the first stored-program computer in France will not be manufactured until 1956. The government agency where Couffignal works, Centre National de la Recherche Scientifique (CNRS), does not obtain a stored-program computer (a British model) until 1955.
	Design of Whirlwind I begins at MIT.
	Working at the IAS, Andrew D. Booth, and Kathleen Britten write the program for realizing a translation dictionary on an electronic computing machine, provided that the necessary storage capacity is available. This may be the earliest work leading toward machine translation.
	The ENIAC is converted into an elementary stored-program computer via the use of function tables.
	The Fotosetter, the first phototypesetter, is invented. The first phototypesetters are mechanical devices that replace the metal type matrices with matrices carrying the image of the letters. They replace the caster with a photographic unit.
January 7–10	The first large conference on electronic and electromechanical digital computers is held at Cambridge, Massachusetts. About 250 people attend. At the conference Samuel H. Caldwell suggests the formation of an organization of people engaged in this new field. In September 1947 the Eastern Association for Computing Machinery will hold its first meeting.
February 20	In a speech at the London Mathematical Society that will remain unpublished until many years after his death, Turing states that "digital computing machines such as the ACE. . . are in fact practical versions of the universal machine."
April	The first part of Goldstine and von Neumann's *Planning and Coding Problems for an Electronic Computing Instrument* is published. The remaining two parts appear on April 15 and August 16, 1948. This is the first theoretical discussion of programming for stored program computers—none of which yet operate. **(See Reading 9.2.)**
April 8	Eckert and Mauchly learn from a patent lawyer that von Neumann's *First Draft of a Report on the EDVAC* is a publication barring their patenting the ENIAC because it was issued more than a year before they planned to apply for a patent.
April 24	Electronic Control Company (Eckert and Mauchly) develops the tentative instruction code C-1 for what they call "a Statistical EDVAC." This is the earliest document on the programming of an electronic digital computer intended for commercial use. **(See Reading 9.3.)**

May 24	The "Statistical EDVAC" is renamed the UNIVAC.
June 26	Eckert and Mauchly apply for the broad ENIAC patent, essentially a patent on the stored-program electronic digital computer, basing their description of the machine to a large extent on the government report they issued on November 30, 1945. **(See Reading 8.10.)**
Summer	Bigelow and his team redesign the IAS machine to include error checking and parallel processing, essential features of what will become known as the "von Neumann architecture".
September 15	The Eastern Association for Computing Machinery, predecessor of the Association for Computing Machinery (ACM), holds its first meeting at Columbia University in New York. Seventy-eight people attend. John H. Curtiss is elected president, Mauchly, vice president, and Berkeley, secretary.
October	Northrop Aviation places the contract for the BINAC (BINary Automatic Computer) with Eckert and Mauchly's Electronic Control Company. The BINAC will consist of two identical serial computers operating in parallel with mercury delay-line memory and magnetic tape as a secondary memory and auxiliary input device.
December	The point-contact transistor is invented at Bell Labs by John Bardeen, Walter Brattain, and William Shockley. Much smaller than vacuum tubes and consuming only a fraction of the energy, the transistor is able to switch currents on and off at substantially higher speeds.
Late 1947	The first brochure advertising UNIVAC is issued by Eckert and Mauchly's Electronic Control Company. This is the first sales brochure ever issued for an electronic digital computer.
1948	A contract is drawn up between Eckert and Mauchly and the United States Census Bureau for the production of UNIVAC.
	IBM produces the 604 multiplying punch based on vacuum-tube technology. The mass-produced 604 features the industry's first assemblage of digital electronics replaceable as a unit. This card tabulator remains a workhorse for scientific and business use, even though it has to be wired with a plugboard.
	Wiener publishes *Cybernetics or Control and Communication in the Animal and the Machine*, a widely read and influential book that applies theories of information and communication to both biological systems and machines. This is also the first conventionally published book to discuss electronic digital computing. Writing as a mathematician rather than an engineer, Wiener's discussion is theoretical rather than specific. Computer-related words with the "cyber" prefix, including "cyberspace," originate from Wiener's book.
	IBM announces its first large-scale digital calculating machine, the Selective Sequence Electronic Calculator (SSEC). The SSEC is the first computer that can modify a stored program. It features 12,000 vacuum tubes and 21,000 electromechanical relays.
	Andrew D. Booth creates a magnetic drum memory, which is two inches long and two inches wide and capable of holding 10 bits per inch. He will offer it for sale in 1952.
	Columbia Records introduces the Long Playing record with 17 minutes of music on each side.
June	John Walston introduces cable television, initially in the mountains of Pennsylvania.
June 21	The Manchester University "Baby" prototype computer runs its first program, written by Kilburn. This small pilot version of a larger computer was built at the University of Manchester in England to demonstrate the Williams-Kilburn CRT memory. The Manchester "Baby" is the first stored-program electronic digital computer. It operates for only a short time.
July–August	Turing writes a report for the National Physical Laboratory entitled "Intelligent Machinery," in which he reasons that a thinking machine should be given the blank mind of an infant instead of an adult mind filled with opinions and ideas. He estimates it will take a battery of programmers fifty years to bring this learning machine from childhood to adult mental maturity.
July and October	Shannon publishes his *Mathematical Theory of Communication*. The theory determines how much information can be sent per unit of time in a system with a given, limited amount of transmission power. Shannon also introduces the term "bit" into the literature and provides its current meaning in the context of information. **(See Reading 12.2.)**

September	Turing joins the computer project at Manchester University as chief programmer.
September 9	With the completion of the second module of the computer (the first was completed in August), the BINAC is operational. Among its numerous innovations are germanium diodes in the logic processing hardware—probably the first application of semiconductors in computers. Until its delivery to Northrop Aviation in September 1949, the BINAC remains in Philadelphia for use in numerous sales demonstrations.
September 20	At the Hixon Symposium in Pasadena, California, von Neumann delivers his *General and Logical Theory of Automata*, the first of a series of five works (some posthumous) in which he attempts to develop a precise mathematical theory allowing comparison of computers and the human brain.
1949	Berkeley publishes *Giant Brains or Machines That Think*, the first popular book on electronic digital computers. This book contains a discussion about a machine called "Simon," which has been called the first personal computer. **(See Reading 8.6.)**
	Hopper leaves Harvard to join Eckert-Mauchly Computer Corporation as a senior mathematician/programmer.
	In his novel *1984,* George Orwell creates a world in which totalitarian bureaucracies use computers to enslave populations.
	René Higonnet and Louis Moyroud invent the Lithomat in France. It is the first successful phototypesetting machine. Later models called Lumitype can print more than 28,000 characters per hour.
	10,000,000 television sets have been sold.
March 15 & March 21	The United States Census Bureau writes test programs for the BINAC. These manuscript programs, dated March 15 and March 21, are possibly among the earliest extant programs for a stored-program computer built in the United States.
May 6	Wilkes's EDSAC is fully operational at Cambridge, England. On May 6 it runs a program written by Wilkes for calculating a table of squares. It also runs a program written by David Wheeler for calculating a sequence of prime numbers, becoming the first easily used, fully functional stored-program computer to run a program.
June 9	Geoffrey Jefferson, a neurological surgeon at Manchester, delivers a speech entitled "The mind of mechanical man," in which he discusses the differences between computers and the human brain. **(See Reading 11.1).**
July 15	Warren Weaver circulates a memorandum entitled "Translation," suggesting that language translation by computer might be possible. **(See Reading 10.1.)**
Summer	Mauchly conceives the Short Code, the first high-level programming language for an electronic computer, to be used with the BINAC. It first runs on UNIVAC I, serial 1, in 1950.

September 20	At the Hixon Symposium in Pasadena, California John von Neumann speaks on "The general and logical theory of automata." Within this speech he compares the functions of genes to self-reproducing automata. "For instance, it is quite clear that the instruction I is roughly effecting the functions of a gene. It is also clear that the copying mechanism B performs the fundamental act of reproduction, the duplication of the genetic material, which is clearly the fundamental operation in the multiplication of living cells. It is also easy to see how arbitrary alterations of the system E, and in particular of I, can exhibit certain typical traits which appear in connection with mutation, which is lethality as a rule, but with a possibility of continuing reproduction with a modification of traits." (pp. 30–31). Sydney Brenner reads and is influenced by this brief discussion of the gene within the context of information when the Hixon Symposium is published in 1951. Jeffress, Lloyd A. (ed.) *Cerebral Mechanisms in Behavior.* The Hixon Symposium. New York: John Wiley, 1951. "The brilliant part of this paper in the *Hixon Symposium* is his description of it takes to make a self-reproducing machine. Von Neumann shows that you have to have a mechanism not only of copying the *machine*, but of copying the *information* that specifies the machine. So he divided the machine—the *automaton* as he called it—into three components; the functional part of the automaton, a decoding section which actually takes a tape, reads the instructions and builds the automaton; and a device that takes a copy of this tape and inserts it into the new automaton." Brenner, *My Life in Science*, p. 33: "I think that because of the cultural differences between most biologists on the one hand, and physicists and mathematicians on the other, it had absolutely no impact at all. Of course I wasn't smart enough to really see then that this is what DNA and the genetic code was all about. And it is one of the ironies of this entire field that were you to write a history of ideas in the whole of DNA, simply from the documented information as it exists in the literature—that is, a kind of Hegelian history of ideas—you would certainly say that Watson and Crick depended upon von Neumann, because von Neumann essentially tells you how it's done. But of course no one knew anything about the other. It's a great paradox to me that in fact this connection was not seen." (Brenner, *My Life* 35–36).
November	The first test program is run on Trevor Pearcey and Maston Beard's CSIRAC, the first stored-program computer in Australia. Excluding the BINAC, which only operated for a short time, this is one of three stored-program computers operating in the world at this time.
1950	Turing publishes *"Computing Machinery and Intelligence,"* in which he describes the "Turing test" for determining whether a machine is "intelligent". **(See Reading 11.2)**
	Jule Charney, Agnar Fjörtoff, and John von Neumann publish "Numerical Integration of the Barotropic Vorticity Equation," the first weather forecast by electronic computer, which takes twenty-four hours of processing time on the ENIAC to calculate a twenty-four hour forecast.
	Engineering Research Associates publishes *High-Speed Computing Devices*, the first textbook on how to build an electronic digital computer. In the form of a "cookbook," it describes available computer components and how they work. It has extensive, up-to-date bibliographies of the American computing literature and some of the English.
	Wilkes, Wheeler, and Stanley Gill issue *Report on the Preparation of Programmes for the EDSAC and the Use of the Library of Subroutines.* This dittoed document is the first treatise on software written for an operational stored-program computer. The book describes "assemblers" and "subroutines" — segments of programs that are frequently used, so they can be kept in "libraries" and reused as needed in many software applications. The Cambridge group thus introduces the concept of reusable code, one of the principal tools for reducing software bugs and improving the productivity of programmers. It will be published as a printed book, with some changes and a new title, in 1951. **(See Reading 9.4.)**
	The Diners' Club issues the first credit card, invented by Diners' Club founder Frank McNamara. It allows members to charge the cost of restaurant bills only.
	Richard W. Hamming publishes *Error Detecting and Error Codes.* **(See Reading 12.3.)**
	11638 new books are published in the United Kingdom.
Early 1950	Project Whirlwind is in limited operation at MIT as a general purpose computer.
February 6	Eckert-Mauchly Computer Corporation is sold to Remington Rand.
March	Shannon publishes "Programming a computer for playing chess," the first technical paper on this topic.**(See Reading 11.3.)**

November	In an article published in *Scientific American* about "Simon," the first personal computer, Berkeley predicts that "some day we may even have small computers in our homes, drawing energy from electric power lines like refrigerators or radios".
1951	IBM decides to produce their first electronic computer, the 701, a machine for scientific applications based on the Princeton IAS design.
	Three-dimensional magnetic-core memory replaces electrostatic memory on the Whirlwind I, leading to increased performance and reliability.
January 8–13	The Paris symposium on "Calculating Machines and Human Thought" takes place. Unlike the other early computer conferences, there is no demonstration of a stored-program electronic digital computer; Couffignal demonstrates the prototype of his non-stored-program machine.
February	The first Ferranti Mark I version of the Manchester University machine is delivered to Manchester University. The Mark I is the first commercially produced electronic digital computer to be delivered to a customer.
March 31	UNIVAC I, serial 1, is signed over to the United States Census Bureau. The official dedication occurs on June 14, 1951. Excluding the unique BINAC, the UNIVAC I is the first electronic computer to be commercially manufactured in the United States. Its development precedes the British Ferranti Mark I, but this British machine is actually delivered to its first customer one month earlier than the UNIVAC I. Though the United States Census Bureau owns UNIVAC I, serial 1, Eckert-Mauchly division of Remington Rand retains it in Philadelphia for sales demonstration purposes, and does not actually install it at government offices for twenty-one months.
April	Whirlwind I begins operation. It includes the first primitive graphics display on its vectorscope screen. **(See Reading 8.7.)**
July 9–12	The second English electronic computer conference is held at Manchester to inaugurate the first Ferranti Mark I. There Wilkes introduces the term "microprogramming," referring to the design of control circuits. The idea is not widely accepted until the following decade. **(See Reading 8.8.)**
July 9–12	Bertram V. Bowden, the first computer salesman in England, discusses "The application of calculating machines to business and commerce" at the second English electronic computer conference. **(See Reading 10.2.)**
July 9–12	At the same conference J. M. Bennett and John Kendrew describe their use of the Cambridge EDSAC for the computation of Fourier Syntheses in the calculation of structure factors of the protein molecule, myoglobin. This is the first application of an electronic computer to computational biology. **(See Reading 10.3.)**
November 1.	LEO I (*Lyons Electronic Office*) is fully operational at J. Lyons and Company in England. This adaptation of the EDSAC is the first electronic digital computer to run business programs on a routine basis.
1952	The EDVAC, planning for which had started in 1944, with development starting in 1947–48, is finally finished at the Moore School. By this time it is essentially obsolete.
	Manufacturers begin producing vacuum tubes specially designed for use in digital circuits.
	Three-dimensional magnetic-core memory replaces electrostatic memory on the Whirlwind I, leading to increased performance and reliability.
	Compagnie des Machines Bull, the first French electronic computer manufacturer, produces its Gamma 3 electronic calculator. It is not a stored-program computer.
	Hopper writes the first compiler (A-0) for UNIVAC.
	Hopper publishes "The Education of a Computer," in which she describes fundamental principles in programming and anticipates future developments. **(See Reading 9.5.)**
January	Sergei Lebedev has MESM, the first Russian stored-program computer, operational.
April 30–May 2	The first electronic computer symposium on the west coast of the United States is held in Los Angeles.

June 10	The IAS computer is fully operational at Princeton.
September	Heinz Billing's G1 is in full operation at the Max Planck Institute in Göttingen, directed by Werner Heisenberg. It is the first electronic computer in Germany. It uses drum memory, but it is not a stored-program machine.
September 8–10	The ACM holds a special meeting in Toronto in honor of the installation of the first electronic digital computer in Canada, installed at the University of Toronto. It is a Ferranti Mark I (FERUT).
October	Berkeley begins publication of *Computing Machinery Field,* the first journal on electronic computing, and the ancestor of all commercially published periodical publications on computing. The first three quarterly issues are mimeographed. By the March 1953 issue the title is changed to *Computers and Automation.*
October 24	The UNIVAC Short Code II is developed. This is the earliest extant version of a high-level programming language actually intended to be used on an electronic digital computer.
November 4	UNIVAC I, serial 5, used by the CBS television network, successfully predicts the election of Dwight D. Eisenhower as president of the United States. This is the first time that millions of people see and hear about an electronic computer. The machine is later installed at Lawrence Livermore Laboratories in Livermore, California.
December	IBM introduces the 701, their first stored-program electronic digital computer for commercial production. Designed by Nathaniel Rochester, and based on the IAS machine at Princeton, it is intended for scientific use. Feeling that the word "computer" is too closely associated with UNIVAC, IBM calls the 701 an "electronic data processing machine." IBM eventually sells nineteen of these machines. **(See Reading 8.9.)**
1953	Bertram V. Bowden, computer salesman for Ferranti Limited, edits *Faster than Thought,* the first widely read English book on electronic digital computing. It will remain in print without change until 1968.
	Richard W. Appel and other students at Harvard Business school issue the first report on the applications of electronic computers to business. The report is issued before any electronic computer is delivered to an American corporation. **(See Reading 10.4.)**
	Charles Townes invents the MASER (Microwave Amplification by Stimulated Emission of Radiation). It is a precursor to the LASER that amplifies light.
April 25	James D. Watson and Francis Crick discover the self-complimentary double-helical structure of the DNA molecule. James D. Watson and Francis H. C. Crick, "Molecular Structure of Nucleic Acids. A Structure for Deoxyribose Nucleic Acid." *Nature* 171 (1953): 737–38. In this paper they state that, "It has not escaped our notice that the specific pairing we have postulated immediately suggests a possible copying mechanism for the genetic material." "We have also been stimulated by a knowledge of the general nature of the unpublished experimental results and ideas of Dr. M.H.F. Wilkins, Dr. R.E. Franklin and their co-workers at King's College, London."
May 30	Watson and Crick publish "Genetical Implications of the Structure of Deoxyribonucleic Acid" in *Nature.* In this paper they propose DNA's means of replication. This discovery has been called as significant, or possibly even more significant, than the original discovery of the structure of the DNA.
September	IBM announces the development of the 702, a version of the 701 designed for business rather than scientific applications.
1954	English Electric constructs a commercial version of Turing's Pilot ACE called DEUCE. Thirty-three of the machines will be sold, the last in 1962.
	George Gamov comes up with the idea of a genetic code: "Possible Mathematical Relation between Deoxyribonucleic Acids and Proteins," *Det. Kongelige Danske Videnskabernes Selskab: Biologiske Meddeleiser* 22, no. 3 (1954): 1–13. In the fall of 1953 Gamov gave Crick an earlier draft of this paper entitled "Protein synthesis by DNA molecules." "Gamov's scheme was decisive, Crick has often said since, because it forced him, and soon others, to begin to think hard and from a particular slant—that of the coding problem—about the next stage now that the structure of DNA was known." (Judson, *Eighth Day of Creation,* 236).

	IBM announces the 704. It is the first commercially available computer to incorporate indexing and floating point arithmetic as standard features. The 704 also features a magnetic core memory, far more reliable than its predecessors' cathode-ray-tube memories. A commercial success, IBM will produce 123 704s between 1955 and 1960.
	UNIVAC I, serial 8, is installed at General Electric Appliance Park outside Louisville, Kentucky. It is the first electronic computer sold to a nongovernmental customer in the United States.
	J. H. Laning and Neil Zierler develop an algebraic compiler for the Whirlwind I, the first high-level algebraic language for a computer.
	IBM develops and builds the fastest, most powerful electronic computer of its time—the Naval Ordnance Research Computer (NORC)—for the U.S. Navy Bureau of Ordnance. The NORC's multiplication unit remains the fastest ever built with vacuum tube technology. IBM introduces the input-output channel as a feature on the NORC. This innovation synchronizes the flow of data into and out of the computer while computation is in progress, relieving the central processor of that task.
	The first commercial transistor radio, Regency, designed by Texas Instruments, is built and marketed by IDEA Corporation.
January	*Journal of the Association of Computing Machinery* begins publication. The ACM has twelve hundred members.
January 22	The Federal Communications Commission approves the National Television Committee's recommendation for a system of color television broadcasting based on RCA's Dot Sequential Color System.
March 24	RCA begins manufacture of its twelve-inch model CT100 color television set. It uses phosphor dots deposited on an internal glass plate. It costs $1,000.00. 5000 of these sets will be produced.
May 10	Texas Instruments manufactures the first silicon transistor.
May 13–14	Hopper organizes the first symposium strictly on software for the Office of Naval Research. **(See Reading 9.6.)**
June 7	Alan Turing dies at the age of forty-two, having eaten cyanide injected into an apple.
October	FACOM, built by Fuji Communications Apparatus Manufacturing Company from forty-five hundred relays, is "the first commercial relay computer in Japan."
November 10	IBM announces the specifications for FORTRAN (FORmula TRANSlation), a computer language based on algebra, grammar and syntax rules. It is the first scientific programming language.
December	The first electronic digital computer in Italy, the FINAC version of Ferranti Mark I, somewhat modified from the English design, arrives at INAC (Istituto Nazionale per le Applicazioni del Calcolo) in Rome.
1955	The first IBM 702, an electronic computer for commercial applications, is delivered.
	IBM introduces the IBM 608 transistor calculator, the first all solid-state computing machine commercially marketed.
	Development begins on the SAGE Air Defense System, using a computer built by IBM after a design based on the Whirlwind. It includes the first light pen. The full SAGE system is completed by 1963.
	IBM develops magnetic core storage units, a dramatic improvement over cathode ray tube memory technology. By successfully adapting pill-making machines for production, IBM greatly improves the manufacture of these tiny, "doughnut" shaped, iron oxide cores, making the cores reliable and cost effective enough to serve as the basic technology behind every computer's main memory until the early 1970s.
	The ENIAC is turned off for the last time. As primitive as it was, it is estimated that the machine did more arithmetic than the entire human race had done up till the time of its invention.

	Frederick Sanger sequences the amino acids of insulin, the first of any protein. His work "revealed that a protein has a definite constant, genetically determined sequence—and yet a sequence with no general rule for its assembly. Therefore it had to have a code" (Judson, *Eighth Day of Creation*, p. 188). Sanger will receive the Nobel Prize in chemistry in 1958.
	Compagnie des Machines Bull launches the first stored-program electronic computer produced for commercial sale in France, the Gamma ET.
	Because of failing health, von Neumann does not finish his last work, *The Computer and the Brain*, in which he compares the functions of computers and the human brain.
August 31	John McCarthy, Marvin Minsky, Nathaniel Rochester, and Claude Shannon invite participants to a summer session at Dartmouth College to conduct research on what they call "Artificial Intelligence" (AI), thereby coining the term. **(See Reading 11.5.)**
September	Stanford Research Institute begins the computerization of the banking industry by demonstrating a prototype electronic accounting machine using its ERMA (Electronic Recording Method of Accounting) system.
October	ETL-Mark-2, the second Japanese electronic computer, is produced by the Electrotechnical Laboratory in Japan. It is built of twenty-one thousand relays and does not store a program.
1956	FUJIC, the first Japanese stored-program electronic computer, is built by the Fuji Photo Film Company, initially for the calculation of optical design problems. It uses sixteen-hundred vacuum tubes and a mercury delay-line memory.
	Ray Dolby, Charles Ginsberg and Charles Anderson of Ampex sell the first video tape recorder. It costs $50,000.
	IBM introduces the RAMAC (Random Access Method of Accounting and Control) disk-storage system, a memory device based on rotating disks. This is the first hard drive. It permits random access to any of the million characters distributed over both sides of 50 two-foot-diameter disks. It stores about 2,000 bits of data per square inch and has a purchase price of about $10,000 per megabyte. By 1997, the cost of storing a megabyte will drop to around ten cents.
Summer	At the Dartmouth summer session on AI Newell and Herbert Simon demonstrate the first AI program, the Logic Theorist, to find the basic equations of logic as defined in *Principia Mathematica* by Whitehead and Russell. For one of the equations, the Logic Theorist surpasses its inventors' expectations by finding a new and better proof. This is the "the first foray by artificial intelligence research into high-order intellectual processes" (Feigenbaum and Feldman).
June 26–29	The First International Congress on Cybernetics is held in Namur, Belgium. Few, if any, of the computer pioneers attend. By this time the field of cybernetics is separated from those of computing and artificial intelligence to emphasize issues of control and communication in learning, automation, and biology. The cybernetics approach expands in Europe and Russia but declines in the United States.
July	MICR (Magnetic Ink Character Reading) is demonstrated to the Bank Management Committee of the American Bankers' Association.
August 21	Sperry Rand agrees to cross-license patents with IBM, thereby turning over strategic technology.
September	Noam Chomsky invents his hierarchy of syntactic forms and transformational-generative grammar— profoundly influential in linguistics and artificial intelligence.
October 17–18	The first Italian computer conference is held in Rome.
November	The first Japanese conference on electronic computers is held at Waseda University in Tokyo.
1957	The Burroughs "Atlas Guidance" computer is used to control the launch of the Atlas missile. It is one of the first computers to use transistors.
	IBM phases out vacuum tubes in computer design: "It shall be the policy of IBM to use solid-state circuitry in all machine developments. Furthermore, no new commercial machines or devices shall be announced which make primary use of tube circuitry." http://www-1.ibm.com/ibm/history/history/year_1955.html

	EDSAC 2, the first large-scale computer with a control unit based on microprogramming, becomes operational in Cambridge, England.
	The first AN/FSQ7 is operational for the SAGE Air Defense System on a limited basis. The system allows online access, in graphical form, to data transmitted to and processed by its computers. Fully deployed by 1963, the IBM-built early warning system will remain operational until 1984. With 23 direction centers situated on the nation's northern, eastern, and western boundaries, SAGE pioneers the use of computer control over large, geographically distributed systems.
	Commercial transistorized computers, including the UNIVAC Solid State 80 and the Philco TRANSAC S-2000, are introduced. These inaugurate the so-called second generation of electronic computers.
	Hopper writes the first English-language data-processing compiler, B-0 (FLOW-MATIC) for the UNIVAC II.
	John Backus and his team at IBM ship FORTRAN for the IBM 704. This software is proprietary to IBM.
February 8	John von Neumann dies at the age of fifty-four.
September	Crick delivers his paper "On Protein Synthesis," published in *Symp. Soc. Exp. Biol.* 12 (1958): 138–63. In it Crick proposes two general principles: 1) The Sequence Hypothesis: "The order of bases in a portion of DNA represents a code for the amino acid sequence of a specific protein. Each 'word' in the code would name a specific amino acid. From the two-dimensional genetic text, written in DNA, are forced the whole diversity of uniquely shaped three-dimensional proteins" (gnn.tigr.org.timeline), and 2) The Central Dogma: "Information is transmitted from DNA and RNA to proteins but information cannot be transmitted from a protein to DNA." This paper "permanently altered the logic of biology." (Judson)
October 4	The Soviet Union launches Sputnik, the first artificial earth satellite.
1958	Zuse produces the Z22, the first commercial electronic digital computer in Germany. It uses vacuum tubes. Zuse KG is the first independent German electronic computer company. It will eventually be purchased by Siemens.
	Seymour Cray of Control Data Corporation builds the first transitorized supercomputer, the CDC 1604.
	Jack Kilby of Texas Instruments conceives of the integrated circuit and constructs a basic prototype.
	Independently of Kilby, Robert Noyce of Fairchild Semiconductor invents a process that makes it practical to manufacture integrated circuits.
	IBM announces their 1401: a relatively inexpensive computer that proves very popular with businesses, and which begins to compete seriously with existing punched-card equipment.
	Researchers at the Bell Labs invent the modem (modulator - demodulator), providing a way to convert digital signals to analog signals and back for transmission over analog telephone lines.
January 31	The U. S. launches its first artificial satellite, Explorer-1. It was built at the Jet Propulsion Lab at Caltech. It ceases transmission on May 23 after less than 4 months. Explorer I is credited with the most important discovery of the International Geophysical Year — the discovery of one of the belts of radiation surrounding the earth, subsequently named the Van Allen Belts after James Van Allen, the scientist who identified them.
February 7	In response to the Soviet Union's launching of Sputnik, President Dwight Eisenhower creates the Advanced Research Planning Agency of the Department of Defense (ARPA).
July	Arthur Lee Samuel first demonstrates that machines can learn from past errors, one of the earliest examples of non-numerical computation.
October	Newell, Clifford Shaw, and Simon invent "game tree pruning," an artificial intelligence technique.
November	Frank Rosenblatt invents the *perceptron,* the first precisely specified, computationally oriented neural network.

November 24–27	The National Physical Laboratory at Teddington, England holds the first international symposium on artificial intelligence, calling it *Mechanisation of Thought Processes.* At this conference McCarthy delivers his paper "Programs with Common Sense." **(See Reading 11.6.)**
December 19	President Eisenhower's Christmas address is transmitted from the PROJECT SCORE satellite. It is the first voice transmission from a satellite.
1959	Wesley Clark designs and builds the TX-2 computer at MIT's Lincoln Laboratories. It has 320 kilobytes of fast memory, about twice the capacity of the biggest commercial machines. Other features are magnetic tape storage, an on-line typewriter, the first Xerox printer, paper tape for program input, and a nine inch CRT screen.
	Gordon Gould files his patent on the LASER (Light Amplification by Stimulated Emission of Radiation) based on a discovery he made in 1957. The patent will not be granted until 1977.
	Based on technology originally developed at the Stanford Research Institute, General Electric delivers the first 32 ERMA (Electronic Recording Method of Accounting) computing systems to the Bank of America. The system uses MICR (Magnetic Ink Character Reading.) ERMA will serve as the Bank's accounting computer and check handling system until 1970.
	Xerox introduces the xerographic copier.
	Lejaren Hiller and Leonard Isaacson publish the first book on computer-generated music: *Experimental Music: Composition with an Electronic Computer*, based on work done on the University of Illinois's ILLIAC computer.
May	A group representing computer users, manufacturers, universities, and the government, meets at the Pentagon to plan COBOL, a nonproprietary computer language designed for business use that can be run on all electronic computers.
July	Arthur Lee Samuel first demonstrates that machines can learn from past errors, one of the earliest examples of non-numerical computation.
Late 1950s	In the late 1950s it becomes recognized that the longevity of paper is a function of its acidity or alkalinity: the lower the acidity and higher the alkalinity, the greater the longevity of paper.
1959–1960	The United States banking industry adopts MICR, (*Magnetic Ink Character Recognition*), which allows computers to read the data printed on checks.
1960	Reflecting the obsolescence of mathematical tables, *Mathematical Tables and Other Aids to Computation* (MTAC), the first computing journal, changes its name to *Mathematics of Computation.*
	The Advanced Research Projects Agency (ARPA) of the United States Defense Department increases funding for computer research.
	IBM introduces a transistorized version of its 709 computer, the 7090. It becomes the most popular large computer of the early 1960s.
	Digital Equipment Corporation (DEC) introduces its first computer, the PDP-1 designed in part by C. Gordon Bell. Selling for $120,000, it is a commercialization of the TX-O and TX-2 computers designed at MIT's Lincoln Laboratories. On advice from the venture-capital firm that financed the company, DEC does not call it a "computer" but a "programmed data processor" instead. Some references will identify this machine as the first minicomputer; however DEC will give either the PDP-5 introduced in 1963 or the PDP-8 introduced in 1965 that designation.
	The United States Department of Defense issues a requirement that all computers supplied to it must be capable of compiling the COBOL programming language.
	William A. Fetter, a researcher at Boeing, coins the term "computer graphics."
	About six thousand computers are operational in the United States, and perhaps ten thousand worldwide.

	Drs. William Chardack and Andrew Gage, and electrical engineer Wilson Greatbatch, report the success of the world's first successful long-term implant in a human patient of a self-contained, internally powered artificial pacemaker in their paper, "A transistorized, self-contained, implantable pacemaker for the long-term correction of complete heart block."
	John McCarthy introduces LISP (*LISt Processor*), the language of choice for AI programming.
March	J. C. R. Licklider publishes "Man-computer symbiosis," postulating that the computer should become an intimate symbiotic partner in human activity, including communication. **(See Reading 10.5.)**
April	The first report on COBOL is published.
September 13–15	The first symposium on bionics (*biological electronics*) takes place at Wright-Patterson Air Force Base in Ohio. **(See Reading 11.7.)**
1961	QUOTRON, a computerized stock-quotation system using a Control Data Corporation computer, is introduced. It becomes popular with stockbrokers, signaling the end of ticker tape.
	Francis Crick, Sydney Brenner and colleagues propose that DNA code is written in "words" called codons formed of three DNA bases. DNA sequence is built from four different bases, so a total of 64 (4 × 4 × 4) possible codons can be produced. They also propose that a particular set of RNA molecules subsequently called transfer RNAs (tRNAs) act to "decode" the DNA. Francis Crick, L. Barnett, Sydney. Brenner and R. J. Watts-Tobin, "General Nature of the Genetic code for Proteins," *Nature* 192 (1961): 1227–32. "There was an unfortunate thing at the Cold Spring Harbor Symposium that year. I said, 'We call this messenger RNA' Because Mercury was the messenger of the gods, you know. And Erwin Chargaff very quickly stood up in the audience and said he wished to point out that Mercury may have been the messenger of the gods, but he was also the god of thieves. Which said a lot for Chargaff at the time! But I don't think that we stole anything from anybody—except from nature. I think it's right to steal from nature, however." (Brenner, *My Life*, 85).
	Edward Zajak at Bell Labs produces the first computer animated film, entitled *Two-Gyro Gravity-Gradient Attitude Control System*.
	Over seven thousand people belong to the ACM.
	Fernando José Corbató and colleagues at MIT describe the first working time-sharing system.
May 1961	Wesley A. Clark, a physicist at MIT, starts building the Linc (*Laboratory instrument computer*). The machine, which some will later call "the first personal computer," will be first used in 1962. It has small table-top size, "low cost" ($43,000), keyboard and display, file system and an interactive operating system. Eventually fifty of the machines will be sold by Digital Equipment Corporation.
May 31	Leonard Kleinrock submits his MIT thesis proposal, *Information Flow in Large Communication Nets*. This is the first paper on what will later come to be known as data communications or data networking theory. **(See Reading 13.2.)**
October 19	Texas Instruments delivers the first integrated circuit computer to the U.S. Air Force. "The advanced experimental equipment has a total volume of only 6.3 cubic inches and weighs only 10 ounces. It provides the identical electrical functions of a computer using conventional components which is 150 times its size and 48 times its weight and which also was demonstrated for purposes of comparison. It uses 587 digital circuits (Solid Circuit™ semiconductor networks) each formed within a minute bar of silicon material. The larger computer uses 8500 conventional components and has a volume of 1000 cubic inches and weight of 480 ounces." http://www.ti.com/corp/docs/company/history/iccomp.shtml
1962	Steve Russell and his team at MIT take about 200 hours to program the first computer game on a PDP-1. It is called "Spacewar!"
	Marshall McLuhan publishes *The Gutenberg Galaxy: The Making of Typographic Man* in which he divides history in four epochs: oral tribe culture, manuscript culture, the Gutenberg galaxy and the electronic age. For the break between the time periods in each case the occurrence of a new medium is responsible. Writing before computing is pervasive, McLuhan is concerned with the influence of radio, television and film on print culture.

April	Kleinrock publishes *Information Flow in Large Communication Nets* in RLE Quarterly Progress Reports. This is the first publication to describe and analyze an algorithm for chopping messages into smaller pieces, later to be known as packets. His MIT doctoral thesis, *Message Delay in Communication Nets with Storage*, filed in December 1962, will elaborate on the impact of this algorithm on data networks. **(See Reading 13.3.)**
Summer	Licklider publishes "Online man-computer communication," calling for time-sharing of computers, and illustrating available graphic displays of information, and the need for an improved graphical interface. **(See Reading 10.6.)**
July 10	A Delta rocket from Cape Canaveral launches the A T & T TELSTAR 1 satellite. It is the first communication satellite. It transmits the first direct television pictures from the United States to Europe, becoming the first satellite to relay signals from the earth to a satellite and back.
October 1	Licklider is appointed Director of the Pentagon's Information Processing Techniques Office (IPTO), a division of ARPA (the Advanced Research Projects Agency).His initial budget is $10,000,000 per year. He eventually initiates the sequence of events leading to ARPANET.
December	Demonstration of DAC-1 (Design Augmented by Computers), a joint development effort between General Motors and IBM begun in 1959. This is the first computer-assisted design (CAD) program.
1963	The ASCII (American Standard Code for Information Interchange) standard is promulgated, specifying the pattern of seven bits to represent letters, numbers, punctuation, and control signals in computers.
	Digital Equipment Corporation introduces the PDP-5, DEC's first 12 bit computer and "the world's first commercially produced minicomputer." (The PDP-8 introduced in 1965 will also be given this designation.)
	Allen M. Cormack shows that changes in tissue density can be computed from x-ray data. No machine is constructed at this time because of limitations in computing power. This is a key discovery, leading in 1972 to the invention of computed tomography (CT).
	Ivan Sutherland, a student at MIT working on the experimental TX-2 computer, creates the first graphical user interface, or first interactive graphics program, in his Ph.D. thesis, *Sketchpad: A Man-Machine Graphical Communication System*. **(See Reading 10.7.)**
April 25	Licklider sends a memo to "members and affiliates of the Intergalactic Computer Network outlining a key part of his strategy to connect all their individual computers and time-sharing systems into a single computer network spanning the continent."(Waldrop)
November	Touch-tone telephone dialing is introduced, enabling calls to be switched digitally.
1964	Kleinrock publishes his 1962 PhD thesis in book form as *Communication Nets: Stochastic Message Flow and Delay*, providing a technology and mathematical theory of data communications. **(See Reading 13.4.)**
	Paul Baran writes *On Distributed Communications Networks*, describing the use of redundant routing and message blocks to send information across a decentralized network topology.
	RCA announces the Spectra series of computers, which can run the same software as IBM's 360 machines. The Spectra computers are the first commercial computers to use integrated circuits.
	SABRE (*Semi-Automatic Business-Related Environment*), an online computerized airline reservation system developed by American Airlines and IBM, becomes operational. It works over telephone lines in "real time" to handle seat inventory and passenger records from terminals in more than 50 cities.
	Installations of the IBM System/360s begin.
	The Internal Revenue Service (IRS) begins using social security numbers as tax ID numbers.
	Thomas Kurtz and John Kenny invent BASIC (*Beginner's All-Purpose Symbolic Instruction Code*) at Dartmouth.
	Systems Development Corporation develops the first computerized encyclopedia.

	William Fetter at Boeing produces the first computer model of a human figure for use in the study of cockpit design. It is called the "First Man."
February 4	Eckert and Mauchly receive patent no. 3,120,606 for the ENIAC, a general patent on the stored-program electronic computer. Sperry Rand Univac, owner of the patent, charges a 1.5 percent royalty for all electronic computers sold by all companies except IBM, with which it had previously cross-licensed patents.
February 14	Texas Instruments in partnership with Zenith Radio introduces the first consumer product containing an integrated circuit—a hearing aid.
April 7	IBM announces the System/360 family of compatible machines. These are the first IBM computers capable of both commercial and scientific applications that are offered at what is considered a "reasonable price." Microprogramming is adopted in their design.
November	The Homestead Meeting between Licklider and Lawrence G. Roberts sparks Roberts to undertake the creation of the ARPANET.
1965	DEC introduces the PDP-8, the first "production model minicomputer." "Small in physical size, selling in minimum configuration for under $20,000."
	William Fetter publishes the first book on computer graphics: *Computer Graphics in Communication*. Fetter coined the term "computer graphics" in 1960.
	Honeywell attempts to open the home computer market with its Kitchen Computer. The H316 is the first under-$10,000 16-bit machine from a major computer manufacturer. It is the smallest addition to the Honeywell "Series 16" line. The H316 is available in three versions: table-top, rack-mountable, and self-standing pedestal. The pedestal version, complete with cutting board, is marketed by Neimann Marcus as "The Kitchen Computer." It comes with some built-in recipes, two weeks' worth of programming, a cookbook, and an apron.
	Ted Nelson coins the terms "hypertext" and "hyperlink" to refer to the features of a computerized information system.
January	J. A. Robinson publishes his resolution principle, a standard of logical deduction in AI applications.
April	James Cooley and John Tukey publish the fast Fourier transform algorithm. Wilkes introduces memory caching.
April 19	Gordon Moore observes the exponential growth in the number of transistors per integrated circuit and predicts that this trend will continue. The press calls this "Moore's Law." **(See Reading 8.10.)**
October	Roberts does the first actual network experiment, tying Lincoln Labs' TX-2 to SDC's Q32. This is the first time that two computers talk to each other and the first time that packets are used to communicate between computers.
1966	The New York Stock Exchange completes automation of its basic trading functions.
	Shipments of semiconductor memory, as a replacement for magnetic-core, begin.
	The IRS completes computerization of income-tax processing, with a central facility in Martinsburg, West Virginia, and satellite locations around the United States.
	Robert H. Dennard of IBM invents Dynamic Random Access Memory (DRAM) cells, one-transistor memory cells that store each single bit of information as an electrical charge in an electronic circuit. The technology permits major increases in memory density.
	Aaron Klug formulates a method for digital image processing of two-dimensional images. A. Klug and D. J. de Rosier, "Optical filtering of electron micrographs: Reconstruction of one-sided images," *Nature* 212 (1966): 29–32.
	Stephen B. Gray founds The Amateur Computer Society, possibly the first personal computer club.
	Data Corporation begins as a contractor to the U.S. Air Force. It will eventually be renamed LexisNexis.

	Roger K. Summit has the DIALOG online information retrieval system operational for Lockheed Aircraft.
October	Roberts writes *Towards a Cooperative Network of Time-Shared Computers*, describing networking research at MIT.
December	Roberts becomes ARPA IPTO (Advanced Research Projects Agency Information Processing Technology Office) Chief Scientist and begins the design of the ARPANET. The ARPANET program as proposed to Congress by Roberts will explore computer resource sharing and packet switching communications to ensure reliability.
1967	National Physical Laboratory (NPL) in Middlesex, England develops the NPL Data Network under Donald Watts Davies. This is an experiment in packet switching.
	The Colleges and universities in the state of Ohio found the Ohio College Library Center (OCLC) to develop a computerized system in which the libraries of Ohio academic institutions can share resources and reduce costs. After the database expands far beyond the state of Ohio it will be renamed Online Computer Library Center.
	Texas Instruments files the patent for the first hand-held calculator. The patent (Number 3,819,921) will be awarded on June 25, 1974. This miniature calculator (the world's first) employs a large-scale integrated semiconductor array containing the equivalent of thousands of discrete semiconductor devices.
March	The United States Senate holds the first hearings on computer privacy.
April	At the ARPANET Design Session held by Roberts at the ARPA IPTO PI meeting in Ann Arbor, Michigan, Wesley Clark suggests the use of mini-computers for network packet switches instead of using the main frame computers themselves for switching. These machines will be called Interface Message Processors.
1967 Spring–Summer	Department of Defense requests Director of Advanced Research Planning Agency (ARPA) to form a Task Force "to study and recommend hardware and software safeguards that would satisfactorily protect classified information in multi-access, resource-sharing computer systems." Their report will be published in 1970.
October	Donald Davies introduces the use of the term "packet" to describe discrete blocks of data sent over networks in his paper "A digital communications network for computers."
October	Lawrence Roberts publishes the first paper on the design of the ARPANET: "Multiple computer networks and intercomputer communication." **(See Reading 13.5)**
1968	Licklider and Robert Taylor publish "The computer as a communication device," in which they describe features of the future ARPANET. **(See Reading 13.6.)**
	The first manned Apollo flights occur, including Apollo 8, which circumnavigates the moon on Christmas Eve.
	Jasia Reichardt publishes *Cybernetic Serendipity: The Computer and the Arts*, based on an exhibition in London. This is the first serious exhibition of computer art.
	Hewlett Packard introduces the desk calculator, HP 9100A.
	Stanley Kubrick, in his film *2001: A Space Odyssey*, captures imaginations with the idea of a computer that can see, speak, hear, and "think."
January	Aaron Klug describes techniques for the reconstruction of three-dimensional structures from electron micrographs, thus founding the processing of three-dimensional digital images. D. J. de Rosier and A. Klug, "Reconstruction of three dimensional structures from electron micrographs," *Nature* 217 (1968) 130–34.
July 18	Robert Noyce, Gordon Moore and Andrew Grove found Intel. The company is originally incorporated under the name of NM Electronics.

December 8	Douglas Engelbart at the Stanford Research Institute demonstrates an "oNLine System" (NLS), the features of which include hypertext, text editing, screen windowing, and email. To make this system operate, Engelbart invents the mouse.
October 7–11	The term "software engineering" is coined at a NATO conference, in response to the perception that computer programming has not kept up with advances in computer hardware.
1969	Kenneth Thompson and Dennis Ritchie develop the UNIX operating system at Bell Labs. This is the first operating system designed to run on computers of all sizes, making open systems possible. UNIX will become the foundation for the Internet.
	IBM adopts a new marketing policy that charges separately for most systems engineering activities, future computer programs, and customer education courses. This "unbundling" will give rise to a multibillion-dollar software and services industry.
	In this year 32,393 books are produced in the United Kingdom.
	Compuserve, the first commercial online service, is established.
May	Advanced Micro Devices is founded by Jerry Sanders and seven others from Fairchild Semiconductor.
July 21	Neil Armstrong and Edwin Aldrin become the first human beings to walk on the moon. Their landing is almost canceled in the final seconds because of an overload of the Apollo Guidance Computer's memory, but on advice from Earth, they ignore the warnings and land safely.
September 2	The First ARPANET node is installed at the UCLA Network Measurement Center. Kleinrock establishes the first network connection between a network switch and a time-shared host computer. ARPANET, sponsored by the U.S. Defense Department's Advanced Research Projects Agency (ARPA), will eventually link computers across the country, and around the world. It will evolve into the Internet. **(See Reading 13.7.)**
October 29	The first message is sent over ARPANET from Kleinrock's UCLA computer to the second node at Stanford Research Institute's computer. The message is simply "Lo."
1970	DEC introduces the PDP-11 minicomputer, which popularizes the notion of a "bus" (i.e. "Unibus" invented by C. Gordon Bell) onto which a variety of additional circuit boards or peripheral products can be placed. 20,000 units will be sold by 1975.
	Xerox opens the Palo Alto Research Center (PARC). It will become the incubator of the Graphical User Interface (GUI), the mouse, the WYSIWYG text editor, the laser printer, the desktop computer, the Smalltalk programming language and integrated development environment, Interpress (a resolution-independent graphical page description language and the precursor to PostScript), and Ethernet.
	IBM announces the 370 series, an upgrade for the 360, using semiconductor memory in place of magnetic cores.
	The first automatic teller machine (ATM) is installed.
	The floppy disk is introduced.
February	The Rand Corporation publishes the classified report of the Defense Science Board Task Force on Computer Security, *Security Controls for Computer Systems*. This is the first systematic review of computer security problems.
March	ARPANET establishes a node at Bolt Beranek and Newman in Cambridge, thereby spanning the U.S.
June	Edgar F. Codd publishes "A relational model of data for large shared data banks." Codd's model becomes widely accepted as the definitive model for relational database management systems. A language, Structured English Query Language ("SEQUEL") was developed by IBM to apply Codd's model. SEQUEL later becomes SQL, presumably because trademark conflicts cause IBM to switch from the original name.
December	Gilbert Hyatt files a patent application entitled *Single Chip Integrated Circuit Computer Architecture* based on work begun in 1968. This is the first general patent on the microprocessor. Twenty years later in 1990, the U.S. Patent Office will award the patent, but it will be overturned in 1995.

1971	Intel announces the 4004 four-bit, central processor logic chip designed by Federico Faggin. It is the first microprocessor.
	IBM's first operational application of speech recognition enables customer engineers servicing equipment to "talk" to and receive "spoken" answers from a computer that can recognize about 5,000 words.
	C. Gordon Bell and Allen Newell publish *Computer Structures: Readings and Examples*, a systematized presentation of the principles governing the design of computer systems.
June	Henri Gouraud of the University of Utah publishes the Gouraud shading method for polygon smoothing, a scheme for continuous shading in computer graphics, in his paper "Computer display of curved surfaces," in *IEEE Transactions in Computers*. The effect makes a surface composed of discrete polygons appear to be continuous.
September 17	"A new standard one-chip MOS/LSI calculator logic circuit has been announced by Texas Instruments. This single chip may make full electronic calculators available to everyone at prices that can put a calculator into every kitchen or businessman's pocket. The chip incorporates all of the logic and memory circuits to perform complete 8-digit 3-register calculator functions, including full precision add, subtract, multiply, and divide operations." http://www.ti.com/corp/docs/company/history/calcchip.shtml
1972	Xerox decides to develop the Alto computer system. Conceptually the first personal computer system, it will eventually employ a bitmapped display, networking through Ethernet, and a mouse.
	ARPANET has 15 nodes (23 hosts).
	Dennis M. Ritchie of Bell Labs writes the C programming language.
	Nolan Bushnell hires Al Alcorn to program the table tennis game "Pong." It is the first video game.
	Godfrey Hounsfield invents computed tomography (CT), the first application of computers to medical imaging.
	The Universal Product Code (UPC)—the familiar barcode—is accepted by a grocer's trade association.
	Intel announces the 8008 microprocessor.
March	Ray Tomlinson at BNN invents email for ARPANET: SNDMSG and READMAIL, chosing the "@" sign as a key email address component.
July	Lawrence Roberts of ARPA writes the first email management program, RD, to list incoming messages and support forwarding, filing, and responding to them.
1972–74	Inexpensive electronic calculators flood the market.
1973	Stanley Cohen, Annie Chang, Robert Helling, and Herbert Boyer demonstrate that if DNA is fragmented with restriction endonucleases and combined with similarly restricted plasmid DNA, the resulting recombinant DNA molecules are biologically active and can replicate in host bacterial cells. Plasmids can thus act as vectors for the propagation of foreign cloned genes. This is the first practical method of cloning a gene and a breakthrough in the development of recombinant DNA technologies and genetic engineering. Cohen, Chang, Boyer and Helling, "Construction of Biologically Functional Bacterial Plasmids *in Vitro*," *Proc. Nat. Acad. Sci.* 70 (1973): 3240–44
	The first ARPANET international connections are established to University College, London and NORSAR (Norway).
October 19	Eckert and Mauchly's ENIAC patent is ruled invalid in the case of Honeywell Inc. v. Sperry Rand Corporation et al. **(See Reading 8.12.)**
1974	The first of the three Cohen-Boyer recombinant DNA cloning patents is granted, leading to the foundation of the biotechnology industry.

	IBM announces Systems Network Architecture (SNA), a networking protocol for computing systems. SNA is a uniform set of rules and procedures for computer communications to free computer users from the technical complexities of communicating through local, national, and international computer networks.
	The term "mainframe" is first used in a *Scientific American* article to distinguish the main computer in a laboratory from other computers.
	IBM builds the first prototype computer employing RISC (Reduced Instruction Set Computer) architecture. Based on an invention by John Cocke, the RISC concept simplifies the instructions given to run computers, making them faster and more powerful. It will be implemented in the experimental IBM 801 minicomputer. The goal of the 801 is to execute one instruction per cycle. (In 1987 John Cocke will receive the A. M. Turing Award for significant contributions in the design and theory of compilers, the architecture of large systems and the development of reduced instruction set computers (RISC); for discovering and systematizing many fundamental transformations now used in optimizing compilers including reduction of operator strength, elimination of common subexpressions, register allocation, constant propagation, and dead code elimination.)
March	Intel announces the 8080 eight-bit microprocessor. It powers the Altair 8800 designed by H. Edward Roberts, the first truly inexpensive personal computer. Within a year it will be designed into hundreds of different products.
May	Vinton Cerf and Robert Kahn publish "A Protocol for Packet Network Intercommunication" in which they describe the Transmission Control Protocol (TCP). **(See Reading 13.8.)**
November 20	The U.S. Department of Justice files an antitrust suit for the breakup of American Telephone and Telegraph (AT&T), alleging anticompetitive behavior.
1975	Bill Gates and Paul G. Allen write a version of the Basic programming language that runs on the MITS Altair. This is the first computer language written for a personal computer.
	Benoit Mandelbrot, a researcher at IBM, conceives fractal geometry — the concept that seemingly irregular shapes can have identical structure at all scales. This new geometry makes it possible to describe mathematically the kinds of irregularities existing in nature. Fractals later make a great impact on engineering, economics, metallurgy, art and health sciences, and are also applied in the field of computer graphics and animation.
	Robert Metcalfe of Xerox invents Ethernet.
	The Federal Government's antitrust suit against IBM goes to trial. It will be dropped in 1982 after thirty million pages of documents are generated.
	This year the first personal computer magazines will begin publication including *Byte, Creative Computing,* and *The Computer Hobbyist.*
	IBM introduces the first laser printer for use with its mainframes.
January	H. Edward Roberts, working in Albuquerque, New Mexico, announces in a *Popular Electronics* article the MITS (Micro Instrumentation Telemetry Systems) Altair personal computer kit, the first personal computer to be offered for sale. It has an "open architecture." The basic Altair 8800 sells for $397.
September	IBM introduces the 5100 Portable Computer for corporate users. More luggable than portable, the machine weighs 50 pounds. The price, fully configured, is $19,975.
1976	Steven Jobs and Stephen Wozniak found Apple Computer Corporation, and introduce the Apple 1 at the price of $666.
	Altair programmer Michael Shrayer writes the first PC word processing program, the Electric Pencil.
	Raymond Kurzweil introduces the Kurzweil Reading Machine, the first print-to-speech reading machine for the blind.
	SATNET, Atlantic packet Satellite network is launched. This network links the United States with Europe. It uses INTELSAT satellites owned by a consortium of countries—not exclusively by the United States.

March	The World Altair Computer Conference, probably the first personal computer conference, takes place in Albuquerque.
1977	Intel introduces the 8086 sixteen-bit microprocessor.
	AT&T and Bell Labs construct a prototype cellular telephone system. The following year the first public trials will occur in Chicago with 2000 users.
	Lawrence Ellison founds Software Development Laboratories. The company will introduce the first Relational Database Management System (see 1970) based on the IBM System/R model and the first database management system utilizing IBM's Structured Query Language (SQL) technology. The company will be renamed Oracle Corporation in 1983.
	Apple introduces the Apple II, the first personal computer sold as a fully assembled product, and the first with color graphics.
	Walter Gilbert and Allan M. Maxam devise technique for sequencing DNA. "The Gilbert-Maxam method involved multiplying, dividing, and carefully fragmenting DNA. A stretch of DNA would be multiplied a millionfold in bacteria. Each strand was radioactively labeled at one end. Nested into four groups, chemical reagents were applied to selectively cleave the DNA strand along its bases—adenine (A), guanine (G), cytosine (C) and thymine (T). Carefully dosed, the reagents would break the DNA into a large number of smaller fragments of varying length. In gel electrophoresis, as a function of DNA's negative charge, the strands would separate according to length—revealing, via the terminal points of breakage, the position of each base." (http://gnn.tigr.org/timeline/timeline_frames.shtml)
	Frederick Sanger and colleagues independently develop the methods for the rapid sequencing of long sections of DNA molecules. Sanger's method, and that developed by Gilbert and Maxam, make it possible to read the nucleotide sequence for entire genes that run from 1000 to 30,000 bases long. Sanger, F., Nicklen, S., and Coulson, A.R. DNA Sequencing with Chain-Terminating Inhibitors. *Proc. Nat. Acad. Sci. (USA)* 74 (1977) 5463–67.
	Formation of the first genetic engineering company, Genentech, specifically founded to use recombinant DNA methods to make medically important drugs. Cohen and Boyer are involved with the company.
	Bill Gates and Paul Allen officially found Microsoft in Albuquerque, New Mexico.
1978	TCP is split into TCP and IP.
	Wang introduces its VS minicomputer system, which becomes one of the most popular office systems, inaugurating the concept of office automation.
	Xerox donates fifty Alto computer systems to various American universities. They have bitmapped displays, networking through Ethernet, and a mouse. Everything fits on the desktop except the disk storage and CPU. Each system costs $32,000.
May 1	A DEC sales representative attempts to send the first intentional commercial spam to every Arpanet address on the West Coast. The sender, Gary Thuerk, thinks that Arpanet users will find it cool that DEC has integrated ARPANET protocol support directly into the new DEC-20 and TOPS-20 OS. http://www.thocp.net/reference/internet/spam.htm
June 11	Texas Instruments announces a speech synthesis monolithic integrated circuit. For the first time the human vocal tract is electronically duplicated on a single chip of silicon.
1979	Compuserve offers personal computer users email communication. The following year it will offer real-time chat online.
	Phillips and Sony develop the compact disc.
	Dan Bricklin and Bob Frankston write *Visicalc*, the first spreadsheet program, for the Apple II. It helps dispel the notion that the Apple II is only a toy for hobbyists.
	The first single-chip digital signal processor (DSP) is developed at Bell Labs, making small portable digital telephones possible.

1980	Tim Berners-Lee writes a program called "Enquire within upon everything," named after the title of a Victorian book on advice. This program allows the user to store information using "random associations." It is a predecessor to the World Wide Web.
	IBM hires Allen and Gates of Microsoft to create an operating system for their new personal computer, then under development. Allen and Gates buy the rights to a simple operating system manufactured by Seattle Computer Products and use it as a template. IBM allows Gates and Allen to keep the marketing rights to the operating system, called DOS.
	Bell Labs develops digital cellular telephone technology, offering better sound quality, greater channel capacity and lower cost than analog.
1981	Intel introduces the 8088 microprocessor, a low-cost version of the 8086 using an eight-bit external bus.
	Xerox introduces the Star computer system, the first with a true graphical user interface.
	Osborne produces the first commercially successful portable computer. It weighs twenty-three pounds and runs the CP/M operating system.
	There are 213 hosts on ARPANET; a new host is added approximately every 20 days.
August 12	IBM introduces their open architecture personal computer based on the Intel 8088 processor. It runs MS-DOS, a 16-bit operating system developed by Microsoft.
August	Sony releases the first commercial electronic camera, the Sony Mavica (Magnetic Video Camera). Not a digital camera, it is actually a video camera that takes video freeze-frames.
1982	The Federal Communications Commission authorizes commercial cellular telephone service for the United States.
	SUN announces its first workstation.
	John Warnock develops the PostScript page description language, enabling the creation of scalable digital type-fonts and desktop publishing. Warnock and Charles Geschke found Adobe Systems. Initially they focus on the creation and sale of Postscript type-fonts and PostScript controllers for laser printers.
	The TRS-80, Model 100, introduces the concept of a "laptop" computer.
	DCA (Defense Communications Agency) and ARPA establish the Transmission Control Protocol (TCP) and Internet Protocol (IP), as the protocol suite, commonly known as TCP/IP, for ARPANET. This leads to one of the first definitions of an "internet" as a connected set of networks, specifically those using TCP/IP, and the "Internet" as connected TCP/IP internets.
	Sony introduces compact disk (CD) players.
	Sanger and colleagues sequence the entire genome of bacteriophage lambda using a random shotgun technique. This is the first whole genome shotgun (WGS) sequence. Sanger, F., "Nucleotide Sequence of Bacteriophage Lambda," *J. Mol. Biol.* 162 (1982): 729–73.
1983	The first commercial analog cellular service is made available in Chicago by Ameritech.
	IBM introduces the DB2 relational database for mainframe computers.
	Six million personal computers are sold in the United States.
	Microsoft Windows is announced.
	ARPANET splits into ARPANET and MILNET. MILNET is integrated into the Defense Data Network created the previous year. The Department of Defense continues to support both networks.
January 1	ARPANET requires that all connected machines use TCP/IP. TCP/IP becomes the core Internet protocol and replaces NCP (Network Control Protocol) entirely.
November	Domain Name System (DNS), designed by Jon Postel, Paul Mockapetris, and Craig Partridge is introduced. The six original domains are .edu, .gov, .com, .mil, .org, .net, and .int.

1984	Apple Computer introduces the Macintosh, with a graphical user interface based on the Xerox Star system.
	William Gibson coins the term "cyberspace" in his novel *Neuromancer.*
	Moderated newsgroups are introduced on USENET.
January 1	American Telephone and Telegraph (AT & T), is officially broken up, ending a long-established monopoly on telephone service.
May 3	Michael Dell founds Dell Computer Corporation at the age of 19 by building PC clones out of his dorm room at the University of Texas at Austin.
December	Len Bosack and Sandy Lerner from Stanford University found Cisco Systems. The company is named for San Francisco, gateway to the Pacific Rim.
1985	Paul Brainerd founds Aldus Corporation to produce PageMaker, the first page layout program for personal computers. Initially it runs on the Apple Macintosh. Brainerd also coins the term "desktop publishing." Aldus will be purchased by Adobe Systems.
	Intel introduces the 386 microprocessor. It features 275,000 transistors — more than 100 times as many as the first Intel microprocessor, the 4004. It is a 32-bit chip with multi tasking.
	Three proposals are made to sequence the human genome. Robert Sinsheimer convenes a meeting in Santa Cruz that develops the idea of complete characterization of the human genome. Renato Dulbecco (Salk Institute) suggests sequencing the genome to help to understand cancer. Charles de Lisi at the Dept of Energy proposes a project to sequence the genome to help understand radiation damage.
March 15	Symbolics.com becomes the first registered domain.
April 1	Stewart Brand and Larry Brilliant found The Whole Earth 'Lectronic Link, perhaps the first online community, latter known as The WELL. It will connect to the Internet in 1992.
May	Quantum Computer Services is founded. In November its first online service, Q-Link, launches on Commodore Business Machines. The company will become America Online in October 1991.
November	Microsoft Windows 1.0 is introduced.
1986	The number of hosts on the ARPANET/Internet exceeds five thousand.
	The National Science Foundation approves funding for the Internet backbone.
	Leroy Hood and Lloyd Smith from the California Institute of Technology develop the first automatic sequencing machine working with a laser that recognizes fluorescing DNA markers.
1987	Applied Biosystems puts the first commercial DNA sequencing machine, based on Hood's technology, on the market.
	Formal proposals by Department of Energy in US to sequence the human genome. Report at Oak Ridge National Laboratory Genome website. Cost predictions for the human genome sequence: It is estimated that one worker can produce about 50,0000 bases of finished DNA sequence per year at a cost of about $1–$2 per base. Thus the human genome would take 60,000 person-years and cost $3–6 billion to complete.
	UUNET sells the first-ever commercial Internet connection.
	The number of hosts on the Internet exceeds ten thousand.

November	C. Gordon Bell, as Chairman of the Subcommittee on Computer Networking, Infrastructure and Digital Communications of the Federal Coordinating Council on Science, Engineering and Technology, publishes *A Report to the Office of Technology Policy on Computer Networks to Support Research in the United States. A Study of Critical Problems and Future Options.* The report states: "Over the next 15 years, there will be a need for a 100,000 times increase in national network capacity to enable researchers to exploit computer capabilities for representing complex data in visual form, for manipulating and interacting with this complex data and for sharing large data bases with other researchers." "As the first step, the current Internet system developed by the Defense Advanced Research Projects Agency and the networks supported by agencies for researchers should be interconnected. These facilities, if coordinated and centrally managed, have the capability to interconnect many computer networks into a single virtual computer network. As the second step, the existing computer networks that support research programs should be expanded and upgraded to serve 200–400 research institutions with 1.5 million bits per second capabilities. "As the third step, network service should be provided to every research institution in the U.S., with transmission speeds of three billion bits per second." (p. 3)
	25,000,000 PC's are sold in the United States.
1988	John and Thomas Knoll develop ImagePro, the prototype of Adobe Photoshop. Photoshop 1.0 will ship in February 1990.
1989	The number of hosts on the Internet exceeds one hundred thousand.
	Sony releases the Sony ProMavica MVC-5000, one of the first digital cameras.
	The first gateways between private e-mail carriers and the Internet are established. CompuServe is connected through Ohio State University, MCI through the Corporation for National Research Initiatives.
	Digital high-definition TV software, based on video compression algorithms, is developed at Bell Labs.
1989–90	Tim Berners-Lee at CERN writes the first software for a World Wide Web server, invents the Hypertext Mark-Up Language (HTML) and writes the first WYSIWYG hypertext text client. On November 12, 1990 he issues "World Wide Web: Proposal for a Hypertext Project" (http://www.w3.org/Proposal) This is originally done to supply information to the high energy physics community. At this time the number of websites in existence is one.
1990	ARPANET discontinues operations.
	ARCHIE, designed to index FTP files, becomes the first search engine.
1991	The first web server on the Internet in North America goes live at Stanford Linear Accelerator (SLAC).
	The National Science Foundation (NSF) lifts restrictions on the commercial use of the NSFNET backbone, clearing the way for electronic commerce.
	Adobe introduces the Portable Document Format (.PDF) to aid in the transfer of documents across platforms. PDF is a file format used to represent a document in a manner independent of the application software, hardware, and operating system used to create it.
	J. Craig Venter describes a fast new approach to gene discovery using Expressed Sequence Tags (ESTs). "Although controversial when first introduced, ESTs are soon widely employed both in public and private sector research. They prove economical and versatile, used not only for rapid identification of new genes, but also for analyzing gene expression, gene families, and possible disease-causing mutations.
1992	CERN releases the World Wide Web.
	Berners-Lee creates the first blog at the first website: http://info.cern.ch./. From this site Berners-Lee points to other new sites as they go online. The original blog is archived as: http://www.w3.org/History/19921103-hypertext/hypertext/WWW/News/9201.html
	The number of hosts on the Internet surpasses 1,000,000.
	Internet Society (ISOC) is chartered.

	Ventor leaves the National Institutes of Health and founds The Institute for Genome Research (TIGR).
1993	The White House and the United Nations launch websites.
	The National Center for Supercomputing Applications (NCSA) introduces Mosaic, the first graphics-based Web browser, and the eventual basis for Netscape.
	IBM pioneers the technology of scalable parallel systems, joining multiple computer processors and breaking down complex, data-intensive jobs to speed their completion.
	Traffic on the Internet expands at a 341,634 percent growth rate.
May	Tim O'Reilly launches the Global Network Navigator, the first web portal and the first true commercial website. It will be sold to America Online in 1995.
1994	The number of websites reaches 10,000. The World Wide Web Consortium (W3C) is founded.
	The NSFNET backbone is upgraded to 155 Mbps as traffic passes 10 trillion bytes per month.
	The first Internet radio station or "cyberstation" broadcasts from InterOp in Las Vegas.
	HTTP (Web) packets surpass FTP traffic as the largest-volume Internet protocol.
	NSFNET reverts back to a research network and the main U. S. backbone traffic now goes through interconnected network providers.
	The first demonstration of wireless Internet access occurs at Bell Labs.
1995 July	Jeff Bezos founds Amazon.com.
September	Pierre M. Omidyar founds eBay as a sole proprietorship.
1996	According to UNESCO, 968,735 new books are produced in the world this year.
	IBM announces the DB2 Universal Database, the first fully scalable, Web-ready database management system. It is called "universal" because it can sort and query alphanumeric data as well as text documents, images, audio, video and other complex objects In 1996 some 70 percent of the world's business information is managed by IBM databases.
	This year more email is sent than regular paper mail.
	There are 14,352,000 Internet hosts and 100,000 websites.
	IBM unveils continuous speech recognition technology for Mandarin Chinese. In developing the product, researchers identified and classified thousand of vocal tones and homonyms, created an algorithm that deconstructs syllables into parts, and developed a new language model to transform spoken words into the right combination drawn from 6,700 Chinese characters. IBM also announces software that gives people a hands-free way to dictate text and navigate the desktop with the power of natural, continuous speech. IBM introduces software that reads aloud information displayed on the computer screen. The software allows the visually impaired to access and use the Internet.
	The Telecommunications Act of 1996 is passed, opening U.S. local and long distance markets to competition.
1997	126,000,000 metric tons of paper are consumed in the world.
May 11	Gary Kasparov resigns 19 moves into Game 6 against Deep Blue, an IBM supercomputer. Deep Blue is an IBM RS/6000 SP supercomputer capable of calculating 200 million chess positions per second. This is the first time that a current world chess champion loses to a computer under tournament conditions.

June	Wireless Application Protocol or WAP is established as a secure specification that allows users to access information instantly via handheld wireless devices such as mobile phones, pagers, two-way radios, smartphones and communicators. WAPs that use displays and access the Internet run what are called microbrowsers — browsers with small file sizes that can accommodate the low memory constraints of handheld devices and the low-bandwidth constraints of a wireless-handheld network.
1998	W3C releases the eXtensible Markup Language (XML) specification, allowing web pages to be tagged with descriptive labels.
	The average person receives 733 pieces of mail per year, half of which is junk mail.
	MP3 (MPEG Audio Layer 3) is introduced. It is an audio compression technology being a part of the MPEG-1 and MPEG-2 specifications. MP3 compresses CD quality sound by a factor of 8–12, while maintaining almost the same high-fidelity sound quality.
April	The Internet Society (ISOC) meets to discuss the growing spam problem.
May	J. Craig Venter founds Celera Genomics with Applera Corporation (Applied Biosystems) to sequence and assemble the human genome.
September 7	Larry Page and Sergey Brin found Google.
1999	64,711 new books are published in the United States in this year.
	It requires about 756,000,000 trees to produce the world's annual paper supply. "The UNESCO Statistical Handbook for 1999 estimates that paper production provides 1,510 sheets of paper per inhabitant of the world on average, although in fact the inhabitants of North America consume 11,916 sheets of paper each (24 reams), and inhabitants of the European Union consume 7,280 sheets of paper annually (15 reams), according to the ENST report. At least half of this paper is used in printers and copiers to produce office documents." http://www.sims.berkeley.edu/research/projects/how-much-info-2003/print.htm
	The U. S. Supreme Court rules that domain names are property.
	U.S. Vice President Al Gore announces *Blue Pacific,* jointly developed by the U.S. Energy Department's Lawrence Livermore National Laboratory and IBM. It can perform 3.9 trillion calculations per second (15,000 times faster than the average desktop computer) and has over 2.6 trillion bytes of memory (80,000 times more than the average PC). It would take a person using a calculator 63,000 years to perform as many calculations as this computer can perform in a single second.
December	IBM announces the start of a five-year effort to build a massively parallel computer, *Blue Gene,* which will be 500 times more powerful than the world's fastest computers at the time of the announcement. Initially *Blue Gene* will be applied to the study of bio-molecular phenomena such as protein folding.
2000	More than 25,000,000 websites have been identified, and over 10,000,000 domain names have been registered.
	There are 3,200,000 new book titles listed for sale in the United States. The number of book titles available in the world may be about 8,000,000.
	Web size estimates by NEC-RI and Inktomi surpass 1 billion pages that can be indexed. (Cisco)
June	Celera Genomics announces its first draft of the human genome.
August	IBM forms a Life Sciences Solutions division, incorporating its Computational Biology Center.
2001	The U.S. Government dedicates the *ASCI White* supercomputer at the Lawrence Livermore National Laboratory in California. An IBM system, it covers a space the size of two basketball courts and weighs 106 tons. It contains six trillion bytes (TB) of memory, almost 50,000 times greater than the average personal computer, and has more than 160 TB of Serial Disk System storage capacity — enough to hold *six times* the information stored in the 29 million books in the Library of Congress.
January 15	*Wikipedia, the Free Encyclopedia* begins as an English language project. As of September 2004 it contained over 350,000 articles in English and over 650,000 in other languages.

February	"In a remarkable special issue, *Nature* includes a 60-page article by the Human Genome Project partners, studies of mapping and variation, as well as analysis of the sequence by experts in different areas of biology. *Science* publishes the article by Celera on the assembly of HGP and Celera data as well as analyses of the use of the sequence." *Nature,* "The human genome." *Science,* "The sequence of the human genome." "Celera Genomics announced the first complete assembly of the human genome. Using whole genome shotgun sequencing, Celera began sequencing in September 1999 and finished in December. Assembly of the 3.12 billion base pairs of DNA, over the next six months, required some 500 million trillion sequence comparisons, and represented the most extensive computation ever undertaken in biology. "The Human Genome Project reported it had finished a "working draft" of the genome, stating that the project had fully sequenced 85 percent of the genome. Five major institutions in the United States and Great Britain performed the bulk of sequencing, together with contributions from institutes in China, France, and Germany." (gnn.tigr.or/timeline/2000)
2002	Babbage's Difference Engine No. 2, designed between 1847 and 1849, but never previously built, is completed and fully operational at the Science Museum, London. Built from Babbage's engineering drawings roughly 150 years after it was originally designed, it weighs 5 tons and consists of 8000 machined parts, equally divided between the calculating and automatic printing and stereotyping apparatus. It is operated by turning hand-cranks.
	There are 147,344,723 Internet hosts and 36,689,008 websites (Cisco)
2004	OCLC (Online Computer Library Center) serves more than 50,540 libraries of all types in the U.S. and 84 countries and territories around the world. OCLC WorldCat contains 56 million records representing 894 million holdings.
	The largest library in the world, the Library of Congress, contains nearly 128 million items on approximately 530 miles of bookshelves. The collections include more than 29 million books and other printed materials, 2.7 million recordings, 12 million photographs, 4.8 million maps, and 57 million manuscripts.
December	Google announces the Google Print project to scan and make searchable on the Internet the texts of more than ten million books from the collections of the New York Public Library, and the libraries of Michigan, Stanford, Harvard and Oxford Universities.

3
Human Computers

3.1

Mental Calculation. A Reminiscence of the late Mr. G. P. Bidder, Past-President

W. Pole, F.R.S., Hon. Sec. Inst. C.E.

From *Minutes of the Proceedings of the Institute of Civil Engineers* 15 (1855–56): 250–56.

INTRODUCTORY NOTE TO READING 3.1:

As I wrote in the Introduction to this book, for centuries before the successful construction in 1943–45 of programmed calculating or computing machines, the term "computer," without the qualifier "human," generally applied to humans rather than machines. During this pre-1945 period the machines were more typically called "calculators," and the word "computer" was more generally applied to people. In the early nineteenth century Charles Babbage called his machines "calculating engines" (Difference Engine or Analytical Engine). In the first decade or so of electronic computing, the word "calculator" was sometimes used for electronic computers. The "C" in the EDSAC, a first generation of stored-program electronic computer developed at Cambridge University, stood for calculator. In the UNIVAC, the first stored-program electronic digital computer sold commercially in the United States, the "C" stood for computer. In the United States the word "computer" first became closely associated in the public mind with the UNIVAC after that computer predicted the election of Dwight D. Eisenhower on nationwide television on November 4, 1953. The effect of this prediction was so dramatic that IBM called their initial commercial offerings of electronic digital computers (IBM 701 and 702) "data processing machines" rather than "computers" to distinguish them from the UNIVAC. Only after electronic digital computers became relatively widespread in the late 1950s or early 1960s did the word "computer" begin to apply exclusively to machines rather than people. Exactly when that transition took place is not clear. In the second edition of the first textbook on software, by Wilkes, Wheeler, and Gill (1957)[1], the authors compare (on page 1) communicating a problem to a digital computer with communicating the same problem to a "human computer," thus indicating that the usage of the word "computer" to describe humans was still alive at this date. This may, however, be one of the later usages of "human computer" in a computing book other than a history of computing.[2]

The readings in this chapter concern the special calculating ability that certain human computers developed in the pre-electronic computing era. During the nineteenth century and earlier some human computers could perform complex mathematical calculations in their heads faster than any mechanical calculating machine. They were known as "lightning calculators." Some were idiot savants, but others were normal people with exceptional mental powers. In thinking about the history of computing we should remember that prior to World War II the term "computer" designated humans rather than machines.

---

1   Maurice Wilkes; David Wheeler; and Stanley Gill. *Programs for an Electronic Digital Computer.* Second edition. Reading, Mass.: Addison-Wesley, 1957.

2   For a detailed history of the origin and use of the word "computer" from Roman times up to the very recent past see Mario Aloisio, "The Calculation of Easter Day, and the Origin and Use of the Word *Computer*," *Annals of the History of Computing* XXVI, number 3 (2004): 42–49.

Of all the human computers on record, the most remarkable may have been George Parker Bidder (1806–1878). The son of a stonemason, George began to manifest his remarkable mathematical powers around the age of five. After an older brother taught him to count, George taught himself arithmetic, learning how to do complex calculations in his head before he could write. His father exhibited George at local fairs, then toured him around England as "The Calculating Prodigy" and "The Calculating Boy." In 1816 George came to the attention of John and Sir William Herschel, who paid for him to attend Wilson's Grammar School (John Herschel was a friend of Charles Babbage, who in 1822 made his first proposal to the Royal Society for support in building a Difference Engine; see reading 4.1 in this anthology). However, George's father pulled him out of school after a few months to continue his public exhibitions. In 1819, when George was thirteen, he came to the attention of Sir Henry Jardine, who had George tutored privately. The following year members of the Royal Society took up a subscription enabling George to attend Edinburgh University, where he studied engineering.

George Bidder's remarkable mathematical abilities contributed to great success in engineering. From 1834 he practiced civil engineering in partnership with his friend Robert Stephenson, son of the pioneering railway engineer George Stephenson. The firm did surveys and engineering for railways, waterworks, docks in England and Europe. In 1845/6 Bidder formed the Electric Telegraph Company, pioneering in the employment of women as telegraph operators. When the British telegraphs were nationalized in 1869 these women became the first female Civil Servants in England. Bidder achieved fame and considerable wealth through his chosen career. He was exceptionally capable at appearing before Parliamentary Committees to gain approval of projects because his prodigious ability at mental calculation made him highly effective in presenting his plans and spotting errors in the plans of others. Bidder's paper on *Mental Calculation*, though a summary of a longer and more detailed speech, is a testimony to the limits of the calculating ability of the unaided human mind. [JMN]

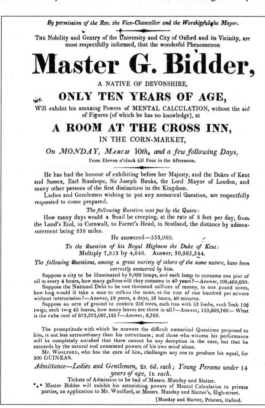

A handbill announcing Bidder's appearances at Oxford in 1817, when he was ten years of age.

Bidder in 1856, at the time he presented his paper on Mental Calculation (from the *Illustrated London News*, March 15, 1856).

TEXT OF READING 3.1

In the year 1855 Mr. Bidder gave to the Institution[1] a most interesting description of the wonderful powers of Mental Calculation with which he was endowed, and he made the Address specially valuable by showing how the methods he used might be taught in ordinary education, and employed in calculations generally. He not only gave examples of his modes of working complicated sums in ordinary arithmetic (as applied to weights and measures, time, and money), but also solved more difficult problems, involving square and cube roots, prime numbers, compound interest and so on, including some special calculations of a mechanical and engineering nature.

In the course of the Address he alluded to still higher feats as possible, particularly to the determination of logarithms, which he appeared to consider the *ne plus ultra* of mental calculation. He said, alluding to the two chief processes by which he worked:—

"Were my powers of registration at all equal to the powers of reasoning or execution, I should have no difficulty, in an inconceivably short space of time, in composing a voluminous table of logarithms; but the power of registration limits the power of calculation, and it is only with great labour and stress of mind, that mental calculation can be carried on beyond a certain extent."

The object of the present Paper is to put on record the fact, that Mr. Bidder subsequently succeeded in performing this astonishing feat, which at the time he spoke he had thought beyond his power. He appears to have considered, in fact, that he had, in the above words, given himself a sort of challenge, and after much further study, he declared his competency to calculate, mentally, and "in an inconceivably short space of time," the logarithm of any number, with the accuracy of the large published tables, extending to seven or eight places of decimals.

The enormous difficulty of this will be evident if any one will consider how he would set to work to calculate, mentally and accurately, the value of x in the equation say—

$$10^x = 369353,$$

or how he would mentally sum up a large number of terms of the series—

$$0.86858896\left\{\frac{n-1}{n+1} + \frac{1}{3}\left(\frac{n-1}{n+1}\right)^3 + \frac{1}{5}\left(\frac{n-1}{n+1}\right)^5 + \&c.\right\}$$

n being a large number whose logarithm is to be found.

Mr. Bidder had often been in communication with the Author of this Paper on the subject of mental calculation, and towards the end of his life he communicated this discovery, and requested the Author to aid him in testing its accuracy. For this purpose the following series of prime numbers was selected by the Author, with the aid of a mathematical friend:—

71, 97, 659, 877, 1297, 6719, 8963, 9973, 115,249, 175,349 290,011, 350,107, 229,847, 369,353.

Each of these was given, separately, to Mr. Bidder, and the logarithm in answer was returned very quickly. The time occupied on each varied from half a minute to four minutes, being generally about two minutes.

The logarithms were given in eight places, but the Author had only Hutton's table of seven places to check them with. The majority were stated at first quite correctly; but in some cases errors occurred (generally of one figure only), which were discovered and corrected on simply announcing that the answer was not exact. The experiment was at any rate amply conclusive as to the real efficiency of the mental power to perform the calculations for any numbers.

After the tests were over Mr. Bidder was good enough to explain fully the manner in which the calculations were made; and as this is quite a unique incident in mathematical history, it may be worth putting on record. Indeed, Mr. Bidder wished it to be published as an addendum to his lecture, and gave it to the Author with that view.

In general terms, it may be stated that his mode of calculation was not based on any of the formulas proper for calculating logarithms in the first instance; for probably no amount of genius and skill would suffice for reducing them to manageable form for mental calculation, when the given number was large. Neither was it a matter of simple memory, for it would be equally impossible for any one to recollect the logarithms, to eight places, of hundreds of thousands of numbers.

It was, however, founded on a power of memory, of a more limited range. Mr. Bidder's process may be said briefly to be this: having stored in his memory the logarithms of a few simple numbers, he was able, by his wonderful skill in dealing with figures, to make use of them, mentally, to calculate accurately the logarithms of any other numbers however large. A brief description will give an idea of the manner in which this was done.

In the first place, as to the mnemonic bases used. He knew by heart the logarithms of a great many *small prime numbers,* nearly all, he said, under 100, and some few above.

Secondly, it will be easily understood that these would enable him to calculate the logarithms of any large numbers which were multiples of those he knew. Thus for the logarithm of 63 he had only to add together the logarithms of 7 and 9; for the logarithm of 3567, he had only to sum up the logarithms of 29, 41, and 3, and so on.

In carrying out this process he had an almost miraculous power of seeing, as it were intuitively, what factors would divide any large given number not a prime. Thus if he was given the number 17,861, he would instantly remark it was = 337 × 53; or he would see as quickly that 1659 was = 79 × 7 × 3. He could not, he said, explain how he did this, it seemed like a natural instinct to him.

These two qualifications, therefore—the knowledge of the logarithms of certain small primes, and the power of reducing large compound numbers to their component factors—constituted the foundation on which Mr. Bidder's operations proceeded. They would suffice for determining the logarithms of a great many numbers by simply adding together the logarithms of their component factors, which he could do mentally with the greatest ease.

But it still remains to be explained how he treated the case of large primes, and this is really the great interest of his process.

His first endeavour was to find some multiple number *very near* the number given, differing from it only in the last place of figures, and if possible only by unity. For example, being given the number 1051, he would easily find the logarithm of 1050 (= 30 × 7 × 5) to which he would then have to make an addition for the difference of 1. This addition would be very important (for the accuracy aimed at), as it would affect the last five figures of the logarithm. The operation is difficult and complicated, and the manner of dealing with it was really the key to Mr. Bidder's success. It is due to him, therefore, to explain it somewhat fully.

His method consisted in the use, as a basis, of the following Table, which he knew by heart (only seven places are given here, he himself used eight):—

For an Addition of any Number n of	There must be added to its Logarithm
n/100	Log. 1.01 = 0.0043214
n/1000	Log. 1.001 = 0.00043407
n/10000	Log. 1.0001 = 0.0000434
n/100000	Log. 1.00001 = 0.0000043

Suppose therefore, as in the above case, there is to be added to the logarithm a sum corresponding to an addition to the number of n/1050 (= 1). Mr. Bidder would take the proportion 1/1000 : 0.0004341 : : 1/1050 : 0.0004134. This calculation would pass through his mind instantaneously, and thus he would get, by mental addition—

Log. 30 . . . =	1.4771213
Log. 5 . . . =	0.6989700
Log. 7 . . . =	0.8450980
Addition for the 1 =	0.0004134
Log. of 1051 . . =	3.0216027

But it would sometimes be necessary to add a larger proportion than above mentioned, say between $n/100$ and $n/1000$. For these he adopted mentally a kind of proportionate sliding scale. Thus, for the number 601, he would see that $n/600$ would require 0.0007232, so that—

Log. 600 . . . =	2.7781513
Addition for the 1 =	0.0007232
Log. of 601 . . =	2.7788745

He preferred that the differences should be less than $n/1000$, and to attain this result he would often multiply the given number by some other. For example, with the number 8771, instead of taking it as—

$$(73 \times 12) + 1$$

he multiplied it by 13, which gave $11{,}401 = (609 \times 19) + 1$ and he found the logarithm thus—

Log. 600	= 2.7781512
Log. 19	= 1.2787536
Addition for 1 = 0.000043428/1.141	= 0.0000381
Log. 11401	= 4.0569429
Deduct log. 13	= 1.1139433
Log. 877	= 2.9429996

Similarly to find the logarithm of 97 (which he could not remember at once), he multiplied it by 33, giving $3{,}201 \; (= 100 \times 2^5 + 1)$ which he worked in the same way, saying that it was more certain than $96 + 1$, and quite as easy to him.

The following statement will illustrate how these principles were applied for each of the test numbers given him:—

71 given by memory;

97 already explained;

$659 = (3 \times 2 \times 11) - 1;$

877 already explained;

$$1297 = \frac{(400 \times 107) + 1}{33};$$

$6719 = (64 \times 105) - 1;$

$8963 = (27 \times 4 \times 83) - 1;$

$$9973 = \frac{(9 \times 41) + 1}{37};$$

$115249 = (25 \times 461) - 1;$ [and $461 = (23 \times 20) + 1$]

$175349 = (25 \times 7014) - 1;$ [and $7014 = 7000 + 14$]

$229847 = 230000 - 153;$

$290011 = (29 \times 10000) + 11;$

$350107 = (7 \times 50000) + 107;$

$369353 = (9 \times 41000) + 369 - 16.$

In these latter cases the calculation of the excess was more complicated, thus—

$$\frac{1}{1000} : 0004341 :: \frac{1.07}{3501} :: 0.0001328$$

In the case of 369,353 he first added for a 1/1000 part and then deducted for the 16—a good example of his readiness in devising the best way of performing the calculation.

It is worth mentioning that Mr. Bidder declared that the logarithms he knew by heart had been all calculated mentally; he had never written them down, nor looked for information into a Table for many years.

Although this great feat is probably far in advance of any other mental calculation on record, it will be seen that, when thus analysed, it is explained on the same principles as are given in Mr. Bidder's lecture of 1855, and which may be classified as follows:—

1. A good memory for retaining certain standard numbers for reference.

2. The power of performing the ordinary simple arithmetical operations of multiplication, division, proportion, &c., on large numbers with great facility, quickness, and accuracy.

3. A remarkable intuitive detection of multiple numbers, and an instantaneous perception of the factors forming them.

4. The power of what Mr. Bidder called "registration," i.e., of keeping a string of successive processes and results clear in the mind, and working accurately upon them.

5. The power of devising instantly the best mode of performing a complicated problem, as regards facility, quickness, and certainty.

All these were undoubtedly the result of natural gifts; the second, third, and fourth, special and phenomenal. The fifth Mr. Bidder considered to be largely improved by practice and experience.

It is obvious that such powers cannot be taught to even the most promising and intelligent pupils; but undoubtedly the processes described may furnish useful hints for improving the power of practical calculation.

NOTE.

Mr. Bidder's son, Mr. G. P. Bidder, Q.C. (himself an accomplished mathematician), has favoured the Author with the following remarks on the above memorandum. They show the truth of the assertion, so confidently made by his father, that many of the principles of labour-saving in calculation which he devised could be taught and made useful.

"I remember very well my father's fondness for calculating logarithms, and the facility with which he performed the operation. We often discussed the subject, and in consequence my own attention was drawn to it, and I eventually became able to calculate them mentally without much trouble, though not at a speed comparable with his, nor with such accuracy. Moreover, I always contented myself with six places of decimals.

"Of course the great desideratum is to devise a method which relieves the mind, as far as possible, of the burthen of performing and registering long calculations. The details of my father's method, as described in the Paper, are new to me, and I think it may be interesting to compare it with my own, which; although in its main lines very similar, yet differs somewhat in form; for having obtained from him an idea of the general principles he adopted, I arrived at my own details independently. My method for numbers not large was as follows:—

"I knew by heart the logarithms of 2, 3, 7, and 11, and also the modulus 0.4343. My rule then was to select some multiple of the prime of the form $m + n$, where m is a multiple of 2, 3, 7, and 11, and n was very small, usually = 1.

Then $\log_{10} (m + n) = \log_{10} m + \log_{10} \left(1 + \dfrac{n}{m}\right)$.

But $\log_{10} \left(1 + \dfrac{n}{m}\right) = 0.4343 \log_e \left(1 + \dfrac{n}{m}\right)$,

and $\log_e \left(1 + \dfrac{n}{m}\right) = \left(\dfrac{n}{m}\right) - 1/2 \left(\dfrac{n}{m}\right)^2 + 1/3 \left(\dfrac{n}{m}\right)^3$, &c.

"This I found quite practicable mentally for primes not very large.

"For very large numbers (not having my father's great power of seizing instantaneously upon component factors), I adopted another method, which I can best illustrate by an example, which recently I worked out mentally, namely, to find the logarithm of 724871.

"The method depends on the use of the powers of 1.1, 1.01, 1.001, &c., of which the logarithms are assumed to be known. It is not difficult to make out that—

$$724871 = 72 \times (1.001)^6 \times (1.0001)^7 \times (1.00001)^{4.5}.$$

"Adding the logarithms together, the result is obtained, .860261. The mental strain is much less than would at first sight appear.
"GEORGE P. BIDDER."

• • •

1. Minutes of Proceedings, vol. xv. p. 255. The memorandum on which the present Paper is

based was prepared during Mr. Bidder's lifetime, and with his approval; but something happened to delay its publication, and it has only recently come to light again.

Notes on the Special Development of Calculating Ability.

W. G. Smith, M.A., Ph.D.

From Ellice M. Horsburgh, ed., *Modern Instruments and Methods of Calculation: A Handbook of the Napier Tercentenary Exhibition* (London: G. Bell and Sons, 1914), pp. 60–68.

INTRODUCTORY TO NOTE TO READING 3.2

"Notes on the Special Development of Calculating Ability" by W. G. Smith remains one of the best historical studies of exceptional calculating ability in people. It was originally published as a chapter in the *Handbook of the Napier Tercentenary Celebration* (Edinburgh, 1914). The Napier tercentenary celebration, marking the three hundredth anniversary of the publication of Napier's *Mirifici logarithmorum canonis descriptio* (1614), was held in Edinburgh from July 24 to July 27, 1914—just five days before the start of World War I. Participants in the exhibition included individuals and companies from Scotland, England, France, and Germany. The meeting was intended to include a colloquium on the mathematics of computation, but this was canceled because war was considered imminent.

A celebration of Napier's pivotal role in the history of calculation, the exhibition featured displays of many different types of calculating machines, as well as exhibits of other aids to calculation such as mathematical tables, the abacus and slide rules, planimeters and other integrating devices, and ruled papers and nomograms. These were described in the *Handbook* to the exhibition, which contained separate sections, with chapters by various contributors, devoted to each type of calculating device. The most widely used tools for calculation at the time of the Napier tercentenary were mathematical tables, a topic thoroughly surveyed, explained, and described in the *Handbook,* which also contained a large illustrated section on calculating machines. The *Handbook* remains the best general survey of calculating machines and related subjects in the period up to World War I. [JMN]

TEXT OF READING 3.2

The growth of calculating ability as it appears within the range of conditions in ordinary life is a matter of interest and importance. But when these conditions are absent, as they have been with not a few calculators, the interest is much heightened. Those who show distinguished ability in mental calculation may be young; they may owe little or nothing to education or to the stimulus of a cultured environment; they may even, while attaining a striking measure of success, be unable to read or write. The psychological problems which are involved are thrown into the clearest relief in the case of those who are quite young; but, while there are important observations on record in regard to such instances, the data which we possess refer, in the main and quite naturally, to the work of mental calculation as carried on in more mature years. We may, however, legitimately assume that whatever insight is gained with respect to the process of calculation in later years, may, with appropriate qualifications, be applied in considering the problems of earlier development.[1]

That precocity is a marked characteristic of calculating ability is clear. Binet, referring to "the natural family of great calculators," estimates the age at which the ability appears as being on the average eight years.[2] A later writer, Mitchell, contends that it should be given as five to five and a half years.[3] Early development is a distinguishing feature of great men in science as in other provinces; but, as Binet remarks, the degree of precocity is perhaps nowhere so marked as it is in mental calculation.

Proceeding to consider the mental features which are presented in various forms by the calculators, and whose recognition may assist in understanding their achievements, we may note in the first place a deep interest in numbers. The presence of this characteristic might perhaps be assumed on general grounds. On the other hand, here, as at other points, it may be well to refer to observations relating directly to the work of calculators. In speaking of his own attainments, Bidder remarks that he has no particular turn of mind beyond a liking for figures, a liking which, he adds, many possess like him.[4] It was towards the age of six years, according to Binet, that Inaudi was seized by the passion for numbers. We learn that Rückle, whose gifts in the way of memory and calculation have been fully studied by Müller, possessed in his youth, and particularly in the period from the twelfth to the fourteenth year, a very intense interest in numbers, their analysis, and other features. It is easy to understand that such interest may form the stimulus to the persistent exercise of mental powers with respect to numbers, and to prolonged and cumulative practice. This result may, in addition, be favoured by the situation in which the boy is placed. Mondeux, Inaudi, and others were occupied in their early youth in tending sheep. Such an employment gives an opportunity for the development of this special form of talent. Even illness, or physical disability, may, as Mitchell points out, form a favourable condition, by preventing the boy from participating in ordinary games. It should, at the same time, be noted that numbers, while presenting certain abstract and universal features of experience, offer relatively simple relations for the work of calculation, and are capable of illustration in various simple forms. Mondeux is reported to have used pebbles in his calculations. Bidder used peas, marbles, and especially shot, in working out numerical relations. Other branches of study do not, it is clear, offer the same opportunities for early unaided progress.

It is obvious that intellectual activity is involved in the attainments of the calculator. But in attempting to formulate it as a definite factor in explanation, one is met by certain difficulties. The concept of this activity is not free from a certain indefiniteness, which we can hardly discuss here. It may perhaps be taken as meaning generally the insight into the relations of objects. Now one is ordinarily not surprised to hear of instances where general intellectual ability is markedly present, but where mathematical ability is not conspicuous. But even the unreflective mind is struck by the circumstance that this calculating ability may be present in a comparatively isolated form. The case of Dase may be cited here. He showed a remarkable power of calculation, yet, as Schumacher writes to Gauss, it was impossible to get him to comprehend the first beginnings of mathematics.[5] We may suppose, in such a case as that of Dase, either an extremely one-sided form of intellectual ability, or a general ability which is limited by lack of interest in any other object in the mathematical sphere except that which is purely numerical. On both suppositions the matter involves difficulty.

Another aspect of this general problem is presented by the case, studied with great care by Wizel,[6] of a woman possessing considerable power of calculation who is in an imbecile condition, the result of an attack of typhus in her seventh year. Her mental life is characterised by alternation between a state of indifference or apathy and one of excitement; apart from arithmetical knowledge, the range of ideas is very limited, the poverty in abstract and general ideas being specially noticeable; her power of judgment is on the level of that of a child of three years. Her abilities in calculation are described by Wizel as follows:—"Apart from addition and subtraction, which she performs slowly and often incorrectly, she manifests unusual abilities in the sphere of multiplication, and partly also in that of division. In spite of her retarded intelligence she carries on these operations rapidly, and, what is more remarkable, with much greater rapidity than an ordinary normal individual." With three-place numbers the results are much poorer: "she multiplies in memory three-place by one-place numbers pretty well, but here her calculating abilities terminate." Wizel suggests that where the problems are solved immediately the memory alone is exercised: where several seconds are required, definite methods, *e.g.* factorising, are employed. Those problems in which the number 16 is involved are solved with special facility, apparently because in earlier years the patient was very fond of collecting objects, *e.g.* coins, which were arranged and counted in groups of sixteen. Referring to the main lines of explanation already mentioned, one may suppose that the phenomena are due to lack of interest in almost everything except numbers,[7] or to the survival, in the midst of extensive pathological impairment, of memory for numbers and the related calculating ability. It is reasonable to consider that both factors are at work, the latter being the more important. It may be noted that the preservation of abilities connected with number is a feature in certain cases of aphasia.

The importance of memory has been justly emphasised in the discussion of the present topic. Its function may be considered here in two main respects, which in practice are inextricably bound together. In the first place, it enables the calculator to keep in permanent possession those properties of numbers which he has already grasped; in the second place, it enables him to retain the actual data, the particular products, or other features of the special problem before him at the moment. These are analogous, on the one hand, to the general memory of a language, and, on the other, to the knowledge at any moment of what has been said at the preceding stages of a conversation. As an illustration of the former, there may be noted the fact, mentioned by Cauchy in the report to the Académie des Sciences,[8] that Mondeux knew almost by heart the squares of all the whole numbers up to 100. Bidder points out the importance of knowing by heart such facts as the number of seconds in a year or the number of inches in a mile. Rückle, in his twelfth year, knew by heart as regards all the numbers up to 1000 whether they were primes or not, and in the latter case what their factors were. As regards the second direction in which memory is active, it may be noted that, according to Bidder, the key to mental calculation lies in registering only one fact at a time, the strain in calculation being due to this work of registration. Thus in a complex multiplication he goes through a series of operations, "the last result in each operation being alone registered by the memory, all the previous results being consecutively obliterated until a total product is obtained",[9] what is thus not kept in view can be recollected when needed. It may be mentioned that, according to Binet, Inaudi could recall at the close of a public exhibition 300 figures involved in the different problems he had dealt with, and, after the lapse of sixteen to eighteen hours, many of the numbers used on the previous evening, though but few of those of the preceding evenings.

With regard to the ability to learn by heart and reproduce immediately a series of numbers, the following data given among others by Binet and Müller are of interest. In order to learn by heart a series of 105 digits read aloud and thereafter to repeat it, Inaudi required twelve minutes; to learn a written series of 100 digits and write it out, Diamandi required twenty-five minutes; to learn a visual series of 102 digits and repeat it by heart, Rückle required, on the average, approximately five minutes and forty seconds; Arnould, using special mnemo-technical devices, required, when tested in the same way as Diamandi, fifteen minutes.

In the investigations described by Binet,[10] a fact of considerable importance was brought out, viz. that Inaudi's imagery is of the auditory, or auditory-motor type, not of the visual type. Rückle's type, on the other hand, is visual, though, when it is advantageous, he can use auditory-motor factors. The fact referred to above is significant in relation to the view that mental calculation is carried out on a visual basis. Thus Bidder junior says:[11]—"If I perform a sum mentally, it always proceeds in a visible form in my mind; indeed, I can conceive no other way possible of doing mental arithmetic." An attempt has been made by Proctor[12] on the basis of his own early experiences to explain mental calculation by a special form of visual imagery. It was suggested that while the reference to ordinary arithmetical processes was inadequate, it was possible to find an explanation in the possession of an enhanced power to picture numbers as an assemblage of spots, or dots, arranged in columns which could be modified with the utmost facility and whose relations could be immediately grasped. At one time Proctor considered this to be the general method; later on he admitted that its use was limited, while contending that it gave the best account of Colburn's feats. The general value of the suggestion may be acknowledged; the recorded observations do not, however, support the view that this method of "mental marshalling" has actually been employed by great calculators. In connection with the visual type, attention may be called to the occasional presence of number forms in which the figures appear in a definite spatial order. It is of interest that Galton,[13] who first studied this topic, had the existence of such forms brought to his notice by Bidder, junior, who inherited, in some measure, his father's gift of calculation. Such a form was detected by Binet in the case of Diamandi. It has been urged by Hennig that "the possessors of number diagrams in general not only have a better memory for numbers, but also are apt to be much better in mental calculation" than those who lack this feature.[14] A wider review of the facts leads, however, to the conclusion that an unqualified assertion of the advantages of this feature cannot reasonably be made.[15]

Whilst with certain calculators the memory for numbers is merely one phase of a general power which shows itself in other directions also, in other cases the memory, while excellent as regards numbers, is relatively poor in other directions. In illustration of the latter case, it may be noted that Mondeux has much difficulty in retaining a name or an address. Inaudi's memory, again, is not in any way remarkable beyond the sphere of number. In attempting to understand this feature, suggestions have been made of an innate mental ability or a special development of memory due to certain assignable conditions. The latter suggestion seems to supply the basis for an adequate explanation of the phenomena. It has been shown by experimental methods that memory can be trained in such a way as to improve markedly its effectiveness both in immediate reproduction and in its more permanent phases. It is not necessary to discuss the question whether such a result is to be interpreted as a real change in power, or as being due to the more efficient and economical use of powers already possessed. Assuming that the latter view is the more probable, one may refer to general conditions which have been recognised, such as the increased ability to concentrate and maintain attention, the diminution of fatigue, and better adjustment of emotional and active tendencies to the work which is being prosecuted. It will be acknowledged that the interest in numbers, to which reference has already been made, forms, when it is persistent, a powerful motive to improvement of memory in this sphere. The admiration readily accorded to unusual attainments in the direction of mental calculation will inevitably assist in reinforcing the original interest. And it is to be observed that growing excellence in this sphere may be accompanied by an actual lessening of power in other subjects, especially in cases where there may be recognised a certain narrowness or poverty of mental content.

Reference may next be made to the influence of attention. In summarising the characteristics of Rückle, who combines a remarkable memory and a high calculating ability with mathematical culture,

Müller points out that he possesses in a high degree the power of concentrating his attention with full intensity, and that after a few introductory words he is ready to devote his full strength to each problem put before him, regardless of movement or experimental preparations in the room where he is working. One may note a similar attitude in the calculator Inaudi, who is not troubled by the noise or conversation going on around him on the stage, and in the case of Mondeux, of whom it is stated, that when his attention is directed to the numbers which have to be combined, his thought can follow the problems "as if he were completely isolated from all that surrounds him." What may be regarded as another aspect of attention is indicated by certain remarks which Schumacher makes regarding Dase. Thus in one instance he writes:[16] "His rapid knowledge of numbers is to me almost the most remarkable thing. If you throw down a handful of peas, the most cursory glance enables him to tell their number." A similar remark is made regarding his ability to grasp a line of figures. We seem to have before us in such facts that feature of attention by which the calculator is able to grasp with the utmost rapidity, and almost in a single act, the significance of a complex group of figures or other connected data which are presented to him. The advance which the child makes in passing from the reading of letters to the unitary grasp of words and higher complexes is made by the skilled calculator in his handling of higher numerical groups. We may say generally of attention that, with regard to memory, it develops concentration on the relevant features of the subject-matter which is presented, and facilitates the learning process by which knowledge of specific relations is built up, as well as the subsequent process in which this knowledge is recalled, while, with regard to intellectual activity, it brings the problem vividly before the calculator, and enables him to grasp the complex relations of what is presented with the utmost rapidity.[17]

A special feature of the calculating process is perhaps to be found in the case of Colburn. To the inquiries made regarding the methods employed in his calculations, he was for some time unable to give any answer, though evidently trying honestly to enlighten his friends. His account of the discovery, in his tenth year, of the method of factorising, which, for upwards of three years, he had been unable to give, may be quoted.[18] "It was on the night of 17th December 1813, while in the City of Edinburgh, that he waked up, and, speaking to his father, said, 'I can tell you how I find out the factors.' His father rose, obtained a light, and, beginning to write, took down a brief sketch, from which the rule was described and the following tables formed." He then proceeds to give a set of tables of the various pairs of factors which, multiplied, give the two-place endings up to 99. Referring to his backwardness in giving explanations several years earlier, he remarks that it was not owing to ignorance of the methods he pursued; "he rather thinks it was on account of a certain weakness of the mind which prevented him from taking at once such a general and comprehensive view of the subject, as to reduce his ideas to a regular system in examination." This explanation is very reasonable, but it may be suggested that it hardly seems to give an adequate account of the suddenness of the discovery in the instance cited above, or in another when he was at dinner with a friend, and, as we learn,—"Suddenly Zerah said he thought he could tell how he extracted roots." The question then may be raised whether such observations do not point to a certain ability to carry on the operations of calculation in a mental region, which, to speak figuratively, is beyond the margin of attentive processes, or is subconscious, if we may introduce this ambiguous term.[19] When the complexity of a cognitive activity is considerable and the rapidity with which it is carried out is great, we may be readily aware of its results, and yet may find it difficult, with even special training, to give a full account of the character of the processes involved. Something of this kind is probably present in rapid expert calculation, and we may perhaps fairly suppose that Colburn's observations indicate a process of this kind. If not carried out originally in this form, his calculations may, owing to some special circumstance, have readily passed into this form in the course of persistent exercise.[20]

Having thus reviewed the chief features of the mental processes involved in the actual work of great calculators, we may turn to the problem of the speed of their activity. There are two sides of this problem—the arithmetical and the psychological. As regards the first, attention may be called to the circumstance that, in the course of their persistent occupation with numbers, the calculators have in fact discovered various procedures and various properties of numbers, by which problems can be solved with greatly increased facility. One instance will suffice—the discovery by Colburn of the significance, with respect to the finding of roots, of two-figure endings together with the first one, two, or more figures in a lengthy number of five, six, or more digits.

Passing to the psychological problem, we may refer again to the calculator's knowledge of many properties of numbers which he possesses permanently by memory, and in respect of which the labour and time of calculation are spared. "It is certain," Binet remarks, "that M. Inaudi knows in advance many of the results of partial calculations which he utilises on each new occasion; his memory has retained the roots of a great number of perfect squares; he knows also the number of hours, minutes, and seconds in the year, the month, and the day." The constant practice carried on by the calculators increases, in addition, the facility with which the appropriate data are recalled. A remark by Bidder is interesting in this connection:—"Whenever, as in calculation, I feel called upon to make use of the stores of my mind, they seem to rise with the rapidity of lightning." Further, continual exercise will enable the intellectual activity, especially in its relations with attention, to be carried on with growing rapidity.[21] One must at the same time keep in mind that there are certain innate, unacquired differences between individuals in the rapidity with which mental activities are carried on.

Scripture calls attention[22] to the great shortening in time which may be attained "if the adding, subtracting, multiplying, etc., can be done before the numbers themselves come into full consciousness," and if all superfluous processes are omitted. He suggests also that this feature may explain Colburn's inability to explain his methods. Binet points out[23] that Inaudi, to whom the subject-matter of a problem is read aloud, begins to calculate while listening to the series of data,

and that Diamandi, in the process of learning a series of numbers, does not keep separate the processes of reading, learning, and of the final writing out, the processes being in reality *enchevêtrées*. Such a union of processes may possibly exist in other cases also, and, if so, it would help to explain the rapidity with which the results are reached. Reference may be made in this connection to observations which indicate the ability to carry on at the same time two distinct series of mental operations. Binet remarks[24] with regard to Inaudi:—"We have seen him sustain a conversation with M. Charcot at the Salpêtrière while he solved mentally a complicated problem; this conversation did not confuse him in his calculations, it simply prolonged their duration." We are told of Buxton,[25] the Derbyshire labourer, whose calculations were not remarkable for their rapidity, that "he would suffer two people to propose different questions, one immediately after the other, and give each his respective answer without the least confusion"; and, again, that "he will talk with you freely whilst he is doing his questions, it being no molestation to him, but enough to confound a penman." It is, of course, clear that such observations do not give a rigid proof of the complete concurrence of the different series of activities. A remark of Bidder, junior, emphasises the importance of the self-reliance which prolonged practice secures:—"I am certain that unhesitating confidence is half the battle. In mental arithmetic it is most true that he who hesitates is lost." Müller mentions an observation of Rückle regarding multiplication, to the effect that one must above all avoid hesitation between different modes of procedure, and that one learns by practice to know at once what method to adopt.

While the various processes indicated in the earlier and later sections of this brief review have of necessity been discussed separately, it is not meant to be suggested that they exist in isolation. The various features are no doubt intimately connected in actual practice. At the same time we have to keep in mind that different individuals may reach a similar result as regards the solution of problems through complex activities which may differ both in their constituent processes and in the varying prominence which certain common elements possess. Recognising the co-operation of factors and the differentiation of the complex activities, we seem to reach a reasonably adequate understanding of the achievements in calculation both in early life and in more mature years.

•••

1. The following works deal more or less comprehensively with the present subject:—"Arithmetical Prodigies," by E. W. Scripture, *American Journal of Psychology,* iv., 1891-92; *Les grand calculateurs et joueurs d'echecs,* by A. Binet, 1894; "Mathematical Prodigies," by F. D. Mitchell, *American Journal of Psychology,* xviii., 1907; *Zur Analyse der Gedächtnistätigkeit und des Vorstellungsverlaufes,* by G. E. Müller, 1911-13.

2. *Op. cit.,* p. 191.

3. *Op. cit.,* p. 97.

4. Here and elsewhere the reference is to G. P. Bidder, senior, whose paper on "Mental Calculation" appears in the *Proceedings of the Institute of Civil Engineers,* xv., 1855-56. His son, J. P. Bidder, will be referred to as Bidder, junior.

5. *Briefwechsel zwischen C. F. Gauss und H. C. Schumacher,* v. S. 295.

6. "Ein Fall von phänomenalen Rechentalent bei einem Imbecillen," *Archiv fur Psychiatrie,* xxxviii., 1904.

7. It is remarked by Wizel (*op. cit.,* S. 128), with reference to the two topics—her supposed persecutions, and calculation:—"Round these subjects the conversation usually turns. Otherwise she is interested in nothing, speaks of nothing, busies herself with nothing."

8. *Comptes rendus,* xi., 1840, p. 953.

9. *Op. cit.,* p. 260.

10. *Op. cit.,* ch. v.; *cf.* J. M. Charcot, *Comptes rendus,* cxiv., 1872.

11. *Spectator,* li., 1878, p. 1634.

12. *Cornhill Magazine,* xxxii., 1875; this article is reprinted in "Science Byways," *Belgravia,* xxxviii., 1879.

13. *Inquiries into Human Faculty and Development,* 1883 (Number Forms).

14. "Entstehung und Bedeutung der Synopsien," *Zeitschrift für Psychologie und Physiologie der Sinnesorgane,* x., 1886, S. 215.

15. *Cf.* Miller, *op. cit.,* Abschnitt 8, Kap. 3.

16. *Op. cit.,* S. 296.

17. Reference may be made to experimental investigations regarding the range, or span, of attention and of consciousness; *cf.* W. Wundt, *Grundzuge der physiol. Psychologie,* iii.

18. *A Memoir of Zerah Colburn written by himself,* 1833, p. 183

19. An observation made by Gauss (*op. cit.,* S. 297) may be cited in this connection. After referring to the great psychological interest which an adequate analysis of Dase's mental processes in calculation would possess, and to the difficulties involved, he proceeds: —"For, indeed, I have had many experiences of my own, which remain puzzling to me. The following is an instance. Sometimes, while I walk along a certain path, I begin in thought to count the steps . . . thus I count on to 100, and then begin again. When, however, this is once started, it is all done unconsciously; I think about quite different things, notice attentively anything remarkable—only I have to avoid speaking meanwhile—and after some time I begin to be aware that I am continuing to count in time."

20. It may be noted here that according to Mitchell (*op. cit.,* pp. 100 ff.) three grades of ability may be distinguished in the great calculators. In the first the operation is one of pure counting, and it is the properties of numbers and series that are thought of, while in the second the interest relates principally to the operations of calculation. In the third real mathematical ability is found. Mental arithmetic grows naturally and independently out of counting.

21. The following remarks by Bidder, junior (*op. cit.,* p. 634), refer to his father's powers. "The second faculty, that of rapid operation, was no doubt congenital, but developed by incessant practice and by the confidence thereby acquired. . . . When I speak of 'incessant practice,' I do not mean deliberate drilling of set purpose; but with my father, as with myself, the mental handling of numbers or playing with figures afforded a positive pleasure and constant occupation of leisure moments."

22. *Op. cit.,* p. 44.

23. *Op. cit.,* pp. 80, 123.

24. *Op. cit.,* p. 37.

25. *Gentleman's Magazine,* xxi., 1751, pp. 61, 347.

4

Mechanizing the Production of Mathematical Tables

124

A Letter to Sir Humphry Davy, Bart. . . . on the Application of Machinery to the Purposes of Calculating and Printing Mathematical Tables

Charles Babbage

London: J. Booth; Baldwin, Cradock & Joy, 1822.

INTRODUCTORY NOTE TO READING 4.1

Attempts to mechanize the production of mathematical tables drove advances in computing from the nineteenth century until the volumes of printed tables were finally replaced by inexpensive hand-held calculators in the 1960s. About 1820 Charles Babbage (1791–1871), a mathematician, economist, and engineer unlike any before him, was motivated to build his first calculating engine, the special-purpose Difference Engine no. 1, in order to mechanize the drudgery of calculation and improve the accuracy of mathematical tables. The problem of producing more accurate mathematical tables remained the central problem faced by human computers in Babbage's day, just as it had in previous centuries. Mathematical tables were the most widely available calculating aids, and they were essential for many purposes, including navigation and astronomy, insurance, and civil engineering. They were also the main work product of human computing, work done entirely by hand. In principle their calculation was not complex, but without the most careful organization, human error at the various stages of production always introduced mistakes. Errors in astronomical and navigational tables sometimes had unfortunate consequences, especially for sea powers like England and the United States. Beginning in 1766, the British government had funded the annual production of navigational tables, known as the *Nautical Almanac*, under the direction of the Astronomer Royal. This was the first permanent table-making project established in the world. Known as the "seaman's bible," this annual publication was credited with substantially improving accuracy in navigation. In the years prior to Babbage's project, production of the tables had fallen into decline, and errors in them had mounted. It was not hard to convince the British Government that mechanical production of tables, and typesetting them by the same machine to avoid introducing typographical errors, would greatly improve their accuracy. Thus Babbage succeeded in receiving generous funding for the project.

In his letter to Sir Humphrey Davy (Reading 4.1), his initial publication on the Difference Engine no. 1, Babbage wrote, "The intolerable labour and fatiguing monotony of similar arithmetic calculations first excited the desire and afterward suggested the idea of a machine which by the aid of gravity or any other moving power, should become a substitute of one of the lowest operations of the human intellect." In proposing this project Babbage was recommending an approach which had no true antecedents. No difference engine had ever been built before.

By designing the Difference Engine no. 1 not only to calculate the tables, but also to produce stereotype printing plates in order to avoid the introduction of typesetting errors, Babbage was attempting to mechanize the production of thought rather than physical labor—the mechanization of what he called "mental labor." To do so required first an analytical process that Babbage called "the division of mental labor," in which a complex process was broken down into its simplest components. When he began developing his ideas for the engine around 1820, hardly anyone thought of what Babbage called "the division of mental labor." Analysis of labor costs and production methods had focused on production of material products. When Babbage addressed these problems, information, such as mathematical table-making, was a cottage industry processed entirely by people, by hand. The mechanization of computation and other clerical work was later called information processing.

Babbage may have been the first to study information processing even if he did not use the term. Only in the rare situations where an enormous volume of transactions needed to be processed accurately and quickly, had the process of mental labor been formally organized on a large scale. One of the only large organizations in Babbage's time that effectively employed the division of mental labor to increase the efficiency of its operations was the Banker's Clearing House in the City of London, about which Babbage wrote the only contemporary account.[1] Within Babbage's lifetime, other efficiently organized information-processing organizations employing "the division of mental labor" arose; these included the Prudential, founded in 1856 as the first of the great industrial insurance companies that would by the later part of the century handle the policies of millions of people. In 1877 it took three hundred clerks working at the Prudential six months to review its 2,500,000 policies with the assistance of twenty-four Thomas de Colmar arithmometers, the first commercially manufactured calculating machines. Within the next two decades, as improved mechanical calculators and electric card-tabulating machinery were developed, the Prudential was able to greatly increase its information-processing efficiency.

In his design for the Difference Engine no. 1, Babbage was influenced by the division of mental labor employed in the production of the famous mathematical tables of de Prony. Thus Babbage designed the Difference Engine to calculate mathematical tables using the most basic processes of addition and subtraction

Roffe's engraving, taken from "an original family painting," shows Babbage in 1833 at the age of forty-one, around the time that his manufacturing engineer, Joseph Clement, completed work on the small working portion of the Difference Engine no. 1. Shortly thereafter Babbage terminated his business relationship with Clement, and was forced to shut down work on the Difference Engine. The hiatus forced him to rethink the project entirely, and by the time he resumed working with Clement he had conceived the plan for his far more advanced general-purpose Analytical Engine.

by the method of finite differences, a process that could be repeated over and over again by a machine. Yet for all of Babbage's creativity and ingenuity, he did not really improve the process of computing mathematical tables. He had the right ideas; the time was not ripe for their implementation.

---

1 Babbage's account can be found in Ch. 14 of his *On the Economy of Machinery and Manufactures* (London: Charles Knight, 1832).

In 1832, after nearly a decade of intermittent work on the project, Babbage had his manufacturing engineer, Joseph Clement, fabricate a small working portion of his Difference Engine no. 1. It stood about two and one-half feet high, two feet wide, and two feet deep. Tooled out of bronze and steel, it represented approximately one-ninth of the full machine, and was the only working portion of any of Babbage's calculating engines constructed during his lifetime. The portion cost the British Treasury £17,478 14s 10d—a staggering sum considering that it was estimated that a family of four could live in reasonable comfort at the time for about £350 per year. Babbage later estimated that he had also spent about £20,000 of his personal funds on the project. In view of the enormous outlay and such limited results, it is not hard to understand why the British government was not enthusiastic about continuing to fund this project, with its endless delays and cost overruns. [JMN]

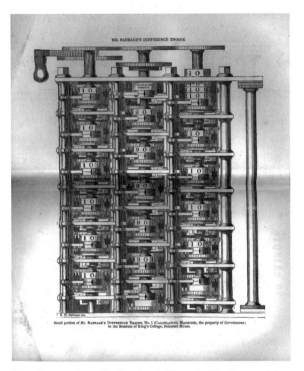

Wood engraving after Benjamin Herschel Babbage of the portion of the Difference Engine no. 1 completed in 1832. This version of B. H. Babbage's illustration, from John Timbs's *Stories of Inventors and Discoverers in Science and the Useful Arts* (1860), shows more of the Engine than the version printed in Babbage's *Passages from the Life of a Philosopher* (1864).

TEXT OF READING 4.1

My Dear Sir,

The great interest you have expressed in the success of that system of contrivances which has lately occupied a considerable portion of my attention, induces me to adopt this channel for stating more generally the principles on which they proceed, and for pointing out the probable extent and important consequences to which they appear to lead. Acquainted as you were with this inquiry almost from its commencement, much of what I have now to say cannot fail to have occurred to your own mind: you will however permit me to re-state it for the consideration of those with whom the principles and the machinery are less familiar.

The intolerable labour and fatiguing monotony of a continued repetition of similar arithmetical calculations, first excited the desire, and afterwards suggested the idea, of a machine, which, by the aid of gravity or any other moving power, should become a substitute for one of the lowest operations of human intellect. It is not my intention in the present Letter to trace the progress of this idea, or the means which I have adopted for its execution; but I propose stating some of their general applications, and shall commence with describing the powers of several engines which I have contrived: of that part which is already executed I shall speak more in the sequel.

The first engine of which drawings were made was one which is capable of computing any table by the aid of differences, whether they are positive or negative, or of both kinds. With respect to the number of the order of differences, the nature of the machinery did not in my own opinion, nor in that of a skilful mechanic whom I consulted, appear to be restricted to any very limited number; and I should venture to construct one with ten or a dozen orders with perfect confidence. One remarkable property of this machine is, that the greater the number of differences the more the engine will outstrip the most rapid calculator.

By the application of certain parts of no great degree of complexity, this may be converted into a machine for extracting the roots of equations, and consequently the roots of numbers: and the extent of the approximation depends on the magnitude of the machine.

Of a machine for multiplying any number of figures (m) by any other number (n) I have several sketches; but it is not yet brought to that degree of perfection which I should wish to give it before it is to be executed.

I have also certain principles by which, if it should be desirable, a table of prime numbers might be made, extending from 0 to ten millions.

Another machine, whose plans are much more advanced than several of those just named, is one for constructing tables which have no order of differences constant.

A vast variety of equations of finite differences may by its means be solved, and a variety of tables, which could be produced in successive parts by the first machine I have mentioned, could be calculated by the latter one with a still less exertion of human thought. Another and very remarkable point in the structure of this machine is, that it will calculate tables governed by laws which have not been hitherto shown to be explicitly determinable, or that it will solve equations for which analytical methods of solution have not yet been contrived.

Supposing these engines executed, there would yet be wanting other means to ensure the accuracy of the printed tables to be produced by them.

The errors of the persons employed to copy the figures presented by the engines would first interfere with their correctness. To remedy this evil, I have contrived means by which the machines themselves shall take from several boxes containing type, the numbers which they calculate, and place them side by side; thus becoming at the same time a substitute for the compositor and the computer: by which means all error in copying as well as in printing is removed.

There are, however, two sources of error which have not yet been guarded against. The ten boxes with which the engine is provided contain each about three thousand types; any box having of course only those of one number in it. It may happen that the person employed in filling these boxes shall accidentally place a wrong type in some of them; as for instance, the number 2 in the boxes which ought only to contain 7s. When these boxes are delivered to the superintendant of the engine, I have provided a simple and effectual means by which he shall in less than half an hour ascertain whether, amongst these 30,000 types, there be any individual misplaced or even inverted. The other cause of error to which I have alluded, arises from the type falling out when the page has been set up: this I have rendered impossible by means of a similar kind.

The quantity of errors from carelessness in correcting the press, even in tables of the greatest credit, will scarcely be believed, except by those who have had constant occasion for their use. A friend of mine, whose skill in practical as well as theoretical astronomy is well known, produced to me a copy of the tables published by order of the French Board of Longitude, containing those of the Sun by Delambre and of the Moon by Burg, in which he had corrected above *five hundred errors:* most of these appear to be errors of the press; and it is somewhat remarkable, that in turning over the leaves in the fourth page I opened we observed a new error before unnoticed. These errors are so much the more dangerous, because independent computers using the same tables will agree in the same errors.

To bring to perfection the various machinery which I have contrived, would require an expense both of time and money which can be known only to those who have themselves attempted to execute mechanical inventions. Of the greater part of that which has been mentioned, I have at present contented myself with sketches on paper, accompanied by short memorandums, by which I might at any time more fully develop the contrivances; and where any new principles are introduced I have had models executed in order to examine their actions. For the purpose of demonstrating the practicability of these views, I have chosen the engine for differences, and have constructed one of them which will produce any tables whose second differences are constant. Its size is the same as that which I should propose for any more extensive one of the same kind: the chief difference would be, that in one intended for use there would be

a greater repetition of the same parts in order to adapt it to the calculation of a larger number of figures. Of the action of this engine, you have yourself had opportunities of judging, and I will only at present mention a few trials which have since been made by some scientific gentlemen to whom it has been shown, in order to determine the rapidity with which it calculates. The computed table is presented to the eye at two opposite sides of the machine; and a friend having undertaken to write down the numbers as they appeared, it proceeded to make a table from the formula $x^2 + x + 41$. In the earlier numbers my friend, in writing quickly, rather more than kept pace with the engine; but as soon as four figures were required, the machine was at least equal in speed to the writer.

In another trial it was found that thirty numbers of the same table were calculated in two minutes and thirty seconds: as these contained eighty-two figures, the engine produced thirty-three every minute.

In another trial it produced figures at the rate of forty-four in a minute. As the machine may be made to move uniformly by a weight, this rate might be maintained for any length of time, and I believe few writers would be found to copy with equal speed for many hours together. Imperfect as a first machine generally is, and suffering as this particular one does from great defect in the workmanship, I have every reason to be satisfied with the accuracy of its computations; and by the few skilful mechanics to whom I have in confidence shown it, I am assured that its principles are such that it may be carried to any extent. In fact, the parts of which it consists are few but frequently repeated, resembling in this respect the arithmetic to which it is applied, which, by the aid of a few digits often repeated, produces all the wide variety of number. The wheels of which it consists are numerous, but few move at the same time; and I have employed a principle by which any small error that may arise from accident or bad workmanship is corrected as soon as it is produced, in such a manner as effectually to prevent any accumulation of small errors from producing a wrong figure in the calculation.

Of those contrivances by which the composition is to be effected, I have made many experiments and several models; the results of these leave me no reason to doubt of success, which is still further confirmed by a working model that is just finished.

As the engine for calculating tables by the method of differences is the only one yet completed, I shall in my remarks on the utility of such instruments confine myself to a statement of the powers which that method possesses.

I would however premise, that if any one shall be of opinion, notwithstanding all the precaution I have taken and means I have employed to guard against the occurrence of error, that it may still be possible for it to arise, the method of differences enables me to determine its existence. Thus, if proper numbers are placed at the outset in the engine, and if it has composed a page of any kind of table, then by comparing the last number it has set up with that number previously calculated, if they are found to agree, the whole page must be correct: should any disagreement occur, it would scarcely be worth the trouble of looking for its origin, as the shortest plan would be to make the engine recalculate the whole page, and nothing would be lost but a few hours' labour of the moving power.

Of the variety of tables which such an engine could calculate, I shall mention but a few. The tables of powers and products published at the expense of the Board of Longitude, and calculated by Dr. Hutton, were solely executed by the method of differences; and other tables of the roots of numbers have been calculated by the same gentleman on similar principles.

As it is not my intention in the present instance to enter into the theory of differences, a field far too wide for the limits of this letter, and which will probably be yet further extended in consequence of the machinery I have contrived, I shall content myself with describing the course pursued in one of the most stupendous monuments of arithmetical calculation which the world has yet produced, and shall point out the mode in which it was conducted and what share of mental labour would have been saved by the employment of such an engine as I have contrived.

The tables to which I allude are those calculated under the direction of M. Prony by order of the French Government,—a work which will ever reflect the highest credit on the nation which patronized and

on the scientific men who executed it. The tables computed were the following.

1. The natural sines of each 10,000 of the quadrant calculated to twenty-five figures with seven or eight orders of differences.

2. The logarithmic sines of each 100,000 of the quadrant calculated to fourteen decimals with five orders of differences.

3. The logarithm of the ratios of the sines to their arcs of the first 5,000 of the 100,000ths of the quadrant calculated to fourteen decimals with three orders of differences.

4. The logarithmic tangents corresponding to the logarithmic sines calculated to the same extent.

5. The logarithms of the ratios of the tangents to their arcs calculated in the same manner as the logarithms of the ratios of the sines to their arcs.

6. The logarithms of numbers from 1 to 10,000 calculated to nineteen decimals.

7. The logarithms of all numbers from 10,000 to 200,000 calculated to fourteen figures with five orders of differences.

Such are the tables which have been calculated, occupying in their present state seventeen large folio volumes. It will be observed that the trigonometrical tables are adapted to the decimal system, which has not been generally adopted even by the French, and which has not been at all employed in this country. But, notwithstanding this objection, such was the opinion entertained of their value, that a distinguished member of the English Board of Longitude was not long since commissioned by our Government to make a proposal to the Board of Longitude of France to print an abridgement of these tables at the joint expense of the two countries; and five thousand pounds were named as the sum our Government was willing to advance for this purpose. It is gratifying to record this disinterested offer, so far above those little jealousies which frequently interfere between nations long rivals, and manifesting so sincere a desire to render useful to mankind the best materials of science in whatever country they might be produced. Of the reasons why this proposal was declined by our neighbours, I am at present uninformed: but, from a personal acquaintance with many of the distinguished foreigners to whom it was referred, I am convinced that it was received with the same good feelings as those which dictated it.

I will now endeavour shortly to state the manner in which this enormous mass of computation was executed; one table of which (that of the logarithms of numbers) must contain about eight millions of figures.

The calculators were divided into three sections. The first section comprised five or six mathematicians of the highest merit, amongst whom were M. Prony and M Legendre. These were occupied entirely with the analytical part of the work; they investigated and determined on the formulae to be employed.

The second section consisted of seven or eight skilful calculators habituated both to analytical and arithmetical computations. These received the formulae from the first section, converted them into numbers, and furnished to the third section the proper differences at the stated intervals.

They also received from that section the calculated results, and compared the two sets, which were computed independently for the purpose of verification.

The third section, on whom the most laborious part of the operations devolved, consisted of from sixty to eighty persons, few of them possessing a knowledge of more than the first rules of arithmetic: these received from the second class certain numbers and differences, with which, by additions and subtractions in a prescribed order, they completed the whole of the tables above mentioned.

I will now examine what portion of this labour might be dispensed with, in case it should be deemed advisable to compute these or any similar tables of equal extent by the aid of the engine I have referred to.

In the first place, the labour of the first section would be considerably reduced, because the formulae used in the great work I have been describing have already been investigated and published. One person,

or at the utmost two, might therefore conduct it.

If the persons composing the second section, instead of delivering the numbers they calculate to the computers of the third section, were to deliver them to the engine, the whole of the remaining operations would be executed by machinery, and it would only be necessary to employ people to copy down as fast as they were able the figures presented to them by the engine. If, however, the contrivances for printing were brought to perfection and employed, even this labour would be unnecessary, and a few superintendents would manage the machine and receive the calculated pages set up in type. Thus the number of calculators employed, instead of amounting to ninety-six, would be reduced to twelve. This number might however be considerably diminished, because when an engine is used the intervals between the differences calculated by the second section may be greatly enlarged. In the tables of logarithms M. Prony caused the differences to be calculated at intervals of two hundred, in order to save the labour of the third section: but as that would now devolve on machinery, which would scarcely move the slower: for its additional burthen, the intervals might properly be enlarged to three or four times that quantity. This would cause a considerable diminution in the labour of the second section. If to this diminution of mental labour we add that which arises from the whole work of the compositor being executed by the machine, and the total suppression of that most annoying of all literary labour, the correction of the errors of the press,[1] I think I am justified in presuming that if engines were made purposely for this object, and were afterwards useless, the tables could be produced at a much cheaper rate; and of their superior accuracy there could be no doubt. Such engines would however be far from useless: containing within themselves the power of generating to an almost unlimited extent tables whose accuracy would be unrivalled, at an expense comparatively moderate, they would become active agents in reducing the abstract inquiries of geometry to a form and an arrangement adapted to the ordinary purposes of human society.

I should be unwilling to terminate this Letter without noticing another class of tables of the greatest importance, almost the whole of which are capable of being calculated by the method of differences. I refer to all astronomical tables for determining the positions of the sun or planets: it is scarcely necessary to observe that the constituent parts of these are of the form $a \sin \theta$; where a is a constant quantity, and θ is what is usually called the argument. Viewed in this light they differ but little from a table of sines, and like it may be computed by the method of differences.

I am aware that the statements contained in this Letter may perhaps be viewed as something more than Utopian, and that the philosophers of Laputa may be called up to dispute my claim to originality. Should such be the case, I hope the resemblance will be found to adhere to the nature of the subject rather than to the manner in which it has been treated. Conscious, from my own experience, of the difficulty of convincing those who are but little skilled in mathematical knowledge, of the possibility of making a machine which shall perform calculations, I was naturally anxious, in introducing it to the public, to appeal to the testimony of one so distinguished in the records of British science. Of the extent to which the machinery whose nature I have described may be carried, opinions will necessarily fluctuate, until experiment shall have finally decided their relative value: but of that engine which already exists I think I shall be supported, both by yourself and by several scientific friends who have examined it, in stating that it performs with rapidity and precision all those calculations far which it was designed.

Whether I shall construct a larger engine of this kind, and bring to perfection the others I have described, will in a great measure depend on the nature of the encouragement I may receive.

Induced, by a conviction of the great utility of such engines, to withdraw for some time my attention from a subject on which it has been engaged during several years, and which possesses charms of a higher order, I have now arrived at a point where success is no longer doubtful. It must however be attained at a very considerable expense, which would not probably be replaced, by the works it might produce, for a long period of time, and which is an undertaking I should

feel unwilling to commence, as altogether foreign to my habits and pursuits.

I remain, my dear Sir,

With the greatest respect,

Faithfully yours,

C. BABBAGE

• • •

1. I have been informed that the publishers of a valuable collection of mathematical tables, now reprinting, pay to the gentleman employed in correcting the press at the rate of three guineas a sheet, a sum by no means too large for the faithful execution of such a laborious duty.

Scheutz's Calculating Machine and its Use in the Construction of the English Life Table No. 3

William Farr

From *English Life Table* (London: H.M.S.O., 1864), cxxxix–cxliv.

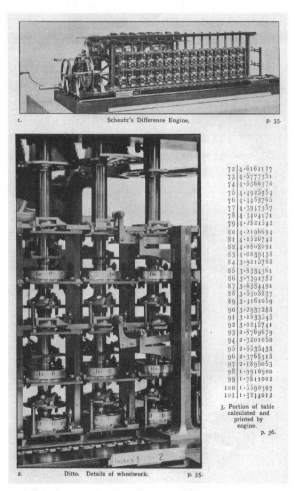

Photographs of the Scheutz difference engine no. 2 together with a portion of a table calculated and printed by the engine. From David Baxandall's *Catalogue of the Collections in the Science Museum, South Kensington* (1926).

INTRODUCTORY NOTE TO READING 4.2

Though Babbage had no close collaborators, there were a few other inventors who followed his work—notably the Swedes Georg and Edvard Scheutz. In 1834 Georg Scheutz read about the Difference Engine in the lengthy account by Dionysius Lardner published in the *Edinburgh Review*.[1] This was the most extensive published description of the actual workings of the machine, though it contained mistakes and left crucial questions unanswered. From Lardner's account, Georg Scheutz, an experienced inventor, set about building what Babbage was never able to complete. He succeeded remarkably in his technological goals, building his first trial device, his difference engine no. 1, in 1843. Scheutz probably succeeded where Babbage did not because Scheutz was not a perfectionist like Babbage: Scheutz allowed some compromises in order to bring the machine to fruition. His first operational difference engine (no. 2) was completed in October 1853.

The Scheutzes worried that Babbage might view them as competitors, but instead he welcomed their contributions, and assisted them in publicizing their machine. Through Babbage's auspices the machine was put on display at the Royal Society in November 1854. It won a gold medal at the Great Exposition in Paris in 1855, and in 1857 the Dudley Observatory in Albany, New York, purchased it for the purpose of calculating astronomical tables, a task for which it was little used. That machine is preserved in the Smithsonian.

---

1 Dionysius Lardner, Babbage's Calculating Engine, *Edinburgh Review* 59 (1834): 263–327.

The Scheutz difference engine no. 3, the last one built, was constructed on the order of William Farr, chief statistician for the General Register Office, with the intention of using it for the *British Life Table*. That machine is preserved in the London Science Museum. It is one of the ironies of history that the British government, which had previously refused to fund completion of Babbage's calculating engines, in 1859 funded a difference engine designed in Sweden. According to Farr the finished machine contained about 4320 separately machined parts. Farr described the problems of working with the machine:

> The Machine required incessant attention. The differences had to be inserted at the proper terms of the various series, checking was required, and when the mechanism got out of order it had to be set right. Of the first watch nothing is known, but the first steam-engine was indisputably imperfect; and here we had to do with the second Calculating Machine as it came from the designs of its constructors and from the workshop of the engineer. The idea had been as beautifully embodied in metal by Mr. Bryan Donkin as it had been conceived by the genius of its inventors; but it was untried. So its work had to be watched with anxiety, and its arithmetical music had to be elicited by frequent tuning and skilful handling, in the quiet most congenial to such productions.

> This volume is the result; and thus—if I may use the expression—the soul of the Machine is exhibited in a series of Tables which are submitted to the criticism of the consummate judges of this kind of work in England and in the world.[2]

At a time when labor was relatively inexpensive and events moved at a slower speed, there seems to have been little justification for using an expensive and troublesome machine to calculate life tables when it did not result in more accurate tables being produced. The most meaningful analysis of the strengths and shortcomings of the Scheutz difference engine may have come from George Biddell Airy, the Astronomer Royal. In charge of the annual production of the tables in the *Nautical Almanac*, Airy might have been the first to confirm the need for a difference engine to compute astronomical tables. But he was always a critic of Babbage's projects, and Babbage resented him. In an article published in 1856, before the third engine was built, Airy wrote, "[T]he demand for such machines has arisen on the side, not of computers, but of mechanists."[3] By computers Airy meant people who computed the tables manually. By mechanists he meant enthusiasts for technology who were driven by passion, such as Babbage, or entrepreneurs, such as the Scheutzes.

Airy listed four stages used to prepare typical tables, and analyzed how each stage might or might not benefit from mechanization. "Airy's arguments finally reveal the technical grounds for his consistent skepticism of the utility of calculating engines, and his views are profoundly damaging to the utopian idea of a handle-cranking solution to the error-free production of mathematical tables so dear to the advocates of the engines. He was a pragmatist whose criterion of usefulness was based almost entirely on the direct benefits to existing tabulation practices at the Royal Observatory, which he ran. Babbage, and to some extent the Scheutzes, were visionaries, intoxicated by ingenuity, intricacy, the mastery of mechanism and the seductive appeal of control over number.

"Airy wrote with extraordinary clearsightedness. He suggested for the first time that the real value of difference engines is not to generate new tables from scratch using repeated addition, but to detect errors in existing tables through repeated subtraction. Babbage seemed to have missed this trick. Indeed, when commercial machines capable of differencing finally became available in the 1920s and 1930s they were used for error-detection in existing tables rather than for the generation of new ones."[4]

---

2   William Farr, *English Life Table* (London: H.M.S.O. & Longman, Green, Longman, Roberts and Green, 1864), cxl.

3   quoted in Doron Swade, *The Cogwheel Brain: Charles Babbage and the Quest to Build the First Computer* (London: Little, Brown, 2000), 201.

When it came to the practical utility of their machines, neither Babbage nor the Scheutzes were ever very clear. They could hardly argue for the machines on the basis of efficiency or cost-effectiveness. These machines were the earliest trial efforts in a revolution in computing that could not be fully realized until the work of Comrie, Aiken, Stibitz, Eckert, von Neumann, Hopper, and others more than one hundred years later. To appreciate the value of these early difference engines invented by Babbage and the Scheutzes, one had to see them for what they promised rather than what they delivered. One had to be an enthusiast for the new. Though he had formerly opposed the machines, George Biddell Airy recommended the purchase of the Scheutz difference engine no. 3 for the General Register Office to be used by William Farr. For a time, even the most critical Airy became an enthusiast for the new technology.

Yet, having invested so much time and money in the project while realizing only token gains, the British government showed little patience with the Scheutz calculating machine. The General Register Office soon reverted to manual calculations by human computers employing logarithms, which they used until the GRO's conversion to mechanical calculation methods in 1911. [JMN]

---

4 Swade, *op. cit.,* 201–2.

TEXT OF READING 4.2

The following description of the Calculating Machine was sent by the Registrar General to the Exhibition of 1862 for distribution, with specimens of its printed work, of stereotyped plates, and of papier-mâché moulds stamped by its printing apparatus.

The Registrar General would have been glad to send the Machine to be exhibited with the Difference Engine of Mr. Babbage; but it was then in use at the General Register Office, and it was a matter of great importance to complete the new Life Tables, for which there was an urgent demand. Upon other grounds the completion of the work was called for.

The first public money was advanced for the Difference Engine of Mr. Babbage in 1823, and it had been so far completed as to show beyond a doubt the practicability of the conception. His Engine was in the Exhibition of 1862; and the first Machine which the Scheutzes, father and son, constructed was exhibited and won the gold medal at the Exhibition of 1855 in Paris. The powers of the Swedish Machine[1] had been displayed in the production of thirty pages of five-figure logarithms for the numbers from 1,000 to 10,000;[2] but it had executed no original work of any extent. Now there are, besides the thousands of machines in the clouds of inventors' brains, many ingenious and beautiful machines in exhibitions of no practical use whatever. How can the spectator know whether they will execute genuine work at all? Who can detect their errors or compare the cost of their work with that of other work of the same kind? A watch to look at is sometimes not a watch to go, according to common observation. Which of these classes of works had we in hand? Here were calculating machines in which everybody was interested, which had existed in pieces or in the state of projects, in which money had been invested for nearly forty years, and which in the completed state had hitherto realized none of the expectations which the country naturally entertained; so it did seem that the time had come for substantial work rather than for exhibition and appeals even to legitimate curiosity.

The Machine consists of more than 4,000 pieces, and it is about ten hundred-weight.[3] It had been shaken out of order on its way from the Factory to Somerset House. It might have been injured or destroyed on its journey to or from the Exhibition, and no one would absolutely guarantee its safety there. Under these circumstances the Machine was not exhibited.

So this work was continued uninterruptedly at the General Register Office until it was completed; and I cannot agree with Mr. Babbage, who thinks that it could have been safely carried on in the midst of the crowds of the Exhibition, with incessant interruptions for explanation, and with the possible clang of musical instruments, discordant sounds, or noises in the ears of the operators.

The Machine required incessant attention. The differences had to be inserted at the proper terms of the various series, checking was required, and when the mechanism got out of order it had to be set right. Of the first watch nothing is known, but the first steam-engine was indisputably imperfect; and here we had to do with the second Calculating Machine as it came from the designs of its constructors and from the workshop of the engineer. The idea had been as beautifully embodied in metal by Mr. Bryan Donkin as it had been conceived by the genius of its inventors; but it was untried. So its work had to be watched with anxiety, and its arithmetical music had to be elicited by frequent tuning and skilful handling, in the quiet most congenial to such productions.

This volume is the result; and thus—if I may use the expression—the soul of the Machine is exhibited in a series of Tables which are submitted to the criticism of the consummate judges of this kind of work in England and in the world.

If their approving testimony be won, it will be some compensation to the "English workmen," the firm of Messrs. Donkin and the Messrs. Scheutz, for the loss of a medal at the Exhibition of 1862.

The Machine, I should add, was seen by many scientific men at the General Register Office during the Exhibition; and it was made known that it was accessible then, as it is now, to any accredited person, on application to the Registrar General.

W. Farr

General Register Office,

5th August 1864.

Pascal, Leibnitz, and other mathematicians conceived the idea of performing numerical operations mechanically; and Mr. Babbage invented a calculating machine, of which, for various reasons, he did not complete the construction. It was, however, lucidly described in the Edinburgh Review for July 1834 by Dr. Lardner. The article inspired Mr. Scheutz, a Swede, with enthusiasm in the cause, and he exclaimed, "I also will make a calculating machine." With his son, after many sacrifices, and many years of labour, he succeeded. The machine was brought to England, and its Inventors were received in the most friendly way by Mr. Babbage, who bore open testimony to the originality of the Swedes. A Committee of the Royal Society reported favourably on the machine, and it was exhibited in the rooms at Somerset House, where Mr. Gravatt, a Fellow of the Society, displayed its powers and uses to some of the principal scientific authorities of the kingdom. The machine won a gold medal for its Inventors at the French Exhibition, and was purchased by a liberal American for an Institution in the United States.

Mr. Babbage's account of the labours of the Inventors, and his son's description of the machine containing several hundred different pieces, in the lucid notation of his father, will be found full of interest and instruction. Those two papers, the Edinburgh Review, Weld's History of the Royal Society, the Preface to Scheutz's Specimen Tables, and the Report of the Committee of the Royal Society, give the history of the two machines.

Scheutz's machine had thus passed its preliminary examination satisfactorily.

At that time it appeared to be desirable to construct a new Life Table from the materials accumulated at the General Register Office by the registration of births and deaths in seventeen years (1838–1854), and by the two enumerations of the population of England and Wales in 1841 and 1851.[4] The Tables for single lives, and the various combinations of joint lives, male and female, involve a great deal of numerical computation; and as it was found that the calculations of the series, thrown into a form which is described elsewhere,[5] could be performed by the machine, the Registrar General was pleased to bring the matter under the notice of Sir George Lewis, then Secretary of State for the Home Department.

And in doing so he pointed out the importance which had been justly attached by the most eminent scientific men of the country, by Her Majesty's Government, and by Parliament, to the machine of Mr. Babbage, for which, though it had not been completed, 17,000*l.* of money had been granted, besides the money expended by Mr. Babbage himself.[6] Here was a machine in working order, suggested to its Inventors by the English machine, and which Mr. Scheutz and the Messrs. Donkin offered to construct, with several improvements, for 1,200*l.*, of which the interest at 5 per cent. was 60*l.* a year. The Astronomer Royal concurred with the Registrar General in advising Her Majesty's Government to order a new machine; and accordingly the contract was entered into, and a machine was constructed by the Messrs. Donkin from Mr. Scheutz's drawings, superior, as it was reported to the Registrar General, to the first machine.

In constructing a new machine of many pieces, to execute a great number of exact movements, several new tools were required, and the workmen had to be specially instructed. This involved expense, from which the Messrs. Donkin, however, did not shrink.

The machine has been extensively tried, and it has, upon the whole, answered every expectation. But it is a delicate instrument, and requires considerable skill in the manipulation. It consists of a multitude of pieces, and some of these occasionally get deranged, so as to print errors, which can, however, by a due system of checks, be almost invariably detected and rectified. It approaches infallibility in certain respects, but it is not infallible, except in very skilful hands. The weakest point of the machine is the printing apparatus, and that admits of evident improvement.

The machine calculates and prints series of a particular kind, and to the execution of these operations its utility is therefore limited. Its scope is less ambitious than the new analytical machine for which Mr. Babbage abandoned his first invention, as that machine seeks to embrace the whole field of analysis.[7]

The machine simply performs the operation of addition, but by various expedients the other arithmetical operations can be reduced to this elementary process. Thus the machine, by adding the arithmetical complement of a number to another, virtually produces the same result as by direct subtraction. For subtracting 0.0293838 from 9.8530811 we have 9.8236973. Now the arithmetical complement of 0.0293838, obtained by subtracting it from 10.0000000, is 9.9706162; so the machine adding this to the number gives the following result:

$$9.8530811$$
$$+ \text{ arithmetical complement of } 0.0293838 = 9.9706162$$
$$19.8236973$$

It is ten more than that obtained by direct subtraction; and the machine does not print the ten, so it disappears from the result. Subtraction by this simple expedient is performed by the same operations as addition; so by introducing logarithms and their complements, with proper Tables, multiplication and division are also reduced to the same operations as addition.

The calculations for the English Life Table are brought within the compass of the machine at the General Register Office by a method which we will now describe as plainly as possible, and which is based on that of finite differences discovered by Newton.

The machine will not calculate the series of double square numbers 1^4; 2^4; 3^4; 4^4; general term x^4; or 1, 16, 81, 256, 625, &c. directly by multiplication; but if the differences of these numbers are taken four times, the fourth order of differences will be found constant. They run thus:

x	(The Function.) $xxxx = x^4$	δ^1	δ^2	δ^3	δ^4
1	1	15	50	60	24
2	16	65	110	84	24
3	81	175	194	108	
4	256	369	302		
5	625	671			
6	1296				

There is a row of calculating wheels for the Function, and a row for each of the four orders of differences; each wheel being figured 0, 1, 2, 3, 4, 5, 6, 7, 8, 9. These are set. And thus this series may be continued to any extent, by adding the constant numbers of δ^4 to those of δ^3; those under δ^3 to δ^2; those under δ^2 to δ^1; those under δ^1 to 1, 16, &c. called the function, or the series of double squares. The machine performs all these additions, and stereoglyphs the series in a leaden or a papier-mâché mould, which serves for stereotyping.

To calculate Interest Tables a series of this kind is required; namely, 1 divided by 1.03, and the quotient again divided by 1.03, &c., so on 100 times. Thus the value of $1l.$ payable at the end of one year, of $1l.$ payable at the end of two years, of three years, four years, &c., is found, reckoning the interest of money at 3 per cent. Now the machine will not perform these divisions, and will not therefore give the numbers directly, but it will calculate the logarithms of these numbers by inserting $0.0000000_{,5000000}$ in the function wheels, and constantly adding to it $\delta^1 - 9.987162[7]_{,7529484}$. The machine prints 0.0000000; 9.9871628; 9.9743256; and the other logarithms in pages 6 and 7 of the volume. It will be observed that the bracketed figure [7] is augmented by the machine, and becomes 8. In truth it is followed by a 7; and as 7.7 is nearer to 8.0 than to 7.0, the correction is necessary to make the approximation as near the truth as is possible, with seven decimals. By a very simple arrangement in the setting— that is, by substituting, as above, 5 for the eighth 0 from the decimal point in the first number of the function—the machine effects all the corrections usual in such cases; thus, 7,0; 7,1; 7,2; 7,3; 7,4 are printed as 7, and 7,5; 7,6; 7,7; 7,8; 7,9 are printed 8 in the seventh decimal place.

The book of logarithms gives, in the corresponding numbers, the value of $1l.$ payable at the end of each year. Thus the value of £1.000 000 payable after the lapse of a year is, .970,874$l.$; payable after the lapse of 2 years, .942,596$l.$; payable after the lapse of 3 years, .915,142$l.$; and so on. The sum of 20 of these successive values is the value of an annuity certain for 20 years, and so on for any other number of years. The interest is here taken at 3 per cent. The values for other rates of interest are calculated in the same way by the machine.

There are many series, of which the fourth difference is not constant; yet the error from the neglect of the subsequent orders of differences is so small, that the series is calculated correctly within required degrees of accuracy, by dividing the long series into periods. This is the case with logarithms, which from given sets of four orders of differences can be calculated by the machine.

Such also is the series of logarithms of the probabilities of living a year after any given age. The chance of living a year increases from birth to the age of 12, 13, or 14; and then it decreases at increasing rates, not like interest, however, in simple geometrical ratios, otherwise the series could be calculated by one order of logarithmic differences. Three orders of logarithmic differences are required; and by making the logarithms of the probability of living a year the first order of differences, the other orders becoming the 2d, 3d, and 4th, we get the series of logarithms corresponding to the numbers out of a given number born, attaining each year of age. The machine has calculated a Table of this kind, showing the numbers living at the end of every quarter of a year of age.

By combining these series for males and females with the interest logarithmic series, and again with each other, the mean duration of life is determined, as well as the value of annuities on one or two lives of the same or of different ages. These Tables have been calculated by the machine, at certain rates of interest.

The art is to shape the formulas and the numerical operations so that they can be executed by the machine.

The following example arranged by Mr. Lewis of this Department displays the method of calculating the Column λl_x Males from the age 20 to 50, and gives some idea of the way in which the Machine has been rendered available in the production of this Volume of Tables.

Referring to the Table of Differences on the next page, it will be seen that the original Differences for the Male ages 20–50 are these:—

Function =	$\lambda l_{20} =$	5.5232361,$_{0000}$
$\lambda p_{20} =$	$\delta^1 =$	9.9963874,$_{0000}$
	$\delta^2 =$	9.9999196,$_{4155}$
	$\delta^3 =$	0.0000026,$_{4330}$
	$\delta^4 =$	9.9999991,$_{6530}$

but when they are ready for the machine they are arranged in the following order:

$u_x =$	$\lambda l_{20} =$	$u_{20} =$	5.5232361,$_{5000}$	
$\delta^1_{x-1} =$	$\lambda p_{19} =$	$\delta^1_{19} =$	9.9964712,$_{3645}$	These two differences are taken from those against age 19
$\delta^2_{x-1} =$		$\delta^2_{19} =$	9.9999161,$_{6355}$	
$\delta^3_{x-2} =$		$\delta^3_{18} =$	0.0000043,$_{1270}$	These two differences are taken from those against age 19
$\delta^4_{x-2} =$		$\delta^4_{18} =$	9.9999991,$_{6530}$	

δ^4 being *constant* remains unchanged.

u_{70} is then placed upon the first or Function row of figure wheels in the machine, δ^1_{19} on the second row, δ^2_{19} on the third row, and so on.

The handle of the machine is then turned, and the effect of the first half-stroke is that the numbers on the third and fifth rows (δ^2 & δ^4) are added to those on the rows immediately above them (δ^1 & δ^3); the second half-stroke adds the *new* numbers on δ^1 & δ^3 to the numbers on the u_2, and δ^2, and thus gives u_{21} as the result of a complete forward and backward motion of the machine.

The way in which the machine adds the differences together will be rendered more intelligible by the example here given:

Figure Wheels.	Machine as set.	After the forward motion.	After the backward motion.
1st row ...	$u_{20} = 5.5232861,_{5000}$	$5.5232361,_{5000}$	$5.5197135,_{5000} = u_{21}$
2d row ...	$\delta^1_{18} = 9.9964712,_{3645}$	$9.9983874,_{0000}$	$9.9983874,_{0000} = \delta^1_{20}$
3d row ...	$\delta^2_{19} = 9.9999161,_{6356}$	$9.9999161,_{6355}$	$9.9999198,_{4155} = \delta^2_{20}$
4th row ...	$\delta^3_{18} = 0.0000043,_{1270}$	$0.0000034,_{7800}$	$0.0000034,_{7800} = \delta^3_{19}$
5th row ...	$\delta^4_{18} = 9.9999991,_{6530}$	$9.9999991,_{6530}$	$9.9999991,_{6530} = \delta^4_{19}$

All that is necessary, therefore, when the differences have been once transferred to the machine, is to turn the handle until the requisite number of values of u_x is obtained.

• • •

1. This first Swedish Machine was bought by Mr. Rathbone, an American, and presented by him to the Dudley Observatory at Albany. No account has reached us of any work executed by it in America.
2. Specimens of Tables calculated, stereo-moulded, and printed by machinery. Longmans, 1857.
3. Mr. Bryan Donkin states that Scheutz's Calculating Machine consists of about 4,320 pieces, of which 2,054 are screws, 364 compose the chain, and 902 are other parts of the mechanism. The weight of the Machine (exclusive of case) is by his estimate about 10 cwt.
4. Deaths 6,470,720, with ages distinguished.
5. Paper presented to the Royal Society, March 17, read April 7, 1859. See Transactions of that year.
6. The following statement occurs in Mr. Babbage's "Passages from the Life of a Philosopher":—"As to the expense actually incurred upon the first Difference Engine, that of the Government was about 17,000l. On my own part and out of my own private resources I have sacrificed upon this and other works of science upwards of 20,000l." (p. 103.)
7. See a Paper in the Transactions of the British Association.

4·3

An Electric Tabulating System

Herman Hollerith

From *The Quarterly*, Columbia University School of Mines, Vol. X, no.16 (Apr. 1889), pp. 238–255.

INTRODUCTORY NOTE TO READING 4.3

In this article, published in 1889, Herman Hollerith (1860–1929) described his invention of the electric punched-card tabulating system for compiling statistics for the United States Census of 1890. This was one of the key inventions in the history of data processing. Using Hollerith's system, the U.S. Census Bureau reduced information processing time by 80% over manual methods.

Electric punched-card tabulators were the first large scale information processing machinery, and they remained the primary means of information processing until about 1960. Gradually the tabulating machines became increasingly sophisticated. By the time of World War II they were capable of limited programming through plug-boards.

In 1896 Hollerith founded the Tabulating Machine Company. For the census of 1890 Hollerith introduced the automatic card feed into his punched-card tabulators. In 1911 Hollerith sold the Tabulating Machine Company to Charles R. Flint. The following year Flint merged the Tabulating Machine Company with the Computing Scale Company, the International Time Recording Company, and the Bundy Manufacturing Company to form the Computing-Tabulating-Recording Company (C-T-R), producing and selling Hollerith tabulating equipment, time clocks, and other business machinery. In 1914 Thomas J. Watson became president of C-T-R, and focused the company on electric punched-card tabulating. Ten years later Watson changed the name of the company from Computing-Tabulating-Recording Company to International Business Machines (IBM). Until about 1960, when the market for electronic computers was established, the leasing of electric punched card tabulators and annual sale of billions of punched cards remained the primary source of income for IBM.[JMN]

TEXT OF READING 4.3

Few, who have not come directly in contact with a census office, can form any adequate idea of the labor involved in the compilation of a census of 50,000,000 persons, as was the case in the last census, or of over 62,000,000, as will be the case in the census to be taken in June, 1890. The fact, however, that Congress at its last session in "An Act to provide for the taking of the eleventh and subsequent censuses," fixes the maximum cost of the next or eleventh census, exclusive of printing and engraving, at $6,400,000, will perhaps impress one with some idea of the magnitude of such an undertaking.

Although our population is constantly increasing, and although at each census more complicated combinations and greater detail are required in the various compilations, still, up to the present time, substantially the original method of compilation has been employed; that of making tally-marks in small squares and then adding and counting such tally-marks.

While engaged in work upon the tenth census, the writer's attention was called to the methods employed in the tabulation of population statistics and the enormous expense involved. These methods were at the time described as "barbarous, some machine ought to be devised for the purpose of facilitating such tabulations.["] This led the writer to a thorough study of the details of the methods used, which were no doubt the most approved ever employed in compiling a census. After a careful consideration of the many problems involved and considerable experimenting on quite a large scale, the method which forms the subject of this paper is confidently offered as a means for facilitating this work.

The work of a census can be divided into two main branches: that of enumeration, and that of compilation or tabulation. In regard to the enumeration, the plan originally adopted at the tenth census, with such splendid results, will substantially be followed in the next census, and is provided for in the Act of Congress above referred to. As under the provisions of this Act the enumerators are paid according to the number of persons, farms, or manufacturing establishments enumerated, and as the rates of compensation are slightly increased, the per capita cost of the enumeration must of necessity be slightly in excess of that of the tenth census. Referring to the records of the tenth census, we find the cost of the enumeration to have been $2,095,563.32.[1]

An increase of population of thirty per cent. during the decade can reasonably be assumed, so that the cost of the enumeration at the eleventh census, at the same per capita rate, would be not less than $2,724,232.32. Adding to this amount the cost of the extra schedules required under the present Act of Congress and allowing for the increased rates of compensation for the enumeration of farms and manufacturing establishments,[2] we see that an estimate of $3,000,000 is not an unreasonable one for the cost of the next enumeration.

From the data thus enumerated are compiled the various reports which form the legitimate work of a census. The expenses of the office of the Superintendent of the Tenth Census at Washington amounted to $2,385,999.50. If the same methods of compilation are to be employed in the next census, the per capita cost of compilation would, of course, remain substantially the same, so that allowing for the increased population, the expenses of this portion of the work would amount to $3,101,799.67. To this ought also be added the cost of compiling the additional data required under the present Act of Congress. If, however, the data enumerated at the next census is compiled with that fullness and completeness which it deserves, and which it ought to receive, these expenses would far exceed the above amount. As will be shown presently, many of the facts enumerated in the tenth census were not compiled at all, or if compiled were treated in so simple and elementary a manner as to leave much to be desired. On the other hand, however, the compilations of the tenth census were so vastly superior to anything that had previously been attempted that it is very likely to be inferred that the tenth census left nothing to be desired. If at the eleventh census no material improvements are adopted in the methods of tabulation, it will probably be found impossible to accomplish more than at the tenth census on account of the time and expense involved.

A census is often spoken of as a photograph of the social and economic conditions of a people. The analogy can be made, not only with reference to the results obtained, but also to the methods of obtaining these results. Thus the enumeration of a census corresponds with the exposure of the plate in photography, while the compilation of a census corresponds with the development of the photographic plate. Unless the photographic plate is properly exposed it is impossible to obtain a good picture, so likewise, in case of a census, a good result is impossible unless the enumeration is made properly and with sufficient detail. As the first flow of the developer brings out the prominent points of our photographic picture, so in the case of a census the first tabulations will show the main features of our population. As the development is continued, a multitude or detail appears in every part, while at the same time the prominent features are strengthened, and sharpened in definition, giving finally a picture full of life and vigor. Such would be the result of a properly compiled and digested census from a thorough enumeration. If this country is to expend $3,000,000 on the exposure of the plate, ought not the picture be properly developed?

The population schedules of the tenth census contained the following inquiries, the replies to which were capable of statistical treatment:

- Race or color: whether white, black, mulatto, Chinese, or Indian.

- Sex.

- Age.

- Relationship of each person enumerated to the head of the family.

- Civil or conjugal condition: whether single, married, widowed, or divorced.

- Whether married during the census year.

- Occupation.

- Number of months unemployed.

- Whether sick or otherwise temporarily disabled so as to be unable to attend to ordinary business or duties on the day of the enumeration; what was the sickness or disability?

- Whether blind, deaf and dumb, idiotic, insane, maimed, crippled, bedridden, or otherwise disabled.

- Whether the person attended school during the census year.

- Cannot read.

- Cannot write.

- Place of birth.

- Place of birth of father.

- Place of birth of mother.

Such an enumeration as this, if made thoroughly, certainly corresponds to a fully timed exposure of our photographic plate. It would scarcely be termed under-exposed.

If it is of interest and value to know the number of males and of females in our population, of how much greater interest is it to know the number of native males and of foreign males; or again, to know the number of native white males, of foreign white males, of colored males, etc.; or still again, the combination of each one of these facts with each single year of age. All this was done in the tenth census. Many other interesting and valuable combinations were compiled, far surpassing anything of the kind that had ever before been attempted, still, on the other hand, many of the facts enumerated were never compiled at all. Thus, for example, it is to-day impossible to obtain the slightest reliable statistical information regarding the conjugal conditions of our people, though the complete data regarding this is locked up in the returns of the enumeration of the tenth census. In other words, the development was not carried far enough to bring out even this most important detail of our picture. The question why this information was not compiled was several times asked during the discussion of the present census bill in the committee of the Senate. A correct and proper answer to this inquiry would probably have been simply, "lack of funds," for a minute that the eminent statistician who planned and directed the tenth census did not fully appreciate the value of such a compilation.

To know simply the number of single, married, widowed, and divorced persons among our people would be of great value, still it would be of very much greater value to have the same information in combination with age, with sex, with race, with nativity, with occupation, or with various sub-combinations of these data. If the data regarding the relationship of each person to the head of the family were properly compiled, in combination with various other data, a vast amount of valuable information would be obtained. So again, if the number of months unemployed were properly enumerated and compiled with reference to age, to occupation, etc., much information might be obtained of great value to the student of the economic problems affecting our wage-earners.

One more illustration will be given. We have in a census, besides the data relating to our living population, records regarding the deaths during the previous year. In both cases we have the information regarding age and occupation. It the living population were tabulated by combinations of age and occupation, and likewise the deaths by ages and occupations, we would then have data from which some reliable inferences might be drawn regarding the effects of various occupations upon length of life. It might even be possible to construct life tables for the various occupations as we now do for the different States and cities. Such information would be of service in relation to life insurance and other problems. Again, it would point out any needed reforms regarding the sanitary conditions and surroundings of any occupation. This is a field of statistical investigation which is as yet almost wholly unexplored.

In this connection it may perhaps be proper to quote from a letter addressed to the writer, in reply to certain inquiries, by General Francis A. Walker, the well-known Superintendent of the Tenth Census:

"In the census of a country so populous as the United States the work of tabulation might be carried on almost literally without limit, and yet not cease to obtain new facts and combinations of facts of political, social, and economic significance.

"With such a field before the statistician, it is purely a question of time and money where he shall stop. Generally speaking, he cannot do less than has been done before in the treatment of the same subject. Generally speaking, also, he will desire to go somewhat beyond his predecessors, and introduce some new features to interest and instruct his own constituency, so that there is a constant tendency to make the statistical treatment of similar material successively more and more complex. It will even frequently happen that these later refinements in the statistics of a country are of greater economic significance than some of the earlier and more elementary grouping of facts."

No one is more competent to speak authoritatively on this question than General Walker, and certainly no one's opinion is more worthy of consideration.

Irrespective of the wishes and desires of those who are in charge of our various statistical inquiries, we often find in this country that public opinion needs and demands certain statistical information. Thus in the present Act of Congress while the main points are left discretionary with the Secretary of the Interior, under whose direction the census is taken, still on certain points direct instructions are given. For example, it is provided that the colored population be enumerated and tabulated with reference to the distinctions of blacks, mulattoes, quadroons, and octoroons. In the census of 1860 the population was compiled under 14 age groups, in 1870 the ages were tallied under 25 groups, while in 1880 the census office, in compliance with numerous requests from many different sources, tabulated the population according to single years of age, making in all over 100 specifications. Thus we see that each year the problem of compiling a census becomes a more difficult one.

Heretofore in census and similar compilations essentially one of two methods has been followed. Either the records have been preserved in their proper relations, and the information drawn off by tallying first one grouping of facts and then the next, or the records have been written upon cards or slips, which are first sorted and counted according to one grouping of facts and then according to the next.

To form some idea of the questions involved in the first plan, let us assume that the record relating to each person at the next census be written in a line across a strip of paper, and that such lines are exactly one-half inch apart, it would then take a strip of paper over 500 miles long to contain such records. These must be gone over, again and again, until all the desired combinations have been obtained. This is practically the method followed in compiling the tenth census. On the other hand, if written cards are to be used the prospect is hardly more encouraging. One hundred comparatively thin cards will form a stack over an inch high.

In the next census, therefore, if such cards are to be used it will require a stack over ten miles high. Imagine for a moment the trouble and confusion which would be caused by a few such cards becoming misplaced. This method of individual cards was employed in the census of Massachusetts for 1885. The 2,000,000 cards there used weighed about 14 tons. Were the same cards to be used in the next United States census it would require about 450 tons of such cards.

In place of these methods it is suggested that the work be done so far as possible by mechanical means. In order to accomplish this the records must be put in such shape that a machine could read them. This is most readily done by punching holes in cards or strips of paper, which perforations can then be used to control circuits through electro-magnets operating counters, or sorting mechanism, or both combined.

Record-cards of suitable size are used, the surfaces of which are divided into quarter-inch squares, each square being assigned a particular value or designation. If, for example, a record of sex is to be made, two squares, designated respectively M and F, are used, and, according as the record relates to a male or a female, the corresponding square is punched. These holes may be punched with any ordinary ticket-punch, cutting a round hole, about three-sixteenths of an inch in diameter. In similar manner other data, such as relate to conjugal condition, to illiteracy, etc., is recorded. It is often found, however, that the data must be recorded with such detail of specification that it would be impracticable to use a separate space for each specification. In such cases recourse is had to combinations of two or more holes to designate each specification. For example, if it is desired to record each single year of age, twenty spaces are used, divided into two sets of ten each, designated, respectively, from 0 to 9. One set of ten spaces is used to record the tens of years of age, while the other set is used to record the units of years of age. Thus, twelve years would be recorded by punching 1 in the first set, and 2 in the second; while 21 years would be recorded by punching 2 in the first set, and 1 in the second set. Occupations may be arranged into arbitrary groups, each such group being designated, for example, by a capital letter, and each specific occupation of that group by a small letter. Thus, Aa would designate one occupation, Ab another, etc. If desired, combinations of two or more letters of the same set may be used. Thus, AB can be used to designate one occupation, AC another, BC another, etc. With such an arrangement, the initial letter may be used to designate groups of occupation as before. In this way it is apparent that a very small card will suffice for an elaborate record. For the work of a census, a card 3" × 5 1/2" would be sufficient to answer all ordinary purposes. The cards are preferably made of as thin manilla stock as will be convenient to handle.

If printed cards are used, the punching may be done with ordinary ticket-punches; more satisfactory results, however, can be obtained with punches designed especially for this work, as will be presently described.

In a census the enumerator's district forms the statistical unit of area, and a suitable combination is arranged to designate each such district. A card is punched with the corresponding combination for each person in such enumeration districts, and the cards of each district are then numbered consecutively, in a suitable numbering machine, to correspond with numbers assigned to the individual records on the enumerator's returns. This combination of holes, and this number, will serve to identify any card. Should any card become misplaced, it is readily detected among a number of cards by the fact that one or more of these holes will not correspond with the holes in the balance of the cards. By means of a suitable wire or needle a stack of a thousand or more cards can be tested in a few seconds, and any misplaced cards detected. When it is remembered that in a census millions of cards must constantly be handled, the importance of this consideration is appreciated. With ordinary written cards it would be practically impossible to detect misplaced cards, and a few such misplaced cards would cause almost endless confusion.

As the combination of holes used for designating the enumerator's district are the same for all the cards of that district, a special machine is arranged for punching these holes. This machine is provided with a number of interchangeable punches, which are placed according to the combination it is desired to punch. Five or six cards are then placed in the punch against suitable stops, and by means of a lever the corresponding holes are punched through these cards at one operation.

The individual records are now transcribed to the corresponding cards by punching according to a prearranged scheme as described above. For this purpose what may be known as a keyboard-punch is arranged, in which the card is held fixed in a frame, while the punch is moved over the card in any direction by means of a projecting lever provided with a suitable knob or handle. Below the knob is a keyboard provided with holes lettered and numbered according to the diagram of the card, and so arranged that when a pin projecting below the knob is over any hole, the punch is over the corresponding space of the card. If the pin is depressed into any hole of the keyboard, the punch is operated and the corresponding space of the card is punched. With such a keyboard-punch it is, of course, apparent that a perfectly blank card may be used, one corner, however, being cut off to properly

locate the card in subsequent operations.

To read such a punched record card, it is only necessary to place it over a printed form, preferably of a different color, when the complete record shows directly through the perforations.

Heretofore, reference has only been made to the compilation of a census, but these methods are equally applicable to many other forms of statistical compilations, as, for example, the various forms of vital statistics. Fig. 1, for example, represents the diagram of the

Card Used in Surgeon-General's Office.

card as at present used in the office of the Surgeon-General U.S.A., for compiling the army health statistics. The data relating to the month, the post, the division, and the region to which the record relates, is recorded by punching a hole in each of the divisions across the end of the card by means of the machine with interchangeable punches as before described. This portion of the record corresponds almost exactly with the record for the enumeration district of a census. The individual record is then transcribed to the card by punching in the remaining spaces with a keyboard-punch as before described.

Such a card allows a complete record, including the following data, for each individual; rank, arm of service, age, race, nationality, length of service, length of residence at the particular post, whether the disease was contracted in the line of duty or not, whether admitted to sick report during the month or during a previous month, the source of admission, the disposition of the case, or whether remaining under treatment, the place of treatment, the disease or injury for which treated, and finally the number of days treated. Between 40,000 and 50,000 such records are received annually, and from these are compiled the various health statistics pertaining to our army.

A card has just been arranged for the Board of Health of New York City to be used in compiling the mortality statistics of that city. The record for each death occurring in the City of New York, as obtained from the physicians' certificates, is transcribed to such a card by punching as before described. This card allows for recording the following data: sex, age, race, conjugal condition, occupation, birthplace, birthplace of parents, length of residence in the city; the ward in which the death occurred, the sanitary subdivision of such ward, the nature of the residence in which the death occurred, whether a tenement, dwelling, hotel, public institution, etc., and finally the cause of death. In the city of New York about 40,000 deaths are recorded annually.

These illustrations will serve to show how readily a card can be arranged to record almost any desired grouping of facts.

With a little practice great expertness is secured in making such transcriptions, and a record can thus be transcribed much more readily than by writing, even if considerable provision is made for facilitating the writing by the use of abbreviations.

From the punched record cards it next becomes necessary to compile the desired statistics. For this purpose the apparatus shown in Figs. 2 to 8 is used.

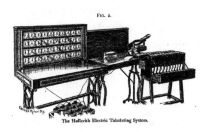

FIG. 2.

The Hollerith Electric Tabulating System.

FIG. 3.

The Press.

The press or circuit-closing device, shown in Figs. 2, 3, and 4, consists of a hard rubber bed plate, as shown in section in Fig. 4, provided with suitable stops or gauges against which the record-cards can be placed. This hard rubber plate is provided with a number of holes or cups corresponding in number and relative position with the centres of the spaces of the card. An iron wire nail is securely driven through a hole in the bottom of each cup, and a wire, connecting at its other end with a binding-post on the back of the press frame, is securely held under the head of each nail. Each cup is partly filled with mercury, which, through the nail and wire, is thus in electrical connection with the corresponding binding-post. Above the hard rubber plate is a reciprocating box provided with a number of projecting spring-actuated points, corresponding in number and arrangement with the centres of the mercury cups. The construction and arrangement of these pins is shown in Fig. 4. If a card

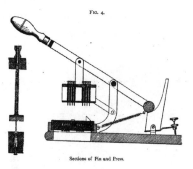

FIG. 4.

Sections of Pin and Press.

is placed on the rubber plate against the stops it is of course apparent that, when the box is brought down by the handle, the pins will all be pressed back, excepting such as correspond with the punched spaces of the card which project into the mercury, and are thus in electrical connection with the corresponding binding-posts on back of the press frame.

A number of mechanical counters are arranged in a suitable frame, as shown in Fig. 5. The face of each

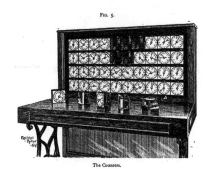

FIG. 5.

The Counters.

counter is three inches square, and is provided with a dial divided into 100 parts and two hands, one counting units the other hundreds. The counter consists essentially of an electro-magnet, the armature of which is so arranged that each time it is attracted by closing the circuit it registers one. A suitable carrying device is arranged so that at each complete revolution of the unit hand the hundred hand registers one, each counter thus registering or counting to one hundred hundred, or 10,000, which will be found sufficient for all ordinary statistical purposes. The counters are so arranged that they can readily be reset at 0, and all are removable and interchangeable, the mere placing of the counter in position in the frame making the necessary electrical connections through the magnet.

For the purpose of sorting the cards according to any group of statistical items or combinations of two or more of such items, the sorting-box, shown in Fig. 6, is used. This consists of a box suitably divided into

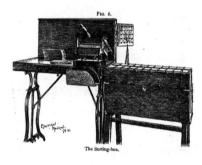

FIG. 6.

The Sorting-box.

compartments, each one of which is closed by a lid. Each lid, L, as shown in Fig. 7, is held closed against

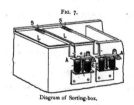

FIG. 7.

Diagram of Sorting-box.

the tension of the spring, S, by the catch, a, in the armature, A. If a circuit is closed through the magnet, E, the armature, A, is attracted, thus releasing the lid, L, which is opened by the springs, and remains open until again closed by hand.

As the cards are punched they are arranged by enumerators' districts, which form our unit of area. The first compilation that would be desired would be to obtain the statistics for each enumeration district according to some few condensed groupings of facts. Thus it might be desired to know the number of males and of females, of native born and of foreign born, of whites and of colored, of single, married, and widowed, the number at each of centre groups of ages, etc., in each enumeration district. In order to obtain such statistics the corresponding binding-posts on the back of the press frame are connected, by means of suitable piece of covered wire, with the binding-posts of the counters upon which it is desired to register the corresponding facts. A proper battery being arranged in circuit, it is apparent that if a card is placed on the hard rubber bed plate, and the box of the press brought down upon the card, the pins corresponding with the punched spaces will close the circuit through the magnets of the corresponding counters which thus register one each. If the counters are first set at 0, and the cards of the given enumeration district then passed through the press one by one, the number of males and of females, of whites and of colored, etc., will be indicated on the corresponding counters.

If it is desired to count on the counters directly, combinations of two or more items, small relays are used to control secondary circuits through the counters. If, for example, it is desired to know the number of native white males, of native white females, of foreign white males, of foreign white females, of colored males, and of colored females; these being combinations of sex, race, and nativity, ordinary relays are arranged as shown in the diagram, Fig. 8, the mag-

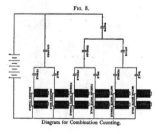

FIG. 8.

Diagram for Combination Counting.

nets of which are connected with the press as indicated. If a card punched for native white, and male is placed in the press, the corresponding relays are actuated, which close a secondary circuit through the counter magnet, native white male, thus registering one on the corresponding counter.

By a suitable arrangement of relays any possible combination of the data recorded on the cards may be counted. When it is desired to count more complicated combinations, however, special relays with multiple contact points are employed.

If it is desired to assort or distribute the cards according to any desired item or combination of items recorded on the card, it is only necessary to connect the magnets of the sorting-box in exactly the same manner as has been described for the counters. When a card is then placed in the press, one of the lids of the sorting-box, according to the data recorded on the card, will open. The card is deposited in the open compartment of the sorting-box and the lid closed with the right hand, while at the same time the next card is placed in position in the press with the left hand.

It is, of course, apparent that any number of items or combinations of items can be counted. The number of such items or combinations, which can be counted at any one time, being limited only by the number of counters, while at the same time the cards are sorted according to any desired set of statistical facts. In a census the cards as they come from the punching machines would, of course, be arranged according to enumeration districts. Each district could then be run through the press, and such facts as it is desired to know in relation to this unit of area could be counted on the counters, while the cards are at the same time assorted according to some other set of facts, arranging them in convenient form for further tabulations. In this manner, by the arrangement of a judicious "scheme," it will be found that a most elaborate compilation may be effected with but a few handlings of the cards.

Two of the most important elements, in almost all statistical compilations, are time which results could be obtained with the present method, in a census, for example, would be dependent upon: 1st, the rate at which a clerk could punch the record-cards, and, 2d,

the number of clerks employed upon this part of the work. The first can readily be determined by experiment, when the second becomes merely a simple arithmetical computation. The work of counting or tabulating on the machines can be so arranged that, within a few hours after the last card is punched, the first set of tables, including condensed grouping of all the leading statistical facts, would be complete. The rapidity with which subsequent tables could be published would depend merely upon the number of machines employed.

In regard to accuracy, it is apparent that the processes of counting and sorting, being purely mechanical, can be arranged, with such checks, that an error is practically impossible. The one possible source of error is in the punching of the cards. If proper precautions are here taken, a census practically free from errors of compilation could be obtained. Even in this respect the present method would have manifest advantages. A card wrongly punched could involve an error of only a single unit, while by all previous methods single errors involving an error in the result of tens, of hundreds, of thousands, or even more, are possible.

It is firmly believed that in regard to cost, time and accuracy, this method would possess very great advantages in doing the work that has heretofore been done, but this is believed to be insignificant in comparison with the fact that a thorough compilation would be possible, within reasonable limits of cost, while such compilation is practically impossible, by the ordinary methods, on account of the enormous expense involved.

• • •

1. The cost of the tenth census was as follows:

Enumerators	$2,095,563.32
Superintendent's Office	2,385,999.50
Special Agents	625,067.29
Printing Reports	678,624.61
Total	$5,785,254.72

2.

Enumerators	Rates of Compensation	
	1890 Cens.	1880 Cens.
For each inhabitant enumerated	2	2
For each death recorded	2	2
For each farm returned	15	10
For each manufacturing industry reported	20	15
For each soldier, sailor, etc.	5	....

The Application of the Hollerith Tabulating Machine to Brown's Tables of the Moon

L. J. Comrie, M.A., Ph.D.

From *Monthly Notices of the Royal Astronomical Society* 92 (1932): 694–707.

INTRODUCTORY NOTE TO READING 4.4

Leslie John Comrie (1893–1950) pioneered the use of commercial accounting machines in scientific applications, especially in the production of mathematical tables for astronomy, navigation, and other purposes. Born in New Zealand, he completed undergraduate and master's degrees in chemistry at University College, Aukland. When World War I broke out Comrie served in France in the New Zealand Expeditionary Force, even though he had a hearing disability. He was invalided out of the service after losing a leg. He resumed his education at St. John's College, Cambridge on a University Expeditionary Force scholarship, receiving a Ph.D. in astronomy. His first academic posts were in the United States as assistant professor of mathematics and astronomy at Swarthmore College (1923–24), and assistant professor of astronomy at Northwestern University (1924–25).

In 1925 Comrie returned to England to join the Nautical Almanac Office, becoming deputy supervisor the following year. He introduced the standard equinox, which provided a fixed frame of reference for the computation of the orbits of comets and minor planets. The annual set of navigational tables published in the *Nautical Almanac* was the direct linear successor of tables issued without interruption from 1767–1831 by the Commissioners of Longitude, and from 1832–1959 by the Lord Commissioners of the Admiralty. It was often called the "seaman's bible."

"The *Nautical Almanac* was not computed directly by the Royal Observatory, but by a number of freelance human computers dotted around Great Britain. The calculations were performed twice, independently, by two computers, and checked by a third 'comparator.' Many of these human computers were retired clerks or clergymen with a facility for figures and a reputation for reliability who worked from home. We know almost nothing of these anonymous drudges. Probably the only one to escape oblivion was the Reverend Malachy Hitchins, an eighteenth-century Cornish clergyman who was a computer and comparator for the *Nautical Almanac* for a period of forty years. A lifetime of computation dedication earned him a place in the *Dictionary of National Biography*. When Astronomer Royal Maskelyne died in 1811—Hitchins had died two years previously—the *Nautical Almanac* 'fell on evil days for about 20 years, and even became notorious for its errors.'"[1] It was during those evil days that Charles Babbage set about finding a mechanical substitute for table production by human computers; see reading 4.1 in this anthology.

In the late 1920s, early in his career at the Nautical Almanac Office, Comrie discovered that the Burroughs accounting machine could be used without modification as a difference engine. This discovery enabled him to revise almost single-handedly the *Nautical Almanac* (which had remained essentially unchanged for nearly a cen-

---

1   Martin Campbell-Kelly and William Aspray. Computer. A History of the Information Machine (New York: Basic Books, 1996), 10.

tury) and to mechanize all of the calculations performed at the Office, which he transformed into the most efficient computing organization of its day.

"Instead of using freelance computers, with their high degree of scientific training, he decided to systematize the work and make use of ordinary clerical labor and standard calculating machines. Almost all of Comrie's human computers were young, unmarried women with just a basic knowledge of commercial arithmetic.

"Comrie's great insight was to realize that one did not need special-purpose machines such as differential analyzers; he thought computing was primarily a question of organization. For most calculations, he found that his 'calculating girls' equipped with ordinary commercial calculating machines did the job perfectly well. Soon the Nautical Almanac Office was fitted out with Comptometers, Burroughs adding machines, and NCR accounting machines. Inside the Nautical Almanac Office, at first glance, the scene could easily have been mistaken for that in any ordinary commercial office. This was appropriate, for the Nautical Almanac Office was simply processing data that happened to be scientific rather than commercial"[2]

In 1928 Comrie became the first to use a punched-card tabulating system in a purely scientific application—calculating the position of the moon at noon and midnight from 1935 to the end of the twentieth century. About the same time, across the Atlantic, Wallace J. Eckert, with the support of IBM, founded the Columbia University Statistical Bureau to promote the use of punched-card tabulating machines in scientific research.[JMN]

---

2 Campbell-Kelly and Aspray, *op. cit.*, 67.

TEXT OF READING 4.4

Introduction.—Positions of the Moon derived from Brown's *Tables of the Motion of the Moon* were first introduced into national ephemerides in 1923. In these *Tables* over 1400 periodic terms with coefficients as large as 00″.003 are tabulated. Some idea of the extent of the *Tables* may be gathered from the fact that they contain 180 separate tables and cover 660 pages. Although they are well arranged, the work of using them is laborious, and, before the advent of the Hollerith machine, represented the continuous work of two skilled computers. The mechanical methods that have been applied to certain portions of the work have eliminated much fatigue, increased tenfold the speed with which results can be obtained, and reduced the cost to one-quarter of its former amount.

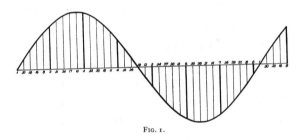

Fig. i.

The Tabulation of Harmonic Functions of the Time.—The inequalities arising in lunar theory are of the form $a \sin (b + ct)$, where a is the amplitude or coefficient, b is the phase angle at the moment when $t = 0$, and c is the movement of the argument in a unit of time. This expression is called a harmonic; it represents a periodic term, of period $2\pi/c$. The *Tables* present values of these terms, and it is their selection and summation, or the synthesis of a series of harmonic terms, that constitutes the principal work of using the *Tables*. Where the periods of various terms are commensurable, for instance if they depend on $(b + ct)$, $2(b + ct)$, $3(b + ct)$, etc., they are combined into one table; it is this power of combination that has enabled 1400 terms to be tabulated in less than 200 tables. The fundamental periods of individual tables are not commensurable, so that, although the entries from each table are used over and over again, combinations of entries from any one group of tables do not recur. It is to be borne in mind that in preparing ephemerides the intervals of t are uniform, and that the period of each term is, in general, short when compared with the lifetime of the *Tables*.

Consider the tabulation of a term in which, for simplicity, $a = 1$, $b = 0°$, $c = 50°$, and the unit of t is 1 day. The values required on successive days are represented by the ordinates 1, 2, 3 . . . in fig. 1. If we superimpose the values for day 9 and subsequent days on the first period of the curve, it is seen that this is eventually divided into 36 equidistant parts, after which the sequence repeats itself. This immediately suggests the procedure actually adopted in tabulation, namely, that a complete period of the harmonic should be subdivided into an integral number of parts, so chosen that the motion in a day (or other unit of time) is an integral number of these parts. In the illustration 1 day = 50°/360° = 5/36 revolutions, so that the constructor of the tables would divide the period into 36 integral parts, the movement per day being 5 of these parts. The order of the final tabular entries would be the order in which they are used.

d		r		r
182	=	1	−	0.003401
183	=	1	+	0.002075
365	=	2	−	0.001326
548	=	3	+	0.000749
913	=	5	−	0.000578
1461	=	8	+	0.000171
5296	=	29	−	0.000065

In this simple illustration the daily motion in revolutions is represented by an exact fraction, but this is not the case in general. Consider the term −10.272 sin 2L in the long-period nutation in longitude, where L is the Sun's mean longitude. The daily motion of 2L (at epoch 1950) is 1°.97129469, or, in revolutions of 360°, 0ʳ.0054758186. This number of revolutions has to be represented by a proper fraction in its lowest terms. With the aid of a calculating machine one finds readily the figures in the accompanying table, the development being made in such a way that the residuals alternate in sign, each being numerically less than the preceding one.

Hence 8/1461 or 29/5296 revolutions are close approximations to the daily motion of 2L. If we adopt the former for our purpose, a table may be constructed giving

$$1.272 \sin \frac{360° \times k}{1461}$$

where k varies from 0 to 1460. By rearranging the 1461 entries in this table in the order, 1, 9, 17 . . . 1449, 1457, 4, 12 . . . 1452, 1460, 7, 15 . . . 1447, 1455, 2, 10 . . . 1450, 1458, 5, 13 . . . 1453, 1461, 8, 16 . . . 1448, 1456, 3, 11 . . . 1451, 1459, 6, 14 . . . 1446, 1454, 1, 9, 17 . . . they will represent the values of the term required at consecutive intervals of 1 day. It is seen that entry No. 1 (corresponding to $k = 0$) is not used a second time until every other entry has been used once. The cycle of entries, when once started at the proper place, could be used indefinitely, except for the fact that 8/1461 is not a perfect representation of the mean daily motion of 2L, while even this mean motion is not constant. The entries are given permanent consecutive numbers representing the order in which they are used.

k	No. used above	2L	Order of use, or card number	Entry in units of $0''.001$
0	1	0000	1	0
1	2	0.246	549	−5
2	3	0.493	1097	−11
3	4	0.739	184	−16
4	5	0.986	732	−22
5	6	1.232	1280	−27
6	7	1.478	367	−33
7	8	1.725	915	−38
8	9	1.971	2	−44

Hence the final table runs thus:—

No.	Entry
1	0
2	−44
3	−87
4	−31
5	−175

Since a revolution has been divided into 1461 parts, the interval between these parts is 0°.2464. The value of 2L will, in general, lie between two of those used in constructing the table. Thus if, at some given date, $2L = 1°.000$, the entry required (see the line $k = 4$ in above table) may be expressed as $732^c.06$, since, as will be seen later, each tabular entry is represented by a card. Similarly the entry for 1°.200 would be $732^c.87$, or $1280^c − 0^c.13$. From the table in which the fraction 8/1461 was developed, it is seen that the adopted value of 2L at the end of 1461 days is $0^r.000171$ too small. Thus the true interval between consecutive days is, in units of 1/1461 revolutions, 8.000171. The advance in card number corresponding to 8 units is 1; hence the card number advances 1.000171 per day, the integral part, by virtue of the final numbering of the cards in the actual order of use, denoting 8 units, and the decimal part denoting units of 1/1461 revolutions. If F be the fraction of the card number required to represent the true entry at any date, it is easily seen that, at any initial time, F need not exceed ± 0.5. It increases by 0.000171 per day, or by 1 every sixteen years. Hence once every sixteen years there must be a discontinuity in the sequence of card numbers to change a value of F just greater than 0.5 to a value just numerically less than − 0.5. From the column "Order of use" it is seen that entries that are adjacent in numerical value, e.g. 732 and 1280, differ by 548 in their assigned numbers. Hence when F exceeds 0.5 an addition of 548 must be made to the card number to obtain the card number corresponding to the nearest tabular entry; or, again, $732^c.50 = 1280^c − 0^c.50$.

The correction required to allow for the fraction or interpolating factor F is

$$-\frac{2\pi F \times 1''.272\cos 2L}{1461} = -0''.0055 F \cos 2L$$

and, since F need not exceed ± 0.5, this will not exceed ± 00.003. In computing nutation all terms with coefficients less than 00.004 are omitted, so that the omission of a correction or proportional part that may attain $\pm 0''.003$ is comparable with omitting a term whose coefficient is 00.003. The proportional parts omitted in the other nutation terms do not exceed 00.001. It would, of course, have been possible to reduce the proportional parts of this term to a maximum of $0''.001$ by adopting $29/5296$ revolutions as the daily motion of $2L$. But this would have involved the making of 5296 tabular entries, and the gain in accuracy would be inappreciable, as a value of the nutation to within 00.01 is ample for the present needs of astronomy.

The single-entry tables (i.e. those that depend on a single argument) of Brown's *Tables* are arranged in the manner described. Hence the user ascertains first the tabular entry corresponding to his initial date; the entries for subsequent consecutive dates are simply subsequent consecutive entries in the table, with occasional discontinuities. These entries may be copied in order from each table, and the transcribed entries added. This becomes laborious, mainly because of the number of entries to be copied and added—about 120,000 a year, as positions are computed for each noon and midnight. Also the risk of errors in copying and adding half a million figures is not inconsiderable. In the process about to be described the copying is done once only, the addition is done mechanically, and the results of the addition are printed.

Hollerith Cards and Punches.[1]—The basic unit in Hollerith equipment is a card $7\,3/4 \times 3\,1/4$ inches in size, divided into 45 vertical columns,[2] as shown in fig. 2. Each column contains 12 vertical positions, named, from top to bottom, Y, X, 0, 1 . . . 9.[3] A group of several columns constitutes a field, and in each field a number (within the capacity of the field) may be entered by

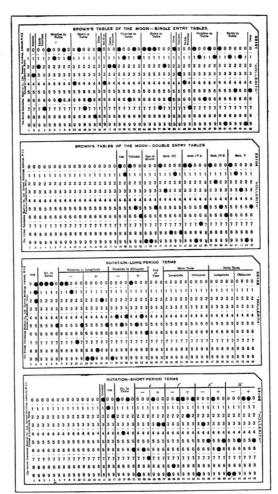

FIG. 2.—*Punched Cards.*

punching a hole in each column. The key-punch is shown in fig. 3. The card is carried by a movable car-

FIG. 3.—*Hand Key-punch.*

riage, each key depression driving a knife through the card, and releasing the carriage so that it moves to the next column. Electrical punches are also available; in these the depression of any key merely actuates a magnet, which drives the appropriate knife through the card. In the electric duplicating punch (fig. 4) a com-

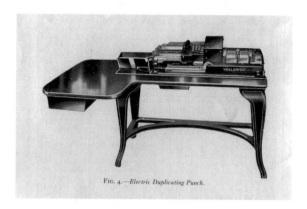

FIG. 4.—*Electric Duplicating Punch.*

pletely punched master-card, if placed in the upper frame, will be automatically copied, at the rate of 10 holes a second, on a card in the lower part of the machine. If any columns of the master-card are unpunched, the machine will naturally stop, and the operator can enter figures by hand in the usual way. As soon as a punched column is reached the duplicating process continues.

A first-class operator will punch 300 cards an hour. The number of errors made in punching is only a fraction of the errors that would be made in copying. The method of checking the punching will be described later.

The Sorter.—The function of the sorter (fig. 5) is

FIG. 5.—*Sorter.*

to separate the cards into groups according to the holes punched in some selected column. Thirteen receptacles are provided for the sorted cards, one corresponding to each of the twelve positions Y . . . 9 in which a hole may be punched, and one for cards in

which no hole is punched. The machine may be used to arrange cards in numerical order. In this case they are first sorted on the units column; the 10 receiving pockets used are then emptied in order from 0 to 9, and the cards once more sorted, this time on the tens column. The process is repeated until the cards have been sorted on every column in which the digits concerned occur. The accuracy of each sort is easily verified by passing a knitting needle through the appropriate holes in all the cards withdrawn from any one pocket, or by holding the cards up to a source of light. The sorter works at the rate of 24,000 cards an hour.

The Tabulator.—The purpose of the tabulator (fig. 6) is to add the items on the cards and print the totals.

FIG. 6.—*Tabulator.*

The process of printing each individual item as well as the totals is known as listing; if totals only are printed the process is tabulating. The cards are fed past a series of 45 brushes, to which direct current is supplied. Behind the cards are 45 insulated blocks, each connected to a plug-socket in a plugboard. The adding mechanism consists of a bank of five counters, each with nine separate adding wheels. Each wheel is represented on the plugboard by a plug-socket, so that any card column may be connected to any adding wheel by plugging across from one hole to another by means of a flexible cord, as on a telephone switchboard. The card acts as an insulator between brush and block; wherever a hole has been punched current passes through, and actuates the adding wheel that has been plugged to the column containing the hole.

The printing mechanism (fig. 7) is on the right of

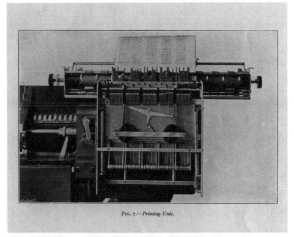

FIG. 7.—*Printing Unit.*

the machine. The type-bars are lifted in phase with the passage of the card past the reading brushes; the current that causes the adding also releases a pawl that arrests the type-bar, holding it at its correct level until the type is struck by the type-hammer. The printing of any individual column may be suppressed by locking its hammer. When totals are printed any counter may be cleared, or it may print only a "progressive total" or "sub-total," retaining its contents intact.

The speed of the machine when listing is 4500 cards an hour, and 9000 when tabulating. A delay of one second occurs each time a total is printed, so that the effective speed depends on the average number of cards per group. There are, of course, operating stops for various causes, *e.g.* placing new cards in the feeding mechanism, or new paper in the printing mechanism, so that the above speeds are not attained in practice.

Automatic Control.—This feature is of the utmost importance in the present application. When the cards corresponding to any one date have been added, the feeding must cease while the total is being printed, the counters must be cleared and then the feeding must be resumed. This sequence is performed automatically, without any attention whatsoever on the part of the operator. Actually the cards are read by two rows of 45 brushes, the lower brushes being responsible for actuating the adding wheels as already described. The upper brushes at the same time read the following card. The control is plugged so that an effort is made

to pass current through corresponding holes at the upper and lower brushes, and then through relays. In fig. 8 the machine is controlling on a 3-column field, both the cards shown being punched 426. If by the time the 0's have passed the brushes the circuit PQ is closed, the machine will continue to feed cards; if not, it will stop feeding, print the total, clear, and then continue feeding. In this case, when the line of 6's reaches the brushes the relay U is closed, when the 4's pass H is closed, and when the 2's pass T is closed, so that the upper card would be passed on to the lower brushes for addition. If the following card were punched 427, the relay U would not be closed, so that the end of the group of numbers 426 would be detected.

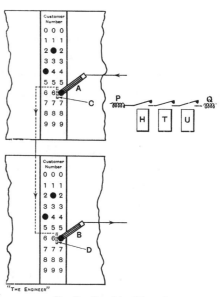

FIG. 8.—*Principle of Control.*

Verification of the Punching.—In commercial practice punching is usually verified by a special verifying punch. In order to place the responsibility for the accuracy of the cards, not on junior punch operators, but on experienced proof-readers, they were listed by means of the tabulator, and these printed lists were then compared with Brown's *Tables.*

Calculation of Long-period Terms of Nutation.—The preparation of a table for the term $-10.272 \sin 2L$ has been described. Each entry of the table is now punched on a card, as shown in fig. 2, the punching of card No. 5 being illustrated. Since the contribution of any term may be positive or negative, two fields are provided; if the contribution is positive it appears in the right-hand field, with its complement in the left-hand field, and *vice versa*. Since the nutation in obliquity depends on the cosines of the arguments on which the nutation in longitude depends, it is included on the same cards, the term in this case being $+0''.551 \cos 2L$.

It is now necessary to determine the starting-point in the table, or rather in the stack of cards. The value of $2L$ is

1936 January $1^d.0$	$198°.96142 = 1015^c.452$
1950 January $1^d.0$	$200°.16244 = 833^c.326$

We have already seen that the card increment per day is $1^c.000171$. Hence $365^d = 365^c.062$, $366^d = 366^c.063$, and 4 years or $1461^d = 1461^c.250 = 0^c.250$. Commencing on 1936 January 1 the card used is 1015, so that, using the cards in sequence, the card to be used on 1937 January 1 is $1015 + 366 = 1381$. Including the fraction, the card required is 1381.515, and, as discontinuities are introduced (when required, as in this case) at the beginning of a year, card 1380 is used on 1936 December 31, and $1380 + 1 + 548 - 1461 = 468$ on 1937 January 1. Thus a table of cards for January 1 of each year is prepared.

1936	1015	1940	102	1944	162	1948	102
1937	468	1941	468	1945	468	1949	468
1938	833	1942	833	1946	833	1950	833
1939	1198	1943	1198	1947	1198		

The next discontinuity is made at the beginning of the year 1953.

We may now conceive the cards for each harmonic to be arranged in a stack, with the card required for the initial date on top. The problem is to add together for the first date the entries on the top cards of each stack, then for the next date the numbers on the next cards, and so on. The top cards are picked up by hand, and the groups thus formed constitute another stack, which is fed into the tabulator. The printed result for a portion of 1938 January is shown in fig. 9. The first counter is connected to column 2 and (omitting two wheels) to columns 3–6. The second counter records the date, punched in columns 25–27 of the "main-term" card (depending on the Moon's node, and with a slowly changing coefficient), which is not permanent, but is punched specially for each date. The third and fourth counters contain the nutation in longitude and obliquity respectively. In the year 1938 the nutation in longitude is always positive and that in obliquity always negative, so that columns 12–16 and 17–20 are plugged. In years where either nutation changes sign (they cannot both change sign in the same year) the fifth counter is also used, and both fields of the nutation which passes through zero are plugged. By means of the hammer-blocks only five figures are allowed to print in the longitude totals and four in the obliquity totals, so that carry-over from the complements used does not appear. Thus the nutation, as well as its complement, will be printed; it is easy to distinguish these. The nutation is positive when the right-hand column contains the true value, and *vice versa*.

Reverting to fig. 9, it is seen that on the first day of the month the cards are listed, whereas on the other days only the totals are printed. This gives a printed record of the card numbers in use on that date. It will be seen that card No. 833 has been used for argument 2 (= $2L$), in accordance with the table above. The cards for subsequent days of the month follow in numerical order except those for argument 3, in which they follow in descending order.[4] There are eight numbered cards in each group, so that the total of the card numbers, which is recorded, should progress $+7 - 1 = +6$ from day to day, unless the cards of one argument reach their highest number, to be followed by card No. 1. The "period" of argument 4 (= $L - \pi$) is also 1461 cards (although it cannot be combined with argument 2), and since 1460 is used on January 1 and 1461 on January 2, card No. 1 will be used on January 3, making the difference between the totals for Janu-

Arg. No	Card. No	Month	Day	Longitude	Obliquity
1	0000			15524	4007
2	0833			437	517
3	1213			164	9944
4	1460			99996	
5	0068			16	21
6	0571			99992	9992
7	0157			99992	5
8	1005			99995	
9	0023			2	
45	5330 +6	1	01	16118	4486
45	5336 −1455	1	02	16157	4488
45	3881 +6	1	03	16194	4487
45	3887 +6	1	04	16233	4488
45	3893 +6	1	05	16269	4487
45	3899 +6	1	06	16305	4483
45	3905 +6	1	07	16339	4482
45	3911 +6	1	08	16374	4478
45	3917 +6	1	09	16407	4474
45	3923 +6	1	10	16439	4470

FIG. 9.—*Long-period Nutation.*

ary 2 and January 3 + 6 −1461 = −1455.

It will be seen that the numbers in the first counter provide all the necessary proof that the correct cards have been used. The constant total 45 shows that nine cards have been used, one from each of the arguments 1–9; the list on the first day of the month shows what cards were in use then, and this list can be compared with that prepared beforehand; the progression of the totals shows that the cards subsequently used were in a continuous numerical sequence.

The "control," which enables the tabulator to distinguish the end of one group and the beginning of the next, is on column 2, in which the nine cards of each group are punched

	0	0	0	0	0	0	0	0
1	1	3	4	5	6	7	8	9
	2							

respectively. Towards the end of the group control is being maintained through the 0's, but when the last card punched 0 and 9 is followed by a card punched 1, the control is "split" and the total printed. In the next group the first two cards are connected by their common 1's, and thereafter control is maintained by the 0's. In adding or sorting on a multi-punched column only the highest digit punched is effective.

The cards are finally passed through the sorter, sorting on column 2, so that they are separated into nine groups, each group containing the cards belonging to one argument. These groups are then placed *below* the unused numbers of their stack, in order to maintain the sequence. This replenishes the supply of cards, so that the mixing process, tabulation, sorting and replacement proceed continuously until the entire calculation is completed. Thus each card is used over and over again, although with different partners on each occasion. The tabulation for one year takes less than an hour.

Single-entry Tables.—All of Brown's single-entry tables were added in the manner described for long-period nutation. No complements are required, as all the quantities in the Tables have been rendered positive by the addition of constants, the sum of these constants being disposed of by various means, for example by subtraction from the mean longitude. The proportional parts are not negligible, so they are computed separately by hand, and applied at some convenient stage. Thus the Hollerith handles only the tabular entries, and does not relieve the computer of his interpolation. Actually no reference is made to a table when computing its proportional parts, as these are computed as cosine curves with the same period as the table, but differing by 90° in phase and having a small varying amplitude.

Double-entry Tables.—There are 61 tables each depending on two arguments, one of which is D, the mean elongation of the Moon from the Sun, while the other receives one of the numbers 1–22. These fall into four groups—one for longitude, two for latitude and one for parallax. Hence all the tables depending on any one of the arguments 1–22 are punched on one card (see fig. 2) and are added simultaneously, using four of the adding counters, the remaining counter being used for printing arguments and dates. Here the tabular entries corresponding to each argument are not numbered consecutively, but are divided into "columns," each of which contains 63 entries, one each for every half-day of the synodic period, together with an overlap of two dates at each end of the lunar month. The cards are, of course, punched with argument and column number, together with the day of the lunar month. For each lunation one "column" must be selected from each argument, and corresponding dates added. But since all the cards that have to be added on any one date have a common number, namely, the day of the month, they are brought together, not by hand, but much more expeditiously by the sorter. In tabulation this number becomes the control number. As before, the first date of each month is listed (fig. 10), giving a permanent record of the "column" numbers used. Here the check consists of the constancy of the printed total in the first column. After tabulation the cards are sorted on the columns containing the argument number, and replaced in storage until required again.

Table and Column	Day of Month	III	IV a	IV b	V
1 056	995	3818	975	256	1395
2 026	000	1406	463	60	2302
3 073	000	69	208	184	2056
4 116	000	3799	462	32	605
5 017	000	1398	233	9	341
6 075	000	1188	117	15	143
7 003	000	573	102	14	40
8 035	000	129	21	12	6
9 038	000	140	31	9	30
10 040	000	187	14		
11 031	000	97	7		
12 006	000	39			
13 032	000	89			
14 015	000	74			
15 026	000	25			
20589	995	13031	2633	591	6918
20589	000	13324	2721	587	6967
20589	005	13492	2807	591	6978
20589	010	13532	2883	600	6952
20589	015	13455	2941	618	6884
20589	020	13277	2980	644	6785
20589	025	13023	2993	677	6651
20589	030	12720	2986	705	6492
20589	035	12395	2955	737	6314
20589	040	12081	2906	765	6130
20589	045	11807	2846	789	5946
20589	050	11585	2778	805	5775

FIG. 10.—*Brown's Double-entry Tables.*

It was in this particular section of the work that the greatest efficiency was attained; on the average 20 figures were added per second, and the totals printed. The totals from 44 tables for two years (1460 dates) were done by three girls and the machines in one day.

Calculation of Short period Terms of Nutation.—There are four short-period quantities that depend on the same arguments, namely, the nutation in longitude ($\Delta'\psi$), the independent day-number f', and the two Besselian day-numbers A' and B'. Although f' and A' are constant multiples of $\Delta'\psi$, it was found convenient to compute all four of these quantities independently and simultaneously. The largest coefficient, in the units adopted, which are one-tenth of those in the *Nautical Almanac*, is 405, and the sum of the coefficients is less than 1000 units. The cards are punched in direct and complementary form (fig. 2) as in the case of the long-period nutation. Eleven terms have been included, and a twelfth card (punched in columns 11–14) is necessary in each group in order to be able to list the date. Hence in column 17 (the sorting column) all the available 12 positions are used.

In the specimen for 1948 January, shown in fig. 11, the left-hand group of the first counter is the sum of columns 17–21, and advances 11 each date, except when one of the arguments recommences its cycle. The right-hand group represents the date. The second counter is devoted to $\Delta'\psi$, the left-hand group being the sum of columns 22–24, and the right-hand group the sum of columns 25–27. Figures to the left of these totals, which would result from the carry-over produced by complementary numbers, are suppressed by locking the appropriate hammers. It will be seen that two complementary totals are given for each date. If the right-hand total is smaller than that on the left it is to be taken, with a + sign prefixed; if the left-hand total is smaller it is taken, with a – sign prefixed. In actual practice this leads to taking about seven successive totals from one column, followed by about seven successive totals from the other column. Thus the results in the example are read, after rounding off:—

Card numbers	Date	$\Delta'\psi$ –	$\Delta'\psi$ +	f' –	f' +	A' –	A' +	B' –	B' +
	101								
559	000	833	167	898	102	668	332	50	950
1 0058	000	969	031	981	019	939	061		
2 0406	000	967	033	980	020	935	065	995	005
3 0877	000	987	013	992	008	974	026	10	990
4 0199	000	985	015	991	009	970	030		
5 0293	000	11	989	7	993	23	977	999	001
6 0404	000	994	006	996	004	988	012		
7 0062	000	994	006	996	004	988	012	999	001
8 0246	000	3	997	2	998	5	995	3	997
9 0728	000	2	998	1	999	4	996	2	998
154	000	996	004	998	002	992	008		
53986	101	741	259	842	158	486	514	58	942
+11 53997	102	815	185	888	112	636	364	94	906
-236 53761	103	919	081	950	050	840	160	109	891
+11 53772	104	22	978	13	987	47	953	96	904
-398 53374	105	101	899	62	938	204	796	66	934
+11 53385	106	141	859	86	914	280	720	21	979
-287 53098	107	136	864	84	916	269	731	978	022
+11 53109	108	93	907	57	943	189	811	941	059
+11 53120	109	28	972	17	983	53	947	919	081
+11 53131	110	951	049	972	028	905	095	910	090

FIG. 11.—*Short-period Nutation.*

Jan.	$\Delta'\psi$	f'	A'	B'
	"	s		"
1	+.26	+.016	+.0051	–.06
2	+.18	+.011	+.0036	–.09
3	+.08	+.005	+.0016	–.11
4	–.02	–.001	–.0005	–.10

5	−.10	−.006	−.0020	−.07
6	−.14	−.009	−.0028	−.02
7	−.14	−.008	−.0027	+.02
8	−.09	−.006	−.0019	+.06
9	−.03	−.002	−.0005	+.08
10	+.05	+.003	+.0010	+.09

After the cards are mixed the time required to produce the results for one year is less than an hour, or about one minute for the calculation of each of the four elements for one month.

Work done with the Machines.—A Hollerith installation was used in H.M. Nautical Almanac Office for seven months in 1929; actually punching was started six months before the arrival of the sorter and tabulator, as it was necessary to punch 20,000,000 holes in half a million cards. The work described on long- and short-period nutation, and on double-entry tables, as well as that of most of the single-entry tables, was carried to the year 2000. The greater part of the cost was incurred in doing the first ten years, which would have sufficed for immediate needs. But to continue for the next 55 years with a trained and organised staff added very little to the cost, and was certainly more economical than re-training and re-organising ten years later. Moreover, there is little likelihood of Brown's *Tables* being superseded before the end of the century; any acquisition to our knowledge of the Moon during the next seven decades is almost certain to be expressed in the form of corrections to Brown's *Tables,* not in the form of new tables.

The sorter and tabulator, which may only be hired, cost about £2 a day. The cost of doing by hand what was done on the machines has been estimated at £6000; this estimate probably errs on the low side. The cost with the machines was certainly less than £1500.

Other Applications of the Machines.—The use of Hollerith machines in connection with systematic interpolation to tenths has already been described.[5] The tabulator may be used to produce values of $y = a + bx$ where x varies uniformly. A series of cards, all of which are punched 1 in column (say) 21, 2 in column 22, . . . 9 in column 29, is used. a is first entered into the adding counter. If b is, for example, 40337, column 27 is plugged to the units wheel, column 23 to the tens and hundreds wheels, and column 24 to the fifth wheel. Thus each card adds 40337 to a, and a progressive total may be printed automatically after each addition. If b is large, several counters may be connected together. Thus on one occasion the first thousand multiples of each of four 20-figure numbers were produced in four hours, i.e. in about one-tenth of the time in which they could have been copied by hand.

The machine may be used very efficiently for producing sums of products if the number of products entering into each sum is large. This is applicable in multiple correlation, where characteristics $a, b, c \ldots$ are observed, and $[a^2], [ab], [ac] \ldots [b^2], [bc]$, etc. are required. Suppose $a, b, c \ldots$ to be punched. Sort the cards on the units column of a, and add the various columns for each digit separately, getting totals $a_9, a_8 \ldots a_1, b_9 \ldots b_1, c_9 \ldots c_1$, etc. Now sort on the tens column of a and repeat the adding process, obtaining $a_9 \ldots a_1, b_9 \ldots b_1$, etc. If, for simplicity, a is less than 100, we have

$$[a^2] = 9a_9 + 8a_8 + \ldots a_1 + 90a_9' + \ldots$$
$$10a_1'[ab] = 9b_9 + 8b_8 + \ldots b_1 + 90b_9' + \ldots$$
$$10b_1'$$

and so on. Actually, instead of printing the totals $a_9 \ldots a_1$, etc., progressive totals are printed, i.e.

$$a_9, a_9 + a_8, a_9 + a_8 + a_7 \ldots a_9 + a_8 + a_7 + a_6 + a_5 + a_4 + a_3 + a_2 + a_1.$$

The sum of these is $9a_9 + 8a_8 + \ldots a_1$. In this way, on one occasion 15,000 products of 3-figure numbers were formed and added in about three hours.

The principal method used in tide prediction is the summation of harmonic terms, so that the use of the machine in this connection suggests itself. It would yield the height of the tide at uniform intervals of time, say one hour. As long as tidal predictions are limited, as at present, to the times and heights of high and low water, the method would not be economical. But in busy ports it must surely be an advantage to know the actual height of the tide at any moment, which could be obtained from a table of hourly heights. When the demand for this is felt, the use of the Hollerith may be considered. The apparent difficulty of the varying amplitudes of the constituents for different ports would be easily overcome by using two similar sets of cards for each harmonic; by adjusting the relative phases of these, any amplitude from zero to twice that of either set may be obtained.

· · ·

1. A description of the Hollerith machines, containing more mechanical details, has been given by the writer in an article, "The Hollerith and Powers Tabulating Machines," in Office Machinery Users' Association Transactions, 1929-30.

2. Machines using a card of the same size, but divided into 80 columns, are also in use.

3. The letters Y and X are not printed on the card.

4. This argument is $2\mathcal{S}$. The cards were inadvertently prepared on the assumption that $2\mathcal{S}$ increased, but the error was easily rectified by using the cards in the reverse order.

5. *M.N.* [Monthly Notices of the Royal Astronomical Society], **88**, 518, 1928.

4·5

Scientific Computing Service Limited: A Description of its Activities, Equipment and Staff

L. J. Comrie

London: Scientific Computing Service, 1938.

L. J. Comrie discovered in 1928 how to use ordinary desktop mechanical calculating machines as difference engines. In doing so he developed "programs" for the human computers to follow in using the machines, since these machines could not run programs.

INTRODUCTORY NOTE TO READING 4.5

In 1936 Leslie J. Comrie (see Reading 4.4) left the Admiralty to form the London-based Scientific Computing Service (SCS), the world's first independent service bureau set up to take in outside scientific computing work on a commercial basis. At this time the British Tabulating Machine Company, Limited (BTM), manufacturer of the Hollerith line of tabulating machines, and a subsidiary of IBM, operated punched-card service bureaus for commercial rather than scientific applications all over England. Comrie maintained a consulting relationship with BTM for many years and earned commissions on referrals. This business relationship may help to explain why Comrie always had such superb illustrations of the machines in his various scientific papers.[JMN]

TEXT OF READING 4.5

INTRODUCTION

This is an age of specialists. It is now freely acknowledged that arithmetic, in its various forms, is the work of specialists equipped with a knowledge of mathematical, physical and other sciences, well versed in numerical processes, with access to the calculating and accounting machines constructed primarily to meet the needs of the commercial world, and with the imaginative ingenuity required to adapt these machines to scientific requirements.

To most mathematicians, physicists and others engaged in research, arithmetical operations, especially when they arise in bulk, are irksome; if tackled at all, they are rarely done in the way that an experienced arithmetician would do them. Applied scientists are notoriously averse to calculations that go beyond slide-rule or graphical accuracy, or that involve tables that cannot be interpolated linearly. Also it is frequently impossible to possess even one modern calculating machine—still less the range of machines that enables each stage of a series of computations to be done in the most efficient and economical manner.

Of the greatly increased importance attached to numerical processes in scientific work during the last 15 or 20 years, there is no doubt whatsoever; published papers bear ample testimony to this. Numerous acknowledgments show how frequently the investigator passes on the "donkey-work" of his arithmetic. Yet, until now, there has not been any recognised organisation or institution to which the investigator could turn with the assurance that he would find his language understood, and the confidence that the facilities of experienced computers and mechanical equipment could be put at his disposal.

It was to fill this gap that SCIENTIFIC COMPUTING SERVICE came into being, first in 1937 as a private venture, and later, in 1938, when it was abundantly evident that it had the full support of the scientific public, as a limited company. In the short space of a year the full-time staff grew to 16, most of whom have had academic training. Under the established heads of departments are expanding groups; these are kept in constant touch with each other and with general calculations, so that a powerful team is available for large-scale computations.

The premises at 23 Bedford Square have been chosen and furnished for the specific objects of the company. They are situated in an easily accessible, professional, academic, and cultural neighbourhood, and yet are free from the noise, dust and distraction of a main traffic route. Small, carpeted, well-lighted rooms, each holding three or four workers, tend to reduce disturbances and interference from the noise of machines; the largest and noisiest machine is housed in a room of its own. Generous filing and storage accommodation has been provided; a new type of "House Exchange" telephone enables internal or external communications to be made at will, on a single instrument, without the intervention of an operator. A growing professional library, to include all known modern tables and reference books on computing and calculating machines, is available to the staff and to the company's clients; many periodicals of British and foreign learned societies are taken regularly.

PRINCIPAL ACTIVITIES

The principal activities may be summarised thus :

1. Scientific calculations generally, and particularly those where mechanical computation and mass production methods may be employed. Even the possessor of a small calculating machine may often find it advantageous to have work done on a multi-register or a tabulating machine, which it would not be economical to purchase for a relatively small job.

2. Investigators need not be deterred by the fact that the technicalities of their highly specialised work cannot always be fully understood by computers. "Two heads are better than one", and a successful result may often be the outcome of collaboration between an investigator who contributes the necessary data, analysis, formulae, and typical examples, and a

competent arithmetician who supplies a knowledge of arithmetical processes and tools, and the labour and equipment to carry out the processes.

3. A special feature is made of table making, whether from a given formula, or from existing tables. Much of this work is done on a 6-register National machine, capable of differencing to the fifth difference a function given at equal intervals of the independent variable, or of integrating from sixth differences, with printing of all intermediate differences. This accounting machine (of which a full description is available and will be sent on application), which was first applied to scientific work in 1932, has revolutionised the art of table making, and particularly of subtabulation, i.e. systematic interpolation to smaller intervals. It lends itself also to other summation problems, such as formation of moments from equidistant data, curve fitting, and the numerical solution of differential equations.

4. Mathematical statistics. For correlations, analysis of variance, regressions and allied statistical processes, the formation of the normal equations used in least square solutions, and similar problems, the punched-card machines—particularly the Hollerith—are available. As these machines cannot normally be hired for less than a year, this service enables them to be utilised for any jobs—no matter how short—for which they are suitable. The capacity of these machines is illustrated by the fact that one of them recently formed and summed nearly a million products in two months. A new model, containing more special features than any model so far made, has been built for the work of this company. Other models have been

successfully applied on a large scale to the tabulation of examination results.

5. Analysis of questionnaires. When thousands of answers to a questionnaire have to be handled, as in market research, they are coded and transferred to punched cards, from which the desired analyses and tables are produced by sorting and tabulating machines.

6. Fourier analysis and Fourier synthesis. Here again the punched-card machines, with their facilities for sorting, multiplying and adding in groups as desired, lend themselves to large undertakings that would otherwise be laborious.

7. Survey calculations, especially the determination of latitudes and longitudes from star altitudes, the adjustment of triangulations by least squares, the calculation of map projections, and the conversion of co-ordinates from one system to another.

8. The numerical solution of differential equations and the numerical evaluation of finite integrals. Work of this nature is a common feature of modern mathematical physics. It is greatly facilitated by access to various types of calculating machines, with experience in their application to quadrature problems.

9. An advisory and investigational service relating to the purchase or use of calculating machines. We are familiar with all the calculating machines on sale, and can advise regarding ways of using machines, or on purchase, when all the conditions are specified—e.g. nature of the work, type of operators, amount of money available, etc. Most of the machines suitable for scientific computing may be inspected on our premises, without the embarrassment of the presence of importunate salesmen.

10. Instruction in the art of mechanical computing. Courses of varying length and covering various machines and processes are offered. The length of the course, its scope, and the fees are arranged to suit individual requirements. These courses appeal to institutions installing new machines, and also to Honours students as vacation courses—especially in practical interpolation, table making, subtabulating and the use of the punched-card tabulating machines.

11. The preparation, publication and sale of mathematical tables, notes on calculating machines or computational processes, and computing forms, e.g. for surveying, navigation, etc. As no other booksellers specialise in mathematical tables, we hold a stock for inspection and sale. We are also able to advise where various mathematical functions are tabulated.

12. Press work, e.g. the preparation of printer's copy (particularly of tables), drafting of instructions to printers, and proof-reading, especially where careful attention to typography is essential. A special typewriter (see below) with 135 characters lends itself to the preparation of copy for lithographic printing, or of mathematical or technical articles.

13. The giving of demonstrations and exhibitions of calculating machines, and of lectures on mechanical computing.

MECHANICAL EQUIPMENT

The principal machines in use are:

Adding and Listing Machines

1. A 10-column electric Victor machine with a sexagesimal keyboard, arranged to add to 999 59 59.999, for use with degrees (or hours), minutes, seconds, and decimals of a second. Small decimal numbers can be handled by the degrees or by the seconds columns. This machine was designed for adding and subtracting the angles and times that occur in surveying computations.

2. A 10-column decimal electric Continental machine, with two registers, and a means of transferring a total or subtotal from the first register to the second. This machine lends itself to the summation of numbers in groups, with the simultaneous formation of the grand total of the groups.

3. A 12-column 6-register decimal National machine, built to order. A similar machine is described, and its use illustrated in the publication listed below as number (19). As further improvements on the machine there described, this machine may be split into two 6-column machines; a result derived a complement may be printed in complementary form, or in direct form, or in both forms. A special feeding device permits the use of continuous flat stationery of different sizes. This machine is never idle; its principal work is differencing, mechanical integration, and subtabulation.

Multiplying Machines

1. Brunsviga calculating machines, models 13z ($10 \times 8 \times 13$), 20 ($12 \times 11 \times 20$) and Twin 13z. The model 20 (of which several are in use) is a favourite for general and exploratory calculations, and is valued specially for its ability to transfer from the product register to the setting levers, and for the split clearing of the product register. The twin machine, apart from many general uses, is ideal for the handling of rectangular co-ordinate survey problems, as described in article (23) of the list below.

2. Mercedes electric machine, model 38 MSW, of capacity $8 \times 8 \times 16$. This has all the features available on modern electric machines, including automatic multiplication and division, continued multiplication, a special storage register, and a sliding window in the product register for converting complements into direct numbers.

3. Madas electric machine, of capacity $10 \times 10 \times 20$, with automatic multiplication and division. This particular machine has been specially modified so that it will produce sums of numbers and their squares from a single setting of each number. This feature is particularly valuable in mathematical statistical calculations.

4. Facit electric machine, of capacity $9 \times 8 \times 13$.

Punched-Card Machines

Punches and verifiers only are kept at Bedford Square. By arrangement with the British Tabulating Machine Company Ltd., the heavier machines are installed at Clifton House, in Euston Road, N.W. 1. These comprise a sorter, sorter-counter, reproducer, multiplying punch and a specially constructed tabulator with summary punch. The latter has six 11-wheel decimal counters, which can (for most purposes) be resolved into twelve 5-wheel counters, and a printing bank with 80 type-bars. Descriptions of the Hollerith system and some of its applications are given in articles (14), (16), and (22) of the list below. In correlations and regressions that involve many variables, these machines render possible undertakings that would otherwise be beyond human endurance or patience.

Typewriters

Besides 90-character Imperial typewriters for correspondence, there is a new 135-character Continental machine—the first of this kind to reach England—for the production of printer's copy, whether for composition or for photo-lithography. It has two shifts, 45 keys, and three characters on each key. The vertical spacing is in steps of 1/12-inch, as compared with 1/6-inch on most typewriters; the spacing generally used is 3/12- or 1/4-inch. The lay-out of the keyboard is as follows:

*	§	|	±	°	'	''	/	÷	×	<	>
1	2	3	4	5	6	7	8	9	0	[	]
1	2	3	4	5	6	7	8	9	0	=	•
ψ	ω	ε	ρ	τ	η	Γ	Δ	Π	π	≤	≥
Q	W	E	R	T	Y	U	I	O	P	(	)
q	w	e	r	t	y	u	i	o	p	+	−
α	σ	δ	φ	γ	Σ	Ω	κ	λ	ϖ	∂	
A	S	D	F	G	H	J	K	L		{	}
a	s	d	f	g	h	j	k	l	⌢	_	
ζ	ξ	χ	θ	β	ν	μ	∫	√	~		
Z	X	C	V	B	N	M	?	£	%		
z	x	c	v	b	n	m	,	.	½		

The small numerals may be used either as superiors, as in a^2b^3, or as inferiors, as in a_2b_3 or H_2SO_4.

Staff

In view of the wide range of problems that have to be handled, a highly intelligent and well-qualified staff is essential. The company has been fortunate in securing people temperamentally fitted for computing; all of these have devoted themselves enthusiastically to the task of establishing and consolidating the reputation of the newly created institution. A separate Staff List, giving the names and qualifications of all members of the staff, is issued from time to time.

Certain responsibilities are delegated to heads of departments, particularly the detailed supervision of work that is following established procedures. There is no hard and fast line of demarcation between the departments; in fact a particular job undertaken by the company may easily be shared by all departments. In this way the organisation is flexible, and members of the staff are continually acquiring fresh experience that can be brought to bear on incoming problems. The services of several specialists are also available to the company in a consulting capacity.

The Managing Director, Dr. L. J. Comrie, is a recognised pioneer in mechanical computing. In 1920 he founded the British Astronomical Association Computing Section, and compiled the first *Handbook*. In 1923–25, while on the faculty of two American Universities, he introduced computation as part of the curriculum. During the eleven years of his connection with H.M. Nautical Almanac Office, at the Royal Naval College, Greenwich, first as Deputy Superintendent and later as Superintendent, the *Nautical Almanac* became the foremost of the national ephemerides, and the revolutionary methods of mechanical calculation introduced brought international fame to the Office. No better training ground for the service that is now being given to the professional public could have been found, as the experience of mass production of figures, and of numerical and mechanical processes, is directly applicable wherever computation is involved. It is Dr. Comrie's ambition to transfer to the new

institution he is developing the reputation he built up for the Nautical Almanac Office.

Dr. Comrie has specialised in interpolation, to which he has made many original contributions. In 1928 he put forward the "end-figure" method of sub-tabulation, which has since been widely used in places where expensive machines are not available. In the same year he showed how two commercial machines—the Brunsviga-Dupla and the Burroughs Class 11—could be used for building up functions from their second finite differences. In 1931 he "discovered" that the 6-register National (then called the Ellis) machine could be used for differencing to the fifth difference or integrating from sixth differences; in other words it fulfilled Babbage's dream of a "difference-engine" a century before. This machine has been taken up by the British Association, H.M. Nautical Almanac Office, and the National Physical Laboratory; the latest and most elaborate example, which is in the possession of this company, has rendered possible large programmes of table making that would otherwise have been shirked.

In 1928 appeared the first mention of the "throwback" (although the name was not given till later), a powerful means of allowing for the effect of higher-order differences. In the *British Association Mathematical Tables,* where this device is extensively used, many columns of print have been eliminated, and the user is spared much labour. This was followed in 1934 (published in 1936) by a method of inverse interpolation (using two machines simultaneously) that has now been adopted where this process is required in bulk; here again, a process that was formerly avoided whenever possible can now be faced with equanimity. The tables necessary for this and other methods were included in the *Nautical Almanac* for 1937, and published separately under the title *Interpolation and Allied Tables.*

Another pioneer achievement was the introduction in 1928 of the Hollerith punched-card system for scientific work. This was first applied to the synthesis of the harmonic terms by which the motion of the Moon is represented. With 20,000,000 holes punched in

500,000 cards, large contributions to the Moon's motion up to the year 2000 were evaluated. This system has since been applied to the calculation of correlations and regressions, to various types of Fourier synthesis, to the conversion of spherical and rectangular co-ordinates, to the formation of moments, to the preparation of normal equations in least square solutions, and to the analysis of lines in spectra.

The use of twin machines, such as the Brunsviga Twin 13Z, has also been developed. One spectacular application is to the reduction of prismatic spectrograms by the Hartmann formula; here three constants are held disposed on the machine, while wave-lengths are obtained by introducing varying measures. The machine is ideal for the problems of rectangular co-ordinate survey that arise in military practice, and a description of entirely new methods specially evolved for the machine has been published; these methods have been adopted by the War Office.

Lectures on these subjects have been given on various occasions. Among these may be mentioned courses of six lectures at Imperial College (1929), at University College (the Newmarch Lectures, 1933), and a six weeks' course in 1932 in the University of California, at Berkeley. Other lectures and demonstrations have been given to various learned societies.

Another activity is the preparation or editing of tables. The third edition (1930) of Barlow's *Tables of Squares, Cubes, Square Roots, Cube Roots and Reciprocals of all Integer Numbers up to* 10,000 is well known. This was followed (1931) by the production of *Four-Figure Tables of the Trigonometrical Functions with the Argument in Time,* and (with a collaborator) a volume of *Standard Four-Figure Mathematical Tables;* these tables are now in general use by mathematical physicists and others engaged in original work. A table of 7-figure values of the trigonometrical functions for every second of time is being published by H.M. Stationery Office. In collaboration with Professor Peters, of Berlin, two 900-page volumes giving 7-figure and 8-figure values respectively of the four principal trigonometrical functions were prepared. Considerable contributions have been made to the *British Association*

tion Mathematical Tables; in particular the preparation of Volume VI (Bessel Functions) may be mentioned. A recent table is for use in fitting a Pearson Type IV curve.

The newly established service is carrying on the tradition of table-making. Hughes' *Tables for Sea and Air Navigation,* for determining latitude and longitude by position line methods, may be expected to supersede existing tables. A new edition of Callendar's *Steam Tables* is in preparation. A 400-page volume of tables has been compiled for the War Office.

The statistical work is in charge of Mr. G. B. Hey, B.A., who joined us after a brilliant career at Cambridge which included two years' research work on agricultural and mathematical statistics. He took a leading part in applying Hollerith machines to what is undoubtedly the most extensive series of correlations yet done in this country. His knowledge of the application of the punched-card system to statistical work is second to none.

The work of table making, proof-reading, and general calculations, especially those involving the National machine, is supervised by Miss K. M. Stocks, B.A., who took the Mathematical Tripos at Cambridge in 1932. She is a skilled proof-reader, with a good eye for typography, and has been associated with the preparation and press work of various books and tables recently published or now in the press.

The third main division of our work, which may be broadly termed applied astronomy, as it includes surveying, map-making, and geophysics, is under the care of Mr. R. W. Pring, B.Sc., who took first-class honours in mathematics and astronomy at University College, London. He has a natural aptitude for work of this kind, and brings much originality of thought to it.

Miss S. M. Burrough, B.Sc., was also trained in mathematics and astronomy at University College. She is our most versatile computer, being able to do any calculation or operate any machine.

5
The Earliest Data Networks

Account of the Chappe Optical Telegraph

A. L. Ternant

From *The Story of the Telegraph,* translated by R. Routledge (London: George Routledge and Sons, c. 1885), pp. 4–12. Illustration taken from Alexis Belloc, *La télégraphie historique depuis les temps les plus reculés jusqu'a nos jours* (Paris: Firmin-Didot, 1894), fig. 40.

Letterhead of Abaham Chappe, one of the four brothers who founded the Chappe optical telegraph network, depicting Mercury carrying one of their semaphores. This was fifty years before the Western Union Telegraph Company adopted Mercury as its trademark.

INTRODUCTORY NOTE TO READING 5.1:

The first systems for transmitting information faster than messengers on horseback were telegraph systems that began to be invented at the end of the eighteenth century. These may be considered the first organized data networks. The first telegraph system that had a wide installation was the optical system developed in France by the Chappe family. This system, created by the four Chappe brothers—Claude, Abraham, Ignace, and Pierre—debuted in the 1790s and remained in use until superseded by the electric telegraph in the 1850s. It came into being during a period of considerable unrest—the French Revolution was in full swing and France was at war with several neighboring countries. The times favored the development of an organized, nationwide system of communication that would enable France's central government to receive and transmit intelligence in the shortest possible time. The Chappe optical telegraph could transmit one character in about thirty seconds, although, because optical telegraphy transmission speed was affected by visibility, transmission in rain or snow was significantly slower than transmission on a clear day. Nevertheless, this method was several times faster than a horseback rider carrying a message. Chappe's telegraph spanned the entire country of France, with offshoots to Belgium and Italy. It was said that under optimal conditions a message could be transmitted from Paris to Milan in about thirty minutes.

The chief architect of the Chappe telegraph was Claude Chappe (1763–1805), who began working on designs for the telegraph in 1789. After experimenting successfully with visual signaling devices that used pendulums and modified clock faces, Claude and his brothers devised a semaphore telegraph consisting of a large beam (the regulator) with smaller wings (indicators) mounted at each end. These could be manipulated in various ways to signal alphabetic, numeric, and other coded symbols between stations, at a rate of one symbol every ten to thirty seconds. The first optical telegraph line, consisting of nineteen stations built between Paris and Lille (a distance of 190 km. or about 120 miles) was opened in July 1794. In August 1794 the telegraph was used to report two major

French military victories; this happy news established Claude Chappe's reputation as a benefactor of his country, and insured the French government's continued support of the telegraph. By 1805 there were four main branches extending from Paris into the north, east, west, and south of France. Similar networks soon sprang up throughout Europe, particularly in Sweden, where Abraham Nicolas Edelcrantz's shutter-based optical telegraph was in use until 1888. Chappe's visual telegraph system remained operational in France until 1852, when it was superseded by an electric telegraph; at the time of its replacement, the Chappe telegraph network covered more than three thousand miles and included 556 separate stations.

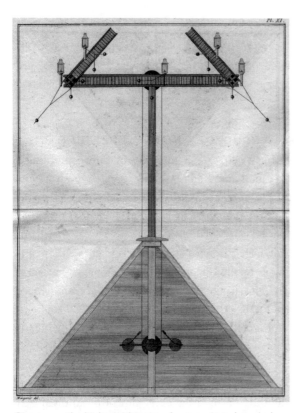

Chappe optical telegraph semaphore system. Located on towers several miles apart, these semaphore signals were read through telescopes located in each tower, and copied by the next tower down the line. The telegrapher in the previous tower would check to see that the following tower copied his signal exactly. If not he would signal an error. Operators in the towers did not know the encryption methods, so that secrecy of the messages was maintained. The system could transmit one character in about thirty seconds. It was claimed that under optimal conditions a message could be transmitted from Paris to Milan in thirty minutes. Weather conditions affected transmission speed.

In the Chappe system messages were encrypted and translated by semaphore signals built on the tops of towers miles apart. A telegrapher in the next tower would read the semaphore signals through a telescope and retransmit the message to the following tower. This process would be repeated, with error-correction checks in place at each repetition, until the message reached the end of the line. Because optical telegraph systems using semaphores required that messages be continually retransmitted from tower to tower, there was no fail-safe way to eliminate error. Furthermore it was necessary to encrypt all messages so that the operators would not be privy to secret information. Thus only the directors of the system and the inspectors were allowed to know the code for message signals. The two operators in each signaling tower knew only the limited set of control codes used for error corrections, clock synchronizations, etc. The actual codes were written in codebooks. Claude Chappe's 1795 codebook had 8,940 words and phrases. By 1799 he had added four supplementary codebooks with additional words and phrases, and names of places and people. Thus each message had to include a citation of the code book employed.

"All signals on the semaphore telegraph were passed one at a time, in strictly synchronous fashion. The operators were required to check [by telescope] their neighboring stations every few minutes for new signals, and reproduce them as quickly as possible. The operator then had to verify that the next station inline reproduced the signal correctly, and set an error signal if it failed to do so. Each symbol had to be recorded in a logbook, as soon as it was carried to completion. Since no symbolic or numeric code system for representing the semaphore positions was described, this was done in the form of little pictograms. . . ."[1]

The official Chappe telegraphy letterhead used on a letter reproduced with this introductory note shows that as early as 1803 the Chappe family was using the figure of Mercury holding one of their semaphores as an emblem of telegraphy. This was more than fifty years before the Western Union Telegraph Company adopted Mercury as its trademark.

Because little written by the Chappe family seems to have been translated into English, I selected this account of the Chappe telegraph from the early history of telegraphy by A. L. Ternant, translated into English in 1885. [JMN]

---

1   Gerard J. Holzmann and Björn Pehrson, *The Early History of Data Networks* (Los Alamitos, CA: IEEE Computer Society Press, 1995), 87.

TEXT OF READING 5.1

In his "Art of Signals," published at Hanau in 1795, Major Boucheroeder states that the art of telegraphy dates from the building of the Tower of Babel in the year B.C. 2247. This structure, he thinks, must have had for its special purpose the establishment of a central point of communication between the different countries then inhabited by mankind.

Scripture also relates that columns of fire and of smoke were used to lead the Israelites across the desert after their flight from Egypt.

The idea of attaching a signification to the appearance of fires on heights is so natural that traces of it are found among various savage tribes in Africa.

History and poetry have preserved certain traditions which prove that the art of telegraphy was used in heroic times.

Hannibal erected watch-towers in Africa and in Spain in order to transmit phrases by signals. The Romans adopted this method, and wherever they extended their conquests, they established rapid communications which enabled them to maintain their power over the conquered nations. Remains of these towers still exist in France. Those of Uzès, Bellegarde, Arles, and of the Valley of Luchon, were occupied by watchmen who rapidly transmitted news from the adjoining countries.

The telegraph represented on Trajan's column is the only description of a Roman telegraphic station that has come down to our days. This station is surrounded by palisades; its second story has a balcony, and the building is surmounted by a small tower.

The Arabs and the Asiatics practised the art of conversing by means of visible signals, and the Chinese erected fire-machines on their great wall of 188 leagues in length, in order that the alarm might be given along the whole frontier that divided them from the Tartars, when some horde of that race were threatening them. They, like the Indians, used lights so brilliant that they penetrated fogs, and neither wind nor rain could extinguish them. The English, having learnt in India the composition of these fireworks, used them in the operations of the great trigonometrical survey by which the observatories of Paris and of Greenwich were connected in 1787.

These operations were conducted on one side by Cassini, Méchain and Legendre, and on the other by Roy and Blagden, and by them not only was a perfect triangulation effected by the use of fireworks, and even of ordinary reflecting lamps, but there was besides an exchange of signals from the opposite shores of the Straits of Dover. The possibility of a telegraphic communication across the Channel was therefore demonstrated as early as 1787.

Francis Kessler, an enthusiastic patron of the occult sciences, was the anticipator of the optical telegraph, now used in the army. He enclosed his telegraph in a barrel containing a lamp with its reflector. In front of the barrel was a moveable screen which could be raised or lowered by means of a lever. The screen raised once indicated the first letter of the alphabet, raised twice the letter B, raised three times the letter C, and so on. We shall presently see how the Morse alphabet signals may be represented by similar methods. The alphabetic system was in vogue at the period of which we are speaking, and it has reached down to the present time. In 1684, the celebrated Robert Hook described before the Royal Society of London, his system of signals formed of planks of various shapes painted black, and which could be raised between slides.

Telegraphy by means of opaque bodies has continued in use for ships, especially as a means of indicating to mariners the heights and movements of the tides in ports. For this purpose balls with black bands are hoisted up on an apparatus formed of a mast and a yard. These balls stand out quite black against the sky. A ball placed at the intersection of the mast and yard indicates a depth of water of three metres throughout the whole length of the channel. Each ball placed on the mast below the first, adds one metre to the depth of water; if placed above it adds two. A ball hoisted at the end of the yard represent a quarter of a metre when it is to the left of the mast, and half a metre when it is to the right. Therefore only six balls are required to indicate the depth of the water, each quarter of a metre from three metres to eight and three-quarters.

These signals may be made at night by substituting lanterns for the balls, and using a coloured light to mark the point at which the yard crosses the mast.

To indicate the flow of the tides, a white flag with a black cross, and a black pendant in the form of a vane are used.

These flags are hoisted as soon as there are two metres of water in the channel, and they are taken away when the water has again come down to that level. During the flow of the tide the pendant is above the flag; at the time of high water the pendant is taken away; and during the ebb the pendant is below the flag.

When the state of the sea prevents entrance to the port, all these signals are replaced by a red flag, also hoisted on the top of the mast.

This digression has withdrawn us a little from the history of visual telegraphs, but we thought the foregoing details would not be without interest.

Bertin, in his "Curiosités de la Littérature," informs us that the Marquis of Worcester laid claim to the invention of a hundred new machines, and asked Charles II of England a certain sum of money to make them known. This was refused. It has been said that the telegraph and the steam-engine were amongst these inventions, but no trace now remains of the results obtained in these researches. Towards the end of the seventeenth century, Amontons and also Marcel made some experiments, as we know, although the machines and the drawings of these inventors have been lost, and Marcel has not left even a description of his plan. He did not wish to have his method made public until it had been adopted by the king; but Louis XIV was then old, and Marcel got no answer to his petition. Dupuis, the author of "L'Origine de Tous les Cultes," in 1723, laid before the government a scheme of alphabetic telegraphy. It was not until ten years afterwards that he made a trial of it at Ménilmontant in order to communicate between his house and that of a friend at Bagneux. When Chappe's telegraph was laid before the Legislative Assembly in 1792, Dupuis,

who was one of the members, abandoned his plan.

In 1783, Linguet offered the French government a method of transmitting to the greatest distance intelligence of any kind, even long sentences, with almost the speed of thought. This plan, which Linguet thought would obtain his release from the Bastille, was tested before commissioners appointed by the government. It was not adopted, and no trace of it remains.

Monge seems also to have proposed, before Chappe, a signal telegraph which was erected on the central pavilion of the Tuileries, but was never used.

It seems therefore that many scientific men studied the art of signalling, before Chappe and his brothers introduced their system of optical telegraphy into France. Nearly all their predecessors were content to communicate a few words from one station to another station, and this is one reason why they failed. But in order to transmit a considerable number of signals to great distances, it is evidently requisite that the stations must be numerous. The brothers Chappe tried experiments among themselves with a rude apparatus for corresponding by signs, consisting of a wooden rule turning on a pivot and carrying two smaller rules of half the size at its extremities. They afterwards made some attempts at transmitting signals by electricity. Claude Chappe, the most ingenious of the five brothers, had contrived a method of corresponding by help of two synchronous pendulums, electrically marking the same figures. He carried insulated conductors to certain distances; but the difficulty of insulating them, the high electrical intensity required, and the dependence of the action on the state of the atmosphere, led him to think that his plan of communicating by electricity could never be realized.

It is curious to observe that Claude Chappe entertained for a short time the idea of utilizing the very agent which was destined to afterwards displace his own telegraph.

After many failures, however, Claude Chappe succeeded at length in perfecting a system of visual telegraphy in which signals were repeated from station to station, by means of an apparatus, the upper portion of which was composed of three pieces each capable of being separately moved (Fig. 1). The largest of these

pieces, having the form of a very elongated parallelogram with two other pieces mounted at its extremities, can be placed in four different positions; namely, horizontal, vertically, or inclined at 45° right or left. Each of the attached moveable pieces, called wings, can be made to assume seven different positions as regards the principal piece, by forming with it, above or below an angle of 45°, a right angle, or an obtuse angle, and by coinciding with it in direction. The three will thus produce 196 different figures, which may be regarded as so many simple signals, to each of which any determined meaning may be attached. It will easily be seen that by placing in any direction a series of such machines, each of which repeats the movements of that which precedes it, the figures made at the first station, are transmitted to the end of the line, as are the ideas that have been attached to them, of which the intermediate agents may however have no knowledge. In order that it may be known that the signal has been properly given from the summit of the cabin, there is placed within, at the lower part of the posts that support the telegraph, a repeater, which serves as handle for giving movement, thus at once taking and giving the figure which has to be formed at the upper part.

Such is the system of Claude Chappe, which he fortunately got adopted, thanks to the good offices of his brother Ignatius, who had been appointed member of the Legislative Assembly in October, 1791. By the aid of his relative Delaunay, formerly Consul of France at Lisbon, Claude Chappe drew up a secret vocabulary of 9,999 words, in which each word was represented by a number. Such were the results presented by Claude Chappe, on the 22nd March, 1792, to the Legislative Assembly, before whom he was admitted. In the speech which he made on this occasion he asked the Assembly that, if the invention should be successful, he should merely be recouped for the expenses of his experiment.

The examination of his machine was referred to a committee; but it was not until the 1st April, 1793, that Romme, the secretary of this committee, reported in favour of the adoption of Claude Chappe's system of telegraphy. Romme ended his report by asking the Assembly for a vote of the money necessary to establish a preliminary experimental line. The Convention voted the insignificant sum of 6,000 francs, at the same time directing the committee to appoint a commission before whom the new apparatus should be worked. The members of this commission were Arbogast, Daunou, and Lakanal, to the last of whom Claude Chappe was indebted for the final adoption of his telegraph by the Convention. An experiment made on the 12th July, 1793, had so distinctly told in favour of Chappe's system that there was no longer room for hesitation. Lakanal, who had been appointed secretary to the commission, made a deep impression on the Assembly when he read his report before it, on the 26th July, 1793. He wound up by proposing to confer on Claude Chappe the title of Telegraph Engineer with the stipend of a lieutenant of engineers, and proposing also that they should consider what lines of communication the Committee of Public Safety required to be formed in the interests of the Republic. The Convention embodied Lakanal's proposals in a decree. Officially adopting Chappe's telegraph, it directed the Committee of Public Safety to cause a line of communication, with the necessary number of stations, to be established. Chappe, thus appointed Telegraph Engineer received the pay of 5 francs 10 sous per day, so that his position was assimilated to that of a lieutenant of engineers.

The Committee of Public Safety, thinking that Chappe's telegraph would enable the commanders of the army to communicate rapidly with each other, decided that the telegraphs should first be established in the vicinity of besieged towns, and that the lines should pass from the limits of the frontiers, that is to say from Lille and from Landau to Paris.

This line was ready for use in *Fructidor, An. II.* (August, 1794), and the circumstances connected with the first despatch deserve to be related.

The town of Conde had just been retaken from the Austrians. On the same day, namely the 1st September, 1794, at noon, a despatch forwarded from the tower of St. Catherine at Lille passed from station to station until it reached the dome of the Louvre at Paris, just at the moment the Convention was about to sit.

Carnot ascended the tribune, and with a sonorous voice, announced that he had just received by the telegraph the following news:

"Conde is restored to the Republic; its surrender took place at six o'clock this morning."

This news was received with thunders of applause, and every voice was raised to honour the new invention, so brilliantly inaugurated for the glory and safety of the country.

Chappe's aerial telegraph underwent divers vicissitudes under the Directory and under the Empire. Nevertheless under these governments, as well as under the Restoration, many lines were established in France; but Chappe was not to witness these developments of his cherished invention; for, disgusted with the little esteem in which his invention was held by the emperor, and suffering acutely from a chronic disease of the bladder, he gave way to despair, and cut his own throat on the 25th January, 1805. Besides the monument which was erected to him in the cemetery of Père Lachaise, there is under the lofty signal-tower in the Rue de Grenelle-Saint-Germain, from which so

many historical despatches have issued, a small memorial to mark the spot where Claude Chappe committed suicide.

Claude's brothers, Ignatius and René, were appointed directors, with salaries of 8,000 francs per annum. They had to resign in 1830, when a royal order appointed M. Marchal provisionary administrator, and from that time to 1848, the aerial telegraph remained stationary. M. Ferdinand Flocon was at that date appointed administrator of telegraphs, but was succeeded in 1849 by M. Alphonse Foy, who had previously held the office under Louis Philippe. It was M. Foy who had the honour of introducing the electric telegraph into France. He entrusted M. Bréguet with the task of constructing a French apparatus for reproducing the signals of the aerial telegraph. This difficult problem was solved by M. Bréguet in the most elegant manner; but the signal apparatus soon became merely alphabetical, that is to say, the signals of the aerial telegraph were speedily reduced to the twenty-five letters of the alphabet, supplemented by the figures and other signals that are met with in all the other systems.

The aerial telegraph was also used by our troops during the Crimean war, and M. Inspector Carette utilized it on this occasion as a field telegraph. Submarine telegraphy, then scarcely two years old, was also brought into the Crimea by the English, who connected Varna and Balaclava by laying in the Black sea a gutta-percha covered wire, which lasted about six months. The new and the old telegraphy were by these circumstances brought face to face. Aerial telegraphy, however, had had its day, and since then it has entirely disappeared.

$$5.2$$

Improvement in the Mode of Communicating Information by Signals by the Application of Electro-Magnetism

Samuel F. B. Morse

Specification forming part of Letters Patent No. 1,647, dated June 20, 1840.

INTRODUCTORY NOTE TO READING 5.2

Samuel F. B. Morse became attracted to the study of electricity while attending Yale College, where he heard lectures by Jeremiah Day and Benjamin Silliman. Although he at first pursued a career as an artist, Morse maintained his interest in electricity and electrical machines. During a trip to Europe in 1830, he observed the Chappe optical telegraph in France, and conceived the idea of transmitting messages by electric spark. On the return voyage aboard the ship *Sully* in October and November 1832, Morse designed his first telegraph, using a simple code of dots and dashes that would later evolve into the Morse code. Morse built a prototype device in 1835, and in 1837, after going into partnership with Leonard Gale and Alfred Vail, he took out his first patent. The best description that Morse ever wrote of his system was the patent number 1647 dated June 20, 1840, entitled *Improvement in the Mode of Communicating Information by Signals by the Application of Electro-Magnetism*. The three illustrations for the patent appear to have been drawn by Morse, who was an accomplished draughtsman as well as a painter.

In developing his electro-magnetic telegraph to greatly improve the speed of communicating information, Morse took advantage of the railroad networks that were in the process of construction around the world. The telegraph wires of Morse's electromagnetic telegraph tended to follow railroad lines, which were actually the first networks to link the world. Railroads carried people, freight, and printed information far faster than before. It took more than fifty years to build the railroad lines that tied the world together, but their construction led to an economic boom and speculation in railroad stock not unlike the speculation in Internet stocks at the end of the twentieth century. Just as the expansion of the Internet was perceived as explosive, the growth of telegraph networks, which to some extent paralleled the growth of railroads, was seen as explosive. And like the Internet, the telegraph caused revolutionary change in the speed of information transfer and in the way business was transacted.

While the telegraph lines tended to follow railroad lines, and paralleled the rapid development of railroads around the world, railroads were also among the primary users of telegraph systems to carry information throughout their networks. Railroad networks also processed amounts of information regarding reservations and railroad schedules unlike anything the world had ever seen. Railroad companies thus became some of the earliest major customers of mechanical information-processing and accounting machines, and continued to use the newer technology in a variety of manifestations as it became available. [JMN]

TEXT OF READING 5.2

To all whom it may concern:

Be it known that I, the undersigned, Samuel F. B. Morse, of the city, county, and State of New York, have invented a new and useful machine and system of signs for transmitting intelligence between distant points by the means of a new application and effect of electro-magnetism in producing sounds and signs, or either, and also for recording permanently by the same means, and application, and effect of electro-magnetism, any signs thus produced and representing intelligence, transmitted as before named between distant points; and I denominate said invention the "American Electro-Magnetic Telegraph," of which the following is a full and exact description, to wit:

It consists of the following parts—first, of a circuit of electric or galvanic conductors from any generator of electricity or galvanism and of electro-magnets at any one or more points in said circuit; second, a system of signs by which numerals, and words represented by numerals, and thereby sentences of words, as well as of numerals, and letters of any extent and combination of each, are communicated to any one or more points in the before-described circuit; third, a set of type adapted to regulate the communication of the above mentioned signs, also cases for convenient keeping of the type and rules in which to set and use the type; fourth, an apparatus called the "straight port-rule," and another called the "circular port-rule," each of which regulates the movement of the type when in use, and also that of the signal-lever; fifth, a signal-lever which breaks and connects the circuit of conductors; sixth, a register which records permanently the signs communicated at any desired points in the circuit; seventh, a dictionary or vocabulary of words to which are prefixed numerals for the uses hereinafter described; eighth, modes of laying the circuit of conductors.

The circuit of conductors may be made of any metal—such as copper, or iron wire, or strips of copper or iron, or of cord or twine, or other substances— gilt, silvered, or covered with any thin metal leaf properly insulated and in the ground, or through or beneath the water, or through the air. By causing an electric or galvanic current to pass through the circuit of conductors, laid as aforesaid, by means of any generator of electricity or galvanism, to one or more electro-magnets placed at any point or points in said circuit, the magnetic power thus concentrated in such magnet or magnets is used for the purposes of producing sounds and visible signs, and for permanently recording the latter at any and each of said points at the pleasure of the operator and in the manner hereinafter described—that is to say, by using the system of signs which is formed of the following parts and variations, viz:

Signs of numerals consist, first, of ten dots or punctures, made in measured distances of equal extent from each other, upon paper or any substitute for paper, and in number corresponding with the numeral desired to be represented. Thus one dot or puncture for the numeral 1, two dots or punctures for the numeral 2, three of the same for 3, four for 4, five for 5, six for 6, seven for 7, eight for 8, nine for 9, and ten for 0, as particularly represented on the annexed drawing marked Example 1, Mode 1, in which is also included a second character, to represent a cipher, if preferred.

Signs of numerals consist, secondly, of marks made as in the case of dots, and particularly represented on the annexed drawing marked Example 1, Mode 2.

Signs of numerals consist, thirdly, of characters drawn at measured distances in the shape of the teeth of a common saw by the use of a pencil or any instrument for marking. The points corresponding to the teeth of a saw are in number to correspond with the numeral desired to be represented, as in the case of dots or marks in the other modes described, and as particularly represented in the annexed drawing marked Example 1, Mode 3.

Signs of numerals consist, fourthly, of dots and lines separately and conjunctively used as follows, the numerals 1, 2, 3, and 4 being represented by dots, as in Mode 1, first given above: The numeral 5 is represented by a line equal in length to the space between the two dots of any other numeral; 6 is represented by the addition of a dot to the line representing 5; 7 is represented by the addition of two dots to said line; 8 is represented by prefixing a dot to said line; 9 is represented by two dots prefixed to said line; and 0 is repre-

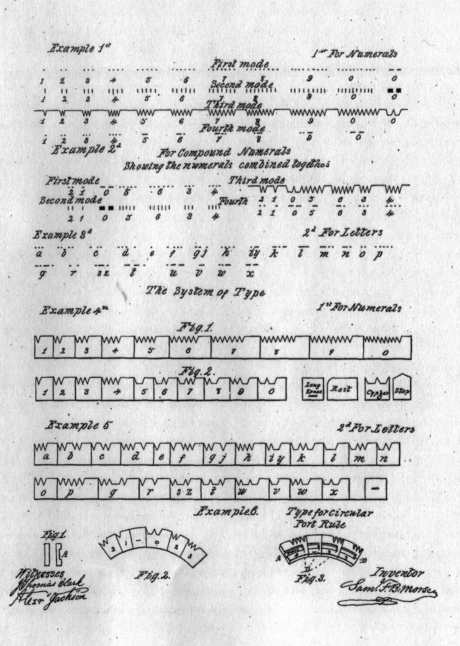

sented by two lines, each of the length of said line that represents the number 5; said signs are particularly set forth in the annexed drawings, marked Example 1, Mode 4.

Either of said modes are to be used as may be preferred or desired and in the method hereinafter described.

The sign of a distinct numeral, or of a compound numeral when used in a sentence of words or of numerals, consists of a distance or space of separation between the characters of greater extent than the distance used in separating the characters that compose any such distinct or compound numeral. An illustration of this sign is particularly exhibited in the annexed drawing marked Example 2.

Signs of letters consist in variations of the dots, marks, and dots and lines, and spaces of separation of the same formation as compose the signs of numerals, varied and combined differently to represent the letters of the alphabet in the manner particularly illustrated and represented in the annexed drawing marked Example 3.

The sign of a distinct letter, or of distinct words, when used in a sentence, is the same as that used in regard to numerals and described above.

Signs of words, and even of set phrases or sentences, may be adopted for use and communication in like manner under various forms, as convenience may suggest.

The type for producing the signs of numerals consist, first, of fourteen pieces or plates of thin metal, such as type-metal, brass, iron, or like substances, with teeth or indentations upon one side or edge of ten of said type, corresponding in number to the dots or punctures or marks requisite to constitute the numerals respectively heretofore described in the system of signs, and having also a space left upon the side or edge of each type, at one end thereof, without teeth or indentations, corresponding in length with the distance or separation desired between each sign of a numeral. Another of said type has two indentations, forming thereby three teeth only, and without any space at either end, to correspond with the size of a cypher, as heretofore described by reference to Exam-

ple 1, Modes 1, 2 3, of drawings in said system of signs. One other of said type is without any indentation on its side or edge, and being in length to correspond with the distance or separation desired between distinct or compound numerals, and with the sign heretofore described for that purpose. One of the remaining two of said type is formed with one corner of it beveled, (system of type, Example 4, Fig. 1,) and is called a "rest," and the other is in a pointed form and called a "stop."

Each of said type is particularly delineated on the annexed drawing marked Example 4, Fig. 1, and numbered or labeled in accordance with the purpose for which they are designed respectively, and are used, in like manner, for producing each of the several signs of numerals heretofore described in the system of signs.

The type for producing the signs of numerals consists, secondly, of five pieces or plates of metal first described above, four of which are the same as are numbered 1, 2, 3, and 4 in the annexed drawing marked Example 4, Fig. 1, and the fifth one being the same as is denominated in the same example "the long space," and heretofore alluded to; also, of six other pieces or plates of said metal, varied in indentations and teeth and spaces, as represented on the annexed drawings marked Example 4, Fig. 2, to produce signs of the denominations described in the fourth mode of the before-mentioned system of signs, Example 1.

The type for producing the signs of letters are of the same denomination with those used in producing signs of numerals, and only varied in form, from one to twenty-three, as exhibited in the annexed drawing marked Example 5.

The type for producing both signs of numerals and signs of letters are adapted for use to either a straight rule, called the "straight port-rule," and are in that case made straight lengthwise, as described in the drawings annexed and heretofore referred to in Example 5, or to a circular port-rule, in which case they are lengthwise circular or formed into sections of a circle, as represented in the drawings annexed marked Example 6, Figs. 2 and 3, and as will be further understood by the descriptions hereinafter contained of the straight and circular port-rules. On the under side of the type for the circular port-rule (which type are of greater thickness than those for the straight port-rule) is a groove (system of type, Example 6, A in Figs. 1 and 3) about midway of their width, and in depth about half the thickness aforesaid, and extending from the space ends, as B, Example 6, Fig. 3—that is, the ends without indentation—of said type, along the length, and conforming to the curve thereof, to a point, D D, equal in distance from the opposite ends to half the width of the pointed teeth cut upon their edges. For a delineation of these type reference is made to sections thereof in Figs. 1 and 3 upon the annexed drawings marked Example 6.

The type cases are wood, or of any other material, with small compartments of the exact length of the type, for greater convenience in distributing, and resembling those in common use among printers.

The type-rules are of wood or metal, or other material that may be preferred, and about three feet in length, with a groove into which the type, when used, are placed. On the under side of each type-rule are cogs, by which they are adapted to a pinion-wheel having corresponding cogs and forming part of a port-rule. The type-rule in use is moved onward as motion is given to the said wheel. A delineation of the type-rule is contained in the annexed drawing marked Example 7.

The straight port-rule consists of a pinion-wheel, before mentioned, turned by a hand-crank attached to a horizontal screw that plays into the cogs of the pinion-wheel as the latter do into the cogs of the type-rule, or by any other power in any of the well-known methods of mechanism. It is connected with a railway or groove, in and by which the type-rule, from the motion imparted to it by said wheel, is conveyed in a direct line beneath a lever that breaks and connects the galvanic circuit in the manner hereinafter mentioned. A delineation of said wheel, crank, and screw is contained in the drawings hereunto annexed marked Example 8, Figs. 1, 2, 3.

The circular port-rule is a substitute, when preferred, for both the type-rule and the straight port-rule, and consists of a horizontal or inclined wheel, Example 9, Fig. 1, A, of any convenient diameter, of wood or metal, having its axis connected on the under side of the wheel, with a pinion-wheel, K, and as in the case of the straight port-rule. It is moved by the motion of the pinion-wheel, as is the type-rule in the former description. On the entire circumference of said horizontal or inclined wheel, and upon its upper surface, is a shoulder or cavity, a, Figs. 1, 2, corresponding in depth with the thickness of the type used, and in width, b, equal to that of the type, exclusive of their teeth or indentations. Near the outer edge of the surface of said shoulder or cavity are cogs c, throughout the circumference of the wheel, projecting upward at a distance from each other equal to one-half of the width of the teeth or indentations of the type, and otherwise corresponding in size to the width and depth of the groove D D, Fig. 4, in the under side of the circular type before described and illustrated by reference to Example 6, Figs, 1 and 3. Directly over said shoulder or cavity and cogs, and at one or more points on the circumference of said wheel, is extended from a fixture outside of the orbit of the wheel a stationary type-feeder, E, Fig. 1, formed of one end, e, and one side, E, perpendicular, of tin or brass plate or other sub stance, and of interior size and shape to receive any number of the type which are therein deposited with their indentations projecting outward, as in Fig. 2, and their grooves downward, as in Fig. 4. Said type-feeder is so suspended from its fixture F F over the shoulder or cavity of the wheel A, before described, as to admit of the passage under it of said wheel in its circuit as near the bottom of the feeder as practicable, without coming in contact therewith. The type deposited in the feeder as before mentioned form a perpendicular column, as in Fig. 2, the lower type of which rests upon the surface of the before-named shoulder of the wheel b, Fig. 2, and the cog of the wheel, projecting upward, enters the groove D D, Fig. 4, of the type hereinbefore described.

The operation of said circular port-rule in regulating the movement of the type in sue is as follows: When the wheel A is set in motion the type resting immediately upon the shoulder of the wheel, in the manner mentioned above, as in Fig. 2, is carried forward on the curvature of the wheel from beneath the

S. F. B. Morse.

Telegraph Signs.

N.º 1647.   Patented Jun. 20, 1840.

Example. 7.

Type Rule.

Example. 8.

Straight Port Rule

Fig. 1.

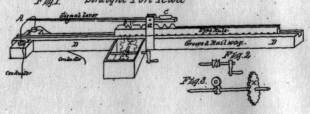

Example. 9.

Circular Port Rule..

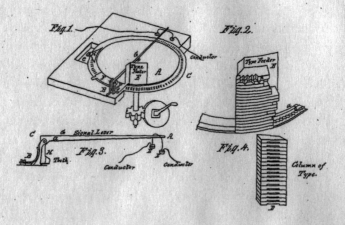

Witnesses.
J. Thomas Clark
Alexr Jackson

Inventor
Saml F. B. Morse

column of type resting upon it in the stationary type-feeder by means of one of the before-named cogs coming in contact with that point D, Fig. 3, Example 6, in the groove of the type, hereinbefore described as forming the termination of said groove, and which is particularly delineated at the points D D in the annexed drawings, marked Example 6, Fig. 3. As by said process the lower type in the column that is held by the stationary feeder is carried forward and removed, the next type settles immediately upon the shoulder of the wheel, and, after the manner of the removed type, is brought in contact with another cog of said shoulder within the groove of the type, and thence carried forward from beneath the incumbent column, as was its predecessor. Then follows consecutively in the same method each type deposited within the feeder so long as the wheel is kept in motion. The deposit of the type in the stationary feeder is regulated by the order in which the letters or numerals or words they represent are designed to be communicated at any distant point or points. After the type are respectively carried forward on the curvature of the wheel in the manner stated above, beyond the point where they are acted upon by the signal-lever, as is hereinafter described, they are lifted, each in its turn, from the shoulder of the wheel A and cast off into a box or packet, G, below the wheel by means of a slender shaft or spindle, H, made of any metal, and resembling in form a common plow-share, extending downward from a fixture, o, placed outside of the wheel, into a groove, K, within the before-named shoulder of said wheel A, and on the inner side of the cogs c, already described. By means of said groove the downward point of said shaft or spindle H is brought within the curvature and below the surface of said shoulder b, Fig. 2, and consequently under the approaching end of the type, so that each type successively, as it is carried forward on said curvature, in the manner before described, is lifted from the shoulder and forced upward on the inclined shaft or spindle by the type in contact with it at the other end until turned off into the before-named box or pocket G below, ready for a redistribution.

For a more particular delineation of the several parts of said circular port-rule reference is made to the annexed drawings marked Example 9, Figs. 1 and 2.

The signal-lever, Example 9, Fig. 3, consists, first, for use with the straight port-rule, Example 8, Fig. 1, A, of a strip of wood of any length from six to twenty-four inches, resting upon a pivot, a, or in a notched pillar formed into a fulcrum by a metal pin, a, passing through it and the lever. At one end of the lever a metallic wire, bent to a semicircular or half-square form, as at A, or resembling the prongs of a fork distended, is attached by its center, as described in the annexed drawings, Example 8, at the point marked A. Between said end of the lever and the fulcrum a, and near the latter, on the under side of the lever A, is inserted a metallic tooth or cog, b, curved on the side nearest to the fulcrum, and in other respects corresponding to the teeth or indentations upon the type already described. On the opposite extremity of the lever is a small weight, C, to balance or offset, in part, when needed, the weight of the lever on the opposite side of the fulcrum. The lever thus formed is stationed directly over the railway or groove D D, heretofore described as forming a connected part of the straight port-rule. The movement of the type-rule brings the tooth of each type therein set in contact with the tooth or cog of the lever, and thereby forces the lever upward until the points of the two teeth in contact have passed each other, when the lever again descends as the teeth of the type proceeds onward from the tooth of the lever. This operation is repeated as frequently as the teeth of the type are brought in contact with the tooth of the lever. By thus forcing the said lever upward and downward the ends of the semicircular or pronged wire are made alternately to rise from and fall into two small cups or vessels of mercury, E E, in each of which is an end or termination of the metallic circuit-conductors, first described above. This termination of the metallic circuit in the two cups or vessels breaks and limits the current of electricity or galvanism through the circuit; but a connection of the circuit is effected or restored by the falling of the two ends of the pronged wire A attached to said lever into the two cups, connecting the one cup with the other in that way. By the rising of the lever, and consequently the wire upon its end, from its connection with said cups, said circuit is in like manner again broken, and the current of electricity or galvanism destroyed. To effect at pleasure these two purposes of breaking and connecting said circuit is the design of said motion that is imparted in the before-mentioned manner to said lever, and to regulate this motion, and reduce it to the system of intelligible signs before described, is the design and use of the variations in the form of the type, also before described. A plate of copper, silver, or other conductor connected with the broken parts of said circuit of conductors, and receiving the contact of the wire attached to said lever, may be substituted, if preferred, for said cups of mercury. For a particular delineation of the several parts of said lever, reference is made to the annexed drawing marked Example 8.

The signal-lever consists, secondly, for use with the circular port-rule, Example 9, Fig. 3, of a strip of wood, G, with a metallic wire, A, at one end, of the form and for the purposes of the lever already described above. It turns on a pivot or fulcrum, a, placed either near the middle of in the end of the lever. At the end of the lever, at C, opposite to the metallic wire A, an elbow, c, is formed on a right angle with the main lever, and extending downward from the level with the pivot or fulcrum sufficiently for a metallic tooth, H, in the end thereof, corresponding with the teeth or indentations of the type, already described, to press against the type projecting from the shoulder or cavity of the wheel A, Fig. 1, that forms the circular port-rule, before described. Said wheel is placed beneath the said lever, as seen at G, Fig. 1, in a position to be reached by the extremity or tooth H of the arm of the lever just mentioned. The tooth H in the arm of the lever is kept in constant contact with the type of the circular port-rule by the pressure of a spring, B, upon it, as described in the annexed drawings marked Example 9, at B. Figs. 1 and 3 in the same example exhibit sections of the said lever. The action thus produced by the contact of the teeth of the type in the port-rule, when said wheel is in motion, with the tooth in the arm of the lever, lifts up and drags down the opposite extremity, A, of said lever, having the metallic wire upon it, as the tooth of said lever passes into or out of the indentations of the type, and in the same manner and to the same effect as the first-described lever rises and falls, and accordingly breaks and closes the circuit of conductors, as in the former instance. In the use of this circular port-rule and its appropriate lever, Fig. 3, type may be used having the points of their teeth and their indentations shaped as counterparts or reverses to those delineated in the annexed drawings heretofore referred to and marked Examples 4, 5, and 6, and thereby the forms of the recorded signs will be changed in a corresponding manner.

The register consists, first, of a lever of the shape of the lever connected with the circular port-rule above described, and is delineated in the annexed drawings marked Example 10, Figs. 1, 2, and 4, at A. Said lever A operates upon a fulcrum, a, that passes through the end that forms the elbow a, upon the lower extremity of which, and facing an electromagnet, is attached the armature of a magnet, f. In the other extreme of the lever, at B, is inserted one or more pencils, fountain-pens, printing-wheels, or other marking-instruments, as may be seen in the Fig. 4 of the example last mentioned, at letter B. The magnet is at letter C in the same figure.

Secondly, of a cylinder or barrel of metal or wood, and covered with cloth or yielding coating, to turn upon an axis and occupying a position directly beneath the pencil, fountain-pen, printing-wheel, or other marking-instrument to be used, as exhibited in the last-mentioned example of drawings, Fig. 4, D. Two rollers, marked b b in said figure of drawings, are connected with said cylinder, on the upper-side curvatures thereof, and being connected with each other by two narrow bands of tape passing over and beneath each, near the ends thereof, and over the intervening surface of the cylinder, in a manner to cause a friction of the bands of tape upon the latter when in motion, as delineated in the last-named example, Fig. 4, at points marked c c c. The distance between said bands of tape on the rollers is such as to admit of the pencil, or other marking instrument in the lever, to drop upon the intervening space of the cylinder. Near by said cylinder is a spool to turn on an axis, and marked d in the said figure, to receive any desired length of paper or other substance formed into slips or a continuous ribbon, and for the purpose, of receiving a record of the signs of intelligence communicated.

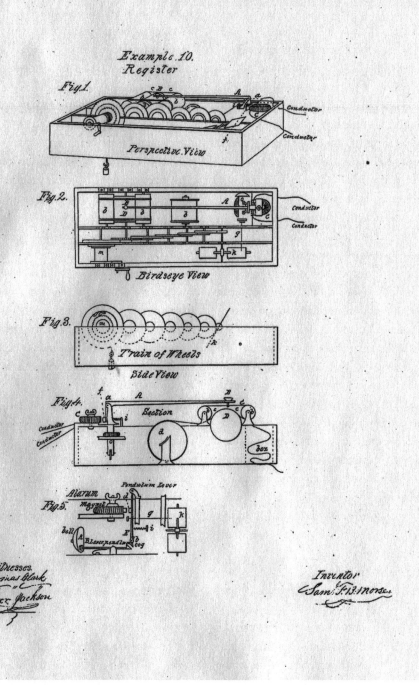

When the register is in motion one end of the paper on said spool being inserted between the under surfaces of said two rollers, under the strips of tape that connect them and the cylinder, it is drawn by the friction or pressure thus caused upon it forward from said spool gradually, and passed over said cylinder, and is thence deposited in a box on the opposite side, or is cut off at any desired length as it passes from the cylinder and rollers.

Thirdly, of an alarm-bell, A, Example 10, Fig. 5, which is struck by means of a lever-hammer, B, that is acted upon by a movable cog, b, placed upon an axis or pin, b, that confines it in the lower extremity of a pendulum-lever, (marked E in Fig. 5 of Example 10,) having an armature of a magnet attached to it at d, and acted upon by an electro-magnet, o, placed near it and the before-named magnet, and in the same circuit of conductors with the latter. Said cog b moves in a quarter-circle only, as the motion of said arm of the lever passes backward and forward in the act of recording, as hereinafter described. When forced into a horizontal position in said quarter-circle it ceases to act upon the hammer; but when moved from a perpendicular position it presses upon the projection in the end of the hammer, causing the opposite end of the hammer to be raised, from which elevation it again falls upon a stationary bell, A, as soon as said cog reaches a horizontal position, and ceases, as before mentioned, to press upon the hammer. Thus a notice, by sound or an alarm, is given at the point to which intelligence is to be communicated as soon as the register begins to act, and such sound may be continued or not, at pleasure, for the purpose mentioned or for any other uses, as the hammer shall be suspended or not from contact with the bell, or with any number of bells that may be employed. Fig. 5 of said example, marked 10 in the annexed drawings, represents sections of said hammer and bell.

Said several parts of the register are set in motion by the communication to or action upon the before-named armature of a magnet, attached to the lever of the register, of the electric or galvanic current in the circuit of conductors, and from an electro-magnet in said circuit, as before described, stationed near the said armature. As said armature is drawn or attracted from its stationary and horizontal position toward the said magnet when the latter is charged from the circuit of conductors, said lever is turned upon its fulcrum, and the opposite end thereof necessarily descends and brings the pen, or marking-instrument which it contains in contact with the paper or other substance on the revolving cylinder directly beneath it. As said armature ceases to be thus drawn or attracted by said magnet, as is the case as soon as said magnet ceases to be charged from the circuit of conductors, or as the current in said circuit is broken in the manner hereinbefore described, the said armature is forced back by its own specific gravity, or by a spring or weight, as may be needed, to its former position, and the pen or marking-instrument in the opposite end of the lever is again raised from its contact with the paper or other substance on the before-named revolving cylinder. This same action is communicated simultaneously from the same circuit of conductors to as many registers as there are corresponding magnets provided within any circuit and at any desired distances from each other.

The cylinder and its two associate rollers are set in motion simultaneously with the first motion of the lever by the withdrawal of a small wire or spindle, g, Example 10, Figs. 2 and 5, from beneath one branch of a fly-wheel, k, that forms a part of the clock machinery hereinafter named. Said wire g is withdrawn by the action upon said wire of a small electro-magnet, o, Figs. 2 and 5, stationed in the circuit and near the large magnet before named, as delineated in Fig. 5 of Example 10. Said cylinder and rollers are subsequently kept in motion by a train of wheels similar to common clock-wheels, as in Figs. 2 and 3, acted upon by a weight, raised as occasion may require by a hand-crank, and their motion is regulated by the same wheels to correspond with the action of the registering-pen or marking-instrument. Said train is represented in Figs. 1, 2, and 3 of said Example 10.

The electro-magnet thus used is made in any of the usual modes, such as winding insulated copper wire, or strips of copper, or tin-foil, or other metal around a bar of soft iron, either straight or bent into a circular form, and having the two extremities of the coils connected with the circuit of conductors, so that the coils around the magnet make part of the circuit.

To extend more effectually the length of any desired circuit of conductors, and to perpetuate the power of the electric or galvanic current equally throughout the same, I adopt the following mode, and also for connecting and using any desired number of additional and intervening batteries or generators of said current, and for connecting progressively any number of consecutive circuits, viz: Place at any point in a circuit an electro-magnet of the denomination already described, with an armature upon a lever of the form and structure, and in the position of that used at the register to hold and operate the marking-instrument, with only a substitution therein for such marking-instrument of a forked wire, A, Example 9, Fig. 3, like that upon the end of the signal-lever heretofore described. Directly beneath the latter wire place two cups of mercury, E E, or two metallic plates joined to terminations of a circuit leading from the fresh or additional battery or generator of said circuit in the same manner as they are to be provided in the first circuit of conductors at the points where the cups of mercury are hereinbefore described. As the current in the first circuit acts upon the magnet thus provided the armature thereof and lever are thereby moved to dip the forked wire A into the cups of the second circuit, as in the circuit first described. This operation instantly connects the break in said second circuit, and thus produces an additional and original power or current of electricity or galvanism from the battery of said second circuit to the magnet or magnets placed at any one or more points in such circuit, to be broken at pleasure, as in the first circuit; and from thence by the same operation the same results may again be repeated, extending and breaking at pleasure such current through yet another and another circuit, *ad infinitum,* and with as many intervening registers for simultaneous action as may be desired, and at any distances from each other.

The dictionary or vocabulary consists of words alphabetically arranged and regularly numbered, beginning with the letters of the alphabet, so that each word in the language has its telegraphic number, and is designated at pleasure, through the signs of numerals.

The modes which I propose of insulating the wires or other metal for conductors, and of laying the circuits, are various. The wires may be insulated by winding each wire with silk, cotton, flax, or hemp, and then dipping them into a solution of caoutchouc, or into a solution of shellac, or into pitch or resin and caoutchouc. They may be laid through the air, inclosed above the ground, in the ground, or in the water. When through the air they may be insulated by a covering that shall protect them from the, weather, such as cotton, flax, or hemp, and dipped into any solution, which is a non-conductor, and elevated upon pillars. When inclosed above the ground they may be laid in tubes of iron or lead, and these again may be inclosed, in wood, if desirable. When laid in the ground they maybe inclosed in iron, leaden, wooden, or earthen tubes, and buried beneath the surface. Across rivers the circuit may be carried beneath the bridges, or, where there are no bridges, inclosed in lead or iron, and sunk at the bottom, or stretched across, where the banks are high, upon pillars elevated on each side of the river.

What I claim as my invention, and desire to secure by Letters Patent, is as follows:

1. The formation and arrangement of the several parts of mechanism constituting the type-rule, the straight port-rule, the circular port-rule, the two signal-levers, and the register-lever, and alarm-lever, with its hammer, as combining respectively with each of said levers one or more armatures of an electromagnet, and as said parts are severally described in the foregoing specification.

2. The combination of the mechanism constituting the recording-cylinder, and the accompanying rollers and train-wheels, with the formation and arrangement of the several parts of mechanism, the formation and arrangement of which are claimed as above, and as described in the foregoing specification.

3. The use, system, formation, and arrangement of type, and of signs, for transmitting intelligence between distant points by the application of electro-magnetism and metallic conductors combined with mechanism described in the foregoing specification.

4. The mode and process of breaking and connecting by mechanism currents of electricity or galvanism in any circuit of metallic conductors, as described in the foregoing specification.

5. The mode and process of propelling and connecting currents of electricity, or galvanism in and through any desired number of circuits of metallic conductors from any known generator of electricity or galvanism, as described in the foregoing specification.

6. The application of electro-magnets by means of one or more circuits of metallic conductors from any known generator of electricity or galvanism to the several levers in the machinery described in the foregoing specification, for the purpose of imparting motion to said levers and operating said machinery, and for transmitting by signs and sounds intelligence between distant points and simultaneously to different points.

7. The mode and process of recording or marking permanently signs of intelligence transmitted between distant points, and simultaneously to different points, by the application and use of electro-magnetism or galvanism as described in the foregoing specification.

8. The combination and arrangement of electro-magnets in one or more circuits of metallic conductors with armatures of magnets for transmitting intelligence by signs and sounds, or either, between distant points and to different points simultaneously.

9. The combination and mutual adaptation of the several parts of the mechanism and system of type and of signs with and to the dictionary or vocabulary of words, as described in the foregoing specification.

In testimony whereof I, the said Samuel F. B. Morse, hereto subscribe my name in the presence of the witnesses whose names are hereto subscribed, on the 7th day of April, A. D. 1838.
SAML. F. B. MORSE.
Witnesses:
B. B. FRENCH,
CHARLES MONROE.

Researches in Telephony

Alexander Graham Bell

From *Proceedings of the American Academy of Arts and Sciences*, n. s., 4 (whole series 12) (1876–77): 1–10.

INTRODUCTORY NOTE TO READING 5.3

Alexander Graham Bell developed his first successful electrical sound-transmission apparatus in 1875. In the early morning of February 14, 1876, Bell filed a patent application at the United States Patent Office for a speaking telephone, only hours before the American inventor Elisha Gray filed a patent caveat (a confidential report of an invention not yet perfected) on a rival device. On March 7, 1876, Bell was granted his first telephone patent, covering broadly the electrical transmission of speech; five days later, the apparatus described in the patent transmitted human speech for the first time. Bell delivered his first report on the telephone before the American Academy of Arts and Sciences on May 10, 1876. That document is reproduced in this anthology as Reading 5.3.

Although not the first to invent a telephone (that honor goes to Philip Reis, who perfected his invention in 1861), Bell was the first to make one that could reproduce intelligible speech at the receiving end. The telephone became commercially viable in 1878, when the invention of the microphone by David Edward Hughes made telephony feasible for general communication.

Bell received a second patent, covering important mechanical features in this apparatus on January 30, 1877. These two patents—among the most valuable ever issued—are known as "the Bell patents." In the summer of 1877 Bell and two partners formed the Bell Telephone Company (the parent of AT&T), and the Bell patents were put into commercial use.

Bell Telephone's chief rival during the early years of telephony was the Western Union Telegraph Company, which had purchased the patents on both Elisha Gray's telephone and a telephone invented by Thomas Edison, and was establishing its own telephone systems throughout the United States using its already-established network of telegraph wires. To increase its advantage over Bell's company, Western Union claimed publicly that Bell had stolen the idea for the telephone from Gray. In 1879 Bell Telephone brought a patent infringement suit against Western Union, which was settled out of court in Bell's favor—the first in a series of legal victories for Bell Telephone. A key piece of evidence in this suit was a letter from Gray to Bell dated March 5, 1877, in which Gray had disclaimed credit for invention of the telephone "as I do not believe a mere description of an idea that has never been *reduced to practice*—in the *strict sense* of that phrase—should be dignified with the name invention." [JMN]

TEXT OF READING 5.3

1. It has long been known that an electro-magnet gives forth a decided sound when it is suddenly magnetized or demagnetized. When the circuit upon which it is placed is rapidly made and broken, a succession of explosive noises proceeds from the magnet. These sounds produce upon the ear the effect of a musical note, when the current is interrupted a sufficient number of times per second. The discovery of "Galvanic Music," by Page,[1] in 1837, led inquirers in different parts of the world almost simultaneously to enter into the field of telephonic research; and the acoustical effects produced by magnetization were carefully studied by Marrian,[2] Beatson,[3] Gassiot,[4] De la Rive,[5] Matteucci,[6] Guillemin,[7] Wertheim,[8] Wartmann,[9] Janniar,[10] Joule,[11] Laborde,[12] Legat,[13] Reis,[14] Poggendorff,[15] Du Moncel,[16] Delezenne,[17] and others.[18]

2. In the autumn of 1874, I discovered that the sounds emitted by an electro-magnet under the influence of a discontinuous current of electricity are not due wholly to sudden changes in the magnetic condition of the iron core (as heretofore supposed), but that a portion of the effect results from vibrations in the insulated copper-wires composing the coils. An electro-magnet was arranged upon circuit with an instrument for interrupting the current,—the rheotome being placed in a distant room, so as to avoid interference with the experiment. Upon applying the ear to the magnet, a musical note was clearly perceived, and the sound persisted after the iron core had been removed. It was then much feebler in intensity, but was otherwise unchanged,—the curious crackling noise accompanying the sound being well marked.

The effect may probably be explained by the attraction of the coils of the wire for one another during the passage of the galvanic current, and the sudden cessation of such attraction when the current is interrupted. When a spiral of fine wire is made to dip into a cup of mercury, so as thereby to close a galvanic circuit, it is well known that the spiral coils up and shortens. Ferguson[19] constructed a rheotome upon this principle. The shortening of the spiral lifted the end of the wire out of the mercury, thus opening the circuit, and the weight of the wire sufficed to bring the end down again,—so that the spiral was thrown into continuous vibration. I conceive that a somewhat similar motion is occasioned in a helix of wire by the passage of a discontinuous current, although further research has convinced me that other causes also conspire to produce the effect noted above. The extra currents occasioned by the induction of the voltaic current upon itself in the coils of the helix no doubt play an important part in the production of the sound, as very curious audible effects are produced by electrical impulses of high tension. It is probable, too, that a molecular vibration is occasioned in the conducting wire, as sounds are emitted by many substances when a discontinuous current is passed through them. Very distinct sounds proceed from straight pieces of iron, steel, retort-carbon, and plumbago. I believe that 1 have also obtained audible effects from thin platinum and German-silver wires, and from mercury contained in a narrow groove about four feet long. In these cases, however, the sounds were so faint and outside noises so loud that the experiments require verification. Well-marked sounds proceed from conductors of all kinds when formed into spirals or helices. I find that De la Rive had noticed the production of sound from iron and steel during the passage of an intermittent current, although he failed to obtain audible results from other substances. In order that such effects should be observed, extreme quietness is necessary. The rheotome itself is a great source of annoyance, as it always produces a sound of similar pitch to the one which it is desired to hear. It is absolutely requisite that it should be placed out of earshot of the observer, and at such a distance as to exclude the possibility of sounds being mechanically conducted along the wire.

3. Very striking audible effects can be produced upon a short circuit by means of two Grove elements. I had a helix of insulated copper-wire (No. 23) constructed, having a resistance of about twelve ohms. It was placed in circuit with a rheotome which interrupted the current one hundred times per second. Upon placing the helix to my ear I could hear the unison of the note produced by the rheotome. The intensity of the sound was much increased by placing a wrought-iron nail inside the helix. In both these cases, a crackling effect accompanied the sound. When the

nail was held in the fingers so that no portion of it touched the helix, the crackling effect disappeared, and a pure musical note resulted.

When the nail was placed inside the helix, between two cylindrical pieces of iron, a loud sound resulted that could be heard all over a large room. The nail seemed to vibrate bodily, striking the cylindrical pieces of metal alternately, and the iron cylinders themselves were violently agitated.

4. Loud sounds are emitted by pieces of iron and steel when subjected to the attraction of an electro-magnet which is placed in circuit with a rheotome. Under such circumstances, the armatures of Morse-sounders and Relays produce sonorous effects. I have succeeded in rendering the sounds audible to large audiences by interposing a tense membrane between the electro-magnet and its armature. The armature in this case consisted of a piece of clock-spring glued to the membrane. This form of apparatus I have found invaluable in all my experiments. The instrument was connected with a parlor organ, the reeds of which were so arranged as to open and close the circuit during their vibration. When the organ was played the music was loudly reproduced by the telephonic receiver in a distant room. When chords were played upon the organ, the various notes composing the chords were emitted simultaneously by the armature of the receiver.

5. The simultaneous production of musical notes of different pitch by the electric current, was foreseen by me as early as 1870, and demonstrated during the year 1873. Elisha Gray,[20] of Chicago, and Paul La Cour,[21] of Copenhagen, lay claim to the same discovery. The fact that sounds of different pitch can be simultaneously produced upon any part of a telegraphic circuit is of great practical importance; for the duration of a musical note can be made to signify the dot or dash of the Morse alphabet, and thus a number of telegraphic messages may be sent simultaneously over the same wire without confusion by making signals of a definite pitch for each message.

6. If the armature of an electro-magnet has a definite rate of oscillation of its own, it is thrown bodily into vibration when the interruptions of the current are timed to its movements. For instance, present an electro-magnet to the strings of a piano. It will be found that the string which is in unison with the rheotome included in the circuit will be thrown into vibration by the attraction of the magnet.

Helmholtz,[22] in his experiments upon the synthesis of vowel sounds caused continuous vibration in tuning-forks which were used as the armatures of electro-magnets. One of the forks was employed as a rheotome. Platinum wires attached to the prongs dipped into mercury.

The intermittent current occasioned by the vibration of the fork traversed a circuit containing a number of electro-magnets between the poles of which were placed tuning-forks whose normal rates of vibration were multiples of that of the transmitting fork. All the forks were kept in continuous vibration by the passage of the interrupted current. By re-enforcing the tones of the forks in different degrees by means of resonators, Helmholtz succeeded in reproducing artificially certain vowel sounds.

I have caused intense vibration in a steel strip, one extremity of which was firmly clamped to the pole of a U-shaped electro-magnet, the free end overhanging the other pole. The amplitude of the vibration was greatest when the coil was removed from the leg of the magnet to which the armature was attached.

7. All the effects noted above result from rapid interruptions of a voltaic current, but sounds may be produced electrically in many other ways.

The Canon Gottoin de Coma,[23] in 1785, observed that noises were emitted by iron rods placed in the open air during certain electrical conditions of the atmosphere ; Beeson[24] produced a sound from an iron wire by the discharge of a Leyden jar; Gore[25] obtained loud musical notes from mercury, accompanied by singularly beautiful crispations of the surface during the course of experiments in electrolysis; and Page[26] produced musical tones from Trevelyan's bars by the action of the galvanic current.

8. When an intermittent current is passed through the thick wires of a Ruhmkorff's coil, very curious audible effects are produced by the currents induced in the secondary wires. A rheotome was placed in circuit with the thick wires of a Ruhmkorff's coil, and the fine wires were connected with two strips of brass (A

and B), insulated from one another by means of a sheet of paper. Upon placing the ear against one of the strips of brass, a sound was perceived like that described above as proceeding from an empty helix of wire during the passage of an intermittent voltaic current. A similar sound, only much more intense, was emitted by a tin-foil condenser when connected with the fine wires of the coil.

One of the strips of brass, A (mentioned above), was held closely against the ear. A loud sound came from A whenever the slip B was touched with the other hand. It is doubtful in all these cases whether the sounds proceeded from the metals or from the imperfect conductors interposed between them. Further experiments seem to favor the latter supposition. The strips of brass A and B were held one in each hand. The induced currents occasioned a muscular tremor in the fingers. Upon placing my forefinger to my ear a loud crackling noise was audible, seemingly proceeding from the finger itself. A friend who was present placed my finger to his ear, but heard nothing. I requested him to hold the strips A and B himself. He was then distinctly conscious of a noise (which I was unable to perceive) proceeding from his finger. In these cases a portion of the induced currents passed through the head of the observer when he placed his ear against his own finger; and it is possible that the sound was occasioned by a vibration of the surfaces of the ear and finger in contact.

When two persons receive a shock from a Ruhmkorff's coil by clasping hands, each taking hold of one wire of the coil with the free hand, a sound proceeds from the clasped hands. The effect is not produced when the hands are moist. When either of the two touches the body of the other a loud sound comes from the parts in contact. When the arm of one is placed against the arm of the other, the noise produced can be heard at a distance of several feet. In all these cases a slight shock is experienced so long as the contact is preserved. The introduction of a piece of paper between the parts in contact does not materially interfere with the production of the sounds, while the unpleasant effects of the shock are avoided.

When a powerful current is passed through the body, a musical note can be perceived when the ear is closely applied to the arm of the person experimented upon. The sound seems to proceed from the muscles of the fore-arm and from the biceps muscle. The musical note is the unison of the rheotome employed to interrupt the primary circuit. I failed to obtain audible effects in this way when the pitch of the rheotome was high. Elisha Gray[27] has also produced audible effects by the passage of induced electricity through the human body. A musical note is occasioned by the spark of a Ruhmkorff's coil when the primary circuit is made and broken sufficiently rapidly. When two rheotomes of different pitch are caused simultaneously to open and close the primary circuit, a double tone proceeds from the spark.

When a voltaic battery is common to two closed circuits, the current is divided between them. If one of the circuits is rapidly opened and closed, a pulsatory action of the current is occasioned upon the other.

All the audible effects resulting from the passage of an intermittent current can also be produced, though in less degree, by means of a pulsatory current.

9. When a permanent magnet is caused to vibrate in front of the pole of an electro-magnet, an undulatory or oscillatory current of electricity is induced in the coils of the electro-magnet, and sounds proceed from the armatures of other electro-magnets placed upon the circuit. The telephonic receiver referred to above (par. 4), was connected in circuit with a single-pole electro-magnet, no battery being used. A steel tuning-fork which had been previously magnetized was caused to vibrate in front of the pole of the electro-magnet. A musical note similar in pitch to that produced by the tuning-fork proceeded from the telephonic receiver in a distant room.

10. The effect was much increased when a battery was included in the circuit. In this case, the vibration of the permanent magnet threw the battery-current into waves. A similar effect was produced by the vibration of an unmagnetized tuning-fork in front of the electro-magnet. The vibration of a soft iron armature, or of a small piece of steel spring no larger than the pole of the electro-magnet in front of which it was placed, sufficed to produce audible effects in the distant room.

11. Two single-pole electro-magnets, each having a

resistance of ten ohms, were arranged upon a circuit with a battery of five carbon elements. The total resistance of the circuit, exclusive of the battery, was about twenty-five ohms. A drum-head of gold-beater's skin, seven centimetres in diameter, was placed in front of each electromagnet, and a circular piece of clock-spring, one centimetre in diameter, was glued to the middle of each membrane. The telephones so constructed were placed in different rooms. One was retained in the experimental room, and the other taken to the basement of an adjoining house.

Upon singing into the telephone, the tones of the voice were reproduced by the instrument in the distant room. When two persons sang simultaneously into the instrument, two notes were emitted simultaneously by the telephone in the other house. A friend was sent into the adjoining building to note the effect produced by articulate speech. I placed the membrane of the telephone near my mouth, and uttered the sentence, "Do you understand what I say?" Presently an answer was returned through the instrument in my hand. Articulate words proceeded from the clock-spring attached to the membrane, and I heard the sentence: "Yes, I understand you perfectly."

The articulation was somewhat muffled and indistinct, although in this case it was intelligible. Familiar quotations, such as, "To be, or not to be; that is the question." "A horse, a horse, my kingdom for a horse." "What hath God wrought," &c., were generally understood after a few repetitions. The effects were not sufficiently distinct to admit of sustained conversation through the wire. Indeed, as a general rule, the articulation was unintelligible, excepting when familiar sentences were employed. Occasionally, however, a sentence would come out with such startling distinctness as to render it difficult to believe that the speaker was not close at hand. No sound was audible when the clock-spring was removed from the membrane.

The elementary sounds of the English language were uttered successively into one of the telephones and the effects noted at the other. Consonantal sounds, with the exception of L and M, were unrecognizable. Vowel-sounds in most cases were distinct. Diphthongal vowels, such as *a* (in ale), *o* (in old), *i* (in isle), *ow* (in now), *oy* (in boy), *oor* (in poor), *oor* (in

door), *ere* (in here), *ere* (in there), were well marked.

Triphthongal vowels, such as *ire* (in fire), *our* (in flour), *ower* (in mower), *ayer* (in player), were also distinct. Of the elementary vowel-sounds, the most distinct were those which had the largest oral apertures. Such were *a* (in far), *aw* (in law), *a* (in man), and *e* (in men).

13. Electrical undulations can be produced directly in the voltaic current by vibrating the conducting wire in a liquid of high resistance included in the circuit.

The stem of a tuning-fork was connected with a wire leading to one of the telephones described in the preceding paragraph. While the tuning-fork was in vibration, the end of one of the prongs was dipped into water included in the circuit. A sound proceeded from the distant telephone. When two tuning-forks of different pitch were connected together, and simultaneously caused to vibrate in the water, two musical notes (the unisons respectively of those produced by the forks) were emitted simultaneously by the telephone.

A platinum wire attached to a stretched membrane, completed a voltaic circuit by dipping into water. Upon speaking to the membrane, articulate sounds proceeded from the telephone in the distant room. The sounds produced by the telephone became louder when dilute sulphuric acid, or a saturated solution of salt, was substituted for the water. Audible effects were also produced by the vibration of plumbago in mercury, a solution of bichromate of potash, in salt and water, in dilute sulphuric acid, and in pure water.

14. Sullivan[28] discovered that a current of electricity is generated by the vibration of a wire composed partly of one metal and partly of another; and it is probable that electrical undulations were caused by the vibration. The current was produced so long as the wire emitted a musical note, but stopped immediately upon the cessation of the sound.

15. Although sounds proceed from the armatures of electro-magnets under the influence of undulatory currents of electricity, I have been unable to detect any audible effects due to the electro-magnets themselves. An undulatory current was passed through the coils of an electromagnet which was held closely against the ear. No sound was perceived until a piece of iron or

steel was presented to the pole of the magnet. No sounds either were observed when the undulatory current was passed through iron, steel, retort-carbon, or plumbago. In these respects an undulatory current is curiously different from an intermittent one. (See par. 2.)

16. The telephonic effects described above are produced by three *distinct* varieties of currents, which I term respectively intermittent, pulsatory, and undulatory. *Intermittent currents* are characterized by the alternate presence and absence of electricity upon the circuit; *pulsatory currents* result from sudden or instantaneous changes in the intensity of a continuous current; and *undulatory currents* are produced by gradual changes in the intensity of a current analogous to the changes in the density of air occasioned by simple pendulous vibrations. The varying intensity of an undulatory current can be represented by a sinusoidal curve, or by the resultant of several sinusoidal curves.

Intermittent, pulsatory, and undulatory currents may be of two kinds,—*voltaic,* or *induced;* and these varieties may be still further discriminated into *direct* and *reversed* currents ; or those in which the electrical impulses are all positive or negative, and those in which they are alternately positive and negative (see table one, below).

17. In conclusion, I would say that the different kinds of currents described above may be studied optically by means of König's manometric capsule.[29] The instrument, as I have employed it, consists simply of a gas-chamber closed by a membrane to which is attached a piece of clock-spring. When the spring is subjected to the attraction of an electro-magnet, through the coils of which a "telephonic" current of electricity is passed, the flame is thrown into vibration.

I find the instrument invaluable as a rheometer, for an ordinary galvanometer is of little or no use when "telephonic" currents are to be tested. For instance, the galvanometer needle is insensitive to the most powerful undulatory current when the impulses are reversed, and is only slightly deflected when they are direct. The manometric capsule, on the other hand, affords a means of testing the amplitude of the electrical undulations; that is, of deciding the difference between the maximum and minimum intensity of the current.

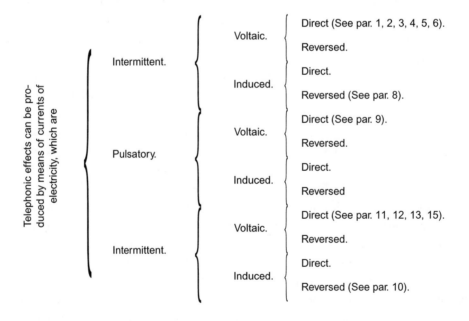

...

1. C. G. Page. "The Production of Galvanic Music." Silliman's Journ., 1837, XXXII., p. 396; Silliman's Journ., July, 1837, p. 354; Silliman's Journ., 1838, XXXIII., p. 118; Bibl. Univ. (new series), 1839, II., p. 398.

2. T. P. Marrian. Phil. Mag., XXV., p. 382; Inst., 1845, p. 20; Arch. de l'Électr., V., p. 195.

3. W. Beatson. Arch. de l'Électr., V., p. 197; Arch. de Sc. Phys. et Nat. (2d series), II., p. 113.

4. Gassiot. See "Treatise on Electricity," by De la Rive, I., p. 300.

5. De la Rive. Treatise on Electricity, I., p. 300; Phil. Mag., XXXV., p. 422; Arch. de l'Électr., V., p 200; Inst., 1846, p. 83; Comptes Rendus, XX., p. 1287; Comp. Rend., XXII., p. 432; Pogg. Ann., LXXVI., p. 637; Ann. de Chim. et de Phys., XXVI., p. 158.

6. Matteucci. Inst., 1845, p. 315; Arch. de l'Électr., V., 389.

7. Guillemin. Comp. Rend., XXII., p. 264; Inst., 1846, p. 30; Arch. d. Sc. Phys. (2d series), I., p. 191.

8. G. Wertheim. Comp. Rend., XXII., pp. 336, 544; Inst., 1846, pp. 65, 100; Pogg. Ann., LXVIII, p. 140; Comp. Rend., XXVI., p.505; Inst., 1848, p. 142; Ann. de Chim. et de Phys., XXIII., p. 302; Arch. d. Sc. Phys. et Nat., VIII, p. 206; Pogg. Ann., LXXVII., p. 43; Berl. Ber., IV., p. 121.

9. Elie Wartmann. Comp. Rend., XXII., p. 544; Phil. Mag. (3d series), XXVIII., p. 544; Arch. d. Sc. Phys. et Nat. (2d series), I., p. 419; Inst., 1846, p. 290; Monatscher. d. Berl. Akad., 1846, p. 111.

10. Janniar. Comp. Rend., XXIII., p. 319; Inst., 1846, p. 269; Arch. d. Sc. Phys. et Nat. (2d series), II., p. 394.

11. J. P. Joule. Phil. Mag., XXV., pp. 76, 225; Berl. Ber., III., p. 489.

12. Laborde. Comp. Rend., L., p. 692; Cosmos, XVII., p. 514.

13. Legat. Brix. Z. S., IX., p. 125.

14. Reis. "Téléphonie." Polytechnic Journ., CLXVIII., p. 185; Böttger's Notizbl., 1863, No. 6.

15. J. C. Poggendorff. Pogg. Ann., XXVIII., p. 192; Berliner Monatsber., 1856, p. 133; Cosmos, IX., p. 49; Berl. Ber., XII., p. 241; Pogg. Ann., LXXXVII., p. 139.

16. Du Moncel. Exposé, II., p. 125; also, III., p. 83.

17. Delezenne. "Sound produced by Magnetization," Bibl. Univ. (new series), 1841, XVI., p. 406.See London Journ., XXXII., p. 402; Polytechnic Journ., CX., p. 16; Cosmos, IV., p. 43; Glösener—Traité général, &c., p.850; Dove. Repert., VI., p. 58 Pogg. Ann., XLIII., p. 411; Berl. Ber., I., p. 144; Arch. d. Sc. Phys. et Nat., XVI., p. 406 ; Kuhn's Encyclopaedia der Physik, pp. 1014-1021.

18. See London Journ., XXXII., p. 402; Polytechnic Journ., CX., p. 16; Cosmos, IV., p. 43; Glösener—Traité général, &c., p.850; Dove. Repert.,VI., p. 58 Pogg. Ann., XLIII., p. 411; Berl. Ber., I., p. 144; Arch. d. Sc. Phys. et Nat., XVI., p. 406 ; Kuhn's Encyclopaedia der Physik, pp. 1014-1021.

19. Ferguson. Proceedings of Royal Scottish Soc. of Arts, April 9, 1866; Paper on "A New Current Interrupter."

20. Elisha Gray. Eng. Pat. Spec., No. 974. See "Engineer," March 26, 1875.

21. Paul la Cour. Telegraphic Journal, Nov. 1, 1875.

22. Helmholtz. Die Lehre von dem Tonempfindungen.

23. See "Treatise on Electricity," by De la Rive, I., p. 800.

24. *Ibid.*

25. Gore. Proceedings of Royal Society, XII., p. 217.

26. Page. "Vibration of Trevelyan's bars by the galvanic current." Silliman's Journal, 1850, IX., pp. 106–108.

27. Elisha Gray. Eng. Pat. Spec., No. 2646, see "Engineer," Aug. 14, 1874.

28. Sullivan. "Currents of Electricity produced by the vibration of Metals." Phil. Mag., 1845, p. 261; Arch. de l'Électr., X., p. 480.

29. König. "Upon Manometric Flames," Phil. Mag., 1873, XLV., No. 297, 298.

5.4
Wireless Telegraphy

Guglielmo Marconi

From *Journal of the Institute of Electrical Engineers*, XXVIII, no. 139 (April 1899): 273–297.

INTRODUCTORY NOTE TO READING 5.4

This is the first paper on wireless telegraphy published by Guglielmo Marconi (1874–1937). "Marconi seems to have learned in 1894 of Hertz's laboratory experiments with electromagnetic waves. He was immediately curious as to how far the waves might travel, and began to experiment, with the assistance of Prof. A. Righi of Bologna. His initial apparatus resembled Hertz's in its use of a Ruhmkorff-coil spark gap oscillator and dipole antennas with parabolic reflectors, but it replaced Hertz's spark-ring detector with the coherer that had been employed earlier by Branly and Lodge. [Lodge was only able to transmit and receive over a distance of 150 yards.] Marconi quickly discovered that increased transmission distance could be obtained with larger antennas, and his first important invention was the use of sizable elevated antenna structures and ground connections at both transmitter and receiver, in place of Hertz's dipoles. With this change he achieved in 1895 a transmission distance of 1.5 miles (the length of the family estate), and at about the same time conceived of 'wireless telegraph' communication through keying the transmitter in telegraph code."[1]

Marconi was the son of Giuseppe Marconi, a wealthy landowner, and his second wife, Annie Jameson, daughter of an Irish whiskey distiller. His education was private, and included special instruction in physics. When Marconi could not interest the Italian government in the potential of his work, he moved to London where one of his Irish cousins, Henry Jameson Davis, helped him to prepare a patent application. Davis also arranged demonstrations of the wireless telegraph for government officials and in 1897 helped form and finance the Wireless Telegraph and Signal Co., Ltd. In 1900 this became Marconi's Wireless Telegraph Co., Ltd.

Due to the great interest in his presentation, Marconi had to read this paper twice, and the journal records two sets of discussions (we have reproduced only the first set here). Within a year after this speech Marconi increased his signaling distance to 150 miles, and decided to attempt to transmit across the Atlantic. In 1901 Marconi succeeded in wireless transmission across the Atlantic. In 1909 he shared the Nobel Prize for physics with K. F. Braun. [JMN]

---

1 Charles C. Gillespie, editor, *Dictionary of Scientific Biography*, IX (1974), 98.

Advances in communication were among the most
notable technological developments of the nineteenth
century.

"Wireless telegraphy," or telegraphy through space without connecting wires, is a subject which has attracted considerable attention since the results of the first experiments I carried out in this country became known. It is not my intention this evening to give my views on or discuss the theory of the system, with which I have carried out so many experiments, and by means of which I have worked various installations, but I hope to put before you some exact information of what has been done by myself and my assistants during the last twelve months, and also some reliable data as to the means employed to obtain such results. Much has been published on the subject, I must say with varying accuracy, and there can hardly be any one here altogether ignorant of the general characteristics of the system.

Before I go into this subject further I wish to state that any success I have met with in the practical application of wireless telegraphy has been in a large measure due to the efficient co-operation which has been rendered by my assistants.

I think it will not be out of place if I give a brief description of the apparatus.

TRANSMITTER.—When long distances are to be bridged over and it is not necessary that the signals should be sent in one definite direction, I employ as transmitter an arrangement as shown in Fig. 1, in

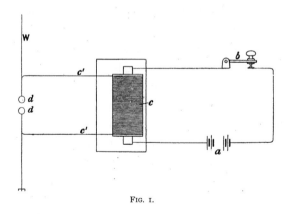

FIG. I.

which two small spheres connected to the terminals of the secondary winding of an induction coil *c* are connected, one to earth and the other to a vertical conductor *W*, which I will call the aerial conductor.

Should it be necessary to direct a beam of rays in one given direction I prefer to use an arrangement similar to a Righi oscillator placed in the focal line of a suitable cylindrical parabolic reflector, *f* Fig. 2. The

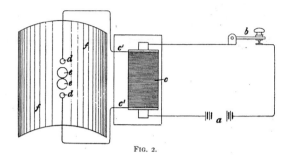

FIG. 2.

transmitter works as follows:—When the key *b* is pressed, the current of the battery is allowed to actuate the spark coil *c* which charges the spheres of the Righi oscillator or the vertical wire *W* which discharges through the spark gap.

This discharge is an oscillating one, and the system of spheres and insulated conductor becomes a radiator of electric waves. It is easy to understand how, by pressing the key for long or short intervals, it is possible to emit a long or short succession of waves, which, when they influence the receiver, reproduce on it a long or short effect, according to their duration, in this way reproducing the Morse or other signals transmitted from the sending station.

RECEIVER.—One of the principal parts in my receiver is the sensitive tube or coherer or radio-conductor, which was discovered, I think I am right in saying, by Professor Calzecchi Onesti, of Fermo,[1] and was improved by Branly, and modified by Professor Lodge and others. The only form of coherer I have found to be trustworthy and reliable for long distance work is one designed by myself as shown in Fig. 3. It consists of a small glass tube, four centimetres long, into which two metal pole pieces, *j*1 *j*2, are tightly fitted. They are separated from each other by a small gap, which is partly filled with a mixture of nickel and silver filings. This coherer forms part of a circuit containing the local cell and a sensitive telegraph relay actuating another circuit, which circuit works a trembler *p* or decoherer and a recording instrument *h*.

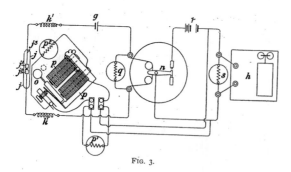

FIG. 3.

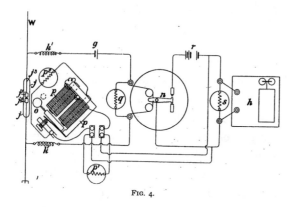

FIG. 4.

In its normal condition the resistance of the filings in the tube j is infinite, or at least very great, but when the filings are influenced by electric waves or surgings, cohesion instantly takes place, and the tube becomes a comparatively good conductor, its resistance falling to between 100 and 500 ohms. This allows the current from the local cell g to actuate the relay n.

One end of the tube is connected to earth and the other to. a vertical conductor similar to that of the transmitter Fig. 1, or if reflectors are used a short strip of copper is connected to each end, Fig. 5. The length

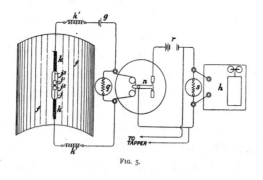

FIG. 5.

of these strips of copper must be carefully determined, as good results cannot be obtained unless they happen to be of the proper length, which will cause them to be

in tune or syntony with the transmitted oscillations.

All the electro-magnetic apparatus in the receiver is shunted by non-inductive resistances in such a manner that there may be no sparking at contacts and no sudden perturbations or jerks caused by the local battery current near the coherer.

I find that the relay tapper and telegraphic instrument, if not properly shunted, produce disturbing effects, the result of which is to prevent the coherer from regaining its sensitive condition after the receipt of electrical oscillations.

No such trouble is experienced when suitable shunts are used, and I attribute to their action in very great measure the success which has been attained with this system.

Small choking coils k' k' are introduced between the coherer and the relay. They compel the oscillating current due to the electric waves to traverse the coherer rather than waste its energy in the alternative path afforded by the relay.

The oscillations induced on the strips k k or aerial conductor W which acts as resonator, by the radiation from the oscillator affect the sensitive tube. This effect on the tube consists, as we have said, in a great increase of its conductivity, thus completing the circuit and allowing the current from the cell to actuate the relay. The relay in its turn causes a larger battery r to pass a current through the tapper or interrupter p, and also through the electro-magnets of the recording instrument h.

The tapper or trembler is so adjusted as to tap the tube and shake the filings in it. If in the instant during which these various actions take place, the electrical oscillations had died out in the resonator, the shake or tap given to the tube by the hammer o would have restored it to its normal high-resistance condition, and the Morse instrument or recorder would have marked a dot on the tape, but if the oscillations continue at very brief intervals, the acquired conductivity of the tube j is destroyed only for an instant by the tap of the trembler, and immediately re-established by the electrical surgings, and therefore the relay tapper and telegraph instrument are again actuated, and so on until the oscillations from the radiator have ceased.

The practical result is that the receiver is actuated

for a time equal to that during which the key is pressed at the transmitting station. For each signal, however short, the armatures of the relay and tapper perform some very rapid vibrations dependent on each other. For it is the action of the relay which starts the tapper, but the tapper by its action interrupts the relay.

The armature of the Morse recording instrument being rather heavy, and possessing a comparatively large inertia, cannot follow the very rapid vibrations of the tongue of the relay, but remains down all the time, during which the rapidly intermittent action of the receiver lasts. In this way the armature of the inker gives a practically exact reproduction of the movements of the key at the transmitting end, dashes coming out as dashes, and dots as dots.

Much has been said and written about coherers being very unreliable and untrustworthy in their action, but I must confess that this has not been in any way my experience. Provided a coherer is properly constructed and used on a suitable receiver, it is just as certain in its action as any other electrical apparatus, such as an electro-magnet or an incandescent lamp. I have coherers which were made three years ago that are now quite as good if not better than they were at that time, and we have had tubes working for months in most important installations without ever giving trouble. At the installation my Company have erected at the South Foreland Lighthouse, which, as you probably know, is working to the East Goodwin Lightship, the coherer was mounted on the receiver when we first started in December of last year, and has done its work in a most satisfactory manner ever since.

I must call your attention to the object and function of the vertical wire W. It has been by means of this addition to the apparatus, that we have been able to telegraph over distances which have been so far unattained, I think I am right in saying, by any other method of space telegraphy. The way I came to appreciate the great importance of the addition of the conductor W and earth connection E to the apparatus was as follows:

(I take this data from a copy of a letter I wrote to Mr Preece in November, 1896.)

When carrying out some experiments in Italy in 1895, I was using an oscillator having one pole earthed and the other connected to an insulated capacity, the receiver also earthed and connected to a similar capacity. The capacities were in this case cubes of tinned iron of 30 centimetres side, and I found that when these were placed on the top of a pole 2 metres high, signals could be obtained at 30 metres from the transmitter. With the same cubes on poles 4 metres high, signals were obtained at 100 metres, and with the same cubes at a height of 8 metres, other conditions being equal, Morse signals were easily obtained at 400 metres. With larger cubes of 100 centimetres side, fixed at a height of 8 metres, reliable signals could be obtained at 2,400 metres all round, equal to about one mile and a half.

These results seemed to point out that a system of transmitter and receiver designed according to the lines on Fig. 1, i.e., a radiator of the Hertzian type having one pole earthed and the other connected to a vertical, or almost vertical, conductor, or to a lofty capacity area, and a resonator consisting of a suitable receiver having similarly one terminal connected to earth and the other to an insulated vertical conductor, constitute a system of transmitter and receiver capable of giving effects at far greater distances than the ordinary systems of Hertzian radiators and resonators.

The results I have referred to also show that the distance at which signals could be obtained varied approximately with the square of the distance of the capacities from earth, or perhaps with the square of the length of the vertical conductors. This law has since been verified by a careful series of experiments and found correct, and has furnished us with a sure and safe means of calculating what length the vertical wire should have in order to obtain results at a given distance. It is well to know that the said law has never failed to give the expected results across clear space in any installation or experiment I have carried out, although it usually seems that the distance obtained is slightly in excess of what one might expect. I find that with parity of other conditions a vertical wire 20 feet long at the transmitter and receiver is sufficient for communicating one mile, 40 feet at each end for 4 miles, and 80 feet for 16 miles and so on. An installation is now working over a distance of 18 miles with a vertical wire 80 feet high at each installation station.

Professor Ascoli[2] has confirmed this law and demonstrated mathematically, using Neumann's formula, that the inductive action is proportional to the square of the length of one of the two conductors if the two are vertical and of equal length, and in simple inverse proportion of the distance between them. Therefore, the intensity of the induced oscillation does not diminish with the increase of distance if the length of the vertical conductors is increased in proportion with the square root of the distance. That is, if the height of the wire is double, the possible distance becomes quadrupled.

Should it be necessary to rig up an installation at a distance of say 32 miles, such as is about the distance between Folkestone and Boulogne, it is easy to find that a vertical wire 114 feet long would be quite sufficient for that purpose.

Such laws are applicable only when apparatus properly constructed is employed. With apparatus in which some or several improved details are omitted I find it quite impossible to obtain anything like the results above mentioned. If, say, the impedance coils $k'k'$ are omitted the distance (other conditions being equal) is reduced to almost half its original value.

I must also call your attention to such cases as when obstacles like hills or mountains, or large metallic objects, happen to intervene between the places between which it is desired to establish communication. With all other forms of Hertzian transmitters and receivers with which I have experimented I find it to be quite impossible to obtain any results if a hill, mountain, or large metallic object intervenes in any way between the two stations. I am not aware whether any satisfactory results have been obtained by others where such obstacles have intervened, but when the vertical wire system is employed it becomes easy to telegraph between positions screened from each other by hills or by the curvature of the earth. In such cases it seems to be a marked advantage if the aerial conductor is thick or if a capacity area is placed at the top of it.

I am rather doubtful as to the correct explanation that can be given to this effect. I think there can be very little doubt as to the complete opacity, to electric waves, of a hill three miles thick, or of, say, several miles of sea-water. A solution of this difficulty might be given by attributing the results to the effect of the diffraction of such long waves as those radiated by a conductor 100 ft. long, but in that case it is difficult to explain why other forms of Hertzian transmitters and receivers, also giving long waves, do not act when such obstacles intervene. A way out of the difficulty may be arrived at if we suppose that the electrical oscillations are transmitted to the earth by the earth wire E of the transmitter and travel in all directions along the surface of the earth till they reach the earth wire of the receiving instrument, and by travelling up the said wire to the coherer thus bring about its action. This was the first explanation I came to during my early experiments. I, however, do not wish to say that I hold entirely to this view at present, although I have not yet found any other perfectly satisfactory explanation of the phenomena.

It is well, also, to note that a horizontal wire, even if supported at a considerable height from earth, seems to be of little or no practical utility in increasing the range of signals. If, say, a vertical wire 30 ft. long is employed at both stations, and to the top of this is added a horizontal length of 300 ft., as shown in Fig. 6,

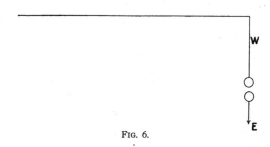

Fig. 6.

the distance obtained is greater with the vertical wire without the horizontal length than it would be if both were employed. These results show that with this system it is not sufficient to use a horizontal radiating or collecting wire, as such a wire would be of no utility for long-distance signalling.

I believe that the exceedingly marked advance made by the adoption of the vertical conductor is due to the fact that the plane of polarisation of the rays radiated is vertical, and that therefore they are not absorbed by the surface of the earth, which acts as a receiving conductor placed horizontally. As the maximum effect is obtainable when the conductors of the transmitter and receiver are parallel, this makes it necessary to have a vertical conductor connected to one pole of the coherer.

Before proceeding to describe the results obtained under various conditions by means of what we may call the vertical wire system, I think it desirable to bring before you some observations and results I have obtained with a system of Hertzian wave telegraphy, which was the first with which I worked, and in which parabolic reflectors are used to control the propagation and intensify the effects obtained when comparatively short electric waves are employed for signalling. As in ordinary optics, so also in the optics of electromagnetic oscillations, it is possible, as has been shown by Hertz, to reflect the waves radiated from the oscillator in one definite direction only. This can be done, as you know, by using convenient reflectors, similar to those used for projectors, but preferably, for economical reasons, made of copper or zinc, instead of silver amalgam or silver. Except when very small radiators of the Righi or Lebedew type are employed, it is desirable to use cylindrical parabolic reflectors, and it is with reflectors such as I here exhibit that the trials to which I am alluding have been carried out. The advantages obtainable by their use are obvious.

In any other system intended for the transmission of telegraphic signals by means of electric waves through space, the waves have been allowed to radiate in all directions, and would affect all suitable receivers within a certain radius, which of course is dependent on the power of the radiator or transmitter and on the sensitiveness of the resonator or receiver. It is, however, possible, by means of syntonising arrangements, to prevent, to a certain extent, messages affecting instruments or receivers for which they are not intended, and therefore to select any receiver by altering the wave length of the transmitter. By means of reflectors it is possible to project the waves in one almost parallel beam which will not affect any receiver placed out of its line of propagation, whether the said receiver is or is not in tune or syntony with the oscilla-

tion transmitted. This would enable several forts, or hill-tops, or islands to communicate with each other without any fear of the enemy tapping or interfering with the signals, for if the forts are on small heights the beam of rays would pass above the positions which might be occupied by the enemy. An illustration of the possibility of directing these waves can be shown by the action of the receiver, which in this case rings a bell only when the radiator in the reflector is directed towards it. These results are much more marked in an open space than in a lecture theatre, as the walls, gilt hangings, &c., tend to reflect the rays in all directions and may alter the results.

In experiments carried out over a distance of 1 3/4 miles, I noticed that only a very small movement of the transmitting reflector was sufficient to stop the signals at the receiving end, which could be only obtained within a latitude of 50 ft. to the right or left of what was believed to be the centre of the beam of reflected radiations.

There exists a most important case to which the reflector system is applicable, namely to enable ships to be warned by lighthouses, light-vessels, or other ships, not only of their proximity to danger, but also of the direction from which the warning comes. If we imagine that A is a lighthouse provided with a transmitter of electric waves, constantly giving a series of intermittent impulses or flashes, and B a ship provided with a receiving apparatus placed in the focal line of a reflector, it is plain that when the receiver is within range of the oscillator the bell will be rung only when the reflector is directed towards the transmitter, and will not ring when the reflector is not directed towards it. If the reflector is caused to revolve by clockwork or by hand, it will therefore give warning only when occupying a certain sector of the circle in which it revolves. It is therefore easy for a ship in a fog to make out the exact direction of point A, whereby, by the conventional number of taps or rings, she will be able to discern either a dangerous point to be avoided or the port or harbour for which she is endeavouring to steer.

I have not up to the present attempted to signal any greater distance than about two miles with reflectors, but I am of opinion that across clear space it will be quite possible to obtain satisfactory results at far greater distances, especially if the reflectors are accurately made any larger than those I have used. By means of the same apparatus exhibited here I have succeeded in signalling over a distance of 2 1/2 miles, without of course the use of any real "base" lines, which were supposed to be essential for any distance greater than a few feet.

It was by means of reflectors I obtained the results over 1 3/4 miles mentioned by Mr. Preece at the British Association meeting of 1896.

I have, however, dedicated more time to the other system *i.e.,* the vertical wire system.

A station at Alum Bay, Isle of Wight, and another at Bournemouth, the distance between them being 14 1/2 miles, were erected at the beginning of last year in order to test the practicability of the system under all conditions of weather, and also to afford an opportunity of proving that "Wireless Telegraphy" was not a myth but a working reality. I believe some details of the special conditions of these stations would be of interest. The installation at Alum Bay is in the Needles Hotel, and the Bournemouth station (which has lately been transferred to the Haven Hotel, Poole, thereby increasing the distance to 18 miles), was at Madeira House, South Cliff. At each station a pole 120 feet high was used, which supported the aerial conductor, usually a stranded conductor of 7/20 copper wire insulated with rubber and tape. A 10″ induction coil is used at each station, worked by a battery of 100 Obach cells "M" size, the current taken by the coil being at 14 volts from 6 to 9 amperes. The spark discharge takes place between two small spheres about 1″ in diameter, this form of transmitter having been found more simple and more effective than the Righi oscillator I had previously used. The length of spark is adjusted to about 1 centimetre; this, being a much shorter spark than the coil can give, allows a good margin over for any irregularity that might be caused by the break. No care is ever taken to polish the spheres *d d* at the place where the spark occurs, as the results seem decidedly better with dull spheres than with polished ones.

The first tests were made between the Isle of Wight and a steamer, the height of the mast on the boat being about 60 ft. Readable signals were obtained up to a distance of 18 miles from Alum Bay. During the course of these experiments, I had the pleasure of the company and assistance of Captain Kennedy, R.E., who was good enough to draw a map showing the course of the steamer. It has apparently been thought that weather or varying conditions of atmospheric electricity may interfere with or stop the signals transmitted by this system, but experience of over fourteen months of continual everyday work has brought me to the conclusion that there is no kind of weather which can stop or seriously interfere with the working of such an installation. We have given demonstrations to several eminent scientists, who came down and wanted a show, often when we did not expect them, but on no occasion have they found any difficulty in the work of transmitting and receiving messages between the two stations.

In September of last year, in consequence of the expiration of our lease at Madeira House, Bournemouth, we transferred that station, as I have said, to the Haven Hotel, Poole, thereby increasing the distance to 18 miles. Experiments and tests are carried out daily between the two stations, the improvement in apparatus having allowed us to reduce the height to 80 ft. at each end. An average of fully 1,000 words are daily transmitted through the ether each way.

In the spring of last year Lord Kelvin inspected our station at Alum Bay, and he was kind enough to express himself as highly pleased with what he saw. He sent several telegrams to his friends, including Mr. Preece and Sir George Stokes, and insisted on paying 1s. royalty on each message, wishing in this way to show his appreciation of what was done and to illustrate its fitness at that time for commercial use.

We are now working at experiments directed towards still further reducing the height necessary for a given distance, and also a good deal on syntonic systems.

In May of last year Lloyds desired to have an illustration of the possibility of signalling between Ballycastle and Rathlin Island in the north of Ireland. My assistants, Mr. Kemp and the late Mr. Glanville, installed the instruments at Ballycastle and at Rathlin Island. The distance between the two positions is 7 1/2 miles, of which about 4 are overland and the remainder across the sea, a high cliff also intervening between the two positions. At Ballycastle a pole 70 ft. high was used to support the wire, and at Rathlin a vertical conductor was supported by the lighthouse 80 ft. high. Signalling was found quite possible between the two points, but it was thought desirable to bring the height of the pole at Ballycastle to 100 ft., as the proximity of the lighthouse to the wire at Rathlin seemed to diminish the effectiveness of that station. At Rathlin we found that the lighthouse-keepers were not long in learning how to work the instruments, and after the sad accident which happened to poor Mr. Glanville that installation was worked by them alone, there being no expert on the island at the time.

Following this, in July we were requested by a Dublin paper, the *Daily Express,* to report from the high seas the results and incidents of the Kingstown Regatta. In order to do this we erected a land station, by the kind permission of the harbour-master at Kingstown, in his grounds, where a pole 100 ft. high was placed. A steamer, the *Flying Huntress,* was chartered to follow the racing yachts, the instruments being placed in the cabin. The height of the vertical wire attainable by the mast was 75 ft. A telephone was fixed from our land station at Kingstown to the *Express* office in Dublin, and as the messages came from the ship they were telephoned to Dublin, and published in succeeding editions of the evening papers.

The relative positions of the various yachts were thus wirelessly signalled while the races were in progress, sometimes over a distance of ten miles, and were published long before the yachts had returned to harbour. During the several days the system was in use between the tug and the land station, over seven hundred messages were sent and received, none requiring to be repeated. On trying longer distances it was found that with a height of 80 ft. on the ship and the same height as already stated on land, it was possible to communicate up to a distance of 25 miles, and it is worthy of note in this case that the curvature of the earth intervened very considerably at such a distance

between the two positions. On one occasion, on a regatta day, I had the pleasure of the company of Professor G. F. Fitzgerald, of Trinity College, Dublin, on the ship, who, as would be expected, took a very great interest in the proceedings.

Immediately after finishing at Kingstown I had the honour of being asked to install wireless telegraph communication between the Royal yacht *Osborne* and Osborne House, Isle of Wight, in order that her Majesty might communicate with H.R.H. the Prince of Wales, from Osborne House to the Royal yacht in Cowes Bay, and during the trips His Royal Highness frequently took. The working of this installation was a very pleasant experience for me, and it afforded also an opportunity of more thoroughly studying the effect of intervening hills.

In this installation induction coils capable of giving a 10-inch spark were used at both stations. The height of the pole supporting the vertical conductor was 100 feet at Osborne House.

On the Royal yacht *Osborne* the top of our conductor was suspended to the main mast at a height of 83 ft. from the deck, the conductor being very near one of the funnels, and in the proximity of a great number of wire stays. The vertical conductor consisted of a 7/20 stranded wire at each station.

The Royal yacht was moored in Cowes Bay at a distance of 1 3/4 miles from Osborne House, the two positions not being in sight of each other, the hills behind East Cowes intervening. This circumstance would have rendered direct signalling between the two positions impossible by means of any flag, semaphore, or heliograph system. Constant and uninterrupted communication was maintained between the Royal yacht and Osborne House during the sixteen days the system was in use, no hitch whatever occurring.

One hundred and fifty messages were sent, being chiefly private communications between the Queen and the Prince. Many of these messages contained over a hundred and fifty words, and the average speed of transmission was about fifteen words per minute.

By kind permission of the Prince of Wales I will now read to you some of the telegrams which passed between the Royal yacht and Osborne House.

August 4th.

From DR. FRIPP *to* SIR JAMES REID.

H.R.H. the Prince of Wales has passed another excellent night, and is in very good spirits and health. The knee is most satisfactory.

August 5th.

From DR. FRIPP *to* SIR JAMES REID.

H.R.H. the Prince of Wales has passed another excellent night, and the knee is in good condition.

The following telegram was sent during a cruise, and while the Royal yacht was under way, as you will see from the context.

August 10th.

From H.R.H. THE PRINCE OF WALES *to* DUKE OF CONNAUGHT.

Will be very pleased to see you on board any time this afternoon when the *Osborne* returns.

This telegram was sent when the yacht was off Bernbridge, at a distance of about seven or eight miles from Osborne.

On August 12th the *Osborne* steamed to the Needles, and communication was kept up with Osborne House until off Newton Bay, a distance of seven miles, the two positions being completely screened from each other (even to the tops of the masts) by the hills lying between. At the same position we found it quite possible to speak with our station at Alum Bay, although Headon Hill, Golden Hill, and over five miles of land lay directly between. The positions were eight and a half miles apart. Headon Hill was 45 ft. higher than the top of our conductor at Alum Bay station, and 314 ft. higher than the vertical wire on the *Osborne*.

The yacht on the same trip proceeded till about three miles past the Needles, communication having been maintained during the whole trip. Another day, when I did not happen to be on board, the yacht went on a cruise round Bembridge and Sandown, communication being maintained with Osborne House, although more than eight miles of land lay between the two positions. The Prince of Wales and other members of the Royal Family, especially the Duke of York, made much use of the system, and expressed themselves as highly satisfied with its practicability.

I consider these results rather interesting, as doubts have been expressed by some as to whether it would be possible by this system to telegraph over long stretches of land.

Results across hills were also obtained near Spezia by officers of the Italian Navy, using my system.

In December of last year my Company thought it desirable to demonstrate that the system was quite practical and available for enabling telegraphic communication to be established and maintained between lightships and the shore. This, as you are probably aware, is a matter of much importance, as all other systems tried so far have failed, and the cables by which some three or four ships are sometimes connected are exceedingly expensive, and require special moorings and fittings, which are troublesome to maintain and liable to break in storms.

The officials of Trinity House offered us the opportunity of demonstrating to them the utility of the system between the South Foreland Lighthouse, and one of the following light-vessels, viz., the *Gull*, the *South Goodwin*, and the *East Goodwin*. We naturally chose the one furthest away—the *East Goodwin*—which is just 12 miles from the South Foreland Lighthouse.

The apparatus was taken on board in an open boat, and rigged up in one afternoon. The installation started working from the very first without the slightest difficulty. The system has continued to work admirably through all the storms, which during this year have been remarkable for their continuance and severity.

On one occasion during a big gale in January, a very heavy sea struck the ship, carrying part of her bulwarks away. The report of this mishap was promptly telegraphed to the Superintendent of Trinity House, with all details of the damage sustained.

The height of the wire on board the ship is 80 ft., the mast being for 60 ft. of its length of iron, and the remainder of wood. The aerial wire is let down among a great number of metal stays and chains, which do not appear to have any detrimental effect on the strength of the signals. The instruments are placed in the aft-cabin, and the aerial wire comes through the framework of a skylight, from which it is insulated by means of a rubber pipe. As usual, a 10-inch coil is used, worked by a battery of dry cells, the current taken being about 6 to 8 amperes at 14 volts.

Various members of the crew learned in two days how to send and receive, and in fact how to run the station, and owing to the assistant on board not being as good a sailor as the instruments have proved to be, nearly all the messages during very bad weather are sent and received by these men, who, previous to our visit to the ship, had probably scarcely heard of wireless telegraphy, and were certainly unacquainted with even the rudiments of electricity. It is remarkable that wireless telegraphy, which had been considered by some as rather uncertain, or that might work one day and not the next, has proved in this case to be more reliable, even under such unfavourable conditions, than the ordinary land wires, very many of which were broken down in the storms of last month.

The instruments at the South Foreland Lighthouse are similar to those used on the ship, but as we contemplate making some long distance tests from the South Foreland to the coast of France, the height of the pole is much greater than would be necessary for the lightship installation.

We found that 80 ft. of height is quite sufficient for speaking to the ship, but I am of opinion that the height available on the ship and on shore would be ample even if the distance to which messages had to be sent were more than double what it is at present.

Service messages are constantly passing between the ship and the lighthouse, and the officials of Trinity House have been good enough to give expression of their entire satisfaction with the result of this installation. The men on board send numerous messages almost daily on their own private affairs; and this naturally tends to make their isolated life less irksome.

My Company has been anxious for some time to establish wireless communication between England and France across the Channel, in order that our French neighbours might also have an opportunity of testing for themselves the practicability of the system, but the promised official consent of the French Government has only been received this evening. Otherwise this communication would have been established

long ago. The positions for the stations chosen were situated at Folkestone and Boulogne, the distance between them being 32 miles. I prefer these positions to Calais and Dover, as the latter are only separated by a distance of about 20 miles, which is only slightly more than we are doing every day at Poole and Alum Bay, and as we find that distance so easy we would naturally prefer further tests to be made at much greater distances.

We did ask for permission to erect a station at Cherbourg, the corresponding station to be at the Isle of Wight, but the French authorities stated that they would prefer us to have our station in that country in some other position on the north coast.

My system has been in use in the Italian Navy for more than a year, but I am not at liberty to give many details of what is done there. Various installations have been erected and are working along the coast, two of these being at Spezia.

Distances of 19 miles have been bridged over in communicating with war vessels, although 10 miles have been found quite sufficient for the ordinary fleet requirements.

Other installations are now contemplated in this country for commercial and military purposes, and I am confident that in a few months many more wireless telegraph stations will be established both here and abroad.

Supplementary Note, added March 30th, 1899.
As the installation in the neighbourhood of Boulogne has been started since I read my paper, if I may I would like to add that France and England were successfully connected on Monday, the 27th of March. The station on the English side is situated at the South Foreland Light-house, near Dover, and that on the French side at the Chalet L'Artois, Wimereux, near Boulogne. The instruments were sent over from London the previous Monday in charge of two assistants, a house having been taken to serve as a station. A suitable pole was then erected, and at 5 o'clock on the 27th, within a week from the time the instruments left London, perfect telegraphic communication was established between the two points. The first messages

passed in the presence of the Committee appointed by the French Government, viz., Colonel Comte du Pontavice de Heussey, Captain Ferrie, and M. Voisenet. The first message was sent from France to England, and the reply was promptly returned by my assistant-in-charge at the South Foreland Lighthouse. There has not been the slightest hitch in the communication since, and it will no doubt be interesting to know that yesterday, the 29th, operations were conducted by two French officers, Captain Ferrie, of the French Engineers, sending from the English side to M. Voisenet, French Telegraph Engineer, on the French side. These gentlemen kept up a telegraphic correspondence for several hours, and they and numerous others have expressed themselves as highly satisfied with the successful start and working of the installation.

The CHAIRMAN: I have the pleasure to announce that, as a great number of people have been turned away from the door this evening owing to there being no room for them, Mr. Marconi has very kindly consented to give his paper again at a date which we hope to be able to fix very soon.

Dr. J. A. FLEMING: I am sure, sir, we shall all desire to present to Mr. Marconi our hearty congratulations on the magnificent success he has obtained in carrying out his most interesting experiments.

He is in such complete possession of the field that there is very little any of us can add in the discussion of his paper except by way of confirmation or questions to elicit more information. There are one or two points, however, on which I should like to make a remark or two. First, as to the transmitter. I believe in his earlier experiments Mr. Marconi made use of a Righi transmitter in which the central spark balls were immersed in oil, but I think he has since abandoned the use of oil. In many experiments tried last summer with various transmitters, I found that the use of oil did not result in much advantage. In the spark transmitter the creation of the wave depends essentially upon being able to produce a great difference of potential between two balls or rods, and then this difference of potential is made suddenly to disappear by the breaking down of the insulation of the dielectric. Although oil, by its dielectric strength, may enable us

to create a greater difference of potential between the balls before the spark passes than would be the case with air, yet after a few sparks have passed the oil becomes full of particles of carbon resulting from the decomposition of the oil, and it seems to cease to give way electrically with the necessary suddenness. Hence what we gain in one way we lose in another. Practically, therefore, the use of oil between the spark balls does not seem to result in any increased wave energy for a given spark gap and spark coil. In the next place as regards the coherer. I think Mr. Marconi still finds it advantageous to employ a glass tube which is exhausted of its air as the container. For purely experimental purposes I have found it convenient to construct the coherer so that one can easily change the metallic filings in nature or quantity. With that aim it is constructed as follows:—

Two pieces of silver or platinoid are bent into the shape of the letter L and placed back to back (see Fig. A). Between them is laid a distance piece of celluloid

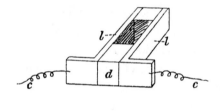

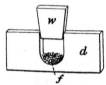

l l. L-shaped metal pieces.
d. Distance piece of celluloid.
w. Wedge, closing cavity.
f. Metallic filings.
c c. Connecting wires.

FIG. A.

or ivory cut out as shown in the diagram. The whole is bound together with silk thread, and a small wedge put into the top as a lid. It will be seen that the result is to construct a small closed box with metallic sides. In this box are placed the metallic filings. I generally use nickel with 5 per cent of finely powdered uranium. The good performance of this coherer depends very much upon the exact quantity and degree of fineness of the filings. This has to be discovered by experiment. I can confirm Mr. Marconi's statement that when once well made the coherer is by no means the uncertain instrument it has been often stated to be.

Passing on next to the question of distance transmission, there is, I think, no doubt that Mr. Marconi's splendid results have been due to his invention of the long vertical wire or rod as an adjunct. I can also confirm what he says about the use of a vertical as against a horizontal wire.

In the course of many experiments I made last year on a small scale, I had abundant opportunity to notice the far greater distances to which we can signal by the use of a vertical wire than by an equal length of receiving wire used horizontally.

I believe also that an important element in his success is due to the earth connection. In his system the spark balls and the coherer are inserted between the earth and the long vertical receiving and transmitting wires.

If the earth acts as a perfect conductor the system may then perhaps be regarded as one conductor in which electrical oscillations are set up. There is, however, much yet to be learnt as to the true function of the earth in these experiments. Mr. Marconi's researches open up a wide vista for future investigations and interesting matter for discussion at present; but as so many others will no doubt desire to speak on the paper, I will not detain you any longer, but conclude by expressing once more our thorough appreciation of all that Mr. Marconi has been able to achieve.

Dr. ERSKINE MURRAY: Four months ago, when I joined the Wireless Telegraph Company as Mr. Marconi's assistant, I was more ignorant, probably, than a good many of those present at the meeting to-night of the subject of Wireless Telegraphy in its practical application. Of course, every one interested in this subject could not but follow the experiments from the outsider's point of view, as they were reported in the newspapers and the technical press—though unfortunately a number of the journals were, at that time, rather hostile to Mr. Marconi, so that the reports were perhaps not quite as full as they might have been. On my first going to Bournemouth and seeing the action

of the telegraph, I was much surprised to find how very ordinary it was in character. It just worked like any other telegraph—not quite as fast as you hear the instruments going in the General Post Office, but working at a very rational speed and with very considerable certainty.

The law governing the relation of the height of the vertical wires and the distance between them is a most interesting point. A somewhat simple illustration may be taken from the ordinary electrical machines. In the frictional and influence-electric machines, the electricity is collected by means of a number of fine points. The "tension," as defined by Clerk Maxwell, is very much greater on the point than it is elsewhere on the more rounded part of the conductor, and therefore the force from the parts near the points (not only from the actual point itself) is greater than it would be nearer to the body of the conductor. Now, in this case the earth forms one large conductor, and the wires standing up are the points. When such a wire is charged the surface density increases with the elevation, probably very nearly in proportion to the distance from the earth. The tension depends on the square of the surface density, and therefore the action at the top will be more or less proportional to the square of the height. This is not perhaps perfectly accurate, but it will serve to indicate what, I think, may be one cause of the action in this case.

Mr. EVERSHED: I have done some work in connection with wireless telegraphy of the electro-magnetic kind, but have never even made a single experiment on Hertzian telegraphy, and it follows therefore that I feel unable to discuss Mr. Marconi's paper. Ever since I heard of Mr. Marconi's work I have been hoping that we should have the advantage of hearing it described by himself in this room, and that hope, I feel sure, was shared by every member of this Institution. During the time he has been carrying out his work, various questions have occurred to me concerning such points as the power used, the law of the variation of distance from which signals can be sent, and the connection between this distance and the length of the vertical wire, but, in his paper, he seems to have anticipated every one of my questions.

I notice that the law connecting the length of vertical wire and the distance to which he can signal is an exceedingly simple one, and I should like to draw attention to the analogy there is between that law and one which I explained in connection with my own system of wireless telegraphy a few weeks ago. I showed that the distance to which signals could be sent by means of electro-magnetic induction depended, among other things, on the product of the areas of two circuits. Now, during that same discussion, Dr. Fleming referred to the analogous case of the vertical or horizontal wire used in Hertzian telegraphy, and suggested that the true function of that wire was to integrate the electric force over a considerable space, and therefore get sufficient energy to work the coheres. That explanation seems exceedingly simple, and I think we might adopt it until some one proposes a better. Now it follows from what Dr. Fleming said during that discussion, that Mr. Marconi's law would almost necessarily be true, because the effect either of the transmitting or the receiving vertical wires should be proportional to its length. Consequently, if the length of the two wires be doubled the effect will be quadrupled, a law which Mr. Marconi appears to find very accurately fulfilled in his experiments, or at least sufficiently accurately to enable him to design new telegraphs for greater distances.

It is well known that I have been working on the subject of telegraphy to lightships for a good many years, and I should like to say, in conclusion, that one proposal that I made for signalling to lightships was submitted to the Royal Commission, which inquired into the subject. It was tried and was a total failure—and I want to be the first to congratulate Mr. Marconi very heartily on having succeeded.

Mr. H. W. SULLIVAN: We have been told that great improvement is effected in signalling by Mr. Marconi's system, by having an earth at both ends—that is to say, both on the transmitter and on the receiver. I think it is very important to know if that earth should be a perfect one, more especially in view of the difficulties, which Mr. Granville so well described lately before the Institution, as being met with at the Fastnet Rock, in establishing and maintaining an earth—difficulties

which will be found in all similar cases of weather-beaten and exposed igneous rocks. Hearing Mr. Granville, one could not but admire the persistent ingenuity which has been applied to overcome that difficulty. The Fastnet is a very difficult case, not only because the rock itself is non-conducting, but because the wire itself is frequently thrown up by the surf.

If, as seems to be the case, Mr. Marconi has successfully solved the problem of communicating with light-ships and lighthouses, he has conferred a great and lasting benefit upon the world.

Mr. W. P. GRANVILLE: Whilst congratulating Mr. Marconi upon the energy and skill with which he has conducted his most interesting experiments, I should like to ask one or two questions. First, with regard to the vertical wire at Alum Bay, the base of the standard on which the wire is erected is on a hill perhaps 100 or 200 feet in height. It is the same at Bournemouth. I should therefore like to know whether the height of the vertical wire above the sea line makes any material difference.

The other question relates to the neighbourhood of conducting masses at the transmitting and also at the receiving end. For instance, in the case in which I have been more particularly interested at the Fastnet light-house, the whole mass of the tower, as I pointed out a little while ago, is of thick iron plate; and the whole of the buildings on the rock are of iron. In a case of that kind, where one cannot get more than ten or twenty feet away from the mass of conducting metal, I should like to ask if Mr. Marconi would find any great difficulty with his apparatus?

Captain W. P. BRETT, R.E.: It is somewhat difficult to discuss the paper, which is mainly a record of facts, which are, however, very interesting from the point of view that success has been obtained over distances unattained as yet by any other system of wireless telegraphy.

With regard to the question of the earth connection, I do not want to anticipate Mr. Marconi's reply, but I happened to be present about a month since at some experiments which he was conducting between the South Foreland and the East Goodwin Lightship. I was at that time most interested in the question as to the extent to which the earth connection affected the receiving of signals, and at my request Mr. Marconi, while signals were being received, suddenly disconnected the earth connection of the receiver. The result was that the signals came just as before. It would therefore appear that, at any rate where there is an open space, the earth connection of the receiver is not a necessity for the working of the apparatus, at least over twelve miles. I am quite prepared to accept that the earth connection in conjunction with a vertical line is a necessity at the *transmitter,* simply because it confers, or, in conjunction with the vertical wire, assists in conferring an oscillating character on the discharge. It does not appear as if good or bad earth comes into the question of receiving at all. No earth at all is necessary so far as the receiving portion of the apparatus is concerned. I should like to ask Mr. Marconi whether he has had an opportunity at Poole of repeating the experiment of disconnecting the earth when messages are being received over the greater distance between that station and Alum Bay. That would probably throw a great deal of light on whether the earth conduction, or waves skimming, as it were, over the surface of the earth, play any part in the transmission, or whether it is due to pure ether waves generated from the vertical wire. I hope Mr. Marconi has followed out that experiment, because I think the result at South Foreland came rather as a surprise to himself.

The CHAIRMAN: Trinity House is represented here this evening. May I ask if any of the Brethren of Trinity House or any representative of Trinity House will be prepared to speak?

Captain VYVYAN (Deputy Master of Trinity House): I am totally unprepared, sir, to enter into any discussion on this subject, of which, an hour ago, I was comparatively ignorant. I have learned a good deal on the subject since, and I congratulate Signor Marconi most heartily upon the success he has obtained and the abnormal gathering and reception he has had here to-night. I should like to confirm everything he has said about the success that has been obtained with regard to the light-ships. For over two months this experiment has been going on, and I can confirm every word that he has said with regard to its success. Had there been any hitch at all I should have heard of it. I congratulate Mr. Marconi very heartily.

Captain J. M. KENNEDY, R.E.: When Mr. Marconi first came to England, through the kindness of Mr. Preece and Mr. Gavey, under whom I was then serving, I was able to attend and take part in the experiments at Weston, Salisbury Plain, and, more recently, those in the Isle of Wight. In a paper which I read just a year ago at the United Service Institution, I dealt chiefly with the military application of this system of wireless telegraphy. As regards communication between fixed stations, such as forts and permanent camps, we may say from what we have seen to-night that the question is solved, but an army in the field—in the Soudan or in Afghanistan, for instance—cannot be expected to carry about with it 100 or 150 feet poles. Some other way must be found for raising the vertical wire. I therefore tried several experiments with kites and balloons, the latter when there was no wind and the former when there was, and experienced no difficulty with them. The balloons were only 4 feet in diameter; they were no trouble to carry about, and could be expanded from a small cylinder. One advantage of these balloons and kites is that they obviate all the difficulties of insulation. No wire stays or boiler plates exist to cause annoyance, and there is no limit to the length of wire that can be used, for it is as easy to put up 1,000 feet of wire as it is 10 feet; other things being equal, this means practically unlimited latitude as regards range. In some experiments I made at Bath, I had two miles of wire up on one of Captain Baden Powell's kites. It is needless to say that the enormous impedance in that long wire was too great for use as a resonator, a much shorter conductor answered our purpose better; but we had very strong, and very painful, atmospheric effects—in the shape of 6-inch sparks.

I think I am right in saying, and I am proud to be able to say it, that about a year ago I was, with the exception of Captain Brett and of Captain Jackson, of the Royal Navy, the only true believer in Mr. Marconi and his system. Consequently it is very easy for me now to join with the multitude in sounding his praise.

The CHAIRMAN: I think that we must now adjourn this discussion. Speaking for myself, as one who has believed in this system of communication with lighthouses and ships ever since he heard of the Hertzian experiments, I should like to ask Mr. Marconi if he could not settle for us experimentally before the date of the adjourned discussion, whether it is really necessary to have the earth connection, because this assumed necessity for an earth connection is one of the most difficult things for me to understand.

• • •

1. See *Nuovo Cimento,* series 3, vol. xvii., Jan.-Feb., 1885; and ditto, Jan.-Feb., 1896.

2. See *Elettricista*, August number, 1897. (Rowe.)

3. See *Nuovo Cimento,* series 3, vol. xvii., Jan.-Feb., 1885; and ditto, Jan.-Feb., 1896.

4. See *Elettricista*, August number, 1897. (Rowe.)

5·5

"Seeing by electricity" in 1880

From *Television* I, No. 2 (April 1928): 8, 37.

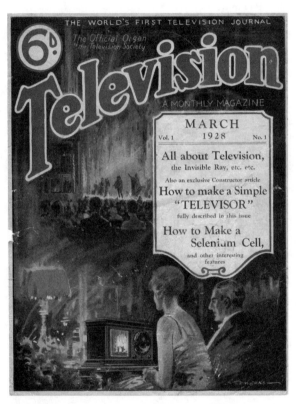

Cover of the first issue of the first television magazine, 1928.

INTRODUCTORY NOTE TO READINGS 5.5 AND 5.6

These two articles are taken from the first published volume of what was self-designated *Television: The World's First Television Journal. A Monthly Magazine Devoted to the Interests and Progress of the Science of Seeing by Wire and Wireless.* The year 1928 marked the beginning of television's transformation from scientific curiosity to commercially viable broadcast medium. The journal served as the official organ of the Television Society. The articles are largely self-explanatory. [JMN]

TEXT OF READING 5.5

The art of transmitting images by means of electric currents is now in about the same state of advancement as the art of transmitting speech by telephone had attained in 1876, and it remains to be seen whether it will develop as rapidly and successfully as the art of telephony. Professor Bell's announcement that he had filed at the Franklin Institute a sealed description of a method of "Seeing by Telegraph" brings to mind an invention for a similar purpose submitted to us some months since by the inventor, Mr. Geo. Carey, of the Surveyors' Office, City Hall, Boston, Mass. By consent of Mr. Carey we present herewith engravings and description of his wonderful instruments.

Figures 1 and 2 are instruments for transmitting

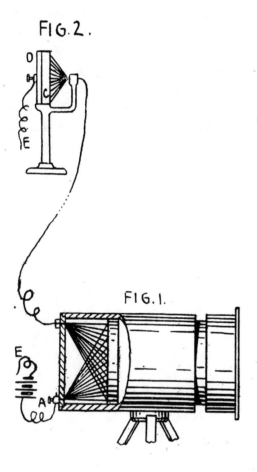

and recording at long distances permanently or otherwise by means of electricity the picture of any object

that may be projected by the lens of camera (Figure 1) upon its disc P. The operation of this device depends upon the changes in electrical conductivity produced by the action of light in the metalloid selenium. The disc P is drilled through perpendicularly to its face with numerous small holes, each of which is filled partly or entirely with selenium, the selenium forming part of an electrical circuit. The wires from the disc P are insulated and are wound into a cable after leaving binding screw B. These wires pass through disc C (Figure 2) in the receiving instrument at a distant point, and are arranged in the same relative position as in disc P (Figure 1).

A chemically-prepared paper is placed between discs C and D for the image of any object projected upon the disc P (Figure 1) to be printed upon.

Figure 3 is a sectional view of Figure 2, showing

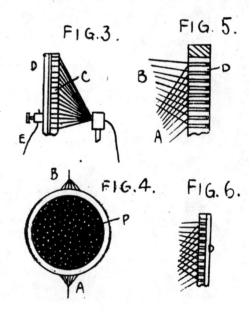

wires and the chemically-prepared paper.

Figure 5 is a sectional view of disc P (Figure 1) showing selenium points and conducting wires.

Figure 6 is a sectional view of another receiving instrument with platinum or carbon points, covered with a glass cap, there being a vacuum between glass cap D and insulating plate or disc C.

These points are rendered incandescent by the passage of electric current, thereby giving a luminous image instead of printing the same. These platinum or carbon points are arranged relatively the same as the selenium points in plate P (Figures 1 and 4); each platinum or carbon point is connected with one of the wires from selenium point in disc P (Figure 1), and forms part of an electric circuit.

The operation of the apparatus is as follows: If a white letter, A, upon a black ground, be projected upon disc P (Figure 1) all parts of disc will be *dark* except where the letter A is, when it will be light; and the selenium points in the light will allow the electric current to pass, and if the wires leading from disc P (Figure 1) are arranged in the same relative position when passing through disc C (Figure 2), the electricity will print upon the chemically-prepared paper between C and D (Figure 2) a copy of the letter A, as projected upon the disc P (Figure 1). By this means any object so projected and so transmitted will be reproduced in a manner similar to that by which the letter A was reproduced.

Figures 7 and 8 are instruments for transmitting

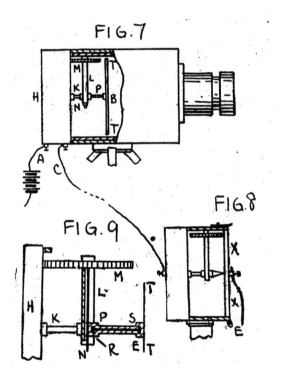

FIG. 7

FIG. 8

FIG. 9

and recording by means of electricity the picture of any object that may be projected upon the glass plate at TT (Figure 7) by the camera lens. The operation of

these instruments depends upon the changes in electrical conductivity produced by the action of light on the metalloid selenium.

The clockwork revolves a shaft K, forcing the arm L and wheel M to describe a circle of revolution. The screen N, being fastened firmly to the wheel M, turns as wheel M revolves on its axis, thus turning the sliding piece P, and selenium pointed disc, or ring B; towards the wheel M (see Figure 9). These two motions cause the point, disc, or ring I, to describe a spiral line upon the glass TT, thus passing over every portion of the picture projected upon glass TT.

The selenium point, disc, or ring, will allow the electrical current to flow through it in proportion to the intensity of the lights and shades of the picture projected upon the glass plate TT. The electric currents enter camera at A and pass directly to the selenium point, disc, or ring B;, thence through the sliding piece P and shaft K by an insulated wire to binding screw C (Figure 7); from this screw by wire to binding screw D (Figure 81 through shaft K and sliding piece P to point E (Figure 8); then through the chemically-prepared paper placed against the inner surface of the metallic plate XX by wire F to the ground, thus completing the circuit and leaving upon the above-mentioned chemically-prepared paper an image or permanent impression of any object projected upon the glass plate TT by the camera lens.

Figure 8 is the receiving instrument, which has a clock movement similar to that of Figure 7, with the exception of the metallic point E, in place of the selenium point, disc or ring (Figure 7) at B. Figure 9 is an enlarged view of clockwork and machinery shown in Figures 1 and 2.

Seeing Round the World: What Television Will Mean to You

Shaw Desmond

From *Television* I, No. 2 (April 1928): 11–14.

Seeing "at a distance" is going to touch the lives of each one of us; take us out of our ruts; bring us fortune and perhaps, sometimes, fortune's maladroit sister "Misfortune"; and, generally, turn our lives upside down. It is going to change the outer lives of men and women as much as the telegraph or telephone. It is going to do more—it is going to make both those instruments of human advance and human torture (perhaps one and the same thing!) infinitely more potent whether for good or evil.

From the moment that you, John Brown, or you, Mrs. John Brown, get out of bed in the morning until you pass into your beauty sleep at night, television is going to haunt you. Nor, indeed, will either of you, separately or together, be able to escape the multitudinous activities of the televisor even when you have retired to your room! The televisor is the eye that sees everywhere . . . *but,* and it is a very big "but," NOT *unless you wish it!* You need not answer the telephone by your bed-side unless you wish. Similarly, you need not be seen by the televisor unless you wish. *But the insistence of the televisor will undoubtedly be as great as that of the telephone.*

Hard Facts of the Future.

Here I shall indulge in no airy prognostication. I shall confine myself strictly to facts, or to things about to become facts. When I speak of buying a beefsteak by the televisor. When I speak of buying a Paris "creation" by the televisor. When I speak of addressing thousands of your constituents to be when running for that incredible talking-shop known as the House of Commons—in all these I shall be dealing with hard facts about to mature or already matured.

You are a business man, Mr. Brown. You telegraph. You telephone. But now you are going to "televise" (patent applied for). You are going to be "televised" (additional patent secured).

You will find that fellow Smith at the other end of your wire—or rather "wireless"—walking and talking as in life. No use for Smith, whom you loathe, to disguise himself behind a mere "voice," as he does now over the telephone. You will be able to mark each flicker of Smith's eye-lashes ("confound the fellow! why can't he smile?"), note each gesture, draw your own conclusions. For you are "televising" Smith.

Smith's usually oily voice, on the 'phone, with Smith's plausibility, but minus Smith's expression, may mislead you to-day when you telephone. It can't mislead you to-morrow. Smith's face has got to "come across with the goods." Smith has to speak something like the truth because Smith's face is there to give the voice the lie, if necessary.

The telephone is probably the world's biggest time-waster! That statement I make without fear of effective contradiction. The last time I made it was to a New York banker who in his time steered America through one of her banking crises—and he admitted the essential truth of it, after consideration.

"Business is Business."

For to-day you, Mr. John Brown, probably send three times as many messages over the 'phone as you need to send . . . just because the 'phone is at your elbow. If you were an American you would send five times as many. I sat once in a New Jersey house where for some hours I listened to forty-eight messages on the 'phone (a most reprehensible proceeding!), and afterwards put it to my host that of these forty-eight messages, thirty-seven need never have been sent. He denied. Thought. Admitted!

But with the televisor automatically put into action with the lifting of the telephone receiver you will think twice before you send a useless message. It is one thing "to talk to a voice." It is another thing "to talk to a man." That is the difference.

With a voice, you can avoid responsibility. You are under no compunction to "watch out." You are not being observed. But when you talk to a man, not in the spirit but in the concrete flesh, you have to watch your step. You will be apt to think twice before you make connection. That is human nature.

Or a contract has been signed in New York whilst you sit in your London office. It purports to be signed by Jones. It has been "wirelessed" that it contains certain clauses. You want to see that signature. You want to see those clauses. You don't want any "funny business," because you are not quite sure of Jones.

So you ask the New York end kindly to hold up the contract before the televisor. To "televise" the contract. You see exactly what is being signed. You know where you are.

But all this drops into nothingness when we come to what I will call "television-advertising." It is going to shake the world to its publicity centres. It is going to revolutionise the sales of everything from chewing-gum, that modern devitamised food, to white elephants, and cures for corns.

As I have already dealt with what I have called "television broadcasting" fairly fully in the columns of various London newspapers, I propose here to leave out the minuter details of the enormous possibilities of wireless-broadcasting if ever the "B.B.C." pass out of the stodgy official stage to be taken over by private enterprise. Yet I will venture to set out the conclusions to which I have arrived after discussing it with various editors of dailies, publicity specialists, and big business leaders.

The Programme of To-morrow.

My conclusions, after these conversations, set out in order of importance are:

1. That television-advertising will probably be a commercial proposition within two to three years and in common use within three to five years.

2. That used with broadcasting and compared with the present use only in advertising of the printed word, in which *sight* alone is used, it will be as much more effective as would be the comparative effects of a play on a man sitting in a theatre with eyes open, and a man sitting in the same theatre blindfolded. When *seeing* is added to the hearing we have a pretty perfect combination.

3. That the day is now fairly close when the great dailies will use "television-broadcasting" as part of their daily work, in a way to be shown later in this article, and that instead of hurting them this new advertising medium will enormously increase their circulations and power. *For nothing can completely replace the printed word.*

4. That the great stores, etc., will be able to reach their millions by the "advertising-televisor" where to-day they reach their thousands.

5. That as television is a British invention, and by virtue of the international strength of the Baird patents, if England be alive to the possibilities of the new medium, it will give her an initial impetus over her competitors, similar to the initial impetus which steam gave her a century ago in the industrial world.

Compressed, we shall see (for steps are now being taken indeed to make it effective) our great dailies broadcast to millions of readers and "listeners-in" the front page of their edition of the *morrow* with, printed across it, the words: "This space has been reserved in to-morrow's edition for Messrs. Blank, the great popular emporium, to advertise their motor-cars," or dresses or hats, as the case may be.

But you will ask: "How shall I be able to see this?"

As Sherlock Holmes would say to his dear Watson: "That is elementary."

There will scarcely be a house in England to-morrow which will not have its own television screen. You will sit in your armchair after you come home from "the city," put a pipe on, switch on your wireless and look at the screen which will be hanging like a picture before your eyes. On that screen you will see perhaps a curtain as in a theatre. The curtain will roll up. And behind the curtain you will see the front page of your favourite daily, to-morrow's issue, with to-morrow's date, and underneath the announcement I have mentioned. C'est tout! After a minute or so, when you have properly tuned in your televisor, the entertainment, both visible and audible, will commence.

It is possible that, if the editor of TELEVISION permits, I may return to this "television-advertising" in a later article. I will now content myself with stating, first, that an invention is now maturing which will certainly make this "home-screen" possible; secondly, that it is considered sufficiently "brass-tacks" to have interested leading business men and newspaper men; and, lastly, that as Edison recently said to me in his laboratories in New Jersey, *"there is practically no limit to the possibilities of power-projection,"* whether that projection takes the form of wireless motors or wireless broadcasting, or television-advertising.

We are only at the beginning. And it is now, as always, the first step, already taken, which costs.

So much for the business side of television and Mr. John Brown. What about John Brown's wife?

"Take Politics."

Woman has come out of her shell—commercially, socially, artistically. But the shell has not yet quite dropped from her. Bits of it are clinging to her still!

She is finding all sorts of difficulties in her new freedom. She finds that "the brutal male" has still to be reckoned with; that sex-war is fact, not fiction; and that she must fight for what she wants, and that she can only hold what she wants so long as she fights!

Television may be described as the midwife of the new society—of that society in which woman will play her part equally with man.

Take politics!

Do you realise that there is actually in existence a televisor which can stand on your table and which takes up little more room than a typewriter? Do you realise that this handy little instrument is about to be used by Mrs. Phillipson, Lady Astor and Mr. Lloyd George, also by Messrs. Winston Churchill and Ramsay MacDonald? They may not know it yet—but they will either have to use it or lose their seats! This is not hyperbole, it is stern fact. *The vote is to be "televised."*

No more meetings in little stuffy halls when the candidate, his halo newly polished, seeks the suffrages of the intelligent electorate! No more tortuous train journeys! No more travelling a hundred miles by outraged constituents to the lobby of the House to call the sitting member over the coals! Not on your life! (I regret this American slang, but would plead that everybody is doing it, from peers to postmen!)

Think of the awful advantage of a beautiful woman would-be M.P. over a plain common or garden male when she takes out her powder puff, does something diabolic with a lip-stick and pencil, and puts on a devastating hat!—to appeal over the televisor to her constituents to be! Think of Jix or Winston in the same position. Where does the mere male come in?

He doesn't!

"An Awful Prospect!"

Nor is this any joke. It is going soon to be hard brute fact for the wretched male politician. For the televisor will be used in every election from Land's End to John o' Groats.

It might even mean a female majority in the House. Awful prospect!

A female Prime Minister. A female War Minister. A female Minister of Morals! The mind baulks. For all these things the televisor may make possible.

But coming from suffrage to sausages.

Has any woman reading these lines known what it is to go out under a broiling sun to see Mr. Diehard's legs of mutton or steaks? Has any unhappy housewife (and we men simply don't know what women go through in the house!), following me thus far, ever had to trust to luck and Mr. Greenheart's honesty for plums or apples or oranges or Brussels sprouts? Why, every daughter of Eve of them all has been through it.

Enter the televisor!

You "televise "Mr. Diehard, the butcher. You tell Mr. Diehard that you don't want any aged meat, nor are you primarily concerned with Mr. Diehard's bank balance—but rather with your own digestion and that of your husband. Has Mr. Diehard any *really tender* beefsteak?

No use Diehard saying he *has!* You want to see what you are buying. Won't he please hold up the piece of meat for your inspection through the televisor?

Mr. Diehard sighs and does so. No chance now to send round a bit of tender and a bit of tough to help each other out. He's got to deliver the goods—the identical goods you have inspected through the televisor. Result: happiness, digestively and maritally. More human happiness turns upon human digestion than most of us are ready to concede!

Or you, Mrs. John Brown, are living in the wilds. Down there in the heart of Devonshire or up in the north-west Highlands from which I have just come after listening to the complaints of all sorts and conditions of women who "won't buy a London dress because they can't first see what they are getting."

The Mannequin Parade.
You want a London, a Paris, or a Viennese dress. You don't order in the dark or "in the blind "as the idiom goes on the continent. You wireless Selfridge or Peter Robinson's or Worth, tell them what you want, and ask them kindly to place the dress before the "exhibition screen." You have the morning of your life enjoying the latest creations a thousand miles away (perhaps to-morrow three thousand miles away when you see and speak with New York as easily as with Balham or Blackfriars) without having to stir a foot from your own home, without exertion, and without that

irritation which I gather from my women friends is inseparable from "buying a dress," which is worse than buying a horse or buying a gun.

"Oh! but," you say, "what about the colour?"

Well, what about it?

Did you not know that we are now well on the high road to solving colour transmission by television, as it has already been solved on the films? That is but a detail—an important and even difficult detail—but a detail now on the point of solution.

You will be able to see the delicate jade in a Paquin dress as clearly as though you were in their Paris showrooms. The costly exquisiteness of the "absolutely simple" dress of the really great designer will be as plain to your eyes as though the mannequin were strutting, before you in your own room—*as she will*. For *I do not doubt that ultimately either a genius like Baird, or another, will bring in the stereoscopic effect into the televisor* which will let those to whom you speak walk, as they certainly will talk, *right out of the screen.*

A Word to the Wise.
You, Mrs. Brown, will be able to indulge your *penchant* for fashionable "At Homes" without going out. Your friends will be able to come into your room without *their* going out. You can have a "Televisor-At Home" hour fixed beforehand when all your friends will touch the switch, let the screen roll up, and find themselves speaking together in that screen, as though in the flesh.

And, of course, I have only touched the fringe of the commercial and social and political potentialities of television. And, of course, as certainly, all sorts of clever-clever people will say: "But that's all in the future. It's not going to be in our lifetime."

For the comfort or dismay of those critics (and no intelligent man objects to intelligent criticism) may the writer, who does not own a television share, and as novelist and publicist has in this no axe to grind, state the following unchallengeable facts:

First, that *a man has sat in a chair in London and his image has been "televised" to New York, his features and personality being recognised there.* Secondly, that cases like that of the wireless operator of the Cunarder

Berengaria in which, when one thousand miles out at sea, he recognised his *fiancée* in a televisor screen, will become each day more common and soon will no more call for comment than a long distance telephone conversation. Lastly, that television in the United States at least is already recognised as one of the most formidable business propositions on that live-wire continent, with already a formidable organisation and revenue of its own, and that what America is doing to-day England will be doing to-morrow (would that it were the other way about!).

If the doubting Thomas or Thomasine (for the feminine doubter does exist) want further hard unassailable facts then let them digest these:

The fact brought to my notice when I was engaged recently in completing the scenario of one of my novels for a leading producer, *that no film of a certain type is being written to-day without consideration of its future television possibilities.* The fact that, as Mr. M. A. Wetherell, the internationally known producer of the "Robinson Crusoe," the "Victory," "Somme," and other films recently stated to me: "Television is going one day to revolutionise the world of pictures from roof-tree to foundation." And that final, hard-headed fact, for "money talks," that Hollywood, which I visited not very long ago, as also the world of the legitimate theatre, are being deeply exercised in their minds by the possible effects of television upon their entirely separate worlds.

If this consensus of evidence will not convince you, Mr. John Brown, and your charming partner, Mrs. John, that television is not something "in the air" but something already with its tentacles set deep into solid earth, then I am afraid nothing will convince you. And if the England for which you both stand will not be convinced—so much the worse for England! But the men who run England are, many of them, already half-way on the road to conviction—to that strange compelling conviction—that we are about "*to see round the world!*"

6

Origins of the General Purpose Programmable Computer—
Babbage's Analytical Engine

6.1

Sketch of the Analytical Engine Invented by Charles Babbage

L. F. Menabrea

With Notes upon the Memoir by the Translator Ada Augusta, Countess of Lovelace

From *Scientific Memoirs* 3 (1843): 666–731.

INTRODUCTORY NOTE TO READING 6.1

A unique personality and avid technologist, Charles Babbage pushed the level of metal-working to the limits of his time, leaving us the comprehensive designs of three magnificent machines: the Difference Engine no. 1 (see Reading 4.1); the Difference Engine no. 2 (first built around 1990 and presently operational in the London Science Museum), and the Analytical Engine, the first programmable digital computer, which might have been the size of a steam locomotive or bigger had it been constructed.

Of Babbage's three calculating engines, by far the most remarkable was the Analytical Engine, which he began developing in 1836. In the design and conception of this machine Babbage pioneered many features of digital computing. The key concept in the Analytical Engine was the separation of arithmetic computation from the storage of numbers. Taking his terminology from the textile industry, one of the first to be mechanized during the Industrial Revolution, Babbage named the computation part of the engine the "Mill" and the storage portion the "Store." In the textile industry yarns were brought from the store to the mill where they were woven into fabric, after which they were brought back to the store. In the Analytical Engine numbers would be brought from the Store to the Mill for processing, after which they would return to the Store.

As a means of organizing the processing Babbage also looked to the textile industry for the solution, borrowing the technology of the Jacquard loom in which the patterns were recorded on punched cards. Jacquard cards were linked together with ribbons to record the method of producing the pattern. Depending upon the intricacy of the designs, large numbers of the cards could be linked together to produce an infinite variety of patterns. When Jacquard cards were linked together in sequence, these linked cards were sometimes called "trains" because the cards were linked much the way railroad cars were connected. Using the trains of punched cards the patterns could be reproduced at will.[1] In adopting Jacquard's technology for organizing the information processing in his Analytical Engine, Babbage envisaged the machine processing information according to logical procedures for which he had no name. He would sometimes refer to the series of logical steps that might be recorded on a sequence of Jacquard cards as "trains," as in trains of thought. He also used the word "procedure." We call this procedure programming.

Swade described the features of the Analytical Engine as follows:

The features Babbage invested in the Engine are astonishing. It could be programmed by the use of punched cards.[2] It had a separate "memory" and "central processor". It was capable of "looping" or "iteration" (the ability to repeat a sequence of operations a programmable number of times) as well as conditional branching (the ability to take one course of action or another, depending on the outcome of a calculation—IF . . . THEN statements). It incorporated "microprogramming" as well as "pipelining" (the preparation of a result in advance of its need) and catered for the use of multiple processors to speed computation by splitting the task—the basis of modern parallel computing. It also featured a range of input and output devices, including graph plotters, printers, and card readers and punches. In short, Babbage had designed what we would now call a general purpose digital computing engine. . . . [3]

Incorporating these features in machined or cast-metal parts would have required an enormous structure. Swade estimated that that the central section of the Mill, or central processing unit, would have been about fifteen feet tall and six feet in diameter. The length of the Store, or memory, depended upon its capacity. Swade estimated that a modest configuration with a capacity for storing one hundred fifty-digit numbers would extend the machine to about twenty feet in length, creating a machine about the size of a steam locomotive. But Babbage thought even bigger than that. "He wrote of machines with a storage capacity of 1,000 numbers. A store of that size would extend the machine to over one hundred feet in length. . . ." [4]

If Babbage could not obtain government funding to complete his Difference Engine no. 1, it is not surprising that funding the Analytical Engine was impossible. It exists only in the very small portion of the "Mill" and printing unit that Henry P. Babbage completed in 1906, long after his father's death, and in the detailed engineering drawings that Charles Babbage left. As it turned out, the main scientific interest in this amazing machine came from Italy, where Babbage was asked to make a scientific presentation on the Analytical Engine. Luigi Menabrea's report of this presentation in Torino was the first publication describing the logical design of the machine. Menabrea's paper contains the earliest published examples of what we now call programs for a digital computer. Not surprisingly Babbage seized the opportunity to further promote the engine when Ada Lovelace, daughter of Lord Byron, expressed interest in translating and annotating Menabrea's paper. The cooperation between Babbage and Byron's daughter, a celebrity in her own right, is one of the more unusual events in the history of Victorian science.

---

1   An excellent explanation of how Babbage intended the Jacquard cards to be used can be found in the historical introduction to Aiken and Hopper's *A Manual of Operation for the Automatic Sequence Controlled Calculator* (1946) from which we quote: "These cards, the precursors of Hollerith's punched cards, were used by the Jacquard weavers to control the looms to produce and reproduce the patterns designed by the artists. The designs were first sketched as they were to appear in the finished product, transferred to squared paper and used as guides for punching the cards. The cards allowed certain needles to be extended through the punched holes, thereby controlling hooks which, in turn, raised particular warp threads to produce the desired pattern. In order to continue the weaving of the same design the cards were interlaced with twine in an endless sequence so that one card was brought into position immediately after another was used. Holes were punched for the lacings as well as for the pegs which guided the cards over a cylinder.

"In adapting these cards for use in his machine, Babbage required two decks; one of variable cards and one of operational cards. The first set was designed to select the particular numbers to be operated upon from the store; the second set, to select the operation to be performed by the mill. The deck of operation cards therefore represented the solution of a mathematical situation independent of the values of the parameters and variables involved. Thus the analytical engine was to have been completely general as regards algebraic operations.

"In order to use selected values of transcendental and other functions, the engine was to be equipped with a mechanism to call for such functions. Having stopped and rung a bell, a certain part of the machine would indicate that a particular value of a particular function was required. The attendant would then insert a punched card containing the desired function and its argument. The machine then checked the card to make sure it was the one requested, by subtracting the argument of the inserted card from the argument standing in the machine. If the difference was zero, the engine would continue its computation. If an incorrect card was supplied the engine would 'ring a louder bell and stop.'

"As in the difference engines, the analytical engine was to print its own results. Further, a mechanism was to have been added for punching numerical results in blank cards for future use. In this way, the engine could compute the tables required and punch its own cards 'entirely free from error'"(pp. 5–6).

Afin de diminuer autant que possible les chances d'erreur dans l'écriture des données numériques du problème, on les écrit successivement sur une des colonnes du moulin ; puis, au moyen de cartons disposés à cet effet, ces mêmes nombres vont se placer sur les colonnes convenables, sans que l'opérateur ait aucunement à s'en inquiéter ; de cette manière toute son attention se reportera sur la simple écriture de ces mêmes nombres.

D'après ce qui vient d'être exposé, on voit que l'ensemble des colonnes des variables peut être considéré comme un *magasin* de nombres qui y sont accumulés par le moulin et qui,

Menabrea's paper, originally published in French, was the first published account of the logical design and operation of Babbage's Analytical Engine. The charts depicting logical procedures, one of which we reproduce here, were the first published computer programs.

Ada inherited from her father both brilliance and mental illness. Her personality and family background was analyzed thoroughly by Woolley in *The Bride of Science* (1999). An upper-class woman who had been tutored in mathematics by Augustus de Morgan, she was extremely unusual, if not unique, for her day. Her correspondence with Babbage suggests that she was self-consciously impressed with her own mathematical abilities. Recent scholars have belittled her mathematical skills, attributing most of the mathematics in her famous account of the Analytical Engine to Babbage's coaching. Nevertheless, Ada was responsible for the first detailed description of the workings of the machine, roughly three times the length of Menabrea's original text, and she brought to the project a fine sense of style that enabled her to describe the logic of the machine in a poetic way. Her annotated translation of Menabrea's paper has been called the most important document in the history of computing before the advent of the electronic digital computer. Babbage believed that this paper proved "that the whole of the developments and operations of Analysis are now capable of being executed by machinery."[5] Ada is identified as the author only by her initials, A.A.L., at the end of each of her notes.

Considering the monumental achievements involved in the design of Babbage's Analytical Engine, it is remarkable how little attention it received during Babbage's lifetime. More than likely the achievements in this design that we considered so remarkable were not much appreciated in Babbage's day. The paper by Menabrea and its translation by the Countess of Lovelace were the only accounts of its method of operation published before Babbage's autobiography. [JMN]

2   Though he was not able to build the actual Analytical Engine, Babbage did experiment with how the punched cards would work. When we wrote this bibliography, samples of Babbage's original punched cards containing mathematical instructions were preserved in the Science Museum, London. One is reproduced in Williams, *A History of Computing Technology* (1985) on page 188.

3   Doron Swade, *The Cogwheel Brain* (London: Little, Brown, 2000), 114–15.

4   Swade, *op. cit.*, 115.

5   Charles Babbage, *Babbage's Calculating Engines...* (Los Angeles: Tomash Publishers, 1982), 7.

TEXT OF READING 6.1

Those labours which belong to the various branches of the mathematical sciences, although on first consideration they seem to be the exclusive province of intellect, may, nevertheless, be divided into two distinct sections; one of which may be called the mechanical, because it is subjected to precise and invariable laws, that are capable of being expressed by means of the operations of matter; while the other, demanding the intervention of reasoning, belongs more specially to the domain of the understanding. This admitted, we may propose to execute, by means of machinery, the mechanical branch of these labours, reserving for pure intellect that which depends on the reasoning faculties. Thus the rigid exactness of those laws which regulate numerical calculations must frequently have suggested the employment of material instruments, either for executing the whole of such calculations or for abridging them; and thence have arisen several inventions having this object in view, but which have in general but partially attained it. For instance, the much-admired machine of Pascal is now simply an object of curiosity, which, whilst it displays the powerful intellect of its inventor, is yet of little utility in itself. Its powers extended no further than the execution of the four first[1] operations of arithmetic, and indeed were in reality confined to that of the first two, since multiplication and division were the result of a series of additions and subtractions. The chief drawback hitherto on most of such machines is, that they require the continual intervention of a human agent to regulate their movements, and thence arises a source of errors; so that, if their use has not become general for large numerical calculations, it is because they have not in fact resolved the double problem which the question presents, that of *correctness* in the results, united with *economy* of time.

Struck with similar reflections, Mr. Babbage has devoted some years to the realization of a gigantic idea. He proposed to himself nothing less than the construction of a machine capable of executing not merely arithmetical calculations, but even all those of analysis, if their laws are known. The imagination is at first astounded at the idea of such an undertaking; but the more calm reflection we bestow on it, the less impossible does success appear, and it is felt that it may depend on the discovery of some principle so general, that, if applied to machinery, the latter may be capable of mechanically translating the operations which may be indicated to it by algebraical notation. The illustrious inventor having been kind enough to communicate to me some of his views on this subject during a visit he made at Turin, I have, with his approbation, thrown together the impressions they have left on my mind. But the reader must not expect to find a description of Mr. Babbage's engine; the comprehension of this would entail studies of much length; and I shall endeavour merely to give an insight into the end proposed, and to develop the principles on which its attainment depends.

I must first premise that this engine is entirely different from that of which there is a notice in the 'Treatise on the Economy of Machinery,' by the same author. But as the latter gave rise[2] to the idea of the engine in question, I consider it will be a useful preliminary briefly to recall what were Mr. Babbage's first essays, and also the circumstances in which they originated.

It is well known that the French government, wishing to promote the extension of the decimal system, had ordered the construction of logarithmical and trigonometrical tables of enormous extent. M. de Prony, who had been entrusted with the direction of this undertaking, divided it into three sections, to each of which was appointed a special class of persons. In the first section the formulæ were so combined as to render them subservient to the purposes of numerical calculation; in the second, these same formulæ were calculated for values of the variable, selected at certain successive distances; and under the third section, comprising about eighty individuals, who were most of them only acquainted with the first two rules of arithmetic, the values which were intermediate to those calculated by the second section were interpolated by means of simple additions and subtractions.

An undertaking similar to that just mentioned having been entered upon in England, Mr. Babbage conceived that the operations performed under the third section might be executed by a machine; and this idea he realized by means of mechanism, which has been in part put together, and to which the name Difference Engine is applicable, on account of the principle upon which its construction is founded. To give some notion of this, it will suffice to consider the series of whole square numbers, 1, 4, 9, 16, 25, 36, 49, 64, &c. By subtracting each of these from the succeeding one, we obtain a new series, which we will name the Series of First Differences, consisting of the numbers 3, 5, 7, 9, 11, 13, 15, &c. On subtracting from each of these the preceding one, we obtain the Second Differences, which are all constant and equal to 2. We may represent this succession of operations, and their results, in the following table.

	A. Column of Square Numbers	B. First Differences	C. Second Differences
	1		
		3	2 b
	4		
		5	2 d
a	9		
		7	2
c	16		
		9	2
	25		
		11	
	36		

From the mode in which the last two columns B and C have been formed, it is easy to see, that if, for instance, we desire to pass from the number 5 to the succeeding one 7, we must add to the former the constant difference 2; similarly, if from the square number 9 we would pass to the following one 16, we must add to the former the difference 7, which difference is in other words the preceding difference 5, plus the constant difference 2; or again, which comes to the same thing, to obtain 16 we have only to add together the three numbers 2, 5, 9, placed obliquely in the direc-

tion *ab*. Similarly, we obtain the number 25 by summing up the three numbers placed in the oblique direction *dc*: commencing by the addition 2 + 7, we have the first difference 9 consecutively to 7; adding 16 to the 9 we have the square 25. We see then that the three numbers 2, 5, 9 being given, the whole series of successive square numbers, and that of their first differences likewise may be obtained by means of simple additions.

Now, to conceive how these operations may be reproduced by a machine, suppose the latter to have three dials, designated as A, B, C, on each of which are traced, say a thousand divisions, by way of example, over which a needle shall pass. The two dials, C, B, shall have in addition a registering hammer, which is to give a number of strokes equal to that of the divisions indicated by the needle. For each stroke of the registering hammer of the dial C, the needle B shall advance one division; similarly, the needle A shall advance one division for every stroke of the registering hammer of the dial B. Such is the general disposition of the mechanism.

This being understood, let us, at the beginning of the series of operations we wish to execute, place the needle C on the division 2, the needle B on the division 5, and the needle A on the division 9. Let us allow the hammer of the dial C to strike; it will strike twice, and at the same time the needle B will pass over two divisions. The latter will then indicate the number 7, which succeeds the number 5 in the column of first differences. If we now permit the hammer of the dial B to strike in its turn, it will strike seven times, during which the needle A will advance seven divisions; these added to the nine already marked by it will give the number 16, which is the square number consecutive to 9. If we now recommence these operations, beginning with the needle C, which is always to be left on the division 2, we shall perceive that by repeating them indefinitely, we may successively reproduce the series of whole square numbers by means of a very simple mechanism.

The theorem on which is based the construction of the machine we have just been describing, is a particular case of the following more general theorem: that if in any polynomial whatever, the highest power of whose variable is m, this same variable be increased by equal degrees; the corresponding values of the polynomial then calculated, and the first, second, third, &c. differences of these be taken (as for the preceding series of squares); the mth differences will all be equal to each other. So that, in order to reproduce the series of values of the polynomial by means of a machine analogous to the one above described, it is sufficient that there be $(m + 1)$ dials, having the mutual relations we have indicated. As the differences may be either positive or negative, the machine will have a contrivance for either advancing or retrograding each needle, according as the number to be algebraically added may have the sign *plus* or *minus*.

If from a polynomial we pass to a series having an infinite number of terms, arranged according to the ascending powers of the variable, it would at first appear, that in order to apply the machine to the calculation of the function represented by such a series, the mechanism must include an infinite number of dials, which would in fact render the thing impossible. But in many cases the difficulty will disappear, if we observe that for a great number of functions the series which represent them may be rendered convergent; so that, according to the degree of approximation desired, we may limit ourselves to the calculation of a certain number of terms of the series, neglecting the rest. By this method the question is reduced to the primitive case of a finite polynomial. It is thus that we can calculate the succession of the logarithms of numbers. But since, in this particular instance, the terms which had been originally neglected receive increments in a ratio so continually increasing for equal increments of the variable, that the degree of approximation required would ultimately be affected, it is necessary, at certain intervals, to calculate the value of the function by different methods, and then respectively to use the results thus obtained, as data whence to deduce, by means of the machine, the other intermediate values. We see that the machine here performs the office of the third section of calculators mentioned in describing the tables computed by order of the French government, and that the end originally proposed is thus fulfilled by it.

Such is the nature of the first machine which Mr. Babbage conceived. We see that its use is confined to cases where the numbers required are such as can be obtained by means of simple additions or subtractions; that the machine is, so to speak, merely the expression of one[3] particular theorem of analysis; and that, in short, its operations cannot be extended so as to embrace the solution of an infinity of other questions included within the domain of mathematical analysis. It was while contemplating the vast field which yet remained to be traversed, that Mr. Babbage, renouncing his original essays, conceived the plan of another system of mechanism whose operations should themselves possess all the generality of algebraical notation, and which, on this account, he denominates the *Analytical Engine*.

Having now explained the state of the question, it is time for me to develop the principle on which is based the construction of this latter machine. When analysis is employed for the solution of any problem, there are usually two classes of operations to execute: firstly, the numerical calculation of the various coefficients; and secondly, their distribution in relation to the quantities affected by them. If, for example, we have to obtain the product of two binomials $(a+bx)$ $(m+nx)$, the result will be represented by $am + (an + bm) x + bnx^2$, in which expression we must first calculate am, an, bm, bn; then take the sum of $an + bm$; and lastly, respectively distribute the coefficients thus obtained amongst the powers of the variable. In order to reproduce these operations by means of a machine, the latter must therefore possess two distinct sets of powers: first, that of executing numerical calculations; secondly, that of rightly distributing the values so obtained.

But if human intervention were necessary for directing each of these partial operations, nothing would be gained under the heads of correctness and economy of time; the machine must therefore have the additional requisite of executing by itself all the successive operations required for the solution of a problem proposed to it, when once the *primitive numerical data* for this same problem have been introduced. Therefore, since, from the moment that the nature of the calculation to be executed or of the problem to be resolved have been indicated to it, the machine is, by its own intrinsic power, of itself to go through all the intermediate operations which lead to the proposed result, it must exclude all methods of trial and guess-work, and can only admit the direct processes of calculation.[4]

It is necessarily thus; for the machine is not a thinking being, but simply an automaton which acts according to the laws imposed upon it. This being fundamental, one of the earliest researches its author had to undertake, was that of finding means for effecting the division of one number by another without using the method of guessing indicated by the usual rules of arithmetic. The difficulties of effecting this combination were far from being among the least; but upon it depended the success of every other. Under the impossibility of my here explaining the process through which this end is attained, we must limit ourselves to admitting that the first four operations of arithmetic, that is addition, subtraction, multiplication and division, can be performed in a direct manner through the intervention of the machine. This granted, the machine is thence capable of performing every species of numerical calculation, for all such calculations ultimately resolve themselves into the four operations we have just named. To conceive how the machine can now go through its functions according to the laws laid down, we will begin by giving an idea of the manner in which it materially represents numbers.

Let us conceive a pile or vertical column consisting of an indefinite number of circular discs, all pierced through their centres by a common axis, around which each of them can take an independent rotatory movement. If round the edge of each of these discs are written the ten figures which constitute our numerical alphabet, we may then, by arranging a series of these figures in the same vertical line, express in this manner any number whatever. It is sufficient for this purpose that the first disc represent units, the second tens, the third hundreds, and so on. When two numbers have been thus written on two distinct columns, we may propose to combine them arithmetically with each other, and to obtain the result on a third column. In general, if we have a series of columns[5] consisting of discs, which columns we will designate as V_0, V_1, V_2, V_3, V_4, &c., we may require, for instance, to divide the number written on the column V_1 by that on the column V_4, and to obtain the result on the column V_7. To effect this operation, we must impart to the machine two distinct arrangements; through the first it is prepared for executing *a division*, and through the second the columns it is to operate on are indicated to it, and also the column on which the result is to be represented. If this division is to be followed, for example, by the addition of two numbers taken on other columns, the two original arrangements of the machine must be simultaneously altered. If, on the contrary, a series of operations of the same nature is to be gone through, then the first of the original arrangements will remain, and the second alone must be altered. Therefore, the arrangements that may be communicated to the various parts of the machine may be distinguished into two principal classes:

First, that relative to the *Operations*.

Secondly, that relative to the *Variables*.

By this latter we mean that which indicates the columns to be operated on. As for the operations themselves, they are executed by a special apparatus, which is designated by the name of *mill*, and which itself contains a certain number of columns, similar to those of the Variables. When two numbers are to be combined together, the machine commences by effacing them from the columns where they are written, that is, it places *zero*[6] on every disc of the two vertical lines on which the numbers were represented; and it transfers the numbers to the mill. There, the apparatus having been disposed suitably for the required operation, this latter is effected, and, when completed, the result itself is transferred to the column of Variables which shall have been indicated. Thus the mill is that portion of the machine which works, and the columns of Variables constitute that where the results are represented and arranged. After the preceding explanations, we may perceive that all fractional and irrational results will be represented in decimal fractions. Supposing each column to have forty discs, this extension will be sufficient for all degrees of approximation generally required.

It will now be inquired how the machine can of itself, and without having recourse to the hand of man, assume the successive dispositions suited to the operations. The solution of this problem has been taken from Jacquard's apparatus,[7] used for the manufacture of brocaded stuffs, in the following manner:—

Two species of threads are usually distinguished in woven stuffs; one is the *warp* or longitudinal thread, the other the *woof* or transverse thread, which is conveyed by the instrument called the shuttle, and which crosses the longitudinal thread or warp. When a brocaded stuff is required, it is necessary in turn to prevent certain threads from crossing the woof, and this according to a succession which is determined by the nature of the design that is to be reproduced. Formerly this process was lengthy and difficult, and it was requisite that the workman, by attending to the design which he was to copy, should himself regulate the movements the threads were to take. Thence arose the high price of this description of stuffs, especially if threads of various colours entered into the fabric. To simplify this manufacture, Jacquard devised the plan of connecting each group of threads that were to act together, with a distinct lever belonging exclusively to that group. All these levers terminate in rods, which are united together in one bundle, having usually the form of a parallelopiped with a rectangular base. The rods are cylindrical, and are separated from each other by small intervals. The process of raising the threads is thus resolved into that of moving these various lever-arms in the requisite order. To effect this, a rectangular sheet of pasteboard is taken, somewhat larger in size than a section of the bundle of lever-arms. If this sheet be applied to the base of the bundle, and an advancing motion be then communicated to the pasteboard, this latter will move with it all the rods of the bundle, and consequently the threads that are connected with each of them. But if the pasteboard, instead of being plain, were pierced with holes corresponding to the extremities of the levers which meet it, then, since each of the levers would pass through the pasteboard during the motion of the latter, they would all remain in their places. We thus see that it is easy so to determine the position of the holes in the pasteboard, that, at any given moment, there shall be a certain number of levers, and consequently of parcels of threads, raised, while the rest remain where they were. Supposing this process is successively repeated according to a law indicated by the pattern to be executed, we perceive that this pattern may be reproduced on the stuff. For this purpose we need merely compose a series of cards according to the law required, and arrange them in suitable order one after the other; then, by causing them to pass over a polygonal beam which is so connected as to turn a new face for every stroke of the shuttle, which face shall then be impelled parallelly to itself against the bundle of lever-arms, the operation of raising the threads will be regularly performed. Thus we see that brocaded tissues may be manufactured with a precision and rapidity formerly difficult to obtain.

Arrangements analogous to those just described have been introduced into the Analytical Engine. It contains two principal species of cards: first, Operation cards, by means of which the parts of the machine are so disposed as to execute any determinate series of operations, such as additions, subtractions, multiplications, and divisions; secondly, cards of the Variables, which indicate to the machine the columns on which the results are to be represented. The cards, when put in motion, successively arrange the various portions of the machine according to the nature of the processes that are to be effected, and the machine at the same time executes these processes by means of the various pieces of mechanism of which it is constituted.

In order more perfectly to conceive the thing, let us select as an example the resolution of two equations of the first degree with two unknown quantities. Let the following be the two equations, in which x and y are the unknown quantities:—

$$\begin{cases} mx + ny = d \\ m'x + n'y = d' \end{cases}$$

We deduce $x = \dfrac{dn' - d'n}{n'm - nm'}$, and for y an analogous expression. Let us continue to represent by V_0, V_1, V_2, &c. the different columns which contain the numbers, and let us suppose that the first eight columns have been chosen for expressing on them the numbers represented by m, n, d, m', n', d', n and n', which implies that $V_0 = m$, $V_1 = n$, $V_2 = d$, $V_3 = m'$, $V_4 = n'$, $V_5 = d'$, $V_6 = n$, $V_7 = n'$.

The series of operations commanded by the cards, and the results obtained, may be represented in the following table:—

Number of the operations	Operation-cards	Cards of the variables		Progress of the operations
	Symbols indicating the nature of the operations	Columns on which operations are to be performed	Columns which receive results of operations	
1	$\times$	$V_2 \times V_4 =$	V_8	$= dn'$
2	$\times$	$V_5 \times V_1 =$	V_9	$= d'n$
3	$\times$	$V_4 \times V_0 =$	V_{10}	$= n'm$
4	$\times$	$V_1 \times V_3 =$	V_{11}	$= nm'$
5	$-$	$V_8 - V_9 =$	V_{12}	$= dn' - d'n$
6	$-$	$V_{10} - V_{11} =$	V_{13}	$= n'm - nm'$
7	$\div$	$\dfrac{V_{12}}{V_{13}}$	V_{14}	$= x = \dfrac{dn' - d'n}{n'm - nm'}$

Since the cards do nothing but indicate in what manner and on what columns the machine shall act, it is clear that we must still, in every particular case, introduce the numerical data for the calculation. Thus, in the example we have selected, we must previously inscribe the numerical values of m, n, d, m', n', d', in the order and on the columns indicated, after which the machine when put in action will give the value of the unknown quantity x for this particular case. To obtain the value of y, another series of operations analogous to the preceding must be performed. But we see that they will be only four in number, since the denominator of the expression for y, excepting the sign, is the same as that for x, and equal to $n'm-nm'$. In the preceding table it will be remarked that the column for operations indicates four successive *multiplications*, two *subtractions*, and one *division*. Therefore, if desired, we need only use three operation-cards; to manage which, it is sufficient to introduce into the machine an apparatus which shall, after the first multiplication, for instance, retain the card which relates to this operation, and not allow it to advance so as to be replaced by another one, until after this same operation shall have been four times repeated. In the preceding example we have seen, that to find the value of x we must begin by writing the coefficients m, n, d, m', n', d', upon eight columns, thus repeating n and n' twice. According to the same method, if it were required to calculate y likewise, these coefficients must be written on twelve different columns. But it is possible to simplify this process, and thus to diminish the chances of errors, which chances are greater, the larger the number of the quantities that have to be inscribed previous to setting the machine in action. To understand this simplification, we must remember that every number written on a column must, in order to be arithmetically combined with another number, be effaced from the column on which it is, and transferred to the *mill*. Thus, in the example we have discussed, we will take the two coefficients m and n', which are each of them to enter into *two* different products, that is m into mn' and md', n' into mn' and $n'd$. These coefficients will be inscribed on the columns V_0 and V_4. If we commence the series of operations by the product of m into n', these numbers will be effaced from the columns V_0 and V_4, that they may be transferred to the mill, which will multiply them into each other, and will then command the machine to represent the result, say on the column V_6. But as these numbers are each to be used again in another operation, they must again be inscribed somewhere; therefore, while the mill is working out their product, the machine will inscribe them anew on any two columns that may be indicated to it through the cards; and as, in the actual case, there is no reason why they should not resume their former places, we will suppose them again inscribed on V_0 and V_4, whence in short they would not finally disappear, to be reproduced no more, until they should have gone through all the combinations in which they might have to be used.

We see, then, that the whole assemblage of operations requisite for resolving the two[8] above equations of the first degree may be definitely represented in the following table:—

Columns on which are inscribed the primitive data	Number of the operations	Cards of the operations		Variable cards				Statement of results
		Number of the operation cards	Nature of each operation	Columns acted on by each operation	Columns that receive the result of each operation	Indication of change of value on any column		
$^1V_0 = m$	1	1	×	$^1V_0 \times {}^1V_4$	$^1V_6$	$\left\{\begin{array}{ccc}{}^1V_0 &=& {}^1V_0 \\ {}^1V_4 &=& {}^1V_4\end{array}\right\}$		$^1V_6 = mn'$
$^1V_1 = n$	2	"	×	$^1V_3 \times {}^1V_1$	$^1V_7$	$\left\{\begin{array}{ccc}{}^1V_3 &=& {}^1V_3 \\ {}^1V_1 &=& {}^1V_1\end{array}\right\}$		$^1V_7 = m'n$
$^1V_2 = d$	3	"	×	$^1V_2 \times {}^1V_4$	$^1V_8$	$\left\{\begin{array}{ccc}{}^1V_2 &=& {}^1V_2 \\ {}^1V_4 &=& {}^0V_4\end{array}\right\}$		$^1V_8 = dn'$
$^1V_3 = m'$	4	"	×	$^1V_5 \times {}^1V_1$	$^1V_9$	$\left\{\begin{array}{ccc}{}^1V_5 &=& {}^1V_5 \\ {}^1V_1 &=& {}^0V_1\end{array}\right\}$		$^1V_9 = d'n$
$^1V_4 = n'$	5	"	×	$^1V_0 \times {}^1V_5$	$^1V_{10}$	$\left\{\begin{array}{ccc}{}^1V_0 &=& {}^0V_0 \\ {}^1V_5 &=& {}^0V_1\end{array}\right\}$		$^1V_{10} = d'm$
$^1V_5 = d'$	6	"	×	$^1V_2 \times {}^1V_3$	$^1V_{11}$	$\left\{\begin{array}{ccc}{}^1V_2 &=& {}^0V_2 \\ {}^1V_3 &=& {}^0V_3\end{array}\right\}$		$^1V_{11} = dm'$
	7	2	−	$^1V_6 \times {}^1V_7$	$^1V_{12}$	$\left\{\begin{array}{ccc}{}^1V_6 &=& {}^0V_6 \\ {}^1V_7 &=& {}^0V_7\end{array}\right\}$		$^1V_{12} = mn' - m'n$
	8	"	−	$^1V_8 \times {}^1V_9$	$^1V_{13}$	$\left\{\begin{array}{ccc}{}^1V_8 &=& {}^0V_8 \\ {}^1V_9 &=& {}^0V_9\end{array}\right\}$		$^1V_{13} = dn' - d'n$
	9	"	−	$^1V_{10} \times {}^1V_{11}$	$^1V_{14}$	$\left\{\begin{array}{ccc}{}^1V_{10} &=& {}^0V_{10} \\ {}^1V_{11} &=& {}^0V_{11}\end{array}\right\}$		$^1V_{14} = d'm - dm'$

1	2	3	4	5	6	7	8
	10	3	÷	$^1V_{13} \times {}^1V_{12}$	$^1V_{15}$	$\left.\begin{array}{l} {}^1V_{13} = {}^0V_{13} \\ {}^1V_{12} = {}^0V_{12} \end{array}\right\}$	$^1V_{15} = \dfrac{dn' - d'n}{mn' - m'n} = x$
	11	"	÷	$^1V_{14} \times {}^1V_{12}$	$^1V_{16}$	$\begin{array}{l} {}^1V_{14} = {}^0V_{14} \\ {}^1V_{12} = {}^0V_{12} \end{array}$	$^1V_{16} = \dfrac{d'm - dm'}{mn' - m'n} = y$
1	2	3	4	5	6	7	8

In order to diminish to the utmost the chances of error in inscribing the numerical data of the problem, they are successively placed on one of the columns of the mill; then, by means of cards arranged for this purpose, these same numbers are caused to arrange themselves on the requisite columns, without the operator having to give his attention to it; so that his undivided mind may be applied to the simple inscription of these same numbers.

According to what has now been explained, we see that the collection of columns of Variables may be regarded as a *store* of numbers, accumulated there by the mill, and which, obeying the orders transmitted to the machine by means of the cards, pass alternately from the mill to the store and from the store to the mill, that they may undergo the transformations demanded by the nature of the calculation to be performed.

Hitherto no mention has been made of the *signs* in the results, and the machine would be far from perfect were it incapable of expressing and combining amongst each other positive and negative quantities. To accomplish this end, there is, above every column, both of the mill and of the store, a disc, similar to the discs of which the columns themselves consist. According as the digit on this disc is even or uneven, the number inscribed on the corresponding column below it will be considered as positive or negative. This granted, we may, in the following manner, conceive how the signs can be algebraically combined in the machine. When a number is to be transferred from the store to the mill, and *vice versâ*, it will always be transferred with its sign, which will effected by means of the cards, as has been explained in what precedes. Let any two numbers then, on which we are to operate arithmetically, be placed in the mill with their respective signs. Suppose that we are first to add them together; the operation-cards will command the addition: if the two numbers be of the same sign, one of the two will be entirely effaced from where it was inscribed, and will go to add itself on the column which contains the other number; the machine will, during this operation, be able, by means of a certain apparatus, to prevent any movement in the disc of signs which belongs to the column on which the addition is made, and thus the result will remain with the sign which the two given numbers originally had. When two numbers have two different signs, the addition commanded by the card will be changed into a subtraction through the intervention of mechanisms which are brought into play by this very difference of sign. Since the subtraction can only be effected on the larger of the two numbers, it must be arranged that the disc of signs of the larger number shall not move while the smaller of the two numbers is being effaced from its column and subtracted from the other, whence the result will have the sign of this latter, just as in fact it ought to be. The combinations to which algebraical subtraction give rise, are analogous to the preceding. Let us pass on to multiplication. When two numbers to be multiplied are of the same sign, the result is positive; if the signs are different, the product must be negative. In order that the machine may act conformably to this law, we have but to conceive that on the column containing the product of the two given numbers, the digit which indicates the sign of that product has been formed by the mutual addition of the two digits that respectively indicated the signs of the two given numbers; it is then obvious that if the digits of the signs are both even, or both odd, their sum will be an even number, and consequently will express a positive number; but that if, on the contrary, the two digits of the signs are one even and the other odd, their sum will be an odd number, and will consequently express a negative number. In the case of division. instead of adding the digits of the discs, they must be subtracted one from the other, which will produce results analogous to the preceding; that is to say, that if these figures are both even or both uneven, the remainder of this subtraction will be even; and it will be uneven in the contrary case. When I speak of mutually adding or subtracting the numbers expressed by the digits of the signs, I merely mean that one of the sign-discs is made to advance or retrograde a number of divisions equal to that which is expressed by the digit on the other sign-disc. We see, then, from the preceding explanation, that it is possible mechanically to combine the signs of quantities so as to obtain results conformable to those indicated by algebra.[9]

The machine is not only capable of executing those numerical calculations which depend on a given algebraical formula, but it is also fitted for analytical calculations in which there are one or several variables to be considered. It must be assumed that the analytical expression to be operated on can be developed according to powers of the variable, or according to determinate functions of this same variable, such as circular functions, for instance; and similarly for the result that is to be attained. If we then suppose that above the columns of the store, we have inscribed the powers or the functions of the variable, arranged according to whatever is the prescribed law of development, the coefficients of these several terms may be respectively placed on the corresponding column below each. In this manner we shall have a representation of an analytical development; and, supposing the position of the several terms composing it to be invariable, the problem will be reduced to that of calculating their coefficients according to the laws demanded by the nature of the question. In order to make this more clear, we shall take the following[10] very simple example, in which we are to multiply $(a + bx^1)$ by $(A + B \cos^1 x)$. We shall begin by writing x^0, x^1, $\cos^0 x$, $\cos^1 x$, above the columns V_0, V_1, V_2, V_3; then since, from the form of the two functions to be combined, the terms which are to compose the products will be of the following nature, $x^0.\cos^0 x$, $x^0.\cos^1 x$, $x^1.\cos^0 x$, $x^1.\cos^1 x$, these will be inscribed above the columns V_4, V_5, V_6, V_7. The coefficients of x^0, x^1, $\cos^0 x$, $\cos^1 x$ being given, they will, by means of the mill, be passed to the columns V_0, V_1, V_2 and V_3. Such are the primitive data of the problem. It is now the business of the machine to work out its solution, that is, to find the coefficients which are to be inscribed on V_4, V_5, V_6, V_7. To attain this object, the law of formation of these same coefficients being known, the machine will act through the intervention of the cards, in the manner indicated by the following table:—[11]

Columns above which are written the functions of the variable	Coefficients		Cards of the operations		Cards of the variables			
	Given	To be formed	Number of the operations	Nature of the operations	Columns on which operations are to be performed	Columns on which are to be inscribed the results of the operations	Indication of change of value on any column submitted to an operation	Results of the operations
$x^{01}V_0$	a	"	"	"	"	"	"	"
$x^{11}V_1$	b	"	"	"	"	"	"	"
$\cos^0 x^1 V_2$	A	"	"	"	"	"	"	"

$\text{Cos}^1x^1V_3$	B	"	"	"	"	"	"	"
$x^0\text{cos}^0x^0V_4$	...	aA	1	×	$^1V_0 \times {}^1V_2$	$^1V_4$	$\left\{\begin{array}{l}{}^1V_0 = {}^1V_0 \\ {}^1V_2 = {}^1V_2\end{array}\right\}$	$^1V_4 = aA$ coefficients of $x^0\text{cos}^0x$
$x^0\text{cos}^1x^0V_5$	...	aB	2	×	$^1V_0 \times {}^1V_3$	$^1V_5$	$\left\{\begin{array}{l}{}^1V_0 = {}^0V_0 \\ {}^1V_3 = {}^1V_3\end{array}\right\}$	$^1V_5 = aB$ coefficients of $x^0\text{cos}^1x$
$x^1\text{cos}^0x^0V_6$	...	bA	3	×	$^1V_1 \times {}^1V_2$	$^1V_6$	$\left\{\begin{array}{l}{}^1V_1 = {}^0V_1 \\ {}^1V_2 = {}^0V_2\end{array}\right\}$	$^1V_6 = bA$ coefficients of $x^1\text{cos}^0x$
$x^1\text{cos}^1x^0V_7$	...	bB	4	×	$^1V_1 \times {}^1V_3$	$^1V_7$	$\left\{\begin{array}{l}{}^1V_1 = {}^0V_1 \\ {}^1V_3 = {}^0V_3\end{array}\right\}$	$^1V_7 = bB$ coefficients of $x^1\text{cos}^1x$

It will now be perceived that a general application may be made of the principle developed in the preceding example, to every species of process which it may be proposed to effect on series submitted to calculation. It is sufficient that the law of formation of the coefficients be known, and that this law be inscribed on the cards of the machine, which will then of itself execute all the calculations requisite for arriving at the proposed result. If, for instance, a recurring series were proposed, the law of formation of the coefficients being here uniform, the same operations which must be performed for one of them will be repeated for all the others; there will merely be a change in the locality of the operation, that is, it will be performed with different columns. Generally, since every analytical expression is susceptible of being expressed in a series ordered according to certain functions of the variable, we perceive that the machine will include all analytical calculations which can be definitively reduced to the formation of coefficients according to certain laws, and to the distribution of these with respect to the variables.

We may deduce the following important consequence from these explanations, viz. that since the cards only indicate the nature of the operations to be performed, and the columns of Variables with which they are to be executed, these cards will themselves possess all the generality of analysis, of which they are in fact merely a translation. We shall now further examine some of the difficulties which the machine must surmount, if its assimilation to analysis is to be complete. There are certain functions which necessarily change in nature when they pass through zero or infinity, or whose values cannot be admitted when they pass these limits. When such cases present themselves, the machine is able, by means of a bell, to give notice that the passage through zero or infinity is taking place, and it then stops until the attendant has again set it in action for whatever process it may next be desired that it shall perform. If this process has been foreseen, then the machine, instead of ringing, will so dispose itself as to present the new cards which have relation to the operation that is to succeed the passage through zero and infinity. These new cards may follow the first, but may only come into play contingently upon one or other of the two circumstances just mentioned taking place.

Let us consider a term of the form ab^n; since the cards are but a translation of the analytical formula, their number in this particular case must be the same, whatever be the value of n; that is to say, whatever be the number of multiplications required for elevating b to the nth power (we are supposing for the moment that n is a whole number). Now, since the exponent n indicates that b is to be multiplied n times by itself, and all these operations are of the same nature, it will be sufficient to employ one single operation-card, viz. that which orders the multiplication.

But when n is given for the particular case to be calculated, it will be further requisite that the machine limit the number of its multiplications according to the given values. The process may be thus arranged. The three numbers a, b and n will be written on as many distinct columns of the store; we shall designate them V_0, V_1, V_2; the result ab^n will place itself on the column V_3. When the number n has been introduced into the machine, a card will order a certain registering-apparatus to mark $(n-1)$, and will at the same time execute the multiplication of b by b. When this is completed, it will be found that the registering-apparatus has effaced a unit, and that it only marks $(n-2)$; while the machine will now again order the number b written on the column V_1 to multiply itself with the product b^2 written on the column V_3, which will give b^3. Another unit is then effaced from the registering-apparatus, and the same processes are continually repeated until it only marks zero. Thus the number b^n will be found inscribed on V_3, when the machine, pursuing its course of operations, will order the product of b^n by a; and the required calculation will have been completed without there being any necessity that the number of operation-cards used should vary with the value of n. If n were negative, the cards, instead of ordering the multiplication of a by b^n, would order its division; this we can easily conceive, since every number, being inscribed with its respective sign, is consequently capable of reacting on the nature of the operations to be executed. Finally, if n were fractional, of the form p/q, an additional column would be used for the inscription of q, and the machine would bring into action two sets of processes, one for raising b to the power p, the other for extracting the qth root of the number so obtained.

Again, it may be required, for example, to multiply an expression of the form $ax^m + bx^n$ by another $Ax^p + Bx^q$, and then to reduce the product to the least number of terms, if any of the indices are equal. The two factors being ordered with respect to x, the general result of the multiplication would be $Aax^{m+p} + Abx^{n+p} + Bax^{m+q} + Bbx^{n+q}$. Up to this point the process pre-

sents no difficulties; but suppose that we have $m = p$ and $n = q$, and that we wish to reduce the two middle terms to a single one $(Ab + Ba)x^{m+q}$. For this purpose, the cards may order $m + q$ and $n + p$ to be transferred into the mill, and there subtracted one from the other; if the remainder is nothing, as would be the case on the present hypothesis, the mill will order other cards to bring to it the coefficients Ab and Ba, that it may add them together and give them in this state as a coefficient for the single term $x^{n+p} = x^{m+q}$.

This example illustrates how the cards are able to reproduce all the operations which intellect performs in order to attain a determinate result, if these operations are themselves capable of being precisely defined.

Let us now examine the following expression:—

$$2 \cdot \frac{2^2 \cdot 4^2 \cdot 6^2 \cdot 8^2 \cdot 10^2 \ldots (2n)^2}{1^2 \cdot 3^2 \cdot 5^2 \cdot 7^2 \cdot 9^2 \ldots (2n-1)^2 \cdot (2n+1)^2}$$

which we know becomes equal to the ratio of the circumference to the diameter, when n is infinite. We may require the machine not only to perform the calculation of this fractional expression, but further to give indication as soon as the value becomes identical with that of the ratio of the circumference to the diameter when n is infinite, a case in which the computation would be impossible. Observe that we should thus require of the machine to interpret a result not of itself evident, and that this is not amongst its attributes, since it is no thinking being. Nevertheless, when the cos of $n = \infty$ has been foreseen, a card may immediately order the substitution of the value of π (π being the ratio of the circumference to the diameter), without going through the series of calculations indicated. This would merely require that the machine contain a special card, whose office it should be to place the number π in a direct and independent manner on the column indicated to it. And here we should introduce the mention of a third species of cards, which may be called *cards of numbers*. There are certain numbers, such as those expressing the ratio of the circumference to the diameter, the Numbers of Bernoulli, &c., which frequently present themselves in calculations. To avoid the necessity for computing them every time they have to be used, certain cards may be combined specially in order to give these numbers ready made into the mill, whence they afterwards go and place themselves on those columns of the store that are destined for them. Through this means the machine will be susceptible of those simplifications afforded by the use of numerical tables. It would be equally possible to introduce, by means of these cards, the logarithms of numbers; but perhaps it might not be in this case either the shortest or the most appropriate method; for the machine might be able to perform the same calculations by other more expeditious combinations, founded on the rapidity with which it executes the first four operations of arithmetic. To give an idea of this rapidity, we need only mention that Mr. Babbage believes he can, by his engine, form the product of two numbers, each containing twenty figures, in *three minutes.*

Perhaps the immense number of cards required for the solution of any rather complicated problem may appear to be an obstacle; but this does not seem to be the case. There is no limit to the number of cards that can be used. Certain stuffs require for their fabrication not less than *twenty thousand* cards, and we may unquestionably far exceed even this quantity.[12]

Resuming what we have explained concerning the Analytical Engine, we may conclude that it is based on two principles: the first consisting in the fact that every arithmetical calculation ultimately depends on four principal operations—addition, subtraction, multiplication, and division; the second, in the possibility of reducing every analytical calculation to that of the coefficients for the several terms of a series. If this last principle be true, all the operations of analysis come within the domain of the engine. To take another point of view: the use of the cards offers a generality equal to that of algebraical formulæ, since such a formula simply indicates the nature and order of the operations requisite for arriving at a certain definite result, and similarly the cards merely command the engine to perform these same operations; but in order that the mechanisms may be able to act to any purpose, the numerical data of the problem must in every particular case be introduced. Thus the same

series of cards will serve for all questions whose sameness of nature is such as to require nothing altered excepting the numerical data. In this light the cards are merely a translation of algebraical formulæ, or, to express it better, another form of analytical notation.

Since the engine has a mode of acting peculiar to itself, it will in every particular case be necessary to arrange the series of calculations conformably to the means which the machine possesses; for such or such a process which might be very easy for a calculator may be long and complicated for the engine, and *vice versâ.*

Considered under the most general point of view, the essential object of the machine being to calculate, according to the laws dictated to it, the values of numerical coefficients which it is then to distribute appropriately on the columns which represent the variables, it follows that the interpretation of formulæ and of results is beyond its province, unless indeed this very interpretation be itself susceptible of expression by means of the symbols which the machine employs. Thus, although it is not itself the being that reflects, it may yet be considered as the being which executes the conceptions of intelligence.[13] The cards receive the impress of these conceptions, and transmit to the various trains of mechanism composing the engine the orders necessary for their action. When once the engine shall have been constructed, the difficulty will be reduced to the making out of the cards; but as these are merely the translation of algebraical formulæ, it will, by means of some simple notations, be easy to consign the execution of them to a workman. Thus the whole intellectual labour will be limited to the preparation of the formulæ, which must be adapted for calculation by the engine.

Now, admitting that such an engine can be constructed, it may be inquired: what will be its utility? To recapitulate; it will afford the following advantages:— First, rigid accuracy. We know that numerical calculations are generally the stumbling-block to the solution of problems, since errors easily creep into them, and it is by no means always easy to detect these errors. Now the engine, by the very nature of its mode of acting, which requires no human intervention during the course of its operations, presents every species of security under the head of correctness: besides, it carries with it its own check; for at the end of every operation it prints off, not only the results, but likewise the numerical data of the question; so that it is easy to verify whether the question has been correctly proposed. Secondly, economy of time: to convince ourselves of this, we need only recollect that the multiplication of two numbers, consisting each of twenty figures, requires at the very utmost three minutes. Likewise, when a long series of identical computations is to be performed, such as those required for the formation of numerical tables, the machine can be brought into play so as to give several results at the same time, which will greatly abridge the whole amount of the processes. Thirdly, economy of intelligence: a simple arithmetical computation requires to be performed by a person possessing some capacity; and when we pass to more complicated calculations, and wish to use algebraical formulæ in particular cases, knowledge must be possessed which presupposes preliminary mathematical studies of some extent. Now the engine, from its capability of performing by itself all these purely material operations, spares intellectual labour, which may be more profitably employed. Thus the engine may be considered as a real manufactory of figures, which will lend its aid to those many useful sciences and arts that depend on numbers. Again, who can foresee the consequences of such an invention? In truth, how many precious observations remain practically barren for the progress of the sciences, because there are not powers sufficient for computing the results! And what discouragement does the perspective of a long and arid computation cast into the mind of a man of genius, who demands time exclusively for meditation, and who beholds it snatched from him by the material routine of operations! Yet it is by the laborious route of analysis that he must reach truth; but he cannot pursue this unless guided by numbers; for without numbers it is not given us to raise the veil which envelopes the mysteries of nature. Thus the idea of constructing an apparatus capable of aiding human weakness in such researches, is a conception which, being realized, would mark a glorious epoch in the history of the sciences. The plans have been arranged for all the various parts, and for all the wheel-work, which compose this immense apparatus, and their action studied; but these have not yet been fully combined together in the drawings[14] and mechanical notation.[15] The confidence which the genius of Mr. Babbage must inspire, affords legitimate ground for hope that this enterprise will be crowned with success; and while we render homage to the intelligence which directs it, let us breathe aspirations for the accomplishment of such an undertaking.

NOTES BY THE TRANSLATOR

Note A

The particular function whose integral the Difference Engine was constructed to tabulate, is

$$\Delta^7 u_z = 0$$

The purpose which that engine has been specially intended and adapted to fulfil, is the computation of nautical and astronomical tables. The integral of

$$\Delta^7 u_z = 0$$

being

$$u_z = a + bx + cx^2 + dx^3 + ex^4 + fx^5 + gx^6,$$

the constants a, b, c, &c. are represented on the seven columns of discs, of which the engine consists. It can therefore tabulate *accurately* and to an *unlimited extent*, all series whose general term is comprised in the above formula; and it can also tabulate *approximatively* between *intervals of greater or less extent*, all other series which are capable of tabulation by the Method of Differences.

The Analytical Engine, on the contrary, is not merely adapted for *tabulating* the results of one particular function and of no other, but for *developing and tabulating* any function whatever. In fact the engine may be described as being the material expression of any indefinite function of any degree of generality and complexity, such as for instance,

$F(x, y, z, \log x, \sin y, x^p, \&c.),$

which is, it will be observed, a function of all other possible functions of any number of quantities.

In this, which we may call the *neutral* or *zero* state of the engine, it is ready to receive at any moment, by means of cards constituting a portion of its mechanism (and applied on the principle of those used in the Jacquard-loom), the impress of whatever *special* function we may desire to develope or to tabulate. These cards contain within themselves (in a manner explained in the Memoir itself) the law of development of the particular function that may be under consideration, and they compel the mechanism to act accordingly in a certain corresponding order. One of the simplest cases would be for example, to suppose that

$F(x, y, z, \&c. \&c.)$

is the particular function

$\Delta^n u_z = 0$

which the Difference Engine tabulates for values of n only up to 7. In this case the cards would order the mechanism to go through that succession of operations which would tabulate

$u_z = a + bx + cx^2 + \ldots + mx^{n-1}$

where n might be any number whatever.

These cards, however, have nothing to do with the regulation of the particular *numerical* data. They merely determine the *operations*[16] to be effected, which operations may of course be performed on an infinite variety of particular numerical values, and do not bring out any definite numerical results unless the numerical data of the problem have been impressed on the requisite portions of the train of mechanism. In the above example, the first essential step towards an arithmetical result would be the substitution of specific numbers for n, and for the other primitive quantities which enter into the function.

Again, let us suppose that for F we put two complete equations of the fourth degree between x and y. We must then express on the cards the law of elimination for such equations. The engine would follow out those laws, and would ultimately give the equation of one variable which results from such elimination. Various *modes* of elimination might be selected; and of course the cards must be made out accordingly. The following is one mode that might be adopted. The engine is able to multiply together any two functions of the form

$a + bx + cx^2 + \ldots + px^n.$

This granted, the two equations may be arranged according to the powers of y, and the coefficients of the powers of y may be arranged according to powers of x. The elimination of y will result from the successive multiplications and subtractions of several such functions. In this, and in all other instances, as was explained above, the particular *numerical* data and the *numerical* results are determined by means and by portions of the mechanism which act quite independently of those that regulate the *operations*.

In studying the action of the Analytical Engine, we find that the peculiar and independent nature of the considerations which in all mathematical analysis belong to *operations*, as distinguished from *the objects operated upon* and from the *results* of the operations performed upon those objects, is very strikingly defined and separated.

It is well to draw attention to this point, not only because its full appreciation is essential to the attainment of any very just and adequate general comprehension of the powers and mode of action of the Analytical Engine, but also because it is one which is perhaps too little kept in view in the study of mathematical science in general. It is, however, impossible to confound it with other considerations, either when we trace the manner in which that engine attains its results, or when we prepare the data for its attainment of those results. It were much to be desired, that when mathematical processes pass through the human brain instead of through the medium of inanimate mechanism, it were equally a necessity of things that the reasonings connected with *operations* should hold the same just place as a clear and well-defined branch of the subject of analysis, a fundamental but yet independent ingredient in the science, which they must do in studying the engine. The confusion, the difficulties, the contradictions which, in consequence of a want of accurate distinctions in this particular, have up to even a recent period encumbered mathematics in all those branches involving the consideration of negative and impossible quantities, will at once occur to the reader who is at all versed in this science, and would alone suffice to justify dwelling somewhat on the point, in connexion with any subject so peculiarly fitted to give forcible illustration of it as the Analytical Engine. It may be desirable to explain, that by the word *operation*, we mean *any process which alters the mutual relation of two or more things*, be this relation of what kind it may. This is the most general definition, and would include all subjects in the universe. In abstract mathematics, of course operations alter those particular relations which are involved in the considerations of number and space, and the *results* of operations are those peculiar results which correspond to the nature of the subjects of operation. But the science of operations, as derived from mathematics more especially, is a science of itself, and has its own abstract truth and value; just as logic has its own peculiar truth and value, independently of the subjects to which we may apply its reasonings and processes. Those who are accustomed to some of the more modern views of the above subject, will know that a few fundamental relations being true, certain other combinations of relations must of necessity follow; combinations unlimited in variety and extent if the deductions from the primary relations be carried on far enough. They will also be aware that one main reason why the separate nature of the science of operations has been little felt, and in general little dwelt on, is the *shifting* meaning of many of the symbols used in mathematical notation. First, the symbols of *operation* are frequently *also* the symbols of the *results* of operations. We may say that these symbols are apt to have both a *retrospective* and a *prospective* signification. They may signify

either relations that are the consequences of a series of processes already performed, or relations that are yet to be effected through certain processes. Secondly, figures, the symbols of *numerical magnitude*, are frequently *also* the symbols of *operations*, as when they are the indices of powers. Wherever terms have a shifting meaning, independent sets of considerations are liable to become complicated together, and reasonings and results are frequently falsified. Now in the Analytical Engine, the operations which come under the first of the above heads are ordered and combined by means of a notation and of a train of mechanism which belong exclusively to themselves; and with respect to the second head, whenever numbers meaning *operations* and not *quantities* (such as the indices of powers) are inscribed on any column or set of columns, those columns immediately act in a wholly separate and independent manner, becoming connected with the *operating mechanism* exclusively, and re-acting upon this. They never come into combination with numbers upon any other columns meaning *quantities*; though, of course, if there are numbers meaning *operations* upon *n* columns, these may *combine amongst each other*, and will often be required to do so, just as numbers meaning *quantities* combine with each other in any variety. It might have been arranged that all numbers meaning *operations* should have appeared on some separate portion of the engine from that which presents numerical *quantities*; but the present mode is in some cases more simple, and offers in reality quite as much distinctness when understood.

The operating mechanism can even be thrown into action independently of any object to operate upon (although of course no *result* could then be developed). Again, it might act upon other things besides *number*, were objects found whose mutual fundamental relations could be expressed by those of the abstract science of operations, and which should be also susceptible of adaptations to the action of the operating notation and mechanism of the engine. Supposing, for instance, that the fundamental relations of pitched sounds in the science of harmony and of musical composition were susceptible of such expression and adaptations, the engine might compose elaborate and scientific pieces of music of any degree of complexity or extent.

The Analytical Engine is an *embodying of the science of operations*, constructed with peculiar reference to abstract number as the subject of those operations. The Difference Engine is the embodying of *one particular and very limited set of operations*, which (see the notation used in Note B) may be expressed thus (+, +, +, +, +, +), or thus, 6(+). Six repetitions of the one operation, +, is, in fact, the whole sum and object of that engine. It has seven columns, and a number on any column can add itself to a number on the next column to its *right-hand*. So that, beginning with the column furthest to the left, six additions can be effected, and the result appears on the seventh column, which is the last on the right-hand. The *operating* mechanism of this engine acts in as separate and independent a manner as that of the Analytical Engine; but being susceptible of only one unvarying and restricted combination, it has little force or interest in illustration of the distinct nature of the *science of operations*. The importance of regarding the Analytical Engine under this point of view will, we think, become more and more obvious as the reader proceeds with M. Menabrea's clear and masterly article. The calculus of operations is likewise in itself a topic of so much interest, and has of late years been so much more written on and thought on than formerly, that any bearing which that engine, from its mode of constitution, may possess upon the illustration of this branch of mathematical science should not be overlooked. Whether the inventor of this engine had any such views in his mind while working out the invention, or whether he may subsequently ever have regarded it under this phase, we do not know; but it is one that forcibly occurred to ourselves on becoming acquainted with the means through which analytical combinations are actually attained by the mechanism. We cannot forbear suggesting one practical result which it appears to us must be greatly facilitated by the independent manner in which the engine orders and combines its *operations*: we allude to the attainment of those combinations into which *imaginary*

quantities enter. This is a branch of its processes into which we have not had the opportunity of inquiring, and our conjecture therefore as to the principle on which we conceive the accomplishment of such results may have been made to depend, is very probably not in accordance with the fact, and less subservient for the purpose than some other principles, or at least requiring the cooperation of others. It seems to us obvious, however, that where operations are so independent in their mode of acting, it must be easy, by means of a few simple provisions, and additions in arranging the mechanism, to bring out a *double* set of *results*, viz.—1st, the *numerical magnitudes* which are the results of operations performed on *numerical data*. (These results are the *primary* object of the engine.) 2ndly, the *symbolical results* to be attached to those numerical results, which symbolical results are not less the necessary and logical consequences of operations performed upon *symbolical data*, than are numerical results when the data are numerical.[17]

If we compare together the powers and the principles of construction of the Difference and of the Analytical Engines, we shall perceive that the capabilities of the latter are immeasurably more extensive than those of the former, and that they in fact hold to each other the same relationship as that of analysis to arithmetic. The Difference Engine can effect but one particular series of operations, viz. that required for tabulating the integral of the special function

$$\Delta^n u_z = 0$$

and as it can only do this for values of n up to 7,[18] it cannot be considered as being the most *general* expression even of *one particular* function, much less as being the expression of any and all possible functions of all degrees of generality. The Difference Engine can in reality (as has been already partly explained) do nothing but *add*; and any other processes, not excepting those of simple subtraction, multiplication and division, can be performed by it only just to that extent in which it is possible, by judicious mathematical arrangement and artifices, to reduce them to a *series of additions*. The method of differences is, in fact, a method of additions; and as it includes within its means a larger number of results attainable by *addition* simply, than any other mathematical principle, it was very appropriately selected as the basis on which to construct *an Adding Machine*, so as to give to the powers of such a machine the widest possible range. The Analytical Engine, on the contrary, can either add, subtract, multiply or divide with equal facility; and performs each of these four operations in a direct manner, without the aid of any of the other three. This one fact implies everything; and it is scarcely necessary to point out, for instance, that while the Difference Engine can merely *tabulate*, and is incapable of *developing*, the Analytical Engine can either *tabulate or develope*.

The former engine is in its nature strictly *arithmetical*, and the results it can arrive at lie within a very clearly defined and restricted range, while there is no finite line of demarcation which limits the powers of the Analytical Engine. These powers are co-extensive with our knowledge of the laws of analysis itself, and need be bounded only by our acquaintance with the latter. Indeed we may consider the engine as the *material and mechanical representative* of analysis, and that our actual working powers in this department of human study will be enabled more effectually than heretofore to keep pace with our theoretical knowledge of its principles and laws, through the complete control which the engine gives us over the *executive manipulation* of algebraical and numerical symbols.

Those who view mathematical science, not merely as a vast body of abstract and immutable truths, whose intrinsic beauty, symmetry and logical completeness, when regarded in their connexion together as a whole, entitle them to a prominent place in the interest of all profound and logical minds, but as possessing a yet deeper interest for the human race, when it is remembered that this science constitutes the language through which alone we can adequately express the great facts of the natural world, and those unceasing changes of mutual relationship which, visibly or invisibly, consciously or unconsciously to our immediate physical perceptions, are interminably going on in the agencies of the creation we live amidst: those

who thus think on mathematical truth as the instrument through which the weak mind of man can most effectually read his Creator's works, will regard with especial interest all that can tend to facilitate the translation of its principles into explicit practical forms.

The distinctive characteristic of the Analytical Engine, and that which has rendered it possible to endow mechanism with such extensive faculties as bid fair to make this engine the executive right-hand of abstract algebra, is the introduction into it of the principle which Jacquard devised for regulating, by means of punched cards, the most complicated patterns in the fabrication of brocaded stuffs. It is in this that the distinction between the two engines lies. Nothing of the sort exists in the Difference Engine. We may say most aptly, that the Analytical Engine *weaves algebraical patterns* just as the Jacquard-loom weaves flowers and leaves. Here, it seems to us, resides much more of originality than the Difference Engine can be fairly entitled to claim. We do not wish to deny to this latter all such claims. We believe that it is the only proposal or attempt ever made to construct a calculating machine *founded on the principle of successive orders of differences*, and capable of *printing off its own results*; and that this engine surpasses its predecessors, both in the extent of the calculations which it can perform, in the facility, certainty and accuracy with which it can effect them, and in the absence of all necessity for the intervention of human intelligence *during the performance of its calculations*. Its nature is, however, limited to the strictly arithmetical, and it is far from being the first or only scheme for constructing *arithmetical* calculating machines with more or less of success.

The bounds of *arithmetic* were however outstepped the moment the idea of applying the cards had occurred; and the Analytical Engine does not occupy common ground with mere "calculating machines." It holds a position wholly its own; and the considerations it suggests are most interesting in their nature. In enabling mechanism to combine together *general* symbols in successions of unlimited variety and extent, a uniting link is established between the operations of matter and the abstract mental processes of the *most abstract* branch of mathematical science. A new, a vast, and a powerful language is developed for the future use of analysis, in which to wield its truths so that these may become of more speedy and accurate practical application for the purposes of mankind than the means hitherto in our possession have rendered possible. Thus not only the mental and the material, but the theoretical and the practical in the mathematical world, are brought into more intimate and effective connexion with each other. We are not aware of its being on record that anything partaking in the nature of what is so well designated the *Analytical Engine* has been hitherto proposed, or even thought of, as a practical possibility, any more than the idea of a thinking or of a reasoning machine.

We will touch on another point which constitutes an important distinction in the modes of operating of the Difference and Analytical Engines. In order to enable the former to do its business, it is necessary to put into its columns the series of numbers constituting the first terms of the several orders of differences for whatever is the particular table under consideration. The machine then works *upon* these as its data. But these data must themselves have been already computed through a series of calculations by a human head. Therefore that engine can only produce results depending on data which have been arrived at by the explicit and actual working out of processes that are in their nature different from any that come within the sphere of its own powers. In other words, an *analysing* process must have been gone through by a human mind in order to obtain the data upon which the engine then *synthetically* builds its results. The Difference Engine is in its character exclusively *synthetical*, while the Analytical Engine is equally capable of analysis or of synthesis.

It is true that the Difference Engine can calculate to a much greater extent with these few preliminary data, than the data themselves required for their own determination. The table of squares, for instance, can be calculated to any extent whatever, when the numbers *one* and *two* are furnished; and a very few differences computed at any part of a table of logarithms would enable the engine to calculate many hundreds or even thousands of logarithms. Still the circumstance of its

requiring, as a previous condition, that any function whatever shall have been numerically worked out, makes it very inferior in its nature and advantages to an engine which, like the Analytical Engine, requires merely that we should know the *succession and distribution* of the operations to be performed; without there being any occasion,[19] in order to obtain data on which it can work, for our ever having gone through either the same particular operations which it is itself to effect, or others. Numerical data must of course be given it, but they are mere arbitrary ones; not data that could only be arrived at through a systematic and necessary series of previous numerical calculations, which is quite a different thing.

To this it may be replied, that an analysing process must equally have been performed in order to furnish the Analytical Engine with the necessary *operative* data; and that herein may also lie a possible source of error. Granted that the actual mechanism is unerring in its processes, the *cards* may give it wrong orders. This is unquestionably the case; but there is much less chance of error, and likewise far less expenditure of time and labour, where operations only, and the distribution of these operations, have to be made out, than where explicit numerical results are to be attained. In the case of the Analytical Engine we have undoubtedly to lay out a certain capital of analytical labour in one particular line; but this is in order that the engine may bring us in a much larger return in another line. It should be remembered also that the cards, when once made out for any formula, have all the generality of algebra, and include an infinite number of particular cases.

We have dwelt considerably on the distinctive peculiarities of each of these engines, because we think it essential to place their respective attributes in strong relief before the apprehension of the public; and to define with clearness and accuracy the wholly different nature of the principles on which each is based, so as to make it self-evident to the reader (the mathematical reader at least) in what manner and degree the powers of the Analytical Engine transcend those of an engine, which, like the Difference Engine, can only work out such results as may be derived from *one restricted and particular series of processes*, such as those included in $\Delta^n u_z = 0$. We think this of importance, because we know that there exists considerable vagueness and inaccuracy in the mind of persons in general on the subject. There is a misty notion amongst most of those who have attended at all to it, that *two* "calculating machines" have been successively invented by the same person within the last few years; while others again have never heard but of the one original "calculating machine," and are not aware of there being any extension upon this. For either of these two classes of persons the above considerations are appropriate. While the latter require a knowledge of the fact that there *are two* such inventions, the former are not less in want of accurate and well-defined information on the subject. No very clear or correct ideas prevail as to the characteristics of each engine, or their respective advantages or disadvantages; and in meeting with those incidental allusions, of a more or less direct kind, which occur in so many publications of the day, to these machines, it must frequently be matter of doubt *which* "calculating machine" is referred to, or whether *both* are included in the general allusion.

We are desirous likewise of removing two misapprehensions which we know obtain, to some extent, respecting these engines. In the first place it is very generally supposed that the Difference Engine, after it had been completed up to a certain point, *suggested* the idea of the Analytical Engine; and that the second is in fact the improved offspring of the first, and *grew out* of the existence of its predecessor, through some natural or else accidental combination of ideas suggested by this one. Such a supposition is in this instance contrary to the facts; although it seems to be almost an obvious inference, wherever two inventions, similar in their nature and objects, succeed each other closely in order of *time*, and strikingly in order of *value*; more especially when the same individual is the author of both. Nevertheless the ideas which led to the Analytical Engine occurred in a manner wholly independent of any that were connected with the Difference Engine. These ideas are indeed in their own intrinsic nature independent of the latter engine, and

might equally have occurred had it never existed nor been even thought of at all.

The second of the misapprehensions above alluded to relates to the well-known suspension, during some years past, of all progress in the construction of the Difference Engine. Respecting the circumstances which have interfered with the actual completion of either invention, we offer no opinion; and in fact are not possessed of the data for doing so, had we the inclination. But we know that some persons suppose these obstacles (be they what they may) to have arisen *in consequence* of the subsequent invention of the Analytical Engine while the former was in progress. We have ourselves heard it even *lamented* that an idea should ever have occurred at all, which had turned out to be merely the means of arresting what was already in a course of successful execution, without substituting the superior invention in its stead. This notion we can contradict in the most unqualified manner. The progress of the Difference Engine had long been suspended, before there were even the least crude glimmerings of any invention superior to it. Such glimmerings, therefore, and their subsequent development, were in no way the original *cause* of that suspension; although, where difficulties of some kind or other evidently already existed, it was not perhaps calculated to remove or lessen them that an invention should have been meanwhile thought of, which, while including all that the first was capable of, possesses powers so extended as to eclipse it altogether.

We leave it for the decision of each individual (*after he has possessed himself* of competent information as to the characteristics of each engine) to determine how far it ought to be matter of regret that such an accession has been made to the powers of human science, even if it *has* (which we greatly doubt) increased to a certain limited extent some already existing difficulties that had arisen in the way of completing a valuable but lesser work. We leave it for each to satisfy himself as to the wisdom of desiring the obliteration (were that now possible) of all records of the more perfect invention, in order that the comparatively limited one might be finished. The Difference Engine would doubtless fulfil all those practical objects which it was originally destined for. It would certainly calculate all the tables that are more directly necessary for the physical purposes of life, such as nautical and other computations. Those who incline to very strictly utilitarian views may perhaps feel that the peculiar powers of the Analytical Engine bear upon questions of abstract and speculative science, rather than upon those involving every-day and ordinary human interests. These persons being likely to possess hut little sympathy, or possibly acquaintance, with any branches of science which they do not find to be *useful* (according to *their* definition of that word), may conceive that the undertaking of that engine, now that the other one is already in progress, would be a barren and unproductive laying out of yet more money and labour; in fact, a work of supererogation. Even in the utilitarian aspect, however, we do not doubt that very valuable practical results would be developed by the extended faculties of the Analytical Engine; some of which results we think we could now hint at, had we the space; and others, which it may not yet be possible to foresee, but which would be brought forth by the daily increasing requirements of science, and by a more intimate practical acquaintance with the powers of the engine, were it in actual existence.

On general grounds, both of an *a priori* description as well as those founded on the scientific history and experience of mankind, we see strong presumptions that such would be the case. Nevertheless all will probably concur in feeling that the completion of the Difference Engine would be far preferable to the non-completion of any calculating engine at all. With whomsoever or wheresoever may rest the present causes of difficulty that apparently exist towards either the completion of the old engine, or the commencement of the new one, we trust they will not ultimately result in this generation's being acquainted with these inventions through the medium of pen, ink and paper merely; and still more do we hope, that for the honour of our country's reputation in the future pages of history, these causes will not lead to the completion of the undertaking by some *other* nation or government. This could not but be matter of just regret; and equally so, whether the obstacles may have originated in pri-

vate interests and feelings, in considerations of a more public description, or in causes combining the nature of both such solutions.

We refer the reader to the 'Edinburgh Review' of July 1834, for a very able account of the Difference Engine. The writer of the article we allude to has selected as his prominent matter for exposition, a wholly different view of the subject from that which M. Menabrea has chosen. The former chiefly treats it under its mechanical aspect, entering but slightly into the mathematical principles of which that engine is the representative, but giving, in considerable length, many details of the mechanism and contrivances by means of which it tabulates the various orders of differences. M. Menabrea, on the contrary, exclusively develops the analytical view; taking it for granted that mechanism is able to perform certain processes, but without attempting to explain *how*; and devoting his whole attention to explanations and illustrations of the manner in which analytical laws can be so arranged and combined as to bring every branch of that vast subject within the grasp of the assumed powers of mechanism. It is obvious that, in the invention of a calculating engine, these two branches of the subject are equally essential fields of investigation, and that on their mutual adjustment, one to the other, must depend all success. They must be made to meet each other, so that the weak points in the powers of either department may be compensated by the strong points in those of the other. They are indissolubly connected, though so different in their intrinsic nature, that perhaps the same mind might not be likely to prove equally profound or successful in both. We know those who doubt whether the powers of mechanism will in practice prove adequate in all respects to the demands made upon them in the working of such complicated trains of machinery as those of the above engines, and who apprehend that unforeseen practical difficulties and disturbances will arise in the way of accuracy and of facility of operation. The Difference Engine, however, appears to us to be in a great measure an answer to these doubts. It is complete as far as it goes, and it does work with all the anticipated success. The Analytical Engine, far from being more complicated, will in many respects be of simpler construction; and it is a remarkable circumstance attending it, that with very *simplified* means it is so much more powerful.

The article in the 'Edinburgh Review' was written some time previous to the occurrence of any ideas such as afterwards led to the invention of the Analytical Engine; and in the nature of the Difference Engine there is much less that would invite a writer to take exclusively, or even prominently, the mathematical view of it, than in that of the Analytical Engine; although mechanism has undoubtedly gone much further to meet mathematics, in the case of this engine, than of the former one. Some publication embracing the *mechanical* view of the Analytical Engine is a desideratum which we trust will be supplied before long.

Those who may have the patience to study a moderate quantity of rather dry details will find ample compensation, after perusing the article of 1834, in the clearness with which a succinct view will have been attained of the various practical steps through which mechanism can accomplish certain processes; and they will also find themselves still further capable of appreciating M. Menabrea's more comprehensive and generalized memoir. The very difference in the style and object of these two articles makes them peculiarly valuable to each other; at least for the purposes of those who really desire something more than a merely superficial and popular comprehension of the subject of calculating engines.

A. A. L.

Note B

That portion of the Analytical Engine here alluded to is called the storehouse. It contains an indefinite number of the columns of discs described by M. Menabrea. The reader may picture to himself a pile of rather large draughtsmen heaped perpendicularly one above another to a considerable height, each counter having the digits from 0 to 9 inscribed on its *edge* at equal intervals; and if he then conceives that the counters do not actually lie one upon another so as to be in contact, but are fixed at small intervals of vertical distance

on a common axis which passes perpendicularly through their centres, and around which each disc can *revolve horizontally* so that any required digit amongst those inscribed on its margin can be brought into view, he will have a good idea of one of these columns. The *lowest* of the discs on any column belongs to the units, the next above to the tens, the next above this to the hundreds, and so on. Thus, if we wished to inscribe 1345 on a column of the engine, it would stand thus:—

$$1$$
$$3$$
$$4$$
$$5$$

In the Difference Engine there are seven of these columns placed side by side in a row, and the working mechanism extends behind them: the general form of the whole mass of machinery is that of a quadrangular prism (more or less approaching to the cube); the results always appearing on that perpendicular face of the engine which contains the columns of discs, opposite to which face a spectator may place himself. In the Analytical Engine there would be many more of these columns, probably at least two hundred. The precise form and arrangement which the whole mass of its mechanism will assume is not yet finally determined.

We may conveniently represent the columns of discs on paper in a diagram like the following:—

V_1	V_2	V_3	V_4	&c.
○	○	○	○	&c.
0	0	0	0	
0	0	0	0	
0	0	0	0	&c.
0	0	0	0	
□	□	□	□	&c.

The V's are for the purpose of convenient reference to any column, either in writing or speaking, and are consequently numbered. The reason why the letter V is chosen for the purpose in preference to any other letter, is because these columns are designated (as the reader will find in proceeding with the Memoir) the *Variables*, and sometimes the *Variable columns*, or the *columns of Variables*. The origin of this appellation is, that the values on the columns are destined to change, that is to *vary*, in every conceivable manner. But it is necessary to guard against the natural misapprehension that the columns are only intended to receive the values of the *variables* in an analytical formula, and not of the *constants*. The columns are called Variables on a ground wholly unconnected with the *analytical* distinction between constants and variables. In order to prevent the possibility of confusion, we have, both in the translation and in the notes, written Variable with a capital letter when we use the word to signify a *column of the engine*, and variable with a small letter when we mean the *variable of a formula*. Similarly, *Variable-cards* signify any cards that belong to a column of the engine.

To return to the explanation of the diagram: each circle at the top is intended to contain the algebraic sign + or −, either of which can be substituted[20] for the other, according as the number represented on the column below is positive or negative. In a similar manner any other purely *symbolical* results of algebraical processes might be made to appear in these circles. In Note A. the practicability of developing *symbolical* with no less ease than *numerical* results has been touched on. The zeros beneath the *symbolic* circles represent each of them a disc, supposed to have the digit 0 presented in front. Only four tiers of zeros have been figured in the diagram, but these may be considered as representing thirty or forty, or any number of tiers of discs that may be required. Since each disc can present any digit, and each circle any sign, the discs of every column may be so adjusted[21] as to express any positive or negative number whatever within the limits of the machine; which limits depend on the *perpendicular* extent of the mechanism, that is, on the number of discs to a column.

Each of the squares below the zeros is intended for the inscription of any *general* symbol or combination of symbols we please; it being understood that the number represented on the column immediately above is the numerical value of that symbol, or combi-

nation of symbols. Let us, for instance, represent the three quantities a, n, x, and let us further suppose that $a = 5, n = 7, x = 98$. We should have—[22]

V_1	V_2	V_3	V_4	&c.
+	+	+	+	&c.
0	0	0	0	
0	0	0	0	
0	0	9	0	&c.
5	7	8	0	
$\boxed{a}$	$\boxed{n}$	$\boxed{x}$		&c.

We may now combine these symbols in a variety of ways, so as to form any required function or functions of them, and we may then inscribe each such function below brackets, every bracket uniting together those quantities (and those only) which enter into the function inscribed below it. We must also, when we have decided on the particular function whose numerical value we desire to calculate, assign another column to the right-hand for receiving the *results*, and must inscribe the function in the square below this column. In the above instance we might have any one of the following functions:—

$$ax^n, x^{an}, a \cdot n \cdot x, \frac{a}{n}x, a + n + x, \&c., \&c.$$

Let us select the first. It would stand as follows, previous to calculation:—

V_1	V_2	V_3	V_4	&c.
+	+	+	+	&c.
0	0	0	0	
0	0	0	0	
0	0	9	0	&c.
5	7	8	0	
$\boxed{a}$	$\boxed{n}$	$\boxed{x}$	$\boxed{ax^n}$	&c.
	ax^n			&c.

The data being given, we must now put into the engine the cards proper for directing the operations in the case of the particular function chosen. These operations would in this instance be,—

Firstly, six multiplications in order to get x^n ($= 98^7$ for the above particular data).

Secondly, one multiplication in order then to get $a \cdot x^n$ ($= 5 \cdot 98^7$).

In all, seven multiplications to complete the whole process. We may thus represent them:—

$$(\times, \times, \times, \times, \times, \times, \times), \text{ or } 7 (\times).$$

The multiplications would, however, at successive stages in the solution of the problem, operate on pairs of numbers, derived from *different* columns. In other words, the *same operation* would be performed on different *subjects of operation*. And here again is an illustration of the remarks made in the preceding Note on the independent manner in which the engine directs its *operations*. In determining the value of ax^n, the *operations* are *homogeneous*, but are distributed amongst different *subjects of operation*, at successive stages of the computation. It is by means of certain punched cards, belonging to the Variables themselves, that the action of the operations is so *distributed* as to suit each particular function. The *Operation-cards* merely determine the succession of operations in a general manner. They in fact throw all that portion of the mechanism included in the *mill* into a series of different *states*, which we may call the *adding state*, or the *multiplying state*, &c. respectively. In each of these states the mechanism is ready to act in the way peculiar to that state, on any pair of numbers which may be permitted to come within its sphere of action. Only *one* of these operating states of the mill can exist at a time; and the nature of the mechanism is also such that only *one pair of numbers* can be received and acted on at a time. Now, in order to secure that the mill shall receive a constant supply of the proper pairs of numbers in succession, and that it shall also rightly locate the result of an operation performed upon any pair, each Variable has cards of its own belonging to it.

It has, first, a class of cards whose business it is to *allow* the number on the Variable to pass into the mill, there to be operated upon. These cards may he called the *Supplying-cards*. They furnish the mill with its proper food. Each Variable has, secondly, another class of cards, whose office it is to allow the Variable to *receive* a number *from* the mill. These cards may be called the *Receiving-cards. They* regulate the location of results, whether temporary or ultimate results. The Variable-cards in general (including both the preceding classes) might, it appears to us, be even more appropriately designated the Distributive-cards, since it is through their means that the action of the operations, and the results of this action, are rightly *distributed*.

There are *two varieties* of the *Supplying* Variable-cards, respectively adapted for fulfilling two distinct subsidiary purposes: but as these modifications do not bear upon the present subject, we shall notice them in another place.

In the above case of ax^n, the Operation-cards merely order seven multiplications, that is, they order the mill to be in the *multiplying state* seven successive times (without any reference to the particular columns whose numbers are to be acted upon). The proper Distributive Variable-cards step in at each successive multiplication, and cause the distributions requisite for the particular case.

For x^{an}	the operations would be	$34(\times)$
$a \cdot n \cdot x$		$(\times, \times), \text{ or } 2(\times)$
$\dfrac{a}{n} \cdot x$		$(\div, \times)$
$a + n + x$		$(+, +), \text{ or } 2(+)$

The engine might be made to calculate all these in succession. Having completed ax^n, the function x^{an} might be written under the brackets instead of ax^n, and a new calculation commenced (the appropriate Operation and Variable-cards for the new function of course coming into play). The results would then appear on V_5. So on for any number of different functions of the quantities a, n, x. Each *result* might either permanently remain on its column during the succeeding calculations, so that when all the functions had been computed, their values would simultaneously exist on V_4, V_5, V_6, &c.; or each result might (after being printed off, or used in any specified manner) be effaced, to make way for its successor. The square under V_4 ought, for the latter arrangement, to have the functions ax^n, x^{an}, anx, &c. successively inscribed in it.

Let us now suppose that we have *two* expressions whose values have been computed by the engine independently of each other (each having its own group of columns for data and results). Let them be ax^n, and bpy. They would then stand as follows on the columns:—

V_1	V_2	V_3	V_4	V_5	V_6	V_7	V_8	V_9
+	+	+	+	+	+	+	+	+
0	0	0	0	0	0	0	0	0
0	0	0	0	0	0	0	0	0
0	0	0	0	0	0	0	0	0
0	0	0	0	0	0	0	0	0
a	n	x	ax^n	b	p	y	bpy	$\dfrac{ax^n}{bpy}$

We may now desire to combine together these two *results*, in any manner we please; in which case it would only be necessary to have an additional card or cards, which should order the requisite operations to be performed with the numbers on the two result-columns V_4 and V_8, and the *result of these further operations* to appear on a new column, V_9. Say that we wish to divide ax^n by bpy. The numerical value of this division would then appear on the column V_9, beneath which we have inscribed $\dfrac{ax^n}{bpy}$. The whole series of operations from the beginning would be as follows (n being $= 7$):

$\{7(\times), 2(\times), \div\}$, or $\{9(\times), \div\}$.

This example is introduced merely to show that we may, if we please, retain separately and permanently any *intermediate* results (like ax^n, $b{\cdot}p{\cdot}y$) which occur in the course of processes having an ulterior and more complicated result as their chief and final object (like $\dfrac{ax^n}{bpy}$).

Any group of columns may be considered as representing a *general* function, until a *special* one has been implicitly impressed upon them through the introduction into the engine of the Operation and Variable-cards made out for a *particular* function. Thus, in the preceding example, V_1, V_2, V_3, V_5, V_6, V_7 represent the *general* function $\phi(a, n, b, p, x, y)$ until the function $\dfrac{ax^n}{bpy}$ has been determined on, and *implicitly* expressed by the placing of the right cards in the engine. The actual working of the mechanism, as regulated by these cards, then *explicitly* develops the value of the function. The inscription of a function under the brackets, and in the square under the result-column, in no way influences the processes or the results, and is merely a memorandum for the observer, to remind him of what is going on. It is the Operation and the Variable-cards only which in reality determine the function. Indeed it should be distinctly kept in mind, that the inscriptions within *any* of the squares are quite independent of the mechanism or workings of the engine, and are nothing but arbitrary memorandums placed there at pleasure to assist the spectator.

The further we analyse the manner in which such an engine performs its processes and attains its results, the more we perceive how distinctly it places in a true and just light the mutual relations and connexion of the various steps of mathematical analysis; how clearly it separates those things which are in reality distinct and independent, and unites those which are mutually dependent.
A. A. L.

Note C

Those who may desire to study the principles of the Jacquard-loom in the most effectual manner, viz. that of practical observation, have only to step into the Adelaide Gallery or the Polytechnic Institution. In each of these valuable repositories of scientific *illustration*, a weaver is constantly working at a Jacquard-loom, and is ready to give any information that may be desired as to the construction and modes of acting of his apparatus. The volume on the manufacture of silk, in Lardner's Cyclopædia, contains a chapter on the Jacquard-loom, which may also be consulted with advantage.

The mode of application of the cards, as hitherto used in the art of weaving, was not found, however, to be sufficiently powerful for all the simplifications which it was desirable to attain in such varied and complicated processes as those required in order to fulfil the purposes of an Analytical Engine. A method was devised of what was technically designated *backing* the cards in certain groups according to certain laws. The object of this extension is to secure the possibility of bringing any particular card or set of cards into use *any number of times successively* in the solution of one problem. Whether this power shall be taken advantage of or not, in each particular instance, will depend on the nature of the operations which the problem under consideration may require. The process is alluded to by M. Menabrea, and it is a very important simplification. It has been proposed to use it for the reciprocal benefit of that art, which, while it has itself no apparent connexion with the domains of abstract science, has yet proved so valuable to the latter, in suggesting the principles which, in their new and singular field of application, seem likely to place *algebraical* combinations not less completely within the province of mechanism, than are all those varied intricacies of which *intersecting threads* are susceptible. By the introduction of the system of *backing* into the Jacquard-loom itself, patterns which should possess symmetry, and follow regular laws of any extent, might be woven by means of comparatively few cards.

Those who understand the mechanism of this loom will perceive that the above improvement is eas-

ily effected in practice, by causing the prism over which the train of pattern-cards is suspended to revolve *backwards* instead of *forwards*, at pleasure, under the requisite circumstances; until, by so doing, any particular card, or set of cards, that has done duty once, and passed on in the ordinary regular succession, is brought back to the position it occupied just before it was used the preceding time. The prism then resumes its *forward* rotation, and thus brings the card or set of cards in question into play a second time. This process may obviously be repeated any number of times.

A. A. L.

Note D

We have represented the solution of these two equations below, with every detail, in a diagram similar to those used in Note B; but additional explanations are requisite, partly in order to make this more complicated case perfectly clear, and partly for the comprehension of certain indications and notations not used in the preceding diagrams. Those who may wish to understand Note G completely, are recommended to pay particular attention to the contents of the present Note, or they will not otherwise comprehend the similar notation and indications when applied to a much more complicated case. (See figure 1.)

In all calculations, the columns of Variables used may be divided into three classes:—

1st. Those on which the data are inscribed:

2ndly. Those intended to receive the final results:

3rdly. Those intended to receive such intermediate and temporary combinations of the primitive data as are not to be permanently retained, but are merely needed for *working with*, in order to attain the ultimate results. Combinations of this kind might properly be called *secondary data*. They are in fact so many *successive stages* towards the final result. The columns which receive them are rightly named *Working-Variables*, for their office is in its nature purely *subsidiary* to other purposes. They develope an intermediate and transient class of results, which unite the original data with the final results.

The Result-Variables sometimes partake of the nature of Working-Variables. It frequently happens that a Variable destined to receive a final result is the recipient of one or more intermediate values successively, in the course of the processes. Similarly, the Variables for data often become Working-Variables, or Result-Variables, or even both in succession. It so happens, however, that in the case of the present equations the three sets of offices remain throughout perfectly separate and independent.

It will be observed, that in the squares below the *Working*-Variables nothing is inscribed. Any one of these Variables is in many cases destined to pass through various values successively during the performance of a calculation (although in these particular equations no instance of this occurs) . Consequently no *one fixed* symbol, or combination of symbols, should be considered as properly belonging to a merely *Working*-Variable; and as a general rule their squares are left blank. Of course in this, as in all other cases where we mention a *general* rule, it is understood that many particular exceptions may be expedient.

In order that all the indications contained in the diagram may be completely understood, we shall now explain two or three points, not hitherto touched on. When the value on any Variable is called into use, one of two consequences may be made to result. Either the value may *return* to the Variable after it has been used, in which case it is ready for a second use if needed; or the Variable may be made zero. (We are of course not considering a third case, of not unfrequent occurrence, in which the same Variable is destined to receive the *result* of the very operation which it has just supplied with a number.) Now the ordinary rule is, that the value *returns* to the Variable; unless it has been foreseen that no use for that value can recur, in which case zero is substituted. At the *end* of a calculation, therefore, every column ought as a general rule to be zero, excepting those for results. Thus it will be seen by the diagram, that when m, the value on V_0, is used for the second time by Operation 5, V_0 becomes 0, since m is not again needed; that similarly, when $(mn' - m'n)$, on V_{12}, is used for the third time by Operation 11, V_{12} becomes zero, since $(mn' - m'n)$ is not again needed. In order to provide for the one or the other of

DIAGRAM BELONGING TO NOTE D.

Number of Operations.	Nature of Operations.	Variables for Data.						Working Variables.									Variables for Results.	
		$^1V_0$	$^1V_1$	$^1V_2$	$^1V_3$	$^1V_4$	$^1V_5$	$^0V_6$	$^0V_7$	$^0V_8$	$^0V_9$	$^0V_1$	$^0V_{11}$	$^0V_{12}$	$^0V_{13}$	$^0V_{14}$	$^0V_{15}$	$^0V_{16}$
		+	+	+	+	+	+	+	+	+	+	+	+	+	+	+	+	+
		0	0	0	0	0	0	0	0	0	0	0	0	0	0	0	0	0
		0	0	0	0	0	0	0	0	0	0	0	0	0	0	0	0	0
		0	0	0	0	0	0	0	0	0	0	0	0	0	0	0	0	0
		0	0	0	0	0	0	0	0	0	0	0	0	0	0	0	0	0
		m	n	d	m'	n'	d'										$\dfrac{dn'-d'n}{mn'-m'n}=x$	$\dfrac{d'm-dm'}{mn'-m'n}=y$
1	×	m				n'		$m n'$										
2	×		n		m'				$m'n$									
3	×			d						$d n'$								
4	×		0				d'				$d'n$							
5	×	0					0					$d'm$						
6	×			0	0								$d m'$					
7	−							0	0					$(mn'-m'n)$				
8	−									0	0				$(d n'-d'n)$			
9	−											0	0			$(d'm-dm')$		
10	÷													$(mn'-m'n)$	0		$\dfrac{dn'-d'n}{mn'-m'n}=x$	
11	÷													0		0		$\dfrac{d'm-dm'}{mn'-m'n}=y$

Figure 1.

the courses above indicated, there are *two* varieties of the *Supplying* Variable-cards. One of these varieties has provisions which cause the number given off from any Variable to *return* to that Variable after doing its duty in the mill. The other variety has provisions which cause *zero* to be substituted on the Variable, for the number given off. These two varieties are distinguished, when needful, by the respective appellations of the *Retaining* Supply-cards and the *Zero* Supply-cards. We see that the primary office (see Note B.) of both these varieties of cards is the same; they only differ in their *secondary* office.

Every Variable thus has belonging to it one class of *Receiving* Variable-cards and *two* classes of *Supplying* Variable-cards. It is plain however that only the *one* or the *other* of these two latter classes can be used by any one Variable for one operation; never *both* simultaneously, their respective functions being mutually incompatible.

It should be understood that the Variable-cards are not placed in *immediate contiguity* with the columns. Each card is connected by means of wires with the column it is intended to act upon.

Our diagram ought in reality to be placed side by side with M. Menabrea's corresponding table, so as to be compared with it, line for line belonging to each operation. But it was unfortunately inconvenient to print them in this desirable form. The diagram is, in the main, merely another manner of indicating the various relations denoted in M. Menabrea's table. Each mode has some advantages and some disadvantages. Combined, they form a complete and accurate method of registering every step and sequence in all calculations performed by the engine.

No notice has yet been taken of the *upper* indices which are added to the left of each V in the diagram; an addition which we have also taken the liberty of making to the V's in M. Menabrea's tables of pages 681, 684 [*sic*], since it does not *alter* anything therein represented by him, but merely *adds* something to the previous indications of those tables. The *lower* indices are obviously indices of *locality* only, and are wholly independent of the operations performed or of the results obtained, their value continuing unchanged during the performance of calculations. The *upper* indices, however, are of a different nature. Their office is to indicate any *alteration* in the value which a Variable represents; and they are of course liable to changes during the processes of a calculation. Whenever a Variable has only zeros upon it, it is called ^{0}V; the moment a value appears on it (whether that value be placed there arbitrarily, or appears in the natural course of a calculation), it becomes ^{1}V. If this value gives place to another value, the Variable becomes ^{2}V, and so forth. Whenever a *value* again gives place to *zero*, the Variable again becomes ^{0}V, even if it have been ^{n}V the moment before. If a *value* then again be substituted, the Variable becomes $^{n+1}$V (as it would have done if it had not passed through the intermediate ^{0}V); &c. &c. Just before any calculation is commenced, and after the data have been given, and everything adjusted and prepared for setting the mechanism in action, the upper indices of the Variables for data are all unity, and those for the Working and Result-variables are all zero. In this state the diagram represents them.[23]

There are several advantages in having a set of indices of this nature; but these advantages are perhaps hardly of a kind to be immediately perceived, unless by a mind somewhat accustomed to trace the successive steps by means of which the engine accomplishes its purposes. We have only space to mention in a general way, that the whole notation of the tables is made more consistent by these indices, for they are able to mark a *difference* in certain cases, where there would otherwise be an apparent *identity* confusing in its tendency. In such a case as $V_n = V_p + V_n$ there is more clearness and more consistency with the usual laws of algebraical notation, in being able to write $^{m+1}V_n = {}^qV_p + {}^mV_n$. It is also obvious that the indices furnish a powerful means of tracing back the derivation of any result; and of registering various circumstances concerning that *series of successive substitutions*, of which every *result* is in fact merely the final consequence; circumstances that may in certain cases involve relations which it is important to observe, either for purely analytical reasons, or for practically adapting the workings of the engine to their occurrence. The series of substitutions which lead to the equations of the diagram are as follow:—

(1.)	(2.)	(3.)	(4.)	
$^1V_{16} =$	$\dfrac{^1V_{14}}{^1V_{12}} =$	$\dfrac{^1V_{10} - {}^1V_{11}}{^1V_6 - {}^1V_7} =$	$\dfrac{^1V_0 \cdot {}^1V_5 - {}^1V_2 \cdot {}^1V_3}{^1V_0 \cdot {}^1V_4 - {}^1V_3 \cdot {}^1V_1} =$	$\dfrac{d'm - dm'}{mn' - m'n}$
(1.)	(2.)	(3.)	(4.)	
$^1V_{15} =$	$\dfrac{^1V_{13}}{^1V_{12}} =$	$\dfrac{^1V_8 - {}^1V_9}{^1V_6 - {}^1V_7} =$	$\dfrac{^1V_2 \cdot {}^1V_4 - {}^1V_5 \cdot {}^1V_1}{^1V_0 \cdot {}^1V_4 - {}^1V_3 \cdot {}^1V_1} =$	$\dfrac{dn' - d'n}{mn' - m'n}$

There are *three* successive substitutions for each of these equations. The formulæ (2.), (3.) and (4.) are *implicitly* contained in (1.), which latter we may consider as being in fact the *condensed* expression of any of the former. It will be observed that every succeeding substitution must contain *twice* as many V's as its predecessor. So that if a problem require n substitutions, the successive series of numbers for the V's in the whole of them will be $2, 4, 8, 16 \ldots 2^n$.

The substitutions in the preceding equations happen to be of little value towards illustrating the power and uses of the upper indices, for, owing to the nature of these particular equations, the indices are all unity throughout. We wish we had space to enter more fully into the relations which these indices would in many cases enable us to trace.

M. Menabrea incloses the three centre columns of his table under the general title *Variable-cards*. The V's however in reality all represent the actual *Variable-columns* of the engine, and not the cards that belong to them. Still the title is a very just one, since it is through the special action of certain Variable-cards (when *combined* with the more generalized agency of the Operation-cards) that every one of the particular relations he has indicated under that title is brought about.

Suppose we wish to ascertain how often any *one* quantity, or combination of quantities, is brought into use during a calculation. We easily ascertain *this*, from the inspection of any vertical column or columns of the diagram in which that quantity may appear. Thus, in the present case, we see that all the data, and all the intermediate results likewise, are used twice, excepting $(mn' - m'n)$, which is used three times.

The *order* in which it is possible to perform the operations for the present example, enables us to effect all the eleven operations of which it consists with only *three Operation cards*; because the problem is of such a nature that it admits of each *class* of operations being performed in a group together; all the multiplications one after another, all the subtractions one after another, &c. The operations are $\{6(\times), 3(-), 2(\div)\}$.

Since the very definition of an operation implies that there must be *two* numbers to act upon, there are of course *two Supplying* Variable-cards necessarily brought into action for every operation, in order to furnish the two proper numbers. (See Note B.) Also, since every operation must produce a *result*, which must be placed *somewhere*, each operation entails the action of a *Receiving* Variable-card, to indicate the proper locality for the result. Therefore, at least three times as many Variable-cards as there are *operations* (not *Operation-cards*, for these, as we have just seen, are by no means always as numerous as the *operations*) are brought into use in every calculation. Indeed, under certain contingencies, a still larger proportion is requisite; such, for example, would probably be the case when the same result has to appear on more than one Variable simultaneously (which is not unfrequently a provision necessary for subsequent purposes in a calculation), and in some other cases which we shall not here specify. We see therefore that a great disproportion exists between the amount of *Variable* and of *Operation*-cards requisite for the working of even the simplest calculation.

All calculations do not admit, like this one, of the operations of the same nature being performed in groups together. Probably very few do so without exceptions occurring in one or other stage of the progress; and some would not admit it at all. The *order* in which the operations shall be performed in every particular case is a very interesting and curious question, on which our space does not permit us fully to enter. In almost every computation a great *variety* of arrangements for the succession of the processes is possible, and various considerations must influence the selection amongst them for the purposes of a Calculating Engine. One essential object is to choose that arrangement which shall tend to reduce to a minimum the *time* necessary for completing the calculation.

It must be evident how multifarious and how mutually complicated are the considerations which the working of such an engine involve. There are frequently several distinct *sets of effects* going on simultaneously; all in a manner independent of each other, and yet to a greater or less degree exercising a mutual influence. To adjust each to every other, and indeed even to perceive and trace them out with perfect correctness and success, entails difficulties whose nature partakes to a certain extent of those involved in every question where *conditions* are very numerous and inter-complicated; such as for instance the estimation of the mutual relations amongst *statistical* phænomena, and of those involved in many other classes of facts.

A. A. L.

Note E

This example has evidently been chosen on account of its brevity and simplicity, with a view merely to explain the *manner* in which the engine would proceed in the case of an *analytical calculation containing variables*, rather than to illustrate the *extent of its powers* to solve cases of a difficult and complex nature. The equations of page 679 [*sic*] are in fact a more complicated problem than the present one.

We have not subjoined any diagram of its development for this new example, as we did for the former one, because this is unnecessary after the full application already made of those diagrams to the illustration of M. Menabrea's excellent tables.

It may be remarked that a slight discrepancy exists between the formulæ

$$(a + bx')$$

$$(A + B \cos' x)$$

given in the Memoir as the *data* for calculation, and the *results* of the calculation as developed in the last division of the table which accompanies it. To agree perfectly with this latter, the data should have been given as

$$(ax^0 + bx')$$

$$(A \cos^0 x + B \cos' x)$$

The following is a more complicated example of the manner in which the engine would compute a trigonometrical function containing variables. To multiply

$$A + A_1 \cos \theta + A_2 \cos 2\theta + A_3 \cos 3\theta + \ldots$$

by

$$B + B_1 \cos \theta$$

Let the resulting products be represented under the general form

$$C_0 + C_1\cos\theta + C_2\cos 2\theta + C_3\cos 3\theta + \ldots . (1.)$$

This trigonometrical series is not only in itself very appropriate for illustrating the processes of the engine, but is likewise of much practical interest from its frequent use in astronomical computations. Before proceeding further with it, we shall point out that there are three very distinct classes of ways in which it may be desired to deduce numerical values from any analytical formula.

First. We may wish to find the collective numerical value of the *whole formula*, without any reference to the quantities of which that formula is a function, or to the particular mode of their combination and distribution, of which the formula is the result and representative. Values of this kind are of a strictly arithmetical nature in the most limited sense of the term, and retain no trace whatever of the processes through which they have been deduced. In fact, any one such numerical value may have been attained from an *infinite variety* of data, or of problems. The values for x and y in the two equations (see Note D.) come under this class of numerical results.

Secondly. We may propose to compute the collective numerical value of *each term* of a formula, or of a series, and to keep these results separate. The engine must in such a case appropriate as many columns to *results* as there are terms to compute.

Thirdly. It may be desired to compute the numerical value of various *subdivisions of each term*, and to keep all these results separate. It may be required, for instance, to compute each coefficient separately from its variable, in which particular case the engine must appropriate *two result-columns* to *every term that contains both a variable and coefficient.*

There are many ways in which it may be desired in special cases to distribute and keep separate the numerical values of different parts of an algebraical formula; and the power of effecting such distributions to any extent is essential to the *algebraical* character of the Analytical Engine. Many persons who are not conversant with mathematical studies, imagine that because the business of the engine is to give its results in *numerical notation*, the *nature of its processes* must consequently be *arithmetical* and *numerical*, rather than *algebraical* and *analytical*. This is an error. The engine can arrange and combine its numerical quantities exactly as if they were *letters* or any other *general* symbols; and in fact it might bring out its results in algebraical *notation*, were provisions made accordingly. It might develope three sets of results simultaneously, viz. *symbolic* results (as already alluded to in Notes A. and B.), *numerical* results (its chief and primary object); and *algebraical* results in *literal* notation. This latter however has not been deemed a necessary or desirable addition to its powers, partly because the necessary arrangements for effecting it would increase the complexity and extent of the mechanism to a degree that would not be commensurate with the advantages, where the main object of the invention is to translate into *numerical* language general formulæ of analysis already known to us, or whose laws of formation are known to us. But it would be a mistake to suppose that because its *results* are given in the *notation* of a more restricted science, its *processes* are therefore restricted to those of that science. The object of the engine is in fact to give the *utmost practical efficiency* to the resources of *numerical interpretations* of the higher science of analysis, while it uses the processes and combinations of this latter.

To return to the trigonometrical series. We shall only consider the first four terms of the factor (A + A$_1$ cos θ + &c.), since this will be sufficient to show the method. We propose to obtain separately the numerical value of *each coefficient* C_0, C_1, &c. of (1.). The direct multiplication of the two factors gives

$$\mathrm{BA} + \mathrm{BA}_1 \cos\theta + \mathrm{B}\,\mathrm{A}_2 \cos 2\theta + \mathrm{BA}_3 \cos 3\theta +$$
$$\ldots + \mathrm{B}_1\mathrm{A}\cos\theta + \mathrm{B}_1\mathrm{A}_1 \cos\theta \cdot \cos\theta + \mathrm{B}_1\mathrm{A}_2$$
$$\cos 2\theta \cdot \cos\theta + \mathrm{B}_1\mathrm{A}_3 \cos 3\theta \cdot \cos\theta \quad (2.)$$

a result which would stand thus on the engine:—

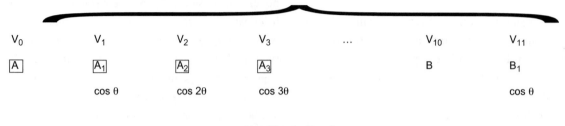

V_0	V_1	V_2	V_3	...	V_{10}	V_{11}
$\boxed{A}$	$\boxed{A_1}$	$\boxed{A_2}$	$\boxed{A_3}$		B	B_1
	$\cos\theta$	$\cos 2\theta$	$\cos 3\theta$			$\cos\theta$

Variables for Results

V_{20}	V_{21}	V_{22}	V_{23}	...	V_{31}	V_{32}	V_{33}	V_{34}
$\boxed{BA}$	$\boxed{BA_1}$	$\boxed{BA_2}$	$\boxed{BA_3}$		$\boxed{B_1A}$	$\boxed{B_1A_1}$	B_1A_2	B_1A_3
	$\cos\theta$	$\cos 2\theta$	$\cos 3\theta$			$(\cos\theta\cdot\cos\theta)$	$(\cos 2\theta\cdot\cos\theta)$	$(\cos 3\theta\cdot\cos\theta)$

The variable belonging to each coefficient is written below it, as we have done in the diagram, by way of memorandum. The only further reduction which is at first apparently possible in the preceding result, would be the addition of V_{21} to V_{31} (in which case B_1A should be effaced from V_{31}). The whole operations from the beginning would then be—

First Series of Operations	Second Series of Operations	Third Series, which contains only one (final) operation
$^1V_{10} \times {}^1V_0 = {}^1V_{20}$	$^1V_{11} \times {}^1V_0 = {}^1V_{31}$	$^1V_{21} \times {}^1V_{31} = {}^2V_{21}$, and V_{31} becomes $= 0$.
$^1V_{10} \times {}^1V_1 = {}^1V_{21}$	$^1V_{11} \times {}^1V_1 = {}^1V_{32}$	
$^1V_{10} \times {}^1V_2 = {}^1V_{22}$	$^1V_{11} \times {}^1V_2 = {}^1V_{33}$	
$^1V_{10} \times {}^1V_3 = {}^1V_{23}$	$^1V_{11} \times {}^1V_3 = {}^1V_{34}$	

We do not enter into the same detail of *every* step of the processes as in the examples of Notes D. and G., thinking it unnecessary and tedious to do so. The reader will remember the meaning and use of the upper and lower indices, &c., as before explained.

To proceed: we know that

$$\cos n\theta \cdot \cos\theta = \frac{1}{2}\cos\overline{n+1}\theta + \frac{1}{2}\overline{(n-1)}\cdot\theta\ldots \quad (3.)$$

Consequently, a slight examination of the second line of (2.) will show that by making the proper substitutions, (2.) will become

BA	$+BA_1$ $\cdot\cos\theta$	$+BA_2$ $\cdot\cos 2\theta$	$+BA_3$ $\cdot\cos 3\theta$	
	$+B_1A$ $\cdot\cos\theta$			
$+\frac{1}{2}B_1A_1$		$+\frac{1}{2}B_1A_1$ $\cdot\cos 2\theta$		
	$+\frac{1}{2}B_1A_2$ $\cdot\cos\theta$		$+\frac{1}{2}B_1A_2$ $\cdot\cos 3\theta$	
		$+\frac{1}{2}B_1A_3$ $\cdot\cos 2\theta$		$+\frac{1}{2}B_1A_2$ $\cdot\cos 4\theta$
C_0	C_1	C_2	C_3	C_4

These coefficients should respectively appear on

V_{20}	V_{21}	V_{22}	V_{23}	V_{24}

We shall perceive, if we inspect the particular arrangement of the results in (2.) on the Result-columns as represented in the diagram, that, in order to effect this transformation, each successive coefficient upon V_{32}, V_{33}, &c. (beginning with V_{32}), must through means of proper cards be divided by *two*;[24] and that one of the halves thus obtained must be added to the coefficient on the Variable which precedes it by ten columns, and the other half to the coefficient on the Variable which precedes it by twelve columns; V_{32}, V_{33}, &c. themselves becoming zeros during the process.

This series of operations may be thus expressed:— [25]

Fourth Series.

$^1V_{32} \div 2 +$ $^1V_{22} =$	$^2V_{22} = BA_2 + 1/2\, B_1A_1$	
$^1V_{32} \div 2 +$ $^1V_{20} =$	$^2V_{20} = BA_2 + 1/2\, B_1A_1$	$= C_0$
$^1V_{33} \div 2 +$ $^1V_{23} =$	$^2V_{23} = BA_3 + 1/2\, B_1A_2$	$= C_3$
$^1V_{33} \div 2 +$ $^2V_{21} =$	$^3V_{21} = BA_1 + B_1A + 1/2\, B_1A_2$	$= C_1$
$^1V_{34} \div 2 +$ $^0V_{24} =$	$^1V_{24} = 1/2\, B_1A_3$	$= C_4$
$^1V_{34} \div 2 +$ $^2V_{22} =$	$^3V_{22} = BA_2 + 1/2\, B_1A_1 + 1/2$ B_1A_3	$= C_2$

The calculation of the coefficients C_0, C_1, &c. of (1.) would now be completed, and they would stand ranged in order on V_{20}, V_{21}, &c. It will be remarked, that from the moment the fourth series of operations is ordered, the Variables V_{31}, V_{32}, &c. cease to be *Result*-Variables, and become mere *Working*-Variables.

The substitution made by the engine of the processes in the second side of (3.) for those in the first side is an excellent illustration of the manner in which we may arbitrarily order it to substitute any function, number, or process, at pleasure, for any other function, number or process, on the occurrence of a specified contingency.

We will now suppose that we desire to go a step further, and to obtain the numerical value of each *complete* term of the product (1.); that is, of each *coefficient and variable united*, which for the $(n + 1)$th term would be $C_n \cdot \cos n\,\theta$.

We must for this purpose place the variables themselves on another set of columns, V_{41}, V_{42}, &c., and then order their successive multiplication by V_{21}, V_{22}, &c., each for each. There would thus be a final series of operations as follows:—

Fifth and Final Series of Operations
$^2V_{20} \times {}^0V_{40} = {}^1V_{40}$
$^3V_{21} \times {}^0V_{41} = {}^1V_{41}$
$^3V_{22} \times {}^0V_{42} = {}^1V_{42}$
$^2V_{23} \times {}^0V_{43} = {}^1V_{43}$
$^1V_{24} \times {}^0V_{44} = {}^1V_{44}$

(N.B. that V_{40} being intended to receive the coefficient on V_{20} which has *no* variable, will only have cos 0θ (= 1) inscribed on it, preparatory to commencing the fifth series of operations.)

From the moment that the fifth and final series of operations is ordered, the Variables V_{20}, V_{21}, &c. then in their turn cease to be *Result*-Variables and become mere *Working*-Variables; V_{40}, V_{41}, &c. being now the recipients of the ultimate results.

We should observe, that if the variables cos θ, cos 2θ, cos 3θ, &c. are furnished, they would be placed directly upon V_{41}, V_{42}, &c., like any other data. If not, a separate computation might be entered upon in a separate part of the engine, in order to calculate them, and place them on V_{41}, &c.

We have now explained how the engine might compute (1.) in the most direct manner, supposing we knew nothing about the *general* term of the resulting series. But the engine would in reality set to work very differently, whenever (as in this case) we *do* know the law for the general term.

The first two terms of (1.) are

$$\left(BA + \frac{1}{2}B_1A_1 \right) + \left(\overline{BA_1 + B_1A + \frac{1}{2}B_1A_2} \cdot \cos\theta \right) \tag{4.}$$

and the general term for all after these is

$$\left(BA_n + \frac{1}{2}B_1 \cdot \overline{A_{n-1} + A_{n-2}} \right) \cos n\theta \tag{5.}$$

which is the coefficient of the $(n + 1)$th term. The engine would calculate the first two terms by means of a separate set of suitable Operation-cards, and would then need another set for the third term; which last set of Operation-cards would calculate all the succeeding terms *ad infinitum*, merely requiring certain new Variable-cards for each term to direct the operations to act on the proper columns. The following would be the successive sets of operations for computing the coefficients of $n + 2$ terms:—

$$(\times, \times, \div, +), (\times, \times, \times, \div, +, +), n(\times, +, \times, \div, +).$$

Or we might represent them as follows, according to the numerical order of the operations:—

$$(1, 2 \ldots 4), (5, 6 \ldots 10), n(11, 12 \ldots 15).$$

The brackets, it should be understood, point out the relation in which the operations may be *grouped*, while the comma marks *succession*. The symbol + might be used for this latter purpose, but this would be liable to produce confusion, as + is also necessarily used to represent one class of the actual operations which are the subject of that succession. In accordance with this meaning attached to the comma, care must be taken when any one group of operations recurs more than once, as is represented above by $n(11 \ldots 15)$, not to insert a comma after the number or letter prefixed to that group. $n, (11 \ldots 15)$ would stand for *an operation n, followed by the group of operations* (11 $\ldots 15$); instead of denoting *the number of groups which are to follow each other.*

Wherever a *general* term exists, there will be a *recurring group* of operations, as in the above example. Both for brevity and for distinctness, a *recurring group* is called a *cycle*. A *cycle* of operations, then, must be understood to signify any *set of operations* which is repeated *more than once*. It is equally a *cycle*, whether it be repeated *twice* only, or an indefinite number of times; for it is the fact of a *repetition occurring at all* that constitutes it such. In many cases of analysis there is a *recurring group* of one or more *cycles*; that is, a *cycle of a cycle*, or a *cycle of cycles*. For instance: suppose

we wish to divide a series by a series,

$$(1.) \quad \frac{a + bx + cx^2 + \ldots}{a' + b'x + c'x^2 + \ldots},$$

it being required that the result shall be developed, like the dividend and the divisor, in successive powers of x. A little consideration of (1.), and of the steps through which algebraical division is effected, will show that (if the denominator be supposed to consist of p terms) the first partial quotient will be completed by the following operations:—

$$(2.) \quad \{(\div), p(\times, -)\} \text{ or } \{(1), p(2, 3)\},$$

that the second partial quotient will be completed by an exactly similar set of operations, which acts on the remainder obtained by the first set, instead of on the original dividend. The whole of the processes therefore that have been gone through, by the time the *second* partial quotient has been obtained, will be,—

$$(3.) \quad 2\{(\div), p(\times, -)\} \text{ or } 2\{(1), p(2, 3)\},$$

which is a cycle that includes a cycle, or a cycle of the second order. The operations for the *complete* division, supposing we propose to obtain n terms of the series constituting the quotient, will be,—

$$(4.) \quad n\{(\div), p(\times, -)\} \text{ or } n\{(1), p(2, 3)\},$$

It is of course to be remembered that the process of algebraical division in reality continues *ad infinitum*, except in the few exceptional cases which admit of an exact quotient being obtained. The number n in the formula (4.) is always that of the number of terms we propose to ourselves to obtain; and the nth partial quotient is the coefficient of the $(n - 1)$th power of x.

There are some cases which entail *cycles of cycles of cycles*, to an indefinite extent. Such cases are usually very complicated, and they are of extreme interest when considered with reference to the engine. The algebraical development in a series of the nth function of any given function is of this nature. Let it be proposed to obtain the nth function of

(5.) $\phi(a, b, c, \ldots, x)$, x being the variable.

We should premise, that we suppose the reader to understand what is meant by an nth function. We suppose him likewise to comprehend distinctly the difference between developing *an nth function algebraically*, and merely *calculating an nth function arithmetically*. If he does not, the following will be by no means very intelligible; but we have not space to give any preliminary explanations. To proceed: the law, according to which the successive functions of (5.) are to be developed, must of course first be fixed on. This law may be of very various kinds. We may propose to obtain our results in successive *powers* of x, in which case the general form would be

$$C + C_1x + C_2x^2 + \&c.;$$

or in successive powers of n itself, the index of the function we are ultimately to obtain, in which case the general form would be

$$C + C_1n + C_2n^2 + \&c.;$$

and x would only enter in the coefficients. Again, other functions of x or of n instead of *powers* might be selected. It might be in addition proposed, that the coefficients themselves should be arranged according to given functions of a certain quantity. Another mode would be to make equations arbitrarily amongst the coefficients only, in which case the several functions, according to either of which it might be possible to develope the nth function of (5.), would have to be determined from the combined consideration of these equations and of (5.) itself.

The *algebraical* nature of the engine (so strongly insisted on in a previous part of this Note) would enable it to follow out any of these various modes indifferently; just as we recently showed that it can distribute and separate the numerical results of any one prescribed series of processes, in a perfectly arbitrary manner. Were it otherwise, the engine could merely *compute the arithmetical nth function*, a result which, like any other purely arithmetical results,

would be simply a collective number, bearing no traces of the data or the processes which had led to it.

Secondly, the *law* of development for the nth function being selected, the next step would obviously be to develope (5.) itself, according to this law. This result would be the first function, and would be obtained by a determinate series of processes. These in most cases would include amongst them one or more *cycles* of operations.

The third step (which would consist of the various processes necessary for effecting the actual substitution of the series constituting the *first function*, for the *variable* itself) might proceed in either of two ways. It might make the substitution either wherever x occurs in the original (5.), or it might similarly make it wherever x occurs in the first function itself which is the equivalent of (5.). In some cases the former mode might be best, and in others the latter.

Whichever is adopted, it must be understood that the result is to appear arranged in a series following the law originally prescribed for the development of the nth function. This result constitutes the second function; with which we are to proceed exactly as we did with the first function, in order to obtain the third function, and so on, $n - 1$ times, to obtain the nth function. We easily perceive that since every successive function is arranged in a series *following the same law*, there would (after the *first* function is obtained) be a *cycle of a cycle of a cycle*, &c. of operations,[26] one, two, three, up to $n - 1$ times, in order to get the nth function. We say, *after the first function is obtained*, because (for reasons on which we cannot here enter) the *first* function might in many cases be developed through a set of processes peculiar to itself, and not recurring for the remaining functions.

We have given but a very slight sketch of the principal *general* steps which would be requisite for obtaining an nth function of such a formula as (5.). The question is so exceedingly complicated, that perhaps few persons can be expected to follow, to their own satisfaction, so brief and general a statement as we are here restricted to on this subject. Still it is a very important case as regards the engine, and suggests ideas peculiar to itself, which we should regret to pass wholly without allusion. Nothing could be more interesting than to follow out, in every detail, the solution by the engine of such a case as the above; but the time, space and labour this would necessitate, could only suit a very extensive work.

To return to the subject of *cycles* of operations: some of the notation of the integral calculus lends itself very aptly to express them: (2.) might be thus written:—

(6.) $(4), \Sigma(+1)^p (\times, -)$ or $(1) \Sigma(+1)^p (2, 3)$,

where p stands for the variable; $(+1)^p$ for the function of the variable, that is, for ϕp; and the limits are from 1 to p, or from 0 to $p-1$, each increment being equal to unity. Similarly, (4.) would be,—

(7.) $\Sigma(+1)^n \{(4), \Sigma(+1)^p (\times, -)\}$

the limits of n being from 1 to n, or from 0 to $n-1$,

(8.)   or $\Sigma(+1)^n \{(1), \Sigma(+1)^p (2, 3)\}$.

Perhaps it may be thought that this notation is merely a circuitous way of expressing what was more simply and as effectually expressed before; and, in the above example, there may be some truth in this. But there is another description of cycles which *can* only effectually be expressed, in a condensed form, by the preceding notation. We shall call them *varying cycles*. They are of frequent occurrence, and include successive cycles of operations of the following nature:—

(9.)
$$p(\overline{1, 2, \ldots m}), \overline{p - 1}(1, 2, \ldots m), \overline{p - 2}(1, 2, \ldots m)$$
$$\ldots p - n(1, 2, \ldots m)$$

where each cycle contains the same group of operations, but in which the number of repetitions of the group varies according to a fixed rate, with every cycle. (9.) can be well expressed as follows:—

(10.)
$(p\,(1, 2 \ldots m)$, the limits of p being from $p -$
n to p.

Independent of the intrinsic advantages which we thus perceive to result in certain cases from this use of the notation of the integral calculus, there are likewise considerations which make it interesting, from the connections and relations involved in this new application. It has been observed in some of the former Notes, that the processes used in analysis form a logical system of much higher generality than the applications to number merely. Thus, when we read over any algebraical formula, considering it exclusively with reference to the processes of the engine, and putting aside for the moment its abstract signification as to the relations of quantity, the symbols +, ×, &c. in reality represent (as their immediate and proximate effect, when the formula is applied to the engine) that a certain prism which is a part of the mechanism (see Note C.) turns a new face, and thus presents a new card to act on the bundles of levers of the engine; the new card being perforated with holes, which are arranged according to the peculiarities of the operation of addition, or of multiplication, &c. Again, the *numbers* in the preceding formula (8.), each of them really represents one of these very pieces of card that are hung over the prism.

Now in the use made in the formulæ (7.), (8.) and (10.), of the notation of the integral calculus, we have glimpses of a similar new application of the language of the *higher* mathematics. Σ, in reality, here indicates that when a certain number of cards have acted in succession, the prism over which they revolve must *rotate backwards*, so as to bring those cards into their former position; and the limits 1 to n, 1 to p, &c., regulate how often this backward rotation is to be repeated.
A. A. L.

Note F

There is in existence a beautiful woven portrait of Jacquard, in the fabrication of which 24,000 cards were required.

The power of *repeating* the cards, alluded to by M. Menabrea on page 680 [*sic*], and more fully explained in Note C., reduces to an immense extent the number of cards required. It is obvious that this mechanical improvement is especially applicable wherever *cycles* occur in the mathematical operations, and that, in preparing data for calculations by the engine, it is desirable to arrange the order and combination of the processes with a view to obtain them as much as possible *symmetrically* and in cycles, in order that the mechanical advantages of the *backing* system may be applied to the utmost. It is here interesting to observe the manner in which the value of an *analytical* resource is *met* and *enhanced* by an ingenious *mechanical* contrivance. We see in it an instance of one of those mutual *adjustments* between the purely mathematical and the mechanical departments, mentioned in Note A. as being a main and essential condition of success in the invention of a calculating engine. The nature of the resources afforded by such adjustments would be of two principal kinds. In some cases, a difficulty (perhaps in itself insurmountable) in the one department would be overcome by facilities in the other; and sometimes (as in the present case) a strong point in the one would be rendered still stronger and more available by combination with a corresponding strong point in the other.

As a mere example of the degree to which the combined systems of cycles and of backing can diminish the *number* of cards requisite, we shall choose a case which places it in strong evidence, and which has likewise the advantage of being a perfectly different *kind* of problem from those that are mentioned in any of the other Notes. Suppose it be required to eliminate nine variables from ten simple equations of the form—

$$ax_0 + bx_1 + cx_2 + dx_3 + \ldots = p \qquad (1.)$$

$$a^1x_0 + b^1x_1 + c^1x_2 + d^1x_3 + \ldots = p^1 \qquad (2.)$$

&c.   &c.   &c.   &c.

We should explain, before proceeding, that it is not our object to consider this problem with reference to the actual arrangement of the data on the Variables of the engine, but simply as an abstract question of the *nature* and *number* of the *operations* required to be performed during its complete solution.

The first step would be the elimination of the first unknown quantity x_0 between the first two equations.

This would be obtained by the form—

$$(a^1a - aa^1)x_0 + (a^1b - ab^1)x_1 + (a^1c - ac^1)x_2 + \\ (a^1d - ad^1)x_3 + \ldots = a^1p - ap^1,$$

for which the operations 10 ($\times, \times, -$) would be needed. The second step would be the elimination of x_0 between the second and third equations, for which the operations would be precisely the same. We should then have had altogether the following operations:—

$$10(\times, \times, -), 10(\times, \times, -) = 20(\times, \times, -)$$

Continuing in the same manner, the total number of operations for the complete elimination of x_0 between all the successive pairs of equations would be—

$$9 \cdot 10(\times, \times, -) = 90(\times, \times, -)$$

We should then be left with nine simple equations of nine variables from which to eliminate the next variable x_1, for which the total of the processes would be

$$8 \cdot 9(\times, \times, -) = 72(\times, \times, -)$$

We should then be left with eight simple equations of eight variables from which to eliminate x_2, for which the processes would be—

$$7 \cdot 8(\times, \times, -) = 56(\times, \times, -)$$

and so on. The total operations for the elimination of all the variables would thus be—

$$9 \cdot 10 + 8 \cdot 9 + 7 \cdot 8 + 6 \cdot 7 + 5 \cdot 6 + 4 \cdot 5 + 3 \cdot 4 \\ + 2 \cdot 3 + 1 \cdot 2 = 330.$$

So that *three* Operation-cards would perform the office of 330 such cards.

If we take *n* simple equations containing $n - 1$ variables, *n* being a number unlimited in magnitude, the case becomes still more obvious, as the same three cards might then take the place of thousands or millions of cards.

We shall now draw further attention to the fact, already noticed, of its being by no means necessary that a formula proposed for solution should ever have been actually worked out, as a condition for enabling the engine to solve it. Provided we know the *series of operations* to be gone through, that is sufficient. In the foregoing instance this will be obvious enough on a slight consideration. And it is a circumstance which deserves particular notice, since herein may reside a latent value of such an engine almost incalculable in its possible ultimate results. We already know that there are functions whose numerical value it is of importance for the purposes both of abstract and of practical science to ascertain, but whose determination requires processes so lengthy and so complicated, that, although it is possible to arrive at them through great expenditure of time, labour and money, it is yet on these accounts practically almost unattainable; and we can conceive there being some results which it may be *absolutely impossible* in practice to attain with any accuracy, and whose precise determination it may prove highly important for some of the future wants of science, in its manifold, complicated and rapidly-developing fields of inquiry, to arrive at.

Without, however, stepping into the region of conjecture, we will mention a particular problem which occurs to us at this moment as being an apt illustration of the use to which such an engine may be turned for determining that which human brains find it difficult or impossible to work out unerringly. In the solution of the famous problem of the Three Bodies, there are, out of about 295 coefficients of lunar perturbations given by M. Clausen (Astro^e. Nachrichten, No. 406) as the result of the calculations by Burg, of two by Damoiseau, and of one by Burckhardt, fourteen coefficients that differ in the nature of their algebraic sign; and out of the remainder there are only 101 (or about one-third) that agree precisely both in signs and in amount. These discordances, which are generally small in individual magnitude, may arise either from an erroneous determination of the abstract coefficients in the development of the problem, or from discrepancies in the data deduced from observation, or from both causes combined. The former is the most ordinary source of error in astronomical computations, and this the engine would entirely obviate.

We might even invent laws for series or formulæ in an arbitrary manner, and set the engine to work upon them, and thus deduce numerical results which we might not otherwise have thought of obtaining; but this would hardly perhaps in any instance be productive of any great practical utility, or calculated to rank higher than as a philosophical amusement.

A. A. L.

Note G

It is desirable to guard against the possibility of exaggerated ideas that might arise as to the powers of the Analytical Engine. In considering any new subject, there is frequently a tendency, first, to *overrate* what we find to be already interesting or remarkable; and, secondly, by a sort of natural reaction, to *undervalue* the true state of the case, when we do discover that our notions have surpassed those that were really tenable.

The Analytical Engine has no pretensions whatever to *originate* anything. It can do whatever we *know how to order it* to perform. It can *follow* analysis; but it has no power of *anticipating* any analytical relations or truths. Its province is to assist us in making *available* what we are already acquainted with. This it is calculated to effect primarily and chiefly of course, through its executive faculties; but it is likely to exert an *indirect* and reciprocal influence on science itself in another manner. For, in so distributing and combining the truths and the formulæ of analysis, that they may become most easily and rapidly amenable to the mechanical combinations of the engine, the relations and the nature of many subjects in that science are necessarily thrown into new lights, and more profoundly investigated. This is a decidedly indirect, and a somewhat *speculative*, consequence of such an invention. It is however pretty evident, on general principles, that in devising for mathematical truths a new form in which to record and throw themselves out for actual use, views are likely to be induced, which should again react on the more theoretical phase of the subject. There are in all extensions of human power, or additions to human knowledge, various *collateral* influences, besides the main and primary object attained.

To return to the executive faculties of this engine: the question must arise in every mind, are they *really* even able to *follow* analysis in its whole extent? No reply, entirely satisfactory to all minds, can be given to this query, excepting the actual existence of the engine, and actual experience of its practical results. We will however sum up for each reader's consideration the chief elements with which the engine works:—

1. It performs the four operations of simple arithmetic upon any numbers whatever.

2. By means of certain artifices and arrangements (upon which we cannot enter within the restricted space which such a publication as the present may admit of), there is no limit either to the *magnitude* of the *numbers* used, or to the *number of quantities* (either variables or constants) that may be employed.

3. It can combine these numbers and these quantities either algebraically or arithmetically, in relations unlimited as to variety, extent, or complexity.

4. It uses algebraic *signs* according to their proper laws, and developes the logical consequences of these laws.

5. It can arbitrarily substitute any formula for any other; effacing the first from the columns on which it is represented, and making the second appear in its stead.

6. It can provide for singular values. Its power of doing this is referred to in M. Menabrea's memoir, page 685 [*sic*] where he mentions the passage of values through zero and infinity. The practicability of causing it arbitrarily to change

its processes at any moment, on the occurrence of any specified contingency (of which its substitution of

$$\left(\frac{1}{2}\cos\overline{n+1}\theta + \frac{1}{2}\cos\overline{n-1}\theta\right)$$

for $(\cos n\theta \cos\theta)$, explained in Note E., is in some degree an illustration), at once secures this point.

The subject of integration and of differentiation demands some notice. The engine can effect these processes in either of two ways:—

First. We may order it, by means of the Operation and of the Variable-cards, to go through the various steps by which the required *limit* can be worked out for whatever function is under consideration.

Secondly. It may (if we know the form of the limit for the function in question) effect the integration or differentiation by direct[27] substitution. We remarked in Note B., that any *set* of columns on which numbers are inscribed, represents merely a *general* function of the several quantities, until the special function have been impressed by means of the Operation and Variable-cards. Consequently, if instead of requiring the value of the function, we require that of its integral, or of its differential coefficient, we have merely to order whatever particular combination of the ingredient quantities may constitute that integral or that coefficient. In ax^n, for instance, instead of the quantities

V_0	V_1	V_2	V_3
a	n	x	ax^n
ax^n			

being ordered to appear on V_3 in the combination ax^n, they would be ordered to appear in that of

anx^{n-1}

They would then stand thus:—

V_0	V_1	V_2	V_3
a	n	x	ax^{n-1}
	anx^{n-1}		

Similarly, we might have $\frac{a}{n}x^{(n+1)}$, the integral of ax^n.

An interesting example for following out the processes of the engine would be such a form as

$$\int \frac{x^n dx}{\sqrt{a^2 - x^2}},$$

or any other cases of integration by successive reductions, where an integral which contains an operation repeated n times can be made to depend upon another which contains the same $n-1$ or $n-2$ times, and so on until by continued reduction we arrive at a certain *ultimate* form, whose value has then to be determined.

The methods in Arbogast's *Calcul des Dérivations* are peculiarly fitted for the notation and the processes of the engine. Likewise the whole of the Combinatorial Analysis, which consists first in a purely numerical calculation of indices, and secondly in the distribution and combination of the quantities according to laws prescribed by these indices.

We will terminate these Notes by following up in detail the steps through which the engine could compute the Numbers of Bernoulli, this being (in the form in which we shall deduce it) a rather complicated example of its powers. The simplest manner of computing these numbers would be from the direct expansion of

$$\frac{x}{\varepsilon^x - 1} = \frac{1}{1 + \frac{x}{2} + \frac{x^2}{2 \cdot 3} + \frac{x^3}{2 \cdot 3 \cdot 4} + \text{etc.}} \qquad (1.)$$

which is in fact a particular case of the development of

$$\frac{a + bx + cx^2 + \&c.}{a' + b'x + c'x^2 + \&c.}$$

mentioned in Note E. Or again, we might compute them from the well-known form

$$B_{2n-1} = 2 \cdot \frac{1 \cdot 2 \cdot 3 \ldots 2n}{(2\pi)^{2n}} \cdot \left\{ 1 + \frac{1}{2^{2n}} + \frac{1}{3^{2n}} + \ldots \right\} \qquad (2.)$$

or from the form

$$B_{2n-1} = \frac{\pm 2n}{(2^{2n-1})2^{n-1}} \begin{cases} \frac{1}{2}n^{2n-1} \\ -(n-1)^{2n-1}\left\{1 + \frac{1}{2} \cdot \frac{2n}{1}\right\} \\ +(n-2)^{2n-1}\left\{1 + \frac{2n}{1} + \frac{1}{2} \cdot \frac{2n \cdot (2n-1)}{1 \cdot 2}\right\} \\ -(n-3)^{2n-1}\left\{1 + \frac{2n}{1} + \frac{2n \cdot 2n-1}{1 \cdot 2} + \frac{1}{2} \cdot \frac{2n \cdot (2n-1) \cdot (2n+1)}{1 \cdot 2 \cdot 3}\right\} \\ + \quad \ldots \quad \ldots \quad \ldots \quad \ldots \end{cases}$$

$$(3.)$$

or from many others. As however our object is not simplicity or facility of computation, but the illustration of the powers of the engine, we prefer selecting the formula below, marked (8.) This is derived in the following manner:—

If in the equation

$$\frac{x}{\varepsilon^x - 1} = 1 - \frac{x}{2} + B_1\frac{x^2}{2} + B_3\frac{x^4}{2 \cdot 3 \cdot 4} + B_5\frac{x^6}{2 \cdot 3 \cdot 4 \cdot 5 \cdot 6} + \ldots$$

$$(4.)$$

(in which B_1, B_3 . . . , &c. are the Numbers of Bernoulli), we expand the denominator of the first side in powers of x, and then divide both numerator and denominator by x, we shall derive

$$1 = \left(1 - \frac{x}{2} + B_1\frac{x^2}{2} + B_3\frac{x^4}{2 \cdot 3 \cdot 4} + \ldots\right)\left(1 + \frac{x}{2} + \frac{x^2}{2 \cdot 3} + \frac{x^3}{2 \cdot 3 \cdot 4}\ldots\right)$$

$$(5.)$$

If this latter multiplication be actually performed, we shall have a series of the general form

$$1 + D_1 x + D_2 x^2 + D_3 x^3 + \ldots \qquad (6.)$$

in which we see, first, that all the coefficients of the powers of x are severally equal to zero; and secondly, that the general form for D_{2n}, the coefficient of the $2n+1$th *term* (that is of x^{2n} any *even* power of x), is the following:—

$$\frac{1}{2 \cdot 3 \ldots 2n+1} - \frac{1}{2} \cdot \frac{1}{2 \cdot 3 \ldots 2n} + \frac{B_1}{2} \cdot \frac{1}{2 \cdot 3 \ldots 2n-1} + \frac{B_3}{2 \cdot 3 \cdot 4} \cdot \frac{1}{2 \cdot 3 \ldots 2n-3} +$$

$$\frac{B_5}{2 \cdot 3 \cdot 4 \cdot 5 \cdot 6} \cdot \frac{1}{2 \cdot 3 \ldots 2n-5} + \ldots + \frac{B_{2n-1}}{2 \cdot 3 \ldots 2n} \cdot 1 = 0$$

$$(7.)$$

Multiplying every term by $(2 \cdot 3 \ldots 2^n)$ we have

$$0 = -\frac{1}{2} \cdot \frac{2n-1}{2n+1} + B_1\left(\frac{2n}{2}\right) + B_3\left(\frac{2n \cdot 2n-1 \cdot 2n-2}{2 \cdot 3 \cdot 4}\right)$$

$$+ B_5\left(\frac{2n \cdot 2n-1 \ldots 2n-4}{2 \cdot 3 \cdot 4 \cdot 5 \cdot 6}\right) + \ldots + B_{2n-1}$$

$$(8.)$$

which it may be convenient to write under the general form:—

$$0 = A_0 + A_1B_1 + A_3B_3 + A_5B_5 +$$
$$\ldots + B_{2n-1} \qquad (9.)$$

A_1, A_3, &c. being those functions of n which respectively belong to B_1, B_3, &c.

We might have derived a form nearly similar to (8.), from D_{2n-1} the coefficient of any *odd* power of x in (6.); but the general form is a little different for the coefficients of the *odd* powers, and not quite so convenient.

On examining (7.) and (8.), we perceive that, when these formulæ are isolated from (6.), whence they are derived, and considered in themselves separately and independently, n may be any whole number whatever; although when (7.) occurs as *one of the* D's in (6.), it is obvious that n is then not arbitrary, but is always a certain function of the *distance of that* D *from the beginning*. If that distance be $=d$, then

$2n + 1 = d$, and $n = \dfrac{d-1}{2}$ (for any *even* power of x)

$2n = d$, and $n = \dfrac{d}{2}$ (for any *odd* power of x)

It is with the *independent* formula (8.) that we have to do. Therefore it must be remembered that the conditions for the value of n are now modified, and that n is a perfectly *arbitrary* whole number. This circumstance, combined with the fact (which we may easily perceive) that whatever n is, every term of (8.) after the $(n + 1)$th is $=0$, and that the $(n + 1)$th term itself is always $B_{2n-1} \cdot \dfrac{1}{1} = B_{2n-1}$, enables us to find the value (either numerical or algebraical) of any nth Number of Bernoulli B_{2n-1}, *in terms of all the preceding ones*, if we but know the values of $B_1, B_3 \ldots B_{2n-3}$. We append to this Note a Diagram and Table, containing the details of the computation for B_7 (B_1, B_3, B_5 being supposed given).

On attentively considering (8.), we shall likewise perceive that we may derive from it the numerical value of *every* Number of Bernoulli in succession, from the very beginning, *ad infinitum*, by the following series of computations:—

1st Series.—Let $n = 1$, and calculate (8.) for this value of n. The result is B_1.

2nd Series.—Let $n = 2$. Calculate (8.) for this value of n, substituting the value of B_1 just obtained. The result is B_3.

3rd Series.—Let $n = 3$. Calculate (8.) for this value of n, substituting the values of B_1, B_3 before obtained. The result is B_5. And so on, to any extent.

The diagram[28] represents the columns of the engine when just prepared for computing B_{2n-1} (in the case of $n = 4$); while the table beneath them presents a complete simultaneous view of all the successive changes which these columns then severally pass through in order to perform the computation. (The reader is referred to Note D. for explanations respecting the nature and notation of such tables.)

Six numerical *data* are in this case necessary for making the requisite combinations. These data are 1, 2, $n(=4)$, B_1, B_3, B_5. Were $n = 5$, the additional datum B_5 would be needed. Were $n = 6$, the datum B_9 would be needed; and so on. Thus the actual *number of data* needed will always be $n + 2$, for $n = n$; and out of these $n + 2$ data, $(\overline{n + 2} - 3)$ of them are successive Numbers of Bernoulli. The reason why the Bernoulli Numbers used as data are nevertheless placed on *Result*-columns in the diagram, is because they may properly be supposed to have been previously computed in succession by the *engine* itself; under which circumstances each B will appear as a *result*, previous to being used as a *datum* for computing the succeeding B. Here then is an instance (of the kind alluded to in Note D.) of the same Variables filling more than one office in turn. It is true that if we consider our computation of B_7 as a perfectly isolated calculation, we may conclude B_1, B_3, B_5 to have been arbitrarily placed on the columns; and it would then perhaps be more consistent to put them on V_4, V_5, V_6 as data and not results. But we are not taking this view. On the contrary, we suppose the engine to be *in the course of* computing the Numbers to an indefinite extent, from the very beginning; and that we merely single out, by way of example, *one amongst* the successive but distinct series of computations it is thus performing. Where the B's are fractional, it must be understood that they are computed and appear in the notation of *decimal* fractions. Indeed this is a circumstance that should be noticed with reference to all calculations. In any of the examples already given in the translation and in the Notes, some of the *data*, or of the temporary or permanent results, might be fractional, quite as probably as whole numbers. But the arrangements are so made, that the nature of the processes would be the same as for whole numbers.

In the above table and diagram we are not considering the *signs* of any of the B's, merely their numerical magnitude. The engine would bring out the sign for each of them correctly of course, but we cannot enter on *every* additional detail of this kind as we might wish to do. The circles for the signs are therefore intentionally left blank in the diagram.

Operation-cards 1, 2, 3, 4, 5, 6 prepare $-\dfrac{1}{2} \cdot \dfrac{2n-1}{2n+1}$.

Thus, Card 1 multiplies *two* into n, and the three *Receiving* Variable-cards belonging respectively to V_4,

V_5, V_6, allow the result $2n$ to be placed on each of these latter columns (this being a case in which a triple receipt of the result is needed for subsequent purposes); we see that the upper indices of the two Variables used, during Operation 1, remain unaltered.

We shall not go through the details of every operation singly, since the table and diagram sufficiently indicate them; we shall merely notice some few peculiar cases.

By Operation 6, a *positive* quantity is turned into a *negative* quantity, by simply subtracting the quantity from a column which has only zero upon it. (The sign at the top of V_8 would become - during this process.)

Operation 7 will be unintelligible, unless it be remembered that if we were calculating for $n = 1$ instead of $n = 4$, Operation 6 would have completed the computation of B_1 itself, in which case the engine instead of continuing its processes, would have to put B_1 on V_{21}; and then either to stop altogether, or to begin Operations 1, 2 ... 7 all over again for value of $n(= 2)$, in order to enter on the computation of B_3; (having however taken care, previous to this recommencement, to make the number on V_3 equal to *two*, by the addition of unity to the former $n = 1$ on that column). Now Operation 7 must either bring out a result equal to zero (if $n = 1$); or a result *greater* than *zero*, as in the present case; and the engine follows the one or the other of the two courses just explained, contingently on the one or the other result of Operation 7. In order fully to perceive the necessity of this *experimental* operation, it is important to keep in mind what was pointed out, that we are not treating a perfectly isolated and independent computation, but one out of a series of antecedent and prospective computations.

Cards 8, 9, 10 produce $-\frac{1}{2} \cdot \frac{2n-1}{2n+1} + B_1 \frac{2n}{2}$. In Operation 9 we see an example of an upper index which again becomes a value after having passed from preceding values to zero. V_{11} has successively been $^0V_{11}$, $^1V_{11}$, $^2V_{11}$, $^0V_{11}$, $^3V_{11}$; and, from the nature of the office which V_{11} performs in the calculation, its index will continue to go through further changes of the same description, which, if examined, will be found to be regular and periodic.

Card 12 has to perform the same office as Card 7 did in the preceding section; since, if n had been = 2, the 11th operation would have completed the computation of B_3.

Cards 13 to 20 make A_3. Since A_{2n-1} always consists of $2n - 1$ factors, A_3 has three factors; and it will be seen that Cards 13, 14, 15, 16 make the second of these factors, and then multiply it with the first; and that 17, 18, 19, 20 make the third factor, and then multiply this with the product of the two former factors.

Card 23 has the office of Cards 11 and 7 to perform, since if n were = 3, the 21st and 22nd operations would complete the computation of B_5. As our case is B_7, the computation will continue one more stage; and we must now direct attention to the fact, that in order to compute A_7 it is merely necessary precisely to repeat the group of Operations 13 to 20; and then, in order to complete the computation of B_7, to repeat Operations 21, 22.

It will be perceived that every unit added to n in B_{2n-1}, entails an additional repetition of operations (13 ... 23) for the computation of B_{2n-1}. Not only are all the *operations* precisely the same however for every such repetition, but they require to be respectively supplied with numbers from the very *same pairs of columns*; with only the one exception of Operation 21, which will of course need B_5 (from V_{23}) instead of B_3 (from V_{22}). This identity in the *columns* which supply the requisite numbers must not be confounded with identity in the *values* those columns have upon them and give out to the mill. Most of those values undergo alterations during a performance of the operations (13 ... 23), and consequently the columns present a new set of values for the *next* performance of (13 ... 23) to work on.

At the termination of the *repetition* of operations (13...23) in computing B_7, the alterations in the values on the Variables are, that

V_6	=	$2n - 4$ instead of $2n - 2$.
V_7	=	6............4.
V_{10}	=	0............1.
V_{13}	=	$A_0 + A_1B_1 + A_3B_3 + A_5B_5$ instead of $A_0 + A_1B_1 + A_3B_3$.

In this state the only remaining processes are, first, to transfer the value which is on V_{13} to V_{24}; and secondly, to reduce V_6, V_7, V_{13} to zero, and to add[29] *one* to V_3, in order that the engine may be ready to commence computing B_9. Operations 24 and 25 accomplish these purposes. It may be thought anomalous that Operation 25 is represented as leaving the upper index of V_3 still = unity; but it must be remembered that these indices always begin anew for a separate calculation, and that Operation 25 places upon V_3 the *first* value *for the new calculation.*

It should be remarked, that when the group (13 . . . 23) is *repeated*, changes occur in some of the *upper* indices during the course of the repetition: for example, $^3V_6$ would become $^4V_6$ and $^5V_6$.

We thus see that when $n = 1$, nine Operation-cards are used; that when $n = 2$, fourteen Operation-cards are used; and that when $n > 2$, twenty-five Operation-cards are used; but that no *more* are needed, however great n may be; and not only this, but that these same twenty-five cards suffice for the successive computation of all the Numbers from B_1 to B_{2n-1} inclusive. With respect to the number of *Variable*-cards, it will be remembered, from the explanations in previous Notes, that an average of three such cards to each *operation* (not however to each Operation-*card*) is the estimate. According to this, the computation of B_1 will require twenty-seven Variable-cards; B_3 forty-two such cards; B_5 seventy-five; and for every succeeding B after B_5, there would be thirty-three additional Variable-cards (since each repetition of the group (13 . . . 23) adds eleven to the number of operations required for computing the previous B). But we must now explain, that whenever there is a *cycle of operations,* and if these merely require to be supplied with numbers from the *same pairs of columns,* and likewise each operation to place its *result* on the *same* column for every repetition of the whole group, the process then admits of a *cycle of Variable-cards* for effecting its purposes. There is obviously much more symmetry and simplicity in the arrangements, when cases do admit of repeating the Variable as well as the Operation-cards. Our present example is of this nature. The only

exception to a *perfect identity* in *all* the processes and columns used, for every repetition of Operations (13 . . . 23), is, that Operation 21 always requires one of its factors from a new column, and Operation 24 always puts its result on a new column. But as these variations follow the same law at each repetition (Operation 21 always requiring its factor from a column *one* in advance of that which it used the previous time, and Operation 24 always putting its result on the column *one* in advance of that which received the previous result), they are easily provided for in arranging the recurring group (or cycle) of Variable-cards.

We may here remark, that the average estimate of three Variable-cards coming into use to each operation, is not to be taken as an absolutely and literally correct amount for all cases and circumstances. Many special circumstances, either in the nature of a problem, or in the arrangements of the engine under certain contingencies, influence and modify this average to a greater or less extent; but it is a very safe and correct *general* rule to go upon. In the preceding case it will give us seventy-five Variable-cards as the total number which will be necessary for computing any B after B_3. This is very nearly the precise amount really used, but we cannot here enter into the minutiæ of the few particular circumstances which occur in this example (as indeed at some one stage or other of probably most computations) to modify slightly this number.

It will be obvious that the very *same* seventy-five Variable-cards may be repeated for the computation of every succeeding Number, just on the same principle as admits of the repetition of the thirty-three Variable-cards of Operations (13 . . . 23) in the computation of any *one* Number. Thus there will be a *cycle of a cycle* of Variable-cards.

If we now apply the notation for cycles, as explained in Note E., we may express the operations for computing the Numbers of Bernoulli in the following manner:—

(1...7), (24, 25) gives B$_1$	= 1st number; (n being = 1)
(1...7), (8...12), (24, 25) gives B$_3$	= 2nd number; (n being = 2)
(1...7), (8...12), (13...23), (24, 25) gives B$_5$	= 3rd number; (n being = 3)
(1...7), (8...12), 2(13...23), (24, 25) gives B$_7$	= 4th number; (n being = 4)
....	
....	
(1...7), (8...12), $\sum(+1)^{n-2}$(13...23), (24, 25) gives B$_{2n-1}$	= nth number; (n being = n)

Again,

$$(1...7), (24, 25), \sum_{\text{limits 1 to } n}(+1)^n \left\{ (1...7), (8...12), \sum_{\text{limits 0 to } (n+2)}(n+2) \right.$$

$$(13...23), (24, 25)$$

represents the total operations for computing every number in succession, from B$_1$ to B$_{2n-1}$ inclusive.

In this formula we see a *varying cycle* of the *first* order, and an ordinary cycle of the *second* order. The latter cycle in this case includes in it the varying cycle.

On inspecting the ten Working-Variables of the diagram, it will be perceived, that although the *value* on any one of them (excepting V$_4$ and V$_5$) goes through a series of changes, the *office* which each performs is in this calculation *fixed* and *invariable*. Thus V$_6$ always prepares the *numerators* of the factors of any A; V$_7$ the *denominators*. V$_8$ always receives the $(2n - 3)$th factor of A$_{2n-1}$, and V$_9$ the $(2n - 1)$th. V$_{10}$ always decides which of two courses the succeeding processes are to follow, by feeling for the value of n through means of a subtraction; and so on; but we shall not enumerate further. It is desirable in all calculations so to arrange the processes, that the *offices* performed by the Variables may be as uniform and fixed as possible.

Supposing that it was desired not only to tabulate B$_1$, B$_3$, &c., but A$_0$, A$_1$, &c.; we have only then to appoint another series of Variables, V$_{41}$, V$_{42}$, &c., for

receiving these latter results as they are successively produced upon V$_{11}$. Or again, we may, instead of this, or in addition to this second series of results, wish to tabulate the value of each successive *total* term of the series (8.), viz. A$_0$, A$_1$B$_1$, A$_3$B$_3$, &c. We have then merely to multiply each B with each corresponding A, as produced, and to place these successive products on Result-columns appointed for the purpose.

The formula (8.) is interesting in another point of view. It is one particular case of the general Integral of the following Equation of Mixed Differences:—

$$\frac{d^2}{dx^2}(z_{n+1}x^{2n+2}) = (2n+1)(2n+2)z^n x^{2n}$$

for certain special suppositions respecting z, x and n.

The *general* integral itself is of the form,

$$z_n = f(n) \cdot x + f_1(n) + f_2(n) \cdot x^{-1} + f_3(n) \cdot x^{-3} + \cdots$$

and it is worthy of remark, that the engine might (in a manner more or less similar to the preceding) calculate the value of this formula upon most *other* hypotheses for the functions in the integral with as much, or (in many cases) with more ease than it can formula (8.).

A. A. L.

No. of Op.	Nature of Op.	Variables acted upon.	Variables receiving results.	Indication of change in the value on any Variable.	Statement of Results.	$^1V_1$ ○ 0 0 0 1 — 1	$^1V_2$ ○ 0 0 0 2 — 2	$^1V_3$ ○ 0 0 0 4 — n	$^0V_4$ ○ 0 0 0 0 — □	$^0V_5$ ○ 0 0 0 0 — □	$^0V_6$ ○ 0 0 0 0 — □
1	×	$^1V_2 \times ^1V_3$	$^1V_4, ^1V_5, ^1V_6$	$\left\{\begin{array}{l}^1V_2=^1V_2\\^1V_3=^1V_3\end{array}\right\}$	$= 2n$	...	2	n	$2n$	$2n$	$2n$
2	−	$^1V_4 - ^1V_1$	$^2V_4$	$\left\{\begin{array}{l}^1V_4=^2V_4\\^1V_1=^1V_1\end{array}\right\}$	$= 2n-1$	1	...	...	$2n-1$		
3	+	$^1V_5 + ^1V_1$	$^2V_5$	$\left\{\begin{array}{l}^1V_5=^2V_5\\^1V_1=^1V_1\end{array}\right\}$	$= 2n+1$	1	...	...	...	$2n+1$	
4	÷	$^2V_5 \div ^2V_4$	$^1V_{11}$	$\left\{\begin{array}{l}^2V_5=^0V_5\\^2V_4=^0V_4\end{array}\right\}$	$= \dfrac{2n-1}{2n+1}$	...	...	...	0.	0	...
5	÷	$^1V_{11} \div ^1V_2$	$^2V_{11}$	$\left\{\begin{array}{l}^1V_{11}=^2V_{11}\\^1V_2=^1V_2\end{array}\right\}$	$= \dfrac{1}{2}\cdot\dfrac{2n-1}{2n+1}$	...	2	...	...	...	...
6	−	$^0V_{13} - ^2V_{11}$	$^1V_{13}$	$\left\{\begin{array}{l}^2V_{11}=^0V_{11}\\^0V_{13}=^1V_{13}\end{array}\right\}$	$= -\dfrac{1}{2}\cdot\dfrac{2n-1}{2n+1}=A_0$	...	...	...	...	...	...
7	−	$^1V_3 - ^1V_1$	$^1V_{10}$	$\left\{\begin{array}{l}^1V_3=^1V_3\\^1V_1=^1V_1\end{array}\right\}$	$= n-1(=3)$	1	...	n	...	...	...
8	+	$^1V_2 + ^0V_7$	$^1V_7$	$\left\{\begin{array}{l}^1V_2=^1V_2\\^0V_7=^1V_7\end{array}\right\}$	$= 2+0=2$	...	2	...	...	...	...
9	÷	$^1V_6 \div ^1V_7$	$^3V_{11}$	$\left\{\begin{array}{l}^1V_6=^1V_6\\^0V_{11}=^3V_{11}\end{array}\right\}$	$= \dfrac{2n}{2}=A_1$	...					$2n$
10	×	$^1V_{21} \times ^3V_{11}$	$^1V_{12}$	$\left\{\begin{array}{l}^1V_{21}=^1V_{21}\\^3V_{11}=^3V_{11}\end{array}\right\}$	$= B_1\cdot\dfrac{2n}{2}=B_1A_1$	...	...	...	...	...	...
11	+	$^1V_{12} + ^1V_{13}$	$^2V_{13}$	$\left\{\begin{array}{l}^1V_{12}=^0V_{12}\\^1V_{13}=^2V_{13}\end{array}\right\}$	$= -\dfrac{1}{2}\cdot\dfrac{2n-1}{2n+1} + B_1\cdot\dfrac{2n}{2}$	...	...	...	...	...	...
12	−	$^1V_{10} - ^1V_1$	$^2V_{10}$	$\left\{\begin{array}{l}^1V_{10}=^2V_{10}\\^1V_1=^1V_1\end{array}\right\}$	$= n-2(=2)$	1	...	...	...	...	...
13	−	$^1V_6 - ^1V_1$	$^2V_6$	$\left\{\begin{array}{l}^1V_6=^2V_6\\^1V_1=^1V_1\end{array}\right\}$	$= 2n-1$	1	...	...	...	...	$2n-1$
14	+	$^1V_1 + ^1V_7$	$^2V_7$	$\left\{\begin{array}{l}^1V_1=^1V_1\\^1V_7=^2V_7\end{array}\right\}$	$= 2+1=3$	1	...	...	...	...	...
15	÷	$^2V_6 \div ^2V_7$	$^1V_8$	$\left\{\begin{array}{l}^2V_6=^2V_6\\^2V_7=^2V_7\end{array}\right\}$	$= \dfrac{2n-1}{3}$	...	...	...	...	...	$2n-1$
16	×	$^1V_8 \times ^3V_{11}$	$^4V_{11}$	$\left\{\begin{array}{l}^1V_8=^0V_8\\^3V_{11}=^4V_{11}\end{array}\right\}$	$= \dfrac{2n}{2}\cdot\dfrac{2n-1}{3}$	...	...	...	...	...	...
17	−	$^2V_6 - ^1V_1$	$^3V_6$	$\left\{\begin{array}{l}^2V_6=^3V_6\\^1V_1=^1V_1\end{array}\right\}$	$= 2n-2$	1	...	...	...	...	$2n-2$
18	+	$^1V_1 + ^2V_7$	$^3V_7$	$\left\{\begin{array}{l}^2V_7=^3V_7\\^1V_1=^1V_1\end{array}\right\}$	$= 3+1=4$	1	...	...	...	...	...
19	÷	$^3V_6 \div ^3V_7$	$^1V_9$	$\left\{\begin{array}{l}^3V_6=^3V_6\\^3V_7=^3V_7\end{array}\right\}$	$= \dfrac{2n-2}{4}$	...	...	...	...	...	$2n-2$
20	×	$^1V_9 \times ^4V_{11}$	$^5V_{11}$	$\left\{\begin{array}{l}^1V_9=^0V_9\\^4V_{11}=^5V_{11}\end{array}\right\}$	$= \dfrac{2n}{2}\cdot\dfrac{2n-1}{3}\cdot\dfrac{2n-2}{4}=A_3$	...	...	...	...	...	...
21	×	$^1V_{22} \times ^5V_{11}$	$^0V_{12}$	$\left\{\begin{array}{l}^1V_{22}=^1V_{22}\\^0V_{12}=^2V_{12}\end{array}\right\}$	$= B_3\cdot\dfrac{2n}{2}\cdot\dfrac{2n-1}{3}\cdot\dfrac{2n-2}{3}=B_3A_3$	...	...	...	...	...	...
22	+	$^2V_{12} + ^2V_{13}$	$^3V_{13}$	$\left\{\begin{array}{l}^2V_{12}=^0V_{12}\\^2V_{13}=^3V_{13}\end{array}\right\}$	$= A_0 + B_1A_1 + B_3A_3$	...	...	...	...	...	...
23	−	$^2V_{10} - ^1V_1$	$^3V_{10}$	$\left\{\begin{array}{l}^2V_{10}=^3V_{10}\\^1V_1=^1V_1\end{array}\right\}$	$= n-3(=1)$	1	...	...	...	...	...
					Here follows a repetition						
24	+	$^4V_{13} + ^0V_{24}$	$^1V_{24}$	$\left\{\begin{array}{l}^4V_{13}=^0V_{13}\\^0V_{24}=^1V_{24}\end{array}\right\}$	$= B_7$	...	...	...	...	...	...
25	+	$^1V_1 + ^1V_3$	$^1V_3$	$\left\{\begin{array}{l}^1V_1=^1V_1\\^1V_3=^1V_3\\^5V_6=^0V_6\\^5V_7=^0V_7\end{array}\right.$	$= n+1=4+1=5$ .... by a Variable-card. by a Variable-card.	1	...	$n+1$	...	...	0

		Working Variables.						Result Variables.		
$^0V_7$	$^0V_8$	$^0V_9$	$^0V_{10}$	$^0V_{11}$	$^0V_{12}$	$^0V_{13}$	$^1V_{21}$ B_1 in a decimal fraction.	$^1V_{22}$ B_3 in a decimal fraction.	$^1V_{23}$ B_5 in a decimal fraction.	$^0V_{24}$
							B_1	B_3	B_5	B_7
...	...	...	...	$\dfrac{2n-1}{2n+1}$						
...	...	...	...	$\dfrac{1}{2}\cdot\dfrac{2n-1}{2n+1}$						
...	...	...	...	0	....	$-\dfrac{1}{2}\cdot\dfrac{2n-1}{2n+1}=A_0$				
...	...	...	$n-1$							
2										
2	...	...	...	$\dfrac{2n}{2}=A_1$						
...	...	...	...	$\dfrac{2n}{2}=A_1$	$B_1.\dfrac{2n}{2}=B_1A_1$	....	B_1			
...	...	...	...	....	0	$\left\{-\dfrac{1}{2}\cdot\dfrac{2n-1}{2n+1}+B_1.\dfrac{2n}{2}\right\}$				
...	...	...	$n-2$							
3										
3	$\dfrac{2n-1}{3}$									
...	0	...	...	$\dfrac{2n}{2}\cdot\dfrac{2n-1}{3}$						
4										
4	...	$\dfrac{2n-2}{4}$	...	$\left\{\begin{array}{c}\dfrac{2n}{2}\cdot\dfrac{2n-1}{3}\cdot\dfrac{2n-2}{3}\\ =A_3\end{array}\right\}$						
...	...	0								
...	...	...	...	0	B_3A_3	....	......	B_3		
...	...	...	...	....	0	$\left\{A_3+B_1A_1+B_3A_3\right\}$				
...	...	...	$n-3$							

of Operations thirteen to twenty-three.

$^0V_7$	$^0V_8$	$^0V_9$	$^0V_{10}$	$^0V_{11}$	$^0V_{12}$	$^0V_{13}$	$^1V_{21}$	$^1V_{22}$	$^1V_{23}$	$^0V_{24}$
...	...	...	...	....	....	....	......	......	......	B_7
0										

1. This remark seems to require further comment, since it is in some degree calculated to strike the mind as being at variance with the subsequent passage, where it is explained that *an engine which can effect these four* operations can in fact effect *every species of calculation*. The apparent discrepancy is stronger too in the translation than in the original, owing to its being impossible to render precisely into the English tongue all the niceties of distinction which the French idiom happens to admit of in the phrases used for the two passages we refer to. The explanation lies in this: that in the one case the execution of these four operations is the *fundamental starting-point*, and the object proposed for attainment by the machine is the *subsequent combination of these* in every possible variety; whereas in the other case the execution of some *one* of these four operations, selected at pleasure, is the *ultimatum*, the sole and utmost result that can be proposed for attainment by the machine referred to, and which result it cannot any further combine or work upon. The one *begins* where the other *ends*. Should this distinction not now appear perfectly clear, it will become so on perusing the rest of the Memoir, and the Notes that are appended to it.—NOTE BY TRANSLATOR.

2. The idea that the one engine is the offspring and has grown out of the other, is an exceedingly natural and plausible supposition, until reflection reminds us that no *necessary* sequence and connexion need exist between two such inventions, and that they may be wholly independent. M. Menabrea has shared this idea in common with persons who have not his profound and accurate insight into the nature of either engine. In Note A. (see the Notes at the end of the Memoir) it will be found sufficiently explained, however, that this supposition is unfounded. M. Menabrea's opportunities were by no means such as could be ade-

quate to afford him information on a point like this, which would be naturally and almost unconsciously *assumed*, and would scarcely suggest any inquiry with reference to it.—NOTE BY TRANSLATOR.

3. See Note A.

4. This must not be understood in too unqualified a manner. The engine is capable under certain circumstances, of feeling about to discover which of two or more possible contingencies has occurred, and of then shaping its future course accordingly.—NOTE BY TRANSLATOR.

5. See Note B.

6. Zero is not *always* substituted when a number is transferred to the mill. This is explained further on in the memoir, and still more fully in Note D.—NOTE BY TRANSLATOR.

7. See Note C.

8. See Note D.

9. Not having had leisure to discuss with Mr. Babbage the manner of introducing into his machine the combination of algebraical signs, I do not pretend here to expose the method he uses for this purpose; but I considered that I ought myself to supply the deficiency, conceiving that this paper would have been imperfect if I had omitted to point out one means that might be employed for resolving this essential part of the problem in question.

10. See Note E.

11. For an explanation of the upper left-hand indices attached to the V's in this and in the preceding Table, we must refer the reader to Note D, amongst those appended to the memoir.—NOTE BY TRANSLATOR.

12. See Note F.

13. See Note G.

14. This sentence has been slightly altered in the translation in order to express more exactly the present state of the engine.—NOTE BY TRANSLATOR

15. The notation here alluded to is a most interesting and important subject, and would have well deserved a separate and detailed Note upon it amongst those appended to the Memoir. It has, however, been impossible, within the space allotted, even to touch upon so wide a field.—NOTE BY TRANSLATOR.

16. We do not mean to imply that the *only* use made of the Jacquard cards is that of regulating the algebraical *operations*; but we mean to explain that *those* cards and portions of mechanism which regulate these *operations* are wholly independent of those which are used for other purposes. M. Menabrea explains that there are *three* classes of cards used in the engine for three distinct sets of objects, viz. *Cards of the Operations, Cards of the Variables*, and certain *Cards of Numbers*.

17. In fact, such an extension as we allude to would merely constitute a further and more perfected development of any system introduced for making the proper combinations of the signs *plus* and *minus*. How ably M. Menabrea has touched on this restricted case is pointed out in Note B.

18. The machine might have been constructed so as to tabulate for a higher value of n than seven. Since, however, every unit added to the value of n increases the extent of the mechanism requisite, there would on this account be a limit beyond which it could not be practically carried. Seven is sufficiently high for the calculation of all ordinary tables.

    The fact that, in the Analytical Engine, the same extent of mechanism suffices for the solution of $\Delta^n u_z = 0$, whether $n = 7$, $n = 100,000$, or $n =$ any number whatever, at once suggests how entirely distinct must be the *nature of the principles* through whose application matter has been enabled to become the working agent of abstract mental operations in each of these engines respectively, and it affords an equally obvious pre-

sumption, that in the case of the Analytical Engine, not only are those principles in themselves of a higher and more comprehensive description, but also such as must vastly extend the *practical* value of the engine whose basis they constitute.

19. This subject is further noticed in Note F.

20. A fuller account of the manner in which the signs are regulated is given in M. Menabrea's Memoir. He himself expresses doubts (in a note of his own) as to his having been likely to hit on the precise methods really adopted; his explanation being merely a conjectural one. That it *does* accord precisely with the fact is a remarkable circumstance, and affords a convincing proof how completely M. Menabrea has been imbued with the true spirit of the invention. Indeed the whole of the above Memoir is a striking production, when we consider that M. Menabrea had had but very slight means for obtaining any adequate ideas respecting the Analytical Engine. It requires however a considerable acquaintance with the abstruse and complicated nature of such a subject, in order fully to appreciate the penetration of the writer who could take so just and comprehensive a view of it upon such limited opportunity.

21. This adjustment is done by hand merely.

22. It is convenient to omit the circles whenever the signs + or – can be actually represented.

23. We recommend the reader to trace the successive substitutions backwards from (1) to (4), in M. Menabrea's Table. This he will easily do by means of the upper and lower indices, and it is interesting to observe how each V successively ramifies (so to speak) into two other V's in some other column of the Table, until at length the V's of the original data are arrived at.

24. This division would be managed by ordering the number 2 to appear on any separate new column which should be conveniently situated for the

purpose, and then directing this column (which is in the strictest sense a *Working*-Variable) to divide itself successively with V_{32}, V_{33}, &c.

25. It should be observed, that were the rest of the factor $(A + A \cos \theta + \&c.)$ taken into account, instead of *four* terms only, C_3 would have the additional term $1/2B_1A_4$; and C_4 the two additional terms, BA_4, $1/2B_1A_5$. This would indeed have been the case had even *six* terms been multiplied.

26. A cycle that includes n other cycles, successively *contained one within another*, is called a cycle of the $n + 1$th order. A cycle may simply *include* many other cycles, and yet only be of the second order. If a series follows a certain law for a certain number of terms, and then another law for another number of terms, there will be a cycle of operations for every new law; but these cycles will not be *contained one within another*,—they merely *follow each other*. Therefore their number may be infinite without influencing the *order* of a cycle that includes a repetition of such a series.

27. The engine cannot of course compute limits for perfectly *simple* and *uncompounded* functions, except in this manner. It is obvious that it has no power of representing or of manipulating with any but *finite* increments or decrements, and consequently that wherever the computation of limits (or of any other functions) depends upon the *direct* introduction of quantities which either increase or decrease *indefinitely*, we are absolutely beyond the sphere of its powers. Its nature and arrangements are remarkably adapted for taking into account all *finite* increments or decrements (however small or large), and for developing the true and logical modifications of form or value dependent upon differences of this nature. The engine may indeed be considered as including the whole Calculus of Finite Differences; many of whose theorems would be especially and beautifully fitted for development by its processes, and would offer peculiarly interesting considerations.

We may mention, as an example the calculation of the Numbers of Bernoulli by means of the *Differences of Zero*.

28. See the diagram at the end of these Notes.

29. It is interesting to observe, that so complicated a case as this calculation of the Bernoullian Numbers, nevertheless, presents a remarkable simplicity in one respect; viz., that during the processes for the computation of *millions* of these Numbers, no other arbitrary modification would be requisite in the arrangements, excepting the above simple and uniform provision for causing one of the data periodically to receive the finite increment unity.

6.2

Of the Analytical Engine

Charles Babbage

From *Passages from the Life of a Philosopher* (London: Longman, Green, Longman, Roberts & Green, 1864), ch.8.

Obituary portrait of Babbage from *The Illustrated London News*.

INTRODUCTORY NOTE TO READING 6.2

In viewing Babbage's achievements, one is struck by his originality. There is no one else like him in the history of science and technology. Even though Babbage had many friends, one is impressed by how much he worked alone. His calculating engines were his creations, executed in metal or simply on paper by his collaborating engineers. Even if he had wanted other collaborators, there was no other scientist in his day with his particular interests and such iron-willed determination. The Analytical Engine, had it been built, might have been the most complex mechanical device ever constructed. Babbage's character and originality come through in his autobiographical account entitled *Passages from the Life of a Philosopher*. Just like Babbage, the book does not fit into a standard mold. Too rambling and thematic for a conventional autobiography, it is an invaluable record of his unconventional point of view on his highly original life. It is also the best account of his calculating engines that Babbage published. [JMN]

TEXT OF READING 6.2

Man wrongs, and Time avenges.

BYRON—The Prophecy of Dante

The circular arrangement of the axes of the Difference Engine round large central wheels led to the most extended prospects. The whole of arithmetic now appeared within the grasp of mechanism. A vague glimpse even of an Analytical Engine at length opened out, and I pursued with enthusiasm the shadowy vision. The drawings and the experiments were of the most costly kind. Draftsmen of the highest order were necessary to economize the labour of my own head; whilst skilled workmen were required to execute the experimental machinery to which I was obliged constantly to have recourse.

In order to carry out my pursuits successfully, I had purchased a house with above a quarter of an acre of ground in a very quiet locality. My coach-house was now converted into a forge and a foundry, whilst my stables were transformed into a workshop. I built other extensive workshops myself, and had a fire-proof building for my drawings and draftsmen. Having myself worked with a variety of tools, and having studied the art of constructing each of them, I at length laid it down as a principle—that, except in rare cases, I would never do anything myself if I could afford to hire another person who could do it for me.

The complicated relations which then arose amongst the various parts of the machinery would have baffled the most tenacious memory. I overcame that difficulty by improving and extending a language of signs, the Mechanical Notation, which in 1826 I had explained in a paper printed in the "Phil. Trans." By such means I succeeded in mastering trains of investigation so vast in extent that no length of years ever allotted to one individual could otherwise have enabled me to control. By the aid of the Mechanical Notation, the Analytical Engine became a reality: for it became susceptible of demonstration.

Such works could not be carried on without great expenditure. The fluctuations in the demand and supply of skilled labour were considerable. The railroad mania withdrew from other pursuits the most intellectual and skilful draftsmen. One who had for some years been my chief assistant was tempted by an offer so advantageous that in justice to his own family he could scarcely have declined it. Under these circumstances I took into consideration the plan of advancing his salary to one guinea per day. Whilst this was in abeyance, I consulted my venerable surviving parent. When I had fully explained the circumstances, my excellent mother replied: "My dear son, you have advanced far in the accomplishment of a great object, which is worthy of your ambition. You are capable of completing it. My advice is—pursue it, even if it should oblige you to live on bread and cheese."

This advice entirely accorded with my own feelings. I therefore retained my chief assistant at his advanced salary.

The most important part of the Analytical Engine was undoubtedly the mechanical method of carrying the tens. On this I laboured incessantly, each succeeding improvement advancing me a step or two. The difficulty did not consist so much in the more or less complexity of the contrivance as in the reduction of the *time* required to effect the carriage. Twenty or thirty different plans and modifications had been drawn. At last I came to the conclusion that I had exhausted the principle of successive carriage. I concluded also that nothing but teaching the Engine to foresee and then to act upon that foresight could ever lead me to the object I desired, namely, to make the whole of any unlimited number of carriages in one unit of time. One morning, after I had spent many hours in the drawing-office in endeavouring to improve the system of successive carriages, I mentioned these views to my chief assistant, and added that I should retire to my library, and endeavour to work out the new principle. He gently expressed a doubt whether the plan was *possible*, to which I replied that, not being able to prove its impossibility, I should follow out a slight glimmering of light which I thought I perceived.

After about three hours' examination, I returned to the drawing-office with much more definite ideas upon the subject. I had discovered a principle that proved the possibility, and I had contrived mechanism which, I thought, would accomplish my object.

I now commenced the explanation of my views, which I soon found were but little understood by my assistant; nor was this surprising, since in the course of my own attempt at explanation, I found several defects in my plan, and was also led by his questions to perceive others. All these I removed one after another, and ultimately terminated at a late hour my morning's work with the conviction that *anticipating* carriage was not only within my power, but that I had devised one mechanism at least by which it might be accomplished.

Many years after, my assistant, on his return from a long residence abroad, called upon me, and we talked over the progress of the, Analytical Engine. I referred back to the day on which I had made that most important step, and asked him if he recollected it. His reply was that he perfectly remembered the circumstance; for that on retiring to my library, he seriously thought that my intellect was beginning to become deranged. The reader may perhaps be curious to know how I spent the rest of that remarkable day.

After working, as I constantly did, for ten or eleven hours a day, I had arrived at this satisfactory conclusion, and was revising the rough sketches of the new contrivance, when my servant entered the drawing-office, and announced that it was seven o'clock—that I dined in Park Lane—and that it was time to dress. I usually arrived at the house of my friend about a quarter of an hour before the appointed time, in order that we might have a short conversation on subjects on which we were both much interested. Having mentioned my recent success, in which my host thoroughly sympathized, I remarked that it had produced an exhilaration of the spirits which not even his excellent champagne could rival. Having enjoyed the society of Hallam, of Rogers, and of some few others of that delightful circle, I retired, and joined one or perhaps two much more extensive reunions. Having thus forgotten science, and enjoyed society for four or five hours, I returned home. About one o'clock I was asleep in my bed, and thus continued for the next five hours.

This new and rapid system of carrying the tens when two numbers are added together, reduced the actual time of the addition of any number of digits, however large, to nine units of time for the addition, and one unit for the carriage. Thus in ten's units of time, any two numbers, however large, might be added together. A few more units of time, perhaps five or six, were required for making the requisite previous arrangements.

Having thus advanced as nearly as seemed possible to the minimum of time requisite for arithmetical operations, I felt renewed power and increased energy to pursue the far higher object I had in view.

To describe the successive improvements of the Analytical Engine would require many volumes. I only propose here to indicate a few of its more important functions, and to give to those whose minds are duly prepared for it some information which will remove those vague notions of wonder, and even of its impossibility, with which it is surrounded in the minds of some of the most enlightened.

To those who are acquainted with the principles of the Jacquard loom, and who are also familiar with analytical formulae, a general idea of the means by which the Engine executes its operations may be obtained without much difficulty. In the Exhibition of 1862 there were many splendid examples of such looms.

It is known as a fact that the Jacquard loom is capable of weaving any design which the imagination of man may conceive. It is also the constant practice for skilled artists to be employed by manufacturers in designing patterns. These patterns are then sent to a peculiar artist, who, by means of a certain machine, punches holes in a set of pasteboard cards in such a manner that when those cards are placed in a Jacquard loom, it will then weave upon its produce the exact pattern designed by the artist.

Now the manufacturer may use, for the warp and weft of his work, threads which are all of the same colour; let us suppose them to be unbleached or white threads. In this case the cloth will be woven all of one colour; but there will be a damask pattern upon it such as the artist designed.

But the manufacturer might use the same cards, and put into the warp threads of any other colour.

Every thread might even be of a different colour, or of a different shade of colour; but in all these cases the *form* of the pattern will be precisely the same—the colours only will differ.

The analogy of the Analytical Engine with this well-known process is nearly perfect.

The Analytical Engine consists of two parts:

1. The store in which all the variables to be operated upon, as well as all those quantities which have arisen from the result of other operations, are placed.

2. The mill into which the quantities about to be operated upon are always brought.

Every formula which the Analytical Engine can be required to compute consists of certain algebraical operations to be performed upon given letters, and of certain other modifications depending on the numerical value assigned to those letters.

There are therefore two sets of cards, the first to direct the nature of the operations to be performed—these are called operation cards: the other to direct the particular variables on which those cards are required to operate—these latter are called variable cards. Now the symbol of each variable or constant, is placed at the top of a column capable of containing any required number of digits.

Under this arrangement, when any formula is required to be computed, a set of operation cards must be strung together, which contain the series of operations in the order in which they occur. Another set of cards must then be strung together, to call in the variables into the mill, the order in which they are required to be acted upon. Each operation card will require three other cards, two to represent the variables and constants and their numerical values upon which the previous operation card is to act, and one to indicate the variable on which the arithmetical result of this operation is to be placed.

But each variable has below it, on the same axis, a certain number of figure-wheels marked on their edges with the ten digits: upon these any number the machine is capable of holding can be placed. When-

ever variables are ordered into the mill, these figures will be brought in, and the operation indicated by the preceding card will be performed upon them. The result of this operation will then be replaced in the store.

The Analytical Engine is therefore a machine of the most general nature. Whatever formula it is required to develop, the law of its development must be communicated to it by two sets of cards. When these have been placed, the engine is special for that particular formula. The numerical value of its constants must then be put on the columns of wheels below them, and on setting the Engine in motion it will calculate and print the numerical results of that formula.

Every set of cards made for any formula will at any future time recalculate that formula with whatever constants may be required.

Thus the Analytical Engine will possess a library of its own. Every set of cards once made will at any future time reproduce the calculations for which it was first arranged. The numerical value of its constants may then be inserted.

It is perhaps difficult to apprehend these descriptions without a familiarity both with analytical forms and mechanical structures. I will now, therefore, confine myself to the mathematical view of the Analytical Engine, and illustrate by example some of its supposed difficulties.

An excellent friend of mine, the late Professor Mac-Cullagh, of Dublin, was discussing with me, at breakfast, the various powers of the Analytical Engine. After a long conversation on the subject, he inquired what the machine could do if, in the midst of algebraic operations, it was required to perform logarithmic or trigonometric operations.

My answer was, that whenever the Analytical Engine should exist, all the developments of formula would be directed by this condition—that the machine should be able to compute their numerical value in the shortest possible time. I then added that if this answer were not satisfactory, I had provided means by which, with equal accuracy, it might compute by logarithmic or other Tables.

I explained that the Tables to be used must, of

course, be computed and punched on cards by the machine, in which case they would undoubtedly be correct. I then added that when the machine wanted a tabular number, say the logarithm of a given number, that it would ring a bell and then stop itself. On this, the attendant would look at a certain part of the machine, and find that it wanted the logarithm of a given number, say of 2303. The attendant would then go to the drawer containing the pasteboard cards representing its table of logarithms. From amongst these he would take the required logarithmic card, and place it in the machine. Upon this the engine would first ascertain whether the assistant had or had not given him the correct logarithm of the number; if so, it would use it and continue its work. But if the engine found the attendant had given him a wrong logarithm, it would then ring a louder bell, and stop itself. On the attendant again examining the engine, he would observe the words, "Wrong tabular number," and then discover that he really had given the wrong logarithm, and of course he would have to replace it by the right one.

Upon this, Professor MacCullagh naturally asked why, if the machine could tell whether the logarithm was the right one, it should have asked the attendant at all? I told him that the means employed were so ridiculously simple that I would not at that moment explain them; but that if he would come again in the course of a few days, I should be ready to explain it. Three or four days after, Bessel and Jacobi, who had just arrived in England, were sitting with me, inquiring about the Analytical Engine, when fortunately my friend MacCullagh was announced. The meeting was equally agreeable to us all, and we continued our conversation. After some time Bessel put to me the very same question which MacCullagh had previously asked. On this Jacobi remarked that he, too, was about to make the same inquiry when Bessel had asked the question. I then explained to them the following very simple means by which that verification was accomplished.

Besides the sets of cards which direct the nature of the operations to be performed, and the variables or constants which are to be operated upon, there is another class of cards called number cards. These are much less general in their uses than the others, although they are necessarily of much larger size.

Any number which the Analytical Engine is capable of using or of producing can, if required, be expressed by a card with certain holes in it; thus—

Number				Table						
2	3	0	3	3	6	2	2	9	3	9
●	●	○	●	●	●	●	●	●	●	●
●	●	○	●	●	●	●	●	●	●	●
○	●	○	●	●	●	○	○	●	●	●
○	○	○	○	○	●	○	○	●	○	●
○	○	○	○	○	●	○	○	●	○	●
○	○	○	○	○	●	○	○	●	○	●
○	○	○	○	○	○	○	○	●	○	●
○	○	○	○	○	○	○	○	●	○	●
○	○	○	○	○	○	○	○	●	○	●

The above card contains eleven vertical rows for holes, each row having nine or any less number of holes. In this example the tabular number is 3 6 2 2 9 3 9, whilst its number in the order of the table is 2 3 0 3. In fact, the former number is the logarithm of the latter.

The Analytical Engine will contain,

1. Apparatus for printing on paper, one, or, if required, two copies of its results.

2. Means for producing a stereotype mould of the tables or results it computes.

3. Mechanism for punching on blank pasteboard cards or metal plates the numerical results of any of its computations.

Of course the Engine will compute all the Tables which it may itself be required to use. These cards will therefore be entirely free from error. Now when the Engine requires a tabular number, it will stop, ring a bell, and ask for such number. In the case we have assumed, it asks for the logarithm of 2 3 0 3.

When the attendant has placed a tabular card in the Engine, the first step taken by it will be to verify the *number* of the card given it by subtracting its number from 2 3 0 3, the number whose logarithm it asked for. If the remainder is zero, then the engine is certain that the logarithm must be the right one, since it was computed and punched by itself.

Thus the Analytical Engine first computes and punches on cards its own tabular numbers. These are brought to it by its attendant when demanded. But the Engine itself takes care that the *right* card is brought to it by verifying the *number* of that card by the number of the card which it demanded. The Engine will always reject a wrong card by continually ringing a loud bell and stopping itself until supplied with the precise intellectual food it demands.

It will be an interesting question, which time only can solve, to know whether such tables of cards will ever be required for the Engine. Tables are used for saving the time of continually computing individual numbers. But the computations to be made by the Engine are so rapid that it seems most probable that it will make shorter work by computing directly from proper formulae than by having recourse even to its own Tables.

The Analytical Engine I propose will have the power of expressing every number it uses to fifty places of figures. It will multiply any two such numbers together, and then, if required, will divide the product of one hundred figures by number of fifty places of figures.

Supposing the velocity of the moving parts of the Engine to be not greater than forty feet per minute, I have no doubt that

Sixty additions or subtractions may be completed and printed in one minute.

One multiplication of two numbers, each of fifty figures, in one minute.

One division of a number having 100 places of figures by another of 50 in one minute.

In the various sets of drawings of the modifications of the mechanical structure of the Analytical Engines, already numbering upwards of thirty, two great principles were embodied to an unlimited extent.

1st. The entire control over *arithmetical* operations, however large, and whatever might be the number of their digits.

2nd. The entire control over the *combinations* of algebraic symbols, however lengthened those processes may be required. The possibility of fulfilling these two conditions might reasonably be doubted by the most accomplished mathematician as well as by the most ingenious mechanician.

The difficulties which naturally occur to those capable of examining the question, as far as they relate to arithmetic, are these,

a. The number of digits in *each constant* inserted in the Engine must be without limit.

b. The number of constants to be inserted in the Engine must also be without limit.

c. The number of operations necessary for arithmetic is only four, but these four may be repeated an *unlimited* number of times.

d. These operations may occur in any order, or follow an *unlimited* number of laws.

The following conditions relate to the algebraic portion of the Analytical Engine:

e. The number of *literal* constants must be *unlimited.*

f. The number of *variables* must be *without limit.*

g. The combinations of the algebraic signs must *be unlimited.*

h. The number *of functions* to be employed must be *without limit.*

This enumeration includes eight conditions, each of which is absolutely *unlimited* as to the number of its combinations.

Now it is obvious that no *finite* machine can include infinity. It is also certain that no question *necessarily* involving infinity can ever be converted into any other in which the idea of infinity under some shape or other does not enter.

It is impossible to construct machinery occupying unlimited space; but it is possible to construct finite machinery, and to use it through unlimited time. It is this substitution of the *infinity of time* for the *infinity of space* which I have made use of, to limit the size of the engine and yet to retain its unlimited power.

(*a*). I shall now proceed briefly to point out the means by which I have effected this change.

Since every calculating machine must be constructed for the calculation of a definite number of figures, the first datum must be to fix upon that number. In order to be somewhat in advance of the greatest number that may ever be required, I chose fifty places of figures as the standard for the Analytical Engine. The intention being that in such a machine two numbers, each of fifty places of figures, might be multiplied together and the resultant product of one hundred places might then be divided by another number of fifty places. It seems to me probable that a long period must elapse before the demands of science will exceed this limit. To this it may be added that the addition and subtraction of numbers in an engine constructed for *n* places of figures would be equally rapid whether *n* were equal to five or five thousand digits. With respect to multiplication and division, the time required is greater:

Thus if $a \cdot 10^{50} + b$ and $a' \cdot 10^{50} + b'$ are two numbers each of less than a hundred places of figures, then each can be expressed upon two columns of fifty figures, and *a, b, a', b'* are each less than fifty places of figures: they can therefore be added and subtracted upon any column holding fifty places of figures.

The product of two such numbers is—

$$aa' \, 10^{100} + (ab' + a'b) \, 10^{50} + bb'.$$

This expression contains four pairs of factors, *aa', ab', a'b, bb'*, each factor of which has less than fifty places of figures. Each multiplication can therefore be executed in the Engine. The time, however, of multiplying two numbers, each consisting of any number of digits between fifty and one hundred, will be nearly four times as long as that of two such numbers of less than fifty places of figures.

The same reasoning will show that if the numbers of digits of each factor are between one hundred and one hundred and fifty, then the time required for the operation will be nearly nine times that of a pair of factors having only fifty digits.

Thus it appears that whatever may be the number of digits the Analytical Engine is capable of holding, if it is required to make all the computations with *k* times that number of digits, then it can be executed by the same Engine, but in an amount of time equal to k^2 times the former. Hence the condition (*a*), or the unlimited number of digits contained in each constant employed, is fulfilled.

It must, however, be admitted that this advantage is gained at the expense of diminishing the number of the constants the Engine can hold. An engine of fifty digits, when used as one of a hundred digits, can only contain half the number of variables. An engine containing *m* columns, each holding *n* digits, if used for computations requiring *kn* digits, can only hold *m/k* constants or variables.

(*b*). The next step is therefore to prove (*b*), *viz.*: to show that a finite engine can be used as if it contained an unlimited number of constants. The method of punching cards for tabular numbers has already been alluded to. Each Analytical Engine will contain one or more apparatus for printing any numbers put into it, and also an apparatus for punching on pasteboard cards the holes corresponding to those numbers. At another part of the machine a series of number cards, resembling those of Jacquard, but delivered to and computed by the machine itself, can be placed. These can be called for by the Engine itself in any order in which they may be placed, or according to *any law* the Engine may be directed to use. Hence the condition (*b*) is fulfilled, namely: an *unlimited number of constants* can be inserted in the machine in an *unlimited* time.

I propose in the Engine I am constructing to have places for only a thousand constants, because I think it will be more than sufficient. But if it were required to have ten, or even a hundred times that number, it would be quite possible to make it, such is the simplicity of its structure of that portion of the Engine.

(*c*). The next stage in the arithmetic is the number of times the four processes of addition, subtraction, multiplication, and division can be repeated. It is obvious that four different cards thus punched

would give the orders for the four rules of arithmetic.

Now there is no limit to the number of such cards which may be strung together according to the nature of the operations required. Consequently the condition (*c*) is fulfilled.

(*d*). The fourth arithmetical condition (*d*), that the order of succession in which these operations can be varied, is itself *unlimited*, follows as a matter of course.

The four remaining conditions which must be fulfilled, in order to render the Analytical Engine as general as the science of which it is the powerful executive, relate to algebraic quantities with which it operates.

The thousand columns, each capable of holding any number of less than fifty-one places of figures, may each represent a constant or a variable quantity. These quantities I have called by the comprehensive title of variables, and have denoted them by V_n, with an index below. In the machine I have designed, *n* may vary from 0 to 999. But after any one or more columns have been used for variables, if those variables are not required afterwards, they may be printed upon paper, and the columns themselves again used for other variables. In such cases the variables must have a new index; thus, $^mV^n$. I propose to make *n* vary from 0 to 99. If more variables are required, these may be supplied by Variable Cards, which may follow each other in unlimited succession. Each card will cause its symbol to be printed with its proper indices.

For the sake of uniformity, I have used *V* with as many indices as may be required throughout the Engine. This, however, does not prevent the printed result of a development from being represented by any

letters which may be thought to be more convenient. In that part in which the results are printed, type of any form may be used, according to the taste of the proposer of the question.

It thus appears that the two conditions, (*e*) and (*f*), which require that the number of constants and of variables should be unlimited, are both fulfilled.

The condition (*g*) requiring that the number of combinations of the four algebraic signs shall be unlimited, is easily fulfilled by placing them on cards in any order of succession the problem may require.

The last condition (*h*), namely, that the number of functions to be employed must be without limit, might seem at first sight to be difficult to fulfil. But when it is considered that any function of any number of operations performed upon any variables is but a combination of the four simple signs of operation with various quantities, it becomes apparent that any function whatever may be represented by two groups of cards, the first being signs of operation, placed in the order in which they succeed each other, and the second group of cards representing the variables and constants placed in the order of succession in which they are acted upon by the former.

Thus it appears that the whole of the conditions which enable a *finite* machine to make calculations of *unlimited* extent are fulfilled in the Analytical Engine. The means I have adopted are uniform. I have converted the infinity of space, which was required by the conditions of the problem, into the infinity of time. The means I have employed are in daily use in the art of weaving patterns. It is accomplished by systems of cards punched with various holes strung together to any extent which may be demanded. Two large boxes, the one empty and the other filled with perforated cards, are placed before and behind a polygonal prism, which revolves at intervals upon its axis, and advances through a short space, after which it immediately returns.

A card passes over the prism just before each stroke of the shuttle; the cards that have passed hang down until they reach the empty box placed to receive them, into which they arrange themselves one over the other.

When the box is full, another empty box is placed to receive the coming cards, and a new full box on the opposite side replaces the one just emptied. As the suspended cards on the entering side are exactly equal to those on the side at which the others are delivered, they are perfectly balanced, so that whether the formulae to be computed be excessively complicated or very simple, the force to be exerted always remains nearly the same.

In 1840 I received from my friend M. Plana a letter pressing me strongly to visit Turin at the then approaching meeting of Italian philosophers. In that letter M. Plana stated that he had inquired anxiously of many of my countrymen about the power and mechanism of the Analytical Engine. He remarked that from all the information he could collect the case seemed to stand thus:—

> "Hitherto the *legislative* department of our analysis has been all powerful—the *executive* all feeble.

> "Your engine seems to give us the same control over the executive which we have hitherto only possessed over the legislative department."

Considering the exceedingly limited information which could have reached my friend respecting the Analytical Engine, I was equally surprised and delighted at his exact prevision of its powers. Even at the present moment I could not express more clearly, and in fewer terms, its real object. I collected together such of my models, drawings, and notations as I conceived to be best adapted to give an insight into the principles and mode of operating of the Analytical Engine. On mentioning my intention to my excellent friend the late Professor MacCullagh, he resolved to give up a trip to the Tyrol, and join me at Turin.

We met at Turin at the appointed time, and as soon as the first bustle of the meeting had a little abated, I had the great pleasure of receiving at my own apartments, for several mornings, Messrs. Plana, Menabrea, Mossotti, MacCullagh, Plantamour, and others of the most eminent geometers and engineers of Italy.

Around the room were hung the formula, the drawings, notations, and other illustrations which I had brought with me. I began on the first day to give a short outline of the idea. My friends asked from time to time further explanations of parts I had not made sufficiently clear. M. Plana had at first proposed to make notes, in order to write an outline of the principles of the engine. But his own laborious pursuits induced him to give up this plan, and to transfer the task to a younger friend of his, M. Menabrea, who had already established his reputation as a profound analyst.

These discussions were of great value to me in several ways. I was thus obliged to put into language the various views I had taken, and I observed the effect of my explanations on different minds. My own ideas became clearer, and I profited by many of the remarks made by my highly-gifted friends.

One day Mossotti, who had been unavoidably absent from the previous meeting, when a question of great importance had been discussed, again joined the party. Well aware of the acuteness and rapidity of my friend's intellect, I asked my other friends to allow me five minutes to convey to Professor Mossotti the substance of the preceding sitting. After putting a few questions to Mossotti himself, he placed before me distinctly his greatest difficulty.

He remarked that he was now quite ready to admit the power of mechanism over numerical, and even over algebraical relations, to any extent. But he added that he had no conception how the machine could perform the act of judgment sometimes required during an analytical inquiry, when two or more different courses presented themselves, especially as the proper course to be adopted could not be known in many cases until all the previous portion had been gone through.

I then inquired whether the solution of a numerical equation of any degree by the usual, but very tedious proceeding of approximation would be a type of the difficulty to be explained. He at once admitted that it would be a very eminent one.

For the sake of perspicuity and brevity I shall confine my present explanation to possible roots.

I then mentioned the successive stages:

Number of Operation Cards used	
1 a.	Ascertain the number of possible roots by applying Sturm's theorem to the coefficients.
2 b.	Find a number greater than the greatest root.
3 c.	Substitute the powers of ten (commencing with that next greater than the greatest root, and diminishing the powers by unity at each step) for the value of x in the given equation. Continue this until the sign of the resulting number changes from positive to negative. The index of the last power of ten (call it n), which is positive, expresses the number of digits in that part of the root which consists of whole numbers. Call this index $n + 1$.
4 d.	Substitute successively for x in the original equation 0×10^n, 1×10^n, 2×10^n, 3×10^n, ... 9×10^n, until a change of sign occurs in the result. The digit previously substituted will be the first figure of the root sought.
5 e.	Transform the original equation into another whose roots are less by the number thus found. The transformed equation will have a real root, the digit, less than 10^n.
6 f.	Substitute $1 \times 10^{n-1}$, $2 \times 10^{n-1}$, $3 \times 10^{n-1}$, &c., successively for the root of this equation, until a change of sign occurs in the result, as in process 4. This will give the second figure of the root. This process of alternately finding a new figure in the root, and then transforming the equation into another (as in process 4 and 5), must be carried on until as many figures as are required, whether whole numbers or decimals, are arrived at.
7 g.	The root thus found must now be used to reduce the original equation to one dimension lower.
8 i.	This new equation of one dimension lower must now be treated by sections 3, 4, 5, 6, and 7, until the new root is found.
9 k.	The repetition of sections 7 and 8 must go on until all the roots have been found.

Now it will be observed that Professor Mossotti was quite ready to admit at once that each of these different processes could be performed by the Analytical Machine through the medium of properly-arranged sets of Jacquard cards.

His real difficulty consisted in teaching the engine to know when to change from one set of cards to another, and back again repeatedly, at intervals not known to the person who gave the orders.

The dimensions of the algebraic equation being known, the number of arithmetical processes necessary for Sturm's theorem is consequently known. A set of operation cards can therefore be prepared. These must be accompanied by a corresponding set of variable cards, which will represent the columns in the store, on which the several coefficients of the given equation, and the various combinations required amongst them, are to be placed.

The next stage is to find a number greater than the greatest root of the given equation. There are various courses for arriving at such a number. Any one of these being selected, another set of operation and variable cards can be prepared to execute this operation.

Now, as this second process invariably follows the first, the second set of cards may be attached to the first set, and the engine will pass on from the first to the second process, and again from the second to the third process.

But here a difficulty arises: successive powers of ten are to be substituted for x in the equation, until a certain event happens. A set of cards may be provided to make the substitution of the highest power of ten, and similarly for the others; but on the occurrence of a certain event, namely, the change of a sign from + to −, this stage of the calculation is to terminate.

Now at a very early period of the inquiry I had found it necessary to teach the engine to know when any numbers it might be computing passed through zero or infinity.

The passage through zero can be easily ascertained, thus: Let the continually-decreasing number which is being computed be placed upon a column of wheels in connection with a carrying apparatus. After each process this number will be diminished, until at last a number is subtracted from it which is greater than the number expressed on those wheels.

Thus let it be   00000,00000,00000,00423
Subtract   00000,00000,00000,00511
                 99999,99999,99999,99912

Now in every case of a carriage becoming due, a certain lever is transferred from one position to another in the cage next above it.

Consequently in the highest cage of all (say the fiftieth in the Analytical Engine), an arm will be moved or not moved accordingly as the carriages do or do not run up beyond the highest wheel.

This arm can, of course, make any change which has previously been decided upon. In the instance we have been considering it would order the cards to be turned on to the next set.

If we wish to find when any number, which is increasing, exceeds in the number of its digits the number of wheels on the columns of the machine, the same carrying arm can be employed. Hence any directions may be given which the circumstances require.

It will be remarked that this does not actually prove, even in the Analytical Engine of fifty figures, that the number computed has passed through infinity; but only that it has become greater than any number of fifty places of figures.

There are, however, methods by which any machine made for a given number of figures may be made to compute the same formulae with double or any multiple of its original number. But the nature of this work prevents me from explaining that method.

It may here be remarked that in the process, the cards employed to make the substitutions of the powers of ten are *operation* cards. They are, therefore, quite independent of the numerical values substituted. Hence the same set of operation cards which order the substitutions 1×10^n will, if backed, order the substitution of 2×10^n, &c. We may, therefore, avail ourselves of mechanism for backing these cards, and call it into action whenever the circumstances themselves require it.

The explanation of M. Mossotti's difficulty is this:—Mechanical means have been provided for backing or advancing the operation cards to any extent. There exist means of expressing the conditions under which these various processes are required to be called into play. It is not even necessary that two courses only should be possible. Any number of courses may be possible at the same time; and the choice of each may depend upon any number of conditions.

It was during these meetings that my highly valued friend, M. Menabrea, collected the materials for that lucid and admirable description which he subsequently published in the Bibli. Univ. de Geneve, t. xli. Oct. 1842.

The elementary principles on which the Analytical Engine rests were thus in the first instance brought before the public by General Menabrea.

Some time after the appearance of his memoir on the subject in the "Bibliotheque Universelle de Geneve," the late Countess of Lovelace[1] informed me that she had translated the memoir of Menabrea. I asked why she had not herself written an original paper on a subject with which she was so intimately acquainted? To this Lady Lovelace replied that the thought had not occurred to her. I then suggested that she should add some notes to Menabrea's memoir; an idea which was immediately adopted.

We discussed together the various illustrations that might be introduced: I suggested several, but the selection was entirely her own. So also was the algebraic working out of the different problems, except, indeed, that relating to the numbers of Bernoulli, which I had offered to do to save Lady Lovelace the trouble. This she sent back to me for an amendment, having detected a grave mistake which I had made in the process.

The notes of the Countess of Lovelace extend to about three times the length of the original memoir. Their author has entered fully into almost all the very difficult and abstract questions connected with the subject.

These two memoirs taken together furnish, to those who are capable of understanding the reasoning, a complete demonstration—That *the whole of the developments and operations of analysis are now capable of being executed by machinery.*

There are various methods by which these developments are arrived at:—1. By the aid of the Differential and Integral Calculus. 2. By the Combinatorial Analysis of Hindenburg. 3. By the Calculus of Derivations of Arbogast.

Each of these systems professes to expand any function according to any laws. Theoretically each method may be admitted to be perfect; but practically the time and attention required are, in the greater number of cases, more than the human mind is able to bestow. Consequently, upon several highly interesting questions relative to the Lunar theory, some of the ablest and most indefatigable of existing analysts are at variance.

The Analytical Engine is capable of executing the laws prescribed by each of these methods. At one period I examined the Combinatorial Analysis, and also took some pains to ascertain from several of my German friends, who had had far more experience of it than myself, whether it could be used with greater facility than the Differential system. They seemed to think that it was more readily applicable to all the usual wants of analysis.

I have myself worked with the system of Arbogast, and if I were to decide from my own limited use of the three methods, I should, for the purposes of the Analytical Engine, prefer the Calcul des Derivations.

As soon as an Analytical Engine exists, it will necessarily guide the future course of the science. Whenever any result is sought by its aid, the question will then arise—By what course of calculation can these results be arrived at by the machine in the *shortest time?*

In the drawings I have prepared I proposed to have a thousand variables, upon each of which any number not having more than fifty figures can be placed. This machine would multiply 50 figures by other 50, and print the product of 100 figures. Or it would divide any number having 100 figures by any other of 50 figures, and print the quotient of 50 figures. Allowing but a moderate velocity for the machine, the time occupied by either of these operations would be about one minute.

The whole of the *numerical* constants throughout the works of Laplace, Plana, Le Verrier, Hansen, and other eminent men whose indefatigable labours have brought astronomy to its present advanced state, might easily be recomputed. They are but the numerical coefficients of the various terms of functions developed according to certain series. In all cases in which these numerical constants can be calculated by more than one method, it might be desirable to compute them by several processes until frequent practice shall have confirmed our belief in the infallibility of mechanism.

The great importance of having accurate Tables is admitted by all who understand their uses; but the multitude of errors really occurring is comparatively little known. Dr. Lardner, in the "Edinburgh Review," has made some very instructive remarks on this subject.

I shall mention two within my own experience: these are selected because they occurred in works where neither care nor expense were spared on the part of the Government to insure perfect accuracy. It is, however, but just to the eminent men who presided over the preparation of these works for the press to observe, that the real fault lay not in them but in *the nature of things.*

In 1828 I lent the Government an original MS. of the table of Logarithmic Sines, Cosines, &c., computed to every second of the quadrant, in order that they might have it compared with Taylor's Logarithms, 4to., 1792, of which they possessed a considerable number of copies. Nineteen errors were thus detected, and a list of these errata was published in the Nautical Almanac for 1832: these may be called

Nineteen errata of the first order   1832

An error being detected in one of these errata, in the following Nautical Almanac we find an

Erratum of the errata in N. Alm. 1832   1833

But in this very erratum of the second order a new mistake was introduced larger than any of the original mistakes. In the year next following there ought to have been found

Erratum in the erratum of the errata in N. Alm. 1832   1834

In the "Tables de la Lune," by M. P. A. Hansen, 4to, 1857, published at the expense of the English Government, under the direction of the Astronomer Royal, is to be found a list of errata amounting to 155. In the 21st of these original errata there have been found *three* mistakes. These are duly noted in a newly-printed list of errata discovered during computations made with them in the "Nautical Almanac"; so that we now have the errata of an erratum of the original work.

This list of errata from the office of the "Nautical Almanac" is larger than the original list. The total number of errors at present (1862) discovered in Hansen's "Tables of the Moon" amounts to above three hundred and fifty. In making these remarks I have no intention of imputing the slightest blame to the Astronomer Royal, who, like other men, cannot avoid submitting to inevitable fate. The only circumstance which is really extraordinary is that, when it was demonstrated that all tables are capable of being computed by machinery, and even when a machine existed which computed certain tables, that the Astronomer Royal did not become the most enthusiastic supporter of an instrument which could render such invaluable service to his own science.

In the Supplementary Notices of the Astronomical Society, No. 9, vol. xxiii., p. 259, 1863, there occurs a Paper by M. G. de Ponteculant, in which forty-nine numerical coefficients relative to the Longitude, Latitude, and Radius vector of the Moon are given as computed by Plana, Delaunay, and Ponteculant. The computations of Plana and Ponteculant agree in thirteen cases; those of Delaunay and Ponteculant in two; and in the remaining thirty-four cases they all three differ.

I am unwilling to terminate this chapter without reference to another difficulty now arising, which is calculated to impede the progress of Analytical Science. The extension of analysis is so rapid, its domain so unlimited, and so many inquirers are entering into its fields, that a variety of new symbols have been introduced, formed on no common principles. Many of these are merely new ways of expressing well-known functions. Unless some philosophical principles are generally admitted as the basis of all notation, there appears a great probability of introducing the confusion of Babel into the most accurate of all languages.

A few months ago I turned back to a paper in the Philosophical Transactions, 1844, to examine some analytical investigations of great interest by an author who has thought deeply on the subject. It related to the separation of symbols of operation from those of quantity, a question peculiarly interesting to me, since the Analytical Engine contains the embodiment of that method. There was no ready, sufficient and simple mode of distinguishing letters which represented quantity from those which indicated operation. To understand the results the author had arrived at, it became necessary to read the whole Memoir.

Although deeply interested in the subject, I was obliged, with great regret, to give up the attempt; for it not only occupied much time, but placed too great a strain on the memory.

Whenever I am thus perplexed it has often occurred to me that the very simple plan I have adopted in my *Mechanical Notation* for lettering drawings might be adopted in analysis.

On the geometrical drawings of machinery every piece of matter which represents framework is invariably denoted by an *upright* letter; whilst all letters indicating moveable parts are marked by *inclined* letters.

The analogous rule would be

Let all letters indicating operations or modifications be expressed by *upright* letters;

Whilst all letters representing quantity should be represented by *inclined* letters.

The subject of the principles and laws of notation is so important that it is desireable, before it is too late, that the scientific academies of the world should each contribute the results of their own examination and conclusions, and that some congress should assemble to discuss them. Perhaps it might be still better if each academy would draw up its own views, illustrated by examples, and have a sufficient number printed to send to all other academies.

• • •

1. Ada Augusta, Countess of Lovelace, only child of the Poet Byron.

6.3
Automatic Calculating Machines

Percy E. Ludgate

From Ellice M. Horsburgh, ed., *Modern Instruments and Methods of Calculation: A Handbook of the Napier Tercentenary Exhibition* (London: G. Bell and Sons, 1914), pp. 124–27.

INTRODUCTORY NOTE TO READING 6.3

Between the time of Babbage and the 1930s, Percy Ludgate (1883–1922) may have been the only person to attempt to build a general-purpose programmable computer. Ludgate wrote this account for the *Handbook of the Napier Tercentenary Celebration* (1914); this compendium, issued at the beginning of World War I, is the best record of calculating machines up to that date. Little is known about Ludgate except that he was an accountant working in Ireland who developed programmable calculating machines in his spare time. Apart from this survey article, Ludgate published an account of his own proposed machine in 1909 in the *Scientific Proceedings, Royal Dublin Society*. Like Babbage, Ludgate was never able to obtain funding for construction of his machine, and he died at the age of only 39. According to Lee, Ludgate's machine represented advances over Babbage's ideas in program control, and "all three main components of Ludgate's analytical machine—the store, the arithmetic unit, and the sequencing mechanism—show evidence of considerable ingenuity and originality."[1] Unfortunately the drawings of the machine that Ludgate mentions in his 1914 article seem to have disappeared. [JMN]

---

1   J. A. N. Lee, *Computer Pioneers* (Los Alamitos, CA: IEEE Computer Society Press, 1995), 446–48.

Automatic calculating machines on being actuated, if necessary, by uniform motive power, and supplied with numbers on which to operate, will compute correct results without requiring any further attention. Of course many adding machines, and possibly a few multiplying machines, belong to this category; but it is not to them, but to machines of far greater power, that this article refers. On the other hand, tide-predicting machines and other instruments that work on geometrical principles will not be considered here, because they do not operate arithmetically. It must be admitted, however, that the true automatic calculating machine belongs to a possible rather than an actual class; for, though several were designed and a few constructed, the writer is not aware of any machine in use at the present time that can determine numerical values of complicated formulae without the assistance of an operator.

The first great automatic calculating machine was invented by Charles Babbage. He called it a "difference-engine," and commenced to construct it about the year 1822. The work was continued during the following twenty years, the Government contributing about £17,000 to defray its cost, and Babbage himself a further sum of about £6000. At the end of that time the construction of the engine, though nearly finished, was unfortunately abandoned owing to some misunderstanding with the Government. A portion of this engine is exhibited in South Kensington Museum, along with other examples of Babbage's work. If the engine had been finished, it would have contained seven columns of wheels, with twenty wheels in each column (for computing with six orders of differences), and also a contrivance for stereotyping the tables calculated by it. A machine of this kind will calculate a sequence of tabular numbers automatically when its figure-wheels are first set to correct initial values.

Inspired by Babbage's work, Scheutz of Stockholm made a difference-engine, which was exhibited in England in 1854, and subsequently acquired for Dudley Observatory, Albany, U.S.A. Scheutz's engine had mechanism for calculating with four orders of differences of sixteen figures each, and for stereotyping its results; but as it was only suitable for calculating tables having small tabular intervals, its utility was limited. A duplicate of this engine was constructed for the Registrar General's Office, London.

In 1848 Babbage commenced the drawings of an improved difference-engine, and though he subsequently completed the drawings, the improved engine was not made.

Babbage began to design his "analytical engine" in 1833, and he put together a small portion of it shortly before his death in 1871. This engine was to be capable of evaluating any algebraic formula, of which a numerical solution is possible, for any given values of the variables. The formula it is desired to evaluate would be communicated to the engine by two sets of perforated cards similar to those used in the Jacquard loom. These cards would cause the engine automatically to operate on the numerical data placed in it, in such a way as to produce the correct result. The mechanism of this engine may be divided into three main sections, designated the "Jacquard apparatus," the "mill," and the "store." Of these the Jacquard apparatus would control the action of both mill and store, and indeed of the whole engine.

The store was to consist of a large number of vertical columns of wheels, every wheel having the nine digits and zero marked on its periphery. These columns of wheels Babbage termed "variables," because the number registered on any column could be varied by rotating the wheels on that column. It is important to notice that the variables could not perform any arithmetical operation, but were merely passive registering contrivances, corresponding to the pen and paper of the human computer. Babbage originally intended the store to have a thousand variables, each consisting of fifty wheels, which would give it capacity for a thousand fifty-figure numbers. He numbered the variables consecutively, and represented them by the symbols $V_1, V_2, V_3, V_4 \ldots V_{1000}$. Now, if a number, say 3.14159, were placed on the 10th variable, by turning the wheels until the number appeared in front, reading from top to bottom, we may express the fact by the equation $V_{10} = 3.14159$ or $V_{10} = \pi$. We may equate the symbol of the variable either to the actual number the variable contains, or to the algebraic equivalent of that number. Moreover, in theoretical work it is often convenient to use literal instead of numerical indices for the letters V, and therefore $V_n = ab$ means that the nth variable registers the numerical value of the product of a and b.

The mill was designed for the purpose of executing all four arithmetical operations. If V_n and V_m were any two variables, whose sum, difference, product, or quotient was required, the numbers they represent would first be automatically transferred to the mill, and then submitted to the requisite operation. Finally, the result of the operation would be transferred from mill to store, being there placed on the variable (which we will represent by V_z) destined to receive it. Consequently the four fundamental operations of the machine may be written as follows:

1. $V_n + V_m = V_z.$
2. $V_n - V_m = V_z.$
3. $V_n \times V_m = V_z.$
4. $V_n \div V_m = V_z.$

Where n, m, and z may be any positive integers, not exceeding the total number of variables, n and m being unequal.

One set of Jacquard cards, called "directive cards," (also called "variable cards") would control the store, and the other set, called "operation cards," would control the mill. The directive cards were to be numbered like the variables, and every variable was to have a supply of cards corresponding to it. These cards were so designed that when one of them entered the engine it would cause the Jacquard apparatus to put the corresponding variable into gear. In like manner every operation card (of which only four kinds were required) would be marked with the sign of the particular operation it could cause the mill to perform. Therefore, if a directive card bearing the number 16 (say) were to enter the engine, it would cause the number on V_{16} to be transferred to the mill or *vice versa*; and an operation card marked with the sign $\div$ would, on entering the engine, cause the mill to divide one of the numbers transferred to it by the other. It will be observed that the choice of a directive card would be represented in the notation by the substitution of a numerical for a literal index of a V; or, in other words, the substitution of an integer for one of the indices n, m, and z in the foregoing four examples. Therefore three directive cards strung together would give definite values to n, m, and z, and one operation card would determine the nature of the arithmetical operation, so that four cards in all would suffice to guide the machine to select the two proper variables to be operated on, to subject the numbers they register to the desired operation, and to place the result on a third variable. If the directive cards were numbered 5, 7, and 3, and the operation card marked +, the result would be $V_5 + V_7 = V_3$.

As a further illustration, suppose the directive cards are strung together so as to give the following successive values to n, m, and z:

Sequence of values for n . . .	2, 6, 4, 7.
Sequence of values for m . . .	3, 1, 5, 8.
Sequence of values for z . . .	6, 7, 8, 9.

Let the sequence of operation cards be

$+ \times - \div$

When the cards are placed in the engine, the following results are obtained in succession:

1st operation,	$V_2 + V_3 = V_6.$
2nd operation,	$V_6 \times V_1 = V_7.$
3rd operation,	$V_4 - V_5 = V_8.$
4th operation,	$V_7 \div V_8 = V_9.$

From an inspection of the foregoing it appears that V_1, V_2, V_3, V_4 and V_5 are independent variables, while V_6, V_7, V_8, and V_9 have their values calculated by the engine, and therefore the former set must contain the data of the calculation.

Let $V_1 = a$, $V_2 = b$, $V_3 = c$, $V_4 = d$, and $V_5 = e$, then we have

1st operation,	$V_2 + V_3 = b + c = V_6$.
2nd operation,	$V_6 \infty V_1 = (b + c)a = V_7$.
3rd operation,	$V_4 - V_5 = d - e = V_8$.
4th operation,	$V_7 \div V_8 = \dfrac{(b+c)a}{d-e} = V_9$.

Consequently, whatever numerical values of a, b, c, d, and e are placed on variables V_1 to V_5 respectively, the corresponding value of $\dfrac{a(b+c)}{d-e}$ will be found on V_9, when all the cards have passed through the machine. Moreover, the same set of cards may be used any number of times for different calculations by the same formula.

In the foregoing very simple example the algebraic formula is deduced from a given sequence of cards. It illustrates the converse of the practical procedure, which is to arrange the cards to interpret a given formula, and it also shows that the cards constitute a mathematical notation in themselves.

Seven years after Babbage died a Committee of the British Association appointed to consider the advisability and to estimate the expense of constructing the analytical engine reported that: "We have come to the conclusion that in the present state of the design it is not possible for us to form any reasonable estimate of its cost or its strength and durability." In 1906 Charles Babbage's son, Major-General H. P. Babbage, completed the part of the engine known as the "mill," and a table of twenty-five multiples of π to twenty-nine figures, was published as a specimen of its work, in the *Monthly Notices of the Royal Astronomical Society*, April 1910.

I have myself designed an analytical machine, on different lines from Babbage's, to work with 192 variables of 20 figures each. A short account of it appeared in the *Scientific Proceedings, Royal Dublin Society*, April 1909. Complete descriptive drawings of the machine exist, as well as a description in manuscript, but I have not been able to take any steps to have the machine constructed.

The most pleasing characteristic of a difference-engine made on Babbage's principle is the simplicity of its action, the differences being added together in unvarying sequence; but notwithstanding its simple action, its structure is complicated by a large amount of adding mechanism—a complete set of adding wheels with carrying gear being required for the tabular number, and every order of difference except the highest order. On the other hand, while the best feature of the analytical engine or machine is the Jacquard apparatus (which, without being itself complicated, may be made a powerful instrument for interpreting mathematical formulae), its weakness lies in the diversity of movements the Jacquard apparatus must control. Impressed by these facts, and with the desirability of reducing the expense of construction, I designed a second machine in which are combined the best principles of both the analytical and difference types, and from which are excluded their more expensive characteristics. By using a Jacquard I found it possible to eliminate the redundancy of parts hitherto found in difference-engines, while retaining the native symmetry of structure and harmony of action of machines of that class. My second machine, of which the design is on the point of completion, will contain but *one* set of adding wheels, and its movements will have a rhythm resembling that of the Jacquard loom itself. It is primarily intended to be used as a difference-machine, the number of orders of differences being sixteen. Moreover, the machine will also have the power of automatically evaluating a wide range of miscellaneous formulae.

7
The Theory of the Universal Machine

7.1
On Computable Numbers

Alan M. Turing

Extract from "On Computable Numbers, with an Application to the *Entscheidungsproblem*," *Proc. Lond. Math. Soc.,* 2nd series, 42 (1936): 231–235, 241–244. Reprinted by permission of the London Mathematical Society.

INTRODUCTORY NOTE TO READING 7.1

Alan Turing's theoretical paper "On Computable Numbers" (1936) is undoubtedly the most famous theoretical paper in the history of computing. It is a mathematical description of what Turing called a universal machine—an imaginary computing device designed to replicate the mathematical "states of mind" and symbol-manipulating abilities of a human computer. Turing conceived of the universal machine as a means of answering the last of the three questions about mathematics posed by David Hilbert in 1928: (1) is mathematics *complete*; (2) is mathematics *consistent*; and (3) is mathematics *decidable.*

Hilbert's final question, known as the *Entscheidungsproblem,* concerns whether there exists a definite method—or, in the suggestive words of Turing's teacher Max Newman, a "mechanical process"—that can be applied to any mathematical assertion, and which is guaranteed to produce a correct decision as to whether that assertion is true.[1] The Czech logician Kurt Gödel had already shown that arithmetic (and by extension mathematics) was both inconsistent and incomplete. Turing showed, by means of his universal machine, that mathematics was also undecidable.

To demonstrate this, Turing came up with the concept of "computable numbers," which are numbers defined by some definite rule, and thus calculable on the universal machine. These computable numbers "would include every number that could be arrived at through arithmetical operations, finding roots of equations, and using mathematical functions like sines and logarithms—every number that could possibly arise in computational mathematics."[2] Turing then showed that these computable numbers could give rise to *uncomputable* ones—ones that could not be calculated using a definite rule—and that therefore there could be no "mechanical process" for solving all mathematical questions, since an uncomputable number was an example of an unsolvable problem. Turing's idea of a "universal machine" was given the name "Turing machine" by Alonzo Church (see Reading 7.2).

Turing spent from September 1936 to 1938 at Princeton University, where he studied with Alonzo Church, and came into contact with John von Neumann. Concerned about what he perceived was an inevitable war with Germany, in 1937 Turing built an electromechanical cryptanalysis machine to multiply binary numbers in a Princeton machine shop—an early confirmation of his parallel interests in both the theory of computing and its expression in concrete devices. In 1938 Turing returned to Cambridge. The following year he designed an analog machine to calculate the Riemann zeta-function, and also worked on an analog tide-predicting machine. On September 4, 1939, one day after England declared war with Germany, Turing reported to the Government Code and

---

1   Andrew Hodges, *Alan Turing: The Enigma* (New York: Simon & Schuster, 1983), 91.

2   Hodges, *op. cit.,* 100.

Cypher School at Bletchley Park. There, as part of the British government's huge wartime cryptanalysis project, he designed an improved Bombe, and helped develop the Heath Robinson machine and the Colossus special-purpose electronic computers that deciphered the Germans' Enigma code. In November 1942 Turing crossed the Atlantic to consult on the world's first totally unbreakable speech encipherment system, intended for communication of speech signals between Roosevelt and Churchill.[3] He worked in Washington, DC, briefly, and in New York with Claude Shannon and Harry Nyquist at Bell Laboratories before returning to Bletchley Park.

After the war Turing turned his attention to the new field of large-scale electronic digital computers, designing the National Physical Laboratory's Automatic Computing Engine (ACE), programming the prototype of the University of Manchester's Mark I, and assisting Ferranti in programming the commercial version of this machine. Speaking in February 1947 Turing stated that "digital computing machines such as the ACE . . . are in fact practical versions of the universal machine."[4] In 1952, at the age of forty, Turing was arrested and convicted for committing homosexual acts, then a criminal offense in England. As punishment he was forced to undergo a year-long course of estrogen therapy, otherwise known as chemical castration, which rendered him impotent for the duration of the treatment. The treatment did not affect his productivity, however, as he continued to conduct research and to publish during this period. He died at the age of forty-two from eating cyanide injected into an apple.

Though Turing's paper may have had little direct influence on the other designers and builders of the first electronic computers, his concept of the "universal machine" was adapted to theories of brain function by McCulloch and Pitts (see Reading 7.4). McCulloch and Pitts's ideas in turn exerted a considerable influence on von Neumann's *First Draft of a Report on the EDVAC* (see Reading 8.1), a theoretical description of the stored-program machine that was read by all the designers of first-generation computers. In showing that a universal machine was possible, Turing's paper was highly influential in the theory of computation, and it remained a powerful expression of the virtually unlimited adaptability of electronic digital computers.

For the purposes of this anthology we have chosen not to include some of the most abstract and theoretical portions of Turing's paper. Those who want to read the complete text will find that on the Internet.[JMN]

---

3   Hodges, *op. cit.,* 246.

4   Martin Davis, *The Universal Computer: The Road from Leibniz to Turing* (New York: W. W. Norton, 2000), 189.

TEXT OF READING 7.1

. . . 1. COMPUTING MACHINES.

We have said that the computable numbers are those whose decimals are calculable by finite means. This requires rather more explicit definition. No real attempt will be made to justify the definitions given until we reach §9. For the present I shall only say that the justification lies in the fact that the human memory is necessarily limited.

We may compare a man in the process of computing a real number to a machine which is only capable of a finite number of conditions $q_1, q_2, \ldots, q_R$ which will be called "m-configurations". The machine is supplied with a "tape", (the analogue of paper) running through it, and divided into sections (called "squares") each capable of bearing a "symbol". At any moment there is just one square, say the r-th, bearing the symbol $\mathbf{S}(r)$ which is "in the machine". We may call this square the "scanned square". The symbol on the scanned square may be called the "scanned symbol". The "scanned symbol" is the only one of which the machine is, so to speak, "directly aware". However, by altering its m-configuration the machine can effectively remember some of the symbols which it has "seen" (scanned) previously. The possible behaviour of the machine at any moment is determined by the m-configuration q_n and the scanned symbol $\mathbf{S}(r)$. This pair q_n, $\mathbf{S}(r)$ will be called the "configuration": thus the configuration determines the possible behaviour of the machine. In some of the configurations in which the scanned square is blank (i.e. bears no symbol) the machine writes down a new symbol on the scanned square: in other configurations it erases the scanned symbol. The machine may also change the square which is being scanned, but only by shifting it one place to right or left. In addition to any of these operations the m-configuration may be changed. Some of the symbols written down will form the sequence of figures which is the decimal of the real number which is being computed. The others are just rough notes to "assist the memory". It will only be these rough notes which will be liable to erasure.

It is my contention that these operations include all those which are used in the computation of a number. The defence of this contention will be easier when the theory of the machines is familiar to the reader. In the next section I therefore proceed with the development of the theory and assume that it is understood what is meant by "machine," "tape", "scanned," etc.

2. DEFINITIONS.

Automatic machines.

If at each stage the motion of a machine (in the sense of §1) is *completely* determined by the configuration, we shall call the machine an "automatic machine" (or a-machine). For some purposes we might use machines (choice machines or c-machines) whose motion is only partially determined by the configuration (hence the use of the word "possible" in §1). When such a machine reaches one of these ambiguous configurations, it cannot go on until some arbitrary choice has been made by an external operator. This would be the case if we were using machines to deal with axiomatic systems. In this paper I deal only with automatic machines, and will therefore often omit the prefix a-.

Computing machines.

If an a-machine prints two kinds of symbols, of which the first kind (called figures) consists entirely of 0 and 1 (the others being called symbols of the second kind), then the machine will be called a computing machine. If the machine is supplied with a blank tape and set in motion, starting from the correct initial m-configuration, the subsequence of the symbols printed by it which are of the first kind will be called the *sequence computed by the machine*. The real number whose expression as a binary decimal is obtained by prefacing this sequence by a decimal point is called the *number computed by the machine*.

At any stage of the motion of the machine, the number of the scanned square, the complete sequence of all symbols on the tape, and the m-configuration will be said to describe the *complete configuration* at that stage. The changes of the machine and tape between successive complete configurations will be called the *moves* of the machine.

Circular and circle-free machines.

If a computing machine never writes down more than a finite number of symbols of the first kind it will be called *circular*. Otherwise it is said to be *circle free*.

A machine will be circular if it reaches a configuration from which there is no possible move, or if it goes on moving, and possibly printing symbols of the second kind, but cannot print any more symbols of the first kind. The significance of the term "circular" will be explained in §8.

Computable sequences and numbers.

A sequence is said to be computable if it can be computed by a circle-free machine. A number is computable if it differs by an integer from the number computed by a circle-free machine.

We shall avoid confusion by speaking more often of computable sequences than of computable numbers.

3. EXAMPLES OF COMPUTING MACHINES.

I. A machine can be constructed to compute the sequence 010101.... The machine is to have the four *m*-configurations "$\mathbf{b}$", "$\mathbf{c}$", "$\mathbf{k}$" "$\mathbf{e}$" and is capable of printing "0", and "1". The behaviour of the machine is described in the following table in which "R" means "the machine moves so that it scans the square immediately on the right of the one it was scanning previously". Similarly for "L". "E" means the scanned symbol is "erased" and "P" stands for "prints". This table (and all succeeding tables of the same kind) is to be understood to mean that for a configuration described in the first two columns the operations in the third column are carried out successively, and the machine then goes over into the *m*-configuration described in the last column. When the second column is left blank, it is understood that the behaviour of the third and fourth columns applies for any symbol and for no symbol. The machine starts in the *m*-configuration b with a blank tape.

Configuration		Behaviour	
b	None	P0, R	c
c	None	R	e
k	None	P1, R	k
e	None	R	b

If (contrary to the description in §1) we allow the letters L, R to appear more that once in the operations column we can simplify the table considerably.

m-config.	Symbol	Operations	Final m-config.
b	None	P0	b
	0	R, R, P1	b
	1	R, R, P0	b

II. As a slightly more difficult example we can construct a machine to compute the sequence 001011011101111011111.... The machine is to be capable of five *m*-configurations, viz. "$\mathbf{o}$", "$\mathbf{q}$", "$\mathbf{p}$" "$\mathbf{f}$", "$\mathbf{b}$" and of printing "∂", "x", "0", "1". The first three symbols on the tape will be "∂ ∂ 0"; the other figures follow on alternate squares. On the intermediate squares we never print anything but "x". These letters serve to "keep the place" for us and are erased when we have finished with them. We also arrange that in the sequence of figures on alternate squares there shall be no blanks.

Configuration		Behaviour	
m-configuration	Symbol	Operations	Final *m*-configuration
b		$P\partial$, R, $P\partial$, R, P0, R, R, P0, L, L	o
o	1	R, Px, L, L, L	o
	0		q
q	Any (0 or 1)	R, R	q
	None	P1, L	p

	x	E, R	q
p	ə	R	f
	None	L, L	p
	Any	R, R	f
f	None	P0, L, L	o

To illustrate the working of this machine a table is given below of the first few complete configurations. These complete configurations are described by writing down the sequence of symbols which are on the tape, with the *m*-configuration written below the scanned symbol. The successive complete configurations are separated by colons.

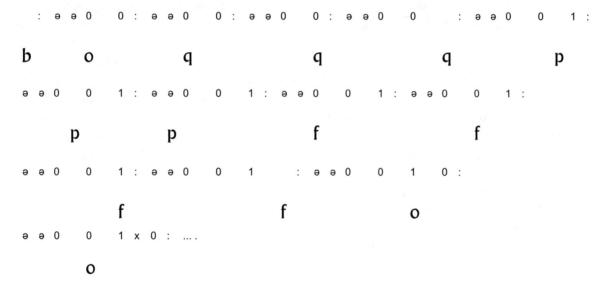

This table could also be written in the form

$$\mathbf{b} : ə ə \mathbf{0} 0 \quad 0 : ə ə \mathbf{q} 0 \quad 0 : \ldots, \quad \text{(C)}$$

in which a space has been made on the left of the scanned symbol and the *m*-configuration written in this space. This form is less easy to follow, but we shall make use of it later for theoretical purposes.

The convention of writing the figures only on alternate squares is very useful: I shall always make use of it. I shall call the one sequence of alternate squares *F*-squares and the other sequence *E*-squares. The symbols on *E*-squares will be liable to erasure. The symbols on *F*-squares form a continuous sequence. There are no blanks until the end is reached. There is no need to have more than one *E*-square between each pair of F-squares: an apparent need of more E-squares can be satisfied by having a sufficiently rich variety of symbols capable of being printed on E-squares. If a symbol β- is on an F-square S and a symbol α is on the E-square next on the right of S, then S and β and will be said to be marked with α. The process of printing this α will be called marking β (or S) with α. . . .

6. THE UNIVERSAL COMPUTING MACHINE.

It is possible to invent a single machine which can be used to compute any computable sequence. If this machine $\mathcal{U}$ is supplied with a tape on the beginning of which is written the S.D [standard description] of some computing machine $\mathcal{M}$, then $\mathcal{U}$ will compute the same sequence as $\mathcal{M}$. In this section I explain in outline the behavior of the machine. The next section is devoted to giving the complete table for $\mathcal{U}$.

Let us first suppose that we have a machine $\mathcal{M}'$ which will write down on the F-squares the successive complete configurations of $\mathcal{M}$. These might be expressed in the same form as on p. 235, using the second description, (C), with all symbols on one line. Or, better, we could transform this description (as in §5) by replacing each m-configuration by "D" followed by "A" repeated the appropriate number of times, and by replacing each symbol by "D" followed by "C" repeated the appropriate number of times. The numbers of letters "A" and "C" are to agree with the numbers chosen in §5, so that, in particular, "0" is replaced by "DC", "1" by "DCC", and the blanks by "D" . These substitutions are to be made after the complete configurations have been put together, as in (C). Difficulties arise if we do the substitution first. In each complete configuration the blanks would all have to be replaced by "D", so that the complete configuration would not be expressed as a finite sequence of symbols.

If in the description of the machine II of §3 we replace "O" by "DAA", "ə" by "DCCC", "ꝗ" by "DAAA", then the sequence (C) becomes:

DA : DCCCDCCCDAADCDDC :
    DCCCDCCDAAADCDDC : . . . (C₁).

(This is the sequence of symbols on F-squares.)

It is not difficult to see that if $\mathcal{M}$ can be constructed, then so can $\mathcal{M}'$. The manner of operation of $\mathcal{M}'$ could be made to depend on having the rules of operation (i.e., the S.D) of it written somewhere within itself (i.e. within $\mathcal{M}'$); each step could be carried out by referring to these rules. We have only to regard the rates as being capable of being taken out and exchanged or others and we have something very akin to the universal machine.

One thing is lacking: at present the machine $\mathcal{M}'$ prints no figures. We may correct this by printing between each successive pair of complete configurations the figures which appear in the new configuration but not in the old. Then (C₁) becomes

DDA : 0 : 0 : DCCCDCCCDAADCDDC :
    DCCC. . . . (C₂)

It is not altogether obvious that the E-squares leave enough room for the necessary "rough work", but this is, in fact, the case.

The sequences of letters between the colons in expressions such as (C₁) may be used as standard descriptions of the complete configurations. When the letters are replaced by figures, as in §5, we shall have a numerical description of the complete configuration, which may be called its description number. . . .

[Review of] A. M. Turing. On Computable Numbers, with an Application to the *Entscheidungsproblem*

Alonzo Church

From *Journal of Symbolic Logic* 2 (1937): 42–43.

INTRODUCTORY NOTE TO READING 7.2

Alonzo Church, professor of mathematics at Princeton, and one of Turing's teachers, was the first to coin the term "Turing machine" for Turing's universal machine. Church coined the term in his relatively brief review of "On Computable Numbers." With regard to Turing's proof of the unsolvability of Hilbert's *Entscheidungsproblem,* Church acknowledged that "computability by a Turing machine . . . has the advantage of making the identification with effectiveness in the ordinary (not explicitly defined) sense evident immediately—i.e. without the necessity of proving preliminary theorems." Church, working independently of Turing, had arrived at his own answer to the *Entscheidungsproblem* a few months earlier.[JMN]

TEXT OF READING 7.2

The author proposes as a criterion that an infinite sequence of digits 0 and 1 be "computable", that it shall be possible to devise a computing machine, occupying a finite space and with working parts of finite size, which will write down the sequence to any desired number of terms if allowed to run for a sufficiently long time. As a matter of convenience, certain further restrictions are imposed on the character of the machine, but these are of such a nature as obviously to cause no loss of generality—in particular, a human calculator, provided with pencil and paper and explicit instructions, can be regarded as a kind of Turing machine. It is thus immediately clear that computability, so defined, can be identified with (especially, is no less general than) the notion of effectiveness as it appears in certain mathematical problems (various forms of the Entscheidungsproblem, various problems to find complete sets of invariants in topology, group theory, etc., and in general any problem which concerns the discovery of an algorithm).

The principal result is that there exist sequences (well-defined on classical grounds) which are not computable. In particular the *deducibility problem* of the functional calculus of first order (Hilbert and Ackermann's engere Funktionenkalkül) is unsolvable in the sense that, if the formulas of this calculus are enumerated in a straightforward manner, the sequence whose nth term is 0 or 1, according as the nth formula in the enumeration is or is not deducible, is not computable. (The proof here requires some correction in matters of detail.)

In an appendix the author sketches a proof of equivalence of "computability" in his sense and "effective calculability" in the sense of the present reviewer (*American journal of mathematics,* vol. 58 (1936), pp. 345–363, see review in this Journal, vol. 1, pp. 73–74). The author's result concerning the existence of uncomputable sequences was also anticipated, in terms of effective calculability, in the cited paper. His work was, however, done independently, being nearly complete and known in substance to a number of persons at the time that the paper appeared.

As a matter of fact, there is involved here the equivalence of three different notions: computability by a Turing machine, general recursiveness in the sense of Herbrand-Gödel-Kleene, and X-definability in the sense of Kleene and the present reviewer. Of these, the first has the advantage of making the identification with effectiveness in the ordinary (not explicitly defined) sense evident immediately—i.e. without the necessity of proving preliminary theorems. The second and third have the advantage of suitability for embodiment in a system of symbolic logic.

Letter Covering the Memorandum on the Scope, etc., of a Suggested Computing Machine (September 21, 1940) & Memorandum on the Mechanical Solution of Partial Differential Equations

Norbert Wiener

From Norbert Wiener, *Collected Works with Commentaries*, ed. P. Masani (Cambridge, MA: MIT Press, 1976–85), vol. IIB, 122–34.

INTRODUCTORY NOTE TO READING 7.3.

In *Cybernetics, or Control and Communication in the Animal and the Machine* (1948), Norbert Wiener made his first published reference to a confidential report that he had written for Vannevar Bush in 1940, describing a general purpose electronic computer. In the Introduction to *Cybernetics* Wiener mentioned that the machine would have the following theoretical requirements:

1. That the central adding and multiplying apparatus of the computing machine should be numerical, as in ordinary adding machine, rather than on a basis of measurement, as in the Bush differential analyzer;

2. That these mechanisms, which are essentially switching devices, should depend on electronic tubes rather than on gears or mechanical relays, in order to secure quicker action;

3. That, in accordance with the policy adopted in some existing apparatus of the Bell Telephone Laboratories, it would probably be more economical in apparatus to adopt the scale of two for addition and multiplication, rather than the scale of ten;

4. That the entire sequence of operations be laid out on the machine itself so that there should be no human intervention from the time the data were entered until the final results should be taken off; and that all logical decisions necessary for this should be built into the machine itself;

5. That the machine contain an apparatus for the storage of data which should record them quickly, hold them firmly until erasure, read them quickly, erase them quickly, and be immediately available for the storage of new material (Wiener, *Cybernetics* [1948], 10–11).

Wiener's confidential memorandum, prepared for Vannevar Bush and his Rapid Arithmetical Machine Project at MIT, was probably influenced by Wiener's reading of Turing's "On Computable Numbers" (1936). It was inspired by Wiener's attendance on September 11, 1940 of a meeting of the American Mathematical Association in Dartmouth, New Hampshire. There George Stibitz's Complex Number Calculator, an electromechanical relay machine located in New York that Stibitz had developed for Bell Labs, was demonstrated via a remote teletype terminal. Both Wiener and John Mauchly, who would later contribute to the design of the ENIAC, spent a lot of time experimenting with the system.

Wiener's memorandum is probably the earliest dated document in English describing a theoretical electronic computer, except for John Atanasoff's more detailed report on the Atanasoff-Berry Computer, dated August 1940, which remained unpublished until 1973. Wiener's report must have seemed impractical to Bush, who was preoccupied with developing more elaborate versions of his differential analyzer for military applications. Bush filed away the report without taking any action. Remarkably, the brief report and the correspondence related to it turned up during the editing of Wiener's collected papers. It was published in that set with the following editorial comments:

[The machine] exhibits every characteristic of the modern digital computer except for the stored program. The proposed machine employs:

A discrete quantized numerical algorithm for solution of the PDE.

A classical Turing machine architecture.

Binary arithmetic and data storage.

An electronic arithmetic logic unit.

A multitrack magnetic tape.

It is interesting to wonder how much von Neumann and Wiener influenced each other. Their paths had crossed on several occasions . . . prior to 1940, at which time both von Neumann and Wiener were consultants to the joint War Preparedness Committee of the American Mathematical Society and the Mathematical Association of America, but it was Wiener who was consultant on computation. It is hard to estimate how much cross-fertilization occurred between these two men. Yet, had Bush circulated the Wiener memorandum, we might today be talking about the limitations of the Wiener-von Neumann, if not the Wiener machine instead of the von Neumann machine" (Wiener, *Collected Works* [1976–85], vol. IIB, 137, 139).

The letter and memorandum were published for the first time in Norbert Wiener's *Collected Works*, Vol. IIB, pp. 122–34. [JMN]

TEXT OF READING 7.3

September 21, 1940

Dr. Vannevar Bush

Carnegie Institution

Washington, D.C.

Dear Bush:

In response to your suggestion of this morning, I am sending you a memorandum concerning my proposed computing machine for the solution of boundary value problems in partial differential equations.

This device solves a partial difference equation involving the time, and asymptotically equivalent to a partial differential equation involving the time, yielding for infinite time a purely space partial differential equation which may be of very different forms. This partial difference equation is solved by an apparatus which repeatedly scans a collection of data recorded on some very inexpensive device and replaces these data by new data. This replacement is done by an apparatus which, as there is only one of it, may be reasonably elaborate without making the entire apparatus too costly.

I shall take up as a particular example a method for solving the boundary value problem for the Laplace equation

$$\frac{\partial^2 u}{\partial x^2} + \frac{\partial^2 u}{\partial y^2} = 0$$

We replace this by the difference equation

$$u(x+1, y) + u(x-1, y) + u(x, y+1) + u(x, y-1) = 0,$$

and obtain the solution of this difference equation as the limit for infinite values of time of the solution of the difference equation

$$1/4\{u(x+1, y; t) + u(x-1, y; t) + u(x, y+1; t) + u(x, y-1; t)\} = u(x, y, t+1).$$

It will be seen that in this last equation the step of moving forward one unit in time corresponds to the step of replacing numerical values at the meshes of a net by their average. In this replacement the boundary of the net is left untouched. We thus require an apparatus which will record a function at all the meshes of the net, combined with the scanning apparatus which will read the values at the four meshes surrounding a given point, average them, and replace the average value as the new value for this point. I propose that the values be recorded in the binary system on an endless steel tape in the usual magnetic manner. That is, this tape will contain ten parallel lines marked and scanned magnetically, and these lines will indicate a number between 0 and 1024, according to the lines which are printed or left blank at a particular cross-section of the tape. There are scanning apparatus placed slightly before and slightly after a given point as well as apparatus removed from this point by a fixed distance before and after it, to indicate points above it and below it when a pattern of equispaced lines on a two-dimensional figure are placed consecutively on the tape. These four values are read by an apparatus leading to a rapid electrical adding machine on the binary scale, and after discarding the last two digits the sum is printed magnetically on the binary system on the tape after a distance equivalent to the sum of the lengths of all the lines covering the figure. It will probably be advantageous to slightly modify this arrangement by carrying printing and reading at the same level of the tape—printing on one side of a broad tape while reading on the other and *vice-versa*. The boundary values are to be carried on still a third width of tape and are to be switched in at the appropriate points by an appropriate signal, in place of the running values on the tape. The boundary values are never erased, but the rest of the tape is swept clean magnetically after it has been used.

Now for an estimate of the speed of this apparatus. Taking a network of 100 by 100 points and replacing the difference equation of the apparatus by the closely related differential equation, the problem of determining the speed of the apparatus is equivalent to that of determining the rate at which a solution of the differential equation

$$\frac{\partial^2 u}{\partial x^2} + \frac{\partial^2 u}{\partial y^2} = -4\frac{\partial u}{\partial t}$$

tends to 0 when the boundary values are 0 and the boundary is interior to the square

$$x = 0; x = 100; y = 0; y = 100.$$

We can estimate this by taking the extreme case of the complete square and initial values

$$\sin\frac{\pi x}{100} \sin\frac{\pi y}{100}$$

The solution of this problem is

$$\sin\frac{\pi x}{100} \sin\frac{\pi y}{100} \exp\left(-\frac{\pi^2}{2(100)^2}t\right)$$

so that the error is reduced by the factor e in a single scanning. If we are aiming at an accuracy of one part in 1,000, this means that 1.4 scannings are necessary and therefore that on each line 140,000,000 impulses must be recorded before the scanning is complete. Assuming a rate of scanning of 10,000 impulses per second, this yields a time not exceeding 3.89 hours for the final answer to be obtained.

If we can record 100 impulses per inch, the steel tape need not be over 100" long; furthermore, it must be wide enough to record, without confusion, thirty lines of impulses. Certainly a 6" tape will not be out of the question. The linear speed of the tape will be such that it makes a complete circuit in a second. When the scanning is complete, as the tape contains all the numerical values of the potential function for all the meshes inside the boundary, it will be perfectly practicable to devise a machine for printing the results in the form of a table.

Let it be noticed that the rapidity of the machine varies inversely as the fourth power of the number of meshes.

I have here assumed a magnetical printing and scanning. It is perfectly possible to replace this by a photoelectric scanning combined with a printing by some such device as an electric spark. The difficulty in this latter case is that erasure is impossible and excessive quantities of paper tape must go to waste. However, you will see that the variations in method keeping the same idea are enormous.

To vary the setup for partial differential equations, whether linear or not, we have to modify the number of pickup points in accordance with the order of the equation, and the electrical apparatus between the scanning and the printing devices in accordance with the form and degree of the equation. Notice that no apparatus repeated more than a small number of times is changed by this. Thus the expense of the apparatus is only slightly increased. Of course, for more complicated boundary value questions a more complicated method for indicating and putting in the boundary values is needed. In any event this apparatus is primarily adapted for equations of the *elliptic type*.

I repeat the main contribution which I have here to make to the problem of the mechanical solution of partial differential equations is the consistent use of the idea of scanning; this is economically important as it allows expensive apparatus to be used repeatedly and efficiently.

I can think of many problems to which the method could be applied. For example, there are problems concerning the flow around airplane wings and problems concerning the field around condensers and there are hydrodynamical problems, problems from the theory of elasticity, problems concerning sound waves of finite amplitude, problems from interior ballistics, and so on. I can't say from the outside just which, if any, of these, are of more importance.

There is another quite different matter which I mentioned to you in private conversation and which I would like to repeat for purposes of record. It has to do with the idea of making an anti-aircraft barrage by bursting in the air containers of liquified ethylene or propane or acetylene gases so that an appreciable region will be filled with an explosive mixture of these in the air. The idea is that in such a way a region of the air may be interdicted to enemy aircraft—a matter of tens of seconds or of minutes instead of the fraction of a second during which a high explosive burst is continuing, and that thereby the efficiency of a barrage from a small number of anti-aircraft guns may be appreciably increased.

I enjoyed very much the chance to talk with you on your visit here and hope you can find some corner of activity in which I may be of use during the emergency.

Very sincerely yours,

Norbert Wiener

MEMORANDUM ON THE MECHANICAL SOLUTION OF PARTIAL DIFFERENTIAL EQUATIONS

The projected machine will solve boundary value problems in the field of partial differential equations. In particular, it will determine the equipotential lines and lines of flow about an airfoil section given by determining about 200 points on its profile, to an accuracy of one part in a thousand, in from three to four hours. It will also solve three-dimensional potential problems, problems from the theory of elasticity, etc. It is not confined to linear problems, and may be used in direct attacks on hydrodynamics. It will also solve the problem of determining the natural modes of vibration of a linear system.

1. Certain Typical Partial Differential Equation Problems

Partial differential equation problems of the second order belong to several different types, among which the following are particularly important:

A. Hyperbolic problems. Otherwise known as wave problem. Example:

$$\frac{\partial^2 u}{\partial x^2} + \frac{\partial^2 u}{\partial y^2} = \frac{\partial^2 u}{\partial t^2}; \quad u \text{ and } \frac{\partial u}{\partial t} \text{ are given for } t = 0$$

If region studied is finite, some boundary condition such as $u = 0$ or $\partial u/\partial n = 0$ given along boundary.

B. Parabolic problem. Otherwise known as heat flow problem. Example:

$$\frac{\partial^2 u}{\partial x^2} + \frac{\partial^2 u}{\partial y^2} = \frac{\partial u}{\partial t}; \quad u \text{ alone is given for } t = 0$$

Boundary conditions as in A.

C. Elliptic problem. Example:

$$\frac{\partial^2 u}{\partial x^2} + \frac{\partial^2 u}{\partial y^2} = 0$$

Time does not enter into this problem. Boundary conditions as in A. Can be solved by letting $t \to \infty$ in B.

All of these, as well as many non-linear problems such as those of hydrodynamics, and many problems of higher order, such as those of elasticity, may be put in the following form:

a. We start with a time variable t, a number of space variables, $x_1, \ldots, x_n$, and a number of dependent variables, $u_1, \ldots, u_m$,

b. We have a number of equations of the form

$$(1) \quad \frac{\partial u_j}{\partial t} = f_j\left(t, x_1, \ldots, x_n, u_1, \ldots, u_m, \frac{\partial u_1}{\partial x_1}, \ldots, \frac{\partial u_m}{\partial x_n}, \frac{\partial^2 u_1}{\partial x_1^2}, \ldots\right)$$

c. We know the initial values of $u_1, \ldots, u_m$ as functions of x for $t = 0$.

d. We know certain auxiliary boundary conditions for the u_j in space. For example, B is already in this form, and A becomes

$$\frac{\partial u}{\partial t} = v; \frac{\partial v}{\partial t} = \frac{\partial^2 u}{\partial x^2} + \frac{\partial^2 u}{\partial y^2}.$$

C is merely the limit of B as $t \to \infty$, and may so be solved. We ask for $u_1, \ldots, u_m$ as functions of $x_1, \ldots, x_n$ and t.

2. The Approximation to differential Equations by Difference Equations

A system of equations very close to (1), and yielding (1) as a limiting case, is

$$(1') \quad \Delta_t u_j = f_j\left(t, x_1, \ldots, x_n, u_1, \ldots, u_m, \Delta x_1 u_1, \ldots, \Delta x_n u_m, \Delta^2 x_1 u_1, \ldots\right),$$

where the quantities u_j are determined only for values of $t, x_1, \ldots, x_n$ lying in arithmetical progressions, which we may restrict without loss of generality to the arithmetical progression of the integers. This system of equations is equivalent to a system

$$(2) \quad u_j(x_1, \ldots, x_n, t + 1) = \phi_j(t, x_1, \ldots, x_n, u_1(x_1, \ldots, x_n, t), \ldots, u_m(x_1, \ldots, x_n, t), u_1(x_1 + 1, x_2, \ldots, x_n, t), \ldots).$$

Conditions c are not much altered by the transition from differential to difference equations, and conditions d become conditions holding on the discrete points forming the boundary of a region of n-dimensional meshwork.

We propose to obtain an approximate solution to system of equations (1) by approximating to them by a system (2) of a finite number of simultaneous equations, which we shall solve by an appropriate mechanism, taking full account of boundary and initial conditions.

An example is the equation $\partial^2 u/\partial x^2 + \partial^2 u/\partial y^2 = 4\partial u/\partial t$, which corresponds to the difference equation

(3) $u(x + 1, y, t) - 2u(x, y, t) + u(x - 1, y, t) +$
$u(x, y + 1, t) - 2u(x, y, t) + u(x - 1, y, t) =$
$4u(x, y, t + 1) - 4u(x, y, t)$

or

(4) $u(x + 1, y, t) + u(x - 1, y, t) + u(x, y + 1,$
$t) + u(x, y - 1, t) = 4u(x, y, t + 1)$

The initial conditions are of the form

(5) $u(x, y, 0) = U(x, y),$

and the boundary conditions may be $u = 0$ at a certain specified set of points (μ, ν) of the net.

If we consider the solution of this problem for large values of t, then irrespective of the function assumed for $v(x, y)$, if we put

(6) $v(x, y) = \lim_{t \to \infty} u(x, y, t)$

we shall have

(7) $v(x + 1, y) + v(x - 1, y) + v(x, y + 1) + v(x,$
$y - 1) = 4v(x, y),$

corresponding to the differential equation $\partial^2 v/\partial x^2 + \partial^2 v/\partial y^2 = 0$.

Again, let us consider the equation

$$\left(\frac{\partial^2}{\partial x^2} + \frac{\partial^2}{\partial y^2}\right)\left(\frac{\partial^2 u}{\partial x^2} + \frac{\partial^2 u}{\partial y^2}\right) = -20\frac{\partial u}{\partial t}$$

The corresponding difference equation will be

$u(x + 2, y, t) + u(x - 2, y, t) + u(x, y + 2, t) +$
$u(x, y - 2, t) + 2\{u(x + 1, y + 1, t) + u(x + 1,$
$y - 1, t) + u(x - 1, y + 1, t) + u(x - 1, y - 1,$
$t)\} - 8\{u(x + 1, y, t) + u(x - 1, y, t) + u(x, y$
$+ 1, t) + u(x, y - 1, t)\} + 20u(x, y, t + 1) = 0$

As $t \to \infty$, this will give the equilibrium equation of the elastic plate

$$\left(\frac{\partial^2}{\partial x^2} + \frac{\partial^2}{\partial y^2}\right)\left(\frac{\partial^2 u}{\partial x^2} + \frac{\partial^2 u}{\partial y^2}\right) = 0$$

Appropriate boundary conditions will fix the values of u around two consecutive lines of boundary nodes. This will correspond to fixing u and its normal derivative on the boundary in the differential equation, and to a fixed edge in the sense of elasticity theory. As an example, in the following network, u is given at the points marked by circles and is to be determined at the points marked by crosses:

In the equation $\partial^2 u/\partial x^2 + \partial^2 u/\partial y^2 = 0$, a common form of boundary condition is

$$au + b\frac{\partial u}{\partial x} = C, \text{ or } au + b\cos\alpha\frac{\partial u}{\partial x} + b\sin\alpha\frac{\partial u}{\partial x} = C$$

The analogue in the difference equation case is a condition of the form

(8) $au(x, y) + b\cos\alpha\{u(x + 1, y) - u(x, y)\} +$
$b\sin\alpha\{u(x, y + 1) - u(x, y)\} = C$

or

$Au(x, y) + Bu(x + 1, y) + Cu(x, y + 1) = D,$

for a boundary point $u(x, y)$ such that $u(x + 1, y)$ and $u(x, y + 1)$ are interior or boundary points of the net. Similar conditions may be found when $u(x - 1, y)$ and $u(x, y + 1)$ are interior or boundary points, etc. Every effective boundary point has either $u(x - 1, y)$ or $u(x + 1, y)$ and either $u(x, y - 1)$ or $u(x, y + 1)$ on the net. Thus in scanning a boundary point of the type for which (8) is applicable, we put

(9)
$$u(x, y, t + 1) = -\frac{B}{A}u(x + 1, y, t) - \frac{C}{A}u(x, y + 1, t) + \frac{D}{A}$$

Let us now consider a net of v^2 points, some of which are boundary points. Let us develop this set, row after row, into a single sequence. Calling the nth point in this sequence P_n the process of averaging by which we obtain $u(P_n, t + 1)$ from $u(P_n, t)$ will be represented as follows:

1. If P_n is an interior point of the mesh region over which we wish to determine the potential function,

$$\text{(10)} \quad u(P_n, t + 1) = \pi\{u(P_{n-1}, t) + u(P_{n-v}, t) + u(P_{n+1}, t) + u(P_{n+v}, t)\}$$

2. If P_n is a boundary point,

$$\text{(11)} \quad u(P_n, t + 1) = u(P_n, t).$$

3. If P is neither an internal point nor a boundary point, how we determine $u(P_n, t + 1)$ is indifferent.

Thus if we have a record of the values of $u(P_n, t)$ on a linear tape, if we can scan these values so as to obtain $u(P_{n\pm1}, t)$, $u(P_{n\pm v}, t)$, if we have a rapid mechanism for adding these values together and dividing by four, and if we can imprint this on the tape for the next run, leaving all boundary values unaltered, say by some switch-off mechanism, we can solve the system of equations (4) mechanically.

3. The Component Elements Required

A. A quick mechanism for imprinting numerical values on a running tape. I suggest that these values be carried in the binary scale, as a number of lines on which a signal may be turned on or off, to represent a digit 1 or 0 in the corresponding place in the binary scale. The signal might be magnetic—either a DC mark or an AC hum; mechanical—a puncture in paper made by a spark; phosphorescent—stimulated by light, cathode rays, or X-rays; a state of ionization in the tape—stimulated by cathode rays, light, or an electrostatic field; or it might be none of these.

B. A mechanism for reading four such imprinted values simultaneously at fixed stations on the tape as it moves by. Again, the reading may be magnetic, photo-electric, dielectric, or something still different.

C. A rapid adding mechanism for adding the values given in B to a single number for reimprinting on the tape as in A. I am told that vacuum tube-capacitance mechanisms of this type exist with an overall speed of 1/50,000 sec. per operation.

D. The number given by C should be reimprinted as in A, with the last two digits dropped, to signify division by four.

E. A special switching apparatus should be provided which will exempt the values at the boundary points from any alteration under the operations of the mechanism.

F. It is highly desirable in the interest of conserving material that after the data on the tape have been read, the tape can be cleanly erased to receive new numerical data. Otherwise the amount even of cheap paper tape consumed may be excessive.

Almost the complete set of data for $u(P_n, t)$ should be retained while $u(P_n, t + 1)$ is printing. Perhaps a desirable tape should be in three widths, one for boundary values, and the other two alternating between reading on one width and erasing and printing on the other.

With magnetic scanning and printing, it does not seem too much to hope that an entire set of reading, adding, and printing operations may be completed in 10^{-4} sec. To avoid blurring, the separate channels in the tape had better be wires of magnetic material, held together in a non-magnetic matrix. Under these circumstances, it does not seem hopeless to get a sharp signal in from one hundredth to one tenth of an inch of length of the tape. Thus with ten thousand points to be scanned, the length of tape would be from eight to eighty feet. If readings are required to a tenth of a percent, each of the three sections of the tape should contain ten channels, or thirty in all—perhaps three to six inches of tape in width. For an accuracy of a hundredth of a percent, the tape need only be a third wider.

The number of complete scannings needed is easy to compute roughly. Subtracting the function which fits the boundary values and goes initially on the tape, which may be arbitrary, from the final value, we obtain a function vanishing on the boundary, and serving as the initial value for the difference equation system

$$(12) \quad w(P_n, t+1) = \pi\{w(P_{n-v}, t) + w(P_{n-1}, t) + w(P_{n+1}, t) + w(P_{n+v}, t)\}$$

with zero boundary values. The number of scannings needed is the value of t for which the solution of this latter system becomes less than some agreed standard of accuracy. The most unfavorable case is that in which the boundary is that of the complete square. The solution of the differential equation problem for the complete square is

$$(13)$$
$$\sum_m \sum_n A_{mn} \sin \frac{m\pi x}{v} \sin \frac{n\pi y}{v} e^{-[(m^2+n^2)/4](\pi^2 t/v^2)}$$

where the initial values are given by

$$(14) \quad \sum_m \sum_n A_{mn} \sin \frac{m\pi x}{v} \sin \frac{n\pi y}{v}$$

The slowest term in (13) to vanish [as $t\to\infty$] is the term $m = n = 1$, and we are justified in taking $e^{(-\pi^2)/2}$ as the factor by which the error is reduced in v^2 time-steps. Thus in $(1.4)v^2$ time-steps the original error is divided by a factor of more than 1000. In other words, this will take place after $1.4v^4$ scannings of individual points, or on our time assumption, in $.00014v^4$ sec. If $v = 100$, this will be about 3.9 hr.

Mutatis mutandis, the argument given here applies to the three dimensional potential problem. For a cube of v^3 points, the number of points to be scanned to reduce the original error by a factor of 1000 is about $2v^5$.

4. The Use of the Machine to Determine Flow about an Airplane Wing

The flow of air about an airplane wing has lines of flow which are equipotential lines of the following function u:

1. $\dfrac{\partial^2 u}{\partial x^2} + \dfrac{\partial^2 u}{\partial y^2} = 0$ outside the wing

2. $u = 0$ on the wing.

3. u is asymptotically $y +$ const. at infinity.

Now let us put

$$\xi = \frac{x}{x^2+y^2}; \eta = \frac{y}{x^2+y^2}; u(x,y) = v(\xi, \eta);$$

then

$$x = \frac{\xi}{\xi^2+\eta^2}; y = \frac{\eta}{\xi^2+\eta^2}.$$

The contour of the wing maps into a certain curve in (ξ, η) space, and the exterior of the contour to the interior of this curve. The point at infinity goes into the origin, and it is well known that within the boundary curve except at the origin, $v(\xi, \eta)$ satisfies the differential equation

$$\frac{\partial^2 v}{\partial \xi^2} + \frac{\partial^2 v}{\partial \eta^2} = 0$$

Thus if $w(\xi, \eta)$ is the solution of this equation free from singularities in the interior and satisfying

$$w = \frac{\eta}{\xi^2+\eta^2}$$

on the curve, then

$$v(\xi, \eta) = \frac{\eta}{\xi^2+\eta^2} - w.$$

In other words, we may replace the external potential problem of flow about a wing by an internal problem much more suitable for setting up on the machine, in which the number of boundary points for a net of 100 × 100 points will easily exceed 200.

The operation of inversion and the determination of the boundary in the inverted problem will be greatly facilitated by the use of paper on which the families of curves

$$\frac{x}{x^2 + y^2} = \xi, \frac{y}{x^2 + y^2} = \eta$$

are printed.

In this formulation of the problem, we have availed ourselves of the duality between the lines of flow and the equipotential lines of a two-dimensional potential problem. The direct attack on the wing problem would be to solve the boundary value problem for zero potential gradient normal to the wing and asymptotic potential of x at infinity. Like the other problem, this may be reduced to an internal problem by an inversion. Unlike the method of the other problem, this method may be extended directly to three-dimensional problems, such as that of the flow of air about an airplane model. In this case, the boundary value conditions, though linear, are like those in (9), and need more elaborate methods to take them off the tape.

5. General Considerations Concerning Mechanical Solution of Partial Differential Equations

The fundamental difficulty in the solution of partial differential equations by mechanical methods lies in the fact that they presuppose a method of representing functions of two or more variables. Here television technique has shown the proper way: *scanning,* or *the approximate mapping of such functions as functions of a single variable,* the time. This technique depends on very rapid methods of recording, operating on, and reading quantities or numbers.

All computing machines are composed of parts to perform certain specified operations. These parts may be used in conjunction in such a way as to carry on a process of successive approximation, in which number of parts is proportional to accuracy, measured on a logarithmic scale, or to solve more problems of a given sort. The speeding up of the pace of a machine leads to a directly proportional increase in the number of operations which can be performed in a given time, and is thus indirectly equivalent to an improvement in accuracy.

There are thus three equivalent ways of improving computing apparatus: improvement in accuracy, number of parts, and speed. Of these, at our present stage of progress, improvement in speed is incomparably the cheapest. By giving up our present dependence on mechanical parts of high inertia and friction, and resorting to electrical devices of low impedance, it is easy to perform arithmetical operations at several thousand times the present speed, with but a slight increase over the present cost. Where operations are so multiplied in number as is the case with partial differential equations as distinguished from ordinary differential equations, the economic advantage of high-speed electronic arithmetical machines, combined with scanning processes, over the multiplication of mechanical parts, becomes so great that it is imperative.

Every such apparatus must combine with the high speed arithmetical machines adequate high-speed devices for the storage and reproductions of data. Steel tape and other similar devices for this purpose are almost independent of the particular nature of the problem to be solved. The data taken off these recording devices must be recombined by fast arithmetical machines adapted to the particular equation or set of equations in question.

If machines of this sort can be devised, they will be of particular use in many domains in which the present theory is computationally so complex as to be nearly useless. This is true of all but a few of the simplest problems in hydro-dynamics. Turbulence theory, the study of waves of shock, the theory of explosions, internal ballistics, the study of the motion of a projectile above the speed of sound, etc., suffer greatly for the lack of computational tools. There are many cases where our computational control is so incomplete that we have no way of telling whether our theory agrees with our practice.

However, even where existing machines function well, there is scope for machines such as are described in this memorandum. Ordinary differential equations may be solved by scanning as well as partial differential equations, and for boundary value or characteristic function problems, these methods are preferable to the methods of search which are necessary on the differential analyser until conditions at the two ends of an interval can be pieced together.

For a machine of general applicability, we must
have:

1. a tape apparatus like that of the potential
    machine, only perhaps with more wires
    for more internal functions and bound-
    ary data;

2. scanning and recording apparatus for
    scanning and recording in more places;
    and

3. electronic machines capable of perform-
    ing rapid sequences of operations such
    as addition and multiplication on the
    data read off, before printing the result
    on the binary scale.

The machines in (3), while perhaps expensive, are
not often repeated, and their total cost need not be
excessive.

A Logical Calculus of the Ideas Immanent in Nervous Activity

Warren S. McCulloch and Walter Pitts

Extract from *Bulletin of Mathematical Biophysics* 5 (1943): 115–33.

INTRODUCTORY NOTE TO READING 7.4.

McCulloch and Pitts's paper contains the first mathematical model of neural networks. Written before the invention of the stored-program electronic computer, it was highly influential on the theory of the stored-program computer and on the development of cybernetics, and may be considered the foundation of neurocomputing. Based on an amalgam of Rudolf Carnap's logical calculus and Bertrand Russell and Alfred North Whitehead's *Principia mathematica*, the paper presented a logical model of neuron nets, showing their functional similarity to Turing's universal machines. Published in a relatively obscure journal, the paper was generally ignored until it came to the notice of John von Neumann, author of the pioneering theory of the stored-program electronic computer (*First Draft of a Report on the EDVAC* [1945]; see Reading 8.1). Von Neumann was the first to realize that the switches of a stored-program computer could be described in McCulloch and Pitts notation. This observation led him to the logical equivalence of finite nets and the state tables and delays describing Turing machines.

"A Logical Calculus of the Ideas Immanent in Nervous Activity" was a collaboration of two extraordinary individuals. Warren S. McCulloch majored in philosophy and psychology at Haverford and Yale, earned a master's degree at Columbia in psychology for work in experimental aesthetics, and received his M.D. at Columbia Medical School, where he studied the physiology of the nervous system. He worked at Bellevue and Rockland State Hospital for the Insane, returned to Yale where he worked with the neurologist Dusser de Barenne, then left Yale for the University of Illinois at Chicago where he came into contact with Walter Pitts. An autodidact without a high school or college degree, Pitts had nevertheless studied mathematical logic under Carnap at Chicago and was a highly original mathematical logician. After the two wrote this paper, Pitts moved to the Research Laboratory of Electronics at MIT, where he collaborated with Norbert Wiener and others. McCulloch followed him to MIT in 1952. While Pitts may have been a typical scholarly introvert, McCulloch was extroverted and dramatic in his appearance and his language.

Very little seems to be known about Walter Pitts. Howard Rheingold recounted the following story:

At the age of fifteen, Walter Pitts ran away from home when his father wanted him to quit school and get a job. He arrived in Chicago, and met a man in a park who knew a little about logic. This man, "Bert" by name, suggested that Pitts read a book by the logician Carnap, who was then teaching in Chicago. Bert turned out to be Bertrand Russell, and Pitts introduced himself to Carnap in order to point out a mistake the great logician had made in his book.

Pitts studied with Carnap, and eventually came into contact with McCulloch, who was interested in consulting with logicians in regard to his neurophysiological research. Pitts helped McCulloch understand how certain kinds of networks—the kinds of circuits that might be important parts of nervous systems as well as electrical devices—could embody the logical devices known as Turing machines.[1]

In the historical introduction to *Cybernetics*, Wiener had this to say about Pitts:

At that time Mr. Pitts was already thoroughly acquainted with mathematical logic and neurophysiology but had not had the chance to make very many engineering contacts. In pacticular, he was not acquainted with Dr. Shannon's work, and he had not had much experience with the possibilities of electronics. He was very much interested when I showed him examples of modern vacuum tubes and explained to him these were ideal means for realizing in the metal the equivalents of his neuronic circuits and systems. From that time, it became clear to us that the ultra-rapid computing machine, depending as it does on consecutive switching devices, must represent almost an ideal model of the problems arising in the nervous system.[2]

"As von Neumann emphasized in his *General and Logical Theory of Automata* (1951), the essence of McCulloch and Pitts's contribution was to show how any function of the brain that could be described clearly and unambiguously in a finite number of words could be expressed as one of their formal neuron nets. The close relationship between Turing machines and neuron nets was one of the goals of the authors; by 1945 they understood that neuron nets, when supplied with an appropriate analog of Turing's infinite tape, were equivalent to Turing machines. With Turing machines providing an abstract characterization of thinking in the machine world and McCulloch and Pitts's neuron nets providing one the biological world, the equivalence result suggested a unified theory of thought that broke down barriers between the physical and biological worlds. Their paper not only pointed out the similarity in abstraction function between the human brain and computing devices; it also provided a way of conceiving of the brain as a machine in a more precise way than had been available before. It provided a means for further study of the brain, starting from a precise mathematical formulation."[3]

Because of the technical complexity of McCulloch and Pitts's paper, we have chosen not to reproduce it in its entirety. Those who wish to read the complete paper can find it in McCulloch's *Embodiments of Mind* (Cambridge, MA: MIT Press, 1965). [JMN]

---

1   Howard Rheingold, *Tools for Thought. The History and Future of Mind-Expanding Technology* (Cambridge, MA: MIT Press, 2000), 107–8.

2   Norbert Wiener, *Cybernetics or Control and Communication in the Animal and the Machine* (Paris: Hermann et Cie.; New York: Wiley & Sons, 1948), 22

3   William Aspray, The Scientific Conceptualization of Information: A Survey, *Annals of the History of Computing* 7 (1985): 117–40. The quotation can be found on p. 130.

TEXT OF READING 7.4

Because of the "all-or-none" character of nervous activity, neural events and the relations among them can be treated by means of propositional logic. It is found that the behavior of every net can be described in these terms, with the addition of more complicated logical means for nets containing circles; and that for any logical expression satisfying certain conditions, one can find a net behaving in the fashion it describes. It is shown that many particular choices among possible neurophysiological assumptions are equivalent, in the sense that for every net behaving under one assumption, there exists another net which behaves under the other and gives the same results, although perhaps not in the same time. Various applications of the calculus are discussed.

I. INTRODUCTION

Theoretical neurophysiology rests on certain cardinal assumptions. The nervous system is a net of neurons, each having a soma and an axon. Their adjunctions, or synapses, are always between the axon of one neuron and the soma of another. At any instant a neuron has some threshold, which excitation must exceed to initiate an impulse. This, except for the fact and the time of its occurrence, is determined by the neuron, not by the excitation. From the point of excitation the impulse is propagated to all parts of the neuron. The velocity along the axon varies directly with its diameter, from less than one meter per second in thin axons, which are usually short, to more than 150 meters per second in thick axons, which are usually long. The time for axonal conduction is consequently of little importance in determining the time of arrival of impulses at points unequally remote from the same source. Excitation across synapses occurs predominantly from axonal terminations to somata. It is still a moot point whether this depends upon irreciprocity of individual synapses or merely upon prevalent anatomical configurations. To suppose the latter requires no hypothesis *ad hoc* and explains known exceptions, but any assumption as to cause is compatible with the calculus to come. No case is known in which excitation through a single synapse has elicited a nervous impulse in any neuron, whereas any neuron may be excited by impulses arriving at a sufficient number of neighboring synapses within the period of latent addition, which lasts less than one quarter of a millisecond. Observed temporal summation of impulses at greater intervals is impossible for single neurons and empirically depends upon structural properties of the net. Between the arrival of impulses upon a neuron and its own propagated impulse there is a synaptic delay of more than half a millisecond. During the first part of the nervous impulse the neuron is absolutely refractory to any stimulation. Thereafter its excitability returns rapidly, in some cases reaching a value above normal from which it sinks again to a subnormal value, whence it returns slowly to normal. Frequent activity augments this subnormality. Such specificity as is possessed by nervous impulses depends solely upon their time and place and not on any other specificity of nervous energies. Of late only inhibition has been seriously adduced to contravene this thesis. Inhibition is the termination or prevention of the activity of one group of neurons by concurrent or antecedent activity of a second group. Until recently this could be explained on the supposition that previous activity of neurons of the second group might so raise the thresholds of internuncial neurons that they could no longer be excited by neurons of the first group, whereas the impulses of the first group must sum with the impulses of these internuncials to excite the now inhibited neurons. Today, some inhibitions have been shown to consume less than one millisecond. This excludes internuncials and requires synapses through which impulses inhibit that neuron which is being stimulated by impulses through other synapses. As yet experiment has not shown whether the refractoriness is relative or absolute. We will assume the latter and demonstrate that the difference is immaterial to our argument. Either variety of refractoriness can be accounted for in either of two ways. The "inhibitory synapse" may be of such a kind as to produce a substance which raises the threshold of the neuron, or it may be so placed that the local disturbance produced by its excitation opposes the alteration induced by the otherwise excitatory synapses. Inasmuch as position is already known to have such effects in the case of electrical stimulation, the first hypothesis is to be excluded unless and until it be substantiated, for the second involves no new hypothesis. We have, then, two explanations of inhibition based on the same general premises, differing only in the assumed nervous nets and, consequently, in the time required for inhibition. Hereafter we shall refer to such nervous nets as *equivalent in the extended sense*. Since we are concerned with properties of nets which are invariant under equivalence, we may make the physical assumptions which are most convenient for the calculus.

Many years ago one of us, by considerations impertinent to this argument, was led to conceive of the response of any neuron as factually equivalent to a proposition which proposed its adequate stimulus. He therefore attempted to record the behavior of complicated nets in the notation of the symbolic logic of propositions. The "all-or-none" law of nervous activity is sufficient to insure that the activity of any neuron may be represented as a proposition. Physiological relations existing among nervous activities correspond, of course, to relations among the propositions; and the utility of the representation depends upon the identity of these relations with those of the logic of propositions. To each reaction of any neuron there is a corresponding assertion of a simple proposition. This, in turn, implies either some other simple proposition or the disjunction or the conjunction, with or without negation, of similar propositions, according to the configuration of the synapses upon and the threshold of the neuron in question. Two difficulties appeared. The first concerns facilitation and extinction, in which antecedent activity temporarily alters responsiveness to subsequent stimulation of one and the same part of the net. The second concerns learning, in which activities concurrent at some previous time have altered the net permanently, so that a stimulus which would previously have been inadequate is now adequate. But for nets undergoing both alterations, we can substitute equivalent fictitious nets composed of neurons whose connections and thresholds are unaltered. But one point must be made clear: neither of us conceives the formal equivalence to be a factual explanation. *Per contra!*—we regard facilitation and extinction as dependent upon continuous changes in threshold

related to electrical and chemical variables, such as after-potentials and ionic concentrations; and learning as an enduring change which can survive sleep, anaesthesia, convulsions and coma. The importance of the formal equivalence lies in this: that the alterations actually underlying facilitation, extinction and learning in no way affect the conclusions which follow from the formal treatment of the activity of nervous nets, and the relations of the corresponding propositions remain those of the logic of propositions.

The nervous system contains many circular paths, whose activity so regenerates the excitation of any participant neuron that reference to time past becomes indefinite, although it still implies that afferent activity has realized one of a certain class of configurations over time. Precise specification of these implications by means of recursive functions, and determination of those that can be embodied in the activity of nervous nets, completes the theory.

II. THE THEORY: NETS WITHOUT CIRCLES

We shall make the following physical assumptions for our calculus.

1. The activity of the neuron is an "all-or-none" process.

2. A certain fixed number of synapses must be excited within the period of latent addition in order to excite a neuron at any time, and this number is independent of previous activity and position on the neuron.

3. The only significant delay within the nervous system is synaptic delay.

4. The activity of any inhibitory synapse absolutely prevents excitation of the neuron at that time.

5. The structure of the net does not change with time. . . .

IV. CONSEQUENCES

Causality, which requires description of states and a law of necessary connection relating them, has appeared in several forms in several sciences, but never, except in statistics, has it been as irreciprocal as in this theory. Specification for any one time of afferent stimulation and of the activity of all constituent neurons, each an "all-or-none" affair, determines the state. Specification of the nervous net provides the law of necessary connection whereby one can compute from the description of any state that of the succeeding state, but the inclusion of disjunctive relations prevents complete determination of the one before. Moreover, the regenerative activity of constituent circles renders reference indefinite as to time past. Thus our knowledge of the world, including ourselves, is incomplete as to space and indefinite as to time. This ignorance, implicit in all our brains, is the counterpart of the abstraction which renders our knowledge useful. The role of brains in determining the epistemic relations of our theories to our observations and of these to the facts is all too clear, for it is apparent that every idea and every sensation is realized by activity within that net, and by no such activity are the actual afferents fully determined.

There is no theory we may hold and no observation we can make that will retain so much as its old defective reference to the facts if the net be altered. Tinitus, paraesthesias, hallucinations, delusions, confusions and disorientations intervene. Thus empiry confirms that if our nets are undefined, our facts are undefined, and to the "real" we can attribute not so much as one quality or "form." With determination of the net, the unknowable object of knowledge, the "thing in itself," ceases to be unknowable.

To psychology, however defined, specification of the net would contribute all that could be achieved in that field—even if the analysis were pushed to ultimate psychic units or "psychons," for a psychon can be no less than the activity of a single neuron. Since that activity is inherently propositional, all psychic events have an intentional, or "semiotic," character. The "all-or-none" law of these activities, and the conformity of their relations to those of the logic of propositions, insure that the relations of psychons are those of the two-valued logic of propositions. Thus in psychology, introspective, behavioristic or physiological, the fundamental relations are those of two-valued logic.

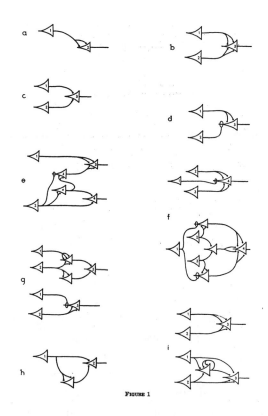

FIGURE 1

EXPRESSION FOR THE FIGURES

In the figure the neuron c_i is always marked with the numeral i upon the body of the cell, and the corresponding action is denoted by 'N' with i as subscript, as in the text.

Figure 1a	$N_2(t) .[. N_1(t-1)$
Figure 1b	$N_3(t) .[. N_1(t-1) \mathbf{v} N_2(t-1)$
Figure 1c	$N_3(t) .[. N_1(t-1) . N_2(t-1)$
Figure 1d	$N_3(t) .[. N_1(t-1) . ; N_2(t-1)$
Figure 1e	$N_3(t) :[: N_1(t-1) .v. N_2(t-3) . ; N_2(t-2)$ $N_4(t) .[. N_2(t-2) . N_2(t-1)$
Figure 1f	$N_4(t) :[: ; N_1(t-1) . N_2(t-1) \mathbf{v} N_3(t-1) .v.$ $N_1(t-1) . N_2(t-1) . N_3(t-1)$ $N_4(t) :[: ; N_1(t-2) . N_2(t-2) \mathbf{v} N_3(t-2) .v.$ $N_1(t-2) . N_2(t-2) . N_3(t-2)$
Figure 1g	$N_3(t) .[. N_2(t-2) ; N_1(t-3)$
Figure 1h	$N_2(t) .[. N_1(t-1) . N_1(t-2)$
Figure 1i	$N_3(t) :[: N_2(t-1) .v. N_1(t-1) . (Ex) t-1 .$ $N_1(x) . N_2(x)$

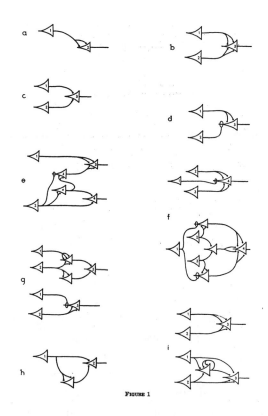

Hence arise constructional solutions of holistic problems involving the differentiated continuum of sense awareness and the normative, perfective and resolvent properties of perception and execution. From the irreciprocity of causality it follows that even if the net be known, though we may predict future from present activities, we can deduce neither afferent from central, nor central from efferent, nor past from present activities—conclusions which are reinforced by the contradictory testimony of eye-witnesses, by the difficulty of diagnosing differentially the organically diseased, the hysteric and the malingerer, and by comparing one's own memories or recollections with his contemporaneous records. Moreover, systems which so respond to the difference between afferents to a regenerative net and certain activity within that net, as to reduce the difference, exhibit purposive behavior; and organisms are known to possess many such systems, subserving homeostasis, appetition and attention. Thus both the formal and the final aspects of that activity which we are wont to call *mental* are rigorously deduceable from present neurophysiology. The psychiatrist may take comfort from the obvious conclusion concerning causality—that, for prognosis, history is never necessary. He can take little from the equally valid conclusion that his observables are explicable only in terms of nervous activities which, until recently, have been beyond his ken. The crux of this ignorance is that inference from any sample of overt behavior to nervous nets is not unique, whereas, of imaginable nets, only one in fact exists, and may, at any moment, exhibit some unpredictable activity. Certainly for the psychiatrist it is more to the point that in such systems "Mind" no longer "goes more ghostly than a ghost." Instead, diseased mentality can be understood without loss of scope or rigor, in the scientific terms of neurophysiology. For neurology, the theory sharpens the distinction between nets necessary or merely sufficient for given activities, and so clarifies the relations of disturbed structure to disturbed function. In its own domain the difference between equivalent nets and nets equivalent in the narrow sense indicates the appropriate use and importance of temporal studies of nervous activity: and to mathematical biophysics the theory contributes a tool for rigorous symbolic treatment of known nets and an easy method of constructing hypothetical nets of required properties.

LITERATURE

Carnap, R. 1938. *The Logical Syntax of Language.* New York: Harcourt, Brace and Company.

Hilbert, D., and Ackerman, W. 1927. *Grundzüge der Theoretischen Logik.* Berlin: J. Springer.

Russell, B., and Whitehead, A. N. 1925. *Principia Mathematica.* Cambridge: Cambridge University Press.

8

Logical Design and Production of the First Electronic Digital Computers

8.1

First Draft of a Report on the EDVAC

John von Neumann

Excerpt from *First Draft of a Report on the EDVAC* ([Philadelphia:] Moore School of Electrical Engineering, University of Pennsylvania, June 30, 1945), pp. 1–14.

INTRODUCTORY NOTE TO READING 8.1:

Of the mathematical geniuses who made their mark in the twentieth century, John von Neumann was arguably the most versatile. He invented game theory, and made notable contributions to algebra, set theory, quantum mechanics, mathematical logic, and other related fields. A native of Hungary, von Neumann received his doctorate in mathematics (with minors in experimental physics and chemistry) from the University of Budapest in 1926. When the Institute for Advanced Study was founded at Princeton in 1933, he was appointed one of the institute's six professors of mathematics, a position that he held for the rest of his life.

Von Neumann's intelligence was legendary. He was a mathematical prodigy who at the age of six could divide eight-digit numbers in his head. He also had extraordinary ability with languages. Among his other remarkable talents was total recall of entire novels or other book-length texts, which he enjoyed reciting for the entertainment of his friends. The same memory allowed him to retain an inexhaustible supply of jokes and humorous anecdotes, yet he was also notorious for not being able to find a drinking glass in his own kitchen, a place where he virtually never ventured. Herman Goldstine provided several anecdotes about von Neumann in his *The Computer from Pascal to von Neumann*. In this work Goldstine pointed out that it was typical for von Neumann to be presented with equations that other students or colleagues could not solve. Von Neumann was famous for retiring to a corner of a busy room where he would stand and calculate the solution in record time entirely in his head. It was also von Neumann's habit to jot down a flood of creative ideas very rapidly and to pass them on to collaborators to put the ideas into publishable form. That is one reason why von Neumann rarely published anything without a co-author.

Even before the ENIAC was completed members of the Moore School group, including Eckert and Mauchly, recognized the limitations of its programming methodology, which required plugging in patch cords from buses to panels for the solution of each problem. As early as January 29, 1944, Eckert left a memorandum briefly discussing the stored-program concept that would eventually be realized in a machine to be called the EDVAC. While working on the ENIAC project during the summer of 1944, Goldstine happened to run into von Neumann at a train station. Prior to this Goldstine had attended von Neumann's lectures but they had never met. When Goldstine explained that the machine he was working on would be capable of 333 multiplications per second, von Neumann became intensely interested.

"Soon thereafter the two of us went to Philadelphia so that von Neumann could see the ENIAC. At this period the two accumulator tests were well underway. I recall with amusement Eckert's reaction to the impending visit. He said that he could tell whether von Neumann was really a genius by his first question. If this was about the logical structure of the machine, he would believe in von Neumann, otherwise not. Of course, this *was* von Neumann's first query."[1]

The United States Army began funding development of the stored-program EDVAC at the Moore School in October, 1944. Von Neumann's *First Draft* was a product of regular discussions he held with members of the Moore School EDVAC project, including Eckert and Mauchly. Both Von Neumann and Goldstine (who had the typed report prepared from materials sent to him by von Neumann) considered the *First Draft* to be an internal working paper, unintended for publication. Its purpose, according to Goldstine, was to clarify and coordinate the thinking of those working on the EDVAC project.[2] For this reason neither von Neumann nor Goldstine took care to assign credit for the ideas it contained. Because it was just a working paper and they deliberately avoided the specifics of hardware in order not to compromise the value of the theory, the document was not given a security classification.

J. Robert Oppenheimer, director of the Princeton Institute for Advanced Studies, with John von Neumann in front of the Princeton IAS computer. The cylinders in the lower left corner are CRT memories of the Williams-Kilburn type. (Photograph by Alan W. Richards, courtesy of the Archives of the Institute for Advanced Study.)

---

1 Herman H. Goldstine, *The Computer from Pascal to von Neumann* (Princeton: Princeton University Press, 1972), 182.

2 Goldstine, *op. cit.*, 196.

A preliminary version of the *First Draft* was circulated in May 1945 to a few members of the Moore School staff for review.[3] Between the circulation of the preliminary draft and the appearance of the final version, Von Neumann wrote several letters to Goldstine containing information and ideas that he wanted to incorporate into the report. On June 25, 1945, copies of the *First Draft's* final version were distributed to twenty-four people closely connected to the EDVAC project. The report's importance was immediately recognized, and as its fame spread copies were sent to interested people outside the Moore School—a circumstance made possible by the report's non-classified status.

The stated purpose of the report was as follows:

to deal with the structure of a very high speed automatic digital computing system, and in particular with its logical control. . . .

An automatic computing system is a (usually highly composite) device which can carry out instructions to perform calculations of a considerable order of complexity—e.g., to solve a non-linear partial differential equation in 2 or 3 independent variables numerically.

The instructions which govern this operation must be given to the device in absolutely exhaustive detail. They include all numerical information which is required to solve the problem. . . . These instructions must be given in some form which the device can sense [e.g., punched cards, paper tape, etc.]. . . . All these procedures require the use of some code, to express the logical and the algebraical definition of the problem under consideration. . . .

Once these instructions are given to the device, it must be able to carry them out completely and without any need for further intelligent human intervention. At the end of the required operations the device must record the results again in one of the forms referred to above. The results are numerical data. . . (pp. 1–2).

Arthur Burks, in his introduction to von Neumann's posthumously published *Theory of Self-Reproducing Automata,* cited the salient features of the *First Draft* as "the separation of logical from circuit design, the comparison of the machine to the human nervous system, the general organization of the machine, and the treatment of programming and control."[4] Von Neumann based the logical construction of his proposed machine on idealized switch-delay elements derived from the idealized neural elements described in McCulloch and Pitts's *A Logical Calculus of the Ideas Immanent in Nervous Activity* (Reading 7.4). Burks described the advantages of this approach as follows:

The use of idealized computing elements has two advantages. First, it enables the designer to separate the logical design from the circuit design of the computer. . . . With idealized computing elements one can distinguish the purely logical (memory and truth-functional) requirements for a computer from the requirements imposed by the state of technology and ultimately by the physical limitations of the material and components from which the computer is made. . . . Second, the use of idealized computing elements is a step in the direction of a theory of automata. Logical design in terms of these elements can be done with the rigor of mathematical logic, whereas engineering design is necessarily an art and a technique in

3   William Aspray, *John von Neumann and the Origins of Modern Computing* (Cambridge, Mass.: MIT Press, 1990), 263, n. 63.

4   Arthur W. Burks, Editor's introduction. In J. von Neumann, *Theory of Self-Reproducing Automata* (Urbana: U. of Illinois Press, 1966), 9.

part. Moreover, this approach facilitates a comparison and contrast between different types of automata elements, in this case, between computer elements on the one hand and neurons on the other. Von Neumann made such comparisons in First Draft of a Report on the EDVAC, noting the differences as well as the similarities.[5]

Von Neumann's idealized computer was composed of six basic units: high-speed memory, a central arithmetic unit, an outside recording medium, an input organ, an output organ, and a central control. These are described in detail in the *First Draft*, using a quasi-physiological terminology derived from McCulloch and Pitts. The stored-program concept can be found in the repertoire of instructions proposed for EDVAC.

Although the Moore School staff's reaction to von Neumann's report was initially favorable, by 1946 the report had become the center of a bitter dispute, one that caused Eckert and Mauchly to sever relations with Goldstine and von Neumann, and led to the breakup of the Moore School computer group. At stake were two closely related issues—intellectual credit for the ideas expressed in the *First Draft*, and patent rights for the ideas embodied in EDVAC. It is generally agreed that the ideas expressed in the *First Draft* were conceived jointly in a series of discussions held by the core members of the Moore School computer group; moreover, it is also known that Eckert and Mauchly had begun considering the concept of a stored-program computer in late 1943 or early 1944, prior to von Neumann's involvement.[6] Von Neumann's supporters have argued that even though the raw material for the *First Draft* might have been the common property of the Moore School group, von Neumann was able to "crystallize thinking in the field of computers as no other person ever did,"[7] and thus gave these new ideas credibility in the scientific world. Supporters of Eckert and Mauchly cast von Neumann in the role of opportunist, claiming that von Neumann's report merely described in idealized fashion a set of physical computer structures and data-processing ideas already proposed by Eckert and Mauchly, which von Neumann appropriated without properly crediting their source.[JMN]

---

5 Burks, *op. cit.*, 9–10.

6 Michael R. Williams, *A History of Computing Technology* (Englewood Cliffs, N.J., Prentice-Hall, 1985), 302. See also Scott McCartney, *ENIAC: The Triumphs and Tragedies of the World's First Computer* (New York: Walker & Co., 1999), 119–20.

7 Goldstine, *op. cit.*, 197–98.

TEXT OF READING 8.1.

1.0 DEFINITIONS

1.1.   The considerations which follow deal with the structure of a *very high speed automatic digital computing system,* and in particular with its *logical control.* Before going into specific details, some general explanatory remarks regarding these concepts may be appropriate.

1.2.   An *automatic computing system* is a (usually highly composite) device, which can carry out instructions to perform calculations of a considerable order of complexity—e.g. to solve a non-linear partial differential equation in 2 or 3 independent variables numerically.

The instructions which govern this operation must be given to the device in absolutely exhaustive detail. They include all numerical information which is required to solve the problem under consideration: Initial and boundary values of the dependent variables, values of fixed parameters (constants), tables of fixed functions which occur in the statement of the problem. These instructions must be given in some form which the device can sense: Punched into a system of punch cards or on teletype tape, magnetically impressed on steel tape or wire, photographically impressed on motion picture film, wired into one or more, fixed or exchangeable plugboards—this list being by no means necessarily complete. All these procedures require the use of some code; to express the logical and the algebraical definition of the problem under consideration, as well as the necessary numerical material (cf. above).

Once these instructions are given to the device, it must be able to carry them out completely and without any need for further intelligent human intervention. At the end of the required operations the device must record the results again in one of the forms referred to above. The results are numerical data; they are a specified part of the numerical material produced by the device in the process of carrying out the instructions referred to above.

1.3   It is worth noting, however, that the device will in general produce essentially more numerical material (in order to reach the results) than the (final) results mentioned. Thus only a fraction of its numerical output will have to be recorded as indicated in 1.2, the remainder will only circulate in the interior of the device, and never be recorded for human sensing. This point will receive closer consideration subsequently, in particular in [sentence left uncompleted].

1.4   The remarks of 1.2 on the desired automatic functioning of the device must, of course, assume that it functions faultlessly. Malfunctioning of any device has, however, always a finite probability—and for a complicated device and a long sequence of operations it may not be possible to keep this probability negligible. Any error may vitiate the entire output of the device. For the recognition and correction of such malfunctions intelligent human intervention will in general be necessary.

However, it may be possible to avoid even these phenomena to some extent. The device may recognize the most frequent malfunctions automatically, indicate their presence and location by externally visible signs, and then stop. Under certain conditions it might even carry out the necessary correction automatically and continue.

2.0 MAIN SUBDIVISION OF THE SYSTEM

2.1   In analyzing the functioning of the contemplated device, certain classificatory distinctions suggest themselves immediately.

2.2   First: Since the device is primarily a computer, it will have to perform the elementary operations of arithmetics most frequently. These are addition, subtraction, multiplication and division: $+, -, \times, \div$. It is therefore reasonable that it should contain specialized organs for just these operations.

It must be observed, however, that while this principle as such is probably sound, the specific way in which it is realized required close scrutiny. Even the above list of operations: $+, -, \times, \div$, is not beyond doubt. It nay be extended to include such operations as $\sqrt{}$, $\sqrt[3]{}$, sgn, 1 1, also $^{10}\log$, $^{2}\log$, ln, sin and their inverses, etc. One might also consider restricting it, e.g. omitting $\div$ and even $\times$. One might also consider more elastic arrangements. For some operations radically different procedures are conceivable, e.g. using successive approximation methods or function tables.

These matters will be gone into in [sentence left uncompleted]. At any rate a *central arithmetical* part of the device will probably have to exist, and this constitutes *the first specific part: CA.*

2.3 Second: The logical control of the device, that is the proper sequencing of its operations can be most efficiently carried out by a central control organ. If the device is to be *elastic*, that is as nearly as possible *all purpose*, then a distinction must be made between the specific instructions given for and defining a particular problem, and the general control organs which see to it that these instructions—no matter what they are—are carried out. The former must be stored in some way—in existing devices this is done as indicated in 1.2—the latter are represented by definite operating parts of the device. By the *central control* we mean this latter function only, and the organs which perform it form *the second specific part: CC.*

2.4 Third: Any device which is to carry out long and complicated sequences of operations (specifically of calculations) must have a considerable memory. At least the four following phases of its operation require a memory:

    a.   Even in the process of carrying out a multiplication or a division, a series of intermediate (partial) results must be remembered. This applies to a lesser extent even to additions and subtractions (when a carry digit may have to be carried over several positions), and to a greater extent to $\sqrt{}$, $\sqrt[3]{}$, if these operations are wanted.

    b.   The instructions which govern a complicated problem may constitute a considerable material, particularly so, if the code is circumstantial (which it is in most arrangements). This material must be remembered.

    c.   In many problems specific functions play an essential role. They are usually given in form of a table. Indeed in some cases this is the way in which they are given by experience (e.g. the equation of

state of a substance in many hydrodynamical problems), in other cases they may be given by analytical expressions, but it may nevertheless be simpler and quicker to obtain their values from a fixed tabulation, than to compute them anew (on the basis of the analytical definition) whenever as value is required. It is usually convenient to have tables of a moderate number of entries only (100-200) and to use interpolation. Linear and even quadratic interpolation will not be sufficient in most cases, so it is best to count on a standard of cubic or biquadratic (or even higher order) interpolation, cf. [sentence left unfinished].

Some of the functions mentioned in the course of 2.2 may be handled in this way: $^{10}\lg$, $^{2}\lg$, $\ln$, $\sin$ and their inverses, possibly also $\sqrt{}$, $\sqrt[3]{}$. Even the reciprocal might be treated in this manner, thereby reducing $\div$ to $\times$.

    d.   For partial differential equations the initial conditions and the boundary conditions may constitute an extensive numerical material, which must be remembered throughout a given problem.

    e.   For partial differential equations of the hyperbolic or parabolic type, integrated along a variable t, the (intermediate) results belonging to the cycle t must be remembered for the calculation of the cycle $t + dt$. This material is much of the type (d), except that it is not put into the device by human operators, but produced (and probably subsequently again removed and replaced by the corresponding data for $t + dt$) by the device itself, in the course of its automatic operation.

f. For total differential equations (d), (e) apply too, but they require smaller memory capacities. Further memory requirements of the type (d) are required in problems which depend on given constants, fixed parameters, etc.

g. Problems which are solved by successive approximations (e.g. partial differential equations of the elliptic type, treated by relaxation methods) require a memory of the type (e). The (intermediate) results of each approximation must be remembered, while those of the next one are being computed.

h. Sorting problems and certain statistical experiments (for which a very high speed device offers an interesting opportunity) require a memory for the material which is being treated.

2.5 To sum up the third remark: The device requires a considerable memory. While it appeared, that various parts of this memory have to perform functions which differ somewhat in their nature and considerably in their purpose, it is nevertheless tempting to treat the entire memory as one organ, and to have its parts even as interchangeable as possible for the various functions enumerated above. This point will be considered in detail cf. [sentence left unfinished].

At any rate the total *memory* constitutes *the third specific part of the device: M.*

2.6 The three specific parts CA, CC together C; and M correspond to the *associative* neurons in the human nervous system. It remains to discuss the equivalents of the *sensory* or *afferent* and the motor or *efferent* neurons. These are the *input* and the *output* organs of the device, and we shall now consider them briefly.

In other words: All transfers of numerical (or other) information between the parts C and M of the device must be effected by the mechanisms contained in these parts. There remains, however, the necessity of getting the original definitory information from outside into the device, and also of getting the final information, the *results,* from the device into the outside.

By the outside we mean media of the type described in 1.2: Here information can be produced more or less directly by human action (typing, punching, photographing light impulses produced by keys of the same type, magnetizing metal tape or wire in some analogous manner, etc.), it can be statically stored, and finally sensed more or less directly by human organs.

The device must be endowed with the ability to maintain the input and output (sensory and motor) contact with some specific medium of this type (cf. 1.2): That medium will be called the *outside recording medium of the device: R.* Now we have:

2.7 Fourth: The device must have organs to transfer (numerical or other) information from R into its specific parts C and M. These organs form its input, the fourth specific part: *I.* It will be seen, that it is best to make all transfers from R (by I) into M, and never directly into C.

2.8 Fifth: The device must have organs to transfer (presumably only numerical information) from its specific parts C and M into R. These organs form its *output*, the *fifth specific part*: O. It will be seen that it is again best to make all transfers from M (by O) into R, and never directly from C.

2.9 The output information, which goes into R, represents, of course, the final results of the operation of the device on the problem under consideration. These must be distinguished from the intermediate results, discussed e.g. in 2.4, (e)-(g), which remain inside M. At this point an important question arises: Quite apart from its attribute of more or less direct accessibility to human action and perception R has also the properties of a memory. Indeed, it is the natural medium for long time storage of all the information obtained by the automatic device on various problems. Why is it then necessary to provide for another type of memory within the device M? Could not all, or at least some functions of M—preferably those which involve great bulks of information—be taken over by R?

Inspection of the typical functions of M, as enumerated in 2.4, (a)-(h), shows this: It would be convenient to shift (a) (the short-duration memory required while an arithmetical operation is being carried out) outside the device, i.e. from U into R. (Actually (a) will be inside the device, but in CA rather than in M. Cf. the end of 12.2.) All existing devices, even the existing desk computing machines, use the equivalent of M at this point. However (b) (logical instructions) might be sensed from outside, i.e. by I from R, and the same goes for (c) (function tables) and (e), (g) (intermediate results). The latter may be conveyed by O to R when the device produces them, and sensed by I from R when it needs them. The same is true to some extent of (d) (initial conditions and parameters) and possibly even of (f) (intermediate results from a total differential equation). As to (h) (sorting and statistics), the situation is somewhat ambiguous: In many cases the possibility of using M accelerates matters decisively, but suitable blending of the use of M with a longer range use of R may be feasible without serious loss of speed and increase the amount of material that can be handled considerably.

Indeed, all existing (fully or partially automatic) computing devices use R—as a stack of punchcards or a. length of teletype tape—for all these purposes (excepting (a), as pointed out above). Nevertheless it will appear that a really high speed device would be very limited in its usefulness, unless it can rely on M, rather than on R, for all the purposes enumerated in 2.4, (a)-(h), with certain limitations in the case of (e), (g), (h).

3.0 PROCEDURE OF DISCUSSION

3.1   The classification of 2.0 being completed, it is now possible to take up the five specific parts into which the device was seen to be subdivided, and to discuss them one by one. Such a discussion must bring out the features required for each one of these parts in itself, as well as in their relations to each other. It must also determine the specific procedures to be used in dealing with numbers from the point of view of the device, in carrying out arithmetical operations, and providing for the general logical control. All ques-

tions of timing and of speed, and of the relative importance of various factors, must be settled within the framework of these considerations.

3.2   The ideal procedure would be, to take up the five specific parts in some definite order, to treat each one of them exhaustively and go on to the next one only after the predecessor is completely disposed of. However, this seems hardly feasible. The desirable features of the various parts, and the decisions based on them, emerge only after a somewhat zigzagging discussion. It is therefore necessary to take up one part first, pass after an incomplete discussion to a second part, return after an equally incomplete discussion of the latter with the combined results to the first part, extend the discussion of the first part without yet concluding it, then possibly go on to a third part, etc. Furthermore, these discussions of specific parts will be mixed with discussions of general principles, of arithmetical procedures, of the elements to be used, etc.

In the course of such a discussion the desired features and the arrangements which seem best suited to secure them will crystallize gradually until the device and its control assume a fairly definite shape. As emphasized before, this applies to the physical device as well as to the arithmetical and logical arrangements which govern its functioning.

3.3   In the course of this discussion the viewpoints of 1.4, concerned with the detection, location, and under certain conditions even correction, of malfunctions must also receive some consideration. That is, attention must be given to facilities for *checking* errors. We will not be able to do anything like full justice to this important subject, but we will try to consider it at least cursorily whenever this seems essential.

4.0 ELEMENTS, SYNCHRONISM NEURON ANALOGY

4.1   We begin the discussion with some general remarks:

Every digital computing device contains certain relay like *elements*, with discrete equilibria. Such an element has two or more distinct states in which it can exist indefinitely. These may be perfect equilibria, in each of which the element will remain without any outside support, while appropriate outside stimuli will transfer it from one equilibrium into another. Or, alternatively, there may be two states, one of which is an equilibrium which exists when there is no outside support, while the other depends for its existence upon the presence of an outside stimulus. The relay action manifests itself in the emission of stimuli by the element whenever it has itself received a stimulus of the type indicated above. The emitted stimuli must be of the same kind as the received one, that is, they must be able to stimulate other elements. There must, however, be no energy relation between the received and the emitted stimuli, that is, an element which has received one stimulus, must be able to emit several of the same intensity. In other words: Being a relay the element must receive its energy supply from another source than the incoming stimulus.

In existing digital computing devices various mechanical or electrical devices have been used as elements: Wheels, which can be locked into any one of ten (or more) significant positions, and which on moving from one position to another transmit electric pulses that may cause other similar wheels to move; single or combined telegraph relays, actuated by an electromagnet and opening or closing electric circuits; combinations of these two elements;—and finally there exists the plausible and tempting possibility of using vacuum tubes, the grid acting as a valve for the cathode-plate circuit. In the last mentioned case the grid may also be replaced by deflecting organs, i.e. the vacuum tube by a cathode ray tube—but it is likely that for some time to come the greater availability and various electrical advantages of the vacuum tubes proper will keep the first procedure in the foreground.

Any such device may time itself autonomously, by the successive reaction times of its elements. In this case all stimuli must ultimately originate in the input. Alternatively, they may have their timing impressed by a fixed clock, which provides certain stimuli that are necessary for its functioning at definite periodically recurrent moments. This clock may be a rotating axis in a mechanical or a mixed, mechanico-electrical device; and it may be an electrical oscillator (possibly crystal controlled) in a purely electrical device. If reli-

ance is to be placed on synchronisms of several distinct sequences of operations performed simultaneously by the device, the clock impressed timing is obviously preferable. We will use the term *element* in the above defined technical sense, and call the device *synchronous* or *asynchronous*, according to whether its timing is impressed by a clock or autonomous, as described above.

4.2   It is worth mentioning, that the neurons of the higher animals are definitely elements in the above sense. They have all-or-none character, that is two states: Quiescent and excited. They fulfill the requirements of 4.1 with an interesting variant: An excited neuron emits the standard stimulus along many lines (axons). Such a line can, however, be connected in two different ways to the next neuron: First: In an *excitatory synapsis*, so that the stimulus causes the excitation of that neuron. Second: In an *inhibitory synapsis,* so that the stimulus absolutely prevents the excitation of that neuron by any stimulus on any other (excitatory) synapsis. The neuron also has a definite reaction time, between the reception of a stimulus and the emission of the stimuli caused by it, the *synaptic delay.*

Following W. Pitts and W. S. MacCulloch ("A logical calculus of the ideas immanent in nervous activity", *Bull. Math. Biophysics*, Vol. 5 (1943), pp. 115-133) we ignore the more complicated aspects of neuron functioning: Thresholds, temporal summation, relative inhibition, changes of the threshold by after effects of stimulation beyond the synaptic delay, etc. It is, however, convenient to consider occasionally neurons with fixed thresholds 2 and 3, that is neurons which can be excited only by (simultaneous) stimuli on 2 or 3 excitatory synapses (and none on an inhibitory synapsis).

It is easily seen, that these simplified neuron functions can be imitated by telegraph relays or by vacuum tubes. Although the nervous system is presumably asynchronous (for the synaptic delays), precise synaptic delays can be obtained by using synchronous setups.

4.3   It is clear, that a very high speed computing device should ideally have vacuum tube elements. Vacuum tube aggregates like counters and scalers have been used and found reliable at reaction times (synaptic delays) as short as a microsecond ($= 10^{-6}$ seconds), this is a performance which no other device can approximate. Indeed: Purely mechanical devices may be entirely disregarded and practical telegraph relay reaction times are of the order of 10 milliseconds ($= 10^{-2}$ seconds) or more. It is interesting to note that the synaptic time of a human neuron is of the order of a milliseconds ($= 10^{-3}$ seconds).

In the considerations which follow we will assume accordingly, that the device has vacuum tubes as elements. We will also try to make all estimates of numbers of tubes involved, timing, etc. on the basis, that the types of tubes used are the conventional and commercially available ones. That is, that no tubes of unusual complexity or with fundamentally new functions are to be used. The possibilities for the use of new types of tubes will actually become clearer and more definite after a thorough analysis with the conventional types (or some equivalent elements) has been carried out.

Finally it will appear that a synchronous device has considerable advantages.

8.2

Description of the ENIAC and Comments on Electronic Digital Computing Machines

J. Presper Eckert, John W. Mauchly, Herman H. Goldstine and John G. Brainerd

Applied Mathematics Panel, National Defense Research Committee, November 30, 1945.

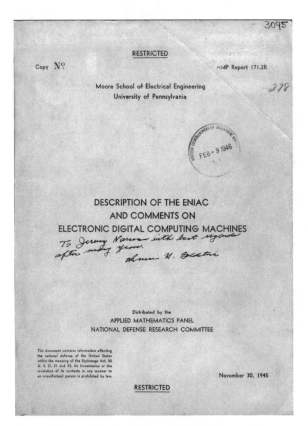

Cover of the original report inscribed by Herman H. Goldstine, from the editor's collection.

INTRODUCTORY NOTE TO READING 8.2

This is the first published report on the operational ENIAC, the world's first general purpose large-scale electronic digital computer. In the spring of 1945 the National Defense Research Committee (NDRC) was becoming very interested in electronic computers, and Warren Weaver, head of the NDRC's Applied Mathematics Panel, asked John von Neumann to write a report on the Moore School's ENIAC and EDVAC projects. Von Neumann was unable to fulfill Weaver's request, so Weaver assigned the task to John Grist Brainerd, director of the ENIAC project. Brainerd was eager to have the report appear under his name, but Eckert and Mauchly objected, since Brainerd was largely unfamiliar with the scientific aspects of the project. After some internal dispute, it was agreed that the report's authors should be listed on the title as Eckert, Mauchly, Goldstine, and Brainerd. The report was issued with a "Restricted" classification and 91 copies were distributed to military, Office of Scientific Research and Development and NDRC personnel, as indicated by the distribution list on the inside front cover.

Although confidential progress reports on the ENIAC had been issued in 1944, this report of November 30, 1945, was the first account of the completed machine. As stated in the title, the report contained a detailed description of the ENIAC, as well as chapters on the need for high-speed computing machines, the advantages of electronic digital machines, design principles for high-speed computing machines, and reliability and checking. At the end are three appendices discussing the ENIAC's arithmetic operations, programming methods, and general construction data. This may have been the earliest published report on how the first electronic digital computer was programmed. Even though the ENIAC was not a stored-program computer its design and mode of operation involved numerous programming firsts.

The report also provided information on the planned stored-program EDVAC, which was then in an early design stage. For the three years between May 1945 and June 1948 the ENIAC remained the only functioning electronic general purpose digital computer in the world.[JMN]

Setting up a program on the ENIAC. The so-called "portable" function table was only portable to the extent that it was on wheels, and could be pushed around the room by two or three people.

TEXT OF READING 8.2

INTRODUCTION

In recent years various large machines have been devised for carrying out in more or less automatic fashion the numerical solution of mathematical problems which could hardly be undertaken without such machines. The Moore School of Electrical Engineering of the University of Pennsylvania has, for the past two and one-half years, been engaged in the development of such machines for the Ballistic Research Laboratory of the Aberdeen Proving Ground.

The ENIAC, described in this report, is the first general purpose automatic electronic digital computing machine. Its speed considerably exceeds that of any non-electronic machine, and its accuracy is in general superior to that of any non-digital machine (such as a differential analyzer).

The ENIAC is extremely flexible, and is not fundamentally restricted to any given class of problems. However, there are problems for which its speed is limited by the input and output devices, so that it is impossible to derive the full benefit of its high computing speed in such cases. The ENIAC carries out its entire computing schedule automatically, but the sequence which it is to follow must be set up manually beforehand. The intended use of the ENIAC is to compute large families of solutions all based on the same program of operations, in which case the time spent in manual set up can be disregarded.

A second electronic digital machine, the EDVAC, is now being planned. It will be of larger capacity than the ENIAC, have a somewhat higher computing speed, and will be completely automatic, including set up. Despite these features, it will require considerably *less* equipment than the ENIAC, since the electronic components will be used in a quite different and much more efficient way.

The nature of the problems which these machines bring within the range of computation, and the real necessity for speed in carrying out such computations, are covered in the first chapter of this report. Following this, chapter 2 points out that to attain the speed, accuracy and flexibility required, electronic digital machines must be used.

A description of the ENIAC in Chapter 3 is intended to give the reader a rather complete account of the general features of the ENIAC and also provide him with some information on the way in which the various units can be used. The important function of control is considered first, then various kinds of memory or storage facilities, then the arithmetic units, and finally the input and output devices. (Specific explanations of some arithmetic and programming techniques will be found in the appendices; there is also an appendix giving constructional data.)

The later chapters of this report are concerned with a discussion of some general principles which seem pertinent to computing machine design and which have been used in formulating the plans for the EDVAC.

It should be noted in this introductory section that it is recognized that the object of computing machine design is not merely to speed up arithmetic processes, but to attain a high overall speed, including the problem set-up and the preparation of results in useful form. It is desirable to have as much as possible done automatically.

It is also to be observed that a great deal of the equipment in non-electronic machines is "in multiple", that is, concurrent operation of many parts is used to increase computing speed. Electronic devices are inherently so fast that it is unnecessary to achieve speed in this way. By resorting to "serial operation", a considerable saving in equipment may be secured. However, the consequent loss in speed is tolerable only when electronic components having high inherent speed are employed. Reliability and maintenance are aided by this equipment reduction, and serial operation also has important advantages both from the point of view of checking and because it simplifies the work of planning the computational program.

CHAPTER 1: THE NEED FOR HIGH SPEED GENERAL PURPOSE COMPUTING MACHINES

1.1 Need for General Purpose Computing Machines

Before proceeding to a description of the ENIAC there will first be given a brief indication of the need for truly high-speed computing machines in the applied sciences and specifically the needs of the Ballistic Research Laboratory, Aberdeen Proving Ground, for such machines. The discussion of these points will be brief since it is believed that von Neumann is planning to devote considerable space to them in an AMP report soon to appear.

An examination of the literature of the physical sciences shows that the principal emphasis in these fields has been in the solution of linear problems (those which can be formulated in terms of linear equations) which can be handled by analytic techniques. Physical problems different from these are not necessarily more difficult from a physical point of view, but they have been bypassed in favor of the problems whose analytic solutions are possible of attainment.

Those problems which cannot be solved analytically have been handled by computational methods or through the use of specific analogy machines. As an illustration of the computational approach we might mention the truly remarkable work of Hartree on the structure of the atom, a series of calculations extending over a period of about 15 years. An exemplification of the latter technique is found in the use of wind tunnels. At present, the supersonic wind tunnel at the Ballistic Research Laboratory is used about 30% of the time as an analogy machine to solve two-dimensional steady state aerodynamical problems. Industrial companies frequently resort to highly specific analogy machines to solve, for example, linear equations of electric circuit theory or the partial differential equations which enter into electron-optics problems. It may be noted that much of present experimental work consists essentially of the solution of mathematical problems by analogy methods. If one had a computing machine of sufficient flexibility the necessity for these experiments would be obviated provided that it was sufficiently rapid to solve the problems in a length of time competitive with that of experimentation. Furthermore, with computing machines whose speeds were orders of magnitude faster than experimental methods, not only would progress in mathematical physics and engineering be accelerated, but, undoubt-

edly, research would also be extended into fields as yet unexplored.

To handle efficiently large classes of problems which can be mathematically formulated, automatically sequenced general purpose computing machines are needed. The machines thus far developed or, at present, contemplated are sufficiently general to solve problems whose complexity is comparable to those of two-dimensional transient or three-dimensional steady state aerodynamical motion. Such machines will stimulate the investigation of many problems, otherwise computationally unapproachable, in many other fields. We mention only a few of the more obvious: quantum mechanical and electrodynamical studies, molecular and statistical studies in chemistry, astrophysical applications, exploratory investigations in theoretical meteorology as well as researches in mathematical statistics and mathematics itself.

1.2 Need for Speedy Computing Machines

In discussing the speed of computing machines it is perhaps desirable to distinguish between so-called continuous variable and digital machines. Although existing continuous variable machines such as the differential analyzer and the a-c network analyzer are exceedingly rapid, the class of problems which they can solve is limited. Since both of these machines perform all operations of a computation in parallel, the size and complexity of the problems they can solve is limited by the number of arithmetic organs they contain. In addition, these machines are necessarily restricted in their accuracy due to their inherent nature. We will, therefore, confine our attention to digital computing machines.

The time required to carry out a multiplication provides a rather good index of the speed of a digital computing machine inasmuch as the time spent in multiplication usually represents the major part of the computing time when such machines are used. In general, the computing time for a given problem can be estimated roughly as 2 or 3 times the amount spent in multiplications. The multiplication time for the ENIAC is about 3 msec, for the EDVAC, about one msec. For electromechanical digital machines, the multiplication time ranges from about 1/2 second to 5 seconds.

To give some idea of the time consumed in carrying out an extensive computation, it might be well to consider a typical aerodynamical problem of interest to the Ballistic Research Laboratory, which involves the solution of quasi-linear hyperbolic differential equations.

I. E. Segal has formulated the partial differential equations for describing the pressure on a high-speed, sharply pointed and non-yawing projectile. The knowledge of this pressure enables one to compute the head drag, the air flow between the projectile and the head wave, and of course, the head shape of lowest drag in a given group of head shapes. If the mathematical solution of this problem is successful, it will evidently point the way to the solution of many problems now handled in wind tunnels or precision firing ranges as experimental problems. We shall then describe Segal's problem and his method of solution as a typical example in mathematical physics illustrating the need for high-speed computing equipment.

We assume as given the shape of the head wave and compute from this the shape of the projectile as well as the flow. The partial differential equations describing the motion of the fluid are quasi-linear hyperbolic partial differential equations wherever the flow is supersonic, and they are solved by the introduction of characteristic parameters. It is assumed by Segal in the derivation of his equations that the air is a compressible and non-viscous, as well as an isentropic, fluid. The considerable simplification brought about by taking the head wave as given, however, results in the inconvenience of having to interpolate in a family of previously computed head waves to determine the flow around the given projectile head at a given Mach number. Segal estimates the number of head waves needed for this interpolation to be in the order of 25.

Before the introduction of characteristic parameters the form of equations to be solved is

$$(a^2 - u^2)\, u_y - uv\, (u_y + v_x) + (a^2 - v^2)\, v_y + a^2 v/y = o,\ v_x - u_y = o,$$

where a is the local velocity of sound; u, v are the components of the fluid velocity at the point (x, y), and where the subscripts denote the partial differentiation.

Without going into the details of the step-by-step integration method used by Segal, we can say that there are approximately 90 multiplications to be performed at each point in the field of integration, and that there will be about a thousand such points. Consequently, on the ENIAC the pure computing time, apart from reading or printing, will be about 5 minutes. As will be seen in the subsequent discussion, the ENIAC has at least two types of memory; a fairly high-speed memory, used locally in connection with the arithmetic operations, and an indefinitely large memory capacity on IBM cards. The machine is equipped both to read and punch such cards. In this problem it appears necessary to use this slow-speed memory to store the results of previous computations and then to reintroduce these data at a later time for subsequent calculations. In fact, it may be necessary to read 2 cards and to print 2 others for each point. The reading and printing however, can probably be done concurrently. It is therefore sufficient to consider the printing time alone. Inasmuch as there will be 2000 cards printed at a rate of 100 cards per minute, the printing time is of the order of 20 minutes. It is thus seen that the total solution for Segal's problem for a given Mach number and a given head wave will be, with ideal ENIAC operation, about a half hour.

As was remarked earlier, it will probably be desirable to do about 25 solutions of this problem for different head waves and possibly about 10 solutions for different Mach numbers so that the total problem will be of the order of 250 solutions of the equations. This would represent, under ideal operating conditions, about 125 hours of total computing to provide a reasonably complete table for the determination of the drag on an ordinary shaped projectile head moving at supersonic speeds. The memory of the EDVAC is planned to be much larger than that of the ENIAC, and the calculated solution time of Segal's problem on the EDVAC is about two minutes for each head wave and Mach number. It is thus seen that on the EDVAC, the total time of solution for the complete problem will be of the order of 8 or 9 hours. This great speed is possible primarily because of the very large high-speed memory of the machine.

Let us contrast this computing time with that on a hypothetical electromechanical machine. Assuming a multiplication time on such a machine of about one second and a printing time of 5 characters per second, there would be spent 25 hours for the pure computing time and about 8 hours for printing making a total computing time of about 33 hours. Consequently, the total time of solution, about 8,000 hours, is sufficiently long so that one would not handle the problem by computational means, but rather would be forced to handle the problem by experimental techniques either in supersonic wind tunnels or precision firing ranges of the sort in use at the Ballistic Research Laboratory.

We should perhaps next inquire into the reasons why one is not content to take extremely long times to carry out a numerical computation. The three arguments on this point are cost per problem, the necessity for getting a solution quickly, and the scope and range of problems which one could and would be willing to undertake. The second point is important not only because of deadline considerations but also because the high-speed machine can be used as a tool of the physicist or engineer, much as his other laboratory equipment is used. The importance of this consideration cannot be over-emphasized since it will allow the scientist to undertake investigations which he would otherwise not even attempt.

1.3 The Needs of the Ballistic Research Laboratory

The Ballistic Research Laboratory is charged by the Ordnance Department with the two responsibilities of carrying out research leading to the development of better gun-projectile-propellant combinations and of producing firing and bombing tables for proposed or existing combinations. In general, the former activity results in computational problems of an aero- or hydro-dynamical nature, whereas the latter gives rise to simple but exceedingly laborious and extensive calculations. This dichotomy in the computing work of

the Laboratory has been reflected in the designs of the ENIAC and the EDVAC, as we shall indicate later.

Although the Laboratory utilized both its own and the Moore School of Electrical Engineering's differential analyzers, assembled a staff of about 200 computers and organized an extensive IBM group, it was felt that even this computing facility would be inadequate to provide the combat services with the firing and bombing tables that were so urgently needed. Accordingly every effort was made to seek entirely new tools for this purpose.

In August, 1942, J. W. Mauchly had summarized briefly, in memorandum form, the advantages to be expected from an electronic high-speed computer of the type that could reasonably be developed at that time. Early in the spring of 1943, Captain Herman H. Goldstine of the Ballistic Research Laboratory, and Colonel Paul N. Gillon of the Office of the Chief of Ordnance, became interested in the possibilities of such a device for carrying out the preparation of firing and bombing tables. At Goldstine's request, Mauchly and J. P. Eckert, Jr. wrote a tentative technical outline of a machine which would be capable of numerically integrating trajectories for firing tables and which would handle other computing jobs of similar complexity. This material was then, April, 1943, included by J. G. Brainerd in a report which formed the basis for a contract between the University of Pennsylvania and the Government to develop an electronic device along these lines. The project was set up under the supervision of Brainerd, with Eckert as chief engineer and Mauchly as principal consultant; Goldstine was appointed resident representative to take technical cognizance of the project for the Ordnance Department.

Under this contract a staff of the Moore School has, since 1 July 1943, worked continuously on the design and construction of the ENIAC. The construction of this machine is at the present time just completed and an acceptance test is in process. It is worth remarking that the final form of the ENIAC represents a change from the initial plans which contemplated primarily a device for solving non-linear total differential equations. These changes were intended to increase the generality of the device so that the ENIAC could be used as a (reasonably) all-purpose digital device. It is still, however, most efficiently usable as a machine for handling fairly simple computations which must be repeated many times, as is the case in making firing tables.

This property stems, to some extent, from the pioneering nature of the work. To make possible simple calculations with a unit, as it was completed, each was designed so that it contained not only its arithmetic facilities but also an extensive group of logical controls. Possibly another factor which limits the generality of the ENIAC is the type of high-speed memory used. It was not until early in 1944 that Eckert and Mauchly invented a device which permitted in a practical manner an increase in memory of two orders of magnitude.

When this new advance in the art was made, a new contract was entered into between the Government and the University for the development of the EDVAC (Electronic Discrete Variable Calculator), an automatically sequenced, all-purpose electronic computing machine. It is expected that this new machine will be useful as a basic research tool for the Laboratory's investigations, e.g., in aerodynamics and interior ballistics.

The development of this machine is still in its early stages since the staff, until recently occupied with the construction of the ENIAC, is also designing the EDVAC. They are being assisted by von Neumann in planning the logical aspects of the EDVAC. The administrative supervision is being handled by Dr. S. R. Warren, Jr.

1.4 Scope of Problems That Can Be Handled on the EDVAC.

It might be well here to clarify the "all-purpose" character of the EDVAC. It is expected that this machine will make possible an exploration of the purely mathematical theory of non-linear differential equations. It will also make possible a computational approach to the various physical theories which were mentioned above in Section 1.1.

Of particular importance to the Laboratory is the possibility of considering non-viscous, isentropic and compressible hydro- and aero-dynamical problems, as well as the more difficult problems in the theory of shook waves. Also of great importance to the Laboratory is the studying of elastic and plastic properties of materials.

It is probable that these machines will necessitate a complete reorientation of thinking about computational techniques. The current techniques of numerical approximation are based on an "economy" of numerical operations which may not be pertinent in selecting; the procedures to be followed on the ENIAC or the EDVAC.

CHAPTER 2: ADVANTAGES OF ELECTRONIC DIGITAL MACHINES

2.1 Purpose of This Chapter

The ENIAC and the EDVAC are *electronic digital* machines. The purpose of this chapter is to indicate reasons for believing that machines of this type have important advantages. A digital machine has more *flexibility* and *accuracy* than is possible or practical in a continuous variable machine. A digital machine which is electronic can have a very decided *speed* advantage over one which is non-electronic. The question of *reliability* is deferred to Chapter 5; it will be sufficient now to say that it is believed that electronic digital machines can be made as reliable as others.

2.2 The Value of Speed, Flexibility and Accuracy

For the type of problem outlined in Chapter 1, it has already been emphasized that speed is an essential, not a secondary, consideration. The value of a result is strongly affected by its timeliness. It may not be easy to assess the value of timeliness in any specific case, but undoubtedly timeliness can be extremely important. Higher speed is therefore worth attaining even if its attainment increases costs. As Sec. 2.6 will indicate, the use of electronic elements to increase speed may actually reduce costs.

Flexibility and accuracy also are valuable from this point of view. With specialized machines, specific problems may be solved rapidly, but time may be lost when new problems require either a new machine or the modification of an old one. Further, even if time is no object, the cost of a group of specialized devices can easily total more than the cost of one flexible all-purpose machine.

2.3 Ultimate Design Aim

The ultimate aim of computing machine design may be taken to be the reduction of the *overall cost* of carrying out numerical solutions to mathematical problems. This point of view will be amplified in Chapter 4. No attempt is made to discuss the actual cost of equipment or operation, but some general comparisons which are relevant to such costs can be made. Actual machine operation is only one of several items contributing to the total cost. It is, however, the major item when a large problem is being done on a slow machine. It is logical, therefore, to give this item first consideration. Since analogy machines (continuous variable or non-digital machines) are capable of producing solutions rather rapidly in some cases, it is necessary first to point out why digital machines are advocated. If digital machines are accepted for reasons of flexibility and accuracy, then the most significant reduction in overall cost can be secured by the use of electronic components to increase speed without increasing equipment.

2.4 Accuracy

The accuracy obtainable with continuous variable machines depends upon the accuracy with which the component parts are constructed. However, exactly the same statement may be made about a digital machine, The essential difference is in the kind of dependence which holds in each case. In a digital machine, minor inaccuracies of components can be made to have no effect at all upon the accuracy of the computations. In continuous variable machines, there is a continuous (though not necessarily simple) relationship between the accuracy of the parts and the accuracy of the results (before translation into digital form). Increased computational accuracy can be attained only by increased precision of the parts. Not only are there practical limits to the precision with which the parts can be manufactured, but the maintenance of such precision during subsequent operation is extremely difficult. For instance, mechanical parts will lose precision through wear. On the other hand, digital machines require only that the accuracy of the parts be kept within certain tolerances, and the tolerance band can be made very wide. The accuracy of a digital machine is then limited only by the amount of equipment which can be used in it. This limitation is more often an economic one than a physical one.

2.5 Flexibility

Analogy computing devices vary greatly in flexibility. Scale models and fixed electrical networks which are completely specialized represent an extreme which is of no interest here. Large network analyzers and differential analyzers are usually considered typical examples of highly flexible analogy devices. Nevertheless, these machines are somewhat specialized and restricted in application.

A digital machine which can be directed to carry out any of the common arithmetic operations in any desired sequence on any given set of numbers has all the generality and flexibility required for any practical purpose. (It cannot compute the "exact" value of pi, but it can compute in a finite number of steps any desired approximation to pi.) Therefore, it can, for example, compute to any desired approximation the solutions of non-linear partial differential equations which are not obtainable from any existing analogy computer. This greater generality might be taken as sufficient justification for a digital machine.

Whether a digital machine is to be preferred for solving problems which can be solved on existing specialized machines depends on the speed (or cost) considerations which will now be discussed.

2.6 Digital Computing Speed

The preceding sections have indicated that advantages of accuracy and flexibility recommend digital rather than continuous variable computing devices. Even moderately large problems which are within the range of existing analogy machines require an enormous number of arithmetic operations when handled by digital machines. The cost of digital computing must be low if such calculations are to be undertaken.

Only very rough comparisons need to be made to demonstrate that digital computation by electronic devices should be a great deal faster than by the electromechanical devices used in existing large computers. Typical electromechanical devices are relays and electrically controlled counter wheels. Five or ten milliseconds is about the operating time for reliable high speed relays. Analogous operation of a vacuum tube can take place in 0.5 to 1 microsecond. The electronic device is therefore capable of operating about 10,000 times faster. (It may be observed that faster tube circuits can be developed at least as readily as faster relays can be designed.)

A vacuum tube and its associated circuit components costs approximately the same amount as a relay. This indicates that an electronic digital computer costing about the same as a non-electronic digital computer should certainly be a great deal faster, and might possibly be faster by a factor of 10,000. For various reasons, the actual factor for the ENIAC is something like 100, and for the EDVAC will, it is hoped, probably be more nearly 1000.

Moderately large computing problems are already being done by digital electromechanical devices. If digital computing costs can be divided by several powers of ten by appropriate use of electronic elements, it seems clear that electronic digital machines should find extensive application.

2.7 Comments on the ENIAC Design

Essentially, the preceding sections of this chapter have presented the point of view which led to the development of the ENIAC. It will be appreciated that the ENIAC design was also influenced in other ways which may be mentioned briefly. During the war, speed was the main object—for reasons of timeliness rather than reduction of cost. Not only was emphasis put on computing speed, but also on constructing the machine as soon as possible. For this reason, extended research and development were curtailed in favor of employing ready methods which could be put into production quickly. The emphasis on computing speed came about because the principal use contemplated for the ENIAC was the calculation of firing tables. In such work, only a small quantity of numerical information has to be introduced and withdrawn during a long computational process. Hence, no effort was made to achieve high input or output speeds. Also, for such work, the same schedule of operations might be followed for several days. Hence it was reasonable to have this operating sequence set up manually before the calculations were started, even though this might require several hours. It is therefore evident that the ENIAC is well suited for highly repetitive calculations, but that its high computing speed may be limited by the input and output devices when large quantities of numerical information are put through rather simple arithmetic processes.

The description of the ENIAC in Chapter 3 must be consulted to obtain a clear picture of the capabilities and limitations of the ENIAC. However, an idea of the computing speed can be given very briefly: additions may be done at the rate of 5000 per second, and 10-digit numbers may be multiplied together at the rate of 360 multiplications per second. Punch card devices introduce numbers at the approximate rate of 200 decimal digits per second. The rate at which numbers may be withdrawn (coming out on punched cards) is somewhat less. Since additions, multiplications, divisions and other processes can be carried on simultaneously, the contrast between computing speed and input and output speed is obvious.

2.8 Comments on the EDVAC Design

As the preceding section has briefly indicated, the ENIAC design has emphasized high computing speed to avoid what has heretofore been the most severe limitation on large computing problems, but has neglected other aspects of the overall computing job. If the time required for purely arithmetic operations is sufficiently reduced by electronic methods, other contributions to the overall time and cost of numerical mathematics may need reduction to preserve an efficient balance. In designing the EDVAC, all parts of the overall computing job are being considered. A discussion along these lines is given in Chapter 4.

CHAPTER 3: DESCRIPTION OF THE ENIAC

3.1 Introduction

In order to describe such digital computing machines as the ENIAC, it is desirable to set up a classification into which the different elements of the machine may be placed. The classification which we will employ is one which is particularly suited to large scale digital computing machines. It is probably not the best system for classifying the elements of continuous variable machines. However, even here, some interesting comparisons can be made using the following system of classification.

We divide the various units of the ENIAC into three classes—arithmetic elements, memory elements, and control elements. The arithmetic elements of the computing machine are those which form the basic operations of arithmetic—addition, subtraction, multiplication, division, and perhaps, square rooting. There should be added to this list another operation which we classify as being arithmetic. This is "magnitude discrimination" or simply "comparison." In this operation we expect to obtain a result which is dependent upon which of two numbers is the larger. This operation is essential in any automatic computing machine and is used to make decisions between alternative possibilities which exist in many problems.

The memory elements of the machine may be divided into two groups—the "internal memory" and the "external memory." The internal memory includes all memory devices within the machine and is thus finite, while the external memory exists outside of the machine in such a form as punched cards or perforated tape. This memory may be increased indefinitely but has the limitation that it must be associated with the machine by an input and output mechanism which is usually comparatively slow.

It is convenient to divide the internal memory into three classes—first, memory for numerical data which can be altered by the operation of the machine (usually rapidly); second, memory for numerical data such as empirical data which are known before the machine is started and may, therefore, be introduced into the memory device slowly, but must be withdrawn rapidly during the computing of the problem; and third, there

must be a memory for instructions—those manifestations which cause transfer between the various memory and arithmetic units and cause the arithmetic units to do the various operations on the numbers. This form of memory, like the second class, may be set up slowly since the necessary information is available before the computation is started and likewise, it must produce its effect rapidly since it must control the operation at all points of the computation.

The discussion of the ENIAC will thus be divided into four parts—first, timing relations and program control; second, memory; third, arithmetic units; and fourth, input and output equipment. The general constructional data are included in the appendix.

The important arithmetic units of the ENIAC are: twenty accumulators, one multiplier, and one combination divider and square rooter.

The accumulators provide facilities for storing numbers computed in the course of a problem and further allowing the addition or subtraction of a second number to or from the stored number. They are capable of performing these operations with up to ten decimal digits and the associated plus or minus sign.

The multiplier computes the product of two decimal numbers of up to ten digits each.

The combination divider and square rooter computes the quotient of two nine digit decimal numbers or finds the square root of one nine digit decimal number.

Electrical connections are established between the units of the ENIAC by connecting them to trunk or transfer lines with plug or cable assemblies in order to provide the intercommunication of numbers. A number of input and output circuits from different units of the ENIAC may be connected to a single trunk provided the number of units is not greater than forty or fifty depending on the length of the trunk. The decimal digits are transmitted into, and received from, these trunks in the form of groups of pulses having a number of evenly spaced pulses, equal in number to the value of the digit represented. Thus, such a group may have from zero to nine pulses. In order to obtain high speed, the trunks have eleven wires in them to enable simultaneous transmission to the ten digits and the sign. It is not possible to transmit signals from more than one unit into a trunk at the same time. Many units may, however, receive signals simultaneously from the same trunk.

3.2 Timing Relations and Program Control

Since the ENIAC contains a number of trunk circuits, operations between various pairs of ENIAC units can be carried out simultaneously. This is possible not only because of this multiple trunk system, but because all units are synchronized by permanent electrical connections with the "cycling unit". Therefore if several operations are started simultaneously between various units of the ENIAC, and since all of these are timed from one and the same circuit, the various operations will end at known times relative to one another. Thus it is possible to plan the next group of simultaneous operations with the assurance that all of the prerequisite steps of the first group have been completed. If the timing of the various operations were not known, interlock circuits would be required to insure the completion of those various operations which are prerequisite to the next group.

The cycling unit supplies a number of specially shaped signals to the other units. It contains an oscillator or "clock" which generates impulses at the rate of one hundred thousand per second, each pulse having a duration of two microseconds. These pulses are fed into a twenty position electronic stepping switch or "counter", which enables the cycling unit to put out a special impulse or "program pulse" at every twentieth pulse of the "clock". These program pulses form the basis of the programming system and mark the beginning and end of the addition cycles which are the basic arithmetical intervals of the machines. The addition cycles are thus repeated at one twentieth of the clock rate, or at five thousand per second. An addition, therefore, takes 1/5000 of a second, or two hundred microseconds.

Between these uniformly recurrent program pulses, groups of pulses are supplied to the other units of the ENIAC so that when called upon to transmit or receive numbers, the required signals will be available to enable the carrying out of the operation.

When one unit is required to transmit numbers to another, the pulses are transmitted through a trunk to the other unit. These pulses originate in the cycling unit and are simply relayed as a whole or in part by that unit.

A switch on the cycling unit enables the operator to suspend continuous operation. The twenty steps of an addition cycle are then carried out every time a push button is pressed. This allows the machine to operate in a normal way during the addition, but permits the operator to advance the problem step by step allowing whatever time is required to check the results of the previous operation. Another position of the switch suspends this type of operation and allows a similar examination of the twenty steps that occur in an addition cycle. This ability to stop the machine at any or all stages of its operation is possible since all of the memory elements are able to retain their state as long as desired, assuming the electric power supply is not interrupted. Each memory element is connected to a small neon lamp which lights up when the element is in the "on" position. Since all the circuits except some of those carrying pulses are directly coupled, any lower clock frequency can be used.

The program pulses previously mentioned as the means of sequencing the machine serve to initiate circuits called "program controls" on the various units. These units, when initiated by a program pulse, cause the unit on which they are located to operate in accordance with the settings of several switches which are part of the program control. When the operation is completed, the program control may transmit another program pulse through special program trunk circuits of one wire each. The program controls are connected to the trunks by a plug and cable assembly, in some respects similar to those previously mentioned for the digits. A program control capable of transmitting a program pulse is known as a "transceiver". A transceiver program control may repeat its operation as many as nine times in accordance with the setting of an associated switch before terminating its operation and transmitting its output program pulse. Some of the units are provided with program controls called "receivers" which operate only once upon reception of a program pulse and do not transmit a pulse when the operation is terminated. Transceivers, with their switches set to positions which do not operate the associated units, can be used to provide delays and isolating of "buffing" action.

It is now seen that one can set up sequences or chains of operations simply by connecting the output of one program control to the input of another program control, making connections through the program trunk lines using plug and cable assemblies. A special control, on a panel known as the "initiating unit", gives out a pulse upon operation of a manual push button, and this pulse can be introduced into such chains to initiate their operation.

In brief, the program control units known as transceivers and receivers remember, with their switches, what processes are to be done. They also time the operations, allow operation from a single terminal input, and permit signals from the cycling unit to cause the required operation to take place in the unit to be controlled.

If it were sufficient in most problems simply to go through a sequence of operations, the above chain system would suffice. However, two difficulties arise in practice. The number of steps in most interesting problems is so large that the group of about three hundred program controls in the ENIAC would be entirely inadequate. Secondly, it is sometimes desirable to make a choice between two or more sets or chains of operations, this choice depending upon some numbers which are the result of an earlier computation. If this choice were to occur only a few times in the course of a computation, one could allow the sequences to run out, thus stopping the computation. At this point the operator could make the choice manually. If this situation occurs a large number of times in a computation, manual choice would be impractical. Both of these difficulties may be overcome by the use of a unit in the ENIAC called the "master programmer".

The master programmer consists of ten units, each of which may be employed in various ways to count program pulses and to switch program connections. Each unit contains a six-position electronic stepping switch and an associated counter. For each unit there is one input channel and any program pulse entering this unit is registered in the counter and also causes the transmission of a program pulse from one of six possible output terminals. The position of the stepper determines which output terminal is so activated. A group of manual switches is associated with each counter-stepper unit, and when the number of pulses received by the unit has advanced the counter to a number corresponding to the switch setting, the stepper is moved to its next position and the counter is cleared to zero. Separate switches are provided for each stepper position. The intervals between transfer from one output channel to the next can therefore be determined in terms of the number of pulses received, and a different number may be used for each stepper position. If less than six outputs are desired, a special switch can be set to cause the stepper to return to its first position after reaching any chosen position.

An input terminal allows the counters to be set directly from a pulse group. Another input terminal allows the stepper to be stepped directly from a pulse group. Finally, an input is provided to allow direct resetting of the stepper. Thus, there are altogether nine terminals—one program input, six program outputs, one direct stepper input, and one stepper re-setting input terminal.

To return to the two difficulties previously mentioned which the master programmer is to overcome, it is clear that since most problems may be separated into a large number of repeated routines, each with a comparatively few steps, the master programmer will allow the ENIAC to cope with these problems in spite of having only three hundred program controls.

The master programmer temporarily forms program chains into "rings". This would be impossible without the master programmer, since the number of program cycles around these rings would be uncontrollable if such a ring were established manually.

It is very important to understand that this far from exhausts the possible improvements which the master programmer makes in the ENIAC. It is possible to have the main routine divided into sub-routines, in which case one stepper is used to feed another stepper, thus allowing the proper sub-routine to be chosen in the course of a regular routine. This process can be carried even further, and thus an elaborate hierarchy of program sequences can be established. The saving in program controls accomplished by such arrangements is enormous.

The second difficulty, that of having to make a number of numerically determined choices as to what routine to do next, can also be overcome by using the master programmer. It is simply necessary to use an accumulator as a magnitude comparing device and to have it signal a stepper through its direct input to change to a new routine.

In the ENIAC, the master programmer does not serve as the sole governing unit, but coordinates many small decentralized control units.

3.3 Memory

The ENIAC has its memory divided into four fundamental classes. It is our present purpose to discuss three of these classes and to postpone the discussion of the fourth until later.

The first class is the one in which the information can be introduced and withdrawn at extremely high speeds, preferably in one addition time (1/5000 second). As was previously noted, this is the type of memory provided by the accumulators. This type of memory is necessary to hold the information computed in the course of a problem while some further calculation is made upon it, or until the time when some operation is to be done which requires it.

The second class of memory consists of three function tables or constant storing units. This class of memory differs from the type of storage employed in the accumulator, mainly in that the tabular values are introduced manually which requires considerable time. These values, however, may be withdrawn at the relatively high speed of five addition times (1/1000 second). The function table provides a hundred tabular values of twelve digits each—each tabular value having, however, two sign indications. The digits, as well as the sign indications, are all set by separate manually operated rotary switches.

Thus, there are fourteen switches for each tabular

value. The two sign indications are provided so that the twelve digits of a tabular value may be assigned to two separate numbers. By dividing the twelve digits into two equal groups, two functions of one hundred tabular values, or one function with two hundred tabular values, can be stored in a single table. The hundred tabular values of the function table are designated by the successive decimal integers from zero to ninety-nine. Thus, the first two digits of an argument may be used to choose the correct tabular value, while the remaining digits are used in an interpolating routine which makes use of the regular arithmetic functions of the machine to obtain the value of the function corresponding to the argument. Thus, the function table supplies only the nearby tabular values that are to be used in an interpolation and does not itself do any interpolation. Any desired interpolation formula is set up as a sequence of operations, using the accumulators and multipliers in the same way as is done with any other arithmetic problem. In order to obtain the nearby values which are required in the interpolation, the program controls of the function table also produce arguments which are one or two integers above or below the argument introduced.

Four tabular values, in addition to the one hundred mentioned above, have been added—two at each end of the table so that those extra arguments required above will be present in the table when the argument value is either zero or ninety-nine. These tabular values are designated by the decimal integers –2, –1, 100, and 101 respectively. Thus in reality, the table contains 104 entries. Since each entry has fourteen switches, there are 1456 switches to be set. If the switch settings are read to the person setting the switches, they can all be set in approximately half an hour. This comparatively long set-up time is partially mitigated by having three such function tables in the machine and by providing the switch assemblies with wheels and easily disconnected cable connections so that several banks of switches can be left set up and plugged in when required. In fact, where a function is required frequently, it is practical to replace the switch assemblies by permanently wired assemblies which can be plugged in when needed.

Several additional uses of the function tables are possible. They may be used for the storage of any group of constants which must be introduced into the machine at a high speed. In problems where the ordinary program controls of the ENIAC are insufficient, it is possible to employ the table as a 104 position program selecting device using its outputs to initiate program circuits rather than feeding the outputs into digit channels. A function table may be used, therefore, to sequence operations, or chains of operations, which may be initiated in sequence or chosen at random depending on the value of the two pulse groups introduced as argument into the table. These pulse groups may be obtained either from the program circuits or from the digit circuits of the machine.

To sum up, three function tables are provided, of a hundred and four entries each, with facilities for dividing the entries into two numbers where twelve digit accuracy is not required for one function. The most notable feature of this type of memory is its large capacity and high speed. Unfortunately, this is coupled with the necessity for manual, and therefore slow, introduction of the data.

The third class of memory is the program equipment which was previously described. The program circuits remember what processes are in progress, what these processes are, how long these processes take, and what processes are to be done next. The actual physical memory is made up of the many tube circuits, switches, trunk circuits, and plug and cord assemblies which make up the programming system in the ENIAC.

The fourth class of memory will be covered later when we discuss the introduction and withdrawal of data from the ENIAC.

3.4 Arithmetic Units

The accumulators are the basic arithmetic units of the ENIAC. They are able to add a number to a number already stored in them. This ability to add is inherent in the ten stage ring counters which serve as the memory elements. In order that numbers may be simultaneously added into all ten counters which provide the memory of an accumulator, a special circuit inserts pulses corresponding to any carry-overs which may take place after the ordinary transfer process. Since subtraction is carried out by a system of complements with respect to 10^{10}, an extra pulse is required to simplify the mechanism for transmitting numbers. Seven pulse times are required for the carry-over process. This additional time must be added to the ten pulse times required to transfer the number, and the three additional pulse times required to allow the program equipment to operate prior to the transfer. A total of twenty pulses is obtained which corresponds to the twenty stages of the cycling unit. Thus, an accumulator requires twenty pulses spaced at ten microseconds, or 1/5000 of a second to do an addition. The complement system of subtraction was used to avoid the necessity for having counter rings which could advance in either direction.

The accumulators are provided with two output circuits—one for positive numbers and one for their complements. It is thus possible to transmit simultaneously a number from an accumulator into one channel and its complement into another. If both output circuits are connected to the same channel, it is of course impossible to do more than one of these operations at a time. Five input circuits are provided which allow the accumulator to receive from five different channels, This is a necessity if several simultaneous operations are to be carried out between different pairs of units. These input channels are also useful in that they provide a simple method of multiplying numbers by powers of ten.

The accumulator contains eight transceiver program controls and four receiver program controls. Since the transceiver program controls allow an operation to be repeated up to nine times a simple method of multiplication by small constants is possible. A program control can, if desired, by the setting of one of its switches cause an accumulator to clear its counters to zero following a transmission. A round-off switch is provided on each accumulator which enables it to clear and leave a five, instead of a zero, in any one of the decades. This five, in conjunction with a special plug device to delete the undesired digits, allows retention of as few significant figures as may be required. If more than ten significant figures are required, it is possible to connect two accumulators in tandem by means of special plug and cable assemblies and to obtain as many as twenty significant figures. The accumulators indicate the numbers which they contain on a bank of neon lamps, which provide a very convenient facility in checking the operation of the ENIAC.

As previously stated, signals may be taken from the sign indicating circuits of the accumulator to provide magnitude discrimination which permits computed numbers to control the program sequence of the machine.

In addition to the two outputs previously mentioned, the accumulators have a set of "static" outputs which provide a ten wire circuit from each counter ring, one from each stage. Thus, since there are ten counter rings, a hundred output circuits are available. These circuits provide all the information about a number simultaneously and are essential in the multiplier.

The multiplier is fed by static outputs from the two accumulators which receive and hold the multiplier and multiplicand respectively. The multiplier contains an internal multiplication table which allows the multiplication of one digit of the multiplier by ten digits of the multiplicand simultaneously. Since pairs of single decimal digits have, in general, two decimal digits in their product, it is necessary to provide two accumulators to receive the twenty digits which result from the multiplication of one digit simultaneously by ten digits. This is true because it is desirable in the interest of speed, to add all of these "partial products" simultaneously to the accumulated partial products of the preceding steps. These two accumulators can conveniently accumulate the "units set" and the "tens set" of these partial products without any interference in the normal carry-over. Since each set of the successive partial products requires ten channels to receive them, and since every set corresponding to the different digits of the multiplier times all of the multiplicand digits must be shifted by one channel with respect to the preceding one, the product accumulators require twenty input channels. These twenty digit accumula-

tors are made by coupling two ordinary accumulators in the manner previously described. Therefore, two sets of double accumulators, or four ordinary accumulators, are required to collect the partial products from the multiplier. After this collection has been accomplished, the final product is obtained by adding the units set and the tens set with a single shift between the channels to obtain the proper relation between the two sets.

If one of the numbers is a complement, the product obtained will be in error by a number whose magnitude is 10^{10} times the other number. If both numbers are complements, the product obtained will be in error by a number whose magnitude is 10^{10} times the sum of the two numbers. Following the collection of partial products, but before the final product is obtained, a special sign-indicating circuit causes appropriate corrections to be made, transmitting them from the multiplier and multiplicand accumulators into the product accumulators.

The multiplier is equipped with twenty-four transceiver program control units, any one of which can control the above process. These program controls each contain a switch which allows the multiplication to be carried out with any number of digits in the multiplier between the maximum of ten and a minimum of two. In addition, other switches in each program control are available which allow the multiplier to cause the reception of numbers into the multiplier and multiplicand accumulators and which allow transmission and rounding-off by the product accumulators.

The time required for multiplication is computed as follows:

(a) one addition time to operate the multiplication table, (b) one addition time for each digit of the multiplier, (c) one addition time for complement correction terms, (d) one addition time to add the units and tens parts of the partial products, and finally, (e) one addition time to transmit the product and receive the next multiplier and multiplicand. Therefore, the maximum time of a multiplication will be obtained with a ten digit multiplier and is fourteen addition times or 1/360 of a second.

The third, and last, arithmetic unit of the ENIAC is a combination divider and square-rooter. This unit can either divide or take a square root, but cannot do both at the same time. This compromise seems desirable since square rooting is fairly infrequent, and is so similar to division, that very little additional equipment was required to make a combination unit. The method employed to do these processes was chosen so as to require a minimum of equipment since neither of these processes are as frequent as the other arithmetic processes, and, therefore, would not justify a large expenditure of equipment.

Division is carried out by the conventional method of successive subtractions. The only uncommon feature is that the shifting operation is accomplished by transmitting the dividend back and forth between the dividend-accumulator and a special shifting accumulator. This, unfortunately, limits single divisions to nine decimal places. However, since the remainder can be retained, the process can be carried further by a special program arrangement if greater accuracy is desired. Another feature of this divider is that, after successive subtraction of the divider from the dividend has produced an overdraft, the remainder is shifted one place to the left and the divisor is added instead of subtracted in obtaining the next digit of the quotient. This turns out to be somewhat simpler to mechanize than the ordinary method of restoring the overdraft.

Square rooting is accomplished essentially by the method of subtracting successive odd numbers and is carried out by a method otherwise analogous to division. As in division, the overdraft is not restored before shifting. The combination divider-square rooter makes use of the ability of the accumulators to provide magnitude control and is in itself, therefore, merely a permanent assemblage of program equipment and circuits for supplying the various constants required to build up the answers. This unit requires several addition times to set up and round off its results. The main computational time is that required for the successive additions and subtractions. An addition time is required between each trial addition or subtraction to sense the sign of the remainder. Since five and a half trials are required on the average, one can estimate the total number of addition times required by lumping the computational time with the set-up and round-off time in a simple formula which gives the total addition times as approximately 13 multiplied by one more than the number of digits required in the answer. Thus, for nine digit answers, the average time required for division or square root is 130 addition times (approximately 1/38 second). Since this time is variable, depending upon the numbers employed, and may be as high as 210 addition times (1/23 second), considerable saving in time may result in carrying out parallel operations.

In order to make possible such parallel operations, an interlock circuit is arranged so that the output pulse, which signifies the end of dividing or square rooting, is not transmitted until both the parallel operation and the division or square root have been completed. This unit is equipped with eight transceiver program controls, each having its own interlock input as well as its own regular input and output.

3.5 Input and Output Equipment

Since the actual computing process is a highly automatic and rapid one, there must be some system for introducing or withdrawing numerical data which is considerably faster than setting switches or copying down numbers from a bank of neon bulbs, which are the only means so far described for doing this.

In order to save the time required to develop any special apparatus, automatic business machines which operate with Hollerith punched cards are employed. Comparatively simple modifications of standard machines of this type give higher speed for introducing or withdrawing data, than appear possible with any other type of commercial equipment. This speed results from the simultaneous use of eighty channels.

Paper tapes are also used in this field by others, and have the advantage of being more easily handled and thus less likely to lose their proper sequence. They have an additional advantage in that they can easily be run forward and backward, and can introduce and withdraw data onto different parts of the same tape simultaneously. Tapes have an inherent disadvantage when used for sorting, since a considerable waste of tape is involved.

Paper cards were chosen because of the economy with which they could be sorted, because no fast tape machines were available, and further, because few of the desirable auxiliary machines that are so necessary to scientific computing were available for handling paper tapes.

On the other hand, card machines were available which would punch, verify, and reproduce the cards, which would print the information upon the cards themselves or upon other sheets of paper, and which would sort and collate the cards. Standard card machines were supplied by the International Business Machine Company, who also kindly cooperated by supplying a special machine for taking information from their standard cards and putting it in a form which could be used in the ENIAC. Also, IBM supplied a standard machine suitably modified to permit punching standard cards from information taken from the ENIAC. Various plugs and cables used for attaching the portable function table switch panels to the function table control panels were also supplied by IBM.

It is, of course, evident that some intermediate memory, such as the cards provide, is necessary if the transition from slow manual operations to fast mechanical operations is to be made. In addition, however, these cards play a very important role in providing the machine with an auxiliary memory of infinite capacity. It is this memory which was referred to earlier as the fourth class. While the absolute speed of introducing and withdrawing data from this type of memory is quite fast (approximately 1/12 second for a ten digit number), it must be considered as a slow memory compared to the electronic equipment in respect to both the putting in and the taking out of data. Since the card machines, both in reading data from the cards and in punching data onto the cards, scan across one dimension of the card, some auxiliary memory is required to hold these numbers.

Rather than use some of the expensive and limited electronic memory which the accumulators provide for this rather slow operation, a number of telephone relays, of a very reliable type, were employed for this purpose. These relays and the equipment for testing them were supplied by the Western Electric Company. The relays were designed by the Bell Laboratories.

Relays are employed not only because they provide an inexpensive memory of adequate speed, but also because they constitute the simplest method of transition from the electromechanical card machines to the electronic circuits. This is especially true in the printer where, because a number of contacts may be put on a single relay, it is possible to have a simple mechanism for converting negative numbers expressed as compliments (in the electronic circuits) to their true negative form (on punched cards). This latter form is preferred on the cards both to facilitate examination and printing of the numbers and because it fits in with the system which is used by the standard auxiliary card machines.

The machine which reads the cards is able to store eighty decimal digits in a group of relays. By means of special holes punched in the cards, it is possible to designate them as "master" and "detail" cards. Some of the eighty digits may be taken from one of these types, and the rest of the eighty digits from the other types. The master-detail card arrangement is very useful when it is desired to do problems in which several constants are required for a considerably larger number of cycles than those which are introduced on the regular or detail cards. These constants are put on special master cards on which a special punched hole causes information from these cards to be retained until another master card appears. The master cards are then used for the less frequently changed numbers or constants while the detail cards are used for those which change frequently. The numbers are stored in the relays, which are associated with the input machine. These in turn control tube circuits associated with thirty transceiver program controls and allow any group of five or ten of the eighty digits to be transmitted at any one time into the rest of the machine. Such a transmission requires only one addition time (1/5000 second). Twenty additional digits and four sign indications, which can be set by hand switches, are provided for constants which do not require alteration in the course of a problem.

This input unit, called the "constant transmitter", can receive cards at the rate of 120 per minute. The output or card punching unit, which we call the "printer", operates from a group of relays which are controlled by the static outputs of the counters in the accumulators and master programmer. Semi-permanent cable connections allow the printer to have its eighty columns controlled from any eighty of the two-hundred and twenty counters which the machine has, with the exception of those which already have their outputs employed in the multiplier and multiplicand accumulators. The printer is capable of punching cards at the rate of one hundred per minute.

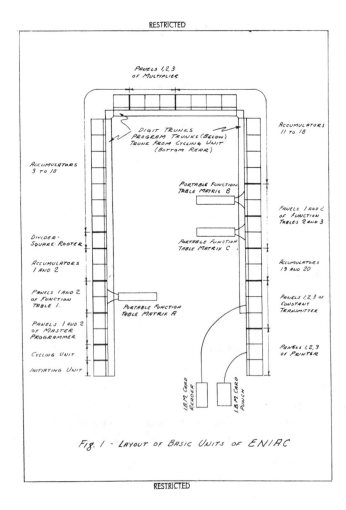

Fig. 1 - Layout of Basic Units of ENIAC

ENIAC Timing Chart			
OPERATION	TIMING		
	Seconds	Micro-seconds	Addition Times
Addition, Subtraction or Transfer Including transfer from constant transmitter	1/5000	200	1
Transfer repeated "n" times in the accumulator (n = 1 to 9)	(1/5000)n	200 n	n
Multiplication By "n" digit multiplier (n = 2 to 10)	(1/1250) + (1/5000)n	800 + 200 n	4 + n
By ten digit multiplier	1/360	2,800	14
Division or Square Rooting Average time for nine digit result	1/38	26,000	130
Average time for "n" digit result (n = 3, 6, 7, 8 or 9)	13(n + 1) (1/5000)		
Maximum time for nine digit result	1/23	42,000	210
Maximum time for "n" digit result (n = 3, 6, 7, 8 or 9)	21n (n + 1) (1/5000)	21(n + 1) (200)	21 (n + 1)
Obtaining a Functional Value Once	1/1000	1000	5
Repeated "n" times (n = 1 to 9)	1/1250 + 1/5000n	500 + 200n	4 + n

CHAPTER 4: DESIGN PRINCIPLES FOR HIGH SPEED COMPUTING MACHINES

4.1 The ENIAC and the EDVAC

As was said in Sec. 2.7, the principal aim in designing the ENIAC was to achieve high speed in the computation of firing tables. There is no essential or fundamental restriction imposed by the ENIAC design on the character or complication of the problems which it can do. Practical limitations on internal memory capacity, both for numerical data and for programming sequences, serve to limit the efficiency and speed of the ENIAC when used for problems beyond its intended scope. Nevertheless, the ENIAC should be able to solve many of these larger problems faster than they can be done on any other existing machine. Undoubtedly, the ENIAC will be used in this way until the EDVAC or some other machine with better facilities for handling non-linear partial differential equations can be built.

In the design of the EDVAC it is hoped to achieve a great deal of flexibility in the handling of both large and small problems, and to do this at a reasonable cost —that is, in a reasonable time with reasonable amounts of equipment. Reasons for believing the reliability will be good are given in Chapter 5. Since the EDVAC will be a digital machine, any desired accuracy can be attained.

Some principles which have guided the design of the EDVAC will now be discussed.

4.2 The Overall Computing Problem

A general aim of computing machine design should be to increase the speed and lessen the cost of scientific computations. This implies much more than high-speed arithmetic. For purposes of discussion, it will be useful to sub-divide the overall computing job into these four steps:

1. Preparation of the problem in a symbolism and form appropriate to the machine.

2. Actual physical preparation of the machine to carry out the work of obtaining the solution.

3. Machine operations such as computing or sorting to achieve the solution.

4. Preparation of the solution in a form suitable for examination and use.

There is no particular advantage in reducing the time and cost of any one of these steps if the overall time and cost are largely controlled by the other steps. It is also important to recognize that all four steps are affected by the design of the computing machine and therefore the designer of a machine should carefully consider the way in which each step is influenced by his design.

4.3 Automatic Operation Desired

It is reasonable to try to make all operations as automatic as possible. Manual operations cannot compete with machine operations in speed, and even unskilled or routine clerical labor is expensive when compared to the cost of automatic machine processes.

Since step 3, the machine computation, can be done automatically and at high speed by electronic digital machines, it becomes important to reduce the time and cost of steps 2 and 4 by rendering them automatic. This is possible, although it is not immediately evident what this will cost in terms of equipment. The point which is desired to emphasize in this section is that one can afford to spend a great deal of equipment in this way.

In making steps 2, 3, and 4 all automatic, however, a greater burden is thrown on step 1, because the operator must plan all subsequent steps beforehand and be able to specify, in some sort of symbols, all the instructions needed to carry them out. For almost all problems of any complexity at all, step 1 will be the most time-consuming and costly. When this fact is recognized, it is seen that an important object of computing machine design is to simplify step 1. Further discussion of this objective will be given in Section 4.14.

4.4 Speed Versus Equipment

Computing speed and amount of computing equipment are to some extent interdependent. The designer is faced with many choices which involve this relationship. If a designer is restricted to the use of but one type of element or component, the computing speed which he may achieve is more or less fixed by the amount of equipment he can use. By using more equipment, and carrying out many operations at once, he can effectively increase the computing speed. Conversely, he may prefer to sacrifice speed in order to reduce equipment. This exchange has limitations, of course, since all operations of a long calculation cannot be done concurrently, nor can equipment be reduced to the vanishing point by going to the other extreme.

It is obvious that excessive equipment is undesirable from the point of view of both first cost and maintenance. It would therefore be unwise to multiply equipment unless the speed so gained in the automatic processes serves to materially reduce the overall computing time.

4.5 Levels of Serial or Multiple Operation

At this point it is convenient to distinguish various levels at which the designer may choose to gain speed by use of more equipment or may choose to sacrifice speed to save equipment. The terms "multiple" and "serial" will be applied to these choices.

LEVEL		SERIAL	MULTIPLE
(a)	Representation of numbers	Digits of the same number follow each other through same channels and devices.	Separate channels and devices operate on all digits of a number at once.
(b)	Standard arithmetic processes, such as multiplication	Digits are passed in sequence through the same adder. Multiplication is done by repeated addition.	A large number of adders act on all digits at once. (Partial products may be used—if so, they are all summed by multiple adders.)
(c)	Combination of standard processes by programming.	Never more than one standard operation is done at one time. All steps are arranged in a single sequence.	Several standard arithmetic processes may be carried on at the same time. This is subject to the operator's control.

It is assumed, in level (c), that the various standard operations which may be put in either serial or multiple order are all part of the same computing problem. The process of doing many problems on as many different machines operating simultaneously might be thought of as a fourth category of multiple operation, but this is of no interest to the designer.

4.6 Multiple Operation in Non-electronic Machines

For non-electronic computing machines, the computing time for complicated problems may be quite large compared to the time spent in step 1 or other non-automatic steps. Multiple operation to gain speed therefore seems desirable. In fact, multiple operation at level (a) is quite customary, and various degrees of multiple operation at level (b) are often used. Any attempt to gain speed by multiple operation at level (c) has a disadvantage not shared by the other two levels. Here the operator must plan his problems carefully so as to make use of the speed which is afforded him. To some extent, then, the gain in computing speed is offset by the additional burden which is transferred to the non-automatic step 1.

4.7 Serial Operation in Electronic Machines

The situation is quite different when electronic machines are considered. In this case computing speeds are so high that often many numerical solutions can be obtained in less time than may be required for carrying out step 1. It is therefore reasonable to examine the possibility of sacrificing some of this speed in order to reduce equipment. The sacrifice in speed need not be as drastic as one might suppose, however, for the following reason. There is no sharply defined limiting speed for electronic equipment, and the design of electronic computing circuits has not yet reached "speed saturation". As the total amount of electronic equipment is reduced, intensive circuit design becomes easier and more practicable, so that each element may be able to operate at a higher rate. (Thus, the fundamental pulse rate for the EDVAC is expected to be ten times that for the ENIAC.)

It does not appear unreasonable to insist on serial operation at all levels. Specifically, this means that

a. Numbers are to be represented by timed pulse trains, all of the digits for any one number following each other in time sequence through the same channels and circuits.

b. All of the simple elements of a standard arithmetic process are performed in serial order. Thus, successive digits are added by the same adding circuit, and multiplications are carried out by performing a number of additions in sequence.

c. There is never more than one standard arithmetic operation being carried out at any one time. All arithmetic steps follow each other serially.

4.8 Serial Operation in Analogy Machines

It is of interest to note that analogy machines also employ serial operation for certain processes. Network analyzers, once they are set up, produce the desired solutions serially with only a few measuring instruments. The alternative, that of using many instruments distributed over the network and reading all of them at once, would be a multiple process which can hardly be justified.

Also, differential analyzers scan continuously by variation of the independent variable (usually referred to as "time"). In this way, a relatively small number of integrators are able to produce a continuum of results.

Nevertheless, these machines do not employ scanning (or serial operation) to the fullest possible extent. In a differential analyzer, each integrator must, during a given problem, be continuously associated with just one integral process. As more complicated problems are devised, more integrators must be used. A similar remark holds for the network analyzer. Each branch of the network has certain impedances associated with it, and as problems become more complicated, more impedance elements must be used. To solve a non-linear problem on a network analyzer numerous non-linear impedances are required. If, by some scanning process, a single non-linear element could be "switched" from place to place in the network, scanning all the positions where such an element is required, the network analyzer would in effect be able to reduce equipment by serial operation.

4.9 Memory Scanning by a Computer

Although the notion of a serially operated network analyzer may not appear practical, such an idea is closely connected with a practical and quite flexible scheme for a computing machine. Let this machine have a single arithmetic device and a great many number registers, or memory elements, so that it may receive numbers from the memory and also store numbers which it computes in the memory. The arithmetic unit is the single "non-linear element" which scans the various points in the "memory network." Because it is completely flexible, however, this unit must be told how to scan and what sort of computations to do as it proceeds.

4.10 Instruction Memory

For high-speed computation, not only must the arithmetic organ compute at high speed, but the memory elements must be able to supply and receive numbers at high speed. Obviously, a further requirement is that the instructions to the arithmetic unit must keep pace with it. The faster the instructions can be carried out, the faster must new instructions be supplied.

This requirement as to instruction speed can be met in a direct and simple fashion by storing instructions (in numerical code, so to speak) in memory elements or registers of the same type as those used to store the numerical data. The function of receiving such instructions from the memory, interpreting them, and causing the instructions to be carried out, can then be vested in a "control unit" which is also a part of the computing machine.

4.11 Function Table Memory

If high-speed electronic memory elements are used for numerical data produced in the course of operation, and are also used for storing operating instructions; it appears that empirical or mathematical functions which are necessary to a computation should be accommodated in the same way. By so doing, all memory elements are made identical, and a very desirable unification is achieved.

4.12 Flexibility of Memory

By unifying all memory functions through the use of similar memory elements for both operating instructions and numerical data (including function tables), it is possible to obtain new flexibility. All memory elements can be interchangeable. Consequently there is no need to specialize any memory element. Any portion of the total memory may be allotted to operating instructions, and any portion to function tables. This allotment is in no way fixed, so that any part of the memory may be used for any purpose. The same memory element may be used in various ways during the same problem, in fact.

4.13 Memory Capacity Needed

No matter how much high-speed memory capacity is provided, interesting problems are bound to arise which could profitably use even more. Such problems must then be handled by making use of an infinite exterior memory capacity of which IBM punched cards are one example. There would be no need at all for an internal memory if such an infinite external memory could operate at electronic speeds. Since this does not seem possible, some compromise must be made. Some form of permanent and inexpensive infinite memory must be provided. Any improvement in the rate at which numbers and instructions can be transferred from this memory into the internal memory, or vice versa, is greatly to be desired. Obviously, high rates can be achieved by use of multiple equipment, but this does not lower the cost. Any simple and practical form of external memory so far considered cannot compare in speed to the electronic internal memory speed. The internal memory capacity must therefore be chosen with reference to the kind of problems which are to be done at high speed (that is, at speeds not limited by the input and output rates). For instance, an internal memory capacity equivalent to about 2000 ten-digit decimal numbers may be considered a minimum for handling numerical solutions of partial differential equations having two independent variables.

4.14 Simplification of Step 1

It is believed that serial operation at level (c) is of extreme value in simplifying the planning and layout of a problem which comes under step 1. The operator has no parallel timing problems to worry about. Since the machine can do but one operation at a time, his attention can likewise be put on only one thing at a time.

The machine must be capable of carrying out any numerical operation required by the mathematician. It is evident that only a few basic or standard operations could be built up from these. Certain operations, although expressible in terms of more elementary ones, are used so frequently that it is advisable to have the machine "know how" to do these processes. An example of this is multiplication, which should be handled as a basic operation for which no elaborate instructions need be given. On the other hand, the temptation to provide a great variety of standard operations must be resisted. More of these requires more control equipment, but the main reason for limiting the number of basic operations is that step 1 is not simplified but rendered more difficult by having too many operations to remember and to choose among. An instruction code must be simple enough and compact enough to be easily memorized and used without need for constant reference to a dictionary. It is believed that adequate flexibility and easy coding is provided by restricting the arithmetic operations to addition, subtraction, multiplication, division and possibly square root.

A general machine needs also the ability to alter its program of instructions in accordance with the outcome of some numerical calculation. In punched card computing machines, this function can be performed by "digit control." One form which this can take is that of an instruction which causes the machine to choose between two courses of action when two numbers, a and b, are specified. One program is followed if $a - b$ is positive or zero, and the other if $a - b$ is negative. Such an order can obviously be applied to programming identity checking (see Section 5.3), but it has many other applications. Digit control is easily carried out in the ENIAC, and the instruction code for the EDVAC is to contain this essential operation.

Another most important requirement on the programming or instruction possibilities of any large and general machine is that it must be possible to set up hierarchies of control. This may be expressed by saying that it must be possible to set up a given program routine just once, and call upon it as often as required in the course of some other program routine. If this facility is not provided, the same instructions might have to be set up many times. This would be wasteful of memory equipment and wasteful of the operator's time. It is impossible to overemphasize the extreme limitation which lack of this facility would impose. In the ENIAC, the master programmer serves the desired purpose. Instruction orders which operate upon other instruction orders will make this procedure logically possible, in the EDVAC.

One further desirable characteristic for programming systems should be pointed out. Any sequence of instructions which define a problem should be capable of rapid and easy modification by the operator when he desires to make slight variations in his problem. This is obviously possible in the ENIAC, since the operator has immediate access to all of the manual program controls. In a machine which is automatically set up from tape, for instance, it is not obvious that this condition is fulfilled. In the design of the EDVAC, it is hoped to meet this condition.

In conclusion, it maybe remarked that for any large machine it is desirable to establish a "library" of standard program routines. In the case of the ENIAC, such a compilation can sometimes avoid duplication of effort in the planning stage of a new problem which has parts resembling old problems, but it can hardly do much to reduce manual set-up time. For machines which are automatically set up, a great deal of time and effort can be saved by such a library. Electromechanical machines now make extensive use of such libraries, which include function tables as well as program routines. Exactly the same techniques can obviously be applied to the EDVAC.

CHAPTER 5: RELIABILITY AND CHECKING

5.1 Relationship of Reliability and Checking

The need for checking depends greatly on the inherent reliability of the device being checked. A device which fails extremely often is not worth checking, and one which never fails needs no checking. In practice, failures can never be eliminated completely, and some method of controlling and recognizing failures is highly desirable.

In a digital computing machine, the failure of almost any component can vitiate the entire computation. Even a momentary failure of any part may therefore be considered as a failure of the whole machine. Since a large computing machine contains many parts, its failure frequency may be high even though the individual components have a low failure rate.

5.2 Detection and Localization of Failures

Checking devices or methods detect rather than prevent failures. Since the checking device or process may also fail, it might seem that there is no end to checking. It must be recognized, however, that no system can really detect all errors; the true aim of checking is to reduce the probability of undetected failures to an extremely low value which is deemed tolerable.

A secondary, but by no means trivial, function which may be served by checking is to localize the failure. The importance of this feature increases with the size of the machine and the complexity of the calculations. Suppose a long and involved problem is done by two different methods on two different machines. If the results agree, there is very little chance that they are wrong; but if they fail to agree, there may be no clue as to which is right or where the error was made. To avoid having this situation recur frequently, either checking must be done more frequently on smaller parts of the problem, or the machine components must have exceedingly high reliability.

5.3 Types and Levels of Checking

It is convenient in discussing checking methods and devices to use the following terminology:

Repeat checking	The same operation is done again in the same way with the same equipment.
Multiple checking	The same operation is done in the same way, but using entirely separate pieces of equipment of the same construction.
Identity checking	Two equivalent but different methods of doing the same operation are employed, and the results compared. The two methods may make use of different equipment, or the same equipment in different ways.
Test checking	A test problem, for which the correct answer is known, is run through the machine before and after new problems are done. Presumably this problem can be designed to reveal most of the possible failures, and perhaps can help localize these failures.
Smoothness checking	The smoothness of a series of calculated values is examined, usually by higher order differences.
Programmed checking	Checking which is carried out in accordance with specific instruction orders (at the control of the operator).
Built-in checking	Checking which is not at the discretion of the operator, but is always done by the machine without instruction.

These categories are not all-exclusive, nor exhaustive. The first five are types which are usually programmed, not built-in. There are numerous types of built-in checking which are hard to classify. One of the best is that used by certain relay computers which detect whether the proper number of relays have operated in each step of the problem, allowing no operation to proceed until the immediately prior operation has been checked in this way. This method is notable for the nicety with which it localizes errors, and for the high reliability which it achieves.

It is convenient to speak of various "levels" of checking. At the lowest level, every unit operation is checked, while at the highest level an entire problem might be multiple checked or identity checked on two distinct machines. Except for the relay check just mentioned, both of these extremes are unduly expensive, since intermediate methods can usually be found to insure adequate reliability combined with reasonable localization of failures.

It is obvious that a digital computing machine which has any claim to flexibility will certainly permit programmed checking of any sort desired. Smoothness checking, for instance, can be aided by automatic calculation of the required differences. The designer is concerned, however, with the question of what checking devices should be built-in. In answering this question, careful consideration should be given to the kind of failures which are likely to occur.

5.4 Character of Failures

Equipment failures can be broadly classified into these two groups:

Type 1—*lasting failures,* which persist until corrected by the operator or maintenance personnel.

Type 2—*transient failures,* for which the apparatus passes back and forth between correct and incorrect operation, usually but not necessarily at irregular intervals. Type 2 failures are often called "intermittents."

Type 2 faults are more difficult to detect and locate. If not detected immediately, there is no way of knowing how many calculations have been spoiled.

Probably one reason why relays have been preferred to vacuum tubes for use in large computing machines is that more is known about their failure characteristics. Type 1 faults are extremely improbable in good relays. Most failures are type 2, caused by dust particles fouling contacts for a few operations only, being shaken cut by subsequent operations. Those failures are reduced by using two contacts in parallel, but they still predominate over type 1. The step-by-step built-in checking circuit mentioned in Section 5.3 is therefore quite essential for computing reliability.

For vacuum tubes, quantitative information on

failures is very rough, and comparisons are difficult because conditions of usage are not standardized. Some general facts about their failure characteristics are of considerable importance to any discussion of checking. Suitably tested tubes operated under proper conditions can have a useful life of about 10,000 hours. Type 2 failures are rare, and type 1 failures are high during the first few hours of operation, becoming low thereafter. Type 2 failures may arise from mechanical vibrations, loose connections, and such things, but the period or interval associated with these is usually long enough to cover many operations at the high electronic computing speeds. Extremely low-level checking is not needed to detect these.

As tubes age, their signal output gradually decreases, until at some time an occasional pulse may not affect the device it is supposed to operate. For this reason it is important to design computing circuits so they are insensitive to rather large changes in signal strength. The likelihood of type 2 failures from aging effects can then be greatly reduced by periodically testing all tubes. By other methods, potential type 2 failures can be forced into becoming type 1 failures which are readily located. There is no comparable procedure for relay machines.

5.5 ENIAC Checking and Reliability

The ENIAC has not been provided with any built-in checking devices in any strict sense of the term. However, there are circuits which see to it that all of the numerous power supplies are operating within certain tolerance limits, and other circuits which shut down the whole machine if certain fuses are blown. Another feature, described in Chapter 3, is also related to checking and localization of failures. The cycling unit is capable of operating the machine by single addition time steps, or by single pulse steps, each step controlled by a push button. All counters and other flip-flops are equipped with neon indicating lamps, so that many details of circuit operations can be followed visually during a manually-controlled step-by-step check. It is also possible to operate the machine, either "continuously" or step by step, at any pulse repetition rate lower than the standard 100,000 per sec., or even

somewhat above this rate. Thus certain timing tolerances can be investigated.

Since the ENIAC has no built-in checking, careful attention has been given to improving reliability by circuit design. Tubes and other components are operated at very conservative ratings. Tubes are used as binary elements, being either on or off. Large safety factors are provided, both in signal strength and in timing. In general, all tolerances have been made consistently large.

Any kind of programmed checking may, of course, be used, except that there is no way of multiple checking operations such as multiplication, division and square root, for which duplicate equipment does not exist. Identity checking and smoothness checking appear to be reasonable methods. Considering the character of vacuum tube failures, as discussed in the preceding section, repeat checking is probably of no value at all since the same errors will probably be made during the second run. For exactly the same reason, test checking is very likely to be quite successful, and if this turns out to be the case, this will be the most efficient sort of general purpose checking. Only after considerable operating experience will it be known how frequently (or infrequently) test checking will have to be done. Whenever the nature of the problem allows it, smoothness checking should also be done, but this method does not reveal systematic errors.

5.6 Advantages of Serial Operation

From the standpoint of checking and reliability, completely serial machines have important advantages. In the first place, since less equipment is involved, there is less likelihood of a machine failure. The time lost when a failure occurs is also reduced, since both diagnosis and repair are easier with less equipment.

Quite apart from this, however, serial machines have a considerable advantage with respect to checking. Since there is less equipment to be checked, less equipment is needed to do the checking. In fact, a number of components can sometimes be checked by a single checking device. Test checking is easier to work out for a machine having fewer components and proportionately more of them used in each operation. Since many parts of a serial machine are in almost continuous operation, there is also more opportunity for detection and location of type 2 failures.

A very significant fact is that all of the digits for any number must pass through the same channel. This means that a type 1 failure in such a channel will affect all the digits of every number that uses that channel. It is quite probable that the calculations will be so completely upset that the failure will be obvious when the results are inspected, presuming that no built-in checking catches this failure. This is to be contrasted with the possibility, in a multi-channel machine, of a single digit failure causing only a very small error in the results. Such an error might be sufficiently systematic as to go undetected by smoothness checks.

When type 2 failures are considered, the fact that all digits must pass through the same channel is even more important. In a serial machine any type 2 failure will be almost certainly cause a gross error, and again might be noticed without the aid of built-in checking devices. In a multiple machine, if a type 2 failures occurs in a place where it does not cause a gross error, the faulty component may cause errors only infrequently and thus go undetected during the course of many problems, unless identity checking or ingenious test checking is employed.

Although all failures in a serial machine are likely to cause gross errors, and would probably be noticed without built-in checking devices, it seems reasonable to build in any checking device which does not require a great deal of equipment.

5.7 Checking in the EDVAC

For the EDVAC, it is expected that most of the equipment will be associated with the memory. This means that the arithmetic organ and the control unit could be multiple checked by having duplicate equipment for these parts, and yet not increase the total equipment very much. The circuit which compares the results from the two computers can also be checked by having a duplicate comparing circuit, thus guarding against failure of this checking device.

To check the unit operations of the computer within any standard arithmetic process seems unnecessary. Reliability is sufficiently assured by the multiple checking of complete arithmetic processes, and checking at a lower level would involve much more equipment and serve only to localize failures. It is believed that such extreme localization is not necessary, since once a computing failure has been noticed either diagnostic test checking or electrical service instruments can be used to locate the fault more precisely.

Methods for checking the memory and switches will not be described here except in very general terms. It is probable that a kind of built-in test checking, requiring only a small amount of equipment, will be found suitable. Sufficient input and output equipment can he provided so that multiple checking can be used.

It is hoped that these built-in checking devices will improve the reliability to such an extent that the operator will not ordinarily have to devote much attention to programmed checking. If, after the EDVAC is put into operation, it is found that this hope is not entirely justified, then a certain amount of programmed checking might have to be done. In any event, all of the failures which are noticed by the built-in checking system will be to some extent localized and service problems will thereby be simplified.

APPENDIX A
Remarks on Arithmetic Operation of the ENIAC

The purpose of this appendix is to present in more detail the arithmetic operation of the multiplier and divider. To do this let us first describe the system for handling negative numbers in the ENIAC. Since the ring counters in the accumulators cycle in but one direction it is desirable to treat subtraction as a form of addition by the introduction of a system of complements.

Let us focus attention on the 10 decade counters of an accumulator. Any integer between 1 and $10^{10} - 1$ inclusive, is uniquely representable on the counters but the numbers zero and 10^{10} are indistinguishable. Hence the sum $(10^{10} - N) + N$ appears as zero on the decade counters. The number $10^{10} - N$ is referred to as the complement of N with respect to 10^{10}.

To permit a unique representation both of positive numbers N with $0 < N < 10^{10} - 1$ and of the complements of such numbers there is a so-called PM counter to the left of the decade counters. This counter is a binary one since its function is to distinguish between positive numbers (which carry sign P) and their complements (which carry sign M). In the transmission of a positive number no pulses are sent along the PM lead in a digit tray, whereas nine sign pulses are sent for a complement. The PM counter can receive as its input either the sign pulses or a carry-over pulse from the extreme left hand decade. The reception of an even number of pulses leaves the counter in its original state, the reception of an odd number of pulses has the effect of cycling the PM counter to its other stage. It is now easy to verify that all the usual arithmetic properties of addition and subtraction are obeyed in the system described. There follow a few illustrative examples: The sum of 801 and 527 appears as

P 0,000,000,801
P 0,000,000,527
P 0,000,001,328 ;

the difference 801 minus 527 as

P 0,000,000,801
M 9,999,999,473
P 0,000,000,274;

and the difference 527 minus 801 as

P 0,000,000,527
M 9,999,999,199
M 9,999,999,726

The ENIAC is so constructed that the complement of a number is formed by subtracting each digit of the number from 9 and then transmitting an additional pulse over the lead associated with the extreme right hand digit as specified by the setting of the significant figures switch. This additional pulse has the effect of subtracting the right hand digit from 10 so that a complement with respect to 10^{10} is thus formed.

As was mentioned earlier, the divider-square rooter is essentially a mechanism for automatically sequencing the behavior of a number of associated accumulators. It performs this sequencing by generating at various times special programming pulses which are transmitted to the appropriate accumulators. The operation cycle, whether for division or square rooting, divides itself into four distinct phases; phase I in which the stage is set for the following phases; phase II during which the operation is performed; phase III, the round-off period; and phase IV the interlock and clear period.

In phase I the divider emits signals which stimulate the numerator and denominator accumulators to receive their arguments and sets up certain programming circuits. During phase II the basic division and shifting sequences are performed. When the numerator and denominator have like signs, the denominator is subtracted from the numerator and the quotient is increased by one in a particular decade; when the signs are unlike, the denominator is added to the numerator and the quotient is decreased by one in a particular decade. When the remainder changes sign, the basic division sequence is interrupted. The remainder is then transmitted from the numerator accumulator to the shift accumulator, shifted one place to the left and returned to the numerator accumulator. The basic division sequence is then resumed. After a shift, however, the unit, added or subtracted from the quotient, is put into the next decade to the right of the place in which it was previously accommodated. Phase II ceases and phase III starts when an overdraft occurs and when the specified number of answer places have been found. We shall not further discuss phases III and IV, but consider a numerical example of division on the ENIAC. See Problem 1, p. A-4.

The multiplier, as was remarked above, carries out its operation by forming successively partial products consisting of the entire multiplicand by one digit at a time of the multiplier. Arrays built into the multiplier store the multiplications tables for numbers between zero and nine in two parts: the tens digit and the units digit. For example, the product of 4 × 9 is remembered as a tens digit of 3 and units digit of 6. During the multiplication process, the tens digits of the partial products are stored in the so-called left-hand partial product accumulators and the units digits in the right-hand partial product accumulators. Upon the completion of the multiplication cycle the process of correction for multiplication by complements is effected. At the end of this phase the left-hand product is trans-ferred into the right-hand accumulators. See Problem 2, p. A-5.

Phase	Quotient Accumulator		Numerator Accumulator		Denominator Accumulator	Shift Accumulator	
	Receives	Stores after receiving	Receives	Stores after receiving	Receives and stores thereafter	Receives	Stores after receiving
I			P0 209 070 000	P0 209 070 000	P0 230 000 000		
II			M9 770 000 000	1 M9 979 070 000			
	P0 100 000 000	P0 100 000 000					
						M9 790 700 000	M9 790 700 000
			M9 790 700 000	M9 790 700 000			
			P0 230 000 000	P0 020 700 000			
	M9 990 000 000	P0 090 000 000					
					P0 207 000 000		P0 207 000 000
			P0 207 000 000	P0 207 000 000			
			M9 770 000 000	M9 977 000 000			
	P0 001 000 000	P0 091 000 000					
						M9 770 000 000	M9 770 000 000

Problem 1

To perform the division P0 209 070 000 ÷ P0 230 000 000 to four figures without round-off.

Multiplier Digit	Left-hand Partial Product Accumulator		Right-hand Partial Product Accumulator	
	Receives	Stores after Receiving	Receives	Stores after Receiving
2	P1 000 010 000	P1 000 010 000	P0 226 046 000	P0 226 046 000
0	P0 000 000 000	P1 000 010 000	P0 000 000 000	P0 226 046 000
8	P0 040 201 600	P1 040 211 600	P0 008 840 640	P0 234 886 640
Complement Correction	M7 920 000 000	M8 960 211 600		
Final Product Collection			M8 960 211 600	M9 195 098 240

APPENDIX B

Remarks on Programming the ENIAC

Inasmuch as the problem of programming the ENIAC has not been discussed in much detail above it is desirable to devote more space to this subject. Let us first consider an extremely simple problem as an illustration of an elementary programming procedure. In planning a set-up for the ENIAC it is desirable to link the elementary programming sequences into a complex whole by means of the master programmer. Hence we first consider the problem of programming the elementary steps and then plan the over-all connection of these steps by hierarchies of program sequences in the master programmer.

It is desired to form in two accumulators a tabulation of the function n^2 against n (cf. Fig. 1). Let us proceed inductively and assume that one accumulator contains n and another n^2. We then wish to program the first accumulator to transmit its contents twice into the second one, which must then also be programmed to receive twice. Hence we need to use one transceiver program control on accumulator one to cause the transmission and one such control on the second accumulator for the reception. In addition, we must use a program pulse to stimulate simultaneously each of these controls and we shall indicate below the origin of this pulse. The output signal from either control will then be used to stimulate a unit such as the constant transmitter to send the digit one into each of the accumulators. We need therefore to use one receiver program control on each of the two accumulators to receive this digit. Upon the reception by each accumulator of the unit there appear the numbers $(n + 1)$ and $n^2 + 2n\ 1 = (n + 1)^2$. Finally the program output of the constant transmitter may be fed into the transceiver controls mentioned above to stimulate the reiteration of this process. It remains only to describe the inception of the entire cycle. Initially the accumulators contain the number zero, and the initiating pulse is sent to the constant transmitter for the purpose of stimulating the emission of the digit one and to the accumulators to stimulate reception of the digit. Fig. 1 shows a schematic diagram for the set-up of this problem.

Suppose it is desired to form the above tabulation for $n < 13246$ and to stop at $n = 13246$. We then wish to make use of the master programmer to count the number of times we carry out our process. To use the master programmer for this purpose we associate with, for example, the C stepper five decades. The five decade switches associated with the first stage of the stepper are set to 1, 3, 2, 4, 5 respectively. The program output of accumulator 2 in Fig. 2 is now routed to the stepper input and the output of stage 1 is then sent to the program pulse input terminals on accumulators 1, 2 and the constant transmitter (cf. Fig. 2). After the computation of n^2 has been stimulated 13246 times (once by the initiating pulse and 13245 times from the output of stage 1 of the stepper), the stepper cycles to stage 2. The program output pulse from stage 2 of the stepper does not cause any further computations since the output terminal for this stage of the stepper is not connected to any program line.

Evidently we could have used the output of stage 2 to initiate a new and different sequence of events. It is therefore clear that one can, by such simple measures, order the execution of a sequence of subsequences of operations and by suitably interconnecting steppers achieve considerable programming complexity in this manner.

Instead of pursuing this obvious topic further let us discuss other uses of the master programmer. The use of the master programmer is being stressed since it is the mechanism in the ENIAC which enables one to link the simple sequences of instructions given the other units of the computer into a complex whole.

To illustrate another important function of the master programmer, let us consider the problem of programming the ENIAC to discriminate between two program sequences depending on the relative sizes of two numbers a and b. For example, in the integration of a differential equation it may be desired to reiterate a given step if the third difference, a, of a certain quantity is not less than a fixed number, b, and to proceed to the next step in the contrary case. After completing a step of the integration we accordingly wish to form the difference $a - b$ and to examine its sign indication. Recall that if a number is non-negative, no pulses are sent to indicate the sign, whereas, if it is negative, nine pulses are transmitted. Let us now connect the output of stage 1 of a stepper to the program line which carries the stimulating pulse for the sequence of computations involved in reiterating, and the output of its second stage to the line which carries the stimulating pulse for the next step. We now connect the sign indication lead from the accumulator storing the difference $a - b$ to a transceiver whose output is fed to the direct input of our stepper, and connect a program line to the stepper's input. We shall send a program pulse along this line in the same addition time as the transceiver's output will occur. If ($a - b$) is non-negative, no pulses are applied to the direct input of the stepper since no pulses reach the transceiver. Moreover, the pulse applied to the stepper

input causes an output pulse on its stage 1 output, thereby stimulating the reiteration program. If $a - b$ is negative, the stepper is advanced to stage 2 since the transceiver is stimulated. The pulse applied to the stepper input, in this case, causes an output from stage 2, which results in the next line's being computed. Finally a program pulse is sent to the stepper clear direct input so that the stepper returns to stage 1 for the next magnitude discrimination (cf. Fig. 3).

As an extremely simple example of the way in which one may compound sequences of program instructions consider the following problem: Suppose it is desired to read certain data, such as initial conditions from an IBM card, carry out a computational routine of m line steps, print the final results, and then perform the same routine n times. We could then use stage 1 of stepper (with the stage one decade switch set at 1) to signal for the card reading, stage 2 to order the computations to be performed while its associated decade switches count the m repetitions, and stage 3 to control the printing operation (cf. Fig. 4).

Still another master programmer stepper is used to stimulate n repetitions of the read-compute-print sequence. The initiating pulse is sent to this stepper, and the resulting output pulse from stage 1 stimulates the first read-compute-print sequence. The terminal pulse of the read-compute-print sequence is also delivered to this stepper.

In closing let us consider the means at our disposal for performing a large number of multiplications. It is clear that in planning a problem one must determine what is a basic group of elementary arithmetic operations. By this is meant a group of operations, which cannot be built up by iteration of any of its subgroups. An illustration of this notion can be gained by considering a pair of differential equations. The integration performed on one variable is essentially the same as that performed on the other. Hence it suffices to arrange the computation so that only one of the integrations is set up on the arithmetic units and to have the master programmer provide for the iteration. In this fashion, problems involving numbers of multiplications far in excess of 24 can be programmed.

If, however, the basic group of operations itself

requires more than 24 multiplications, it is necessary to resort to other techniques to obtain the necessary freedom. These other techniques require the expenditure of a number of transceivers for non-arithmetic purposes. As will be seen below, to achieve six multiplications in the basic group at the expense of but one multiplier control necessitates the use of about 30 of these transceivers, i.e., about 10 per cent of the program control capacity. In general, in planning a set-up of a problem for the ENIAC the inner economy of the machine must be considered in allocation program facilities to various parts of the problem.

In closing let us consider the means at our disposal for performing a number of multiplications in our basic group, which are essentially alike in the following sense: the multipliers a_i $(i = 1, 2, \ldots, n)$ and multiplicands b_i are received on the same channels; the products $c_i = a_i b_i$ are transmitted on the same lines; there are the same number of digits in the multipliers; the products c_i are rounded-off to the same number of places; and the multiplier, multiplicand and product accumulators require the same clearing or holding instructions. Evidently the simplest procedure for handling the problem is to devote one multiplier program control to each of the n multiplications. This technique is, however, not always possible as, for example, in the case of a problem requiring more than 24 multiplications.

An alternative procedure is to use but $[n/6] + 1$ multiplier controls, where $[x]$ is the largest integer $< x$, and the same number of steppers.

We illustrate by showing how to achieve six products $c_i = a_i b_i$ $(i = 1, 2, \ldots, 6)$ by the use of one stepper and one multiplier control and a number of dummy program controls. We first define a dummy program control as any transceiver which is used to perform no arithmetic operation but serves only to give an output signal after one or more addition time delays. To return now to our problem let us send the initiating pulse into three dummy controls and use their outputs to stimulate the transmission of a_1 b_1 and to stimulate the multiplier to produce c_1. By means of these dummy controls we have isolated the order to the multiplier from the orders calling for the constants a_1, b_1.

We now send the output signal from the multiplier into our stepper and send the output pulse of stage one to four more dummy controls which stimulate the disposal of the product c_1, the transmission a_2, b_2 and the multiplication a_2, b_2 by the same multiplier control. The output signal of the last multiplication is sent to the stepper and output of stage 6 can be used, as indicated above, to stimulate a new multiplier control (cf. Fig. 5).

As a closing illustration let us consider the previous problem but let us set the problem up in a different way eliminating the use of the master programmer. For simplicity we suppose that our multipliers are always five digit numbers. This time we send our initiating pulse to four dummy controls, the first three of which are used as before and the last of which gives a nine addition time delay. When the multiplication is completed, we do not use the multiplier output pulse. Instead we take the delayed signal from our fourth dummy and use that signal to stimulate five more dummy controls in the obvious way. (cf. Fig. 6.)

APPENDIX C
General Construction Data on the ENIAC

The ENIAC is a very large and complicated machine. The electronic and relay apparatus, exclusive of the portable function tables and the auxiliary card machines, which are separate units mounted on wheels and plugged into the ENIAC, is mounted in forty panels each of which is two feet wide and eight and one-half feet high. Including the cases which house the tubes and air filters, the units are about two and one-half feet deep. Over thirty thousand cubic feet of air is forced per minute through the air filters and around the tubes by ten two-horsepower blowers. The hot exhaust air, which is between ten and twenty degrees Fahrenheit above room temperature, is passed through sheet metal ducts out of the building in which the machine is housed. In addition to the forty panels above, six similar panels of greater depth and two of smaller depth house the power supply equipment.

The forty main panels of the ENIAC are arranged in a large U with sixteen of the panels on each leg of the U and eight panels on the end. This U, together with the eight power supply panels, the three portable

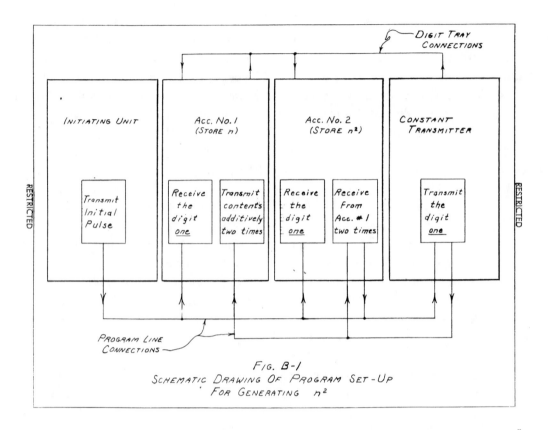

FIG. B-1
SCHEMATIC DRAWING OF PROGRAM SET-UP
FOR GENERATING n²

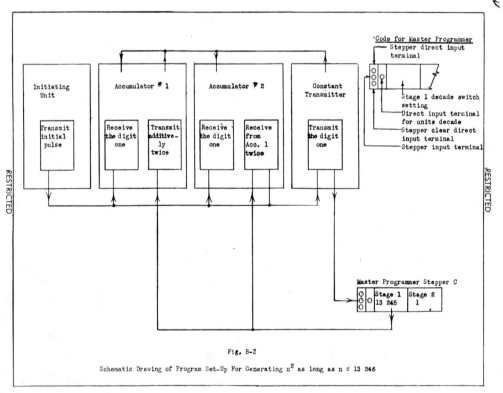

Fig. B-2

Schematic Drawing of Program Set-Up For Generating n^2 as long as n ≤ 13 246

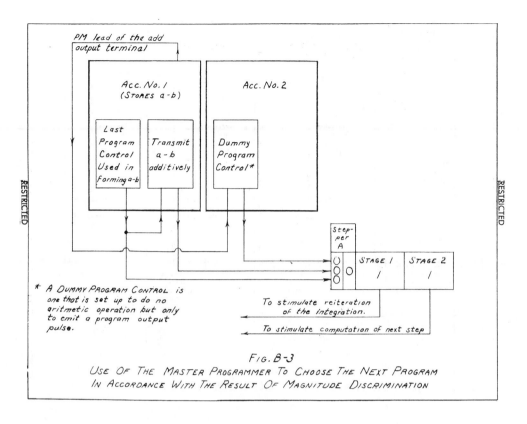

PM lead of the add output terminal

Acc. No. 1
(Stores a-b)

Last Program Control Used in Forming a-b

Transmit a-b additively

Acc. No. 2

Dummy Program Control*

Step-per A

Stage 1 /   Stage 2 /

* A DUMMY PROGRAM CONTROL is one that is set up to do no aritmetic operation but only to emit a program output pulse.

To stimulate reiteration of the integration.

To stimulate computation of next step

FIG. B-3
USE OF THE MASTER PROGRAMMER TO CHOOSE THE NEXT PROGRAM IN ACCORDANCE WITH THE RESULT OF MAGNITUDE DISCRIMINATION

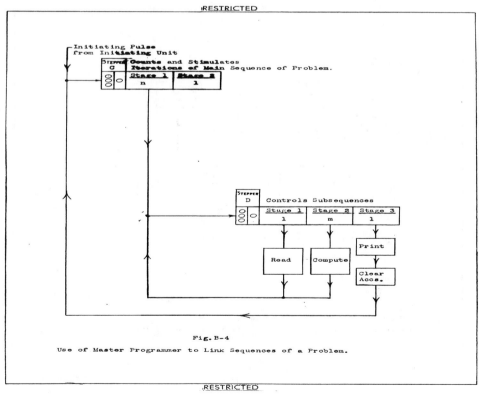

Initiating Pulse from Initiating Unit

Stepper C — Counts and Stimulates Iterations of Main Sequence of Problem.

Stage 1	Stage 2
n	1

Stepper D — Controls Subsequences

Stage 1	Stage 2	Stage 3
1	m	1

Read   Compute   Print

Clear Accs.

Fig. B-4
Use of Master Programmer to Link Sequences of a Problem.

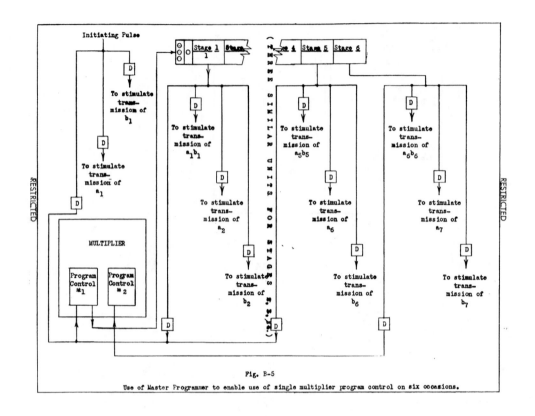

Fig. B-5

Use of Master Programmer to enable use of single multiplier program control on six occasions.

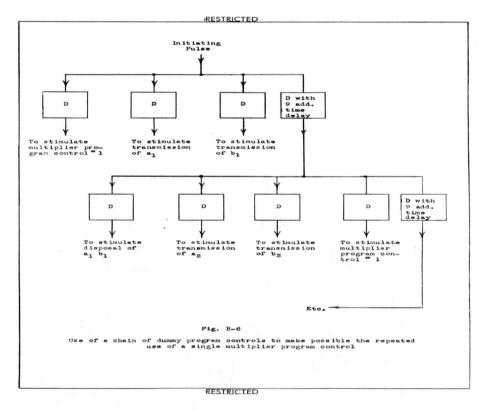

Fig. B-6

Use of a chain of dummy program controls to make possible the repeated use of a single multiplier program control

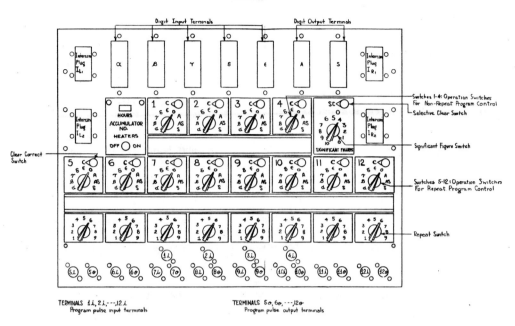

Digit Input Terminals   Digit Output Terminals

Switches 1-4: Operation Switches
For Non-Repeat Program Control

Selective Clear Switch

Significant Figure Switch

Clear Correct
Switch

Switches 5-12: Operation Switches
For Repeat Program Control

Repeat Switch

TERMINALS 1i, 2i, --- 12i
Program pulse input terminals

TERMINALS 5o, 6o, --- 12o
Program pulse output terminals

ACCUMULATOR
FRONT PANEL
PX-5-301R

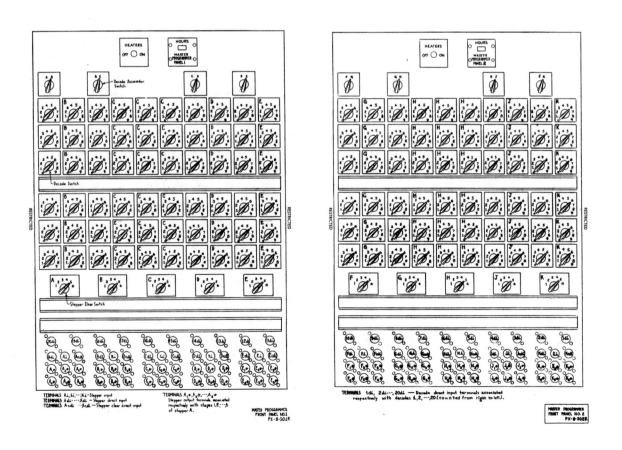

Decade Associator
Switch

Decade Switch

Stepper Clear Switch

TERMINALS Ai, bi, --- Ki — Stepper input
TERMINALS Adi --- Kdi — Stepper direct input
TERMINALS Acdi --- Kcdi — Stepper clear direct input

TERMINALS Ao, bo, --- Ao —
Stepper output terminals associated
respectively with stages 1,2, ---,6
of stepper A.

MASTER PROGRAMMER
FRONT PANEL NO.1
PX-8-301R

TERMINALS 1di, 2di, ---, 20di — Decade direct input terminals associated
respectively with decades 1,2, ---,20 (counted from right to left).

MASTER PROGRAMMER
FRONT PANEL NO.2
PX-8-302R

Reading 8.2: Description of the ENIAC   371

function tables, and some of the auxiliary card machines, are arranged in a room thirty feet by fifty feet. Since the room has a ceiling which is over eleven feet high, the blower motors and ventilating ducts are suspended from the ceiling over the machine in order to save floor space. Viewing the U from the inside, the forty main panels of the ENIAC arranged from left to right are:

1.	Control and Initiating Unit
2.	Cycling Unit
3.	Master Programmer (a two-panel unit)
4.	
5.	First Function Table (a two-panel unit)
6.	
7.	Accumulators 1 and 2 (two one-panel units)
8.	
9.	Divider and Square Rooter
10.	
11.	
12.	
13.	Accumulators 3, 4, 5, 6, 7, 8, 9, and 10 (Eight one-panel units)
14.	
15.	
16.	
17.	
18.	Multiplier (a three-panel unit)
19.	
20.	
21.	
22.	
23.	
24.	Accumulators 11, 12, 13, 14, 15, 16, 17 and 18 (Eight one-panel units)
25.	
26.	

27.	
28.	
29.	Second Function Table (a two-panel unit)
30.	
31.	Third Function Table (a two-panel unit)
32.	
33.	Accumulators 19 and 20 (two one-panel units)
34.	
35.	
36.	Constant Transmitters (a three-panel unit)
37.	
38.	
39.	Printer (a three-panel unit)
40.	

Nine digit trunks of eleven wires each and ninety-nine program trunks of one wire each are mounted in trays which are stacked on shelves at the front of the machine. The digit trays are placed on a centrally located shelf, while the program trays are stacked at the base of the machine. Both sets of trays as well as the frame of the machine are made in eight foot, or four panel sections. Front panels containing the input and output terminals and the various program control switches are mounted between the two tray assemblies. The connecting plug and cable assemblies are plugged into sockets on the front panels and on the trays. The neon bulbs on the accumulators are visible above the digit trays, while other neon bulbs, arranged to show the state of the programming equipment, are visible just below and above the front panels.

If more than nine digit channels or ninety-nine program channels are required, they can be obtained by removing the plug and cable assemblies between one or more adjacent pairs of trays, thus giving a greater number of total channels some of which will no longer extend around the entire machine. At the base of the machine, running along the back of the panels, a single trunk constructed of digit trays is provided to connect the cycling unit to the other machines. This is ordinarily a semi-permanent connection—a connection which is only changed for servicing the equipment.

The panel of the control and initiating unit contains two meters and a small oscilloscope for measuring the filament voltages, the DC voltages, and the AC or hum component of the DC voltages. The cycling unit contains a larger oscilloscope which may be used to examine the various signals which are generated by this unit.

The ENIAC contains between seventeen and eighteen thousand vacuum tubes which are mounted along the back surface of thirty-seven of the forty panels. They are mounted horizontally just inside the dust covers which support the air filters.

The other three panels of the ENIAC contain over fifteen hundred automatic telephone exchange relays mounted in a similar manner. Thus each main panel contains either about five hundred vacuum tubes or about five hundred relays. Over seventy thousand resistors, about ten thousand condensers and five thousand switches comprise, with the vacuum tubes, the numerous elements or components of the ENIAC.

The ENIAC consumes one hundred and fifty kilowatts. This power is supplied by a three phase regulated two hundred and forty volt, sixty cycle power line. The power consumption may be broken up as follows: eighty kilowatts for heating the tubes, forty five kilowatts for generating DC voltages, twenty kilowatts for driving the ventilating blowers, and five kilowatts for the auxiliary card machines.

While the ENIAC does not contain any built-in checking equipment, a number of points were given special attention in its design. First, very conservative tube ratings, well below those of the manufacturer, were used. Second, more than sixty per cent of the tubes were mounted in small units which can be easily removed for repair. This was done in all of the more complicated circuits. Third, the signal or voltage level of the circuits was generally maintained at approximately forty volts and in practically all circuits in which sharp pulses were transmitted, shielded conductors were employed. A few exceptions to this rule were made under extenuating circumstances. Fourth, the ventilating system not only cools the room in which the machine is housed (which is only a few degrees warmer than normal) but also insures that the many resistors, which are already operating well under their rating, are functioning at a conservative temperature. Fifth, and finally, not only was great care given to the selection of such parts as switches and plugs, which have their contact surfaces silver plated, but all components and tubes were carefully tested before being installed.

In addition, special test equipment allows many of the circuits to be easily tested. This equipment includes a special test bench with its own power supply and electronic and oscillographic equipment so that the small spare units may be tested without interfering with the operation of the machine.

Preliminary Discussion of the Logical Design of an Electronic Computing Instrument

Arthur W. Burks, Herman H. Goldstine and John von Neumann

Extract from Arthur W. Burks, Herman H. Goldstine and John von Neumann, *Preliminary Discussion of the Logical Design of an Electronic Computing Instrument* ([Princeton: Institute for Advanced Study,] 1947), pp. 1–10.

INTRODUCTORY NOTE TO READING 8.3

A few months after the ENIAC had its first public demonstration (in February 1946), John von Neumann, Arthur Burks, and Herman Goldstine, the three chief members of the Institute for Advanced Study's Electronic Computer Project, issued their *Preliminary Discussion of the Logical Design of an Electronic Computing Instrument,* a report to the Army Ordnance Department that represents the first published formal conceptual paper on the stored-program computer, if we call von Neumann's informal *First Draft* (Reading 8.1) a privately circulated working paper. The first edition of the *Preliminary Report* appeared in June 1946; a revised second edition, containing an expanded account of the arithmetic processes and a report of further experimental work, was issued in September 1947. This was followed by the three-part *Planning and Coding of Problems for an Electronic Computing Instrument,* written by von Neumann and Goldstine with contributions by Burks, who by this time had left the IAS project to take a professorship at the University of Michigan. The three parts of *Planning and Coding* were issued in 1947–48; a fourth part was promised but never published. According to Burks, the *Preliminary Discussion* and *Planning and Coding* "were conceived as a single work dealing with the two inextricably intertwined sides of the design of a stored-program computer: the 'hard' side of logical design and architecture and the 'soft' side of program languages and their use."[1]

The *Preliminary Report* contains the first technical description of what is known as the von Neumann architecture, in which programs and data are stored in a comparatively slow-to-access storage medium, such as a hard disk; and work is performed on them in a fast, volatile random-access memory. A single bit-parallel switch is used to process instructions one at a time (this last, a concession to the limitations of late 1940s technology, became known later as the "von Neumann bottleneck"). According to Burks, this was a great improvement over the EDVAC's serial design since "because the memory was random access, the programmer did not have to be concerned with the timing problems associated with storage lines holding numbers in series. And although a parallel processor uses more equipment than a serial processor, this was to a large extent counterbalanced by the elimination of the EDVAC equipment required for timing and controlling the sequence of bits in a word."[2] The von Neumann architecture, with some additions and refinements, remained the logical basis for the design of most computers built since the *Preliminary Report's* publication. For excerpts from the *Planning and Coding* section of this report see Reading 9. 2. [JMN]

---

1   W. Aspray and A. Burks, editors, *The Papers of John von Neumann on Computing and Computer Theory* (Cambridge: MIT Press; Los Angeles: Tomash Publishers, 1987), 146.

2   Aspray and Burks, *op. cit.,* 14.

John von Neumann, Julian Bigelow, James Pomerene, and Herman Goldstine
(Photograph courtesy of Herman H. Goldstine.)

TEXT OF READING 8.3

PART I

1. Principal Components of the Machine

1.1. Inasmuch as the completed device will be a general-purpose computing machine it should contain certain main organs relating to arithmetic, memory-storage, control and connection with the human operator. It is intended that the machine be fully automatic in character, i.e. independent of the human operator after the computation starts. A fuller discussion of the implications of this remark will be given in Chapter 3 below.

1.2. It is evident that the machine must be capable of storing in some manner not only the digital information needed in a given computation such as boundary values, tables of functions (such as the equation of state of a fluid) and also the intermediate results of the computation (which may be wanted for varying lengths of time), but also the instructions which govern the actual routine to be performed on the numerical data. In a special-purpose machine these instructions are an integral part of the device and constitute a part of its design structure. For an all-purpose machine it must be possible to instruct the device to carry out any computation that can be formulated in numerical terms. Hence there must be some organ capable of storing these program orders. There must, moreover, be a unit which can understand these instructions and order their execution.

1.3. Conceptually we have discussed above two different forms of memory: storage of numbers and storage of orders. If, however, the orders to the machine are reduced to a numerical code and if the machine can in some fashion distinguish a number from an order, the memory organ can be used to store both numbers and orders. The coding of orders into numeric form is discussed in 6.3 below.

1.4. If the memory for orders is merely a storage organ there must exist an organ which can automatically execute the orders stored in the memory. We shall call this organ the *Control*.

1.5. Inasmuch as the device is to be a computing machine there must be an arithmetic organ in it which can perform certain of the elementary arithmetic operations. There will be, therefore, a unit capable of adding, subtracting, multiplying and dividing. It will be seen in 6.6 below that it can also perform additional operations that occur quite frequently.

The operations that the machine will view as elementary are clearly those which are wired into the machine. To illustrate, the operation of multiplication could be eliminated from the device as an elementary process if one were willing to view it as a properly ordered series of additions. Similar remarks apply to division. In general, the inner economy of the arithmetic unit is determined by a compromise between the desire for speed of operation—a non-elementary operation will generally take a long time to perform since it is constituted of a series of orders given by the control—and the desire for simplicity, or cheapness, of the machine.

1.6. Lastly there must exist devices, the input and output organ, whereby the human operator and the machine can communicate with each other. This organ will be seen below in 4.5, where it is discussed, to constitute a secondary form of automatic memory.

2. First Remarks on the Memory

2.1. It is clear that the size of the memory is a critical consideration in the design of a satisfactory general-purpose computing machine. We proceed to discuss what quantities the memory should store for various types of computations.

2.2. In the solution of partial differential equations the storage requirements are likely to be quite extensive. In general, one must remember not only the initial and boundary conditions and any arbitrary functions that enter the problem but also an extensive number of intermediate results.

a. For equations of parabolic or hyperbolic type in two independent variables the integration process is essentially a double induction. To find the values of the dependent variables at time $t + \Delta t$ one integrates with respect to x from one boundary to the other by utilizing the data at time t as if they were coefficients which contribute to defining the problem of this integration.

Not only must the memory have sufficient room to store these intermediate data but there must be provisions whereby these data can later be removed, i.e. at the end of the $(t + \Delta t)$ cycle, and replaced by the corresponding data for the $(t + 2\Delta t)$ cycle. This process of removing data from the memory and of replacing them with new information must, of course, be done quite automatically under the direction of the control.

b. For total differential equations the memory requirements are clearly similar to, but smaller than, those discussed in (a) above.

c. Problems that are solved by iterative procedures such as systems of linear equations or elliptic partial differential equations, treated by relaxation techniques, may be expected to require quite extensive memory capacity. The memory requirement for such problems is apparently much greater than for those problems in (a) above in which one needs only to store information corresponding to the instantaneous value of one variable [t in (a) above], while now entire solutions (covering all values of all variables) must be stored. This apparent discrepancy in magnitudes can, however, be somewhat overcome by the use of techniques which permit the use of much coarser integration meshes in this case, than in the cases under (a).

2.3.   It is reasonable at this time to build a machine that can conveniently handle problems several orders of magnitude more complex than are now handled by existing machines, electronic or electro-mechanical. We consequently plan on a fully automatic electronic storage facility of about 4,000 numbers of 40 binary digits each. This corresponds to a precision of $2^{-40} \sim 0.9 \times 10^{-12}$, i.e. of about 12 decimals. We believe that this memory capacity exceeds the capacities required for most problems that one deals with at present by a factor of about 10. The precision is also safely higher than what is required for the great majority of present day problems. In addition, we propose that we have a subsidiary memory of much larger capacity, which is also fully automatic, on some medium such as magnetic wire or tape.

3. First Remarks on the Control and Code

3.1.   It is easy to see by formal-logical methods that there exist codes that are *in abstracto* adequate to control and cause the execution of any sequence of operations which are individually available in the machine and which are, in their entirety, conceivable by the problem planner. The really decisive considerations from the present point of view, in selecting a code, are more of a practical nature: simplicity of the equipment demanded by the code, and the clarity of its application to the actually important problems together with the speed of its handling of those problems. It would take us much too far afield to discuss these questions at all generally or from first principles. We will therefore restrict ourselves to analyzing only the type of code which we now envisage for our machine.

3.2.   There must certainly be instructions for performing the fundamental arithmetic operations. The specifications for these orders will not be completely given until the arithmetic unit is described in a little more detail.

3.3.   It must be possible to transfer data from the memory to the arithmetic organ and back again. In transferring information from the arithmetic organ back into the memory there are two types we must distinguish: Transfers of numbers as such and transfers of numbers which are parts of orders. The first case is quite obvious and needs no further explication. The second case is more subtle and serves to illustrate the generality and simplicity of the system. Consider, by way of illustration, the problem of interpolation in the system. Let us suppose that we have formulated the necessary instructions for performing an interpolation of order n in a sequence of data. The exact location in the memory of the $(n + 1)$ quantities that bracket the desired functional value is, of course, a function of the argument. This argument probably is found as the result of a computation in the machine. We thus need an order which can substitute a number into a given order—in the case of interpolation the location of the argument or the group of arguments that is nearest in our table to the desired value. By means of such an order the results of a computation can be introduced into the instructions governing that or a different computation. This makes it possible for a sequence of instructions to be used with different sets of numbers located in different parts of the memory.

To summarize, transfers into the memory will be of two sorts: *Total substitutions,* whereby the quantity previously stored is cleared out and replaced by a new number. *Partial substitutions* in which that part of an order containing a *memory location-number*—we assume the various positions in the memory are enumerated serially by memory location-numbers—is replaced by a new memory location-number.

3.4.   It is clear that one must be able to get numbers from any part of the memory at any time. The treatment in the case of orders can, however, be more methodical since one can at least partially arrange the control instructions in a linear sequence. Consequently the control will be so constructed that it will normally proceed from place n in the memory to place $(n + 1)$ for its next instruction.

3.5.   The utility of an automatic computer lies in the possibility of using a given sequence of instructions repeatedly, the number of times it is iterated being either preassigned or dependent upon the results of the computation. When the iteration is completed a different sequence of orders is to be followed, so we must, in most cases, give two parallel trains of orders preceded by an instruction as to which routine is to be followed. This choice can be made to depend upon the sign of a number (zero being reckoned as plus for machine purposes). Consequently, we introduce an order (*the conditional transfer order*) which will, depending on the sign of a given number, cause the proper one of two routines to be executed.

Frequently two parallel trains of orders terminate in a common routine. It is desirable, therefore, to order the control in either case to proceed to the beginning point of the common routine. This *unconditional transfer* can be achieved either by the artificial use of a conditional transfer or by the introduction of an explicit order for such a transfer.

3.6.   Finally we need orders which will integrate the input-output devices with the machine. These are discussed briefly in 6.8.

3.7.   We proceed now to a more detailed discussion of the machine. Inasmuch as our experience has shown that the moment one chooses a given component as the elementary memory unit, one has also more or less determined upon much of the balance of the machine, we start by a consideration of the memory organ. In attempting an exposition of a highly integrated device like a computing machine we do not find it possible, however, to give an exhaustive discussion of each organ before completing its description. It is only in the final block diagrams that anything approaching a complete unit can be achieved.

The time units to be used in what follows will be:

$$1 \ \mu sec = 1 \ \text{microsecond} = 10^{-6} \ \text{seconds},$$
$$1 \ msec = 1 \ \text{millisecond} = 10^{-3} \ \text{seconds}.$$

4. The Memory Organ

4.1.   Ideally one would desire an indefinitely large memory capacity such that any particular aggregate of 40 binary digits, or *word* (cf. 2.3), would be immediately available—i.e. in a time which is somewhat or considerably shorter than the operation time of a fast electronic multiplier. This may be assumed to be practical at the level of about 100 μsec. Hence the availability time for a word in the memory should be 5 to 50 μsec. It is equally desirable that words may be replaced with new words at about the same rate. It does not seem possible physically to achieve such a capacity. We are therefore forced to recognize the possibility of constructing a hierarchy of memories, each of which has greater capacity than the preceding but which is less quickly accessible.

The most common forms of storage in electrical circuits are the flip-flop or trigger circuit, the gas tube, and the electro-mechanical relay. To achieve a memory of n words would, of course, require about $40n$ such elements, exclusive of the switching elements. We saw earlier (cf. 2.2) that a fast memory of several thousand words is not at all unreasonable for an all-purpose instrument. Hence, about 10^5 flip-flops or analogous elements would be required! This would, of course, be entirely impractical.

We must therefore seek out some more fundamental method of storing electrical information than has been suggested above. One criterion for such a storage medium is that the individual storage organs, which accommodate only one binary digit each, should not be macroscopic components, but rather microscopic elements of some suitable organ. They would then, of course, not be identified and switched to by the usual macroscopic wire connections, but by some functional procedure in manipulating that organ.

One device which displays this property to a marked degree is the iconoscope tube. In its conventional form it possesses a linear resolution of about one part in 500. This would correspond to a (two-dimensional) memory capacity of $500 \times 500 = 2.5 \times 10^5$. One is accordingly led to consider the possibility of storing electrical charges on a dielectric plate inside a cathode-ray tube. Effectively such a tube is nothing more than a myriad of electrical capacitors which can be connected into the circuit by means of an electro beam.

Actually the above mentioned high resolution and concomitant memory capacity are only realistic under the conditions of television-image storage, which are much less exigent in respect to the reliability of individual markings than what one can accept in the storage for a computer. In this latter case resolutions of one part in 20 to 100, i.e. memory capacities of 400 to 10,000, would seem to be more reasonable in terms of equipment built essentially along familiar lines.

At the present time the Princeton Laboratories of the Radio Corporation of America are engaged in the development of a storage tube, the *Selectron, of* the type we have mentioned above. This tube is also planned to have a non-amplitude-sensitive switching system whereby the electron beam can be directed to a given spot on the plate within a quite small fraction of a millisecond. Inasmuch as the storage tube is the key component of the machine envisaged in this report we

are extremely fortunate in having secured the cooperation of the RCA group in this as well as in various other developments.

An alternate form of rapid memory organ is the acoustic feed-back delay line described in various reports on the EDVAC. (This is an electronic computing machine being developed for the Ordnance Department, U.S. Army, by the University of Pennsylvania, Moore School of Electrical Engineering.) Inasmuch as that device has been so clearly reported in those papers we give no further discussion. There are still other physical and chemical properties of matter in the presence of electrons or photons that might be considered, but since none is yet beyond the early discussion stage we shall not make further mention of them.

4.2.   We shall accordingly assume throughout the balance of this report that the Selectron is the modus for storage of words at electronic speeds. As now planned, this tube will have a capacity of $2^{12} = 4,096 \approx 4,000$ binary digits. To achieve a total electronic storage of about 4,000 words we propose to use 40 Selectrons, thereby achieving a memory of 2^{12} words of 40 binary digits each. (Cf. again 2.3).

4.3.   There are two possible means for storing a particular word in the Selectron memory—or, in fact, in either a delay line memory or in a storage tube with amplitude-sensitive deflection. One method is to store the entire word in a given tube and then to get the word out by picking out its respective digits in a serial fashion. The other method is to store in corresponding places in each of the 40 tubes one digit of the word. To get a word from the memory in this scheme requires, then, one switching mechanism to which all 40 tubes are connected in parallel. Such a switching scheme seems to us to be simpler than the technique needed in the serial system and is, of course, 40 times faster. We accordingly adopt the parallel procedure and thus are led to consider a so-called *parallel machine,* as contrasted with the serial principles being considered for the EDVAC. (In the EDVAC the peculiar characteristics of the acoustic delay line, as well as various other considerations, seem to justify a serial procedure. For more details, cf. the reports referred to in 4.1.) The essential difference between these two systems lies in the method of performing an addition; in a parallel machine all corresponding pairs of digits are added simultaneously, whereas in a serial one these pairs are added serially in time.

4.4. To summarize, we assume that the fast electronic memory consists of 40 Selectrons which are switched in parallel by a common switching arrangement. The inputs of the switch are controlled by the control.

4.5. Inasmuch as a great many highly important classes of problems require a far greater total memory than 2^{12} words, we now consider the next stage in our storage hierarchy. Although the solution of partial differential equations frequently involves the manipulation of many thousands of words, these data are generally required only in blocks which are well within the 2^{12} capacity of the electronic memory. Our second form of storage must therefore be a medium which feeds these blocks of words to the electronic memory. It should be controlled by the control of the computer and is thus an integral part of the system, not requiring human intervention.

There are evidently two distinct problems raised above. One can choose a given medium for storage such as teletype tapes, magnetic wire or tapes, movie film or similar media. There still remains the problem of automatic integration of this storage medium with the machine. This integration is achieved logically by introducing appropriate orders into the code which can instruct the machine to read or write on the medium, or to move it by a given amount or to a place with given characteristics. We discuss this question a little more fully in 6.8.

Let us return now to the question of what properties the secondary storage medium should have. It clearly should be able to store information for periods of time long enough so that only a few per cent of the total computing time is spent in re-registering information that is "fading off." It is certainly desirable, although not imperative, that information can be erased and replaced by new data. The medium should be such that it can be controlled, i.e. moved forward and backward, automatically. This consideration makes certain media, such as punched cards, undesirable. While cards can, of course, be printed or read by appropriate orders from some machine, they are not well adapted to problems in which the output data are fed directly back into the machine, and are required in a sequence which is non-monotone with respect to the order of the cards. The medium should be capable of remembering very large numbers of data at a much smaller price than electronic devices. It must be fast enough so that, even when it has to be used frequently in a problem, a large percentage of the total solution time is not spent in getting data into and out of this medium and achieving the desired positioning on it. If this condition is not reasonably well met, the advantages of the high electronic speeds of the machine will be largely lost.

Both light- or electron-sensitive film and magnetic wires or tapes, whose motions are controlled by servomechanisms integrated with the control, would seem to fulfil our needs reasonably well. We have tentatively decided to use magnetic wires since we have achieved reliable performance with them at pulse rates of the order of 25,000/sec and beyond.

4.6. Lastly our memory hierarchy requires a vast quantity of dead storage, i.e. storage not integrated with the machine. This storage requirement may be satisfied by a library of wires that can be introduced into the machine when desired and at that time become automatically controlled. Thus our dead storage is really nothing but an extension of our secondary storage medium. It differs from the latter only in its availability to the machine.

4.7. We impose one additional requirement on our secondary memory. It must be possible for a human to put words on to the wire or other substance used and to read the words put on by the machine. In this manner the human can control the machine's functions. It is now clear that the secondary storage medium is really nothing other than a part of our input-output system, cf. 6.8.4 for a description of a mechanism for achieving this.

4.8. There is another highly important part of the input-output which we merely mention at this time, namely, some mechanism for viewing graphically the results of a given computation. This can, of course, be achieved by a Selectron-like tube which causes its screen to fluoresce when data are put on it by an electron beam.

4.9.   For definiteness in the subsequent discussions we assume that associated with the output of each Selectron is a flip-flop. This assemblage of 40 flip-flops we term the *Selectron Register*.

5. The Arithmetic Organ

5.1.   In this chapter we discuss the features we now consider desirable for the arithmetic part of our machine. We give our tentative conclusions as to which of the arithmetic operations should be built into the machine and which should be programmed. Finally, a schematic of the arithmetic unit is described.

5.2.   In a discussion of the arithmetical organs of a computing machine one is naturally led to a consideration of the number system to be adopted. In spite of the longstanding tradition of building digital machines in the decimal system, we feel strongly in favor of the binary system for our device. Our fundamental unit of memory is naturally adapted to the binary system since we do not attempt to measure gradations of charge at a particular point in the Selectron but are content to distinguish two states. The flip-flop again is truly a binary device. On magnetic wires or tapes and in acoustic delay line memories one is also content to recognize the presence or absence of a pulse or (if a carrier frequency is used) of a pulse train, or of the sign of a pulse. (We will not discuss here the ternary possibilities of a positive-or-negative-or-no-pulse system and their relationship to questions of reliability and checking, nor the very interesting possibilities of carrier frequency modulation.) Hence if one contemplates using a decimal system with either the iconoscope or delay-line memory one is forced into a binary coding of the decimal system—each decimal digit being represented by at least a tetrad of binary digits. Thus an accuracy of ten decimal digits requires at least 40 binary digits. In a true binary representation of numbers, however, about 33 digits suffice to achieve a precision of 10^{10}. The use of the binary system is therefore somewhat more economical of equipment than is the decimal.

The main virtue of the binary system as against the decimal is, however, the greater simplicity and speed with which the elementary operations can be performed. To illustrate, consider multiplication by repeated addition. In binary multiplication the product of a particular digit of the multiplier by the multiplicand is either the multiplicand or null according as the multiplier digit is 1 or 0. In the decimal system, however, this product has ten possible values between null and nine times the multiplicand, inclusive. Of course, a decimal number has only $\log_{10}2 \sim 0.3$ times as many digits as a binary number of the same accuracy, but even so multiplication in the decimal system is considerably longer than in the binary system. One can accelerate decimal multiplication by complicating the circuits, but this fact is irrelevant to the point just made since binary multiplication can likewise be accelerated by adding to the equipment. Similar remarks may be made about the other operations.

An additional point that deserves emphasis is this: An important part of the machine is not arithmetical, but logical in nature. Now logics, being a yes-no system, is fundamentally binary. Therefore a binary arrangement of the arithmetical organs contributes very significantly towards producing a more homogenous machine, which can be better integrated and is more efficient.

The one disadvantage of the binary system from the human point of view is the conversion problem. Since, however, it is completely known how to convert numbers from one base to another and since this conversion can be effected solely by the use of the usual arithmetic processes there is no reason why the computer itself cannot carry out this conversion. It might be argued that this is a time consuming operation. This, however, is not the case. (Cf. 9.6 and 9.7 of Part II. Part II is a report issued under the title *Planning and Coding of Problems for an Electronic Computing Instrument.*) Indeed a general-purpose computer, used as a scientific research tool, is called upon to do a very great number of multiplications upon a relatively small amount of input data, and hence the time consumed in the decimal to binary conversion is only a trivial percentage of the total computing time. A similar remark is applicable to the output data.

In the preceding discussion we have tacitly assumed the desirability of introducing and withdrawing data in the decimal system. We feel, however, that the base 10 may not even be a permanent feature in a scientific instrument and consequently will probably attempt to train ourselves to use numbers base 2 or 8 or 16. The reason for the bases 8 or 16 is this: Since 8 and 16 are powers of 2 the conversion to binary is trivial; since both are about the size of 10, they violate many of our habits less badly than base 2. (Cf. Part II, 9.4.)

5.3.   Several of the digital computers being built or planned in this country and England are to contain a so-called "floating decimal point". This is a mechanism for expressing each word as a characteristic and a mantissa—e.g. 123.45 would be carried in the machine as (0.12345, 03), where the 3 is the exponent of 10 associated with the number. There appear to be two major purposes in a "floating" decimal point system both of which arise from the fact that the number of digits in a word is a constant, fixed by design considerations for each particular machine. The first of these purposes is to retain in a sum or product as many significant digits as possible and the second of these is to free the human operator from the burden of estimating and inserting into a problem "scale factors"—multiplicative constants which serve to keep numbers within the limits of the machine.

There is, of course, no denying the fact that human time is consumed in arranging for the introduction of suitable scale factors. We only argue that the time so consumed is a very small percentage of the total time we will spend in preparing an interesting problem for our machine. The first advantage of the floating point is, we feel, somewhat illusory. In order to have such a floating point one must waste memory capacity which could otherwise be used for carrying more digits per word. It would therefore seem to us not at all clear whether the modest advantages of a floating binary point offset the loss of memory capacity and the increased complexity of the arithmetic and control circuits.

There are certainly some problems within the scope of our device which really require more than 2^{-40} precision. To handle such problems we wish to

plan in terms of words whose lengths are some fixed integral multiple of 40, and program the machine in such a manner as to give the corresponding aggregates of 40 digit words the proper treatment. We must then consider an addition or multiplication as a complex operation programmed from a number of primitive additions or multiplications (cf. §9, Part II). There would seem to be considerable extra difficulties in the way of such a procedure in an instrument with a floating binary point.

The reader may remark upon our alternate spells of radicalism and conservatism in deciding upon various possible features for our mechanism. We hope, however, that he will agree, on closer inspection, that we are guided by a consistent and sound principle in judging the merits of any idea. We wish to incorporate into the machine—in the form of circuits—only such logical concepts as are either necessary to have a complete system or highly convenient because of the frequency with which they occur and the influence they exert in the relevant mathematical situations.

5.4.   On the basis of this criterion we definitely wish to build into the machine circuits which will enable it to form the binary sum of two 40 digit numbers. We make this decision not because addition is a logically basic notion but rather because it would slow the mechanism as well as the operator down enormously if each addition were programmed out of the more simple operations of "and", "or", and "not". The same is true for the subtraction. Similarly we reject the desire to form products by programming them out of additions, the detailed motivation being very much the same as in the case of addition and subtraction. The cases for division and square-rooting are much less clear.

It is well known that the reciprocal of a number a can be formed to any desired accuracy by iterative schemes. One such scheme consists of improving an estimate X by forming $X' = 2X - aX^2$. Thus the new error $1 - aX'$ is $(1 - aX)^2$, which is the square of the error in the preceding estimate. We notice that in the formation of X', there are two bona fide multiplications—we do not consider multiplication by 2 as a true product since we will have a facility for shifting right or left in one or two pulse times. If then we somehow could guess $1/a$ to a precision of 2^{-5}, 6 multiplications—3 iterations—would suffice to give a final result good to 2^{-40}. Accordingly a small table of 2^4 entries could be used to get the initial estimate of $1/a$. In this way a reciprocal $1/a$ could be formed in 6 multiplication times, and hence a quotient b/a in 7 multiplication times. Accordingly we see that the question of building a divider is really a function of how fast it can be made to operate compared to the iterative method sketched above: In order to justify its existence, a divider must perform a division in a good deal less than 7 multiplication times. We have, however, conceived a divider which is much faster than these 7 multiplication times and therefore feel justified in building it, especially since the amount of equipment needed above the requirements of the multiplier is not important.

It is, of course, also possible to handle square roots by iterative techniques. In fact, if X is our estimate of $a^{1/2}$, then $X' = 1/2(X + a/X)$ is a better estimate. We see that this scheme involves one division per iteration. As will be seen below in our more detailed examination of the arithmetic organ we do not include a square-rooter in our plans because such a device would involve more equipment than we feel is desirable in a first model. (Concerning the iterative method of square-rooting, cf. 8.10 in Part II.)

5.5.   The first part of our arithmetic organ requires little discussion at this point. It should be a parallel storage organ which can receive a number and add it to the one already in it, which is also able to clear its contents and which can transmit what it contains. We will call such an organ an *Accumulator*. It is quite conventional in principle in past and present computing machines of the most varied types, e.g. desk multipliers, standard IBM counters, more modern relay machines, the ENIAC. There are of, course, numerous ways to build such a binary accumulator. We distinguish two broad types of such devices: static, and dynamic or pulse-type accumulators. These will be discussed in 5.11, but it is first necessary to make a few remarks concerning the arithmetic of binary addition. In a parallel accumulator, the first step in an addition is to add each digit of the addend to the corresponding digit of the augend. The second step is to perform the carries, and this must be done in sequence since a carry may produce a carry. In the worst case, 39 carries will occur. Clearly it is inefficient to allow 39 times as much time for the second step (performing the carries) as for the first step (adding the digits). Hence either the carries must be accelerated, or use must be made of the average number of carries or both.

Babbage's Dream Comes True [review of *A Manual of Operation for the Automatic Sequence Controlled Calculator* (1946)]

L. J. Comrie

From *Nature* 158 (1946): 567–68.

INTRODUCTORY NOTE TO READING 8.4

In this review of the Harvard Computation Laboratory's manual for the Automatic Sequence Controlled Calculator, designed and constructed by Howard Aiken in collaboration with IBM (see Reading 9.1), Leslie J. Comrie (see Readings 4.5 and 4.5) stated that this machine finally realized the dream of Charles Babbage (see Readings 6.1 and 6.2) to build a general purpose programmable computer. He suggested that Britain's failure to continue funding Babbage's calculating engines had cost her the leading place in the nineteenth century world of mechanical computing, and implied that this failure might have been responsible for Babbage's dream being first realized in the United States rather than England.

Though Aiken claimed that the Automatic Sequence Controlled Calculator, also known as the Harvard Mark I, was one hundred times as fast as a well-equipped human computer with an electric mechanical calculator, Comrie insisted in his review that the particular calculations that Aiken used for benchmarking could be done almost as fast by a human computer using a Brunsviga or a National mechanical calculator. He argued that in order to justify its existence the machine must be used to do calculations that were impossible with prior technology. [JMN]

The black mark earned by the government of the day more than a hundred years ago for its failure to see Charles Babbage's difference engine brought to a successful conclusion has still to be wiped out. It is not too much to say that it cost Britain the leading place in the art of mechanical computing. Babbage then conceived and worked on his "analytical engine", designed to store numbers and operate on them according to a sequence of processes conveyed to the machine by cards similar to those used in the Jacquard loom. This, however, was never completed.

The machine now described, "The Automatic Sequence Controlled Calculator", is a realisation of Babbage's project in principle, although its physical form has the benefit of twentieth century engineering and mass-production methods. Prof. Howard H. Aiken (also Commander, U.S.N.R.) of Harvard University inspired the International Business Machines Corporation (I.B.M.) to collaborate with him in constructing a new machine, largely composed of standard Hollerith counters, but with a superimposed and specially designed tape sequence control for directing the operations of the machine. The foremost I.B.M. engineers were assigned to the task; many of their new inventions are incorporated as basic units. When the machine was completed, Thomas J. Watson, on behalf of the Corporation, presented it to Harvard University—yet another token of the interest I.B.M. has shown in science. Would that this example were followed by their opposite numbers in Great Britain! One notes with astonishment, however, the significant omission of "I.B.M." in the title and in Prof. Aiken's preface, although President Conant's foreword carefully refers always to the "I.B.M. Automatic Sequence Controlled Calculator".

The machine contains seventy-two storage counters, each capable of holding twenty-three digits and a sign. For smaller numbers each counter can be split into two, while for larger numbers they can be teamed up. There are also sixty switch-set 24-figure registers, for holding constants; these likewise can be split. There are several special units, two being for multiplying and dividing; these first form nine multiples of the multiplicand or divisor. In multiplication the multiples directed by the multiplier are chosen and added step by step. In division the dividend or remainder is compared with the multiples in succession; that which is just less than the dividend is subtracted, and the appropriate figure of the quotient recorded. When working to the full 23-figure capacity of the machine, multiplication takes about six seconds, and division twice as long; additions and subtractions are done at the rate of three a second, whatever their length.

Three special units (which share many of the machine components) are for calculating logarithms, antilogarithms (or exponentials) and sines (or cosines). The process of calculating a 21-figure logarithm is a combination of the factor method and of the series $\log(1 + x) = M(x - x^2/2 + x^3/3 - x^4/4 \ldots)$. The machine first finds four factors, one each from the groups $2 \ldots 9$, $1.1 \ldots 1.9$, $1.01 \ldots 1.09$ and $1.001 \ldots 1.009$, the logarithms of which are specially stored. In the fifth factor x is less than 10^{-3}, so that six terms of the above series suffice, in the form

$$(((((-M/6x + M/5)x - M/4)x + M/3)x - M/2)x + M)x.$$

To find a number from its logarithm, if a, b, c are the first three digits of the mantissa, and d the remaining digits, we have a power of 10 (depending on the characteristic) multiplied by

$$10^{.1a} . 10^{.01b} . 10^{.001c} . 10^d$$

The first three of these factors are obtained from a store in the machine for the 27 values corresponding to a, b or $c = 1 \ldots 9$. The last is computed from

$$1 + D + D^2/2! + D^3/3! \; D^4/4! + \ldots \text{ where } D = d/M.$$

This unit is known as the exponential unit.

The sine unit first ascertains in which octant x (which must be in radians) lies. This determines the sign of the function, and instructs the machine whether to use the series for sin x or cos x for x less than $1/4\pi$. In the worst possible case, 11 terms suffice to give 23 decimals.

It will be seen that these three traits give access to all logarithmic, exponential, circular and hyperbolic functions without tables, although other functions can be entered via tapes or cards. Each logarithm, antilogarithm (or exponential) or sine, if to the full capacity of the machine, takes about a minute, which is comparable with the time required by a good computer to look up and interpolate a linear table with ten decimals only.

The brains of the machine lie in the control tape, which is code-punched in three sections. The first instructs the machine where to find its data; the second gives the destination of the data or answer; the third dictates the process. Very often these tapes, being simply a sequence of processes and independent of the actual figures used, as in the evaluation of integrals by quadrature, can be stored in a tape library, and used over and over again.

A problem that has been solved is that of conveying computed results to many users. Tables produced by the machine can be typed by an electromatic typewriter, with vertical and horizontal spaces as required. Reproduction by photolithography eliminates many fruitful sources of error and much drudgery, transcription, composition and proof-reading. Volume 2 of this series is such a table of Hankel functions of order one third, and other tables are in the press.

Prof. Aiken estimates that the calculator is nearly a hundred times as fast as a well-equipped manual computer; running twenty-four hours a day, as it does, it may do six months' work in a day. Perhaps his examples, chosen for their simplicity, do not do the machine justice, because they could be done almost as quickly, and certainly more economically, with a Brunsviga and a National.

The question naturally arises: Does the calculator open up new fields in numerical and mathematical analysis—especially in such pressing problems as the solution of ordinary and partial differential equations, and the solution of large numbers of simultaneous linear equations? It is disappointing to have to record

that the only output of the machine of which we are informed consists of tables of Bessel functions, which are not difficult (to the number of figures required in real life) by existing methods and equipment. If the machine is to justify its existence, it must be used to explore fields in which the numerical labour has so far been prohibitive.

A useful 65-page bibliography of numerical analysis will be welcomed by all interested in computation.

8.5

Remarks on the Realization of Large Memory Capacity

Julian H. Bigelow, James H. Pomerene, Ralph J. Slutz and Willis H. Ware

Excerpt from *Interim Progress Report on the Physical Realization of an Electronic Computing Instrument* (Princeton: Institute for Advanced Study, 1947), pp. 20–32.

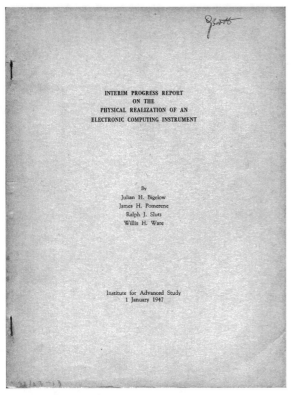

INTERIM PROGRESS REPORT
ON THE
PHYSICAL REALIZATION OF AN
ELECTRONIC COMPUTING INSTRUMENT

By
Julian H. Bigelow
James H. Pomerene
Ralph J. Slutz
Willis H. Ware

Institute for Advanced Study
1 January 1947

The first progress report on the design and construction of the Princeton IAS computer. This copy once belonged to computing pioneer A. D. Booth.

INTRODUCTORY NOTE TO READING 8.5

This excerpt is from the first in a series of progress reports describing the design and construction of the Princeton Institute for Advanced Studies (IAS) computer, written by the IAS electronic computer project engineering staff. The IAS computer owed its existence to the efforts of John von Neumann, who persuaded the Institute for Advanced Study to accept his Electronic Computing Project—a major departure from the IAS's traditional orientation toward theoretical science. Von Neumann obtained funding for the project from RCA, the Army Ordnance Department, and the Navy Office of Research (the military support was supplanted later in the project by funding from the Atomic Energy Commission). The project was headed by von Neumann and Herman Goldstine, with Arthur Burks serving as a part-time consultant and Julian Bigelow as chief engineer. About twenty engineers worked on the IAS computer from the project's inception in March 1946 until the machine's public dedication in June 1952.

The IAS computer was planned as a parallel machine—a reversal of von Neumann's earlier opinion, expressed in the *First Draft of a Report on the EDVAC* (see Reading 8.1), that any first machine should be serial in nature. The reason for this change was that RCA had convinced von Neumann that their Selectron digital electrostatic tube—then in the planning stages—could serve as the basis for a reliable parallel memory system. The Selectron tube turned out to be quite difficult to manufacture, and the IAS engineers ended up using the Williams tube memory system instead. The IAS machine's hardware was completed in January 1951, and it began running programs in the middle of that year, beginning with a long series of calculations connected with the design of the hydrogen bomb that supposedly took sixty continuous days of computer time. The machine was officially dedicated on June 10, 1952, and remained in operation until 1960, working primarily on problems in numerical mathematics, numerical meteorology, and engineering.

The IAS computer served as the model for a number of quaintly-named computers built during the 1950s: the Aberdeen Proving Ground's ORDVAC; the University of Illinois's ILLIAC; the Rand Corporation's JOHNNIAC (named after von Neumann); Los Alamos's MANIAC; the Argonne National Laboratory's AVIDAC, ORACLE, and GEORGE machines; and several others constructed both in the United States and abroad. The logical basis for its design—known as the "von Neumann architecture"—became an industry standard. For this anthology we decided to reproduce material relating to the Princeton group's research on electronic memory design—the central problem facing early builders of stored-program electronic digital computers.[JMN]

III.1 DISCUSSION OF PERFORMANCE CRITERIA

The most basic technological problem in the realization of the computing instrument is clearly the problem of large memory capacity. Considerable thought has been given this problem both by our group and others, no wholly satisfactory answer having materialized. It may be of passing interest to indicate the chief performance criteria and qualifications by which such a memory would be judged.

III.11 Information Storage per Unit Volume

This is the number of binary digits per cubic inch stored in the memory. Any device making possible about a million binary digits per cubic inch would certainly fill the need beautifully; in fact one tenth this density would suffice, since contained in a cabinet 8 feet × 8 feet × 1 foot would be about 10^{10} binary digits.

III.12 Inscription Speed Range

It would be desirable that this memory be capable of receiving binary digits at any speed no matter how low, and at high speeds up to perhaps 40 binary digits per microsecond: although a top speed of 1/100 this figure would be acceptable. (This goal is far in excess of that of M_2 as proposed in Section VI.1, which is capable of about one 40 binary digit word per thousand microseconds.)

III.13 Reproduction Speed Range

The memory should be capable of supplying information to a teletype at perhaps 40 binary digits per second, and of transferring into various electrical components at the same maximum speeds as inscription (III.12).

III.14 Accessibility

This is an extremely important attribute for a memory to possess, and implies that the entire memory be anywhere immediately inscribable and reproducable upon demand. It is this ability which makes the Selectron memory (M_1) desirable and not replaceable without some sacrifice by the serially accessible magnetic ribbon memory (M_2). However, by subdivision, a serial memory may be made to approximate an immediately accessible memory. (See III.34)

III.15 Verifiability

This implies that it should be possible to read the memory without clearing it, so that checking systems can be developed. It is a very desirable property of any memory in which failure of type A or B (II.63) may occur. (See Sec. VII.2–VII.23)

III.16 Erasability

This is an important attribute of a satisfactory memory, particularly where iterative routines involving partial substitutions are to occur. Both magnetic ribbon and Selectron memories have this property; photographic film does not.

III.17 Permanence

Eventually it is expected that a library of calculations, tabulated functions, procedures, etc. will have been accumulated by use of the machine; it is desirable that these be on some permanent record having a life of months or years. Magnetic wire seems to fill this need well, and any otherwise satisfactory memory could be unloaded onto wire to fill this need.

III.18 Durability

The memory should be capable of many millions of operations; or should be easily and quickly reproduced, in case of wear or deterioration.

III.19 Convenience and Economy

Certain schemes for realizing large storage capacity require processing between the inscription and reproduction operations; chief among these are photographic techniques. This is a considerable disadvantage, since the memory cannot then be erased nor can it be immediately re-read as required in many iterative techniques. Further, intervening processes of chemical variety are certain to prove a great inconvenience in the procedure of operating the machine. It would seem that the only feasible sort of non-erasable memory would be one immediately reproducible and on a medium cheap enough to be consumed and discarded in large quantities, so that the operation of reading and re-writing can replace erasure. Even then, the quantity of medium consumed in most lengthy problems would render the accessibility (cf. III.14) of the memory unacceptably slow.

III.2 MEDIA AND ENERGY STORAGE

Broadly speaking, any physical medium is potentially suitable for memory if it can be quickly and locally modified in a detectable way, and can thereafter be scanned. The local modification can be of a physical sort, as in the case of embossing a plastic, or in the nature of energy storage such as local thermal, electromagnetic or electrostatic charge. Various schemes were considered; for example, mechanically embossing wax cylinders, as in a Dictaphone, is a possibility. Such rolls are approximately ten inches circumference and six inches long; they could be embossed at about 100 digits to the inch at perhaps a five kilocycle repetition rate. If the tracking pitch were .010 inch this would produce a capacity of about half a million binary digits in each roll, serially scannable and immediately reproducible. The plastic nature of the wax might make erasure possible, and the cost of the medium is certainly low since by facing off the surface, each cylinder may be re-used about a hundred times. However, several disadvantages remain: The embossed cylinder cannot be re-read many times without deterioration, and also the material is sensitive to accidental impressions, and (it is thought) likely to contain a statistically significant number of local mechanical defects producing false signals.

Also considered were schemes involving local energy storage on areas of some material, such as local charge on sheets of dielectric; local magnetization of surface areas; local temperature on chalk or other suitable surfaces, etc. Such schemes become feasible if suitable inscribing and scanning means can be developed. Electron streams can be used to charge, read and revive capacitive systems; this is essentially the technique of the Selectron and has the advantage of high-speed non-serial scan without use of moving parts. Similarly, electron streams could be used to detect local magnetic charge on surfaces, but are not suitable for inscribing, which requires heavy currents and implies electromagnetic devices. The combination of electronic detection with requirements as to vacuum, plus the electromagnetic recording requirement does not suggest any practical combination of these two; so that the only alternative is both recording and detecting by (moving) electromagnetic means; this is essentially what is used in M_2 to be discussed in detail below. Regarding the possibilities of thermal storage, no careful studies have been made; the suggestion results merely from the fact that heat may be deposited and detected by essentially optical means. Techniques of this variety may also be developed using fluorescence; this avenue is being explored by Eastman Kodak Company.

If schemes for developing non-erasable memory are to be given serious consideration it would seem worthwhile to investigate less elegant media than photographic film. That is, photographic film is capable of all tones of light sensitivity from black to transparent; this is unnecessary if binary digits are to be recorded, and simpler "binary" chemistry could be used. For example, enough photo or electrical energy will turn white paper black by charring; a more practical example is ordinary radio-facsimile paper which changes from white to black by passage of a slight electric current. Conceivably something of this sort could be made fast enough and cheap enough to be reproduced and discarded rather than erased; however, no efforts have been made to explore this possibility.

III.21 Energy Level; Fundamental Role of Non-Linearity

For many practical reasons the most desirable memory medium would be one having two stable states at low energy level; this would lend itself to recording without excessive power amplification, and to reading with minimum risk of indecision due to the occurrence of borderline values. Experimentally it may be observed that the existence of two stable states in a given medium is usually evidenced by non-linearity in the susceptibility of the medium to recording stimulus; media evidencing such non-linearity being often stable for long periods of time, while those not evidencing non-linearity often tend to one or the other "normal" state. This is particularly true of magnetic media.

III.22 Memory transfer; Amplification

In addition to the ability to "hold" and "clear" all memories must be able to transfer and receive information. Consider the problem of transferring from one memory cell to another; clearly this can be accomplished only with less of energy, and some means of amplification must exist. Such amplification may actually be a buffer stage between cells, or it may be accomplished by de-stabilizing the recipient cell relative to the transmitting cell. This last technique has the advantage that it can often be done by a single device to a whole bank of cells which are to be simultaneously transferred, so that a multiplicity of individual amplifiers may be avoided (see X.5 and X.6). This technique can nearly always be made effective if the medium is sufficiently non-linear; never if it is strictly linear.

III.23 Sensitivity Ratio Criteria

The time-stability of an energy-storing medium could therefore be expressed as the ratio of the energy necessary to erase a digit to that necessary to record the digit; and this ratio may, of course, fall off with time. These values are measured at the same terminals; in the case of elements combining two stable states in each cell with amplification in that cell there are clearly two such ratios, one at the input and one at the output end. In such a case the ratio of input energy to the output energy at any time gives something in the nature of a transfer sensitivity.

III.3 CELLULAR AND CONTINUOUS MEDIA

Certain technical points connected with the realization of large memory capacity do not depend on the particular medium used, but are rather more fundamental. In attempting to realize large capacity the urge is to avoid fabricating individual cells having individual connections and instead to use mass-produced cellular or even continuous media having cells defined by the recording process. This raises problems of scanning and of registration.

III.31 Problem of Scanning

All methods of seeking information located in a medium appear reducible to two; switching and traversing or "scanning"; occasionally combinations of these are used. Switching implies connector leads corresponding to each cell; scanning implies hunting by relative motion of a ray or some physical device.

In order that a switching system have capacity enough to make possible the identification of individual cells in a memory of 10^{10}, without involving an unmanageable number of leads, it is essential that the combinational possibilities of the leads be used. If this be done, memory capacity can grow factorially relative to the number of connectors, and there is some hope that the switching problem could be handled.

The technique of scanning implies switching by relative motion of some sort; about the only non-mechanical way of doing this is to use deflected electron beams either directly on the geometry of the medium, which is to say as an electronic switch; or the electronic beam may be used to produce fluorescence, affording an optical scanner. Either of these two schemes can be made extremely rapid compared to methods involving the motion of structural parts. Light may be used to some advantage to magnify mechanical motion; as by rotating mirrors or prisms; the oil damped Duddel galvanometer, for example, can traverse ten inches with a small spot of light in about one tenth millisecond and is reproducible in deflection to about 1/2 percent.

III.32 Problem of Registration

Associated with the means for relative scanning motion must be some system of registration, or of identifying cell areas in the medium. This may conceivably be accomplished more simply than by the construction of sets of leads together with a switch; for example, it may be realized by a single cartesian grill over which the scanner travels, counting the bars to locate cells. In this case the identifying wires could be replaced by a grill and a single lead wire, together with a counter. If a further assumption can be made — that the deflection of the scanning ray is reproducible (not necessarily linear), than a further simplification can be made; the grill can be replaced by remotely situated reference scales, such as stepped voltage dividers, one corresponding to each coordinate of the medium.

III.33 Three-Dimensional Continuous Media

Although the efficiency of a storing medium is properly expressed volumetrically, no essentially three-dimensional practical storage medium has been disclosed. The capacity of various filaments and sheets can be expressed in one or two coordinates, as next described.

III.34 Two-Dimensional Continuous Media

Among those considered were paper sheets coated with powdered magnetic material, formed into cylinders and scanned by rotation; spiral tracks of magnetic wire wound on cylinders and scanned by rotation; optically sensitive sheets scanned by light spots from prisms or mirrors, or electron beam spots, etc. A representative scheme of this sort, and one which may require further investigation is the following: Consider a cylinder about 3 inches in diameter and 10 inches long; its circumference is 10 inches and if a wire capable of holding 100 binary digits to the linear inch were wound in a groove of .010 pitch this would give a total memory capacity of 10^6 binary digits. If this were rotated at 6000 RPM (it certainly could be rotated at many times this speed) each turn would require 10 milliseconds, which would be the longest waiting time for any digit. The average wait would be 5 milliseconds and by increasing speed and/or using several sensing stations this could certainly be reduced to 1 millisecond. The digit rate would be about 10^5 per second.

III.35 One-Dimensional Continuous Media

Under this heading come storage-delay devices such as transmission lines, acoustic tanks, etc., also various magnetic ribbons, perforated tapes, films, etc. Of these, the magnetic ribbons appear to us to offer far greater potentialities than any of the others toward realization of large digit capacity, and in addition are simple, erasable, immediately reproducible, free from temperature coefficients, chemical processes, etc. Accordingly, our main experimental effort was in this direction, and in what follows all references to serially scanned storage media imply this type.

III.4 VARIOUS "MAGNETIC RIBBONS"

Since about five years before the war, and particularly during the last few years, various magnetic ribbons for speech and music recording have been developed. Among these are wires of ferrous and magnetic alloy types, flat tapes formed by rolling such wires, evaporated metallic layers on plastic threads and ribbons, and paper and plastic tapes coated with powdered ferrous alloys, of colloidal grain-size. Various claims are advanced for these ribbons, primarily centered on their performance in reproducing speech and music. Essential to such performance is the property of amplitude linearity, or at least something in the nature of amplitude proportionality, and much effort and ingenuity has been applied toward accentuating this property.

It is clear that for the recording of binary information this property is not essential; in fact is very undesirable. The ideal observed response curve for binary recording would be (as already indicated) sharply S-shaped having little or no response over a certain region, then a very short transition to a "saturated" or completely activated state. Certain of the magnetic ribbons do in fact have this sort of response, of which full advantage will be taken in the final design of the memory component.

III.41 Performance Criteria; Head Design, orientation, amplification

The "best" magnetic recording ribbon for M_2 will be determined by a combination of properties rather than by any single virtue, including those listed in Section III (III.1–III.19). It is very difficult experimentally to separate the performance of the ribbon in these respects from that of the recording head, and most of our measurements represent their joint performance. It is quite possible that the rank of the ribbon samples reported in our tests would be affected by a change in head design, but it is unlikely that a radically different ranking would result.

There is also the question of head orientation relative to the medium; various experimenters (particularly the flat tape advocates) recommended transverse or crosswise magnetic orientation as opposed to the longitudinal arrangement used in our tests. We have no knowledge as to the merits of these schemes for binary recording, and intend to investigate them at some later date.

Again there is the question of reproduced signal voltage; this is certainly greatly affected by head design, so that the required amplification will be affected by this factor. It is believed that considerable improvement can be made; by merely re-winding the pick-up coil; a gain of five to ten-fold may easily be possible.

III.42 Density of Information

One of the most important figures of merit is the maximum linear density with which information can be packed on the ribbon or wire without (1) interference by adjacent pulses in such a way that the signal level of a given pulse is appreciably affected by the presence and polarity of its neighbors, and (2) reducing the signal level to the vicinity of the noise level. This figure, together with the cross-sectional dimensions of the sample, determine its volumetric storage capacity.

III.43 Positive and Negative Sequences; Signal Integration

As indicated elsewhere in this report (VII.2–VII.28) it is desirable for checking and other reasons to avoid using the absence of signal as representing anything except failure; in particular, it is desirable to represent both 1 and 0 by voltages, of opposite sign. Hence the magnetic medium will be inscribed with both positive-sequence and negative-sequence magnetic pulses, and when reproduced by motion relative to an electro-magnetic pickup, this by differentiation will produce pairs of voltage pulses, +− for one recording polarity and −+ for the opposite. These voltage outputs could be distinguished by any (or a combination) of four reading methods: 1) By rectifying and excluding either the first or second pulse; 2) By a rectifying and adding switch whereby the second pulse is changed in sign and added to the first (or vice versa); 3) By differentiation; relying upon the observed fact that the rate of voltage change is greater between pairs of voltage pulses than the initial or final slope; 4) By simply integrating with respect to time, so that the summation of area of the first pulse is cancelled by the summation of the second. Scheme 3) requires further investigation to determine whether it may increase the usable pulse density on the medium; scheme 4) is the simplest and since it appears to have a favorable effect upon the signal-to-noise ratio, will probably be adopted.

III.44 Inscription Speed Range

It is essential that the magnetic ribbon be capable of inscription at relatively high speeds, so that the Selectron memory (M_1) can be emptied in very short time; also that the medium be capable of inscription at very low (typewriter) speeds; further, the play-back voltage of signal inscribed at either of these two extremes should be essentially the same at high reproduction rates, such that a single reading unit can read (without adjustment or prejudiced reliability) data of either sort. This point requires particular attention, and may in itself (there are other advantages) justify the use of some type of high speed rotating recording and reading head to be associated with the keyboard transcribing operation (see VII.4–VII.44).

III.45 Reproduction Speed Range

As in the case of inscription, and for essentially the same reasons, reproduction must be possible at speeds from those corresponding to a keyboard to perhaps

1000 times this rate, and the same techniques should be applicable (see VII.4–VII.44).

III.46 Durability and Wear

It may be anticipated that in relatively long problems involving many sub-routines reversals, read-backs and substitutions (local erasure and re-recording) may occur hundreds of times; and that furthermore several miles of record may pass over a given recording or reading station. This must clearly be possible without appreciable mechanical wear and danger of mechanical failure, and also without alteration of the magnetic properties of the medium, or serious reduction in signal-to-noise ratio. If, in addition to the hazards of this sort resulting from mechanically moving the medium from one storage spool to another over various pulleys and sliding over the recording head, there is the added factor of a rotating head acting while the wire is stationary, the question of durability and wear will require very careful attention in design.

III.47 Retentivity

This is a specific property of the magnetic medium, indicating the stable level to which the magnetization fall upon removal of the recording excitation. A high value of retentivity is desirable since the reading voltage will thereby be increased and consequently the need for amplification decreased. However, high retentivity is not desirable at the expense of other properties, for example coercive force, and of S-shaped magnetization curve in the vicinity of the origin.

III.48 Coercive Force

This is the energy (per pulse) necessary to cause erasure (or reversal of the polarity) of a signal; a high value of this parameter is desirable since it implies a very stable recording medium in the sense of III.25. This property is practically the most important in that it tends to suppress background noise, the risk of accidental transfer between turns on a spool (shadow printing) and the accidental loss of signal level. However, the happy circumstance is that many wires combine high coercive force with high retentivity, and furthermore possess the desired S-shaped curve, although their availability in quantity is in some cases not yet assured (see V.1–V.13). Many of the media optimizing these properties do so at the expense of very special alloys, heat-treating and cold-working techniques, the result being frangible and less durable than the more usual alloys.

Benchmarking the Earliest Electro-Mechanical and Electronic Computers

Edmund C. Berkeley

Extract from *Giant Brains or Machines that Think* (New York: John Wiley & Sons; London: Chapman & Hall, 1949), pp. 109, 126.

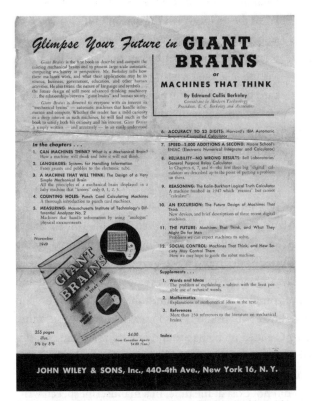

Advertising flyer for Berkeley's *Giant Brains*, laid into his personal copy of the first edition.

In a discussion with Maurice V. Wilkes, designer of the Cambridge EDSAC, and pioneer in software, I learned how difficult it was to benchmark the performance of the earliest electronic computers. Since none of the earliest machines remains operational, any comparison of processing speeds must remain anecdotal. Perhaps the best accessible comparison of the speed of Howard Aiken's electromechanical Harvard Mark I with the world's first electronic computer—Eckert and Mauchly's ENIAC, which used vacuum tubes as switches—comes from Edmund Berkeley's *Giant Brains or Machines that Think* (1949). This was the first book on electronic computers written for a general audience, and it remains a useful non-technical explanation of how the earliest machines worked.

The basic data processing unit in the Harvard Mark I was the relay. Relays were automatic electric switches that turned circuits on and off. The fastest relay available during the 1940s could turn on and off (switch from 0 to 1) in about 1/100 of a second. According to Berkeley, processing speed of the Harvard Mark I could be measured as follows:

The time required in the machine for adding, subtracting, transferring, or clearing numbers is 3/10 of a second. This is the time of one machine cycle or reading one coding line. Multiplication takes at the most 6 seconds, and an average of 4 seconds. Division takes at the most 16 seconds, and an average of 11 seconds. Each, however, requires only 3 lines of coding, or 9/10 of a second's attention from the sequence mechanism; interposed operations fill the rest of the time. To calculate a logarithm, an exponential, or a sine to the full number of digits obtainable by means of the automatic subroutine takes at the most 90, 66, and 60 seconds respectively. To get three 24 digit numbers from feeding a punch card takes 1/3 second. To punch a number takes from 1/2 second up to 3 seconds. To print a number takes from 1 1/2 seconds up to 7 seconds.[1]

The dust jacket for Berkeley's *Giant Brains* (1949), printed in black ink on a bright yellow background.

Later in the same work, Berkeley provided similar numbers for the ENIAC:

> Eniac adds or subtracts very swiftly at the rate of 5000 a second. Eniac multiplies at the rate of 360 to 500 a second. Division, however, is slow, relatively; the rate is about 50 a second. Reading numbers from punched cards, 12 a second for 10-digit numbers, is even slower. As a result of these rates, you find, when you put a problem on Eniac, that one division delays you as long as 100 additions or 8 multiplications. Division might have been speeded up somewhat by (1) rapidly convergent approximation . . . to the reciprocal of the divisor and (2) multiplying by the dividend; this might have taken 5 or 6 multiplication times instead of 8. Also, the use of a standard IBM punch-card feed and card punch slows the machine greatly. One way to overcome this drawback might be to install one or two additional sets of such equipment, which increase input and output speed.[2]

A fundamental difference between Eckert and Mauchly's ENIAC, sponsored by the United States Army, and Aiken's Harvard Mark I, sponsored by the United States Navy, was that the ENIAC used eighteen thousand vacuum tubes for processing data, employing relays only in several registers associated with input and output equipment. Fulfilling the same purpose as the more complex relay, a vacuum tube could switch on and off, from 0 to 1, in about one millionth of a second, or roughly ten thousand times faster than a relay. But other complicated factors slowed the machine down, so that ENIAC ended up being around one thousand times faster than the electromechanical Harvard Mark I. For three or four years the ENIAC was the world's only electronic computer. It was initially used for classified computation of problems relating to nuclear weapons. We might consider it the world's first supercomputer, though the concept did not exist at the time. In a manuscript speech written in 1970 Pres Eckert, co-inventor of the ENIAC, stated that the Harvard Mark I was "over 100 times faster than an unaided man in doing arithmetic, but it was electro-mechanical. It could have led to relay machines 100 times faster than itself or 10,000 times faster than man. However, Mauchly and I decided to leapfrog such developments and to build a self-operating machine to be called ENIAC. It was 1000 times the speed of Mark I or 100,000 times the speed of man."[3] [JMN]

---

1   Edmund Berkeley, *Giant Brains or Machines that Think* (New York: John Wiley & Sons; London: Chapman & Hall, 1949), 109.

2   Berkeley, *op. cit.*, 126.

3   Quoted in Diana H. Hook and Jeremy M. Norman, *Origins of Cyberspace: A Library on the History of Computing, Networking and Telecommunications* (Novato, CA: historyofscience.com, 2002), 625.

Whirlwind I: A High-Speed Electronic Digital Computer

Digital Computer Laboratory, Massachusetts Institute of Technology

INTRODUCTORY NOTE TO READING 8.7:

Jay Forrester, the head of MIT's Whirlwind Computer Project, received his B.S. in engineering from the University of Nebraska in 1939 and his master's degree in science from MIT in 1945. In 1940, the year after Hitler's invasion of Poland, he joined MIT's new Servomechanisms Laboratory, founded that year in response to the increased technical demands of a world at war. The laboratory specialized in the development of feedback circuits, mechanical and electrical analog devices, and powerful servomechanisms responsive to remote control. In his six years there, Forrester attained extensive familiarity with these machines, as well as with associated problems of integrated system design and development.

In late 1944 the United States Navy asked the Servomechanisms Laboratory to develop an analog flight simulation system, dubbed the Aircraft Stability and Control Analyzer (ASCA). The project was assigned to Forrester, who spent a year on the problem before determining that the available analog techniques were too slow to function as control devices for a real-time flight simulator. In January 1946, acting on a suggestion made by fellow graduate student Perry O. Crawford, Forrester proposed using digital computer technology to solve the real-time speed problem—this may have been the first time that digital techniques were chosen to implement a major control function. Forrester's proposal was accepted by the Navy's Office of Research and Inventions, and the project was given the name "Whirlwind."

During the next few years Forrester and his team designed and began constructing the Whirlwind I, a parallel machine with sixteen-bit word length and an electrostatic memory, using a special variant of the Williams tube. In 1948 the flight-simulator portion of the Whirlwind Project was dropped, the navy deciding instead to concentrate on producing a general-purpose digital computer. By 1949 the Whirlwind Project had become too expensive for the Navy to fund, and the project was taken over by the United States Air Force, which was in urgent need of a digital computer to manage its air-defense system. For this new project, the Whirlwind was outfitted with a cathode-ray-tube (CRT) display screen, a light pen for selecting display elements, and a magnetic drum for recording and storing data from radar installations. This was the first computer with a graphical display. To meet the air defense system's need for high-speed main memory, and to eliminate the maintenance difficulties and high cost associated with electrostatic tubes, Forrester and his team began to work on developing a three-dimensional, random-access, magnetic-core storage unit to replace the Whirlwind's CRT memory. The Whirlwind's magnetic-core memory, installed in 1953, represented "a fundamental turning point in the development of computer architectures. With the replacement of the electrostatic memory by Forrester's magnetic cores in 1952 [*sic*], the reliability of the machine reached such a high standard that it was possible to consider using it for actual air traffic control, and the basic speed of the machine had increased to reach its original design of 50,000 operations per second."[1]

The Whirlwind Project was responsible for many advances in computer technology. Apart from its magnetic-core memory, the Whirlwind I also featured self-checking procedures, sophisticated visual display facilities, feedback control loops, and techniques for sending digital data over telephone lines. "Last, and of profound influence upon subsequent computer design, was the working out for Whirlwind of the intricate systemic details of 'synchronous parallel logic'—that is, the transmitting of electronic pulses, or digits, simultaneously within the computer rather than sequentially, while maintaining logical coherence and control. This feature accelerated enormously (compared to other computers of that day) the speeds with which the computer could process its information."[2]

The brochure on the Whirlwind I, which we reproduce in its entirety, was published in 1951, shortly after the machine became fully operational. It is one of the earliest brochures published for the general public about an electronic computer. [JMN]

---

1 Williams, *A History of Computing Technology* (Englewood Cliffs, N. J.: Prentice-Hall, 1985), 386.

2 Kent C. Redmond and Thomas M. Smith, *Project Whirlwind: The History of a Pioneer Computer* (Bedford, Mass.: Digital Press, 1980), 217.

Whirlwind 1

A HIGH-SPEED ELECTRONIC DIGITAL COMPUTER

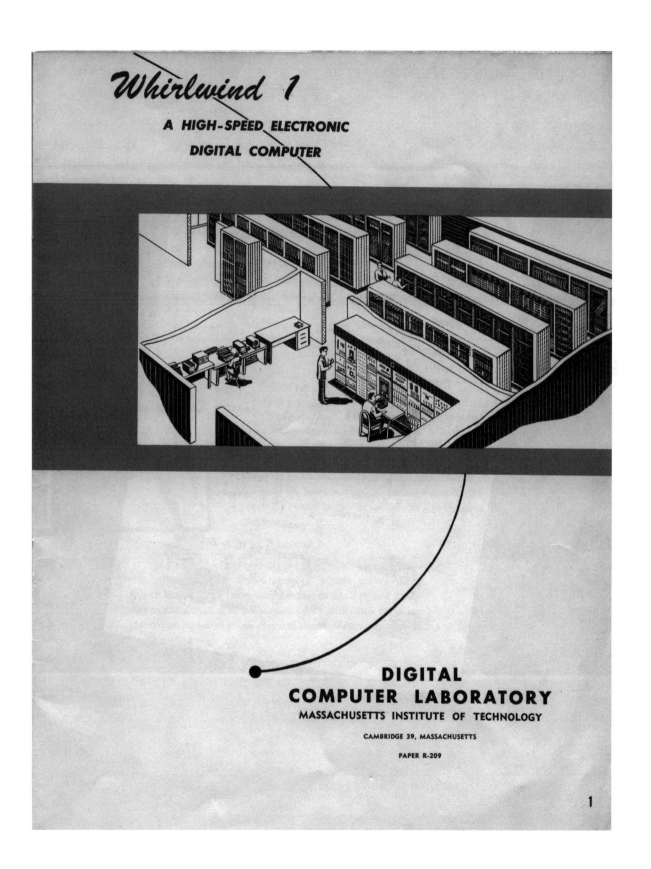

**DIGITAL
COMPUTER LABORATORY**
MASSACHUSETTS INSTITUTE OF TECHNOLOGY

CAMBRIDGE 39, MASSACHUSETTS

PAPER R-209

1

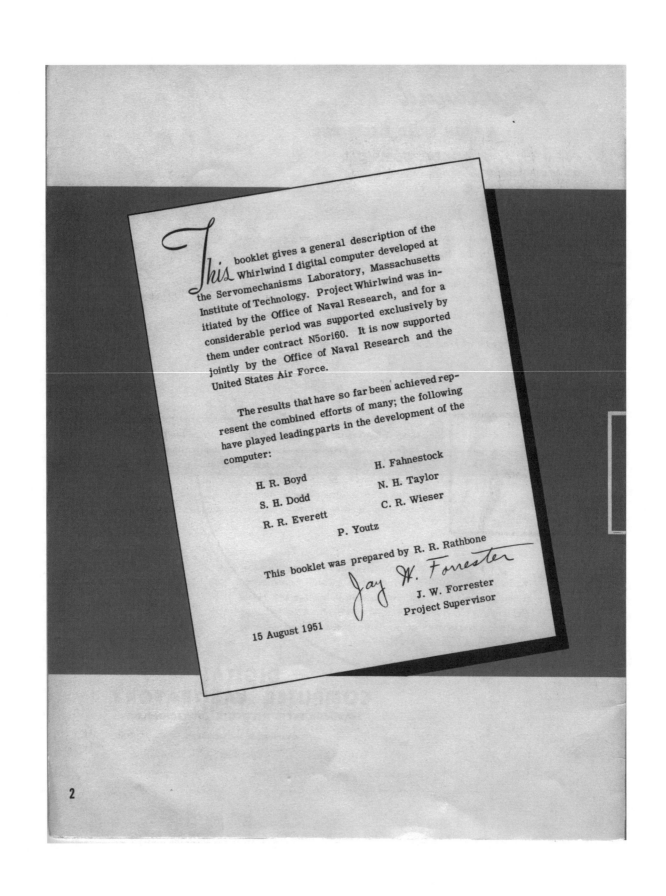

This booklet gives a general description of the Whirlwind I digital computer developed at the Servomechanisms Laboratory, Massachusetts Institute of Technology. Project Whirlwind was initiated by the Office of Naval Research, and for a considerable period was supported exclusively by them under contract N5ori60. It is now supported jointly by the Office of Naval Research and the United States Air Force.

The results that have so far been achieved represent the combined efforts of many; the following have played leading parts in the development of the computer:

H. R. Boyd   H. Fahnestock

S. H. Dodd   N. H. Taylor

R. R. Everett   C. R. Wieser

P. Youtz

This booklet was prepared by R. R. Rathbone

Jay W. Forrester

J. W. Forrester
Project Supervisor

15 August 1951

2

Computing Devices

$\mathcal{A}$ digital computer counts. Only discrete quantities are used by the machine during a computation, and these are represented numerically. For example, the abacus is a simple digital device on which calculations are performed by sliding counters along digit rods. The precision of a digital computer is determined by the number of digits in the machine (in the case of the abacus, the number of rods and counters), and may be increased by the addition of more digits.

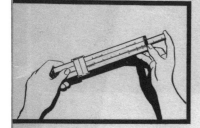

$\mathcal{I}$n contrast, an analog computer measures; the quantities it uses are continuous. For example, the slide rule, an analog device, provides continuous mathematical measurements. The precision of any particular analog computer, however, has a definite upper limit, determined by the precision of its fabricated parts, and once this limit is reached, precision cannot be increased without a redesign of the whole machine.

$\mathcal{M}$odern electronic digital computers operate automatically. Usually, high-frequency pulses travel along transmission lines from one element to another and cause electronic circuits to be turned on or off. The resulting electronic states of these circuits represent the numbers in the problem.

3

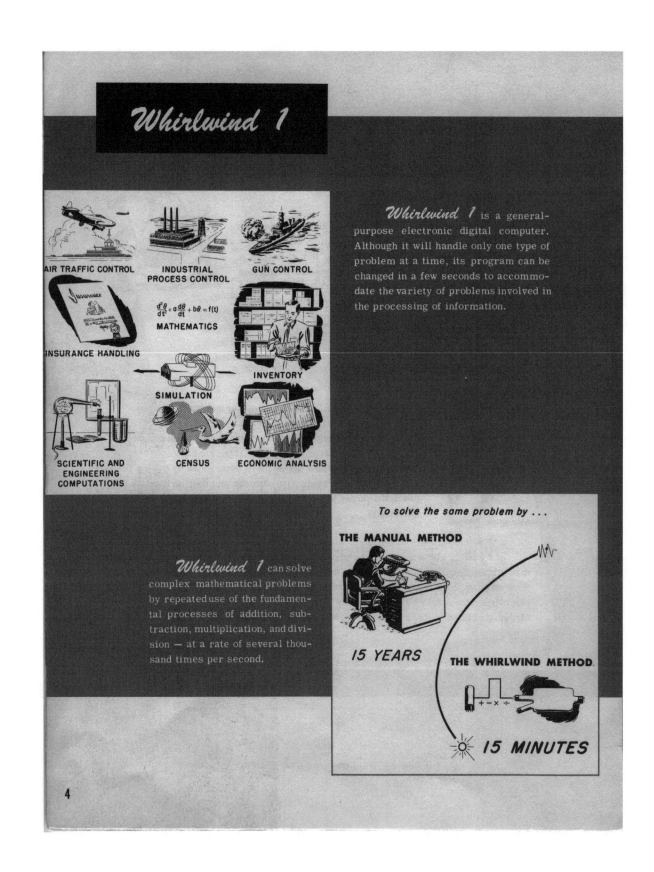

Whirlwind 1

AIR TRAFFIC CONTROL

INDUSTRIAL PROCESS CONTROL

GUN CONTROL

INSURANCE HANDLING

$$\frac{d^2\theta}{dt^2} + a\frac{d\theta}{dt} + b\theta = f(t)$$

MATHEMATICS

INVENTORY

SIMULATION

SCIENTIFIC AND ENGINEERING COMPUTATIONS

CENSUS

ECONOMIC ANALYSIS

Whirlwind 1 is a general-purpose electronic digital computer. Although it will handle only one type of problem at a time, its program can be changed in a few seconds to accommodate the variety of problems involved in the processing of information.

Whirlwind 1 can solve complex mathematical problems by repeated use of the fundamental processes of addition, subtraction, multiplication, and division — at a rate of several thousand times per second.

To solve the same problem by ...

THE MANUAL METHOD

15 YEARS

THE WHIRLWIND METHOD

15 MINUTES

4

Whirlwind 1

is a parallel computer...

In a *PARALLEL* computer, all the digits of a number are stored, selected, and operated on *SIMULTANEOUSLY*

In a *SERIAL* computer, the digits of a number are stored, selected, and operated on *SEQUENTIALLY*

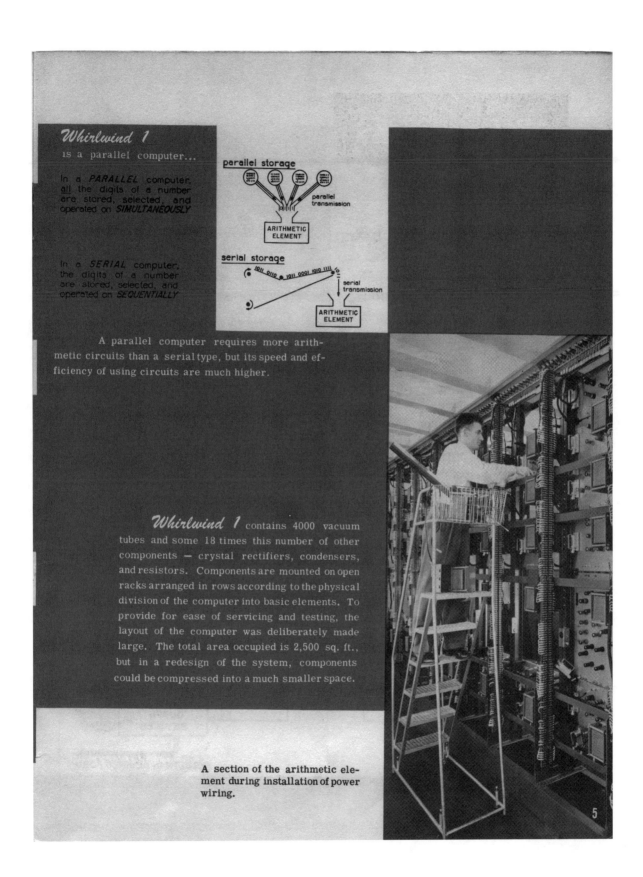

parallel storage

parallel transmission

ARITHMETIC ELEMENT

serial storage

serial transmission

ARITHMETIC ELEMENT

A parallel computer requires more arithmetic circuits than a serial type, but its speed and efficiency of using circuits are much higher.

Whirlwind 1 contains 4000 vacuum tubes and some 18 times this number of other components — crystal rectifiers, condensers, and resistors. Components are mounted on open racks arranged in rows according to the physical division of the computer into basic elements. To provide for ease of servicing and testing, the layout of the computer was deliberately made large. The total area occupied is 2,500 sq. ft., but in a redesign of the system, components could be compressed into a much smaller space.

A section of the arithmetic element during installation of power wiring.

5

Basic Elements of Whirlwind 1

Every computing system has certain basic elements. In the manual system portrayed below, these elements are the messenger who brings in the problem, the operator, the notebook in which he enters incoming data and records answers, the calculating machine, and the messenger who takes the results.

In the WHIRLWIND I system, the operator becomes CONTROL; the desk calculator, the ARITHMETIC ELEMENT; the notebook, STORAGE; and the messengers, the INPUT and OUTPUT devices.

COMPARISON BETWEEN...

MANUAL COMPUTATION

INCOMING PROBLEM

OPERATOR

OUTGOING RESULTS

AND

Whirlwind 1 COMPUTATION

STORAGE	CONTROL	ARITHMETIC ELEMENT

INPUT DEVICES

OUTPUT DEVICES

PROBLEMS TO BE DONE

RESULTS IN DESIRED FORM

6

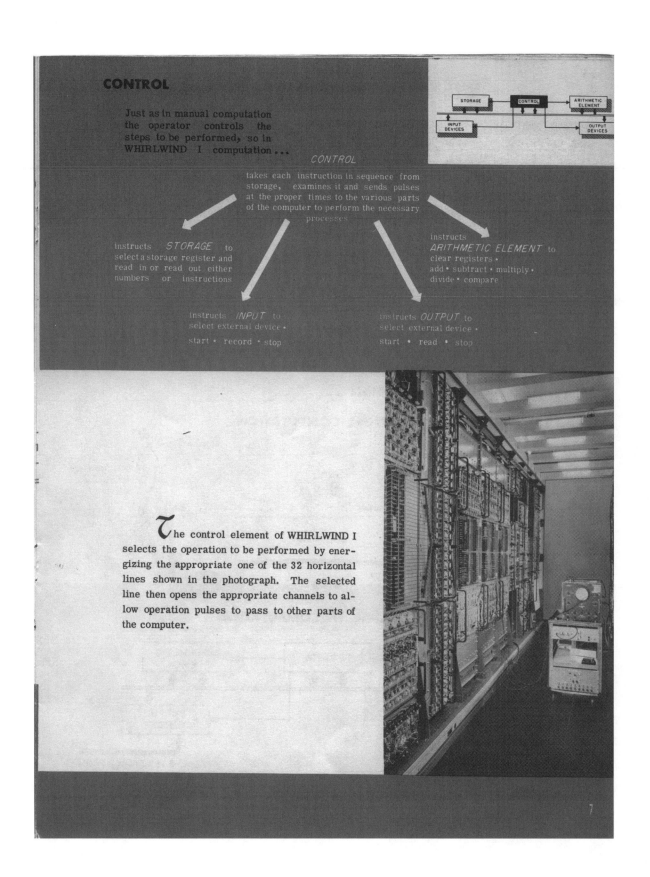

CONTROL

Just as in manual computation the operator controls the steps to be performed, so in WHIRLWIND I computation...

CONTROL

takes each instruction in sequence from storage, examines it and sends pulses at the proper times to the various parts of the computer to perform the necessary processes

instructs *STORAGE* to select a storage register and read in or read out either numbers or instructions

instructs *INPUT* to select external device • start • record • stop

instructs *ARITHMETIC ELEMENT* to clear registers • add • subtract • multiply • divide • compare

instructs *OUTPUT* to select external device • start • read • stop

The control element of WHIRLWIND I selects the operation to be performed by energizing the appropriate one of the 32 horizontal lines shown in the photograph. The selected line then opens the appropriate channels to allow operation pulses to pass to other parts of the computer.

ARITHMETIC ELEMENT
Digits 8 through 15.

THE COMPUTER PROPER
First row, Input-Output; second row,
Electrostatic Storage; third row, Arithmetic
Element; fourth row, Control.

8

TEST CONTROL

A test center which provides facilities for monitoring computations, determining sources of trouble, and coordinating maintenance procedures.

The computer proper may be seen at the left.

9

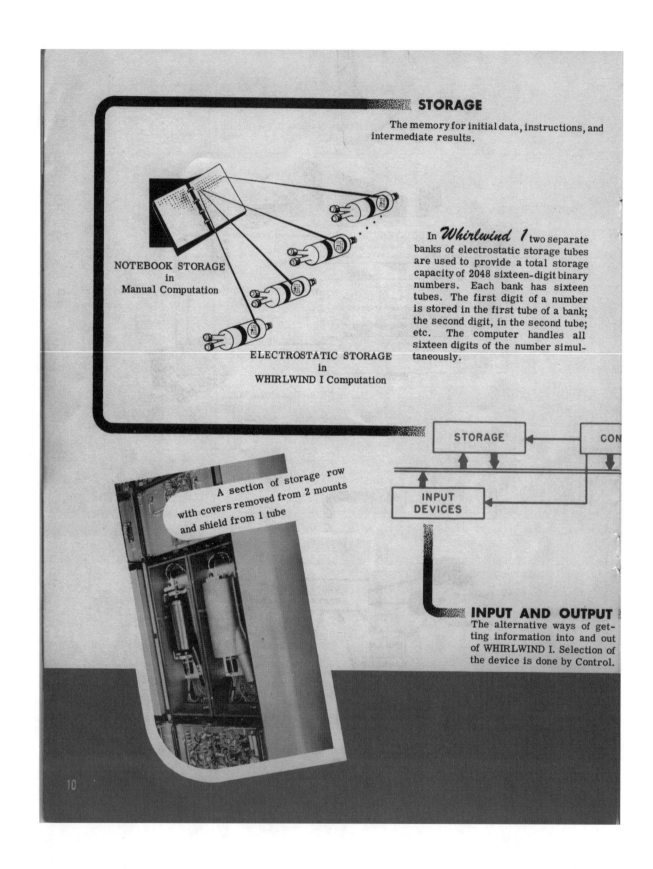

STORAGE

The memory for initial data, instructions, and intermediate results.

NOTEBOOK STORAGE
in
Manual Computation

ELECTROSTATIC STORAGE
in
WHIRLWIND I Computation

In *Whirlwind 1* two separate banks of electrostatic storage tubes are used to provide a total storage capacity of 2048 sixteen-digit binary numbers. Each bank has sixteen tubes. The first digit of a number is stored in the first tube of a bank; the second digit, in the second tube; etc. The computer handles all sixteen digits of the number simultaneously.

A section of storage row with covers removed from 2 mounts and shield from 1 tube

STORAGE

CON

INPUT
DEVICES

INPUT AND OUTPUT

The alternative ways of getting information into and out of WHIRLWIND I. Selection of the device is done by Control.

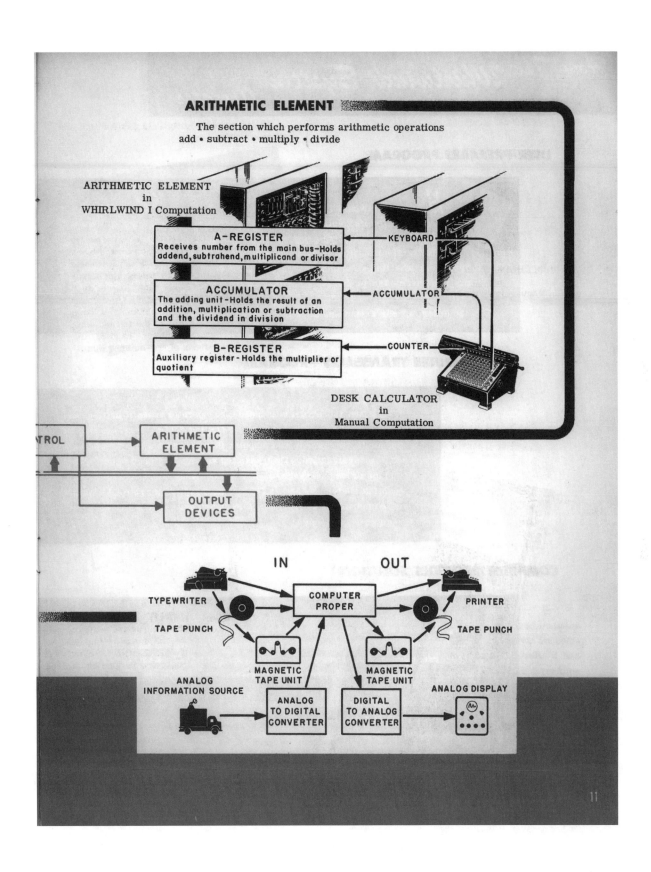

ARITHMETIC ELEMENT

The section which performs arithmetic operations
add • subtract • multiply • divide

ARITHMETIC ELEMENT
in
WHIRLWIND I Computation

A–REGISTER
Receives number from the main bus–Holds
addend, subtrahend, multiplicand or divisor

KEYBOARD

ACCUMULATOR
The adding unit–Holds the result of an
addition, multiplication or subtraction
and the dividend in division

ACCUMULATOR

B–REGISTER
Auxiliary register–Holds the multiplier or
quotient

COUNTER

DESK CALCULATOR
in
Manual Computation

...TROL

ARITHMETIC
ELEMENT

OUTPUT
DEVICES

IN   OUT

TYPEWRITER

TAPE PUNCH

COMPUTER
PROPER

PRINTER

TAPE PUNCH

ANALOG
INFORMATION SOURCE

MAGNETIC
TAPE UNIT

MAGNETIC
TAPE UNIT

ANALOG DISPLAY

ANALOG
TO DIGITAL
CONVERTER

DIGITAL
TO ANALOG
CONVERTER

USER PREPARES PROGRAM

Before Whirlwind I can solve a problem, the user must break down the general processes for its solution into steps which the machine can handle. These steps must then be coded into a program as instructions and numbers.

Instructions, written in a special code of letters and decimal figures, tell the computer what to do; numbers are simply the decimal equivalents of the quantities involved in the problem. Each instruction and number is assigned to a specific storage register in the computer: instructions to consecutive registers, in the order of their execution; numbers to any remaining registers.

COMPUTER TRANSLATES PROGRAM

When the program is ready, an operator types it into special input equipment which converts the letters and decimal numbers into an intermediate code which the computer then translates into its own language — binary notation. The translated version is stored on perforated paper tape or magnetic tape, as the case demands, and may be fed to the computer at a later time and at a faster-than-typewriter rate. All Whirlwind I computations are performed in binary arithmetic which uses only the digits zero and one.

COMPUTER PROVIDES SOLUTION

As soon as the program is in computer storage, Whirlwind I is ready to begin the solution of the problem. Control takes the first instruction from Storage, examines it, and sends the appropriate command pulses to carry it out. Control then goes on to each instruction sequentially, and causes it to be performed.

The last instruction tells the computer how to deliver its results. These may be in the form of a table, an oscilloscope display, or a stream of impulses that will control a machine or any other device.

12

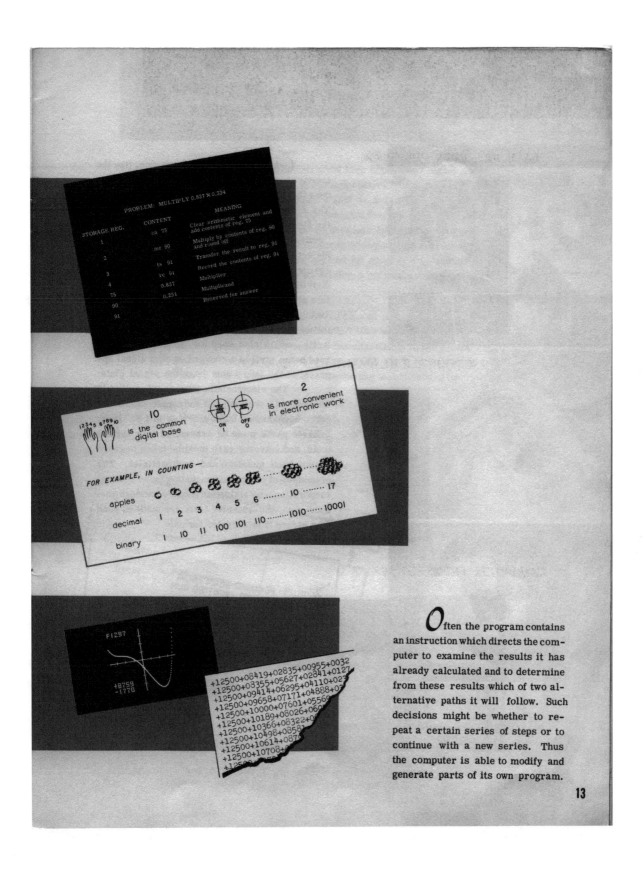

PROBLEM: MULTIPLY 0.837 × 0.234

STORAGE REG.	CONTENT	MEANING
1	ca 75	Clear arithmetic element and add contents of reg. 75
2	mr 90	Multiply by contents of reg. 90 and round off
3	ts 91	Transfer the result to reg. 91
4	rc 51	Record the contents of reg. 91
75	0.837	Multiplier
90	0.234	Multiplicand
91		Reserved for answer

10 is the common digital base

1 2 3 4 5 6 7 8 9 10

ON 1 / OFF 0 **2** is more convenient in electronic work

FOR EXAMPLE, IN COUNTING —

apples									
decimal	1	2	3	4	5	6	......	10	....	17
binary	1	10	11	100	101	110	....	1010	....	10001

F1297

+8759
−1770

+12500+08419+02835+00955+0032
+12500+03355+05627+02841+0127
+12500+09414+06295+04110+023
+12500+09658+07171+04888+0
+12500+10000+07601+0556
+12500+10189+08026+060
+12500+10366+08322+0
+12500+10498+0858
+12500+10614+087
+12500+10708
+1250

*O*ften the program contains an instruction which directs the computer to examine the results it has already calculated and to determine from these results which of two alternative paths it will follow. Such decisions might be whether to repeat a certain series of steps or to continue with a new series. Thus the computer is able to modify and generate parts of its own program.

13

Electrostatic Storage Tubes

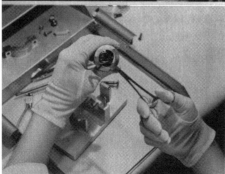

*T*he electrostatic storage tube, like the television picture tube, uses a movable electron beam to distribute information over a surface. The diagram below illustrates the operation of the storage tube. A high-velocity electron gun "writes" a binary digit as a charged spot on a dielectric storage surface. Whether the spot is charged positively (for digit 1) or negatively (for digit 0) depends on the voltage level of the surface at the time of writing. A holding gun, producing an electron flood, keeps digits "in storage" for as long a period as desired. The high-velocity gun is also used to "read." When the read beam strikes a charged spot, a signal appears on the output line from the signal plate.

The electrostatic storage tubes used in Whirlwind I were designed and constructed in the Servomechanisms Laboratory at M.I.T. Many delicate parts must be assembled with special tools, and extreme care must be taken to guard against hand moisture and dust particles. The processes of component mounting, tube sealing, evaporation, and activation require patience plus know-how, and extensive tests are made on each tube before it is accepted for use.

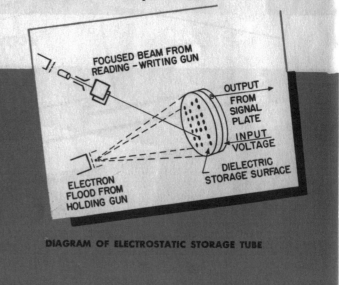

DIAGRAM OF ELECTROSTATIC STORAGE TUBE

Principal Electronic Circuits

The computations of Whirlwind I are executed by high-frequency pulses in electronic circuits. The principal circuits are the FLIP-FLOP and the GATE TUBE. The FLIP-FLOP is a two-position electronic switch. Two vacuum tubes are so connected that one tube or the other is conducting — but not both. The FLIP-FLOP is capable of maintaining either position indefinitely until it is switched by a command pulse. Thus, if we interpret one position as a 1 and the other as a 0, we may store intelligence in the FLIP-FLOP by sending a command pulse to establish the desired position.

The GATE TUBE is used to control pulse travel. A sensing pulse arriving at one grid of the GATE TUBE will appear at the output only when a gating voltage is applied simultaneously to the second grid. By connecting the output of one tube of the FLIP-FLOP to the second grid of the GATE TUBE, we can control the opening and closing of the "gate."

Whirlwind I uses about 275 FLIP-FLOPS and 1500 GATE TUBES in its Control and Arithmetic Element.

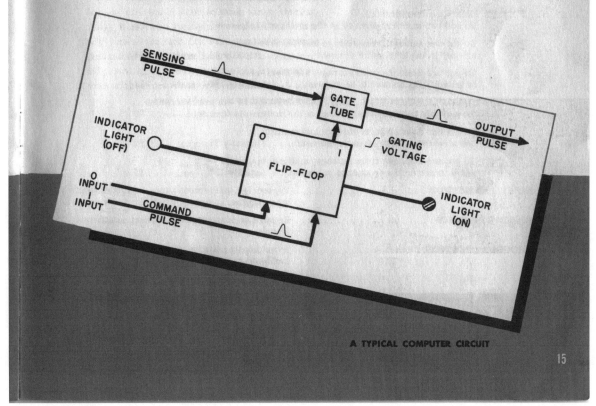

A TYPICAL COMPUTER CIRCUIT

15

Summary of Whirlwind 1 Specifications

TYPE OF COMPUTER . . . . General purpose, high-speed

DESIGN . . . . Electronic, digital

NUMBER SYSTEM USED . . . . Binary

REGISTER LENGTH (basic) . . . . 16 Binary digits

METHOD of HANDLING NUMBERS . . . . Parallel digit transmission, addition, and storage

TYPE of INTERNAL STORAGE . . . . Electrostatic storage tubes

CAPACITY of INTERNAL STORAGE . . . . Initially 256 registers; when complete, 2048 registers

ACCESS TIME to INTERNAL STORAGE . . . . . . Initially 25 microseconds; when complete, 6 microseconds

BASIC FUNCTIONAL DESIGN . . . . 0.1-microsecond pulses, representing instructions or numbers, are distributed via gate tubes, which pass pulses only when a coincidence signal from a memory device, such as a flip-flop, is present

PULSE REPETITION FREQUENCY . . . . 2 megacycles in arithmetic element, 1 megacycle elsewhere

ADDITION TIME (in microseconds)
　　To add two numbers already in the arithmetic element 2

　　To get one number from storage and add it to one already in the arithmetic element . . . . . . Initially 60, goal 24

　　To get two numbers from storage, add them, and to transfer the answer to storage . . . . . Initially 180, goal 72

AVERAGE MULTIPLICATION TIME, INCLUDING ROUNDOFF (in microseconds)
　　To multiply two numbers already in the arithmetic element 20

　　To get one number from storage and multiply it by one already in the arithmetic element . . . . Initially 75, goal 39

　　To get two numbers from storage, multiply them, and to transfer the product to storage . . . Initially 195, goal 87

INPUT AND OUTPUT . . . . Typewriter, perforated paper tape, magnetic tape, magnetic drum, oscilloscope display

ERROR DETECTION . . . . By built-in identity checks and miscellaneous alarms

TROUBLE LOCATION . . . . By automatic marginal-checking system which locates deteriorating components during test periods

16

The Best Way to Design an Automatic Calculating Machine

Maurice V. Wilkes

From Manchester University, *Manchester University Computer. Inaugural Conference* [Bolton: Tillotson's, 1951], pp. 16–18.

INTRODUCTORY NOTE TO READING 8.8

Maurice V. Wilkes directed the design and construction of the EDSAC, the first readily usable, full-scale stored-program computer. The EDSAC was preceded in operation by the Manchester "Baby" prototype stored-program machine, which ran for only a short time in 1948. In the United States, Eckert and Mauchly's BINAC was probably running programs about the same time, but it too was a very short-lived machine.

In addition to developing the EDSAC, Wilkes was responsible for a number of programming innovations, such as labels, macros, and microprogramming, that became standard in the computer industry. He studied physics at Cambridge University, where he received his Ph.D. in 1936 with a thesis based on work performed in the Cavendish Laboratory on the propagation of very long radio waves in the ionosphere. While engaged in postgraduate research on this topic, he was allowed to use Cambridge University's model differential analyzer to solve a difficult equation. This machine, which Wilkes found "irresistible," inspired an abiding interest in automatic computing. At the end of 1936, Wilkes was put in charge of Cambridge's model differential analyzer, and the following year he joined the staff of the university's newly founded Mathematical Laboratory, becoming its director after the close of World War II. The Mathematical Laboratory (renamed the Computing Laboratory in the 1960s) played a critical role in the development of the electronic computer.

In this paper presented at the second English Computer Conference in 1951 Wilkes introduced the term "microprogramming," referring to the design of the control circuits of a digital computer. The paper marks his first public discussion of the subject other than at an informal Cambridge seminar in 1949. "In Wilkes' seminal paper, he described an implementation of a control store using a diode matrix. The microinstructions held in the control store had a simple format: the unencoded control signals were stored with a next-address field. Initial selection of the appropriate microprogram was handled by using the opcode value appended with zeros as a starting address in the control store, and normal sequencing used the contents of the next-address fields thereafter. Conditional transfers were handled by allowing conditions to modify bits in the next-address fields."[1] Although Wilkes first suggested the use of microprogramming in the early 1950s, and implemented it in the successor to EDSAC, EDSAC 2, the idea was not widely adopted until the following decade, when the development of semiconductor devices was sufficiently advanced. It was adopted in the IBM System/360.[JMN]

---

1 Mark Smotherman, *A Brief History of Microprogramming* [1999]. www.cs.clemson.edu/~mark/upprog.html.

TEXT OF READING 8.8

I would like to begin by adding my congratulations to the many others which have been received by Professor Williams, Manchester University and Ferranti Ltd., on the construction of the machine which has just been inaugurated. In the face of this beautifully engineered machine, the title I have chosen for my opening remarks in this discussion may sound a little impertinent. But, as Dr. Kilburn remarked yesterday, the designer of an electronic calculating machine must continually take decisions, and he does not know when he takes them whether they are right or wrong. I might put it by saying that in a mathematical sense the solution to the problem of designing an electronic calculating machine is unstable. Two similar groups of engineers with similar backgrounds and assisted by similar groups of mathematicians will, if working independently, produce quite different machines. Moreover, the machines finally built will depend on the scale on which the projects are conducted, the experience and background of the teams, and the state of technical developments at the time. The last item is important since new developments in electron tubes, or in non-linear devices of the germanium type, might well affect even so fundamental a decision as the choice between the serial or parallel modes of operation for the machine. It is desirable, therefore, to keep under review the considerations which underlie the design of calculating machines and to try to examine them in the light of general principles as well as of current technical developments. I am aware that in doing this one is in danger of saying things which are sufficiently obvious without being said, but I am in the fortunate position of having been asked to open a discussion rather than to give a paper. I shall not, therefore, attempt to present a logical thesis but shall allow myself to raise issues rather than settle them.

I think that most people will agree that the first consideration for a designer at the present time is how he is to achieve the maximum degree of reliability in his machine. Amongst other things the reliability of the machine will depend on the following:

a. The amount of equipment it contains.

b. Its complexity.

c. The degree of repetition of units.

By the complexity of a machine I mean the extent to which cross-connections between the various units obscure their logical inter-relation. A machine is easier to repair if it consists of a number of units connected together in a simple way without cross-connections between them; it is also easier to construct since different people can work on the different units without getting in each other's way.

As regards repetition I think everyone would prefer to have in a particular part of the machine a group of five identical units rather than a group of five different units. Most people would prefer to have six identical units rather than five different units. How far one ought to be prepared to go in the direction of accepting a greater quantity of equipment in order to achieve repetition is a matter of opinion. The matter may be put as follows. Suppose that it is regarded as being equally desirable to have a particular part of the machine composed of a group of n different units, or composed of a group of kn identical units, all the units being of similar size. What is the value of k? My conjecture is that $k > 2$. I should say that I am thinking of a machine which has about 10 groups of units and that n is approximately equal to 10.

The remarks I have just made are of general application. I will now try to be more specific. If one builds a parallel machine one has a good example, in the arithmetical unit, of a piece of equipment consisting of identical units repeated many times. Such an arithmetical unit is, however, much larger than that in a serial machine. On the other hand I think it is true to say that the control in a parallel machine is simpler than in a serial machine. I am using the word *control* here in a very general sense to include everything that does not appertain to the store proper (i.e., it includes the access circuits) or to the registers and adders in the arithmetical unit. That the control can be simpler in a parallel machine may I think be seen by comparing the waveforms which must be produced in order to effect the transfer of a number from one register to another in a serial synchronous machine and in a parallel asynchronous machine. These are the two extreme cases. In the case of a serial synchronous machine the waveform must rise at some critical moment relative to the clock and must fall at another critical moment, and its edges must be sharp. In a parallel asynchronous machine all that is needed is a single pulse whose time of occurrence, length, and shape are all non-critical (see Fig. 9).

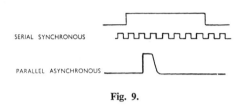

SERIAL SYNCHRONOUS

PARALLEL ASYNCHRONOUS

Fig. 9.

The arithmetical unit of a parallel machine is often shown diagrammatically as in Fig. 10.

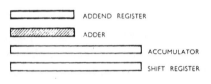

ADDEND REGISTER

ADDER

ACCUMULATOR

SHIFT REGISTER

Fig. 10.

At the beginning of a multiplication the multiplier is placed in the right-hand half of the accumulator register. The right-hand half of the shift register may be dispensed with if shifting is done in two stages. Showing the right-hand half of the accumulator as a separate register we then have the diagram of Fig. 11.

We are thus led to think of an arithmetical unit composed of a number of standard units each containing four flip-flops (one belonging to each of four registers) together with an adder. Gates would be provided to make possible the transfer of numbers from one register to another, through the adder when necessary. These transfers would be effected by pulsing one or more of a set of wires emerging from the arithmetical unit.

Fig. 11.

It is also necessary to have registers in the control of a machine. These, with the names given to them respectively in the Manchester machine and in the E.D.S.A.C., are as follows:

Register for holding the address of the next order due to be executed (control, or sequence control tank).

Register holding order at present being executed (current instruction register, or order tank).

Register for counting the number of steps in a multiplication or shifting operation (not needed with the fast multiplier on the Manchester machine, timing control tank in the E.D.S.A.C.).

In addition the Manchester machine has a number of *B* registers.

If one *B* register is considered to be sufficient the parallel machine we are considering can use the same unit (containing 4 flip-flops and 1 adder) for the control registers as for arithmetical registers. In this way an extreme degree of repetition can be achieved.

It remains to consider the control proper, that is, the part of the machine which supplies the pulses for operating the gates associated with the arithmetical and control registers. The designer of this part of a machine usually proceeds in an *ad hoc* manner, drawing block diagrams until he sees an arrangement which satisfies his requirements and appears to be reasonably economical. I would like to suggest a way in which the control can be made systematic, and therefore less complex.

Each operation called for by an order in the order code of the machine involves a sequence of steps which may include transfers from the store to control or arithmetical registers, or *vice versa*, and transfers from one register to another. Each of these steps is achieved by pulsing certain of the wires associated with the control and arithmetical registers, and I will refer to it as a "micro-operation." Each true machine operation is thus made up of a sequence or "micro-programme" of micro-operations.

Fig. 12 shows the way in which pulses for performing the micro-operations may be generated. The timing pulse which initiates a micro-operation enters the decoding tree and is routed to one of the outputs according to the number set on the register R. It passes into the rectifier matrix A and gives rise to pulses on certain of the output wires of this matrix according to the arrangement of the rectifiers. These pulses operate the gates associated with the control and arithmetical registers, and cause the correct micro-operation to be performed. The pulse from the decoding tree also passes into matrix B and gives rise to pulses on certain of the output wires of this matrix. These pulses are conducted, via a short delay line, to the register R and cause the number set up on it to be changed. The result is that the next initiating pulse to enter the decoding tree will emerge from a different outlet and will consequently cause a different micro-operation to be performed. It will thus be seen that each row of rectifiers in matrix A corresponds to one of the micro-orders in the sequence required to perform a machine operation.

The system as described would enable a fixed cycle of operations only to be performed. Its utility can be greatly extended by making some of the micro-orders conditional in the sense that they are followed by one of two alternative micro-orders according to the state of the machine. This can be done by making the output of the decoding tree branch before it enters matrix B. The direction the pulse takes at the branch is controlled by the potential on a wire coming from another part of the machine; for example, it might come from the sign flip-flop of the accumulator. The bottom row of matrix A in Fig. 12 corresponds to a conditional micro-order.

The matrix A contains sequences of micro-orders for performing all the basic operations in the order code of the machine. All that is necessary to perform a particular operation is that "micro-control" shall be switched to the first micro-order in the appropriate sequence. This is done by causing the function digits of the order to be set up on the first four or five flip-flops of the register R, zero being set on the others.

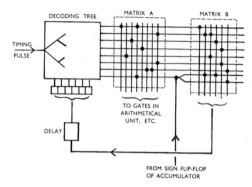

Fig. 12.

A control system designed in this way is certainly very logical in structure but two comments, slightly contradictory in their implications, might be made. In the first place it might be said that there is nothing very new about the arrangement since it makes use of flip-flops, gates, and mixing diodes which are the elements out of which any control is built. With this criticism I would agree. In fact, the controls of various machines now in existence or being constructed could no doubt be drawn in some way closely resembling Fig. 12. The other objection is that the scheme appears to be rather extravagant in equipment. This I think is not true, particularly if some departures from the precise form of Fig. 12 are allowed. I think that by starting with a logical layout one is likely to arrive at a final arrangement which is both logical and economical. Moreover, one is able to see at each stage what one is sacrificing in the way of logical layout in order to achieve economy and *vice versa*.

In order to get some idea of the number of micro-orders required I have constructed a micro-programme for a simple machine with the following orders: add, subtract, multiply (two orders, one for the multiplier, one for the multiplicand), right and left shift (any number of places), transfer from the accumulator to the store, conditional operation depending on the sign of the number in the accumulator, conditional operation depending on the sign of the number in the B register (one B register is assumed), transfer from the store to the B register, input, and output. The micro-programme also provides for the preliminary extraction of the order from the store (Stage 1 in E.D.S.A.C. terminology). Only 40 micro-orders are required to perform all these operations.

The considerations involved in drawing-up a micro-programme resemble those involved in drawing-up an ordinary programme. The final details of the control are thus settled by a systematic process instead of by the usual *ad hoc* procedures based on the use of block diagrams. Of course, sound engineering would be necessary to produce designs for the decoding tree and the matrices which could be used for any desired micro-programme by arranging the rectifiers suitably in the matrices. One important advantage of this method of designing the control is that the order code need not be decided on finally until a late stage in the construction of the machine; it would even be possible to change it after the machine had been put into operation simply by rewiring the matrices.

If desired some of the micro-orders can be made conditional in their action as well as (or instead of) conditional as regards the switching of micro-control. This can be done by making the output of the decoding tree branch before it enters matrix *A*. I doubt if much economy can be achieved this way and if it is done to any extent the advantage that micro-programming resembles ordinary programming is lost. Other variants of the scheme as I have described it will no doubt occur to you.

The matrices may be regarded as very high-speed stores holding fixed information. If they could be replaced by an erasable store to which information could be transferred from the main store of the machine when required we should have a machine with no fixed order code; the programmer would, in fact, be able to choose his order code to suit his own requirements and to change it during the course of the programme if he considered it desirable. Such a machine would have a number of fascinating possibilities but I doubt whether, in view of the amount of equipment it would doubtless involve, its construction could be justified.

8.9

Principles of Operation: Type 701 and Associated Equipment

International Business Machines Corporation

Extract from *Principles of Operation: Type 701 and Associated Equipment* (New York: IBM, ©1953), pp. 11–27.

INTRODUCTORY NOTE TO READING 8.9

In 1952 IBM entered the commercial electronic computer market with its 701 system, designed for scientific applications, and described by IBM president Thomas J. Watson Jr., as "the machine that carried us into the electronics business".[1] The 701, also known as the "Defense Calculator," had originally been developed to meet the high-speed calculating needs of the United States Defense Department during the Korean War. The machine was designed by an engineering team led by Jerrier Haddad and Nathaniel Rochester with an architecture based on John von Neumann's IAS computer, employing a binary number system and a parallel-memory device capable of retrieving all the digits of a "word" at once. For storage, it used three-inch "Williams tubes." The 701's processor performed multiplications at a rate of two thousand per second—four times faster than UNIVAC—and the machine could read data from both punched cards and magnetic tape. The 701 was referred to in company literature as an "electronic data processing machine"—IBM deliberately avoided using the word "computer," which was too closely associated with the rival UNIVAC since the UNIVAC I successfully predicated the election of Dwight Eisenhower on nationwide television.

The first 701, consisting of twelve separate units, was installed in December 1952 at IBM's headquarters in New York City. Eighteen more 701 systems were manufactured, most of them leased by the Defense Department or military aerospace firms for $15,000 per month; the last 701 was shipped to the United States Weather Bureau in the spring of 1955. The 701's success was critical in persuading the initially reluctant IBM to commit itself to electronic computers: "Prior to [the 701] experience, planning and marketing executives could speculate endlessly on whether data could safely be entrusted to invisible tape recording or control entrusted to the ethereal stored program. But when it had been demonstrated that 701s could be manufactured, programmed, maintained, and relied upon for useful results as promised . . . the question thereafter was not *whether* to build new computers but *which* machines to introduce and *when* . . . ."[2]

In the brochure from which this reading was selected, IBM emphasizes the significance of the stored program: "In order to achieve maximum versatility, every function of the machine is under control of the stored program. This versatility allows the machine to execute instructions at the rate of about 14,000 per second on typical problems. Also, functions such as input-output operation, which are determined by fixed circuitry on some computers, are under complete control of the program, and, hence, under complete control of the operator. The great advantage of this system lies in the fact that a customer may build up a library of programs which will accomplish

---

1 Quoted in Cuthbert C. Hurd, Prologue, *Annals of the History of Computing* 5 (1983): 110.

2 Charles J. Bashe *et al. IBM's Early Computers* (Cambridge, MA: MIT Press, 1986), 164.

his special applications at peak machine efficiency. No compromise in efficiency is necessary in the design of the machine to accommodate an *average* application. Furthermore, a customer may efficiently calculate on *any* 701 installation simply by using his own library of programs." [JMN]

This IBM 702 Electronic Data-Processing Machine is installed at the company's headquarters in New York City. In the background are eight magnetic tape units through which information is fed to and delivered from the machine. Each 2,400-foot reel of tape may contain over 5,000,000 characters (either letters, digits, or symbols), so the total "memory capacity" of the units shown is in excess of 40,000,000 characters, all of which are available to the machine at the rate of 15,000 characters per second.

Superb photograph of the commercial version of the IBM 702 system, a version of the 701 designed for commercial applications. From Arthur D. Little's *The Electronic Data Processing Industry* (1956).

TEXT OF READING 8.9
GENERAL

The 701 is a large-scale electronic digital computer controlled by a stored program of the one-address type, and utilizing various types of internal storage.

The internal high-speed memory is on cathode-ray tubes and will be referred to as the "electrostatic memory." When the amount of storage available in the electrostatic memory is not large enough, magnetic drums are used to store and supply large blocks of information for ready access at frequent intervals. The "drum memory" is also capable of retaining its contents while the power is turned off, so that intermediate results remain available overnight when the machine is shut down. Any part of the information on the drums may be selectively altered by the machine at any time.

If a larger secondary memory is needed, or if information is to be filed away for future reference, magnetic tapes may be used instead of magnetic drums. Magnetic tape is a storage and input-output medium that provides compactness, allows rapid reading and writing and can be re-used many times.

To achieve a greater computing efficiency, the machine works internally in the binary-number system. The input and output, however, may be accomplished on standard IBM cards in the familiar decimal-number system by programming that does not interfere with maximum reading, punching, and printing speeds.

Results of a computation are printed on a modified Type 407 accounting machine operating at a speed of over 10,000 characters per minute. Control of the automatic tape-controlled carriage may be accomplished either manually, by control panel wiring, or by the stored program itself. Output can also take the form of cards punched in either binary or decimal; this again depends on the programming.

The programs may be written and introduced into the computer in various ways. Usually the instructions are key-punched on cards in their original form and read into the machine. If the program is to be preserved for future use, it can then be recorded on tape and filed away in a compact form. To prepare the machine for calculation the appropriate magnetic tapes are inserted in the tape units, cards are placed in the punch hopper, if necessary, and the cards containing the instructions and data of the problem are placed in the hopper of the card reader. By pushing one button the machine may be made to store the program and data of the problem and start calculating. From then on, operation of the computer is fully automatic, with all of the components being under the complete control of the program, although it is possible for the operator to interrupt the calculation manually at any time.

The primary unit of information is defined as a full word which consists of 35 bits (binary digits) and a sign, or 36 bits in all. However, any of these full words can be split into two "half words," each having 17 bits and a sign, or 18 bits in all. Since 3 1/3 bits are about equivalent in information content to one decimal digit, the full word has a precision of about ten decimal digits, and the half-word corresponds to about five decimal digits.

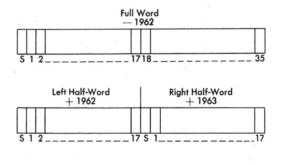

FIGURE 1

Figure 1 shows schematically a full word and the two half-words contained in the full word. The position of each of the 35 binary bits within the full word is numbered 1 through 35 from left to right. The sign bit of the number is represented on the extreme left and is labeled S. If this full word is divided between the 17th and 18th positions, the positions in the left half-word are designated exactly as in the full word. However, the 18th position of the full word now becomes the sign position of the *right* half-word, while the remaining positions are numbered 1 through 17. A word is considered negative if the binary digit 1 occupies the sign position; it is considered positive if the sign position contains the digit 0.

STORAGE

Information may be stored in electrostatic storage, on magnetic drums, on magnetic tape, and on punched cards.

The purpose of this section is simply to point out, in general terms, the types and extent of storage available on the 701. Punched cards are a well-known form of permanent storage and will receive extensive discussion in the input-output section of this manual. Details of the instructions necessary for manipulation of information contained on drums and tapes will also be found in the same section.

Electrostatic

The heart of the machine is the electrostatic storage unit, through which all information to and from all other components of the machine must pass. Electrostatic storage consists of a bank of cathode-ray tubes. Information is stored on the screen of each tube through the presence or absence of charged spots at certain locations on the screen. In this way, a certain number of binary digits (or "bits") may be stored on each tube. One electrostatic storage unit can accommodate 1024 full words or 2048 half words. However, two such units may be used to provide a maximum storage of 2048 full words or 4096 half words. It is assumed in what follows that maximum electrostatic storage has been provided for this installation.

Principal advantages of electrostatic storage over other types is the very small time necessary to extract information from any given location and send it to the computing unit and the fact that the programmer has random access to any electrostatic storage location. Information is lost when the power is turned off.

Magnetic Drums

Additional storage capacity is provided by four magnetic drums. These drums are rotating cylinders surfaced with a material that can be magnetized locally. Binary digits are stored on a drum through the presence or absence of small magnetized areas at certain locations on the surface of the drum. Each drum has a storage capacity of 2048 full words. Information is transmitted to and from drum storage only through electrostatic storage. When such a transfer of information occurs, the machine is said to write on or read from the drum. Any part of the information on a drum can be selectively altered by the machine at any time. Because access to individual words on a drum is slow in relation to electrostatic storage access, it is more efficient to use the drums for storing large blocks of information. After the first word of such a block has been located, the remaining words are read at the rate of 800 per second. Magnetic drums will retain stored information after the power is off.

Magnetic Tapes

There is also a tape-storage section which includes four magnetic tape units. Each tape, which may be up to 1400 feet long, is wound on a reel. The tape itself is a non-metallic, oxide coated band one-half inch wide. Binary information is recorded on tape by means of magnetized spots. A block of words recorded consecutively on a tape is called *a record* or *unit record*. The amount of information contained on each tape depends on the lengths of the individual records, since there is a certain amount of space between each record to allow for starting and stopping the tape. It is possible to store upwards of 200,000 words on each tape. The machine can read or write information on a tape only through the medium of electrostatic storage. It takes, on the average, about 10 milliseconds for the tape to accelerate to its reading or writing speed after which the reading or writing of a unit record takes places at the rate of 1250 words per second. Since the tapes are removable, a library of standard programming and mathematical tables may be kept on tapes.

ADDRESS SYSTEM

Memory Locations

Full and half-word locations in electrostatic storage, together with the tapes, drums, printer, card reader, and punch, are identified by a system of numerical addresses. By means of a number, then, we may tell the machine to refer to any information contained in electrostatic storage or to any component of the machine, provided only that we use the system to be described.

Electrostatic   The 2048 different locations for full words in electrostatic storage are identified by the negative even integers from –0000 to –4094. The 4096 possible locations for half-words in electrostatic storage are distinguished by the positive integers from +0000 to +4095. The relation between full and half-word addresses is as follows: if $-2n$ refers to a full-word location, then $+2n$ identifies the left half-word, and $+(2n+1)$ the right half-word, into which the full-word location may be split.

For example, if the full-word address is –1962, then the left half-word address is +1962 and refers to the sign position and positions 1 to 17 of the full word. The right half-word address is +1963 and refers to positions 18 to 35 of the full-word location, position 18 being the sign position of the right half word (Figure 1). If a full word is to be obtained from or supplied to electrostatic storage and, through error, a negative odd address is given (e.g., –1963), the result will be the same as if the next lower (in absolute value) negative even address (–1962) were given.

Magnetic Drums   As mentioned before, there are four magnetic drums on which information can be stored. Each drum is capable of storing 2048 full words of information. Each full word on a drum is identified by a system of addresses analogous to the system used for electrostatic memory, except that there is no provision for recognizing half-words. Thus, information must be used or stored on a drum in units of full words. An address of –1962 may then refer to the full word stored in location 1962 in electrostatic storage or any one of the four drums. This address usually refers to a location in electrostatic storage. An address will refer to a drum location only under specific conditions. These conditions are described under *Input-Output Components*.

Magnetic Tapes   Information is recorded on magnetic tapes in blocks of full words. The size of this block of words is optional with the programmer and is limited only by the length of the tape itself. A series of these blocks is said to compose a file of information.

By programming we can locate any particular full word in any unit record on any one of the four tapes. Usually, however, we are interested in obtaining a complete record, or even an entire file, at one time.

There is no way by which an address can be made to refer automatically to a particular location on tape, as was possible both in electrostatic storage and on the drums. This is because we normally use magnetic tapes to store a complete block of information at one time. If we want to refer to a particular word among a block of words, it is usually best to use the drum storage where this can easily be done. The exact method by which words are transferred to and from tape is discussed later under *Input-Output Components*.

Component Identification

There are four tape units, four drums, one card reader, one printer, and one card punch—all of which must be given identifying numbers. These identifying numbers are placed in the address part of an instruction whenever the programmer wants the machine to operate one of these units. Table I gives the system of addresses. Note in Table I that identifications coincide with those of certain electrostatic storage locations. Whether the address part of an instruction refers to electrostatic storage or to one of the components depends on the operation part. Some operations will make no sense if the address is interpreted as an electrostatic location; other operations make no sense if the address is interpreted as a component identification. Thus, an address is automatically interpreted by the machine in the light of what it is asked to do by the operation part of the instruction (*see Operations*).

TABLE I

	1	2	3	4
Tape Units	0256	0257	0258	0259
Drums	0128	0129	0130	0131
Printer	0512			
Card Reader	2048			
Card Punch	1024			

COMPUTING

Calculation is done by directing information to the computing section, causing operations to be performed on this information, and by storing the results of these operations in the memory. To understand these processes, we must first realize that the computing section is composed of three internal registers called (1) memory register, (2) accumulator register, and (3) multiplier-quotient register. Each of these registers is capable of holding a full word. Their exact capacities:

Memory register: 35 bits and sign
Accumulator register: 37 bits and sign
MQ register :   35 bits and sign

(The two extra positions of the accumulator register, called the overflow positions of this register, will be explained later; these positions are designated as P and Q.) Figure 2 shows a schematic representation of these registers.

The flow of information from the electrostatic memory to these registers is shown in Figure 3. Note that all information must pass through the memory register before entering either of the other two registers. In this flow of information, three cases are to be explained (Figure 4) :

1. If an instruction calls for a full word from electrostatic storage, the word first appears unchanged in the memory register before it goes to either of the other registers.

2. If an instruction calls for the left half-word of a full word, positions 1 through 17 of the full word and the associated sign are transmitted as shown. Note particularly that the least significant 18 bits of the memory register are set to zeros.

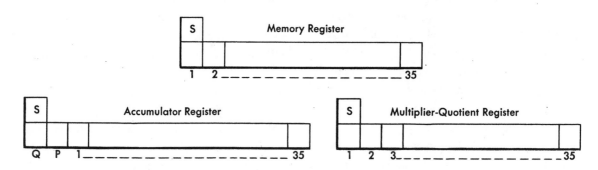

FIGURE 2

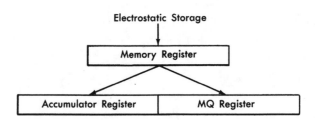

FIGURE 3

3. If an instruction calls for the right half-word of a full word, positions 19 through 35 of the full word are transmitted to the left half of the memory register. If there is a binary digit of 1 or 0 in the 18th position of the electrostatic location, the right half-word is recognized in the memory register as negative or positive, respectively. The 18 rightmost positions of the memory register are set to zero.

Once the word is in the memory register, it is a simple step for the word to be transmitted, bit for bit, to either the accumulator register or multiplier-quotient register. The programmer does not have to concern himself with the fact that the memory register is an intermediate step in the flow of words from electrostatic memory to the accumulator register or MQ (multiplier-quotient) register. It is of interest here, because at any time during machine calculation the operator can display the contents of all three registers on the operator's panel (see *Control*). For example, one instruction tells the machine to transmit a word from a given electrostatic location to the MQ register. Note that this is done with no explicit reference to the memory register.

There are also instructions that cause information to be transmitted *from* the accumulator register or MQ register *to* an electrostatic location. In these cases, the memory register plays *no part whatsoever*.

When storing a result in a half-word location, only the sign and the first 17 bits of the accumulator register are stored. The remaining 18 bits on the right of the accumulator and the two overflow bits on the left are ignored. The same is true when storing the contents of the MQ register in a half-word location of electrostatic memory.

Before beginning a discussion of the arithmetic operations, it should be stated that all numbers in the 701 are expressed in the form of a magnitude and a sign. The results of any operation performed in the computing unit are always returned to this form. Results are never expressed as complements.

In the following paragraphs a description of possible operations will be stated in general terms. The actual methods and instructions necessary for performing these operations are explained later.

Accumulation

A schematic representation of the accumulator register was given in Figure 2. Note that there are the usual 35 positions to accommodate a full word, plus two overflow positions, P and Q. Note also that the sign is

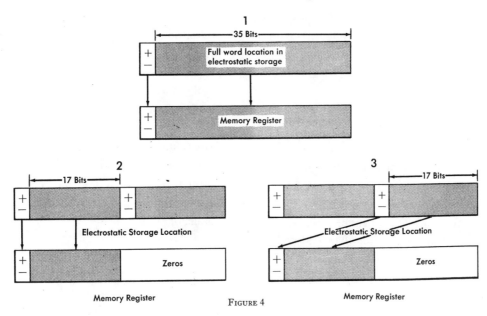

FIGURE 4

not located to the left of the bits as is done for both full and half-words in the electrostatic memory. The sign of a register is indicated separately and is schematically represented in Figure 2 by the block labeled S.

The accumulator register, together with the basic circuits for adding and subtracting, form what will be called the "accumulator." The accumulator is capable of adding a number (coming from memory via the memory register) to its contents, of subtracting an incoming number from its contents, of shifting its contents right or left, and of resetting itself to zero before entering a new word. The contents of the accumulator can also be stored in memory.

Accumulation is performed as follows:

Suppose, for example, we wish to calculate

$$A + B = C$$

where A and B may have either sign. A is first placed in the accumulator. Then B is called in from memory and is added to the contents of the accumulator. The sum, C, remains in the accumulator replacing A. Finally, C can be stored in memory or used for another operation in the accumulator.

A similar situation arises in subtraction, where the number to be subtracted is the one that comes from memory.

It is also possible to add to or subtract from the contents of the accumulator the absolute value of a number stored in memory, the sign of this number being ignored.

Rounding

When the machine is instructed to round, the process is as follows :

If a 1 is in the first position of the MQ register, the contents of the accumulator are increased by a 1 in the 35th position. If a zero is in the first position of the MQ register, the contents of the accumulator are unchanged. In either case the contents of the MQ register are unchanged.

Thus it will be seen how the rounding process, in conjunction with a shifting process to be described later, enables the programmer to round and truncate a number to any desired number of bits.

Multiplication

Multiplication in the 701 provides for the multiplication of two 35 bit factors to produce a maximum size product of 70 bits in one operation.

To multiply $A \times B$, we first must place the multiplier, A, in the MQ register. Then we simply call out B from memory and, at the same time, tell the machine to multiply. After the multiplication is complete, the most significant bits of the product are found in the accumulator, while the least significant bits are placed in the MQ. It should be noted that before any multiplication begins, the accumulator is automatically reset to zero. Also, the number in the MQ register is destroyed during the multiplication process. Both of these features are necessitated by the way in which the machine multiplies internally. Thus, it is seen that cumulative multiplication cannot take place in the accumulator, but the summation is very easily programmed.

Placing of the binary point in the factors is completely arbitrary. A simple familiar rule to remember with regard to placing the binary point in the resulting product follows:

Rule: Add the number of binary bits to the right of the binary point in each factor. This sum is the number of bits appearing to the right of the binary point in the product as defined above.

We can also tell the machine to multiply and round in one operation. In this case, an ordinary multiplication is followed by the rounding process. The result is a rounded product of 35 bits at most in the accumulator.

Division

Just as multiplication may result in a 70 bit product, so division may start with a 70 bit dividend. The more significant half of the dividend is placed in the accumulator, and the less significant half is put into the MQ register. The divisor is called in from memory, and the machine is instructed to divide.

The quotient is developed in the MQ register, displacing the part of the dividend which was in that register. After the division, the accumulator contains the remainder. This remainder has the same sign as the dividend. Preservation of this remainder makes double precision division particularly convenient.

If only a full-sized 35-bit dividend is available, we may want to reset the MQ register to zero before division, because the contents of this register are considered to be part of the dividend. The magnitude of the number in the MQ register, in relation to the accumulator, however, is less than one in the 35th position of the accumulator. If this error is not tolerable, we must remember to reset the MQ register to zero before division.

These properties of the MQ register may be used conveniently to obtain a rounded quotient. With a 35-bit dividend the procedure is :

1. Place the divisor in the accumulator.

2. Shift it 36 places to the right into the MQ register, so that one-half the value of the divisor appears in the MQ register.

3. Place the dividend in the accumulator.

4. Divide.

The resultant quotient in the MQ register is then properly rounded to 35 bits. If a 70-bit dividend is to be used, the absolute value of the less-significant half must first be increased by one-half the absolute value of the divisor before shifting into the MQ register.

The effect of this procedure is the same as if a 36-bit quotient had first been developed, a 1 had been added to the 36th bit, and this bit had been dropped after any carries had been propagated.

As in multiplication, something must be said with regard to where the binary point is assumed to be in division. What will be called the "standard" case will be stated first followed by two rules necessary to determine the location of the binary point in any other case. The machine will perform division only if the divisor is larger than the dividend as defined below.

"Standard" Case. Assume that the binary point of the dividend is located between the 35th position of the accumulator and the first position of the MQ register. Also assume that the divisor being called in from memory has its binary point located to the right of the 35th position. [Caution: *If, with the binary points assumed to be in these positions, the dividend is larger than or equal to the divisor (in absolute value), the machine will stop, and a division check light will turn on to warn the operator.*] With these assumptions, the 35-bit quotient developed in the MQ register will have its point located to the left of the first position. The remainder, if any, which is developed in the accumulator, has its binary point located between positions P and 1.

The following rules are based on changes of the binary points from the standard case.

RULE 1: A change in the binary point of the dividend results in a change equal in magnitude and in the same direction in the points of both the quotient and remainder.

RULE 2: A change in the point of the divisor results in a corresponding change in the opposite direction of the point of the quotient. The point of the remainder is unchanged.

Shifting

Shifting is a process by which the binary bits of a word may be moved to the right or left with respect to the positions of a register in the computing section. There have been references to these paragraphs in previous sections as a means of programming calculations so that the binary point may be arbitrarily located at the discretion of the programmer.

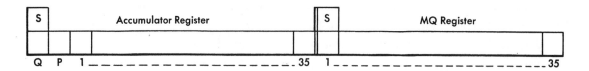

FIGURE 5

Two kinds of shifts are possible:

Accumulator Shift. The 37 bits that may be standing in the accumulator register can be shifted one or more places, either to the right or left. Digits shifted beyond the capacity of the register are lost. Vacated positions are filled with zeros.

Long Shift. Both the multiplier-quotient register and the accumulator take part in the long shift. They behave as if the MQ register were connected to the right of the accumulator as shown schematically in Figure 5. For instance, a long right shift by 69 places causes the bit in position 1 of the accumulator to be shifted all the way over to position 35 in the MQ register, the intervening bits having dropped off the end. The process is similar for a long left shift. On a long *right* shift the sign of the MQ register is changed to the sign of the accumulator register. On a long *left* shift, the sign of the accumulator register is changed to the sign of the MQ register. A useful device is to specify a long shift of zero places which produces no actual shift but merely changes the sign of the MQ register or the accumulator as described above.

If the shift is far enough, with either the accumulator shift or the long shift, nothing will be left but zeros. Thus, shifting may be used to reset the accumulator or MQ register to zero. For convenience in certain programs, such as floating-point calculations, we can specify a shift of as many as 255 places in a single operation, although only zeros are produced by long shifts in excess of 71 places. However, no provisions have been made for permitting shifts by more than 255 places. An attempted shift of more than 255 places

gives the results described under *Operations.*

It should be noted that the overflow positions of the accumulator participate in both kinds of shift. The signs of the registers, however, do not participate in the shift except as specifically noted above.

Sign of Zero

It is possible for a zero in this calculator to have either a plus or a minus sign. For instance, a negative number in the accumulator may be shifted so far to the right or left that all numerical bits are zeros. This still leaves the minus sign, so that technically the result is "–0". Arithmetic operations may also result in zeros of either sign. The arithmetic circuits are designed so that if the result of an addition or subtraction is zero, the sign of the result will be that of the number which was in the accumulator immediately before the addition or subtraction took place. In numerical work no distinction need be made between a +0 and a –0 result, because either zero can be used in further arithmetic operations.

This characteristic of the machine is sometimes very convenient ; there are ways the machine can be made to recognize either type of zero. It is also possible for the machine to ignore the sign entirely and test to see only if the result is zero. Such controls are discussed in a following section.

Overflow Indication

This section covers the accumulator overflow positions, P and Q.

During such operations as adding, subtracting, and shifting left, it is possible for non-zero binary bits to enter into or be shifted completely through the overflow positions of the accumulator. This can happen by means of a left shift or as the result of a carry in addition or subtraction. Whenever a non-zero binary bit enters position P from position 1, an overflow indicator within the machine is turned on. Associated with the activation of this indicator is an overflow light on the operator's panel. This overflow indication occurs even in a shift that sends a binary bit completely through the overflow positions. Overflow may indicate an error in setting up the program for a given set of data. Frequently, however, operations are planned deliberately to produce overflow. Hence, the machine will continue to operate after an overflow, but an instruction is available to test the condition of the overflow indicator and to program the desired action after an overflow. This may include stopping the machine on overflow, performing a special set of operations, or simply ignoring overflow. Testing the overflow indicator turns it off.

Examples of the operation of the overflow indicator follow. In these examples we assume the binary point to be to the left of position 1. For convenience and abbreviation only the first three bits to the right of the binary point are shown.

In the addition

Overflow Positions		
+.100	+00.110	= +01.010
Word from Memory	Accumulator	Accumulator

there is a carry that produces an overflow and causes the overflow light to go on. If now the indicator is turned off (by use of the test instruction) and a second addition

$$+.100 + 01.010 = +01.110$$

is performed, the overflow indicator does not come on again, because there was no carry past the binary point this time. A further addition

$$+.100 + 01.110 = +10.010$$

again gives an overflow indication, because a carry was propagated through the binary point.

If shifts or carries go beyond Q, the excess bits are dropped. Thus +00.010 shifted left by two places in the accumulator gives +01.000 with an overflow. But if +00.010 is shifted left by four places, the result is +00.000, again with an overflow indication. In the first case, the process may be reversed by shifting right, but in the second case, bit 1 has been lost, and any shifting to the right still gives a zero result.

The extra two bits in the accumulator enable the programmer to make full use of the 35 numerical bits in memory for such operations as double-precision arithmetic. When a possible overflow must be allowed for in a program, the extra bits make it considerably easier to shift and return the result to a standard form.

The overflow bits do not enter into multiplication, because the product of two 35-bit numbers cannot exceed 70 bits. Neither can they be part of a dividend, because the dividend cannot be greater than the divisor as defined earlier in the "standard" case.

CONTROL

Stored Program

Completely automatic and flexible control of the calculator requires use of a stored program. The procedure generally used by 701 programmers with the stored program system is as follows:

1. The mathematician analyzes his problem and breaks its solution down into basic steps of which the 701 is capable.

2. By means of a number code, determined by the design of the computer, he translates these steps into a numerical form which can be interpreted by the machine. Each of these steps is then stored in the electrostatic memory. Each step, which later will be seen to consist of an operation part and an address part, will hereafter be referred to as an instruction to the machine.

3. Data necessary for solution of the problem are stored in the memory of the machine.

By means of a control, the programmer tells the machine in which memory location he has stored the first instruction to be executed. After receiving this information, the 701 is able to find all succeeding instructions and execute them automatically.

A complete analysis of the instruction system of the 701 follows.

Instruction Sequencer   The numerical representation of an instruction to the machine occupies the space of a half-word in the electrostatic memory. Instructions may temporarily be stored on drum, tape, or cards, but at the time they are to be used, they must be in electrostatic storage.

A program contains a set of instructions, usually to be executed in sequence, to produce a particular result. The instructions are ordinarily introduced into consecutively-numbered half-word locations of memory in the order in which they were written. The reasons for this follow.

Each time an operation is to be performed, the machine looks up the instruction in the electrostatic memory, executes it, and then goes back to the memory for the next instruction. The order in which instructions are executed is controlled by a unit known as the instruction sequencer. This unit contains a counter known as the instruction counter, which contains the address of the instruction currently being executed. After each execution, the number in this counter is automatically increased by 1. Consequently, the machine will automatically take its next instruction from a location whose half-word address is one higher than the address from which the current instruction was obtained. In this way the machine continues to execute instructions in the sequence in which they were stored in memory.

This normal sequence of instructions can be altered by means of certain "transfer" operations to be explained below. By means of these operations, any half-word location in electrostatic storage can be designated as the source of the next instruction. The address of this location is placed in the instruction counter by the transfer instruction; thereafter, execution of the program again proceeds sequentially.

An important observation with regard to this stored-program technique should be noted. Instructions are stored in the machine just like numerical data; the only distinction between the two is the way in which they are interpreted by the machine. If for any reason the address of a half-word of data is entered into the program counter, the data will be interpreted as an instruction. Conversely, an instruction may be caused to enter the computing unit just as data are caused to enter the computing unit. Thus, one instruction may call for the modification of another instruction by directing the machine to compute a new address part or to substitute another operation part. One program may operate on itself and compute one of its own instructions. A program may choose between several alternatives, depending on results obtained in the course of the problem. The ability of the machine to modify and to relocate instructions at high speed lends great flexibility to its operation and enlarges the scope of its application.

Instruction Layout   Each operation the machine can execute—including arithmetic operations, shifting, rounding, reading, writing, and others—is assigned a numerical code. An operation in conjunction with the address of an appropriate operand constitutes an *instruction* and is written and stored as a single binary number. The two components of an instruction are, referred to as the *operation part* and the *address part*. A schematic diagram of an instruction is shown in Figure 6.

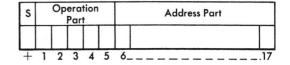

FIGURE 6

Note that the 17 bits of information and associated sign require exactly a half-word of storage space.

The operation part of an instruction determines the nature of the operation the machine is to execute. The numerical code for the operation is located in positions 1 through 5 of the instruction itself. The 701 is capable of performing exactly 32 distinct operations divided into four categories: (1) arithmetic operations, (2) logical operations, (3) input-output operations, (4) sense operations. These operations will be explained in detail later.

The address part of an instruction specifies a number that usually refers to a location in electrostatic storage. In such cases, the address will be a positive or negative integer as defined previously under *Address*

System. The sign of the integer in positions 6 through 17 of the instruction is determined by the sign of the instruction itself. Thus, the sign of an instruction applies only to the address part. For some instructions, however, the address part designates a certain input-output unit; with shift instructions it indicates the number of places to be shifted. But the name "address part" for the 12 rightmost bits of an instruction is retained, although these bits do not always represent an address in the true sense of the word. It will be seen later that the sign of some instructions is immaterial.

The machine interprets the numbers in the operation part and the address part as integers. In other words, the binary point of the binary digits occupying positions 1 through 5 is considered to be immediately to the right of position 5. Similarly, the binary point of the digits occupying the address part is considered to be immediately to the right of position 17.

For example, an instruction which designates 05 as the operation and −0013 as the address, will actually look in binary form as follows:

Operation part   Address part

$\overbrace{-00101}$ $\overbrace{000000001101}$

Operator's Panel

The various buttons, keys, switches, and signal lights by means of which the operator can control and communicate with the machine are assembled to form the operator's panel. The only control panels on the machine which require wiring are those for the card reader, printer, and card punch. These panels are discussed later in a separate section.

Description of the Panel   Components of the operator's panel are listed below with a brief explanation of their functions. Some of these functions will not be completely understood without reading later sections.

Power-On Button. Turns on the power for the entire calculator and automatically performs the resetting functions of the reset and clear-memory button.

Power-Off Button. Turns off the power for the entire calculator immediately, but leaves the blowers on for 10 minutes.

DC-Off Button. Turns off the direct-current power for servicing the machine.

DC-On Button. Turns the direct-current power on after it has been turned off with the DC-off button.

Power-On Light. Indicates that the main AC power is on.

Ready Light. Indicates that the AC and DC power is on and that the calculator is stopped but is ready to run. When the power is turned on, there is a delay before the ready light comes on.

Operating Light. Indicates that the calculator is running. When the calculator is started, the operating light goes on and the ready light goes off. When the calculator stops, the operating light goes off and the ready light goes on, if the power is still on.

Automatic-Manual Switch. When this switch is set to automatic, the calculator may be operated at full speed. When it is set to manual, the calculator may be operated manually by means of the half-step and multiple-step keys and the enter MQ, enter instruction, and memory display buttons; the load button is inoperative, and the start button cannot start the calculator. The calculator cannot be advanced manually while the stored program is using any input-output device.

Manual Light. Goes on when the automatic-manual switch is set to manual.

Start Button. If the automatic-manual switch is set to automatic, the start button resets the various machine interlocks and then starts the calculator. The program begins with the instruction whose address is contained in the instruction counter.

Reset Button. Resets the accumulator, MQ and memory registers, the instruction counter as well as certain internal input-output and check interlocks which are not discussed in this manual. It does not affect electrostatic storage.

Reset and Clear-Memory Button. Changes every bit in electrostatic storage to a 1 and, in addition, performs certain resetting functions not discussed in this manual.

Register Lights. Groups of small neon lights that indicate the contents of the following registers:

Memory register

Accumulator register

MQ register

Instruction counter

Instruction register

    a. Sign register

    b. Operation-part register

    c. Address-part register

A light being on indicates a binary digit of 1 located in that position of the register. A light being off indicates a zero.

MQ-Entry Keys. These 18 keys are used to set up a half-word for manual entry into the **MQ register.** Depressing a key represents a binary 1.

Enter-MQ Button. If the automatic-manual switch is set to MANUAL, the enter-MQ button enters the half-word set up on the 18 MQ-entry keys in the left 18 positions of the MQ register. The rightmost 18 positions of the MQ register are reset to zero.

Instruction-Entry Keys. There are 18 instruction entry keys, consisting of a sign-entry key, five operation-part entry keys, and twelve address-part entry keys. They are used to set up instructions for manual entry of an instruction into the control section of the calculator.

Enter-Instruction Button. If the automatic-manual switch is set to manual, the enter instruction button enters the instruction set up on the instruction entry keys into the instruction register and causes this instruction to be executed. The calculator then stops. Instructions, pertaining to input-output devices which must follow each other at high speed, cannot be executed manually with the enter instruction button. If the stored program calls on an input-output device which must receive its instructions in rapid succession, the calculator will automatically go into high-speed operation until this section of the program is completed.

Memory-Display Button. If the automatic-manual switch is set to manual, the memory-display button causes the full word stored at the address set up on the address part of the instruction-entry, keys to be displayed on the memory-register lights. Only full words are displayed in this way.

Half-Step Key. If the automatic-manual switch is set to manual, the half-step key advances the program one half-step at a time, provided the machine interlocks do not prevent the advance of the program. Half-steps are of two kinds : interpretation half-step, during which an instruction is interpreted, and execution half-step, during which the instruction is executed. Repeatedly pressing the half-step key causes the calculator to alternate between interpreting and executing an instruction. If a READ or WRITE instruction is executed, the calculator will go into automatic operation until the stored program is through using the particular input-output unit selected by the READ or WRITE instruction.

Multiple-Step Key. Holding down the multiple-step key is equivalent to pressing the half-step key repeatedly about ten times a second. Releasing the multiple-step key stops this action.

Machine Cycle Button. Advances the program one machine cycle at a time. It is intended only for servicing the machine and is not used by the operator. The half-step or multiple-step keys should be used to advance a program manually.

Load Selector Switch. Selects either the card reader, or the first tape unit (address 0256), or the first drum unit (address 0128), from which a unit record is to be read by means of the load button.

Load Button. If the automatic-manual switch is set to automatic, the load button initiates the reading of a unit record from the input unit selected by the load selector switch. It causes the first full word of the unit record to be read and to be stored at the address set up on the address-part entry keys. The calculator then starts automatically, using as the first instruction the left half-word at the same address. Pressing the load button is in effect the same as giving the following instructions:

READ	(Address of input-output unit specified by load selector)
SET DR 0000	(Relevant for drum only)
COPY	(Address set up on address-part entry keys)
TR	(Address set up on address-part entry keys)

Thus it is seen that the calculator will go into automatic operation starting with the instruction located at the address set up on the instruction entry keys.

Sense-Input Switches. There are 6 two-position sense-input switches, identified by addresses 0069 to 0074. They can be sensed by means of a SENSE instruction with the corresponding address part and used to cause the calculator to skip an instruction.

Sense-Output Lights. These four lights may be turned on individually by means of SENSE instructions, as explained above. Another SENSE instruction turns all four off together. The lights are used by the programmer to indicate the progress of a problem and to signal various conditions.

Instruction-Time Light. For half-step operation this light indicates that the calculator is ready to perform the next interpretation half-step.

Execution-Time Light. For half-step operation this light indicates that the calculator is ready to perform the next execution half-step.

Overflow Light. Turns on when the overflow indicator turns on. It is turned off by execution of a TR OV instruction or by the reset and clear-memory button.

Input-Output Light. Indicates that one of the input-output units is selected by the calculator.

Program-Stop Light. Indicates that the calculator has stopped as a result of executing a STOP instruction. It is reset by the start button, or the reset button, or the reset and clear-memory button.

Copy-Check Light. Indicates that the calculator has stopped because a copy instruction was given at the wrong time. It is reset by the start button, or the reset button, or the reset and clear-memory button.

Tape-Check Light. Indicates that the calculator has stopped because of a discrepancy in the tape group count or the redundancy check while a tape was being read. It is reset by the start button, or the reset button, or the reset and clear-memory button.

Divide-Check Light. Indicates that the calculator has stopped because the dividend is not less than the divisor. It is reset by the start button or the reset button, or the reset and clear-memory button.

Calculator-Fuse Light. Indicates that a fuse for the main calculator unit, or electrostatic storage, or a tape or drum unit has burned out. After replacement of the fuse, the light is reset by the start button or the reset button, or the reset and clear-memory button.

Input-Output Fuse Light. Indicates that a fuse has burned out in the card reader, punch, or printer. After replacement of the fuse, the light is reset by the start button or the reset button, or the reset and clear-memory button.

Basic Manipulations

Entering Information into Storage   Information may be entered manually into electrostatic storage from the operator's panel one half-word at a time. The procedure:

1. Set up the automatic-manual switch to manual.

2. Set up the half-word on the MQ-entry keys.

3. Set up the instruction + STORE MQ xxxx on the instruction entry keys, where xxxx represents the address (in binary form) at which the half-word is to be stored.

4. Press the enter-MQ button to enter the half-word into the MQ register.

5. Press the enter-instruction button to execute the instruction (set up under 3), thus storing the half-word in memory.

6. Press the memory-display button to check that the half-word has been stored correctly.

A full word can be entered into electrostatic storage from the operator's panel only by splitting it into two half-words and entering each separately.

Starting Machine with a Given Instruction   Assume the operator wants the machine to begin calculating with an instruction located in address xxxx of electrostatic memory.

1. Set automatic-manual switch to manual.

2. Set up the instruction TRANSFER xxxx on the instruction entry keys.

3. Press the enter-instruction button.

4. Set automatic-manual switch to automatic.

5. Press the start button.

If there is a program stored in memory, the machine will start calculating with the instruction located at xxxx and continue automatically.

8.10

Electronic Numerical Integrator and Computer

J. Presper Eckert and John W. Mauchly

Patent no. 3,120,606, filed June 26, 1947.

INTRODUCTORY NOTE TO READING 8.10

Who invented the stored-program electronic digital computer? Could this invention be patented? The stored-program computer could not have been invented without memory in which to store the program and process data. It also required a method of processing the data within the memory. Maurice Wilkes provided a useful three-part definition of the stored-program concept, which we excerpt from a larger discussion:

Serial execution of instructions: instructions were to be executed one at a time, those concerned with the organization of the flow of control taking their turn with those calling for arithmetic operations.

Single memory: the memory would contain addressable words each composed of the same number of binary digits; addresses would consist of integers running consecutively through the memory. If a word were sent to the control unit it would be interpreted as an instruction, and if sent to the arithmetic unit it would be interpreted as an item of data.

Modification and construction of instructions: the programmer would be able to modify addresses, or indeed whole instructions, by performing arithmetical or logical operations on them in the arithmetic unit. Similarly, he would have the power to construct new instructions and plant them in a program.

The last three items constitute the stored program principle which, when used as a term of art, means something more than that the program is stored in a memory.[1]

Pres Eckert invented the first operational electronic memory and the first operational means for data processing within it. As he wrote in 1991:

My big idea was the idea of the *stored instruction sequence* or program, using a single fast memory for both data and instruction, with no distinction between registers used for many purposes.

At the time I first thought of this idea, (in January 1944), I knew of no good way to provide the required memory registers. My first idea was to use a magnetic disc such as Bell Laboratories had used in some telephone sound recording work. But first let me tell you how I thought of the idea itself.

While we were building and testing the ENIAC there were periods, usually waiting for some wiring to be completed by a technician or some circuit to be debugged, when I had time to think. My thoughts usually turned to what the next machine should be like. I thought it should have a magnetic wire or tape for input

---

1 Maurice V. Wilkes, *Computer Perspectives* (San Francisco: Morgan Kaufmann Publishers, 1995), 18.

and output and probably a greater use of binary as opposed to decimal or coded decimal arithmetic. If we were free of punch cards there was no longer a good reason to stick to the decimal system.

The problem on which I always got stuck was the question of how to spend money on the various high speed electronic memories. In ENIAC we had one type of memory for numbers or data, another for instructions, another for fixed set of numbers and another for input output buffering. The problem was that each different problem in the future would require a different mix of these things. It occurred to me that most of the great mathematicians and scientists tried to avoid solving specific problems and tried to find general solutions to broad areas of problems. I felt we had to find a general, rather than a specific solution to the memory problem. Once you take this position you have no choice but to say let's have only one kind of memory for almost all our high speed purposes, except for some very few "working registers."

I wrote, in January 1944, a memo proposing magnetic discs as memory for all forms of storage required. I later realized that a variation of a "mercury tank" which I had invented and developed for several radar problems at M.I.T. and Harvard could be modified to be a random access memory and would be the best bet for our first stored program machine, the BINAC and our first commercial machine, the UNIVAC I. We also performed considerable work on an electrostatic storage tube approach.[2]

Few people disputed Eckert's major role in the discovery of the stored-program concept. What was disputed was the completeness of his and Mauchly's discovery, and their right to patent it. Eckert and Mauchly applied for the ENIAC patent in 1947; this was a general patent on the stored-program electronic digital computer. The patent was finally granted in 1964, but was thrown out in the famous case of Honeywell v. Sperry Rand in 1973 for two fundamental reasons: (1) John von Neumann's *First Draft of a Report on the EDVAC* (see Reading 8.1), an incomplete theoretical description of a stored-program computer, published essential parts of the invention two years before Eckert and Mauchly applied for the patent; and (2) the special-purpose ABC computer invented by John Atanasoff in Iowa during World War II, but never properly operational, represented prior discovery of key concepts. This litigation will remain among the most famous in the history of computing. Reading 8.10 reproduces excerpts from the ENIAC patent. Reading 8.12 reproduces excerpts from Judge Earl R. Larson's ruling that eventually invalidated the patent. [JMN]

---

2 Diana H. Hook and Jeremy M. Norman, *Origins of Cyberspace. A Library on the History of Computing, Networking, and Telecommunications* (Novato, CA: historyofscience.com, 2002), 638–39.

TEXT OF READING 8.10

This invention relates to methods and apparatus for performing computations involving arithmetical operations, at extremely high speeds, and with minimum use of mechanical elements, as generally so termed, and more particularly, relates to the art of electrical computing machines, with particular reference to a machine utilizing electronically produced pulses (i.e., sharp voltage changes not greater than five microseconds in duration) to represent digits and numbers, and using such pulses for control and programming operations, thus obviating the need for mechanically moving parts for these purposes. The present invention also relates to the method of using such pulses for computational purposes.

In the progress of development of computing machines from the time of the use of pebbles or grains, and the application of the abacus, to the extensive mechanical or partly mechanical and partly electrical machines of the present day, the aim has been to remove from the mind of man as much as possible of the responsibility of remembering numbers, remembering the necessary computations to be performed, remembering and writing the results of parts of computations, and how and when to use such results of such parts in complete equations, as well as to effect the necessary operations more rapidly and without physical labor.

The art and technique of aids to computation and calculation have been the subject of extensive development, extending through simple adding machines to present day complex computing machines, which include electric devices, in part in answer to the need and demand for greater speed and the elimination of moving mechanisms whose inertia sets a definite limit to the practicable speed of operation.

With the advent of everyday use of elaborate calculations, speed has become paramount to such a high degree that there is no machine on the market today capable of satisfying the full demand of modern computational methods. The most advanced machines have greatly reduced the time required for arriving at solutions to problems which might have required months or days by older procedures. This advance, however, is not adequate for many problems encountered in modern scientific work and the present invention is intended to reduce to seconds such lengthy computations.

In automatic machines the manner of controlling the storing in memory devices of the necessary numerical components and the "programming" of the pickup of these numbers and their transfer to particular operating units, as well as the special programming of peculiar internal arithmetic operations in the units, has involved a problem of foremost importance which it is here sought to advance. In such machines it is convenient to designate as "memories" those parts or elements which are so constituted as to predetermine and cause definite effects from signals transmitted to the system. External memories may consist of switches and coupling between units, arbitrarily made in accordance with the planned use of the apparatus for the solution of a given problem, and of means such as tapes or punched cards and reading machines by which numerical data (numbers pulses) and program instructions (characteristic control pulse signals) are introduced into the apparatus. Functions of the machine by which numbers are stored and control pulse signals stored for subsequent transmission or collection from storage, as well as any automatically generated or guided to particular units, may be termed internal memories.

It is an especial aim to reduce the requirement of external memories in such machines, and to provide for the replacement thereof by internal memories, so that approach to more fully automatic operation is attained by the mere insertion of data in pulse form and the automatic generation within the machine of the necessary further data, including control pulses.

A machine has been constructed at the University of Pennsylvania which embodies our invention. This machine, hereinafter referred to as ENIAC (from the initials of its name, "Electronic Numerical Integrator and Computer") is the first general purpose automatic electronic digital computing machine known to us. Its speed considerably exceeds that of any non-electronic machine, and its accuracy is in general superior to that of any non-digital machine (such as a differential analyzer).

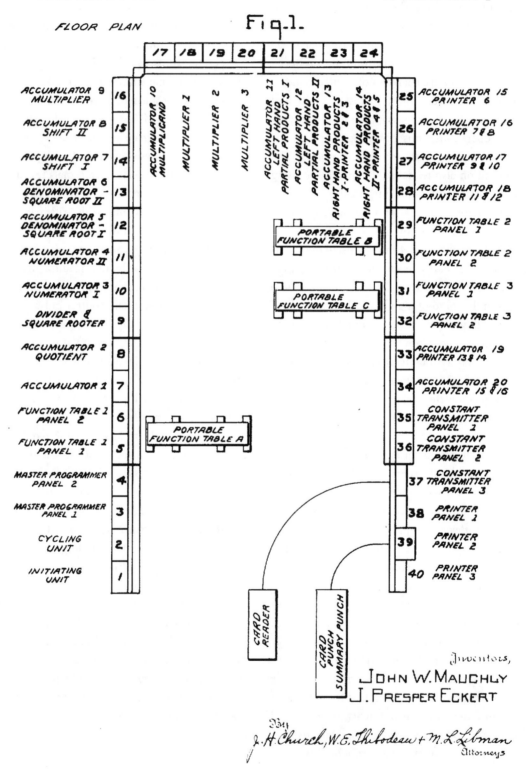

The ENIAC is extremely flexible, and is not fundamentally restricted to any given class of problems. However, there are problems for which its speed is limited by the input and output devices, so that it is impossible to derive the full benefit of its high computing speed in such cases. The ENIAC carries out its entire computing schedule automatically, but the sequence which it is to follow must be set up manually beforehand. The primary intended use of the ENIAC is to compute large families of solutions all based on the same program of operations, in which case the time spent in manual set-up is relatively unimportant.

It should be noted in this introductory section that it is recognized that the object of computing machine design is not merely to speed up arithmetic processes, but to attain a high overall speed, including the problem set-up and the preparation of results in useful form. It is desirable to have as much as possible done automatically.

It is also to be observed that a great deal of the equipment in non-electronic machines is "in multiple," that is, concurrent operation of many parts is used to increase computing speed. Electronic devices are inherently so fast that it is unnecessary to achieve speed in this way. By resorting to "serial operation," a considerable saving in equipment may be effected. However, the consequent loss in speed is tolerable only when electronic components having high inherent speed are employed. Reliability and maintenance are aided by this equipment reduction, and serial operation also has important advantages both from the point of view of checking and because it simplifies the work of planning the computational program.

An examination of the literature of the physical sciences shows that the principal emphasis in these fields has been in the solution of linear problems (those which can be formulated in terms of linear equations) which can be handled by analytic techniques. Physical problems other than those above mentioned are not necessarily more difficult from a physical science point of view, but they have prior to this invention been by-passed in favor of the problems whose analytic solutions are possible of attainment.

Those problems which cannot be solved analytically have been handled by computational methods or through the use of specific analogy machines. As an illustration of the computational approach we might mention the truly remarkable work of Hartree on the structure of the atom, a series of calculations extending over a period of about 15 years. An exemplification of the latter technique is found in the use of wind tunnels. At present, the supersonic wind tunnel at the Ballistic Research Laboratory, at Aberdeen, Maryland, is used about 30% of the time as an analogy machine to solve two-dimensional steady state aerodynamical problems. Industrial companies frequently resort to highly specific analogy machines to solve, for example, linear equations of electric circuit theory or the partial differential equations which enter into electron-optics problems. It may be noted that much of present experimental work consists essentially of the solution of mathematical problems by analogy methods. If one had a computing machine of sufficient flexibility the necessity for these experiments would be obviated. Our invention makes available such a machine.

In discussing the speed of computing machines it is desirable to distinguish between so-called continuous variable and digital machines. Although existing continuous variable machines such as the differential analyzer and the A.-C. network analyzer are exceedingly rapid, the class of problems which they can solve is limited. Since both of these machines perform all operations of a computation in parallel, the size and complexity of the problems they can solve is limited by the number of arithmetic organs they contain. In addition, these machines are necessarily restricted in their accuracy due to their inherent nature. We have therefore chosen to direct our endeavors to the perfection of a digital computing machine.

The time required to carry out a multiplication provides a rather good index of the speed of a digital computing machine inasmuch as the time spent in multiplication usually represents the major part of the computing time when such machines are used. In general, the computing time for a given problem can be estimated roughly as 2 or 3 times the amount spent in multiplications. The multiplication time for the ENIAC is about 3 milliseconds. For electromechanical digital machines, the multiplication time ranges from about $1/2$ second to 5 seconds.

To give some idea of the time consumed in carrying out an extensive computation, we may consider a typical aerodynamical problem of interest in ballistic research, which involves the solution of quasilinear hyperbolic differential equations.

I. E. Segal has formulated the partial differential equations for describing the pressure on a high-speed, sharply pointed and non-yawing projectile. The knowledge of this pressure enables one to compute the head drag, the air flow between the projectile and the head wave, and of course, the head shape of lowest drag in a given group of head shapes. If the mathematical solution of this problem is successful, it will evidently point the way to the solution of many problems now handled in wind tunnels or precision firing ranges as experimental problems. Segal's procedure above is a typical example in mathematical physics illustrating the need for high-speed computing equipment. It involves partial differential equations describing the motion of the fluid which are quasi-linear hyperbolic partial differential equations wherever the flow is supersonic, and they are solved by the introduction of characteristic parameters. The Segal formula requires interpolation in a family of previously computed head waves to determine the flow around the given projectile head at a given Mach number. Segal estimates the number of head waves needed for this interpolation to be in order of 25.

Before the introduction of characteristic parameters the form of equations to be solved is

$$(a^2 - u^2)u_y - uv(u_y + v_z) + a^2 - v^2)v_y + a^2 v/y = 0$$

$$v_x - u_y = 0$$

where a is the local velocity of sound; u, v are the components of the fluid velocity at the point (x, y), and where subscripts denote the partial differentiation.

Without going into details, we can say that there are approximately 90 multiplications to be performed at each point in the field of integration, and that there will be about a thousand such points. Consequently, on the ENIAC the pure computing time, apart from reading or printing, will be about 5 minutes. Inasmuch as there will be 2000 cards printed at the rate of 100 cards per minute, the printing time is of the order of 20 minutes. It is thus seen that the total solution for Segal's problem for a given Mach number and a given head wave will be, with ideal ENIAC operation, about a half hour.

For the 25 solutions of this problem with respective head wave values, and possibly about 10 solutions for different Mach numbers the total problem will represent about 125 hours of total computing time with the ENIAC.

Contrasting this with the use of a hypothetical electromechanical machine corresponding to such as have been developed and therefore assuming a multiplication time on such a machine of about one second and a printing time of 5 characters per second, there would be spent 25 hours for the pure computing time and about 8 hours for printing, making a total computing time of about 33 hours, or a total time for the 25 solutions of about 8,000 hours. It would then be preferable to handle the problem by experimental techniques either in supersonic wind tunnels or precision firing ranges of the sort in use at the Ballistic Research Laboratory.

The question arises, why not be content with long time numerical computations? The three arguments on this point are, cost per problem, urgency for getting a solution quickly, and the scope and range of problems which could profitably be undertaken. The second point is important not only because of deadline considerations but also because the high-speed machine can be used as a tool of the physicist or engineer, much as his other laboratory equipment is used. The latter attainment of the ENIAC will allow the scientist to undertake investigations which he would otherwise not even attempt.

Objects, advantages and features of invention in the present disclosure may be understood from the foregoing and in conjunction with the detailed description and illustration hereinafter. Among the objects and advantages contemplated, some are outlined herein, although others equally important may be recognized in the embodiment of the invention or its parts disclosed and in the results and benefits attendant on practice of the invention.

A serious obstacle to the successful construction of

an electronic computing machine of satisfactory accuracy and reliability has been the tendency for parasitic signals and other manifestations to develop, due to the reactances inherent in interconnection circuits, and it is an important aim of this invention to prevent such parasitic impairment of the proper response of the machine to the significant pulses for either numerical effect, or for control and timing of computative operations.

An object of the invention is to so organize an intricate and extensive system of intimately associated circuits that liability of feed-back responses or capacitative or inductive effects which would change the essential significance of the functioning of electron emission tubes in the system is eliminated.

Another difficulty which it is a purpose of the invention to overcome in a novel way, is the tendency for signals to become distorted as to potential, duration, and shape (as recorded by the oscilloscope) by interferences capacitative or inductive. In this direction a novel approach has been effected by not transmitting properly timed pulses of numerical or control significance directly through the various conductors from the initiating device directly to the one which is to respond, but instead producing a program pulse which serves only as part of the potential necessary to operate a gate or pulse former device of very definite pulse forming characteristics, the remainder of the necessary stimulating potential being derived from a constantly repeated frame of pulses having a definite order. This frame has a duration called an addition time, which is a multiple of a pulse time, that is, the interval from the beginning of one pulse to the beginning of the next pulse.

As a consequence of the foregoing, in our invention at each introduction of data to an arithmetic unit, an original shaping of the pulse received by that unit is effected by the unit itself.

It is an important aim of the invention to devise a novel means of preserving the definite and highly effective form of signal information transmitted to or through the various parts of the system and which will have standard pulse forms and potentials at all stages of operations and registering caused by such pulses.

In a related sense it is an aim to offer a novel means

by which the foregoing may be attained by maintaining at all operating units a frame of pulses occurring in timed sequence related to an overall time beat, so that at each unit a series of pulses is available in fully effective form for numerical entries, and for control functions, and by which, when such pulses are properly selected and made effective, several units may be caused to function together with exactitude.

In the same connection it is a purpose to enable the transmission of signals of both numerical significance and control significance in such manner that they become adequately effective at selected units to cause reception of predetermined pulses of the said frame of pulses with the desired numerical or control significance, whereby the initial signal is not required to maintain a high effectiveness as to form and potential by transmission past the functioning apparatus.

An important desideratum in the invention is the production by means of a simple constantly operating oscillator circuit of clock pulses having the basic frequency determined for effective operation of the various electronic elements of the machine, and to derive in a novel way from each of an arbitrary recurrent number or cycle of such clock pulses, a variety of pulses in a plurality of circuits in a coordinated relation so that some of the pulses so derived will control the utilization of other pulses derived in the same or other cycles and other sources, for arithmetic functioning of units of the machine. In the same direction it is sought to reduce to a minimum the number of the clock pulses required in such cycle, so that a number of numerical signals and control signals greatly exceeding the number of pulses in such a cycle, but all occurring in the same cycle as the clock pulses with which they are associated, may be produced.

Among the objects of the invention either additional or contributory to the foregoing, are the following:

a.   To enable the performance of mathematical equivalents of differential equations by mathematical representations of the variables by discrete numbers, with such certainty that the introduction of the same data at different times will give the identical numerical result, as distinct from such machines as the differential analyzer.

b. In the control of the arithmetical functions of the machine, to eliminate the repeating routines of instructions in external memory material.

c. Futher, where sub-routines of arithmetical procedure are required, it is a purpose to cause automatic origination of sub-routine controls and selection of these as an internal function of the machine, so that the material required to be prepared as external data to be fed into the machine is further minimized.

d. To organize the elements of the machine so as to eliminate functions of such nature that they might be materially affected by variations of operating conditions such as often occur. The machine is thus adapted to practically infallible operation under varying conditions which extensive experience has shown may be expected to be manifest in such machines over a reasonable period of operation.

For instance, it is an attainment of the invention that electron emission high vacuum tubes such as common triodes or pentodes, used in radio receivers, are made use of as switching devices in such manner that their operation occurs in a condition far from the critical point between conduction and non-conduction, and so that deterioration in the tube elements or the state of the space therein over a period of months, will not materially affect the response of the tube to control potentials applied to the grids as pulses or potentials of substantial values.

It is a related aim to use such tubes as switches or other kinetic equivalents in such manner that their function will be either conducting or non-conducting, accompanying this by use of the tubes at or close to saturation for their conducting state, and with a grid bias well below the critical point for their non-con-

ducting state. This also permits use of tubes of high $m\mu$ and low capacitance in order to establish great certainty of operation and response generally. In this way aggregated reactances between trunk lines and ether conductors and between electrodes of the tubes are not sufficient to distort transmitted signals materially or to set up parasitic pulses of sufficient degree to cause malfunction.

Associated with, and as a part of this relation of circuits and the objects in view, the potentials of circuits having mutually adjacent conductors or other relation in which relatively high reactance values are unavoidable, have been so organized in relation to their greatest possible reactances, their potential levels so fixed relatively to such liabilities and the operating pulses produced at potential levels so antagonistic to such liabilities, that impairment of signal pulses, or production of equivalent or intervening parasitic pulses, will be inconsequential.

A further aim is to present a novel means of determining the selection of predetermined pulses forming part of an arbitrary arrangement or frame of pulses being automatically transmitted in trunk conductors, by the timing of energization of plural grid tubes, so that a control pulse of long or short duration may be utilized to partially establish the necessary grid potential for changing the stable state of a tube having an adequate B potential for initiating a desired pulse on such change, and another pulse either for control or with numerical significance, forming part of a frame of pulses which are being manifest on another grid of such tube at the same time, will cause it to transmit to an appropriate conductor a pulse of a desired characteristic and significance with functional value effective at a unit conditioned to receive it.

In the attainment of functions necessary in an electronic system, by which arithmetically significant results may be produced, it is a salient object of the invention to enable the use of standard high vacuum electron radio tubes.

It is also an important aim of the invention to enable the use of such tubes for producing control actions in the system by which various parts may be caused to receive electrical impulses of numerical significance and hold a corresponding condition such that they may cooperate with other units to integrate two or more such storage equivalents of sums or digits, or to produce control responses by which the intercommunication of units may be effected as required, as well as effecting the clearing of the units of conditions representing stored numbers of controls.

While electronic ring counters have been evolved utilizing such tubes in relations known as trigger circuits and flip-flops, and the present invention utilizes an adaptation of a flip-flop ring to its use where the reception and counting of pulses of numerical significance is desired, it is a special aim of the invention to evolve novel means by which such ring counters are embodied so as to operate with great certainty and effectiveness, and to organize such counters in a correlated system whereby novel arithmetical computations are attained not heretofore conceived or possible with available apparatus.

In ring counters of the familiar prior art an output from the counter numerically significant of its stage of operation at a given time has heretofore only been obtained by operating the counter in such manner that the number value contained is erased. The present invention seeks to enable the repetition of such output successively at basic times intervals, or to repeat the output at irregular intervals, while preserving the information in the storing clement until required or purposely erased or "cleared."

It is further sought to present a novel means to take from a matrix such as a punched card a record significant of numbers and instructions, by mechanical means, and to establish a set-up significant of such numbers and instructions in such manner that pulse equivalents of these numbers and instructions will automatically by made effective electronically and transmitted through the system in the desired order required for arithmetical procedures in units properly responsive thereto.

It is a highly important purpose of the invention to provide a novel electronic means for carrying out the arithmetical process of multiplications very rapidly and to devise a novel system whereby the product may be secured through an automatic electronic operation of the system.

To this end it is sought to evolve a novel circuit system and associated tube organization whereby there may be effected the equivalent of the necessary off-set or shift of the product of the multiplicand by a digit of the multiplier in relation to the product of the same multiplicand by another digit of the same multiplier.

Another object related to the multiplication procedure in the system is to construct and coordinate a resistance grid system in which signals applied to the cross elements of one direction in the grid system may cause potentials on intersecting transverse members to select pulses to he transmitted to the counters of an accumulator in the necessary decades to effect the desired result.

An object subordinate to the last mentioned is to devise a novel and effective means for transmitting to the shifter device pulses significant of a treatment of input to the multiplier corresponding to the multiplication of one number by another.

Another important aim is to construct a novel organization of the multiplier grid work of conductors and resistance couplings at significant intersections with input electronic valves and pulse supplying means and output electronic valves in controlled relation to conductors signals by which the second named valves are energized by coincidence results to transmit pulses significant of results of factors represented in the input.

A purpose related to the last named object is to so organize the grid work and valve devices in the form of radio tubes that feedback and cross couplings are obviated and so as to avoid sufficient partial or complete diverted transmissions of pulses to set up or initiate output effects other than the numerical product or result equivalents corresponding to the computational procedure of multiplication.

It is an important aim of the invention to simplify the apparatus required in securing interaction between two or more computing or arithmetic units, by utilizing a novel coordination of an arbitrary clock frame, work of pulses effective in all units alike and recurrent either at fixed intervals automatically, or at will and requiring only a small number of selectively transmitted pulses, so that the requirement of interlock coupling of circuits is eliminated to a large degree, and the amount of a apparatus greatly minimized.

It is an important aim of the invention to enable the utilization in a novel way of a cyclically repeated frame of pulses of uniform interval in the cycle to effect the communication to the storing and computing units of the machine of pulses of numerical significance, either plus or minus, and all necessary operating pulses by which the various adding, multiplying, dividing, subtracting, and square rooting operations of the system are carried out.

A further object related to the foregoing is to establish a number of categories of control and numerically significant pulses with standard pulse times within the predetermined cycle, but wherein the number of control and numerically significant pulses included in such categories greatly exceed the number of pulse times included within the cycle.

A related object is to enable the derivation from a frame of successive pulses cyclically repeated and communicated to parts of each unit in the machine, of numerically significant pulses communicated on one or more of a plurality of channels to units conditioned and intended to receive such data and / or to function computatively therewith and with other data previously or subsequently transmitted.

An important aim of the invention contributing to its successful operation with a minimum of impairment or malfunction mathematically, is to effect intercommunication between units having pulse-responsive circuits which are maintained at widely different potentials for their normal conditions, by the communication of pulses from one such unit to another such unit without mutual disturbance of their normal potentials, yet in a most definite manner taking full advantage of the before mentioned operations of tubes well below or above cut off, or well above minimum conductance conditions (that is close to the saturation state of conductance).

A specific object of the invention is to present a novel organization of electron valve tubes and circuits for communicating control signals and effecting the transmission of complements of nine. A related purpose is to enable the derivation of both decimal digits and / or their complements from the same clock pulses, in a novel and simple manner.

It is also sought to fix the value of transmitted number data as plus or minus, by novel means, which will be effective both in the functioning of computing units of the machine, and in the optically observable condition of the units.

A novel attainment of the invention is a means for the derivation of the complement of ten of a number. This means is further distinguished by functioning in such manner that the transmitted complement is obtained by transmission originally of the principal number itself, and a derivation of the complement by an automatic internal routine of the machine.

A further object is to provide a novel means of communicating pulses of positive potential from one circuit to another with a high rise and good form. That is to say, in usual methods of producing positive pulses with vacuum tubes it has been difficult to produce a pulse of a rise of fifty volts or more which can be limited to approximately two microseconds in duration and which will have a sharp rise and sharp fall at termination. In accomplishing this it is an object to utilize a vacuum tube in a novel way for the production of pulses by deriving the pulse from the cathode in an efficient manner.

Another important object of the invention is to provide a novel automatic means for producing the quotient of two digital quantities represented by electric pulses in terms of a digital quantity also represented by electric pulses. A subsidiary object to the above is to provide an electronic digital divider capable of handling digital quantities of either positive or negative sign, with the correct sign in the quotient.

Another object is to provide automatic means for electronically evaluating the square root of a digitally represented quantity.

An important feature of the invention is the provision of an electrical function table capable of storing digital values in tabular form for transmission to the computer at electronic speeds. An object subsidiary to the above is to provide, in such a function table, means for automatically transmitting at electronic speeds not only the value of the function corresponding to a given argument, but also a sequence of function values bracketing the one corresponding to the argument, for use in interpolation or any other desired mathematical purpose.

Another object is to provide means enabling the automatic transfer to the computer at electronic speeds of any one of a number of digital values stored in an external memory or recording device, in any desired predetermined sequence.

Another object is to provide means for automatically repeating any operation of the computer at electronic speeds for any exact predetermined number of times.

A particularly important object is the provision of means and method enabling the automatic choice by the computer, at electronic speeds, of any one of a plurality of possible computational operations in response to the value of the result of a previous computational operation, in accordance with a predetermined standard of selection.

Another object is to enable the transfer of a digital number from a static mechanical representation thereof by the positional arrangement of switching elements, such as switches or relays, into a dynamic electronic representation thereof by means of coded and suitably channeled electrical pulses of extremely short duration, at electronic speeds.

ADVANTAGES OF ELECTRONIC DIGITAL MACHINES

A digital machine has more *flexibility* and *accuracy* than is possible or practical in a continuous variable machine. A digital machine which is electronic can also have a very decided *speed* advantage over one which is non-electronic. The evidence of many months' operation is that electronic digital machines can be made at least as reliable as any others.

Flexibility and accuracy also are important economic considerations in this invention. With specialized machines, specific problems may be solved rapidly, but time may be lost when new problems require either a new machine or the modification of an old one. Further, even if time is no object, the cost of a group of specialized devices can easily total more than the cost of one flexible all-purpose machine.

Accuracy

The accuracy obtainable with continuous variable machines depends upon the accuracy with which the component parts are constructed. However, exactly the same statement may be made about a digital machine. The essential difference is in the kind of dependence which holds in each case. In a digital machine, minor inaccuracies of components can be made to have no effect at all upon the accuracy of the computation. In continuous variable machines, there is a continuous (though not necessarily simple) relationship between the accuracy of the parts and the accuracy of the results (before translation into digital form). Increased computational accuracy can be attained only by increased precision of the parts. Not only are there practical limits to the precision with which the parts can be manufactured, but the maintenance of such precision during subsequent operation is extremely difficult. For instance, mechanical parts will lose precision through wear. On the other hand, digital machines require only that the accuracy of parts be kept within certain tolerances, and the tolerance band can be made very wide. The accuracy of a digital machine is then limited only by the amount of equipment which can be used in it. This limitation is more often an economic one than a physical one.

Flexibility

Analogy computing devices vary greatly in flexibility. Scale models and fixed electrical networks which are completely specialized represent an extreme which is of no interest here. Large network analyzers and differential analyzers are usually considered typical examples of highly flexible analogy devices. Nevertheless, these machines are somewhat specialized and restricted in application.

A digital machine which can be directed to carry out any of the common arithmetic operations in any desired sequence on any given set of numbers has all the generality and flexibility required for any practical purpose. (It cannot compute the "exact" value of pi, but it can compute in a finite number of steps any desired approximation of pi.) Therefore, it can, for example, compute to any specified definite approximation the solutions of non-linear partial differential equations which are not obtainable from any existing analogy computer. This attainment is one of the important objects of our invention.

Digital Computing Speed and Cost

The preceding sections have indicated that advantages of accuracy and flexibility recommend digital rather than continuous variable computing devices. Even moderately large problems which are within the range of existing analogy machines require an enormous number of arithmetic operations when handled by digital machines. The cost of digital computing must be low if such calculations are to be undertaken.

Only very rough comparisons need to be made to demonstrate that digital computation by electronic devices should be a great deal faster than by the electro-mechanical devices used in existing large computers. Typical electro-mechanical devices are relays and electrically controlled counter wheels. Five or ten milliseconds is about the operating time for reliable high speed relays. Analogous operation of a vacuum tube can take place in 0.5 to 1 microsecond. The electronic device is therefore capable of operating about 10,000 times faster. (It may be observed that faster tube circuits can be developed.)

A vacuum tube and its associated circuit components costs approximately the same amount as a relay. This indicates that generally for a given cost the ENIAC gains time by a factor of 10,000, when compared to the non-electronic electromechanical digital computer.

For various reasons, the actual factor for the ENIAC is something like 100, and for our future electronic machines will probably be more nearly 1000. Since moderately large computing problems are already being done by digital electromechanical devices, it seems clear that the ENIAC will find much more extensive application than practicable with the electromechanical machine.

Cramming More Components onto Integrated Circuits

Gordon E. Moore

From *Electronics* 38 (1965).

INTRODUCTORY NOTE TO READING 8.11

In 1965, four years after the integrated circuit was invented, Gordon Moore observed the exponential growth in the number of transistors per integrated circuit, and predicted that this trend would continue. The press called this observation "Moore's Law." The rule has successfully predicted the exponential growth of transistors in microprocessors, beginning with the Intel 4004 in 1971 (2,250 transistors) and continuing to the present: the Pentium 4 processor, introduced in 2000, had 42,000,000 transistors. A major goal of research on microprocessors has been to break down technical barriers to allow further exponential advances in the complexity of microprocessors, reflective of Moore's Law. As an evidence of continuing success in this regard, Intel announced on August 31, 2004, while I was editing this book, that it had built a fully functional 70Mb static random access memory (SRam) chip with more than half a billion transistors, using 65 nanometer (nm) process technology. SRam chips are used as test vehicles for new manufacturing processes.[1] [JMN]

---

1 http://www.vnunet.com/news/1157714

TEXT OF READING 8.11

The future of integrated electronics is the future of electronics itself. The advantages of integration will bring about a proliferation of electronics, pushing this science into many new areas.

Integrated circuits will lead to such wonders as home computers—or at least terminals connected to a central computer—automatic controls for automobiles, and personal portable communications equipment. The electronic wristwatch needs only a display to be feasible today.

But the biggest potential lies in the production of large systems. In telephone communications, integrated circuits in digital filters will separate channels on multiplex equipment. Integrated circuits will also switch telephone circuits and perform data processing.

Computers will be more powerful, and will be organized in completely different ways. For example, memories built of integrated electronics may be distributed throughout the machine instead of being concentrated in a central unit. In addition, the improved reliability made possible by integrated circuits will allow the construction of larger processing units. Machines similar to those in existence today will be built at lower costs and with faster turnaround.

PRESENT AND FUTURE

By integrated electronics, I mean all the various technologies which are referred to as microelectronics today as well as any additional ones that result in electronics functions supplied to the user as irreducible units. These technologies were first investigated in the late 1950's. The object was to miniaturize electronics equipment to include increasingly complex electronic functions in limited space with minimum weight. Several approaches evolved, including microassembly techniques for individual components, thin-film structures and semiconductor integrated circuits.

Each approach evolved rapidly and converged so that each borrowed techniques from another. Many researchers believe the way of the future to be a combination of the various approaches.

The advocates of semiconductor integrated circuitry are already using the improved characteristics of thin-film resistors by applying such films directly to an active semiconductor substrate. Those advocating a technology based upon films are developing sophisticated techniques for the attachment of active semiconductor devices to the passive film arrays.

Both approaches have worked well and are being used in equipment today.

THE ESTABLISHMENT

Integrated electronics is established today. Its techniques are almost mandatory for new military systems, since the reliability, size and weight required by some of them is achievable only with integration. Such programs as Apollo, for manned moon flight, have demonstrated the reliability of integrated electronics by showing that complete circuit functions are as free from failure as the best individual transistors.

Most companies in the commercial computer field have machines in design or in early production employing integrated electronics. These machines cost less and perform better than those which use "conventional" electronics.

Instruments of various sorts, especially the rapidly increasing numbers employing digital techniques, are starting to use integration because it cuts costs of both manufacture and design.

The use of linear integrated circuitry is still restricted primarily to the military. Such integrated functions are expensive and not available in the variety required to satisfy a major fraction of linear electronics. But the first applications are beginning to appear in commercial electronics, particularly in equipment which needs low-frequency amplifiers of small size.

RELIABILITY COUNTS

In almost every case, integrated electronics has demonstrated high reliability. Even at the present level of production—low compared to that of discrete components—it offers reduced systems cost, and in many systems improved performance has been realized.

Integrated electronics will make electronic techniques more generally available throughout all of society, performing many functions that presently are done inadequately by other techniques or not done at all. The principal advantages will be lower costs and greatly simplified design—payoffs from a ready supply of low-cost functional packages.

For most applications, semiconductor integrated circuits will predominate. Semiconductor devices are the only reasonable candidates presently in existence for the active elements of integrated circuits. Passive semiconductor elements look attractive too, because of their potential for low cost and high reliability, but they can be used only if precision is not a prime requisite.

Silicon is likely to remain the basic material, although others will be of use in specific applications. For example, gallium arsenide will be important in integrated microwave functions. But silicon will predominate at lower frequencies because of the technology which has already evolved around it and its oxide, and because it is an abundant and relatively inexpensive starting material.

COSTS AND CURVES

Reduced cost is one of the big attractions of integrated electronics, and the cost advantage continues to increase as the technology evolves toward the production of larger and larger circuit functions on a single semiconductor substrate. For simple circuits, the cost per component is nearly inversely proportional to the number of components, the result of the equivalent piece of semiconductor in the equivalent package containing more components. But as components are added, decreased yields more than compensate for the increased complexity, tending to raise the cost per component. Thus there is a minimum cost at any given time in the evolution of the technology. At present, it is reached when 50 components are used per circuit. But the minimum is rising rapidly while the entire cost curve is falling (see graph below). If we

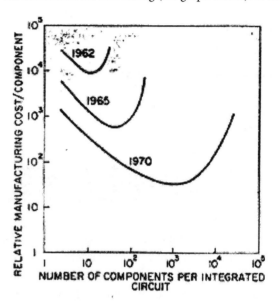

look ahead five years, a plot of costs suggests that the minimum cost per component might be expected in circuits with about 1,000 components per circuit (providing such circuit functions can be produced in

moderate quantities.) In 1970, the manufacturing cost per component can be expected to be only a tenth of the present cost.

The complexity for minimum component costs has increased at a rate of roughly a factor of two per year (see graph). Certainly over the short term this rate can

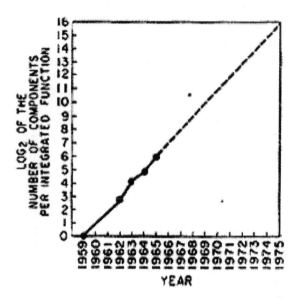

be expected to continue, if not to increase. Over the longer term, the rate of increase is a bit more uncertain, although there is no reason to believe it will not remain nearly constant for at least 10 years. That means by 1975, the number of components per integrated circuit for minimum cost will be 65,000.

I believe that such a large circuit can be built on a single wafer.

TWO-MIL SQUARES
With the dimensional tolerances already being employed in integrated circuits, isolated high-performance transistors can be built on centers two thousandths of an inch apart. Such a two-mil square can also contain several kilohms of resistance or a few diodes. This allows at least 500 components per linear inch or a quarter million per square inch. Thus, 65,000 components need occupy only about one-fourth a square inch.

On the silicon wafer currently used, usually an inch or more in diameter, there is ample room for such a structure if the components can be closely packed with no space wasted for interconnection patterns.

This is realistic, since efforts to achieve a level of complexity above the presently available integrated circuits are already underway using multilayer metalization patterns separated by dielectric films. Such a density of components can be achieved by present optical techniques and does not require the more exotic techniques, such as electron beam operations, which are being studied to make even smaller structures.

INCREASING THE YIELD
There is no fundamental obstacle to achieving device yields of 100%. At present, packaging costs so far exceed the cost of the semiconductor structure itself that there is no incentive to improve yields, but they can be raised as high as is economically justified. No barrier exists comparable to the thermodynamic equilibrium considerations that often limit yields in chemical reactions; it is not even necessary to do any fundamental research or to replace present processes. Only the engineering effort is needed.

In the early days of integrated circuitry, when yields were extremely low, there was such incentive. Today ordinary integrated circuits are made with yields comparable with those obtained for individual semiconductor devices. The same pattern will make larger arrays economical, if other considerations make such arrays desirable.

HEAT PROBLEM
Will it be possible to remove the heat generated by tens of thousands of components in a single silicon chip?

If we could shrink the volume of a standard high-speed digital computer to that required for the components themselves, we would expect it to glow brightly with present power dissipation. But it won't happen with integrated circuits. Since integrated electronic structures are two-dimensional, they have a surface available for cooling close to each center of heat generation. In addition, power is needed primarily to drive the various lines and capacitances associated with the system. As long as a function is confined to a small area on a wafer, the amount of capacitance which must be driven is distinctly limited. In fact, shrinking dimensions on an integrated structure makes it possible to operate the structure at higher speed for the same power per unit area.

DAY OF RECKONING

Clearly, we will be able to build such component-crammed equipment. Next, we ask under what circumstances we should do it. The total cost of making a particular system function must be minimized. To do so, we could amortize the engineering over several identical items, or evolve flexible techniques for the engineering of large functions so that no disproportionate expense need be borne by a particular array. Perhaps newly devised design automation procedures could translate from logic diagram to technological realization without any special engineering.

It may prove to be more economical to build large systems out of smaller functions, which are separately packaged and interconnected. The availability of large functions, combined with functional design and construction, should allow the manufacturer of large systems to design and construct a considerable variety of equipment both rapidly and economically.

LINEAR CIRCUITRY

Integration will not change linear systems as radically as digital systems. Still, a considerable degree of integration will be achieved with linear circuits. The lack of large-value capacitors and inductors is the greatest fundamental limitations to integrated electronics in the linear area.

By their very nature, such elements require the storage of energy in a volume. For high Q it is necessary that the volume be large. The incompatibility of large volume and integrated electronics is obvious from the terms themselves. Certain resonance phenomena, such as those in piezoelectric crystals, can be expected to have some applications for tuning functions, but inductors and capacitors will be with us for some time.

The integrated r-f amplifier of the future might well consist of integrated stages of gain, giving high performance at minimum cost, interspersed with relatively large tuning elements.

Other linear functions will be changed considerably. The matching and tracking of similar components in integrated structures will allow the design of differential amplifiers of greatly improved performance. The use of thermal feedback effects to stabilize integrated structures to a small fraction of a degree will allow the construction of oscillators with crystal stability.

Even in the microwave area, structures included in the definition of integrated electronics will become increasingly important. The ability to make and assemble components small compared with the wavelengths involved will allow the use of lumped parameter design, at least at the lower frequencies. It is difficult to predict at the present time just how extensive the invasion of the microwave area by integrated electronics will be. The successful realization of such items as phased-array antennas, for example, using a multiplicity of integrated microwave power sources, could completely revolutionize radar.

8.12

Findings of Fact, Conclusions of Law and Order for Judgment, File no. 4–67 Civ. 138, Honeywell Inc. v. Sperry Rand Corporation and Illinois Scientific Developments, Inc. Decided Oct. 19, 1973

Earl R. Larson

Extract from 180 *United States Patent Quarterly* 673 (n.d.): 677–702.

INTRODUCTORY NOTE TO READING 8.12

After Eckert and Mauchly succeeded in 1964 in obtaining the ENIAC patent for which they had applied in 1947, Honeywell filed a lawsuit against Sperry Rand, the company to which Eckert and Mauchly had assigned the patent. In my introductory notes to Reading 8.10 I discussed the background and scope of the ENIAC patent. Reading 8.12 reproduces excerpts from the actual ruling that invalidated the patent. These excerpts from 180 *United States Patent Quarterly* 673 include some of the most important historical summaries of the evidence pertaining to the invention of the electronic computer. The *United States Patent Quarterly* publishes judicial opinions and administrative decisions relating to patents, trademarks and other intellectual property issues. This publication was the sole official publication resulting from the litigation over the ENIAC patent. The litigation "lasted six years and involved testimony by over 150 witnesses and 30,000 pieces of evidence, ranging from a single sheet of paper to a file cabinet-full."[1] [JMN]

---

1   J. A. N. Lee, *Computer Pioneers* (Los Alamitos, CA: IEEE Computer Society Press, 1995), 151.

TEXT OF READING 8.12

Action by Honeywell Inc. against Sperry Rand Corporation and Illinois Scientific Developments, Inc., for violation of antitrust laws and for declaratory judgment of patent invalidity and noninfringement in which defendants counterclaim for patent infringement. Judgment for plaintiff in part and for defendants in part. . . .

0. INTRODUCTION

0.1 This case is a consolidation of two actions which were commenced simultaneously on May 26, 1967 before this Court and the District Court for the District of Columbia:

Honeywell Inc. v. Sperry Rand Corporation, U. S. District Court for the District of Minnesota, File No. 4–67 Civ. 138 (hereinafter the Minnesota action).

Illinois Scientific Developments, Inc. v. Honeywell, Inc., U. S. District Court for the District of Columbia, Civil Action No. 1373–67 (hereinafter the District of Columbia action).

0.1.1 Honeywell Inc. (hereinafter Honeywell or plaintiff) is a Delaware corporation with its principal office and place of business in Minneapolis, Minnesota.

0.1.2 Sperry Rand Corporation (hereinafter SR) is a Delaware corporation with its principal office and place of business in New York, New York, and is authorized to do and does business in Minnesota.

0.1.3 Illinois Scientific Developments, Inc. (hereinafter ISD) is an Illinois corporation with its principal office and place of business at that of SR. ISD is a wholly owned subsidiary of SR.

0.1.4 Honeywell's Complaint in the Minnesota action as originally filed raised two causes of action:

.1 Count One charged SR with violation of Section 2 of the Sherman Act by reason of the maintenance and enforcement of an allegedly fraudulently procured patent (the so-called "ENIAC patent"). The ENIAC patent was alleged to have the exclusionary power to effectively dominate the entire electronic data processing industry. Injunctive relief and damages were sought.

.2 Count Two sought declaratory judgment of invalidity and unenforceability of the ENIAC patent for the antitrust misconduct complained of in Count One, and for failure to comply with the legal prerequisites of the Patent Statute.

0.1.5 ISD's Complaint in the District of Columbia action charged infringement by Honeywell of the ENIAC patent. Injunctive relief and damages were sought.

0.1.6 On March 5, 1968, the District of Columbia action was transferred to the District of Minnesota and consolidated by order of Judge Nordbye on May 1, 1968, with the Minnesota action as a counterclaim by ISD, which was realigned as a defendant.

0.1.7 On May 1, 1968, Honeywell filed its First Amended Complaint, in the consolidated action, adding expanded allegations that SR and ISD's conduct had violated Section 1 as well as Section 2 of the Sherman Act, and adding Count Three charging that the acquisition of the ENIAC patent was a violation of Section 7 of the Clayton Act.

0.1.8 On August 29, 1969, Honeywell filed its Second Amended Complaint, adding a paragraph 30A under which other patents and pending patent applications, in addition to the ENIAC patent, were alleged to be subject to the same infirmities as those with respect to the ENIAC patent, and their procurement, licensing, and attempted enforcement were alleged to constitute a further part of a pattern of conduct of defendants in restraint of trade in violation of the Sherman Act.

0.2 Based upon statements of claims as presented by the parties, the Court's pre-trial understanding of the issues to be tried was expressed to counsel for the parties at a hearing on July 1, 1970 to the following effect:

0.2.1 Honeywell claims that the basic issue as far as it is concerned is whether the activities of SR and ISD and their predecessors in obtaining, maintaining, and enforcing their EDP patent portfolio, including knowhow, violate the antitrust laws particularly Sections 1 and 2 of the Sherman Act and Section 7 of the Clayton Act.

0.2.2 Honeywell claims that SR and ISD engaged in illegal activities as follows:

.1 The fraudulent procurement and enforcement of ENIAC, EDVAC, and other patents and patent applications.

.2 The illegal acquisition of the ENIAC patent application.

.3 The use of the claimed illegal patent portfolio to induce IBM and BTL to give up meritorious attacks on the validity of the ENIAC patent and other of defendants' EDP patents.

.4 Irrespective of the ENIAC patent's validity, the entering into of a total cross-license of EDP patents and EDP knowhow with IBM in 1956.

.5 The attempted enforcement of the ENIAC patent known by defendants to be subject to infirmities.

.6 Demanding discriminatory royalties for the ENIAC patent license.

0.2.3 Honeywell claims that if it prevails on any of the foregoing that it is then entitled to damages and injunctive relief.

0.2.4 Honeywell states further that if its allegations of conspiracy and combination in violation of the antitrust laws are not sustained, then certain subsidiary issues must be reached:

.1 Whether or not the ENIAC patent is valid under the technical aspects of the Patent Laws.

.2 If the ENIAC patent is technically valid, has Honeywell infringed.

.3 If infringement is proved, what damages has ISD sustained.

0.2.5 SR and ISD take the position that this is basically a lawsuit by ISD charging Honeywell with infringement of the ENIAC patent, and a suit by Honeywell against SR and ISD for a declaratory judgment that the ENIAC patent is invalid.

0.2.6 SR and ISD claim that Honeywell has admitted the infringement if the ENIAC patent is valid, but will nevertheless select a limited number of claims to litigate this question.

0.2.7 In response to the ENIAC patent infringement claim, SR and ISD claim that Honeywell has raised a number of affirmative defenses:

.1 Public use prior to the critical date of June 26, 1946.

.2 That Mauchly and Eckert were not the sole inventors of the ENIAC patent.

.3 Derivation from Dr. John V. Atanasoff.

.4 Fraudulent procurement.

.5 Fraudulent conduct to delay the issuance of the ENIAC patent.

0.2.8 With respect to the antitrust issues, SR and ISD claim that the issues relate to:

.1 Fraudulent procurement which has been raised by Honeywell as a defense, but has also been raised by Honeywell as an affirmative antitrust allegation.

.2 Discriminatory licensing by SR in making IBM its favored licensee.

.3 SR's acquisition of title to the ENIAC patent application alleged in Count Three of the Complaint in 1955, which Honeywell claims substantially lessened competition.

0.2.9 In response to the Count Three claim of Honeywell's complaint, SR and ISD claim that a private party does not have standing under Section 7 of the Clayton Act, and also that the statute of limitations has run.

0.2.10 At the close of plaintiff's case, defendants moved to dismiss Counts One and Three of the Amended Complaint. The motion was denied as to Count One, but granted as to Count Three with entry of judgment stayed until final decision or otherwise ordered.

0.3 Pursuant to pretrial order on March 29, 1971, trial was set on the issues of liability under Honeywell's claims of antitrust violation and ISD's claim of patent infringement.

0.3.1 Pending determination of the issues of liability, Honeywell's testimony as to damages on its antitrust claims, and ISD's testimony as to patent infringement damages or accounting, were deferred.

0.3.2 Honeywell's evidence as to impact or injury was received in the trial on the liability issues.

0.4 Trial commenced before the Court without a jury on June 1, 1971 and continued with few interruptions until it closed on March 13, 1972, consuming over 135 days or parts of days. During this long course of trial, the Court heard and received extensive evidence. The statistics are impressive.

0.4.1 Seventy-seven witnesses presented oral testimony in the courtroom, and the testimony of an additional eighty witnesses was presented by deposition transcripts.

0.4.2 The Court's attention was directed to 25,686 exhibits marked by Honeywell as Plaintiff's Trial Exhibits (PX).

0.4.3 The Court's attention was directed to 6,968 exhibits marked by SR and ISD as Defendants' Trial Exhibits (DX).

0.4.4 Many of the exhibits were extremely voluminous, including both documents of great length and also collections of multiple documents designated as single exhibits. For example, PX-1 is a 496 page book describing the 19th century work of Charles Babbage relating to early digital computing, and DX-2 is a collection of documents relating to the ENIAC patent application, occupying a four-drawer legal filing cabinet; DX-1, the ENIAC patent itself, comprises 91 sheets of drawings and 232 columns of closely printed text.

0.4.5 About 500 additional exhibits were marked and referred to during the trial.

0.4.6 The trial transcript extends to over 20,667 pages.

0.5 The trial afforded the Court a comprehensive view of complex technical and economic evidence involving the electronic data processing industry and relevant history before and about automatic electronic digital computing and computers.

0.5.1 The Court was aided by extensive tutorial testimony and demonstrative exhibit presentations. The courtroom demonstrations included the copious use of charts, photographs, slides, physical devices, mechanical and electronic machines operated in the courtroom, and a movie film.

0.5.2 The Court had a view of both Honeywell and SR electronic data processing systems in computing operation at their respective Twin City facilities.

0.5.3 The Court had the assistance of explanatory courtroom testimony by knowledgeable fact and expert witnesses called by both parties in the course of the trial and in the presentation of demonstrative and physical exhibits.

0.5.4 The Court had the benefit of excellent and well documented briefs of both parties.

0.5.4.1 Pursuant to a pretrial conference held on July 1, 1970, the Court suggested and counsel adopted the format of Sample Pretrial Order No. 5 of the Manual for Complex and Multidistrict Litigation for the submission of final pretrial briefs.

0.5.4.2 The pretrial briefs submitted by the parties set forth, in separately numbered declarative sentences, the narration of facts relied upon in support of each claim for relief. Legal contentions and authorities in support of the claims for relief which were the subject of the narrative statement of facts were separately stated in separately numbered paragraphs. Similarly, opposing briefs set forth separate factual statements admitting or denying those of the adverse party, or presenting affirmative matters of a factual nature, and a statement of legal contentions and authorities in defense against the claim for relief to which the response was made.

0.5.4.3 Honeywell found that the separately numbered factual sentence format of the pretrial briefs lent itself to a computerized data storage and retrieval system. In this way, Honeywell's numbered narrative statement, with designated supporting evidence, and SR and ISD's admissions or denials, together with designated opposing evidence or affirmative narrative statement, were available in computer printout form (sometimes referred to by the parties as Honeywell's Computerized Brief or "CB").

0.5.4.4 During the course of the trial, Honeywell's computerized data storage and retrieval enabled the updating and annotating of its narrative statement in accordance with the trial evidence. In addition, cumulative lists and indices of exhibits and testimony were also subject to this computerized data storage and retrieval and were made available after the close of the trial.

0.5.4.5 After trial, extensive and comprehensive post-trial briefs of both parties were submitted, following the narrative statement format of the pretrial briefs but further supplemented by so-called "conventional" briefs containing strong advocacy by which counsel have been less than kind to each other. The Court has not lacked for thorough presentation by both parties on all issues in their pretrial and post-trial briefs.

0.5.5 The Court further had the benefit of numerous documentary aids in dealing with the special terminology and content of complex electronic and financial evidence, as well as rules and customs of patent practice, involved in the reconstruction of over three decades of past history underlying the modern day computer industry. For example:

0.5.5.1 Glossary of Principal Terms, Appendix A to Volume I of Plaintiff's Trial Brief.

0.5.5.2 General Information Concerning Patents, Appendix B to Volume I of Plaintiff's Trial Brief.

0.5.5.3 Plaintiff's Exhibit 21755.7, Abstract of the Patent Office History, U. S. Patent Application Serial Number 757,158 [the ENIAC patent application], and defendants' response thereto in their Appendix to Request or Findings.

0.6 On April 9, 1973, the Court advised counsel for the parties of ultimate Findings made upon the evidence of record. The decision reached is a mixed one, and the aid of both parties has been sought through the submission of more detailed Findings on those issues where plaintiff or defendants have prevailed.

0.6.1 The Court's ultimate Findings are grouped under twenty-five numbered topics, substantially in the order treated by counsel in their briefs. The ulti-

mate and detailed supportive Findings are set forth below under these topics by decimal sub-numbering.

0.6.2 The nature and complexity of the issues upon which the facts have been found has resulted in an intermingling, where appropriate, of related conclusions of law under ultimate Finding topics.

0.6.3 The Findings are therefore both an amalgamation of findings of fact and conclusions of law, and an amalgamation of the supportive contributions of each party as to the respective issues upon which they have prevailed in whole or in part.

0.6.4 Findings 1 through 12 below are concerned primarily with the validity and enforceability of defendants' electronic data processing (EDP) or so-called "computer" patent rights against plaintiff. Findings 13 through 23 below deal more particularly with the antitrust issues arising out of the procurement, licensing and enforcement of those patent rights, and other business conduct of SR in the EDP industry. Findings 24 through 26 pertain to legal matters and relief.

0.6.5 All legal citations which support the Findings and Conclusions herein are located in the Appendix hereto at the corresponding decimalized number.

0.6.6 In reaching these Findings, the Court has weighed the evidence relating to defendants' patent rights and business activities against the background evidence which was presented to show:

0.6.6.1 the history of technical evolution of automatic electronic digital computing from the earliest mechanical aids to the modern day computer;

0.6.6.2 the history of development of the EDP industry, from the early business efforts of SR's predecessors, and of International Business Machine Corporation (IBM) and others, including Honeywell, to the time of this lawsuit;

0.6.6.3 the history of design and construction of the earliest automatic electronic digital computers and, particularly, the so-called "ABC" (Atanasoff-Berry Computer) at Iowa State College, and the "ENIAC" machine (Electronic Numerical Integrator and Computer) of Army Ordnance at the Moore School of the University of Pennsylvania;

0.6.6.4 the work of Dr. John W. Mauchly (Mauchly or sometimes simply M), J. Presper Eckert, Jr., (Eckert or sometimes simply E) and many others in connection with the ENIAC machine, and in connection with their subsequent business activities for Electronic Control Company (ECC) and Eckert-Mauchly Computer Corporation (EMCC) and Remington Rand, Inc. (RR), as predecessors of SR;

0.6.6.5 the procurement of a patent describing and claiming "the invention" embodied in the ENIAC machine (the ENIAC patent), and the history of its lengthy prosecution before the Patent Office, including interference proceedings, controversies with IBM, and litigation with Bell Telephone Laboratories, Inc. (BTL);

0.6.6.6 the history of use of the ENIAC machine, including such important use as: calculations for the Los Alamos Scientific Laboratory of the University of California (Los Alamos Laboratory) and Dr. Edward Teller relating to the hydrogen bomb and calculations by Dr. Douglas R. Hartree relating to supersonic airfoils and projectiles;

0.6.6.7 the history of commercialization and further evolution of the ENIAC and computer machine work, including: the activities of the Moore School in the development of an "EDVAC" (Electronic Discrete Variable Automatic Computer) machine, and the description of a design for such a machine by Dr. John von Neumann; and the activities of Eckert and Mauchly and the ECC and EMCC, RR business enterprise predecessors of SR in the development of EDVAC, BINAC, and UNIVAC machines;

0.6.6.8 the procurement and continuing prosecution of patents and applications (referred to at Paragraph 30A of the Second Amended Complaint) on developments arising out of the commercialization and further business activities of Eckert and Mauchly based on the work on the ENIAC and EDVAC machines;

0.6.6.9 a detailed technological, financial and economic survey of the EDP industry's major or so-called "main frame" manufacturers who are the producers of full EDP systems, including such matters as gross dollar values of EDP sales, rentals and research and development expenditures by SR, IBM, Honeywell, Radio Corporation of America (RCA), National Cash Register Company (NCR). Burroughs Corporation (Burroughs), General Electric Company (GE), Control Data Corporation (CDC), and Philco-Ford Corporation (Philco-Ford); and

0.6.6.10 the convergence of all of these historical and evolving forces upon the extraordinary automatic electronic digital computer and the EDP industry today: an industry producing EDP systems which perform an almost limitless variety of electronic data processing operations at the seemingly incredible speed of a millionth of a second (microsecond) or even a billionth of a second (nanosecond) and of persisting in the work for hours on end, and thus completing tasks beyond the capacity of human bodies and minds.

0.7 The Findings, as an amalgamation as aforesaid, are nonetheless the result of as careful and detailed attention as could be given to a most fascinating, albeit burdensome lawsuit. Where conflicts existed in the testimony, facts have been found on the basis of close observation of the appearance, conduct and demeanor of the witnesses and to contemporaneous documentation or exhibits, wherever available.

0.8 Hence, the Findings, hereinafter set forth, represent the final culmination of an extraordinary part of history such as this Court has seldom confronted; the Findings are an effort at summation of a truly complex lawsuit in a relatively condensed form.

0.9 The Findings which follow, therefore, constitute the Court's decision in compliance with Rule 52 and all applicable provisions of the Rules of Civil Procedure and of law.

1. PUBLIC USE

1.1 The claimed invention disclosed in the ENIAC ('606) patent was in public use prior to the critical date.

1.1.1 The ENIAC patent, No. 3,120,606, discloses and claims the ENIAC machine constructed at the Moore School of Electrical Engineering of the University of Pennsylvania.

1.1.1.1 The ENIAC machine was an electronic computer of monstrous size, built during wartime with government funds by a team of Moore School employees. It employed some 18,000 vacuum tubes, hundreds of switches, thousands of relays, and miles of wiring. Defendants contend that the ENIAC machine is properly regarded as the pioneer electronic computer from which all others evolved.

1.1.1.2 The ENIAC machine is described in a Final Report which was prepared by the Moore School team, transmitted to and accepted by Army Ordnance by about June 6, 1946. There are no significant differences between the ENIAC machine as constructed and placed in operation, and the ENIAC machine as described in the Final Report.

1.1.1.3 The descriptive content of the ENIAC patent disclosure was extracted from and based upon corresponding portions of the Final Report description of the ENIAC machine. There are no significant differences between the subject matter described in the Final Report and the claims of the ENIAC patent.

1.1.1.4 The patentees of the ENIAC patent state therein that the ENIAC machine "embodies our invention" and are bound thereby. Conduct with respect to that ENIAC machine is, therefore, conduct with respect to "the invention."

1.1.1.5 SR and ISD have further characterized the subject matter of the ENIAC patent as "the invention of the Automatic Electronic Digital Computer," and are bound thereby. Conduct with respect to an automatic electronic digital computer is, therefore, conduct with respect to "the invention."

1.1.1.6 Each of the claims of the ENIAC patent reads on the ENIAC machine as it was constructed and placed in operation at the Moore School and described in the Final Reports.

1.1.1.7 The ENIAC machine which was represented by Eckert and Mauchly to be that which "embodies our invention" is identical with the ENIAC invention, however claimed.

1.1.1.8 Counsel for defendants did not object to the Court's statement at trial that there was no dispute about the fact that Eckert and Mauchly claimed to be the two sole joint inventors of the ENIAC, from input all the way through to output.

1.1.1.9 For the foregoing reasons, there is no necessity to make specific reference to the individual claims of the ENIAC patent where conduct barring the valid

issuance of a patent is conduct involving either the same ENIAC machine (as will be set forth hereinafter with respect to the bars of public use and on sale), or involving a prior automatic electronic digital computer (as will be set forth hereinafter with respect to the bars of derivation from Atanasoff and prior publication by von Neumann).

1.1.1.10 Where an additional bar to less than the all-inclusive entirety of "the invention" has also been found herein, specific selected claims of the ENIAC patent have been applied and essentially cumulative further findings particularized by claims are also hereinafter included.

1.1.1.11 The entire subject matter of the ENIAC machine, represented by Eckert and Mauchly to be that which "embodies our invention," is barred from valid patentability since that machine was in public use in this country more than one year prior to the date of the application for patent on June 26, 1947. The one-year-prior or statutory bar date is referred to as the "critical date," and is June 26, 1946.

1.1.2 The ENIAC machine was constructed by mid-November, 1945.

1.1.2.1 The design for the ENIAC machine was frozen prior to the end of 1944 so that the construction of the machine could be completed as rapidly as possible to confirm the usefulness of electronic computation with such large machines.

1.1.2.2 By mid-1945, the construction of the various ENIAC units was complete and testing of the completed units had commenced.

1.1.2.3 The ENIAC was placed in operation as a system in mid-November, 1945.

1.1.2.4 Moore School and Army Ordnance representatives considered that the ENIAC machine was being operated rather than tested after December 1, 1945.

1.1.3 The ENIAC machine which embodied "the invention", claimed by the ENIAC patent was in public and non-experimental use for the following purposes, and at times prior to the critical date:

Los Alamos calculations December, 1945-February, 1946

International publicity

1. Press demonstration use February 1, 1946

2. Newsreel use February 8, 1946

3. Formal dedication use February 15, 1946

4. Open house use February 16, 1946 Hartree calculations April, 1946–July, 1946

Constant practical use December, 1945–June, 1946
Commercial solicitation uses February, 1946–April, 1946

1.1.3.1 The Court finds that PX 4245, a March 19, 1946 letter from Major W. J. Stephens, Jr., to Mr. A. Borbeck, Artillery Branch, which was never previously called to the attention of either the Patent Office or the late judge Archie O. Dawson in the case of Sperry Rand Corporation et al. v. Bell Telephone Laboratories, Inc. (hereinafter SR v. BTL) before the Southern District of New York, clearly indicates that prior to March, 1946 the ENIAC machine was "completed with the performance of research and experimental work in connection with the development of an Electronic Numerical Integrator and Computer."

1.1.3.2 SR and ISD contend that the correspondence of November, 1946, between the Moore School and the Army Ordnance patent section responsible for preparation of the ENIAC patent application (referred to by the names of the writers as the "Sharpless/Libman letters") has no probative value. Despite an error in the date of the press demonstration as recited in PX 5374, the Sharpless/Libman letters otherwise have great probative value and clearly indicated to Army Ordnance attorney Max L. Libman, who was then preparing the ENIAC patent application, that the completed ENIAC machine was first put to work for practical purposes on December 10, 1945, on a set of partial differential equations for the Manhattan Engineering District (hereinafter "the Los Alamos calculations or problem"). That initial work was not considered experimental since the letter states that "when the first problem was put on the machine it was the first time that the machine as a whole was being used, it was fully expected that the problem would be solved and it was."

1.1.4 The Los Alamos calculations which commenced December 10, 1945, were the first problem placed on the ENIAC machine. When the first problem was put on the machine it was the first time that the machine as a whole was being used. It was fully expected that the problem would be solved. It was.

1.1.4.1 The ENIAC machine, and hence any invention claimed in the ENIAC patent, was reduced to practice no later than the date of commencement of the use of the machine for the Los Alamos calculations, December 10, 1945.

1.1.4.2 The ENIAC project for the development of a high-speed electronic computer was made known to Dr. John von Neumann (Army Ordnance scientific consultant) by Dr. Herman H. Goldstine (Army Ordnance liaison officer on the ENIAC project) in the summer of 1944, after the ENIAC design had been frozen. Von Neumann visited the Moore School in July, 1944, and witnessed two ENIAC accumulator units and a cycling unit wired to function as a small ENIAC machine. By early 1945, von Neumann had begun consideration of how the ENIAC machine could be organized and operated to solve complex problems.

1.1.4.3 By the summer of 1945, Dr. Edward Teller, Dr. Stanislaw Ulam and other scientists of the Los Alamos Laboratory had already recognized the urgent need for large-scale numerical calculations designed to verify the feasibility of a hydrogen bomb design concept having several parameters including various mixtures of deuterium and tritium. Teller discussed his computational needs with von Neumann who indicated his belief that the ENIAC machine would be suitable for performing certain calculations regarding the feasibility of the hydrogen bomb, called the "Super."

1.1.4.4 The calculations to be performed were complex and required a large number of arithmetical computations. They were not intended to provide a particular numerical answer or series of answers, but rather were contemplated to provide, and did provide, the basis for a yes or no answer on the utility of continued scientific exploration of the "Super."

1.1.4.5 Useful results could be and were obtained from such calculations on the ENIAC machine even though calculational errors may have occurred in some of the primary and intermediate calculations.

1.1.4.6 Army Ordnance agreed, in 1945, to allow the use of the ENIAC by Los Alamos Laboratory personnel at the Moore School for the Los Alamos calculations.

1.1.4.7 At or about the time in December, 1945, when the Los Alamos calculations were placed on the ENIAC machine at the Moore School in Philadelphia, the machine had passed all component and system tests and was operating quite satisfactorily. The Los Alamos calculations employed 99 percent of the capacity of the ENIAC machine.

1.1.4.8 The satisfactory operation of the ENIAC machine was verified during the Los Alamos calculations by:

.1 repeating a particular production run twice and then verifying that the results obtained for each repetition were identical;

.2 stepping the ENIAC through a calculation and checking all answers after each add time;

.3 running a test problem between successive runs and checking the answer obtained to determine that it corresponded to the known answer of the test problem.

1.1.4.9 After satisfactory operation of the ENIAC machine was verified by comparing a hand calculated answer to the ENIAC machine answer for selected calculations, various conditions of the Los Alamos problem were changed to obtain production runs for which the answer had not been previously hand calculated.

1.1.4.10 By January, 1946, many production runs for the Los Alamos calculations were completed. The calculations continued in progress for considerably over one month.

1.1.4.11 Any difficulties encountered were not with the machine but with the mathematical nature of the problem and mistakes of the mathematicians who had designed the problem for the machine.

1.1.4.12 The use of the ENIAC machine by the Los Alamos Laboratory personnel was not under the con-

trol of Eckert and Mauchly, nor under any condition of secrecy for their private benefit. The Moore School also had no control over the use of Army Ordnance's ENIAC machine by the Los Alamos personnel.

1.1.4.13 The ENIAC machine was used to perform numerous production runs for the Los Alamos calculations beginning in December, 1945, and continuing in January-February, 1946, and the consequences of these calculations were far-reaching and thoroughly practical.

1.1.4.14 The results of the Los Alamos calculations using the ENIAC machine were included in three Los Alamos reports which show or state in substance that without the ENIAC machine, important work on nuclear energy release problems could not have been done at the time. The Court concurs with Dr. Teller that one of the reports, in April, 1946, delivered a verdict on the feasibility of a thermo-nuclear bomb: difficult, but with hard work and concentrated effort, hopeful.

1.1.4.15 The contribution of the ENIAC machine in performing the Los Alamos calculations was acknowledged on March 18, 1946, by Dr. Norris Bradbury, Director of the Los Alamos Laboratory, as being of very great value in the work on the project. The Los Alamos calculations using the ENIAC machine were a substantial effort which successfully and satisfactorily solved specified problems, and the results were useful and did not lie dormant.

1.1.4.16 The use of the ENIAC machine for the Los Alamos calculations was a non-experimental public use in this country prior to the critical date of the claimed invention disclosed in the ENIAC patent, and an absolute statutory bar to the valid issuance of the ENIAC patent.

1.1.4.17 The Court credits the live testimony of distinguished scientists who were contemporaneous participants in these events including Drs. Teller, Ulam, Mark, Metropolis and Frankel of the Los Alamos Laboratory and Dr. Goldstine of Army Ordnance. The testimony of Eckert and Mauchly did not contradict such testimony or the contemporaneous circumstances.

1.1.5 Upon completion of the construction of the ENIAC machine by mid-November, 1945, and commencement of its full-scale operating use by December, 1945, Army Ordnance generated international publicity to show to all the world the developments in computing which had been proved operational.

1.1.5.1 The general principles of the ENIAC design and the machine's operational and functional characteristics were unclassified after December 17, 1945.

1.1.5.2 Only certain design details and circuits of the ENIAC remained classified Confidential after December 17, 1945, and this designation:

.1 was not made for the benefit or protection of Eckert and Mauchly;

.2 was not made at the request of Eckert and Mauchly;

.3 but was made by Army Ordnance to protect circuits of the machine being used by other military departments, including the Army Signal Corps.

1.1.5.3 The security classification of the ENIAC circuits and design details was not a matter under the control of Eckert and/or Mauchly. After the declassification in 1945, the design details and circuits of the ENIAC were left confidential until February, 1947, solely at the discretion of and for the benefit of the Government, and not for the commercial business interest and private benefit of Eckert and Mauchly.

1.1.5.4 The Army Ordnance international publicity program for the ENIAC machine was extensive and well planned, and Eckert and Mauchly as participants therein had been warned that the display of the machine would foreclose any of their private patent rights if not promptly pursued.

1.1.5.5 In January, 1946, formal press releases were prepared by Army Ordnance for release immediately following the dedication ceremony which was scheduled to be held on February 15, 1946. Mauchly's diary entries attest to his role in personally editing the Army Ordnance press releases to insure specific recognition of Eckert and him.

1.1.5.6 Eckert and Mauchly cooperated in the preparation and planning of the efforts of Army Ordnance and the Moore School to achieve saturation publicity for the completion of the ENIAC, including press releases, interviews, speeches, newsreels, press demon-

strations, formal dedication and the Moore School open house, such as:

.1 Eckert and Mauchly delivered prepared remarks on the utility and speed of the ENIAC machine to reporters who attended the press demonstration;

.2 Mauchly prepared and delivered a speech to the reporters at the press demonstration explaining that the ENIAC machine demonstrated that it was possible to utilize electronic computers to solve many problems never previously solved; and

.3 Eckert delivered a speech at the press demonstration and informed reporters that the ENIAC machine had sounded the death knell to the era of electro-mechanical computing devices, and that the advent of the ENIAC machine had made electronic computers a part of the concrete present rather than a vague promise of the future.

1.1.5.7 The ENIAC machine was operated at the press demonstration on February 1, 1946, for publicity purposes, and in a manner calculated to be impressive through the press to the general public.

1.1.5.8 One of the calculations illustratively demonstrated was the use of the ENIAC machine to add the number 97,367 to itself 5,000 times, as was visible on the face of the accumulators. After the 5,000 additions were completed, the result was checked and it was determined that the ENIAC machine had properly performed the calculation.

1.1.5.9 As another demonstration calculation, the ENIAC machine multiplier was used to multiply 13,975 times 13,975 500 times, and the product was checked and found to have been properly calculated.

1.1.5.10 As another demonstration calculation, the ENIAC machine was used to produce a table of squares and cubes of the numbers from 1 to 100. The ENIAC machine functioned properly during the preparation of the table, and the results were error free.

1.1.5.11 As another demonstration calculation, the ENIAC machine was used to compute the sines and cosines for 100 different angles, and the table prepared was punched on so-called tab cards, printed on paper, and distributed to members of the press. The ENIAC machine functioned properly during the preparation of the table of sines and cosines, and correct results were obtained for each computation.

1.1.5.12 As another demonstration calculation, the ENIAC machine performed representative calculations arising out of the Los Alamos Laboratory work. A printed copy of the results or so-called printout of a number of Los Alamos-type calculations was prepared and distributed to the attendees at the press demonstration. These calculations utilized substantially the full capacity of the ENIAC machine, and contained no errors attributable to malfunction of the ENIAC machine.

1.1.5.13 Although the demonstration calculations performed on the ENIAC machine for the press were not intended by Army Ordnance or the Moore School to be for the private benefit or on behalf of Eckert and Mauchly, they were in fact later relied upon by them for that financial purpose. In no event were the calculations performed in order to enable Eckert and Mauchly to complete or perfect the making of "the invention" embodied in the ENIAC machine.

1.1.5.14 The use of the ENIAC machine in public during the press demonstration was not an experimental use, but was a publicity exercise in joint behalf of the Moore School and Army Ordnance, and was intended to impress the scientific community and the general public with the capabilities of the machine and the fact of its completion.

1.1.5.15 The use of the ENIAC machine to perform calculations during the February 1, 1946, press demonstration was a non-experimental public use of the claimed invention disclosed in the ENIAC patent, prior to the critical date and an absolute statutory bar to the valid issuance of the ENIAC patent.

1.1.5.16 The ENIAC machine was filmed in staged operation in February, 1946, for the benefit of newsreel photographers, for publicity purposes, and in a manner calculated to provide a motion picture demonstration to be shown nationally to the general public.

1.1.5.17 The use of the ENIAC machine for the newsreel photographers was not an experimental use,

but was part of the large-scale international publicity program calculated to impress the public with the capabilities of the machine and the fact of its completion.

1.1.5.18 The ENIAC machine was formally dedicated on February 15, 1946, for publicity purposes, at a ceremony involving preeminent representatives of government, military, university, industrial and scientific establishments, and in a manner calculated to achieve maximum recognition of and to stimulate interest in the completed and operating ENIAC machine.

1.1.5.19 As of the date of the dedication and demonstration of the ENIAC machine at the Moore School on February 15, 1946, the ENIAC machine was represented to be, and was in fact, completed and successful.

1.1.5.20 During the dedication demonstration of the ENIAC machine, a ballistic trajectory problem was run as a simple means for impressing observers with what the machine could do. Although the trajectory data was simplified for the demonstration, the basic arithmetical operations of adding, subtracting, multiplying and dividing which would be done in a complete trajectory problem were performed. Any variance between the trajectory calculations performed during the dedication and an actual trajectory occurred as a result of programming simplifications rather than as a result of any operating defects in the ENIAC machine.

1.1.5.21 Although complete ballistic firing tables were not prepared during the dedication, the demonstration was intended to and did show that such tables could be prepared by repeating the trajectory calculations as performed with different input conditions. The data used was real and had been verified beforehand. The ENIAC machine did not err.

1.1.5.22 None of the calculations performed on the ENIAC machine at the dedication were performed for the private benefit or on behalf or under the control of Eckert and Mauchly to enable them to complete or perfect the making of "the invention" embodied in the ENIAC machine. Instead, their private interest was one of commercial exploitation (see 1.1.5.6 and .13 above).

1.1.5.23 The use of the ENIAC machine in public at the formal dedication was not an experimental use, but was part of the large-scale publicity program calculated to impress the public with the capabilities of the machine and the fact of its completion.

1.1.5.24 The use of the ENIAC machine to perform calculations during the dedication was a non-experimental public use of the claimed invention disclosed in the ENIAC patent, prior to the critical date, and an absolute statutory bar to the valid issuance of the ENIAC patent.

1.1.5.25 The ENIAC machine was publicly exhibited and demonstrated in operation on February 16, 1946, at an "open house" for the invited entirety of the Moore School staff and student body. At the open house, the same ballistic trajectory calculations that were performed at the dedication were again performed. The ENIAC machine operated satisfactorily at the open house.

1.1.5.26 The use of the ENIAC machine in public at the open house was a non-experimental public use of the claimed invention of the ENIAC patent, prior to the critical date, and an absolute statutory bar to the valid issuance of the ENIAC patent.

1.1.5.27 The Court has heard from numerous live witnesses regarding the international publicity regarding the completion and successful operation of the ENIAC machine and saw the ENIAC newsreel exhibited during the testimony of Dr. Goldstine. The Court credits this testimony.

1.1.6 Dr. Douglas R. Hartree, a highly regarded British scientist, used the completed ENIAC machine in 1946 prior to the critical date to perform complex and fundamental calculations relating to the performance of airfoils at supersonic speeds in air.

1.1.6.1 As early as 1939 Hartree had begun his study of methods for the solution of equations involved in laminar boundary layers in compressible flow. The equations are applicable to the field of supersonic aircraft design, as well as to the design of various projectiles.

1.1.6.2 Hartree's study of the laminar boundary layer in compressible flow was not a single problem for which a single answer was to be calculated, but was instead a broad investigation involving numerous computations using the ENIAC machine, each of which resulted in large groups or families of calculations or solutions which were to be compiled in the form of tables. The ENIAC patent states that the primary intended use of the ENIAC machine is to compute such large families of solutions.

1.1.6.3 Hartree visited the United States in 1945, saw the nearly completed ENIAC machine, and was furnished copies of the ENIAC progress reports. He commented on the ENIAC machine in an article published in Nature magazine in England on April 20, 1946.

1.1.6.4 Because of his knowledge of the ENIAC project gained from viewing the ENIAC machine in 1945 and the material in the progress reports, Hartree, when he arrived in the United States in April, 1946, had already reduced laminar boundary layer equations to a form suitable for solution by using the ENIAC machine. Hartree also brought working charts to the United States which described how the ENIAC machine was to be programmed by plug wiring and set up to perform the calculations required.

1.1.6.5 Prior to his visit to the United States in the spring of 1946, Hartree had already studied some special cases of the boundary layer equations which are described as null (or zero) order functions and had hand-calculated five-figure solutions to some of the families of calculations. The other cases of the study of the laminar boundary layer in compressible flow are described as the higher order functions. At the time that Hartree arrived in the United States, he brought with him the hand calculations of the null-order functions of the boundary layer equations.

1.1.6.6 Mauchly's present wife, then Kathleen McNulty, was assigned by Army Ordnance to plug in wires on the ENIAC machine according to the programming charts which Hartree had brought with him to the United States.

1.1.6.7 Hartree began his work on the ENIAC machine by evaluating the null-order equations. Calculation of the null-order equations using the ENIAC involved the basic operations of adding, multiplying and dividing. The calculation of the null-order functions on the ENIAC machine required a number of production runs, each of which produced results in the form of a stack of punched cards.

1.1.6.8 Hartree's calculations using the ENIAC machine were complex and carefully planned, and required the operating capacity of the entire machine.

1.1.6.9 Hartree's use of the ENIAC machine began in April, 1946, and he successfully used the machine. to perform useful calculations and produce large families of solutions of the null-order functions. Hartree checked the results by comparing solutions obtained from the ENIAC machine with corresponding five-figure solutions which had been hand-calculated by him prior to his arrival in the United States. Hartree completed his evaluation of the null-order functions prior to the critical date for the ENIAC patent application. Completion of these null-order functions was a substantial independent portion of Hartree's intended complete study of the laminar boundary layer in compressible flow. Also prior to the critical date for the ENIAC patent application, Hartree had successfully used the ENIAC machine to provide useful answers to practical study of the laminar boundary layer in compressible flow.

1.1.6.10 Hartree's use of the ENIAC machine in 1946 on his own boundary layer problem was as a consultant employed and paid by Army Ordnance. Hartree was neither an agent nor employee of either Eckert, Mauchly or the Moore School, nor under any obligation of secrecy or otherwise to any thereof.

1.1.6.11 Prior to the critical date, Hartree described to Mauchly in detail the nature of the calculations that he had performed using the ENIAC machine, and Mauchly made notes of the discussion. Mauchly testified that he knew at the time of Hartree's visit that Hartree was working at the time on a problem in fluid dynamics which had to do with boundary layers and that this made sense because Mauchly had dealt with similar problems in the wind tunnel at the Bureau of Standards in the 1930's. Mauchly testified that he attended a lecture at the Moore School given by Hartree in which the boundary layer calculations were described.

1.1.6.12 Mauchly and Eckert, who had by then resigned from the Moore School, did not evaluate the results of the calculations run by Hartree to learn or to decide if any design changes to the ENIAC machine were necessary. They were not authorized to make any changes and did not make any. Although Eckert and Mauchly were aware of the fact of Hartree's use of the ENIAC machine, they neither allowed, participated in nor exercised any control over that use or over any of its consequences.

1.1.6.13 Hartree's calculations were of scientific importance and the subject of significant published papers, upon which Eckert and Mauchly later relied for their private business advantage. Hartree left the United States to return to England on July 20, 1946. In October, 1946, Nature magazine published a further article by Hartree on the ENIAC machine and his calculations on the laminar boundary layer problem. The Hartree October Nature article briefly described the method used for solving the three simultaneous, linear, ordinary, differential equations which were said by Hartree to arise from the theory of the laminar boundary layer in a compressible fluid. Eckert and Mauchly's partnership, Electronic Control Company, later reprinted the article in an advertising brochure in which it was stated that "the article represented here is based on his [Hartree's] first hand experience in using the ENIAC."

1.1.6.14 The use of the ENIAC machine by Hartree was a non-experimental public use in this country of the claimed invention disclosed in the ENIAC patent, prior to the critical date, and an absolute statutory bar to the valid issuance of the ENIAC patent.

1.1.6.15 This Court has considered Hartree's article in the 1948 Philosophical Transactions of the Royal Society and the testimony of Dr. Goldstine and Dr. Clippinger (a former Army Ordnance employee with contemporaneous knowledge of the ENIAC machine, and a present Honeywell employee), as against the conflicting testimony by defendants' counsel Hall, and holds that the Hartree article is a description of the pre-critical-date work and includes a tabulation of some of the families of solutions which he obtained prior to the critical date. Clippinger also testified that a recheck of the results on a high speed modern computer had demonstrated the correctness of Hartree's result. The Court has considered and credits the testimony of Dr. Clippinger to the effect that the Hartree article indicates that the ENIAC machine gave Hartree correct results.

1.1.7 The use of the ENIAC machine by Army Ordnance after December 1, 1945 and prior to the critical date, involved no question of whether the machine worked or how it could be improved by Eckert and Mauchly as claimant inventors for their own private advantage, but was instead a program of production operation under the sole control of Army Ordnance entirely for governmental uses, purposes and benefits.

1.1.7.1 Beginning with the Los Alamos calculations in December, 1945, and extending to the ENIAC patent critical date, the ENIAC machine entered a period of constant practical use under the control of Army Ordnance.

1.1.7.2 In addition to the public use of the ENIAC machine for the Los Alamos calculations and the Hartree problem, there are other uses which cumulatively confirm the public use of the ENIAC machine, prior to the critical date.

1.1.7.3 None of the specific instances of ENIAC machine operation between December 10, 1945, and the critical date, comprising, in sum, a history of constant practical use of the ENIAC machine by Army Ordnance, were carried out under the control of, or in any way for the private benefit of, Eckert and Mauchly, or under any obligation of secrecy to Eckert and Mauchly.

1.1.7.4 None of these other examples of the use of the ENIAC machine were carried out for the purpose of completing or perfecting the making of "the invention" of Eckert and Mauchly embodied in the ENIAC machine.

1.1.7.5 After the Los Alamos calculations, the ENIAC was in more or less continuous use being set up for or in actual work in solving problems. All so-called testing, debugging and troubleshooting was normal operation and continued throughout the useful life of the ENIAC machine.

1.1.7.6 When Eckert's connection with the ENIAC project was terminated in March of 1946, the machine had been completed and running for some time and was in use by Army Ordnance, and Eckert so testified in 1954. At least by January, 1946, the ENIAC machine was a complete and operable calculating instrument, and Mauchly so testified in 1954. Neither Eckert nor Mauchly testified to the contrary before this Court.

1.1.7.7 There were no long periods of maintenance or repair shutdown, and the general practice was to operate in a continuous schedule and shut down only when a fault became apparent. The percentage of hours used for computing time was quite high, and Eckert and Mauchly so testified, so that Sperry Rand's attorney Wobensmith summarized Mauchly's testimony to that effect in 1954.

1.1.7.8 Harry Huskey, of the Moore School staff, operated the ENIAC machine, from April 15 to April 19, 1946, to generate a table of sines and cosines and this use was called to the attention of Libman, the Army Ordnance attorney who prepared and filed the ENIAC patent application for Eckert and Mauchly, prior to that filing. Eckert and Mauchly did not evaluate the results of Huskey's calculations to determine whether or not any changes in the ENIAC design were necessary in the light of the results obtained, nor were any changes ever recommended or made by them or for them.

1.1.7.9 The constant practical use of the ENIAC machine after December 1, 1945, was a non-experimental public use of the claimed invention disclosed on the ENIAC patent prior to the critical date, and an absolute statutory bar to the valid issuance of the ENIAC patent.

1.1.8 Eckert and Mauchly took commercial advantage of Army Ordnance's public uses of the ENIAC machine and also placed the ENIAC machine in public use themselves by demonstrating it to potential customers as a part of their attempts to commercialize the ENIAC machine subject matter prior to the critical date.

1.1.8.1 Eckert and Mauchly intended that the widespread publicity to be gained for them personally from the ENIAC press demonstration, dedication and open house in February, 1946, would advance their private commercial business interests.

1.1.8.2 More than one year prior to the June 26, 1947 filing date of the ENIAC patent, beginning at least as early as the fall of 1944, Eckert and Mauchly placed the claimed invention disclosed in the ENIAC patent in public use and on sale by describing and demonstrating the ENIAC machine to their intended customers for their own commercial gain.

1.1.8.3 Eckert and Mauchly took full private business advantage of the publicity and dedication activities as a convenient forum for their solicitation of future computing machine contracts from government agencies.

1.1.8.4 During the fall of 1944, Mauchly called on various potential customers to determine the business prospects for selling high-speed computing or data processing machines. Prior to October, 1944, the ENIAC two-accumulator system had been successfully built and operated. The completion of the ENIAC two-accumulator system gave Eckert and Mauchly a tool by which they could convince potential customers that a high-speed computing or data processing machine could in fact be successfully built.

1.1.8.5 Army Ordnance's contract (W-670-ORD-4926) for the ENIAC project work required the University of Pennsylvania to grant the U. S. Government a royalty-free license under all patents arising from the work done under the contract. However, since the employment agreements of the engineers working on the ENIAC project did not clearly require any assignment of their invention rights to the University of Pennsylvania, the University was not in a position to grant the Government such a license.

1.1.8.6 Prior to March, 1945, Eckert and Mauchly sought advice from George A. Smith, a patent attorney, on methods of securing for themselves the commercial invention rights arising from the work under the Army Ordnance contract. Pursuant to his advice, Eckert and Mauchly asked the University of Pennsylvania for the right to have their own patent attorney file patent applications in their names on ideas arising

out of the work on the project. During March, 1945, Eckert and Mauchly pressed for recognition of their commercial interests by the University of Pennsylvania in return for assurances that they would help the University fulfill its obligations under the contract. Facing the fact that it would require the cooperation of Eckert and Mauchly to fulfill its contractual obligations to the U. S. Government, the University yielded the commercial rights to any patents they might obtain based on the work on the contract.

1.1.8.7 Mauchly was in personal contact with personnel of the U. S. Weather Bureau as early as April, 1945, to learn their computing needs and to discuss the ENIAC and future work with them. Eckert and Mauchly also followed up their interest in business prospects at the U. S. Census Bureau throughout the summer of 1945.

1.1.8.8 On other occasions during 1945, Eckert and Mauchly called on about a dozen Census Bureau officials including Everett Kimball, Jr., Dr. Madow, Morris H. Hansen, and James L. McPherson, in order to interest them in high-speed computing or data processing machines. Hansen assigned McPherson the task of evaluating Eckert and Mauchly's proposals regarding such a high-speed computing or data processing machine. As a result of this assignment, McPherson held meetings from time to time with Eckert and Mauchly at the Census Bureau. During the meetings with McPherson and other census officials, Eckert and Mauchly described the ENIAC and sought a contract to develop a similar but more advanced machine for the Census Bureau.

1.1.8.9 In order to interest potential financial backers Earnest Cuneo and Lazar Teper in the financial backing of an Eckert-Mauchly computer company, Eckert and Mauchly displayed the ENIAC machine to them in January, 1946.

1.1.8.10 Eckert and Mauchly early sought private business advantage from the fact of the ENIAC machine's completion by the Moore School in 1945 and its constant practical use thereafter by Army Ordnance. For example, on February 15, 1946, Commander Reichelderfer of the U. S. Weather Bureau attended the ENIAC dedication and dinner on behalf of the U. S. Weather Bureau, being seated at Mauchly's table at Mauchly's request. Mauchly's purpose in having Reichelderfer present was one of private self-interest to advance his business enterprise plans, held jointly with Eckert, by using the occasion of the ENIAC dedication as a business promotion effort: During the dedication, Reichelderfer and the other guests witnessed a demonstration of the ENIAC machine. Thereafter, on February 21, 1946, Eckert and Mauchly again demonstrated the ENIAC machine for Reichelderfer's associates Dr. Harry Wexler and Jerome Namias of the U. S. Weather Bureau, and discussed with them the possible construction of a similar computer for weather purposes. The contacts with and demonstrations for Reichelderfer, Namias and Wexler were attempts to commercialize the invention embodied in the ENIAC machine prior to the critical date, and resulted in non-experimental public uses of the claimed invention disclosed in the ENIAC patent prior to the critical date, constituting an absolute bar to the valid issuance of the ENIAC patent.

1.1.8.11 By mid-March, 1946, Eckert and Mauchly had put out a number of commercial feelers, and were actively pursuing them. For example, on March 20, 1946, in order to promote their sale of a high-speed computing or data processing machine, Eckert and Mauchly made a presentation to the Committee on Tabulation Methods and Mechanical Equipment of the U. S. Census Bureau.

1.1.8.12 On March 22, 1946, Dean Pender of the University of Pennsylvania demanded that Eckert and Mauchly either subjugate their personal commercial interests to the interests of the University or have their employment by the University terminated. On or about March 22, 1946, Eckert and Mauchly submitted their resignations from the University of Pennsylvania to take effect March 31, 1946.

1.1.8.13 On April 2, 1946, two days after their resignations from the University of Pennsylvania became effective, Eckert and Mauchly met with representatives of the Weather Bureau, Census Bureau, and Bureau of Standards. During that meeting, Eckert again described the ENIAC machine.

1.1.8.14 In order to promote their proposed sale of a computing machine, Eckert and Mauchly invited representatives of the Census Bureau and National Bureau of Standards to witness a demonstration of the ENIAC machine. The demonstration, held April 11, 1946, was attended by Eckert and Mauchly, Dr. John H. Curtiss representing the National Bureau of Standards, and Messrs. A. A. Berlinsky, J. F. Rosen, Morris H. Hansen, and James L. McPherson, representing the Census Bureau. During the April 11, 1946, demonstration, the ENIAC machine was set up and running while its operation was explained. The April 11, 1946, ENIAC demonstration was an essential part of Eckert and Mauchly's implementation of the plan to exploit electronic computing or data processing machines commercially.

1.1.8.15 Following the April 11, 1946, ENIAC machine demonstration, Eckert and Mauchly agreed to submit to the Census Bureau a set of specifications which could be included in any contract which the Bureau would award to them. The April 11, 1946, ENIAC demonstration and Eckert and Mauchly's descriptions of the ENIAC machine were Curtiss' principal sources of information about electronic computing and Eckert and Mauchly's principal credentials for competence and credibility. On or about April 30, 1946, Eckert and Mauchly submitted some tentative specifications of a proposed computing machine to the Census Bureau, as requested during the April 11 demonstration.

1.1.8.16 Based on Curtiss' recommendation, Eckert and Mauchly were awarded contract CST-7964 in the fall of 1946 to conduct a design study, including the construction of components, and prepare a report based thereon proposing a computer to be built for the Census Bureau. Contract CST-7964 directly followed from the ENIAC machine demonstration and the sequence of visits and evaluations of the technical competence of Eckert and Mauchly by the Bureau of Standards.

1.1.8.17 Eckert and Mauchly's demonstration of the ENIAC machine on April 11, 1946, was a commercialization by Eckert and Mauchly of the claimed invention disclosed in the ENIAC patent and embodied in the ENIAC machine prior to the critical date, and resulted in a non-experimental public use of "the invention" of the ENIAC patent prior to the critical date, constituting an absolute bar to the valid issuance of the ENIAC patent.

1.1.8.18 Eckert and Mauchly, in attempting to gain commercial and private business advantage from the pre-critical date early practical operation of the ENIAC machine, and the massive publicity thereof, advertised in their Eckert-Mauchly Computer Corporation literature in 1949 that the ENIAC machine had been put into operation in January, 1946.

1.1.8.19 With regard to the issue of Eckert and Mauchly's commercialization of the ENIAC machine subject matter prior to the critical date, the Court has considered the conflict between, on the one hand, the disinterested testimony of Mr. James L. McPherson and related contemporaneous documentary evidence, and, on the other hand, the testimony of Eckert and Mauchly. The Court credits the testimony of McPherson and corroborating documentary evidence, and holds that Eckert and Mauchly knowingly sought to and did commercialize the ENIAC machine and any invention embodied therein prior to the critical date.

[1] 1.2 The usual standard in civil cases of proof by a fair preponderance of the evidence is easily and clearly satisfied.

1.3 I do not believe that the standard to be applied is that of clear and satisfactory proof or clear and convincing proof or proof beyond a reasonable doubt.

1.4 If necessary for decision, I find that the more stringent standards have been satisfied.

1.4.1 The Court has heard 22 live witnesses over many weeks of the trial relating to the history and facts surrounding the use of the ENIAC machine prior to the critical date. The Court has seen the newsreel film made in February, 1946, showing the ENIAC machine actually being used for its intended purpose in a clearly publicly intended setting.

1.4.2 Thousands of the documents received by the Court bearing on the public use issue originated contemporaneously with the relevant events and were obtained from independent and disinterested sources.

1.4.3 The Court credits this heavy weight of evi-

dence, fully revealed for the first time upon this record, as compelling a finding that the plaintiff has shown by clear and satisfactory proof, or clear and convincing proof, or proof beyond a reasonable doubt, that the claimed invention disclosed in the ENIAC patent was in public use in this country prior to the critical date.

1.5 The use of ENIAC after December 1, 1945, was clearly not experimental in nature.

1.5.1 Defendants contend that all uses of the ENIAC machine prior to the critical date are exempted from their otherwise clear barring effect because they constitute experimental uses under Eckert and Mauchly's control, or for their benefit, and were necessary and essential to the completion or perfecting of the making of "the invention" claimed by them. The facts are clearly to the contrary.

1.5.1.1 By December, 1945, Army Ordnance was using its ENIAC machine under an operating contract W-18-001-ORD-1706 (separate from contract 4926 under which the ENIAC machine was built) which provided for the Moore School to furnish services for the initial operation of the ENIAC machine at the Moore School pending completion of the building at the Aberdeen Proving Ground where the machine was to be later housed.

1.5.1.2 After the ENIAC machine was put into constant practical use by Army Ordnance in December, 1945, the ENIAC group or team, including Eckert and Mauchly, turned their attention to the commencement of work on the next generation of computer design, the EDVAC.

1.5.1.3 Eckert and Mauchly resigned from the Moore School in March, 1946, and had no further official contact with any of the work with the ENIAC machine after April 1, 1946.

[2] 1.52 The pre-critical date uses of the ENIAC machine were not made under the surveillance of Eckert and Mauchly, and for the purpose of enabling them to test the machine and ascertain whether it would answer the purpose intended and to make such alterations and improvements as experience demonstrates to be necessary, and therefore are not excused as experimental uses within the meaning of Elizabeth

v. Pavement Co., 97 U.S. 126 (1877). The ENIAC machine demonstrated that it would answer its intended purpose in December 1945 when it was used for production runs on the Los Alamos calculations.

1.5.3 By December 1, 1945, the ENIAC machine was under the custody, dominion and control of the customer, Army Ordnance, and the relationship to the machine of Eckert, Mauchly and the other engineers at the Moore School involved in the ENIAC team effort was not one of continuing inventorship and experimentation.

1.5.4 The uses of the ENIAC machine from December, 1945, to the critical date were for its intended purpose of performing automatic electronic digital computation, and were not for the experimental purpose of the completion or perfection of the making of "the invention."

1.5.4.1 The uses of the ENIAC machine between December 1, 1945, and the critical date were not in the nature of testing, checking, or experimentation, but rather were uses of the ENIAC machine for its intended practical purpose.

1.5.4.2 The Court has considered the ENIAC Service Log and the testimony concerning the various entries which were made in it. The evidence is clear and convincing that the Service Log is a record showing routine maintenance on the ENIAC machine. The fact that such maintenance was performed does not in any way detract from the non-experimental nature of the various ENIAC public uses. The Court has considered the assertion of defendants that the ENIAC Service Log shows that changes to the machine were made. The evidence is clear and convincing that, without exception, the changes recorded in the Service Log were not design changes of any significance to "the invention," but were instead minor and routine refinements or adjustments of a non-inventive nature. This work on the ENIAC machine was done by Homer Spence, the maintenance engineer for ENIAC, after December 1, 1945, and was routine maintenance unrelated to the completion or perfection of "the invention."

[3] 1.5.4.3 The burden of proof of any exemption from the public use bar, such as by reason of experi-

mentation essential to the completion of the making or perfecting of "the invention" by or for Eckert and Mauchly, rests with SR & ISD, and has not been carried. Instead, Honeywell has proven such use to be non-experimental and clearly practical. . . .

3. ATANASOFF

3.1 The subject matter of one or more claims of the ENIAC was derived from Atanasoff, and the invention claimed in the ENIAC was derived from Atanasoff.

3.1.1 SR and ISD are bound by their representation in support of the counterclaim herein that, the invention claimed in the ENIAC patent is broadly "the invention of the Automatic Electronic Digital Computer."

3.1.2 Eckert and Mauchly did not themselves first invent the automatic electronic digital computer, but instead derived that subject matter from one Dr. John Vincent Atanasoff.

3.1.3 Although not necessary to the finding of derivation of "the invention" of the ENIAC patent, Honeywell has proved that the claimed subject matter of the ENIAC patent relied on in support of the counterclaim herein is not patentable over the subject matter derived by Mauchly from Atanasoff. As a representative example, Honeywell has shown that the subject matter of detailed claims 88 and 89 of the ENIAC patent corresponds to the work of Atanasoff which was known to Mauchly before any effort pertinent to the ENIAC machine or patent began.

3.1.4 Between 1937 and 1942, Atanasoff, then a professor of physics and mathematics at Iowa State College, Ames, Iowa, developed and built an automatic electronic digital computer for solving large systems of simultaneous linear algebraic equations.

3.1.5 In December, 1939, Atanasoff completed and reduced to practice his basic conception in the form of an operating breadboard model of a computing machine.

3.1.6 This breadboard model machine, constructed with the assistance of a graduate student, Clifford Berry, permitted the various components of the machine to be tested under actual operating conditions.

3.1.7 The breadboard model established the soundness of the basic principles of design, and Atanasoff and Berry began the construction of a prototype or pilot model, capable of solving with a high degree of accuracy a system of as many as 29 simultaneous equations having 29 unknowns.

3.1.8 By August, 1940, in connection with efforts at further funding, Atanasoff prepared a comprehensive manuscript which fully described the principles of his machine, including detail design features.

3.1.9 By the time the manuscript was prepared in August, 1940, construction of the machine, destined to be termed in this litigation the Atanasoff-Berry computer or "ABC," was already far advanced.

3.1.10 The description contained in the manuscript was adequate to enable one of ordinary skill in electronics at that time to make and use an ABC computer.

3.1.11 The manuscript was studied by experts in the art of aids to mathematical computation, who recommended its financial support, and these recommendations resulted in a grant of funds by Research Corporation for the ABC's continued construction.

3.1.12 In December, 1940, Atanasoff first met Mauchly while attending a meeting of the American Association for the Advancement of Science in Philadelphia, and generally informed Mauchly about the computing machine which was under construction at Iowa State College. Because of Mauchly's expression of interest in the machine and its principles, Atanasoff invited Mauchly to come to Ames, Iowa, to learn more about the computer.

3.1.13 After correspondence on the subject with Atanasoff, Mauchly went to Ames, Iowa, as a houseguest of Atanasoff for several days, where he discussed the ABC as well as other ideas of Atanasoff's relating to the computing art.

3.1.14 Mauchly was given an opportunity to read, and did read, but was not permitted to take with him, a copy of the comprehensive manuscript which Atanasoff had prepared in August, 1940.

3.1.15 At the time of Mauchly's visit, although the ABC was not entirely complete, its construction was sufficiently well advanced so that the principles of its operation, including detail design features, was explained and demonstrated to Mauchly.

3.1.16 The discussions Mauchly had with both Atanasoff and Berry while at Ames were free and open and no significant information concerning the machine's theory, design, construction, use or operation was withheld.

3.1.17 Prior to his visit to Ames, Iowa, Mauchly had been broadly interested in electrical analog calculating devices, but had not conceived an automatic electronic digital computer.

3.1.18 As a result of this visit, the discussions of Mauchly with Atanasoff and Berry, the demonstrations, and the review of the manuscript, Mauchly derived from the ABC "the invention of the automatic electronic digital computer" claimed in the ENIAC patent.

3.1.19 The Court has heard the testimony at trial of both Atanasoff and Mauchly, and finds the testimony of Atanasoff with respect to the knowledge and information derived by Mauchly to be credible. . . .

7. THE FIRST DRAFT REPORT

7.1 The First Draft Report was a printed publication prior to the critical date, and was an anticipatory publication, and contains an enabling disclosure of the ENIAC.

7.1.1 In 1944, Dr. John von Neumann, a mathematician of international distinction, was serving as a consultant with the Ballistics Research Laboratory of Army Ordnance. During this same period, he also was serving as scientific advisor and counselor to the Los Alamos Laboratories in nuclear weapons research matters.

7.1.1.1 Dr. Herman H. Goldstine, of the Ballistics Research Laboratory ("BRL"), sparked von Neumann's interest in the ENIAC during a train ride which the two took to Philadelphia in late summer 1944. Almost immediately thereafter, von Neumann viewed the ENIAC two-accumulator system in operation and became deeply involved in the ENIAC project, meeting frequently with Eckert, Mauchly, Burks and Goldstine.

7.1.1.2 Von Neumann's dual roles BRL and Los Alamos led him to recommend the use of high-speed computing machines as an aid to the computations of the Los Alamos Laboratories and to Dr. Edward Teller in particular.

7.1.1.3 Goldstine and von Neumann agreed that a report should be prepared to summarize the general ideas regarding the art of high-speed automatic electronic digital computers discussed at the Moore School and, as a result, von Neumann prepared a document entitled "First Draft of a Report on the EDVAC". This First Draft Report was authored by von Neumann between February and June of 1945 and was a substantial and major part of the total report he intended to write.

7.1.1.4 Von Neumann's First Draft Report, a comprehensive document of one hundred one pages, contains fifteen chapters, each having subsections, and deals in detail with the logical organization and makeup of a high-speed automatic electronic digital computer. Included in the report are definitions of report terminology and a chapter devoted to the procedure used by the author for discussion. Specific hardware was not detailed, in order to avoid governmental security classification and, in Eckert's and Mauchly's words, to avoid raising engineering problems which might detract from the logical considerations under discussion.

7.1.2 Goldstine, with the approval of von Neumann, circulated a large number of mimeographed copies of the First Draft Report for the express purpose of making the knowledge therein publicly available to advance the state of the computer art.

7.1.2.1 The purpose of early publication of the First Draft Report was to further the development of the art of building high-speed automatic electronic digital computers, and to advance scientific engineering thinking on this subject as widely and as early as feasible.

7.1.2.2 After its completion in mimeographed form, the Draft Report, which was unclassified with the knowledge and approval of Army Ordnance, was immediately distributed to members of the technical staff in the Moore School, and thereafter, to other persons in the United States and England variously representing: the Ballistics Research Laboratory; the Princeton Institute for Advanced Study; the Applied Mathematics Panel of the National Defense Research Committee; the Radiation Laboratory at the Massachusetts Institute of Technology; Scientific Computing Ltd. in London, England; United States Army Ordnance; United States Naval Ordnance; the Computing Laboratory at Cambridge University in England; the Mathematics Institute at New York University; and the University of Chicago.

7.1.2.3 The First Draft Report was a printed publication, within the meaning of 35 U.S.C. §102, by June 30, 1945, prior to the ENIAC patent critical date.

7.1.2.4 The distribution of the First Draft Report had an important influence on the continuing development of electronic computers.

7.1.2.5 The computing system described by von Neumann in the First Draft Report featured the use of the computer's high-speed memory to store not only numbers but operating instructions as well. Called "stored programming," this concept introduced new dimensions in the speed, flexibility and usefulness of automatic electronic digital computers.

7.1.3 While the First Draft Report does not include a detailed disclosure of the specific hardware to mechanize the machine disclosed within the report, it does include a disclosure sufficient to teach one skilled in the art how to accomplish the logical control of a high-speed automatic digital computing system.

7.1.3.1 Each of the logic elements (referred to as "organs") disclosed in the First Draft Report had existing physical counterparts and/or could have been constructed by the exercise of ordinary skill in the art at the time the report was published, before the critical date for the ENIAC patent. Experts in the field testified at trial that the report is, and was at the time of its publication, sufficient to enable persons skilled in the art to make and use the computer set forth in the report.

7.1.3.2 Plaintiff's tutorial expert witness, Kenneth Rose, read and understood the First Draft Report and presented an in-court demonstration model of the stored program technique taught in the First Draft Report:

7.1.3.3 The Court also heard the testimony of plaintiff's expert witness Paul Winsor, who studied the First Draft Report extensively with a view toward determining whether or not a computer could have been constructed at the time (1945) from the report's teachings. He examined the wartime technology available, when the report was published, to construct the elements referred to in the report. As a result of his study, Winsor concluded, and this Court concurs, that the report was sufficient to enable persons skilled in the art in 1945 to construct the computer set forth therein with the available technology. Moreover, documents written by persons concerned with the report, contemporaneous with its publication, corroborate this testimony. For example, ENIAC patent attorney Church commented on the First Draft Report:

"I think the broad conception is there and to one skilled in the art it is sufficient to put them on the road of accomplishing a development."

Von Neumann's attorney Townsend agreed, despite the fact that his conclusion prejudiced any possible patent rights his client might have sought. The Court credits this testimony.

7.1.4 The claims of the ENIAC patent asserted in this suit are anticipated by or obvious in view of the First Draft Report. The Court reaches this finding through an independent study of the record, including the testimony of plaintiff's expert, Winsor.

7.1.4.1 Claims 8, 9, 52, 55, 56, 57, 65, 75 and 78 are each anticipated by the First Draft Report.

7.1.4.2 The inventive subject matter of "the Automatic Electronic Digital Computer" is either anticipated by or obvious in view of the First Draft Report.

7.1.5 The finding that the First Draft Report disclosed the basic concepts of the ENIAC invention is supported by statements of those who considered the same issue prior to the time the ENIAC application was filed.

7.1.5.1 The applicants for the ENIAC patent were informed before the ENIAC patent application was filed, by Army Ordnance patent lawyers who prepared and prosecuted the ENIAC application, that the First Draft Report was a barring publication. [See also Findings 13.31 et seq. herein]

7.1.5.2 Defendants have admitted that by April 8, 1947, Eckert and Mauchly had been advised that the Army Ordnance patent lawyers considered the First Draft Report to be a printed publication within the meaning of the patent statute.

7.1.5.3 On April 8, 1947, a meeting including the patentees, Eckert and Mauchly, and Libman (the principal active lawyer who prepared and filed the ENIAC application on behalf of Eckert and Mauchly) and Church (later an attorney of record for Eckert and Mauchly in the ENIAC application), was held to consider the impact of the First Draft Report on the patentability of inventions theretofore made by them. During this meeting, Church stated:

"It is our firm belief from the facts that we have now that this report of yours dated 30 June 1945 is a publication and will prohibit you or anyone else from obtaining a patent on anything it discloses because it has been published more than a year and statute provides that if you don't file disclosures within a year it constitutes a bar to patenting that device."

7.1.5.4 During the April 8, 1947 meeting, Eckert admitted that the report was a barring publication, and it was clearly and unequivocally established, in the presence of the patentees Eckert and Mauchly and their patent lawyers Church and Libman, that the report was an enabling publication dated more than one year before the ENIAC patent application was filed.

7.1.6 It is apparent from the distribution list of the June 30, 1945 First Draft Report that Mauchly was charged with the duty of delivering the report to the Army Ordnance Patent Department. The list also makes clear the report's relevance to Eckert's and Mauchly's patent matters. On the list, it is stated:

"Dr. J. W. Mauchly (2) (to be given to patent lawyer and patent Dept. of Ordnance)"

There is no evidence that Mauchly ever carried out this duty, and the First Draft Report did not come to the attention of the Army Ordnance Patent Department until it was later submitted by von Neumann. . . .

9
The Origins of Computer Programming

9.1
Solution of Examples

Howard H. Aiken and Grace Hopper

Extract from *A Manual of Operation for the Automatic Sequence Controlled Calculator* (Cambridge, MA: Harvard University Press, 1946), pp. 287–300.

INTRODUCTORY NOTE TO READING 9.1

We reproduce excerpts from the manual for the electromechanical Harvard Mark I, the first programmable calculating machine to actually produce mathematical tables, that was the first to fulfill the dream of Charles Babbage originally set out in print in 1822 (see Reading 3.1). Aiken saw himself as Babbage's intellectual successor, and he and Hopper placed the Harvard Mark I in its historical context in an excellent historical introduction to this technical manual. In his biography of Aiken, I. Bernard Cohen[1] pointed out that Aiken was not well informed about the actual design of Babbage's Analytical Engine when he was designing the Mark I; otherwise Aiken probably would have included conditional branch facilities in its original design. Before designing the machine Aiken seems to have read Babbage's autobiography rather than the posthumous *Babbage's Calculating Engines*, in which more details of the design of the Analytical Engine were given.

An imposing thick quarto with large photographs of the very modernistic looking Mark I, this technical volume full of computer programs must have been perceived as radically new when it was published. The computer historian Paul Ceruzzi, in his introduction to the 1985 reprint of the Mark I's manual, implies as much in the following description:

> [The Harvard Mark I] manual was a milepost that marked the state of the art of machine computation at one of its critical places: where, for the first time, machines could automatically evaluate arbitrary sequences of arithmetic operations. Most of this volume (pp. 98–337, 406–557) consists of descriptions of the Mark I's components, its architecture, and operational codes for directing it to solve typical problems. ... The *Manual* is one of the first places where sequences of arithmetic operations for the solution of numeric problems *by machine* were explicitly spelled out. It is furthermore the first extended analysis of what is now known as computer programming since Charles Babbage's and Lady Lovelace's writings a century earlier. The instruction sequences, which one finds scattered throughout this volume, are thus among the earliest examples anywhere of digital computer programs.[2]

The Harvard Mark I, also known as the IBM Automatic Sequence Controlled Calculator, was the brainchild of Howard Aiken, who first conceived of building a powerful, large-scale calculating machine in 1935 while pursuing graduate studies in physics at Harvard University. In 1937, after Aiken had become a professor of applied mathe-

---

1   I. Bernard Cohen, *Howard Aiken: Portrait of a Computer Pioneer* (Cambridge, MA: MIT Press, 1999).

2   Paul Ceruzzi, Introduction to *A Manual of Operation for the Automatic Sequence Controlled Calculator* (Cambridge, MA: MIT Press; Los Angeles: Tomash Publishers, 1985), xv-xvii.

The Automatic Sequence Controlled Calculator, also known as the Harvard Mark I, in its futuristic cabinets designed by Norman Bel Geddes.

matics at Harvard's Graduate School of Engineering, he proposed his idea to a number of calculating-machine manufacturers, receiving several rejections before finally convincing IBM to undertake the project. The project was partly funded by money from the United States Navy; the remainder came from IBM, whose president, Thomas J. Watson, viewed the undertaking as good publicity and as a showcase for IBM's talents.

Aiken's machine began construction in May 1939 at IBM's North Street Laboratory in Endicott, New York. The chief engineers on the project were Clair D. Lake, James W. Bryce, Francis E. Hamilton, and Benjamin Durfee; these men were responsible for translating Aiken's design ideas into workable machinery, and Aiken never hesitated to acknowledge them as co-inventors of the Mark I. To give the machine a beautiful appearance, Watson commissioned the avant-garde industrial designer Norman Bel Geddes to design a metal cabinet for the machine. Geddes's work gave the machine a very modernistic look.

Construction of the Mark I was completed in early 1943, and a year later the machine was dismantled and shipped to Harvard, where it became operational in May 1944. The machine was officially presented to Harvard by IBM at a dedication ceremony held on August 7. Unfortunately, the press release announcing the event slighted IBM by describing Aiken as the machine's sole inventor, ignoring the crucial role IBM had played in its creation. This regrettable faux pas infuriated Watson, who was in attendance at the ceremony, and put an end to any hopes of a continuing partnership between IBM and Harvard.

The Mark I was an electromechanical machine, based largely on existing IBM punched-card technology. Ceruzzi describes it as follows:

Howard Aiken, Grace Hopper and Robert Campbell, all wearing their US Navy uniforms, in front of the Harvard Mark I. Grace Hopper, chief programmer for the machine, holds a punched paper tape. Hopper wrote the bulk of the *Manual*. Campbell co-authored chapters 5 and 6 with Aiken. (Photograph courtesy of Harvard University Archives.)

The architecture of the Mark I was unlike that of any modern computer. Its basic units were a set of seventy-two accumulators that could both store and add 23-digit signed decimal numbers. There was no clear separation of the storage and arithmetic functions. Besides the accumulators there were sixty constant registers whose contents could be read but not altered during a program run, a multiply-divide unit, and paper tape readers for reading numbers and sequences of operations....

The basic computing element was a multipole rotary switch, connected by a clutch to a drive shaft, by which decimal units, carry, and timing information were stored. Banks of twenty-four switches (holding twenty-three decimal digits and the sign of a number), made up one accumulator. The drive shaft rotated continuously; electrically activated clutches engaged the wheels of an accumulator whenever a number was to be transferred. The clutches were in turn driven by double-throw relays. The Mark I was an electromechanical calculator: it held numbers in mechanical elements (the rotary switches), which were electrically controlled (by the clutch relays). Electrical pulses traveling along a common bus conveyed numbers to and from the accumulators....

Getting the Mark I to execute a desired sequence of operations involved a combination of two processes: preparing a sequence tape fed into the Sequence Control Unit (coding) and plugging cables into plugboards located at several places on the machine (setup).... The Sequence Tape reader had no provision for backing up the tape or for skipping steps. This meant that the Mark I executed only simple, linear sequences of instructions. Sequence (and Value) tapes could be cemented into endless loops, however, and this was frequently done. After 1947 a Subsidiary Sequence mechanism was attached to the Calculator that allowed such endless loops of tape to supply sub-sequences to the main sequence control.[3]

After the Mark I was set up at Harvard in 1944 it was immediately commandeered for war work by the United States Navy. Aiken, a commander in the United States Naval Reserve (USNR), was put in charge of the navy's computation project, and he later joked that he was first naval officer ever to command a computer. Most of Aiken's staff at the Computation Laboratory also held commissions in the USNR. One of these was Lieutenant (later Admiral) Grace M. Hopper, a mathematician who, in her own words, had "never met a digit" until joining the Computation Laboratory; she would go on to become one of the most famous of the postwar computer pioneers, making fundamental contributions to the development of the first compilers. The operating manual for the Mark I calculator—published as Volume 1 of the *Annals of the Computation Laboratory of Harvard University*—was written largely by Hopper, who was the chief author of chapters 1–3 and the eight appendices following chapter 6. [JMN]

---

3 Ceruzzi, *op. cit.*, xxi–xxvi

TEXT OF READING 9.1

In most cases there are several methods of adapting a problem for machine computation. After all methods of attack have been considered, one usually will show distinct advantages as regards speed and ease of operation and reliability of the checking procedures employed.

Since machine time is extremely valuable, the first consideration in planning a sequence tape is to reduce the computation time to a minimum consistent with the required accuracy. However, a fine balance must be maintained between computation time and the ensuing complexity of the coding. The conservation of one or two cycles of machine time will, for example, not be profitable if it means that the counters containing essential parts of a computation must be reset before the results are checked.

The second consideration in planning a computation is ease of operation. If switches must be altered or sequence tapes interchanged at relatively short intervals of time, these operations will constitute not only a loss of time but also a source of error.

Ease of rerunning a computation in the wake of an error and the possibility of computing for specific values of the independent variables must also be considered. Machine failures occur from time to time. The amount of time consumed in detecting the source of an error is usually dependent upon the complexity of the coding. The time required to resume operation after an error, which is dependent upon the number of manipulations the attendant must perform, should be reduced to a minimum in a well planned sequence tape. Specifically, no decisions or computations should be required on the part of the attendant. The operating instructions and the values printed or punched should provide all the information necessary for rerunning any part of the computation.

Finally, of paramount importance in the design of a sequence control tape are the checks on the computation. These must insure positive proof that the output values obtained are precisely those required and that they are correct to the desired accuracy. Four classes of errors must be taken into account: (1) errors inherent in the mathematical formulae; (2) errors produced by a repetition of the four fundamental operations of arithmetic; (3) errors introduced by manual operations; (4) errors due to mechanical or electrical failures within the calculator itself.

The errors inherent in the mathematical formulae must be evaluated during the preliminary analysis before the coding is begun. Decisions must be made as regards the number of terms of an infinite series to be retained, the number of times an iterative process must be applied and the order of interpolation required. These decisions are dependent upon the interval and increment of the independent variable and the accuracy desired in the computed results.

The loss of accuracy due to the repetition of the four basic arithmetical operations in a finite digital calculator must be subjected to a detailed analysis. For each operation, the maximum error must be assumed and the error of the final result computed. The simple expedient of using a certain number of extra computing columns will, in general, nullify errors from this source. Thus the choice of the operating decimal position will in part be dictated by the number of extra columns so allowed.

The two sources of human error mentioned in Chapter V, incorrect switch settings and incorrect plugging, are perhaps the most serious of all. If the mathematical nature of a problem permits a check of the final results, independent of the method of computation, the errors of the manual operations will be detected. If, however, the only checks which may be applied are those of an operational character; i.e., substantiating the fact that the desired sequence of operations has been correctly performed by the calculator, such errors as incorrect switch settings may not be detected. Hence meticulous precision on the operator's part and careful checking of all manual operations are essential.

Mechanical and electrical failures within the calculator itself are the final source of errors which must be checked. If a problem is properly coded, either operational or end result checks must be provided to detect such failures. In no case should the calculator be permitted to run more than twenty minutes without checks.

Although the probability is exceedingly small, a failure in the checking circuits of the machine may occur. To provide for the detection of such an event, all check quantities should be printed and kept under observation. If the check quantities are printed before the checking operation is performed, in case of failure, the magnitude and conformation of the error may provide a clue to its source. If possible, all quantities essential to the computation of the value being checked should be preserved in the calculator until the check is completed. These quantities may then be printed or punched and manual computation used to aid in tracing the source of the error. If the length of a computation is not too great, a rerun after a failure, with the tolerances set arbitrarily low so that the machine will stop even though the computation is correct, may provide correct values for comparison with those in error. Such a comparison will often lead directly to the particular source of difficulty.

Before the actual coding is begun, the storage counters should be allocated to the various parts of the computation. Then as the coding proceeds, a diagram should be prepared showing the lines of coding by which the counters are reset and the quantities they contain at every cycle of the computation.

A clear copy of the coding must be provided before an attempt is made to run a sequence tape on the calculator, The lines of perforations in the tape should be numbered to correspond to the lines of coding. In the coding sheets, colored indicators should call attention to all prints, interpolations and checks. All functional operations should be separated by horizontal rulings.

Before a sequence tape is run on the machine, a manual computation of a degenerate case, of the first point to be evaluated or of some arbitrary point, should be made. Comparison of the results of this manual computation with the results yielded by the tape will serve to check the coding and punching of the tape. The manual computation should parallel the operations dictated by the tape so that intermediate results may be compared if the final results fail to check.

Every sequence control tape must be accompanied by operating instructions. These instructions must be sufficiently complete to enable an experienced attendant to set up the problem and operate the calculator. All value and functional tapes and cards supplied with a problem must be thoroughly checked before a problem is ready to run. The only remaining source of input values, the switch settings, must be checked just before the machine is started. Directions for checking the switch settings must be given in the operating instructions. The quantities standing in the switches must be printed or punched for checking, either under control of a sequence tape or under manual control of the keyboard ordinarily used in the preparation of sequence tapes. If blank tape is placed across the reading pins of the sequence mechanism, this keyboard maybe connected to the calculator to transmit successive single lines of coding to the machine. Only an experienced attendant should attempt to use the keyboard, however, because of the rapid manipulations necessary in using automatic codes. The keyboard is most frequently used for printing and punching quantities when testing to locate a source of error.

It is often necessary to make preliminary computations and to set certain values in storage counters before a computation is begun. In such an event a starting tape is used. It is usually a short two-ended control tape and may well include printing quantities from the switches, checking plugging and resetting storage counters. If possible starting tapes should be used only at the beginning of a problem or to re-establish operation after failure to check. In general, they should not be used at the start of each individual run since too much time would be wasted in changing control tapes.

The operating instructions accompanying a sequence tape must include all of the following information.

1. Switches.
    All quantities to be set in switches must be listed. Both symbols and numerical values must be stated. All tolerances must be accompanied by a reference to the quantity to be checked.

2. Tapes.

All value and functional tapes, together with a statement of the interpolator on which they are to be placed, must be listed. All tapes must be clearly labeled and starting lines indicated. On the sequence tape itself, the starting line and all rerun lines must be marked.

3. Card Feeds.

The cards required by each feed must be identified by their serial numbers. The relationship of the serial numbers to the argument and function being computed must be clearly stated. In the instructions for reruns or any other special runs, further instructions for the replacement of cards must be given.

4. Card Punch.

The quantities being punched and the printed values with which they may be compared must be identified. The composition of serial numbers in relation to the argument and function must be made clear. Instructions must be given for the labeling, filing and storing of all cards punched.

5. Typewriters.

The mathematical symbols of the quantities printed and their relative positions must be stated. Sample headings of pages or rolls should be cited. It must also be stated whether or not the typewriter reverse switches may be used since these switches do not reverse the half pick-up coding.

6. Storage Counters.

All manual resets of storage counters must be listed. In particular, if a counter is used to accumulate for each quantity or group of quantities printed, and stop the machine at the end of a page, this counter must be identified.

7. Functional Counters.

All manual resets required must be listed.

8. Checks.

All checks must be listed and the following information supplied for each check:

(a) quantity checked;

(b) amount of tolerance and switch from which it is derived;

(c) line of coding containing the check procedure;

(d) procedure in case of failure to check.

9. Rerun Instructions.

In general, these will be of two types:

(a) rerun of the point on which the failure occurred;

(b) rerun of any other point.

Complete plugging instructions must also accompany every sequence control tape. These instructions must include all of the following information: (1) a statement of the position of the operating decimal point of the calculator and of the typewriter and punch decimal points, if these differ; (2) a list of the units of the calculator employed in the computation and diagrams of their plugging; (3) the switch settings for division, logarithms and interpolation must be listed if these functions are to be used; (4) for each typewriter, the horizontal grouping of the digits to be printed must be stated, the vertical grouping of the lines of the tabular values must be given, plugging diagrams for each typewriter must be provided.

If the logarithm, exponential, sine or interpolator units are to be used by a sequence tape, these units should be tested on known arguments before the tape itself is tested. Such known arguments must include, for the exponential and sine units, both positive and negative values. In the case of the sine unit, arguments from each of the four quadrants using both the sine and cosine series should be chosen. The reading pins of the interpolators should be tested by reading known values such as diagonal numbers.

If a sequence tape is of such general interest that it will be preserved in the tape library, its starting tape should be designed with care in order to check all switch settings, all plugging and all of the functional units employed, as well as to compute the initial values required by the main control tape. However, for problems to be run but once on the calculator, the starting tape should be as simple as is consistent with adequate provision for setting up the problem and rerunning in case of failures.

In the preparation of control tapes and operating instructions, a standard practice is necessary since the operation of large scale calculating machinery on a continuous basis is of necessity a group enterprise. The methods and techniques employed must be standardized in order that the required results may be obtained with a minimum of special instructions. The foregoing discussion covers the more important rules of coding developed in nearly two years of operation of the calculator. However, so brief a description cannot be expected to cover all the details involved. These will be illustrated by means of examples chosen for mathematical simplicity in order that the coding and checking may be the focal points of the discussion.

Example 1. It is required to evaluate the polynomial,

$$F(x) = x^4 + 3x^3 - 3x^2/4 - 22x + 3,$$

by successive multiplications, in the interval $5 \le x \le 10$, with $x = 0.01$. The values of $F(x)$ are to be punched in tabulating machine cards for use in further computation. Each card must be identified by a serial number consisting of the argument, x_n, punched with decimal point between card columns 75 and 76 (machine columns 5 and 6) and a one in the 80th card column (1 in 1st machine column). It is not required to print the values of $F(x)$. One value of $F(x)$ is to be computed during each revolution of the control tape. The tape is to be designed so that it may be rolled back and rerun without any additional manipulations. The starting tape is to be designed so that it may be used to re-establish the computation for any arbitrary value of the argument.

If $F(x)$ is written in the form,

$$F(x) = (((x_n + 3)x_n - 3/4)x_n - 22)x_n + 3,$$

it should be clear that only three multiplications will be required to evaluate the given polynomial. In general a polynomial of nth degree will require not more than n multiplications. The constants will be supplied from switches. Since $F(x) < 2 \times 10^4$ in the interval under consideration, the standard position of the operating decimal point, between columns 15 and 16, may be assumed.

No.	Code	Setting and Purpose
1	741	$\Delta x = 1$ in 14th machine column; increment of argument for computing
2	742	$\Delta x = 1$ in 4th machine column; increment of argument for punch card serial numbers
4	743	1 in 1st machine column; punch card code for $F(x)$; zero check tolerance
5	7431	0.75
6	7432	22
7	74321	3
9	751	x_{n-1} = argument for computing; decimal point between columns 15 and 16; used in starting tape only
10	752	$x_{n-1} + 3$; decimal point between columns 15 and 16; used in starting tape only
11	7521	x_{n-1} = argument for punch card serial numbers; decimal point between columns 5 and 6; used in starting tape only

Since the argument is always ≥ 5, containing at least one non-zero digit, and is always used as the multiplier, four lines of coding may be interposed between the read-in of MP and the read-out of the product. The resets of the counters receiving the products, and the additions of the successive constants, are interposed in the multiplications.

Starting Tape

Description	Line	OUT	IN	MISC
reset ctr. 1	1	1	1	7
x_{n-1} from sw. 9 to ctr. 1; argument for computing	2	751	1	7
reset ctr. 2	3	2	2	7
x_{n-1} + 3 from sw. 10 to ctr. 2	4	752	7	7
reset ctr. 64	5	7	7	7
x_{n-1} from sw. 11 to ctr. 64; argument for punch card serial number	2	7521	7	7

Main Control Tape

Description	Line	OUT	IN	MISC.
Δx from sw. 1 to ctr. 1; ctr. 1 = x_{n-1} + Δ = x_n; argument for computing	1	741	1	7
Δx from sw. 2 to ctr. 64; ctr. 64 = x_{n-1} + Δ = x_n; argument for punch card serial number	2	742	7	7
Δx from sw. 1 to ctr. 2; ctr. 2 = x_{n-1} + Δx + 3 = x_n + 3	3	741	2	7
x_n + 3 from ctr. 2 to MC Rerun line	4	2	761	7
	5			7
	6			
x_n from ctr. 1 to MP	7	1		7
	8			7
	9			7
reset ctr. 3	10	21	21	7
− 0.75 from sw. 5 to ctr. 3	11	7431	21	32
$(x_n + 3)x_n$ to ctr. 3; ctr. 3 = $(x_n + 3)x_n$ − 0.75	12		21	7
$(x_n + 3)x_n$ − 0.75 from ctr. 3 to MC	13	21	761	7
	14			7
	15			
x_n from ctr. 1 to MP	16	1		7
	17			7
	18			7
reset ctr. 4	19	3	3	7
− 22 from sw. 6 to ctr. 4	20	7432	3	32
$((x_n + 3)x_n − 0.75)x_n$ to ctr. 4; ctr. 4 = $((x_n + 3)x_n − 0.75)x_n$ − 22	21		3	7
$((x_n + 3)x_n − 0.75)x_n$ − 22 from ctr. 4 to MP	22	3	761	7
	23			7
	24			
x_n from ctr. 1 to MP	25	1		7
	26			7
	27			7
reset cir. 5	28	31	31	7
3 from sw. 7 to ctr. 5	29	74321	31	
$(((x_n + 3)x_n − 0.75)x_n − 22)x_n$ to ctr. 5; ctr. 5 = $F(x_n)$	30		31	7
$F(x_n)$ to punch ctr.	31	31	753	
initiate punching and wait until punching is completed	32			51
x_n from ctr. 64 to punch ctr. for serial number	33	7	753	
1 in 1st machine column to punch ctr.; code for F(x)	34	743	753	
initiate punching and continue operation	35			75
	36			87

OPERATING INSTRUCTIONS

1. Set switches as listed. Punch the values set in the switches and compare the punched values with the list of switch settings.

2. The quantities punched under control of the main tape are the values of $F(x_n)$. Each card is to be identified by a serial number consisting of the argument, x_n, punched in card columns 74–77 and a one, the code for $F(x)$, in card column 80. All cards punched are to be placed in the drawer provided for this purpose.

3. Run starting tape.

4. Run main control tape. If no failures occur, continue running until card for $x_n = 9.99$ has been punched, then press stop key.

5. If a failure occurs during the computation for the argument, x_n, roll the tape back to line 4, marked "Rerun line", and repeat the computation for this value.

6. If tests are made and counters disturbed, or if it is desired to compute for any arbitrary value of the argument, repeat the starting procedure with switches 9, 10 and 11 reset as listed.

7. Since the maximum number of non-zero digits in any argument is three, the maximum time for any multiplication is ten cycles. Hence, the maximum time for each revolution of the control tape may be computed as follows:

accumulate arguments	3
three multiplications	30
punching of results	10
punching of serial number	3
Total:	46 cycles = 13.8 seconds.

If further computations are added to this tape, it will be possible to interpose thirteen of these cycles

reducing the computation time to 9.9 seconds.

8. The first card punched under control of the main tape will be $F(x) = 874.25$ with the serial number 500001.

PLUGGING INSTRUCTIONS

1. Plug the multiply unit for the standard position of the operating decimal point (see page 247).

2. Plug the punch as shown in the diagram below.

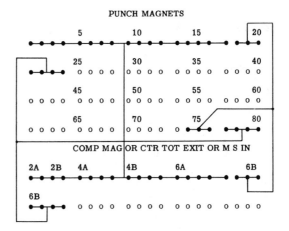

Example 2. It is required to evaluate the polynomial of example 1 using difference engine techniques.

Suppose five values of the function, F_{n-5}, F_{n-4}, F_{n-3}, F_{n-2}, F_{n-1}, to be available in punched cards. A starting tape will be designed to feed these five cards, and compute the differences associated with the argument x_{n-1}. Switch 8 will contain $\Delta 4F = 0.000\ 000\ 24$ and this quantity will be used to check the differences computed by the starting tape. Before beginning the computation with the calculator, $F(4.95)$, $F(4.96)$, $F(4.97)$, $F(4.98)$ and $F(4.99)$ must be computed manually and punched in tabulating machine cards. Thereafter, $F(x)$ must be punched in cards by the main control tape. Hence, in the event of a machine error, any five successive values of the function, known to be correct, may be used to re-establish the computation with the aid of the starting tape.

The main control tape is to be designed so that the value of the function and its differences computed in the $m - 1$st revolution of the tape will be used in the mth revolution of the tape to compute the next succeeding value of the function and its differences. The standard decimal position will be used.

Starting Tape	Line	OUT	IN	MISC.
reset ctr. 1	1	1	1	7
F_{n-5} to ctr. 1 from card feed I	2		1	7632
reset ctr. 2	3	2	2	7
F_{n-4} to ctr. 2 from card feed I	4		2	7632
reset ctr. 3	5	21	21	7
F_{n-3} to ctr. 3 from card feed I	6		21	7632
reset ctr. 4	7	3	3	7
F_{n-2} to ctr. 4 from card feed I	8		3	7632
reset ctr. 8	9	4	4	7
F_{n-1} to ctr. 8 from card feed I	10		4	7632
reset ctr. 9	11	41	41	7
F_{n-1} from ctr. 8 to ctr. 9	12	4	41	7
$- F_{n-2}$ from ctr. 4 to ctr. 9; ctr. 9 = ΔF_{n-2}	13	3	41	732
$- F_{n-3}$ from ctr. 3 to ctr. 4; ctr. 4 = ΔF_{n-3}	14	21	3	732
$- F_{n-4}$ from ctr. 2 to ctr. 3; ctr. 3 = ΔF_{n-4}	15	2	21	732
$- F_{n-5}$ from ctr. 1 to ctr. 2; ctr. 2 = ΔF_{n-5}	16	1	2	732
reset ctr. 10	17	42	42	7
ΔF_{n-2} from ctr. 9 to ctr. 10	18	41	42	7
$- \Delta F_{n-3}$ from ctr. 4 to ctr. 10; ctr. 10 = $\Delta^2 F_{n-3}$	19	3	42	732
$- \Delta F_{n-4}$ from ctr. 3 to ctr. 4; ctr. 4 = $\Delta^2 F_{n-4}$	20	21	3	732
$- \Delta F_{n-5}$ from ctr. 2 to ctr. 3; ctr. 2 = $\Delta^2 F_{n-5}$	21	2	21	732
reset ctr.11	22	421	421	7
$\Delta^2 F_{n-3}$ from ctr. 10 to ctr. 11	23	42	421	7
$\Delta^2 F_{n-4}$ from ctr. 4 to ctr. 11; ctr. 11 = $\Delta^3 F_{n-4}$	24	3	421	732
$\Delta^2 F_{n-5}$ from ctr. 3 to ctr. 4; ctr. 4 = $\Delta^3 F_{n-5}$	25	21	3	732
reset ctr. 12	26	43	43	7
$\Delta^3 F_{n-4}$ from ctr. 11 to ctr. 12	27	421	43	7
$\Delta^3 F_{n-5}$ from ctr. 4 to ctr. 12; ctr. 12 = $\Delta^4 F_{n-5}$	28	3	43	732
reset comparison ctr. 5	29	31	31	7
$\Delta^4 F$ from sw. 8 to ctr. 5	30	75	31	7
$-\Delta^4 F_{n-5}$ from ctr. 12 to ctr. 5	31	43	31	732
reset check ctr. 72	32	74	74	7
zero check tolerance from sw. 4 to check ctr. 72	33	743	74	7
$|\Delta^4 F - \Delta^4 F|$ to check ctr. 72	34	31	74	71
check; reset check ctr. 72	35	74	74	64
reset ctr. 64	36	7	7	7
x_{n-1} from sw. 11 to ctr. 64; argument for punch card serial number	37	7521	7	7

Main Control Tape	Line	OUT	IN	MISC.
reset working counters for differences computation	1	43	43	7
	2	431	431	7
	3	432	432	7
	4	4321	4321	7
transfer differences from storage to working counters F_{n-1} from ctr. 8 to ctr. 12	5	4	43	7
ΔF_{n-2} from ctr. 9 to ctr. 13	6	41	431	7
$\Delta^2 F_{n-3}$ from ctr.10 to ctr. 14	7	42	432	7
$\Delta^3 F_{n-4}$ from ctr. 11 to ctr. 15	8	421	4321	7
$\Delta^4 F$ from sw. 8 to ctr. 15; ctr. 15 = $\Delta^3 F_{n-3}$	9	75	4321	7
$\Delta^3 F_{n-3}$ from ctr. 15 to ctr. 14; ctr. 14 = $\Delta^2 F_{n-2}$	10	4321	432	7
$\Delta^2 F_{n-2}$ from ctr. 14 to ctr. 13; ctr. 13 = ΔF_{n-1}	11	432	431	7
ΔF_{n-1} from ctr. 13 to ctr. 12; ctr. 12 = F_n	12	431	43	7
F_n from ctr. 12 to punch ctr.	13	43	753	7
reset ctr. 8; initiate punching; continue operation but complete punching before reading into punch ctr.	14	4	4	751
reset ctr. 9	15	41	41	7
reset ctr. 10	16	42	42	7
reset ctr. 11	17	421	421	7

	Line	OUT	IN	MISC.
Δx from sw. 2 to ctr. 64; ctr. 64 = $x_{n-1} + \Delta x = x_n$; argument for punch card serial number	18	742	7	
F_n from ctr. 12 to ctr. 8	19	43	4	7
ΔF_{n-1} from ctr. 13 to ctr. 9	20	431	41	7
$\Delta^2 F_{n-2}$ from ctr. 14 to ctr. 10	21	432	42	7
$\Delta 3 F_{n-3}$ from ctr. 15 to ctr. 11	22	4321	421	7
x_n from ctr. 64 to punch ctr. for serial number	23	7	753	
1 in 1st machine column to punch ctr.; code for $F(x)$	24	743	753	
initiate punching and continue operation	25			75
	26			87

OPERATING INSTRUCTIONS

1. Set switches as listed on page 293, adding switch 8 = 0.000 000 24. Punch the values set in the switches and compare the punched values with the list of switch settings.

2. The quantities punched under control of the main tape are the values of $F(x_n)$. Each card is to be identified by a serial number consisting of the argument, x_n, punched in card columns 74–77 and a one, the code for $F(x)$, in card column 80. All cards punched are to be placed in the drawer provided for this purpose.

3. Five cards, labeled "starting cards", must be placed in card feed I. These cards are identified by the serial numbers 495001, 496001, 497001, 498001 and 499001.

4. Run starting tape. When cards run out, turn off card feed control switch and restart calculator. If the starting tape is completed correctly, the sequence mechanism will stop on a blank line of tape.

5. If the check, on line 35 of the starting tape fails, the calculator will stop on line 36, reading $(7, 7, 7)$. The starting cards must be refed and the starting tape rerun. If the check continues to fail, the counters used in the difference computation (ctrs. 1 through 15) and switch 8 must be tested.

6. Run main control tape. If no failures occur, continue running until the card for $x_n = 9.99$ has been punched, then press the stop key.

7. If it is necessary to rerun the computation, or to run it for an arbitrary value of the argument, x_n:

    (a) five cards from those punched under control of the main tape must be placed in card feed I; these cards are identified by the arguments $x_{n-5}, x_{n-4}, x_{n-3}, x_{n-2}, x_{n-1}$, in that order, punched in card columns 74–77 and a one in card column 80;

    (b) switch 11 must be set to x_{n-1};

    (c) the starting procedure must be repeated and the computation continued under control of the main tape.

8. The maximum time for each revolution of the main tape may be computed as follows:

computation of $F(x_n)$	12
punching $F(x_n)$	10
punching serial number	3
Total	25 cycles = 7.5 seconds.

9. The first card punched under control of the main sequence tape will be $F(5.00) = 874.25$ with the serial number 500001.

PLUGGING INSTRUCTIONS

1. Plug the card punch as in example 1 (see page 296).

2. Plug card feed I direct (see page 272). . . .

9.2

General Principles of Coding and Flow-Diagramming

Herman H. Goldstine and John von Neumann

Extract from *Planning and Coding Problems for an Electronic Computing Instrument* ([Princeton: Institute for Advanced Study,] 1947–48), ch. 7.

INTRODUCTORY NOTE TO READING 9.2

A continuation of Burks, Goldstine and von Neumann's *Preliminary Discussion of the Logical Design of an Electronic Computing Instrument* (see Reading 8.3), *Planning and Coding Problems for an Electronic Computing Instrument* represents the first major account of computer-programming methodology for a stored-program computer, even though no such machine was operational at the time the report was written. The report was the only work on computer programming available until the private distribution in 1950 and publication in 1951 of Wilkes, Wheeler, and Gill's *Preparation of Programs for an Electronic Digital Computer* (see Reading 9.4). *Planning and Coding* was issued in three parts in 1947–48; a fourth part was promised but never published.

Because the new electronic computers were so much faster than previously available calculating technology—up to 10^5 times as fast as a manual desk calculator—von Neumann recognized that new programming procedures would have to be devised to enable users to take full advantage of the machines' speed. Thus in *Planning and Coding* particular emphasis is laid upon

disabus[ing] readers of the notion that programming is a straightforward, linear, almost mechanical translation of a mathematical problem into instructions that can be executed by the computer, as programming had been for earlier devices. . . .

The authors point out that in the execution of orders, the computer does not simply pass through them a single time in a linear fashion. To gain its full flexibility, the computer must be able to execute transfer orders (which allow it to jump backward or forward to some specified place in the instruction sequence) and substitution sequences (which allow the coded sequence of instructions to be modified in the course of a computation), and these changes may be conditioned on the results obtained earlier in the computation. They described programming as involving two aspects: writing the static code that is entered into the machine and understanding the dynamic process by which the machine executes these orders. . . .

To aid in this dynamic analysis Goldstine and von Neumann invented a logical tool known as a flow diagram: a labeled graph for tracking the dynamic flow as the computer executes orders and changes values of variables.[1]

---

1 William Aspray, *John von Neumann and the Origins of Modern Computing* (Cambridge, MA: MIT Press, 1990), 69–70.

The final part of the report describes a programming methodology built around the use of variable addressing and a library of subroutines—a methodology designed to eliminate the need for programming the computer "from scratch" each time it was given a new problem. This variable-address computing machine language was an invention of von Neumann. "The importance of being able to do this [write subroutines rather than recode the machine each time] is very great. It is likely to have a decisive influence on the ease and the efficiency with which a computing automaton of the type that we contemplate will be operable. This possibility should, more than anything else, remove a bottleneck at the preparing, setting up, and coding of problems, which might otherwise be quite dangerous."[2] [JMN]

---

2 *Planning and Coding Problems for an Electronic Computing Instrument*, part II, vol. III, AB 287.

TEXT OF READING 9.2

7.1. In the first part of this report we discussed in broad outline our basic point of view in regard to the electronic computing machine we now envision. There is included in that discussion a tabulation of the orders the machine will be able to obey. In this, the second part of the report, we intend to show how the orders may be used in the actual programming of numerical problems.

Before proceeding to the actual programming of such problems, we consider it desirable to discuss the nature of coding *per se* and in doing this to lay down a *modus operandi* for handling specific problems. We attempt therefore in this chapter to analyze the coding of a problem in a detailed fashion, to show where the difficulties lie, and how they are best resolved.

The actual code for a problem is that sequence of coded symbols (expressing a sequence of words, or rather of half words and words) that has to be placed into the Selectron memory in order to cause the machine to perform the desired and planned sequence of operations, which amount to solving the problem in question. Or to be more precise: This sequence of codes will impose the desired sequence of actions on C by the following mechanism: C scans the sequence of codes, and effects the instructions, which they contain, one by one. If this were just a linear scanning of the coded sequence, the latter remaining throughout the procedure unchanged in form, then matters would be quite simple. Coding a problem for the machine would merely be what its name indicates: Translating a meaningful text (the instructions that govern solving the problem under consideration) from one language (the language of mathematics, in which the planner will have conceived the problem, or rather the numerical procedure by which he has decided to solve the problem) into another language (that one of our code).

This, however, is not the case. We are convinced, both on general grounds and from our actual experience with the coding of specific numerical problems, that the main difficulty lies just at this point. Let us therefore describe the process that takes place more fully.

The control scans the coded instructions in the selectron memory as a rule linearly, i.e. beginning, say, with word No. 0, and proceeding from word No. y to word No. $y + 1$ (and within each word from its first half to its second half), but there are exceptions: The transfer orders xC, xC', xCc, xCc' (cf. Table 1 at the end of the first part of the report, or Table 2 below) cause C to jump from word y to the arbitrarily prescribed word x (unconditionally or subject to the fulfillment of certain conditions). Also, these transfer orders are among the most critical constituents of a coded sequence. Furthermore, the substitution orders xSp, xSp' (and also xS, cf. as above) permit C to modify any part of the coded sequence as it goes along. Again, these substitution orders are usually of great importance.

To sum up: C will, in general, not scan the coded sequence of instructions linearly. It may jump occasionally forward or backward, omitting (for the time being, but probably not permanently) some parts of the sequence, and going repeatedly through others. It may modify some parts of the sequence while obeying the instructions in another part of the sequence. Thus when it scans a part of the sequence several times, it may actually find a different set of instructions there at each passage. All these displacements and modifications may be conditional upon the nature of intermediate results obtained by the machine itself in the course of this procedure. Hence, it will not be possible in general to foresee in advance and completely the actual course of C, its character and the sequence of its omissions on one hand and of its multiple passages over the same place on the other, as well as the actual instructions it finds along this course, and their changes through various successive occasions at the same place, if that place is multiply traversed by the course of C. These circumstances develop in their actually assumed forms only during the process (the calculation) itself, i.e. while C actually runs through its gradually unfolding course.

Thus the relation of the coded instruction sequence to the mathematically conceived procedure of (numerical) solution is not a statical one, that of a translation, but highly dynamical: A coded order stands not simply for its present contents at its present location, but more fully for any succession of passages of C through it, in connection with any succession of modified contents to be found by C there, all of this being determined by all other orders of the sequence (in conjunction with the one now under consideration). This entire, potentially very involved, interplay of interactions evolves successively while C runs through the operations controlled and directed by these continuously changing instructions.

These complications are, furthermore, not hypothetical or exceptional. It does not require a deep analysis of any inductive or iterative mathematical process to see that they are indeed the norm. Also, the flexibility and efficiency of our code is essentially due to them, i.e. to the extensive combinatorial possibilities which they indicate. Finally, those mathematical problems, which by their complexity justify the use of the machine that we envision, require an application of these control procedures at a rather high level of complication and of multiplicity of the course of C and of the successive changes in the orders.

All these assertions will be amply justified and elaborated in detail by the specific coded examples which constitute the bulk of this report, and by the methods that we are going to evolve to code them.

Our problem is, then, to find simple, step-by-step methods, by which these difficulties can be overcome. Since coding is not a static process of translation: but rather the technique of providing a dynamic background to control the automatic evolution of a meaning, it has to be viewed as a logical problem and one that represents a new branch of formal logics. We propose to show in the course of this report how this task is mastered.

The balance of this chapter gives a rigorous and complete description of our method of coding, and of the auxiliary concepts which we found convenient to introduce in order to expound this method. (The subsequent chapters of the report deal with specific examples, and with the methods of combining already existing coded sequences.) Since this is the first report on this subject, we felt justified to stress rigor and completeness rather than didactic simplicity. A later presentation will be written from the didactic point of view, which, we believe, will show that our methods are fairly easy to learn.

Table 2			
	Symbolization		Operation
	Complete	Abbreviation	
1	S(x) → Ac	x	Clear accumulator and add number located at position x in the Selectrons into it
2	S(x) → Ac −	x−	Clear accumulator and subtract number located at position x in the Selectrons into it
3	S(x) → AcM	xM	Clear accumulator and add absolute value of number located at position x in the Selectrons into it
4	S(x) → Ac − M	x − M	Clear accumulator and subtract absolute value of number located at position x in the Selectrons into it
5	S(x) → Ah	xh	Add number located at position x in the Selectrons into the accumulator
6	S(x) → Ah −	xh −	Subtract number located at position x in the Selectrons into the accumulator
7	S(x) → AhM	xhM	Add absolute value of number located at position x in the Selectrons into the accumulator
8	S(x) → Ah − M	xh − M	Subtract absolute value of number located at position x in the Selectrons into the accumulator
9	S(x) → R	xR	Clear register[1] and add number located at position x in the Selectrons into it

10	R → A	A	Clear accumulator and shift number held in register into it
11	S(x) × R → A	x ×	Clear accumulator and multiply the number located at position x in the Selectrons by the number in the register, placing the left-hand 39 digits of the answer in the accumulator and the right-hand 39 digits of the answer in the register. The sign digit of the register is to be made equal to the extreme left (non-sign) digit. If the latter is 1, then 2^{-39} is to be added into the accumulator
12	A 4 S(x) → R	x 4	Clear register and divide the number in the accumulator by the number located in position x of the Selectrons, leaving the remainder in the accumulator and placing the quotient in the register
13	Cu → S(x)	xC	Shift the control to the left-hand order of the order pair located at position x in the Selectrons
14	Cu' → S(x)	xC'	Shift the control to the right-hand order of the order pair located at position x in the Selectrons
15	Cc → S(x)	xCc	If the number in the accumulator is ≥ 0, shift the control as in Cu → S(x)
16	Cc' → S(x)	xCc'	If the number in the accumulator is ≥ 0, shift the control as in Cu' → S(x)
17	At → S(x)	xS	Transfer the number in the accumulator to position x in the Selectrons
18	Ap → S(x)	xSp	Replace the left-hand 12 digits of the left-hand order located at position x by the 12 digits 9 to 20 (from the left) in the accumulator
19	Ap' → S(x)	xSp'	Replace the left-hand 12 digits of the right-hand order located at position x by the 12 digits 29 to 40 (from the left) in the accumulator
20	R	R	Replace the contents $\xi_0 \xi_1 \xi_2 \ldots \xi_{38} \xi_{39}$ of the accumulator by $\xi_0 \xi_0 \xi_1 \ldots \xi_{37} \xi_{38}$
21	L	L	Replace the contents $\xi_0 \xi_1 \xi_2 \ldots \xi_{38} \xi_{39}$ and $\eta_0 \eta_1 \eta_2 \ldots \eta_{38} \eta_{39}$ of the accumulator and the register by $\xi_0 \xi_2 \xi_3 \ldots \xi_{39} 0$ and $\eta_1 \eta_2 \eta_3 \ldots \eta_{39} \eta_1$

[1] Register means arithmetic register.

7.2. Table 2 is essentially a repetition of Table 1 at the end of Part I of this report, i.e. it is a table of orders with their abbreviations and explanations. We found it convenient to make certain minor changes. They are as follows:

First: 11 has been changed, so as to express the round off rule discussed in 5.11 in Part 1 of this report. In accord with the discussion carried out *loc. cit.*, we use the first round off rule described there. As far as the left-hand 39 digits are concerned, this consists of adding one to digit 40, and effecting the resulting carries thereby possibly modifying the left-hand 39 digits. Since we keep track of the right-hand 39 digits, too, it is desirable to compensate for this within the extreme left (nonsign) digit of the right-hand 39 digits. This amounts to adding 1/2 in the register. The number there is ≥ 0 (sign digit 0), hence a carry results if and only if that number is ≥ 1/2, i.e. if its extreme left (nonsign) digit is 1. In this case the carry adds 2^{-39} in the accumulator and subtracts 1 in the register.

Hence instead of adding 1/2 in the register we actually subtract 1/2 there. However, the aggregate result (on the 78 digit number) is in any event the addition of 1/2 in the register (i.e. of one to digit 40), hence it must be compensated by subtracting 1/2 in the register. Consequently we do nothing or subtract 1 in the register, according to whether its extreme left (non-sign) digit is 0 or 1. And, as we saw above, we correspondingly do nothing or add 2^{-39} in the accumulator. Note, that the operation $+2^{-39}$, which may cause carries, takes place in the accumulator, which can indeed effect carries; while the operation -1, which can cause no carries, takes place in the register, which cannot effect carries. Indeed: Subtracting 1 in the register, where the sign digit is 0 (cf. above) merely amounts to replacing the sign digit by 1. The new formulation of 11 expresses exactly these rules.

Second: 18, 19 have been changed somewhat for reasons set forth in 8.2 below. We note that 18, 19 assume, both in their old form (Table 1) and their new form (Table 2), that in each order the memory position number x occupies the 12 left digits (cf. 6.6.5. in Part I of this report).

Third: 20, 21 have also been changed. The new form of 20 is a right shift, which is so arranged that it halves the number in the accumulator, including an arithmetically correct treatment of the sign digit. The new form of 21 is a left shift, which is so arranged that it doubles the number in the accumulator (provided that that number lies between $-1/2$ and $1/2$), including an arithmetically correct treatment of the sign digit. At the same time, however, 21 (in its new form) is so arranged that the extreme left digit (after the sign digit) in the accumulator is not lost, but transferred into the register. It is inserted there at the extreme right, and the original contents of the register are shifted left correspondingly. The immediate uses of 20, 21 are arithmetical, but the last mentioned features of 21 are required for other, rather combinatorial uses of 20, 21. For these uses there will be some typical examples in 9.5 and 9.6.

It should be added that various elaborations and refinements of 20, 21 might be considered. Shifts by a given number of places, shifts until certain sizes have been reached, etc. We do not consider the time mature as yet as to make any definite choices in this respect, although some variants would have certain advantages in various situations. We will, for the time being, use the simplest forms of 20, 21 as given in Table 2.

7.3. We now proceed to analyze the procedures by which one can build up the appropriate coded sequence for a given problem—or rather for a given numerical method to solve that problem. As was pointed out in 7.1, this is not a mere question of translation (of a mathematical text into a code), but rather a question of providing a control scheme for a highly dynamical process, all parts of which may undergo repeated and relevant changes in the course of this process.

Let us therefore approach the problem in this sense.

It should be clear from the preliminary analysis of 7.1, that in planning a coded sequence the thing that one should keep primarily in mind is not the original (initial) appearance of that sequence, but rather its functioning and continued changing while the process that it controls goes through its course. It is therefore advisable to begin the planning at this end, i.e. to plan first the course of the process and the relationship of its successive stages to their changing codes, and to extract from this the original coded sequence as a secondary operation. Furthermore, it seems equally clear, that the basic feature of the functioning of the code in conjunction with the evolution of the process that it controls, is to be seen in the course which the control C takes through the coded sequence, paralleling the evolution of that process. We therefore propose to begin the planning of a coded sequence by laying out a schematic of the course of C through that sequence, i.e. through the required region of the Selectron memory. This schematic is the *flow diagram of C*. Apart from the above *a priori* reasons, the decision to make the flow diagram of C the first step in code-planning appears to be extensively justified by our own experience with the coding of actual problems. The exemplification of this kind of experience on a number of selected typical examples forms the bulk of this report.

In drawing the flow diagram of C the following points are relevant:

First: The reason why C may have to move several

times through the same region in the Selectron memory is that the operations that have to be performed may be repetitive. Definitions by induction (over an integer variable); iterative processes (like successive approximations); calculations of sums or of products of many addends or factors all formed according to the same law (but depending on a variable summation or multiplication index); stepwise integrations in a simple quadrature or a more involved differential equation or system of differential equations, which approximate the result and which are iterative in the above sense; etc.—these are typical examples of the situation that we have in mind. To simplify the nomenclature, we will call any simple iterative process of this type an *induction* or a *simple induction*. A multiplicity of such iterative processes, superposed upon each other or crossing each other will be called a *multiple induction.*

When a simple induction takes place, C travels during each step of the induction over a certain path, at the end of which it returns to its beginning. Hence this path may be visualized as a loop. We will call it an *induction loop* or a *simple induction loop*. A multiple induction gives rise to a multiplicity of such loops; they form together a pattern which will be called a *multiple induction loop.*

We propose to indicate these portions of the flow diagram of C by a symbolism of lines oriented by arrows. Thus a linear sequence of operations, with no inductive elements in it, will be denoted by symbols like those in Figs. 7.1 (a-c), while a simple induction loop is shown in (d), eod., and multiple induction loops are shown in (e-f), eod.

Second: It is clear that this notation is incomplete and unsatisfactory. Figures 7.1 (d-f) fail to indicate how C gets into these loops, how many times it circles each loop, and how it leaves it. (e-f), eod. also leave it open what the hierarchy of the loops is, in what order they are taken up by C, etc.

Actually the description of an induction is only complete if a criterion is specified which indicates whether the iterative step should be repeated, i.e. the loop circled once more, or whether the iterations are completed and a new path is to be entered. Accord-

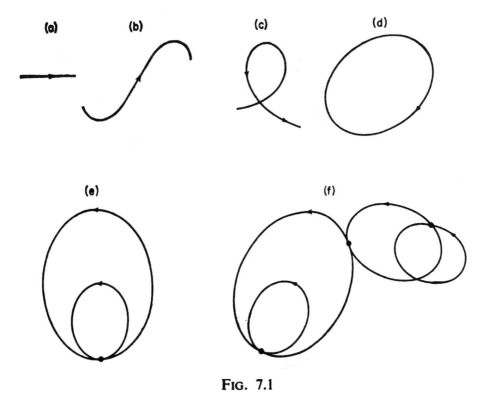

Fig. 7.1

ingly a simple induction loop, like the one shown in Fig. 7.1 (d), needs an indication of the path on which C enters it at the beginning of the induction, the path on which C leaves it at the end of the induction, and the area in which the criterion referred to above is applied, i.e. where it is determined whether C is to circle the loop again, or whether it is to proceed on the exit path. We will denote this area by a box with one input arrow and two output arrows, and we call this an *alternative box*. Thus Fig. 7.1 (d), becomes the more complete Fig. 7.2 (b). The alternative box may also be used to bifurcate a linear, non-looped piece of C's course. Indeed, alternative procedures may be required in non-inductive procedures, too. This is shown in Fig. 7.2 (a). Finally multiple induction loops, completed in this sense, are shown on (c-d), eod. It will be noted that in these inductions in (c) the small loop represents an induction that is subordinate to that one on the big loop, i.e. part of its inductive

step. Similarly in (d) the two small loops that are attached to the big loop are in the same subordinate relation to it, while the loop at the extreme right is again subordinate to the loop to which it is attached.

Third: The alternative boxes which we introduced correspond to the conditional transfer orders xCc, xCc'. That is, the intention that they express will be effected in the actual code by such an order. Of the two output branches (cf., for example, Fig. 7.2 (a)) one leads to the order following immediately in the Selectron memory upon the last order on the input branch, while the other leads to the left- or the right-hand order in $S(x)$. If at the moment at which this decision is made the number u is in A, then $u < 0$ causes the first branch to be taken. We will place the u which is thus valid into the alternative box, and mark the two branches representing the two alternatives $u \geq 0$ and $u < 0$ by + and by − respectively. In this way Figs. 7.2 (a-b) become Figs. 7.3 (a-b). Figure 7.3 (b) may be

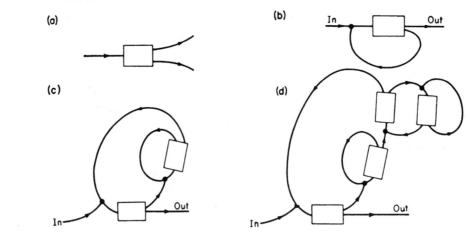

FIG. 7.2

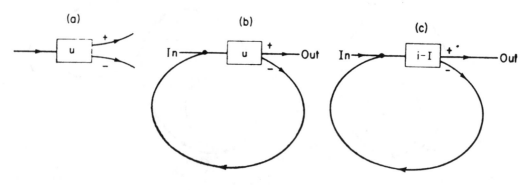

FIG. 7.3

made still more specific: If the induction variable is i, and if the induction is to end when i reaches the value I (if i's successive values are 0, 1, 2, . . . , then this means that I iterations are wanted), and if, as shown in Fig. 7.3 (b), the – branch is in the induction loop while the + branch leaves it, then the u of this figure may be chosen as $i - I$, and the complete scheme is that shown in Fig. 7.3 (c). (In many inductions the natural ending is defined by $i + 1$, having reached a certain value I. Then the above $i - I$ is to be replaced by $i - I + 1$.)

Fourth: Two or more paths of the flow diagram may merge at certain points. This takes place of necessity at the input of the alternative box of an induction loop (cf. Figs. 7.2 (b-d) and 7.3 (b-c)), but it can also happen in a linear, non-looped piece of C's course, as shown in Fig. 7.4. This corresponds to two alternative procedures leading up to a common continuation.

7.4. The flow diagram of C, as described in 7.3 is only a skeleton of the process that is to be represented. We pass therefore to examining the additions which have to be made in order to complete the scheme.

First: Our flow diagram in its present form does not indicate what arithmetical operations and transfers of numbers actually take place along the various parts of its course. These, however, represent the properly mathematical (as distinguished from the logical) activities of the machine, and they should be shown as such. For this reason we will denote each area in which a coherent group of such operations takes place by a special box which we call an *operation box*. Since a box of this category is an insertion into the flow diagram at a point where no branching or merger takes place, it must have one input arrow and one output arrow. This distinguishes it clearly from the alternative boxes of Fig. 7.3. Figures 7.5 (a-c) show the positions of operation boxes in various looped and unlooped flow diagrams.

Second: While C moves along the flow diagram, the contents of the alternative boxes (which we have indicated) and of the operation boxes (which we have not indicated yet) will, in general, keep changing—and so will various other things that have to be associated with these in order to complete the picture (and which we have not yet indicated either). This whole *modus*

procedendi assumes, however, that the flow diagram itself (i.e. the skeleton of Fig. 7.3) remains unchanged. This, however, is not unqualifiedly true. To be specific: The transfer orders xC, xC' (unconditional), and also xCc, xCc' (conditional), can be changed in the course of the process by substitution orders xSp, xSp'. This changes the connections between various parts of the flow diagram. When this happens, we will terminate the corresponding part of the flow diagram with a circle marked with a Greek letter, and originate the alternative continuations from circles marked with properly indexed specimens of the same Greek letter, as shown in Fig. 7.6 (b). We call this arrangement a *variable remote connection*. The circle $\rightarrow \bigcirc$ is the *entrance* to this remote connection, the circles $\bigcirc \rightarrow$ are the *exits* from it.

NOTE 1. The lettering with Greek letters $\alpha, \beta, \gamma, \ldots$ need neither be monotone nor uninterrupted, and decimal fractions following the Greek letters may be used for further subdivisions or in order to interpolate omissions, etc. All of this serves, of course, to facilitate modifications and corrections on a diagram which is in the process of being drawn up. The same principles will be applied subsequently to the enumerations of other entities: Constancy intervals (cf. the last part of 7.6, the basic Greek letters being replaced by Arabic numerals), storage positions (cf. the beginning of 7.7, the basic Greek letters being replaced by English capitals), operation boxes and alternative boxes (cf. the last part of 7.8, the basic Greek letters being replaced by Roman numerals).

NOTE 2. In the case of an unconditional transfer order which is never substituted, the flow diagram can be kept rigid, and no remote connection need be used. It is nevertheless sometimes convenient to use one even in such a case as shown in Fig. 7.6 (a). Indeed, this device may be used at any point of the flow diagram, even at a point where no transfer order is located and C scans linearly (i.e. from one half-word to the next). This is so when the flow diagram threatens to assume an unwieldy form (e.g. grow off the paper) and it is desired to dissect it or to rearrange it. An arrangement of this type will be called a *fixed remote connection*.

The circles $\rightarrow \bigcirc$ and $\bigcirc \rightarrow$ are again the *entrance* and the *exit* of this connection. The Greek letter at the exit need, of course, not be indexed now. It is sometimes convenient to give a remote connection of either type more than one entrance. These are then equivalent to a pre-entrance confluence. They may be used when the geometry of the flow diagram makes the explicit drawing of the confluence inconvenient.

7.5. We pointed out at the beginning of the second remark in 7.4, that our present form of the flow dia-

gram is still incomplete in two major respects: First, the contents of the operation boxes have not yet been indicated. Second, certain further features of the process that accompanies the course of C have not yet been brought out. Let us begin by analyzing the latter point.

No complicated calculation can be carried out without *storing* considerable numerical material while the calculation is in progress. This *storage* problem has been considered in considerable detail in Part I of this

FIG. 7.4

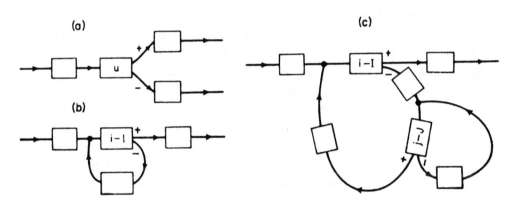

FIG. 7.5

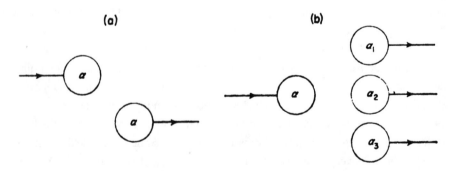

FIG. 7.6

report (cf. in particular 1.3, 2, 4 there). The storage may involve data which are needed for the entire duration of the procedure, and are therefore never changed by that procedure, as well as data which play a role only during part of the procedure (i.e. during one circling of an induction loop, or during a part of the course over a linear piece or an induction loop) and may therefore be changed (i.e. replaced by other data) at the end of their usefulness. These changes serve, of course, the very important purpose of making it possible to use the same storage (Selectron memory) space successively for changing and different ends. We will talk accordingly of *fixed* and of *variable storage*. These concepts are to be understood as being meaningful only relatively to the procedure which we are coding. Occasionally it will also be found useful to use them relatively to certain parts of that procedure.

Before we develop the means to indicate the form and contents of the (fixed and variable) storage that is required, it is necessary to go into another matter.

A mathematical-logical procedure of any but the lowest degree of complexity cannot fail to require *variables* for its description. It is important to visualize that these variables are of two kinds, namely: First, a kind of variable for which the variable that occurs in an induction (or more precisely: with respect to which the induction takes place) is typical. Such a variable exists only within the problem. It assumes a sequence of different values in the course of the procedure that solves this problem, and these values are successively determined by that procedure as it develops. It is impossible to substitute a value for it and senseless to attribute a value to it "from the outside". Such a variable is called (with a term borrowed from formal logics) a *bound variable*. Second, there is another kind of variable for which the parameters of the problem are typical—indeed it is essentially the same thing as a parameter. Such a variable has a fixed value throughout the procedure that solves the problem, i.e. a fixed value for the entire problem. If it is treated as a variable in the process of planning the coded sequence, then a value has to be substituted for it and attributed to it ("from the outside"), in order to produce a coded sequence that can actually be fed into the machine.

Such a variable is called (again, borrowing a term from formal logics) a *free variable*.

In discussing the ways to indicate the form and contents of the storage that is required, there is no trouble in dealing with free variables: They are as good as constants, and the fact that they will acquire specific values only after the coding process is completed does not influence or complicate that process. Also, fixed storage offers no problems. The real crux of the matter is the variable storage and its changes. An item in the variable storage changes when it is explicitly replaced by a different one. (This is effected by the operation boxes, cf. 7.4 and the detailed discussion in 7.7, 7.8.) When the value of a bound variable changes (this is effected by the substitution boxes, cf. the last part of 7.6), this should also cause indirectly a change of those variable storage items in whose expression this variable occurs. However, we prefer to treat these variable value changes merely as changes in notation which do not entail any actual change in the relevant variable storage items. On the contrary, their function is to establish agreement between preceding and following expressions (occupying identical storage positions), which differ as expressions, but whose difference is removed by the substitution in question. (For details cf. the third rule relative to storage in 7.8.)

7.6. After these preparations we can proceed to an explicit discussion of storage and of bound variables.

In order to be able to give complete indications of the state of these entities, it is necessary to keep track of their changes. We will, therefore, mark along the flow diagram the points where changes of the content of any variable storage or of the value or domain of variability of any bound variable takes place. These points will be called the *transition points*. The transition points subdivide the flow diagram into connected pieces, along each of which all changing storages have constant contents and all bound variables have constant values. (The remote connections of the second remark in 7.4 rate in this respect as if they were unbroken paths. For a variable remote connection all possible branches are regarded in this way.) We call these *constancy intervals*. Clearly a constancy interval is bounded by the transition points on its endings.

NOTE. The constant contents and values attached to a constancy interval may, of course, vary from one passage of C over that interval to another.

Let us now consider the transition points somewhat more closely. We have introduced so far three kinds of interruptions of the flow diagram: alternative boxes, operation boxes, remote connections. Of these the first and the third effect no changes of the type under consideration, they influence only the course of C. The second, however, performs arithmetical operations, therefore it may require storage, and hence effect changes in the variable storage. In fact, all variable storage originates in such operations, and all operations of this type terminate in consigning their results to storage, which storage, just by virtue of this origin, must be variable. Accordingly the operation boxes are the transition points inasmuch as the changing of variable storage is concerned. Thus we are left to take care of those transition points which change the values or delimit the domains of variability of bound variables. Changing the value of a bound variable involves arithmetical operations which must be indicated. An inductive variable i, which serves to enumerate the successive stages of an iteration, undergoes at each change an increase by one. We denote this substitution by $i + 1 \rightarrow i$. It is, however, neither necessary nor advisable to permit no other substitutions. Indeed, even an induction or iteration begins with a different substitution, namely that one assigning to i the value 0 [or 1] i.e. $0 \rightarrow i$ [or $1 \rightarrow i$]. In many cases, of which we will present examples, it is necessary to substitute with still more freedom, e.g. $f(i, j, k, \dots) \rightarrow i$, where f is a function of i itself as well as of other variables $j, k, \dots$. (For details cf. the first part of 7.7.) For this reason we will denote each area in which a coherent change or group of such changes takes place, by a special box, which we call a *substitution box*. Next we consider the changes, actually limitations, of the domains of variability of one or more bound variables, individually or in their interrelationships. It may be true, that whenever C actually reaches a certain point in the flow diagram, one or more bound variables will necessarily possess certain specified values, or possess certain properties, or satisfy certain relations with each other. Furthermore, we may, at such a point, indicate the validity of these limitations. For this reason we will denote each area in which the validity of such limitations is being asserted, by a special box, which we call an *assertion box*.

The boxes of these two categories (substitutions and assertions) are, like the operation boxes, insertions into pieces of the flow diagram where no branchings or mergers take place. They have, therefore, one input arrow and one output arrow. This necessitates some special marks to distinguish them from operation boxes. In drawing these boxes in detail, certain distinguishing marks of this type will arise automatically (cf. as above), but in order to clarify matters we will also mark every substitution and assertion by a cross #. In addition, we will, for the time being, also mark substitution boxes with an s, followed by the bound variable that is being changed and assertion boxes with an a.

Thus the operation boxes, the substitution boxes and the assertion boxes produce together the dissection of the flow diagram into its constancy intervals. We will number the constancy intervals with Arabic numerals, with the rules for sequencing, subdividing, modifying and correcting as given in Note 1 in 7.4.

To conclude, we observe that in the course of circling an induction loop, at least one variable (the induction variable) must change, and that this variable must be given its initial value upon entering the loop. Hence the junction before the alternative box of an induction loop must be preceded by substitution boxes along both paths that lead to it: along the loop and along the path that leads to the loop. At the exit from an induction loop the induction variable usually has a (final) value which is known in advance, or for which at any rate a mathematical symbol has been introduced. This amounts to a restriction of the domain of variability of the induction variable, once the exit has been crossed—indeed, it is restricted from then on to its final value, i.e. to only one value. Hence this is usually the place for an assertion box.

A scheme exhibiting all the features discussed in this section is shown in Fig. 7.7.

7.7. We now complete the description of our method to indicate the successive stages and the functioning of storage.

The areas in the Selectron memory that are used in the course of the procedure under consideration will be designated by capital letters, with the rules for sequencing, subdividing, modifying and correcting as given in Note I in 7.4.

The changes in the contents of this storage are effected by the operation boxes, as described in 7.6. An operation box should therefore contain the following indications: First, the expressions which have to be calculated. Second, the storage positions to which these expressions have to be sent subsequently. The latter are stated by an affix "to ...". For example, if the expression $\sqrt{(xy + z)}$ (x, y, z are variables or other expressions) is to be formed and then stored at C.2, then the indication will be "$\sqrt{(xy + z)}$ to C.2". It may also be desired to introduce a new symbol for this expression, i.e. to define one, e.g. $w = \sqrt{(xy + z)}$. Then the indication will be "$w = \sqrt{(xy + z)}$ to C.2".

It should be added that an expression that has been calculated in an operation box may also be sent to a variable remote connection (i.e. to its entrance, cf. the last part of 7.4). The expression must, of course, be the designation of one of the exits of that connection, and the operation consists of equating the designation of the entrance to it. The latter is the Greek letter (possibly with decimals, cf. Note 1 in 7.4), the former is this Greek letter with a definite index. No affix "to ..." is needed in this case, since the designation of the entrance determines the connection that is meant. Hence such an operation looks like this: "$\alpha = \alpha_2$". One or more indications of this kind make up the contents of every operation box.

NOTE 1. An affix "to ..." may also refer to several positions. For example: "to A, C.1, 2".

NOTE 2. The optional procedure of defining a new symbol by an expression formed in an operation box becomes mandatory when that box is followed by a point of confluence of several paths. Indeed, consider the two operation boxes from which the constancy interval 7 issues in Fig. 7.7. Assume that their contents are intended to be "$x + y$ to C.1" and "$x - y$ to C.1", respectively. In order that C.1 have a fixed content throughout the constancy interval 7, as required by our definitions, it is necessary to give the alternative expressions $x + y$ and $x - y$ a common name, say z. Then the contents of the two operation boxes in question will be "$z = x + y$ to C.1" and "$z = x - y$ to C.1".

NOTE 3. A variant of the procedure of defining a new symbol is to define an expression involving a new symbol, which will afterwards only occur as a whole, or to define the value of a function for a new value of its variable (usually in an induction). For example: "$f(i + 1) = 1/2f(i)\{1 - f(i)\}$ to A.2".

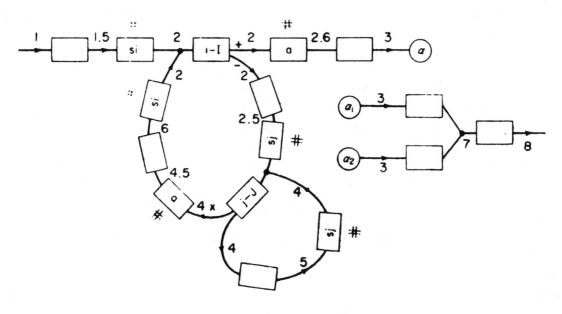

FIG. 7.7

The contents of a substitution box are one or more substitutions of the type described in 7.6, in connection with the definition of the concept of a substitution box. Such a substitution is written like this: "$f(i, j, k, \ldots) \to i$". Here i is a bound variable, the one whose value is being changed (substituted), while $f = f(i, j, k, \ldots)$ is an expression which may or may not contain i itself as well as any other bound variables $j, k, \ldots$ (and any free variables or constants).

The contents of an assertion box are one or more relations. These may be equalities, or inequalities, or any other logical expressions.

The successive contents of the storage positions referred to above (A, B, C, . . . with decimal fractions) must be shown in a separate table, the *storage table*. In conjunction with this table a list of the free variables should be given (in one line) and a list of the bound variables (in the next line).

The storage table is a double entry table with its lines corresponding to the storage positions, and its columns to the constancy intervals. Columns and lines are to be marked with the symbols and numbers of the entities to which they correspond. Each field of this table should show the contents of the position that corresponds to its line throughout the constancy interval corresponding to its column. These contents are expressions which may contain bound variables as well as free variables and constants. It should be noted that the bound variables must appear as such, without any attempt to substitute for them their actual values, since only the former are attached to a given constancy interval as such, while the latter depend also on the specific stage in the course of C, in which C passes at a particular occasion through that constancy interval.

It is obviously convenient to fill in a field in the storage table only if it represents a change from the preceding constancy interval. Therefore we reserve the right (without making it an obligation) to leave a field empty if it represents no such change. In this case the field must be thought of as having the same content as its line had in the column (or columns) of the constancy interval (or intervals) immediately preceding it along the flow diagram. (In the plural case, which occurs at a junction of the flow diagram, these columns [constancy intervals] must all have the same content as the line in question. Indeed, without observing this rule, it would not be possible to treat all incoming branches of a junction as one constancy interval. Compare, for example, the constancy intervals 2 and 7 in Fig. 7.7.) If this antecedent column is not the one immediately to the left of the column in question, it may be advisable to indicate its number in brackets in the field in question.

Certain storage positions (lines) possess no relevance during certain constancy intervals (columns), i.e. their contents are changed or produced and become significant at other stages of the procedure (in other columns). The corresponding field may then be marked with a dash. The repetition rules given above apply to these fields with dashes too.

A scheme exhibiting all these features is shown in Fig. 7.8.

In certain problems it is advantageous to represent several storage positions, i.e. several lines, by one line which must then be marked by a generic variable, or by an expression containing one or more such variables, and not by a definite number. This variable will replace one or more (or all) of the decimal digits (or, rather, numbers) following after the capital letter that denotes the storage area in which this occurs, or these variables may enter into an expression replacing those digits (numbers). In a line which is marked in this way the fields will also be occupied by expressions containing that generic variable or variables. "Expressions" include, of course, also explanations which state what expression should be formed depending on various alternative possibilities.

It may be desirable to use such variable-marked lines only in a part of the storage table, i.e. only for certain columns (constancy intervals). Or, one may want to use different systems of variable markings in different parts. This necessitates breaking the storage table up accordingly and grouping those columns (constancy intervals) together for which the same system of variable markings is being used.

Since the flow diagram is fixed and explicitly drawn, therefore, the columns of the storage table are fixed, too, and there can be no question of variable markings for them.

In actual practice it may be preferable to distribute all or part of this table over the flow diagram. This can be done by attaching every field at which a change takes place to that constancy interval to which it (i.e. its column) belongs, with an indication of the storage position that it represents. (This applies to fields whose line has fixed markings, as well as to those whose line has variable markings, cf. above). Since the immediately preceding constancy intervals are at once seen in this arrangement, there is here no need to give any of the indications suggested by our repetition rules. For mnemotechnical reasons it may be occasionally worthwhile to indicate at a constancy interval the contents of certain fields at which no changes are taking place at that stage (e.g. because no change took place there over a long run, and the original indication is at a remote point in the flow diagram). These two methods, the *tabular* and the *distributed* indication of the storage, may also be used together, in mixed forms. Thus, if the distributed method is used in principle, there may be constancy intervals at which more fields have to be described than convenient (e.g. for reasons of space). Such an interval may then be marked by an asterisk, and a *partial storage table* made, which covers by its columns only the constancy intervals with asterisks. Figure 7.8 is the tabular form of the storage table of a flow diagram which is part of that one of Fig. 7.7 (without the portion along the

constancy intervals 7, 8, and part of 3), and which will be given in full in Fig. 7.10. The distributed form is shown in Fig. 7.9.

7.8. The only constituents of the flow diagram about which more remains to be said are the operation boxes, the substitution boxes and the assertion boxes—although, even for these, short descriptions were given in 7.7. We will now discuss them exhaustively.

An operation box contains one or more expressions, and it indicates that these expressions have to be calculated. Every expression may or may not be preceded by a symbol to which it is equated and which it is defining (cf. also Note 3 in 7.7.); and it may or may not be followed by an affix "to ...", the ... being occupied by the symbol of a definite position, at which the expression in question is to be stored. If the affix "to ..." is missing, this means that the expression in question may be stored in the accumulator or the arithmetical register or otherwise, but that at any rate it will not be needed at a more remote future stage.

A substitution box contains one or more expressions of the type "$f \rightarrow i$", where i is a bound variable, and f is an expression which may or may not contain i and any other bound variables, as well as any free variables and constants. A substitution box is always marked with a cross #.

An assertion box contains one or more relations (cf. the corresponding discussion in 7.7). It is always marked with a cross #.

		1	1.5	2	2.5	2.6	3	4	4.5	5	6
I, J	A.1	–	1	i	–	I	–	[2]	–	–	$i + 1$
	2	–	1	$g(i)$	–	$g(I)$	p	[2]	–	–	$g(i + 1)$
i, j	B.1	–	–	–	1	–	–	j	J	$j + 1$	–
	2	–	–	–	$\frac{1}{2}$	–	–	$f(j, i)$	$f(J, i)$	$f(i + 1, i)$	–

FIG. 7.8

The three categories of boxes that have just been described, express certain actions which must occur, or situations which must exist, when C passes in its actual course through the regions which they represent. We will call these the *effects* of these boxes, but it must be realized, that these are effects in a symbolic sense only.

The effects in question are as follows:

The bound variables occurring in the expressions of an operation box must be given the values which they possessed in the constancy interval immediately preceding that box, at the stage in the course of C immediately preceding the one at which that box was actually reached. The calculated expression must then be substituted in a storage position corresponding to the immediately following constancy interval, as indicated.

A substitution box never requires that any specific calculation be made, it indicates only what the value of certain bound variables will be from then on. Thus if it contains "$f \rightarrow i$", then it expresses that the value of the bound variable i will be f in the immediately following constancy interval, as well as in all subsequent constancy intervals, which can be reached from there without crossing another substitution box with a "$g \rightarrow$

i" in it. The expression f is to be formed with all bound variables in it having those values which they possessed in the constancy interval immediately preceding the box, at the stage in the course of C immediately preceding the one at which that box was actually reached. (This is particularly significant for i itself, if it occurs in f.)

An assertion box never requires that any specific calculations be made, it indicates only that certain relations are automatically fulfilled whenever C gets to the region which it occupies.

The contents of the various fields of the storage table (tabulated or distributed), i.e. the various storage positions at the various constancy intervals must fulfill certain conditions. It should be noted that these remarks apply to the contents of the field in the flow diagrams, and not to the contents of the corresponding positions in the actual machine at any actual moment. The latter obtain from the former by substituting in each case for every bound variable its value according to the actual stage in the course of C—and of course for every free variable its value corresponding to the actual problem being solved. Now the conditions referred to above are as follows:

First: The interval in question is immediately pre-

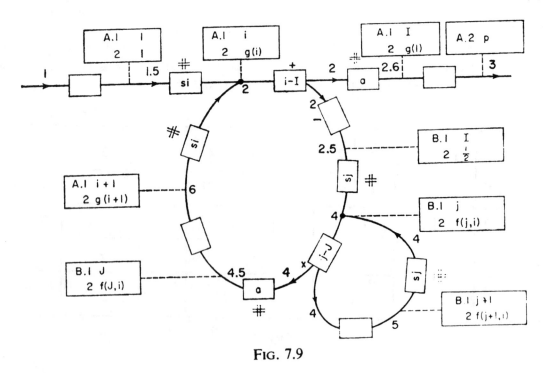

FIG. 7.9

ceded by an operation box with an expression in it that is referred "to . . ." this field: The field contains the expression in question, unless that expression is preceded by a symbol to which it is equated and which it is defining (cf. also Note 3 in 7.7), in which case it contains that symbol.

Second: The interval in question is immediately preceded by a substitution box containing one or more expressions "$f \to i$", where i represents any bound variable that occurs in the expression of the field: Replace in the expression of the field every occurrence of every such i by its f. This must produce the expression which is valid in the field of the same storage position at the constancy interval immediately preceding this substitution box.

Third: The interval in question is immediately preceded by an assertion box: It must be demonstrable, that the expression of the field is, by virtue of the relations that are validated by this assertion box, equal to the expression which is valid in the field of the same storage position at the constancy interval immediately preceding this assertion box. If this demonstration is not completely obvious, then it is desirable to give indications as to its nature: The main stages of the proof may be included as assertions in the assertion box, or some reference to the place where the proof can be found may be made either in the assertion box or in the field under consideration.

Fourth: The interval in question is immediately preceded by a box which falls into neither of the three above categories. The field contains a repetition of what the field of the same storage position contained at the constancy interval immediately preceding this box.

Fifth: If the interval in question contains a merger (of several branches of the flow diagram), so that it is immediately preceded by several boxes, belonging to any or all of the four above categories, then the corresponding conditions (as stated above) must hold with respect to each box.

Finally: The contents of a field need not be shown if it is felt that the omission (or rather the aggregate of simultaneously effective omissions of this type) will not impose a real strain on the reader, due to the amount of implicitly given material that he must remember. Such omissions will be indicated in many cases where mere repetitions of previous contents are involved. (Cf. the remarks made in this connection in 7.7, in the course of the discussion of the distributed form of storage.)

The storage table need not show all the storage positions actually used. The calculations that are required by the expressions of an operation box or of an alternative box may necessitate the use of additional storage space. This space is then specifically attached to that box, i.e. its contents are no longer required and its capacity is available for other use as soon as the instructions of that box have been carried out.

Figure 7.10 shows a complete flow diagram. It differs from that one of Fig. 7.9 only inasmuch that the operation boxes and the storage boxes were left empty then. It is easily verified that it represents the (doubly inductive) procedure defining the number p, which is described under it.

Among the boxes shown on this flow diagram the operation boxes and the alternative boxes and the variable remote connections require further, detailed coding. The substitution boxes and the assertion boxes (i.e. the boxes which are marked by a cross #) are purely explanatory, and require no coding, as pointed out earlier in 7.8. The storage boxes have to be coded essentially as they stand. (For all this, cf. the details given in 7.9.) Thus the remaining problem of coding is attached to the operation boxes, the alternative boxes and the variable remote connections, and it will prove to be in the main only a process of static translation (cf. the end of 7.1 as well as 7.9). In order to prepare the ground for this final process of detailed (static) coding, we enumerate the operation boxes and the alternative boxes by Roman numerals, with the rules for sequencing, subdividing, modifying and correcting as given in Note 1 in 7.4. Figure 7.10 shows such an enumeration. The variable remote connections are already enumerated.

Finally, we indicate the beginning and the end of the completed flow diagram by two circles, $\textcircled{i} \to$ and $\to \textcircled{e}$ cf. Fig. 7.10.

7.9. We can now describe the actual process of coding. It is a succession of steps in the following order.

First: Coding is, of course, preceded by a mathematical stage of preparations. The mathematical or mathematical-physical process of understanding the problem, of deciding with what assumptions and what idealizations it is to be cast into equations and conditions, is the first step in this stage. The equations and conditions thus obtained are rigorous, with respect to the system of assumptions and idealizations that has been selected. Next, these equations and conditions, which are usually of an analytical and possibly of an implicit nature, must be replaced by arithmetical and explicit procedures. (These are usually step-by-step processes or successive approximation processes, or processes with both of these characteristics —and they are almost always characterized by multiple inductions.) Thus a procedure obtains, which is approximate in that sense in which the preceding one was rigorous. This is the second step in this stage.

It should be noted that the first step has nothing to do with computing or with machines: It is equally necessary in any effort in mathematics or applied mathematics. Furthermore, the second step has, at least, nothing to do with mechanization: It would be equally necessary if the problems were to be computed "by hand".

Finally, the precision of the approximation process, introduced by the second step, must be estimated. This includes the errors due to the approximations introduced by the second step, as well as the errors due to the machine's necessarily rounding off to a fixed number of digits (in our projected machine to a sign plus 39 binary digits, cf. Part I of this report) after every intermediate operation (specifically: after every multiplication and division). These are, of course, the well-known categories of *truncation errors* and of *round-off errors,* respectively. In close connection with these it is also necessary to estimate the sizes to which the numbers that occur in any part and at any stage of the calculation, may grow. After these limits have been established, it is necessary to arrange the calculation so that every number is represented by a multiple (by a fixed power of 2) which lies in the range in which the machine works (in our projected machine between −1 and 1, cf. Part I of this report). This is the third and

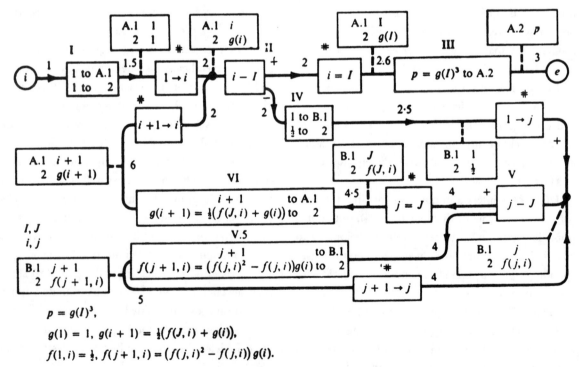

$$p = g(I)^3,$$
$$g(1) = 1, \ g(i + 1) = \tfrac{1}{4}(f(J, i) + g(i)),$$
$$f(1, i) = \tfrac{1}{2}, \ f(j + 1, i) = (f(j, i)^2 - f(j, i)) \, g(i).$$

FIG. 7.10

last step of this stage. Like the second step, it is necessary because of the computational character of the problem, rather than because of the use of a machine.

In our case there exists an alternative with respect to this third step: It may be carried out by the planner, "mathematically", or it may be set up for computation, in which case it may be advantageous to have it, too, carried out by the machine.

After these preliminaries are completed, the coding proper can begin.

Second: Coding begins with the drawing of the flow diagrams. This is the *dynamic* or *macroscopic* stage of coding. The flow diagram must be drawn on the basis of the rules and principles developed in 7.3–7.8. It has been our invariable experience, that once the problem has been understood and prepared in the sense of the preceding first remark, the drawing of the flow diagram presents little difficulty. Every mathematician, or every moderately mathematically trained person should be able to do this in a routine manner, if he has familiarized himself with the main examples that follow in this report, or if he has had some equivalent training in this method.

It is advisable to draw a (usually partial) storage table for the main data of the problem, and use from then on either purely distributed, or mixed distributed and tabular storage, *pari passu* with the evolution of the diagram. The flow diagram is, of course, best started with one of the lowest (innermost) inductions, proceeding to the higher inductions which contain it, reverting (after these are exhausted) to another lowest induction (if any are left), etc. No difficulty will be found in keeping the developing flow diagram complete at every stage, except for certain enumerations which are better delayed to the end (cf. below).

It is difficult to avoid errors or omissions in any but the simplest problems. However, they should not be frequent, and will in most cases signalize themselves by some inner maladjustment of the diagram, which becomes obvious before the diagram is completed. The flexibility of the system of 7.3–7.8 is such that corrections and modifications of this type can almost always be applied at any stage of the process without throwing out of gear the procedure of drawing the diagram, and in particular without creating a necessity of "starting all over again".

The enumeration of the distributed storage and of the remote connections and of the constancy intervals should be done *pari passu* with the drawing of the diagram. The enumeration of the operation boxes and of the alternative boxes, on the other hand, is best done at the end after the flow diagram has been completed.

After a moderate experience has been acquired, many simplifications and abbreviations will suggest themselves to almost any coder. These are best viewed as individual variants. We wish to mention only one here. If distributed storage is extensively used, only a few (if any) among the constancy intervals will have to be enumerated.

Third: The next stage consists of the individual coding of every operation box, alternative box and variable remote connection. This is the *static* or *microscopic* stage of coding. Its main virtue is that the boxes in question can now be taken up one by one, and that the work on each one of them is essentially unaffected by the work on the others. (With one exception, cf. below.)

We feel certain that a moderate amount of experience with this stage of coding suffices to remove from it all difficulties, and to make it a perfectly routine operation. The actual procedure will become amply clear by reading the examples that follow in this report. We state here only general principles which govern the procedure.

The coding of a variable remote connection is best attached to the immediately preceding box. If it is preceded by several such boxes, either of these may be used; if no suitable box is available, it may be given a Roman numeral and treated as a separate box.

The coding of the (operation or alternative) boxes remains. The coding of each box is a separate operation, and we called it, as such, static. This is justified in this sense: The course of C during such a period of coding is strictly linear, i.e. there are no jumps forward or backward (by the Cu or Cc type transfer orders—the orders 13–16 in Table 2)—except possibly at the end of the period—C moves without omitting anything and without ever going twice over the same ground (within one period of this type). It is in this sense only that the process is static: Substitutions, i.e. changes in the memory (hence either in the storage or in the orders), occur at every step. In addition, partial substitutions (by the Sp type substitution orders—the orders 18-19 in Table 2) cause a slight deviation from strict linearity: They affect orders (the ones which are to be modified by substitution) which may not have been coded yet. In this situation it is best to leave in the substitution order the space reserved for the position mark of the order to be substituted (in the preliminary enumeration, cf. below) empty, and mark the substitution order as incomplete. After all orders have been coded, all these vacancies can be filled in. These filling-in operations can be effected within a single linear passage over the entire coded sequence.

The coding of such a box occurs accordingly as a simple linear sequence, and it is therefore necessary to define a system for the enumeration of the code orders within the sequence (of this box). We call it the *preliminary enumeration*, because the numbers which we assign at this stage are not those that will be the x's of the actual position in the Selectron memory. The latter form the *final enumeration* to be discussed further below. The preliminary enumeration is defined as follows: The symbol of the box under consideration is to be shown, then a comma, and then an Arabic numeral—the latter being used to enumerate the code orders of this sequence. (We might again allow the rules for sequencing, subdividing, modifying and correcting as given in Note 1 in 7.4, for this enumeration, too. It will, however, hardly ever be necessary to have recourse to these—there will almost never be any difficulty in carrying out a simple linear numbering of the entire sequence *pari passu* with its coding.)

Thus the enumeration for a box II.1 might be II.1, 1; II.1, 2; . . . . Actually these symbols will be written under each other, and the box symbol (II.1 in the above case) need be shown only the first time. In every order the expression $S(x)$ will have to be written with the full preliminary symbol of x, e.g. ; S (II.1, 3). (This example must, of course, be thought of as referring to a Selectron position x containing an order. If x contained a number, an expression like S (A.2, 2) would be typical.)

References to a variable remote connection are best made by its Greek letter (possibly with decimals, cf. Note 1 in 7.4, and with or without indexing according to whether the entrance or the exit is meant), since it may not be feasible or convenient to determine at this stage the identifications of its parts with the appropriate (Roman numeral) boxes.

Any storage that becomes necessary in the course of this coding (in excess of the tabulated or distributed storage of the flow diagram, i.e. the storage attached to the box, cf. the last part of 7.8), has to be shown separately, as *local storage*. The local storage should be enumerated in the same way as indicated above, but with a symbols after the comma, e.g.: II.1, *s*.l; II.1, *s*.2; . . . . [For an $S(x)$ which refers to such a position one might write, e.g. S (II.1, *s*.2), in the sense of the suggestion in the preceding paragraph. However, since the reference is by its nature to the box under consideration at the time, it is legitimate to abbreviate by omitting the box symbol, writing e.g. S (*s*.2).]

The coding itself should be done in a column of its own, enumerated as indicated above. It is advisable to parallel it with another, explanatory, column, which shows for each order the effect of the substitution that it causes. This effect appears, of course, in one of the following places: The accumulator (symbol: Ac), or the arithmetical register (symbol: R), or some storage position or coded order (symbols as described up to now). The explanatory column then shows each time the symbol of the place where the substitution takes place, and its contents after the substitution. The C*u* or C*c* type transfer orders (the orders 13–16 in Table 2) cause no substitution, they transfer C instead (and they occur only at the end of the sequence)—hence they require no explanation.

An order in the sequence, which becomes effective in a substituted form (substituted by an earlier order in the sequence), should be shown in its original form and then, in brackets, in its substituted form. The original form may have a –, the sign of irrelevance, or any other symbol (e.g. the number 0, of course, as a 12 digit binary), in place of its x (in its $S(x)$). It is this form which matters in the actual coding. (In writing out a code, it is best to use the sign of irrelevance in such a case. When it comes to real coding, however, an actual number must be used, e.g. 0.) The substituted form, on the other hand, is clearly the one which will actually control the functioning of the machine, and it is the one to which the explanation should be attached.

We repeat: We feel certain that direct, linear coding according to this principle presents no difficulties after a moderate amount of experience has been acquired.

Fourth: The last stage of coding consists of assigning all storage positions and all orders their final numbers. The former may be enumerated in any order, say linearly. The latter may then follow, also in a linear order, but with the following restriction: The flow diagram indicates that a certain box must follow immediately after another operation box, or immediately after the – branch of an alternative box (– is the case where the transfer of C by a conditional transfer order—type C*c*—does not become effective). In this case the sequence of the former box must begin immediately following the end of the sequence of the latter box: It can happen, that this principle requires that a box be the immediate successor of several boxes. In this case all of the latter boxes (except one) must be terminated by (unconditional) transfer orders to the former box. Such a transfer order is also necessary if a box requires as its immediate successor a non-initial order of another box.

At this stage the identification of every part (entrance and exits) of every variable remote connection with appropriate (Roman numeral) boxes (i.e. orders in them) must be established. The Greek letter references to these connections will then be rewritten accordingly.

These principles express all the restrictions that need be observed in the final, linear ordering of the boxes. To conclude, we note that it must be remembered, that two orders constitute together a word, i.e. that they have together one final number, and are distinguished from each other as its "left" or "right" order.

After this final enumeration has been completed, one more task remains: In every order, in the expression $S(x)$ the preliminary number x must be replaced by the final number x, and for those orders which substitute positions that are occupied by orders (orders

without or with primes—these are the orders 13–16 and 18, 19 in Table 2) the distinction between "left" and "right" must be made (i.e. the order must not be primed or it must be primed, respectively). In the case of positions which correspond to the exits of one variable remote connection it is clearly necessary that they be all "left" or all "right". This must be secured; the ways to achieve this are obvious.

When the coding is thus completed, the positions where the sequence of orders begins and ends (corresponding to *i* and *e*, cf. the end of 7.8), should be noted. There will be more to say about these when we get to the questions of subroutines and of combining routines, to which reference will be made further below, but we will not go into this matter now.

All these things being understood, it is indicated to state this in addition: There are still some things which have to be discussed in connection with the coding of problems, and which we have neglected to consider in this chapter, and will also disregard in the chapters which follow in this Part II of the report. We refer to the orders which stop the machine, to the orders which control the magnetic wire or tape and the oscilloscopic output of the machine, and to the logical principles and practical methods applying to the use of the magnetic wire or tape inputs and outputs as a subsidiary memory of the machine.

We made brief references to these matters in the paragraphs 4.5, 4.8, 6.8 (and the sub-paragraphs of the latter) in Part I of this report. They require, of course, a much more detailed consideration. That we neglect to take them up here, in Part II of our report, is nevertheless deliberate. The main reason for this neglect is that they depend on parts of the machine where a number of decisions are still open. These are decisions which lead only to minor engineering problems either way, but they do affect the treatment of the three subjects mentioned above (stop orders, output orders, use of the input-output as a subsidiary memory) essentially. So the corresponding discussion is better withheld for a later report.

Furthermore, the two first items are so simple, that they do not seriously impair the picture that we are going to present in what follows. The potentialities of the third item are much more serious, but we do not know as yet, to what an extent such a feature will be part of the first model of our machine.

There are further important general principles affecting the efficient use of coding and of routines. These are primarily dealing with *general routines* and *sub-routines* and with their use in *combining routines* to new routines. These matters will be taken up, as far as the underlying principles are concerned in Chapter 12, and put to practical use in various examples, with further discussion in the subsequent Chapters 13 and 14. In the immediately following Chapters 8–11, we will give examples of coding individual routines, on the basis of the general principles of this Chapter 7.

Tentative Instruction Code for a Statistical EDVAC (Code C-1, April 24, 1947) & Instructional Code C-1 for Statistical Machine (EDVAC II)

Electronic Control Company

INTRODUCTORY NOTE TO READING 9.3

In late September 1946, Pres Eckert and John Mauchly's fledgling Electronic Control Company, the world's first electronic computer company, formally contracted to supply the United States Census Bureau with an EDVAC-type machine, for which the Bureau would pay $300,000. This would be the first electronic computer ever sold. Since the Census Bureau was forbidden by law to enter into any research and development contracts, a complex financing arrangement was worked out between ECC (renamed the Eckert-Mauchly Computer Corporation in 1947), the Census Bureau, and the National Bureau of Standards (NBS), in which the money, supplied by the Army Ordnance Department, was funneled via the Census Bureau to the NBS, which then used it to fund the development of an electronic digital computer for use by all the involved parties. The design and construction of this computer—the first UNIVAC I—took longer than anticipated, largely due to the ECC/EMCC's continuing financial difficulties. The Census Bureau did not take possession of its computer until 1951, by which time the EMCC had been acquired by Remington Rand.

We reproduce here, for the first time, two of the earliest programming documents issued by Eckert and Mauchly's Electronic Control Company. Existing only in mimeograph typescript, these are probably the earliest extant documents concerning the programming of an electronic digital computer intended for commercial applications. The documents refer to a "statistical EDVAC" or "EDVAC II"; the name "UNIVAC" (for *UNIV*ersal *A*utomatic *C*omputer) was formally adopted on May 24, 1947.[1] The *Tentative Instruction Code*, dated April 24, 1947, discusses the aspects and requirements of a workable machine code, including reconciliation of the two "somewhat competitive considerations" of ease of use and the need to limit the number of instructions. *Instruction Code C-1*, dated May 1, 1947, contains the program itself, an explanation of abbreviations, and a list of binary equivalents of alphanumeric characters and symbols.

When Eckert, Mauchly, and their staff at ECC were thinking about the design of UNIVAC, they had to devise a basic instruction set for the computer. Eckert and Mauchly's machine differed from the other electronic digital machines of the time—ENIAC, the Manchester "Baby," EDVAC, EDSAC, etc.—in that it was intended for business and statistical purposes rather than for scientific work. It would thus require a different type of architecture, consisting of short memory elements for representing decimal digits and characters (although the underlying technology would still be binary). This was unexplored territory, and the ECC staff were unsure of what UNIVAC might be required to do in the future. The author or authors of this report thus suggested that programs be written using the C-1 instruction set to see if they might be able to simplify it for the final design of the machine. This instruction set contained thirty different instructions, including some being set aside for division (not yet considered at this time), graphical output to an oscilloscope, square roots, and true binary (rather than decimal) subtraction to compare values which were not "digits."

---

1 Nancy Stern, *The BINAC* (*Annals of the History of Computing* 1 [1979]: 9–20), 11.

The document shows that some thought had already been put into the programming system. For example, it had been decided that two instructions would fit into one "word" (actually twelve digits) and that some of the digits would be left as zeros so that larger addresses could be used for potential future expansion of the memory size from the current one thousand "words." The discussion of subroutines includes the fact that that provision had been considered for modifying addresses within subroutines to make them relocatable in memory, a problem that was later solved by the use of index registers (first called B-lines by the Manchester group that invented the idea). The advanced concept (for the time) of subroutine jumps—pioneered by David Wheeler of Cambridge ("the Wheeler jump")—would indicate that Eckert and Mauchly were intimately familiar with developments in Britain. (My thanks to Michael R. Williams for contributing to this note.—JMN)

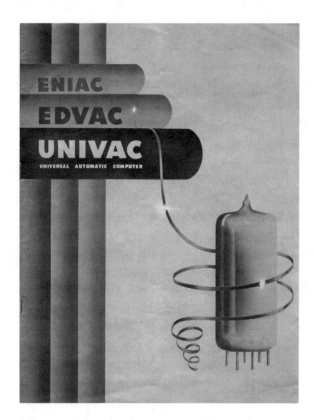

Upper cover of the first sales brochure ever published for an electronic digital computer. Selling the concept of a radically new and very expensive machine that did not yet exist was a formidable marketing challenge. Eckert and Mauchly's approach was to explain how UNIVAC had evolved out of the ENIAC, and the EDVAC which was then also under development. In the brochure they rightly took credit for much of the design of the ENIAC, and for the planning of the EDVAC prior to their departure from the University of Pennsylvania. The brochure suggested that the EDVAC was in existence at the time, though it was just in developmental stages, hardly much further along than UNIVAC. The brochure explained that EDVAC would be much faster than ENIAC, and UNIVAC would be far faster than EDVAC. The brochure contained an overview of the plans for UNIVAC, but most of it was given over to a reprint of Douglas Hartree's "The ENIAC, an electronic computing machine," which had originally been published in *Nature* in 1946. Hartree's article added authority to this brochure from Eckert and Mauchly's virtually unknown start-up company. Throughout the brochure the team is referred to as Mauchly and Eckert, perhaps reflecting Mauchly's seniority to Eckert who was then only twenty-eight. The front cover of the brochure prominently features a vacuum tube, emphasizing the then-advanced feature of using vacuum tubes, rather than electromechanical relays, as switches.

1. GENERAL CONSIDERATIONS

There are two somewhat competitive considerations which affect the choice of an instruction code. On the one hand, it is desirable to give great weight to the ease with which the code can be used. To simplify the task of the personnel who must prepare problems for the machine is highly important unless such a machine is to be used almost entirely for a limited number of constantly recurring problems. On the other hand, too large a number and variety of instructions can complicate the structure of the machine, appreciably increase the amount of equipment involved, and require an undue amount of additional design and construction effort. Compound operations, whereby several elementary steps are carried out in sequence when initiated by a single instruction, are particularly likely to cause difficulties of this sort. The simplest machine design is achieved when relatively few orders, each relating to a single quite elementary operation, are provided.

Less than a dozen instructions, each for a simple elementary machine operation, would provide for all the possibilities which can be achieved by machines with much more elaborate codes. A more extensive set of instructions can serve only two purposes: (1) convenience to the coding personnel, and (2) saving of memory space by making the instructions more compact and saving of machine operation time in certain cases. For a machine using delay line registers, the time required for locating both orders and the numbers which are the subject of the operations to be performed is by no means negligible, and time-saving by compounding several elementary steps in one order deserves serious consideration, even though this may require more control equipment.

In formulating tentative code C-1, described below, the aim has been to provide a set of instructions which would include most of the items which would contribute to ease and compactness of coding, together with saving of machine operating time. Exclusive of the digits for "memory address," each order has a letter (or two decimal digits) for which a group of eight pulses is required. By this system 225 (15^2 rather than 2^8, because certain zero combinations are excluded) different orders could be represented. If no mnemonic

devices for associating symbols with the various orders were used, this would be many more than an operator could become facile with in any reasonable time. It is possible, however, to allocate the symbols so that the "system" can be easily learned.

Code C-1 is to be considered, then, as one toward which machine design might aim. If complexity of design and equipment should impose limitations, the code ultimately adopted may not be as extensive as C-1. Trial coding of problems may also reveal that C-1 should be modified for reasons of convenience. Suggestions for such modification will be greatly appreciated.

2. PULSE CODE FOR NUMERIC AND ALPHABETIC CHARACTERS.

The pulse code must be capable of representing both alphabetic and numerical characters. Since numerical information is expected to predominate in most applications, compactness is of greater importance in the numerical part of the code.

We may describe the pulse code in terms of binary digits. The presence or absence of a pulse in a particular code group will be denoted by 0 or 1, respectively. The pulse groups for all numerical characters (decimal digits) are to be the same size, for timing reasons. The smallest set of binary digits capable of representing the ten different decimal digits is a group of four. Such a group of four binary digits will be called a "*machine digit.*"

Sixteen different machine digits are thus possible, but only fifteen will be used. The combination, 0000, is discarded so that at least one pulse will appear in every machine digit.

Ten of the machine digits are used for the decimal digits from 0 to 9. These are assigned so that addition by modified binary processes are possible, and so that "nines complements" are obtained by interchanging 0 and 1 in the machine digits. The code satisfying these requirements is known as the "excess three" code, since the decimal digit, d, is represented by the binary number which is equal to $d + 3$.

Plus and minus signs are to be used with numerical data in the computer, and these too should have a compact code, Therefore, each of these is represented by a single machine digit. Printers and key-operated input devices will have type-bars and keys for these characters.

Thus, twelve machine digits are assigned to the ten decimal digits and the symbols for + and –. It will be found that this permits a compact duodecimal code when such is required for statistical purposes.

Of the fifteen machine digits, three remain for use in connection with alphabetic characters. These three will be designated as Zone indicators I, II, and III. They will be used in combination with a second machine digit. Since the second machine digit may take on any one of fifteen values, forty-five different combinations are possible. This is more than sufficient, since this is approximately the number of keys on a standard typewriter including numerals. (Should upper and lower case letters be required, this can be managed by using two code groups for "shift to upper case" and "shift to lower case," similar to the system used with a teletypewriter.)

On a key device for preparing magnetic tape, actuation of an alphabetic key will place two machine digits on the tape, one of which is a zone indicator. When a zone indicator is read from a tape into a printer, the printer will examine the next machine digit coming from the tape and operate the single type-bar which such a pair of machine digits will select.

The correspondence between alphabetic characters and such pairs of machine digits is arranged so that the eight-digit binary numbers formed by such pairs increase in value through the alphabet from A to Z. This facilitates the sorting and ordering of alphabetic information by methods similar to those used with purely numerical data.

Spaces, periods and commas may appear together with letters in a list of names. For sorting purposes, these are to be regarded as alphabetic characters prefixed to the usual alphabet. They are therefore given digit groups of lower value than that for A. Thus, the name, "Brook, S. D." would appear ahead of the name, "Brooks, D." automatically as a result of any standard procedure for putting these names in alphabetic order. Also, by proper coding, the machine can recognize the comma and place the last name last for mailing, check-writing or similar purposes.

3. WORD LENGTH AND ORDER STRUCTURE.

The machine now under design is to have 1000 registers, each storing one "word" consisting of 12 machine digits (48 binary digits), One word of numerical information is to consist of one machine digit specifying the algebraic sign of the number, and 11 machine digits representing 11 decimal digits. When alphabetic characters and punctuation are stored in a register, only six such symbols can be accommodated in a register, since each requires a pair of machine digits.

Only five machine digits would be needed to specify one instruction. Thus two, but not three, instructions can be stored in one register. To make each instruction exactly one-half of a word, a zero is inserted in the instruction, just preceding the digits which refer to a memory register. This digit can then be used as part of the register address if, at some later time, machines having more than 1000 registers are built.

As a result, each instruction is six machine digits in length. In most instructions, the first two machine digits correspond to an alphabetic symbol, and these two machine digits are obtained by the actuation of a single key on the key input device. Tape orders and shift orders are an exception to this, since the first part of these orders consists of a combination of two of the numeric or sign indicating symbols.

Not all instructions necessarily refer to a memory register. That some instructions do not is partly a matter of operational convenience and partly a matter of being able to carry out certain operations quickly without introducing a time loss associated with waiting for a specific minor cycle for insertion or removal of numbers from a long delay register. For example, consider the operation of shifting in order to multiply a number by some power of 10. If the number on which this operation is to be performed is already in the accumulator and the result is to be placed in the accumulator, then it would be unhandy from the operator's point of view to have to send this to a memory register first and then bring it back to the accumulator later. Time losses due to waiting are also avoided by an order which makes no use of the long delay lines in the memory. For instructions of this sort, then, the three digits otherwise used to specify a memory register are not needed in this way and could be used for some other purpose.

There is a temptation, in the case of orders which need not specify a memory position, to use the digits thus made available in some other way so as to increase the variety of possible orders. It is believed, however, that there is a strong reason for avoiding instructions which use these digits for other than memory position indicators. This reason has to do with the use of subroutines and the way in which subroutines are to be modified when they are placed in one position or another in the internal memory. Code C-1 has been devised with the idea that such modification should be possible by the use of an extremely simple routine. In general this routine will merely add a constant to the memory position indicators of every order which a subroutine contains. For those orders which do not use the memory switch it will be immaterial whether or not anything is added to the positions which specify the register number, since for such orders the machine will disregard these digits. The only point that then remains to be considered, in constructing a subroutine, is to segregate the orders from any numerical data which may occur in such a subroutine, and this is an extremely easy condition to satisfy.

Certain restrictions have been put on the memory addresses which may be used in a few of the instructions. In transferring the entire contents of one long tank to another, it is expected that the operator will use a memory address which is a multiple of 20, and in subroutines which contain orders of this type the addresses will be modified. by multiples of 20 so that the resulting addresses will also satisfy this condition. The same assumptions and restrictions apply to the tape orders.

Likewise there is a restriction on the address number to be used when the control is shifted to a new register. Only addresses corresponding to even numbers are to be used for such purposes. Consequently subroutines should always have their addresses modified by even numbers. The reason for this restriction has to do with a method for reducing the waiting time which is associated with reading instructions from the memory. It is assumed that 4 instructions, or 2 words, are read from the memory to the control as a group. If an even larger group were used, there would be additional savings in some problems, but it is likely that other problems in which the control was shifted frequently would suffer as a result. For instance, if the machine were to read 4 words from the memory to the control, then the addresses which were suitable for transfer of control would have to be multiples of 4. This would mean that some memory positions in an order sequence would need to be left unused, and also that the coding personnel would have to distinguish whether a given address satisfied the requirement. While it is not difficult to see if a given number is divisible by 4 or not, it is certainly much easier to distinguish whether it is odd or even.

If this restriction to even-numbered addresses is considered unsatisfactory and it is still desired to reduce the waiting time associated with obtaining orders from the memory, this can, of course, be done by the introduction of more equipment. This equipment would consist of a number of short registers holding either single orders or single words, all of which would be filled from successive registers in the main memory. This would be necessary because of the fact that different orders require different lengths of time for their execution. A single long tank in the control organ to hold a series of orders would not avoid the problem of waiting time, but merely transfer it from the main memory to the long tank memory associated with the control.

4. CONTROL ORDERS AND SUBROUTINES.

Some considerations pertinent to this topic have already been dealt with in the preceding section. It was pointed out that the instruction code C-1 has been designed to permit the modification of a subroutine simply by adding a constant to every address in every order which the subroutine contains. This whether a subroutine is placed in one part of the internal memory or another, all addresses which refer to the subroutine itself will be modified by the same constant and the effect will be as if a relative numbering system were used.

There is one occasion on which every subroutine must necessarily refer to a standard position which must not be modified when the subroutine is given a different position in the memory. That is when the operations governed by the subroutine have been completed and it is necessary to return to a main routine. The control order T*m* in Code C-1 provides a convenient method for accomplishing this result. In this order the address *m* is disregarded and the control is transferred to the 000 register. Thus no matter how *m* is modified when the subroutine as a whole is modified, this instruction will always refer to that 000 register.

The V*m* order of Code C-1 provides a convenient method for transferring from a main routine to a subroutine, preserving the information as to the position in the main routine to which the control should later be returned. Before leaving the main routine, the control register is advanced one unit, and this number is then stored in register 000, where it becomes the address of an order U*m* to which the control will later be referred by an instruction T*m*. The order V*m* must always be placed in an odd-numbered register in order that the U*m* order in the 000 register will have an even number. The 000 register is not otherwise different from other registers in the memory. The U*m* order in this register would normally be established by the very first instruction read into the machine.

One possibility which suggests itself is to have a separate one-word register to be used for this purpose instead of the register 000. This would, however, require additional orders to be introduced into the instruction code to permit the access to this register which is required for the following reason. When a subroutine makes use of still another subroutine as a part of its program, then the information in the 000 register relating to the position in the main routine must be temporarily removed so that this register, will be available to be used by the V order which calls in the secondary subroutine. The need for doing this can always be foreseen, since when a subroutine is being laid out it is always known whether or not it makes use of other subroutines.

One other control instruction has been included in code C-1 particularly to facilitate collation of alphabetic data. Such data contains machine digits (zone indicators) which fall outside the decimal digit code and which cannot be subtracted by the arithmetic orders so far provided using a "decimal adder." Equality or inequality of the various machine digits can, however, be sensed by *binary* subtraction.

The instruction $*m* will test, by binary subtraction, whether the number in A is less than the number in L. If so, no transfer of control will be made, but if (A) is equal to or greater than (L), the control will be transferred to *m* (See Section 8 for a suggested application).

5. MODIFICATION OF INSTRUCTIONS.

Code C-1 provides an instruction K*m* to be used in modifying other instructions. From a combination of other orders the effect of this single instruction could be secured. However, four or five other instructions would be needed to accomplish the same purpose, and since there will probably be frequent need for modifying instructions (in order to express rather general sets of operations in compact form) it is desirable to make this process as simple and as convenient as possible from the operator's point of view. The time required for modification of an order would also be considerably greater if four or five instructions had to be used rather than this single one, and occasions would arise in which the operating time of the machine would be appreciably increased if the K order were not available.

6. ELEMENTARY ORDERS TO AND FROM ACCUMULATOR.

Algebraic sums may be formed in the accumulator by use of the orders A*m* and S*m* for addition and subtraction. Only one instruction for disposing of accumulator contents is strictly necessary. O*m*, which transfers the accumulator contents to the memory register *m* and clears the accumulator, would probably be the one retained if only one transfer from A were to be used. The order H*m*, which holds the number in A while storing it in *m*, is not only a help to the coding personnel but also reduces waiting time. Otherwise, there would be a waiting time required in bringing the number back from the memory after the C order was used, and there would also be a waiting time involved in obtaining the A order itself.

Still another method of disposing of the contents of A is provided by the B*m* order. Occasionally the B order might be useful in the course of arithmetic computations when a new number is to be brought into A. If there is no reason why the previous contents of A need go in any particular place, and the new number being brought into A is no longer to be held in the memory, then the number previously in A might just as well be deposited in the register from which the new number comes. This again is an economy device, enabling one instruction to handle what would otherwise require two, and cutting the waiting time by a factor of 2. It is not believed, however, that occasions for its use in arithmetic processes would be sufficiently numerous to justify including the B order for this purpose alone.

The B order is intended primarily for use in the sorting of data and in the systematic rearrangement of words which may be required in the course of computing routines. Suppose, for example, it is desired to interchange the words in memory positions 100 to 104 with those in positions 105 to 109. This could be done by a series of A and C orders. However, by proper use of the B order, almost half the required time can be saved.

7. MULTIPLICATION ORDERS.

Code C-1 contains five different kinds of multiplication orders and two other orders, L and W, which are needed in connection with some of these.

The P order provides for a complete and exact 22-digit product, the more significant half of which is stored in the accumulator and the less significant half in W, which is a one-word register associated with the memory switch. The order in then provides for storing the latter part in any chosen memory register. The other part can, of course, be returned to the memory through a B, C, or H order.

The multiplication orders N, N, and P all require that the multiplicand be stored in a register L provided for this purpose. The instruction L*m* is used to send the multiplicand this register. The multiplier is specified within the multiplication order itself by the memory address which that order contains.

The summation of products can be readily achieved by using the orders *m* and N. When the *m* order is used, the product (rounded off to 11 digits) is formed from the multiplier and multiplicand and added to the previous contents of the accumulator. When the N order is used, the same product is formed, but is subtracted from the contents of the accumulator.

The instructions *m* and N do not alter the contents of L. Hence these orders are also convenient when a constant factor is to be used in forming a number of products. In statistical work, for instance, the same weight factor may have to be applied to a number of variables.

Two cases arise in which it is unnecessary to specify both multiplier and multiplicand by their memory addresses. One of these is when a square is to be formed, so that the two factors are identical. A special order Q*m* has been included in Code C-1 for this purpose. This order is not, of course, a necessary one, since the same effect could have been obtained through the use of an L and *m* order, but again this order is both a convenience to the coding personnel and a device for reducing the waiting time.

Essentially the same remarks apply to instruction X*m*: In this case the multiplicand is the result of a previous operation and exists only in the accumulator. The X order transfers the contents of the accumulator to the multiplicand register L, clears A, following which it behaves like an *m* instruction. Again, although this order is not a necessary one, it does provide convenience and reduce waiting time. Almost the same convenience and saving could be secured if, instead of the X order, an order transferring from A to L, leaving A clear, were provided.

8. EXTRACTION (LOGICAL MULTIPLICATION)

The orders E and F are used for "digit extraction" by a process which is equivalent, in some ways, to logical multiplication. The same effects could be secured by combinations of other orders, but relatively simple electronic means can be used to obtain the desired results directly.

By means of the order, Fm, a number from register m is stored in a one-word tank, F, for use by the Em order. The Em order then clears A, and transfers to A from register m, deleting, however, these digits for which the corresponding digit in F is even. Deleted digits are replaced by zeros. Thus, if the number in F consists entirely of zeros, the Em order would merely clear A to contain all zeros, including the digit position normally occupied by the sign indicator, if the corresponding position in P were zero. If the number in F were + followed by 11 zeros, A would receive only the sign of the number in m, followed by zeros, since the + in F would act in the same manner as an *odd* number. If F were +11111000000, then A would receive the sign and the five most significant digits from m, followed by six zeros. If the number in m is negative, it will be sent through the complementer before selection. In no case does it pass through the adder, however, when this order is used.

The fact that words brought into A with the Em order do not pass through the adder is important when alphabetic information is being treated. The decimal adder for the "excess three" numerical code will alter zone indicators unless special precautions are taken, For sorting alphabetic information, the Em order is used in preparation for the comparison by binary subtraction, for which the instruction, m, is used.

The word stored in F remains there until another F order substitutes a new word. Since the F register is not used in other operations, it may be set up for a given type of selection which is to be used a number of times, and this selection will be available whenever required, even though all sorts of other operations may intervene in the program sequence.

A useful sequence in which the L and F registers alternately take part, while continuing to store words which are needed each time the sequence is repeated, may be suggested: assume that information in compactly coded form is to be collated, and only certain digits of a particular word constitute the key according to which the collation is to be carried out. These may not even be consecutive digits, so that isolation by only a few shift orders is not possible. F is then set up to select the relevant digits. An Em order brings into A the relevant digits selected from a word from one of the two monotonic groups to be collated. This is then transferred to L (directly if such an order, already suggested in the preceding suggestion, were provided; otherwise through a memory register as an intermediate). Then another word, from the other monotonic group, is brought into A by an Em order. This is followed by a binary subtraction comparison, m. If the comparison does not transfer the control, F is left unchanged, and after various operations concerned with transferring data based on the inequality just ascertained, and various steps needed to revise instructions for the next stage of the work, another word from the second monotonic group is brought into A by an Em order. During such a program, F is never altered, and the contents of L are changed only when the m finds an inequality of the sort which causes it to transfer the control.

9. SHIFT ORDERS.

In Code C-1 +n and −n are used for shift orders. +n the effect of multiplying the number in the accumulator by 10^n. −n has the effect of introducing a factor of 10^{-n} in the accumulator contents. The memory address of these orders is disregarded. It is felt that there is much more occasion to shift a result already in the accumulator to a new position in the accumulator than there is to shift a number being brought into the accumulator for the first time or to shift a number which is being sent from the accumulator back to the memory. If the shift order had been coupled with a transfer to or from the memory, then a waiting time would have been incurred every time that the shift order was employed. With the shift order as it stands in Code C-1 no such waiting time is incurred, and should it be desired to couple this shift with a transfer to or from the memory, the only inconvenience which results is that of writing down one other order such as A, B, C, or H.

If the number in A before the shift operation has 11 significant digits and a sign indication, then the shift to the right when −n is used will result in the loss of the *n* right hand digits. The position of the sign will not be affected, Likewise, if the +*n* order is used, *n* digits will be lost from the left of the 11 digit number, but the sign will remain unaffected.

This means that the extraction of a *sequence* of digits from an 11 digit number can be accomplished by an appropriate combination of shift orders instead of using the E order. Thus if it were desired to isolate the 10's and 100's digits of an 11 digit number, this may he done by the order to shift –1; which would lose the original units digit, followed by the order +9, which would lose all digits to the left of the two desired digits. Still another shift order, –8, would be required to bring these two digits back to their original position if that were necessary. For some purposes, however, any final position would be satisfactory. For instance, if the purpose is to discriminate whether the two digit number so formed is greater or less than some other number, that number can be properly placed so that no further shift is required.

In the shift orders discussed above, machine digits corresponding to the "excess three" code for zero are introduced at the right during the left shift and at the left during a right shift.

The order R*m* provides for a different kind of shift, which is in reality a cyclical rearrangement of the 12 machine digits which occur in the word held in the accumulator. The principal use of this order may be in conjunction with the E order. When alphabetic material is being handled in the computer, the position which would be occupied by a sign indication in a numerical order would instead be occupied by a zone indicator. The ordinary shift orders do not shift this machine digit, so that some other method must be used when it is necessary to rearrange such data. It will be seen that a cyclical rearrangement of the machine digits in a word may also have other uses when applied to statistically coded data and can also be used in sorting routines.

10. TRANSFERS BETWEEN LONG TANKS.

The orders Y and Z provide for wholesale transfer of data from one long tank to another. The single memory switch that the machine will contain does not allow the direct interchange between two long tanks which are both in the main memory system. Neither does the order structure permit the specification of two different tank numbers within the same instruction. In order to rearrange large blocks of data within the memory, it would be desirable to make such transfers. The Y and Z orders provide for an alternative which is a reasonable approach to the ideal. Tanks designated by Y and Z are already included as a part of the machine equipment associated with the input and output tapes. Also the order to transfer from tank Z to the memory is essential to the process of running input and output devices simultaneously. Hence orders Y and Z add very little to the complexity of the machine.

Their use may be illustrated by an example. Suppose that, for sorting purposes or other reasons, it is desired to transfer the data occurring in registers 100 to 119 to registers 260 to 279. The order Y 0100 will take the data from registers 100–119 into the Y tank. The order Y 0260 following this will place the information just transferred to the Y tank into registers 260–279. At the same time the information from registers 260–279 will go into the Y tank. The order Y 0100 will then place this information in registers 100–119, where it was desired, and will at the same time return to the Y tank the data which it was storing previous to the initiation of these three orders and which was temporarily held in registers 100–119 after the first Y order.

11. INSTRUCTIONS FOR INPUT AND OUTPUT.

Three types of input and output devices may be associated with the computer. These are magnetic tape devices, a combination typewriter and printer, and an oscilloscope. The oscilloscope may be regarded as quite optional, depending on the use to be made of the machine. It is believed that four tape devices and one typewriter-printer are desirable for general operation. So far as the instructions are concerned, the typewriter and printer combination is to be treated as closely equivalent to a tape device. Each tape device operates either as an input or as an output, assuming either function in accordance with the instructions by which the machine is operating. The tapes have an additional facility in that any tape may be run either forward or backward. (Reversing a tape is, however, a rather infrequent requirement, and therefore orders for changing the direction of tape motion can be executed rather slowly). In Code C-1 the order to reverse a tape is given by specifying the tape number followed by a + or −. When the machine is originally started, all tapes are set to move forward when a tape order occurs. The occurrence of an order 3− will reverse the direction of tape number 3, and tape number 3 will run backward whenever it is given a tape order until an order 3+ is given. Automatic methods for sensing when any tape device has reached the end of its tape can be provided, but for most problems it will be easy to know beforehand how much tape will be required and to be assured that the tape capacity and the problem requirements are compatible. For many statistical problems and particularly those of sorting and collation it is known that about the same volume of data must pass onto output tapes as is read from input tapes.

Often the rate at which data can be fed into and removed from the computer will be the limiting factor in determining the speed of operation. Hence simultaneous operation of input and output devices can effectively increase the operating speed by almost a factor of 2. Code C-1 contains a single instruction which directs the simultaneous operation of one tape used as an input and another tape used as an output. The tape order also contains an address specifying the memory register from which the first output word is obtained.

For example, the order 130200 calls for the following operations. First the words in registers 200–219 are transferred to tank Y. Then these words are transferred from Y to tape number 3. Simultaneously with the operation of tape 3, tank Z is filled from tape 1. When both of these tape operations are completed, the order has been executed. In the meantime following the transfer of 20 words from the registers 200–219 to tank Y, the machine control proceeds to read and execute other instructions provided they are not associated with tape operation or with tanks Y and Z. In the course of such computation or other work

orders Y or Z or another tape order may occur, in which case the internal operation of the machine is suspended until the tape orders which were initiated earlier have been completed.

As was stated above, the typewriter and printer associated with the computer can be controlled by much the same kind of order. It is not intended that the same tape shall be capable of acting both as input and output at the same time, and the same remark applies to the typewriter-printer. Assuming that the tapes are designated as 1, 2, 3, and 4, the typewriter keyboard input could be designated zero. It seems desirable, however, to have the printer designated by a different number so that the order $00m$ can be used as a stop order which directs the machine to obtain an input from the keyboard without directing it to print. In this case the memory address should designate where the information which is typed in is to be transferred after it is stored in the Z tank. Some other digit such as 9 can be used to control printing, so that the order $99m$ would cause the printer to produce the sequence of 20 words obtained from registers beginning with register m.

It is to be emphasized that this suggestion with respect to the typewriter and printer order is extremely tentative, and some other arrangement may be found more desirable. In any event, however, it is intended that some order such as $00m$ shall be available so that at suitable places throughout the routine of a given problem the machine may (if desired) be made to stop, permitting an operator to check the progress of the computations or alter the program by manual input.

The instruction Gm is to be used when an oscilloscope is coupled with the computer and will have the effect of transferring the word stored in register m to the circuits which control the scope. To simplify these control circuits, it is planned that the computer be used to prepare the data to be exhibited in a special form. A tentative form (subject to alteration when the scope circuits are more fully designed) would be to use 9 of the 11 numerical digits in a word to specify to 3 decimal digit accuracy the 3 coordinates which are to be used in plotting a point on the screens. Two or these coordinates are the horizontal and vertical positions, and the third governs the intensity of the spot.

12. CONCLUDING REMARKS.

The tentative nature of Code C-1 must be kept in mind. As stated in Section 1, considerations of machine design may make it necessary or at least highly desirable to alter and also reduce the instruction code. It is believed, however, that Code C-1 should be tried out by coding personnel in order to evaluate it. Those who attempt to use it may very likely discover ways in which its convenience can be improved, or may become convinced that some of the instructions contribute very little toward operational facility. Discussion of this code or possible modifications will be welcome.

INSTRUCTION CODE C-1 FOR STATISTICAL MACHINE (EDVAC II)

Use of parentheses: (m) means "contents of m," etc.

Am	Add (m) to A, result in A.
Bm	Exchange (m) and (A) (clearing A before (m) is put in).
Cm	Transfer (A) to m and clear A.
Dm	Not used—reserved for division.
Em	Extract from (m) the digits specified by (F). When a digit of (F) is 0 (or 2, 4, 6, 8) and 0 is inserted in A. When a digit of (F) is 1 (or 3, 5, 7, 9) the corresponding digit of (m) is inserted in A, without passing through either the complementer or adder. A is cleared of previous contents.
Fm	Transfer (m) to F, first clearing F.
Gm	Graphical output. Send (m) to scope. (m) must be in special form.
Hm	Transfer (A) to m without clearing A (i.e., *hold* (A) in A).
Km	Add (A) to the memory position indicators of the two orders in m, placing the modified orders back in m and leaving A clear.
Lm	Transfer (m) to L, first clearing L.
Mm	Multiply (m) and (L), rounding off to 11 digits, and add this product to (A), result in A.
Nm	Multiply (m) and (L), rounding off to 11 digits, and subtract this product from (A), result in A.

Pm	Multiply (m) and (L), storing the least significant half in W, and adding the more significant half to (A), storing the sum in A.
Qm	Square (m), rounding off to 11 digits, adding the result to (A) and leaving the sum in A.
Rm	Cyclically shift (A) one digit to the right, operating on all digits including that usually used for sign. Digit originally at right is placed at left. Disregard m.
Sm	Subtract (m) from A, result in A.
\$$m$	Comparison by true binary subtraction of all 12 machine digits, if (L) − (A) is negative, control is transferred to m. Result of subtraction is not stored.
Tm	Transfer control to 000 memory register. Disregard m.
?m	Transfer control to m (m even) if sign of (A) is negative.
Um	Transfer control to m (m even).
Vm	Transfer control to m (m even), first transferring (C) + 1 to m = 000. This order is to be placed in odd-numbered registers only.
Wm	Transfer (W) to (m).
Xm	Multiply (A) by (m), rounding off to 11 digits, result in A.
Ym	Exchange (Y) with contents of a series of memory positions, beginning with m (here m must be an integral multiple of 20), proceeding cyclically through one memory tank.
Zm	Exchange (A) with contents of a memory tank (as in order Y).
+nm	Shift (A) n digits to left, that is obtain 10^n(A), result in A. Disregard m.
−nm	Shift (A) n digits to right, that is obtain 10^{-n}(A), result in A. Disregard m.
n+m	Cause tape to run forward. Disregard m.
n−m	Cause tape to run in reverse. Disregard m.
$nn'm$	Transfer to tape tank Y one block of data, beginning with register m, and write this block on tape n', while reading a block from tape n into tape tank Z (Y and Z are tape tanks). Other orders may be executed while this is proceeding, except that orders Ym and Zm interlock with this and cannot be executed until the $nn'm$ order is completed. n = 00 is keyboard or typewriter input. 00m acts as a "stop order," waiting for key input. In this order m must be an integral multiple of 20.

ABBREVIATIONS USED IN ORDER CODE

A	Accumulator, consisting of a one-word tank with an adder in its recirculating loop, so that additional data fed into it will be added to the previous contents. Associated with A is a sign senser, which causes the number in A to be sent through a complementer if negative, before being returned to the memory by a B, C, or H order.
C	Control counter, consisting of a one-word tank with an adder connected to add one to its contents every time an order is executed; thus the number in C at any time indicates the position in the main routine of a problem or the position in a subroutine, as the case may be.
m	Indicates a memory position. The memory can store 1000 words of 12 digits each; hence m always lies in the range 000 to 999 inclusive.
L	Multiplicand register, consisting of a one-word tank for storage of the multiplicand. It is arranged so that whenever a number is fed into it, the previous contents are automatically cleared out first.
W	Input-output register of the memory. Except in operations involving transfers between the memory and tanks Y and Z, and instructions taken from the memory for control purposes, every word coming out of the memory goes first to W; a sign-sensing device is associated with W, so that if necessary the word can be caused to go through a complementer before going to A. Before a word is sent into the memory, it goes to W, where it circulates until the memory is ready to receive it in the proper location.
X	Tape writing tank, consisting of a 20 word tank. Data to be transferred from memory to tape is first read into Y; as soon as this transfer is complete, computation proceeds independently while data are being transferred from Y to the tape. Exchange of information between the memory and Y can also be made independently of the tape for sorting purposes.
Z	Tape reading tank, consisting of a 20 word tank. Data to be read from a tape are transferred to Z, where they are held until a Z order transfers them to the memory. Transfer from the tape to Z proceeds independently of other computation; hence an interlock is provided so that if a Z order is given before the Z tank has been filled with data from the tape, its execution is delayed until that process is complete. Both Y and Z are arranged so that whenever a word is read in, the word previously occupying that position is cleared out.
F	One word register, similar to L, but used to control extraction (Em).

NUMBER AND ALPHABET CODE

0000	not used
0001	−
0010	+
0011	0
0100	1
0101	2
0110	3
0111	4
1000	5
1001	6
1010	7
1011	8
1100	9
1101	Zone 1 indicator
1110	Zone 2 indicator
1111	Zone 3 indicator

Zone 1			Zone 2			Zone 3		
1101	0100	A	1110	0100	J	1111	0100	$
	0101	B		0101	K		0101	S
	0110	C		0110	L		0110	T
	0111	D		0111	M		0111	U
	1000	E		1000	N		1000	V
	1001	F		1001	O		1001	W
	1010	G		1010	P		1010	X
	1011	H		1011	Q		1011	Y
	1100	I		1100	R		1100	Z
	0011	Space		0011	?		0011	Tab.
	0010	, (comma)						
	0001	. (period)						

Word length: 12 digits, including sign. 6 alphabetic characters or combinations of numeric and alphabetic data totaling 12 digits.

Order structure: two orders to a work, each consisting of one alphabetic or two numeric characters, followed by a zero, and then three digits representing a memory location.

The Design of Programs for Electronic Computing Machines

Maurice V. Wilkes, David Wheeler and Stanley Gill

Extract from *The Preparation of Programs for an Electronic Digital Computer* (Cambridge, MA: Addison-Wesley Press, 1951), pp. 1–14.

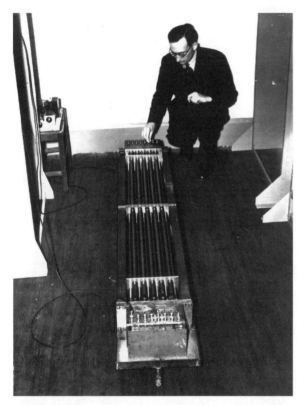

Maurice V. Wilkes with the first battery of mercury tanks, or ultrasonic delay memories, built for the EDSAC. The battery contained sixteen tanks (tubes), of which the top row of five can be seen. The metal box at the end near the foot of the picture contains matching sections used to interface the quartz crystals at the ends of the tanks to the coaxial cables connecting them with the electronic chassis. (© Computer Laboratory, University of Cambridge. Reproduced by permission.)

INTRODUCTORY NOTE TO READING 9.4

We reproduce the first chapter of the first textbook on computer programming. "The [EDSAC] model was well explained by one of the most influential textbooks of this early era, *The Preparation of Programs for an Electronic Digital Computer.* . . . The form of constructing programs and how they should be linked together to form a load module, as described in this book, reappears many times for different computers being constructed in different countries. It provided the basic ideas as to how one should go about creating a computing system rather than simply providing a bit of hardware to be used only by a few specialists."[1]

Wilkes, Wheeler, and Gill's work had its genesis in the privately issued *Report on the Preparation of Programmes for the EDSAC* (1950), a dittoed typescript prepared by the Cambridge University Mathematics Laboratory and distributed to a small number of computer researchers. Wilkes believed that the report deserved a wider publication, and through an American colleague was put in touch with the then-small Addison-Wesley Press, which offered to publish the report after some necessary revision. In his autobiography, Wilkes states that "[Addison-Wesley] must have felt that they were taking a great risk in publishing a book on so obscure a subject as computer programming, and in order to minimize their risk in the event that no-one bought it, they offered the following terms. There were to be no royalties on the first

1   Michael R. Williams, *A History of Computing Technology* (Englewood Cliffs, NJ: Prentice-Hall, 1985), 337.

1,000 copies sold, 20% on the second 1,000 and after that 10% royalties. I am glad to say that the 1,000 mark was passed within fifteen months of the book's being published in July 1951.... I like to think that its success contributed in a small way to the growth of Addison-Wesley from being a very small concern to its present large size."[2] Because Addison-Wesley was then a small publisher with no offices in England, Scientific Computing Service, founded by Leslie. J. Comrie (see Reading 4.5), handled the English distribution. [JMN]

---

2   Maurice V. Wilkes, *Memoirs of a Computer Pioneer* (Cambridge, MA: MIT Press, 1985), 149.

TEXT OF READING 9.4
1-1 INTRODUCTION.

A digital computing machine can perform only the basic operations of arithmetic, namely, addition, subtraction, multiplication, and division. In order to be able to solve a mathematical problem such as the integration of a differential equation it is first necessary to express the problem as a sequence of such operations. This may call merely for some expenditure of labor or it may involve considerable mathematical manipulation; for example, where derivatives or integrals are involved it may be necessary to replace the continuous variables by variables which change in discrete steps.

If the computation were to be performed by a human computer it would be possible to communicate the problem to him in a series of instructions or orders, each specifying an elementary arithmetical operation. It is convenient to use the same nomenclature when speaking of a machine but here the "instructions," or "orders," are groups of symbols punched on a paper tape or prepared in some other form which can be fed into a machine. A sequence of orders for performing some particular calculation is called the program. It must contain everything necessary to cause the machine to perform the require calculations and every contingency must be foreseen. A human computer is capable of reasonable extension of his instructions when faced with a situation which has not been fully envisaged in advance, and he will have past experience to guide him. This is not the case with a machine.

Since an automatic computing machine can perform only a very limited number of basic operations, the simplest mathematical calculation requires an extended sequence of orders. The labor of drawing up a program for a particular problem is often reduced if short, ready-made programs for performing the more common computing operations are available. These short programs are usually called subroutines, and they may be incorporated as they stand in the program, thus reducing the amount of work which has to be done *ab initio*. If it is intended that an electronic computing machine shall be used on a wide variety of problems it is worthwhile to spend much effort on the establishment of an extensive library of such subroutines, together with a workable system whereby selected subroutines may be combined to form a program.

This book contains a detailed description of the library of subroutines used in the Mathematical Laboratory of the University of Cambridge in conjunction with the EDSAC (Electronic Delay Storage Automatic Calculator) and of the way in which programs can be constructed with its aid. There will be some discussion of the best way to construct subroutines for numerical quadrature, the integration of differential equations, and other processes, but the more theoretical problems that arise in numerical analysis are outside the scope of this book. Some of these, for instance those concerned with the convergence of iterative processes and with the accumulation of rounding-off errors, are of great importance and interest and are likely to arise in acute form when planning the large-scale computing operations which an electronic machine makes possible. The present book, however, is concerned with the steps which must be taken to make the machine perform the numerical processes necessary to solve a problem when once it has been decided what those processes are.

There are naturally many ways, all similar in principle but differing in detail, in which subroutines may be used to construct programs, and no attempt will be made here to discuss all the possible alternative methods. It is hoped, however, that the account given of those at present being used with the EDSAC will be of general interest. The ideas and techniques described are applicable, with suitable adaptation, to other electronic calculating machines designed on the same general principles,

1-2 TYPES OF AUTOMATIC COMPUTING MACHINES.

In large automatic computing machines which depend for their action on electromechanical devices the orders are usually punched in coded form on paper tape, one group of holes corresponding to each order. These holes are read by a sensing device and cause the machine to perform the operation called for; the tape is then advanced so that the next group of holes is under the reading head and the next order is similarly executed. In addition to a sensing mechanism for the main program tape, several other sensing mechanisms are usually provided. These can be used to read endless loops of tape which contain orders for performing parts of the program which have to be repeated a number of times. Control of the machine is passed from one tape to another as required. Machines which work in this manner are the Automatic Sequence Controlled Calculator at Harvard University, relay calculators built by the Bell Telephone Laboratories, the Aiken relay computer at Dahlgren, Md., and the IBM Selective Sequence Electronic Calculator.

Such a system, while admirable for controlling a relay machine, would not be fast enough for a machine in which the computation is performed by electronic means and in which it is desired to realize the very high speed which this makes possible. The ENIAC, which was the first purely electronic machine to be built, therefore used a system in which the various steps of the program were initiated by "program pulses" passed from one unit of the machine to another. For example, to cause a number standing in one register or "accumulator" to be added to the number standing in another accumulator, both accumulators needed to be stimulated by a program pulse, one to transmit and one to receive. When the operation was finished both accumulators emitted a pulse, and one of these (it did not matter which, since they both occurred at the same time) was used to stimulate the next action. Putting a problem on the machine consisted, therefore, of making a large number of connections by means of plugs and sockets and setting a number of switches. The main objection to this system is that it takes some time to change over from one problem to another. In all later machines, proposed or completed, the orders are expressed in a coded form and placed in advance in a quick-access store, or memory, from which they are subsequently taken and executed one by one. The orders are usually passed into the machine by means of a punched tape, or some similar medium, but this is used simply as an intermediary in the process of transferring the program to the store, and does not control the computing action of the machine directly.

A store, or memory, is needed in automatic computing machines for the purpose of holding numbers, and in the EDSAC the same store is used to hold the orders; this is made possible by the device of expressing the orders in a numerical code. Several machines working on the same principles as the EDSAC are now in operation in the United States and in England. These principles derive from a report drafted by J. von Neumann in 1946 in connection with a new machine (the EDVAC) then projected by the Moore School of Electrical Engineering (University of Pennsylvania) where the ENIAC had been built. It is found that machines designed along the lines laid down in this report are much smaller and simpler than the ENIAC and at the same time more powerful. The methods by which programs are prepared for all these machines are, as might be expected, similar, although the details vary according to the different order codes used. Anyone familiar with the use of one machine will have no difficulty in adapting himself to another. All machines so far completed use the binary system for internal calculations but this is not an essential feature and several machines under construction use the decimal system. Even if the binary scale is used inside the machine, it is only rarely that the programmer needs to take notice of this fact, since input and output can be performed in the scale of ten, the necessary conversion being done by the machine itself as part of the program.

1-3 DESCRIPTION OF THE EDSAC.

In order to be able to construct programs, some knowledge of the main units of the machine and their interconnection is required, although it is not necessary to understand the precise mode of functioning of the various electronic circuits. There are, from the point of view of the programmer, four main parts to the machine: the *store,* or memory, the *arithmetical unit,* the *input,* and the *output* mechanisms. There is also the control unit which emits the electrical signals that control the action of the other units. Fig. 1 shows the connections between the various units. The store of the EDSAC, which is of the ultrasonic variety, was designed to have capacity for 1024 numbers of 17 binary digits each, although so far only half this capacity has been available. Negative numbers are represented inside the machine by their true complements and the most significant digit of any number is treated in the arithmetical unit as a sign digit. The sign digit is a zero if the number is positive and a one if it is negative. The 512 numbers are held in 512 "storage locations" numbered serially from 0 to 511 for reference purposes. The reference number of the storage location holding a number x is sometimes called the address of x. A special feature of the EDSAC is the possibility of combining any two consecutive storage locations (provided that the first has an even serial number) into a single long storage location capable of holding a number with 35 binary digits, one of which is a sign digit. Such a number is called a "long number" to distinguish it from a "short number" of 17 binary digits. It is possible to accommodate 35 digits in a long storage location, and not 34 only, since in the ultrasonic store of the EDSAC the digits of successive numbers are stored end to end and one digital position between each is left unused; when two storage locations are combined this position can be used to contain an extra digit (sometimes called the "sandwich" digit). It may be noted that a long number contains the equivalent of about ten decimals and a short number the equivalent of about five decimals.

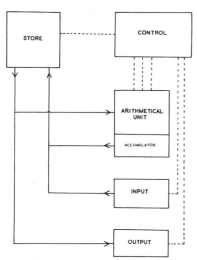

Fig. 1 Schematic diagram of the EDSAC

The arithmetical unit may best be described as being an electronic version of an ordinary desk-type calculating machine. In it the operations of addition, subtraction, and multiplication may be performed; there

is no divider in the EDSAC and the means used for performing division will be described later. The arithmetical unit contains an accumulator register, in which the results of additions, subtractions, and multiplications appear and in which a series of such results may be accumulated. There is another register which is used to hold the multiplier during the process of multiplication. The multiplier is so constructed that numbers are treated as though they lie in the range $-1 \leq x < 1$, that is, the binary point is assumed to come immediately to the right of the sign digit. The programmer should, therefore, rearrange the formulas before drawing up the program, so that all the quantities which need to be handled inside the machine are within the range $-1 \leq x < 1$. This may always be done if suitable positive or negative powers of two are introduced as multiplying constants; in the program these constants are represented by shift orders. An alternative procedure, although not one to be generally recommended, is for the programmer to adopt some other convention as to the position of the binary point and to program a shift after each multiplication; for example, if the binary point is assumed to be between the second and third digits to the right of the sign digit, each multiplication must be followed by a shift of 2 places to the left.

Five-hole punched tape, read by a photoelectric tape reader, is used for input to the EDSAC. All the orders and numbers required for the solution of a problem are punched on a single tape, which may, however, be divided into two or more pieces for insertion in the tape reader one after the other. Library subroutines are stored on separate short lengths of tape and copied mechanically on to the program tape. The output mechanism is a teleprinter. Further information about the engineering of the EDSAC will be found in the papers listed on page 21.

1-4 THE EDSAC ORDER CODE.

The action of the machine proceeds in two stages; in stage I an order passes from the store into the control unit; in stage II the order is executed. The machine then proceeds automatically to repeat stage I, in general taking the order from the storage location following that containing the order just executed. An exception to this rule will be discussed in Section 1-6. Each order calls for one simple operation to be performed; for example, it may cause some number to be extracted from the store and added to whatever happens to be in the accumulator, the sum being left in the accumulator, or it may cause the contents of the accumulator to be transferred to the store. Some orders, for example left or right shift orders, do not involve the use of the store at all.

There are in the EDSAC code eighteen orders from which the programmer can build up his program. They are written in the form of a letter indicating the function of the order, and a number (the address) specifying the location (if any) in the store concerned. The address is followed by the code letter F if it refers to a short storage location, and by the code letter D if it refers to a long storage location. The full order code for the EDSAC is as follows:

Order Code

Where the code letter terminating an order is not shown it may be either F or D.

A n	Add the number in storage location n into the accumulator.
S n	Subtract the number in storage location n from the accumulator.
H n	Copy the number in storage location n into the multiplier register.
V n	Multiply the number in storage location n by the number in the multiplier register and add the product into the accumulator.
N n	Multiply the number in storage location n by the number in the multiplier register and subtract the product from the accumulator.
T n	Transfer the contents of the accumulator to storage location n and clear the accumulator.
U n	Transfer the contents of the accumulator to storage location n and do not clear the accumulator.
C n	Collate the number in storage location n with the number in the multiplier register and add the result into the accumulator; that is, add a "1" into the accumulator in digital positions where both numbers have a "1", and add a "0" in other digital positions.

*R D	Shift the number in the accumulator one place to the right; that is, multiply it by 2^{-1}.
**R 2^{p-2} F	Shift the number in the accumulator p places to the right; that is, multiply it by 2^{-p} ($2 \le p \le 12$).
R F	Shift the number in the accumulator 15 places to the right; that is, multiply it by 2^{-15}
*L F	Shift the number in the accumulator one place to the left; that is, multiply by 2.
**L 2^{p-2} F	Shift the number in the accumulator p places to the left; that is, multiply by 2^p ($2 \le p \le 12$).
L F	Shift the number in the accumulator 13 places to the left; that is, multiply by 2^{13}.
E n F	If the number in the accumulator is greater than or equal to zero, execute next the order which stands in storage location n; otherwise proceed serially.
G n F	If the number in the accumulator is less than zero, execute next the order which stands in storage location n; otherwise proceed serially.
I n	Read the next row of holes on the input tape and place the resulting integer, multiplied by 2^{-16}, in storage location n.
O n	Print the character now set up on the teleprinter and set up on the teleprinter the character represented by the five most significant digits in storage location n.
F n	Place the five digits which represent the character now set up on the teleprinter in the five most significant places in storage location n, clearing the remainder of this location.
*X	Ineffective; machine proceeds to next order.
*Y	Round-off the number in the accumulator to 34 binary digits; that is, add 2^{-35} into the accumulator.
*Z	Stop the machine.

  *   The addresses in these orders need not be zero.

**   The addresses in these orders *may* be $k \cdot 2^{p-2}$ where k is odd, provided that the addresses do not exceed 2047.

1-5 NOTES ON THE ORDER CODE.

As a simple example of the use of this code, suppose that it is required to evaluate the expression $x + y + xy$, taking x and y to be the contents of the short storage locations 50 and 51, and to place the result in the long storage location 52. A program for doing this is as follows (it is assumed that the accumulator is clear at the beginning):

A 50 F

A 51 F

H 50 F

V 51 F

T 52 D

The accumulator has sufficient capacity to hold a number having 71 binary digits, of which one is regarded as a sign digit. As in the store, the binary point is immediately to the right of the sign digit. When two long numbers are multiplied together the resulting 69 digits are all available in the accumulator. A U order or a T order will, however, transfer only the 35 most significant digits (or if the order is terminated by an F, the 17 most significant digits) to the store, although a T order always clears the whole of the accumulator. If it is desired to retain all the 69 digits which are obtained by multiplying two long numbers together, then the 35 most significant digits must first be transferred to the store by means of a U order and the contents of the accumulator shifted 34 places to the left; the 34 least significant digits are then in a suitable position to be transferred to the store by a T order. Note that it is necessary to use three left shift orders, since in the EDSAC the number in the accumulator cannot be shifted more than 13 places to the left by a single shift order.

If an A order is used to add a number x from the store to the number y standing in the accumulator the correct answer will be obtained only if $x + y$ satisfies the condition $-1 \le x + y < 1$. If this condition is violated the number appearing in the accumulator will be $x + y - 2$ if $x + y \ge 1$, and $x + y + 2$ if $x + y < -1$. In a similar way, if the effect of any other order is to cause the capacity of the accumulator to be exceeded, the number which actually appears in the accumulator is that obtained by adding or subtracting a suitable multiple of 2 from the correct result.

The C order (collation) is useful when it is required to pick out specified groups of digits from a number. For example, the first four binary digits, not including the sign digit, of a given number may be isolated by collating the given number with the number 01111000000000000000000000000000000, that is, 15/16.

The number placed in the multiplier register by an H order remains there until it is replaced by another number introduced by another H order. Thus if a series of numbers are to be multiplied by a constant, one H order only is necessary to transfer the constant to the multiplier register at the beginning of the operation.

1-6 THE USE OF CONDITIONAL ORDERS.

An exception to the rule that the machine executes orders in the sequence in which they stand in the store occurs when a conditional order (E or G) is encountered. The action then depends on the sign of the number in the accumulator; if this is negative an E order causes the machine to pass straight on to the next order, while if it is positive or zero the next order is taken from some other location in the store. In the latter case control is said to be transferred to the new storage location. The action of a G order is similar, except that control is transferred if the number in the accumulator is negative. The following program for finding the absolute value of the number in storage location 123 illustrates the use of a conditional order.

Location of order	Order		Notes
			the accumulator is assumed to be clear at the start
301	A 123 F		the number in 123 is added into the accumulator
302	E 305 F		the sign is tested
303	T	F	if negative, the number in the accumulator is changed in sign
304	S	F	
305	T	F	the result is placed in location 0

Conditional orders, however, are much more important than this example would indicate, since they enable the programmer to cause a group of orders to be repeated a number of times and to transfer control from one section of the program to another. Conditional orders thus provide facilities equivalent to those obtained by the use of endless loops of tape on the machines mentioned earlier. The following example shows how the operations called for by the sequence of orders held in storage locations 100 to 109 may be repeated six times.

Method. A number in the store is arranged to have the values $-5, -4, \ldots 0$ units after the group of orders has been obeyed once, twice, ... six times. Thus when this counting number becomes zero, the process has been performed six times.

It is assumed that storage location 0 can be used to hold the counter, and that storage locations 1 and 2 contain $6 \cdot 2^{-15}$ and 2^{-15} respectively.

Location of order	Order			Notes
				the accumulator is assumed clear at the start
97	S	1	F	
98	A	2	F	places new value of counting number in storage location 0 (initially $-5 \cdot 2^{-15}$)
99	T		F	
100				
.				orders to be repeated. It is assumed that they leave the accumulator empty
109				
110	A		F	test whether the counting number is zero
111	G	98		

In many cases it is not known in advance how many times the sequence of orders must be repeated. An example occurs in the calculation of a reciprocal root $a^{-1/2}$ from the iterative formula

$$x^{n+1} = \frac{1}{2} x_n \left(3 - a x_n^2 \right).$$

The iteration is to be started with a first approximation x_0 and stopped when $|x_{n-1} - x_n| < \varepsilon$, where ε is a positive quantity given in advance. This may be done by means of a sequence of orders which, given the value of x, in a certain storage location, say m, calculates x_{n+1} and transfers it to m, where it replaces x_n. In addition, the quantity $|x_{n+1} - x_n| - \varepsilon$ is computed and left in the accumulator. If this quantity is positive or zero, the next order, which is an E order, transfers control back to the beginning of the sequence; otherwise control passes straight on. If storage location m contained x_0 before the sequence of orders was operated for the first time, this storage location will now contain $a^{-1/2}$.

1-7 MODIFICATION OF ORDERS BY THE PROGRAM.

It has been explained that orders are expressed inside the machine in a numerical code, and that the numbers which represent them are held in the same store as other numbers needed in the calculation. If a number which stands for an order is modified, for example by having a constant added to it, it then stands for a different order, and if the section of the program containing it is operated twice, once before and once after the modification, different operations will be performed. This facility of being able to modify the orders in the program by performing arithmetical operations on the numbers representing them is of great importance, and it is perhaps the feature most characteristic of program design for machines like the EDSAC. The operations required for this purpose are performed in the arithmetical unit in the same way as other arithmetical operations.

Some examples of the use which can be made of this facility are given below. It is first necessary, however, to explain the numerical code by which orders are represented inside the EDSAC. The order $\bar{X}$ n F (where $\bar{X}$ stands for any letter in the order code) is represented by the number $2^{-4} + 2^{-15} n$, where the value of $\bar{x}$ for the various orders is given in the table below. The order $\bar{X}$ n D is represented by $2^{-4} \bar{x} + 2^{-15} n + 2^{-16}$.

$\bar{X}$	$\bar{x}$
A	-4
C	-2
E	3
F	-15
G	-5
H	-11
I	8
L	-7
N	-10
O	9
R	4
S	12
T	5
U	7
V	-1
X	-6
Y	6
Z	13

Thus A 50 F would be represented by the number $2^{-4}(-4) + 2^{-15} \cdot 50$; this may be converted into the number representing A 51 F by adding 2^{-15} to it.

It is often convenient to drop the distinction between orders and the numbers representing them, and to speak, for example, of "the order contained in storage location n," and of orders being modified by having constants added to them.

A sequence of orders designed to be repeated a number of times may contain a group of orders which modify other orders in the same sequence. Each time the sequence is operated it will then cause a different set of calculations to be performed. In this way it is possible to use repetitive cycles to perform calculations which do not at first sight appear to lend themselves to such treatment. The advantage of doing this is that programs can often be constructed with many fewer orders than would otherwise be necessary, and

therefore require less space in the store. As an example, suppose that the sum of the contents of storage locations 100, 101, ... 149 is to be added to the contents of storage location 5.

Method. The contents of storage location 100 are added to those of storage location 5 by means of a group of orders containing the order A 100 F. The address specified in this particular order is then increased by one, and the group of orders repeated. Thus the contents of storage locations 100, 101, ... are added in succession to the contents of storage location 5. It is necessary to terminate this process, and a counter is used as in the previous example.

It is assumed that storage location 0 can be used to hold the counter, and that storage locations 1 and 2 contain $50 \cdot 2^{-15}$ and 2^{-15} respectively.

Location of order	Order			Notes
200	S	1	F	set counter (initially $-49 \cdot 2^{-15}$)
201	A	2	F	
202	T		F	
203	A	100	F	the address in this order is increased by one each time the cycle is repeated
204	A	5	F	
205	T	5	F	
206	A	203	F	increase by one the address specified in order 203
207	A	2	F	
208	T	203	F	
209	A		F	test for end of process
210	G	201	F	

This program may be shortened by using the variable order for counting. It then appears as below. Storage location 1 contains the number equivalent to the order A 150 F and storage location 2 contains 2^{-15}.

Location of order	Order			Notes
200	T		F	clears accumulator
201	A	5	F	add appropriate number to the contents of storage location 5
202	A	100	F	
203	T	5	F	
204	A	202	F	increase the address specified in order 202 by one
205	A	2	F	
206	U	202	F	
207	S	1	F	test if the order contained in location 202 has become A 150 F; if not, repeat the process.
208	G	200	F	

This example contains nine orders. If it were written out in full, that is, if a repetitive cycle were not used, 52 orders would be necessary. A more complete discussion of methods of counting will be found in Appendix F.

Occasionally, where there are very few repetitions, it is better to write out the orders in full. This reduces the machine time taken by the process, since no time is consumed in modifying orders or in counting the number of repetitions, and this fact may be important if the whole process has to be performed a large number of times. Moreover, if the accumulator is not required for counting and for modifying orders, the program can often be further shortened by making use of the facility of accumulating sums and products. The total number of orders may even be fewer than if a cycle is used.

1-8 MULTIADDRESS CODES.

In the EDSAC order code each order has reference to, at the most, one location in the store; it is thus described as a single-address code. Other machines have multiaddress codes in which each order may refer to several locations in the store. For example, one order in such a code might be

$A\ r\ s\ t$ add the number in storage location r to the number in storage location s and transfer the result to storage location t.

This is an example of a three-address code. One order in such a code takes up more space in the store than an order in a single-address code (in the EDSAC it would require a long storage location instead of a short one) but it causes a more complicated set of operations to be carried out. Thus the single order $A\ r\ s\ t$ has the same effect as the group of orders $A\ r$, $A\ s$, $T\ t$ in the EDSAC order code, and requires one long storage location instead of three short ones. However, use of a three-address code does not always enable a similar saving to be made; for example, to add the four numbers in storage locations r, s, p, and t together and to place the result in storage location q the following three orders are required:

$A\ r\ s\ q$

$A\ q\ p\ q$

$A\ q\ t\ q.$

In the EDSAC order code the following group would be required:

$A\ r$

$A\ s$

$A\ p$

$A\ t$

$T\ q$

In this case the orders in the single-address code actually take less space than those in the three-address code, the reason being that when using the single-address code the programmer can take advantage of the fact that sums can be accumulated in the accumulator. On the whole it is doubtful whether more than a slight saving in the storage capacity required to hold the orders can be obtained by using a three-address code. Its use does, however, enable the speed of the machine to be increased slightly, since the number of orders which have to be extracted from the store is reduced. On the other hand, the complexity of the control section of the machine is increased.

From the point of view of the programmer there is very little to choose between the convenience of using single- and three-address codes; in particular, counting operations can be performed and orders modified in a three-address code by methods exactly analogous to those described in this chapter for use with a single-address code. The decision as to whether a machine should have a single-address or a three-address code should rest rather with the designer than with the prospective mathematical user.

In most machines the orders are executed, as in the EDSAC, in the serial order in which they stand in the store, except when transfer of control is brought about by the action of a transfer order. An alternative system is to include in each order a specification of the location from which the next order is to be taken. This leads to a four-address code in which three of the addresses are used as in a three-address code and the fourth contains the address of the next order to be executed. This has advantages in the case of a machine which uses ultrasonic tanks (mercury memory) or a magnetic drum for its main store. With either of these stores numbers are available only at certain times in a fixed cycle. If a number or order is to be extracted from a random location there will therefore be a delay, equal on the average to half the circulation time in the case of the ultrasonic store and to half the rotation time in the case of the magnetic drum. If, however, the programmer has control over the location from which the next order is to be obtained, he can reduce this delay by placing the orders and numbers as far as possible in locations chosen so that they become available at the moment they are required. He is assisted in doing this if he is provided with a number of special storage registers which have an access time short compared with that of the main store; for example, a machine using an ultrasonic store may have a number of short mercury tanks, each accommodating a single number in addition to the long tanks of the main store, each of which holds 16 or 32 numbers. This procedure is sometimes called optimum programming and the first machine to be specially designed with a view to its adoption was the ACE (Automatic Computing Engine), of which a pilot model is now working at the National Physical Laboratory at Teddington, Middlesex, England. Optimum programming makes the work of the programmer more complicated, because it introduces considerations concerned with the timing of operations in the machine and thus confuses the essentially arithmetical nature of programming as stressed in this book. However, a compromise can be reached if it is possible for the library subroutines to be constructed in accordance with the principles of optimum programming and for the programmer to construct the other parts of the program in the ordinary way. In this way a high proportion of the gain in speed made possible by the use of optimum programming can be obtained without complicating the task of the programmer unduly. It should be especially noted that the provision of a four-address code of the kind described here and its use in conjunction with optimum programming technique are devices for mitigating the fundamental disadvantages of a delay-type store, and are of no assistance if a store of the electrostatic variety is used.

1-9 BINARY-DECIMAL CONVERSION.

It has already been mentioned that conversion of numbers to and from the binary system is performed by the machine. Full details of how this is done may be found by examining the input and output subroutines in Part III of this book; a general explanation of the principles used will be given in the present section.

The paper tape used for input to the machine is prepared by means of a keyboard perforator. There are five positions across the tape in which holes may or may not be punched and one row of holes may therefore be said to represent a five-digit binary number. The keyboard perforator has 32 keys, labeled with combinations of letters, figures, and other symbols, as in the case of an ordinary teleprinter keyboard. Each key causes one row of holes to be punched on the tape according to the code given in Appendix A. The corresponding five-digit binary numbers are also given in this Appendix.[1] It will be seen that the figures from 0 to 9 are represented by their binary equivalents. For example, 5 is represented by 00101, 6 by 00110, etc.

Suppose that it is required to put the number 0.21973 into the machine. The successive digits of this number are punched in order on the input tape. When the tape is read by the machine acting under the control of a succession of I orders in the program, the binary equivalents of the following numbers will be transferred to the store in succession:

$$2 \times 2^{-16}$$

$$1 \times 2^{-16}$$

$$9 \times 2^{-16}$$

$$7 \times 2^{-16}$$

$$3 \times 2^{-16}$$

The program contains orders which cause the first of these numbers to be multiplied by 10^4, the second by 10^3, the third by 10^2, the fourth by 10, the last by 1, and the results to be added together. This calculation is carried out in the binary scale so that the binary equivalent of 21973.2^{-16} is now to be found in the store. A further multiplication by $10^{-5} \cdot 2^{16}$ forms the required number in its binary form. It will be seen that the decisive step in the conversion of the number to the binary scale takes place in the keyboard perforator, which converts the individual decimal digits of the number to their binary form.

In drawing up the program for this conversion it is necessary to avoid the use of numbers that lie outside the range $-1 \le x < 1$. For example, it is not possible to multiply by 10 directly; instead, it is necessary to multiply by 10/16 and to shift the result four places to the left.

Conversion of binary numbers to their decimal form during output is done in an analogous manner. The teleprinter accepts a five-digit binary number (actually the five most significant digits in the storage location specified in the output order) and prints the corresponding character. Here again the code is so chosen that the binary numbers from 0 to 9 are printed as the corresponding decimal figures; for example, 00101 is printed as 5, 00110 as 6, etc. The program must therefore cause the successive decimal digits of the given number to be calculated in their

binary form; final conversion to decimal form can then take place in the teleprinter.

The principle of the method used to obtain successive decimal digits is to multiply the number (which is assumed to be positive and less than unity) repeatedly by ten and to remove the integral part each time. If the number is expressed as a decimal fraction this method clearly isolates the successive digits, beginning with the most significant. The same is true if the number is expressed as a binary fraction (the multiplication being by ten in its binary form, that is, by the binary number 1010), except that the digits are then obtained in the form of the corresponding binary numbers. When this method is programmed for the EDSAC it is necessary, in order to avoid using numbers outside the range $-1 \le x < 1$, to multiply by 10/16 instead of by 10 and to take the four digits which come immediately after the binary point. The remainder is shifted four places to the left before a further multiplication is performed.

1-10 CHECKING FACILITIES.

The EDSAC was designed with the understanding that the programmer would incorporate in his program such mathematical checks as he might consider necessary, or arrange for them to be carried out afterwards. No special checking devices are therefore provided inside the machine. It is, however, desirable that there should be some means available whereby the programmer can verify that a number computed and held in the store of the machine has been correctly transferred to the teleprinter. For this reason there is an order (the F order) which enables the number transferred to the teleprinter by the last output order to be read back into the store. By making use of this order it is possible to arrange that an indicating symbol, for example a question mark, shall be printed if the number has been incorrectly transferred to the teleprinter. Examples of how this is done will be found in the output subroutines given in detail in Part III of this book. It is of course possible that even though the correct number has been transferred to the teleprinter a wrong character will be printed. The design of the Creed teleprinters used in conjunction with the

EDSAC is such, however, that the possibility of an error occurring beyond the point at which the check is made is remote.

. . .

1. A hole in the tape represents the binary digit 1, except in the case of the most significant digit, where a "1" is represented by the absence of a hole. This is done in order to avoid having to represent the number 0 by blank tape.

9.5

The Education of a Computer

Grace Murray Hopper

From Association for Computing Machinery, *Proceedings* (Pittsburgh: Richard Rimbach Associates for the Association for Computing Machinery, 1952): 243–49.

Grace Murray Hopper in 1960. The third and most influential programmer on Howard Aiken's Harvard Mark I, Hopper later worked for Eckert and Mauchly at Remington Rand, starting in 1949. Through her work with Flow-matic at Remington Rand, Hopper exerted an indirect but enormous influence on the development of the early programming language COBOL, which took Flow-matic as its model. She stands in front of later versions of the UNIVAC reel tapes in their drives. (Photograph reprinted by permission of Unisys Corporation. All rights reserved.)

INTRODUCTORY NOTE TO READING 9.5

Grace Murray Hopper (1906–1992), "first lady of software and first mother-teacher of all computer programmers,"[1] was introduced to computing in 1944, when she was assigned to the Bureau of Ordnance's Computation Project at Harvard University, run by Howard Aiken. During the first decades of the postwar computer industry, Hopper became an innovator and developer of high-level computer languages, writing the first compiler (the A-0) in 1952 and the first English-language data-processing compiler, B-0 (Flow-matic) in 1957. Through her work with Flow-matic, Hopper exerted an indirect but enormous influence on the development of the early programming language COBOL, which took Flow-matic as its model.

Hopper was affiliated with the United States Navy for most of her adult life, attaining the rank of rear admiral in 1985. She was also a senior mathematician and head of UNIVAC programming at the Eckert-Mauchly Computer Corporation, joining the company in 1949 and remaining with it (and its successors, Remington-Rand and Sperry-Rand) until her retirement in 1971. She regarded herself primarily as an educator, and her untiring efforts to advance the cause of automatic programming significantly helped to accelerate the rate of progress in this field.

In her paper on "The Education of a Computer," delivered at the May 1952 meeting of the Association for Computing Machinery in Pittsburgh, Hopper dis-

---

1   J. A. N. Lee, *Computer Pioneers* (Los Alamitos, CA: IEEE Computer Society Press, 1995), 382.

cussed the compiling routines (such as A-0) and other programming tools then being developed at Remington-Rand so that "the programmer may return to being a mathematician." She also expressed her views on computing and programming in general, anticipating a number of future developments: that programming—i.e., software—would become more expensive than hardware, and that computer programming would have commercial as well as mathematical applications. "On a more technical level, there are glimmerings of many tools and techniques concerning compilers that we now accept as commonplace: the subroutine library, complete with specifications; the translation of a formula into its elementary components, the prime function of a compiler; the subroutine interface and relative addressing, which obviates the need to recompile it for each use; the linking loader; and code optimization. Hopper even anticipates symbolic manipulation."[2][JMN]

---

2 David Gries, Introduction to G. M. Hopper, "The Education of a Computer," *Annals of the History of Computing* 9 (1988): 271.

TEXT OF READING 9.5

While the materialization is new, the idea of mechanizing mathematical thinking is not new. Its lineage starts with the abacus and descends through Pascal, Leibnitz, and Babbage. More immediately, the ideas here presented originate from Professor Howard H. Aiken of Harvard University, Dr. John W. Mauchly of Eckert-Mauchly and Dr. M. V. Wilkes of the University of Cambridge. From Professor Aiken came, in 1946, the idea of a library of routines described in the Mark I manual, and the concepts embodied in the Mark III coding machine; from Dr. Mauchly, the basic principles of the "short-order code" and suggestions, criticisms, and untiring patience in listening to these present attempts; from Dr. Wilkes, the greatest help of all, a book on the subject. For those of their ideas which are included herein, I most earnestly express my debt and my appreciation.

INTRODUCTION

To start at the beginning, Fig. 1 represents the configuration of the elements required by an operation: input to the operations; controls, even if they be only start and stop; previously prepared tools supplied to the operation; and output of products, which may, in turn, become the input of another operation. This is the basic element of a production line; input of raw materials, controlled by human beings, possibly through instruments; supplied with machine tools; the operation produces an automobile, a rail, or a can of tomatoes.

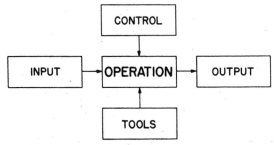

Fig. 1 – AN OPERATION

The armed services, government, and industry are interested not only in creating new operations to pro-

duce new results, but also in increasing the efficiency of old operations. A very old operation, Fig. 2, is the solution of a mathematical problem.

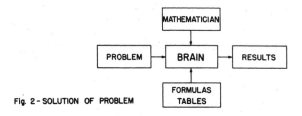

Fig. 2 – SOLUTION OF PROBLEM

It fits the operational configuration: input of mathematical data; control by the mathematician; supplied with memory, formulas, tables, pencil, and paper; the brain carries on the arithmetic, and produces results.

It is the current aim to replace, as far as possible, the human brain by an electronic digital computer. That such computers themselves fit this configuration maybe seen in Fig. 3. (With your permission, I shall use UNIVAC as synonymous with electronic digital computer; primarily because I think that way, but also because it is convenient.)

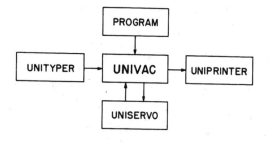

Fig. 3 – UNIVAC SYSTEM

Adding together the configurations of the human being and the electronic computer, Fig. 4 shows the solution of a problem in two levels of operation. The arithmetical chore has been removed from the mathematician, who has become a programmer, and this duty assigned to the UNIVAC. The programmer has been supplied with a "code" into which he translates his instructions to the computer. The "standard knowledge" designed into the UNIVAC by its engineers, consists of its elementary arithmetic and logic.

This situation remains static until the novelty of inventing programs wears off and degenerates into the dull labor of writing and checking programs. This duty now looms as an imposition on the human brain. Also, with the computer paid for, the cost of programming and the time consumed, comes to the notice of vice-presidents and project directors. Common sense dictates the insertion of a third level of operation, Fig. 5.

The programmer may return to being a mathematician. He is supplied with a catalogue of subroutines. No longer does he need to have available formulas or tables of elementary functions. He does not even need to know the particular instruction code used by the computer. He needs only to be able to use the catalogue to supply information to the computer about his problem. The UNIVAC, on the basis of the information supplied by the mathematician, under the control of a "compiling routine of type A", using subroutines and its own instruction code, produces a program. This program, in turn directs the UNIVAC through the computation on the input data and the desired results are produced. A major reduction in time consumed and in sources of error has been made.

If the library is well-stocked, programming has been reduced to a matter of hours, rather than weeks. The program is no longer subject either to errors of transcription or of untested routines.

Specifications for computer information, a catalogue, compiling routines, and subroutines will be given after adding another level to the block diagram. As Fig. 5 stands the mathematician must still perform all mathematical operations, relegating to the UNIVAC programming and computational operations. However, the computer information delivered by the mathematician no longer deals with numerical quantities as such. It treats of variables and constants in symbolic form together with operations upon them, The insertion of a fourth level of operation is now possible, Fig. 6. Suppose, for example, the mathematician wishes to evaluate a function and its first n derivatives. He sends the information defining the function itself to the UNIVAC. Under control of a "compiling routine of type B", in this case a differentiator, using task routines, the UNIVAC delivers the information necessary to program the computation of the function and its derivatives. From the formula for the function, the UNIVAC derives the formulas of the

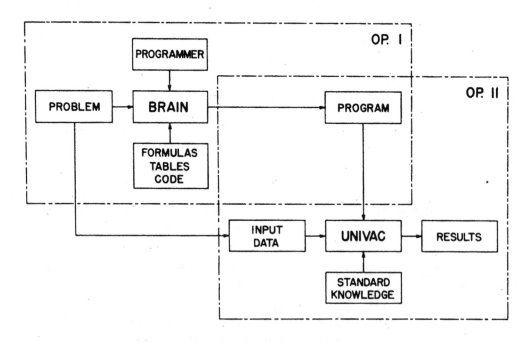

Fig. 4 - SOLUTION OF A PROBLEM

successive derivatives. This information processed under a compiling routine of Type A yields a program to direct the computation.

Expansion makes this procedure look, and seem, long and complicated. It is not. Reducing again to the two-component system, the mathematician and the computer, Fig. 7 presents a more accurate picture of the computing system.

Presuming that code, program, input data, and results are familiar terms, it remains to define and specify the forms of information and routines acceptable to this system. These include

> catalogue,
>
> computer information,
>
> subroutine,
>
> compiling routines, type A and B, and
>
> task routines.

CATALOGUE AND COMPUTER INFORMATION

As soon as the purpose is stated to make use of subroutines, two methods arise. In one, the program refers to an immediately available subroutine, uses it, and continues computation. For a limited number of subroutines, this method is feasible and useful. Such a

system has been developed under the nickname of the "short-order code" by members of the staff of the Computational Analysis Laboratory.

The second method not only looks up the subroutine, but translates it, properly adjusted, into a program. Thus, the completed program maybe run as a unit whenever desired, and may itself be placed in the library as a more advanced subroutine.

Each problem must be reduced to the level of the available subroutines. Suppose a simple problem, to compute

$$y = e^{-x^2} \sin cx$$

using elementary subroutines. Each step of the formula falls into the operational pattern, Fig. 8 ; that is,

$$u = x^2$$

$$U = e^{-u}$$

$$v = cx$$

$$V = \sin v$$

$$Y = UV.$$

As presented in Fig. 9, however, this information is not yet sufficiently standardized to be acceptable to a compiling routine. Several problems must be considered and procedures defined.

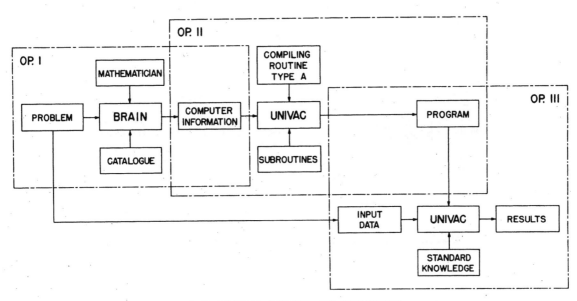

Fig. 5 - COMPILING ROUTINES AND SUBROUTINES

The operations are numbered in normal sequence and this number becomes part of the computer information. Thus when it is desired to change the normal sequence, the alternate destination is readily identified. The compiling routine translates these operation numbers into instructions in the coded program. Two fundamental situations arise, the alternate destination either precedes the operation under consideration or follows it, bypassing several intermediate operations. In both cases, it is necessary only to have the compiling routine remember where it has placed each subroutine or that a transfer of control to operation k has been indicated. In any event the mathematician need only state, "go to operation k", and the compiling routine does the rest.

The symbols to be used for the arguments and results, as well as for the operations, are of next concern. One mathematician might write

$$y = e^{-x^2} \sin cx$$

and another

$$u = e^{-v^2} \sin gv$$

The obvious solution proves best. Make a list of arguments and results and number them. (This amounts to writing all constants and variables as x_i.) The order is immaterial, so that forgotten quantities can be added at the end.

1	x	x_1	6	c	x_6
2	Δx	x_2	7	v	x_7
3	Lx	x_3	8	V	x_8
4	u	x_4	9	y	x_9
5	U	x_5	10	n	x_{10}

As symbols for the operations and sub-routines, a system of "call-numbers" is used. These alphabetic characters represent the class of subroutines. Following Dr. Wilkes, example, these symbols are partially phonetic; that is, a = arithmetic, t = trigonometric, and x = exponential, amc = arithmetic, multiplication by a constant, $x - e = e^{-u}$, $ts0$ = trigonometric, sine. Placed with the call-numbers, $n, f,$ or s, indicates normal, floating, or stated (fixed) decimal point. Other letters and digits indicate radians or degrees for angles, complex numbers, etc. These call-numbers are listed in the catalogue together with the order in which arguments, controls, and results are to be stated. The general rules for the description of an operation are:

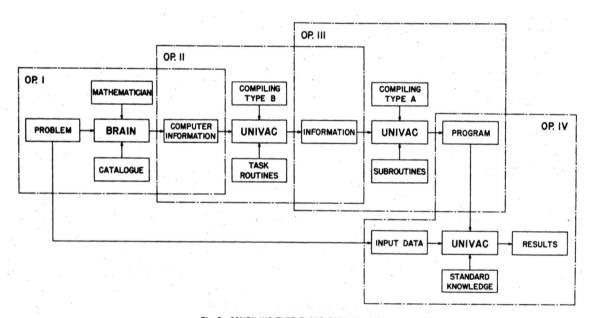

Fig. 6.- COMPILING TYPE B AND TASK ROUTINES

1. call-numbers,

2. number of operation,

3. arguments in order of appearance in formula, variables preceding constants,

4. controls, normal exit if altered, followed by alternate exits in order of appearance in subroutine,

5. results, in order of appearance.

All exceptions to the general rules are listed in the catalogue.

The problem has been reduced to computer information. The exact positions of characters in words as submitted to the UNIVAC has been omitted since it hardly seems of general interest. The preparation of information might be called creating a "multiple-address code", by which any number of arguments may enter an operation, to produce any number of results, and to proceed directly to the next operation unless routed to anyone of several other operations.

SUBROUTINES

Each subroutine in the library is expressed in coding relative to its entrance line considered as 001. They

are, in general, programmed and coded for maximum accuracy and minimum computing time. They may store within themselves constants peculiar to themselves. They may also make use of certain "permanent constants" read in with every program. These permanent constants occupy a reserved section of the memory and are called for by alphabetic memory locations, a trick, at present peculiar to UNIVAC. Thus, these addresses are not modified in the course of positioning the subroutine in a program. They include such quantities as $1/2\pi$, $\pi/4$, $\log_{10}e$, ±0, .2, .5, and the like.

Each subroutine is preceded by certain information, matching and supplementing that supplied by the mathematician:

1. call-number;

2. arguments, the destination of the arguments within the subroutine, expressed in the relative coding of the subroutine;

3. non-modification indicators locating constants embedded in the subroutine which are not to be altered;

4. results, the positions of the results within the subroutine, expressed in relative coding.

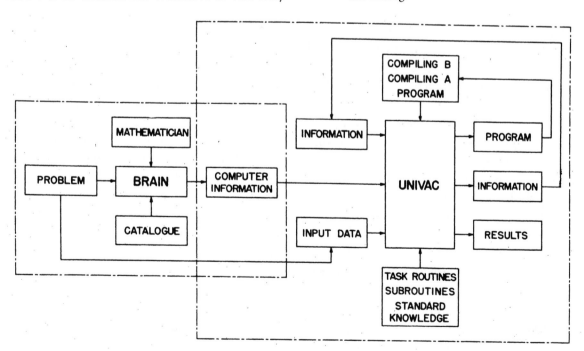

Fig. 7 - COMPUTING SYSTEM

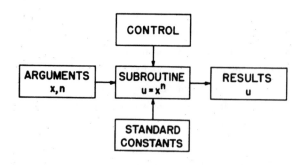

Fig. 8 - OPERATION

Each subroutine is arranged in a standard pattern.

Entrance line—The first line of a subroutine is its entrance line, thus in relative coding it is number one. It is the first line of the subroutine transferred to a program, and it contains an instruction transferring control to the first action line.

Exit lines—The second line of a subroutine is its normal exit line. This contains an instruction transferring control to the line following the last line of the subroutine. Unless an alternate transfer of control is desired, all exits from the subroutine are referred to the normal exit line. Alternate exit lines, involving transfers of control from the usual sequence, follow the normal exit line in a predetermined order as listed in the catalogue.

Arguments—The exit lines are followed by spaces reserved for the arguments arranged in predetermined order.

Results—The results, also in specified order, follow the arguments.

Constants—The results are followed, when possible, by any arbitrary constants peculiar to the subroutine. When the subroutine has been compounded from other subroutines, groups of constants may also appear embedded in the subroutine. These are cared for by the non modification information.

The *first action line* appears next in the subroutine. Its position in the relative coding is defined by the entrance line. No instruction line may precede this line.

The sequence assigned to the entrance and exit lines, arguments, results, and constants is arbitrary. It is convenient. All that is required is that a sequence be established and that the computer recognize this sequence.

For convenience in manipulation, a certain number of elementary subroutines have been combined to form a sub-library. These include

a = arithmetic
b = transfer of data
c = counters
h = hyperbolic functions
i = input routines
l = logarithmic functions
o = output routines
p = polynomials
r = roots and fractional exponents
t = trigonometric functions
u = control transfers
w = storage routines
x = exponential functions
y = editing routines

As subroutines are added to extend the library, it becomes more useful and programming time is further reduced. Indeed, the day may come when the elementary subroutines are rarely used and the computer information will contain but seven or eight items calling into play powerful subroutines.

CONSTRUCTION OF SUBROUTINES

It is not necessary, nor is it advisable, that the inexperienced programmer tamper with the coding within a subroutine. It is usually minimum latency coding using every trick and device know to the experienced programmer. It has been tested by operation on the computer. However, in order to speed the original construction, on paper, of the elementary routines, *kernel* routines and *threading* routines have been devised.

A kernel routine computes a mathematical function or carries out an elementary process for a limited range of the variable concerned; for example, $\sin x$, for $0 < x < \pi/4$ and 10^{-x} for $0 < x < 1$. A kernel routine is always entered and left by way of a threading routine.

Threading routines, incomplete without kernels, remove from the arguments and store, such quantities as algebraic signs, integral parts, and exponents, deliver the reduced arguments to the kernel routine, receive results from the kernel, and adjust algebraic signs and exponents. For example, the threading routines for sin y remove the algebraic sign of y, reduce y by multiples of 2π, reduce the remainder to a quantity x less than $\pi/4$, store the information and select the sin x or cos x kernel routine. The kernel routine returns sin x or cos x. The threading routine adjusts the sign, exponent, and decimal point completing the computation.

Threading routines recognize and give special treatment to such values as zero and infinity, and provide signals and printed information when the capacity of the computer is exceeded.

An elementary subroutine consists of a threading routine accompanied by one or more kernel routines. Hence, the threading routines are similar to the subroutines in form having at the beginning an entrance line, exit lines, (usually undetermined until the kernel routine is supplied), arguments, results, and constants. At the end of a threading routine are certain lines prepared to "overlap" the first section of the kernel routine. This overlap contains

1. the entrance line of the kernel routine;

2. the exit line of the kernel routine set-up by threading routine;

3. arguments; and

4. results.

OPERATION NUMBER	OPERATION	ARGUMENTS	RESULTS	CONTROL
	\multicolumn — $y = e^{-x^2} \sin cx$			

OPERATION NUMBER	OPERATION	ARGUMENTS	RESULTS	CONTROL
0	TRANSFER bOi	0, 01, 99, 2, .5 I (1, 2, 3, 4, 5)	$x, \Delta x, L_x, n, c$ 1, 2, 3, 10, 6	
1	x^n apn	$x, 2$ 1, 10	$u = x^2$ 4	
2	e^{-u} x-e	u 4	$U = e^{-u}$ 5	
3	$c \otimes$ amc	c, x 6, 1	$u = cx$ 7	
4	$\sin v$ tsO	v 7	$V = \sin v$ 8	
5	$\otimes$ amO	U, V 5, 8	$y = UV$ 9	
6	EDIT yrs	x, y 1, 9	$\bar{x}, \bar{y}$ O(1, 2)	
7	$\oplus \to L$ aaL	$x, \Delta x, L_x$ 1, 2, 3	$x + \Delta x \to x$ 1	$x \leq L_x \to 1, x \leq L_x \to 8$ 8, 1
8	STOP ust			

Fig. 9 - EXAMPLE

Compiling Routines Type A are designed to select and arrange subroutines according to information supplied by the mathematician or by the computer. Basically, there is but one Type A routine. However, since the UNIVAC code contains instructions transferring two neighboring quantities simultaneously, a second compiling routine has been designed to care for floating decimal, complex number, and double precision programs. For each operation listed by the mathematician, a type A routine will perform the following services:

1. locate the subroutine indicated by the call-number;

2. from the computer and subroutine information combined with its record of the program, fabricate and enter in the program the instructions transferring the arguments from working storage to the subroutine;

3. adjust the entrance and normal exit lines to the position of the subroutine in the program and enter them in the program;

4. according to the control information supplied by the programmer, adjust alternate exit lines and enter them in the program (this process involves reference to the record);

5. according to the control information supplied with previous operations adjust auxiliary entrance lines and enter them in the program;

6. modify all addresses in the subroutine instructions and enter these instructions in the program;

7. according to information supplied by the subroutine, leave unaltered all constants embedded in the subroutine and transfer them to the program;

8. from the computer and the subroutine information fabricate and enter in the program the instructions transferring the results to

9. maintain and produce a record of the program including the call-number of each subroutine and the position of its entrance line in the program.

The compiling routines also contain certain instructions concerning input tapes, tape library, and program tapes, peculiar to the UNIVAC. All counting operations such allocation of temporary storage and program space, and control of input and output are carried on steadily by the compiling routine. Stated bluntly, the compiling routine is the programmer and performs all those services necessary to the production of a finished program.

Compiling Routines of Type B, will for each operation, by means of "task routines", replace or supplement the given computer information with new information. Thus, compiling routine B-1 will, for each operation, copy the information concerning that operation and call in the corresponding task routine. The task routine will generate the formula, and derive the information, necessary to compute the derivative of the operation. Compiling routine B-1 then records this information in a form suitable for submission to a Type A routine.

Since information may be re-submitted to a type B routine, it is obvious that in order to obtain a program to compute $f(x)$ and its first n derivatives, only the information defining $f(x)$ and the value of n need be given. The formulas for the derivatives of $f(x)$ will be derived by repeated applications of B-1 and programmed by a type A routine.

It is here that the question can best be answered concerning a liking for or an aversion to subroutines. Since the use of subroutines in this fashion increases the abilities of the computer, the question becomes meaningless and transforms into a question of how to produce better subroutines faster. However, balancing the advantages and disadvantages of using subroutines, among the advantages are

1. relegation of mechanical jobs such as memory allocation, address modification, and transcription to the UNIVAC;

2. removal of error sources such as programming errors and transcription errors;

3. conservation of programming time;

4. ability to operate on operations;

5. duplication of effort is avoided, since each program in turn may become a subroutine.

Only two disadvantages are immediately evident. Because of standardization, a small amount of time is lost in performing duplicate data transfers which could be eliminated in a tailor-made routine. In base load problems, this could become serious. Even in this case, however, it is worthwhile to have UNIVAC produce the original program and then eliminate such duplication before rerunning the problem. The second disadvantage should not long remain serious. It is the fact that, if a desired subroutine does not exist, it must be programmed and added to the library. This will be most likely to occur in the case of input and output editing routines until a large variety is accumulated. This situation also emphasizes the need for the greatest generality in the construction of subroutines.

Several directions of future developments in this field can be pointed out. It is to be hoped that reports will be presented on some of them next September.

More type A compiling routines will be devised; those handling commercial rather than mathematical programs; some special purpose compiling routines such as a routine which will compute approximate magnitudes as it proceeds and select sub-routines accordingly. Compiling routines must be informed of the average time required for each sub-routine so that they can supply estimates of running time with each program. Compiling routines can be devised which will correct the computational procedure submitted to produce the most efficient program. For example, if both $\sin \theta$ and $\cos \theta$ are called for in a routine, they will be computed more rapidly simultaneously. This will involve sweeping the computer information once to examine its structure.

Type B routines at present include linear operators. More type B routines must be designed. It can scarcely be denied that type C and D routines will be found to exist adding higher levels of operation. Work is already in progress to produce the formulas developed by type B routines in algebraic form in addition to producing their computational programs.

Thus by considering the professional programmer (not the mathematician), as an integral part of the computer, it is evident that the memory of the programmer and all information and data to which he can refer is available to the computer subject only to translation into suitable language. And it is further evident that the computer is fully capable of remembering and acting upon any instructions once presented to it by the programmer.

With some specialized knowledge of more advanced topics, UNIVAC at present has a well grounded mathematical education fully equivalent to that of a college sophomore, and it does not forget and does not make mistakes. It is hoped that its undergraduate course will be completed shortly and it will be accepted as a candidate for a graduate degree.

9.6
Automatic Programming—Definitions

Grace Murray Hopper

From *Symposium on Automatic Programming for Digital Computers* (Washington, DC: Office of Naval Research, Department of the Navy, 1954), pp. 1–5.

INTRODUCTORY NOTE TO READING 9.6

In 1954 Hopper helped to organize the first symposium on automatic programming, the first symposium specifically on software. She also delivered the symposium's first paper, entitled "Automatic programming—definitions" (reproduced here), and gave a summary of the proceedings at the end. Over two hundred people attended the symposium, which also featured papers by John Backus, inventor of FORTRAN, and Stanley Gill, co-author of the first textbook on computer programming. [JMN]

TEXT OF READING 9.6

In the ten years since Mark I first ran, the terms programmer and programming have come into being. The world is so accustomed to talk of automatic computers—large-scale, high-speed, automatically sequenced, digital, computing devices—that the adjective automatic has been dropped and only the term computer is required. Instead, the word automatic now has been attached to programming and coding.

In the early days, some nine or ten years ago, a programmer was, of necessity, many things. Numerical analyst, encoder-decoder, electrical or electronic technician, detective and bug-hunter, and finally, evaluator. The increase in the number and speed of computers gave rise to specialization and with this specialization, the definition of various types of languages for communication among the specialists. As the analyst, programmer, coder, operator, and maintenance man were separated, flow diagrams, flow charts and other aids to communication were designed. However, up until some three years ago, the only means of communication with the computer remained the instruction code of the operations built into the hardware.

The distinction between a programmer and a coder has never been clearly made. Coder was probably first used as an intermediate point on the salary scale between trainee and programmer. A "programmer" prepares a plan for the solution of a problem. This plan may or may not include numerical and systems analysis, but it surely includes plans for the handling of the input and output data from source document to useful result. It is a plan for the flow of data and operations by the computer and its auxiliary equipment as a part of a system. A programmer's working tools are flow diagrams, schematic representations of the problem, usually involving fairly gross symbols, and plain English. One of his final results, to be passed on to a coder, will be a flow chart, a detailed graphical representation of the sequence of operations the computer itself is expected to perform.

It is then the task of the coder to reduce this flow chart to coding, to a list in computer code, the code representing the operations built into the hard-ware of the computer, of the successive operations required to solve the problem. It is this function, that of the coder, time-consuming and fraught with mistakes, that is the first human operation to be replaced by the computer itself. The task of automatic coding can be divided into two parts:

1. devising a method for expressing the information contained in a flow chart-devising pseudocodes; and

2. preparing the routines and subroutines to process the pseudo-code and produce computer coding and ultimately results.

A pseudocode is any arbitrary code, independent of the hardware of the computer, used to state a problem. Pseudocodes now in existence and in use extend all the way from simple extensions of computer codes, through mnemonic vocabularies, to plain English. They make use of many kinds of addresses and many kinds of parameters. The pseudocodes themselves form a whole field of study and research.

The decoding and processing of the pseudocodes are carried out by executive routines. These routines seem to fall into four classes: assembly, compiling, conversion, and interpretive. The type developed by a particular computer installation seems to be primarily dependent on the characteristics of the computer available. All four types attempt to make it possible for the "untrained user" to run problems on the computer, to reduce the load on the programmers, and to speed up the attainment of a solution, i.e., to reduce the elapsed time between the question and the answer.

All four types of executive routines recognize the subroutine as the building block. A subroutine consists of the instructions necessary to carry out a well-defined operation. Such an operation may be "cosine x" or it may be "Philadelphia Wage Tax" or "select field m from next input item of n words from input device k and transfer it to working storage location w." It is essential only that the operation be well defined.

Whether the subroutine is stored in the library in relative, abstract, or specific coding, it will be either static or dynamic. When a static subroutine is processed by an executive routine, it remains basically the same, and only addresses are altered. However, when a dynamic or generative subroutine is called for, a jump (control transfer) is made to the stored subroutine, which in turn produces a specific routine for the problem from the given parameters and from skeletal structures stored within it.

All four types of executive routines decode the pseudocode. However, they differ as to whether computation itself is carried out during the decoding process or after the decoding is completed.

An assembly routine, after decoding each pseudocode and locating the corresponding subroutine, processes the subroutine, suitably altering and entering addresses, to produce a problem routine (perhaps not completely specific because it may still require certain parameters).

A conversion routine aptly describes itself, since its task is to convert pseudocode to computer code or to call suitable subroutines, to convert relative and floating addresses to specific addresses, to convert decimal quantities into binary notation, to deal with floating-point quantities, and to edit. It may produce computer coding or it may contain within itself an interpretive routine.

An interpretive routine processes the pseudocode and the data simultaneously. Having decoded the pseudocode, it locates the subroutine, supplies the data, and carries out the operation before proceeding to the next element of pseudocode.

A compiling routine combines most of the functions of the other three. It employs conversion and editing routines for data as subroutines, it interprets pseudocode, and it assembles a specific program. It differs from the assembly routine in its use of dynamic subroutines.

Sharp lines of demarcation are difficult to draw. One factor stands out—whether or not the executive routine produces a specific routine. Assembly and compiling routines produce specific routines and thus eliminate the reinterpretation of the pseudocode. This seems to be a time-saving of importance in engineering, commercial, and business applications. In scientific applications, the interpretive technique is satisfactory since the problem is usually only solved once. The use of generative subroutines permits one coding job to cover many cases and permits the compiling routines to eliminate 90% of the red-tape operations from the final program.

Thus, it seems possible that the first characteristic to influence the design of an executive routine is the speed of computation required. Reinterpretation of pseudocode, repetition of loop-tests and other red-tape operations cannot be tolerated in most large-scale business problems. Since the mathematical problems will only be run once and interpretations and red tape must be performed at least once, interpretive routines will meet scientific needs equally well.

The computer characteristic most influential in the design of executive techniques seems to be the quantity and availability of storage. At least two kinds of storage are available in all computers; three kinds are distinguishable in many computers; internal, secondary, and external.

Internal storage is, of course, the high-speed storage of the computer. External is that made available from the outside world. Many of the large computers also have available secondary storage, under the control of the computer, from which transfer to internal storage is comparatively rapid. Under this heading fall magnetic drums and tapes.

If no secondary storage is available, and transfer from external to internal is at a speed slow compared to that of the computer, an interpretive routine is the natural solution. If, on the other hand, a large secondary storage is available, and the ratio of transfer speed to computer speed is comparatively favorable, the compiler is advantageous.

Finally, if latency or access-time enters the situation, the compiling technique again has the advantage because a final sweep of the coded program can be added to reduce it to minimal-access coding for production running.

Whether or not conversion routines are required is dictated by whether the computer is binary or decimal, its range, and its acceptance of alphabetic data. There are some mathematicians willing to think in binary but it is a moot question whether businessmen and the general public are willing to do so. For commercial applications, it is likely that the binary computer will demand very complete conversion routines.

Finally, if the computer is not automatically checked, an interpretive routine may be safer. Programming is difficult enough to check on paper, but when the computer generates it, it is a little more than difficult to check it. It is probably best to immediately run numbers through it and check the results. However, if the subroutines and compiler have been checked out, and a checked computer is used, all resultant mistakes can be referred back to the mathematician who stated the problem.

Thus, three things seem to govern the type of executive routine prepared for a given computer:

1. the storage distribution and the input-output and transfer rates;

2. binary, decimal, alpha-decimal; and

3. checking.

In addition, the type of problem, one-shot as against many times repeated will influence the decision.

So far, only the direct coding for computation or data-processing has been mentioned. Automatic techniques are finding further application in other types of routines such as diagnostic, test, and post-mortem routines, and even in translators and "universal codes."

With more and more computers able to interpret pseudocodes and produce their own computer codes, it is not too much to ask that a pseudocode be defined which can be taught to mathematicians and that each computer installation prepare an interpreter or compiler which will process such a universal code into coding for that computer. I am looking forward to what Dr. Gorn will tell us of this work.

With coding accumulating for existing computers, and engineers designing more computers with new and different instruction codes, translators to make available "old" coding to new computers will conserve programming time. Since this will be a mechanical operation, we shall look to the computers to do this job for us.

Among the earliest and most useful automatic routines were diagnostic routines designed to track down mistakes and malfunctions; test routines designed to demonstrate that a computer was in working order and arbitrate the eternal debate as to whether "it" stopped on a computer malfunction or a programming mistake. When the decision fell on the latter, post-mortem routines were designed to inform the programmer of what had been going on inside just before "it" stopped. In this connection, I like to quote Professor Adams that numerical analysis has errors, computers malfunction, and programmers make mistakes.

In order to set your minds in a way of thinking, I shall steal from tomorrow. As you listen to these papers watch for two things that, I think, they all point toward—two developments we shall want to discuss in the future in the light of what we will learn here. One is the very evident possibility and likelihood that just as compilers control generators to produce programs to process data, we shall soon be talking of systems containing computers controlling and directing computers. The second trend that is appearing, more evident perhaps in the commercial programs, is that the incoming data will itself determine the program to be applied.

The first time I heard of a library of subroutines was from Professor Howard Aiken when Mark I started running. The earliest "relatively coded subroutine" I have found is one for sine x written in August 1944 for Mark I. However, it was necessary to wait until 1951 for a working system and a book to read, that prepared by Wheeler, Wilkes, and Gill for the EDSAC. As computer development has speeded up in the last half of the first decade, let us hope that the production of automatic programming techniques, most of them less than one year old, will also speed up. It is primarily to means of communications such as this meeting, sponsored by the Navy, that we will look for help toward future developments.

10

Early Applications of Electronic Computers

10.1
Translation

Warren Weaver

Memorandum dated July 15, 1949.

INTRODUCTORY NOTE TO READING 10.1

Warren Weaver's twelve-page memorandum entitled *Translation,* written on July 15, 1949 and originally circulated privately to about two hundred people, was the first suggestion that most had ever seen that language translation by electronic computer might be possible. Because Weaver was director of the division of natural sciences at the Rockefeller Foundation from 1932–55, he was in a unique position to fund scientific research in areas that he considered worthwhile. In calling attention to a topic for future development in computing Weaver also tacitly indicated that he was prepared to fund selected research in this area. Thus his report carried special weight among researchers who might be applying for Rockefeller grants. [JMN]

TEXT OF READING 10.1

There is no need to do more than mention the obvious fact that a multiplicity of languages impedes cultural interchange between the peoples of the earth, and is a serious deterrent to international understanding. The present memorandum, assuming the validity and importance of this fact, contains some comments and suggestions bearing on the possibility of contributing at least something to the solution of the worldwide translation problem through the use of electronic computers of great capacity, flexibility, and speed.

The suggestions of this memorandum will surely be incomplete and naive, and may well be patently silly to an expert in the field—for the author is certainly not such.

A WAR ANECDOTE—
LANGUAGE INVARIANTS

During the war a distinguished mathematician whom we will call P, an ex-German who had spent some time at the University of Istanbul and had learned Turkish there, told W. W. the following story.

A mathematical colleague, knowing that P had an amateur interest in cryptography, came to P one morning, stated that he had worked out a deciphering technique, and asked P to cook up some coded message on which he might try his scheme. P wrote out in Turkish a message containing about 100 words; simplified it by replacing the Turkish letters ç, ğ, ı, ö, ş and ü by c, g, i, o, s, and u respectively; and then, using something more complicated than a simple substitution cipher, reduced the message to a column of five-digit numbers. The next day (and the time required is significant) the colleague brought his result back, and remarked that they had apparently not met with success. But the sequence of letters he reported, when properly broken up into words, and when mildly corrected (not enough correction being required really to bother anyone who knew the language well), turned out to be the original message in Turkish.

The most important point, at least for present purposes, is that the decoding was done by someone who did not know Turkish, and did not know that the message was in Turkish. One remembers, by contrast, the well-known instance in World War I when it took our cryptographic forces weeks or months to determine that a captured message was coded from Japanese; and then took them a relatively short time to decipher it, once they knew what the language was.

During the war, when the whole field of cryptography was so secret, it did not seem discreet to inquire concerning details of this story; but one could hardly avoid guessing that this process made use of frequencies of letters, letter combinations, intervals between letters and letter combinations, letter patterns, etc., *which are to some significant degree independent of the language used.* This at once leads one to suppose that, in the manifold instances in which man has invented and developed languages, there are certain invariant properties which are, again not precisely but to some statistically useful degree, common to all languages.

This may be, for all I know, a famous theorem of philology. Indeed the well-known *bow-wow, woof-woof,* etc. theories of Müller and others, for the origin of languages, would of course lead one to expect common features in all languages, due to their essentially similar mechanism of development. And, in any event, there are obvious reasons which make the supposition a likely one. All languages—at least all the ones under consideration here—were invented and developed *by men;* and all men, whether Bantu or Greek, Islandic or Peruvian, have essentially the same equipment to bring to bear on this problem. They have vocal organs capable of producing about the same set of sounds (with minor exceptions, such as the glottal click of the African native). Their brains are of the same general order of potential complexity. The elementary demands for language must have emerged in closely similar ways in different places and perhaps at different times. One would expect wide superficial differences; but it seems very reasonable to expect that certain basic, and probably very nonobvious, aspects be common to all the developments. It is just a little like observing that trees differ very widely in many characteristics, and yet there are basic common characteristics—certain essential qualities of "tree-ness,"—

that all trees share, whether they grow in Poland, or Ceylon, or Colombia. Furthermore (and this is the important point), a South American has, in general, no difficulty in recognizing that a Norwegian tree is a tree.

The idea of basic common elements in all languages later received support from a remark which the mathematician and logician Reichenbach made to W. W. Reichenbach also spent some time in Istanbul, and, like many of the German scholars who went there, he was perplexed and irritated by the Turkish language. The grammar of that language seemed to him so grotesque that eventually he was stimulated to study its logical structure. This, in turn, led him to become interested in the logical structure of the grammar of several other languages; and, quite unaware of W. W.'s interest in the subject, Reichenbach remarked, "I was amazed to discover that, for (apparently) widely varying languages, the basic logical structures have important common features." Reichenbach said he was publishing this, and would send the material to W. W.; but nothing has ever appeared.

One suspects that there is a great deal of evidence for this general viewpoint—at least bits of evidence appear spontaneously even to one who does not see the relevant literature. For example, a note in *Science,* about the research in comparative semantics of Erwin Reifler of the University of Washington, states that "the Chinese words for 'to shoot' and 'to dismiss' show a remarkable phonological and graphic agreement." This all seems very strange until one thinks of the two meanings of "to fire" in English. Is this only happenstance? How widespread are such correlations?

TRANSLATION AND COMPUTERS

Having had considerable exposure to computer design problems during the war, and being aware of the speed, capacity, and logical flexibility possible in modern electronic computers, it was very natural for W. W. to think, several years ago, of the possibility that such computers be used for translation. On March 4, 1947, after having turned this idea over for a couple of years, W. W. wrote to Professor Norbert Wiener of Massachusetts Institute of Technology as follows:

One thing I wanted to ask you about is this. A most serious problem, for UNESCO and for the constructive and peaceful future of the planet, is the problem of translation, as it unavoidably affects the communication between peoples. Huxley has recently told me that they are appalled by the magnitude and the importance of the translation job.

Recognizing fully, even though necessarily vaguely, the semantic difficulties because of multiple meanings, etc., I have wondered if it were unthinkable to design a computer which would translate. Even if it would translate only scientific material (where the semantic difficulties are very notably less), and even if it did produce an inelegant (but intelligible) result, it would seem to me worth while.

Also knowing nothing official about, but having guessed and inferred considerable about, powerful new mechanized methods in cryptography—methods which I believe succeed even when one does not know what language has been coded—one naturally wonders if the problem of translation could conceivably be treated as a problem in cryptography. When I look at an article in Russian, I say: "This is really written in English, but it has been coded in some strange symbols. I will now proceed to decode."

Have you ever thought about this? As a linguist and expert on computers, do you think it is worth thinking about?

Professor Wiener, in a letter dated April 30, 1947, said in reply:

Second—as to the problem of mechanical translation, I frankly am afraid the boundaries of words in different languages are too vague and the emotional and international connotations are too extensive to make any quasimechanical translation scheme very hopeful. I will admit that basic English seems to indicate that we can go further than we have generally done in the mechanization of speech, but you must remember that in certain respects basic English is the reverse of mechanical and throws upon such words as *get* a burden which is much greater than most words carry in conventional English. At the present time, the mechanization of language, beyond such a stage as the design of photoelectric reading opportunities for the blind, seems very premature. . . .

To this, W. W. replied on May 9, 1947:

I am disappointed but not surprised by your comments on the translation problem. The difficulty you mention concerning Basic seems to me to have a rather easy answer. It is, of course, true that Basic puts multiple use on an action verb such as *get*. But, even so, the two-word combinations such as *get up, get over, get back,* etc., are, in Basic, not really very numerous. Suppose we take a vocabulary of 2,000 words, and admit for good measure all the two-word combinations as if they were single words. The vocabulary is still only four million: and that is not so formidable a number to a modern computer, is it?

Thus this attempt to interest Wiener, who seemed so ideally equipped to consider the problem, failed to produce any real result. This must in fact be accepted as exceedingly discouraging, for, if there are any real possibilities, one would expect Wiener to be just the person to develop them.

The idea has, however, been seriously considered elsewhere. The first instance known to W. W., subsequent to his own notion about it, was described in a memorandum dated February 12, 1948, written by Dr. Andrew D. Booth who, in Professor J. D. Bernal's department in Birkbeck College, University of London, had been active in computer design and construction. Dr. Booth said:

A concluding example, of possible application of the electronic computer, is that of translating from one language into another. We have considered this problem in some detail, and it transpires that a machine of the type envisaged could perform this function without any modification in its design.

On May 25, 1948, W. W. visited Dr. Booth in his computer laboratory at Welwyn, London, and learned that Dr. Richens, Assistant Director of the Bureau of Plant Breeding and Genetics, and much concerned with the abstracting problem, had been interested with Dr. Booth in the translation problem. They had, at least at that time, not been concerned with the problem of multiple meaning, word order, idiom, etc., but only with the problem of mechanizing a dictionary. Their proposal then was that one first "sense" the letters of a word, and have the machine see whether or not its memory contains precisely the word in question. If so, the machine simply produces the translation (which is the rub; of course "the" translation doesn't exist) of this word. If this exact word is not contained in the memory, then the machine discards the last letter of the word, and tries over. If this fails, it discards another letter, and tries again. After it has found the largest initial combination of letters which is in the dictionary, it "looks up" the whole discarded portion in a special "grammatical annex" of the dictionary. Thus confronted by *running*, it might find *run* and then find out what the ending (*n*)*ing* does to *run*.

Thus their interest was, at least at that time, confined to the problem of the mechanization of a dictionary which in a reasonably efficient way would handle *all forms* of all words. W. W. has no more recent news of this affair.

Very recently the newspapers have carried stories of the use of one of the California computers as a translator. The published reports do not indicate much more than a word-into-word sort of translation, and there has been no indication, at least that W. W. has seen, of the proposed manner of handling the problems of multiple meaning, context, word order, etc.

This last-named attempt, or planned attempt, has already drawn forth inevitable scorn, Mr. Max Zeldner, in a letter to the *Herald Tribune* on June 13, 1949, stating that the most you could expect of a machine translation of the fifty-five Hebrew words which form the 23d Psalm would start out *Lord my shepherd no I will lack*, and would close *But good and kindness he will chase me all days of my life; and I shall rest in the house of Lord to length days*. Mr. Zeldner points out that a great Hebrew poet once said that translation "is like kissing your sweetheart through a veil."

It is, in fact, amply clear that a translation procedure that does little more than handle a one-to-one correspondence of words cannot hope to be useful for problems of *literary* translation, in which style is important, and in which the problems of idiom, multiple meanings, etc., are frequent.

Even this very restricted type of translation may, however, very well have important use. Large volumes of technical material might, for example, be usefully, even if not at all elegantly, handled this way. Technical writing is unfortunately not always straightforward and simple in style; but at least the problem of multiple meaning is enormously simpler. In mathematics, to take what is probably the easiest example, one can very nearly say that each word, within the general context of a mathematical article, has one and only one meaning.

THE FUTURE OF COMPUTER TRANSLATION

The foregoing remarks about computer translation schemes which have been reported do not, however, seem to W. W. to give an appropriately hopeful indication of what the future possibilities may be. Those possibilities should doubtless be indicated by persons who have special knowledge of languages and of their comparative anatomy. But again, at the risk of being foolishly naive, it seems interesting to indicate four types of attack, on levels of increasing sophistication.

Meaning and Context

First, let us think of a way in which the problem of multiple meaning can, in principle at least, be solved.

If one examines the words in a book, one at a time as through an opaque mask with a hole in it one word wide, then it is obviously impossible to determine, one at a time, the meaning of the words. "Fast" may mean "rapid"; or it may mean "motionless"; and there is no way of telling which.

But, if one lengthens the slit in the opaque mask, until one can see not only the central word in question but also say N words on either side, then, if N is large enough one can unambiguously decide the meaning of the central word. The formal truth of this statement becomes clear when one mentions that the middle word of a whole article or a whole book is unambiguous if one has read the whole article or book, providing of course that the article or book is sufficiently well written to communicate at all.

The practical question is: "What minimum value of N will, at least in a tolerable fraction of cases, lead to the correct choice of meaning for the central word?"

This is a question concerning the statistical semantic character of language which could certainly be answered, at least in some interesting and perhaps in a useful way. Clearly N varies with the type of writing in question. It may be zero for an article known to be about a specific mathematical subject. It may be very low for chemistry, physics, engineering, etc. If N were equal to 5, and the article or book in question were on some sociological subject, would there be a probability of 0.95 that the choice of meaning would be correct 98% of the time? Doubtless not: but a statement of this sort could be made, and values of N could be determined that would meet given demands.

Ambiguity, moreover, attaches primarily to nouns, verbs, and adjectives; and actually (at least so I suppose) to relatively few nouns, verbs, and adjectives. Here again is a good subject for study concerning the statistical semantic character of languages. But one can imagine using a value of N that varies from word to word, is zero for *he, the,* etc., and needs to be large only rather occasionally. Or would it determine unique meaning in a satisfactory fraction of cases, to examine not the $2N$ adjacent *words*, but perhaps the $2N$ adjacent *nouns*? What choice of adjacent words maximizes the probability of correct choice of meaning, and at the same time leads to a small value of N?

Thus one is led to the concept of a translation process in which, in determining meaning for a word, account is taken of the immediate ($2N$ word) context. It would hardly be practical to do this by means of a generalized dictionary which contains all possible phases $2N + 1$ words long: for the number of such phases is horrifying, even to a modern electronic computer. But it does seem likely that some reasonable way could be found of using the micro context to settle the difficult cases of ambiguity.

A more general basis for hoping that a computer could be designed which would cope with a useful part of the problem of translation is to be found in a theorem which was proved in 1943 by McCulloch and Pitts.[1] This theorem states that a robot (or a computer) constructed with regenerative loops of a certain formal character is capable of deducing any legitimate conclusion from a finite set of premises.

Now there are surely alogical elements in language (intuitive sense of style, emotional content, etc.) so that again one must be pessimistic about the problem of *literary* translation. But, insofar as written language is an expression of logical character, this theorem assures one that the problem is at least formally solvable.

Translation and Cryptography

Claude Shannon, of the Bell Telephone Laboratories, has recently published some remarkable work in the mathematical theory of communication.[2] This work all roots back to the statistical characteristics of the communication process. And it is at so basic a level of generality that it is not surprising that his theory includes the whole field of cryptography. During the war Shannon wrote a most important analysis of the whole cryptographic problem, and this work is, W. W. believes, also to appear soon, it having been declassified.

Probably only Shannon himself, at this stage, can be a good judge of the possibilities in this direction; but, as was expressed in W. W.'s original letter to Wiener, it is very tempting to say that a book written in Chinese is simply a book written in English which was coded into the "Chinese code." If we have useful methods for solving almost any cryptographic problem, may it not be that with proper interpretation we already have useful methods for translation?

This approach brings into the foreground an aspect of the matter that probably is absolutely basic—namely, the statistical character of the problem. "Perfect" translation is almost surely unattainable. Processes, which at stated confidence levels will produce a translation which contains only X per cent "error," are almost surely attainable.

And it is one of the chief purposes of this memorandum to emphasize that *statistical semantic* studies should be undertaken, as a necessary preliminary step.

The cryptographic-translation idea leads very naturally to, and is in fact a special case of, the fourth and most general suggestion: namely, that translation make deep use of language invariants.

Indeed, what seems to W. W. to be the most promising approach of all is one based on the ideas expressed on pages 16–17—that is to say, an approach that goes so deeply into the structure of languages as to come down to the level where they exhibit common traits.

Think, by analogy, of individuals living in a series of tall closed towers, all erected over a common foundation. When they try to communicate with one another, they shout back and forth, each from his own closed tower. It is difficult to make the sound penetrate even the nearest towers, and communication proceeds very poorly indeed. But, when an individual goes down his tower, he finds himself in a great open basement, common to all the towers. Here he establishes easy and useful communication with the persons who have also descended from their towers.

Thus may it be true that the way to translate from Chinese to Arabic, or from Russian to Portuguese, is not to attempt the direct route, shouting from tower to tower. Perhaps the way is to descend, from each language, down to the common base of human communication—the real but as yet undiscovered universal language—and then re-emerge by whatever particular route is convenient.

Such a program involves a presumably tremendous amount of work in the logical structure of languages before one would be ready for any mechanization.

This must be very closely related to what Ogden and Richards have already done for English—and perhaps for French and Chinese. But it is along such general lines that it seems likely that the problem of translation can be attacked successfully. Such a program has the advantage that, whether or not it lead to a useful mechanization of the translation problem, it could not fail to shed much useful light on the general problem of communication.

• • •

1. Warren S. McCulloch and Walter Pitts, *Bull. math. Biophys.*, no 5, pp. 115–133, 1943.

2. For a very simplified version, see "The Mathematics of Communication," by Warren Weaver, *Sci. Amer.*, vol. 181, no. 1, pp. 11–15, July 1949. Shannon's original papers, as published in the *Bell Syst. tech. J.*, and a longer and more detailed interpretation by W. W. are about to appear as a memoir on communication, published by the University of Illinois Press. A book by Shannon on this subject is also to appear soon.

10.2

The Application of Calculating Machines to Business and Commerce

B. V. Bowden

From Manchester University, *Manchester University Computer. Inaugural Conference* [Bolton: Tillotson's, 1951]: 30–32.

INTRODUCTORY NOTE TO READING 10.2

Bertram Vivien Bowden (1910–89), who worked for the nascent computer division of the British electronics firm Ferranti Ltd., was probably the first computer salesman in England. He delivered this address on the anticipated business applications of computers at the second English computer conference held at Manchester University in July 1951 under the sponsorship of Ferranti who had delivered the first Ferranti Mark I to Manchester in February of that year. This was the first delivery of an electronic computer to a customer, predating Remington Rand UNIVAC's delivery of the UNIVAC I, serial number 1 to the U. S. Census Bureau by about one month. Bowden's address at the conference to publicize the new Ferranti Mark I may have been the first of its kind published in England.

Commercial application of electronic computing occurred very early in England. By November 1951 the LEO I (*Lyons Electronic Office*) was fully operational at J. Lyons and Company in England. This adaptation of the Cambridge EDSAC was the first electronic digital computer to run business programs on a routine basis. In 1953 Bowden, who had received a Ph.D. from Cambridge, edited *Faster than Thought* (London: Sir Isaac Pitman and Sons, 1953). Begun as a sales brochure, this book, which boasted a stellar list of contributors that included Alan Turing, became the most widely read early introduction to computers in English, remaining in print without change until 1968. [JMN]

TEXT OF READING 10.2

Far more arithmetic is done every day for the purposes of business and commerce than is done in all the scientific and mathematical laboratories of the world. It is reasonable to enquire if these computing machines, which have been designed so far for purely scientific use, can be applied to the general problems of business and commerce. It is as well to remind ourselves of the speed of which these machines are capable; for example, experience shows that the average comptometer operator will perform and check about four hundred 10×10 decimal digit multiplications in an average eight-hour working day. The Manchester University machine on the other hand will multiply two 10-digit numbers together in less than three milliseconds, which means that it will, in a few seconds, do as much work as a comptometer operator does in a day. Furthermore, the machine is capable of remembering several hundred thousand digits, which is equivalent to the contents of a small filing system, all of this information being available to the machine almost instantaneously whenever required.

Experience has shown that the most difficult and expensive operations which arise in ordinary office routine are not the actual computations themselves, but the routing of information from one part of the office to another so that each girl has available to her at all times the data which she needs to do her calculations. Information is routed from one part of the machine to another along its internal wiring, so this problem would not arise if a digital computer were being used.

In order to obtain some idea of the potentialities of these machines, we have attempted to analyse the problems which would be involved in adapting the machine in the University to work out the wages for the Ferranti factory at Hollinwood, which employs about 3,500 people engaged in the manufacture of transformers and electrical machinery of all kinds. There are approximately eighty separate bonus schemes in operation in the factory, and it now takes about 840 man-hours every week to work out the wages with all the appropriate deductions for P.A.Y.E., Savings Schemes and so on. Our analysis has shown

that it will be possible to do the computations themselves on the University machine in about 48 minutes.

This is only a very small part of the story; this quoted time does not allow for putting the data into the machine every week, or for printing out the results. For example, it would take approximately thirty hours to transcribe the information on the clock cards, which are used to record the times the operatives have worked, into a form which the machine would be capable of absorbing. There is, of course, no reason at all why the clocks which print each operator's card as he enters the factory should not be made to record the information directly in the form of punchings which the machine itself would interpret.

A similar problem has to be faced when one feeds to the machine the data on such things as stock cards and work sheets. They too would at the moment need transcription before the machine could read them, but they too could be modified in all probability so that the machine could interpret them directly.

An analysis of the total amount of information which is necessary in Hollinwood to carry the wage computations forward from week to week shows that about two complete drums would be required. The drums are too expensive to be used in this way; it would be necessary to devise a special store which would be more economical but might forego some of the special advantages of the drums.

Finally we come to output. Here we find again that the present teleprinter output is intolerably slow. It would take at least twelve or fourteen hours to print out the necessary data on the P.A.Y.E. slips. It would be possible to devise a parallel type output similar to that which is now being used on the punched card tabulating machines, which would print the necessary output in about half-an-hour.

Our simple analysis shows, therefore, that it would be uneconomical to use the machine for computing wages since the input and output times will both be very much longer than the computation times, and the memory which the machine has available is not really adequate for the purpose. In other words, it appears as if our computing machine is only going to be part of a much larger installation which will have to be devised specially for this kind of work. It is interesting to speculate, therefore, on what we may foresee as reasonable developments in the near future along these lines.

In the first place we have already considered the possibility of using a special type of automatic record of clock figures which the machine itself would be able to interpret. It may also be possible to modify many of the Works' documents so that the machine can directly interpret their contents. This is possible if the numerical data involved can be expressed by the position of marks on a piece of paper. We see at the moment no possibility of making the machine read ordinary manuscript figures but if all documents were written on a special typewriter, it could simultaneously prepare copy which would be suitable for the machine.

It is necessary now to consider the possible developments of very large capacity stores. We may for one moment diverge from our main theme in order to analyse the relationship between the storage of numerical data and the storage of music on a gramophone disc or a magnetic tape. The information contained in the gramophone record is sufficient to ensure that the movement of the cone of the loudspeaker will at all times reproduce the music with adequate fidelity. If this is to be done, it is necessary to specify the position of the cone itself sufficiently frequently to ensure the transmission of the highest frequency in which one is interested (this determines the number of groups of numbers which will be needed). The precision with which the cone position has to be specified, is determined by the ratio of the amplitude of the music to that of the residual background, which determines the number of digits which are necessary in each group. It can be shown that the amount of information which is contained in an ordinary high-quality gramophone record is equivalent to the transmission of over 200,000 binary digits per second. Although it is quite impracticable to pack a disc so tightly with numerical data as with music, it is nevertheless clear, in principle at least, that it will be possible to store very large quantities of data. The whole contents of the Encyclopaedia Britannica could be stored in approximately two thousand million binary digits and it is likely that the magnetic tape which would be needed for this purpose could be contained in an ordinary filing cabinet.

It should, therefore, be quite possible to store the equivalent of the total books of quite a large firm without undue difficulty, although no one has yet faced the serious problems which would arise when an attempt is made to analyse, catalogue and classify such large quantities of data. Many of the computations which are necessary and which have to be recorded are not required in the final balance-sheets, and are merely used in interim stages of the calculations; such data need never be transcribed from the magnetic tape on to paper, but it is important to stress the fact that any data which is subsequently required in printed form by the accountant could be transcribed direct from the tape to paper.

Perhaps we may conclude our preliminary analysis of the problems by saying that these machines will in future have a great influence on business computations. Furthermore, the overall problem is much more difficult than might appear at first sight. It is obvious that the machine will be part of the total system, and that specially fast input/output mechanisms will be needed, in addition to an auxiliary memory of much greater capacity than anything which has been so far proposed. It would furthermore be of great advantage if some at least of the documents with which the machine will be concerned could be written in such a form that the machine could interpret them directly without the necessity of a preliminary transcription, for example, on to punched cards. It appears, however, that all these problems are capable of solution and that, in the fullness of time, machines for commercial purposes will be produced which will have a material influence on the course of events.

We may perhaps speculate for one moment on the kind of thing which they may do. We may be guided to some extent by the comparable effect of the introduction of high-speed automatic machine tools. There was originally a widespread fear that unemployment might result from their introduction but, in the event, after a temporary dislocation of industry, there is a very much greater total of production than before, and the standard of living of all persons engaged in the industry has very much increased. Similarly, it is probably safe to forecast that the effect of introducing automatic business machinery of this type will be not so much a reduction in the total number of white-collar workers as an increase in the amount and quality of the work which they do and a resultant improvement in the understanding, on the part of the executives who control the business, and perhaps of the Government departments which are responsible for controlling the economic destinies of the country, of the very complex mechanism, on the efficient working of which the economic future of the country as a whole will ultimately depend.

DISCUSSION CONTRIBUTIONS

Mr. J. A. Stafford

I have in the past had contact with Dr. Bowden about the help which a machine of this kind may conceivably give to an office such as mine. If our problems are to be intelligible, I should indicate quite briefly the kind of troubles we face.

Not all of you may have filled in a Census of Production form. The forms ask for information under a wide variety of economic headings, e.g., sales of a number of different products—perhaps as many as 500 or 600 from a particular industry, though no one firm would require so great a number—the purchase of materials, stocks of materials, stocks of finished products, wages paid, employment by sex and age, capital expenditure incurred during the financial year, analysis of sales according to the channels through which the sales are effected, etc. On any particular form from a large concern, you have a great deal of information.

When an establishment has sent in its return, we face the problem of ascertaining whether it is reasonable, i.e., whether to accept it as being a true record, or whether to go back to the firm for some kind of explanation. Experience in the 1948 census has shown it very necessary to examine them all. We do have a lot of imperfect returns—something like 25% of all the

returns sent by large establishments employing over 10 persons have to be queried to the firm. The 1948 census was the first full postwar census, and firms may have been unaware of the kind of thing expected of them. Before the war, the percentage of imperfect returns was much less.

We have to check the information supplied—one important feature being to check the internal consistency: that output of a unit of sales is reasonable in relation to materials used, or that the value of a unit of sales is reasonable in relation to returns by similar firms: that total output of the establishment is reasonable in relation to the wages bill or number employed: so that you can compute, say, for a large schedule, some hundreds of ratios which will help you to judge whether it is a satisfactory return or not. In addition, you can refer back to the return of previous years and see that it flows reasonably.

There are a certain number of key criteria against which you can judge the accuracy of the return. At the moment we have to compute these criteria. When we get in some of the schedules, we compute the average value returned for specified provinces. After that, all the schedules coming in are examined against these criteria. Every schedule goes through a computing room so that the ratios can be computed, and officers examine the individual schedule against the criteria. This is a laborious job, and not always an accurate one.

This machine offers a gleam of hope that this process can be done more efficiently and more certainly. As we feed the information in from one establishment, we could ask the machine to answer 'Yes' or 'No' to our questions. If the answers do not correspond, I have no doubt that it could throw the schedule out, and we could examine it for further action. The advantages of this process would depend upon the proportion of defective returns.

One of our problems is to feed the information in to our present machines. We put everything on to punched cards. If you do this before the accuracy of the document is examined, a lot of work will be done for nothing if you have a high proportion of defective returns. We should like to see a machine which would sort out the sheep from the goats. I would like to put in a plea for a cheap and efficient method of feeding information into the machine: will Dr. Bowden please look into that?

The other problem we have is getting information out. We get our information from the tabulator, then have to prepare fair copies so that the final result can be examined, and a fair copy is sent to the printer. As well as a good deal of necessary delay under the present system in examining schedules, time also disappears as we surmount various kinds of obstacles: getting the man to send in the return, getting sufficient returns to create the criteria, examining against them the rest of the returns, then the actual tabulation (which doesn't take as much time as you would think). If we could reduce tabulating time to 10% of what it is at present, this would not make a tremendous difference in the time taken to get out results.

Another point is that we have to be sure, when we publish a report on a trade, that we are not disclosing information about an individual firm. Any one figure must relate to more than one establishment. At the moment this again is a time-consuming process and perhaps the machine could be of some help. We should not have extravagant hopes that the cutting down of the actual computing and tabulating time would result in tremendous speeding-up in our process. This machine offers the most considerable help to us on examination. The machine, as at present designed, is really much cleverer than it needs to be for our purpose, and a more simple model would do our job.

Mr. R. L. Michaelson

The application of electronic computers, exemplified by this University machine, to commercial and industrial organisations is a very wide subject. There is no time to be deep so all I propose to do is to throw out a few random but I trust, not idle, thoughts.

The most important consideration in commercial applications is reliability. If the discovery of the next largest prime number is delayed a week because of machine trouble it is not catastrophic. However if the machine is due to produce a payroll on Friday after-noon a delay until Tuesday might be cataclysmic in a striking manner. Reliability is due to be discussed this afternoon, I mention it now only to emphasise its importance.

There are two dangers which underlie the present stage of development of these computers, one springs from the Manufacturers and the other from the potential users.

Take a representative of the Manufacturers who last week sold a machine to a University and is now calling on the President of a large industrial organisation. In time he is passed to a Vice-President who passes him to an Executive Officer. Eventually he reaches someone who knows how the business is run.

She says that they would like to mechanise the production of invoices. After studying a few specimen invoices the representative is confident and returns to the President and says 'Our machine can do your invoices, for the calculation required is the formation of the product of price and quantity vectors and our machines can multiply vectors. Nor does it matter that the scales of notation are denary, binary, and duodenary.' This danger, then, is over simplification and concentration on computing to the exclusion of practical matters such as printing names and addresses and creating the actuating medium such as tape or card.

The other danger is the inverse of the above and is due to the potential user considering his work too difficult for the machine. The range of items or thought processes which can be coded into rules a machine can understand is much wider than is generally believed. As examples of progressively more complicated rules consider what is required if you wish to make a private telegraphic code. It is not surprising that the Manchester Computer can take care of the following rules:

1. Each group shall comprise 5 letters.

2. A single letter corruption in one group shall not produce another meaningful group.

Suppose now you stipulate for ease of communication that each group of 5 letters shall give a pronounceable word. Our first reaction is that this is not mathematics and the computer can't do it. The truth is that the computer could be readily programmed to observe this rule.

Suppose now we say that none of our 5-letter pronounceable words shall sound like a rude word. This I believe is beyond the capabilities of the general purpose machine in this University.

My trivial example is intended to show that more is translatable into a language the machine can understand than is usually thought, but nevertheless human beings can still and will continue to use their brains to do things a machine can't.

10.3

The Computation of Fourier Syntheses with a Digital Electronic Calculating Machine

J. M. Bennett and J. C. Kendrew

From Manchester University, *Manchester University Computer. Inaugural Conference* [Bolton: Tillotson's, 1951], pp. 35–37.

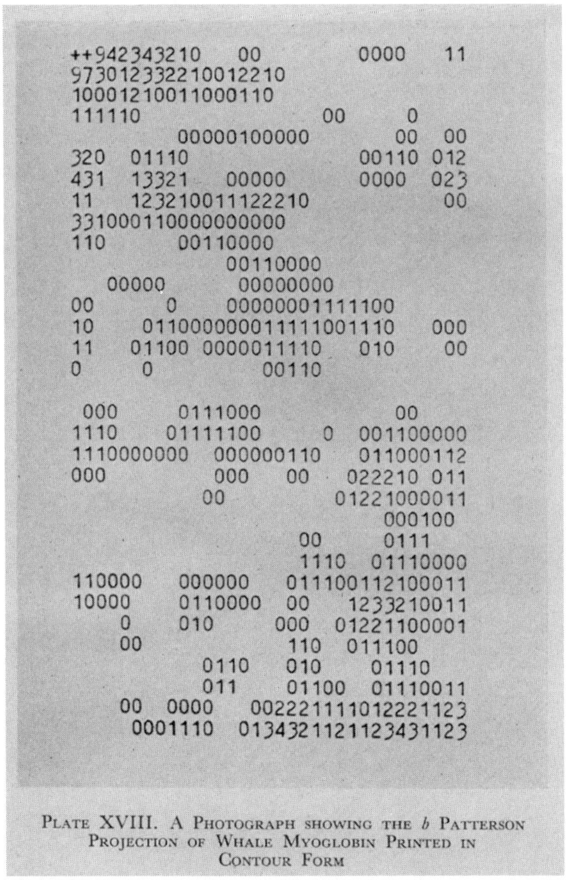

PLATE XVIII. A PHOTOGRAPH SHOWING THE *b* PATTERSON PROJECTION OF WHALE MYOGLOBIN PRINTED IN CONTOUR FORM

Patterson projection of whale myoglobin produced on the EDSAC, from B. V. Bowden's *Faster than Thought* (1953).

INTRODUCTORY NOTE TO READING 10.3

At the second English electronic computer conference at Manchester in July 1951 J. M. Bennett and John Kendrew presented the first report on the application of an electronic digital computer to computational biology, foreshadowing the interdependence that would evolve between electronic computing and molecular biology.

Bennett and Kendrew wrote the first programs for computing Patterson and Fourier syntheses in two and three dimensions with the EDSAC—essential for Kendrew's solution of the molecular structure of the protein myoglobin. This was the first protein for which the structure was solved.

Without electronic computing, solution of the structures of proteins would have been impossible. Andrew D. Booth described the extent of the problem as it existed during the 1940s:

> the production of electron density maps for structure analysis involves very heavy calculations on large quantities of numerical data, and the state of the art during the early 1940s was such that the limits of human ability in this area were reached at structures containing not more than about 10 crystallographically distinct atoms. The determination of a 10-atom-type structure involved, in the early 1940s, about six weeks of experimental work

followed by anything up to three years of hand computation for a group of human "slaves" and, even during wartime, I was trying to design equipment to mechanize parts of the crystallographic process.[1]

Using the EDSAC, a two-dimensional summation of about 400 independent terms for about 2000 points took $1^{1}/_{2}$ hours of processing; a three-dimensional summation of 2000 terms for 18,000 points took 9 hours. This processing time, while absurdly slow compared to current processing, must be compared to the years that might have been required if the calculations had to be done by hand. It is fair to say that the structure of proteins and their interaction would never have been solved without electronic computing, since individual protein molecules may contain as many as 10,000 distinct atoms, and there are estimated to be about 100,000 distinct proteins in the human body.

For his solution of the molecular structure of myoglobin, Kendrew shared the 1962 Nobel Prize in chemistry with Max Perutz, who received his share of the prize for his introduction of the heavy atom method, and for his solution of the more complex structure of hemoglobin at 5.5Å. This was the same year that Watson and Crick received the Nobel Prize for the discovery of the structure of DNA. J. C. Bennett, Kendrew's collaborator in this pioneering computing application, had been on the staff of the Cambridge Computing Laboratory that designed and built the EDSAC before becoming an employee of the British computer firm Ferranti. [JMN]

---

1   Andrew D. Booth, Computers in the University of London, 1945-1962. In Metropolis *et al.*, eds., *A History of Computing in the Twentieth Century* (Orlando, Fla.: Academic Press, 1980), 551.

TEXT OF READING 10.3

The basic task of the crystallographer is to determine the structure of molecules, organic and inorganic, from photographic patterns which result when regular arrangements of these molecules, i.e., crystals, are irradiated with X-rays. He may be given by the chemist several possible structures for a substance, and asked to choose from among them the one which will give the X-ray photographic pattern met with in experiment—or alternatively, from a single crystal of a substance, he may be asked to deduce the structure of the molecules composing it, with little advance information other than a very general idea of some of the atomic groupings.

The geometrical form of a crystal is the consequence of the regular arrangement of the molecules of which it is built up; the regularity is that of a three-dimensional pattern which is repeated over and over again in space. It has been recognised for many years that the geometry of such space patterns, together with the observed facts of crystal form and symmetry, could give much information about the internal structure of the molecules of which the crystal is built up; but it was not until the development of X-ray crystallography that it became possible to obtain information which could lead to the determination of the actual arrangement of the molecular units. Following the work of Von Laue and the classic analyses of crystal structure by W. L. Bragg, this approach has now become standard, although unfortunately it does not supply quite as much information as we would wish.

If a crystal is irradiated correctly with a parallel beam of X-rays, the intensity of diffracted radiation will vary in a regular manner as a function of the cosines (which we shall call h, k and l) of angles θ, Φ, Ψ: the axes chosen are related to the regular form of the crystal structure. If then, we expose a photographic plate to this diffracted radiation, the intensity of exposure will also be a function of h, k and l—and it is these intensities which are measured. The crystallographer must now unravel from these measurements the desired information about the units of which his crystal is built.

The sort of computation which is involved is generally a triple or double Fourier summation of the form

$$h = h_{max}, k = k_{max}, l = l_{max}$$

$$\Sigma \Phi(h, k, l) \cos 2\pi \left(\frac{hx}{a} + \frac{ky}{b} + \frac{lz}{c} \right)$$

$$h = k = l = 0$$

where h, k and l are the direction cosines mentioned above; the $\Phi(h, k, l)$ are functions of the intensities measured for each value of h, k and l; and a, b, c are known constants, which depend on the crystal we are measuring.

We shall first give an outline of the programme required for a single one-dimensional Fourier synthesis. The example chosen[1] is the summation of

$$\sum_{o}^{h_{max}} F_h \cos 2\pi \frac{hx}{a}$$

at equal intervals (x/a) basic from $x = o$ to $x = a$.

We shall suppose that the $(h_{max} + 1)$ values of F_h are contained in storage positions m, $(m + 1)$, ... $(m + h_{max})$. Consider the situation at some point during the synthesis when the variables have the values h, x. We arrange to retain in convenient storage locations three 'counters' which will contain at this point

a. x/a

b. hx/a

c. $-(h_{max} + 1) + h$

Then the next instructions given to the machine are the following:

1. Take the current value of hx/a from (b) and find $\cos 2\pi hx/a$.

2. Find F_h by means of an order which selects the contents of storage positions $(m + h)$.

3. Multiply F_h by $\cos 2\pi hx/a$ and add the results to a running total kept somewhere in the store.

4. Add (a) to (b), i.e., add x/a to hx/a, giving $(h + 1) x/a$, and place in (b) instead of hx/a.

5. Change the order at (c) so that in the next cycle of operations it selects storage position $(m + h + 1)$ thus finding F_{h+1}.

6. Increase (c) by unity, so that it becomes $-(h_{max} + 1) + h + 1$. Test the sign of this number—if it is still negative, return to (1) and repeat the cycle. If it is zero (as it will be after the $(h_{max} + 1)$th cycle), the summation has been completed; in this case proceed to (7).

7. Print out running total.

8. Reset (b) to zero and (c) to $-(h_{max} + 1)$. Set the order at (2) to select storage position m. Clear running total (set to zero).

9. Add (x/a) basic to (a). Test (a)—if still < 1, return to (1) and repeat cycles. If (a) = 1, the programme is finished.

An actual routine designed to carry out this programme on the E.D.S.A.C. will consist of about 100 orders. In addition the store must contain a short routine to take the F_h's from teleprinter tape and place them in a suitable form into positions m, $(m + 1) \ldots \ldots$.; and also a print routine which takes the sums, converts them into decimal notation, and prints out the result with sign to the desired number of significant figures. These routines need about 25 and 50 orders respectively.

One important matter which we have not yet discussed is the method of calculating $\cos 2\pi\, hx/a$. Three main methods are available, and were tried on the E.D.S.A.C.

1. Each term of the type $\left.\begin{array}{c}\cos\\\sin\end{array}\right\} 2\pi \dfrac{hx}{a}$ was obtained as required from the previous

   term $\left.\begin{array}{c}\cos\\\sin\end{array}\right\} 2\pi \dfrac{(h-1)x}{a}$ by means of the

standard addition formulae for

$$\left.\begin{array}{c}\cos\\\sin\end{array}\right\} (a + b) . \left.\begin{array}{c}\cos\\\sin\end{array}\right\} 2\pi \dfrac{x}{a} \text{ must be known,}$$

and can be obtained in each outer (x) cycle by the same formulae (from the previous value, and $\left.\begin{array}{c}\cos\\\sin\end{array}\right\} 2\pi \dfrac{x}{a}$ basic).

2. By means of a short sub-routine introduced at the beginning of the programme a table of values of $\cos 2\pi x/a$ from 0° to 90° was prepared and stored, the intervals chosen being those normally used in crystallography, i.e. $(90/15)°$ or $(90/30)°$. This method has the disadvantage that these intervals do not readily fit in with techniques using binary-scale counters—in fact, two separate counters are required, one taking account of the quadrant, and the other, of the position of the angle in the quadrant. The necessity for re-writing these counters is avoided in the method described in (3).

3. A similar sub-routine was used to compute a table of cosines from 0° to 90°, but this time at intervals of $(90/2^m)°$, where m is an integer (in our programmes the value $m = 5$ was chosen; i.e., $2^m = 32$, giving 33 entries in the table). In this case, the hx/a counter merely records the number of basic intervals (of $(90/32)°$); then the ordinal number of the position in the table at which the required cosine is to be found ($=hx/a$ mod 32) can be obtained from the five least significant digits, and the quadrant from the next two. For example, if $hx/a = 36$ ($= 36 \times 90/32)°$ ($=90° + 4/32. 90°$) the counter will contain 36 in binary form, viz 0100100; the five least significant digits are 00100, giving 4 for

the position in the table; and the next two are 01, i.e., 0100000, which on right shift gives 0000001, or 1; this is interpreted as meaning the second quadrant (00 represents the first quadrant). In the first quadrant the table position is used direct; in the second it is subtracted from 33 and the value obtained from this position in the table is given a minus sign $(\cos (90 + \theta) = -\cos (90 - \theta))$. Cosines in other quadrants, and sines, can be found by minor modifications of the basic procedure.

As an example of the relative speeds of the three methods, a two-dimensional Patterson synthesis for which $(h_{max} + 1) (k_{max} + 1) = 176$ was computed at the following rates:

Calculation of cosines by method (1) 15 secs per (x, y) value.

Calculation of cosines by method (2) 12 secs per (x, y) value.

Calculation of cosines by method (3) 10.5 secs per (x, y) value.

Method (1) is more economical of storage space than (2) and (3) since in the latter a table of cosine values must be stored throughout the programme. Part of this space may be recovered since, once the table has been prepared, the sub-routines introduced for the purpose of computing it may be removed, and the space occupied by it used for other purposes (e.g., the print sub-routine). The routine which reads the F_h's from the tape and stores them away may be similarly over-written once all the F_h's have been taken in.

A change in the arrangement of the calculation to one which is equivalent to that described by Lipson and Beevers, resulted in a further reduction in the time taken per (x, y) value to 2.5 seconds, in the example cited above.

Normally the detailed results will be printed out by the machine, but for many purposes it is unnecessary to know accurately the values of the function at every point in the final summation; all that is required is to draw approximate contours of electron or vector density in positive regions. It was suggested to us by Mr. R. A. Brooker that the E.D.S.A.C. could be made to print out the results in contour form directly, to the required degree of accuracy. It was arranged that:

a. For every negative value of the function the machine prints a space.

b. For every positive value between 0 and 31 the number 0 is printed.

c. 1 is printed for values $32 - 63$, 2 for $64 - 95$, etc., up to 9 for values $288 - 319$.

d. '+' is printed for values exceeding 319.

Contours may rapidly be drawn in at intervals of 32. Moreover, the programme is so arranged that, by changing two parameters, contours at any other interval 2^m (where m is a positive integer) may be printed.

If we use this simple scheme the accuracy with which contours can be drawn is less than in the conventional method of plotting the actual values of the function on a grid. However, greater accuracy may be obtained by printing at closer intervals, making use of letters in addition to the digits $0 - 9$.

At the present stage, it does not seem possible to assess the relative values for crystallographic purposes of general purpose digital machines, and of special purpose analogue machines (see, for example, Pepinsky, 1947; Pepinsky and Sayre, 1948), though it would appear that some crystallographic problems may be more economically tackled by the one and some by the other type. Digital machines have the great advantages of accuracy (which is becoming increasingly important in crystallography), and of versatility, which enables the capital cost and running expenses of a general purpose digital machine to be shared among a number of users with very different problems to solve.

REFERENCES

Beevers, C. A. and Lipson, H., 1936. *Proc. Phys. Soc.* 48. 772.

Pepinsky, R., 1947. *J. App. Phys.* 18. 601.

Pepinsky, R. and Sayre, D., 1948. *Nature.* Lond. 162. 22.

Gill, S., Wheeler, D. J. and Wilkes, M. V., 1951. The preparation of programmes for an electronic digital computer, with special reference to the EDSAC and the use of a library of sub-routines. Addison-Wesley Press Inc., Cambridge, Mass. 1951.

• • •

1. F is used throughout as the coefficient of a Fourier term irrespective of whether it represents the amplitude or the intensity of an X-ray reflection.

Electronic Business Machines: A New Tool for Management

Richard W. Appel et al.

From *Electronic Business Machines: A New Tool for Management . . . A report submitted to Professor Georges F. Doriot in partial fulfillment of the requirements for the second-year course in Manufacturing at the Harvard Graduate School of Business Administration* (Boston, June 1953), pp. 7–59.

Television news anchorman Walter Cronkite (center), Itha Doorhammer, and UNIVAC operator Harold Sweeny in one of the tamer of the out-take photographs taken during CBS television's use of UNIVAC I to predict the outcome of the 1952 Presidential election. This was the first time that millions of people learned about an electronic digital computer.

INTRODUCTORY NOTE TO READING 10.4:

This was a very early independent report written by people outside the computer industry on the application of electronic computers to business needs. It may be the first published report on this topic in the United States. When this report was published, no electronic computer had been delivered to an American corporation. The first UNIVAC I delivered to a private rather than governmental customer was serial number 8, sold to General Electric in 1954. In England the Leo I adaptation of EDSAC had been operational at J. Lyons and Company since November 1951.

The first large general-purpose computers such as ENIAC and EDVAC were originally developed for scientific and engineering applications, and this report discusses the necessity of modifying both computers and business procedures to take advantage of the great computing power and speed offered by the new machines. Chapter VI, titled "Business Machines in 1970," attempts to predict the future evolution of business machines "as they relate to manufacturing companies, department stores, insurance companies, banks and public utilities" (p. 37). Written by a group of seven Harvard Business School students, about whom I have found no information, the report was prepared "in partial fulfillment of the requirements for the second-year course in Manufacturing at the Harvard Graduate School of Business Administration." [JMN]

SEC. 2.   THE COMPONENT PARTS OF UNIVAC

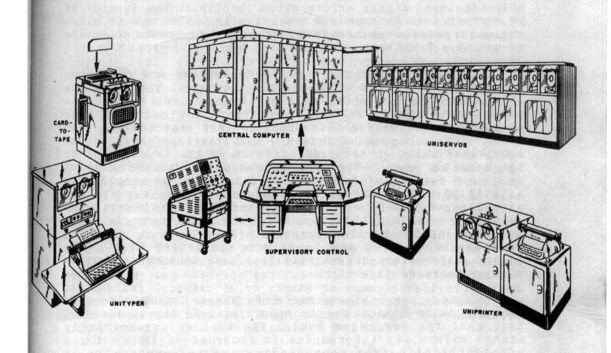

The name "UNIVAC" refers to an assemblage of equipment which includes a computing unit and several auxiliary devices to provide a communication train between the computer and the human inquirer. Information is represented in the central computer by a train of electrical or acoustic pulses. Three auxiliary devices, UNITYPER, UNISERVOs, and UNIPRINTER are used to translate information between the printed page and the computer's language medium.

The component parts of the UNIVAC I system, from the
first revised version of its programming manual 1953).

Superb photograph of the UNIVAC I system. The
mercury delay lines are visible as circular devices in the
open door of the central computer unit in the background.
From Arthur D. Little's *The Electronic Data Processing
Industry* (1956).

CHAPTER III: REQUIREMENTS OF ELECTRONIC BUSINESS MACHINES

Business Problems

The need for electronic business machines arises from a desire for more profitable operation through greater efficiency. The machine improves the efficiency of business operation if it performs its tasks with less expense than required by clerical personnel and/or if it handles and organizes data more accurately and more rapidly than can clerical personnel. Rapid and accurate handling of data aids business in efficiently handling its resources of cash, goods, and plant and equipment.

Substitution for Clerical Personnel: If we look at the problems of a durable goods manufacturer—problems of sales prediction, purchasing, scheduling, inventory control, and accounting—it is clear that a great amount of manual effort is required to obtain in readable and usable form information necessary for conducting the business. Needs for even more clerical personnel or a reasonable substitute that can perform the same functions will be even greater in the future if present trends continue. In 1951 there were 7,800,000 clerical workers employed in the United States as compared to only 4,500,000 in 1940, or an increase of over 70%.[1] A good portion of this increase is undoubtedly attributable to the growing complexity of business operations, the demands of management for more effective means of judging performance, and increasing demands for reports and records by government agencies. In addition, the increased interest of unions in organizing clerical and office workers can eventually result in higher cost for this type of personnel. Electronic business machines will certainly fill a need of business if they provide a lower cost substitute for clerical personnel.

Increased Efficiency of Operation: Perhaps the greatest potential saving to result from electronic business machines will be brought about by more efficient operation of business enterprises. The intelligent application of electronic business machines will provide more information more rapidly than was previously obtainable. For example, through immediate and continuous control of inventory, a retail store could reduce its investment in inventory and increase its sales by having fewer items out of stock. One person acquainted with department store operation estimated that a store could increase its sales volume 10% and decrease inventories 10% by properly applying an electronic business machine to its inventory control.

Need for Reliability: While providing more information to improve the operating efficiency of a company, the electronic business machine must have one quality that is of utmost importance—reliability. The business machine must be technically capable of performing with a high degree of accuracy and reliability. Although a computation in the research laboratory may be held up a few days without significant consequences, a computation in the business field, such as a payroll preparation, must be accurately completed within the time limit. For example, a company that customarily pays its employees on Friday cannot afford to inform them that their checks will not be forthcoming until the following Tuesday, without serious repercussions. In developing more rapid output mechanisms, the problem of reliability becomes of major significance. A single machine which can print at a phenomenal rate makes the company extremely vulnerable in the event of a breakdown, for output would cease completely. Thus it seems that, rather than having a single complex printing device, a more practical alternative would be to utilize a battery of smaller output devices like electric typewriters, one of which could fail without serious consequences.

Needs Created by the Machines: Although electronic computers are expected to help meet many present and future needs of business they are likely to create some needs of their own. These needs will primarily be for personnel for the maintenance and operating of the machines.

The more complicated are the problems that the computer is designed to solve, the more complicated is the machine. This is especially true for scientific applications. As the use of these machines becomes more widespread, it is foreseen that a mounting difficulty will be encountered in training enough people to effectively maintain and operate the machines. Electronic business computers, on the other hand, need not be as complex, but still will require trained personnel for effective maintenance.

Summary: In business there is a great need for quicker processing of a greater volume of information. Because of increasing clerical costs and for greater efficiency and other savings, this increased speed and magnitude of operation should be obtained with a minimum of personnel. Electronic business machines offer a means of meeting these needs.

Design Requirements

The term "electronic business machines" includes a large number of devices doing a great number of types of work. Speaking generally, there are two typical kinds of business machines; the first is primarily a calculator and the second is primarily a memory. Large as well as small installations of each kind may be made.

The electronic business machine that is primarily a calculator is a problem solving machine. It is meant to solve problems like those found in production scheduling, sales forecasting, and engineering design applications. The mathematical and engineering computers built to date have been this kind. (See Exhibit 1.) They typically need only a small memory

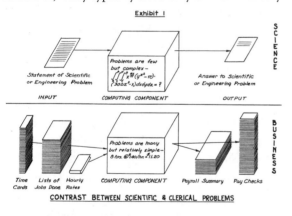

Exhibit 1

CONTRAST BETWEEN SCIENTIFIC & CLERICAL PROBLEMS

and only a relatively small input and output capacity. The take in and put out relatively little data but do a large amount of computation with the data; therefore the problem-solving business machine needs a great arithmetic capacity. Generally the problems will be one of a kind, or at least the same problem will not be given to the computer very often. Therefore the prob-

lem of programming (determining and making available to the computer a detailed and exact step-by-step procedure for solving the problem) is a big job, requiring the services of very highly trained and skilled technicians and mathematicians. Control in the business problem computer is most important; the control must be able to draw upon a fair-sized, fast memory for instructions and some data.

The calculating business machine is usually quite expensive. UNIVAC, a general-purpose machine, attempts to be both a computing and a memory machine and has been estimated to cost upward of $700,000, complete. (Estimates from several sources disagreed somewhat, but all were in excess of $700,000.) The large scientific computers built at various universities and for the government have cost over a million dollars each.

The business machine that is primarily a memory has very wide possible applications. A machine of this type can store detailed inventory records, insurance office records, and accounts receivable and payable. Machines of this type may have small arithmetic capacity for making some calculations for sales and costs, for example, but this is only a small part of the machine. Most of its large memory must be accessible in a random manner but need not be very fast; only a relatively small part of the internal memory need be extremely fast. For some applications the input, usually directly through a keyboard type input, should be of fairly high capacity. The control component of the memory business machine is relatively simple.

The size and cost of the memory business machine may vary widely. While there may be some installations whose costs may go as high as several million dollars, a great number of installations may be made whose cost would be less than $100,000 at the present, still high, prices.

Summary: Since the application of computers to office procedures often requires a substantially different balance of components than is found in the problem-solving business machines, machines developed for these purposes are not readily applicable to most business situations. It has been estimated that the need for large computing machines would constitute about 10% of the potential business machine market, whereas small mechanical desk machines, which might be used in smaller businesses or to perform some functions in large operations, would comprise about 20% of the market.[2] The remaining 70% of the market waits for the machines to be designed to meet the individual needs of companies or types of operations.

CHAPTER IV: ELECTRONIC BUSINESS MACHINE CHARACTERISTICS

Before attempting to discuss the development of computer components and how they may be adapted to business uses, it is well to know something of the basic characteristics of electronic computers and how they operate. This chapter discusses some of these basic characteristics. In doing so the chapter contrasts the electronic business machine with the human brain and illustrates computer operation with a description of UNIVAC, an existing business computer.

Functions

These are the basic functions, common to all electronic digital computers, including business machines: information enters the machine and is transformed so that it can be acted upon; the machine remembers previous instructions and information which it uses to act upon the information it has just received; the machine initiates and carries out action in accordance with instructions it has previously stored which apply to the situation at hand; it grinds out the answers—does the actual arithmetic; it usually knows when it has made a mistake and so will give no wrong answers; and it will divulge answers or store them.

Analog v. Digital Computers

Large-scale computers are divided into two categories, analog and digital. An analog computer deals with physical quantities such as voltages, lengths, or angles. The digital computer, on the other hand, uses pure numbers and is not tied to physical processes. The large-scale analog computer shows its promise principally in the control of physical operations (such as the control of chemical plants and machine tools) and in the computation of some types of mathematical and engineering problems. Because business uses pure numbers rather than physical quantities, it is the digital computer which is well suited for business applications.

Switching

Switching is the important characteristic which distinguishes electronic computers from desk calculators. The desk calculator, once it has come up with an answer, must divulge it immediately, and in a set manner. The electronic business machine can switch numbers (which represent instructions, partial solutions, information, or final answers) from one part of the machine to another; from one arithmetic or control unit to another, between the arithmetic and control units and storage, or between the storage and the input or output equipment.

Binary Numbers

Computers tend naturally to deal in terms of two stable states, yes or no, on or off, zero or one. Examples of elements which display this are: the relay, which is either actuated or not; magnetic material, which is either magnetized in one direction or the other; paper tape or cards, which is either punched or not; and flip-flop circuits.

A flip-flop circuit is basically represented by two electron tubes. If the one tube is on, the other is off and vice versa. Thus the circuit has only two states, both of them stable. That is, the circuit will not change of its own accord, but will change only when a pulse enters from outside the circuit.

The characteristic of having two states is typical of computers in many ways. This is why the binary system of numbers, which is also two-valued, is so well adapted to computers. It is one of the basic characteristics of most large-scale computers that they employ the binary system of digits instead of the decimal system. Binary refers to a system having a base of two, while decimal refers to a system having a base of ten. In the binary system the largest digit is one (the other digit being zero), while in the decimal system the largest digit is 9 (the other digits being zero through 8).

In the decimal system, when the digits in one column add up to more than 9 we know we must carry over to the next column to the left because 9 is the largest digit in the decimal system. Similarly, in the binary system, when the digits add up to more than one in a given column, the machine must carry over to the next column because one is the largest digit in the binary system. Here are the numbers written in the two systems:

Decimal Number	Equivalent Binary Number
0	0
1	1
2	10
3	11
4	100
5	101
6	110
7	111
8	1000
9	1001
10	1010
11	1011
100	1100100
101	1100101

The value of a binary number may be determined by reading from right to left; a one in the first position has a value of one (2^0), a one in the next position has a value of two (2^1); a one in the next position has a value of four (2^2) or twice that of the preceding position. Writing numbers in the binary system takes more than three times as many digits as in the decimal system.

Machines could be built with a decimal base instead of a binary base but they would not be as efficient. Ten positions which are only on or off can represent only the numbers from zero through 9 in the decimal system whereas ten such positions can represent from zero through 1023 in the binary system.

Nearly twice as much information can be stored using the same circuits by using the binary system. It is not necessary for the clerk to know anything about the binary system in order to operate a business machine; the clerk will put in decimal numbers and the machine will do its own conversion.

Measures of Capacity

It is natural for businessmen to want to have some idea of the capacity of a machine, if only to compare it with other machines. One measure of capacity which has been proposed for computing machines is storage capacity times speed. This is analogous to the power of a motor (another measure of capacity) which equals torque times speed. However, there are other significant factors, such as speed in itself, capacity in itself, the maximum length of a number that can be used, and reliability.

Unfortunately, none of these factors, singly or collectively, will adequately serve to measure all electronic business machines. This is true simply because each application of a business machine has different requirements. We have seen that there are two basic types of business machines, problem-solving and information-storage; each individual application will also have its own requirements for speed, storage, and types of input and output.

Comparison with the Human Brain

Large-scale electronic computers are frequently referred to as "giant brains." This description is appropriate in that they share with humans the ability to do arithmetic (although the computer is much faster), and are similar in their facility for communication and recollection and in their facility for perceiving external circumstances and acting accordingly when so instructed. We may well begin to wonder how far computers can go. Can they actually "think"?

Similarities of Communication: There are obvious similarities of communication in that information is absorbed and remembered by both human and electronic brains, the information processing is at least partially controlled by both kinds of brains themselves, and, finally, the information is given out. However, there are other similarities of communication which are not so obvious. Humans show some similarity to machines both in communication between people and in the human nervous system.

Communication between individuals is one of the most distinguishing characteristics of man, in view of the extent that man's achievements are tied up with his language. Because of the very high speed at which the machine works, it too needs systems of communication between its components. What makes computers seem superior to man (aside from their greater speed at arithmetic) is that as the size of the human work group is increased the inefficiency of communication becomes so great that some problems of high complexity become impossible; those working on a problem would have to spend all their time telling each other what they were doing and would have no time to actually make progress in solving the problem itself. Computers, with their much higher speed and efficiency of communication between components, offer the solution to such problems.

Computers also have some similarity to the nervous system used by humans for internal communication. One of the basic principles underlying computer design is the on-off principle. Another corollary principle is that of switching; depending on the magnitude of a certain quantity which controls a switch, the switch will be either "on" or "off." Both of these principles are strikingly similar to the principles of the human nervous system. A nerve will carry a certain impulse or not, depending on whether or not the impulse is above a certain threshold. And, if the impulse is sufficiently strong to be carried by the nerve, it proceeds through a complicated series of switching devices.

Actions Based on External Perception: Human beings can see and hear and regulate their actions according to the external conditions they perceive. Although the business computer does not do this at present, it might in the future if so instructed. For example, a future office computer might be tied in with shipping and packaging and might have to know how full a package was in order to determine whether to continue filling it or not. In other words, it would

be receiving external conditions as a human does when he sees and hears.

What Can't Computers Do? Although we have mentioned some extraordinary ways in which computers can compete with humans, computers cannot do the following: (1) think intuitively or originally, (2) determine all their own instructions, (3) perceive and absorb information without explicit instructions. In these respects, in fact, the machine is inferior to the lower animals. Take, for example, a housecat. (1) He can jump to conclusions about the intentions of a nearby dog without ever having been told to steer clear of this particular dog—he can make up his own mind this is a wise course. (2) He can come up with an original plan of action, such as "Proceed behind the hedge until coming to the tree, then reappraise the situation." (3) He can notice things about the dog that he never has been taught to notice. In other words, in comparison, the computers do an unimaginative, mechanical, black-and-white sort of reasoning.

If human beings are ever inclined to feel inferior to business machines, they shouldn't. Business machines are not brains but merely reflect the intelligence of the men who built them. The machines will do what man has told them to do and nothing more. For a computer to have the capacity of even a very low grade human brain, it would have to be larger than Rockefeller Center, would require all of the power generated at Niagara Falls to run it, and all the water of Niagara to cool it.

Electronic business machines are no substitute for humans in most respects. The business machine can do only a very few tasks; these tasks it does very well. The electronic computer is a specialist, and to a very high degree; it is destined to do menial tasks.

UNIVAC: A Large-Scale Business Computer

To get a picture of an electronic business machine and its components, we will examine the UNIVAC, developed by Remington-Rand.[3] The UNIVAC system is a system with a high-speed electronic computer using mercury-delay-line and magnetic-tape storage.

One of the important differences between UNIVAC and the desk calculator is the difference in speed of operation. The desk calculator goes slowly enough so that the operator can exercise continuous judgment; it might do 400 multiplications during an eight-hour working day. UNIVAC, on the other hand, can do a multiplication in less than .0025 second. If it were allowed to do nothing but multiply, it could do more than 12,000,000 multiplications in an eight-hour day. At such a speed, the machine must control its own operation, for it goes too fast for continuous human supervision. Input and output of information are also major problems at such speeds.

The large-scale computer also differs greatly from the desk calculator in that it is a very complicated electronic device. The Mark I computer of Ferranti, Ltd., has 2,500 condensers, 15,000 resistors, 100,000 soldered joints, and 6 miles of wire. To house this, a large-scale computer must be big. UNIVAC, for example, would require a space 25 feet by 50 feet, 10 feet high, for a typical installation.

We will now discuss the basic components of UNIVAC: Input, Output, Memory, Control, and the Arithmetic element. (Exhibit 2 shows the relationship of the components of a typical electronic business machine.)

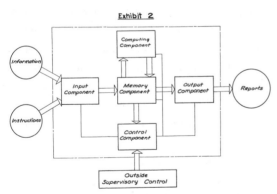

Exhibit 2

COMPONENTS OF THE ELECTRONIC BUSINESS MACHINE

Input and Output: The input of information to UNIVAC is accomplished primarily through a keyboard, much like a typewriter keyboard, which impresses magnetic charges on a tape. The keyboard, being restricted by the human being which operates it, feeds information to the tape slowly. Once the information is on the tape, the tape can feed the information into the computer at very high speeds.

Information, as used in this sense, includes both raw data and instructions to the machine. In addition to introducing information through the keyboard, another method of input is the card-to-tape converter which transfers information on punched cards to the magnetic tape.

Output is accomplished in a manner somewhat the reverse of input. A device puts the answers which the computer has delivered on a magnetic tape, the tape running at 100 inches per second. Since the information must be in printed form to be useful, the information is taken off the magnetic tape at a comparatively slow speed and printed by an electric typewriter. While typing 10 characters per second, the printing device is a great deal slower in printing information than the computer element is in delivering it. For this reason, the output of information, like the input uses magnetic tape as an intermediate medium.

Memory: The magnetic tape serves as one kind of memory—an external kind. A 1,500 foot roll of magnetic tape will store 1,400,000 characters (a character requires 6 binary digits). However, this is not enough to fill all the computer's needs for memory. It must have certain information at its fingertips; certain data and instructions must be held for immediate access. The magnetic tape provides information in a sequence which is fixed by the order in which it was originally put on the tape. This other kind of memory, the internal memory, must provide random access to all information it contains. This internal memory, UNIVAC's mercury-delay-line storage, has a much smaller capacity, holding 1,000 groups of 12 characters each.

Control: Just as in manual computation where the operator controls the steps to be performed, so does UNIVAC's control element take instructions from storage, examine them and send pulses at the proper times to the various parts of the computer to perform the necessary processes. The control instructs the memory to select a certain storage register and read in or read out either numbers or instructions. It instructs the input to start, read, and stop, and instructs the output to start, record, and stop. It instructs the arithmetic element to clear registers, to add, subtract, multiply, divide, and compare.

Arithmetic Element: The arithmetic element is the element that actually does the computing. One might say that it listens through the input element, is under the jurisdiction of the control, speaks through the output, and uses the memory to hold information. It is amazingly rapid. Addition or subtraction is done in less than 600 microseconds (a microsecond is millionth of a second). Division, comparatively a much longer process, takes 4,000 microseconds.

Reliability: The UNIVAC system is not infallible; therefore it checks itself to find any error. One check is accomplished by testing every transfer of information from the memories on an odd-even basis. If the sum of a group of digits is supposed to be odd and turns out even, the machine indicates the error and stops. Another check is accomplished by doing the same arithmetic operations simultaneously on two different circuits and comparing the results. If they do not agree, the machine stops. These checks virtually eliminate the possibility of undetected errors being made and make the UNIVAC system very reliable.

Summary: This chapter has been devoted to aiding the reader to better understand the basic characteristics of electronic computers or business machines. An existing large-scale business computer, UNIVAC, was explained to give the reader a picture of how such machines operate, and computer operation was contrasted with the functioning of the human brain.

CHAPTER V: ELECTRONIC BUSINESS MACHINE COMPONENTS: PRESENT AND FUTURE

This chapter will discuss the five basic components of the electronic business machine, considering both the devices presently available and those which will probably become available in the future. Aspects of performance, suitability, and cost will be considered. In addition, a section of the chapter will be devoted to the topic of reliability of the electronic business machine.

Input

The fundamental function of input devices is to change data which comes from human beings in a slow, irregular manner into data which can be fed into the computing unit at high speeds when the information is completely assembled. An input system is simply a storage system so arranged that recording can be actuated by the external element, human or otherwise, and reading can be actuated by the computer. This storage element is a necessity, at least at present, because of the need of the computer for complete, high-speed information.

A problem faced by input devices is the inevitable errors that humans are liable to make before putting the data into the machine. To avoid these, input data should be used in its original form as much as possible and the closer future developments in input devices come to putting original data in the machine, the greater will be the reduction of errors from this source.

The most important methods of input are next described.

Punched Cards and Punched Tape: A form of input that can take advantage of presently installed equipment in many offices is the card-to-tape converter, which converts the information on punched cards into a tape, which can then be fed into the computing element. The original input device, if card-to-tape converters are used, is the card punch, a device that usually involves fairly substantial manual labor. This sort of input has a serious inherent drawback: the machine which reads the cards is limited inherently in the speed which it can separate the cards for reading. Improvements along this line are not expected to be important.

Perforated paper tape is another form of input that is fairly well developed at present. It can be handled and stored easily and can be discarded without much waste of money. The fact that it cannot be punched at a high rate of speed may not be a handicap, since a human being usually punches the tape through a special typewriter. Being made of paper, such tape is subject to wear. However, checks against inaccuracy are made, and when a tape is worn out another can be made from a previously prepared master. The reliability of tape-punching devices is quite high; Western Union has been using them for some time.

The speed of perforation is inherently limited by the inertia of the mechanical devices that produce the holes. Although electric arcs have been used to perforate the tape (which would eliminate the problem of inertia), they do not seem too promising because of difficulty in controlling them.

Punched tape can be read by two means: electrical devices such as those presently used for IBM cards and photo-electric devices. The top speed expected from the IBM type of device is about 100 digits per column per second; photo-electric sensing, on the other hand, has been used by the British to attain a speed of 5,000 digits per column per second.

So far only punched cards and punched tape have been discussed. But, there is another widely used and promising medium—magnetic tape.

Magnetic Tape: Information is recorded on magnetic tape by moving it past a recording head which impresses one of two magnetic states on it. Later, when the tape is read, it is moved past a reading head. Since a binary system is used, the reading device need only distinguish between one of two states. This tape consists of powdered magnetic iron oxide (magnetite) which is either dispersed uniformly through plastic tape or used as a coating for paper tape.

Although magnetic tape is a method of input and output, it is also a method of permanent external storage. For example, information can be removed from the machine and filed or shipped on the tape.

One of the biggest problems to be faced with magnetic tape is reliability. Remington Rand's UNIVAC has an extra channel in which information is recorded to give an odd-even check; it will indicate an error if there should be an odd number and there is an even one instead.

It is worth while to compare magnetic tapes with punched tapes since these two are the commonest kinds of input devices. Of the two, punched tape has probably been developed further, but magnetic tape is faster. Although photoelectric sensing of punched tape has been done at a speed of 5,000 binary digits per column per second, magnetic tapes have been read at 10,000 digits per column per second. The fact that humans handle the tape gives punched tape an advantage in that it is more rugged than magnetic tape.

Although the foregoing analysis might favor punched tape, the decision is certainly not clear-cut. The makers of UNIVAC use magnetic tape both for input and output. Magnetic tape probably will see increased use in the future.

Other Forms of Input: There are certain other interesting forms of specialized input which have not been discussed so far, such as analog-to-digital converters. These will be important in the automatic control of chemical plants and machine tools. Also, in the future, when (and if) accounting data is given to large-scale computers from outside the accounting department, other devices may become important. For example, data could be given to a machine from pressure gauges and thermocouples scattered throughout the plant. Finally, it is conceivable that sometime in the far future spoken commands and information may be given to the machine, as well as printed information.

In summary, magnetic tapes seem to hold the greatest promise for use in the future as an input medium. Punched tapes will also be used and punched cards will be used to a slight extent. Other methods of input, such as direct introduction through a keyboard are possible but are much slower.

Output

The function of output devices is the reverse of input devices; that is, output devices take information which the computer element has delivered suddenly and at a great rate and record it so that it can be read by human beings at much slower speeds in a convenient form. This definition excludes output which is used to control processes, such as air traffic at an airport or processes in a chemical plant, where instant physical action is taken by the machine.

Output raises the issue of human errors, as does input; there is no point in having a very expensive machine produce results if they are copied with errors and provide false information. In designing a computer, it is usually desirable to have it reduce the output data as far as possible to the final form to avoid such errors and to save the labor of the comparatively slow human. This raises the question of just how good are output devices. In an attempt to answer this, various devices will be discussed. First, some of the basic characteristics of output devices will be mentioned.

Basic Characteristics: With output devices, speed is generally considered to be one of the most important characteristics. For, although input devices are frequently limited by the speed at which a human can put information onto the tape, the faster an output printer works the better. However, speed itself is not as important as the ratio of speed to cost. The example was mentioned of the possible use of a battery of electric typewriters to make up for the inherent lack of speed of a single typewriter and to provide greater reliability. Although speed is very important and cost is also important, other factors must be considered. Unfortunately, no single output device presently available or probably available in the near future seems to be outstandingly qualified on the basis of the ratio of speed to cost.

Reliability and its corollary, the cost of maintenance, are very important and will be discussed later in this chapter. Permanence of the output medium may also be important. If the output medium (e.g., a magnetic tape) is going to be reused repeatedly, its lack of permanence may be notable. Another characteristic worthy of mention is adaptability to intermittent use. Some output devices must run continuously, and consequently the arithmetic element, when not putting forth information, will cause stretches of the output medium to be blank, wasting much time of the printing device when it takes information from the medium.

Output printing devices include the electric typewriter, the matrix printer, the multibar printer, the rotating wheel printer, and others.

The Electric Typewriter: Electric typewriters can be operated from tapes at a speed up to 20 characters per second. That this comparatively slow speed can be overcome by using a number of typewriters has been mentioned. The problem this raises, of how to coordinate the typewriters, must be given consideration. Is the recorded tape to be cut into sections and spread around among several typewriters? Can the printed results be recombined in the correct sequence? The answers to these questions depend on the particular application involved. But, whatever disfavor they may reflect on electric typewriters may be counterbalanced by the ease of maintenance and reliability of this means of printing. Such typewriters are receiving commercial distribution, as they are also used for writing form letters from a punched tape. They are presently available in a well-developed form and cost around $500.

The Multibar Printer: The multibar printer is already well known to users of IBM equipment, for it is used to print numbers on desk calculators and IBM tapes. The printers on IBM machines operate at a speed of 200 digits per second (still much slower than the computer element). There are several inherent disadvantages to this method. Time is required to accelerate and decelerate the type; this problem would be much greater if letters were printed as well as numbers. Another inherent disadvantage is that there must be an element which remembers the incoming information long enough for a complete line of information to be gathered.

The Rotating Wheel Printer: The rotating wheel printer consists of a constantly rotating wheel (or wheels) in place of the type bars of the multibar printer. This kind of printer can print up to 15 lines of information a second, each line having 80 characters. Since two printers have been used satisfactorily together, greater speed from each printer is not so important. The characters created by this method are equivalent in appearance to those of a typewriter.

This device has the advantage of not having to accelerate and decelerate the type (as is necessary with the multibar printer) but is limited by the acceleration of the hammers which strike the rotating wheel through the paper and by the feeding of the paper. This sort of output device still has the disadvantage of requiring a unit to remember all the characters to be printed in a line until the last character of the line has been received. It is estimated that a printer of this type would cost around $25,000.

The Matrix Printer: One example of a very fast output device is the Kodak Printer, officially called the Eastman Kodak Multiple-Stylus Electronic Printer. It can be operated from punched cards, magnetic tape, or any other storage medium which might be used in connection with a computer. It forms characters by printing little squares. These squares combine to form the character as do the light bulbs in some theatre marquees. A rectangle is divided into 35 little squares, these forming the matrix. Each of these little squares is blackened or not, depending on the character being printed, as the paper passes under the styli. Actual printing is accomplished by the styli striking a carbon which strikes the paper. The carbon impressions are then fixed by heat, so they will not easily rub off. Either thin paper or thick cards can be printed.

The machine can print paper at a rate of 50 inches per second. That is, in one hour of operation, nearly 3 miles of tape will be used. This printing speed is equivalent to 300 to 400 characters per second, up to 20 times the maximum speed of an automatic typewriter. Six hundred magazine labels with 4 lines each can be printed in one minute.

The disadvantages of the matrix printer are its substantial cost (about $100,000) as well as the inherent need for some kind of memory to hold information until it can be printed. Because of its high cost this device does not appear to have much promise for use as an output of information from business machines.

Other Output Printing Devices: Photographic output is a rapid means of output which, however, has the disadvantage of recording its results on a rather inconvenient medium (photographic film). This is accomplished by having a cathode-ray tube (similar to the picture tube on a television set) register the output information. The information is then recorded by photographing the face of the tube. If the time required for the data to flash on the picture tube is short in comparison with the time required for the film to travel the width of the tube, then the film can move continuously without causing serious blurring. This eliminates the difficulties arising from accelerating and decelerating the film. By this method, using 50 parallel channels, 500,000 numbers per second can be recorded. These must be read either by enlarging them or by scanning them photoelectrically; however, they cannot be read directly.

Although photographic recording of output is fast, it is inconvenient and will have little or no use in business applications.

Comparative Speeds: For the sake of comparison, the following speeds are listed:

Device	Speed per Second (Maximum Attained)
Electric Typewriters	20 characters
Multibar Printers	200 decimal digits
Rotating Wheel	1,200 characters
Matrix Printer	400 characters
Photographic Output	500,000 decimal digits
Photoelectric Sensing	5,000 decimal digits/column

Summary: At present, electric typewriters and rotating wheel printers seem to be the most promising output devices. Although one typewriter or rotating wheel printer may be too slow, a number of such devices may be used simultaneously if output is first recorded on magnetic tape.

Arithmetic Element

The arithmetic element of the business machine performs the actual arithmetic operations of adding, subtracting, multiplying, and dividing. It receives and holds the numbers to be used, performs the operation required, and holds the answer until the operation is complete, when it dispatches it to the output or storage. The basic parts of the arithmetic element are flip-flop circuits. This element is quite well developed and is the fastest component of the business machine. It is capable of fulfilling all the foreseeable demand that future business needs may put on it. Transistors probably will be used to a great extent in the future, their simpler circuits replacing the more complicated vacuum tube circuits. (Transistors are discussed further under Reliability.)

Control

The control component provides the overall intelligence required to direct the computer. It is not a physical unit by itself, but is a combination of circuits, switches, and memory units positioned throughout the machine. The control component directs each operation of the machine. These directions and instructions may be introduced in the input or stored in a rapid access memory or both. For most business machines, almost all these instructions would be stored in the internal memory, only a few elementary instructions (such as telling the machine to print out something or to record a sale or a receipt of goods) would be put through the input. These elementary instructions would cause certain sets of stored instructions to be used by the control component. In these business machines the programming would be built in. By keeping the possible external instructions to a minimum the need for many high paid technicians would be eliminated and low-paid clerks could operate such a business machine; also, the possibility for error would substantially be lessened.

Problem-solving business machines require trained mathematicians to program each problem before it is given to the machine; these people are not necessary for the memory business machine.

Storage

The fact that computers can remember information is often quite startling to the businessman. Actually, there is nothing mysterious about it. Just as paper stores information expressed in a relatively complex form as writing marks and just as punched cards store information in a relatively simple form as punched or unpunched holes, so do business machine storage devices store information in relatively simple forms. The memory or storage device is simply a piece of equipment into which information can be introduced and from which the same information can be extracted at a later time.

In the scientific and engineering problem-solving computers now in use, the storage usually costs about one-quarter of the total cost of the computer. In computers built for business purposes for control and accounting, the memory will be a very much greater part of the whole; the heart of the business machine is in the storage of information.

In this section we will mention a few of the criteria which influence the choice of a storage, describe briefly the types of storage presently being used, and discuss the direction which developments will take in the next 20 years.

Speaking generally, the criteria used in comparing memory devices are the cost, reliability, and size of the medium and its associated equipment, the ease with which information may be switched to and from the other components of the machine, and the speed and ease with which a particular piece of information may be selected. Each business machine has its own requirements for storage and usually requires more than one kind of a storage device to fulfill these different storage requirements.

There are two general types of storage devices, internal and external. Internal storage is the retention of data within the computer. In a business machine, as in a scientific computer, there are three types of data to be stored internally: tables of data and general information, instructions, and partial results. Generally, the greatest part of the internal storage will be the storage of tables of data and general information such as inventory and sales figures, insurance policy holders' names and other data, accounts receivable and payable, purchases, and specifications. This type of stored information does not need to be reached extremely quickly; it does need to be reliable, cheap, erasable, and preferably nonvolatile. Retention of instructions and partial results require a memory which can reach the data much more rapidly. However, in the business machine, used primarily for retention of information rather than computation of problems, this "fast" memory will be a relatively small part of the whole internal memory.

In addition to the information stored within the business machine, considerable information may be stored in external storage. The punched card is a well-known example of this type of storage.

Magnetic Drum Storage: This storage is characterized by large capacity, moderate cost, and long access time. Magnetic drum storage gives random access to information; that is, upon direction, the memory unit will go directly to any piece of information. Magnetic drums are a non-volatile form of static storage and so retain their memory throughout a period of power loss. At the present time, it appears that magnetic drums offer the most reliable form of internal memory.

This device is a drum whose surface is coated with a magnetic material. (See Exhibit 3.) The drum is

Exhibit 3

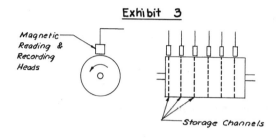

MAGNETIC DRUM STORAGE (SIMPLIFIED)

mounted on its axis and rotates at speeds of 2,000 to 8,000 RPM. Information is stored on channels around the drum in spots, the magnetic polarity of which stores the information. The density is high: more than 1,000 digits may be stored per square inch of surface. The recording and reading of information on these spots is done by heads, one for each channel along the length of the drum. When a particular piece of information is desired the correct reading-recording head must wait until the correct spot rotates to the head. The time required to reach the information is called the access time. For magnetic drums, the average access time is generally of the magnitude of 10,000 to 20,000 microseconds (millionths of a second). Compared with electrostatic tubes, for example, whose access time is around 10 microseconds, this is very slow; however, for the great bulk of the storage needs of a business machine this speed of access is more than adequate. The total storage of a drum may be of the order of several million binary digits. In general, higher capacities are obtained by increasing the size of the drum and reducing its speed, which also increases the access time.

To give an idea of the general size and specifications of magnetic drums, here is an example of one of the larger ones considered: The drum would be 34 inches in diameter and 33 inches long, would have an average access time of 32,000 microseconds, would have 1,240 tubes, and would store almost 2 million binary digits.

Of the internal memory devices developed so far, magnetic drum storage is the least expensive, the cost being about 10¢ per binary digit, including circuitry. The bulk of the cost is in the control and associated circuitry. The drum itself does not wear out, since there is no contact between the reading head and the drum. This storage is erasable and unaffected by temperature, humidity, or small amounts of dust. Magnetic drums have been developed and used successfully; and from a production viewpoint, about all that must be done before drums are widely available is the freezing of specifications and tooling. There are no unknowns which require development work.

Mercury Delay Lines: The mercury delay line storage device was one of the first storage devices to be well developed. However, the cost of a mercury delay line is about $1.50 per digit stored, including circuitry. It is fairly compact: about 20,000 binary digits per cubic foot. This storage is volatile. While mercury delay lines have proved successful in the past, it does not seem likely that they will be widely used in business machines, mainly because of their higher cost.

Electrostatic Tubes: Electrostatic tube storage has been developed but holds little promise for business machines of the future because of its high cost. Though fairly expensive, it is quite effective. Its access time is fast, about 10 microseconds, and the tubes are used for the temporary retention of results and instructions.

The tube itself is about 2 feet long and 8 inches in diameter and holds 1024 binary digits in the form of charged spots on a plate at one end of the tube. The control and auxiliary equipment required is greater than that required for mercury delay lines and the tubes do wear out. The cost per binary digit, including circuitry, runs around $5. Electrostatic tube storage is volatile; if the power to the tubes should be turned off for more than about 20 seconds there is likely to be loss of information. In addition, the tube life is only a year or so.

Magnetic Cores: Magnetic core storage is the most promising of the newer storage systems under consideration. The magnetic core is a tiny donut with an outside diameter of about 3/32″. Each core holds one binary digit; information is determined by the magnetic polarity of the core. The cores are arranged in a grid, each core being around the intersection of two wires. Current is passed through two of the wires going through the cores so that only one core, the one at the intersection of the two wires, is in a magnetic field strong enough to change the polarity of the core; this core is the one that has been selected for reading or recording. (See Exhibit 4.)

Exhibit 4

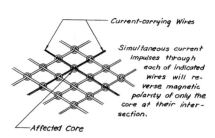

Current-carrying Wires

Simultaneous current impulses through each of indicated wires will reverse magnetic polarity of only the core at their intersection.

Affected Core

PORTION OF A MAGNETIC CORE STORAGE DEVICE

Magnetic cores are compact; probably around 75,000 could be stored per cubic foot in a three-dimensional array. Magnetic cores do not deteriorate or wear. They offer a non-volatile, erasable form of storage. The access time to information stores in magnetic cores is very rapid, on the order of 5 microseconds; this is most satisfactory for retention of instructions and partial results. Magnetic cores are inherently more costly than magnetic drum storage. At present, it costs about 40¢ to make, test, and install a single core. We can expect that this price will decrease to around 5¢ per core in about five years, according to several persons connected with computer development. These prices do not include the cost of the circuitry and control which is said to be about 50¢ per digit. Magnetic cores are still far from being perfected; much development work is being done. When the difficulties are overcome, magnetic core storage is likely to displace electrostatic storage; the former will be able to handle high speed internal storage better and more cheaply.

Several other methods have been used successfully for internal storage, but have no promise for the future because of high cost and high space requirements. The simple flip-flop circuit used in the computing element and circuits using mechanical relays are examples.

External Storage: Magnetic and paper tapes and punched cards have been used for external storage. Magnetic tape storage has performed successfully; it is cheap and reliable. Its main disadvantage is that the information is stored in a sequential order; in order to get at data in a roll of tape it is necessary to go through the whole roll. In other words, switching of information from the tape memory to the other components of the business machine is a slow and difficult process. In order to make a change in a tape memory, it is usually necessary to re-record the whole tape. Magnetic tape costs less than one mil per foot and stores more than 5,000 binary digits per foot—very compact storage. Magnetic tape is also erasable and non-volatile.

Paper tape is also quite cheap and up to now has been used more than has magnetic tape. It is slower than magnetic tape. It is also non-erasable, but this is not very important because paper tape is inexpensive.

Most of the storage requirements for business machines call for random access to the stored information. Tape storage does not provide this so its value lies primarily as temporary storage for input and output mechanisms and for some external storage for the business machine.

Punched cards have been used for storage of information for years. The cards are cheap, about 0.4 cents per card, and hold 1,000 digits per card. Cards have an advantage in that it is easy to read the card visually and it is easy to change a single card once that card has been found. However, access to data on cards is relatively slow and the cards are bulky compared to magnetic tape.

Because the computer can read and record on magnetic tape very rapidly, this type of external storage will probably be of greater significance in the future than punched tapes and punched cards.

Looking to the future, the great need is for cheaper random access memories. The memory unit is a most important part of the business machine in terms of cost; if the installed cost per binary digit could be reduced by a factor of 10 the effect on the introduction of business machines would be marked, since the cost of the memory is a large portion of the total cost of most electronic business machines.

Much work has been done with various types of storage devices. Of the ones considered, at least 14 have been used in computers. While we can hope for a new, cheap, reliable random access storage, the probability of finding a new method does not appear great. Most of the work seems directed toward improving the devices now available. Magnetic cores still need much development work but seem very promising. Magnetic drums are most promising for the storage of information and will probably be the future automatic file. Greatly increasing the number of binary digits stored per square inch on a drum without a proportional increase in the number of vacuum tubes and the circuitry required would be a great stride toward the general use of business machines. This seems to be the direction that research is taking. In addition, quantity production of magnetic drums, like quantity production of magnetic cores, will bring down the cost per binary digit.

In summary, very satisfactory memory devices have been produced. Work in the next 15 years will be aimed at reducing the cost of internal storage.

Reliability

Accuracy and reliability are absolutely essential in an electronic business machine. Even a single unchecked error, caused by a single faulty tube or other element, may throw off control or a calculation completely. For a memory machine to lose part of its memory would be like destroying the inventory records of a company. For a business machine to break down when working against a deadline as, for example, when computing payrolls, would be disastrous. It is believed that this need for reliability has been successfully met through the accuracy which has been built into the components of business machines.

Electron Tubes: Computer tubes and other elements do wear out and fail. To find and remove these failing elements before they result in an error improves the accuracy of the business machine. To know immedi-

ately when and where an error has been made improves the reliability of the machine. Although preventive maintenance testing of tubes before installation has proved economically feasible, it is still very difficult to test new equipment effectively anywhere but in the business machine. Therefore the machines are built to check themselves. The memory usually checks itself through an odd-even check, and the arithmetic element has parallel circuits which perform the operation simultaneously and compare the results. Should the results be different the machine may stop or try the operation over again. Another method of checking the machine is to give it a problem, the answer for which is known.

Statistics show that the weakest link in a high speed automatic computing system is invariably the vacuum tube. The malfunctioning or failure of these electron tubes reduces safety margins considerably, and replacement of tubes is a large item in the overall cost of the operation of a computer. Many of the errors made by tubes show up as random or intermittent errors, a type which is particularly hard to trace down. Tube failures have been found to occur most often in the first 1,000 hours of tube life, and life ranges of tubes have been found to be on the order of 6,000 to 12,000 hours, depending on the type and the use to which the tube is put.

Transistors: A most promising new development which may circumvent some of the problems of the vacuum tube is the point contact transistor. A transistor is a semiconductor power amplifier of small size. In many electronic business machine circuits a single transistor may replace two vacuum tubes and a lot of connecting circuitry.

Essentially, the transistor is a speck of germanium (an uncommon metallic element) with three hair-like wires making contact with it. The cover or container is the largest part of the assembly, but the whole is only about the size of an eraser on the tip of a pencil. Transistors are promising because they are rugged, resistant to mechanical shock, much smaller, and last much longer than do vacuum tubes. Because the oldest transistors have only been in use about four years and improvements have been made continually, it is difficult to say what the life expectancy of a transistor will be. It does appear, however, that the average life will be at least 70,000 hours (eight years). This long life will greatly simplify the maintenance problem of business machines.

Another advantage of transistors over vacuum tubes is that they generate considerably less heat. The vacuum tube works on the principle of heating the cathode hot enough to boil off electrons. This causes the computer installation to be made very large to provide ample space for air to circulate and cool the tubes. Thus, circuits utilizing transistors cannot only be made much smaller because the circuits themselves are much smaller than the circuits utilizing vacuum tubes, but also because they can be made much more compact since there is less heat to be dissipated. Nevertheless, temperature control is still of some importance since the physical mechanism by which transistors work makes them unable to operate at temperatures much higher than 160 degrees F. A further advantage of transistors is that they do not need any warm-up time.

Transistors have been found especially useful in business machines in the switching circuits. Circuits using transistors probably never will completely replace those using vacuum tubes, but each will be used to its own best advantage.

Because the transistor is still a relatively new device, both in theory and in practice, prices are high relative to vacuum tubes, quality control is not yet good but is getting better, and there still is a great deal to be learned about the characteristics and best uses of transistors. At present the cost of transistors varies widely around $10 each. As greater knowledge is attained, greater volume is produced, and more germanium is obtained, this price may be cut by a factor of 10. The transistor promises to be a very reliable and valuable new element.

In summary, the present accuracy of computers is quite satisfactory for almost all business uses; it is only for a use such as air traffic control, where absolute and instantaneous accuracy is required, that the present reliability is not yet good enough. The business machine is designed so that it knows when it has made a mistake by providing built-in checks and comparisons. Although satisfactory, reliability can and will be improved, decreasing the importance of the maintenance problem.

Summary

This chapter has discussed the technical aspects of large-scale electronic business machines in order to get a better idea of what these components are and what they can do now and in the future.

Punched and magnetic tapes seem to be the most promising forms of input. Speed of input to the tape was not considered too important, since the information can be fed into the machine very rapidly.

The most promising kinds of printers for output seemed to be electric typewriters (20 characters per second) and rotating wheel printers (1,200 characters per second). Although output is frequently regarded as a bottleneck, the problem can be solved satisfactorily by using a transfer medium such as magnetic tape in conjunction with several printers in parallel.

The arithmetic and control elements are quite capable of doing the work required of them, although the initial programming and design of the control element requires a combined knowledge of business and computers.

Very satisfactory memory devices have been developed. Consequently, most of the research and development work in this area in the next 15 years is expected to be devoted to cost reduction and the better application of known devices and principles. Cost reduction will be aided considerably by quantity production as well as by development work.

The present-day reliability of business machines for almost all uses is satisfactory. Maintenance is still somewhat of a problem, but with greater experience and newer, longer lasting elements, this problem will be solved.

CHAPTER VI: BUSINESS MACHINES IN 1970

In an attempt to interest businessmen in electronic computers, many articles and books have been written which give the impression that the completely automatic office will be here in the immediate future.

Many of these writings have probably been the result of over-enthusiastic extrapolations of computer applications to the fields of science and engineering. Such future thinking is good in that it tends to stimulate a demand for many of the devices suggested (which otherwise probably would be unknown to the businessman). However, oversimplification of the problems of developing electronic business machines has one bad effect; because some businessmen feel the electronic age in the office is so close they tend either to ask too much of existing electronic office equipment or to refuse to use existing equipment, fearing that it will be made obsolete very shortly by revolutionary developments.

In presenting our conception of electronic business machines in 1970 we wish to point out that, in our opinion, these machines of the future will come about only as the result of gradual evolution—changes will not be of an immediate and revolutionary nature.

By considering some present applications of electronic computers and making reasonable extensions of these applications we have attempted to arrive at a picture of electronic business machines 15 to 20 years hence. These future applications will be discussed as they relate to manufacturing companies, department stores, insurance companies, banks, and public utilities. These categories were thought to be reasonably representative of the possible future applications of electronic business machines.

Manufacturing Companies

A field for many and varied future applications of electronic business machines is that of manufacturing. The oil refining and other process flow industries may well have need for a large-scale electronic digital computer to exercise control over their automatized operations within the next 5 or 10 years; however, the time when discrete unit manufacturing plants will be completely controlled by electronic computing equipment appears to be quite far in the future (perhaps 60 to 70 years).[4] Thus electronic aids to management in fields of market analysis, sales prediction, production control, inventory control, and accounting probably will be independent units, each to be utilized at the discretion of management, rather than one business machine unit which would perform all of the above functions. It must be remembered that whether or not to use an electronic business machine is dependent on circumstances surrounding the particular application.

Market Analysis: The management of a manufacturing company contemplating a new item for their line would be interested in an analysis of the market for their new product. This is a field to which electronic business machines could be effectively applied. An examination of the way in which the United States Department of Commerce, Bureau of the Census, utilized Remington Rand's UNIVAC computer to help produce the second series population tables in 1950 indicates how this type of machine could be used to handle the data involved in market research. This series contains thirty types of tables covering the age, sex, race, location of birth, occupation, education, employment, and income of our population by counties and also for every city, rural farm, and rural nonfarm area within counties. Information obtained by the census taker from each individual was transferred to a punched card. These cards in turn were transcribed onto magnetic tapes which were fed into the computer. Instructions, previously stored in the computer, acted upon the data to arrange it in the order and grouping desired. This process eliminated the handling and sorting of 11,000,000 punched cards and resulted in much greater speed and efficiency in getting results.[5] The storage of this information in a memory unit makes it possible to obtain large numbers of breakdowns, cross-classifications and tabulations of large quantities of random data.

The use of a large-scale computer to process data of this type into meaningful tables with significant savings in time, as demonstrated in the census proceedings, indicates the possible use of computers in the field of market research for a company. Answers to a standard series of questions asked of many prospective customers could be transcribed to magnetic tapes from the original questionnaires.

Instructions previously stored in the computer's memory unit would then proceed to cross-classify and tabulate the reactions of prospective customers, as determined by the interviews, to a new product or possible changes in an old product. Continuing current statistics of this type would allow the management to keep abreast of the consumer demand for the company products.

Companies specializing in market research and opinion polls could, through the use of large-scale computers, perform their services more quickly and at a lower cost and by so doing enable small manufacturers to use this service and to obtain information which would be of help in planning sales and advertising programs more effectively. Already one of the largest market research firms has made application for one of Remington-Rand's large-scale computers as soon as they are available. An electronic business machine for this application would have both a large memory and considerable calculating capacity.

Sales Prediction: Soon after the product goes on the market, the company would be interested in interpreting and analyzing sales trends. The possibility of utilizing computers in this way is suggested by the use of UNIVAC to predict final results of the recent national election as the returns came in. The success of this application had far-reaching effects upon the minds of businessmen, leading them to wonder if the possibility of predicting sales volume on the basis of historical trends was really feasible.

With regard to the election, the procedure and the results are very interesting, for these same procedures can be applied to the everyday business situation. Preparations for UNIVAC's one-night stand were extensive. The Columbia Broadcasting System, which used the UNIVAC, operated on the theory that the election returns from the 1944 and 1948 election, broken down to represent the hour-by-hour and district by district status of the popular vote, would provide a sufficient trend against which the 1952 votes could be compared. This information was fed into the memory unit of the giant computer through the use of magnetic tapes. In addition, other significant data and trends from former elections was stored on the memory drums. As the votes rolled in to CBS in New York City, they were teletyped to Philadelphia and fed into the computer. All the stored data was then drawn upon and the resulting information translated into the

popular margin of victory, the probable electoral votes by states, and odds on the outcome. This task was done at lightning speed giving almost instantaneous comparisons with the past two presidential elections.

The final answers and the effect upon the operators of the UNIVAC are interesting and significant. The computer foresaw the final results long before anything like a definite trend was seen by the experts. On the basis of 3,400,000 returns, the machine predicted an overwhelming Eisenhower victory. It gave Eisenhower 438 electoral votes and Stevenson 93 votes. The actual figures were 442 to 89 respectively.

The effect of the speed and accuracy on the operators of UNIVAC is somewhat typical of sudden developments of this sort. The statisticians refused to believe what the prediction said. There seemed to be an inherent distrust in the machine. As Lowell Thomas said: ". . . UNIVAC was correct, meaning that the calculation of the probabilities was mathematical, cold-blooded, while human beings like ourselves were distracted by various emotional factors, caution, recollection, which is how forecasters have gone wrong in the past." This distrust is understandable for this was the first time that such an instrument was used for this purpose—and there were a myriad of electronic and mechanical parts that could have failed. In an attempt to rule out any faulty information fed into the computer's memory unit, the operators decreased the amount of historical information to be used in making calculations from then on but the same end product, an Eisenhower victory, again resulted.[6]

The ability of the computer, as evidenced by the election results, to make use of historical data and current findings and come up with an accurate prediction, could seemingly be applied to the business situation. Past sales data compiled from the experience of related products could be fed into the memory unit. In addition such variables as weather, the economic trend, style factors, competitors' actions and seasonal fluctuations could also be introduced. After the new product had been put on the market, the incoming sales results, having been broken down to a basis comparable with the stored information, would be fed into the computer and the resulting information plotted or tabulated in some usable fashion. This information would then be available as a basis for production scheduling, inventory control, sales promotion and other management functions.

Inventory and Production Control: This leads us to a consideration of the problems of inventory and production. If we consider the case of a company selling a variety of items from stocks of finished goods, several problems immediately arise. The first of these is need for always having sufficient finished items of the proper type on hand to satisfy customer needs without tying up excessive amounts of capital in inventories or risking losses caused by obsolescence. Second, there is the problem of scheduling production in a manner which will best utilize the equipment available, including a method of following up and controlling production in case actual production differs from that scheduled. Maintaining adequate levels of raw materials and work-in-process to meet production needs is also a large problem as is that of standardizing on various items to be carried in inventory and used in the company's products.

(*Standardization of Inventory*): Before a company can consider setting inventory levels it should be decided what items are to be carried. Standardization of inventories is especially important when a number of different sizes of a particular item are to be carried in raw material or work-in-process inventory. For example, the initial design for an item to be produced in a factory may specify 1/2″ long copper rivets in five different diameters, and designs for other items produced in the factory may specify this same length in even other diameters. In the initial designs, which were probably calculated on the basis of strength requirements, were followed, perhaps copper rivets 1/2″ in length would be stocked in a dozen diameters, each differing from each other by 1/32″. On the other hand, considerable savings might be realized if design and stock departments of the company were to decide upon a series of say four standard sizes of copper rivets 1/2″ long which would be specified in designs and carried in stock. Some cost savings could be realized from ordering a larger quantity of rivets in fewer sizes and also through the reduction of total inventory requirements of 1/2″ length copper rivets.

Such standardization of inventory items in complicated situations could be carried out by the electronic computer. The different sizes of the item in question specified in the initial design, the numbers required, the cost and possible quantity discounts could be entered into the computer. By considering the advantages of using a minimum of sizes (with possible quantity discounts and lower inventory levels) vs. the cost saving to be made by using an item just adequate for the purpose (and not purchasing excess strength or capacity), the computer would be able to indicate the optimum distribution of sizes of particular items which should be stocked by the company. Such information could then be transmitted to the design department to be incorporated in all existing and future designs.

(*Establishing Inventory Levels*): Once raw material and work-in-process inventory items have been standardized and finished goods inventory items have been established, the company must then determine how much of each item to stock. Maximum and minimum inventory levels are often established for this purpose; an attempt generally is made to have sufficient stocks to meet needs but, at the same time, to keep the capital invested at a minimum.

A great number of factors affect the inventory levels to be set. Most of these factors apply to finished goods as well as raw material inventories. They are as follows:

1. Average and peak rates of consumption by use or sales.

2. The time required to replenish the supply plus a safety factor to take into account reasonable delays.

3. The amount of cash available for investment in inventories and the cost of tying up that cash or obtaining additional cash.

4. Discounts available when purchasing raw materials in large quantities or even lots.

5. The storage capacity available and cost of additional storage.

6. Risk that the item stocked will become obsolete.

7. Possible government controls on amounts and prices.

8. Possible wastage or spoilage resulting from extended storage.

In cases where speculative buying predominates, various factors of the market have effect in addition to the items mentioned above.

With eight or more factors affecting inventory maximums and minimums, it can be seen that a large job of multiple correlation exists. For the human mind to take each of the factors into account in their proper relationship is difficult, indeed. However, with proper computer programming techniques, the result or series of results of the optimum combinations of many factors can be determined.

Another point in favor of eventually applying the electronic computer to this type of work is the possibility that many of the above-mentioned factors may vary with time. A minimum inventory level that is suitable at one time may be unsuitable at another. One company that established maximum and minimum stock levels years ago just has not had the time nor the manpower to keep the stock levels up-to-date. This, we feel, is typical of many manufacturing concerns. If the establishing of inventory levels were reduced to application of computer programs, the levels could be revised easily and frequently. A computer suitable for this application would need considerable calculating capacity to consider the many factors involved.

(*Maintaining Inventory Levels*): Once maximum and minimum inventory levels are established, they can be used effectively only if an accurate check is kept on actual inventory levels to see how they compare to the maximum and minimum levels. A large capacity memory unit of an electronic computer would be well suited to this type of operation. Limited applications of this type have already been made but a major drawback seems to be the lack of a memory capacity large enough for all applications.

One segment of a computer's memory unit, say a large magnetic drum storage unit, could be used to keep the actual count of items on hand, while another segment of the memory could record minimum (and possibly maximum) levels desired. These maximum and minimum levels would have been obtained as described in the previous section. Small keyboards at inventory control points could be used to give the computer information on stock additions or withdrawals. Since the computer is capable of comparing two numbers, determining which is greater, and taking action, an automatic inventory check could be made periodically as often as desirable with the actual balances in inventory accounts being compared to the established minimum levels. A number of procedures might be followed when an inventory level has been detected to be below minimum. As computer and programming techniques progress, the point may be reached where upon detecting a below minimum inventory level, the computer would call upon another segment of its memory to determine how many of the items should be re-ordered and then automatically prepare and transmit either a raw, material or production order to the proper source.

The first steps in developing computers and memory units for the handling of this type of problem have already been taken. A large corporation has with the help of computer experts devised a system to aid in handling its complex problems in inventory control. The company manufactures approximately 15,000 items and stores them on a nationwide basis in about a dozen warehouses. The problem of keeping stock records current and making the information available in any one or all of the locations including the central office is apparent. Many times information as to the status of one particular item in the various warehouse locations is necessary. Requesting this information and receiving a reply often involves as much as two to three weeks, during which time the customer may have an opportunity to fulfill his needs elsewhere. The following control system has been established as being feasible and the installation has been estimated to cost about $250,000, including the costs of development.

The system would work in the following manner. At the home office would be located a computer with a magnetic drum memory unit. At each of the warehouse locations there would be a keyboard connected by teletype to the computer in the central office. Into the memory unit would be fed stock number, number of parts on hand, last date an item was withdrawn, last date an item was put into stock, and a minimum inventory level for each of the items in each of the warehouses. When an inquiry was received at any branch and the required number of items was not available at that branch, the operator would feed the coded stock number and another warehouse number into the keyboard and wait for a reply. Almost instantaneously a signal will be received indicating the quantity of the desired item on hand at that particular location. He then would punch in the number of the item required and the balance on the drum would be automatically reduced; the item would be shipped from the second warehouse. At the end of each day the central office would have the machine print off the stock order numbers and the balance on hand throughout the system. In addition, the machine could be set to print out those items below the minimum inventory level or those items on which no activity had occurred for a designated number of days. Such reports would serve as useful controls for production planning and scheduling and sales analysis.

(*Production Scheduling*): Another field that will be open to the application of computer techniques in the future is that of production scheduling, which may also be thought of as a type of operations analysis. It is the desire of the management of a factory to utilize all of the production facilities in the most efficient manner, producing the desired output on time and at a minimum cost. With adequate programming techniques, the following procedures could conceivably be accomplished by the use of an electronic computer.

A portion of the computer memory would be capable of recording and retaining the production load for each machine or facility in the factory, noting the amount of work to be done, the job order number, and the time when the work is scheduled. In the case of standard products, another portion of the memory (perhaps an external source such as a magnetic tape, which could be attached to the computer when needed) would have recorded the procedures to be fol-

lowed in producing the product, including the types of machines, operations, and time required. The computer would be programmed to schedule the new job on the machines of the factory, of course taking into account all previously scheduled work. In scheduling the job, the computer might be called upon to make decisions as to which of several machines to use to perform the same operation in order to obtain the optimum combination of cost and delivery time. In the case of an emergency or rush order, it might even be possible for the computer to "reconsider" decisions it had made in scheduling previous jobs and revise the scheduling of several jobs in order to accommodate the emergency job. The output of the computer could take the form of printed production orders, schedules, and production load reports which would be passed on to the factory's supervisory personnel for their use in carrying on production.

(*Following-up Production Scheduling*): If the production were always carried on in exactly the way scheduled, the operation of follow-up would be of little importance. However, in most practical cases, unanticipated factors such as machine breakdown, illness of workers, and late deliveries of raw materials can disrupt the production schedule. The electronic computer used for production scheduling would also be equipped to receive reports of actual production, compare these reports with schedules, and make necessary schedule revisions. If a particular machine were behind its scheduled work load, the computer might even decide whether or not it would be cheaper to work that machine overtime, revise the machine's production schedule, or shift some of the work load to other machines. Of course, in some cases the machine might produce an item ahead of schedule and be standing idle for a time, in which case the computer might revise the production load to use the idle time.

The potential for electronic business machines in this area of inventory and production control lies in the advantage that electronic computers have over the human brain when a large number of factors must be considered in the light of specified criteria in order to determine an optimum combination of these factors. The greatest savings in these cases will come not necessarily from savings in clerical manpower, but rather from more efficient utilization of production facilities and inventory investment.

Accounting: It is in the area of accounting and control that we look for the more immediate development and availability of electronic computers, because of the work already done in refining and mechanizing accounting procedures. In examining the various journals of original entry in the accounting department (such as cash, payroll, receivables, payables, purchases, sales, and miscellaneous), it can be seen that these records as they are kept today and the help required to keep them could be eliminated through the use of electronic computers. Control over the operations of the company would be increased because of the availability of instant information and adequate reports.

One of the areas where considerable savings could be made is that of payroll, the preparation of which has become increasingly complicated each year. Twenty years ago take-home pay equaled the number of hours worked times the hourly wage. Nowadays even the pay checks of straight salaried employees are complicated by withholding taxes, social security, retirement fund deductions, savings bonds, and bonuses based upon departmental efficiency or other considerations. In the case of employees working on a piece-rate basis, the computations are even more complicated because of variable rates and overtime considerations. Because of its versatility, the computer could calculate the payroll quickly and more economically than could present methods. Stored in its memory unit would be the following:

1. Tables of information relating to deductions and additions. This information would be used to compute the proper amounts to be added or subtracted from earnings.

2. Information relating to the individual such as his name, address, and base pay.

Daily or weekly information from job tickets and overtime slips would be fed into the computer, the "control" information would be drawn upon and in a very short period of time the payroll sheets would be forthcoming along with completed pay checks, statements showing deductions, labor variances, and the total payroll broken down by individuals, departments and products.

The electronic business machine could also be applied to the accounts receivables, handling them quickly and at low cost keeping the situation current. The machine would be given information relating to the products sold, such as name and address, former balance of customer, terms of payments, credit rating, price and freight rates. The computer would then receive a control impulse which would set it for computing accounts receivable. It would also receive input data as to the quantity of each product to be charged to a customer and the payments made. At the output end of the machine the following information would be available: balance due by customer, rate of payment, a sales breakdown, and a comparison between budgeted and actual sales.

A similar procedure could be established for accounts payable. This would be integrated with the inventory situation in order to inform the company as to what and when to reorder. The machine would be supplied with information relating to the product, such as price and specifications, and to the suppliers, such as reliability, promptness of delivery, and terms. The supplies and raw materials data would then be put into the machine, along with payments to the suppliers. The machine could then be called upon to find the best supplier, issue an order, and upon receipt of the goods compute the new balance.

Once these various elements of the accounting function are mechanized in an electronic business machine, it would be possible to contemplate a more comprehensive system in which all functions would be carried on by the machine. The storage unit would be a type of general ledger but each individual account would be carried separately. Another part of the machine, referred to as the control, would contain all the necessary instructions. These instructions would be set up as routines which could be controlled from a switchboard. Depending upon the information required, the operator would depress a button and the necessary statements would be forthcoming.

Department Stores

One distinct type of business that was investigated in order to determine how its record keeping time and expense might be reduced through the use of electronic business machines was the department store. There are several reasons why department stores would be especially receptive to any new methods which might yield them meaningful reports at a reasonable cost. These reasons include the conditions under which department stores typically operate:

1. A large number of departments contain hundreds of different items necessitating separate records for each department in order to determine which items are profitable. Furthermore, markdowns, shortages, direct and indirect expenses must be computed for individual departments.

2. Sales records must be kept for each of the individual items and its characteristics in order for the store to control its inventory and replenish it intelligently. The breadth of merchandise in a department store makes this difficult and defining the particular characteristic of merchandise which it is selling well necessitates elaborate records.

    A store must handle an enormously large number of relatively small sales in doing business. In 1951 department stores reporting their operating figures to the Harvard Business School indicated an average of 870,000 transactions per store[7] which had to be rung-up and charged to the proper sales person and department and, in addition, perhaps had to be deducted from the proper unit control by size, classification, color, and price.

3. Numerous services which stores offer their customers, such as charge accounts and deliveries, require additional control because they involve a great number of different customers.

4. Department stores purchase their merchandise from a large number of manufacturers which are spread throughout different markets and which have different discount schedules and delivery rates. The store must be constantly shifting and changing sources in order to keep up with those manufacturers whose goods are selling best; this type of operation necessitates many calculations in accounts payable and the maintenance of large files of active and inactive accounts.

The above points represent only those operations which are generally peculiar to department stores and which make their record-keeping more complicated than that of most businesses. Department stores must, at the same time, keep records (such as payrolls) which are common to all businesses. It might also be mentioned at this point that many of these problems are being magnified today by the expansion of many departments into branch stores. This will increase the problems of controlling inventory because it is necessary to keep track of goods not only in the main store departments but also in departments of the branches.

In order to overcome the particular difficulties of many small transactions which need minute control (both by departments and within departments), a completely new approach to the complex problems of department store record-keeping is indicated. This approach will have to keep in mind first what information department stores can use to operate most efficiently and, secondly, what systems and machines can obtain that information most quickly and economically. Development of these systems will have to be in conjunction with the development of improved and revised electronic business machines.

The memory function of an electronic calculator should prove especially helpful in the storage of different discounts and terms for paying a department store's many merchandise resources. In the area of inventory, magnetic drum memories should enable department stores to determine more quickly the level and contents of their inventory, both for individual departments and for the store as a whole. Billing charge account customers monthly now constitutes an elaborate and costly job to which a computer might give a useful contribution in terms of increased speed and decreased costs.

However, all these advances will take considerable research and development, both by computer manufacturers and department stores themselves, in the revision of record-keeping systems and in the advancement of machines to do the work. Many practical problems of getting information into and out of the machine will have to be solved. It will be necessary either to develop systems that might cut down the bulk of many small transactions or else find input mechanisms which can do it quickly and inexpensively. The information coming out of the machine must also be quickly transcribable into meaningful terms to department store management, especially in the case of inventory where a slow decision may often mean costly markdowns and obsolete stock.

Fortunately for this purpose many department stores are now grouped in organizations (among them Allied Stores and Federated Stores) which allows them to command greater financial resources and make such cooperative research among department stores feasible. In contacting these groups we found that for competitive reasons they were reluctant to discuss anything they were doing outside of admitting that they were working on the adaption of computers to their operations.

Insurance Companies

The characteristics of an insurance company's operations make this type of business a likely one to benefit from the use of electronic business machines. Since each customer has his own particular insurance situation, the file of information on any individual customer is large and the servicing of his account is complicated. Considerable handling of data by a large clerical force is involved. Premiums must be accounted for, dividends calculated, and new policies and settlements of claims quickly handled. The accounting for premiums is complicated by the fact that premiums from different policyholders may be

received at different intervals: weekly, monthly, quarterly, or yearly. Dividends create a problem because they must be calculated for each policyholder, who may or may not wish to apply the dividends to his premium.

Currently a great deal of punched card equipment is utilized by these companies. Information as to each policyholder is transferred to an individual card. This facilitates the premium billing operation and dividend computation, since the cards can be sorted and tabulated very quickly saving many man-hours of clerical help. However, the fundamental objections to punched cards still holds in that they can be used only a limited number of times before becoming worn and require considerable storage space.

With the advent of electronic business machines, it would be possible to store all necessary information on magnetic drums. While the savings in input time would be negligible, the advantages would accrue in the shorter time necessary for sorting, actual calculation of information, and in the preparation of billings; this presumably could be accomplished in one operation directly from the memory through standard printing mechanisms. In addition, there is always the advantage of having current information available in various tabulated forms depending upon the needs and desires of management.

To date, as nearly as can be determined, only one insurance company has actually done any experimenting with large-scale computers. However, many companies are devoting a great deal of time to the investigation of possible applications of these machines. It is generally felt that considerable research is still necessary in this area and that it will be at least ten years before any widespread use of electronics can be expected in this type of operation. This does not preclude the early use of electronic computers in the actuarial field where much statistical work must be done.

Banks

In the quest for the elimination of clerical help, paper handling, and repetitive calculations our attention turns to the commercial bank, where much work of this type can be found. The question arises—Can a computer take over much of this time-consuming work feasibly and economically?

It has been suggested that computer units would be useful in commercial banks for the purpose of recording customer checking and savings account balances. Each account would be carried on the memory drum so that daily debits and credits would be entered by means of a keyboard type of input. At any instant the balance in any individual account could be obtained by simply entering the customer's code number into the keyboard and depressing the proper key. A simple printing output mechanism could be used to indicate the customer's balance. In addition, daily customer deposit balances could be obtained in order to determine the bank's deposit position. Such current information might prove helpful in maintaining the necessary reserve balance with the Federal Reserve. Having the customer's balance current would seemingly facilitate the preparation of monthly statements as the whole job would be accomplished in a very short period of time, especially when compared to the man-hours required in banks at the present time. This would indeed eliminate much of the tedious clerical work associated with end-of-the-month statement distribution.

However, it is inherent in present-day banking operations that considerable manual handling of supporting documents in the form of checks, notes, and agreements is necessary because of problems of identification, legal requirements of negotiable instruments, customer insistence, and tradition. Currently much punched card equipment is used in mortgage loan departments of commercial banks and the incremental gain from the use of an electronic business machine could be measured only in the increased rapidity with which the operations could be performed. This is true because the problem does not involve the possibility of obtaining more varied types of information, but rather one of obtaining end results with a stereotyped method in which the difference in speed between the punched card sorting and tabulating and the electronic computer may not be significant.

It is our opinion that the nature of banking operations make it one which can benefit to a much lesser degree through the installation of electronic computers. Unless substantial changes in the relations between the bank and its customers come about, it seems impossible to escape the fact that person to person contact is necessary. In the future a logical first step in the mechanization of banking procedures would be the standardization of check sizes in order to utilize the most efficient sorting equipment. The problem of identification still remains and it is difficult to foresee how this human requirement could be obviated.

Public Utilities

The possibilities of the application of computers to public utility billing has been suggested. Meters in service could be directly connected to the central office and data accumulated in memory units. Billing could be performed through computer units which would draw from the information stored in the memory, apply the rate of charge, and print the resulting information on the bill. Payments whether partial or full could be run into the memory as credits with unpaid balances remaining on the memory drum.

Conclusion

The above-mentioned applications of the electronic business machines of the future are but a few examples of what might be done. Although we feel that electronic business machines are well suited to problems such as inventory control, market analysis, sales prediction, and accounting (to mention only a few), the reader should bear in mind that the practicability of using a machine in a particular situation is dependent upon the particular characteristics of that situation.

In considering future applications of electronic business machines we hope that the reader bears in mind that a gradual process of evolution rather than a sudden revolution is the means of reaching the state described in this chapter. In Chapter VII we hope to bring out more of how these changes will come about and what the businessman can do to assist in the development of electronic business machines.

CHAPTER VII: CONCLUSION: BUSINESS MACHINE DEVELOPMENT AND MANAGEMENT'S ROLE

Speculation has been carried on about future applications of electronics in many articles and books aimed at management. Some businessmen have been led to believe that the completely automatic office controlled only by a few push buttons will be available in the near future. However, little space has been devoted to writing about how these results can be achieved. Because of this type of thinking and promotion the businessman has been reluctant to accept and apply the fundamental techniques so far developed. He has been inclined to delay applications of electronic business machines to simple phases of his operations in expectation of the time when he can completely automatize his entire office procedure. Professor Howard H. Aiken, Director of the Computation Laboratory, Harvard University, emphasized this point when he said, "Businessmen have become even more optimistic than we have given them cause to be. They have expected more than we promised—and we promised too much."[8]

Professor Aiken and other experts in the computer field have pointed out that the completely automatic office is still very far off. Much work remains to be done in adapting electronic business machines to business—and also in adapting business to electronic machines. We cannot expect that the completely automatic office will evolve from computers much more rapidly than did the present mechanical desk calculators evolve from the first adding machine. It is probable that electronic business machines capable of performing a myriad of office functions without outside intervention will come as the result of a slow process of evolution. This evolution can be hastened by the businessman now if he will accept those electronic office helps that have already been perfected and apply them properly to some phases of his office operations rather than try to automatize everything at once.

What Electronic Business Machines Can Do for Business

Chapter III pointed out the needs of business: (1) the means for obtaining more information more rapidly and thus increasing the efficiency of business operations and (2) the substitution for clerical personnel in view of the increasing complexity of clerical operations and rising costs of personnel.

One of the great difficulties encountered in writing this report was the absence of adequate experience or even estimates from which reasonable generalizations of cost savings or payoff periods could be estimated. It does seem reasonable that electronic business machines with their great speed and large capacities will have cost advantages. At present only a few reports of actual installations are available. Using a small electronic computer, the Shell Oil Company now calculates owners' crude oil royalties in 3 1/2 hours; this job previously required 17 hours using conventional office machines. In another application a daily job which requires the efforts of 5 clerks could be performed by Shell in a total weekly time of 16 hours—four hours of this time being on the small electronic computer and the rest being time spent on auxiliary conventional machines.[9]

A representative of Remington Rand, Inc., has indicated that if centralized processing of data for a company annually cost $250,000 and were of a nature that could be done by an electronic computer like UNIVAC, such a computer could have a payoff period of 5 years or less in that installation.[10]

The immediate savings in clerical time are the savings which are always obvious; however, there are other savings associated with labor savings which are also very important—savings in fringe benefits, working facilities, and office space, for example.

When the businessman first considers the possibilities of electronic business machines in his business, it is natural that he thinks of the cash savings mentioned above. Actually, these obvious savings are the least important to him. Facts, figures, and information can be obtained immediately or daily; instead of using guesses or impressions, the businessman can use facts as a basis for decisions, making his job easier. Instead of waiting weeks for reports to be sent from warehouses around the country, inventory information can be made available instantly. Chapter III mentioned an estimate that department stores could realize a 10% increase in sales volume and a 10% decrease in investment in inventory by effectively applying electronic business machines to inventory control.

In addition to obtaining information more quickly, management can obtain a greater amount of useful information. As profit margins narrow, greater emphasis is placed upon tracing down of excessive costs and unfavorable cost trends; if so designed, the electronic business machine will give sales, cost, and other information daily.

Quite aside from the amount of useful information and the speed with which it is obtained is the fact that electronic business machines are much more reliable than are office personnel. Machines do not get bored and are particularly good at repetitive, monotonous operations. Although people are still called upon to operate the business machine, there is far less chance for human error and no chance for any show of emotions by the machine.

It is difficult to place a cash value on the greater efficiencies of operation of a company; nevertheless, the savings resulting from greater efficiency of operation will usually be the most important savings brought about by the effective use of electronic business machines.

State of Technological Development

Chapter V pointed out that existing computer components have been perfected to the point where computers could satisfy most business needs. Both the arithmetic and control components are entirely adequate for present and expected future needs. The two most promising types of storage are magnetic drum storage and magnetic core storage. The former has been developed satisfactorily while the latter still needs development work. At present, the big drawback of the memory component, which causes the same drawback of the whole business machine, is its high cost. Through the use of built-in checks the reliability of the machines can be made very high; machines have been produced that are practically incapable of producing mistakes. From a technological point of view, the electronic business machine is ready for use.

Types of Electronic Business Machines to be Developed

As the electronic business machine continues to evolve, the type of business machine produced will change. We feel that emphasis will be away from a general-purpose machine and definitely toward machines which, although basically similar, are designed and built for a particular job in a particular company.

Problem-Solving Machines: Almost all the large, general-purpose scientific computers are located at universities or at government research centers; most of these computers were financed by the government. Although several of these computers have been used extensively for the solution of engineering problems, most of the time and effort expended on these scientific computers has been for the further development of computers themselves and their applications to scientific uses. There has been no effort directed primarily at solving industrial problems, problems of design, and inventory and production control. A definite need now exists for machines and men (mainly men) to handle the computing problems of business; the demand will grow rapidly as one businessman sees how another has made successful use of the facilities.

Few, if any, companies in the country will want to or be able to set up their own large problem-solving business machines. The cost (a million dollars and up) is high, and obtaining and directing the top-notch men required would be a very great problem. The logical and probable development will be several large, general-purpose problem-solving business machines, built by the major business machine companies primarily for business applications, and only secondarily for further development of computer components. The required staff would be large and of varied backgrounds and would not be subject to the varying workloads likely if the machine were used only by one industrial company. The direction of this staff would be much less a problem for the business machine company than it would be for other companies not closely connected with the machines.

At present, there are several standard small computers (less than $100,000) available. Some large companies with the need for the frequent solution of the similar short calculations will find these computers most useful. However, the market for these machines is quite limited. Setting up a problem for the computer requires some training. Installations of this type do not need the constant attendance of a maintenance man; should a circuit go bad there is no great need for putting the machine back into operation instantaneously. Speed is the advantage of this type of installation; no time is lost waiting for results to come back from a central computation laboratory.

Information Storage Machines: It is the use of electronic business machines for storage of information which provides the businessman with the tool for more efficient operation and cash savings. There is a wide and large market for information storage machines.

Compared to the present scientific computers, the size of electronic business machines for memory use will be small. A company will not have one big unit to handle all its storage of inventory, accounts receivable, accounts payable, and other information. Instead it will have smaller machines, each designed for its own function. These machines will be basically similar; the basic circuits and the magnetic drums will probably be standard units for ease of maintenance and produced in volume for economy of manufacture. However, the design and internal programming of each machine will be done expressly for a certain function in a certain company. The machines probably will not be easily interchangeable.

In designing the machine for the company, the businessman will have to work very closely with the representative of the business machine company. The responsibility for the design and installation of the effective electronic business machine lies equally on the businessman and the business machine company.

Once the memory has been installed, there will be no need for mathematicians or highly trained operating personnel. Procedures will have been standardized so that the operator is required to do little reasoning. However, there will be a need for trained and skilled technical men for the continuous maintenance of the machine; a company cannot afford to wait all afternoon for a vacuum tube to be replaced.

Although most units will be small ($50,000 down), the size range will be great with some machines being quite large. An inventory control system for 15,000 items might require a storage with about 2,000,000 binary digits. The installation for a central office of a very large mail order firm might require storage for about 100,000,000 binary digits. A very large insurance company would use about 1000 binary digits per policy for storage of current information or perhaps 10,000,000,000 binary digits. As a rule of thumb, the present cost per binary digit of internal storage is about 10 cents. In the next 20 years we can look for this cost being gradually decreased down to 0.8 cents per binary digit or slightly less.

Remington Rand's UNIVAC system has been successfully used. It is a general-purpose system designed in units so that varying requirements could be met by the same basic system. However, its future use will be limited to the relatively few general applications for business machines requiring a large machine with large computing capacity and fairly large tape memories. It will be replaced by relatively more specialized, more economical, and cheaper electronic business machines.

What the Businessman Must Do

The initiative for the business application of electronic machines must come from the businessman himself. He must also realign his thinking to the capabilities of the electronic business machine and not expect too much from it.

The electronic business machine industry is still much too young to have company sales representatives knocking on most businessmen's doors. It is up to the individual to dig into the problem, to find out how he can best use this new tool, and to get an extra advantage over his competitors.

It may be difficult for the businessman to completely realign his thinking toward his problem in accounting or control or some other field. The electronic business machine is a new medium; it requires new approaches and new procedures. When a business machine is designed to produce a type of information or kind of control, the procedures it will use probably will not resemble previously used procedures.

As a minor example of what this realignment will be, consider the use of a business machine in an inventory control problem. Orthodox accounting would call for records that are accurate to the last unit in inventory. However, if there are usually about 1000 units of an item in stock, the importance of the last decimal digit is insignificant for control purposes but represents one-third of the business machine storage necessary for that item. (Besides, the actual physical inventory probably would only rarely agree with an "accurate" perpetual inventory.) The logical thing to do is to maintain the physical inventory figure accurate only to the 10's column rather than the units column.

Businessmen should not expect the electronic business machine to do everything. A machine designed for one basic purpose is reasonably simple. As soon as the machine is asked to do a little more, the design becomes much more complicated; the added construction and operation generally becomes complicated out of all proportion to the additional information obtained.

The Airlines Reservisor, developed by the Teleregister Corporation and installed in the New York offices of American Airlines, is an example of a machine that was designed simply and is successfully fulfilling the purpose for which it was designed. The Reservisor has a large central magnetic drum memory unit which is connected to input-output units at each ticket agent's window. By properly operating his input-output unit, the agent can tell whether or not any seats remain on a particular flight to a particular destination up to 10 days in advance. He then may depress a button-to indicate the sale of one or more seats, in which case the seats are subtracted from the inventory record on the central magnetic drum. The operations are performed in duplicate and automatically compared for accuracy by the machine. To date this system has functioned satisfactorily. This same type of system has been considered for application to the problem of Pullman reservations for railroads. However, several obstacles to its immediate use exist. Railroads want to continue selling Pullman space by specific type and location in each car. They also want to record reservations more than 10 days in advance (the advance period used by airlines). A memory unit for a railroad reservation unit such as proposed would be very complex and costly. It does not appear that any progress will be made on the problem unless railroads revise downward the number of variables involved in recording reservations. There seems no doubt that if railroads were willing to use a device similar to the Airline Reservisor the result would be more efficient reservation services at lower cost for each railroad.

Necessity for Analyzing Systems: Application of electronic machines to business is greatly handicapped by a lack of men capable of analyzing business systems and procedures in the light of computer developments. The businessman generally knows little about the technical aspects of computers, and the computer expert generally knows nothing of business methods. A definite need exists for individuals who possess dual aptitudes and understand both business and computer problems. Perhaps manufacturers of computers can provide this training, which is so badly needed.

To prepare both the company and the personnel for the coming of the electronic business machine, it would be most prudent for the businessman to start organizing the control functions of the company along the black and white, detailed, step by step, methods which the business machine must use. Such attention paid to organization probably would be worth while even if not aimed at the eventual application of electronic business machines. Since electronic business machines appear to be on the way, the wise businessman will begin now to prepare.

Conclusion

High-speed electronic digital computers developed initially for scientific uses are slowly being adapted to business applications. Computer components are now satisfactory for use in electronic business machines; further developments will be toward reducing costs and increasing memory capacities. Consequently these new machines are ready for application to business. However, businessmen must be willing to alter some of their procedures if they are to make best use of the new data handling techniques. In this field, there is much room for persons having combined backgrounds in business and computer technology to aid in application work.

The completely automatic office is very far in the future. However, in a short time business will be able to gain much from the proper application of electronic business machines. The partially automatic office utilizing these new machines to perform many routine functions is expected within the next 15 years.

• • •

1.   U.S. Department of Commerce, Bureau of Census, *Current Population Reports: Labor Force,* May 19, 1952, p. 26, and *16th Census of the U.S., Population: Labor Force,* p. 81.

2.   John S. Coleman, *Electronics for Business—Luxury or Necessity,* p. 6.

3.   Technical information on UNIVAC was obtained from various Remington Rand publications.

4.   M. David Moross, et al, *Automation Challenge to Management.*

5.   Remington Rand, Inc., *UNIVAC Fac-tronic System,* p. 14.

6.   A. C. Hancock, "UNIVAC Beats Statisticians on Election Night," *Systems* Magazine, December, 1952, pp. 4-5.

7.   Derived from Malcolm P. McNair, *Operating Results of Department and Specialty Stores in 1951.*

8.   Speech at Office Management Conference of American Management Association, October 16, 1952.

9.   Matt W. Box, Assistant Manager, Methods and Statistical Dept., Shell Oil Co., at Office Management Conference of American Management Association, October 16–17, 1952.

10. David N. Savidge, Sales Manager, UNIVAC Fac-Tronic System, at Office Management Conference of the American Management Association, October 16–17, 1952.

10.5
Man-Computer Symbiosis

J. C. R. Licklider

INTRODUCTORY NOTE TO READING 10.5

In this paper published in 1960, the psychologist J. C. R. Licklider (1915–1990), who M. Mitchell Waldrop called "computing's Johnny Appleseed,"[1] first postulated that computers should become intimate symbiotic partners in human activity, including communication. Like Vannevar Bush, who imagined the Memex (Reading 13.1), Licklider promoted ideas rather than worked out their implementation. The main idea of "Man-Computer Symbiosis" was that computers should be developed with the goal "to enable men and computers to cooperate in making decisions and controlling complex situations without inflexible dependence on predetermined programs." Man-computer symbiosis would augment human intellect by freeing it from mundane tasks. Computing would eventually not just run programs for scientists, business or government. In the days of batch processing, long before anyone imagined personal computing, real time interactive computing, to which Licklider referred, was a revolutionary idea. Perhaps because Licklider was a comparative newcomer to computing who came to the field from teaching psychology at MIT rather than from a background in electrical engineering or computer science, he was able to formulate these ideas with remarkable clarity. [JMN]

---

1 Mitchell Waldrop, "Computing's Johnny Appleseed." *Technology Review*, Jan/Feb 2000.

TEXT OF READING 10.5

SUMMARY

Man-computer symbiosis is an expected development in cooperative interaction between men and electronic computers. It will involve very close coupling between the human and the electronic members of the partnership. The main aims are 1) to let computers facilitate formulative thinking as they now facilitate the solution of formulated problems, and 2) to enable men and computers to cooperate in making decisions and controlling complex situations without inflexible dependence on predetermined programs. In the anticipated symbiotic partnership, men will set the goals, formulate the hypotheses, determine the criteria, and perform the evaluations. Computing machines will do the routinizable work that must be done to prepare the way for insights and decisions in technical and scientific thinking. Preliminary analyses indicate that the symbiotic partnership will perform intellectual operations much more effectively than man alone can perform them. Prerequisites for the achievement of the effective, cooperative association include developments in computer time sharing, in memory components, in memory organization, in programming languages, and in input and output equipment.

1 INTRODUCTION

1.1 Symbiosis

The fig tree is pollinated only by the insect *Blastophaga grossorun*. The larva of the insect lives in the ovary of the fig tree, and there it gets its food. The tree and the insect are thus heavily interdependent: the tree cannot reproduce without the insect; the insect cannot eat without the tree; together, they constitute not only a viable but a productive and thriving partnership. This cooperative "living together in intimate association, or even close union, of two dissimilar organisms" is called symbiosis [27].

"Man-computer symbiosis" is a subclass of man-machine systems. There are many man-machine systems. At present, however, there are no man-computer symbioses. The purposes of this paper are to present the concept and, hopefully, to foster the development of man-computer symbiosis by analyzing some problems of interaction between men and computing machines, calling attention to applicable principles of man-machine engineering, and pointing out a few questions to which research answers are needed. The hope is that, in not too many years, human brains and computing machines will be coupled together very tightly, and that the resulting partnership will think as no human brain has ever thought and process data in a way not approached by the information-handling machines we know today.

1.2 Between "Mechanically Extended Man" and "Artificial Intelligence"

As a concept, man-computer symbiosis is different in an important way from what North [21] has called "mechanically extended man." In the man-machine systems of the past, the human operator supplied the initiative, the direction, the integration, and the criterion. The mechanical parts of the systems were mere extensions, first of the human arm, then of the human eye. These systems certainly did not consist of "dissimilar organisms living together . . ." There was only one kind of organism—man—and the rest was there only to help him.

In one sense of course, any man-made system is intended to help man, to help a man or men outside the system. If we focus upon the human operator within the system, however, we see that, in some areas of technology, a fantastic change has taken place during the last few years. "Mechanical extension" has given way to replacement of men, to automation, and the men who remain are there more to help than to be helped. In some instances, particularly in large computer-centered information and control systems, the human operators are responsible mainly for functions that it proved infeasible to automate. Such systems ("humanly extended machines," North might call them) are not symbiotic systems. They are "semi-automatic" systems, systems that started out to be fully automatic but fell short of the goal.

Man-computer symbiosis is probably not the ultimate paradigm for complex technological systems. It seems entirely possible that, in due course, electronic or chemical "machines" will outdo the human brain in most of the functions we now consider exclusively within its province. Even now, Gelernter's IBM-704 program for proving theorems in plane geometry proceeds at about the same pace as Brooklyn high school students, and makes similar errors.[12] There are, in fact, several theorem-proving, problem-solving, chess-playing, and pattern-recognizing programs (too many for complete reference [1, 2, 5, 8, 11, 13, 17, 18, 19, 22, 23, 25]) capable of rivaling human intellectual performance in restricted areas; and Newell, Simon, and Shaw's [20] "general problem solver" may remove some of the restrictions. In short, it seems worthwhile to avoid argument with (other) enthusiasts for artificial intelligence by conceding dominance in the distant future of cerebration to machines alone. There will nevertheless be a fairly long interim during which the main intellectual advances will be made by men and computers working together in intimate association. A multidisciplinary study group, examining future research and development problems of the Air Force, estimated that it would be 1980 before developments in artificial intelligence make it possible for machines alone to do much thinking or problem solving of military significance. That would leave, say, five years to develop man-computer symbiosis and 15 years to use it. The 15 may be 10 or 500, but those years should be intellectually the most creative and exciting in the history of mankind.

2 AIMS OF MAN-COMPUTER SYMBIOSIS

Present-day computers are designed primarily to solve preformulated problems or to process data according to predetermined procedures. The course of the computation may be conditional upon results obtained during the computation, but all the alternatives must be foreseen in advance. (If an unforeseen alternative arises, the whole process comes to a halt and awaits the necessary extension of the program.) The requirement for preformulation or predetermination is sometimes no great disadvantage. It is often said that programming for a computing machine forces one to think clearly, that it disciplines the thought process. If the user can think his problem through in advance,

symbiotic association with a computing machine is not necessary.

However, many problems that can be thought through in advance are very difficult to think through in advance. They would be easier to solve, and they could be solved faster, through an intuitively guided trial-and-error procedure in which the computer cooperated, turning up flaws in the reasoning or revealing unexpected turns in the solution. Other problems simply cannot be formulated without computing-machine aid. Poincaré anticipated the frustration of an important group of would-be computer users when he said, "The question is not, 'What is the answer?' The question is, 'What is the question?'" One of the main aims of man-computer symbiosis is to bring the computing machine effectively into the formulative parts of technical problems.

The other main aim is closely related. It is to bring computing machines effectively into processes of thinking that must go on in "real time," time that moves too fast to permit using computers in conventional ways. Imagine trying, for example, to direct a battle with the aid of a computer on such a schedule as this. You formulate your problem today. Tomorrow you spend with a programmer. Next week the computer devotes 5 minutes to assembling your program and 47 seconds to calculating the answer to your problem. You get a sheet of paper 20 feet long, full of numbers that, instead of providing a final solution, only suggest a tactic that should be explored by simulation. Obviously, the battle would be over before the second step in its planning was begun. To think in interaction with a computer in the same way that you think with a colleague whose competence supplements your own will require much tighter coupling between man and machine than is suggested by the example and than is possible today.

3 NEED FOR COMPUTER PARTICIPATION IN FORMULATIVE AND REAL-TIME THINKING

The preceding paragraphs tacitly made the assumption that, if they could be introduced effectively into the thought process, the functions that can be performed by data-processing machines would improve or facilitate thinking and problem solving in an important way. That assumption may require justification.

3.1 A Preliminary and Informal Time-and-Motion Analysis of Technical Thinking

Despite the fact that there is a voluminous literature on thinking and problem solving, including intensive case-history studies of the process of invention, I could find nothing comparable to a time-and-motion-study analysis of the mental work of a person engaged in a scientific or technical enterprise. In the spring and summer of 1957, therefore, I tried to keep track of what one moderately technical person actually did during the hours he regarded as devoted to work. Although I was aware of the inadequacy of the sampling, I served as my own subject.

It soon became apparent that the main thing I did was to keep records, and the project would have become an infinite regress if the keeping of records had been carried through in the detail envisaged in the initial plan. It was not. Nevertheless, I obtained a picture of my activities that gave me pause. Perhaps my spectrum is not typical—I hope it is not, but I fear it is:

About 85 per cent of my "thinking" time was spent getting into a position to think, to make a decision, to learn something I needed to know. Much more time went into finding or obtaining information than into digesting it. Hours went into the plotting of graphs, and other hours into instructing an assistant how to plot. When the graphs were finished, the relations were obvious at once, but the plotting had to be done in order to make them so. At one point, it was necessary to compare six experimental determinations of a function relating speech-intelligibility to speech-to-noise ratio. No two experimenters had used the same definition or measure of speech-to-noise ratio. Several hours of calculating were required to get the data into comparable form. When they were in comparable form, it took only a few seconds to determine what I needed to know.

Throughout the period I examined, in short, my "thinking" time was devoted mainly to activities that were essentially clerical or mechanical: searching, calculating, plotting, transforming, determining the logical or dynamic consequences of a set of assumptions or hypotheses, preparing the way for a decision or an insight. Moreover, my choices of what to attempt and what not to attempt were determined to an embarrassingly great extent by considerations of clerical feasibility, not intellectual capability.

The main suggestion conveyed by the findings just described is that the operations that fill most of the time allegedly devoted to technical thinking are operations that can be performed more effectively by machines than by men. Severe problems are posed by the fact that these operations have to be performed upon diverse variables and in unforeseen and continually changing sequences. If those problems can be solved in such a way as to create a symbiotic relation between a man and a fast information-retrieval and data-processing machine, however, it seems evident that the cooperative interaction would greatly improve the thinking process.

It may be appropriate to acknowledge, at this point, that we are using the term "computer" to cover a wide class of calculating, data-processing, and information-storage-and-retrieval machines. The capabilities of machines in this class are increasing almost daily. It is therefore hazardous to make general statements about capabilities of the class. Perhaps it is equally hazardous to make general statements about the capabilities of men. Nevertheless, certain genotypic differences in capability between men and computers do stand out, and they have a bearing on the nature of possible man-computer symbiosis and the potential value of achieving it.

As has been said in various ways, men are noisy, narrow-band devices, but their nervous systems have very many parallel and simultaneously active channels. Relative to men, computing machines are very fast and very accurate, but they are constrained to perform only one or a few elementary operations at a time. Men are flexible, capable of "programming themselves contingently" on the basis of newly received information. Computing machines are single-minded, constrained by their "pre-program-ming." Men naturally speak redundant languages organized around unitary objects and coherent actions and employing 20 to 60 elementary symbols. Computers "naturally" speak nonredundant languages, usually with only two elementary symbols and no inherent appreciation either of unitary objects or of coherent actions.

To be rigorously correct, those characterizations would have to include many qualifiers. Nevertheless, the picture of dissimilarity (and therefore potential supplementation) that they present is essentially valid. Computing machines can do readily, well, and rapidly many things that are difficult or impossible for man, and men can do readily and well, though not rapidly, many things that are difficult or impossible for computers. That suggests that a symbiotic cooperation, if successful in integrating the positive characteristics of men and computers, would be of great value. The differences in speed and in language, of course, pose difficulties that must be overcome.

4 SEPARABLE FUNCTIONS OF MEN AND COMPUTERS IN THE ANTICIPATED SYMBIOTIC ASSOCIATION

It seems likely that the contributions of human operators and equipment will blend together so completely in many operations that it will be difficult to separate them neatly in analysis. That would be the case if, in gathering data on which to base a decision, for example, both the man and the computer came up with relevant precedents from experience and if the computer then suggested a course of action that agreed with the man's intuitive judgment. (In theorem-proving programs, computers find precedents in experience, and in the SAGE System, they suggest courses of action. The foregoing is not a far-fetched example.) In other operations, however, the contributions of men and equipment will be to some extent separable.

Men will set the goals and supply the motivations, of course, at least in the early years. They will formulate hypotheses. They will ask questions. They will think of mechanisms, procedures, and models. They will remember that such-and-such a person did some possibly relevant work on a topic of interest back in 1947, or at any rate shortly after World War II, and they will have an idea in what journals it might have been published. In general, they will make approximate and fallible, but leading, contributions, and they will define criteria and serve as evaluators, judging the contributions of the equipment and guiding the general line of thought.

In addition, men will handle the very-low-probability situations when such situations do actually arise. (In current man-machine systems, that is one of the human operator's most important functions. The sum of the probabilities of very-low-probability alternatives is often much too large to neglect.) Men will fill in the gaps, either in the problem solution or in the computer program, when the computer has no mode or routine that is applicable in a particular circumstance.

The information-processing equipment, for its part, will convert hypotheses into testable models and then test the models against data (which the human operator may designate roughly and identify as relevant when the computer presents them for his approval). The equipment will answer questions. It will simulate the mechanisms and models, carry out the procedures, and display the results to the operator. It will transform data, plot graphs ("cutting the cake" in whatever way the human operator specifies, or in several alternative ways if the human operator is not sure what he wants). The equipment will interpolate, extrapolate, and transform. It will convert static equations or logical statements into dynamic models so the human operator can examine their behavior. In general, it will carry out the routinizable, clerical operations that fill the intervals between decisions.

In addition, the computer will serve as a statistical-inference, decision-theory, or game-theory machine to make elementary evaluations of suggested courses of action whenever there is enough basis to support a formal statistical analysis. Finally, it will do as much diagnosis, pattern-matching, and relevance-recognizing as it profitably can, but it will accept a clearly secondary status in those areas.

5 PREREQUISITES FOR REALIZATION OF MAN-COMPUTER SYMBIOSIS

The data-processing equipment tacitly postulated in the preceding section is not available. The computer programs have not been written. There are in fact several hurdles that stand between the nonsymbiotic present and the anticipated symbiotic future. Let us examine some of them to see more clearly what is needed and what the chances are of achieving it.

5.1 Speed Mismatch Between Men and Computers

Any present-day large-scale computer is too fast and too costly for real-time cooperative thinking with one man. Clearly, for the sake of efficiency and economy, the computer must divide its time among many users. Time-sharing systems are currently under active development. There are even arrangements to keep users from "clobbering" anything but their own personal programs.

It seems reasonable to envision, for a time 10 or 15 years hence, a "thinking center" that will incorporate the functions of present-day libraries together with anticipated advances in information storage and retrieval and the symbiotic functions suggested earlier in this paper. The picture readily enlarges itself into a network of such centers, connected to one another by wide-band communication lines and to individual users by leased-wire services. In such a system, the speed of the computers would be balanced, and the cost of the gigantic memories and the sophisticated programs would be divided by the number of users.

5.2 Memory Hardware Requirements

When we start to think of storing any appreciable fraction of a technical literature in computer memory, we run into billions of bits and, unless things change markedly, billions of dollars.

The first thing to face is that we shall not store all the technical and scientific papers in computer memory. We may store the parts that can be summarized most succinctly—the quantitative parts and the reference citations—but not the whole. Books are among the most beautifully engineered, and human-engineered, components in existence, and they will continue to be functionally important within the context of man-computer symbiosis. (Hopefully, the computer will expedite the finding, delivering, and returning of books.)

The second point is that a very important section of memory will be permanent: part indelible *memory* and part *published memory*. The computer will be able to write once into indelible memory, and then read back indefinitely, but the computer will not be able to erase indelible memory. (It may also overwrite, turning all the 0's into 1's, as though marking over what was written earlier.) Published memory will be "read-only" memory. It will be introduced into the computer already structured. The computer will be able to refer to it repeatedly, but not to change it. These types of memory will become more and more important as computers grow larger. They can be made more compact than core, thin-film, or even tape memory, and they will be much less expensive. The main engineering problems will concern selection circuitry.

In so far as other aspects of memory requirement are concerned, we may count upon the continuing development of ordinary scientific and business computing machines There is some prospect that memory elements will become as fast as processing (logic) elements. That development would have a revolutionary effect upon the design of computers.

5.3 Memory Organization Requirements

Implicit in the idea of man-computer symbiosis are the requirements that information be retrievable both by name and by pattern and that it be accessible through procedure much faster than serial search. At least half of the problem of memory organization appears to reside in the storage procedure. Most of the remainder seems to be wrapped up in the problem of pattern recognition within the storage mechanism or medium. Detailed discussion of these problems is beyond the present scope. However, a brief outline of one promising idea, "trie memory," may serve to indicate the general nature of anticipated developments.

Trie memory is so called by its originator, Fredkin [10], because it is designed to facilitate retrieval of information and because the branching storage structure, when developed, resembles a tree. Most common memory systems store functions of arguments at locations designated by the arguments. (In one sense, they do not store the arguments at all. In another and more realistic sense, they store all the possible arguments in the framework structure of the memory.) The trie memory system, on the other hand, stores both the functions and the arguments. The argument is introduced into the memory first, one character at a time, starting at a standard initial register. Each argument register has one cell for each character of the ensemble (e.g., two for information encoded in binary form) and each character cell has within it storage space for the address of the next register. The argument is stored by writing a series of addresses, each one of which tells where to find the next. At the end of the argument is a special "end-of-argument" marker. Then follow directions to the function, which is stored in one or another of several ways, either further trie structure or "list structure" often being most effective.

The trie memory scheme is inefficient for small memories, but it becomes increasingly efficient in using available storage space as memory size increases. The attractive features of the scheme are these: 1) The retrieval process is extremely simple. Given the argument, enter the standard initial register with the first character, and pick up the address of the second. Then go to the second register, and pick up the address of the third, etc. 2) If two arguments have initial characters in common, they use the same storage space for those characters. 3) The lengths of the arguments need not be the same, and need not be specified in advance. 4) No room in storage is reserved for or used by any argument until it is actually stored. The trie structure is created as the items are introduced into the memory. 5) A function can be used as an argument for another function, and that function as an argument for the next. Thus, for example, by entering with the argument, "matrix multiplication," one might retrieve the entire program for performing a matrix multiplication on the computer. 6) By examining the storage at a given level, one can determine what thus-far similar items have been stored. For example, if there is no citation for Egan, J. P., it is but a step or two backward to pick up the trail of Egan, James . . . .

The properties just described do not include all the desired ones, but they bring computer storage into

resonance with human operators and their predilection to designate things by naming or pointing.

5.4 The Language Problem

The basic dissimilarity between human languages and computer languages may be the most serious obstacle to true symbiosis. It is reassuring, however, to note what great strides have already been made, through interpretive programs and particularly through assembly or compiling programs such as FORTRAN, to adapt computers to human language forms. The "Information Processing Language" of Shaw, Newell, Simon, and Ellis [24] represents another line of rapprochement. And, in ALGOL and related systems, men are proving their flexibility by adopting standard formulas of representation and expression that are readily translatable into machine language.

For the purposes of real-time cooperation between men and computers, it will be necessary, however, to make use of an additional and rather different principle of communication and control. The idea may be highlighted by comparing instructions ordinarily addressed to intelligent human beings with instructions ordinarily used with computers. The latter specify precisely the individual steps to take and the sequence in which to take them. The former present or imply something about incentive or motivation, and they supply a criterion by which the human executor of the instructions will know when he has accomplished his task. In short: instructions directed to computers specify courses; instructions-directed to human beings specify goals.

Men appear to think more naturally and easily in terms of goals than in terms of courses. True, they usually know something about directions in which to travel or lines along which to work, but few start out with precisely formulated itineraries. Who, for example, would depart from Boston for Los Angeles with a detailed specification of the route? Instead, to paraphrase Wiener, men bound for Los Angeles try continually to decrease the amount by which they are not yet in the smog.

Computer instruction through specification of goals is being approached along two paths. The first involves problem-solving, hill-climbing, self-organizing programs. The second involves real-time concatenation of pre-programmed segments and closed subroutines which the human operator can designate and call into action simply by name.

Along the first of these paths, there has been promising exploratory work. It is clear that, working within the loose constraints of predetermined strategies, computers will in due course be able to devise and simplify their own procedures for achieving stated goals. Thus far, the achievements have not been substantively important; they have constituted only "demonstration in principle." Nevertheless, the implications are far-reaching.

Although the second path is simpler and apparently capable of earlier realization, it has been relatively neglected. Fredkin's trie memory provides a promising paradigm. We may in due course see a serious effort to develop computer programs that can be connected together like the words and phrases of speech to do whatever computation or control is required at the moment. The consideration that holds back such an effort, apparently, is that the effort would produce nothing that would be of great value in the context of existing computers. It would be unrewarding to develop the language before there are any computing machines capable of responding meaningfully to it.

5.5 Input and Output Equipment

The department of data processing that seems least advanced, in so far as the requirements of man-computer symbiosis are concerned, is the one that deals with input and output equipment or, as it is seen from the human operator's point of view, displays and controls. Immediately after saying that, it is essential to make qualifying comments, because the engineering of equipment for high-speed introduction and extraction of information has been excellent, and because some very sophisticated display and control techniques have been developed in such research laboratories as the Lincoln Laboratory. By and large, in generally available computers, however, there is almost no provision for any more effective, immediate man-machine communication than can be achieved with an electric typewriter.

Displays seem to be in a somewhat better state than controls. Many computers plot graphs on oscilloscope screens, and a few take advantage of the remarkable capabilities, graphical and symbolic, of the charactron display tube. Nowhere, to my knowledge, however, is there anything approaching the flexibility and convenience of the pencil and doodle pad or the chalk and blackboard used by men in technical discussion.

1. *Desk-Surface Display and Control:* Certainly, for effective man-computer interaction, it will be necessary for the man and the computer to draw graphs and pictures and to write notes and equations to each other on the same display surface. The man should be able to present a function to the computer, in a rough but rapid fashion, by drawing a graph. The computer should read the man's writing, perhaps on the condition that it be in clear block capitals, and it should immediately post, at the location of each hand-drawn symbol, the corresponding character as interpreted and put into precise type-face. With such an input-output device, the operator would quickly learn to write or print in a manner legible to the machine. He could compose instructions and subroutines, set them into proper format, and check them over before introducing them finally into the computer's main memory. He could even define new symbols, as Gilmore and Savell [14] have done at the Lincoln Laboratory, and present them directly to the computer. He could sketch out the format of a table roughly and let the computer shape it up with precision. He could correct the computer's data, instruct the machine via flow diagrams, and in general interact with it very much as he would with another engineer, except that the "other engineer" would be a precise draftsman, a lightning calculator, a mnemonic wizard, and many other valuable partners all in one.

2. *Computer-Posted Wall Display:* In some technological systems, several men share responsibility for controlling vehicles whose behaviors interact. Some information must be presented simultaneously to all the men, preferably on a common grid, to coordinate their actions. Other information is of relevance only to one or two operators. There would be only a confusion of uninterpretable clutter if all the information were presented on one display to all of them. The

information must be posted by a computer, since manual plotting is too slow to keep it up to date.

The problem just outlined is even now a critical one, and it seems certain to become more and more critical as time goes by. Several designers are convinced that displays with the desired characteristics can be constructed with the aid of flashing lights and time-sharing viewing screens based on the light-valve principle.

The large display should be supplemented, according to most of those who have thought about the problem, by individual display-control units. The latter would permit the operators to modify the wall display without leaving their locations. For some purposes, it would be desirable for the operators to be able to communicate with the computer through the supplementary displays and perhaps even through the wall display. At least one scheme for providing such communication seems feasible.

The large wall display and its associated system are relevant, of course, to symbiotic cooperation between a computer and a team of men. Laboratory experiments have indicated repeatedly that informal, parallel arrangements of operators, coordinating their activities through reference to a large situation display, have important advantages over the arrangement, more widely used, that locates the operators at individual consoles and attempts to correlate their actions through the agency of a computer. This is one of several operator-team problems in need of careful study.

3. *Automatic Speech Production and Recognition:* How desirable and how feasible is speech communication between human operators and computing machines? That compound question is asked whenever sophisticated data-processing systems are discussed. Engineers who work and live with computers take a conservative attitude toward the desirability. Engineers who have had experience in the field of automatic speech recognition take a conservative attitude toward the feasibility. Yet there is continuing interest in the idea of talking with computing machines. In large part, the interest stems from realization that one can hardly take a military commander or a corporation president away from his work to teach him to type. If computing machines are ever to

be used directly by top-level decision makers, it may be worthwhile to provide communication via the most natural means, even at considerable cost.

Preliminary analysis of his problems and time scales suggests that a corporation president would be interested in a symbiotic association with a computer only as an avocation. Business situations usually move slowly enough that there is time for briefings and conferences. It seems reasonable, therefore, for computer specialists to be the ones who interact directly with computers in business offices.

The military commander, on the other hand, faces a greater probability of having to make critical decisions in short intervals of time. It is easy to overdramatize the notion of the ten-minute war, but it would be dangerous to count on having more than ten minutes in which to make a critical decision. As military system ground environments and control centers grow in capability and complexity, therefore, a real requirement for automatic speech production and recognition in computers seems likely to develop. Certainly, if the equipment were already developed, reliable, and available, it would be used.

In so far as feasibility is concerned, speech production poses less severe problems of a technical nature than does automatic recognition of speech sounds. A commercial electronic digital voltmeter now reads aloud its indications, digit by digit. For eight or ten years, at the Bell Telephone Laboratories, the Royal Institute of Technology (Stockholm), the Signals Research and Development Establishment (Christchurch), the Haskins Laboratory, and the Massachusetts Institute of Technology, Dunn [6], Fant [7], Lawrence [15], Cooper [3], Stevens [26], and their coworkers, have demonstrated successive generations of intelligible automatic talkers. Recent work at the Haskins Laboratory has led to the development of a digital code, suitable for use by computing machines, that makes an automatic voice utter intelligible connected discourse [16].

The feasibility of automatic speech recognition depends heavily upon the size of the vocabulary of words to be recognized and upon the diversity of talkers and accents with which it must work. Ninety-eight per cent correct recognition of naturally spoken decimal digits was demonstrated several years ago at the Bell Telephone Laboratories and at the Lincoln Laboratory [4], [9]. Togo a step up the scale of vocabulary size, we may say that an automatic recognizer of clearly spoken alphanumerical characters can almost surely be developed now on the basis of existing knowledge. Since untrained operators can read at least as rapidly as trained ones can type, such a device would be a convenient tool in almost any computer installation.

For real-time interaction on a truly symbiotic level, however, a vocabulary of about 2000 words, e.g., 1000 words of something like basic English and 1000 technical terms, would probably be required. That constitutes a challenging problem. In the consensus of acousticians and linguists, construction of a recognizer of 2000 words cannot be accomplished now. However, there are several organizations that would happily undertake to develop an automatic recognize for such a vocabulary on a five-year basis. They would stipulate that the speech be clear speech, dictation style, without unusual accent.

Although detailed discussion of techniques of automatic speech recognition is beyond the present scope, it is fitting to note that computing machines are playing a dominant role in the development of automatic speech recognizers. They have contributed the impetus that accounts for the present optimism, or rather for the optimism presently found in some quarters. Two or three years ago, it appeared that automatic recognition of sizeable vocabularies would not be achieved for ten or fifteen years; that it would have to await much further, gradual accumulation of knowledge of acoustic, phonetic, linguistic, and psychological processes in speech communication. Now, however, many see a prospect of accelerating the acquisition of that knowledge with the aid of computer processing of speech signals, and not a few workers have the feeling that sophisticated computer programs will be able to perform well as speech-pattern recognizes even without the aid of much substantive knowledge of speech signals and processes. Putting those two considerations together brings the estimate of the time required to achieve practically significant speech recognition down to perhaps five years, the five years just mentioned.

REFERENCES

1. A. Bernstein and M. deV. Roberts, "Computer versus chess-player," *Scientific American,* vol. 198, pp. 96–98; June, 1958.

2. W. W. Bledsoe and I. Browning, "Pattern Recognition and Reading by Machine," presented at the Eastern Joint Computer Conf., Boston, Mass., December, 1959.

3. F. S. Cooper, et al., "Some experiments on the perception of synthetic speech sounds," *J. Acoust. Soc. Amer.,* vol. 24, pp. 597– 606; November, 1952.

4. K. H. Davis, R. Biddulph, and S. Balashek, "Automatic recognition of spoken digits," in W. Jackson, *Communication Theory,* Butterworths Scientific Publications, London, Eng., pp. 433–441; 1953.

5. G. P. Dinneen, "Programming pattern recognition," *Proc. WJCC,* pp. 94–100; March, 1955.

6. H. K. Dunn, "The calculation of vowel resonances, and an electrical vocal tract," *J. Acoust. Soc. Amer.,* vol. 22, pp. 740–753; November, 1950.

7. G. Fant, "On the Acoustics of Speech," paper presented at the Third Internatl. Congress on Acoustics, Stuttgart, Ger.; September, 1959.

8. B. G. Farley and W. A. Clark, "Simulation of self-organizing systems by digital computers." *IRE Trans. on Information Theory,* vol. IT-4, pp.76–84; September, 1954.

9. J. W. Forgie and C. D. Forgie, "Results obtained from a vowel recognition computer program," *J. Acoust. Soc.* Amer., vol. 31, pp. 1480–1489; November, 1959.

10. E. Fredkin, "Trie memory," *Communications of the ACM,* Sept. 1960, pp. 490–499.

11. R. M. Friedberg, "A learning machine: Part I," *IBM J. Res. & Dev.,* vol. 2, pp. 2–13; January, 1958.

12. H. Gelernter, "Realization of a Geometry Theorem Proving Machine." Unesco, NS, ICIP, 1.6.6, Internatl. Conf. on Information Processing, Paris, France; June, 1959.

13. P. C. Gilmore, "A Program for the Production of Proofs for Theorems Derivable Within the First Order Predicate Calculus from Axioms," Unesco, NS, ICIP, 1.6.14, Internatl. Conf. on Information Processing, Paris, France; June, 1959.

14. J. T. Gilmore and R. E. Savell, "The Lincoln Writer," Lincoln Laboratory, M. I. T., Lexington, Mass., Rept. 51–8; October, 1959.

15. W. Lawrence, et al., "Methods and Purposes of Speech Synthesis," Signals Res. and Dev. Estab., Ministry of Supply, Christchurch, Hants, England, Rept. 56/1457; March, 1956.

16. A. M. Liberman, F. Ingemann, L. Lisker, P. Delattre, and F. S. Cooper, "Minimal rules for synthesizing speech," *J. Acoust. Soc. Amer.,* vol. 31, pp. 1490–1499; November, 1959.

17. A. Newell, "The chess machine: an example of dealing with a complex task by adaptation," *Proc. WJCC,* pp. 101–108; March, 1955.

18. A. Newell and J. C. Shaw, "Programming the logic theory machine." *Proc. WJCC,* pp. 230–240; March, 1957.

19. A. Newell, J. C. Shaw, and H. A. Simon, "Chess-playing programs and the problem of complexity," *IBM J. Res. & Dev.,* vol. 2, pp. 320–335; October, 1958.

20. A. Newell, H. A. Simon, and J. C. Shaw, "Report on a general problem-solving program," Unesco, NS, ICIP, 1.6.8, Internatl. Conf. on Information Processing, Paris, France; June, 1959.

21. J. D. North, "The rational behavior of mechanically extended man", Boulton Paul Aircraft Ltd., Wolverhampton, Eng.; September, 1954.

22. O. G. Selfridge, "Pandemonium, a paradigm for learning," *Proc. Symp. Mechanisation of Thought Processes,* Natl. Physical Lab., Teddington, Eng.; November, 1958.

23. C. E. Shannon, "Programming a computer for playing chess," *Phil. Mag.,* vol. 41, pp. 256–75; March, 1950.

24. J. C. Shaw, A. Newell, H. A. Simon, and T. O. Ellis, "A command structure for complex information processing," *Proc. WJCC,* pp. 119–128; May, 1958.

25. H. Sherman, "A Quasi-Topological Method for Recognition of Line Patterns," Unesco, NS, ICIP, H.L.5, Internatl. Conf. on Information Processing, Paris, France; June, 1959.

26. K. N. Stevens, S. Kasowski, and C. G. Fant, "Electric analog of the vocal tract," *J. Acoust. Soc. Amer.,* vol. 25, pp.734–742; July, 1953.

27. *Webster's New International Dictionary,* 2nd ed., G. and C. Merriam Co., Springfield, Mass., p. 2555; 1958.

10.6

On-Line Man-Computer Communication

J. C. R. Licklider and Welden E. Clark

INTRODUCTORY NOTE TO READING 10.6

As a psychologist Licklider (Reading 10.5) had a particular interest in the human-computer interface. Among the features of this paper is its discussion and reproduction of screen shots of early graphical displays. "Lick had always loved graphics. Indeed, he considered high-resolution graphics to be as critical to human-computer symbiosis as communications or even real-time interactivity. Humans are visual animals, he would muse to anyone who would listen. Our eyes are 'a high-bandwidth data channel' capable of absorbing information at the equivalent of millions of bits per second. Our brains are organized to recognize patterns and sense complex relationships at a glance. . . ."[1] Licklider became especially interested in Ivan Sutherland's *Sketchpad* (Reading 10.7). [JMN]

---

1 Mitchell Waldrop, *The Dream Machine. J. C. R. Licklider and the Revolution that Made Computing Personal* (New York: Viking, 2001), 255.

TEXT OF READING 10.6

SUMMARY

On-line man-computer communication requires much development before men and computers can work together effectively in formulative thinking and intuitive problem solving. This paper examines some of the directions in which advances can be made and describes ongoing programs that seek to improve man-machine interaction in teaching and learning, in planning and design, and in visualizing the internal processes of computers. The paper concludes with a brief discussion of basic problems involved in improving man-computer communication.

INTRODUCTION

On-line communication between men and computers has been greatly impeded, during the whole of the short active history of digital computing, by the economic factor. Large-scale computers have been so expensive that—in business, industrial, and university applications—there has been great pressure to take full advantage of their speed. Since men think slowly, that pressure has tended to preclude extensive on-line interaction between men and large-scale computers. Inexpensive computers, on the other hand, have been severely limited in input-output facilities. Consequently, the main channel of on-line man-computer interaction, in the world of commerce and in the universities, has been the electric typewriter.

In critical military systems such as SAGE, the economic factor has been less restrictive and the need for man-computer interaction greater or more evident. However, the SAGE System, the pioneer among computerized military systems, is "computer-centered"—less so in operation than in initial design, but still clearly computer-centered—and that fact has had a strong influence upon man-computer interaction in military contexts. The computers and their programs have tended to dominate and control the patterns of activity. The scope for human initiative has not been great. Men have been assigned tasks that proved difficult to automate more often than tasks at which they are particularly adept.

For the kind of on-line man-computer interaction required in computer-centered military systems, a console featuring a Charactron display tube, a "light gun," and arrays of display lights and push buttons proved effective. At one time, about four years ago, at least 13 different companies were manufacturing such consoles—different in minor respects but all alike in basic concept. Until recently, therefore, on-line man-computer communication could be summed up in the phrase: electric typewriters and SAGE consoles.

INCREASING NEED FOR MAN-COMPUTER SYMBIOSIS

During the last year or two, three trends that bear upon on-line man-computer interaction have become clear. First, the cost of computation is decreasing; it is no longer wholly uneconomic for a man to think in real time with a medium-scale computer. Second, time-sharing schemes are beginning to appear in hardware form; the economic obstacle fades as the cost of a computer is divided among several or many users. Third, more and more people are sensing the importance of the kinds of thinking and problem solving that a truly symbiotic man-computer partnership might accomplish:

1. Military officers are eager to regain the initiative and flexibility of command they feel they lost to the computers in computer-centered command and control systems, but they want to retain the storage and processing services of the computers.

2. A few mathematicians are finding computers very helpful in exploratory mathematical thinking.

   Working closely with powerful computers and graphic displays, they are able to see at once the consequences of experimental variations in basic assumptions and in the formulation of complex expressions.

3. Several persons responsible for the programming of computerized systems are beginning to believe that the only way to develop major programs rapidly enough to meet hardware time scales is to substitute, for the large crews of programmers, coders, and clerks, small teams of men with sophisticated computer assistance—small teams programming "at the console." With statement-by-statement compiling and testing and with computer-aided book-keeping and program integration, a few very talented men may be able to handle in weeks programming tasks that ordinarily require many people and many months.

4. In war gaming and even to some extent in management gaming, there is a growing feeling that the value of exercises will increase greatly if the pace can be speeded. On-line interaction between the gamers and computers is required to speed the pace.

5. In the planning and design of systems of many kinds, digital simulation is recognized as a valuable technique, even though the preparation and execution of a simulation program may take weeks or months. There is now a growing interest in bringing the technique under direct and immediate control of planners and designers—in achieving the availability and responsiveness of a desk calculator without losing the power and scope of the computer.

6. In the field of education, some of the far-reaching possibilities inherent in a meld of "programmed instruction" and digital computers have become evident to many.

7. The complex equipment used in exploratory research, now in scientific laboratories and perhaps shortly in space, requires overall guidance by scientists but, at the same time, detailed control by computers. Several groups are currently interested in "semi-automatic laboratories."

The foregoing considerations suggest that man-computer communication will be an active field during the next few years and that efforts to facilitate productive interaction between men and computers will receive wide appreciation.

MAN-COMPUTER COMPLEMENTATION

The fundamental aim in designing a man-computer symbiosis is to exploit the complementation that exists between human capabilities and present computer capabilities:

a. To select goals and criteria—human;

b. To formulate questions and hypotheses—human;

c. To select approaches—human;

d. To detect relevance—human;

e. To recognize patterns and objects—human;

f. To handle unforeseen and low-probability exigencies—human;

g. To store large quantities of information—human and computer; with high precision—computer;

h. To retrieve information rapidly—human and computer; with high precision—computer;

i. To calculate rapidly and accurately—computer;

j. To build up progressively a repertoire of procedures without suffering loss due to interference or lack of use—computer.

It seems to us that the functions listed, (a) through (j), are the essential ingredients of creative, intellectual work. In most such work, they are not strung together in simple temporal sequence, but intimately interrelated, often operating simultaneously with much reciprocal interaction. For that reason, the conventional computer-center mode of operation, patterned after that of the neighborhood dry cleaner ("in by ten, out by five"), is inadequate for creative man-computer thinking; a tight, on-line coupling between human brains and electronic computers is required. We must amalgamate the predominately human capabilities and the predominately computer capabilities to create an integrated system for goal-oriented, on-line-inventive information processing.

In associating capabilities (a) through (f) primarily with human beings and capabilities (g) through (j) primarily with computers, we are of course describing the present state of affairs, the technology in which we now must work, and not asserting any essential discontinuity between the domains of human and machine information processing. There is always the possibility that human competence in (g) through (j) can be significantly increased, and it is almost certain that machine competence in (a) through (f) will develop rapidly during the next decades. At present, however, we think that man and computer complement each other, and that the intellectual power of an effective man-computer symbiosis will far exceed that of either component alone.

STEPS TOWARD MAN-COMPUTER SYMBIOSIS

To bring men and computers together in tight synergic interaction, we must make advances in several contributory fields. Among the most important appear to be: time sharing and other possible solutions to the economic problem; memory and processor organization for contingent retrieval of information and programming of procedures; programming and control languages; and on-line input-out equipment, including integrated displays and controls. The groups with which we are associated have been working in those areas. It is disappointing to find that the areas appear to grow more rapidly than we can explore them and to realize how trivial are our

accomplishments relative to the requirements. However., we are beginning to have some tangible results, and it may be worthwhile to illustrate briefly the following three:

1. A system for computer-aided teaching and computer-facilitated study.

2. A man-computer system for use in the planning and design phases of architectural and constructional problems.

3. Two programs that display aspects of the internal processes of a computer during execution of programs.

COMPUTER-AIDED TEACHING AND LEARNING

Exploration of ways in which a computer can facilitate teaching and learning raises several problems in man-computer communication. Effective teacher-student relations involve nearly continuous interchange of information, and anything that interferes with the communication is likely to impair effectiveness.

The importance of rapid, convenient student-teacher communication has demonstrated itself quite clearly in experiments with a simple, automated, language-vocabulary-teaching system. One version of the system, *Tutor 1*, uses a computer typewriter as the communication link between the student and the machine. Let us examine first the procedure briefly and then the problem of typewriter communication between student and computer.

The typescript of the sample German-English lesson, shown in Fig. 1, illustrates the procedure. In a session with *Tutor 1*, the student initiates activity by typing "0." The computer then asks him whether or not the student wants detailed instructions. The student replies by typing "s" for "No, start the lesson." The computer selects a German word at random and presents it. The student then types an English word that he thinks is equivalent in meaning and terminates his response by hitting the "centered-dot" key. If the response is acceptable to the computer, the computer types "+" for "correct." (Brevity is crucial.) If it wants another English equivalent, the computer then types the German word again. If it does not want another English equivalent, it types the item score and the cumulative score to date and offers a comment on the student's performance. When the student misses a word, the computer types "–" for "incorrect" and "ta" for "Do you want to try again?" If the student replies "y" for "yes," the computer presents the missed German word again. If the student replies "n" for "no," the computer types an English equivalent and requires the student to copy it. And so forth, as illustrated.

```
0

Good afternoon.  This will be
your German-English Lesson No. 4.
If you are ready to start at
once, please type "s."  If you
would like to review the
procedure, please type "p."

s

reichen         to hand•  +
reichen         to pass•  +
        64              64    good
öffnen          to offer• – ta    n
to open         to open°
     -120             -56    poor
arbeiten        to arbitrate° – ta    y
arbeiten        to look° – ta    n
to work         to work•
     -184            -240    Dumbkopf!
kochen          to cook• – ta    y
kochen          to boil•  +
        0            -240    okay
öffnen          to open•  +
        64           -176    hot dog
rauchen         to smoke•  +
        64           -112    admirable
arbeiten        to work•  +
        64            -48    good
kochen          to boil•  +
        64             16    very good
machen          to make•  +
        64             80    Keep it up.
        80

That's it.  You did well.  I'll
be looking forward to the next
lesson.
```

Fig. 1 -- Typescript of a short illustrative lesson in which a computer plays the role of instructor in language-vocabulary drill. The student typed "0" to start the session, "s" to start the lesson, the English words (and terminating dots) in right-hand column, and the abbreviations of "yes" and "no" in response to the computer's "ta" ("Do you want to try again?"). The computer typed the remainder, including scores and comments. The procedure is explained in the text.

The first thing we found out about *Tutor 1* was that students (children and adults) who type well like to use it, whereas students who do not type well may be attracted at first but soon tire of the lesson. During the development of the program, several variations were tried out. Those that speeded the pace of presentation or streamlined the procedure of response were the most successful. A version that eliminated the requirement that the student type the response—that allowed him to respond vocally or subvocally and then trusted him to score his answer—was greatly preferred by students who typed only fairly well or poorly; good typists liked "type-the-answer" versions better. With one type-the-answer program, designed to avoid all possible interruptions, students who type well sat for two or three hours at a time, industriously adding new German, French, or Latin words to their vocabularies, occasionally checking their cumulative scores, but never asking for coffee breaks.

Twenty years from now, some form of keyboard operation will doubtless be taught in kindergarten, and forty years from now keyboards may be as universal as pencils, but at present good typists are few. Some other symbolic input channel than the typewriter is greatly needed.

We make some use of the light pen and "light buttons" associated with multiple-choice questions and answers displayed on the oscilloscope. When the alternative courses of action can be laid out in a tree-like branching structure, it is convenient to let the computer ask a multiple-choice question via the oscilloscope display and to arrange the program in such a way that touching the light pen to the button associated with particular response brings forth a subordinate question appropriate to that response. With four familiar alternatives, the operator can make a selection every second or two (i.e., select at a rate of 1 or 2 bits per second), which is adequate for some purposes, though not truly competitive with talking or expert typing (up to 20 and 40, respectively, bits per second in situations in which the pace is not limited by judgmental processes).

In computer-aided teaching, the restriction to a small ensemble of multiple-choice responses sometimes precludes truly convenient, natural communication, and it leads into controversy with those who think that the "constructed response" methods are inherently superior. In our work thus far, it appears that the difference in effectiveness between constructed-response and multiple-choice procedures is small compared with the difference between a convenient, fast response mode and an inconvenient, slow one. Convenience and speed influence markedly the student's enjoyment of his interaction with the computer and the lesson. The most important sub-goal, we believe, is to maximize the amount of enjoyment, satisfaction, and reinforcement the student derives from the interaction. And good student-teacher communication appears to be absolutely essential to that maximization.

Good man-computer communication is important, also, in systems in which the computer serves to facilitate learning without taking the initiative characteristic of most human teachers. We are working on a system, *Graph Equation*, the aim of which is to facilitate a student's exploration of the relations between the symbolic and graphical forms of mathematical equations.

The program displays, for example, the graph of a parabola (see Fig. 2), and below the graph it displays the equation,

$$y = a(x - b)^2 + c \qquad (1)$$

Associated with each of the parameters, *a*, *b*, and *c*, is a potentiometer that controls the value of the parameter. The student can vary the parameter values at will and see, directly and immediately, the correspondence between the configuration of those values and the shape of the parabola. We are in the process of substituting, for the potentiometers, "light scales" with pointers operated by the light pen and of displaying numerical coefficients instead of letter parameters on the oscilloscope. Even in the present crude form, however, the system is an effective aid. It presents the linkage between the symbolic and the graphical representation in a dynamic way. It lets the student explore many more configurations than he could explore if he had to plot graphs on paper. And it lets him see "answers" while he is still thinking about

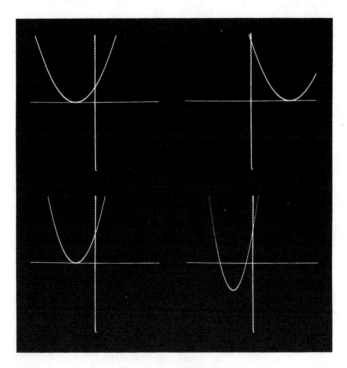

Fig. 2 -- Parabolas displayed by computer to facilitate student's exploration of relations between graphical and symbolic representations of mathematical expressions.

"questions"—something we think may be very important in learning.

We plan, of course, to have the *Graph Equation* system operate dynamically in the other direction, also. The student will draw a rough parabola. The computer will fit an accurate parabola to the rough one and display the accurate one. At the same time, the computer will calculate and display the coefficients. The completed system, we hope, will provide the student with a flexible, responsive study tool. It will not have much practical value as long as it is restricted to parabolas, of course, but it should be possible, with a faster machine, to handle Fourier transforms, convolution integrals, and the like.

Often the student must manipulate characters of text with reference to pictorial or graphical information. We have been able to handle some of these functions but still lack an integrated system for communication of interrelated symbolic and pictorial information between the student and the computer.

COMPUTER-AIDED PLANNING AND DESIGN

In starting to explore the field of computer-aided planning and design of systems, we have focused on hospitals. Hospitals pose very interesting and difficult—and we believe to a large extent typical—system problems because the relative importance of the various planning factors varies from one local context to another, because so many kinds of interest and experience are relevant and eager to make themselves felt, and because tangibles and intangibles are so intimately interrelated. One of the main aims in setting up a computer system to facilitate hospital planning is therefore to provide a means through which general guide lines and local constraints can interact. Another is to permit several persons with various backgrounds and interests to look at tentative plans from their own differing points of view and to manipulate and transform the plans during the course of their discussion. A third (since the intangible factors must ultimately be converted into tangible, physical form) is to give the planners a way of sketching out their suggestions and then relating them, quickly and conveniently, to all the other considerations that have been introduced.

Coplanner, a computer-oriented planning system with which we have been working, is essentially:

1. The PDP-1 computer with type-writer, oscilloscope, light gun, and magnetic-tape unit.

2. An ensemble of empirical data describing the commerce (communication of information, transportation of objects, and movement of personnel) that goes on in typical hospitals.

3. An ensemble of programs for accepting, storing, retrieving, processing and displaying information.

In our work thus far with *Coplanner*, we have experimented with hypothetical hospital situations, using two or three members of our own group and an outside expert or two as the planning team. In preparation for a team planning session, we load into core the programs most likely to be wanted first and make ready the tapes containing the rest of the programs, the ensemble of empirical data, and the material generated in previous planning sessions.

The members of the planning team then sit before the oscilloscope. They start to discuss, for example, a hospital that is expanding its plant and must relocate and enlarge its X-Ray Department. They come to the question: Where should the X-Ray Department be located, relative to the other departments and facilities, in order to minimize the cost of its interdepartmental commerce?

One of the members of the team retrieves, through the computer, a record of previous analyses that provides data on the major components of X-Ray commerce:

a. transport of patients,

b. trips by doctors and internes to supervise x-ray examinations, to study x-ray films, and to consult with

c. personnel of the X-Ray Department,

d. communication not involving movement of personnel, and

e. routine personnel activities such as entering or leaving duty stations and taking meals and breaks.

In response to typewriter commands, the computer then prepares and displays several graphs to summarize the quantitative commerce data. The graphs are mainly distribution graphs and histograms. Since they refer to hospitals of the same type and size, but not to precisely the one being planned, intuitive judgment suggests modifications to take into account various features of the local context. Members of the team make the adjustments in the process of discussion. All they have to do to increase the height of a bar in a histogram is to touch the top of the bar with the light pen and lift it to the desired level. Usually there will be discussion of the change and several successive adjustments of the graph. If the graph is a frequency histogram, raising one bar automatically lowers the others. Efforts have been made to create a favorable context for exercise of the planners' intuitive judgment. Provision is made for labeling, filing, and later processing alternative quantitative summaries if the planners do not agree fully on a single summary.

Figure 3 shows two graphs of the type developed in this phase of the planning discussion.

The planners of course have several different ideas concerning the new layout of the hospital. To make these ideas concrete, they display prepared floor plans—a separate plan for each floor of each version—or sketch them directly on the screen of the oscilloscope, using the light pen as a stylus. Sketching is facilitated by the computer, which posts a background outline plan having the proper dimensions and showing existing structures that cannot readily be altered. In its "straight-line" mode, the computer plots straight lines even if the sketchers lines are wavy. In its "preferentially-parallel-to-axes" mode, the computer plots lines precisely parallel to the x axis if the sketcher makes them approximately so, etc. On their sketches, which they can readily file away and recall for revision, the planners label the various departments and the

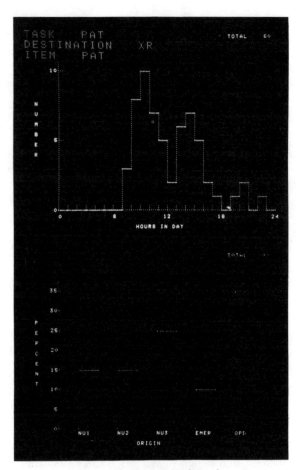

Fig. 3 -- Oscilloscope displays of several aspects of a projected interdepartmental "commerce" pattern in a hypothetical hospital. The upper graph shows the anticipated time distribution of patient transport trips to the X-Ray Department. The lower graph shows the conditional distribution of those trips among departments of origin.

stairs, elevators, dumbwaiters, etc. Each label, typed on the typewriter, appears at the top of the oscilloscope screen, and then is adjusted to desired size, trapped by the light pen, moved to its proper location on the plan, and dropped there. Each label serves as a storage and retrieval tag for the sketch to which it is attached. The plan can therefore be made up in small parts and displayed as a whole. Within a few months, the program will be capable of filing and retrieving assemblies by name.

Having tentatively worked out their ideas about X-Ray commerce and sketched several physical arrangements, the planners now turn to the problem of evaluation. First, they select one of the commerce-distribution hypotheses and one of the physical lay-

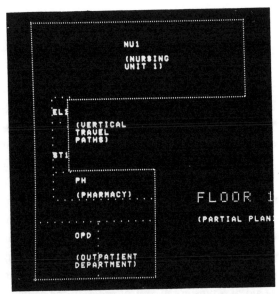

Fig. 4 -- Oscilloscope display of an outline planning sketch of one floor in a hypothetical hospital.

outs for examination and designate them as input data to a fast-time simulation program that converts the commerce pattern from a set of statistical distributions to a sequence of individual trips and calls. Then they apply a program that finds the best routes for the trips and calls and computes expected durations and costs. In calculating cost, the amounts of time spent by various categories of personnel are weighted appropriately. The weighting function can, of course, be discussed and varied by the planning team. The calculated cost provides an evaluative measure for the selected layout under the selected commerce hypothesis. Actually, several different evaluative formulas are ordinarily used. The corresponding cost figures are saved for later use.

The evaluative procedure is then applied to other combinations of layout and commerce hypothesis. When all the combinations have been treated, the planners recall the cost figures and compare them. On

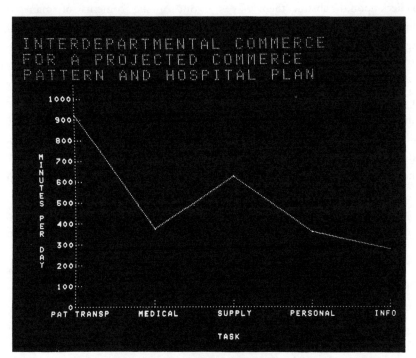

Fig. 5 -- Oscilloscope display of the performance, in respect of "commerce," of a proposed hospital plan. Scale time is defined as man-minutes spent in transit. The contributions of individuals to this quantity are weighted by coefficients associated with their personnel categories.

the basis of this comparison, they usually discard all but the best two or three schemes. They modify the best ones, introduce new considerations developed as a result of the study, and make further simulation and evaluation runs.

Figure 5 shows an output-display prepared by the evaluation program.

If the planners are inclined to go into detail in certain areas, *Coplanner* is prepared to assist them. An elevator-simulation routine, for example, provides a dynamic display of elevator operation under the loads specified by a selected commerce-distribution hypothesis and a determination of best routes. Direct dynamic simulation has important roles to play in work of this kind because it appeals to non-mathematical planners more directly than does queuing-theory analysis performed with the aid only of symbolic assumptions and equations. Sometimes dynamic simulation is a substitute for the abstract theory; sometimes it is an introduction to the abstract theory; sometimes it is a check upon the abstract theory.

In the preceding discussion, one small facet of the hospital planning problem was used to illustrate the approach we are advocating. We have developed a fairly powerful system to facilitate planning in the area discussed and in related areas. In other areas, the system is only starting to develop. The computer parts of the system are not intended, we should emphasize, to calculate optimal plans or designs; they are intended to provide memory, manipulative, computing, and display functions in such a way that they can be integrated with the more intuitive functions supplied by the human parts of the system.[1]

VISUALIZING THE OPERATION OF COMPUTER PROGRAMS

The covertness of the operation of the programs of electronic computers makes it difficult for us to develop of them the same direct, perceptual kind of comprehension that most of us have of familiar mechanisms, the moving parts of which we can see and touch. The great speed with which the programs run adds to the difficulty, of course, but we are in the habit of solving the speed problem—for example, through

"slow motion." Unless a window or a plastic model will provide solution, however, we are in the habit of letting the problem of covertness go unsolved. We tend to be satisfied with extremely indirect procedures for interrogation and for drawing inferences. In the case of the human brain, for example, a neurophysiologist may try to construct a model of an internal process on the basis of waveforms recorded from 10 or 100 of the million or billion neurons involved, plus microscopic inspection of several slices of the tissue prepared in such a way as to render visible one or another feature of its architecture. Our approach to computers is comparable: When trouble arises and the results do not turn out as we expect them to, we may try to figure out what is going on by examining with the aid of a typewriter control program the contents of supposedly critical registers, one register at a time, even though we cannot hope to look at more than a hundred of the thousands or tens of thousands of registers involved. Alternatively, we may ask for a print-out of the contents of many registers at some particular point in the running of the program, hoping to reconstruct the dynamic pattern of events from the static view provided by the printout.

Considering the problem posed by covertness leads one to think about the procedure, *introspection*, used as the basic experimental tool in such early psychological laboratories as Wundt's and Titchener's, and still widely employed in the development, if not in the formal testing, of psychological hypotheses. Human introspection is a useful procedure despite its severe shortcomings. How much more useful it would be if those shortcomings were overcome—if all the processes of the brain were accessible to the reporting mechanism; if the reporting mechanism could describe all the aspects of those processes; if the reports were detailed and accurate; if introspecting did not interfere with the process under examination.

That thought leads immediately to the idea of a computer analogy to, or improvement upon, human introspection. Clearly, computer introspection can be freed of all the shortcomings mentioned, except the last, and the last one can be turned to advantage. Displaying its own internal processes will of course interfere with the computer's execution of its substantive programs, but only by appropriating memory space and time. Often, there is memory space to spare, and programs normally run too fast for the operator to follow them perceptually. The conclusion, therefore, is that it might be interesting to experiment with programs that display various aspects of the internal operation of the running computer.

Two such programs, written for the PDP-1 computer, are *Program Graph* and *Memory Course. Program Graph* was written with the hope that it would facilitate the introduction to computer programming and provide displays through which certain individual or "personality" characteristics of programming style may be seen. *Memory Course* was intended mainly for use in "debugging" computer programs. Both programs make use of a trace routine that executes the instructions of the object program in normal, running sequence and, after each execution, (a) records in core registers the contents of the accumulator, input-output register, and program counter, (b) does some incidental bookkeeping, and (c) turns control over to the display routines. The display routines develop graphs of types to be illustrated.

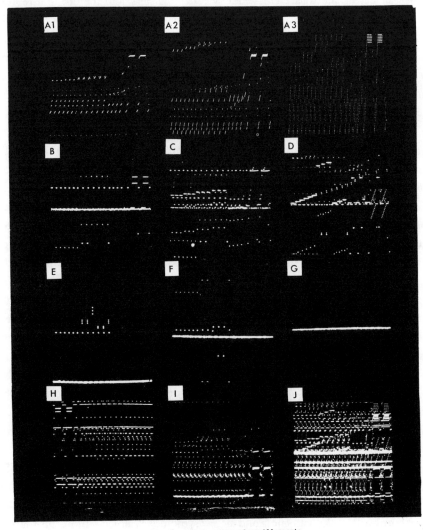

Fig. 6 -- Photographs of oscilloscopic displays made by Program Graph. See text for interpretation.

The graphs displayed by *Program Graph* are illustrated in Fig. 6. In Fig. 6A, as each instruction of the object program is executed, its location is plotted as ordinate, and the cumulative number of executions is plotted as abscissa. (Roughly speaking, therefore, the graph represents active memory location versus time.) Both the ordinate and the abscissa scales run from 0 to 1777 (octal). The interpretation of the graph is quite direct: straight-line parts of the graph represent straight-line parts of the program; jumps represent jumps or subroutine calls; serrations represent loops. The subroutine structure is revealed clearly. If the operator knows the general course the program should follow, he can detect and locate gross faults readily.

Figures 6B-6D show, for the same object program, the contents of the accumulator as a function of time. The abscissa scale again runs from 0 to 1777. In Fig. 6B, the ordinate scale covers the range from -2^{17} to 2^{17}; in Fig. 6C, it runs from -2^{13} to 2^{13}; and in Fig. 6D, it runs from -2^7 to 2^7. Evidently, the accumulator is heavily engaged in computations involving small numbers.

Figures 6E-6G show, for the input-output register, what Figs. 6B-6D showed for the accumulator.

Figure 6H displays the instruction codes. Each instruction code is a two-digit octal number. The ordinate scale extends from 02 (*and*) to 76 (*operate*, which is an augmented instruction, the augmentation not shown). The most heavily used instructions are 20 (*load accumulator with contents of*) and 24 (*deposit contents of accumulator into*).

Figure 6I displays the memory references and the augmentations. Both are shown here; either class may be suppressed.

In Fig. 6J, all the graphs of Figs. 6A-6I are displayed simultaneously. Because the points are shape-coded, it is possible, though difficult, to reconstruct in detail the sequential pattern of a program from graphs of this type. They might therefore find application in historical documentation of very critical computations, such as those concerned with rocket launching and air defense. In any event, the composite representation conveys an impression of the great capability comput-

ers have to introspect upon their internal processes and report about them in detail.

As we leave this topic, we should perhaps mention the phenomenon that appears when *Program Graph* is equipped for recursive operation and set to display its own operation. The result, of course, is only a recursion of beginnings, terminated by overflowing of the pushdown list. This effect is not entirely foreign to human introspection.

The routine, *Memory Course*, plots a grid-like map of memory and displays, against the background of the grid, the course through memory taken by the object program. The dots of the grid represent memory registers, and the dot that represents the register containing the instruction presently being executed is encircled. As control passes from one instruction to another of the object program, a line is drawn connecting the corresponding registers. The effect is hard to illustrate in a still photograph because its effectiveness depends largely upon the kinetic character of the display. However, Fig. 7 may convey an approximate impression. Because the photograph integrates over time, it shows a longer segment of the program's course through memory than one sees when he views the oscilloscope directly. *Program Graph* and *Memory Course* are but two of many possible schemes for displaying the internal processes of the computer. We are working on others that combine graphical presentation with symbolic presentation. Symbolic presentation is widely used, of course, in "debugging" routines. If many symbols are displayed, however, it is not possible to proceed through the program rapidly enough to find errors in reasonable time. By combining graphical with symbolic presentation, and putting the mode of combination under the operator's control via light pen, we hope to achieve both good speed and good discrimination of detailed information.

PROBLEMS TO BE SOLVED IN MAN-COMPUTER COMMUNICATION

Among the problems toward which man-computer symbiosis is aimed—problems that men and computers should attack in partnership—are some of great intellectual depth and intrinsic difficulty. The main

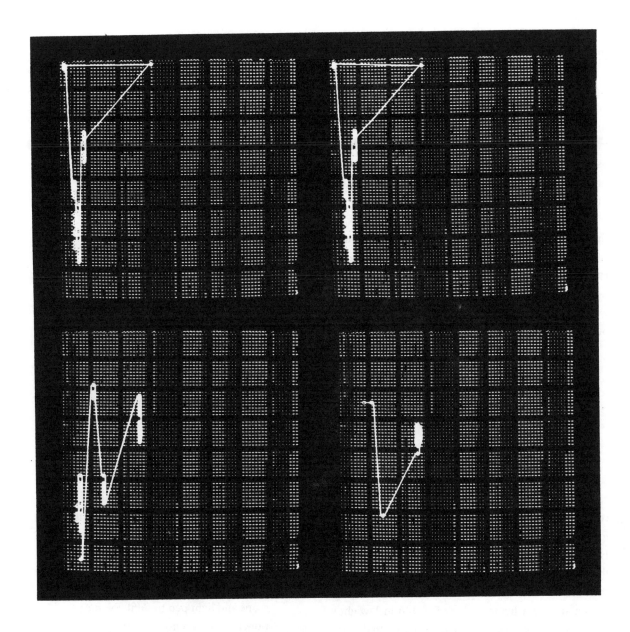

Fig. 7 -- Photograph of oscilloscopic
display made by Memory Course. See text
for interpretation.

problems that must be solved to bring man-computer symbiosis into being, however, appear not to be of that kind. They are not easy, but their difficulty seems due more to limitations of technology than to limitations of intelligence.

What we would like to achieve, at least as a sub-goal, is a mechanism that will couple man to com-puter as closely as man is now coupled to man in good multidisciplinary scientific or engineering teams.

For a psychologist to telephone a mathematician and ask him, "How can I integrate $\int(dx/(1 - x))$?" required, in one empirical test, 105 seconds, including 65 seconds devoted to dialing and formalities with the mathematician's secretary plus 32 seconds of preamble with the mathematician. To ask the mathematician that particular question is, of course, wantonly to waste his time—170 seconds of it, in this case, since all he needed to say was: "Look it up in any table of integrals," and all he did say was that sentence embedded in a context of encouragement and courtesy. (To find a table of integrals and then to locate the entry took the psychologist, who missed the relevant formula on his first pass and started over at the beginning after scanning 569 entries, 7 minutes and 25 seconds.)

What we would like the computer to do for us, in the context of the foregoing example, does not require such a deep solution as an algorithm for formal differentiation; it requires merely good communication and retrieval. We would like to have an arrangement that would let the psychologist write on his desk input-output surface:

$$\int \frac{dx}{1-x^2} = \text{what?} \qquad (2)$$

and then let the computer replace the "what?"—in perhaps 2 or even 20 seconds—by the expression:

$$\frac{1}{2} \log \frac{|1+x|}{|1-x|} \qquad (3)$$

In the example, our aspiration would not stop, of course, with the display of expression (3) in symbolic form. The psychologist would surely want elucidation. His next request might be "Please plot a graph," or, if the novelty were worn off, simply "Graph." We would then like to have the computer display on the input-output surface a figure such as Fig. 140 in Dwight's *Tables*. The figure would, of course, be plotted from computed points, not retrieved from storage. It would be no trouble for the computer to calculate and present it in a few seconds. (For the psychologist to plot a rough graph of the integral took 12 minutes. For another person to locate a published figure (Dwight's) took 17 minutes: a little more than 16 to get to the document room and thumb through books that did not contain the figure, and then a little less than 1 to pick up Dwight's book and scan as far as page 29, where the figure is.)

Five Immediate Problems

Consideration of many such examples as the foregoing and of what would have to be done to put the computer's clerical power conveniently and responsively under the control of human initiative suggests that the main essential steps to man-computer symbiosis are the following:

1. For the economic reason mentioned in the Introduction, develop systems for sharing the time of digital computers among many users on a split-millisecond basis. With J. McCarthy and S. Boilen one of us is working on a small-scale prototype of such a system with five user stations.

2. Devise an electronic input-output surface on which both the operator and the computer can display, and through which they can communicate, correlated symbolic and pictorial information. The surface should have selective persistence plus selective erasability; the computer should not have to spend a large part of its time maintaining the displays. The entire device should be inexpensive enough for incorporation into a remote console. An interesting approach to the man-to-machine part of, this problem is being taken by Teagher. We are employing an oscilloscope and light pen to fulfill the function, but they do not meet the cost and selective-persistence requirements.

3. Develop a programming system that will facilitate real-time contingent selection and shaping of information-processing procedures. The system must permit trial-and-error operation based upon "tentative computation": it will often be necessary to go back to the beginning or to an intermediate point and to try a different attack. We are experimenting with interpretive systems

for on-line assembly of procedures from sub-procedures,[2] and we are planning work on console compiling, intermeshed with testing and contingent application of procedures as they are required by the human components of the man-computer partnership.

4. Develop systems for storage and retrieval of the vast quantities of information required to support, simultaneously at several user stations, creative thinking in various areas of investigation. For economic reasons, such systems must almost certainly be hierarchical, moving information from large-capacity, fast-access storage as (or shortly before) the information is needed. To achieve the desired effectiveness, it will probably be necessary to make advances in the direction of parallel-access, associative memory with preliminary activation based upon apperceptive relevance. In this area, we believe, much fundamental study of information indexing and of memory organization will be necessary before truly satisfactory hardware can be designed, but it appears that quite a bit can be accomplished directly through development of memories—probably read-only memories—with very large capacity and moderately fast access and through the application of existing keyword or descriptor techniques.

5. Solve the problem of human cooperation in the development of large program systems. It appears that the development of effective human cooperation and the development of man-computer symbiosis are "chicken-and-egg" problems. It will take unusual human teamwork to set up a truly workable man-computer partnership, and it will take man-computer partnerships to engender and facilitate the human cooperation. For that reason, the main tasks of the first time-sharing computer system with many remote stations may well be in the areas of language and procedure development.

In the five problem areas just mentioned, "to begin is everything," even if it is necessary at first to build research systems along lines that would be uneconomic for widespread application. If we neglect the arguments of economics and elegance we can think at once of ways of solving, or at least starting to solve, the problems. These ways will probably be adequate to test the premise that man-computer symbiosis will be able to achieve intellectual results beyond the range of men alone or of computers programmed and operated in conventional ways.

Four Long-Term Problems

In four other areas, the problems to be solved appear—if they are not simplified beyond recognition in the effort to make them tractable—to be deep and intrinsically difficult. The first of these areas is computer appreciation of natural written languages, in their semantic and pragmatic as well as in their syntactic aspects. The second is computer recognition of words spoken in context by various and unselected talkers. The third is the theory of algorithms, particularly their discovery and simplification. The fourth is heuristic programming. We believe that these four areas will in the long term be extremely important to man-computer symbiosis, but that man-computer partnerships of considerable effectiveness and value can be achieved without them. We suspect that solutions in these areas will be found with the aid of early man-computer symbioses, rather than conversely.

An Intermediate Problem

A system combining an elementary form of computer speech recognition, computer recognition of carefully hand-printed characters, and simple light-pen editing techniques, would provide, we think, a very convenient and effective communication link between man and computer. The problems involved in creating such a system seem to us to be intermediate between the five and the four. They may be solved in time to permit the use of correlated voice-hand input in the earliest man-computer partnerships, but, if the required solutions are not ready, it would not be good to wait for them.

REFERENCES

1. James J. Souder, Madison Brown, Weldon Clark and Jerome Elkind, *Collaborative Research in Hospital Planning*, United States Public Health Service, Project W-59, to be published in the spring of 1962.

2. B. O. Peirce, *A Short Table of Integrals*, 3rd edition, Boston: Ginn and Company, 1929.

3. H. B. Dwight, *Table of Integrals and other Mathematical Data*, 3rd edition, New York: The Macmillan Company, 1957

4. H. M. Teagher, Semi-Annual Progress Reports dated January 1961, June 1961 and January 1962, M.I.T. Computation Center. Also, Quarterly Progress Reports 2, 3, 4 and 5 of the Real-Time Time-Sharing Project, M.I.T. Computation Center.

•••

1. Coplanner was developed under USPHS Project W-59, Collaborative Research in Hospital Planning. J. J. Souter, A.I.A., and M. B. Brown, M.D., past and present Project Directors, and J. I. Elkind and W. E. Fletcher participated in the formulation of the system.

2. One of the systems is based on a typewriter control program, *Process Control*, written by D. Park.

Sketchpad, a Man-Machine Graphical Communication System. Introduction

Ivan Edward Sutherland

From "Sketchpad, a Man-Machine Graphical Communication System" (Ph.D. diss., MIT, January 1963), pp. 8–23.

INTRODUCTORY NOTE TO READING 10.7

The first, primitive graphical display on a computer was the Vectorscope display on the Whirlwind I, which became operational at MIT in April, 1951. Reading 10.7 concerns *Sketchpad,* the first "Graphical User Interface" (GUI), invented by Ivan Sutherland in 1963. As a graduate student at MIT, Sutherland had the lowest priority to use the TX-2 computer. Thus he had to do all his research on the computer from between three and five AM. [JMN]

TEXT OF READING 10.7

The Sketchpad system makes it possible for a man and a computer to converse rapidly through the medium of line drawings. Heretofore, most interaction between men and computers has been slowed down by the need to reduce all communication to written statements that can be typed; in the past, we have been writing letters to rather than conferring with our computers. For many types of communication, such as describing the shape of a mechanical part or the connections of an electrical circuit, typed statements can prove cumbersome. The Sketchpad system, by eliminating typed statements (except for legends) in favor of line drawings, opens up a new area of man-machine communication.

The decision actually to implement a drawing system reflected our feeling that knowledge of the facilities which would prove useful could only be obtained by actually trying them. The decision actually to implement a drawing system did not mean, however, that brute force techniques were to be used to computerize ordinary drafting tools; it was implicit in the research nature of the work that simple new facilities should be discovered which, when implemented, should be useful in a wide range of applications, preferably including some unforeseen ones. It has turned out that the properties of a computer drawing are entirely different from a paper drawing not only because of the accuracy, ease of drawing, and speed of erasing provided by the computer, but also primarily because of the ability to move drawing parts around on a computer drawing without the need to erase them. Had a working system not been developed, our thinking would have been too strongly influenced by a lifetime of drawing on paper to discover many of the useful services that the computer can provide.

As the work has progressed, several simple and very widely applicable facilities have been discovered and implemented. They provide a *subpicture* capability for including arbitrary symbols on a drawing, a *constraint* capability for relating the parts of a drawing in any computable way, and a *definition copying* capability for building complex relationships from combinations of simple atomic constraints. When combined with the ability to point at picture parts given by the demonstrative light pen language, the subpicture, constraint, and definition copying capabilities produce a system of extraordinary power. As was hoped at the outset, the system is useful in a wide range of applications, and unforeseen uses are turning up.

AN INTRODUCTORY EXAMPLE

To understand what is possible with the system at present let us consider using it to draw the hexagonal pattern of Figure 1.1. We will issue specific com-

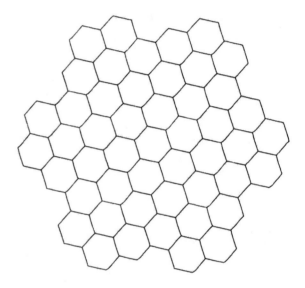

FIGURE 1.1. HEXAGONAL PATTERN

mands with a set of push buttons, turn functions on and off with switches, indicate position information and point to existing drawing parts with the light pen, rotate and magnify picture parts by turning knobs, and observe the drawing on the display system. This equipment as provided at Lincoln Laboratory's TX-2 computer is shown in Figure 1.2. When our drawing is complete it may be inked on paper, as were all the drawings in the thesis, by the plotter shown in Figure 1.3. It is our intent with this example to show what the computer can do to help us draw while leaving the details of how it performs its functions for the chapters which follow.

Figure 1.2

Figure 1.3

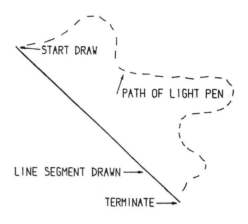

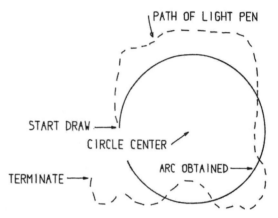

FIGURE 1.4.
LINE AND CIRCLE DRAWING

If we point the light pen at the display system and press a button called "draw," the computer will construct a straight line segment[1] which stretches like a rubber band from the initial to the present location of the pen as shown in Figure 1.4. Additional presses of the button will produce additional lines until we have made six, enough for a single hexagon. To close the figure we return the light pen to near the end of the first line drawn where it will "lock on" to the end exactly. A sudden flick of the pen terminates drawing, leaving the closed irregular hexagon shown in Figure 1.5A.

To make the hexagon regular, we can inscribe it in a circle. To draw the circle we place the light pen where the center is to be and press the button "circle center," leaving behind a center point. Now, choosing a point on the circle (which fixes the radius,) we press the button "draw" again, this time getting a circle arc whose length only is controlled by light pen position as shown in Figure 1.4.

Next we move the hexagon into the circle by pointing to a corner of the hexagon and pressing the button "move" so that the corner follows the light pen, stretching two rubber band line segments behind it. By pointing to the circle and giving the termination flick we indicate that the corner is to lie on the circle. Each corner is in this way moved onto the circle at roughly equal spacing around it as shown in Figure 1.5D.

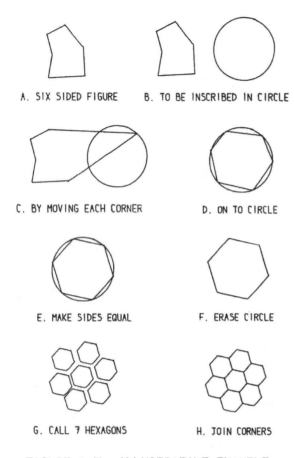

A. SIX SIDED FIGURE   B. TO BE INSCRIBED IN CIRCLE

C. BY MOVING EACH CORNER   D. ON TO CIRCLE

E. MAKE SIDES EQUAL   F. ERASE CIRCLE

G. CALL 7 HEXAGONS   H. JOIN CORNERS

FIGURE 1.5. ILLUSTRATIVE EXAMPLE

We have indicated that the vertices of the hexagon are to lie on the circle, and they will remain on the circle throughout our further manipulations. If we also insist that the sides of the hexagon be of equal length, a regular hexagon will be constructed. This we can do by pointing to one side and pressing the "copy" button, and then to another side and giving the termination flick. The button in this case copies a definition of equal length lines and applies it to the lines indicated. We have said, in effect, make *this* line equal in length to *that* line. We indicate that all six lines are equal in length by five such statements. The computer satisfies all existing conditions (if it is possible) whenever we turn on a toggle switch. This done, we have a complete regular hexagon in-scribed in a circle. We can erase the entire circle by pointing to any part of it and pressing the "delete" button. The completed hexagon is shown in Figure 1.5F.

To make the hexagonal pattern of Figure 1.1 we wish to attach a large number of hexagons together by their corners, and so we designate the six corners of our hexagon as attachment points by pointing to each and pressing a button. We now file away the basic hexagon and begin work on a fresh "sheet of paper" by changing a switch setting. On the new sheet we assemble, by pressing a button to create each hexagon as a subpicture, six hexagons around a central seventh in approximate position as shown in Figure 1.5G. Subpictures may be positioned, each in its entirety, with the light pen, rotated or scaled with the knobs and fixed in position by the pen flick termination signal; but their internal shape is fixed. By pointing to the corner of one hexagon, pressing a button, and then pointing to the corner of another hexagon we can fasten those corners together, because these corners have been designated as attachment points. If we attach two corners of each outer hexagon to the appropriate corners of the inner hexagon, the seven are uniquely related, and the computer will reposition them as shown in Figure 1.5H. An entire group of hexagons, once assembled, can be treated as a symbol. The entire group can be called up on another "sheet of paper" as a subpicture and assembled with other groups or with single hexagons to make a very large pattern. Using Figure 1.5H seven times we get the pattern of Figure 1.1. Constructing the pattern of Figure 1.1 takes less than five minutes with the Sketchpad system.

INTERPRETATION OF INTRODUCTORY EXAMPLE

In the introductory example above we have seen how to draw lines and circles and how to move existing parts of the drawing around. We used the light pen both to position parts of the drawing and to point to existing parts. For example, we pointed to the circle to erase it, and while drawing the sixth line, we pointed to the end of the first line drawn to close the hexagon. We also saw in action the very general *subpicture, constraint,* and *definition copying* capabilities of the system.

Subpicture: The original hexagon might just as well have been anything else: a picture of a transistor, a roller bearing, an airplane wing, a letter, or an entire figure for this report. Any number of different symbols may be drawn, in terms of other simpler symbols if desired, and any symbol may be used as often as desired.

Constraint: When we asked that the vertices of the hexagon lie on the circle we were making use of a basic relationship between picture parts that is built into the system. Basic relationships (atomic constraints) to make lines vertical, horizontal, parallel, or perpendicular; to make points lie on lines or circles; to make symbols appear upright, vertically above one another or be of equal size; and to relate symbols to other drawing parts such as points and lines have been included in the system. It is so easy to program new constraint types that the set of atomic constraints was expanded from five to the seventeen listed in Appendix A in a period of about two days; specialized constraint types may be added as needed.

Definition Copying: In the introductory example above we asked that the sides of the hexagon be equal in length by pressing a button while pointing to the side in question. Here we were using the definition copying capability of the system. Had we defined a composite operation such as to make two lines both parallel and equal in length, we could have applied it just as easily. The number of operations which can be defined from the basic constraints applied to various picture parts is almost unlimited. Useful new definitions are drawn regularly; they are as simple as horizontal lines and as complicated as dimension lines complete with arrowheads and a number which indicates the length of the line correctly. The definition copying capability makes using the constraint capability easy.

IMPLICATIONS OF INTRODUCTORY EXAMPLE

As we have seen in the introductory example, drawing with the Sketchpad system is different from drawing with an ordinary pencil and paper. Most important of all, the Sketchpad drawing itself is entirely different from the trail of carbon left on a piece of paper. Information about how the drawing is tied together is

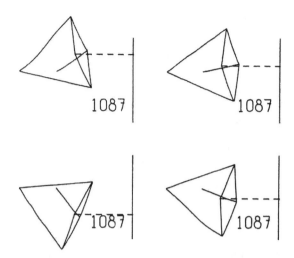

FIGURE 1.6.
FOUR POSITIONS OF LINKAGE
NUMBER SHOWS LENGTH OF DOTTED LINE

stored in the computer as well as the information which gives the drawing its particular appearance. Since the drawing is tied together, it will keep a useful appearance even when parts of it are moved. For example, when we moved the corners of the hexagon onto the circle, the lines next to each corner were automatically moved so that the closed topology of the hexagon was preserved. Again, since we indicated that the corners of the hexagon were to lie on the circle they remained on the circle throughout our further manipulations.

It is this ability to store information relating the parts of a drawing to each other that makes Sketchpad most useful. For example, the linkage shown in Figure 1.6 was drawn with Sketchpad in just a few minutes. Constraints were applied to the linkage to keep the length of its various members constant. Rotation of the short central link is supposed to move the left end of the dotted line vertically. Since exact information about the properties of the linkage has been stored in Sketchpad, it is possible to observe the motion of the entire linkage when the short central link is rotated. The value of the number in Figure 1.6 was constrained to indicate the length of the dotted line, comparing the actual motion with the vertical line at the right of the linkage. One can observe that for all positions of the linkage the length of the dotted line is constant, demonstrating that this is indeed a straight line linkage. Other examples of moving drawings made with Sketchpad may be found in the final chapter.

As well as storing how the various parts of the drawing are related, Sketchpad stores the structure of the subpicture used. For example, the storage for the hexagonal pattern of Figure 1.1 indicates that this pattern is made of smaller patterns which are in turn made of smaller patterns which are composed of single hexagons. If the master hexagon is changed, the entire appearance of the hexagonal pattern will be changed. The structure of the pattern will, of course, be the same. For example, if we change the basic hexagon into a semicircle, the fish scale pattern shown in Figure 1.7 instantly results.

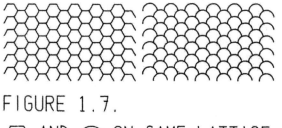

FIGURE 1.7.
⌒\ AND ⌒ ON SAME LATTICE

Since Sketchpad stores the *structure* of a drawing, a Sketchpad drawing explicitly indicates similarity of symbols. In an electrical drawing, for example, all transistor symbols are created from a single master transistor drawing. If some change to the basic transistor symbol is made, this change appears at once in all transistor symbols without further effort. Most important of all, the computer "knows" that a "transistor" is intended at that place in the circuit. It has no need to interpret the collection of lines which we would easily recognize as a transistor symbol. Since Sketchpad stores the *topology* of the drawing as we saw in closing the hexagon, one indicates both what a circuit looks like and its electrical connections when one draws it with Sketchpad. One can see that the circuit connections are stored because moving a component automatically moves any wiring on that component to maintain the correct connections. Sketchpad circuit

drawings will soon be used as inputs for a circuit simulator. Having drawn a circuit one will find out its electrical properties.

SKETCHPAD AND THE DESIGN PROCESS

Construction of a drawing with Sketchpad is *itself* a model of the design process. The locations of the points and lines of the drawing model the variables of a design, and the geometric constraints applied to the points and lines of the drawing model the design constraints which limit the values of design variables. The ability of Sketchpad to satisfy the geometric constraints applied to the parts of a drawing models the ability of a good designer to satisfy all the design conditions imposed by the limitations of his materials, cost, etc. In fact, since designers in many fields produce nothing themselves but a drawing of a part, design conditions may well be thought of as applying to the drawing of a part rather than to the part itself. If such design conditions were added to Sketchpad's vocabulary of constraints the computer could assist a user not only in arriving at a nice looking drawing, but also in arriving at a sound design.

PRESENT USEFULNESS

At the outset of the research no one had ever drawn engineering drawings directly on a computer display with nearly the facility now possible, and consequently no one knew what it would be like. We have now accumulated about a hundred hours of experience actually making drawings with a working system. As is shown in the final chapter, application of computer drawing techniques to a variety of problems has been made. As more and more applications have been made it has become clear that the properties of Sketchpad drawings make them most useful in four broad areas:

For Making Small Changes to
Existing Drawings:
Each time a drawing is made, a description of that drawing is stored in the computer in a form that is readily transferred to magnetic tape. Thus, as time passes, a library of drawings will develop, parts of

which may be used in other drawings at only a fraction of the investment of time that was put into the original drawing. Since a drawing stored in the computer may contain explicit representation of design conditions in its constraints, manual change of a critical part will automatically result in appropriate changes to related parts.

For Gaining Scientific or Engineering Understanding of Operations That Can Be Described Graphically:

The description of a drawing stored in the Sketchpad system is more than a collection of static drawing parts, lines and curves, etc. A drawing in the Sketchpad system may contain explicit statements about the relations between its parts so that as one part is changed the implications of this change become evident through-out the drawing. It is possible, as we saw in Figure 1.6, to give the property of fixed length to lines so as to study mechanical linkages, observing the path of some parts when others are moved.

As we saw in Figure 1.7 any change made in the definition of a subpicture is at once reflected in the appearance of that subpicture wherever it may occur. By making such changes, understanding of the relationships of complex sets of subpictures can be gained. For example, one can study how a change in the basic element of a crystal structure is reflected throughout the crystal.

As a Topological Input Device for Circuit Simulators, etc.:

Since the ring structure storage of Sketchpad reflects the topology of any circuit or diagram, it can serve as an input for many network or circuit simulating programs. The additional effort required to draw a circuit completely from scratch with the Sketchpad system may well be recompensed if the properties of the circuit are obtainable through simulation of the circuit drawn.

For Highly Repetitive Drawings:

The ability of the computer to reproduce any drawn symbol anywhere at the press of a button, and to recursively include subpictures within subpictures makes it easy to produce drawings which are composed of huge numbers of parts all similar in shape. Great interest in doing this comes from people in such fields as memory development and micro logic where vast numbers of elements are to be generated at once through photographic processes. Master drawings of the repetitive patterns necessary can be easily drawn. Here again, the ability to change the individual element of the repetitive structure and have the change at once brought into all sub-elements makes it possible to change the elements of an array without redrawing the entire array.

• • •

1. The terms "circle" and "line" may be used in place of "circle arc" and "line segment" respectively since a full circle in Sketchpad is a circle arc of 360 or more degrees and no infinite line can be drawn.

11

Computing and Intelligence

11.1

The Mind of Mechanical Man

Sir Geoffrey Jefferson

From *Selected Papers* (London: Pittman, 1960), pp. 10–23.

INTRODUCTORY NOTE TO READING 11.1

Sir Geoffrey Jefferson (1886–1961) was a distinguished British neurological surgeon with a strong literary, philosophical, and historical bent who practiced at the Manchester Royal Infirmary. In June 1949, when Jefferson delivered this paper on the differences between the new electronic computers and the human brain at the Royal College of Surgeons, he was aware of the work of F. C. Williams on the Manchester "Baby" stored-program computer that was operational for a short time in 1948. Jefferson described Williams as a professor of "electro-technics," since at this early date the concept of computer science hardly existed. Jefferson referred to the ENIAC in his paper, but he seems to have confused it with the Institute for Advanced Study computer at Princeton. Jefferson also indicated that he had read the early discussion of machines and biological systems in Norbert Wiener's *Cybernetics*, published in 1948. He also refers to English research in cybernetics by J. Z. Young and Grey Walter. It is likely that Jefferson was already aware of the work of Alan Turing, who had moved to Manchester at chief programmer on the Manchester computer project in September, 1948. The serious historical and philosophical discussion presented in this paper stimulated Turing to write his famous response, "Computing Machinery and Intelligence," which is reproduced as Reading 11.2. It is especially interesting to compare and contrast the literary styles and viewpoints of Turing and Jefferson.

When Jefferson wrote a postscript to this paper in 1960 the issues that he had originally raised in 1949 had been further explored but not resolved. Here are some of his comments:

Mine was the first paper by a neurologist faced with the new electronic computing machines, for which much greater identification with the action of the brain was claimed than was in my opinion justifiable. It was a protest against jumping to conclusions and I am sure that it has many imperfections. These machines are much more familiar than they were ten years ago, at which time the address excited a good deal of newspaper comment. My friend and most ingenious mathematical colleague, the late Alan Turing, F.R.S., believed passionately that the computing machines had all but solved at once the intricacies of the mind-brain problem. He said that although a machine might not write a sonnet that I could understand, he was sure that it would write one soon that another computor would enjoy! An American scientist wrote to me that he had shown my pages to his machine and it had been so upset that it had blown its valves. Since then, by making numbers represent words the Burrough's computing machine in New York (1956) has written songs. That should be easy to do by making figures represent musical and verbal phrases. The feat is not what I meant when I asked for the springs of emotion, for the workings of individual experience to sublimate in artistic expression. Perhaps one could build emotion into a machine, for it is not produced only by endocrines. A deal of ink could be spilled by letting one's fancy roam on these possibilities—roam to end where? [JMN]

TEXT OF READING 11.1

No better example could be found of man's characteristic desire for knowledge beyond, and far beyond, the limits of the authentic scientific discoveries of his own day than his wish to understand in complete detail the relationship between the brain and mind—the one so finite, the other so amorphous and elusive. It is a subject which at present awakes a renewed interest, because we are invaded by the physicists and mathematicians—an invasion by no means unwelcome, bringing as it does new suggestions for analogy and comparison. We feel perhaps that we are being pushed, gently not roughly pushed, to accept the great likeness between the actions of electronic machines and those of the nervous system. At the same time we may misunderstand this invitation, and go beyond it to too ready an affirmation that there is identity. We should be wise to examine the nature of this concept and to see how far the electro-physicists share with us a common road. Medicine is placed by these suggestions in a familiar predicament. I refer to the dangers of our being unintentionally misled by pure science. Medical history furnishes many examples, such as the planetary and chemical theories of disease that were the outcome of the Scientific Renaissance. We are the same people as our ancestors and prone to their mistakes. We should reflect that if we go too far and too fast no one will deride us more unashamedly than the scientists who have tempted us.

Discussion of mind-brain relations is, I know well, premature, but I suspect that it always will be premature, taking heart from a quotation that I shall make from Hughlings Jackson—not one of his best-known passages—because it may have been thought to be a sad lapse on his part. I believe it myself to be both true and useful, and so I repeat it.

"It is a favourite popular delusion that the scientific inquirer is under a sort of moral obligation to abstain from going beyond the generalization of the observed facts, which is absurdly called 'Baconian induction.' But anyone who is practically acquainted with scientific work is aware that those who refuse to go beyond fact rarely get as far as fact; and anyone who has studied the history of science knows that almost every great step therein has been made by the 'anticipation of Nature'—that is, by the invention of hypotheses which, though not verifiable, often had very little foundation to start with."

He concludes by saying that even erroneous theories can do useful service temporarily. He was no doubt thinking of his own early clinical researches on local epilepsy, the theory of which necessitated crisp localization of motor function, although when first he proposed it the physiological world could not as yet support him. Had he waited for certainty he would never have got near it as early as he did.

So Jackson hinted, and Darwin in comparable words agreed with him. In more recent times K. J. W. Craik rightly drew attention to the real method of scientists, which is to see whether some idea can be substantiated by experiment. Robert Boyle was not interested in making a law but in finding out what happened when gases were compressed. The results happened to be generalizable in a formula. It is the philosophers who insist on logical definitions which are the more perfect the more they leave out of the vast realms of human striving and usefulness. The so-called Laws of Science had generally no very tidy beginnings. They are no more than science recollected in tranquillity, and not the conscious aim of the eponymous makers of the crucial and revelatory experiment. It may be that the poet who tries to crystallize a moving experience into an immortal line is using his wits in a very similar manner. We must beware of making science too rigid, self-conscious, and pontifical. A. N. Whitehead confessed to me once that he found that he had escaped from the certainty and dogma of the ecclesiastics only in the end to find that the scientists, from whom he had expected an elastic and liberal outlook, were the same people in a different setting. I am encouraged, therefore, to proceed in the hope that, although we shall not arrive at certainty, we may discover some illumination on the way.

ANCIENT AUTOMATA

Before we glance at the new vistas of mechanization opening before us, let us spare a few moments to look at the past, where we shall find that the possibility of building automata has been one of man's dreams since the days of the Trojan horse—a simile more metaphorical than strictly accurate. In the 17th century, that era of scientific awakening, there was great interest in possible replicas of animals and men. Florent Schuyl, in 1664, gives several instances, such as the wooden pigeon of Archytas of Tarentum which flew through the air, suspended by counterweights. There was a wooden eagle, that of Regiomontanus, that showed an Emperor the way to Nuremberg, and a flying fly by the same maker. There was an earthen head that spoke; but, above all, a marvellous iron statue that knelt before the Emperor of Morocco and presented him with a request for a pardon for the man who had made him. There were even greater marvels, such as that incomparable statue the Venus of Daedalus, that had quicksilver in its veins and seemed to be alive, and "an infinity of other similar automata, moving and even speaking machines which Coelius Rodiginus mentions in his book on antiquities, and Kircher and many others describe." Gafford, in 1629, had written of statues of men and women which moved and spoke and played musical instruments, birds that flew and sang, lions that leaped, and a thousand other marvels of the inventions of man which astonished the people.

That most of the foregoing examples were no more than fables, or huge exaggerations of a grain of truth, we may be very sure. But there was some foundation for them in the many marvels which the traveller might see with his own eyes at that day, or soon after, such as the water gardens of Tivoli and Pratelino, at Saint Germain-en-Laye, at Fontainebleau, at Augsburg and Salzburg. Water- or wind-power and clockwork were the only sources of energy available, but they caused movement in some pretty toys, and although the figures moved clumsily, yet move they did. As the traveller approached a grotto, for instance, and as he stood admiring, he pressed unwittingly a lever hidden beneath a stone, causing Neptune to come forward with his trident raised to defend a water-nymph, while the bathing Diana withdrew among the reeds.

If such wonders had already been constructed for the pleasure of noblemen and the entertainment of their guests, how much more perfectly might not the serious scientist contrive a cunning replica of a living thing. As only too often happens, to conceive it possible was as good as its conversion into fact. It could be, therefore it was. I am sure that that is our own temptation.

DESCARTES' POSTULATION

The first convincing postulation of mechanical perfection was of course that of Descartes, who believed that animals, though live things because their hearts were hot (Galen's idea), were entirely reflex in their complicated actions, doing all that they did because their construction compelled them. They had no souls, no minds, and therefore no free will. He expressed himself in a manner which could scarcely be bettered as a fair exposition, up to that moment, of the problem of automata. His views are very apposite to the present day, which has become more Cartesian than it realizes. It should, he thought, be perfectly possible to construct an automaton that would behave not only like an animal but, in so far as he was an animal, like a man because the organs of man and animal were in the main the same. There was an eventual difference: he saw plainly that it reposed in the highest qualities of man's mind and soul.

Descartes made the point, and a basic one it is, that a parrot repeated only what it had been taught and only a fragment of that; it never used words to express its own thoughts. If, he goes on to say, on the one hand, one had a machine that had the shape and appearance of a monkey or other animal without a reasoning soul (i.e. without a human mind) there would be no means of knowing which was the counterfeit. On the other hand, if there was a machine that appeared to be a man, and imitated his actions so far as it would be possible to do so, we should always have two very certain means of recognizing the deceit. First, the machine could not use words as we do to declare our thoughts to others. Secondly, although like some animals they might show more industry than we do, and do some things better than we, yet they would act without knowledge of what they were about simply by the arrangement of their organs, their mechanisms, each particularly designed for each particular action (*cf.* Karel Čapek's Robots). Descartes concluded—

> "From which it comes that it is morally impossible that there be enough diversity in a machine for it to be able to act in all the occurrences of life in the same way that our reason would cause us to act. By these means we can recognize the difference between man and beasts."

He could even conceive a machine that might speak and, if touched in one spot, might ask what one wanted—if touched in another that it would cry out that it hurt, and similar things. But he could not conceive of an automaton of sufficient diversity to respond to the sense of all that could be said in its presence. It would fail because it had no mind.

Apart from this difference—a vital one indeed—the body seemed undeniably to be a sum of mechanisms. It was so crystal-clear to Borelli and the new scientists that both animal and human bodies were nothing more than a collection of pumps, reservoirs, bellows, fires, cooling and heating systems, tubes, conduits, kitchens, girders, levers, pulleys and ropes, that there was little left to marvel at. Let the vulgar gape, let the devout feel gratitude to God—it was all very plain to the scientist of that age. It was not as plain as they thought. Time has shown that hidden in the materials of which this body is composed are all kinds of biochemical ingenuities. It is a chemical engine such as would have astonished the mechanics. Give a man, to take the simplest of all examples, a beautifully efficient set of aluminium bones in place of his original skeleton and he will die of some unpleasant blood disease because bones are living organs as well as props.

There certainly are things to marvel at, and no small wonders they are. One is the truly extraordinary efficiency of the living organism as judged by weight, energy output, and fuel consumption by comparison with any machine whatever; another is its ability to carry on with its own feed-back controls for decades, without adjustments or repair. In the long run, of course, scientific method made great use of the mechanical likenesses that so impressed the savants of the scientific Renaissance. A great service had been done by destroying mystery and by discrediting Platonic and Aristotelian essences and humours. Most of our advances have been made by use of technical methods common both to machines and to living things. But all our advances have depended on observation of the thing itself, accepting likeness to mechanism only as analogy and not as identity.

I fancy that no one will disagree in summary of the foregoing that, however like the various processes are to other things in physical nature, however amenable they are to examination as physico-chemical processes, they remain unmistakably themselves. We shall reach the same conclusion about the brain—that, however its functions may be mimicked by machines, it remains itself and is unique in Nature. Descartes solved the difficulty by making mind supernatural, placing an immaterial mind independent of organism in the pineal. This was the age-old refuge of those faced with the inexplicable in Nature, as we still see in primitive peoples and in the superstitious. We may well doubt today whether a supernatural agency is the basis of mental process. But it was doubted in Lister's time. In 1870 T. H. Huxley reluctantly concluded

> "I can find no intelligible ground for refusing to say that the properties of protoplasm result from the nature and disposition of its molecules . . . and if so, it must be true, in the same sense and to the same extent, that the thoughts to which I am now giving utterance, and your thoughts regarding them, are the expression of molecular changes in the matter of life which is the source of other vital phenomena."

The passage of time which has led us to accept so much has done little to make this conclusion either less true or much more acceptable than it was to Huxley himself. To admit it seems to confess to a certain ordinariness about mind, an ordinariness to which the richness and plasticity or its powers seem to give the lie and in revenge to demand a stupendous physical explanation. And there is something more. Since no thinking man can be unaware of his fellows and of the political scene he will find that the concept of thinking like machines lends itself to certain political dogmas inimical to man's happiness. Furthermore, it erodes religious beliefs that have been mainstays of social conduct and have brought happiness and serenity of mind to many. These possibilities would have leaped to the forefront of Joseph Lister's mind but we shall do best just now to avoid theological reflections.

MODERN AUTOMATA

Ingenuity of invention at the present time confronts our more sophisticated eyes with models as seductive as were the cruder automata of old. By means of electric motors, thermo-couples, photo-electric cells, radio tubes, sound receptors, and electrical resistances variable to moisture it should be possible to construct a simple animal such as a tortoise (as Grey Walter ingeniously did) that would show by its movements that it disliked bright lights, cold, and damp, and be apparently frightened by loud noises, moving towards or away from such stimuli as its receptors were capable of responding to. In a favourable situation the behaviour of such a toy could appear to be very lifelike—so much so that a good demonstrator might cause the credulous to exclaim "This is indeed a tortoise." I imagine, however, that another tortoise would quickly find it a puzzling companion and a disappointing mate.

It is the infinite variety of the behaviour of the world of animals that confuses us. The stage is too vast, the cast too numerous, the qualities of their performances too varied. We should not show any hesitation in attributing conscious mental processes to animals today. Greatly though information has increased, the field study of animals in their natural state is with difficulty pursued over long periods, so that we have but short chapters from their lives, and some are too shy, too evasive, or too episodic in their sojourns to allow of continuous recording. We should find great difficulty in grading animal minds. Such

knowledge as we have is enough to teach us that even among creatures of the same genera there are great differences in the cleverness of individuals. There are not only clever dogs and dull ones, but clever hens and stupid hens, attractive hens (to the cock) and plain ones, and, for all we know, clever and lovely flies, clever elephants, clever snakes and fish, with dull-witted brothers and ugly sisters. Obstinacy, no doubt, varies in the mule.

At what level in the animal scale something that can be called mind appears for the first time we do not know. J. Z. Young's experiments show that even an octopus can learn, be so puzzled by problems set it as to be made what we might be allowed to call neurotic. That this could happen to dogs and monkeys we already knew from ingenious experiment, and now the reproduction of bewilderment that paralyses action in such low forms of life is singularly interesting. The child, confused by its teachers and unable to grasp the logic of its lessons, is but a more complex example of the puzzled octopus. It seems to me likely that the number of synapses in a nervous system is the key to the possible variations in its behaviour. Provided the neurones are not too numerous and, consequently, the synaptic patterns of alternative routes for impulses not too varied, it is not difficult to imagine that some, though not all except the simplest, animal behaviour is the result of a pattern of reflexes, much more complicated, it is true, than the plain push-button-and-answer of some spinal reflexes.

But neither animals nor men can be explained by studying nervous mechanics in isolation, so complicated are they by endocrines, so coloured is thought by emotion. Sex hormones introduce peculiarities of behaviour often as inexplicable as they are impressive (as in migratory fish). We should not have any real idea how to make a model electronic salmon however simple relatively its nervous system is, while birds would be as far beyond us again. I can see that, although a good deal of instruction might be got from varying the proportion of, say, photo-electric cells, thermo-couples, and sound-receivers perhaps above and below the range of human hearing to see how variations affected the antics of a model, it remains uncertain how far we should be truly enlightened on the obscurities of animal behaviour. Olfaction, which plays so large a part in some creatures, would be particularly difficult to mimic. So would the effects of satisfaction of appetites of all kinds and of fatigue—such important influences.

When all is said—and much more could be said on both sides—we emerge with the conviction that, although much can be properly explained by conditioned reflexes and determinism (in which idea mechanism lurks in the background), there is a fringe left over in which free will may act (*i.e.* choice not rigidly bound to individual precedent), a fringe that becomes larger and larger the more complex the nervous system. Both views are correct in their own spheres; neither is wholly correct for everything. I accept here the emendation of Niels Bohr, who sees this as the counterpart of the impossibility of fully describing the electron either as a point or as a wave. It is either, according to how it is examined or in what circumstances. This paradox the mathematicians call the Law of Complementarity, and are not afraid to regard the same thing as true in two different guises. We may do well to follow their example.

THE NERVOUS IMPULSE

The electronic computing machine works as a logical system, making a choice between "yes" and "no" at a great number of points in a vast chain, with the speed of electricity. Because it uses wireless valves, wired circuits, mercury tubes, capacitors, and all the paraphernalia of electricity it works thousands of times faster than can the human brain. Before we proceed further in considering machines we must see how far we can go in saying that our own nervous system is electrical. We shall see that it is not so, in the layman's meaning of the term, but the electrical processes that accompany its actions afford problems of absorbing interest. The fastest known nerve impulses in mammalian nerve or spinal cord travel at about 140 metres per second, the slowest anything down to 0.3 metre per second. What their speed may be in the brain we do not know, but very likely perhaps it does not differ much from these figures. The passage of impulses

through single synapses is known by the work of Lorente de Nó and others to cause a delay of 0.75 millisecond. Such delays, and there are sure to be many in the cortex, impose a certain additional slowness on nervous actions.

The flashing speed of thought which so much impresses us is, it seems, a rather slow affair, but in view of the short distances that impulses have to travel in the brain the rate is fast enough to appear instantaneous to us. It is true that, although the electrical current cannot itself be slowed down from its normal 1,000 ft per microsecond, it is possible to slow down the arrival of an impulse by devices such as delay systems, and especially by the trigger systems, in which each component excites the next, at a rate that can be made inferior to conduction in nerve. There is, it seems, no limit to the slowing which could be imposed, down even to 1 ft per hour. This would entail complex apparatus. For many years nothing recognizably the counterpart of such systems could be found in the structure of the nerve fibre, but there are those who believe now that the retardation is at the nodes of Ranvier, with high-speed leaps between each node (the "saltatory theory" of conduction). Significantly, nodes of Ranvier have been found in the tracts of the spinal cord.

It remains an anomaly that the speed of the nervous impulse is usually slower in the bare fibres of non-medullated than in medullated nerve, as if the nerve sheath increased the speed. In nerve recovering after injury physiological conduction demands more than anatomical continuity, the axons must be a certain size and the sheath a certain thickness, as Young shows, and it is conceivable that the sheath needs to acquire certain physical properties proper for polarization. Whichever way one looks at it the speed of the nervous impulse presents us with a problem in electricity as a biological fact that is so special as to be unique.

Lastly, although electronic methods permit of much more local, more individual questioning of elements in the nervous system, we must not overlook the chemical agencies which transmission demands and from which nerve cells derive their energy. It seems very plain that if the nervous system is examined by electrical methods answers must be obtained in terms of electricity. But if it is examined in terms of chemistry, as Sir Henry Dale and G. L. Brown have done, the same thing now appears as a wonderfully implemented electro-chemical machine. There may be other methods of investigation still to be discovered.

It would probably be wrong to say that electrical methods are more delicate than chemical, yet it is certainly much easier to render an account of nervous actions and to represent the results of understandable diagrams by the former than by the latter means. A one-sided view is only too easily acquired, but let the artificers remember chemistry, for metabolic disorders can block transmission—the "invisible lesions" of clinical neurology of which Sir Charles Symonds has written. The recollection that chemical agencies and enzyme actions are no doubt eventually explicable in physical terms does not entirely remove the force of this reminder.

CALCULATING MACHINES

These lines of thought, however elementary, seemed to me a necessary prologue before we come to consider systems which have a purely electronic structure. We shall be right in concluding that it does not greatly matter what the nervous impulse really is, except that, vastly multiplied, it is part of a communication system, a self-controlled information system (self-controlled because of its integrating feed-backs), and could therefore be compared with man-made systems in these classes. Such systems happen to be a peculiarly rich development of our own times. But we shall be quite wrong if we approach the subject on any other terms except those of analogy.

To be just, nothing more than analogy is claimed by most of their constructors (some, like Professor Williams, do not go so far even as that), but there is a grave danger that those not so well informed will go to great lengths of fantasy. If we see that some nervous tissues behave like some electronic circuits we must all the time remember that the resemblance is with fragments of the nervous system and not with the whole

integrated nervous system of man. It is only right when we do so that we recollect something else, that we cannot be sure that the highest intellectual processes are still carried out in the same way. Something quite different, as yet undiscovered, may happen in those final processes of brain activity that result in what we call, for convenience, mind.

The histological pattern of the human cortex leaves us with a host of questions unanswered. We may be in the familiar position that I sketched in earlier passages, of stretching our knowledge to cover something to which it does not apply. Abstract thinking may not be a matter of neurone mechanics as we know them at lower levels. But let us proceed for the moment by supposing that the system remains the same throughout—and a large assumption it is—and that it is for the moment comparable with something of a different material composition but with a similar plan. The mechanisms of calculating machines are outside the province of neurologist or surgeon, and I have to rely upon and gratefully acknowledge the assistance of Professor F. C. Williams, professor of electro-technics in my own university, and the information gleaned from Dr. Wiener, of Boston, in his entertaining book on the new science that he has christened "Cybernetics" (1948).

Computing machines use very many fewer "neurones" than has the brain. One may compare the 10,000,000,000 cells of Thompson's estimate with the 20,000 valves of the first big American machine ENIAC at Princeton, and the 1,000 of Professor Williams's newer and more efficient experimental and most ingenious instrument in Manchester. McCulloch, of Chicago, was reported as saying that a model that contained valves and wiring anything approaching in number the neurones in the human nervous system would require a building the size of the Empire State Building to house it and the complete electrical output of Niagara Falls to run it. Calculating machines certainly consume great quantities of electricity and generate considerable heat. It is probable that McCulloch's estimate is lavish because the brain almost certainly sends out and receives the same message through several fibres and cells so that we have more nervous tissue than a machine would need and more, certainly, than we use if the meagre effects of excisions from some areas mean what we think they mean.

Wherein do any analogies lie? They lie in certain likenesses between wireless valves and nerve cells in this way, that the valves can be so wired as to store messages, to show the Sherringtonian principles of "convergence" and "divergence," can be inhibited from action, and may be arranged so as only to transmit a message (a symbol in terms of electricity) if they are receiving impulses from one or several other valves and not to transmit if other excitations fail to come in. The likeness between such an arrangement and that of the impulses arriving in a nerve cell through its dendrites and the behaviour of neurone pools is so close as to convince us that in these actions some nervous tissues with simple patterns behave extremely like some electronic circuits. It gives additional support to the belief that human tissues behave according to some physical laws discoverable elsewhere in Nature, without surrendering their own individuality. This is a belief old enough to be both useful and respectable.

The fact that calculating machines can be made to store electrical charges representing numbers for long periods of time suggests that there is "memory" in the machine, which must in fact "remember" how far it has got with a calculation in order to be able to proceed, just as we do ourselves. It must also "remember" all the data and the procedure leading to solution. It retains its "memory" until it is cleared of its charges. Using electronic instead of nervous impulses it can carry out calculations with such great rapidity that it will solve a simple calculation in milliseconds, and in an hour one that would employ a mathematician several months. We are invited to consider that the memory that the machine has in the form of stored charges is perhaps the same as memory in man or in animal, as a "charge" in a cell or groups of those millions of cells whose individual uses we do not know.

All that one is entitled to say is that it could be something of that kind, but that the electrical machine offers no proof that it is so. We might guess so much without a machine, nor does it tell us what the nature of the "charge" in a nerve cell is, except to assume that

it is electrical. Damage to large parts of the human brain, entailing vast cell losses, can occur without serious loss of memory, and that is not true of calculating machines so far, though so large a one might be imagined that parts of it might be rendered inoperative without total loss of function. It can be urged, and it is cogent argument against the machine, that it can answer only problems given to it, and, furthermore, that the method it employs is one prearranged by its operator. The "facilities" are provided and can be arranged in any order by "programming" without rebuilding.

It may be objected that the second argument is equally true of man; our difficulty is in his case that we have not seen the blue-print from which he was constructed, and that we have been baffled by our attempts to reconstruct it. The first objection can be met by the counter-proposition that man himself answers only such propositions as are put to him by his environment, and takes us back indeed to Aristotle's "Nihil est in mente quod non," etc., that our minds are built by education and experience data, processed by the machine, our brain. But the calculating machine which man makes himself throws no new light on this problem; it merely reminds us.

There is another analogy of which Wiener has made interesting use. It is this: that computing machines with complicated circuits may develop spontaneous functional faults in which the operation circles endlessly in a closed loop instead of proceeding in the way intended. This is a not uncommon disease of electronic computing machines. It can be cured by cutting off the current, by shaking the machine, or by putting into it a "shock" charge. Wiener makes much of the likeness between this functional machine-illness and the methods employed in curing obsessional diseases in man (sleep or narcosis, leucotomy or E.C.T.). The likeness stands or falls on the acceptance of Moniz's suggestion, and it is no more, that an obsession is a chain reaction in neurone mechanisms by which a dominant idea blocks the normal functioning of mind and behaviour. It is a good analogy, but it neither proves nor disproves the theory that obsessions are in fact exactly of that kind. They are certainly vastly more complicated than the abnormal "circulation disease" in a calculating machine. I repeat that it is again only analogy, but it is one which the impulsive may much too easily accept as ambivalent proof of identity, simple and diagrammatic.

Wiener made the suggestion that the searching process in automatic telephone exchanges, by which unoccupied circuits are looked for by the electrical equivalents of incoming number combinations, is very likely the counterpart of what happens in the nervous system. This may be true, but the alternative pathways in the cord and brain are so great that "engaged" signals will be rare. "Previous engagement" might, however, account for the failure of some messages to reach consciousness, or explain in different language our inability to do several things at the same time. Comparisons with the scanning processes of television may yet prove instructive. Ideas such as these remind us that we do not need to accept exact similarity for us to look with renewed interest at old problems. They remind us how far we have advanced since we could be satisfied by comparing the nervous system with a hand-operated telephone exchange.

THINKING

The activity of the nerve cells in the grey matter even of an isolated segment of the spinal cord can be demonstrated by electronic detectors. The activity is greater when the cord is in continuity with the brain and falls to a minimum when the roots are divided. Of the vast stream of sense data that pour into our nervous systems we are aware of few and we name still fewer. For it is the fact that even percepta are wordless. Only by necessity do we put a vocabulary to what we touch, see, taste, and smell, and to such sounds as we hear that are not themselves words. We look at a landscape, at the rich carving and majestic architecture of a cathedral, listen to the development of harmonies in a symphony, or admire special skill in games and find ourselves woefully lacking in ability to describe our percepts. Words, as we very rightly say, fail us either to describe the plain facts of these experiences or to impart to others our feelings. Gesture at times speaks more tellingly than tongues.

From these plain truths has arisen the profession of the critic, who has himself to learn and to teach the public to accept a conventional paraphrasis, sometimes taking refuge in describing painting in terms of music and *vice versa*. The variety of the visual and general perceptual scene alone is too great for those frail instruments—words—and it is because of this that literature flourishes. But without using words, though richer in the variety of our experience and with words only just below the surface, our minds are not very dissimilar from those of animals, and it is not difficult to conjecture that a Trappist existence might, for a brief period, be not unpleasant. The development of this theme would take me too far, but it is necessary for us to bear it in mind in considering mechanism and thinking. Granted that much that goes on in our heads is wordless (for if it is not, then we must concede words, an internal vocabulary, to animals), we certainly require words for conceptual thinking as well as for expression. It is here that there is the sudden and mysterious leap from the highest animal to man, and it is in the speech areas of the dominant hemisphere rather than in the pineal that Descartes should have put the soul, the highest intellectual faculties.

It is almost boring to repeat that it is because he has a vocabulary that man's intellectual progress has been made possible—by the day-by-day record of how far he has gone in his pilgrimage towards finite knowledge, that journey without an end. We remember more, that language is not static, but that neologisms continually mark our progress not only in general ideas but in science. We use today scores of scientific terms that men who lived as recently as Priestley, Lavoisier, and Darwin would not understand. It is not enough, therefore, to build a machine that could use words (if that were possible), it would have to be able to create concepts and to *find for itself* suitable words in which to express additions to knowledge that it brought about. Otherwise it would be no more than a cleverer parrot, an improvement on the typewriting monkeys which would accidentally in the course of centuries write *Hamlet*. A machine might solve problems in logic, since logic and mathematics are much the same thing. In fact some measures to that end are on foot in my university's department of philosophy. If the machine typewrites its answers, the cry may rise that it has learned to write, when in fact it would be doing no more than telegraphic systems do already.

Nor must we overlook the limitations of the machines. They need very intelligent staffs to feed them with the right problems, and they will attempt the insoluble and continue at it until the current is switched off. Their great advantage is their speed compared with a human mind, and I have given reasons for that. But, it may be asked, is that so very much more marvellous than the crane that can lift so much more than can a man or than an automobile that can move so much quicker?

The great difference in favour of the calculating machine as compared with the crane, and I willingly allow it, is that the means employed are basically so similar to some single nervous lay-outs. As I have said, the schism arises over the use of words and lies above all in the machines' lack of opinions, of creative thinking in verbal concepts. I shall be surprised, indeed, if that gap is bridged, for even supposing that electrical charges could be made to represent words, what then? I cannot see that anything but jargon would result. Not until a machine can write a sonnet or compose a concerto because of thoughts and emotions felt, and not by the chance fall of symbols, could we agree that machine equals brain—that is, not only write it but know that it has written it. No mechanism could feel (and not merely artificially signal, an easy contrivance) pleasure at its successes, grief when its valves fuse, be warmed by flattery, be made miserable by its mistakes, be charmed by sex, be angry or depressed when it cannot get what it wants.

CONCLUSION

I conclude, therefore, that although electronic apparatus can parallel some of the simpler activities of nerve and spinal cord, for we can already see the parallelism between mechanical feed-backs and Sherringtonian integration, and may yet assist us in understanding better the transmission of the special senses, it still does not take us over the blank wall that confronts us when we come to explore thinking, the ultimate in mind. I am quite sure that the extreme variety, flexibility, and complexity of nervous mechanisms are greatly underestimated by the physicists, who naturally omit everything unfavourable to a point of view. What I fear is that a great many airy theories will arise in the attempt to persuade us against our better judgment. We have had a hard task to dissuade man from reading qualities of human mind into animals. I see a new and greater danger threatening—that of anthropomorphizing the machine. When we hear it said that wireless valves think, we may despair of language. As well say that the cells in the spinal cord below a transverse lesion "think," a heresy that Marshall Hall destroyed 100 years ago. I venture to predict that the day will never dawn when the gracious premises of the Royal Society have to be turned into garages to house the new Fellows.

I end by ranging myself with the humanist Shakespeare believing that the mechanists lag derisorily far behind in their models of Nature's greatest creation, the human nervous system. I recall Hamlet's lines: "What a piece of work is a man! How noble in reason! how infinite in faculty; in form, in moving, how express and admirable! in action, how like an angel! in apprehension, how like a god! the beauty of the world! the paragon of animals!"

In that conclusion, if not always in my approach to it, I feel confident that I should have won the approval of that bold experimenter and noble character in whose remembrance this oration was founded.

POSTSCRIPT

Looking back, 1949 strikes me as roughly a turning point. Since then the British people have been made increasingly alive to and interested in Science. Mine was the first paper by a neurologist faced with the new electronic computing machines, for which much greater identification with the action of the brain was claimed than was in my opinion justifiable. It was a protest against jumping to conclusions and I am sure that it has many imperfections. These machines are much more familiar than they were ten years ago, at which time the address excited a good deal of newspaper comment. My friend and most ingenious mathematical colleague, the late Alan Turing, F.R.S., believed passionately that the computing machines had all but solved at once the intricacies of the mind-brain problem. He said that although a machine might not write a sonnet that I could understand, he was sure that it would write one soon that another computor would enjoy! An American scientist wrote to me that he had shown my pages to his machine and it had been so upset that it had blown its valves. Since then, by making numbers represent words the Burrough's computing machine in New York (1956) has written songs. That should be easy to do by making figures represent musical and verbal phrases. The feat is not what I meant when I asked for the springs of emotion, for the workings of individual experience to sublimate in artistic expression. Perhaps one could build emotion into a machine, for it is not produced only by endocrines. A deal of ink could be spilled by letting one's fancy roam on these possibilities—roam to end where?

Recently, experimental physiologists have made more studies of the chemistry of the nervous impulse. A. L. Hodgkin in his Croonian lecture (1957) presented his studies on the alterations in membrane permeability during the passage of the nervous impulse. He observed the inward passage of Na, and outward passage of K. Some metabolic activity goes on in the nerve fibre designed to pump the Na out again, ready for the next burst of activity.

11.2

Computing Machinery and Intelligence

A. M. Turing

From *Mind* 59 (1950): 433–460.

INTRODUCTORY NOTE TO READING 11.2

In this paper, written in response to the paper delivered by his acquaintance at Manchester, Sir Geoffrey Jefferson (Reading 11.1), Turing considered the question of computational intelligence from a behavioristic standpoint, proposing an experiment, later called the Turing test, that would allow the unbiased comparison of a machine's "thinking behavior" with that of a normal human being. The test involves two parties, "X" and "Y", who engage in a conversation by teletype. Human X cannot know whether Y is a machine or a person. If X believes that Y is responding like a person after a specified period of time, and Y turns out to be a machine, then that machine may be defined as having the capacity to "think."

From the time Turing wrote his paper on computable numbers (1936; see Reading 7.1), in which he modeled his universal machine after the way people carry out computations, Turing believed that every human thought that could be expressed in language could be mimicked by a computer, if it was suitably programmed. Concerning the future of artificial or computational intelligence, Turing wrote, "I believe that in about fifty years' time it will be possible to programme computers with a storage capacity of about 10^9, to make them play the imitation game so well that an average interrogator will not have more than 70 per cent chance of making the right identification after five minutes of questioning. The original question, 'Can machines think?' I believe to be too meaningless to deserve discussion. Nevertheless I believe that at the end of the century the use of words and general educated opinion will have altered so much that one will be able to speak of machines thinking without expecting to be contradicted" (p. 442).

"Turing's work at Manchester [from 1948 onward] was among the earliest investigations of the use of electronic computers for artificial-intelligence research. He was among the first to believe that electronic machines were capable of doing not only numerical computations, but also general-purpose information processing. He was convinced computers would soon have the capacity to carry out any mental activity of which the human mind is capable. He attempted to break down the distinctions between human and machine intelligence and to provide a single standard of intelligence, in terms of mental behavior, upon which both machines and biological organisms could be judged. In providing his standard, he considered only the information that entered and exited the automata. Like Shannon and Wiener, Turing was moving toward a unified theory of information and information processing applicable to both the machine and the biological worlds. . . ."[1] [JMN]

---

1   William Aspray, The Scientific Conceptualization of Information: A Survey, *Annals of the History of Computing* 7 (1985) 132.

1. THE IMITATION GAME

I propose to consider the question, "Can machines think?" This should begin with definitions of the meaning of the terms "machine" and "think." The definitions might be framed so as to reflect so far as possible the normal use of the words, but this attitude is dangerous, If the meaning of the words "machine" and "think" are to be found by examining how they are commonly used it is difficult to escape the conclusion that the meaning and the answer to the question, "Can machines think?" is to be sought in a statistical survey such as a Gallup poll. But this is absurd. Instead of attempting such a definition I shall replace the question by another, which is closely related to it and is expressed in relatively unambiguous words.

The new form of the problem can be described in terms of a game which we call the "imitation game." It is played with three people, a man (A), a woman (B), and an interrogator (C) who may be of either sex. The interrogator stays in a room apart front the other two. The object of the game for the interrogator is to determine which of the other two is the man and which is the woman. He knows them by labels X and Y, and at the end of the game he says either "X is A and Y is B" or "X is B and Y is A." The interrogator is allowed to put questions to A and B thus:

C: Will X please tell me the length of his or her hair?

Now suppose X is actually A, then A must answer. It is A's object in the game to try and cause C to make the wrong identification. His answer might therefore be:

"My hair is shingled, and the longest strands are about nine inches long."

In order that tones of voice may not help the interrogator the answers should be written, or better still, typewritten. The ideal arrangement is to have a teleprinter communicating between the two rooms. Alternatively the question and answers can be repeated by an intermediary. The object of the game for the third player (B) is to help the interrogator. The best strategy for her is probably to give truthful answers. She can add such things as "I am the woman, don't listen to him!" to her answers, but it will avail nothing as the man can make similar remarks.

We now ask the question, "What will happen when a machine takes the part of A in this game?" Will the interrogator decide wrongly as often when the game is played like this as he does when the game is played between a man and a woman? These questions replace our original, "Can machines think?"

2. CRITIQUE OF THE NEW PROBLEM

As well as asking, "What is the answer to this new form of the question," one may ask, "Is this new question a worthy one to investigate?" This latter question we investigate without further ado, thereby cutting short an infinite regress.

The new problem has the advantage of drawing a fairly sharp line between the physical and the intellectual capacities of a man. No engineer or chemist claims to be able to produce a material which is indistinguishable from the human skin. It is possible that at some time this might be done, but even supposing this invention available we should feel there was little point in trying to make a "thinking machine" more human by dressing it up in such artificial flesh. The form in which we have set the problem reflects this fact in the condition which prevents the interrogator from seeing or touching the other competitors, or hearing their voices. Some other advantages of the proposed criterion may be shown up by specimen questions and answers. Thus:

Q: Please write me a sonnet on the subject of the Forth Bridge.

A : Count me out on this one. I never could write poetry.

Q: Add 34957 to 70764.

A: (Pause about 30 seconds and then give as answer) 105621.

Q: Do you play chess?

A: Yes.

Q: I have K at my K1, and no other pieces. You have only K at K6 and R at R1. It is your move. What do you play?

A: (After a pause of 15 seconds) R-R8 mate.

The question and answer method seems to be suitable for introducing almost any one of the fields of human endeavour that we wish to include. We do not wish to penalise the machine for its inability to shine in beauty competitions, nor to penalise a man for losing in a race against an aeroplane. The conditions of our game make these disabilities irrelevant. The "witnesses" can brag, if they consider it advisable, as much as they please about their charms, strength or heroism, but the interrogator cannot demand practical demonstrations.

The game may perhaps be criticised on the ground that the odds are weighted too heavily against the machine. If the man were to try and pretend to be the machine he would clearly make a very poor showing. He would be given away at once by slowness and inaccuracy in arithmetic. May not machines carry out something which ought to be described as thinking but which is very different from what a man does? This objection is a very strong one, but at least we can say that if, nevertheless, a machine can be constructed to play the imitation game satisfactorily, we need not be troubled by this objection.

It might be urged that when playing the "imitation game" the best strategy for the machine may possibly be something other than imitation of the behaviour of a man. This may be, but I think it is unlikely that there is any great effect of this kind. In any case there is no intention to investigate here the theory of the game, and it will be assumed that the best strategy is to try to provide answers that would naturally be given by a man.

3. THE MACHINES CONCERNED IN THE GAME

The question which we put in §1 will not be quite definite until we have specified what we mean by the word "machine." It is natural that we should wish to

permit every kind of engineering technique to be used in our machines. We also wish to allow the possibility than an engineer or team of engineers may construct a machine which works, but whose manner of operation cannot be satisfactorily described by its constructors because they have applied a method which is largely experimental. Finally, we wish to exclude from the machines men born in the usual manner. It is difficult to frame the definitions so as to satisfy these three conditions. One might for instance insist that the team of engineers should be all of one sex, but this would not really be satisfactory, for it is probably possible to rear a complete individual from a single cell of the skin (say) of a man. To do so would be a feat of biological technique deserving of the very highest praise, but we would not be inclined to regard it as a case of "constructing a thinking machine." This prompts us to abandon the requirement that every kind of technique should be permitted. We are the more ready to do so in view of the fact that the present interest in "thinking machines" has been aroused by a particular kind of machine, usually called an "electronic computer" or "digital computer." Following this suggestion we only permit digital computers to take part in our game.

This restriction appears at first sight to be a very drastic one. I shall attempt to show that it is not so in reality. To do this necessitates a short account of the nature and properties of these computers.

It may also be said that this identification of machines with digital computers, like our criterion for "thinking," will only be unsatisfactory if (contrary to my belief), it turns out that digital computers are unable to give a good showing in the game.

There are already a number of digital computers in working order, and it may be asked, "Why not try the experiment straight away? It would be easy to satisfy the conditions of the game. A number of interrogators could be used, and statistics compiled to show how often the right identification was given." The short answer is that we are not asking whether all digital computers would do well in the game nor whether the computers at present available would do well, but whether there are imaginable computers which would do well. But this is only the short answer. We shall see this question in a different light later.

4. DIGITAL COMPUTERS

The idea behind digital computers may be explained by saying that these machines are intended to carry out any operations which could be done by a human computer. The human computer is supposed to be following fixed rules; he has no authority to deviate from them in any detail. We may suppose that these rules are supplied in a book, which is altered whenever he is put on to a new job. He has also an unlimited supply of paper on which he does his calculations. He may also do his multiplications and additions on a "desk machine," but this is not important.

If we use the above explanation as a definition we shall be in danger of circularity of argument. We avoid this by giving an outline of the means by which the desired effect is achieved. A digital computer can usually be regarded as consisting of three parts:

 i. Store.

 ii. Executive unit.

 iii. Control.

The store is a store of information, and corresponds to the human computer's paper, whether this is the paper on which he does his calculations or that on which his book of rules is printed. In so far as the human computer does calculations in his head a part of the store will correspond to his memory.

The executive unit is the part which carries out the various individual operations involved in a calculation. What these individual operations are will vary from machine to machine. Usually fairly lengthy operations can be done such as "Multiply 3540675445 by 7076345687" but in some machines only very simple ones such as "Write down 0" are possible.

We have mentioned that the "book of rules" supplied to the computer is replaced in the machine by a part of the store. It is then called the "table of instructions." It is the duty of the control to see that these instructions are obeyed correctly and in the right order. The control is so constructed that this necessarily happens.

The information in the store is usually broken up into packets of moderately small size. In one machine, for instance, a packet might consist of ten decimal digits. Numbers are assigned to the parts of the store in which the various packets of information are stored, in some systematic manner. A typical instruction might say—

"Add the number stored in position 6809 to that in 4302 and put the result back into the latter storage position."

Needless to say it would not occur in the machine expressed in English. It would more likely be coded in a form such as 6809430217. Here 17 says which of various possible operations is to be performed on the two numbers. In this case the operation is that described above, viz., "Add the number. . . ." It will be noticed that the instruction takes up 10 digits and so forms one packet of information, very conveniently. The control will normally take the instructions to be obeyed in the order of the positions in which they are stored, but occasionally an instruction such as

"Now obey the instruction stored in position 5606, and continue from there"

may be encountered, or again

"If position 4505 contains 0 obey next the instruction stored in 6707, otherwise continue straight on."

Instructions of these latter types are very important because they make it possible for a sequence of operations to be replaced over and over again until some condition is fulfilled, but in doing so to obey, not fresh instructions on each repetition, but the same ones over and over again. To take a domestic analogy. Suppose Mother wants Tommy to call at the cobbler's every morning on his way to school to see if her shoes are done, she can ask him afresh every morning. Alternatively she can stick up a notice once and for all in the hall which he will see when he leaves for school and which tells him to call for the shoes, and also to destroy the notice when he comes back if he has the shoes with him.

The reader must accept it as a fact that digital computers can be constructed, and indeed have been constructed, according to the principles we have described, and that they can in fact mimic the actions of a human computer very closely.

The book of rules which we have described our human computer as using is of course a convenient fiction. Actual human computers really remember what they have got to do. If one wants to make a machine mimic the behaviour of the human computer in some complex operation one has to ask him how it is done, and then translate the answer into the form of an instruction table. Constructing instruction tables is usually described as "programming." To "programme a machine to carry out the operation A" means to put the appropriate instruction table into the machine so that it will do A.

An interesting variant on the idea of a digital computer is a "digital computer with a random element." These have instructions involving the throwing of a die or some equivalent electronic process; one such instruction might for instance be, "Throw the die and put the resulting number into store 1000." Sometimes such a machine is described as having free will (though I would not use this phrase myself), It is not normally possible to determine from observing a machine whether it has a random element, for a similar effect can be produced by such devices as making the choices depend on the digits of the decimal for π.

Most actual digital computers have only a finite store. There is no theoretical difficulty in the idea of a computer with an unlimited store. Of course only a finite part can have been used at any one time. Likewise only a finite amount can have been constructed, but we can imagine more and more being added as required. Such computers have special theoretical interest and will be called infinitive capacity computers.

The idea of a digital computer is an old one. Charles Babbage, Lucasian Professor of Mathematics at Cambridge from 1828 to 1839, planned such a machine, called the Analytical Engine, but it was never completed. Although Babbage had all the essential ideas, his machine was not at that time such a very attractive prospect. The speed which would have been available would be definitely faster than a human computer but something like 100 times slower than the Manchester machine, itself one of the slower of the modern machines, The storage was to be purely mechanical, using wheels and cards.

The fact that Babbage's Analytical Engine was to be entirely mechanical will help us to rid ourselves of a superstition. Importance is often attached to the fact that modern digital computers are electrical, and that the nervous system also is electrical. Since Babbage's machine was not electrical, and since all digital computers are in a sense equivalent, we see that this use of electricity cannot be of theoretical importance. Of course electricity usually comes in where fast signalling is concerned, so that it is not surprising that we find it in both these connections. In the nervous system chemical phenomena are at least as important as electrical. In certain computers the storage system is mainly acoustic. The feature of using electricity is thus seen to be only a very superficial similarity. If we wish to find such similarities we should took rather for mathematical analogies of function.

5. UNIVERSALITY OF DIGITAL COMPUTERS

The digital computers considered in the last section may be classified amongst the "discrete-state machines." These are the machines which move by sudden jumps or clicks from one quite definite state to another. These states are sufficiently different for the possibility of confusion between them to be ignored. Strictly speaking there, are no such machines. Everything really moves continuously. But there are many kinds of machine which can profitably be *thought of* as being discrete-state machines. For instance in considering the switches for a lighting system it is a convenient fiction that each switch must be definitely on or definitely off. There must be intermediate positions, but for most purposes we can forget about them. As an example of a discrete-state machine we might consider a wheel which clicks round through 120° once a second, but may be stopped by a lever which can be operated from outside; in addition a lamp is to light in one of the positions of the wheel. This machine could be described abstractly as follows. The internal state of the machine (which is described by the position of the wheel) may be q_1, q_2 or q_3. There is an input signal i_0 or i_1 (position of lever). The internal state at any moment is determined by the last state and input signal according to the table

		Last State		
		q_1	q_2	q_3
Input	i_0	q_2	q_3	q_1
	i_1	q_1	q_2	q_3

The output signals, the only externally visible indication of the internal state (the light) are described by the table

State	q_1	q_2	q_3
Output	o_0	o_0	o_1

This example is typical of discrete-state machines. They can be described by such tables provided they have only a finite number of possible states.

It will seem that given the initial state of the machine and the input signals it is always possible to predict all future states, This is reminiscent of Laplace's view that from the complete state of the universe at one moment of time, as described by the positions and velocities of all particles, it should be possible to predict all future states. The prediction which we are considering is, however, rather nearer to practicability than that considered by Laplace. The system of the "universe as a whole" is such that quite small errors in the initial conditions can have an overwhelming effect at a later time. The displacement of a single electron by a billionth of a centimetre at one moment might make the difference between a man being killed by an avalanche a year later, or escaping. It is an essential property of the mechanical systems which we have called "discrete-state machines" that

this phenomenon does not occur. Even when we consider the actual physical machines instead of the idealised machines, reasonably accurate knowledge of the state at one moment yields reasonably accurate knowledge any number of steps later.

As we have mentioned, digital computers fall within the class of discrete-state machines. But the number of states of which such a machine is capable is usually enormously large. For instance, the number for the machine now working at Manchester is about $2^{165,000}$, i.e., about $10^{50,000}$. Compare this with our example of the clicking wheel described above, which had three states. It is not difficult to see why the number of states should be so immense. The computer includes a store corresponding to the paper used by a human computer. It must be possible to write into the store any one of the combinations of symbols which might have been written on the paper. For simplicity suppose that only digits from 0 to 9 are used as symbols. Variations in handwriting are ignored. Suppose the computer is allowed 100 sheets of paper each containing 50 lines each with room for 30 digits. Then the number of states is $10^{100 \times 50 \times 30}$ i.e., $10^{150,000}$. This is about the number of states of three Manchester machines put together. The logarithm to the base two of the number of states is usually called the "storage capacity" of the machine. Thus the Manchester machine has a storage capacity of about 165,000 and the wheel machine of our example about 1.6. If two machines are put together their capacities must be added to obtain the capacity of the resultant machine. This leads to the possibility of statements such as "The Manchester machine contains 64 magnetic tracks each with a capacity of 2560, eight electronic tubes with a capacity of 1280. Miscellaneous storage amounts to about 300 making a total of 174,380."

Given the table corresponding to a discrete-state machine it is possible to predict what it will do. There is no reason why this calculation should not be carried out by means of a digital computer. Provided it could be carried out sufficiently quickly the digital computer could mimic the behavior of any discrete-state machine. The imitation game could then be played with the machine in question (as B) and the mimicking digital computer (as A) and the interrogator would be unable to distinguish them. Of course the digital computer must have an adequate storage capacity as well as working sufficiently fast. Moreover, it must be programmed afresh for each new machine which it is desired to mimic.

This special property of digital computers, that they can mimic any discrete-state machine, is described by saying that they are universal machines. The existence of machines with this property has the important consequence that, considerations of speed apart, it is unnecessary to design various new machines to do various computing processes. They can all be done with one digital computer, suitably programmed for each case. It will be seen that as a consequence of this all digital computers are in a sense equivalent.

We may now consider again the point raised at the end of §3. It was suggested tentatively that the question, "Can machines think?" should be replaced by "Are there imaginable digital computers which would do well in the imitation game?" If we wish we can make this superficially more general and ask "Are there discrete-state machines which would do well?" But in view of the universality property we see that either of these questions is equivalent to this, "Let us fix our attention on one particular digital computer C. Is it true that by modifying this computer to have an adequate storage, suitably increasing its speed of action, and providing it with an appropriate programme, C can be made to play satisfactorily the part of A in the imitation game, the part of B being taken by a man?"

6. CONTRARY VIEWS ON THE MAIN QUESTION

We may now consider the ground to have been cleared and we are ready to proceed to the debate on our question, "Can machines think?" and the variant of it quoted at the end of the last section. We cannot altogether abandon the original form of the problem, for opinions will differ as to the appropriateness of the substitution and we must at least listen to what has to be said in this connexion.

It will simplify matters for the reader if I explain first my own beliefs in the matter. Consider first the more accurate form of the question. I believe that in about fifty years' time it will be possible, to programme computers, with a storage capacity of about 109, to make them play the imitation game so well that an average interrogator will not have more than 70 per cent chance of making the right identification after five minutes of questioning. The original question, "Can machines think?" I believe to be too meaningless to deserve discussion. Nevertheless I believe that at the end of the century the use of words and general educated opinion will have altered so much that one will be able to speak of machines thinking without expecting to be contradicted. I believe further that no useful purpose is served by concealing these beliefs. The popular view that scientists proceed inexorably from well-established fact to well-established fact, never being influenced by any improved conjecture, is quite mistaken. Provided it is made clear which are proved facts and which are conjectures, no harm can result. Conjectures are of great importance since they suggest useful lines of research.

I now proceed to consider opinions opposed to my own.

(1) The Theological Objection

Thinking is a function of man's immortal soul. God has given an immortal soul to every man and woman, but not to any other animal or to machines. Hence no animal or machine can think.

I am unable to accept any part of this, but will attempt to reply in theological terms. I should find the argument more convincing if animals were classed with men, for there is a greater difference, to my mind, between the typical animate and the inanimate than there is between man and the other animals. The arbitrary character of the orthodox view becomes clearer if we consider how it might appear to a member of some other religious community. How do Christians regard the Moslem view that women have no souls? But let us leave this point aside and return to the main argument. It appears to me that the argument quoted above implies a serious restriction of the omnipotence of the Almighty. It is admitted that there are certain things that He cannot do such as making one equal to two, but should we not believe that He has freedom to confer a soul on an elephant if He sees fit? We might expect that He would only exercise this power in conjunction with a mutation which provided the elephant with an appropriately improved brain to minister to the needs of this soul. An argument of exactly similar form may be made for the case of machines. It may seem different because it is more difficult to "swallow." But this really only means that we think it would be less likely that He would consider the circumstances suitable for conferring a soul. The circumstances in question are discussed in the rest of this paper. In attempting to construct such machines we should not be irreverently usurping His power of creating souls, any more than we are in the procreation of children: rather we are, in either case, instruments of His will providing mansions for the souls that He creates.

However, this is mere speculation. I am not very impressed with theological arguments whatever they may be used to support. Such arguments have often been found unsatisfactory in the past. In the time of Galileo it was argued that the texts, "And the sun stood still . . . and hasted not to go down about a whole day" (Joshua x. 13) and "He laid the foundations of the earth, that it should not move at any time" (Psalm cv. 5) were an adequate refutation of the Copernican theory. With our present knowledge such an argument appears futile. When that knowledge was not available it made a quite different impression.

(2) The "Heads in the Sand" Objection

"The consequences of machines thinking would be too dreadful. Let us hope and believe that they cannot do so."

This argument is seldom expressed quite so openly as in the form above. But it affects most of us who think about it at all. We like to believe that Man is in some subtle way superior to the rest of creation. It is best if he can be shown to be necessarily superior, for then there is no danger of him losing his commanding position. The popularity of the theological argument is clearly connected with this feeling. It is likely to be quite strong in intellectual people, since they value the power of thinking more highly than others, and are more inclined to base their belief in the superiority of Man on this power.

I do not think that this argument is sufficiently substantial to require refutation. Consolation would be more appropriate: perhaps this should be sought in the transmigration of souls.

(3) The Mathematical Objection

There are a number of results of mathematical logic which can be used to show that there are limitations to the powers of discrete-state machines. The best known of these results is known as Gödel's theorem (1931) and shows that in any sufficiently powerful logical system statements can be formulated which can neither be proved nor disproved within the system, unless possibly the system itself is inconsistent. There are other, in some respects similar, results due to Church (1936), Kleene (1935), Rosser, and Turing (1937). The latter result is the most convenient to consider, since it refers directly to machines, whereas the others can only be used in a comparatively indirect argument: for instance if Gödel's theorem is to be used we need in addition to have some means of describing logical systems in terms of machines, and machines in terms of logical systems. The result in question refers to a type of machine which is essentially a digital computer with an infinite capacity. It states that there are certain things that such a machine cannot do. If it is rigged up to give answers to questions as in the imitation game, there will be some questions to which it will either give a wrong answer, or fail to give an answer at all however much time is allowed for a reply. There may, of course, be many such questions, and questions which cannot be answered by one machine may be satisfactorily answered by another. We are of course supposing for the present that the questions are of the kind to which an answer "Yes" or "No" is appropriate, rather than questions such as "What do you think of Picasso?" The questions that we know the machines must fail on are of this type, "Consider the machine specified as follows. . . . Will this machine ever answer 'Yes' to any question?" The dots are to be replaced by a description of some machine in a standard form, which could be something like that used in §5. When the machine described bears a certain comparatively simple relation to the machine which is under interrogation, it can be shown that the answer is either wrong or not forthcoming. This is the mathematical result: it is argued that it proves a disability of machines to which the human intellect is not subject.

The short answer to this argument is that although it is established that there are limitations to the powers of any particular machine, it has only been stated, without any sort of proof, that no such limitations apply to the human intellect. But I do not think this view can be dismissed quite so lightly. Whenever one of these machines is asked the appropriate critical question, and gives a definite answer, we know that this answer must be wrong, and this gives us a certain feeling of superiority. Is this feeling illusory? It is no doubt quite genuine, but I do not think too much importance should be attached to it. We too often give wrong answers to questions ourselves to be justified in being very pleased at such evidence of fallibility on the part of the machines. Further, our superiority can only be felt on such an occasion in relation to the one machine over which we have scored our petty triumph. There would be no question of triumphing simultaneously over all machines. In short, then, there might be men cleverer than any given machine, but then again there might be other machines cleverer again, and so on.

Those who hold to the mathematical argument would, I think, mostly be willing to accept the imitation game as a basis for discussion. Those who believe in the two previous objections would probably not be interested in any criteria.

(4) The Argument from Consciousness

This argument is very well expressed in Professor Jefferson's Lister Oration for 1949, from which I quote. "Not until a machine can write a sonnet or compose a concerto because of thoughts and emotions felt, and not by the chance fall of symbols, could we agree that machine equals brain—that is, not only write it but know that it had written it. No mechanism could feel (and not merely artificially signal, an easy contrivance) pleasure at its successes, grief when its valves fuse, be warmed by flattery, be made miserable by its mistakes, be charmed by sex, be angry or depressed when it cannot get what it wants."

This argument appears to be a denial of the validity of our test. According to the most extreme form of this view the only way by which one could be sure that machine thinks is to be the machine and to feel oneself thinking. One could then describe these feelings to the world, but of course no one would be justified in taking any notice. Likewise according to this view the only way to know that a man thinks is to be that particular man. It is in fact the solipsist point of view. It may be the most logical view to hold but it makes communication of ideas difficult. A is liable to believe "A thinks but B does not" whilst B believes "B thinks but A does not." Instead of arguing continually over this point it is usual to have the polite convention that everyone thinks.

I am sure that Professor Jefferson does not wish to adopt the extreme and solipsist point of view. Probably he would be quite willing to accept the imitation game as a test. The game (with the player B omitted) is frequently used in practice under the name of *viva voce* to discover whether some one really understands something or has "learnt it parrot fashion." Let us listen in to a part of such a *viva voce*:

Interrogator: In the first line of your sonnet which reads "Shall I compare thee to a summer's day," would not "a spring day" do as well or better?

Witness: It wouldn't scan.

Interrogator: How about "a winter's day," That would scan all right.

Witness: Yes, but nobody wants to be compared to a winter's day.

Interrogator: Would you say Mr. Pickwick reminded you of Christmas?

Witness: In a way.

Interrogator: Yet Christmas is a winter's day,

and I do not think Mr. Pickwick would mind the comparison.

Witness: I don't think you're serious. By a winter's day one means a typical winter's day, rather than a special one like Christmas.

And so on. What would Professor Jefferson say if the sonnet-writing machine was able to answer like this in the *viva voce*? I do not know whether he would regard the machine as "merely artificially signalling" these answers, but if the answers were as satisfactory and sustained as in the above passage I do not think he would describe it as "an easy contrivance." This phrase is, I think, intended to cover such devices as the inclusion in the machine of a record of someone reading a sonnet, with appropriate switching to turn it on from time to time.

In short then, I think that most of those who support the argument from consciousness could be persuaded to abandon it rather than be forced into the solipsist position. They will then probably be willing to accept our test.

I do not wish to give the impression that I think there is no mystery about consciousness. There is, for instance, something of a paradox connected with any attempt to localise it. But I do not think these mysteries necessarily need to be solved before we can answer the question with which we are concerned in this paper.

(5) Arguments from Various Disabilities

These arguments take the form, "I grant you that you can make machines do all the things you have mentioned but you will never be able to make one to do X." Numerous features X are suggested in this connexion. I offer a selection:

Be kind, resourceful, beautiful, friendly, have initiative, have a sense of humour, tell right from wrong, make mistakes, fall in love, enjoy strawberries and cream, make some one fall in love with it, learn from experience, use words properly, be the subject of its own thought, have as much diversity of behaviour as a man, do something really new.

No support is usually offered for these statements. I believe they are mostly founded on the principle of scientific induction. A man has seen thousands of machines in his lifetime. From what he sees of them he draws a number of general conclusions. They are ugly, each is designed for a very limited purpose, when required for a minutely different purpose they are useless, the variety of behaviour of any one of them is very small, etc., etc. Naturally he concludes that these are necessary properties of machines in general. Many of these limitations are associated with the very small storage capacity of most machines. (I am assuming that the idea of storage capacity is extended in some way to cover machines other than discrete-state machines. The exact definition does not matter as no mathematical accuracy is claimed in the present discussion.) A few years ago, when very little had been heard of digital computers, it was possible to elicit much incredulity concerning them, if one mentioned their properties without describing their construction. That was presumably due to a similar application of the principle of scientific induction. These applications of the principle are of course largely unconscious. When a burnt child fears the fire and shows that he fears it by avoiding it, I should say that he was applying scientific induction. (I could of course also describe his behaviour in many other ways.) The works and customs of mankind do not seem to be very suitable material to which to apply scientific induction. A very large part of space-time must be investigated, if reliable results are to be obtained. Otherwise we may (as most English children do) decide that everybody speaks English, and that it is silly to learn French.

There are, however, special remarks to be made about many of the disabilities that have been mentioned. The inability to enjoy strawberries and cream may have struck the reader as frivolous. Possibly a machine might be made to enjoy this delicious dish, but any attempt to make one do so would be idiotic. What is important about this disability is that it contributes to some of the other disabilities, e.g., to the difficulty of the same kind of friendliness occurring between man and machine as between white man and white man, or between black man and black man.

The claim that "machines cannot make mistakes" seems a curious one. One is tempted to retort, "Are they any the worse for that?" But let us adopt a more sympathetic attitude, and try to see what is really meant. I think this criticism can be explained in terms of the imitation game. It is claimed that the interrogator could distinguish the machine from the man simply by setting them a number of problems in arithmetic. The machine would be unmasked because of its deadly accuracy. The reply to this is simple. The machine (programmed for playing the game) would not attempt to give the right answers to the arithmetic problems. It would deliberately introduce mistakes in a manner calculated to confuse the interrogator. A mechanical fault would probably show itself through an unsuitable decision as to what sort of a mistake to make in the arithmetic. Even this interpretation of the criticism is not sufficiently sympathetic. But we cannot afford the space to go into it much further. It seems to me that this criticism depends on a confusion between two kinds of mistake. We may call them "errors of functioning" and "errors of conclusion." Errors of functioning are due to some mechanical or electrical fault which causes the machine to behave otherwise than it was designed to do. In philosophical discussions one likes to ignore the possibility of such errors; one is therefore discussing "abstract machines." These abstract machines are mathematical fictions rather than physical objects. By definition they are incapable of errors of functioning. In this sense we can truly say that "machines can never make mistakes." Errors of conclusion can only arise when some meaning is attached to the output signals from the machine. The machine might, for instance, type out mathematical equations, or sentences in English. When a false proposition is typed we say that the machine has committed an error of conclusion. There is clearly no reason at all for saying that a machine cannot make this kind of mistake. It might do nothing but type out repeatedly "0 = 1." To take a less perverse example, it might have some method for drawing conclusions by scientific induction. We must expect such a method to lead occasionally to erroneous results.

The claim that a machine cannot be the subject of its own thought can of course only be answered if it can be shown that the machine has some thought with some subject matter. Nevertheless, "the subject matter of a machine's operations" does seem to mean something, at least to the people who deal with it. If, for instance, the machine was trying to find a solution of the equation $x^2 - 40x - 11 = 0$ one would be tempted to describe this equation as part of the machine's subject matter at that moment. In this sort of sense a machine undoubtedly can be its own subject matter. It may be used to help in making up its own programmes, or to predict the effect of alterations in its own structure. By observing the results of its own behaviour it can modify its own programmes so as to achieve some purpose more effectively. These are possibilities of the near future, rather than Utopian dreams.

The criticism that a machine cannot have much diversity of behaviour is just a way of saying that it cannot have much storage capacity. Until fairly recently a storage capacity of even a thousand digits was very rare.

The criticisms that we are considering here are often disguised forms of the argument from consciousness, Usually if one maintains that a machine *can* do one of these things, and describes the kind of method that the machine could use, one will not make much of an impression. It is thought that the method (whatever it may be, for it must be mechanical) is really rather base. Compare the parentheses in Jefferson's statement quoted on page 22.

(6) Lady Lovelace's Objection

Our most detailed information of Babbage's Analytical Engine comes from a memoir by Lady Lovelace (1842). In it she states, "The Analytical Engine has no pretensions to *originate* anything. It can do *whatever we know how to order it* to perform" (her italics). This statement is quoted by Hartree (1949) who adds: "This does not imply that it may not be possible to construct electronic equipment which will 'think for itself,' or in which, in biological terms, one could set up a conditioned reflex, which would serve as a basis for 'learning.' Whether this is possible in principle or not is a stimulating and exciting question, suggested by some of these recent developments. But it did not seem that the machines constructed or projected at the time had this property."

I am in thorough agreement with Hartree over this. It will be noticed that he does not assert that the machines in question had not got the property, but rather that the evidence available to Lady Lovelace did not encourage her to believe that they had it. It is quite possible that the machines in question had in a sense got this property. For suppose that some discrete-state machine has the property. The Analytical Engine was a universal digital computer, so that, if its storage capacity and speed were adequate, it could by suitable programming be made to mimic the machine in question. Probably this argument did not occur to the Countess or to Babbage. In any case there was no obligation on them to claim all that could be claimed.

This whole question will be considered again under the heading of learning machines.

A variant of Lady Lovelace's objection states that a machine can "never do anything really new." This may be parried for a moment with the saw, "There is nothing new under the sun." Who can be certain that "original work" that he has done was not simply the growth of the seed planted in him by teaching, or the effect of following well-known general principles. A better variant of the objection says that a machine can never "take us by surprise." This statement is a more direct challenge and can be met directly. Machines take me by surprise with great frequency. This is largely because I do not do sufficient calculation to decide what to expect them to do, or rather because, although I do a calculation, I do it in a hurried, slipshod fashion, taking risks. Perhaps I say to myself, "I suppose the voltage here ought to he the same as there: anyway let's assume it is." Naturally I am often wrong, and the result is a surprise for me for by the time the experiment is done these assumptions have been forgotten. These admissions lay me open to lectures on the subject of my vicious ways, but do not throw any doubt on my credibility when I testify to the surprises I experience.

I do not expect this reply to silence my critic. He will probably say that the surprises are due to some creative mental act on my part, and reflect no credit on the machine. This leads us back to the argument from consciousness, and far from the idea of surprise. It is a line of argument we must consider closed, but it is perhaps worth remarking that the appreciation of something as surprising requires as much of a "creative mental act" whether the surprising event originates from a man, a book, a machine or anything else.

The view that machines cannot give rise to surprises is due, I believe, to a fallacy to which philosophers and mathematicians are particularly subject. This is the assumption that as soon as a fact is presented to a mind all consequences of that fact spring into the mind simultaneously with it. It is a very useful assumption under many circumstances, but one too easily forgets that it is false. A natural consequence of doing so is that one then assumes that there is no virtue in the mere working out of consequences from data and general principles.

(7) Argument from Continuity in the Nervous System
The nervous system is certainly not a discrete-state machine. A small error in the information about the size of a nervous impulse impinging on a neuron, may make a large difference to the size of the outgoing impulse. It may be argued that, this being so, one cannot expect to be able to mimic the behaviour of the nervous system with a discrete-state system.

It is true that a discrete-state machine must be different from a continuous machine. But if we adhere to the conditions of the imitation game, the interrogator will not be able to take any advantage of this difference. The situation can be made clearer if we consider some other simpler continuous machine. A differential analyser will do very well. (A differential analyser is a certain kind of machine not of the discrete-state type used for some kinds of calculation.) Some of these provide their answers in a typed form, and so are suitable for taking part in the game. It would not be possible for a digital computer to predict exactly what answers the differential analyser would give to a problem, but it would be quite capable of giving the right sort of answer. For instance, if asked to give the value of π (actually about 3.1416) it would be reasonable to choose at random between the values 3.12, 3.13, 3.14, 3.15, 3.16 with the probabilities of 0.05, 0.15, 0.55, 0.19, 0.06 (say). Under these circumstances it would be very difficult for the interrogator to distinguish the differential analyser from the digital computer.

(8) The Argument from Informality of Behaviour

It is not possible to produce a set of rules purporting to describe what a man should do in every conceivable set of circumstances. One might for instance have a rule that one is to stop when one sees a red traffic light, and to go if one sees a green one, but what if by some fault both appear together? One may perhaps decide that it is safest to stop. But some further difficulty may well arise from this decision later. To attempt to provide rules of conduct to cover every eventuality, even those arising from traffic lights, appears to be impossible. With all this I agree.

From this it is argued that we cannot be machines. I shall try to reproduce the argument, but I fear I shall hardly do it justice. It seems to run something like this. "if each man had a definite set of rules of conduct by which he regulated his life he would be no better than a machine. But there are no such rules, so men cannot be machines." The undistributed middle is glaring. I do not think the argument is ever put quite like this, but I believe this is the argument used never-theless. There may however be a certain confusion between "rules of conduct" and "laws of behaviour" to cloud the issue. By "rules of conduct" I mean precepts such as "Stop if you see red lights," on which one can act, and of which one can be conscious. By "laws of behaviour" I mean laws of nature as applied to a man's body such as "if you pinch him he will squeak." If we substitute "laws of behaviour which regulate his life" for "laws of conduct by which he regulates his life" in the argument quoted the undistributed middle is no longer insuperable. For we believe that it is not only true that being regulated by laws of behaviour implies being some sort of machine (though not necessarily a discrete-state machine), but that conversely being such a machine implies being regulated by such laws.

However, we cannot so easily convince ourselves of the absence of complete laws of behaviour as of complete rules of conduct. The only way we know of for finding such laws is scientific observation, and we certainly know of no circumstances under which we could say, "We have searched enough. There are no such laws."

We can demonstrate more forcibly that any such statement would be unjustified. For suppose we could be sure of finding such laws if they existed. Then given a discrete-state machine it should certainly be possible to discover by observation sufficient about it to pre-dict its future behaviour, and this within a reasonable time, say a thousand years. But this does not seem to be the case. I have set up on the Manchester computer a small programme using only 1,000 units of storage, whereby the machine supplied with one sixteen-figure number replies with another within two seconds. I would defy anyone to learn from these replies suffi-cient about the programme to be able to predict any replies to untried values.

(9) The Argument from Extrasensory Perception

I assume that the reader is familiar with the idea of extrasensory perception, and the meaning of the four items of it, viz., telepathy, clairvoyance, precognition and psychokinesis. These disturbing phenomena seem to deny all our usual scientific ideas. How we should like to discredit them! Unfortunately the statistical evidence, at least for telepathy, is overwhelming. It is very difficult to rearrange one's ideas so as to fit these new facts in. Once one has accepted them it does not seem a very big step to believe in ghosts and bogies. The idea that our bodies move simply according to the known laws of physics, together with some others not yet discovered but somewhat similar, would be one of the first to go.

This argument is to my mind quite a strong one. One can say in reply that many scientific theories seem to remain workable in practice, in spite of clashing with ESP; that in fact one can get along very nicely if one forgets about it. This is rather cold comfort, and one fears that thinking is just the kind of phenomenon where ESP may be especially relevant.

A more specific argument based on ESP might run as follows: "Let us play the imitation game, using as witnesses a man who is good as a telepathic receiver, and a digital computer. The interrogator can ask such questions as 'What suit does the card in my right hand belong to?' The man by telepathy or clairvoyance gives the right answer 130 times out of 400 cards. The machine can only guess at random, and perhaps gets 104 right, so the interrogator makes the right identification." There is an interesting possibility which opens here. Suppose the digital computer contains a random number generator. Then it will be natural to use this to decide what answer to give. But then the random number generator will be subject to the psychokinetic powers of the interrogator. Perhaps this psychokinesis might cause the machine to guess right more often than would be expected on a probability calculation, so that the interrogator might still be unable to make the right identification. On the other hand, he might be able to guess right without any questioning, by clairvoyance. With ESP anything may happen.

If telepathy is admitted it will be necessary to tighten our test up. The situation could be regarded as analogous to that which would occur if the interrogator were talking to himself and one of the competitors was listening with his ear to the wall. To put the competitors into a "telepathy-proof room" would satisfy all requirements.

7. LEARNING MACHINES

The reader will have anticipated that I have no very convincing arguments of a positive nature to support my views. If I had I should not have taken such pains to point out the fallacies in contrary views. Such evidence as I have I shall now give.

Let us return for a moment to Lady Lovelace's objection, which stated that the machine can only do what we tell it to do. One could say that a man can "inject" an idea into the machine, and that it will respond to a certain extent and then drop into quiescence, like a piano string struck by a hammer. Another simile would be an atomic pile of less than critical size: an injected idea is to correspond to a neutron entering the pile from without. Each such neutron will cause a

certain disturbance which eventually dies away. If, however, the size of the pile is sufficiently increased, tire disturbance caused by such an incoming neutron will very likely go on and on increasing until the whole pile is destroyed. Is there a corresponding phenomenon for minds, and is there one for machines? There does seem to be one for the human mind. The majority of them seem to be "subcritical," i.e., to correspond in this analogy to piles of subcritical size. An idea presented to such a mind will on average give rise to less than one idea in reply. A smallish proportion are supercritical. An idea presented to such a mind that may give rise to a whole "theory" consisting of secondary, tertiary and more remote ideas. Animals minds seem to be very definitely subcritical. Adhering to this analogy we ask, "Can a machine be made to be supercritical?"

The "skin-of-an-onion" analogy is also helpful. In considering the functions of the mind or the brain we find certain operations which we can explain in purely mechanical terms. This we say does not correspond to the real mind: it is a sort of skin which we must strip off if we are to find the real mind. But then in what remains we find a further skin to be stripped off, and so on. Proceeding in this way do we ever come to the "real" mind, or do we eventually come to the skin which has nothing in it? In the latter case the whole mind is mechanical. (It would not be a discrete-state machine however. We have discussed this.)

These last two paragraphs do not claim to be convincing arguments. They should rather be described as "recitations tending to produce belief."

The only really satisfactory support that can be given for the view expressed at the beginning of §6, will be that provided by waiting for the end of the century and then doing the experiment described. But what can we say in the meantime? What steps should be taken now if the experiment is to be successful?

As I have explained, the problem is mainly one of programming. Advances in engineering will have to be made too, but it seems unlikely that these will not be adequate for the requirements. Estimates of the storage capacity of the brain vary from 10^{10} to 10^{15} binary digits. I incline to the lower values and believe that only a very small fraction is used for the higher types of thinking. Most of it is probably used for the retention of visual impressions, I should be surprised if more than 10^9 was required for satisfactory playing of the imitation game, at any rate against a blind man. (Note: The capacity of the *Encyclopaedia Britannica*, 11th edition, is 2×10^9) A storage capacity of 10^7 would be a very practicable possibility even by present techniques. It is probably not necessary to increase the speed of operations of the machines at all. Parts of modern machines which can be regarded as analogs of nerve cells work about a thousand times faster than the latter. This should provide a "margin of safety" which could cover losses of speed arising in many ways. Our problem then is to find out how to programme these machines to play the game. At my present rate of working I produce about a thousand digits of programming a day, so that about sixty workers, working steadily through the fifty years might accomplish the job, if nothing went into the wastepaper basket. Some more expeditious method seems desirable.

In the process of trying to imitate an adult human mind we are bound to think a good deal about the process which has brought it to the state that it is in. We may notice three components.

    a.   The initial state of the mind, say at birth,

    b.   The education to which it has been subjected,

    c.   Other experience, not to be described as education, to which it has been subjected.

Instead of trying to produce a programme to simulate the adult mind, why not rather try to produce one which simulates the child's? If this were then subjected to an appropriate course of education one would obtain the adult brain. Presumably the child brain is something like a notebook as one buys it from the stationer's. Rather little mechanism, and lots of blank sheets. (Mechanism and writing are from our point of view almost synonymous.) Our hope is that there is so little mechanism in the child brain that something like

it can be easily programmed. The amount of work in the education we can assume, as a first approximation, to be much the same as for the human child.

We have thus divided our problem into two parts. The child programme and the education process. These two remain very closely connected. We cannot expect to find a good child machine at the first attempt. One must experiment with teaching one such machine and see how well it learns. One can then try another and see if it is better or worse. There is an obvious connection between this process and evolution, by the identifications

Structure of the child machine	= Hereditary material
Changes of the child machine	= Mutations
Natural selection	= Judgment of the experimenter

One may hope, however, that this process will be more expeditious than evolution. The survival of the fittest is a slow method for measuring advantages. The experimenter, by the exercise of intelligence, should he able to speed it up. Equally important is the fact that he is not restricted to random mutations. If he can trace a cause for some weakness he can probably think of the kind of mutation which will improve it.

It will not be possible to apply exactly the same teaching process to the machine as to a normal child. It will not, for instance, be provided with legs, so that it could not be asked to go out and fill the coal scuttle. Possibly it might not have eyes. But however well these deficiencies might be overcome by clever engineering, one could not send the creature to school without the other children making excessive fun of it. It must be given some tuition. We need not be too concerned about the legs, eyes, etc. The example of Miss Helen Keller shows that education can take place provided that communication in both directions between teacher and pupil can take place by some means or other.

We normally associate punishments and rewards with the teaching process. Some simple child machines can be constructed or programmed on this sort of principle. The machine has to be so constructed that events which shortly preceded the occurrence of a punishment signal are unlikely to be repeated, whereas a reward signal increased the probability of repetition of the events which led up to it. These definitions do not presuppose any feelings on the part of the machine, I have done some experiments with one such child machine, and succeeded in teaching it a few things, but the teaching method was too unorthodox for the experiment to be considered really successful.

The use of punishments and rewards can at best be a part of the teaching process. Roughly speaking, if the teacher has no other means of communicating to the pupil, the amount of information which can reach him does not exceed the total number of rewards and punishments applied. By the time a child has learnt to repeat "Casabianca" he would probably feel very sore indeed, if the text could only be discovered by a "Twenty Questions" technique, every "NO" taking the form of a blow. It is necessary therefore to have some other "unemotional" channels of communication. If these are available it is possible to teach a machine by punishments and rewards to obey orders given in some language, e.g., a symbolic language. These orders are to be transmitted through the "unemotional" channels. The use of this language will diminish greatly the number of punishments and rewards required.

Opinions may vary as to the complexity which is suitable in the child machine. One might try to make it as simple as possible consistently with the general principles. Alternatively one might have a complete system of logical inference "built in." In the latter case the store would be largely occupied with definitions and propositions. The propositions would have various kinds of status, e.g., well-established facts, conjectures, mathematically proved theorems, statements given by an authority, expressions having the logical form of proposition but not belief-value. Certain propositions may be described as "imperatives." The machine should be so constructed that as soon as an imperative is classed as "well established" the appropriate action automatically takes place. To illustrate

this, suppose the teacher says to the machine, "Do your homework now." This may cause "Teacher says 'Do your homework now'" to be included amongst the well-established facts. Another such fact might be, "Everything that teacher says is true." Combining these may eventually lead to the imperative, "Do your homework now," being included amongst the well-established facts, and this, by the construction of the machine, will mean that the homework actually gets started, but the effect is very satisfactory. The processes of inference used by the machine need not be such as would satisfy the most exacting logicians. There might for instance be no hierarchy of types. But this need not mean that type fallacies will occur, any more than we are bound to fall over unfenced cliffs. Suitable imperatives (expressed within the systems, not forming part of the rules of the system) such as "Do not use a class unless it is a subclass of one which has been mentioned by teacher" can have a similar effect to "Do not go too near the edge."

The imperatives that can be obeyed by a machine that has no limbs are bound to be of a rather intellectual character, as in the example (doing homework) given above. Important amongst such imperatives will be ones which regulate the order in which the rules of the logical system concerned are to be applied, For at each stage when one is using a logical system, there is a very large number of alternative steps, any of which one is permitted to apply, so far as obedience to the rules of the logical system is concerned. These choices make the difference between a brilliant and a footling reasoner, not the difference between a sound and a fallacious one. Propositions leading to imperatives of this kind might be "When Socrates is mentioned, use the syllogism in Barbara" or "If one method has been proved to be quicker than another, do not use the slower method." Some of these may be "given by authority," but others may be produced by the machine itself, e.g. by scientific induction.

The idea of a learning machine may appear paradoxical to some readers. How can the rules of operation of the machine change? They should describe completely how the machine will react whatever its history might be, whatever changes it might undergo.

The rules are thus quite time-invariant. This is quite true. The explanation of the paradox is that the rules which get changed in the learning process are of a rather less pretentious kind, claiming only an ephemeral validity. The reader may draw a parallel with the Constitution of the United States.

An important feature of a learning machine is that its teacher will often be very largely ignorant of quite what is going on inside, although he may still be able to some extent to predict his pupil's behavior. This should apply most strongly to the later education of a machine arising from a child machine of well-tried design (or programme). This is in clear contrast with normal procedure when using a machine to do computations: one's object is then to have a clear mental picture of the state of the machine at each moment in the computation. This object can only be achieved with a struggle. The view that "the machine can only do what we know how to order it to do," appears strange in face of this. Most of the programmes which we can put into the machine will result in its doing something that we cannot make sense (if at all, or which we regard as completely random behaviour. Intelligent behaviour presumably consists in a departure from the completely disciplined behaviour involved in computation, but a rather slight one, which does not give rise to random behaviour, or to pointless repetitive loops. Another important result of preparing our machine for its part in the imitation game by a process of teaching and learning is that "human fallibility" is likely to be omitted in a rather natural way, i.e., without special "coaching." (The reader should reconcile this with the point of view on pages 23 and 24 [sic].) Processes that are learnt do not produce a hundred per cent certainty of result; if they did they could not be unlearnt.

It is probably wise to include a random element in a learning machine. A random element is rather useful when we are searching for a solution of some problem. Suppose for instance we wanted to find a number between 50 and 200 which was equal to the square of the sum of its digits, we might start at 51 then try 52 and go on until we got a number that worked. Alternatively we might choose numbers at random until we got a good one. This method has the advantage that it is unnecessary to keep track of the values that have been tried, but the disadvantage that one may try the same one twice, but this is not very important if there are several solutions. The systematic method has the disadvantage that there may be an enormous block without any solutions in the region which has to be investigated first, Now the learning process may be regarded as a search for a form of behaviour which will satisfy the teacher (or some other criterion). Since there is probably a very large number of satisfactory solutions the random method seems to be better than the systematic. It should be noticed that it is used in the analogous process of evolution. But there the systematic method is not possible. How could one keep track of the different genetical combinations that had been tried, so as to avoid trying them again?

We may hope that machines will eventually compete with men in all purely intellectual fields. But which are the best ones to start with? Even this is a difficult decision. Many people think that a very abstract activity, like the playing of chess, would be best. It can also be maintained that it is best to provide the machine with the best sense organs that money can buy, and then teach it to understand and speak English. This process could follow the normal teaching of a child. Things would be pointed out and named, etc. Again I do not know what the right answer is, but I think both approaches should be tried.

We can only see a short distance ahead, but we can see plenty there that needs to be done.

11.3

Programming a Computer for Playing Chess

Claude E. Shannon

From *Philosophical Magazine,* 7th series, 41 (1950): 256–75.

INTRODUCTORY NOTE TO READING 11.3

Shannon's paper, written in 1949 and published in 1950, is the first technical paper on computer chess. In their paper on "Chess-playing programs and the problem of complexity," Allen Newell, J. C. Shaw and Herbert Simon had this to say about Shannon's paper:

> The relevant history [of chess-playing programs] begins with a paper by Claude Shannon in 1949. He did not present a particular chess program, but discussed many of the basic problems involved. The framework he introduced has guided most of the subsequent analysis of the problem. . . .

The basic framework introduced by Shannon for thinking about chess problems consists of a series of questions:

1. Alternatives
   Which alternative moves are to be considered?

2. Analysis

   a. Which continuations are to be explored and to what depth?

   b. How are positions to be evaluated strategically—in terms of their patterns?

   c. How are the static evaluations to be integrated into a single value for an alternative?

3. Final choice procedure

What procedure is to be used to select the final preferred move?

We would hazard that Shannon's paper is chiefly remembered for the specific answers he proposed to these questions: consider all alternatives; search all continuations to fixed depth, n; evaluate with a numerical sum; minimax to get the effective value for an alternative; and then pick the best one.[1] [JMN]

---

1   Allen Newell, J. C. Shaw, and Herbert Simon, Chess-playing programs and the problem of complexity. Reprinted in E. A. Feigenbaum and J. Feldman, *Computers and Thought* (New York: McGraw-Hill, 1963), 42–44.

TEXT OF READING 11.3
1. INTRODUCTION.

This paper is concerned with the problem of constructing a computing routine or "program" for a modern general purpose computer which will enable it to play chess. Although perhaps of no practical importance, the question is of theoretical interest, and it is hoped that a satisfactory solution of this problem will act as a wedge in attacking other problems of a similar nature and of greater significance. Some possibilities in this direction are:

1. Machines for designing filters, equalizers, etc.

2. Machines for designing relay and switching circuits.

3. Machines which will handle routing of telephone calls based on the individual circumstances rather than by fixed patterns.

4. Machines for performing symbolic (non-numerical) mathematical operations.

5. Machines capable of translating from one language to another.

6. Machines for making strategic decisions in simplified military operations.

7. Machines capable of orchestrating a melody.

8. Machines capable of logical deduction.

It is believed that all of these and many other devices of a similar nature are possible developments in the immediate future. The techniques developed for modern electronic and relay type computers make them not only theoretical possibilities, but in several cases worthy of serious consideration from the economic point of view.

Machines of this general type are an extension over the ordinary use of numerical computers in several ways. First, the entities dealt with are not primarily numbers, but, rather chess positions, circuits, mathematical expressions, words, etc. Second, the proper procedure involves general principles, something of the nature of judgment, and considerable trial and error, rather than a strict, unalterable computing process. Finally, the solutions of these problems are not merely right or wrong but have a continuous range of "quality" from the best down to the worst. We might be satisfied with a machine that designed good filters even though they were not always the best possible.

The chess machine is an ideal one to start with, since: (1) the problem is sharply defined both in allowed operations (the moves) and in the ultimate goal (checkmate); (2) it is neither so simple as to be trivial nor too difficult for satisfactory solution; (3) chess is generally considered to require "thinking" for skilful play; a solution of this problem will force us either to admit the possibility of mechanized thinking or to further restrict our concept of "thinking"; (4) the discrete structure of chess fits well into the digital nature of modern computers.

There is already a considerable literature on the subject of chess-playing machines. During the late 18th and early 19th centuries, the Maelzel Chess Automaton, a device invented by von Kempelen, was exhibited widely as a chess-playing machine. A number of papers appeared at the time, including an analytical essay by Edgar Allan Poe (entitled Maelzel's Chess Player) purporting to explain its operation. Most of these writers concluded, quite correctly, that the Automaton was operated by a concealed human chess-master; the arguments leading to this conclusion, however, were frequently fallacious. Poe assumes, for example, that it is as easy to design a machine which will invariably win as one which wins occasionally, and argues that since the Automaton was not invincible it was therefore operated by a human, a clear *non sequitur*. For a complete account of the history and method of operation of the Automaton, the reader is referred to a series of articles by Harkness and Battell in *Chess Review*, 1947.

A more honest attempt to design a chess-playing machine was made in 1914 by Torres y Quévedo, who constructed a device which played an end game of king and rook against king (Vigneron, 1914). The machine played the side with king and rook and would force checkmate in a few moves however its human opponent played. Since an explicit set of rules can be given for making satisfactory moves in such an end game, the problem is relatively simple, but the idea was quite advanced for that period.

The thesis we will develop is that modern general purpose computers can be used to play a tolerably good game of chess by the use of a suitable computing routine or "program". While the approach given here is believed fundamentally sound, it will be evident that much further experimental and theoretical work remains to be done.

2. GENERAL CONSIDERATIONS.

A chess "position" may be defined to include the following data:—

1. A statement of the positions of all pieces on the board.

2. A statement of which side, White or Black, has the move.

3. A statement as to whether the kings and rooks have moved. This is important since by moving a rook, for example, the right to castle on that side is forfeited.

4. A statement of, say, the last move. This will determine whether a possible *en passant* capture is legal, since this privilege is forfeited after one move.

5. A statement of the number of moves made since the last pawn move or capture. This is important because of the 50 move drawing rule. For simplicity, we will ignore the rule of draw after three repetitions of a position.

In chess there is no chance element apart from the original choice of which player has the first move. This is in contrast with card games, backgammon, etc. Furthermore, in chess each of the two opponents has "perfect information" at each move as to all previous moves (in contrast with Kriegspiel, for example). These two facts imply (von Neumann and Morgenstern, 1944) that any given position of the chess pieces must be either:—

1. A won position for White. That is, White can force a win, however Black defends.

2. A draw position. White can force at least a draw, however Black plays, and likewise Black can force at least a draw, however White plays. If both sides play correctly the game will end in a draw.

3. A won position for Black. Black can force a win, however White plays.

This is, for practical purposes, of the nature of an existence theorem. No practical method is known for determining to which of the three categories a general position belongs. If there were chess would lose most of its interest as a game. One could determine whether the initial position is won, drawn, or lost for White and the outcome of a game between opponents knowing the method would be fully determined at the choice of the first move. Supposing the initial position a draw (as suggested by empirical evidence from master games[1]) every game would end in a draw.

It is interesting that a slight change in the rules of chess gives a game for which it is provable that White has at least a draw in the initial position. Suppose the rules the same as those of chess except that a player is not forced to move a piece at his turn to play, but may, if he chooses, "pass". Then we can prove as a theorem that White can at least draw by proper play. For in the initial position either he has a winning move or not. If so, let him make this move. If not, let him pass. Black is now faced with essentially the same position that White had before, because of the mirror symmetry of the initial position.[2] Since White had no winning move before, Black has none now. Hence, Black at best can draw. Therefore, in either case White can at least draw.

In some games there is a simple *evaluation function* $f(P)$ which can be applied to a position P and whose value determines to which category (won, lost, etc.) the position P belongs. In the game of Nim (Hardy and Wright, 1938), for example, this can be determined by writing the number of matches in each pile in binary notation. These numbers are arranged in a column (as though to add them). If the number of ones in each column is even, the position is lost for the player about to move, otherwise won.

If such an evaluation function $f(P)$ can be found for a game it is easy to design a machine capable of perfect play. It would never lose or draw a won position and never lose a drawn position and if the opponent ever made a mistake the machine would capitalize on it. This could be done as follows: Suppose

$f(P) = 1$ for a won position,

$f(P) = 0$ for a drawn position,

$f(P) = -1$ for a lost position.

At the machine's turn to move it calculates $f(P)$ for the various positions obtained from the present position by each possible move that can be made. It chooses that move (or one of the set) giving the maximum value to f. In the case of Nim where such a function $f(P)$ is known, a machine has actually been constructed which plays a perfect game.[3]

With chess it is possible, *in principle*, to play a perfect game or construct a machine to do so as follows: One considers in a given position all possible moves, then all moves for the opponent, etc., to the end of the game (in each variation). The end must occur, by the rules of the game, after a finite number of moves[4] (remembering the 50 move drawing rule). Each of these variations ends in win, loss or draw. By working backward from the end one can determine whether there is a forced win, the position is a draw or is lost. It is easy to show, however, that even with the high computing speeds available in electronic calculators this computation is impractical. In typical chess positions there will be of the order of 30 legal moves. The number holds fairly constant until the game is nearly finished as shown in Fig. 1. This graph was constructed from data given by De Groot, who averaged the number of legal moves in a large number of master games (De Groot, 1946, *a*). Thus a move for White and then one for Black gives about 10^3 possibilities. A typical game lasts about 40 moves to resignation of one party. This is conservative for our calculation since the

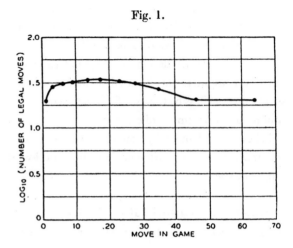

Fig. 1.

machine should calculate out to checkmate, not resignation. However, even at this figure there will be 10^{120} variations to be calculated from the initial position. A machine operating at the rate of one variation per micro-microsecond would require over 10^{90} years to calculate its first move!

Another (equally impractical) method is to have a "dictionary" of all possible positions of the chess pieces. For each possible position there is an entry giving the correct move (either calculated by the above process or supplied by a chess master). At the machine's turn to move it merely looks up the position and makes the indicated move. The number of possible positions, of the general order of $64! \mid 32! \, 8!^2 \, 2!^6$, or roughly 10^{43}, naturally makes such a design unfeasible.

It is clear then that the problem is not that of designing a machine to play perfect chess (which is quite impractical) nor one which merely plays legal chess (which is trivial). We would like it to play a skilful game, perhaps comparable to that of a good human player.

A strategy for chess may be described as a process for choosing a move in any given position. If the process always chooses the same move in the same position the strategy is known in the theory of games as a pure strategy. If the process involves statistical elements and does not always result in the same choice it is a "mixed" strategy. The following are simple examples of strategies:—

1. Number the possible legal moves in the position P, according to some standard procedure. Choose the first on the list. This is a pure strategy.

2. Number the legal moves and choose one at random from the list. This is a mixed strategy.

Both of these, of course, are extremely poor strategies, making no attempt to select good moves. Our problem is to develop a tolerably good strategy for selecting the move to be made.

3. APPROXIMATE EVALUATING FUNCTIONS.

Although in chess there is no known simple and exact evaluating function $f(P)$, and probably never will be because of the arbitrary and complicated nature of the rules of the game, it is still possible to perform an approximate evaluation of a position. Any good chess player must, in fact, be able to perform such a position evaluation. Evaluations are based on the general structure of the position, the number and kind of Black and White pieces, pawn formation, mobility, etc. These evaluations are not perfect, but the stronger the player the better his evaluations. Most of the maxims and principles of correct play are really assertions about evaluating positions, for example:

1. The relative values of queen, rook, bishop, knight and pawn are about 9, 5, 3, 3, 1, respectively. Thus other things being equal (!) if we add the numbers of pieces for the two sides with these coefficients, the side with the largest total has the better position.

2. Rooks should be placed on open files. This is part of a more general principle that the side with the greater mobility, other things equal, has the better game.

3. Backward, isolated and doubled pawns are weak.

4. An exposed king is a weakness (until the end game).

These and similar principles are only generalizations from empirical evidence of numerous games, and only have a kind of statistical validity. Probably any chess principle can be contradicted by particular counter examples. However, from these principles one can construct a crude evaluation function. The following is an example:

$$f(P) = 200(K - K') + 9(Q - Q') + 5(R - R') + 3(B - B' + N - N') + (P - P') - \cdot 5(D - D' + S - S' + I - I') + \cdot 1(M - M') + \ldots$$

in which:

K, Q, R, B, N, P are the number of White kings, queens, rooks, bishops, knights and pawns on the board.

D, S, I are doubled, backward and isolated White pawns.

M = White mobility (measured, say, as the number of legal moves available to White).

Primed letters are the similar quantities for Black.

The coefficients $\cdot 5$ and $\cdot 1$ are merely the writer's rough estimate. Furthermore, there are many other terms that should be included.[5] The formula is given only for illustrative purposes. Checkmate has been artificially included here by giving the king the large value 200 (anything greater than the maximum of all other terms would do).

It may be noted that this approximate evaluation $f(P)$ has a more or less continuous range of possible values, while with an exact evaluation there are only three possible values. This is as it should be. In practical play a position may be an "easy win" if a player is, for example, a queen ahead, or a very difficult win with only a pawn advantage. In the former case there are many ways to win while in the latter exact play is required, and a single mistake often destroys the advantage. The unlimited intellects assumed in the theory of games, on the other hand, never make a mistake and the smallest winning advantage is as good as mate in one. A game between two such mental giants, Mr. A and Mr. B, would proceed as follows. They sit down at the chessboard, draw for colours, and then survey the pieces for a moment. Then either

1. Mr. A says, "I resign" or

2. Mr. B says, "I resign" or

3. Mr. A says, "I offer a draw," and Mr. B replies, "I accept."

4. STRATEGY BASED ON AN EVALUATION FUNCTION.

A very important point about the simple type of evaluation function given above (and general principles of chess) is that they can only be applied in relatively quiescent positions. For example, in an exchange of queens White plays, say, Q × Q (× = captures) and Black will reply P × Q. It would be absurd to calculate the function $f(P)$ after Q × Q while White is, for a moment, a queen ahead, since Black will immediately recover it. More generally it is meaningless to calculate an evaluation of the general type given above during the course of a combination or a series of exchanges.

More terms could be added to $f(P)$ to account for exchanges in progress, but it appears that combinations, and forced variations in general, are better accounted for by examination of specific variations. This is, in fact, the way chess players calculate. A certain number of variations are investigated move by move until a more or less quiescent position is reached and at this point something of the nature of an evaluation is applied to the resulting position. The player chooses the variation leading to the highest evaluation for him when the opponent is assumed to be playing to reduce this evaluation.

The process can be described mathematically. We omit at first the fact that $f(P)$ should only be applied in quiescent positions. A strategy of play based on $f(P)$ and operating one move deep is the following. Let M_1, M_2, M_3, . . ., M_s be the moves that can be made in position P and let M_1P, M_2P, etc. denote symbolically the resulting positions when M_1, M_2, etc. are applied to P. Then one chooses the M_m which maximizes $f(M_mP)$.

A deeper strategy would consider the opponent's replies. Let M_{i1}, M_{i2}, . . ., M_{is} be the possible answers by Black, if White chooses move M_i. Black should play to *minimize* $f(P)$. Furthermore, his choice occurs *after*

White's move. Thus, if White plays M_i Black may be assumed to play the M_{ij} such that

$$f(M_{ij}M_iP)$$

is *a minimum*. White should play his first move such that f is a maximum after Black chooses his best reply. Therefore, White should play to maximize on M_i the quantity

$$\min_{M_{ij}} f(M_{ij}M_iP)$$

The mathematical process involved is shown for a simple case in Fig. 2. The point at the left represents

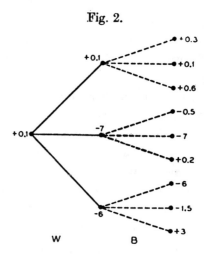

Fig. 2.

the position being considered. It is assumed that there are three possible moves for White, indicated by the three solid lines, and if any of these is made there are three possible moves for Black, indicated by the dashed lines. The possible positions after a White and Black move are then the nine points on the right, and the numbers are the evaluations for these positions. Minimizing on the upper three gives +·1 which is the resulting value if White chooses the upper variation and Black replies with his best move. Similarly, the second and third moves lead to values of −7 and −6. Maximizing on White's move, we obtain +·1 with the upper move as White's best choice.

In a similar way a two-move strategy (based on considering all variations out to 2 moves) is given by

$$\text{Max} \quad \text{Min} \quad \text{Max} \quad \text{Min} \qquad f(M_{ijkl} M_{ijk} M_{ij} M_i P)$$
$$M_i \qquad M_{ij} \qquad M_{ijk} \qquad M_{ijkl} \qquad\qquad \dots (1)$$

The order of maximizing and minimizing this function is important. It derives from the fact that the choices of moves occur in a definite order.

A machine operating on this strategy at the two-move level would first calculate all variations out to two moves (for each side) and the resulting positions. The evaluations $f(P)$ are calculated for each of these positions. Fixing all but the last Black move, this last is varied and the move chosen which minimizes f. This is Black's assumed last move in the variation:—in question. Another move for White's second move is chosen and the process repeated for Black's second move. This is done for each second White move and the one chosen giving the largest final f (after Black's best assumed reply in each case). In this way White's second move in each variation is determined. Continuing in this way the machine works back to the present position and the best first White move. This move is then played. This process generalizes in the obvious way for any number of moves.

A strategy of this sort, in which all variations are considered out to a definite number of moves and the move then determined from a formula such as (1) will be called a type A strategy. The type A strategy has certain basic weaknesses, which we will discuss later, but is conceptually simple, and we will first show how a computer can be programmed for such a strategy.

5. PROGRAMMING A GENERAL PURPOSE COMPUTER FOR A TYPE A STRATEGY.

We assume a large-scale digital computer, indicated schematically in Fig. 3, with the following properties:

1. There is a large internal memory for storing numbers. The memory is divided into a number of boxes each capable of holding, say, a ten-digit number. Each box is assigned a "box number".

Fig. 3.

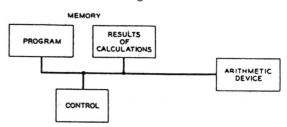

2. There is an arithmetic organ which can perform the elementary operations of addition, multiplication, etc.

3. The computer operates under the control of a "program". The program consists of a sequence of elementary "orders". A typical order is A 372, 451, 133. This means, extract the contents of box 372 and of box 451, add these numbers, and put the sum in box 133. Another type of order involves a decision, for example, C 291, 118, 345. This tells the machine to compare the contents of box 291 and 118. If the first is larger the machine goes on to the next order in the program. If not, it takes its next order from box 345. This type of order enables the machine to choose from alternative procedures, depending on the results of previous calculations. It is assumed that orders are available for transferring numbers, the arithmetic operations, and decisions.

Our problem is to represent chess as numbers and operations on numbers, and to reduce the strategy decided upon to a sequence of computer orders. We will not carry this out in detail but only outline the programs. As a colleague puts it, the final program for a computer must be written in words of one microsyllable.

The rather Procrustean tactics of forcing chess into an arithmetic computer are dictated by economic considerations. Ideally, we would like to design a special computer for chess containing, in place of the arithmetic organ, a "chess organ" specifically designed to perform the simple chess calculations. Although a large improvement in speed of operation would undoubtedly result, the initial cost of computers seems to prohibit such a possibility. It is planned, however, to experiment with a simple strategy on one of the numerical computers now being constructed.

Fig. 4.

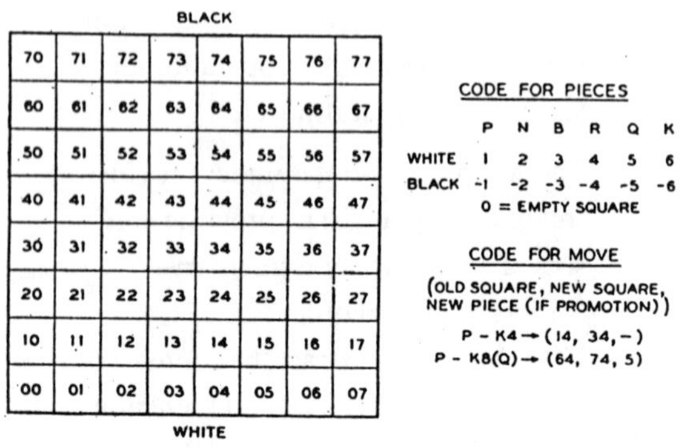

BLACK

70	71	72	73	74	75	76	77
60	61	62	63	64	65	66	67
50	51	52	53	54	55	56	57
40	41	42	43	44	45	46	47
30	31	32	33	34	35	36	37
20	21	22	23	24	25	26	27
10	11	12	13	14	15	16	17
00	01	02	03	04	05	06	07

WHITE

CODE FOR PIECES

	P	N	B	R	Q	K
WHITE	1	2	3	4	5	6
BLACK	-1	-2	-3	-4	-5	-6

0 = EMPTY SQUARE

CODE FOR MOVE

(OLD SQUARE, NEW SQUARE, NEW PIECE (IF PROMOTION))

P – K4 → (14, 34, –)
P – K8(Q) → (64, 74, 5)

A game of chess can be divided into three phases, the opening, the middle game, and the end game. Different principles of play apply in the different phases. In the opening, which generally lasts for about ten moves, development of the pieces to good positions is the main objective. During the middle game tactics and combinations are predominant. This phase lasts until most of the pieces are exchanged, leaving only kings, pawns and perhaps one or two pieces on each side. The end game is mainly concerned with pawn promotion. Exact timing and such possibilities as "Zugzwang", stalemate, etc. become important.

Due to the difference in strategic aims, different programs should be used for the different phases of a game. We will be chiefly concerned with the middle game and will not consider the end game at all. There seems no reason, however, why an end game strategy cannot be designed and programmed equally well.

A square on a chessboard can be occupied in 13 different ways:—either it is empty (0) or occupied by one of the six possible kinds of White pieces (P = 1, N = 2, B = 3, R = 4, Q = 5, K = 6) or one of the six possible Black pieces (P = –1, N = –2, . . ., K = –6). Thus, the state of a square is specified by giving an integer from –6 to +6. The 64 squares can be numbered

according to a co-ordinate system as shown in Fig. 4. The position of all pieces is then given by a sequence of 64 numbers each lying between –6 and +6. A total of 256 bits (binary digits) is sufficient memory in this representation. Although not the most efficient encoding, it is a convenient one for calculation. One further number A will be +1 or –1 according as it is White's or Black's move. A few more should be added for data relating to castling privileges (whether the White or Black kings and rooks have moved), and *en passant* captures (*e.g.*, a statement of the last move). We will neglect these, however. In this notation the starting chess position is given by:—

4, 2, 3, 5, 6, 3, 2, 4; 1, 1, 1, 1, 1, 1, 1, 1;

0, 0, 0, 0, 0, 0, 0, 0; 0, 0, 0, 0, 0, 0, 0, 0;

0, 0, 0, 0, 0, 0, 0, 0; 0, 0, 0, 0, 0, 0, 0, 0;

–1, –1, –1, –1, –1, –1, –1, –1; –4, –2, –3, –5, –6, –3, –2, –4;

+1 $(=\lambda)$.

A move (apart from castling and pawn promotion) can be specified by giving the original and final squares occupied by the moved piece. Each of these squares is a choice from 64, thus 6 binary digits each is sufficient, a total of 12 for the move. Thus the initial move P–K4 would be represented by 1, 4 ; 3, 4. To represent pawn promotion a set of three binary digits can be added specifying the piece that the pawn becomes. Castling is described by giving the king move (this being the only way the king can move two squares). Thus, a move is represented by (a, b, c) where a and b are squares and c specifies a piece in case of promotion.

The complete program for a type A strategy consists of nine sub-programs which we designate T_0, T_1, . . ., T_8 and a master program T_9. The basic functions of these programs are as follows:—

T_0—Makes move (a, b, c) in position P to obtain the resulting position.

T_1—Makes a list of the possible moves of a pawn at square (x, y) in position P.

$T_2, \ldots, T_8$—Similarly for other types of pieces: knight, bishop, rook, queen and king.

T_7—Makes list of all possible moves in a given position.

T_8—Calculates the evaluating function $f(P)$ for a given position P.

T_9—Master program; performs maximizing and minimizing calculation to determine proper move.

With a given position P and a move (a, b, c) in the internal memory of the machine it can make the move and obtain the resulting position by the following program T_0.

1. The square corresponding to number a in the position is located in the position memory.

2. The number in this square x is extracted and replaced by 0 (empty).

3. (*a*) If $x = 1$, and the first co-ordinate of a is 6 (White pawn being promoted) or if $x = -1$, and the first co-ordinate of a is 1 (Black pawn being promoted), the number c is placed in square b (replacing whatever was there).

   (*b*) If $x = 6$ and $a - b = 2$ (White castles, king side) 0 is placed in squares 04 and 07 and 6 and 4 in squares 06 and 05, respectively. Similarly for the cases $x = 6$, $b - a = 2$ (White castles, queen side) and $x = -6$, $a - b = \pm 2$ (Black castles, king or queen side).

   (*c*) In all other cases, x is placed in square b.

4. The sign of λ is changed.

For each type of piece there is a program for determining its possible moves. As a typical example the bishop program, T_3, is briefly as follows. Let (x, y) be the co-ordinates of the square occupied by the bishop.

1. Construct $(x + 1, y + 1)$ and read the contents u of this square in the position P.

2. If $u = 0$ (empty) list, the move (x, y), $(x + 1, y + 1)$ and start over with $(x + 2, y + 2)$ instead of $(x + 1, y + 1)$.

If λu is positive (own piece in the square) continue to 3.
If λu is negative (opponent's piece in the square) list the move and continue to 3.
If the square does not exist continue to 3.

3. Construct $(x + 1, y - 1)$ and perform similar calculation.

4. Similarly with $(x - 1, y + 1)$.

5. Similarly with $(x - 1, y - 1)$.

By this program a list is constructed of the possible moves of a bishop in a given position P. Similar programs would list the moves of any other piece. There is considerable scope for opportunism in simplifying these programs; e. g., the queen program, T_6, can be a combination of the bishop and rook programs, T_3 and T_4.

Using the piece programs $T_1 \ldots T_6$ and a controlling program T_7 the machine can construct a list of *all* possible moves in any given position P. The controlling program T_7 is briefly as follows (omitting details)

1. Start at square 1,1 and extract contents x.

2. If λx is positive start corresponding piece program T_x and when complete return to (1) adding 1 to square number. If λx is zero or negative, return to 1 adding 1 to square number.

3. Test each of the listed moves for legality and discard those which are illegal. This is done by making each of the moves in the position P (by program T_0) and examining whether it leaves the king in check.

With the programs $T_0 \ldots T_7$ it is possible for the machine to play legal chess, merely making a randomly chosen legal move at each turn to move. The level of play with such a strategy is unbelievably bad.[6] The writer played a few games against this random strategy and was able to checkmate generally in four or five moves (by fool's mate, etc.). The following game will illustrate the utter purposelessness of random play:

	White (Random)	Black
(1)	P–KN3	P–K4
(2)	P–Q3	B–B4
(3)	B–Q2	Q–B3
(4)	N–QB3	Q × P mate

We now return to the strategy based on an evaluation $f(P)$. The program T_8 performs the function of evaluating a position according to the agreed-upon $f(P)$. This can be done by the obvious means of scanning the squares and adding the terms involved. It is not difficult to include terms such as doubled pawns, etc.

The final master program T_9 is needed to select the move according to the maximizing and minimizing process indicated above. On the basis of one move (for each side) T_9 works as follows:

1. List the legal moves (by T_7) possible in the present position.

2. Take the first in the list and make this move by T_0, giving position M_1P.

3. List the Black moves in M_1P.

4. Apply the first one giving $M_{11}M_1P$, and evaluate by T_8.

5. Apply the second Black move M_{12} and evaluate.

6. Compare, and reject the move with the smaller evaluation.

7. Continue with the third Black move and compare with the retained value, etc.

8. When the Black moves are exhausted, one will be retained together with its evaluation. The process is now repeated with the second White move.

9. The final evaluations from these two computations are compared and the maximum retained.

10. This is continued with all White moves until the best is selected (*i.e.* the one remaining after all are tried). This is the move to be made.

These programs are, of course, highly iterative. For that reason they should not require a great deal of program memory if efficiently worked out.

The internal memory for positions and temporary results of calculations when playing three moves deep can be estimated. Three positions should probably be remembered: the initial position, the next to the last, and the last position (now being evaluated). This requires some 800 bits. Furthermore, there are five lists of moves each requiring about $30 \times 12 = 360$ bits, a total of 1800. Finally, about 200 bits would cover the selections and evaluations up to the present calculation. Thus, some 3000 bits should suffice.

6. IMPROVEMENTS IN THE STRATEGY.

Unfortunately a machine operating according to this type A strategy would be both slow and a weak player. It would be slow since even if each position were evaluated in one microsecond (very optimistic) there are about 10^9 evaluations to be made after three moves (for each side). Thus, more than 16 minutes would be required for a move, or 10 hours for its half of a 40-move game.

It would be weak in playing skill because it is only seeing three moves deep and because we have not included any conditions about quiescent positions for evaluation. The machine is operating in an extremely inefficient fashion—it computes *all* variations to *exactly* three moves and then stops (even though it or the opponent be in check). A good human player examines only a few selected variations and carries these out to a reasonable stopping-point. A world champion can construct (at best) combinations say, 15 or 20 moves deep. Some variations given by Alekhine ("My Best Games of Chess 1924–1937") are of this length. Of course, only a few variations are explored to any such depth. In amateur play variations are seldom examined more deeply than six or eight moves, and this only when the moves are of a highly forcing nature (with very limited possible replies). More generally, when there are few threats and force-ful moves; most calculations are not deeper than one or two moves, with perhaps half-a-dozen forcing vari-ations explored to three, four or five moves.

On this point a quotation from Reuben Fine (Fine 1942), a leading American master, is interesting: "Very often people have the idea that masters foresee every-thing or nearly everything: that when they played P–R3 on the thirteenth move they foresaw that this would be needed to provide a loophole for the king after the complications twenty moves later, or even that when they play 1 P–K4 they do it with the idea of preventing Kt–Q4 on Black's twelfth turn, or they feel that everything is mathematically calculated down to the smirk when the Queen's Rook Pawn queens one move ahead of the opponent's King's Knight's Pawn. All this is, of course, pure fantasy. The best course to follow is to note the major consequences for two moves, but try to work out forced variations as they go."

The amount of selection exercised by chess masters in examining possible variations has been studied experimentally by De Groot (1946, *b*). He showed var-ious typical positions to chess masters and asked them to decide on the best move, describing aloud their analyses of the positions as they thought them through. In this manner the number and depth of the variations examined could be determined. Fig. 5 shows the result of one such experiment. In this case the chess master examined sixteen variations, ranging in depth from 1/2 (one Black move) to 4–1/2 (five Black and four White) moves. The total number of positions considered was 44.

From these remarks it appears that to improve the speed and strength of play the machine must:—

1. Examine forceful variations out as far as possible and evaluate only at reasonable positions, where some quasi-stability has been established.

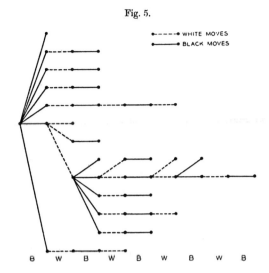

Fig. 5.

2. Select the variations to be explored by some process so that the machine does not waste its time in totally pointless variations.

A strategy with these two improvements will be called a type B strategy. It is not difficult to construct programs incorporating these features. For the first we define a function $g(P)$ of a position which determines whether approximate stability exists (no pieces *en prise*, etc.). A crude definition might be:

$g(P) =$	1 if any piece is attacked by a piece of lower value, or by more pieces than defences or if any check exists on a square controlled by opponent.
	0 otherwise.

Using this function, variations could be explored until $g(P) = 0$, always, however, going at least two moves and never more than say, 10.

The second improvement would require a function $h(P, M)$ to decide whether a move M in position P is worth exploring. It is important that this preliminary screening should *not* eliminate moves which merely look bad at first sight, for example, a move which puts a piece *en prise*; frequently such moves are actually very strong since the piece cannot be safely taken.

"Always give check, it may be mate" is tongue-in-cheek advice given to beginners aimed at their predilection for useless checks. "Always investigate a check, it may lead to mate" is sound advice for any player. A check is the most forceful type of move. The opponent's replies are highly limited—he can never answer by counter attack, for example. This means that a variation starting with a check can be more readily calculated than any other. Similarly captures, attacks on major pieces, threats of mate, etc. limit the opponent's replies and should be calculated whether the move looks good at first sight or not. Hence, $h(P, M)$ should be given large values for all forceful moves (checks, captures and attacking moves), for developing moves, medium values for defensive moves, and low values for other moves. In exploring a variation $h(P, M)$ would be calculated as the machine computes and would be used to select the variations considered. As it gets further into the variation the requirements on h are set higher so that fewer and fewer subvariations are examined. Thus, it would start considering every first move for itself, only the more forceful replies, etc. By this process its computing efficiency would be greatly improved.

It is believed that an electronic computer incorporating these two improvements in the program would play a fairly strong game, at speeds comparable to human speeds. It may be noted that a machine has several advantages over humans:

1. High-speed operation in individual calculations.

2. Freedom from errors. The only errors will be due to deficiencies of the program while human players are continually guilty of very simple and obvious blunders.

3. Freedom from laziness. It is all too easy for a human player to make instinctive moves without proper analysis of the position.

4. Freedom from "nerves". Human players are prone to blunder due to over-confidence in "won" positions or defeatism and self-recrimination in "lost" positions.

5. These must be balanced against the flexibility, imagination and inductive and learning capacities of the human mind.

6. Incidentally, the person who designs the program can calculate the move that the machine will choose in any position, and thus in a sense can play an equally good game. In actual fact, however, the calculation would be impractical because of the time required. On a fair basis of comparison, giving the machine and the designer equal time to decide on a move, the machine might well play a stronger game.

7. VARIATIONS IN PLAY AND STYLE.

As described so far the machine once designed would always make the same move in the same position. If the opponent made the same moves this would always lead to the same game. It is desirable to avoid this, since if the opponent wins one game he could play the same variation and win continuously, due perhaps to some particular position arising in the variation where the machine chooses a very weak move.

One way to prevent this is to have a statistical element in the machine. Whenever there are two or more moves which are of nearly equal value according to the machine's calculations it chooses from them at random. In the same position a second time it may then choose another in the set.

The opening is another place where statistical variation can be introduced. It would seem desirable to have a number of the standard openings stored in a slow-speed memory in the machine. Perhaps a few hundred would be satisfactory. For the first few moves (until either the opponent deviates from the "book" or the end of the stored variation is reached) the machine plays by memory. This is hardly "cheating" since that is the way chess masters play the opening.

It is interesting that the "style" of play of the machine can be changed very easily by altering some of the coefficients and numerical factors involved in the evaluation function and the other programs. By placing high values on positional weaknesses, etc. a positional-type player results. By more intensive examination of forced variations it becomes a combination player. Furthermore, the strength of the play can be easily adjusted by changing the depth of calculation and by omitting or adding terms to the evaluation function.

Finally we may note that a machine of this type will play "brilliantly" up to its limits. It will readily sacrifice a queen or other piece in order to gain more material later or to give checkmate provided the completion of the combination occurs within its computing limits.

The chief weakness is that the machine will not learn by its mistakes. The only way to improve its play is by improving the program. Some thought has been given to designing a program which is self-improving but, although it appears to be possible, the methods thought of so far do not seem to be very practical. One possibility is to have a higher level program which changes the terms and coefficients involved in the evaluation function depending on the results of games the machine has played. Small variations might be introduced in these terms and the values selected to give the greatest percentage of "wins".

8. ANOTHER TYPE OF STRATEGY.

The strategies described above do not, of course, exhaust the possibilities. In fact, there are undoubtedly others which are far more efficient in the use of available computing time on the machine. Even with the improvements we have discussed the above strategy gives an impression of relying too much on "brute force" calculations rather than on logical analysis of a position. It plays something like a beginner at chess who has been told some of the principles and is possessed of tremendous energy and accuracy for calculation but has no experience with the game. A chess master, on the other hand, has available knowledge of hundreds or perhaps thousands of standard situations, stock combinations, and common manoeuvres which occur time and again in the game. There are, for example, the typical sacrifices of a knight at B7 or a bishop at R7, the standard mates such as the "Philidor Legacy", manoeuvres based on pins, forks, discoveries, promotion, etc. In a given position he recognizes some similarity to a familiar situation and this directs his mental calculations along lines with greater probability of success.

There is no reason why a program based on such "type positions" could not be constructed. This would require, however, a rather formidable analysis of the game. Although there are various books analysing combination play and the middle game, they are written for human consumption, not for computing machines. It is possible to give a person one or two specific examples of a general situation and have him understand and apply the general principle involved. With a computer an exact and completely explicit characterization of the situation must be given with all limitations, special cases, etc. taken into account. We are inclined to believe, however, that if this were done a much more efficient program would result.

To program such a strategy we might suppose that any position in the machine is accompanied by a rather elaborate analysis of the tactical structure of the position suitably encoded. This analytical data will state that, for example, the Black knight at B3 is pinned by a bishop, that the White rook at K1 cannot leave the back rank because of a threatened mate on B8, that a White knight at R4 has no move, etc.; in short, all the facts to which a chess player would ascribe importance in analysing tactical possibilities. These data would be supplied by a program and would be continually changed and kept up-to-date as the game progressed. The analytical data would be used to trigger various other programs depending on the particular nature of the position. A pinned piece should be attacked. If a rook must guard the back rank it cannot guard the pawn in front of it, etc. The machine obtains in this manner suggestions of plausible moves to investigate.

It is not being suggested that we should design the strategy in our own image. Rather it should be matched to the capacities and weaknesses of the computer. The computer is strong in speed, and accuracy and weak in analytical ability and recognition. Hence, it should make more use of brutal calculations than humans; but with possible variations increasing by a factor of 10^3 every move, a little selection goes a long way toward improving blind trial and error.

ACKNOWLEDGEMENT.

The writer is indebted to E. G. Andrews, L. N. Enequistand H. E. Singleton for a number of suggestions that have been incorporated in the paper.

October 8, 1948.

APPENDIX.

The Evaluation Function for Chess.

The evaluation function *f*(P) should take into account the "long term" advantages and disadvantages of a position, *i.e.* effects which may be expected to persist over a number of moves longer than individual variations are calculated. Thus the evaluation is mainly concerned with positional or strategic considerations rather than combinatorial or tactical ones. Of course there is no sharp line of division; many features of a position are on the borderline. It appears, however, that the following might properly be included in *f*(P):—

1. Material advantage (difference in total material).

2. Pawn formation:

   a. Backward, isolated and doubled pawns.

   b. Relative control of centre (pawns at K4, Q4, B4).

   c. Weakness of pawns near king (e. g. advanced KNP).

   d. Pawns on opposite colour squares from bishop.

   e. Passed pawns.

3. Positions of pieces:

   a. Advanced knight (at K5, Q5, B5, K6, Q6, B6), especially if protected by pawn and free from pawn attack.

   b. Rook on open file, or semi-open file.

   c. Rook on seventh rank.

   d. Doubled rooks.

4. Commitments, attacks and options:

   a. Pieces which are required for guarding functions and, therefore, committed and with limited mobility.

   b. Attacks on pieces which give one player an option of exchanging.

   c. Attacks on squares adjacent to king.

   d. Pins. We mean here immobilizing pins where the pinned piece is of value not greater than the pinning piece for example; a knight pinned by a bishop.

5. Mobility.

These factors will apply in the middle game: during the opening and end game different principles must be used. The relative values to be given each of the above quantities is open to considerable debate, and should be determined by some experimental procedure. There are also numerous other factors which may well be worth inclusion. The more violent tactical weapons, such as discovered checks, forks and pins by a piece of lower value are omitted since they are best accounted for by the examination of specific variations.

REFERENCES.

Chernev, 1937, *Curious Chess Facts*, The Black Knight Press.

De Groot, A. D., 1946a, *Het Denken van den Schaker* 17-18, Amsterdam; 1946b, *Ibid.*, Amsterdam, 207.

Fine, R., 1942, *Chess the Easy Way,* 79, David McKay.

Furry and Wright, 1938, *The Theory of Numbers*, 116, Oxford.

Von Neumann and Morgenstern, 1944, *Theory of Games,* 125, Princeton.

Vigneron, H., 1914, *Les Automates*, La Natura.

Wiener, N., 1948, *Cybernetics*, John Wiley.

...

1. The world championship match between Capablanca and Alekhine ended with the score Alekhine 6, Capablanca 3, drawn 25.

2. The fact that the number of moves remaining before a draw is called by the 50-move rule has decreased does not affect this argument.

3. Condon, Tawney and Derr, U.S. Patent 2,215,544. The "Nimotron" based on this patent was built and exhibited by Westinghouse at the 1938 New York World's Fair.

4. The longest possible chess game is 6350 moves, allowing 50 moves between each pawn move or capture. The longest tournament game on record between masters lasted 168 moves, and the shortest four moves. (Chernev, *Curious Chess Facts,* The Black Knight Press, 1937.)

5. See Appendix I.

6. Although there is a finite probability, of the order of 10^{-75}, that random play would win a game from Botvinnik. Bad as random play is, there are even worse strategies which choose moves which actually *aid* the opponent. For example, White's strategy in the following game:—1. P–KB3, P–K4. 2. P–KN4, Q–R5 mate.

11.4
Computers and Automata

Claude E. Shannon

Claude Shannon in 1952, showing how an electrical mouse finds its way unerringly through a maze, guided by information "remembered" in the kind of switching relays used in dial telephone systems. Experiments with this mouse helped stimulate Bells Labs researchers to think of new ways to use the logical powers of computers for operations other than numerical calculation (Photograph courtesy of Lucent Technologies, Inc. Used with permission.)

INTRODUCTORY NOTE TO READING 11.4

Shannon's paper "Computers and Automata" is a review of developments in the field of automata and non-numerical computation. It includes descriptions of logic machines, game-playing machines, learning machines, Turing's formulation of computing machines or universal machines, and von Neumann's models of self-reproducing automata. In this paper Shannon posed questions that continue to be of acute interest: "Can a chess playing computer learn from its mistakes? Is it possible to build a machine that can diagnose itself and repair its own malfunctions? Can computer programs ("virtual machines") be created that enable computers to write their own software to the specifications of the human user? Can the way human brains process information (known in some hard-core AI circles as "wetware") ever be effectively simulated by hardware and software?"[1] Shannon's work on automata from this period is especially significant not only for his own contributions, but because his work stimulated the imagination of Marvin Minsky and John McCarthy, who would develop the field of artificial intelligence. See Reading 11.5. [JMN]

---

1 Howard Rheingold, *Tools for Thought* (Cambridge, Mass.: MIT Press, 2000), 128–29.

TEXT OF READING 11.4

Summary—This paper reviews briefly some of the recent developments in the field of automata and non-numerical computation. A number of typical machines are described, including logic machines, game-playing machines and learning machines. Some theoretical questions and developments are discussed, such as a comparison of computers and the brain, Turing's formulation of computing machines and von Neumann's models of self-reproducing machines.

INTRODUCTION

Samuel Butler, in 1871, completed the manuscript of a most engaging social satire, *Erewhon*. Three chapters of *Erewhon*, originally appearing under the title "Darwin Among the Machines," are a witty parody of *The Origin of Species*. In the topsy-turvy logic of satirical writing, Butler sees machines as gradually evolving into higher forms. He considers the classification of machines into genera, species and varieties, their feeding habits, their rudimentary sense organs, their reproductive and evolutionary mechanisms (inefficient machines force men to design more efficient ones), tendencies toward reversion, vestigial organs, and even the problem of free will in machines.

Rereading *Erewhon* today one finds "The Book of the Machines" disturbingly prophetic. Current and projected computers and control systems are indeed assuming more and more the capacities and functions of animals and man, to a far greater degree, in fact, than was envisaged by Butler.

The bread-and-butter work of large-scale computers has been the solution of involved numerical problems. To many of us, however, the most exciting potentialities of computers lie in their ability to perform non-numerical operations—to work with logic, translate languages, design circuits, play games, co-ordinate sensory and manipulative devices and, generally, assume complicated functions associated with the human brain.

Non-numerical computation is by no means an unproven offspring of the more publicized arithmetic calculation. The shoe is rather on the other foot. A hundred years ago Charles Babbage was inspired in the design of his remarkably prescient analytical engine by a portrait woven in silk on a card controlled Jacquard loom—a device then in existence half a century. The largest and most reliable current information processing machine is still the automatic telephone system. Our factories are filled with ingenious and unsung devices performing almost incredible feats of sensing, processing and transporting materials in all shapes and forms. Railway and power systems have elaborate control and protective networks against accidents and human errors.

These, however, are all special-purpose automata. A significant new concept in non-numerical computation is the idea of a general-purpose programmed computer—a device capable of carrying out a long sequence of elementary orders analogous to those of a numerical computer. The elementary orders, however, will relate not to operations on numbers but to physical motions, operations with words, equations, incoming sensory data, or almost any physical or conceptual entities.

This paper reviews briefly some of the research in non-numerical computation and discusses certain of the problems involved. The field is currently very active and in a short paper only a few sample developments can be mentioned.

THE BRAIN AND COMPUTERS

The brain has often been compared, perhaps over-enthusiastically, with computing machines. It contains roughly 10^{10} active elements called neurons. Because of the all or none law of nervous action, neurons bear some functional resemblance to our binary computer elements, relays, vacuum tubes or transistors. The number of elements is six orders of magnitude greater than our largest computers. McCullough has picturesquely put it that a computer with as many tubes as a man has neurons would require the Empire State building to house it, Niagara Falls to power it and the Niagara river to cool it. The use of transistors in such a comparison would improve the figures considerably, power requirements coming down to the hundreds of kilowatt range (the brain dissipates some 25 watts) and size requirements (with close packing) comparable to an ordinary dwelling. It may also be argued that the increased speed of electronic components by a factor of, say, 10^3 might be partially exchangeable against equipment requirements.

Comparisons of this sort should be taken well salted—our understanding of brain functioning is still, in spite of a great deal of important and illuminating research, very primitive. Whether, for example, the neuron itself is the proper level for a functional analysis is still an open question. The random structure at the neural level in number, placement and interconnections of the neurons, suggests that only the statistics are important at this stage, and, consequently, that one might average over local structure and functioning before constructing a mathematical model.

The similarities between the brain and computers have often been pointed out. The differences are perhaps more illuminating, for they may suggest the important features missing from our best current brain models. Among the most important of these are:

1. Differences in size. Six orders of magnitude in the number of components takes us so far from our ordinary experience as to make extrapolation of function next to meaningless.

2. Differences in structural organization. The apparently random local structure of nerve networks is vastly different from the precise wiring of artificial automata, where a single wrong connection may cause malfunctioning. The brain somehow is designed so that overall functioning does not depend on the exact structure in the small.

3. Differences in reliability organization. The brain can operate reliably for decades without really serious malfunctioning (comparable to the meaningless gibberish produced by a computer in trouble conditions) even though the components are probably individually no more reliable than those used in computers.

4. Differences in logical organization. The differences here seem so great as to defy enumeration. The brain is largely self-organizing. It can adapt to an enormous variety of situations tolerably well. It has remarkable memory classification and access features, the ability to rapidly locate stored data via numerous "coordinate systems." It can set up stable servo systems involving complex relations between its sensory inputs and motor outputs, with great facility. In contrast, our digital computers look like idiot savants. For long chains of arithmetic operations a digital computer runs circles around the best humans. When we try to program computers for other activities their entire organization seems clumsy and inappropriate.

5. Differences in input-output equipment. The brain is equipped with beautifully designed input organs, particularly the ear and the eye, for sensing the state of its environment. Our best artificial counterparts, such as Shepard's Analyzing Reader for recognizing and transcribing type, and the "Audrey" speech recognition system which can recognize the speech sounds for the ten digits seem pathetic by comparison. On the output end, the brain controls hundreds of muscles and glands. The two arms and hands have some sixty independent degrees of freedom. Compare this with the manipulative ability of the digitally controlled milling machine developed at M.I.T., which can move its work in but three co-ordinates. Most of our computers, indeed, have no significant sensory or manipulative contact with the real world but operate only in an abstract environment of numbers and operations on numbers.

TURING MACHINES

The basic mathematical theory of digital computers was developed by A. M. Turing in 1936 in a classic paper "On Computable Numbers with an Application to the Entscheidungsproblem." He defined a class of computing machines, now called Turing machines, consisting basically of an infinite paper tape and a computing element. The computing element has a finite number of internal states and is capable of reading from and writing on one cell of the tape and of moving it one cell to the right or left. At a given time, the computing element will be in a certain state and reading what is written in a particular cell of the tape. The next operation will be determined by the current state and the symbol being read. This operation will consist of assuming a new state and either writing a new symbol (in place of the one currently read) or moving to the right or to the left. It is possible for machines of this type to compute numbers by setting up a suitable code for interpreting the symbols. For example, in Turing's formulation the machines print final answers in binary notation on alternate cells of the tape, using the other cells for intermediate calculations.

It can be shown that such machines form an extremely broad class of computers. All ordinary digital computers which do not contain a random or probabilistic element are equivalent to some Turing machine. Any number that can be computed on these machines, or in fact by any ordinary computing process, can be computed by a suitable Turing machine. There are, however, as Turing showed, certain problems that cannot be solved and certain numbers that cannot be computed by any Turing machine. For example, it is not possible to construct a Turing machine which, given a suitably coded description of another Turing machine, can always tell whether or not the second Turing machine will continue indefinitely to print symbols in the squares corresponding to the final answer. It may, at a certain point in the calculation, relapse into an infinite intermediate computation. The existence of mechanically unsolvable problems of this sort is of great interest to logicians.

Turing also developed the interesting concept of a universal Turing machine. This is a machine with the property that if a suitably coded description of any Turing machine is printed on its tape, and the machine started at a suitable point and in a suitable state, it will then act like the machine described, that is, compute (normally at a much slower rate) the same number that the described machine would compute. Turing showed that such universal machines can be designed. They of course are capable of computing any computable number. Most digital computers, provided they have access to an unlimited memory of some sort, are equivalent to universal Turing machines and can, in principle, imitate any other computing machine and compute any computable number.

The work of Turing has been generalized and reformulated in various ways. One interesting generalization is the notion of A computability. This relates to a class of Turing type machines which have the further feature that they can, at certain points of the calculation, ask questions of a second "oracular" device, and use the answers in further calculations. The oracular machine may for example have answers to some of the unsolvable problems of ordinary Turing machines, and consequently enable the solution of a larger class of problems.

LOGIC MACHINES

Boolean algebra can be used as a mathematical tool for studying the properties of relay and switching circuits. Conversely, it is possible to solve problems of Boolean algebra and formal logic by means of simple relay circuits. This possibility has been exploited in a number of logic machines. A typical machine of this kind, described by McCallum and Smith, can handle logical relations involving up to seven classes or truth variables. The required relations among these variables, given by the logical problem at hand, are plugged into the machine by means of a number of "connective boxes." These connective boxes are of six types and provide for the logical connectives "not," "and," "or," "or else," "if and only if," and "if-then." When the connections are complete, starting the machine causes it to hunt through the $2^7=128$ combinations of the basic variables, stopping at all combinations which satisfy the constraints. The machine also indicates the number of "true" variables in each of these states. McCallum and Smith give the following typical problem that may be solved on the machine:

> It is known that salesmen always tell the truth and engineers always tell lies. G and E are salesmen. C states that D is an engineer. A declares that B affirms that C asserts that D says that E insists that F denies that G is a salesman. If A is an engineer, how many engineers are there?

A very suggestive feature in this machine is a selective feedback system for hunting for particular solutions of the logical equations without an exhaustive search through all possible combinations. This is achieved by elements which sense whether or not a particular logical relation is satisfied. If not, the truth variables involved in this relation are caused to oscillate between their two possible values. Thus, variables appearing in unsatisfied relations are continually changing, while those appearing only in satisfied relations do not change. If ever all relations are simultaneously satisfied the machine stops at that particular solution. Changing only the variables in unsatisfied relations tends, in a general way, to lead to a solution more rapidly than methodical exhaustion of all cases, but, as is usually the case when feedback is introduced, leads to the possibility of continual oscillation. McCallum and Smith point out the desirability of making the changes of the variables due to the feedback unbalance as random as possible, to enable the machine to escape from periodic paths through various states of the relays.

GAME PLAYING MACHINES

The problem of designing game-playing machines is fascinating and has received a good deal of attention. The rules of a game provide a sharply limited environment in which a machine may operate, with a clearly defined goal for its activities. The discrete nature of most games matches well the digital computing techniques available without the cumbersome analog-digital conversion necessary in translating our physical environment in the case of manipulating and sensing machines.

Game playing machines may be roughly classified into types in order of increasing sophistication:

1. Dictionary-type machines. Here the proper move of the machine is decided in advance for each possible situation that may arise in the game and listed in a "dictionary" or function table. When a particular position arises, the machine merely looks up the move in the dictionary. Because of the extravagant memory requirements, this rather uninteresting method is only feasible for exceptionally simple games, e.g., tic-tac-toe.

2. Machines using rigorously correct playing formulas. In some games, such as Nim, a complete mathematical theory is known, whereby it is possible to compute by a relatively simple formula, in any position that can be won, a suitable winning move. A mechanization of this formula provides a perfect game player for such games.

3. Machines applying general principles of approximate validity. In most games of interest to humans, no simple exact solution is known, but there are various general principles of play which hold in the majority of positions. This is true of such games as checkers, chess, bridge, poker and the like. Machines may be designed applying such general principles to the position at hand. Since the principles are not infallible, neither are the machines, as indeed, neither are humans.

4. Learning machines. Here the machine is given only the rules of the game and perhaps an elementary strategy of play, together with some method of improving this strategy through experience. Among the many methods that have been suggested for incorporation of learning we have:

a. trial-and-error with retention of successful and elimination of unsuccessful possibilities;

b. imitation of a more successful opponent;

c. "teaching" by approval or disapproval, or by informing the machine of the nature of its mistakes; and finally

d. self-analysis by the machine of its mistakes in an attempt to devise general principles.

Many examples of the first two types have been constructed and a few of the third. The fourth type, learning game-players, is reminiscent of Mark Twain's comment on the weather. Here is a real challenge for the programmer and machine designer.

Two examples of the third category, machines applying general principles, may be of interest. The first of these is a machine designed by E. F. Moore and the writer for playing a commercial board game known as Hex. This game is played on a board laid out in a regular hexagon pattern, the two players alternately placing black and white pieces in unoccupied hexagons. The entire board forms a rhombus and Black's goal is to connect the top and bottom of this rhombus with a continuous chain of black pieces. White's goal is to connect the two sides of the rhombus with a chain of white pieces. After a study of this game, it was conjectured that a reasonably good move could be made by the following process. A two-dimensional potential field is set up corresponding to the playing board, with white pieces as positive charges and black pieces as negative charges. The top and bottom of the board are negative and the two sides positive. The move to be made corresponds to a certain specified saddle point in this field.

To test this strategy, an analog device was constructed, consisting of a resistance network and gadgetry to locate the saddle points. The general principle, with some improvements suggested by experience, proved to be reasonably sound. With first move, the machine won about seventy per cent of its games against human opponents. It frequently surprised its designers by choosing odd-looking moves which, on analysis, proved sound. We normally think of computers as expert at long involved calculations and poor in generalized value judgments. Paradoxically, the positional judgment of this machine was good; its chief weakness was in end-game combinatorial play. It is also curious that the Hex-player reversed the usual computing procedure in that it solved a basically digital problem by an analog machine.

The game of checkers has recently been programmed into a general-purpose computer, using a "general principle" approach. C. S. Strachey used a method similar to one proposed by the writer for programming chess—an investigation of the possible variations for a few moves and a minimax evaluation applied to the resulting positions. The following is a sample game played by the checker program with notes by Strachey. (The white squares are numbered consecutively, 0 – 31, from left to right and top to bottom. Numbers in parentheses indicate captures.)

While obviously no world champion, the machine is certainly better than many humans. Strachey points out various weaknesses in the program, particularly in certain end-game positions, and suggests possible improvements.

Machine	Strachey
11 – 15	23 – 18
7 – 11	21 – 17
8 – 12	20 – 16 *a*
12 – 21 (16)	25 – 16 (21)
9 – 14 !*b*	18 – 9 (14)
6 – 20 (16, 9) *c*	27 – 23
2 – 7 *d*	23 – 18
5 – 8	18 – 14
8 – 13 *e*	17 – 8 (13)
4 – 13 (8)	14 – 9
1 – 5 *f*	9 – 6
15 – 19	6 – 1 (K)
5 – 9	1 – 6 ?*g*

0 – 5 !h	6 – 15 (10)
11 – 25 (22, 15)	30 – 21 (25)
13 – 17	21 – 14 (17)
9 – 18 (14)	24 – 21
18 – 23	26 – 22
23 – 27	22 – 17
5 – 8 i	17 – 14
8 – 13	14 – 9
19 – 23	9 – 6
23 – 26 j	31 – 22 (26)
27 – 31 (K)	6 – 2 (K)
7 – 10	2 – 7
10 – 15	21 – 26 ?k
3 – 10 (7)	16 – 9 (13)
10 – 14	9 – 6
15 – 19	6 – 2 (K)
31 – 27 m	2 – 6
27 – 31 m	6 – 10
31 – 26 n	10 – 17 (14)
19 – 23	29 – 25
26 – 31 p	

Notes [by Strachey]:

a. An experiment on my part—the only deliberate offer I made. I thought, wrongly, that it was quite safe.

b. Not foreseen by me.

c. Better than 5–21 (9, 17).

d. A random move (zero value). Shows the lack of a constructive plan.

e. Another random move of zero value. Actually rather good.

f. Bad. Ultimately allows me to make a King. 10–14 would would have been better.

g. A bad slip on my part.

h. Taking full advantage of my slip.

i. Bad, unblocks the way to a King.

j. Sacrifice in order to get a King (not to stop me Kinging). A good move, but not possible before 19–23 had been made by chance.

k. Another bad slip on my part.

l. Purposeless. The strategy is failing badly in the end game.

m. Too late.

n. Futile. The game was stopped at this point as the outcome was obvious.

LEARNING MACHINES

The concept of learning, like those of thinking, consciousness and other psychological terms, is difficult to define precisely in a way acceptable to the various interested parties. A rough formulation might be framed somewhat as follows. Suppose that an organism or a machine can be placed in, or connected to, a class of environments, and that there is a measure of "success" or "adaptation" to the environment. Suppose further that this measure is comparatively local in time, that is, that one can measure the success over periods of time short compared to the life of the organism. If this local measure of success tends to improve with the passage of time, for the class of environments in question, we may say that the organism or machine is learning to adapt to these environments relative to the measure of success chosen. Learning achieves a quantitative significance in terms of the broadness and complexity of the class of environments to which the machine can adapt. A chess playing machine whose frequency of wins increases during its operating life may be said by this definition to be learning chess, the class of environments being the chess players who oppose it, and the adaptation measure, the winning of games.

A number of attempts have been made to construct simple learning machines. The writer constructed a maze-solving device in which an arbitrary maze can be set up in a five-by-five array of squares, by placing partitions as desired between adjacent squares. A permanently magnetized "mouse," placed in the maze, blunders about by a trial and error procedure, striking various partitions and entering blind alleys until it eventually finds its way to the "food box." Placed in the maze a second time, it will move directly to the food box from any part of the maze that it has visited in its first exploration, without errors or false moves. Placed in other parts of the maze, it will blunder about until it reaches a previously explored part and from there go directly to the goal. Meanwhile it will have added the information about this part of the maze to its memory, and if placed at the same point again will go directly to the goal. Thus by placing it in the various unexplored parts of the maze, it eventually builds up a complete pattern of information and is able to reach the goal directly from any point.

If the maze is now changed, the mouse first tries the old path, but on striking a partition starts trying other directions and revising its memory until it eventually reaches the goal by some other path. Thus it is able to forget an old solution when the problem is changed.

The mouse is actually driven by an electromagnet moving beneath the maze. The motion of the electromagnet is controlled by a relay circuit containing about 110 relays, organized into a memory and a computing circuit, somewhat after that of a digital computer.

The maze-solver may be said to exhibit at a very primitive level the abilities to (1) solve problems by trial and error, (2) repeat the solutions without the errors, (3) add and correlate new information to a partial solution, (4) forget a solution when it is no longer applicable.

Another approach to mechanized learning is that of suitably programming a large-scale computer. A. E. Oettinger has developed two learning programs for the Edsac computer in Cambridge, England. In the first of these, the machine was divided into two parts, one part playing the role of a learning machine and the second its environment. The environment represented abstractly a number of stores in which various items might be purchased, different stores stocking different classes of items. The learning machine faced the problem of learning where various items might be purchased. Starting off with no previous knowledge and a particular item to be obtained, it would search at random among the stores until the item was located. When finally successful, it noted in its memory where the article was found. Sent again for the same article it will go directly to the shop where it previously obtained this article. A further feature of the program was the introduction of a bit of "curiosity" in the learning machine. When it succeeded in finding article number j in a particular shop it also noticed whether or not that shop carried articles $j - 1$ and $j + 1$ and recorded these facts in its memory.

The second learning program described by Oettinger is modeled more closely on the conditioned reflex behavior of animals. A stimulus of variable intensity can be applied to the machine in the form of an input integer. To this stimulus the machine may respond in a number of different ways indicated by an output integer. After the response, it is possible for the operator to indicate approval or disapproval by introducing a third integer at a suitable point. When the machine starts operating, its responses to stimuli are chosen at random. Indication of approval improves the chances for the response immediately preceding; indication of disapproval reduces this chance. Furthermore, as a particular response is learned by conditioning it with approval, the stimulus required for this response decreases. Finally, there is a regular decay of thresholds when no approval follows a response.

Further embellishments of programs of this sort are limited only by the capacity of the computer and the energy and ingenuity of the program designer. Unfortunately, the elementary orders available in most large-scale computers are poorly adapted to the logical requirements of learning programs, and the machines are therefore used rather inefficiently. It may take a dozen or more orders to represent a logically simple and frequently used operation occurring in a learning routine.

Another type of learning machine has been constructed by D. W. Hagelbarger. This is a machine designed to play the game of matching pennies against a human opponent. On the front panel of the machine are a start button, two lights marked + and −, and a key switch whose extreme positions are also marked + and –. To play against the machine, the player chooses + or –, and then pushes the start button. The machine will then light up one of the two lights. If the machine matches the player, that is, lights the light corresponding to the choice of the player, the machine wins; otherwise the player wins. When the play is complete, the player registers by appropriate movement of the key switch the choice he made.

The machine is so constructed as to analyze certain patterns in the players' sequence of choices, and attempt to capitalize on these patterns when it finds them, For example, some players have a tendency if they have won a round, played the same thing and won again, to then change their choice. The machine keeps count of these situations and, if such tendencies appear, plays in such a way as to win. When such patterns do not appear the machine plays at random.

It has been found the machine wins about 55–60 per cent of the rounds, while by chance or against an opponent that played strictly at random it would win only 50 per cent of the time. It appears to be quite difficult for a human being to produce a random sequence of pluses and minuses (to insure the 50 per cent wins he is entitled to by the theory of games) and even more difficult to actually beat the machine by leading it on to suspect patterns, and then reversing the patterns.

A second penny-matching machine was designed by the writer, following the same general strategy but using a different criterion to decide when to play at random and when to assume that an apparent behavior pattern is significant. After considerable discussion as to which of these two machines could beat the other, and fruitless attempts to solve mathematically the very complicated statistical problem involved when they are connected together, the problem was relegated to experiment. A third small machine was constructed to act as umpire and pass the information back and forth between the machines concerning their readiness to make a move and the choices made. The three machines were then plugged together and allowed to run for a few hours, to the accompaniment of small side-bets and loud cheering. Ironically, it

turned out that the smaller, more precipitate of the two machines consistently beat the larger, more deliberate one in a ratio of about 55 to 45.

A still different type of learning machine was devised by W. Ross Ashby who christened it the Homeostat. Homeostasis, a word coined by Walter B. Cannon, relates to an animal's ability to stabilize, by feedback, such biological variables as body temperature, chemical concentrations in the blood stream, etc. Ashby's device is a kind of self-stabilizing servo system. The first model of the Homeostat contained four interconnected servos. The cross-connections of these servos passed through four stepping switches and resistors connected to the points of the steppers. Thus the effect of unbalance in the other three loops on a particular loop depended on the values of the resistors being contacted by the stepper associated with that loop. When any one of the servos was sufficiently out of balance, a corresponding limit relay would operate and cause the corresponding stepping switch to advance one point. Now normally, a servo system with four degrees of freedom and random cross- and self-gain figures will not be stable. If this occurred, one or more of the stepping switches would advance and a new set of resistors would produce a new set of gain figures. If this set again proved unstable, a further advance of the steppers would occur until a stable situation was found. The values of the resistors connected to the stepping switches were chosen by random means (using a table of random numbers). Facilities were provided for introducing many arbitrary changes or constraints among the servos. For example, their connections could be reversed, two of them could be tied together, one of them held at a fixed value, etc. Under all these conditions, the mechanism was able to find a suitable stable position with all the servos in balance. Considering the machine's goal to be that of stabilizing the servos, and the environment to be represented by the various alterations and constraints introduced by the operator, the Homeostat may be said to adapt to its environment.

Certain features of the Homeostat are quite attractive as a basis for learning machines and brain models. It seems in certain ways to do a bit more than was explicitly designed into it. For example, it has been able to stabilize under situations not anticipated when the machine was constructed. The use of randomly chosen resistors is particularly suggestive and reminiscent of the random connections among neurons in the brain. Ashby, in fact, believes that the general principle embodied in the Homeostat, which he calls ultrastability, may underlie the operation of the animal nervous system. One of the difficulties of a too direct application of this theory is that, as Ashby points out, the time required for finding a stable solution grows more or less exponentially with the number of degrees of freedom. With only about 20 degrees of freedom, it would require many lifetimes to stabilize one system. Attempts to overcome this difficulty lead to rather involved conceptual constructions, so involved that it is extremely difficult to decide just how effectively they would operate. Our mathematical tools do not seem sufficiently sharp to solve these problems and further experimental work would be highly desirable.

SELF-REPRODUCING MACHINES

In *Erewhon* the reproduction process in machines was pictured as a kind of symbiotic co-operation between man and machines, the machines using man as an intermediary to produce new machines when the older ones were worn out. Man's part is akin to that of the bee in the fertilization of flowers. Recently von Neumann has studied at an abstract level the problem of true self-reproduction in machines, and has formulated two different mathematical models of such "machines."

The first of these may be pictured somewhat as follows. "Machines" in the model are constructed from a small number (of the order of twenty) types of elementary components. These components have relatively simple functions, for example, girders for structural purposes, elementary logical elements similar to simplified relays or neurons for computing, sensing components for detecting the presence of other elements, joining components (analogous to a soldering iron) for fastening elements together, and so on. From these elements, various types of machines may be "constructed." In particular, it is possible to

design a kind of universal construction machine, analogous to Turing's universal computing machine. The universal constructing machine can be fed a sequence of instructions, similar to the program of a digital computer, which describe in a suitable code how to construct any other machine that can be built with the elementary components. The universal constructing machine will then proceed to hunt for the needed components in its environment and build the machine described on its tape. If the instructions to the universal constructing machine are a description of the universal constructing machine itself, it will proceed to build a copy of itself, and would be a self-reproducing machine except for the fact that the copy is not yet supplied with a set of instructions. By adding to the universal machine what amounts to a tape-copying device and a relatively simple controlling device, a true self-reproducing machine is obtained. The instructions now describe the original universal machine with the addition of the tape reproducer and the controlling device. The first operation of the machine is to reproduce this entity. The controlling device then sends the instruction tape through the tape reproducer to obtain a copy, and places this copy in the second machine. Finally, it turns the second machine on, which starts reading its instructions and building a third copy, and so ad infinitum.

More recently, von Neumann has turned from this somewhat mechanical model to a more abstract self-reproducing structure—one based on a two-dimensional array of elementary "cells." Each cell is of relatively simple internal structure, having, in fact, something like thirty possible internal states, and each cell communicates directly only with its four neighbors. The state of a cell at the next (quantized) step in time depends only on the current state of the cell and the states of its four neighbors. By a suitable choice of these state transitions it is possible to set up a system yielding a kind of self-reproducing structure. A group of contiguous cells can act as an organic unit and operate on nearby quiescent cells in such a way as to organize a group of them into an identical unit.

This second model avoids many of the somewhat extraneous problems of locating, recognizing and positioning components that were inherent in the first model, and consequently leads to a simpler mathematical formulation. Furthermore, it has certain analogies with various chemical and biological problems, such as those of crystal and gene reproduction, while the first scale animal reproduction.

An interesting concept arising from both models is the notion of a critical complexity required for self-reproduction. In either case, only sufficiently complicated "machines" will be capable of self-reproduction. Von Neumann estimates the order of tens of thousands of components or cells to obtain this property. Less complicated structures can only construct simpler "machines" than themselves, while more complicated ones may be capable of a kind of evolutionary improvement leading to still more complicated organisms.

CHALLENGE TO THE READER

We hope that the foregoing sampler of non-numerical computers may have stimulated the reader's appetite for research in this field. The problem of how the brain works and how machines may be designed to simulate its activity is surely one of the most important and difficult facing current science. Innumerable questions demand clarification, ranging from experimental and development work on the one hand to purely mathematical research on the other. Can we design significant machines where the connections are locally random? Can we organize machines into a hierarchy of levels, as the brain appears to be organized, with the learning of the machine gradually progressing up through the hierarchy? Can we program a digital computer so that (eventually) 99 per cent of the orders it follows are written by the computer itself, rather than the few per cent in current programs? Can a self-repairing machine be built that will locate and repair faults in its own components (including components in the maintenance part of the machine)? What does a random element add in generality to a Turing machine? Can manipulative and sensory devices functionally comparable to the hand and eye be developed and coordinated with computers? Can either of von Neumann's self-reproducing models be translated into hardware? Can more satisfactory theories of learning be formulated? Can a machine be constructed which will design other machines, given only their broad functional characteristics? What is a really good set of orders in a digital computer for a computer memory be organized to learn and remember by association, in a manner similar to the human brain?

We suggest these typical questions, and the entire automata field, as a challenge to the reader. Here is research territory ripe for scientific prospectors. It is not a matter of reworking old operations, but of locating the rich new veins and perhaps in some cases merely picking up the surface nuggets.

BIBLIOGRAPHY

W. R. Ashby, *Design for a Brain* (New York, Wiley, 1951).

E. C. Berkeley, *Giant Brains, or Machines That Think* (New York, Wiley, 1949).

S. Butler, *Erewhon and Erewhon Revisited* (New York, Modern Library Edition, 1927).

J. Diebold, *Automation* (New York, Van Nostrand, 1952).

A. S. Householder and H. D. Landahl, *Mathematical Biophysics of the Central Nervous System* (Bloomington, Principia Press, 1945) pp. 103–110.

S. C. Kleene, *Representation of Events in Nerve Nets and Finite Automata,* Rand Corporation Memorandum RM–704, 1951.

D. M. McCallum and J. B. Smith, "Mechanized Reasoning," *Electronic Engineering* (April, 1951).

Warren S. McCulloch, and Walter Pitts, "A Logical Calculus of the Ideas Immanent in Nervous Activity," *Bull. Math. Biophysics,* (1943) vol. 5, pp. 115–133.

W. S. McCulloch, "The Brain as a Computing Machine," *Electrical Engineering* (June, 1949).

John Meszar, Switching Systems as Mechanical Brains *Bell Labs. Record,* (1953) vol. 31, pp. 63–69.

A. Oettinger, "Programming a Digital Computer to Learn," *Phil. Mag.,* (December, 1952) vol. 43, pp. 1243–1263.

W. Pease, "An Automatic Machine Tool," *Scientific American,* (September, 1952) vol. 187, pp. 101–115.

C. E. Shannon, *Presentation of a Maze-Solving Machine,* Transactions of the Eighth Cybernetics Conference, Josiah Macy, Jr. Foundation, New York, 1952, pp. 173–180.

C. E. Shannon, "Programming a Computer for Playing Chess," *Phil. Mag.,* (March, 1950) vol. 41, pp. 256–275.

C. S. Strachey, "Logical or Non-Mathematical Programmes," *Proc. of the Assn. for Computing Machinery,* Toronto (1952), pp. 46– 49.

A. M. Turing, "Computing Machinery and Intelligence," *Mind,* (1950) vol. 59, pp. 433–460.

A. M. Turing, On Computable Numbers, with an Application to the Entscheidungsproblem, *Proc. Lond. Math. Soc.,* (1936) vol. 24, pp. 230– 265.

J. Von Neuman, "The General and Logical Theory of Automata from Cerebral Mechanisms in Behavior," (New York, Wiley, 1951, pp. 1–41.

J. Von Neumann, *Probabilistics Logics,* California Institute of Technology, 1952.

N. Wiener, Cybernetics (New York, Wiley, 1948).

A Proposal for the Dartmouth Summer Research Project on Artificial Intelligence

J. McCarthy, M. L. Minsky, N. Rochester, and C. E. Shannon

August 31, 1955

INTRODUCTORY NOTE TO READING 11.5:

In the summer of 1953 Claude Shannon hired two laboratory assistants, Marvin Minsky and John McCarthy, who would go on to become pioneers in artificial intelligence. On August 31, 1955 Minsky and McCarthy, together with Shannon and IBM's Nathaniel Rochester, sent out an invitation to a summer session at Dartmouth, at which they were planning to conduct research on what they called "Artificial Intelligence." Their invitation named the field and also set out its basic goals. At the Dartmouth summer session on AI, Allen Newell and Herbert Simon demonstrated the first AI program, the Logic Theorist, designed to find the basic equations of logic as defined in *Principia Mathematica* by Whitehead and Russell. For one of the equations, the Logic Theorist surpassed its inventors' expectations by finding a new and better proof. This has been called the "the first foray by artificial intelligence research into high-order intellectual processes." [JMN]

TEXT OF READING 11.5

We propose that a 2 month, 10 man study of artificial intelligence be carried out during the summer of 1956 at Dartmouth College in Hanover, New Hampshire. The study is to proceed on the basis of the conjecture that every aspect of learning or any other feature of intelligence can in principle be so precisely described that a machine can be made to simulate it. An attempt will be made to find how to make machines use language, form abstractions and concepts, solve kinds of problems now reserved for humans, and improve themselves. We think that a significant advance can be made in one or more of these problems if a carefully selected group of scientists work on it together for a summer.

The following are some aspects of the artificial intelligence problem:

1. AUTOMATIC COMPUTERS

If a machine can do a job, then an automatic calculator can be programmed to simulate the machine. The speeds and memory capacities of present computers may be insufficient to simulate many of the higher functions of the human brain, but the major obstacle is not lack of machine capacity, but our inability to write programs taking full advantage of what we have.

2. HOW CAN A COMPUTER BE PROGRAMMED TO USE A LANGUAGE

It may be speculated that a large part of human thought consists of manipulating words according to rules of reasoning and rules of conjecture. From this point of view, forming a generalization consists of admitting a new word and some rules whereby sentences containing it imply and are implied by others. This idea has never been very precisely formulated nor have examples been worked out.

3. NEURON NETS

How can a set of (hypothetical) neurons be arranged so as to form concepts. Considerable theoretical and experimental work has been done on this problem by Uttley, Rashevsky and his group, Farley and Clark, Pitts and McCulloch, Minsky, Rochester and Holland, and others. Partial results have been obtained but the problem needs more theoretical work.

4. THEORY OF THE SIZE OF A CALCULATION

If we are given a well-defined problem (one for which it is possible to test mechanically whether or not a proposed answer is a valid answer) one way of solving it is to try all possible answers in order. This method is inefficient, and to exclude it one must have some criterion for efficiency of calculation. Some consideration will show that to get a measure of the efficiency of a calculation it is necessary to have on hand a method of measuring the complexity of calculating devices which in turn can be done if one has a theory of the complexity of functions. Some partial results on this problem have been obtained by Shannon, and also by McCarthy.

5. SELF-IMPROVEMENT

Probably a truly intelligent machine will carry out activities which may best be described as self-improvement. Some schemes for doing this have been proposed and are worth further study. It seems likely that this question can be studied abstractly as well.

6. ABSTRACTIONS

A number of types of "abstraction" can be distinctly defined and several others less distinctly. A direct attempt to classify these and to describe machine methods of forming abstractions from sensory and other data would seem worthwhile.

7. RANDOMNESS AND CREATIVITY

A fairly attractive and yet clearly incomplete conjecture is that the difference between creative thinking and unimaginative competent thinking lies in the injection of a some randomness. The randomness must be guided by intuition to be efficient. In other words, the educated guess or the hunch include controlled randomness in otherwise orderly thinking.

In addition to the above collectively formulated problems for study, we have asked the individuals taking part to describe what they will work on. Statements by the four originators of the project are attached.

We propose to organize the work of the group as follows.

Potential participants will be sent copies of this proposal and asked if they would like to work on the artificial intelligence problem in the group and if so what they would like to work on. The invitations will be made by the organizing committee on the basis of its estimate of the individual's potential contribution to the work of the group. The members will circulate their previous work and their ideas for the problems to be attacked during the months preceding the working period of the group.

During the meeting there will be regular research seminars and opportunity for the members to work individually and in informal small groups.

The originators of this proposal are:

1. *C. E. Shannon*, Mathematician, Bell Telephone Laboratories. Shannon developed the statistical theory of information, the application of propositional calculus to switching circuits, and has results on the efficient synthesis of switching circuits, the design of machines that learn, cryptography, and the theory of Turing machines. He and J. McCarthy are co-editing an Annals of Mathematics Study on "The Theory of Automata".

2. *M. L. Minsky*, Harvard Junior Fellow in Mathematics and Neurology. Minsky has built a machine for simulating learning by nerve nets and has written a Princeton PhD thesis in mathematics entitled, "Neural Nets and the Brain Model Problem" which includes results in learning theory and the theory of random neural nets.

3. *N. Rochester*, Manager of Information Research, IBM Corporation, Poughkeepsie, New York. Rochester was concerned with the development of radar for seven years and computing machinery for seven years. He and another engineer were jointly responsible for the design of the IBM Type 701 which is a large scale automatic computer in wide use today. He worked out some of the automatic programming techniques which are in wide use today and has been concerned with problems of how to get machines to do tasks which previously could be done only by people. He has also worked on simulation of nerve nets with particular emphasis on using computers to test theories in neurophysiology.

4. *J. McCarthy*, Assistant Professor of Mathematics, Dartmouth College. McCarthy has worked on a number of questions connected with the mathematical nature of the thought process including the theory of Turing machines, the speed of computers, the relation of a brain model to its environment, and the use of languages by machines. Some results of this work are included in the forthcoming "Annals Study" edited by Shannon and McCarthy. McCarthy's other work has been in the field of differential equations.

The Rockefeller Foundation is being asked to provide financial support for the project on the following basis:

1. Salaries of $1200 for each faculty level participant who is not being supported by his own organization. It is expected, for example, that the participants from Bell Laboratories and IBM Corporation will be supported by these organizations while those from Dartmouth and Harvard will require foundation support.

2. Salaries of $700 for up to two graduate students.

3. Railway fare for participants coming from a distance.

4. Rent for people who are simultaneously renting elsewhere.

5. Secretarial expenses of $650, $500 for a secretary and $150 for duplicating expenses.

6. Organization expenses of $200. (Includes expense of reproducing preliminary work by participants and travel necessary for organization purposes.

7. Expenses for two or three people visiting for a short time.

#& # Estimated Expenses 6 salaries of 1200 @ $7200 2 salaries of 700 @ 1400 8 traveling and rent expenses averaging 300 @ 2400 Secretarial and organizational expense @ 850 Additional traveling expenses @ 600 Contingencies @ 550 &—& $13,500

I would like to devote my research to one or both of the topics listed below. While I hope to do so, it is possible that because of personal considerations I may not be able to attend for the entire two months. I, nevertheless, intend to be there for whatever time is possible.

1. Application of information theory concepts to computing machines and brain models. A basic problem in information theory is that of transmitting information reliably over a noisy channel. An analogous problem in computing machines is that of reliable computing using unreliable elements. This problem has been studied by von Neumann for Sheffer stroke elements and by Shannon and Moore for relays; but there are still many open questions. The problem for several elements, the development of concepts similar to channel capacity, the sharper analysis of upper and lower bounds on the required redundancy, etc. are among the important issues. Another question deals with the theory of information networks where information flows in many closed loops (as contrasted with the simple one-way channel usually considered in communication theory). Questions of delay become very important in the closed loop case, and a whole new approach seems necessary. This would probably involve concepts such as partial entropies when a part of the past history of a message ensemble is known.

2. The matched environment-brain model approach to automata. In general a machine or animal can only adapt to or operate in a limited class of environ-

ments. Even the complex human brain first adapts to the simpler aspects of its environment, and gradually builds up to the more complex features. I propose to study the synthesis of brain models by the parallel development of a series of matched (theoretical) environments and corresponding brain models which adapt to them. The emphasis here is on clarifying the environmental model, and representing it as a mathematical structure. Often in discussing mechanized intelligence, we think of machines performing the most advanced human thought activities-proving theorems, writing music, or playing chess. I am proposing here to start at the simple and when the environment is neither hostile (merely indifferent) nor complex, and to work up through a series of easy stages in the direction of these advanced activities.

It is not difficult to design a machine which exhibits the following type of learning. The machine is provided with input and output channels and an internal means of providing varied output responses to inputs in such a way that the machine may be "trained" by a "trial and error" process to acquire one of a range of input-output functions. Such a machine, when placed in an appropriate environment and given a criterion of "success" or "failure" can be trained to exhibit "goal-seeking" behavior. Unless the machine is provided with, or is able to develop, a way of abstracting sensory material, it can progress through a complicated environment only through painfully slow steps, and in general will not reach a high level of behavior.

Now let the criterion of success be not merely the appearance of a desired activity pattern at the output channel of the machine, but rather the performance of a given manipulation in a given environment. Then in certain ways the motor situation appears to be a dual of the sensory situation, and progress can be reasonably fast only if the machine is equally capable of assembling an ensemble of "motor abstractions" relating its output activity to changes in the environment. Such "motor abstractions" can be valuable only if they relate to changes in the environment which can be detected by the machine as changes in the sensory situation, i.e., if they are related, through the structure of the environment, to the sensory abstractions that the machine is using.

I have been studying such systems for some time and feel that if a machine can be designed in which the sensory and motor abstractions, as they are formed, can be made to satisfy certain relations, a high order of behavior may result. These relations involve pairing, motor abstractions with sensory abstractions in such a way as to produce new sensory situations representing the changes in the environment that might be expected if the corresponding motor act actually took place.

The important result that would be looked for would be that the machine would tend to build up within itself an abstract model of the environment in which it is placed. If it were given a problem, it could first explore solutions within the internal abstract model of the environment and then attempt external experiments. Because of this preliminary internal study, these external experiments would appear to be rather clever, and the behavior would have to be regarded as rather "imaginative".

A very tentative proposal of how this might be done is described in my dissertation and I intend to do further work in this direction. I hope that by summer 1956 I will have a model of such a machine fairly close to the stage of programming in a computer.

ORIGINALITY IN MACHINE PERFORMANCE

In writing a program for an automatic calculator, one ordinarily provides the machine with a set of rules to cover each contingency which may arise and confront the machine. One expects the machine to follow this set of rules slavishly and to exhibit no originality or common sense. Furthermore one is annoyed only at himself when the machine gets confused because the rules he has provided for the machine are slightly con-

tradictory. Finally, in writing programs for machines, one sometimes must go at problems in a very laborious manner whereas, if the machine had just a little intuition or could make reasonable guesses, the solution of the problem could be quite direct. This paper describes a conjecture as to how to make a machine behave in a somewhat more sophisticated manner in the general area suggested above. The paper discusses a problem on which I have been working sporadically for about five years and which I wish to pursue further in the Artificial Intelligence Project next summer.

THE PROCESS OF INVENTION OR DISCOVERY

Living in the environment of our culture provides us with procedures for solving many problems. Just how these procedures work is not yet clear but I shall discuss this aspect of the problem in terms of a model suggested by Craik.[1] He suggests that mental action consists basically of constructing little engines inside the brain which can simulate and thus predict abstractions relating to environment. Thus the solution of a problem which one already understands is done as follows:

1. The environment provides data from which certain abstractions are formed.

2. The abstractions together with certain internal habits or drives provide.

3. A definition of a problem in terms of desired condition to be achieved in the future, a goal.

4. A suggested action to solve the problem.

5. Stimulation to arouse in the brain the engine which corresponds to this situation.

6. Then the engine operates to predict what this environmental situation and the proposed reaction will lead to.

7. If the prediction corresponds to the goal the individual proceeds to act as indicated.

The prediction will correspond to the goal if living in the environment of his culture has provided the individual with the solution to the problem. Regarding the individual as a stored program calculator, the program contains rules to cover this particular contingency.

For a more complex situation the rules might be more complicated. The rules might call for testing each of a set of possible actions to determine which provided the solution. A still more complex set of rules might provide for uncertainty about the environment, as for example in playing tic tac toe one must not only consider his next move but the various possible moves of the environment (his opponent).

Now consider a problem for which no individual in the culture has a solution and which has resisted efforts at solution. This might be a typical current unsolved scientific problem. The individual might try to solve it and find that every reasonable action led to failure. In other words the stored program contains rules for the solution of this problem but the rules are slightly wrong.

In order to solve this problem the individual will have to do something which is unreasonable or unexpected as judged by the heritage of wisdom accumulated by the culture. He could get such behavior by trying different things at random but such an approach would usually be too inefficient. There are usually too many possible courses of action of which only a tiny fraction are acceptable. The individual needs a hunch, something unexpected but not altogether reasonable. Some problems, often those which are fairly new and have not resisted much effort, need just a little randomness. Others, often those which have long resisted solution, need a really bizarre deviation from traditional methods. A problem whose solution requires originality could yield to a method of solution which involved randomness.

In terms of Craik's S model, the engine which should simulate the environment at first fails to simulate correctly. Therefore, it is necessary to try various modifications of the engine until one is found that makes it do what is needed.

Instead of describing the problem in terms of an individual in his culture it could have been described in terms of the learning of an immature individual. When the individual is presented with a problem outside the scope of his experience he must surmount it in a similar manner.

So far the nearest practical approach using this method in machine solution of problems is an extension of the Monte Carlo method. In the usual problem which is appropriate for Monte Carlo there is a situation which is grossly misunderstood and which has too many possible factors and one is unable to decide which factors to ignore in working out analytical solution. So the mathematician has the machine making a few thousand random experiments. The results of these experiments provide a rough guess as to what the answer may be. The extension of the Monte Carlo Method is to use these results as a guide to determine what to neglect in order to simplify the problem enough to obtain an approximate analytical solution.

It might be asked why the method should include randomness. Why shouldn't the method be to try each possibility in the order of the probability that the present state of knowledge would predict for its success? For the scientist surrounded by the environment provided by his culture, it may be that one scientist alone would be unlikely to solve the problem in his life so the efforts of many are needed. If they use randomness they could all work at once on it without complete duplication of effort. If they used system they would require impossibly detailed communication. For the individual maturing in competition with other individuals the requirements of mixed strategy (using game theory terminology) favor randomness. For the machine, randomness will probably be needed to overcome the shortsightedness and prejudices of the programmer. While the necessity for randomness has clearly not been proven, there is much evidence in its favor.

THE MACHINE WITH RANDOMNESS

In order to write a program to make an automatic calculator use originality it will not do to introduce randomness without using foresight. If, for example, one wrote a program so that once in every 10,000 steps the calculator generated a random number and executed it as an instruction the result would probably be chaos. Then after a certain amount of chaos the machine would probably try something forbidden or execute a stop instruction and the experiment would be over.

Two approaches, however, appear to be reasonable. One of these is to find how the brain manages to do this sort of thing and copy it. The other is to take some class of real problems which require originality in their solution and attempt to find a way to write a program to solve them on an automatic calculator. Either of these approaches would probably eventually succeed. However, it is not clear which would be quicker nor how many years or generations it would take. Most of my effort along these lines has so far been on the former approach because I felt that it would be best to master all relevant scientific knowledge in order to work on such a hard problem, and I already was quite aware of the current state of calculators and the art of programming them.

The control mechanism of the brain is clearly very different from the control mechanism in today's calculators. One symptom of the difference is the manner of failure. A failure of a calculator characteristically produces something quite unreasonable. An error in memory or in data transmission is as likely to be in the most significant digit as in the least. An error in control can do nearly anything. It might execute the wrong instruction or operate a wrong input-output unit. On the other hand human errors in speech are apt to result in statements which almost make sense (consider someone who is almost asleep, slightly drunk, or slightly feverish). Perhaps the mechanism of the brain is such that a slight error in reasoning introduces randomness in just the right way. Perhaps the mechanism that controls serial order in behavior[2] guides the random factor so as to improve the efficiency of imaginative processes over pure randomness.

Some work has been done on simulating neuron nets on our automatic calculator. One purpose was to see if it would be thereby possible to introduce randomness in an appropriate fashion. It seems to have turned out that there are too many unknown links between the activity of neurons and problem solving for this approach to work quite yet. The results have cast some light on the behavior of nets and neurons, but have not yielded a way to solve problems requiring originality.

An important aspect of this work has been an effort to make the machine form and manipulate concepts, abstractions, generalizations, and names. An attempt was made to test a theory[3] of how the brain does it. The first set of experiments occasioned a revision of certain details of the theory. The second set of experiments is now in progress. By next summer this work will be finished and a final report will have been written.

My program is to try next to write a program to solve problems which are members of some limited class of problems that require originality in their solution. It is too early to predict just what stage I will be in next summer, or just; how I will then define the immediate problem. However, the underlying problem which is described in this paper is what I intend to pursue. In a single sentence the problem is: how can I make a machine which will exhibit originality in its solution of problems?

During next year and during the Summer Research Project on Artificial Intelligence, I propose to study the relation of language to intelligence. It seems clear that the direct application of trial and error methods to the relation between sensory data and motor activity will not lead to any very complicated behavior. Rather it is necessary for the trial and error methods to be applied at a higher level of abstraction. The human mind apparently uses language as its means of handling complicated phenomena. The trial and error processes at a higher level frequently take the form of formulating conjectures and testing them. The English language has a number of properties which every formal language described so far lacks.

1. Arguments in English supplemented by informal mathematics can be concise.

2. English is universal in the sense that it can set up any other language within English and then use that language where it is appropriate.

3. The user of English can refer to himself in it and formulate statements regarding

his progress in solving the problem he is working on.

4. In addition to rules of proof, English if completely formulated would have rules of conjecture.

The logical languages so far formulated have either been instruction lists to make computers carry out calculations specified in advance or else formalization of parts of mathematics. The latter have been constructed so as:

1. to be easily described in informal mathematics,

2. to allow translation of statements from informal mathematics into the language,

3. to make it easy to argue about whether proofs of (???) [sentence left incomplete]

No attempt has been made to make proofs in artificial languages as short as informal proofs. It therefore seems to be desirable to attempt to construct an artificial language which a computer can be programmed to use on problems requiring conjecture and self-reference. It should correspond to English in the sense that short English statements about the given subject matter should have short correspondents in the language and so should short arguments or conjectural arguments. I hope to try to formulate a language having these properties and in addition to contain the notions of physical object, event, etc., with the hope that using this language it will be possible to program a machine to learn to play games well and do other tasks.

The purpose of the list is to let those on it know who is interested in receiving documents on the problem. The people on the list will receive copies of the report of the Dartmouth Summer Project on Artificial Intelligence. [1996 note: There was no report.]

The list consists of people who participated in or visited the Dartmouth Summer Research Project on Artificial Intelligence, or who are known to be interested in the subject. It is being sent to the people on the list and to a few others.

For the present purpose the artificial intelligence problem is taken to be that of making a machine behave in ways that would be called intelligent if a human were so behaving.

A revised list will be issued soon, so that anyone else interested in getting on the list or anyone who wishes to change his address on it should write to:

1996 note: Not all of these people came to the Dartmouth conference. They were people we thought might be interested in Artificial Intelligence.

The list consists of:

Adelson, Marvin
Hughes Aircraft Company
Airport Station, Los Angeles, CA

Ashby, W. R.
Barnwood House
Gloucester, England

Backus, John
IBM Corporation
590 Madison Avenue
New York, NY

Bernstein, Alex
IBM Corporation
590 Madison Avenue
New York, NY

Bigelow, J. H.
Institute for Advanced Studies
Princeton, NJ

Elias, Peter
R. L. E., MIT
Cambridge, MA

Duda, W. L.
IBM Research Laboratory
Poughkeepsie, NY

Davies, Paul M.
1317 C. 18th Street
Los Angeles, CA.

Fano, R. M.
R. L. E., MIT
Cambridge, MA

Farley, B. G.
324 Park Avenue
Arlington, MA.

Galanter, E. H.
University of Pennsylvania
Philadelphia, PA

Gelernter, Herbert
IBM Research
Poughkeepsie, NY

Glashow, Harvey A.
1102 Olivia Street
Ann Arbor, MI.

Goertzal, Herbert
330 West 11th Street
New York, New York

Hagelbarger, D.
Bell Telephone Laboratories
Murray Hill, NJ

Miller, George A.
Memorial Hall
Harvard University
Cambridge, MA.

Harmon, Leon D.
Bell Telephone Laboratories
Murray Hill, NJ

Holland, John H.
E. R. I.
University of Michigan
Ann Arbor, MI

Holt, Anatol
7358 Rural Lane
Philadelphia, PA

Kautz, William H.
Stanford Research Institute
Menlo Park, CA

Luce, R. D.
427 West 117th Street
New York, NY

MacKay, Donald
Department of Physics
University of London
London, WC2, England

McCarthy, John
Dartmouth College
Hanover, NH

McCulloch, Warren S.
R.L.E., M.I.T.
Cambridge, MA

Melzak, Z. A.
Mathematics Department
University of Michigan
Ann Arbor, MI

Minsky, M. L.
112 Newbury Street
Boston, MA

More, Trenchard
Department of Electrical Engineering
MIT
Cambridge, MA

Nash, John
Institute for Advanced Studies
Princeton, NJ

Newell, Allen
Department of Industrial Administration
Carnegie Institute of Technology
Pittsburgh, PA

Robinson, Abraham
Department of Mathematics
University of Toronto
Toronto, Ontario, Canada

Rochester, Nathaniel
Engineering Research Laboratory
IBM Corporation
Poughkeepsie, NY

Rogers, Hartley, Jr.
Department of Mathematics
MIT
Cambridge, MA.

Rosenblith, Walter
R.L.E., M.I.T.
Cambridge, MA.

Rothstein, Jerome
21 East Bergen Place
Red Bank, NJ

Sayre, David
IBM Corporation
590 Madison Avenue
New York, NY

Schorr-Kon, J.J.
C-380 Lincoln Laboratory, MIT
Lexington, MA

Shapley, L.
Rand Corporation
1700 Main Street
Santa Monica, CA

Schutzenberger, M.P.
R.L.E., M.I.T.
Cambridge, MA

Selfridge, O. G.
Lincoln Laboratory, M.I.T.
Lexington, MA

Shannon, C. E.
R.L.E., M.I.T.
Cambridge, MA

Shapiro, Norman
Rand Corporation
1700 Main Street
Santa Monica, CA

Simon, Herbert A.
Department of Industrial Administration
Carnegie Institute of Technology
Pittsburgh, PA

Solomonoff, Raymond J.
Technical Research Group
17 Union Square West
New York, NY

Steele, J. E., Capt. USAF
Area B., Box 8698
Wright-Patterson AFB
Ohio

Webster, Frederick
62 Coolidge Avenue
Cambridge, MA

Moore, E. F.
Bell Telephone Laboratory
Murray Hill, NJ

Kemeny, John G.
Dartmouth College
Hanover, NH

• • •

1. K.J.W. Craik, *The Nature of Explanation*, Cambridge University Press, 1943 (reprinted 1952), p. 92.

2. K.S. Lashley, "The Problem of Serial Order in Behavior", in *Cerebral Mechanism in Behavior, the Hixon Symposium*, edited by L.A. Jeffress, John Wiley & Sons, New York, pp. 112–146, 1951.

3. D. O. Hebb, *The Organization of Behavior*, John Wiley & Sons, New York, 1949.

11.6
Programs with Common Sense

John McCarthy

From National Physical Laboratory, *Mechanisation of Thought Processes; Proceedings of a Symposium Held at the National Physical Laboratory on 24th, 25th, 26th and 27th November 1958* (London: H. M. Stationery Office, 1959), pp. 75–84.

INTRODUCTORY NOTE TO READING 11.6

John McCarthy characterizes this paper on artificial intelligence as "probably the first paper on logical AI, i.e. AI in which logic is the method of representing information in computer memory and not just the subject matter of the program." Logical AI is an approach to the development of symbolic AI. It uses logic to describe the manner in which intelligent machines or people behave. Another way to talk about this is to say that logical AI involves representing knowledge of an agent's world, its goals and the current situation by sentences in logic. The agent decides what to do by inferring that a certain action or course of action is appropriate to achieve the goals. Regarding basic information and definitions underlying artificial intelligence, McCarthy provides very useful information on his website: http://www-formal.stanford.edu/jmc/whatisai/whatisai.html. [JMN]

TEXT OF READING 11.6

SUMMARY

Interesting work is being done in programming computers to solve problems which require a high degree of intelligence in humans. However, certain elementary verbal reasoning processes so simple that they can be carried out by any non-feeble-minded human have yet to be simulated by machine programs.

This paper will discuss programs to manipulate in a suitable formal language (most likely a part of the predicate calculus) common instrumental statements. The basic program will draw immediate conclusions from a list of premises. These conclusions will be either declarative or imperative sentences. When an imperative sentence is deduced the program takes a corresponding action. These actions may include printing sentences, moving sentences on lists, and reinitiating the basic deduction process on these lists.

Facilities will be provided for communication with humans in the system via manual intervention and display devices connected to the computer.

The *advice taker* is a proposed program for solving problems by manipulating sentences in formal languages. The main difference between it and other programs or proposed programs for manipulating formal languages (the *Logic Theory Machine* of Newell, Simon and Shaw and the Geometry Program of Gelernter) is that in the previous programs the formal system was the subject matter but the heuristics were all embodied in the program. In this program the procedures will be described as much as possible in the language itself and, in particular, the heuristics are all so described.

The main advantages we expect the *advice taker* to have is that its behaviour will be improvable merely by making statements to it, telling it about its symbolic environment and what is wanted from it. To make these statements will require little if any knowledge of the program or the previous knowledge of the *advice taker*. One will be able to assume that the *advice taker* will have available to it a fairly wide class of immediate logical consequences of anything it is told and its previous knowledge. This property is expected to have much in common with what makes us describe certain humans as having *common sense*. We shall therefore say that *A program has common sense if it automatically deduces for itself a sufficiently wide class of immediate consequences of anything it is told and what it already knows.*

The design of this system will be a joint project with Marvin Minsky, but Minsky is not to be held responsible for the views expressed here.

Before describing the *advice taker* in any detail, I would like to describe more fully our motivation for proceeding in this direction. Our ultimate objective is to make programs that learn from their experience as effectively as humans do. It may not be realized how far we are presently from this objective. It is not hard to make machines learn from experience to make simple changes in their behaviour of a kind which has been anticipated by the programmer. For example, Samuel has included in his checker program facilities for improving the weights the machine assigns to various factors in evaluating positions. He has also included a scheme whereby the machine remembers games it has played previously and deviates from its previous play when it finds a position which it previously lost. Suppose, however, that we wanted an improvement in behavior corresponding, say, to the discovery by the machine of the principle of the opposition in checkers. No present or presently proposed schemes are capable of discovering phenomena as abstract as this.

If one wants a machine to be able to discover an abstraction, it seems most likely that the machine must be able to represent this abstraction in some relatively simple way.

There is one known way of making a machine capable of learning arbitrary behaviour; thus to anticipate every kind of behaviour. This is to make it possible for the machine to simulate arbitrary behaviours and try them out. These behaviours may be represented either by nerve nets (ref. 2), by Turing machines (ref. 3), or by calculator programs (ref. 4). The difficulty is two-fold. First, in any of these representations the density of interesting behaviours is incredibly low. Second, and even more important, small interesting changes in behaviour expressed at a high level of abstraction do not have simple representations. It is as though the human genetic structure were represented by a set of blue-prints. Then a mutation would usually result in a wart or a failure of parts to meet, or even an ungrammatical blue-print which could not be translated into an animal at all. It is very difficult to see how the genetic representation scheme manages to be general enough to represent the great variety of animals observed and yet be such that so many interesting changes in the organism are represented by small genetic changes. The problem of how such a representation controls the development of a fertilized egg into a mature animal is even more difficult.

In our opinion, a system which is to evolve intelligence of human order should have at least the following features:

1. All behaviours must be representable in the system. Therefore, the system should either be able to construct arbitrary automata or to program in some general purpose programming language.

2. Interesting changes in behaviour must be expressible in a simple way.

3. All aspects of behaviour except the most routine must be improvable. In particular, the improving mechanism should be improvable.

4. The machine must have or evolve concepts of partial success because on difficult problems decisive successes or failures come too infrequently.

5. The system must be able to create subroutines which can be included in procedures as units. The learning of subroutines is complicated by the fact that the effect of a subroutine is not usually good or bad in itself. Therefore, the mechanism that selects subroutines should have concepts of an interesting or powerful subroutine whose application may be good under suitable conditions.

Of the 5 points mentioned above, our work concentrates mainly on the second. We base ourselves on the idea that: In order for a program to be capable of learning something it must first be capable of being told it.

In fact, in the early versions we shall concentrate entirely on this point and attempt to achieve a system which can be told to make a specific improvement in its behaviour with no more knowledge of its internal structure or previous knowledge than is required in order to instruct a human. Once this is achieved, we may be able to tell the advice taker how to learn from experience.

The main distinction between the way one programs a computer and modifies the program and the way one instructs a human or will instruct the advice taker is this: A machine is instructed mainly in the form of a sequence of imperative sentences; while a human is instructed mainly in declarative sentences describing the situation in which action is required together with a few imperatives that say what is wanted. We shall list the advantages of the two methods of instruction.

Advantages of Imperative Sentences

1. A procedure described in imperatives is already laid out and is carried out faster.

2. One starts with a machine in a basic state and does not assume previous knowledge on the part of the machine.

Advantages of Declarative Sentences

1. Advantage can be taken of previous knowledge.

2. Declarative sentences have logical consequences and it can be arranged that the machine will have available sufficiently simple logical consequences of what it is told and what it previously knew.

3. The meaning of declaratives is much less dependent on their order than is the case with imperatives. This makes it easier to have after-thoughts.

4. The effect of a declarative is less dependent on the previous state of the system so that less knowledge of this state is required on the part of the instructor.

5. The only way we know of expressing abstractions (such as the previous example of the opposition in checkers) is in language. That is why we have decided to program a system which reasons verbally.

THE CONSTRUCTION OF THE ADVICE TAKER

The *advice taker* system has the following main features:

1. There is a method of representing expressions in the computer. These expressions are defined recursively as follows: A class of entities called terms is defined and a term is an expression. A sequence of expressions is an expression. These expressions are represented in the machine by list structures (ref. 1).

2. Certain of these expressions may be regarded as declarative sentences in a certain logical system which will be analogous to a universal Post canonical system. The particular system chosen will depend on programming considerations but will probably have a single rule of inference which will combine substitution for variables with modus ponens. The purpose of the combination is to avoid choking the machine with special cases of general propositions already deduced.

3. There is an *immediate deduction routine* which when given a set of premises will deduce a set of immediate conclusions. Initially, the immediate deduction routine will simply write down all one-step consequences of the premises. Later, this may be elaborated so that the routine

will produce some other conclusions which may be of interest. However, this routine will not use semantic heuristics; i.e. heuristics which depend on the subject matter under discussion.

4. The intelligence, if any, of the advice taker will not be embodied in the immediate deduction routine. This intelligence will be embodied in the procedures which choose the lists of premises to which the immediate deduction routine is to be applied. Of course, the program should never attempt to apply the immediate deduction routine simultaneously to the list of everything it knows. This would make the deduction routine take too long.

5. Not all expressions are interpreted by the system as declarative sentences. Some are the names of entities of various kinds. Certain formulas represent *objects*. For our purposes, an entity is an object if we have something to say about it other than the things which may be deduced from the form of its name. For example, to most people, the number 3812 is not an object: they have nothing to say about it except what can be deduced from its structure. On the other hand, to most Americans the number 1776 is an object because they have filed somewhere the fact that it represents the year when the American Revolution started. In the *advice taker* each object has a *property list* in which are listed the specific things we have to say about it. Some things which can be deduced from the name of the object may be included in the property list anyhow if the deduction was actually carried out and was difficult enough so that the system does not want to carry it out again.

6. Entities other than declarative sentences which can be represented by formulas in the system are individuals, functions, and programs.

7. The program is intended to operate cyclically as follows. The immediate deduction routine is applied to a list of premises and a list of individuals. Some of the conclusions have the form of imperative sentences. These are obeyed. Included in the set of imperatives which may be obeyed is the routine which deduces and obeys.

We shall illustrate the way the *advice taker* is supposed to act by means of an example. Assume that I am seated at my desk at home and I wish to go to the airport. My car is at my home also. The solution of the problem is to walk to the car and drive the car to the airport. First, we shall give a formal statement of the premises the *advice taker* uses to draw the conclusions. Then we shall discuss the heuristics which cause the *advice taker* to assemble these premises from the totality of facts it has available. The premises come in groups, and we shall explain the interpretation of each group.

1. First, we have a predicate "*at*". "*at(x,y)*" *is a formalization of* "*x is at y*". Under this heading we have the premises

   1. *at (I, desk)*

   2. *at (desk, home)*

   3. *at (car, home)*

   4. *at (home, county)*

   5. *at (airport, county)*

We shall need the fact that the relation "*at*" is transitive which might be written directly as

   6. *at(x,y), at(y,z) → at(x,z)* or alternatively we might instead use the more abstract premises

   6'. *transitive (at)*

and

   7'. *transitive (u) → (u(x,y), u(yz,z) → u(x,z))*

from which 6. can be deduced.

2. here are two rules concerning the feasibility of walking and driving.

   8. *walkable(x), at(y,x), at(z,x), at(I,y) → can(go(y,z, walking))*

   9. *drivable(x), at(y,x), at(z,x), at(car,y), at(I,car) → can(go(y,z, driving))*

There are also two specific facts

   10. *walkable (home)*

   11. *drivable (county)*

3. Next we have a rule concerned with the properties of going.

   12. *did(go(x,y,z)) → at(I,y)*

4. The problem itself is posed by the premise:

   13. *want (at (I, airport))*

5. The above are all the premises concerned with the particular problem. The last group of premises are common to almost all problems of this sort. They are:

   14. *(x → can(y)), (did(y) → z) → canachult(x,y,z)*

The predicate "*canachult(x,y,z)*" means that in a situation to which x applies, the action y can be performed and brings about a situation to which z applies. A sort of transitivity is described by

   15. *canachult(x,y,z), canachult(z,u,v) → canachult(x,prog(y,u),v)*. Here *prog(u,v)* is the program of first carrying out u and then v. (Some kind of identification of a single action u with the one step program *prog(u)* is obviously required, but the details of how this will fit into the formalism have not yet been worked out).

The final premise is the one which causes action to be taken.

16. x,canachult(x,prog(y,z),w), want(w)
   $\rightarrow$ do(y)

The argument the *advice taker* must produce in order to solve the problem deduces the following propositions in more or less the following order:

1.   at(I,desk) $\rightarrow$ can(go(desk, car, walking))

2.   at (I, car) $\rightarrow$ can (go (home, airport, driving))

3.   did(go(desk, car, walking)) $\rightarrow$ at(I,car)

4.   did(go(home, airport, driving)) $\rightarrow$ at(I, airport)

5.   canachult(at(I, desk), go(desk, car, walking), at(I, car))

6.   canachult(at(I, car), go(home, airport, driving), at(I, airport))

7.   canachult (at (I, desk), program(go (desk, car, walking), go (home, airport, driving)), $\rightarrow$ at(I, airport))

8.   do (go (desk, car, walking))

The deduction of the last proposition initiates action.

The above proposed reasoning raises two major questions of heuristic. The first is that of how the 16 premises are collected, and the second is that of how the deduction proceeds once they are found. We cannot give complete answers to either question in the present paper; they are obviously not completely separate since some of the deductions might be made before some of the premises are collected. Let us first consider the question of where the 16 premises come from.

First of all, we assert that except for the 13th premise (*want* (*at* (*I*, *airport*)) which sets the goal) and the 1st premise (*at* (*I*, *desk*) which we shall get from a routine which answers the question "where am I"), *all the premises can reasonably be expected to be specifically present in the memory* of a machine which has competence of human order in finding its way around. That is, none of them are so specific to the problem at hand that assuming their presence in

memory constitutes an anticipation of this particular problem or of a class of problems narrower than those which any human can expect to have previously solved. We must impose this requirement if we are to be able to say that the *advice taker* exhibits *common sense.*

On the other hand, while we may reasonably assume that the premises are in memory, we still have to describe how they are assembled into a list by themselves to which the deduction routine may be applied. Tentatively, we expect the *advice taker* to proceed as follows: initially, the sentence "*want*($at(I, airport)$)" is on a certain list L, called the main list, all by itself. The program begins with an observation routine which looks at. the main list and puts certain statements about the contents of this list on a list called "observations of the main list". We shall not specify at present what all the possible outputs of this observation routine are but merely say that in this case it will observe that "the only statement on L has the form '*want* (u (x))'." (We write this out in English because we have not yet settled on a formalism for representing statements of this kind). The "deduce and obey" routine is then applied to the combination of the "observations of the main list" list, and a list called the "standing orders list". This list is rather small and is never changed, or at least is only changed in major changes of the advice taker. The contents of the "standing orders" list has not been worked out, but what must be deduced is the extraction of certain statements from property lists. Namely, the program first looks at "*want*($at(I,airport)$)", and attempts to copy the statements on its property list. Let us assume that it fails in this attempt because "*want*($at(I, airport)$)" does not have the status of an object and hence has no property list. (One might expect that if the problem of going to the airport had arisen before, "*want*($at(I, airport)$)" would be an object, but this might depend on whether there were routines for generalizing previous experience that would allow something of general use to be filed under that heading). Next in order of increasing generality the machine would see if anything were filed under "*want*($at(I, x)$)" which would deal with the general problem of getting somewhere. One would expect that premises 6, (or 6' and 7'), 8, 9, 12, would be so filed. There would also be the formula

$$want(at(I, x)) \rightarrow do(observe(where\ am\ I))$$

which would give us premise 1. There would also be a reference to the next higher level of abstraction in the goal statement which would cause a look at the property list of "$want(x)$". This would give us 14, 15, and 16.

We shall not try to follow the solution further except to remark that "$want(at(I, x))$" there would be a rule that starts with the premises "$at(I, y)$" and "$want(I, x)$" and has as conclusion a search for the property list of "$go(y, x, z)$". This would presumably fail, and then there would have to be heuristics that would initiate a search for a y such that "$at(I, y)$" and "$at(airport, y)$". This would be done by looking on the property lists of the origin and the destination and working up. Then premise 9 would be found which has as one of its premises $at(I, car)$. A repetition of the above would find premise 8, which would complete the set of premises since the other "at" premises would have been found as by-products of previous searches.

We hope that the presence of the heuristic rules mentioned on the property lists where we have put them will seem plausible to the reader. It should be noticed that on the higher level of abstraction many of the statements are of the stimulus-response form. One might conjecture that division in man between conscious and unconscious thought occurs at the boundary between stimulus-response heuristics which do not have to be reasoned about but only obeyed, and the others which have to serve as premises in deductions.

We hope to formalize the heuristics in another paper before we start programming the system.

REFERENCES

1. NEWELL, A. and SIMON, H. A. Empirical Explorations of the Logic Theory Machine. A Case Study in Heuristic. *Proceedings of the Western Joint Computer Conference*, p. 218 (February, 1957).

2. MINSKY, M. L. Heuristic Aspects of the Artificial Intelligence Problem. *Lincoln Laboratory Report 34-55*. (December, 1956). (See also his paper for this conference and his Princeton Ph.D. thesis).

3. McCARTHY, J. Inversion of Functions Defined by Turing Machines. In Automata Studies, *Annals of Mathematics Study Number*.

4. FRIEDBERG, R. A Learning Machine, Part I. *IBM Journal of Research and Development*, 1958, 2, No. 1.

DISCUSSION ON THE PAPER BY DR. J. MCCARTHY

PROF. Y. BAR-HILLEL: Dr. McCarthy's paper belongs in the Journal of Half-Baked Ideas, the creation of which was recently proposed by Dr. I. J. Good. Dr. McCarthy will probably be the first to admit this. Before he goes on to bake his ideas fully, it might be well to give him some advice and raise some objections. He himself mentions some possible objections, but I do not think that he treats them with the full consideration they deserve; there are others he does not mention.

For lack of time, I shall not go into the first part of his paper, although I think that it contains a lot of highly unclear philosophical, or pseudo-philosophical assumptions. I shall rather spend my time in commenting on the example he works out in his paper at some length. Before I start, let me voice my protest against the general assumption of Dr. McCarthy—slightly caricatured—that a machine, if only its programme is specified with a sufficient degree of carelessness, will be able to carry out satisfactorily even rather difficult tasks.

Consider the assumption that the relation he designates by "at" is transitive (page 81). However, since he takes both "$at(I, desk)$" and "$at(desk, home)$" as premises, I presume—though this is never made quite clear—that "at" means something like being-a-physical-part-or-in-the-immediate-spatial-neighborhood-of. But then the relation is clearly not transitive. If A is in the immediate spatial neighborhood of B and B in the immediate spatial neighborhood of C, then A need not be in the immediate spatial neighborhood of C. Otherwise, everything would turn out to be in the immediate spatial neighborhood of everything, which is surely not Dr. McCarthy's intention. Of course, starting from false premises, one can still arrive at right conclusions. We do such things quite often, and a machine could do it. But it would probably be bad advice to allow a machine to do such things consistently.

Many of the other 23 steps in Dr. McCarthy's argument are equally or more questionable, but I don't think we should spend our time showing this in detail. My major question is the following: On page 83 McCarthy states that a machine which has a competence of human order in finding its way around will have almost all the premises of the argument stored in its memory. I am at a complete loss to understand the point of this remark. If Dr. McCarthy wants to say no more than that a machine, in order to behave like a human being, must have the knowledge of a human being, then this is surely not a very important remark to make. But if not, what was the intention of this remark?

The decisive question how a machine, even assuming that it will have somehow countless millions of facts stored in its memory, will be able to pick out those facts which will serve as premises for its deduction is promised to receive its treatment in another paper, which is quite alright for a half-baked idea.

It sounds rather incredible that the machine could have arrived at its conclusion—which, in plain English, is "Walk from your desk to your car!"—by sound deduction. This conclusion surely could not possibly follow from the premises in any serious sense. Might it not be occasionally cheaper to call a taxi and have it take you over to the airport: Couldn't you decide to cancel your flight or to do a hundred other things? I don't think it would be wise to develop a programme language so powerful as to make a machine arrive at the conclusion Dr. McCarthy apparently intends it to make.

Let me also point out that in the example the time factor has never been mentioned, probably for the sake of simplicity. But clearly this factor is here so important that it could not possibly be disregarded without distorting the whole argument. Does not the solution depend, among thousands of other things, also upon the time of my being at my desk, the time at which I have to be at the airport, the distance from the airport, the speed of my car, etc.?

To make the argument deductively, sound, its complexity will have to be increased by many orders of magnitude. So long as this is not realized, any discussions of machines able to perform the deductive—and inductive!—operations necessary for treating problems of the kind brought forward by Dr. McCarthy is totally pointless. The gap between Dr. McCarthy's general programme (with which I have little quarrel, after discounting its "philosophical" features) and its execution even in such a simple case as the one discussed seems to me so enormous that much more has to be done to persuade me that even the first step in bridging this gap has already been taken.

DR. O. G. SELFRIDGE: I have a question which I think applies to this. It seems to me in much of that work, the old absolutist Prof. Bar-Hillel has really put his finger on something; he is really worried about the deduction actually made. He seemed really to worry that the system is not consistent, and he made a remark that conclusions should not be drawn from false premises. In my experience those are the only conclusions that have ever been drawn. I have never yet heard of someone drawing correct conclusions from correct premises. I mean this seriously. This, I think, is Dr. Minsky's point this morning. What this leads to is that the notion of deductive logic being something sitting there sacred which you can borrow for particularly sacred uses and producing inviolable results is a lot of nonsense.

Deductive logic is inferred as much as anything else. Most women have never inferred it, but they get on perfectly well, marrying happy husbands, raising happy children, without ever using deductive logic at all. My feeling is that my criticism of Dr. McCarthy is the other way. He assumes deductive logic, whereas in fact that is something to be concocted.

This is another important point which I think Prof. Bar-Hillel ignores in this, the criticism of the programme should not be as to whether it is logically consistent, but only will he be able to wave it around saying "this in fact works the way I want it". Dr. McCarthy would be the first to admit that his programme is not now working, so it has to be changed. Then, can you make the changes in the programme to make it work? That has nothing to do with logic. Can he amend it in such a way that it includes the logic as well as the little details of the programme? Can he manage in such a way that it works the way he does? He said at the beginning of his talk that when he makes an arbitrary change in the programme it will not work usually, and you try to fix that so that it will. He has produced at least some evidence, to me at least, that small changes in his programme will not obviously not make the programme work and might even improve it. His next point is whether he can make small changes that in fact make it work. That is what we do not know yet.

PROF. Y. BAR-HILLEL: May I ask whether you could thrash this out with Dr. McCarthy? It was my impression that Dr. McCarthy's advice taker was meant to be able, among other things, to arrive at a certain conclusion from appropriate premises by faultless deductive reasoning. If this is still his programme, then I think your defence is totally beside the point.

DR. O. G. SELFRIDGE: I am not defending his programme, I am only defending him.

DR. J. MCCARTHY: Are you using the word "programme" in the technical sense of a bunch of cards or in the sense of a project that you get money for?

PROF. Y. BAR-HILLEL: When I uttered my doubts that a machine working under the programme outlined by Dr. McCarthy would be able to do what he expects it to do, I was using "programme" in the technical sense.

DR. O. G. SELFRIDGE: In that case your criticisms are not so much philosophical as technical.

PROF. Y. BAR-HILLEL: They are purely technical. I said that I shall not make any philosophical criticisms, for lack of time.

DR. O. G. SELFRIDGE: A technical objection does not make ideas half-baked.

PROF. Y. BAR-HILLEL: A deductive argument, where you have first to find out what are the relevant premises, is something which many humans are not always able to carry out successfully. I do not see the slightest reason to believe that at present machines should be able to perform things that humans find trouble in doing. I do not think there could possibly exist a programme which would, given any problem, divide all facts in the universe into those which are and those which are not relevant for that problem. Developing such a programme seems to me to be by 10^{10} orders of magnitude more difficult than, say, the Newell-Simon problem of developing a heuristic for deduction in the propositional calculus. This cavalier way of jumping over orders of magnitude only tends to becloud the issue and throw doubt on ways of thinking for which I have a great deal of respect. By developing a powerful programme language you may have paved the way for the first step in solving problems of the kind treated in your example, but the claim of being well on the way towards their solution is a gross exaggeration. This was the major point of my objections.

DR. L. C. PAYNE: First a quick comment on the remark of no woman having ever brought up a child by means of deductive logic, the point surely is obvious. The feedback is very close: if she drops the baby in a disastrous way, she does not get another chance or she gets a great yelp. She learns very quickly by crude techniques of how to achieve precise control. There is direct feedback: If she is trying to win a spouse and tries a move which does not get the right response, she quickly changes her tack. Computer-wise, we have yet to develop an input (sensory system) and data-processing technique that can give even a gesture of such resourcefulness! It is a real-time trial and error process utilizing every bit of every nuance, quickly adapting and re-adapting.

A computer can deal with only a very small amount of information compared with the human brain, and therefore attention has to be concentrated on the efficiency with which this limited amount of information is handled. This is where one may usefully turn to deductive logic, because it will be appreciated that if a person is to benefit from all the studies and knowledge of many people in different places and epochs then synthesis of some sort is essential. Science in general is just this: its laws subsume with great economy the mechanisms of diverse processes. For example the application of deductive logic to Newton's three laws allows us to treat of a multitude of practical applications. Hence if a computer is to have any range of activity, it must be fed with explicit rules, so that by rapid deductions or transformations of data, it can evolve a host of ramifications from a limited amount of information.

The Countess of Lovelace remarked that "a machine can originate nothing: it can only do what we order it to perform". The essence of my contention is that we can only order to perform by means of transformations of data having as their basis existing logical systems. Because of this it might be well to summarize, perhaps boldly before an audience like this, what I think is a summary of existing logics. The first is Formal Logic and consists of statements of the form, if all A are B and C is A, then certainly C is B—the syllogistic type of statement by which one can establish direct connections. This sort of logic is reversible; that is, If you start from a given complex of consistent propositions, then it is possible to take some selection of a derivative statements and from them as a starting complex, derive propositions of the original set. If the original set contains a contradiction then all other contradictions are implied latently. The best example I know of this is one recently cited by Sir Ronald Fisher, which is said to stem from the high table at Trinity College, Cambridge. The late Professor G. H. Hardy was asked, "Do you mean to say, Hardy, that you can prove any contradiction whatsoever if you have got one contradiction?". Hardy replied, "Yes, that is so". The questioner went on, "Well, four equals five, you prove that McTaggart is the Pope". Hardy rejoined at once saying, "If four equals five, then by subtracting three from each, one equals two. McTaggart and the Pope are two, therefore McTaggart and the Pope are one"!

The other important logic is Probability Theory. This consists of statements, that if some well defined proportion of A are B, and if C is A, then only an uncertain inference in the form of a probability statement, can be made about C being B. One has to be especially careful in statements of this kind to see that the total reference set is well defined and also the subset having some specified attribute. This kind of consideration, treated very carefully by Sir Ronald Fisher in his "Statistical Methods and Scientific Inference", nullifies the casual attitude which, to instance an example, can remark that, "statistics means that if you take enough inaccurate statements and put them together then a more accurate statement can be made". The well defined nature of the statistical mode of reasoning, if it is respected, means you can be as logically precise as with Formal Logic, but that the kind of statement you can be logically precise about is less certain, that is, it is a probability statement.

A more restricted logic can be based on what Sir Ronald Fisher calls "mathematical likelihood". This allows quantitative statements to be made on the fullest information available; it is discussed in the reference already given.

Beyond these systems one is very suspicious of the play with random exercises which purport to produce something out of nothing. It seems to me that computers can do nothing beyond applying the existing logics to effect transformations of data, since these are the limits within which exercises can be prescribed explicitly. These limits in fact are very wide and circumscribe most of the rational procedures used by human beings. They are not limited by pure mathematics, where one is constrained to using a limited class functions which lend themselves to analysis. Numerical solutions can certainly explore regions which would bog down a more ponderous mathematical attack. In my opinion higher mathematics can be logically precise and very penetrating only about a very small class of entities, ones that are very abstract in content. Statistics allows one to deal with a wider class with less certainty, and so on down the scale until you reach common sense, where one may be rational about fairly concrete entities. Between common sense and high mathematics one has the whole range of human rationality, but for each refinement in logic one must pay the price of dealing with more restricted classes of entities which become progressively more abstract.

DR. J. McCARTHY (in reply): Prof. Bar-Hillel has correctly observed that my paper is based on unstated philosophical assumptions although what he means by "pseudo-philosophical" is unclear. Whenever we program a computer to learn from experience we build into the programme a sort of epistemology. It might be argued that this epistemology should be made explicit before one writes the programme, but epistemology is in a foggier state than computer programming even in the present half-baked state of the latter. I hope that once we have succeeded in making computer programs reason about the world, we will be able to reformulate epistemology as a branch of applied mathematics no more mysterious or controversial than physics.

On re-reading my paper I can't see how Prof. Bar-Hillel could see in it a proposal to specify a computer programme carelessly. Since other people have proposed this as a device for achieving "creativity", I can only conclude that he had some other paper in mind.

In his criticism of my use of the symbol "at", Prof. Bar-Hillel seems to have misunderstood the intent of the example. First of all, I was not trying to formalize the sentence form, A is at B as it is used in English. "*at*" merely was intended to serve as a convenient mnemonic for the relation between a place and a subplace. Second I was not proposing a practical problem for the program to solve but rather an example intended to allow us to think about the kinds of reasoning involved and how a machine may be made to perform them.

Prof. Bar-Hillel's major point concerns my statement that the premises listed could be assumed to be in memory. The intention of this statement is to explain why I have not included formalizations of statements like, "it is possible to drive from my home to the airport" among my premises. If there were n known places in the country there would be $n (n - 1) / 2$ such sentences and, since we are quite sure that we do not have each of them in our memories, it would be cheating to allow the machine to start with them.

The rest of Prof. Bar-Hillel's criticisms concern ways in which the model mentioned does not reflect the real world; I have already explained that this was not my intention. He is certainly right that the complexity of the model will have to be increased for it to deal with practical problems. What we disagree on is my contention that the conceptual difficulties arise at the present level of complexity and that solving them will allow us to increase the complexity of the model easily.

With regard to the discussion between Prof. Bar-Hillel and Oliver Selfridge—The logic is intended to be faultless although its premises cannot be guaranteed. The intended conclusion is ""*do(go(desk, car, walking))*" not, of course, "*at(I, airport)*". The model oversimplifies but is not intended to oversimplify to the extent of allowing one to deduce one's way to the airport.

Dr. Payne's summary of formal logic does not seem to be based on much acquaintance with it and I think he underestimates the possibilities of applying it to making machines behave intelligently.

11.7

Attitudes toward Intelligent Machines

Paul Armer

From *Bionics Symposium: Living Prototypes—the Key to New Technology, 13–14–15 September 1960* (Wright-Patterson Air Force Base, 1961), pp. 13–39.

INTRODUCTORY NOTE TO READING 11.7

This paper by Paul Armer of the Rand Corporation summarizes the state of research in artificial intelligence in 1961. Delivered at the U. S. government sponsored first symposium on bionics—the application of electronics to biological topics such as artificial limbs or artificial intelligence—Armer's paper is also notable as a reflection of the influence of the cold war on scientific research in the United States. Paul Armer joined Project RAND in 1947 as a mathematician and desk calculator operator when it was still a subsidiary of Douglas Aircraft Corporation. In 1948 Rand incorporated as a non-profit organization, and four years later Armer became head of the Computer Sciences Department at the Rand Corporation. In 1970 Armer left Rand to direct the Stanford University Computation Center. After that he held various positions at Harvard University and at The Center for Advanced Study in the Behavioral Sciences, headed the Charles Babbage Institute Center for the History of Information Technology in Minneapolis, Minnesota, and presided over the American Federation of Information Processing Societies.[JMN]

"A bird is an instrument working according to
mathematical law, which instrument it is
within the capacity of man to reproduce with
all its movements"

—Leonardo da Vinci (1452–1519)

In this paper, I will attempt to analyze some of the attitudes and arguments which have been expressed in dealing with questions like "Can machines think?" or "Can machines exhibit intelligence?" I do so with a single purpose—a hope to improve the climate which surrounds research in the field of machine or artificial intelligence. For those of you who would answer such questions negatively, my goal is *not* to convince you that you are wrong and the positivists are right but merely to attempt to show that most of the disagreement is a matter of semantics. (I will attempt to refute some of the negative arguments.) I do hope to convince those negativists, who argue that research on artificial intelligence is wrong, that they should be tolerant of such research. Those of you who would answer such questions affirmatively need no convincing, but if you share my views concerning the importance of research in this field, then I believe we can profitably spend some time discussing these attitudes, for the negativistic attitudes existent today are inhibiting such research [1].

HISTORY

Before examining the substance of these arguments and attitudes, a look at some of the history of this discussion is in order, for the question of machines exhibiting intelligence is one which has been around for a long time.

Samuel Butler (1835–1902) dealt with the question in *Erewhon* and *Erewhon Revisited* [2], wherein a civil war takes place between the "machinists" and the "anti-machinists." (Incidentally, victory went to the "anti-machinists.") Butler stated "There is no security against the ultimate development of mechanical consciousness in the fact of machines' possessing little consciousness now" and speculated that the time might come when "man shall become to the machines what the horse and dog are to us." Discussion of the question apparently took place in Babbage's time (1792–1871), for the Countess of Lovelace commented on it, negatively, in her writings of Babbage's efforts [3]. The topic came into prominence in the late 1940's when Babbage's dreams became a reality with the completion of the first large digital computers. When the popular press applied the term "giant brains" to these machines, computer builders and users, myself among them, immediately arose, almost to the man, to the defense of the human intellect. We hastened to proclaim that computers did not "think"; they only did arithmetic quite rapidly. Discussion of this question died down (but not out) in the early and mid 1950's but has come back in the last several years stronger than ever before. In fact, it has recently invaded the pages of *Science* [1, 4, 5].

THE NEGATIVE ARGUMENTS

An examination of the arguments advanced by the negativists reveals that many of them are not arguments at all but only statements. Many just dismiss the notion out of hand, saying things like, "Let's settle this once and for all, machines cannot think!" or "A computer is not a giant brain, in spite of what some of the Sunday supplements and science fiction writers would have you believe. It is a remarkably fast and phenomenally accurate moron." [6]

Others have advanced arguments which turn out to be fallacious. Many are of the type "machines will never be able to do this, because they have (or lack) such and such a property." Falsity creeps in from a variety of sources. The attribution of specific properties (or lack thereof) may be in error or it may not logically follow that the presence (or absence) of the specific properties implies that the machine will not be able to do what the arguer states it will never be able to do. Or it may be that the negativist has erroneously assumed that such properties are invariant. Let me give you some examples along these lines.

"The Manchester machine which was set to
solve chess problems presumably proceeded by

this method, namely by reviewing all the possible consequences of all possible moves. This, incidentally, reveals all the strength and weakness of the mechanism. It can review far more numerous possibilities in a given time than can a human player, but it has to review all possibilities. The human player can view the board as a whole and intuitively reject a number of possibilities. The machine cannot do either of these." [7]

The statements about machine behavior in the above are just not true. While it is true that some of the early approaches to chess-playing machines were of the nature of attempting to review *all* possibilities in limited depth [8], this is not the only way in which the problem can be approached. The chess-playing routine of Newell, Shaw, and Simon[9] does *not* examine all possibilities. And those which it does consider it examines in varying detail. The routine rejects moves which appear to be worthless; it selects moves which appear to be good ones and examines them in depth to ascertain that they are indeed good. The earlier routine developed by this same team to prove theorems in logic [10] did not examine all possible proofs — to do so with today's computers would literally take eons of time. Rather, it searched through the maze of possible proofs for ones which looked promising and investigated them. It relied on knowing what approaches had worked before.

An example of an erroneous assumption that machine properties are invariant occurs in an article by John H. Troll:

"The human memory is a filing system that has a far greater capacity than that of the largest thinking machine built. A mechanical brain that had as many tubes or relays as the human brain has nerve cells (some ten billion) would not fit into the Empire State Building, and would require the entire output of Niagara Falls to supply the power and the Niagara River to cool it. Moreover, such a computer could operate but a fraction of a second at a time before several thousand of its tubes would fail and have to be replaced." [11]

His point is tied to the vacuum tube (the article was written in 1954) and has therefore already been weakened by the appearance of the transistor, which requires less space and power and is considerably more reliable than the vacuum tube. An offsetting development is that Troll's estimate of the number of nerve cells is undoubtedly too low. However, on the horizon are techniques involving the use of evaporated films where the details of the machine would not be visible under an optical microscope [12]. It seems reasonable to expect that it will be possible with these techniques to house in one cubic foot of space the same number of logical elements as exist in the human brain. Power requirements will be trivial.

Other negative arguments seem to be semantic in nature. I will not deal with them explicitly but rather implicitly in the following discussion.

THE POSITIVISTS AND A CONCEPT ABOUT THINKING

Of course, there have been many positivists, notably John von Neumann and Norbert Wiener. A. M. Turing was one of the first to expound at length on the question of machines thinking, in an erudite article published in 1950 [13]. Although he discusses the basic question of whether machines can become capable of thinking, he recognizes the difficulty of defining properly the words "machine" and "thinking." To circumvent this problem, he examines instead the question of a game wherein an interrogator, who can communicate with a human and a machine via a teletype but does not know which is which, is to decide which is the machine. Reading of this paper is a must for anyone interested in machine intelligence. Like Turing, I have also avoided defining the word "think." And although I will not attempt to do so explicitly, I would like to advance a concept about thinking which I hope will help resolve some of the semantic difficulties associated with examining the question "Can machines think?" This concept is that thinking is a continuum; an *n*-dimensional continuum. This concept is certainly not new, for it has existed since man first compared his mental abilities with another man and it is implicit in all of the positive arguments on machine intelligence. Psychologists long ago developed "intelligence quotient" as a yardstick in this continuum and their concept of "factors" is indicative of the *n*-dimensionality of the continuum of intelligence. The use of the one-dimensional "I.Q." is obviously an over-simplification of reality. Although this concept is not new, I do not know of an instance in which it has been explicitly stated in the context of machine intelligence. However, I would be surprised if it has not.

Let me draw an analogy with the continuum of the ability to transport. With respect to speed in transporting people from New York to Los Angeles, the jet airplane of today outshines all other existing transportation vehicles. But it does not compare favorably, costwise, with ships for transporting newsprint from British Columbia to California. It cannot transport people from one lake to another. A Cadillac may be the most comfortable vehicle to transport people short distances over a good network of roads, but is hardly a substitute for the jeep in the environment of ground warfare—the jeep's forte is versatility and flexibility. In this dimension in the continuum of the ability to transport, man outshines the jeep, for man can go where jeeps cannot, just as the jeep can go where Cadillacs cannot.

Similarly, we can make comparisons between men and machines in the continuum of thinking. If you object to the use of the word thinking, we can drop it in favor of "information processing," or some similar term. But I believe you must admit to the existence of some continuum of behavior in which men and machines coexist.

And with respect to some of the dimensions, the machine outperforms man; e.g., it can do arithmetic much more rapidly and reliably. In the context of considering the behavior of men and machines in this way, an argument that a machine cannot play chess because "it could only operate on standard-size pieces and could not recognize as chessman the innumerable pieces of different design which the human player recognizes and moves around quite simply" [5] is like

saying that the Wright brothers' airplane could not fly because it could not fly non-stop from Los Angeles to New York nor could it land in a tree like a bird. Why must the test of intelligence be that the machine achieve identically the same point in the continuum as man? Is the test of flying the achievement of the same point in the continuum of transportation as that reached by a bird?

Many of the negativists seem to say that the only evidence of machine intelligence they will accept is an achievement in our continuum seldom achieved by man. For example, they belittle efforts at musical composition by machine because the present output compares miserably with that of Mozart or Chopin. How many *men* can produce music that compares favorably? The ultimate argument of this kind occurred at a recent meeting in England during which a discussant stated that he would not accept the fact that machines could think until one proved the famous conjecture of Fermat, better known as Fermat's last theorem. From his logic one can also conclude that, to this date, no man has been capable of thinking, since the theorem remains unproven. Some negativists want to include in their definition of intelligent behavior the requirement that it be carried out by a living organism. If defined in this way, I must admit that machines do not behave intelligently. This argument seems to me to be centered on semantics. For there does still exist machine behavior which can be compared with human behavior and to conclude that research on the simulation of such human behavior with a machine is wrong is like concluding that research on the simulation of the human heart with an artificial heart is wrong because the artificial organ is not a living one.

Personally, my definition of thinking is such that I admit that machines do think and exhibit intelligent behavior. When a child adds two and two, we usually admit that it is intelligent behavior, particularly when it is our own child. To those of you who would argue that the machine does not know or understand what it is doing, I will use the example of the young child parroting nursery rhymes. Similarly, when an engineer, on the basis of education and experience, designs an electric motor, we ordinarily describe his behavior as intelligent. When machines do a similar job, is it not intelligent? Of course, the machine's capability is very limited compared to the engineer who can do many things besides design motors within a limited framework. Similarly, jeeps cannot scale Mt. Everest and DC-8's cannot land in trees.

The mounting list of tasks which can now be carried out on a computer but which we normally consider requiring intelligence when performed by humans, includes such things as:

Proving theorems in logic and plane geometry [10, 14]

Playing checkers and chess [15, 9]

Assembly line balancing [16]

Composing music [17]

Designing motors [18]

Recognition of manual Morse Code [19]

The collection of capabilities which have been ascribed solely to humans in the past is being slowly chipped away by the application of computers. Time and space precludes my going further into the evidence for machine intelligence; this is well covered in the articles previously cited and in other papers [20, 21, 22]. Such evidence is of course the basis for much of the arguments advanced by the positivists.

To prove that machines *today* do *not* exhibit intelligence it is only necessary to define a lower bound, in our much discussed continuum, which is above the behavior exhibited by the machines of today and then say that behavior above that bound is intelligent and below it is not intelligent. I submit that many of the negativists who use this gambit have been redefining this lower bound so that it is continually above what machines can do today. They may not do so consciously, for, as Marvin Minsky put it so well, "Intelligence is a chimera. You regard an action as intelligent until you understand it. In explaining, you explain away. Conversely, provided you do not understand, it is presumably intelligent." [23] We have all noticed that a skill which seems highly intelligent in others

becomes much less impressive to us when we acquire that skill ourselves. It would be useful to have at hand some milestones for the future, to assign a metric to Minsky's chimera. Turing supplied one such milestone [13] but additional ones are needed. To this end we need a clearly defined task which is at present the exclusive domain of humans (and therefore incontestably "thinking") but which we can hope will eventually yield to accomplishment by machines.

Even if you will admit that both men and machines exhibit intelligence, there still remains the question "is there a boundary in our continuum above which machines can never go?" Personally, I am not prepared to argue either way. Those of you who believe in the immortality of man and the existence of a supreme being, are undoubtedly of a mind that an upper bound for machines must exist. But I strongly submit that with respect to the question of the importance of research on pushing machines further out into the continuum, it is not pertinent whether an upper bound exists or not. If one argues that such a bound does exist, then where it lies is, of course, of some pertinency. But I argue that we have little evidence as to the location of such a bound. It is on the question of the location of this upper bound that I ask for an open mind from those of you who contend that machines will never exhibit intelligence. It is very easy to place that boundary much too low. I am reminded that there were some who objected to further development of the automobile because man was physiologically incapable of tolerating speeds in excess of 15 miles per hour.

Troll, mentioned earlier with regard to a statement about the requirement for the Empire State Building to house ten billion tubes [11], was quite willing to accept the notion that machines can think. But in his article he drew an upper bound, whose location was based on the fallacious assumption that machine properties (size, power, cooling, and reliability) were invariant. Troll apparently did not conceive of the time when we might be able to construct a machine, with the same number of elements as the brain, which was quite small, very reliable and had low power requirements.

Of course, large numbers of elements, high reliability and low power requirements are not enough. Organization of the elements then becomes paramount. But is it not conceivable that we might learn how to organize these elements (or, in the extreme, learn how to have them organize themselves) in such a way that we obtain a machine much further out in the intelligence continuum than machines are today (albeit still below the ultimate boundary)? Might not such a machine be of tremendous value? Consider that today's machines exceed the human brain in some dimensions (e.g., arithmetic speed) and consequently are today of considerable value to man.

Let me illustrate my point with the following incident. We have all had the experience of trying to recall the name of a person we've once met. On a particular occasion Dr. Willis Ware and I were both trying to recall an individual's name. We recounted to one another his physical characteristics, where he worked, what he did, etc. But his name eluded us. After some time, I turned to Dr. Ware and said "His name begins with a 'Z'." At which point Dr. Ware snapped his fingers and said, "That's it, it's Frizell!" The value of machines with the information processing capability exemplified here would obviously be of tremendous value to the fields of information retrieval, military intelligence, etc. Is it not conceivable that we might one day understand the logical processes which went on in Dr. Ware's head and therefore be able to mechanize them on a machine?

We obviously will not achieve such a machine unless somebody believes that it is conceivable and tries to do it. One does not have to believe that the boundary is non-existent in order to try — only that the boundary is much further out than the position occupied by machines today. I cannot rigorously show that the boundary is "way out" but neither have I seen a proof that it is not.

At this point, I would like to paraphrase the quotation of da Vinci's, with which this paper was begun, and also, with the benefit of hindsight, expand on it somewhat. Thus, he might have said:

"When man understands the natural laws which govern the flight of a bird, man will be able to build a flying machine."

Man wasted a good deal of time and effort trying to build a flying machine that flapped its wings like a bird but the important point is that it was the understanding of the law of aerodynamic lift (even though the understanding was imperfect at first) over an airfoil which eventually enabled man to build a flying machine.

There are many facets to this analogy; flight, too, is a continuum; some once thought that there was a boundary (the speed of sound) beyond which flight was impossible, etc. I hope that the more important aspects of the analogy need not be stated explicitly.

RUSSIAN ATTITUDES

Our examination to date has been Western in origin; it might be interesting to look at Soviet attitudes toward artificial intelligence. As one might suspect, Soviet attitudes toward the question of machine intelligence have been quite similar to Western ones. Positivists and negativists exist and they each advance the same sort of arguments as their Western counterparts. For example, there are negativists who do not advance arguments but merely statements. Academician S. A. Lebedev, head of the Institute of Precise Mechanics and Computational Techniques and host to the U. S. exchange delegation in computers (of which I was a member; visiting the USSR the last two weeks of May, 1959) on two occasions dismissed my question concerning his attitude toward intelligent machines with "Machines can do no more than they are instructed to do." He seemed to feel that this settled the issue.

Their literature is filled with discussion of the topic and it was obvious from the questions we received from the Russians about Western attitudes that it is a hotly debated issue. In the USSR, research on artificial intelligence is a part of cybernetics, the term coined by Wiener [24] and now a household word in the Soviet Union. Cybernetics is also used as an umbrella for research in automatic control, automation, computers, programming, information retrieval, language translation, etc. It is universally recognized as an area related to both men and machines and the requirement for an interdisciplinary (engineering, mathematics, computing, biology, psychology, physiology, physics, chemistry, linguistics, etc.) approach to such research is also recognized.

As in the West, the use of the term "giant brains" in the late 1940's resulted in a massive revulsion among the Soviet scientific community and an almost universal rush to the defense of the human mind. The degree of the revulsion was such that several Soviet writers have blamed it for the fact that Russia presently lags the U.S. in the digital computer field [25]. Of course, we are blamed for having used the term "giant brains" and causing them to lag behind. One finds frequent references in the Russian literature to the existence of a negative or nihilistic attitude towards cybernetics and its having persisted for a period of about ten years.

Soviet literature on cybernetics frequently gives credit to Wiener, von Neumann, and other Westerners for pioneering the field. It also contains many references to the work of Pavlov and mixes in much political discussion of communism vs. capitalism, and even of Marx and Lenin. For example, we have:

"Finally, it is particularly necessary to emphasize the importance of the work of Lenin who in elaborating on the ideas of Marx and Engels, developed a materialistic theory of consciousness as a reflection of activity. Attention should also be given to the Lenistic statement of the fact that non-living matter may also possess this property of reflection." [26].

There are some strong positivists in the USSR. For example, we have I. A. Poletayev's statement "nothing except prejudice and superstition allow one to deny with assurance today the possibility that the machine will pass in the end, that limit beyond which consciousness begins." [27] Other strong positivists include S. L. Sobolev (an Academician and a well-known mathematician) and A. A. Lyapunov[28]. We also find

"...Thus, the perfecting of computer machines involuntarily leads us to the need to create a model of the brain. . . . Also, one of the most effective methods of studying intracerebral processes involve experiments carried out on electrical models of the brain.

"But cybernetics has its critics too. These are skeptics. One can find them among scientists and among ordinary citizens, at times also among administrative personnel. These skeptics reject this branch of science and deny it the right of existence. . . . In rejecting this science, they generally state that the very thought of comparing a machine to a human being is an insult.

"And so let us visualize tomorrow's computing machine. It is an invincible chess champion, an alert operator of a chemical combine. It accurately translates fiction from one language into any other; to accomplish this, an intermediary international language will probably be created. The machine writes verses which can already be considered acceptable.

"It can even compose music; let it, for example, listen to something by Chopin and it will create a similar melody—not exactly alike— but if listened to, indistinguishable from. professional music. But this is not all! When carried away, man thinks: 'What if we can make a machine that will reproduce itself?'" [29].

The position now taken by most Soviet writers is positive, although the majority appear, recognizing the continuum, to argue that there does exist an upper bound above which machines cannot go, while admitting to the indeterminacy of the location of that bound.

For example

"As a result we arrive at the conclusion that a machine can perform all the intellectual human functions which can be formalized. . . But what can be formalized? . . . Upon brief reflection we conclude that it is impossible in principle to answer this question." [30]

One point about Soviet attitudes I believe to be most pertinent. I know of no instance in recent years in which the simulation or modelling of human mental activity is considered to be anything but a very legitimate and most interesting area of scientific research. I do not doubt the existence of feelings to the contrary, but they do not seem to be getting into their scientific literature. Most of the negativists seem to be worked up about the "superhuman" aspects of the discussion.

ATTITUDES TOWARD RESEARCH

It is my belief that *proof* that a research goal is attainable should not be a prerequisite to doing research toward that goal. Yet this seems to be the attitude of many negativists toward research in the artificial intelligence area. As I have said, while I cannot rigorously show that the boundary in our continuum, above which machines cannot operate, is "way out," there is no evidence as to its precise location. And as long as its location is not known—and even its very existence uncertain—then research aimed at pushing machines further out into the continuum would seem to be quite legitimate.

RIVALRY BETWEEN MAN AND MACHINES

It is my belief that there is a strong psychological factor in the attitude of many negativists. I'm sure that it was a major factor in my being a negativist ten years ago. To concede that machines can exhibit intelligence is to admit that man has a rival in an area previously held to be within the sole province of man. Troll, in his article mentioned earlier [11] discusses this rivalry at some length. To illustrate this point, let me quote from a letter recently received at RAND:

> ". . . semantics may have a lot to do with the degree of enthusiasm for supporting research in this area [artificial intelligence]. Subjectively, the terms 'intelligent machine' or 'thinking machine' disturb me and even seem a bit threatening: I am a human being, and therefore 'intelligent' and these inhuman devices are going to compete with me and may even beat

me out. On the other hand, if the very same black boxes were labelled 'problem solver,' or even 'adaptive problem solver,' they would seem much more friendly, capable of helping me in the most effective way to do things that I want to do better, but, best of all, I'd still be the boss. This observation is wholly subjective and emotional . . ."

Let me also give you a quotation from a negativist attempting to explain the psychology of the positivists.

> "The use of these expressions [thinking machines and mechanical brains], which imply that such machines in some way possess the power of reasoning, is symptomatic of the existence of a widespread, though unacknowledged, desire to believe that a machine can be something more than a machine." [31]

The answer to the question of why some negativists feel the way they do must be related to what might be called the "sins of the positivists." Exaggerated claims of accomplishments, particularly from the publicity departments of computer manufacturers, have resulted in such a strong reaction within the scientific community that many swing too far in the opposite direction.

INTELLIGENT MACHINES AND TODAY'S DIGITAL COMPUTER

An aspect of a common attitude toward today's computers is that such machines are strictly arithmetic devices. While it is true that machines were first built in order to carry out repetitive arithmetic operations, they are capable of other non-numeric tasks. The essence of the computer is the manipulation of symbols—it is only a historical accident that the first application involved numeric symbols. This incorrect notion that the computer is a numeric device results in the inability of many to conceive of such a device exhibiting intelligent behavior since this would require that the process be reduced to a numerical one. *Please do not misconstrue my remarks to indicate that I equate the human brain with a digital computer as we know it today.* While I do believe that today's digital computers can exhibit intelligent behavior, I do not hold that the intelligent machines of the 1970's will necessarily resemble today's machines, either functionally or physically. In particular, in my desire to see machines pushed further out in the continuum of intelligence, my interests in the dimension of speed are very minor; the organizational aspects are obviously much more important. Likewise, I hold no brief for the strictly digital approach; a combination of analog and digital equipment may prove to be better. I do not mean to disown the digital computer, for, as I will discuss later, it will be a most important tool in the endeavor to push out in our continuum.

THE IMPORTANCE OF RESEARCH IN ARTIFICIAL INTELLIGENCE

I indicated in my introduction that I felt that research aimed at pushing machines further out into the continuum of intelligence was very important. Today's computers are helping to advance the frontiers of man's knowledge in many fields, for computers pervade almost all scientific disciplines. (The fact that they pervade the field of research on artificial intelligent machines means that such research will feed on itself). The use of computers in research has been a key factor in the explosion of knowledge that we have witnessed in the last decade. Their contribution to date has stemmed largely from their speed in doing arithmetic and the reliability with which they do it. As we move out in the continuum of possibilities, new dimensions and contributions will become important. For example, a machine which duplicates (or comes close to) the process inherent in Willis Ware's output of "Frizell" but which exceeds Dr. Ware in speed, reliability and memory capacity may be crucial to perpetuate the present rate of growth of scientific knowledge; without it, scientists may be inundated with research results which they cannot absorb. Even today, many scientists assert that it is often easier to redo research than to determine where it was done before and where the results were recorded. Obviously

then, a "Ware-Frizell" machine would be of tremendous importance to all technological disciplines.

The large amount of money being spent for machines today is evidence of the value we place on the computers' abilities along the dimensions of speed and reliability. If the machine's capabilities can be extended in additional dimensions, will it not be of great importance? Suppose that the boundary beyond which machines cannot go lies fairly close to the human brain in the dimension related to the sophistication of the information processing techniques used. Since we know that we can exceed the human in speed and reliability and probably in amount of memory, such a machine would approach the status of being "super-human." Of course, I only speculate; the boundary may be much lower.

I hope it is obvious that the importance of research on intelligent machines is not dependent on having as a goal the achievement of a "super-human" machine. If you will admit that the limit of man's capability to produce a thinking machine is very far out in our oft-mentioned continuum, then I feel you must admit that research aimed at getting us out there is extremely important.

I have been examining the question of the technological importance of research in artificial intelligence in the context of advancing the frontiers of knowledge for the sake of technological and scientific advancement. In such a context, there is little cause for any concern or action on the part of anyone; progress in the field is being made at a fairly rapid pace in this country. However, in the real world, in which we are engaged in a technological race with the USSR, action becomes important, particularly since, in my opinion, the Russians appear to be putting much more emphasis on research in artificial intelligence than we are. Even if the Russians were not competing in this particular event of the "technological Olympics," it is an event well worth the running.

APPROACHES TO THE PROBLEM OF BUILDING AN INTELLIGENT MACHINE

I think that I can best communicate what I want to say on this topic by the use of an analogy. Suppose that we are given a device which we know exhibits intelligent behavior, because we have observed it in action. We would like to build a machine which approaches it in capability, or better yet, exceeds it. We bring in a group of men to study the basic components of the device. These men study the components, trying to understand how they work. The men apply pulses to subsets of the leads and observe what each component does; they try to understand why the device behaves the way it does in terms of basic physics and chemistry. They also seek to learn how these components function in sub-assemblies.

Meanwhile, we have brought in a second group of men. They approach the problem from the point of view that the device is a "black box" which they are not able to open. They observe that some of the appendages of the device are obviously input devices and others output devices. They observe the device in operation and attempt to theorize how it works. They proceed on the basis that it will not be necessary that the machine they are to construct have the same basic components as exist in the device under study. They believe that if they can understand the logical operation of the existing device, they can duplicate its logic in their own machine, using components they understand and can make.

This group makes conjectures about the logical construction of the device and tries these conjectures out on a computer which they have at hand. These theories are very crude at first and do not mirror the behavior of the "black box" very well, but over time the resemblance improves.

Because we learned a lesson from the effort spent on attempting to build a flying machine that flapped its wings, we set a third group to work studying "intelligence and information processing" per se and building up a science in the area. There is much common ground among all three groups and they keep each other posted on results to date. Further, they all use computers to aid them in their research. All combine their know-how along the way to build better computers (low I.Q. intelligent machines) on which to try out their conjectures. Eventually, the three groups "come together in the middle" and build a machine which is almost as capable as our model. They then turn to the task of building an even better one.

In the real life situation of studying the human brain, the first group, studying components and assemblies thereof, is represented by physiological work. The efforts analogous to the "black box" and "per se" groups are self-evident. This analogy represents, I believe, a plausible scenario for the way things might go in trying to understand the human mind.

WHERE DO THE RUSSIANS STAND?

Earlier I said that I was concerned because I felt that the Russians were putting more emphasis on research in artificial intelligence than we are. Allow me to expand on this topic.

First of all, let us look at what they are doing in some of the disciplines related to such research: computing devices, mathematics, psychology, and physiology. With respect to computers, I can speak with some first-hand knowledge, for, as mentioned earlier, I spent two weeks last year visiting Soviet computer installations. In my opinion, they are somewhat behind us in the actual construction of machines, particularly with respect to input/output equipment and to numbers of machines [32]. However, there is nothing fundamental lacking in their state of the art. There is some indication that they may be having some difficulty in building reliable transistors. The quantity of machines is not as important to research as an offhand comparison of numbers of machines might indicate, since none of their machines is devoted to such things as social security records, subscription fulfillment, or airline reservations. In assessing a comparison of this kind, one always wonders how much of the iceberg we did not see. When visiting the IBM plant in California last summer, Khrushchev said about computers, ". . . for the time being we're keeping them a secret."

The Russians started work on computers after we did but certainly have narrowed the gap. Further, they are giving high priority to the computing field. In their recent announcement concerning the decentralization of responsibility for research, an exception was made for computers, along with fusion, space activities, high temperature metallurgical research and certain areas of chemistry; these remained centralized under the cognizance of the Academy of Sciences. Of course, the Russians are interested in spurring the computer field for reasons other than intelligent machine research. My point is that there is no reason to believe that future Russian research on intelligent machines need be hampered by the computer tools available to them, although machine time is in short supply today.

In mathematics the Russians have had an outstanding reputation for many decades. In computer mathematics I have no doubts that, in general, they excel the West. One of the things which impressed our delegation, and others before us [33], was the number of outstanding mathematicians now working in the computer field. Unfortunately, many of our mathematicians view computers as a glorified slide rule of interest only to engineers or as an expensive sorting device of interest to businesses with clerical problems.

With respect to psychology and physiology, I am ill qualified to comment. Most comparisons I have heard or read fail to take a position on who is ahead. Of course, these fields are also n-dimensional and a one-dimensional statement about who is ahead is difficult or impossible. The question of what percentage of the iceberg is visible is also most pertinent. The one article I've read which stated that the U.S. was behind was written by Gregory Razran and appeared in *Science* [34]. His article indicated that he was much concerned about how we stand because of the possibilities of real breakthroughs in the scientific control of human thought and action. He says,

". . . The need to catch on, catch up, and surpass in vital areas of psychophysiology and the control of men may not be very different from the related requisite in physics and the control of missiles."

Of course, I cannot evaluate his assessment of Russian efforts in these fields nor the connection between psychophysiology and the control of human thought and action, but if Razran's evaluation of the state of U.S. knowledge in psychophysiology, vis-a-vis the S.U., is correct, then I am concerned. Much of the research he reports is of the component type as discussed in my analogy related to approaches to research

on intelligent machines. Change the words "the control of men" in his statement to "the construction of intelligent machines" and it gets my endorsement.

RUSSIAN EMPHASIS ON ARTIFICIAL INTELLIGENCE RESEARCH

I went to the Soviet Union convinced that they were putting a good deal of emphasis on research in artificial intelligence. And I went looking for further evidence—possibly what I was looking for influenced what I thought I found. I also want to emphasize that I was impressed, not by any substantive results, but by their apparent conviction that this was an important research area.

In one institute, in response to my question about the problem of simulating the brain with a computer, I was told that "It is considered *the* number one problem." The emphasis on "the" was the speaker's; the statement was made in English.

At another institute, when Professor L. I. Gutenmacher, head of the Laboratory for Electrical Modeling, told us that the charter of his laboratory was the modeling of human mental processes, I asked him if he had any difficulty getting financial support for such exotic research. His response was "No, not at all; the President of the Academy of Sciences is convinced that this is an important field for research." There is ample evidence that he is being given a lot of support. I was told that his laboratory, formerly and still ostensibly a part of the Institute of Information Sciences, had all the status of an Institute, being separately funded and reporting directly to the Presidium of the Academy of Sciences. Gutenmacher's laboratory is apparently responsible for mechanizing the functions of the Institute of Information Sciences, which is a large, centralized, in-being information retrieval system for scientific information from all over the world.

Despite much effort, our delegation was unable to visit Gutenmacher's laboratory. To my knowledge, no Westerner has done so; in fact none had even met Gutenmacher until our delegation did so. Some in the U.S. have concluded from this denial of entry that there was nothing to be shown. On the other hand, its work may be classified, as Khrushchev indicated. But whether or not they are accomplishing anything is not pertinent to the point that the President of the Soviet Academy of Sciences, a man with much power and resources, believes that modeling human mental activities is possible, that he recognizes the importance of research in this field and he is devoting a lot of resources to it.

What are some of the other indications about Soviet attitudes toward research on intelligent machines? Cybernetics is a household word in Russia. Much is being written on the subject, in journals and in the popular press. There appears to be an effort in the popular writings to legitimatize such research as being in harmony with communism. For example, recall my earlier quote about Lenin [26].

With respect to professional writing, a journal entitled "Problems of Cybernetics" was started in 1958, four hard cover volumes having appeared to date [35]. Since 1955, seminars on cybernetics have been held a the University of Moscow, and on a weekly schedule in 1956. These seminars are aimed at bringing together scientists from the various disciplines involved. Similarly, the editors of *Problems of Cybernetics* state that their aim "is the unification of the scientific interests of those working in different fields of science concerned with cybernetics." There seems to be a widespread recognition of the necessity for an interdisciplinary approach to problems of cybernetics. Article after article appeals for personnel from the various disciplines to get together. How much effect these appeals and seminars are having is unknown. We were told that some 500 physicists had been transferred to the biological sciences. We talked with I. M. Gelfand, a world famous mathematician now working in the physiological field. He began studying the brain but had switched to the heart, which he believes to be much simpler. With the knowledge gained from studying the heart, he will return to the study of the brain. We were also told that other mathematicians were working on psychological and physiological problems. With respect to physiological research, I find the following of interest:

"Essentially, we [the Western World] have not found the physiochemical principles of neural

activity, whereas the Russians have not seriously sought them. However, the current 7-year plan for physiology as presented in a recent editorial by D. A. Biriukev in the *Sechenov Physiological Journal of the USSR* calls for precisely this goal."[36]

Within the Soviet Academy of Sciences, there exists a "Scientific Council on Cybernetics." This council is headed by A. I. Berg and apparently reports directly to the Presidium of the Academy [37]. To my knowledge, there is no evidence of any effect that this Council may be having in coordinating, controlling, or encouraging research in cybernetics, particularly outside of Moscow where individual researchers appear to be entirely on their own with little communication with other such researches and with only meager support. However, one does occasionally encounter references to formation of new groups and laboratories for such work. And a recent visitor to the USSR reports that Soviet physiologists appear to be under pressure to produce explanations for human behavior which can be incorporated into machines. He further reports that their work appears to be under security wraps.

I would like to close this topic with a quotation which appeared in the February 1959 issue of *Fortune*. Frank Pace, Jr., President of General Dynamics Corporation, warning us not to overlook nor be surprised by Russia's capacity to concentrate in specific areas, said:

"If the area has real military or psychological value to them, they'll put massive concentration on it, and achieve results all out of proportion to the general level of their technical ability."

TIMING

Before closing, I'd like to comment on the question "when?" It is one thing to say that it is possible to push machine capabilities way out in the continuum of intelligence, but another to say when. It was over four hundred years from da Vinci to the Wright brothers. But the sands of time in the scientific world have been flowing much more rapidly of late. Advances now made in a decade compare with earlier steps which took a century. Few would have believed in 1950 that man would hit the moon with a rocket before the decade ended. Gutenmacher, when told recently of the Simon and Newell prediction that a machine would be chess champion within ten years [38] said that he thought the prediction conservative; it would happen sooner.

SUMMARY

In summary, I hope that the definition of research on artificial intelligence as an effort to push machines further out in the continuum of intelligence behavior will reduce some of the semantic difficulties surrounding discussions of such research. I feel that such research is very important to our country and that we must expand our efforts therein. To do so implies that more researchers are needed; researchers from the related disciplines. The success of our efforts will depend on how well we do in bringing the various disciplines together and on how many well qualified scientists are attracted to this research area.

ACKNOWLEDGMENTS AND APOLOGIES

I would like to acknowledge many long discussions of this topic with W. H. Ware, E. A. Feigenbaum, F. J. Gruenberger, A. Newell, J. C. Shaw, and H. A. Simon and the influence of the research efforts of the latter three on my thinking. In this paper I have quoted many people. In so doing I have strived to avoid quoting out of context. However, one runs the risk of so doing when only a portion of a man's statement is repeated. If I have misrepresented the intended meaning of anyone in this way, it has been accidental.

REFERENCES

1. MacGowan, R. A., Letter to the Editor, *Science,* July 22, 1960.

2. Butler, Samuel, *Erewhon and Erewhon Revisited,* Modern Library No.136, Random House, New York, 1933.

3. Bowden, B. V. (Editor), *Faster Than Thought,* Pitman, London, 1953.

4. Wiener, Norbert, "Some Moral and Technical Consequences of Automation," *Science,* May 6, 1960.

5. Taube, Mortimer, Letter to the Editor, *Science,* August 26, 1960.

6. Andree, R. V., *Programming the IBM 650 Magnetic Drum Computer and Data Processing Machine,* Holt, 1958.

7. Hugh-Jones, E. M., "Automation Today," *Automation in Theory and Practice,* Oxford, 1956.

8. Kister, J., P. Stein, S. Ulam, W. Welden, and M. Wells, "Experiments in Chess," *Journal of the Association for Computing Machinery,* April *1957.*

9. Newell, A., J. C. Shaw, and H. A. Simon, "Chess-Playing Programs and the Problem of Complexity," *IBM Journal of Research and Development,* October 1958.

10. Newell, A., J. C. Shaw, and H. A. Simon, "Empirical Explorations of the Logic Theory Machine," *Proceedings of the Western Joint Computer Conference,* February 1957.

11. Troll, J. H., "The Thinking of Men and Machines," *Atlantic Monthly,* July 1954.

12. Shoulders, K. R., "On Microelectronic Components, Interconnections, and System Fabrication," *Proceedings of the Western Joint Computer Conference,* May 1960.

13. Turing, A. M., "Computing Machinery and Intelligence," *MIND,* October 1950. Also available in *The World of Mathematics* Vol.4, p. 2099.

14. Gelernter, H. L., "Realization of a Geometry Theorem Proving Machine," *Proceedings of the International Conference on Information Processing,* UNESCO, Paris, France, 1960.

15. Samuel, A. L., "Some Studies in Machine Learning Using The Game of Checkers," *IBM Journal of Research and Development,* Vol. 3, No. 3, July 1959.

16. Tonge, Fred, *A Heuristic Program For Assembly Line Balancing,* The RAND Corporation paper P-1993, May 18, 1960.

17. Hiller, L. A., and L. M. Isaacson, *Experimental Music,* McGraw-Hill, 1959.

18. Goodwin, G. L., "Digital Computers Tap Out Designs for Large Motors, Fast," *POWER,* April 1958.

19. Gold, B., "Machine Recognition of Hand Sent Morse Code," *IRE Transactions on Information Theory,* March 1959.

20. Newell, A., J. C. Shaw, and H. A. Simon, *Problem Solving in Humans and Computers,* The RAND Corporation paper P-987, December 7, 1956.

21. Milligan, Margaret, "Machines Are Smarter Than I Am!" *Data Processing Digest,* October, 1959.

22. McCarthy, J., "Programs With Common Sense," *Proceedings of the Symposium on the Mechanization of Thought Processes, NPL, November 1958,* Her Majesty's Stationery Office, 1959.

23. Minsky, M., "Methods of Artificial Intelligence and Heuristic Programming," *Proceedings of the Symposium on the Mechanization of Thought Processes, NPL, November 1958,* Her Majesty's Stationery Office, 1959.

24. Wiener, Norbert, *Cybernetics,* Wiley, 1948.

25. Shaginyan, M., *In The World of Cybernetics,* Joint Publications Research Service report No. 718-D, 1959, U.S. Department of Commerce, Washington 25, D.C.

26. Braynes, S. N. and A. V. Napalkov, *Certain Problems In The Theory Of Self-Organizing Systems,* Joint Publications Research Service report No.2177-N, 1960, U.S. Department of Commerce, Washington 25, D.C.

27. Poletayev, I. A., *Signal,* Soviet Radio, 1958 (cited in Joint Publications Research Service report No.2211-N, 1960).

28. Lyapunov, A. A. and S. L. Sobolev, "Cybernetics and Natural Science," *Problems of Philosophy,* No.5, 1958.

29. Moiseyev, K., *Man and The "Thinking" Machine,* Joint Publications Research Service report No.2200-N, 1960, U.S. Department of Commerce, Washington 25, D.C.

30. Kolman, E., *Cybernetics,* Joint Publications Research Service report No.5002, 1960, U.S. Department of Commerce, Washington 25, D.C.

31. Wilkes, M. V., *Automatic Digital Computers,* Wiley, 1956.

32. Ware, W. H., (Editor), "Soviet Computer Technology—1959," *IRE Transactions on Electronic Computers,* March 1960.

33. Carr, J. W., et al, "A Visit to Computation Centers in The Soviet Union," *Communications of The Association for Computing Machinery,* June 1959.

34. Razran, Gregory, "Soviet Psychology and Psycho-physiology," *Science,* November 14, 1958.

35. Lyapunov, A. A. (Editor) *Problems of Cybernetics* (Translated by M. Nadler, et al), Pergamon Press, London, 1960.

36. Freeman, W. J., "Review of Textbook of Physiology," *Science,* June 17, 1960.

37. Berg, A. I., "Cybernetics and Society," *Economic Gazette,* June 12, 1960. Translation in *The Soviet Review,* International Arts and Sciences Press, New York, 1960.

38. Newell, A., and H. A. Simon, "Heuristic Problem Solving: The Next Advance in Operations Research," *Journal of the Operations Research Society of* America, Vol. 6, No. 1, January-February 1958.

BIBLIOGRAPHY

1. Adey, W. R., "Instrumentation of Nervous System for Studies of Behavior," *American Rocket Society 14th Annual Meeting,* November 1959.

2. Feigenbaum, E. A., *An Information Processing Theory of Verbal Learning,* The RAND Corporation paper P-1817, October 9, 1959.

3. Gutenmacher, L. I., "The Information Machine Problem," *Izvestiia,* April 1, 1959.

4. Heymann, Hans, Jr., *The USSR In The Technological Race,* The RAND Corporation paper P-1754, July 20, 1959.

5. Krieger, F. J., *Future Science and Technology of the USSR,* The RAND Corporation paper P-1647, March 19, 1959.

6. Licklider, J. C. R., "Man-Computer Symbiosis," *IRE Transactions on Human Factors in Electronics,* March 1960.

7. McCulloch, W. S., "Where Is Fancy Bred?," *Bicentennial Conference on Experimental Psychiatry,* University of Pittsburgh, March 1959.

8. Newell, A., J. C. Shaw, and H. A. Simon, "Report on a General Problem-solving Program," *Proceedings of the International Conference on Information Processing, UNESCO,* Paris, France, 1960.

9. Polya, G., *How To Solve It,* Princeton, 1945.

10. Polya, G., *Mathematics and Plausible Reasoning,* Vols. I, II, Princeton, 1954.

11. Sluckin, W., *Minds and Machines,* Penguin Books, 1954.

12. "Symposium: The Design of Machines to Simulate The Behavior of The Human Brain," *IRE Transactions on Electronic Computers,* December 1955.

13. Beer, Stafford, *Cybernetics and Management,* English Universities Press, London, 1957.

14. Taube, Mortimer, "Man-Machine Relationships," *Datamation,* January/February 1959.

15. von Neumann, J., *Brain and Computer,* Yale University Press, 1958.

12

Communication Theory

12.1

A Symbolic Analysis of Relay and Switching Circuits

Claude E. Shannon

INTRODUCTORY NOTE TO READING 12.1

Claude Shannon's master's thesis, of which we reprint the complete published version, has been frequently called the most important master's thesis of the twentieth century with respect to the influence it had on the development of the electronic and computer industries. Shannon obtained B.S. degrees in mathematics and engineering in 1936 from the University of Michigan, and later that year accepted the post of research assistant at MIT's Department of Electrical Engineering, where he began working toward an advanced degree. As an undergraduate he had studied symbolic logic and Boolean algebra. While working with the Bush differential analyzer at MIT, Shannon became interested in the theory and design of complicated relay and switching circuits like the ones used in telephone systems. Shannon submitted this thesis in 1937 at the age of 21, only one year after Turing published his paper "On Computable Numbers" (Reading 7.1). I decided to place Shannon's thesis in this chapter so that it would be next to his equally famous *Mathematical Theory of Communication*, but it might have been just as logical to place it after Turing's paper in Chapter VII, "The Theory of the Universal Machine."

In his thesis Shannon recognized that the true/false values in Boole's two-valued logic were analogous to the open and closed states of electrical circuits. From this it followed that Boolean algebra could be used to describe or to design electrical circuits. Because Boolean algebra makes it possible to devise a procedure or build a device, the state of which can store specific information, once Shannon showed that electrical circuitry can perform logical and mathematical operations, and can also store the result of these operations, the inference could be drawn that it was possible to design calculating machines using electrical switches. When Shannon wrote his thesis he was thinking of electro-mechanical relays used as switches in telephone technology rather than the vacuum tubes that would be used in electronic computers, but of course the same principles apply to both technologies. During the summer of 1937 in which Shannon wrote his thesis, he was working at Bell Labs in New York City. Thus, it may or may not have been coincidental that George Stibitz at Bell Labs began experimenting with relay calculators about the same time that Shannon submitted his dissertation. [JMN]

TEXT OF READING 12.1

I. INTRODUCTION

In the control and protective circuits of complex electrical systems it is frequently necessary to make intricate interconnections of relay contacts and switches. Examples of these circuits occur in automatic telephone exchanges, industrial motor-control equipment, and in almost any circuits designed to perform complex operations automatically. In this paper a mathematical analysis of certain of the properties of such networks will be made. Particular attention will be given to the problem of network synthesis. Given certain characteristics, it is required to find a circuit incorporating these characteristics. The solution of this type of problem is not unique and methods of finding those particular circuits requiring the least number of relay contacts and switch blades will be studied. Methods will also be described for finding any number of circuits equivalent to a given circuit in all operating characteristics. It will be shown that several of the well-known theorems on impedance networks have roughly analogous theorems in relay circuits. Notable among these are the delta and star-mesh transformations, and the duality theorem.

The method of attack on these problems may be described briefly as follows: any circuit is represented by a set of equations, the terms of the equations corresponding to the various relays and switches in the circuit. A calculus is developed for manipulating these equations by simple mathematical processes, most of which are similar to ordinary algebraic algorisms. This calculus is shown to be exactly analogous to the calculus of propositions used in the symbolic study of logic. For the synthesis problem the desired characteristics are first written as a system of equations, and the equations are then manipulated into the form representing the simplest circuit. The circuit may then be immediately drawn from the equations. By this method it is always possible to find the simplest circuit containing only series and parallel connections, and in some cases the simplest circuit containing any type of connection.

Our notation is taken chiefly from symbolic logic. Of the many systems in common use we have chosen the one which seems simplest and most suggestive for our interpretation. Some of our phraseology, such as node, mesh, delta, wye, etc., is borrowed from ordinary network theory for simple concepts in switching circuits.

II. SERIES-PARALLEL TWO-TERMINAL CIRCUITS

Fundamental Definitions and Postulates

We shall limit our treatment of circuits containing only relay contacts and switches, and therefore at any given time the circuit between any two terminals must be either open (infinite impedance) or closed (zero impedance). Let us associate a symbol X_{ab} or more simply X, with the terminals a and b. This variable, a function of time, will be called the hindrance of the two-terminal circuit $a - b$. The symbol 0 (zero) will be used to represent the hindrance of a closed circuit, and the symbol 1 (unity) to represent the hindrance of an open circuit. Thus when the circuit $a - b$ is open $X_{ab} = 1$ and when closed $X_{ab} = 0$. Two hindrances X_{ab} and X_{cd} will be said to be equal if whenever the circuit $a - b$ is open, the circuit $c - d$ is open, and whenever $a - b$ is closed, $c - d$ is closed. Now let the symbol + (plus) be defined to mean the series connection of the two-terminal circuits whose hindrances are added together. Thus $X_{ab} + X_{cd}$ is the hindrance of the circuit $a - d$ when b and c are connected together. Similarly the product of two hindrances $X_{ab} \cdot X_{cd}$ or more briefly $X_{ab}X_{cd}$ will be defined to mean the hindrance of the circuit formed by connecting the circuits $a - b$ and $c - d$ in parallel. A relay contact or switch will be represented in a circuit by the symbol in Figure 1, the letter being the corresponding hindrance function. Figure 2 shows the interpretation of the plus sign and Figure 3 the multiplication sign. This choice of symbols makes the manipulation of hindrances very similar to ordinary numerical algebra.

It is evident that with the above definitions the following postulates will hold:

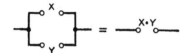

Figure 1 (left). Symbol for hindrance function

$$-\!\!o\ \overset{X}{}\ o\!\!-\!\!o\ \overset{Y}{}\ o\!\!-\ =\ -\!\!o\ \overset{X+Y}{}\ o\!\!-$$

Figure 2 (right). Interpretation of addition

$$= -\!\!o\ \overset{X\cdot Y}{}\ o\!\!-$$

Figure 3 (middle). Interpretation of multiplication

Postulates

1. *a.*	$0 \cdot 0 = 0$	A closed circuit in parallel with a closed circuit is a closed circuit.
b.	$1 + 1 = 1$	An open circuit in series with an open circuit is an open circuit.
2. *a.*	$1 + 0 = 0 + 1 = 1$	An open circuit in series with a closed circuit in either order (i.e., whether the open circuit is to the right or left of the closed circuit) is an open circuit.
b.	$0 \cdot 1 = 1 \cdot 0 = 0$	A closed circuit in parallel with an open circuit in either order is a closed circuit.
3. *a.*	$0 + 0 = 0$	A closed circuit in series with a closed circuit is a closed circuit.
b.	$1 \cdot 1 = 1$	An open circuit in parallel with an open circuit is an open circuit.
4.	At any given time either $X = 0$ or $X = 1$.	

These are sufficient to develop all the theorems which will be used in connection with circuits containing only series and parallel connections. The postulates are arranged in pairs to emphasize a duality relationship between the operations of addition and multiplication and the quantities zero and one. Thus if in any of the *a* postulates the zero's are replaced by one's and the multiplications by additions and vice versa, the corresponding *b* postulate will result. This fact is of great importance. It gives each theorem a dual theorem, it being necessary to prove only one to establish both. The only one of these postulates which differs from ordinary algebra is 1*b*. However, this enables great simplifications in the manipulation of these symbols.

Theorems

In this section a number of theorems governing the combination of hindrances will be given. Inasmuch as any of the theorems may be proved by a very simple process, the proofs will not be given except for an illustrative example. The method of proof is that of "perfect induction," i.e., the verification of the theorem for all possible cases. Since by Postulate 4 each variable is limited to the values 0 and 1, this is a simple matter. Some of the theorems may be proved more elegantly by recourse to previous theorems, but the method of perfect induction is so universal that it is probably to be preferred.

$$X + Y = Y + X, \tag{1a}$$

$$XY = YX, \tag{1b}$$

$$X + (Y + Z) = (X + Y) + Z, \tag{2a}$$

$$X(YZ) = (XY)Z, \tag{2b}$$

$$X(Y + Z) = XY + XZ, \tag{3a}$$

$$X + YZ = (X + Y)(X + Z), \tag{3b}$$

$$1 \cdot X = X, \tag{4a}$$

$$0 + X = X, \tag{4b}$$

$$1 + X = 1, \tag{5a}$$

$$0 \cdot X = 0. \tag{5b}$$

For example, to prove Theorem 4a, note that X is either 0 or 1. If it is 0, the theorem follows from Postulate 2b; if 1, it follows from Postulate 3b. Theorem 4b now follows by the duality principle, replacing the 1 by 0 and the · by +.

Due to the associative laws (2a and 2b) parentheses may be omitted in a sum or product of several terms without ambiguity. The Σ and Π symbols will be used as in ordinary algebra.

The distributive law (3a) makes it possible to "multiply out" products and to factor sums. The dual of this theorem, (3b), however, is not true in numerical algebra.

We shall now define a new operation to be called negation. The negative of a hindrance X will be written X' and is defined to be a variable which is equal to 1 when X equals 0 and equal to 0 when X equals 1. If X is the hindrance of the make contacts of a relay, then X' is the hindrance of the break contacts of the same relay. The definition of the negative of a hindrance gives the following theorems:

$$X + X' = 1, \tag{6a}$$

$$XX' = 0, \tag{6b}$$

$$0' = 1, \tag{7a}$$

$$1' = 0, \tag{7b}$$

$$(X')' = X. \tag{8}$$

Analogue With the Calculus of Propositions

We are now in a position to demonstrate the equivalence of this calculus with certain elementary parts of the calculus of propositions. The algebra of logic,[1,2,3] originated by George Boole, is a symbolic method of investigating logical relationships. The symbols of Boolean algebra admit of two logical interpretations. If interpreted in terms of classes, the variables are not limited to the two possible values 0 and 1. This interpretation is known as the algebra of classes. If, however, the terms are taken to represent propositions, we have the calculus of propositions in which variables are limited to the values 0 and 1,[4] as are the hindrance functions above. Usually the two subjects are devel-

oped simultaneously from the same set of postulates, except for the addition in the case of the calculus of propositions of a postulate equivalent to Postulate 4 above. E. V. Huntington[5] gives the following set of postulates for symbolic logic:

1. The class K contains at least two distinct elements.

2. If a and b are in the class K then $a + b$ is in the class K.

3. $a + b = b + a$.

4. $(a + b) + c = a + (b + c)$.

5. $a + a = a$.

6. $ab + ab' = a$ where ab is defined as $(a' + b')'$.

If we let the class K be the class consisting of the two elements 0 and 1, then these postulates follow from those given in the first section. Also Postulates 1, 2, and 3 given there can be deduced from Huntington's postulates. Adding 4 and restricting our discussion to the calculus of propositions, it is evident that a perfect analogy exists between the calculus for switching circuits and this branch of symbolic logic.[6] The two interpretations of the symbols are shown in Table I.

Due to this analogy any theorem of the calculus of propositions is also a true theorem if interpreted in terms of relay circuits. The remaining theorems in this section are taken directly from this field.

De Morgan's theorem:

$$(X + Y + Z \dots)' = X' \cdot Y' \cdot Z' \dots, \tag{9a}$$

$$(X \cdot Y \cdot Z \dots)' = X' + Y' + Z' + \dots. \tag{9b}$$

This theorem gives the negative of a sum or product in terms of the negatives of the summands or factors. It may be easily verified for two terms by substituting all possible values and then extended to any number n of variables by mathematical induction.

A function of certain variables $X_1, X_2 \dots X_n$ is any expression formed from the variables with the operations of addition, multiplication, and negation. The notation $f(X_1, X_2, \ldots X_n)$ will be used to represent a function. Thus we might have $f(X, Y, Z) = XY + X'(Y' + Z')$. In infinitesimal calculus it is shown that any function (providing it is continuous and all derivatives are continuous) may be expanded in a Taylor series. A somewhat similar expansion is possible in the calculus of propositions. To develop the series expansion of functions first note the following equations:

$$f(X, X_2, \ldots X_n) = X_1 \cdot f(1, X_2 \ldots X_n) + X'_1 \cdot f(0, X_2 \ldots X_n), \quad (10a)$$

$$f(X_1, \ldots, X_n) = [f(0, X_2 \ldots X_n) + X_1] \cdot [f(1, X_2 \ldots X_n) + X'_1]. \quad (10b)$$

These reduce to identities if we let X_1 equal either 0 or 1. In these equations the function f is said to be expanded about X_1. The coefficients of X_1 and X, in 10a are functions of the $(n-1)$ variables $X_2 \ldots X_n$ and may thus be expanded about any of these variables in the same manner. The additive terms in 10b also may be expanded in this manner. Expanding about X_2 we have:

$$f(X_1 \ldots X_n) = X_1 X_2 f(1, 1, X_3 \ldots X_n) + X_1 X'_1 f(1, 0, X_3 \ldots X_n) + X'_1 X_2 f(0, 1, X_3 \ldots X_n) + X'_1 X'_2 f(0, 0, X_3 \ldots X_n) \quad (11a)$$

$$f(X_1 \ldots X_n) = [X_1 + X_2 + f(0, 0, X_3 \ldots X_n)] \cdot [X_1 + X'_2 + f(0, 1, X_3 \ldots X_n)] \cdot [X'_1 + X_2 + f(1, 0, X_3 \ldots X_n)] \cdot [X'_1 + X'_2 + f(1, 1, X_3 \ldots X_n)]. \quad (11b)$$

Continuing this process n times we will arrive at the complete series expansion having the form:

$$f(X_1 \ldots X_n) = f(1, 1, 1 \ldots 1) X_1 X_2 \ldots X_n + f(0, 1, 1 \ldots 1) X'_1 X_2 \ldots X_n + \cdots + f(0, 0, 0 \ldots 0) X'_1 X'_2 \ldots X'_n, \quad (12a)$$

$$f(X_1 \ldots X_n) = [X_1 + X_2 + \cdots X_n + f(0, 0, 0 \ldots 0)] \cdot \ldots \cdot [X'_1 + X'_2 \cdots + X'_n + f(1, 1 \ldots 1)]. \quad (12b)$$

Table I. Analogue Between the Calculus of Propositions and the Symbolic Relay Analysis

Symbol	Interpretation in Relay Circuits	Interpretation in the Calculus of Propositions
X	The circuit X	The proposition X
0	The circuit is closed	The proposition is false
1	The circuit is open	The proposition is true
$X + Y$	The series connection of circuits X and Y	The proposition which is true if either X or Y is true
XY	The parallel connection of circuits X and Y	The proposition which is true if both X and Y are true
X'	The circuit which is open when X is closed and closed when X is open	The contradictory of proposition X
$=$	The circuits open and close simultaneously	Each proposition implies the other

By 12a, f is equal to the sum of the products formed by permuting primes on the terms of $X_1 X_2 \ldots X_n$ in all possible ways and giving each product a coefficient equal to the value of the function when that product is 1. Similarly for 12b.

As an application of the series expansion it should be noted that if we wish to find a circuit representing any given function we can always expand the function by either 10a or 10b in such a way that any given variable appears at most twice, once as a make contact and once as a break contact. This is shown in Figure 4. Similarly by 11 any other variable need appear no more than four times (two make and two break contacts), etc.

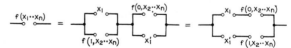

Figure 4. Expansion about one variable

A generalization of De Morgan's theorem is represented symbolically in the following equation:

$$f(X_1, X_2 \ldots X_n, +, \cdot)' = f(X'_1, X'_2 \ldots X'_n, \cdot, +).$$
(13)

By this we mean that the negative of any function may be obtained by replacing each variable by its negative and interchanging the + and symbols. Explicit and implicit parentheses will, of course, remain in the same places. For example, the negative of $X + Y \cdot (Z + WX')$ will be $X' [Y' + Z' (W' + X)]$.

Some other theorems useful in simplifying expressions are given below:

$$X = X + X = X + X + X = \text{etc.,}$$
(14a)

$$X = X \cdot X = X \cdot X \cdot X = \text{etc.,}$$
(14b)

$$X + XY = X,$$
(15a)

$$X(X + Y) + X,$$
(15b)

$$XY + X'Z = XY + X'Z + YZ,$$
(16a)

$$(X + Y)(X' + Z) = (X + Y)(X' + Z)(Y + Z),$$
(16b)

$$Xf(X, Y, Z, \ldots) = Xf(1, Y, Z, \ldots),$$
(17a)

$$X + f(X, Y, Z, \ldots) = X + f(0, Y, Z, \ldots),$$
(17b)

$$X'f(X, Y, Z, \ldots) = X' f(0, Y, Z, \ldots),$$
(18a)

$$X' + f(X, Y, Z, \ldots) = X' + f(1, Y, Z, \ldots).$$
(18b)

All of these theorems may be proved by the method of perfect induction.

Any expression formed with the operations of addition, multiplication, and negation represents explicitly a circuit containing only series and parallel connections. Such a circuit will be called a series-parallel circuit. Each letter in an expression of this sort represents a make or break relay contact, or a switch blade and contact. To find the circuit requiring the least number of contacts, it is therefore necessary to manipulate the expression into the form in which the least number of letters appear. The theorems given above are always sufficient to do this. A little practice in the manipulation of these symbols is all that is required. Fortunately most of the theorems are exactly

the same as those of numerical algebra — the associative, commutative, and distributive laws of algebra hold here. The writer has found Theorems 3, 6, 9, 14, 15, 16a, 17, and 18 to be especially useful in the simplification of complex expressions.

Frequently a function may be written in several ways, each requiring the same minimum number of elements. In such a case the choice of circuit may be made arbitrarily from among these, or from other considerations.

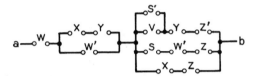

Figure 5. Circuit to be simplified

As an example of the simplification of expressions consider the circuit shown in Figure 5. The hindrance function X_{ab} for this circuit will be:

$$X_{ab} = W + W'(X + Y) + (X + Z)(S + W' + Z)(Z' + Y + S'V) = W + X + Y + (X + Z)(S + 1 + Z)(Z' + Y + S'V) = W + X + Y + Z(Z' + S'V).$$

These reductions were made with 17b using first W, then X and Y as the "X" of 17b. Now multiplying out:

$$X_{ab} = W + X + Y + ZZ' + ZS'V = W + X + Y + ZS'V.$$

The circuit corresponding to this expression is shown in Figure 6. Note the large reduction in the number of elements.

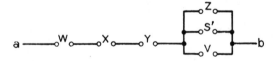

Figure 6. Simplification of figure 5

It is convenient in drawing circuits to label a relay with the same letter as the hindrance of make contacts of the relay. Thus if a relay is connected to a source of voltage through a network whose hindrance function is X, the relay and any make contacts on it would be labeled X. Break contacts would be labeled X'. This assumes that the relay operates instantly and that the make contacts close and the break contacts open simultaneously. Cases in which there is a time delay will be treated later.

III. MULTI-TERMINAL AND NON-SERIES-PARALLEL CIRCUITS

Equivalence of *n*-Terminal Networks

The usual relay control circuit will take the form of Figure 7, where $X_1, X_2, \ldots X_n$, are relays or other devices controlled by the circuit and N is a network of relay contacts and switches. It is desirable to find transformations that may be applied to N which will keep the operation of *all* the relays $X_1, \ldots X_n$ the same. So far we have only considered transformations which may be applied to a two-terminal network keeping the operation of one relay in series with this network the same. To this end we define equivalence of *n*-terminal networks as follows. Definition: Two *n*-terminal networks M and N will be said to be equivalent with respect to these *n* terminals if and only if $X_{jk} = Y_{jk}$; $j, k = 1, 2, 3. \ldots n$, where X_{jk} is the hindrance of N (considered as a two-terminal network) between terminals j and k, and Y_k is that for M between the corresponding terminals. Under this definition the equivalences of the preceding sections were with respect to two terminals.

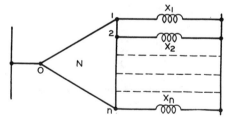

Figure 7. General constant-voltage relay circuit

Star-Mesh and Delta-Wye Transformations

As in ordinary network theory there exist star-to-mesh and delta-to-wye transformations. In imped-

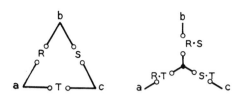

Figure 8. Delta-wye transformation

ance circuits these transformations, if they exist, are unique. In hindrance networks the transformations always exist and are not unique. Those given here are the simplest in that they require the least number of elements. The delta-to-wye transformation is shown in Figure 8. These two networks are equivalent with respect to the three terminals *a*, *b*, and *c*, since by distributive law $X_{ab} = R(S + T) = RS + RT$ and similarly for the other pairs of terminals $a - c$ and $b - c$.

The wye-to-delta transformation is shown in Figure 9. This follows from the fact that $X_{ab} = R + S = (R + S) \cdot (R + T + T + S)$, etc. An *n*-point star also has a mesh equivalent with the central junction point eliminated. This is formed exactly as in the simple three-point star, by connecting each pair of terminals of the mesh through a hindrance which is the sum of the corresponding arms of the star. This may be proved by mathematical induction. We have shown it to be true for $n = 3$. Now assuming it true for $n - 1$, we shall prove it for *n*. Suppose we construct a mesh circuit from the given *n*-point star according to this method. Each corner of the mesh will be an $(n - 1)$-point star and since we have assumed the theorem true for $n - 1$ we may replace the *n*th corner by its mesh equivalent. If Y_{0j} was the hindrance of the original star from the central node 0 to the point *j*, then the reduced mesh will have the hindrance $(Y_{0s} + Y_{or}) \cdot (Y_{0s} + Y_{on} + Y_{0r} + Y_{0n})$ connecting nodes *r* and *s*. But this reduces to $Y_{0s}Y_{0r}$ which is the correct value, since the original *n*-point star with the *n*th arm deleted becomes an $(n - 1)$-point star and by our assumption may be replaced by a mesh having this hindrance connecting nodes *r* and *s*. Therefore the two networks are equivalent with respect to the first $n - 1$ terminals. By eliminating other nodes than the *n*th, or by symmetry, the equivalence with respect to all *n* terminals is demonstrated.

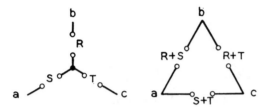

Figure 9. Wye-delta transformation

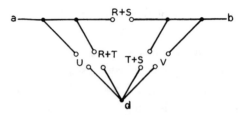

Figure 11. Hindrance function by means of transformations

Hindrance Function of a Non-Series-Parallel Network

The methods of Part II were not sufficient to handle circuits which contained connections other than those of a series-parallel type. The "bridge" of Figure 10, for example, is a non-series-parallel network. These networks will be treated by first reducing to an equivalent series-parallel circuit. Three methods have been developed for finding the equivalent of a network such as the bridge.

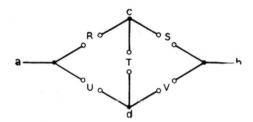

Figure 10. Non-series-parallel circuit

The first is the obvious method of applying the transformations until the network is of the series-parallel type and then writing the hindrance function by inspection. This process is exactly the same as is used in simplifying the complex impedance networks. To apply this to the circuit of Figure 10, first we may eliminate the node c, by applying the star-to-mesh transformation to the star $a - c$, $b - c$, $d - c$. This gives the network of Figure 11. The hindrance function may be written down from inspection for this network:

$$X_{ab} = (R + S)[U(R + T) + V(T + S)].$$

This may be written as

$$X_{ab} = RU + SV + RTV + STU = R(U + TV) + S(V + TU).$$

The second method of analysis is to draw all possible paths through the network between the points under consideration. These paths are drawn along the lines representing the component hindrance elements of the circuit. If any one of these paths has zero hindrance, the required function must be zero. Hence if the result is written as a product, the hindrance of each path will be a factor of this product. The required result may therefore be written as the product of the hindrances of all possible paths between the two points. Paths which touch the same point more than once need not be considered. In Figure 12 this method is applied to the bridge. The paths are shown dotted. The function is therefore given by

$$X_{ab} = (R + S)(U + V)(R + T + V)(U + T + S) =$$
$$RU + SV + RTV + UTS = R(U + TV) +$$
$$S(V + TU).$$

The same result is thus obtained as with the first method.

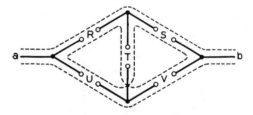

Figure 12. Hindrance function as a product of sums

The third method is to draw all possible lines which would break the circuit between the points under consideration, making the lines go through the hindrances of the circuit. The result is written as a sum, each term corresponding to a certain line. These terms are the products of all the hindrances on the line. The

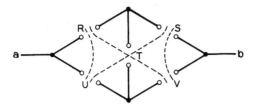

Figure 13. Hindrance function as a sum of products

justification of the method is similar to that for the second method. This method is applied to the bridge in Figure 13.

This again gives for the hindrance of the network:

$$X_{ab} = RU + SV + RTV + STU = R(U+TV) + S(V + TU).$$

The third method is usually the most convenient and rapid, for it gives the result directly as a sum. It seems much easier to handle sums than products due, no doubt, to the fact that in ordinary algebra we have the distributive law $X(Y + Z) = XY + XZ$, but not its dual $X + YZ = (X + Y)(X + Z)$. It is, however, sometimes difficult to apply the third method to nonplanar networks (networks which cannot be drawn on a plane without crossing lines) and in this case one of the other two methods may be used.

Simultaneous Equations

In analyzing a given circuit it is convenient to divide the various variables into two classes. Hindrance elements which are directly controlled by a source external to the circuit under consideration will be called independent variables. These will include hand-operated switches, contacts on external relays, etc. Relays and other devices controlled by the network will be called dependent variables. We shall, in general, use the earlier letters of the alphabet to represent independent variables and the later letters for dependent variables. In Figure 7 the dependent variables are X_1, X_2 ... X_n. X_k will evidently be operated if and only if $X_{0k} = 0$, where X_{0k} is the hindrance function of N between terminals 0 and k. That is,

$$X_k = X_{0k}, k = 1, 2, \ldots n$$

This is a system of equations which completely define the operation of the system. The right-hand members will be known functions involving the various dependent and independent variables and given the starting conditions and the values of the independent variables the dependent variables may be computed.

A transformation will now be described for reducing the number of elements required to realize a set of simultaneous equations. This transformation keeps $X_{0k}(k = 1, 2 \ldots n)$ invariant, but X_{0k} ($j, k = 1, 2 \ldots n$) may be changed, so that the new network may not be equivalent in the strict sense defined to the old one. The operation of all the relays will be the same, however, This simplification is only applicable if the X_{0k} functions are written as sums and certain terms are common to two or more equations. For example, suppose the set of equations is as follows:

$$W = A + B + CW,$$

$$X = A + B + WX,$$

$$Y = A + CY,$$

$$Z = EZ + F.$$

This may be realized with the circuit of Figure 14, using only one A element for the three places where A occurs and only one B element for its two appearances. The justification is quite obvious. This may be indicated symbolically by drawing a vertical line after the terms common to the various equations, as shown below.

$W =$		$B +$	CW
$X =$	$A +$		WX
$Y =$		CY	
$Z =$	$F + EZ$		

It follows from the principle of duality that if we had defined multiplication to represent series connection, and addition for parallel connection, exactly the same theorems of manipulation would be obtained. There were two reasons for choosing the definitions given. First, as has been mentioned, it is easier to

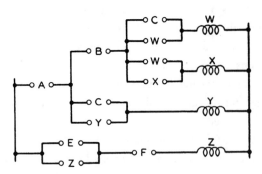

Figure 14. Example of reduction of simultaneous equations

manipulate sums than products and the transformation just described can only be applied to sums (for constant-current relay circuits this condition is exactly reversed), and second, this choice makes the hindrance functions closely analogous to impedances. Under the alternative definitions they would be more similar to admittances, which are less commonly used.

Sometimes the relation $XY' = 0$ obtains between two relays X and Y. This is true if Y can operate only if X is operated. This frequently occurs in what is known as a sequential system. In a circuit of this type the relays can only operate in a certain order or sequence, the operation of one relay in general "preparing" the circuit so that the next in order can operate. If X precedes Y in the sequence and both are constrained to remain operated until the sequence is finished then this condition will be fulfilled. In such a case the following equations hold and may sometimes be used for simplification of expressions. If $XY' = 0$, then

$$X'Y' = Y',$$

$$XY = X,$$

$$X' + Y = 1,$$

$$X' + Y' = X', X + Y = Y.$$

These may be proved by adding $XY' = 0$ to the left-hand member or multiplying it by $X' + Y = 1$, thus not changing the value. For example, to prove the first one, add XY' to $X'Y'$ and factor.

Special Types of Relays and Switches

In certain types of circuits it is necessary to preserve a definite sequential relation in the operation of the contacts of a relay. This is done with make-before-break (or continuity) and break-make (or transfer) contacts. In handling this type of circuit the simplest method seems to be to assume in setting up the equations that the make and break contacts operate simultaneously, and after all simplifications of the equations have been made and the resulting circuit drawn, the required type of contact sequence is found from inspection.

Relays having a time delay in operating, or deoperating may be treated similarly or by shifting the time axis. Thus if a relay coil is connected to a battery through a hindrance X, and the relay has a delay of p seconds in operating and releasing, then the hindrance function of the contacts of the relay will also be X, but at a time p seconds later. This may be indicated by writing $X(t)$ for the hindrance in series with the relay, and $X(t - p)$ for that of the relay contacts.

There are many special types of relays and switches for particular purposes, such as the stepping switches and selector switches of various sorts, multiwinding relays, cross-bar switches, etc. The operation of all these types may be described with the words "or," "and," "if," "operated," and "not operated." This is a sufficient condition that they may be described in terms of hindrance functions with the operations of addition, multiplication, negation, and equality. Thus a two-winding relay might be so constructed that it is operated if the first *or* the second winding is operated (activated) and the first *and* the second windings are not operated. If the first winding is X and the second Y, the hindrance function of make contacts on the relay will then be $XY + X'Y'$. Usually, however, these special relays occur only at the end of a complex circuit and may be omitted entirely from the calculations to be added after the rest of the circuit is designed.

Sometimes a relay X is to operate when a circuit R closes and to remain closed independent of R until a circuit S opens. Such a circuit is known as a lock-in circuit. Its equation is:

$X = RX + S.$

Replacing X by X' gives:

$X' = RX' + S$

or

$X = (R' + X)S'.$

In this case X is *opened* when R closes and remains open until S opens.

IV. SYNTHESIS OF NETWORKS

Some General Theorems on Networks and Functions
It has been shown that any function may be expanded in a series consisting of a sum of products, each product being of the form $X_1 X_2 \ldots X_n$ with some permutation of primes on the letters, and each product having the coefficient 0 or 1. Now since each of the n variables may or may not have a prime, there is a total of 2^n different products of this form. Similarly each product may have the coefficient 0 or the coefficient 1 so there are 2^{2^n} possible sums of this sort. Hence we have the theorem: The number of functions obtainable from n variables is 2^{2^n}.

Each of these sums will represent a different function, but some of the functions may actually involve fewer than n variables (that is, they are of such a form that for one or more of the n variables, say X_k, we have identically $f|_{X_k = 0} = f|_{X_k = 1}$ so that under no conditions does the value of the function depend on the value X_k). Thus for two variables, X and Y, among the 16 functions obtained will be $X, Y, X', Y', 0$, and 1 which do not involve both X and Y. To find the number of functions which actually involve all of the n variables we proceed as follows. Let $\phi(n)$ be the number. Then by the theorem just given:

$$2^{2^n} = \sum_{k=0}^{n} \binom{n}{k} \phi(k),$$

where $\binom{n}{k} = n!/k!(n-k)!$ is the number of combinations of n things taken k at a time. That is, the total number of functions obtainable from n variables is equal to the sum of the numbers of those functions obtainable from each possible selection of variables from these n which actually involve all the variables in the selection. Solving for $\phi(n)$ gives

$$\phi(n) = 2^{2^n} - \sum_{k=0}^{n-1} \binom{n}{k} \phi(k).$$

By substituting for $\phi(n-1)$ on the right the similar expression found by replacing n by $n-1$ in this equation, then similarly substituting for $\phi(n-2)$ in the expression thus obtained, etc., an equation may be obtained involving only $\phi(n)$. This equation may then be simplified to the form

$$\phi(n) = \sum_{k=0}^{n} \binom{n}{k} 2^{2^k} (-1)^{n-k}.$$

As n increases this expression approaches its leading term 2^{2^n} asymptotically. The error in using only this term for $n = 5$ is less than 0.01 percent.

We shall now determine those functions of n variables which require the most relay contacts to realize, and find the number of contacts required. In order to do this, it is necessary to define a function of two variables known as the sum modulo two or disjunct of the variables. This function is written $X_1 \oplus X_2$ and is defined by the equation:

$$X_1 \oplus X_2 = X_1 X'_2 + X'_1 X_2$$

It is easy to show that the sum modulo two obeys the commutative, associative, and the distributive law with respect to multiplication, that is,

$$X_1 \oplus X_2 = X_2 \oplus X_1,$$

$$(X_1 \oplus X_2) \oplus X_3 = X_1 \oplus (X_2 \oplus X_3),$$

$$X_1(X_2 \oplus X_3) = X_1 X_2 \oplus X_1 X_3.$$

Also

$$(X_1 \oplus X_2)' = X_1 \oplus X'_2 = X'_1 \oplus X_2,$$

$$X_1 \oplus 0 = X_1,$$

$$X_1 \oplus 1 = X'_1.$$

Since the sum modulo two obeys the associative law, we may omit parentheses in a sum of several terms without ambiguity. The sum modulo two of the n variables $X_1, X_2 \ldots X_n$ will for convenience be written:

$$X_1 \oplus X_2 \oplus X_3 \ldots \oplus X_n = \mathop{\boldsymbol{\Xi}}_{k=1}^{n} X_k$$

Theorem:[7] The two functions of n variables which require the most elements (relay contacts) in a series-parallel realization are

$$\mathop{\boldsymbol{\Xi}}_{1}^{n} X_k \quad \text{and} \quad \left(\mathop{\boldsymbol{\Xi}}_{1}^{n} X_k \right)',$$

each of which requires $(3 \cdot 2^{n-1} - 2)$ elements.

This will be proved by mathematical induction. First note that it is true for $n = 2$. There are ten functions involving two variables, namely, XY, X + Y, X'Y, X' + Y, XY', X + Y', X'Y' , X' + Y', XY' + X'Y, XY + X'Y'. All of these but the last two require two elements; the last two require four elements and are X $\oplus$ Y and $(X \oplus Y)'$, respectively. Thus the theorem is true for $n = 2$. Now assuming it true for $n - 1$, we shall prove it true for n and thus complete the induction. Any function of n variables may be expanded about the nth variable as follows:

$$f(X_1, X_2 \ldots X_n) = f = X_n f(X_1 \ldots X_{n-1}, 1) + X'_n f(X_1 \ldots X_{n-1}, 0). \tag{19}$$

Now the terms $f(X_1 \ldots X_{n-1}, 1)$ and $f(X_1 \ldots X_{n-1}, 0)$ are functions of $n - 1$ variables and if they individually require the most elements for $n - 1$ variables, then f will require the most elements for n variables, providing there is no other method of writing f so that fewer elements are required. We have assumed that the most elements for $n - 1$ variables are required by

$$\mathop{\boldsymbol{\Xi}}_{1}^{n-1} X_k$$

and its negative. If we, therefore, substitute for $f(X_1 \ldots X_{n-1}, 1)$ the function

$$\mathop{\boldsymbol{\Xi}}_{1}^{n-1} X_k$$

and for $f(X_1 \ldots X_{n-1}, 0)$ the function

$$\left(\mathop{\boldsymbol{\Xi}}_{1}^{n-1} X_k \right)'$$

we find

$$f = X_n \mathop{\boldsymbol{\Xi}}_{1}^{n-1} X_k + X'_n \left(\mathop{\boldsymbol{\Xi}}_{1}^{n-1} X_k \right)' = \left(\mathop{\boldsymbol{\Xi}}_{1}^{n} X_k \right)'.$$

From the symmetry of this function there is no other way of expanding which will reduce the number of elements. If the functions are substituted in the other order we get

$$f = X_n \left(\mathop{\boldsymbol{\Xi}}_{1}^{n-1} X_k \right)' + X'_n \mathop{\boldsymbol{\Xi}}_{1}^{n-1} X_k = \mathop{\boldsymbol{\Xi}}_{1}^{n} X_k.$$

This completes the proof that these functions require the most elements.

To show that each requires $(3 \cdot 2^{n-1} - 2)$ elements, let the number of elements required be denoted by $s(n)$. Then from (19) we get the difference equation

$$s(n) = 2s(n-1) + 2,$$

with $s(2) = 4$. This is linear, with constant coefficients, and may be solved by the usual methods. The solution is

$$s(n) = 3 \cdot 2^{n-1} - 2,$$

as may easily be verified by substituting in the difference equation and boundary condition. Note that the above only applies to a series-parallel realization. In a later section it will be shown that the function

$$\mathop{\boldsymbol{\Xi}}_{1}^{n} X_k$$

and its negative may be realized with $4(n - 1)$ elements using a more general type of circuit. The function requiring the most elements using any type of circuit has not as yet been determined.

Dual Networks

The negative of any network may be found by De Morgan's theorem, but the network must first be transformed into an equivalent series-parallel circuit (unless it is already of this type). A theorem will be developed with which the negative of any planar two-terminal circuit may be found directly. As a corollary a method of finding a constant-current circuit equivalent to a given constant-voltage circuit and vice versa will be given.

Let N represent a planar network of hindrances, with the function X_{ab} between the terminals a and b which are on the outer edge of the network. For definiteness consider the network of Figure 15 (here the hindrances are shown merely as lines).

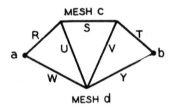

Figure 15 (left). Planar network for illustration of duality theorem

Now let M represent the dual of N as found by the following process; for each contour or mesh of N assign a node or junction point of M. For each element of N, say X_k, separating the contours r and s there corresponds an element X_k connecting the nodes r and s of M. The area exterior to N is to be considered as two meshes, c and d, corresponding to nodes c and d of M. Thus the dual of Figure 15 is the network of Figure 16.

Theorem: If M and N bear this duality relationship, then $X_{ab} = X_{ca}$. To prove this, let the network M be superimposed upon N, the nodes of M within the corresponding meshes of N and corresponding elements crossing. For the network of Figure 15, this is shown in Figure 17 with N solid and M dotted. Incidentally, the easiest method of finding the dual of a network (whether of this type or an impedance network) is to

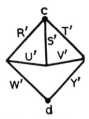

Figure 16 (right).   Dual of figure 15

draw the required network superimposed on the given network. Now, if $X_{ab} = 0$, then there must be some path from a to b along the lines of N such that every element on this path equals zero. But this path represents a path *across M* dividing the circuit from c to d along which every element of M *is* one. Hence $X = 1$. Similarly, if $X_{cd} = 0$, then $X_{ab} = 1$, and it follows that $X_{ab} = X'_{cd}$.

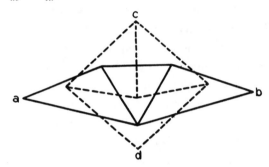

Figure 17.   Superposition of a network and its dual

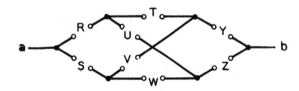

Figure 18.   Nonplanar network

It is evident from this theorem that a negative for any planar network may be realized with the same number of elements as the given network.[8]

In a constant-voltage relay system all the relays are in parallel across the line. To open a relay a series connection is opened. The general constant-voltage system is shown in Figure 19. In a constant-current system the relays are all in series in the line. To de-operate a relay it is short-circuited. The general constant-current circuit corresponding to Figure 19 is shown in Figure 20. If the relay Y_k of Figure 20 is to be operated whenever the relay X_k of Figure 19 is operated and not otherwise, then evidently the hindrance in parallel with Y_k which short-circuits it must be the negative of the hindrance in series with X_k which connects it across the voltage source. If this is true for all the relays, we shall say that the constant-current and constant-voltage systems are equivalent. The above theorem may be used to find equivalent circuits of this sort, for if we make the networks N and M of Figures 19 and 20 duals in the sense described, with Xk and Y_k as corresponding elements, then the condition will be satisfied. A simple example of this is shown in Figures 21 and 22.

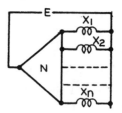

Figure 19 (left). General constant-voltage relay circuit

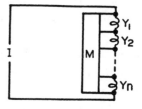

Figure 20 (right). General constant-current relay circuit

Synthesis of the General Symmetric Function

It has been shown that any function represents explicitly a series-parallel circuit. The series-parallel realization may require more elements, however, than some other network representing the same function. In this section a method will be given for finding a circuit representing a certain type of function which in general is much more economical of elements than the best series-parallel circuit. This type of function is known as a symmetric function and appears frequently in relay circuits.

Definition: A function of the n variables $X_1, X_2 \ldots X_n$ is said to be symmetric in these variables if any interchange of the variables leaves the function identically the same. Thus $XY + XZ + YZ$ is symmetric in the variables X, Y, and Z. Since any permutation of variables may be obtained by successive interchanges of two variables, a necessary and sufficient condition that a function be symmetric is that any interchange of two variables leaves the function unaltered.

By proper selection of the variables many apparently unsymmetric functions may be made symmetric. For example, $XY'Z + X'YZ + X'Y'Z'$ although not symmetric in X, Y, and Z is symmetric in X, Y, and Z'. It is also sometimes possible to write an unsymmetric function as a symmetric function multiplied by a simple term or added to a simple term. In such a case the

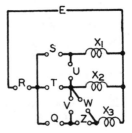

Figure 21 (left). Simple constant-voltage system

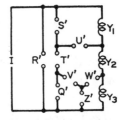

Figure 22 (right). Constant-current system equivalent to figure 21

symmetric part may be realized with the methods to be described, and the additional term supplied as a series or parallel connection.

The following theorem forms the basis of the method of design which has been developed.

Theorem: A necessary and sufficient condition that a function be symmetric is that it may be specified by stating a set of numbers $a_1, a_2 \ldots a_k$ such that if exactly $a_j (j = 1, 2, 3 \ldots,)$ of the variables are zero, then the function is zero and not otherwise. This follows easily from the definition. The set of numbers $a_1, a_2 \ldots a_k$ may be any set of numbers selected from the numbers 0 to n inclusive, where n *is* the number of variables in the symmetric function. For convenience, they will be called the *a*-numbers of the function. The symmetric function $XY + XZ + YZ$ has the *a*-numbers 2 and 3, since the function is zero if just two of the variables are zero or if three are zero, but not if none or if one is zero. To find the *a*-numbers of a given symmetric function it is merely necessary to evaluate the function with 0, 1 $\ldots n$ of the variables zero. Those numbers for which the result is zero are the *a*-numbers of the function.

Theorem: There are 2^{n+1} symmetric functions of n variables. This follows from the fact that there are $n + 1$ numbers, each of which may be taken or not in our selection of *a*-numbers. Two of the functions are trivial, however, namely, those in which all and one of the numbers are taken. These give the "functions" 0 and 1, respectively. The symmetric function of the n variables $X_1, X_2 \ldots X_n$ with the *a*-numbers $a_1, a_2 \ldots a_k$ will be written $S_{a_1 a_2 \ldots a_k}(X_1, X_2, \ldots, X_n)$. Thus the example given would be $S_{2\,3}(X, Y, Z)$. The circuit which has been developed for realizing the general symmetric function is based on the *a*-numbers of the function and we shall now assume that they are known.

Theorem: The sum of two given symmetric functions of the same set of variables is a symmetric function of these variables having for *a*-numbers those numbers common to the two given functions. Thus $S_{1,2,3}(X_1 \ldots X_6) + S_{2,3,5}(X_1 \ldots X_6) = S_{2,3}(X_1 \ldots X_6)$.

Theorem: The product of two given symmetric functions of the same set of variables is a symmetric function of these variables with all the numbers appearing in either or both of the given functions for *a*-numbers. Thus $S_{1,2,3}(X_1 \ldots X_6) \cdot S_{2,3,5}(X_1 \ldots X_6) = S_{1,2,3,5}(X_1 \ldots X_6)$.

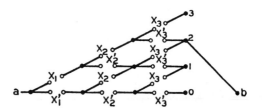

Figure 23.   Circuit for realizing $S_2(X_1, X_2, X_3)$

To prove these theorems, note that a product is zero if either factor is zero, while a sum is zero only if both terms are zero.

Theorem: The negative of a symmetric function of n variables is a symmetric function of these variables having for *a*-numbers all the numbers from 0 to n inclusive which are not in the *a*-numbers of the given function. Thus $S'_{2,3,5}(X_1 \ldots X_6) = S_{0,1,4,6}(X_1 \ldots X_6)$.

Before considering the synthesis of the general symmetric function $S_{a_1 a_2 \ldots a_k}(X_1, X_2, \ldots, X_n)$ a simple example will be given. Suppose the function $S_2(X_1, X_2, X_3)$ is to be realized. This means that we must construct a circuit which will be closed when any two of the variables X_1, X_2, X_3 are zero, but open if none, or one or three are zero. A circuit for this purpose is shown in Figure 23. This circuit may be divided into three bays, one for each variable, and four levels marked 0, 1, 2 and 3 at the right. The terminal b is connected to the levels corresponding to the *a*-numbers of the required function, in this case to the level marked 2. The line coming in at a first encounters a pair of hindrances X_1 and X'_1. If $X_1 = 0$, the line is switched up to the level marked 1, meaning that one of the variables is zero; if not it stays at the same level. Next we come to hindrances X_2 and X'_2. If $X_2 = 0$, the line is switched up a level; if not, it stays at the same level. X_3 has a similar effect. Finally reaching the right-hand set of terminals, the line has been switched up to a level equal to the total number of variables which are zero. Since terminal b is connected to the level marked 2, the circuit $a - b$ will be completed if and only if 2 of the variables are zero. If $S_{0,3}(X_1, X_2, X_3)$ had been desired, terminal b would be connected to both levels 0 and 3. In Figure 23 certain of the elements are evidently superfluous. The circuit may be simplified to the form of Figure 24.

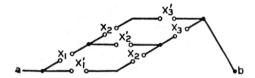

Figure 24. Simplification of figure 23

For the general function exactly the same method is followed. Using the general circuit for *n* variables of Figure 25, the terminal *b* is connected to the levels corresponding to the *a*-numbers of the desired symmetric function. In Figure 25 the hindrances are respected merely by lines, and the letters are omitted from the circuit, but the hindrance of each line may easily be seen by generalizing Figure 23. After terminal *b* is connected, all superfluous elements may be deleted.

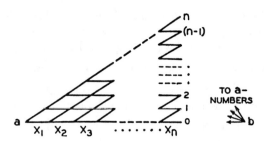

Figure 25. Circuit for realizing the general symmetric function $S_{a_1 a_2 \ldots a_k}(X_1, X_2, \ldots X_n)$

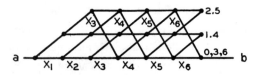

Figure 26. Circuit for $S_{0,3,6}(X_1 \ldots X_6)$ using the "shifting down" process

In certain cases it is possible to greatly simplify the circuit by shifting the levels down. Suppose the function $S_{0,3,6}(X_1 \ldots X_6)$ is desired. Instead of continuing the circuit up to the sixth level, we connect the second level back down to the zero level as shown in Figure 26. The zero level then also becomes the third level and the sixth level. With terminal *b* connected to this level, we have realized the function with a great sav-

ings of elements. Eliminating unnecessary elements the circuit of Figure 27 is obtained. This device is especially useful if the *a*-numbers form an arithmetic progression, although it can sometimes be applied in other cases.

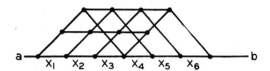

Figure 27. Simplification of figure 26

The functions

$$\mathop{\Xi}_{1}^{n} X_k \quad \text{and} \quad \left(\mathop{\Xi}_{1}^{n} X_k \right)'$$

which were shown to require the most elements for a series parallel realization have very simple circuits when developed in this manner. It can be easily shown that if *n* is even, then

$$\mathop{\Xi}_{1}^{n} X_k$$

is the symmetric function with all the even numbers for *a*-numbers, if *n* is odd it has all the odd numbers for *a*-numbers. The function

$$\left(\mathop{\Xi}_{1}^{n} X_k \right)'$$

is, of course, just the opposite. Using the shifting-down process the circuits are as shown in Figures 28 and 29. These circuits each require $4(n-1)$ elements. They will be recognized as the familiar circuit for controlling a light from *n* points, using $(n-2)$ double-pole double-throw switches and two single-pole double-throw switches. If at any one of the points the position of the switch is changed, the total number of variables which equal zero is changed by one, so that if the light is on, it will be turned off and if already off, it will be turned on.

More than one symmetric function of a certain set of variables may be realized with just one circuit of the

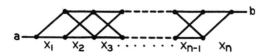

Figure 28. $\overset{n}{\underset{1}{\Xi}}X_k$ for n odd; $(\overset{n}{\underset{1}{\Xi}}X_k)'$ for n even

form of Figure 25, providing the different functions have no *a*-numbers in common. If there are common *a*-numbers the levels may be shifted down, or an extra relay may be added so that one circuit is still sufficient.

The general network of Figure 25 contains $n(n + 1)$ elements. We will show that for any given selection of *a*-numbers, at least *n* of the elements will be superfluous. Each number from 1 to $n - 1$ inclusive which is not in the set of *a*-numbers produces two unnecessary elements; 0 or *n* missing will produce one unnecessary element. However, if two of the *a*-numbers differ by only one, then two elements will be superfluous. If more than two of the *a*-numbers are adjacent, or if two or more adjacent numbers are missing, then more than one element apiece will be superfluous. It is evident then that the worst case will be that in which the *a*-numbers are all the odd numbers or all the even numbers from 0 to *n*. In each of these cases it is easily seen that *n* of the elements will be superfluous. In these cases the shifting down process may be used if $n > 2$ so that the maximum of n^2 elements will be needed only for the four particular functions X, X', $X \oplus Y$, and $(X \oplus Y)'$.

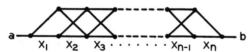

Figure 29. $(\overset{n}{\underset{1}{\Xi}}X_k)$ for n even; $(\overset{n}{\underset{1}{\Xi}}X_k)'$ for n odd

Equations From Given Operating Characteristics

In general, there is a certain set of independent variables A, B, C . . . which may be switches, externally operated or protective relays. There is also a set of dependent variables x, y, z . . . which represent relays, motors or other devices to be controlled by the circuit. It is required to find a network which gives, for each possible combination of values of the independent variables, the correct values for all the dependent vari-

ables. The following principles give the general method of solution.

1. Additional dependent variables must be introduced for each added phase of operation of a sequential system. Thus if it is desired to construct a system which operates in three steps, two additional variables must be introduced to represent the beginning of the last two steps. These additional variables may represent contacts on a stepping switch or relays which lock in sequentially. Similarly each required time delay will require a new variable, representing a time delay relay of some sort. Other forms of relays which may be necessary will usually be obvious from the nature of the problem.

Table II. Relation of Operating Characteristics and Equations

Symbol	In Terms of Operation	In Terms of Nonoperation
X	The switch or relay X is operated	The switch or relay X is not operated
$=$	If	If
X'	The switch or relay X is not operated	The switch or relay X is operated
$\cdot$	Or	And
$+$	And	Or
$(--)'$	The circuit $(--)$ is not closed, or apply De Morgan's theorem	The circuit $(--)$ is closed, or apply De Morgan's theorem
$X(t - p)$	X has been operated for at least p seconds	X has been open for at least p seconds

If the dependent variable appears in its own defining function (as in a lock-in circuit) strict adherence to the above leads to confusing sentences. In such cases the following equivalents should be used.

$X = RX + S$	X is operated when R is closed (providing S is closed) and remains so independent of R until S opens	
$X = (R' + X)S'$		X is opened when R is closed (providing S is closed) and remains so independent of R until S opens

In using this table it is usually best to write the function under consideration either as a sum of pure products or as a product of pure sums. In the case of a sum of products the characteristics should be defined in terms of nonoperation; for a product of sums in terms of operation. If this is not done it is difficult to give implicit and explicit parentheses the proper significance.

2. The hindrance equations for each of the dependent variables should now be written down. These functions may involve any of the variables, dependent or independent, including the variable whose function is being determined (as, for example, in a lock-in circuit). The conditions may be either conditions for operation or for nonoperation. Equations are written from operating characteristics according to Table II. To illustrate the use of this table suppose a relay U is to operate if x is operated and y or z is operated and v or w or z is not operated. The expression for A will be

    $U = x + yz + v'w'z'$.

    Lock-in relay equations have already been discussed. It does not, of course, matter if the same conditions are put in the expression more than once — all superfluous material will disappear in the final simplification.

3. The expressions for the various dependent variables should next be simplified as much as possible by means of the theorems on manipulation of these quanti-

ties. Just how much this can be done depends somewhat on the ingenuity of the designer.

4. The resulting circuit should now be drawn. Any necessary additions dictated by practical considerations such as current-carrying ability, sequence of contact operation, etc., should be made.

V. ILLUSTRATIVE EXAMPLES

In this section several problems will be solved with the methods which have been developed. The examples are intended more to illustrate the use of the calculus in actual problems and to show the versatility of relay and switching circuits than to describe practical devices.

It is possible to perform complex mathematical operations by means of relay circuits. Numbers may be represented by the positions of relays or stepping switches, and interconnections between sets of relays can be made to represent various mathematical operations. In fact, any operation that can be completely described in a finite number of steps using the words "if," "or," "and," etc. (see Table II), can be done automatically with relays. The last example is an illustration of a mathematical operation accomplished with relays.

A Selective Circuit

A relay U is to operate when any one, any three or when all four of the relays w, x, y and z are operated but not when none or two are operated. The hindrance function for U will evidently be:

$$U = wxyz + w'x'yz + w'xy'z + w'xyz' + wx'y'z + wx'yz' + wxy'z'.$$

Reducing to the simplest series-parallel form:

$$U = w[x(yz + y'z') + x'(y'z + yz')] + w'[x(y'z + yz') + x'yz]$$

This circuit is shown in Figure 30. It requires 20 ele-

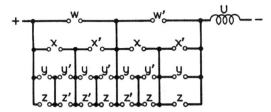

Figure 30. Series-parallel realization of selective circuit

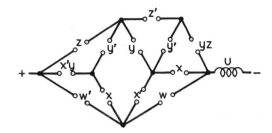

Figure 33. Dual of figure 32

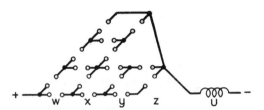

Figure 31. Selective circuit from symmetric-function method

ments. However, using the symmetric-function method, we may write for U:

$$U = S_{1,3,4}(w, x, y, z).$$

This circuit (Figure 31) contains only 15 elements. A still further reduction may be made with the following device. First write

$$U' = S_{0,2}(w, x, y, z).$$

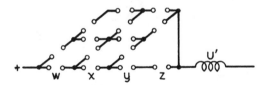

Figure 32. Negative of selective circuit from symmetric-function method

This has the circuit of Figure 32. What is required is the negative of this function. This is a planar network and we may apply the theorem on the dual of a network, thus obtaining the circuit shown in Figure 33. This contains 14 elements and is probably the most economical circuit of any sort.

Design of an Electric Combination Lock

An electric lock is to be constructed with the following characteristics. There are to be five pushbutton switches available on the front of the lock. These will be labeled a, b, c, d, e. To operate the lock the buttons must be pressed in the following order: c, b, a and c simultaneously, d. When operated in this sequence the lock is to unlock, but if any button is pressed incorrectly an alarm U is to operate. To relock the system a switch g must be operated. To release the alarm once it has started a switch h must be operated. This being a sequential system either a stepping switch or additional sequential relays are required. Using sequential relays let them be denoted by w, x, y and z corresponding respectively to the correct sequence of operating the push buttons. An additional time-delay relay is also required due to the third step in the operation. Obviously, even in correct operation a and c cannot be pressed at exactly the same time, but if only one is pressed and held down the alarm should operate. Therefore assume an auxiliary time delay relay v which will operate if either a or c alone is pressed at the end of step 2 and held down longer than time s, the delay of the relay.

When z has operated the lock unlocks and at this point let all the other relays drop out of the circuit. The equations of the system may be written down immediately:

$$w = cw + z' + U',$$

$$x = bx + w + z' + U',$$

$$y = (a + c)y + x + z' + U',$$

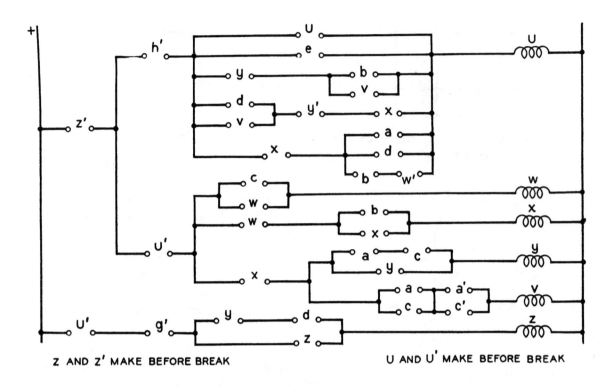

Z AND Z' MAKE BEFORE BREAK   U AND U' MAKE BEFORE BREAK

Figure 34.   Combination-lock circuit

$$z = z(d + y) + g' + U',$$

$$v = x + ac + a'c' + z' + U',$$

$$U = e(w' + abd)(w + x' + ad)[x + y' + dv(t - s)]$$
$$[y + bv(t - s)]\, U + h' + z'.$$

These expressions can be simplified considerably, first by combining the second and third factors in the first term of U, and then by factoring out the common terms of the several functions. The final simplified form is as below. This corresponds to the circuit of Figure 34.

$U =$		$h' + e[ad(b + w') + x']$
		$(x + y' + dv)$
		$(y + vb)U$
$w =$		cw

Electric Adder to the Base Two

A circuit is to be designed that will automatically add two numbers, using only relays and switches. Although any numbering base could be used the circuit is greatly simplified by using the scale of two. Each digit is thus either 0 or 1; the number whose digits in order are $a_k, a_{k-1}, a_{k-2}, \ldots a_2, a_1, a_0$ has the value

$$\sum_{j=0}^{k} a_j 2^j.$$

Let the two numbers which are to be added be represented by a series of switches: $a_k, a_{k-1}, \ldots a_1, a_0$ representing the various digits of one of the numbers and $b_k, b_{k-1}, \ldots b_1, b_0$ the digits of the other number. The sum will be represented by the positions of a set of relays $s_{k+1}, s_k, s_{k-1} \ldots s_1, s_0$. A number which is carried to the jth column from the $(j-1)$th column will be represented by a relay c_j. If the value of any digit is zero, the corresponding relay or switch will be taken to be in the position of zero hindrance; if one, in the position where the hindrance is one. The actual addition is shown below:

c_{k+1}	$c_k\, c_{j+1} c_j\, c_2 c_1$	Carried numbers
	$a_k\, a_{j+1} a_j\, a_2 a_1$	First number
	$b_k\, b_{j+1} b_j\, b_2 b_1$	Second number
	$s_k\, s_{j+1} s_j\, s_2 s_1$	Sum

or

s_{k+1}

Starting from the right, s_0 is one if a_0 is one and b_0 is zero or if a_0 is zero and b_0 one but not otherwise. Hence

$$s_0 = a_0 b'_0 + a'_0 b_0 = a_0 \oplus b_0.$$

c_1 is one if both a_0 and b_0 are one but not otherwise:

$$c_1 = a_0 \cdot b_0.$$

s_j is one if just one a_j, b_j, c_j is one, or if all three are one:

$$s_i = S_{1,3}(a_j, b_j, c_j), j = 1, 2, \ldots k.$$

c_{j+1} is one if two or if three of these variables are one:

$$c_i = S_{2,3}(a_j, b_j, c_j), j = 1, 2, \ldots k.$$

Using the method of symmetric functions, and shifting down for s_j gives the circuits of Figure 35. Eliminating superfluous elements we arrive at Figure 36.

REFERENCES

1. A complete bibliography of the literature of symbolic logic is given in the *Journal of Symbolic Logic*, volume 1, number 4, December 1936. Those elementary parts of the theory that are useful in connection with relay circuits are well treated in the two following references.

2. *The Algebra of Logic*, Louis Cauturat. The Open Court Publishing Company.

3. Universal Algebra, A. N. Whitehead. Cambridge, at the University Press, volume I, book III, chapters I and II, pages 35–42.

4. This refers only to the classical theory of the calculus of propositions. Recently some work has been done with logical systems in which propositions may have more than two "truth values."

5. E. V. Huntington, *Transactions of the American Mathematical Society*, volume 35, 1933, pages 274–304. The postulates referred to are the fourth set, given on page 280.

6. This analogy may also be seen from a slightly different viewpoint. Instead of associating X_{ab} directly with the circuit $a - b$ let X_{ab} represent the proposition that the circuit $a - b$ is open. Then all the symbols are directly interpreted as propositions and the operations of addition and multiplication will be seen to represent series and parallel connections.

7. See the Notes to this paper.

8. This is not in general true if the word "planar" is omitted. The nonplanar network X_{ab} of Figure 18, for example, has no negative containing only eight elements.

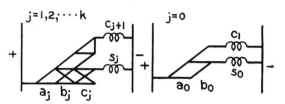

Figure 35.   Circuits for electric adder

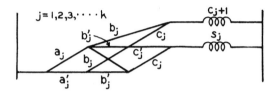

Figure 36.   Simplification of figure 35

12.2

A Mathematical Theory of Communication

C. E. Shannon

Excerpt from *The Bell System Technical Journal* 27 (1948): 379–405.

INTRODUCTORY NOTE TO READING 12.2

Building on research begun during World War II, "Shannon developed a general theory of communication that would treat of the transmission of any sort of information from one point to another in space or time. His aim was to give specific technical definitions of concepts general enough to obtain in any situation where information is manipulated or transmitted—concepts such as information, noise, transmitter, signal, receiver, and message.

"At the heart of the theory was a new conceptualization of information. To make communication theory a scientific discipline, Shannon needed to provide a precise definition of information that transformed it into a physical parameter capable of quantification. He accomplished this transformation by distinguishing information from meaning. He reserved 'meaning' for the content actually included in a particular message. He used 'information' to refer to the number of different possible messages that could be carried along a channel, depending on the message's length and on the number of choices of symbols for transmission at each point in the message. Information in Shannon's sense was a measure of orderliness (as opposed to randomness) in that it indicated the number of possible messages from which a particular message to be sent was chosen. The larger the number of possibilities, the larger the amount of information transmitted, because the actual message is distinguished from a greater number of possible alternatives. . . .

"What began as a study of transmission over telegraph lines was developed by Shannon into a general theory of communication applicable to telegraph, telephone, radio, television, and computing machines—in fact, to any system, physical or biological, in which information is being transferred or manipulated through time or space."[1]

Shannon's paper was also responsible for introducing the term "bit" (for *bi*nary dig*it*) into the published literature, and for giving the term its current meaning of "a unit of information derived from a choice between two equally probable alternatives or 'events'" (*Supplement to the Oxford English Dictionary* [1972]). [JMN]

---

1 William Aspray, The Scientific Conceptualization of Information: A Survey. *Annals of the History of Computing* 7 (1985): 119–22.

INTRODUCTION

The recent development of various methods of modulation such as PCM and PPM which exchange bandwidth for signal-to-noise ratio has intensified the interest in a general theory of communication. A basis for such a theory is contained in the important papers of Nyquist[1] and Hartley[2] on this subject. In the present paper we will extend the theory to include a number of new factors, in particular the effect of noise in the channel, and the savings possible due to the statistical structure of the original message and due to the nature of the final destination of the information.

The fundamental problem of communication is that of reproducing at one point either exactly or approximately a message selected at another point. Frequently the messages have *meaning*; that is they refer to or are correlated according to some system with certain physical or conceptual entities. These semantic aspects of communication are irrelevant to the engineering problem. The significant aspect is that the actual message is one *selected from a set* of possible messages. The system must be designed to operate for each possible selection, not just the one which will actually be chosen since this is unknown at the time of design.

If the number of messages in the set is finite then this number or any monotonic function of this number can be regarded as a measure of the information produced when one message is chosen from the set, all choices being equally likely. As was pointed out by Hartley the most natural choice is the logarithmic function. Although this definition must be generalized considerably when we consider the influence of the statistics of the message and when we have a continuous range of messages, we will in all cases use an essentially logarithmic measure.

The logarithmic measure is more convenient for various reasons:

1. It is practically more useful. Parameters of engineering importance such as time, bandwidth, number of relays, etc., tend to vary linearly with the logarithm of the number of possibilities. For example, adding one relay to a group doubles the number of possible states of the relays. It adds 1 to the base 2 logarithm of this number. Doubling the time roughly squares the number of possible messages, or doubles the logarithm, etc.

2. It is nearer to our intuitive feeling as to the proper measure. This is closely related to (1) since we intuitively measure entities by linear comparison with common standards. One feels, for example, that two punched cards should have twice the capacity of one for information storage, and two identical channels twice the capacity of one for transmitting information.

3. It is mathematically more suitable. Many of the limiting operations are simple in terms of the logarithm but would require clumsy restatement in terms of the number of possibilities.

The choice of a logarithmic base corresponds to the choice of a unit for measuring information. If the base 2 is used the resulting units may be called binary digits, or more briefly *bits*, a word suggested by J. W. Tukey. A device with two stable positions, such as a relay or a flip-flop circuit, can store one bit of information. N such devices can store N bits, since the total number of possible states is $2N$ and $\log_2 2N = N$. If the base 10 is used the units may be called decimal digits. Since

$$\log_2 M = \log_{10} M / \log_{10} 2 = 3.32 \log_{10} M,$$

a decimal digit is about 31 bits. A digit wheel on a desk computing machine has ten stable positions and therefore has a storage capacity of one decimal digit. In analytical work where integration and differentiation are involved the base e is sometimes useful. The resulting units of information will be called natural units. Change from the base a to base b merely requires multiplication by $\log_b a$.

By a communication system we will mean a system of the type indicated schematically in Fig. 1. It consists of essentially five parts:

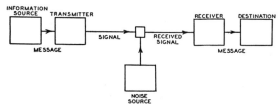

Fig. 1—Schematic diagram of a general communication system.

1. An *information source* which produces a message or sequence of messages to be communicated to the receiving terminal. The message may be of various types: e.g. (a) A sequence of letters as in a telegraph or teletype system; (b) A single function of time $f(t)$ as in radio or telephony; (c) A function of time and other variables as in black and white television—here the message may be thought of as a function $f(x, y, t)$ of two space coordinates and time, the light intensity at point (x, y) and time t on a pickup tube plate; (d) Two or more functions of time, say $f(t)$, $g(t)$, $h(t)$—this is the case in "three dimensional" sound transmission or if the system is intended to service several individual channels in multiplex; (e) Several functions of several variables—in color television the message consists of three functions $f(x, y, t)$, $g(x, y, t)$, $h(x, y, t)$ defined in a three-dimensional continuum—we may also think of these three functions as components of a vector field defined in the region—similarly, several black and white television sources would produce "messages" consisting of a number of functions of three variables; (f) Various combinations also occur, for example in television with an associated audio channel.

2. A *transmitter* which operates on the message in some way to produce a signal suitable for transmission over the channel. In telephony this operation consists merely of changing sound pressure into a proportional electrical current. In

telegraphy we have an encoding operation which produces a sequence of dots, dashes and spaces on the channel corresponding to the message. In a multiplex PCM system the different speech functions must be sampled, compressed, quantized and encoded, and finally interleaved properly to construct the signal. Vocoder systems, television, and frequency modulation are other examples of complex operations applied to the message to obtain the signal.

3. The *channel* is merely the medium used to transmit the signal from transmitter to receiver. It may be a pair of wires, a coaxial cable, a band of radio frequencies, a beam of light, etc.

4. The *receiver* ordinarily performs the inverse operation of that done by the transmitter, reconstructing the message from the signal.

5. The *destination is* the person (or thing) for whom the message is intended.

We wish to consider certain general problems involving communication systems. To do this it is first necessary to represent the various elements involved as mathematical entities, suitably idealized from their physical counterparts. We may roughly classify communication systems into three main categories: discrete, continuous and mixed. By a discrete system we will mean one in which both the message and the signal are a sequence of discrete symbols. A typical case is telegraphy where the message is a sequence of letters and the signal a sequence of dots, dashes and spaces. A continuous system is one in which the message and signal are both treated as continuous functions, e.g. radio or television. A mixed system is one in which both discrete and continuous variables appear, e.g., PCM transmission of speech.

We first consider the discrete case. This case has applications not only in communication theory, but also in the theory of computing machines, the design of telephone exchanges and other fields. In addition the discrete case forms a foundation for the continuous and mixed cases which will be treated in the second half of the paper.

PART I: DISCRETE NOISELESS SYSTEMS

1. The Discrete Noiseless Channel

Teletype and telegraphy are two simple examples of a discrete channel for transmitting information. Generally, a discrete channel will mean a system whereby a sequence of choices from a finite set of elementary symbols $S_1 \ldots S_n$ can be transmitted from one point to another. Each of the symbols S_i is assumed to have a certain duration in time t_i seconds (not necessarily the same for different S_i, for example the dots and dashes in telegraphy). It is not required that all possible sequences of the S_i be capable of transmission on the system; certain sequences only may be allowed. These will be possible signals for the channel. Thus in telegraphy suppose the symbols are: (1) A dot, consisting of line closure for a unit of time and then line open for a unit of time; (2) A dash, consisting of three time units of closure and one unit open; (3) A letter space consisting of, say, three units of line open; (4) A word space of six units of line open. We might place the restriction on allowable sequences that no spaces follow each other (for if two letter spaces are adjacent, it is identical with a word space). The question we now consider is how one can measure the capacity of such a channel to transmit information.

In the teletype case where all symbols are of the same duration, and any sequence of the 32 symbols is allowed the answer is easy. Each symbol represents five bits of information. If the system transmits n symbols per second it is natural to say that the channel has a capacity of $5n$ bits per second. This does not mean that the teletype channel will always be transmitting information at this rate—this is the maximum possible rate and whether or not the actual rate reaches this maximum depends on the source of information which feeds the channel, as will appear later.

In the more general case with different lengths of symbols and constraints on the allowed sequences, we make the following definition: Definition: The capacity C of a discrete channel is given by

$$C = \lim_{T = \infty} \frac{\log N(T)}{T}$$

where $N(T)$ is the number of allowed signals of duration T.

It is easily seen that in the teletype case this reduces to the previous result. It can be shown that the limit in question will exist as a finite number in most cases of interest. Suppose all sequences of the symbols $S_1, \ldots, S_n$ are allowed and these symbols have durations $t_1, \ldots, t_n$. What is the channel capacity? If $N(t)$ represents the number of sequences of duration t we have

$$N(t) = N(t - t_1) + N(t - t_2) + \ldots + N(t - t_n)$$

The total number is equal to the sum of the numbers of sequences ending in $S_1, S_2, \ldots, S_n$ and these are $N(t - t_1) + N(t - t_2) + \ldots + N(t - t_n)$, respectively. According to a well known result in finite differences, $N(t)$ is then asymptotic for large t to X_0^t where X_0 is the largest real solution of the characteristic equation:

$$X^{-t_1} + X^{-t_2} + \ldots + X^{-t_n} = 1$$

and therefore

$$C = \log X_0$$

In case there are restrictions on allowed sequences we may still often obtain a difference equation of this type and find C from the characteristic equation. In the telegraphy case mentioned above

$$N(t) = N(t - 2) + N(t - 4) + N(t - 5) + N(t - 7) + N(t - 8) + N N(t - 10)$$

as we see by counting sequences of symbols according to the last or next to the last symbol occurring. Hence C is $-\log \mu_0$ where μ_0 is the positive root of $1 = \mu^2 + \mu^4 + \mu^5 + \mu^7 + \mu^8 + \mu^{10}$. Solving this we find $C = 0.539$.

A very general type of restriction which may be placed on allowed sequences is the following: We imagine a number of possible states $a_1, a_2, \ldots, a_m$. For each state only certain symbols from the set $S_1 \ldots S_n$ can be transmitted (different subsets for the different states). When one of these has been transmitted the state changes to a new state depending both on the old state and the particular symbol transmitted. The telegraph case is a simple example of this. There are two states depending on whether or not a space was the last symbol transmitted. If so then only a dot or a dash can be sent next and the state always changes. If not, any symbol can be transmitted and the state changes if a space is sent, otherwise it remains the same. The conditions can be indicated in a linear graph as shown in Fig. 2. The junction points correspond to the states and the lines indicate the symbols possible in a state and the resulting state. In Appendix I it is shown that if the conditions on allowed sequences can be described in this form C will exist and can be calculated in accordance with the following result:

Theorem 1: Let $b_{ij}^{(s)}$ be the duration of the sth symbol which is allowable in state i and leads to state j. Then the channel capacity C is equal to log W where W is the largest real root of the determinant equation:

$$\left| \sum_s W^{-b_{ij}^{(s)}} - \delta_{ij} \right| = 0 \, .$$

where $\delta_{ij} = 1$ if $i = j$ and is zero otherwise.

Fig. 2—Graphical representation of the constraints on telegraph symbols.

For example, in the telegraph case (Fig. 2) the determinant is:

$$\begin{vmatrix} -1 & (W^{-2} + W^{-4}) \\ (W^{-3} + W^{-6}) & (W^{-2} + W^{-4} - 1) \end{vmatrix} = 0$$

On expansion this leads to the equation given above for this case.

2. The Discrete Source of Information

We have seen that under very general conditions the logarithm of the number of possible signals in a discrete channel increases linearly with time. The capacity to transmit information can be specified by giving this rate of increase, the number of bits per second required to specify the particular signal used.

We now consider the information source. How is an information source to be described mathematically, and how much information in bits per second is produced in a given source? The main point at issue is the effect of statistical knowledge about the source in reducing the required capacity of the channel, by the use of proper encoding of the information. In telegraphy, for example, the messages to be transmitted consist of sequences of letters. These sequences, however, are not completely random. In general, they form sentences and have the statistical structure of, say, English. The letter E occurs more frequently than Q, the sequence TH more frequently than XP, etc. The existence of this structure allows one to make a saving in time (or channel capacity) by properly encoding the message sequences into signal sequences. This is already done to a limited extent in telegraphy by using the shortest channel symbol, a dot, for the most common English letter E; while the infrequent letters, Q, X, Z are represented by longer sequences of dots and dashes. This idea is carried still further in certain commercial codes where common words and phrases are represented by four- or five-letter code groups with a considerable saving in average time. The standardized greeting and anniversary telegrams now in use extend this to the point of encoding a sentence or two into a relatively short sequence of numbers.

We can think of a discrete source as generating the message, symbol by symbol. It will choose successive symbols according to certain probabilities depending, in general, on preceding choices as well as the particular symbols in question. A physical system, or a mathematical model of a system which produces such a sequence of symbols governed by a set of probabilities is known as a stochastic process.[3] We may consider a discrete source, therefore, to be represented by a stochastic process. Conversely, any stochastic process which produces a discrete sequence of symbols chosen from a finite set may be considered a discrete source. This will include such cases as:

1. Natural written languages such as English, German, Chinese.

2. Continuous information sources that have been rendered discrete by some quantizing process. For example, the

quantized speech from a PCM transmitter, or a quantized television signal.

3. Mathematical cases where we merely define abstractly a stochastic process which generates a sequence of symbols. The following are examples of this last type of source.

   (A) Suppose we have five letters A, B, C, D, E which are chosen each with probability .2, successive choices being independent. This would lead to a sequence of which the following is a typical example.

   BDCBCECCCADCBDDAAECEEA

   ABBDAEECACEEBAEECBCEAD

   This was constructed with the use of a table of random numbers.[4]

   (B) Using the same five letters let the probabilities be .4, .1, .2, .2, .1 respectively, with successive choices independent. A typical message from this source is then:

   AAACDCBDCEAADADACEDA

   EADCABEDADDCECAAAAAD

   (C) A more complicated structure is obtained if successive symbols are not chosen independently but their probabilities depend on preceding letters. In the simplest case of this type a choice depends only on the preceding letter and not on ones before that. The statistical structure can then be described by a set of transition probabilities $p_i(j)$, the probability that letter i is followed by letter j. The indices i and j range over all the possible symbols. A second equivalent way of specifying the structure is to give the "digram" probabilities $p(i, j)$, i.e., the relative frequency of the digram $i\,j$. The letter frequencies $p(i)$, (the probability of letter i), the transition probabilities $p_i(j)$ and the digram probabilities $p(i, j)$ are related by the following formulas.

$$p(i) = \sum_j p(i, j) = \sum_j p(j, i) = \sum_j p(j)p_j(i)$$
$$p(j, i) = p(i)p_i(j)$$
$$\sum_j p_i(j) = \sum_j p_i = \sum_{i, j} p(i, j) = 1$$

As a specific example suppose there are three letters A, B, C with the probability tables:

$p_i(j)$		j	
	A	B	C
A	0	4/5	1/5
i B	1/2	1/2	0
C	1/2	2/5	1/10

i	$p(i)$
A	9/27
B	16/27
C	2/27

$p(i, j)$		j	
	A	B	C
A	0	4/15	1/15
B	8/27	8/27	0
C	1/27	4/135	1/135

A typical message from this source is the following:

ABBABABABABABABBBABBBBBAB

ABABABABBBACACABBABBBBBABB

ABACBBBABA

The next increase in complexity would involve trigram frequencies but no more. The choice of a letter would depend on the preceding two letters but not on the message before that point. A set of trigram frequencies $p(i, j, k)$ or equivalently a set of transition probabilities $p_{ij}(k)$ would be required. Continuing in this way one obtains successively more complicated stochastic processes. In the general n-gram case a set of n-gram probabilities $p(i_1, i_2, \ldots, i_n)$ or of transition probabilities $p_{i_1, i_2, \ldots, i_{n-1}}(i_n)$ is required to specify the statistical structure.

(D) Stochastic processes can also be defined which produce a text consisting of a sequence of "words." Suppose there are five letters A, B, C, D, E and 16 "words" in the language with associated probabilities:

.10 A	.16 BEBE	.11 CABED	.04 DEB
.04 ADEB	.04 BED	.05 CEED	.15 DEED
.05 ADEE	.02 BEED	.08 DAB	.01 EAB
.01 BADD	.05 CA	.04 DAD	.05 EE

Suppose successive "words" are chosen independently and are separated by a space. A typical message might be:

DAB EE A BEBE DEED DEB ADEE ADEE EE DEB BEBE BEBE BEBE ADEE BED DEED DEED CEED ADEE A DEED DEED BEBE CABED BEBE BED DAB DEED ADEB

If all the words are of finite length this process is equivalent to one of the preceding type, but the description may be simpler in terms of the word structure and probabilities. We may also generalize here and introduce transition probabilities between words, etc.

These artificial languages are useful in constructing simple problems and examples to illustrate various possibilities. We can also approximate to a natural language by means of a series of simple artificial languages. The zero-order approximation is obtained by choosing all letters with the same probability and independently. The first-order approximation is obtained by choosing successive letters independently but each letter having the same probability that it does in the natural language.[5] Thus, in the first-order approximation to English, E is chosen with probability .12 (its frequency in normal English) and W with probability .02, but there is no influence between adjacent letters and no tendency to form the preferred digrams such as *TH, ED,* etc. In the second-order approximation, digram structure is introduced. After a letter is chosen, the next one is chosen in accordance with the frequencies with which the various letters follow the first one. This requires a table of digram frequencies $p_i(j)$. In the third-order approximation, trigram structure is introduced. Each letter is chosen with probabilities which depend on the preceding two letters.

3. THE SERIES OF APPROXIMATIONS TO ENGLISH

To give a visual idea of how this series of processes approaches a language, typical sequences in the approximations to English have been constructed and are given below. In all cases we have assumed a 27-symbol "alphabet," the 26 letters and a space.

1. Zero-order approximation (symbols independent and equi-probable).

   XFOML RXKHRJFFJUJ ZLPWCFWK-CYJ FFJEYVKCQSGXYD QPAAMK-BZAACIBZLHJQD

2. First-order approximation (symbols independent but with frequencies of English text).

   OCRO HLI RGWR NMIELWIS EU LL NBNESEBYA TH EEI ALHENHTTPA OOBTTVA NAH BRL

3. Second-order approximation (digram structure as in English).

   ON IE ANTSOUTINYS ARE T INCTORE ST BE S DEAMY ACHIN D ILONASIVE TUCOOWE AT TEA-SONARE FUSO TIZIN ANDY TOBE SEACE CTISBE

4. Third-order approximation (trigram structure as in English).

   IN NO IST LAT WHEY CRATICT FROURE BIRS GROCID PONDE-NOME OF DEMONSTURES OF THE REPTAGIN IS REGOACTIONA OF CRE

5. First-Order Word Approximation. Rather than continue with tetragram, . . . , *n*-gram structure it is easier and better to jump at this point to word units. Here words are chosen independently but with their appropriate frequencies.

   REPRESENTING AND SPEEDILY IS AN GOOD APT OR COME CAN DIF-FERENT NATURAL HERE HE THE A IN CAME THE TO OF TO EXPERT GRAY COME TO FURNISHES THE LINE MESSAGE HAD BE THESE.

6. Second-Order Word Approximation. The word transition probabilities are correct but no further structure is included.

   THE HEAD AND IN FRONTAL ATTACK ON AN ENGLISH WRITER THAT THE CHARACTER OF THIS POINT IS THEREFORE ANOTHER METHOD FOR THE LETTERS THAT THE TIME OF WHO EVER TOLD THE PROBLEM FOR AN UNEX-PECTED

The resemblance to ordinary English text increases quite noticeably at each of the above steps. Note that these samples have reasonably good structure out to about twice the range that is taken into account in their construction. Thus in (3) the statistical process insures reasonable text for two-letter sequence, but four-letter sequences from the sample can usually be fitted into good sentences. In (6) sequences of four or more words can easily be placed in sentences without unusual or strained constructions. The particular sequence of ten words "attack on an English writer that the character of this" is not at all unreasonable. It appears then that a sufficiently complex stochastic process will give a satisfactory representation of a discrete source.

The first two samples were constructed by the use of a book of random numbers in conjunction with (for example 2) a table of letter frequencies. This method might have been continued for (3), (4), and (5), since digram, trigram, and word frequency tables are available, but a simpler equivalent method was used. To construct (3) for example, one opens a book at random and selects a letter at random on the page. This letter is recorded. The book is then opened to another page and one reads until this letter is encountered. The succeeding letter is then recorded. Turning to another page this second letter is searched for and the succeeding letter recorded, etc. A similar process was used for (4), (5), and (6). It would be interesting if further approximations could be constructed, but the labor involved becomes enormous at the next stage.

4. GRAPHICAL REPRESENTATION OF A MARKOFF PROCESS

Stochastic processes of the type described above are known mathematically as discrete Markoff processes and have been extensively studied in the literature.[6] The general case can be described as follows: There exist a finite number of possible "states" of a system; $S_1, S_2, \ldots, S_n$. In addition there is a set of transition probabilities; $p_i(j)$ the probability that if the system is in state S_i it will next go to state S_j. To make this Markoff process into an information source we need only assume that a letter is produced for each transition from one state to another. The states will correspond to the "residue of influence" from preceding letters.

The situation can be represented graphically as shown in Figs. 3, 4 and 5. The "states" are the junction points in the graph and the probabilities and letters produced for a transition are given beside the corresponding line. Figure 3 is for the example B in Section 2, while Fig. 4 corresponds to the example C. In Fig. 3 there is only one state since successive letters are independent. In Fig. 4 there are as many states as letters. If a trigram example were constructed there would be at most n^2 states corresponding to the possible pairs of letters preceding the one being chosen. Figure 5 is a graph for the case of word structure in example D. Here S corresponds to the "space" symbol.

5. ERGODIC AND MIXED SOURCES

As we have indicated above a discrete source for our purposes can be considered to be represented by a Markoff process. Among the possible discrete Markoff processes there is a group with special properties of significance in communication theory. This special class consists of the "ergodic" processes and we shall call the corresponding sources ergodic sources. Although a rigorous definition of an ergodic process is somewhat involved, the general idea is simple. In an ergodic process every sequence produced by the process is the same in statistical properties. Thus the letter frequencies, digram frequencies, etc., obtained from particular sequences will, as the lengths of the sequences increase, approach definite limits independent of the particular sequence. Actually this is not true of every sequence but the set for which it is false has probability zero. Roughly the ergodic property means statistical homogeneity.

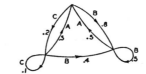

Fig. 3—A graph corresponding to the source in example B.

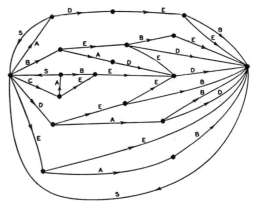

Fig. 4—A graph corresponding to the source in example C.

Fig. 5—A graph corresponding to the source in example D.

dent of the particular sequence. Actually this is not true of every sequence but the set for which it is false has probability zero. Roughly the ergodic property means statistical homogeneity.

All the examples of artificial languages given above are ergodic. This property is related to the structure of the corresponding graph. If the graph has the following two properties[7] the corresponding process will be ergodic:

1. The graph does not consist of two isolated parts A and B such that it is impossible to go from junction points in part A to junction points in part B along lines of the graph in the direction of arrows and also impossible to go from junctions in part B. to junctions in part A.

2. A closed series of lines in the graph with all arrows on the lines pointing in the

same orientation will be called a "circuit." The "length" of a circuit is the number of lines in it. Thus in Fig. 5 the series BEBES is a circuit of length 5. The second property required is that the greatest common divisor of the lengths of all circuits in the graph be one.

If the first condition is satisfied but the second one violated by having the greatest common divisor equal to $d > 1$, the sequences have a certain type of periodic structure. The various sequences fall into d different classes which are statistically the same apart from a shift of the origin (i.e., which letter in the sequence is called letter 1). By a shift of from 0 up to $d - 1$ any sequence can be made statistically equivalent to any other. A simple example with $d = 2$ is the following: There are three possible letters a, b, c. Letter a is followed with either b or c with probabilities 1/3 and 2/3 respectively. Either b or c is always followed by letter a. Thus a typical sequence is

abacacacabacababacac

This type of situation is not of much importance for our work.

If the first condition is violated the graph may be separated into a set of subgraphs each of which satisfies the first condition. We will assume that the second condition is also satisfied for each subgraph. We have in this case what may be called a "mixed" source made up of a number of pure components. The components correspond to the various subgraphs. If $L_1, L_2, L_3, \ldots$ are the component sources we may write

$$L = p_1 L_1 + p_2 L_2 + p_3 L_3 + \ldots$$

where p_i is the probability of the component source L_i.

Physically the situation represented is this: There are several different sources $L_1, L_2, L_3, \ldots$ which are each of homogeneous statistical structure (i.e., they are ergodic). We do not know a priori which is to be used, but once the sequence starts in a given pure component L, it continues indefinitely according to the statistical structure of that component.

As an example one may take two of the processes defined above and assume $p_1 = .2$ and $p_2 = .8$. A sequence from the mixed source

$$L = .2\, L_1 + .8 L_2$$

would be obtained by choosing first L_1 or L_2 with probabilities .2 and .8 and after this choice generating a sequence from whichever was chosen.

Except when the contrary is stated we shall assume a source to be ergodic. This assumption enables one to identify averages along a sequence with averages over the ensemble of possible sequences (the probability of a discrepancy being zero). For example the relative frequency of the letter A in a particular infinite sequence will be, with probability one, equal to its relative frequency in the ensemble of sequences.

If P_1 is the probability of state i and $p_i(j)$ the transition probability to state j, then for the process to be stationary it is clear that the P_i must satisfy equilibrium conditions:

$$P_j = \sum_i P_i p_i(j)$$

In the ergodic case it can be shown that with any starting conditions the probabilities $P_j(N)$ of being in state j after N symbols, approach the equilibrium values as $N \to \infty$.

6. CHOICE, UNCERTAINTY AND ENTROPY

We have represented a discrete information source as a Markoff process. Can we define a quantity which will measure, in some sense, how much information is "produced" by such a process, or better, at what rate information is produced?

Suppose we have a set of possible events whose probabilities of occurrence are $p_1, p_2, \ldots, p_n$. These probabilities are known but that is all we know concerning which event will occur. Can we find a measure of how much "choice" is involved in the selection of the event or of how uncertain we are of the outcome?

If there is such a measure, say $H(p_1, p_2, \ldots, p_n)$, it is reasonable to require of it the following properties:

1. H should be continuous in the p_i.

2. If all the p_i are equal, $p_i = \dfrac{1}{n}$, then H should be a monotonic increasing function of n. With equally likely events there is more choice, or uncertainty, when there are more possible events.

3. If a choice be broken down into two successive choices, the original H should be the weighted sum of the individual values of H. The meaning of this is illustrated in Fig. 6. At the left we have three possibilities $p_1 = 1/2, p_2 = 1/3, p_3 = 1/6$. On the right we first choose between two possibilities each with probability 1/2 and if the second occurs make another choice with probabilities 2/3, 1/3. The final results have the same probabilities as before. We require, in this special case, that

$$H(1/2, 1/3, 1/6) = H(1/2, 1/2) + 1/2H(2/3, 1/3)$$

The coefficient 1/2 is because this second choice only occurs half the time.

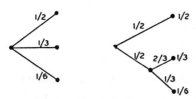

Fig. 6—Decomposition of a choice from three possibilities.

In Appendix II, the following result is established:

Theorem 2: The only H satisfying the three above assumptions is of the form:

$$H = -K \sum_{i=1}^{n} p_i \log p_i$$

where K is a positive constant.

This theorem, and the assumptions required for its proof, are in no way necessary for the present theory. It is given chiefly to lend a certain plausibility to some of our later definitions. The real justification of these definitions, however, will reside in their implications.

Quantities of the form $H = -\sum p_i \log p_i$ (the constant K merely amounts to a choice of a unit of measure) play a central role in information theory as measures of information, choice and uncertainty. The form of H will be recognized as that of entropy as defined in certain formulations of statistical mechanics[8] where p_i is the probability of a system being in cell i of its phase space. H is then, for example, the H in Boltzmann's famous H theorem. We shall call $H = -\sum p_i \log p_i$ the entropy of the set of probabilities $p_1, \ldots, p_n$. If x is a chance variable we will write $H(x)$ for its entropy; thus x is not an argument of a function but a label for a number, to differentiate it from $H(y)$ say, the entropy of the chance variable y.

The entropy in the case of two possibilities with probabilities p and $q = 1 - p$, namely

$$H = -(p \log p + q \log q)$$

is plotted in Fig. 7 as a function of p.

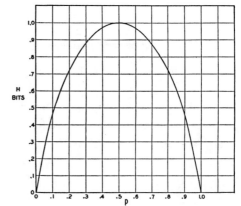

Fig. 7—Entropy in the case of two possibilities with probabilities p and $(1 - p)$.

The quantity H has a number of interesting properties which further substantiate it as a reasonable measure of choice or information.

1. $H = 0$ if and only if all the p_i but one are zero, this one having the value unity. Thus only when we are certain of the outcome does H vanish. Otherwise H is positive.

2. For a given n, H is a maximum and equal to $\log n$ when all the p_i are equal (i.e., $\frac{1}{n}$). This is also intuitively the most uncertain situation.

3. Suppose there are two events, x and y, in question with m possibilities for the first and n for the second. Let $p(i, j)$ be the probability of the joint occurrence of i for the first and j for the second. The entropy of the joint event is

$$H(x, y) = -\sum_{i, j} p(i, j) \log p(i, j)$$

while

$$H(x) = -\sum_{i,j} p(i, j) \log \sum_j p(i, j)$$

$$H(y) = -\sum_{i,j} p(i, j) \log \sum_i p(i, j)$$

It is easily shown that

$$H(x, y) \leq H(x) + H(y)$$

with equality only if the events are independent (i.e., $p(i, j) = p(i)\, p(j)$). The uncertainty of a joint event is less than or equal to the sum of the individual uncertainties.

4. Any change toward equalization of the probabilities $(p_1, p_2, \ldots, p_n)$ increases H. Thus if $p_1 < p_2$ and we increase p_1, decreasing p_2 an equal amount so that p_1 and p_2 are more nearly equal, then H increases. More generally, if we perform any "averaging" operation on the p_i of the form

$$p'_i = \sum_j a_{ij} p_j$$

where $\sum_i a_{ij} = \sum_j a_{ij} = 1$, and all $a_{ij} \geq 0$, then H increases (except in the special case where this transformation amounts to no more than a permutation of the p_j with H of course remaining the same).

5. Suppose there are two chance events x and y as in 3, not necessarily independent. For any particular value i that x can assume there is a conditional probability $p_i(j)$ that y has the value j. This is given by

$$p_i(j) = \frac{p(i, j)}{\sum_i p(i, j)}$$

We define the *conditional entropy* of y, $H_x(y)$ as the average of the entropy of y for each value of x, weighted according to the probability of getting that particular x. That is

$$H_x(y) = -\sum_{i,j} p(i, j) \log p_i(j)$$

This quantity measures how uncertain we are of y on the average when we know x. Substituting the value of $p_i(j)$ we obtain

$$H_x(y) = -\sum_{ij} p(i, j) \log p_i(i, j) + \sum_{ij} p(i, j) \log \sum_j p(i, j) = H(x, y) - H(x)$$

or

$$H(x, y) = H(x) + H_x(y)$$

The uncertainty (or entropy) of the joint event x, y is the uncertainty of x plus the uncertainty of y when x is known.

6. From 3 and 5 we have

$$H(x) + H(y) \geq H(x, y) = H(x) + H_x(y)$$

Hence

$$H(y) \geq H_x(y)$$

The uncertainty of y is never increased by knowledge of x. It will be decreased unless x and y are independent events, in which case it is not changed.

7. THE ENTROPY OF AN INFORMATION SOURCE

Consider a discrete source of the finite state type considered above. For each possible state i there will be a set of probabilities $p_i(j)$ of producing the various possible symbols j. Thus there is an entropy H_i for each state. The entropy of the source will be defined as the average of these H_i weighted in accordance with the probability of occurrence of the states in question:

$$H = \sum_i P_i H_i$$

$$= -\sum_{i,j} P_i p_i(j) \log p_i(j)$$

This is the entropy of the source per symbol of text. If the Markoff process is proceeding at a definite time rate there is also an entropy per second

$$H' = \sum_i f_i H_i$$

where f_i is the average frequency (occurrences per second) of state i. Clearly

$$H' = mH$$

where m is the average number of symbols produced per second. H or H' measures the amount of information generated by the source per symbol or per second. If the logarithmic base is 2, they will represent bits per symbol or per second.

If successive symbols are independent then H is simply $-\sum p_i \log p_i$ where p_i is the probability of symbol i. Suppose in this case we consider a long message of N symbols. It will contain with high probability about $p_1 N$ occurrences of the first symbol, $p_2 N$ occurrences of the second, etc. Hence the probability of this particular message will be roughly

$$p = p_1^{p_1 N} p_2^{p_2 N} \dots p_n^{p_n N}$$

or

$$\log p \doteq N \sum_i p_i \log p_i$$

$$\log p \doteq -NH$$

$$H \doteq \frac{\log 1/p}{N}$$

H is thus approximately the logarithm of the reciprocal probability of a typical long sequence divided by the number of symbols in the sequence. The same result holds for any source. Stated more precisely we have (see Appendix III):

Theorem 3: Given any $\varepsilon > 0$ and $\delta > 0$, we can find an N_0 such that the sequences of any length $N \geq N_0$ fall into two classes:

1. A set whose total probability is less than ε.

2. The remainder, all of whose members have probabilities satisfying the inequality

$$\left| \frac{\log p^{-1}}{N} - H \right| < \delta$$

In other words we are almost certain to have $\dfrac{\log p^{-1}}{N}$ very close to H when N is large.

A closely related result deals with the number of sequences of various probabilities. Consider again the sequences of length N and let them be arranged in order of decreasing probability. We define $n(q)$ to be the number we must take from this set starting with the most probable one in order to accumulate a total probability q for those taken.

Theorem 4:

$$\lim_{N \to \infty} \frac{\log n(q)}{N} = H$$

when q does not equal 0 or 1.

We may interpret $\log n(q)$ as the number of bits required to specify the sequence when we consider only the most probable sequences with a total probability q. Then $\dfrac{\log n(q)}{N}$ is the number of bits per symbol for the specification. The theorem says that for large N this will be independent of q and equal to H. The rate of growth of the logarithm of the number of reasonably probable sequences is given by H, regardless of our interpretation of "reasonably probable." Due to these results, which are proved in appendix III, it is possible for most purposes to treat the long sequences as though there were just 2^{HN} of them, each with a probability 2^{-HN}.

The next two theorems show that H and H' can be determined by limiting operations directly from the statistics of the message sequences, without reference to the states and transition probabilities between states.

Theorem 5: Let $p(B_i)$ be the probability of a sequence B_i of symbols from the source. Let

$$G_N = -\frac{1}{N} \sum_i p(B_i) \log p(B_i)$$

where the sum is over all sequences B_i containing N symbols. Then G_N is a monotonic decreasing function of N and

$$\lim_{N \to \infty} G_N = H$$

Theorem 6: Let $p(B_i, S_j)$ be the probability of sequence B_i followed by symbol S_j and $p_{B_i}(S_j) = p(B_i, S_j)/(pB_i)$] be the conditional probability of S_j after B_i. Let

$$F_N = -\sum_{i,j} p(B_i, S_j) \log p_{B_i}(S_j)$$

where the sum is over all blocks B_i of $N - 1$ symbols and over all symbols S_j. Then F_N is a monotonic decreasing function of N,

$$F_N = NG_N - (N-1)G_{N-1},$$

$$G_N = \frac{1}{N}\sum_1^n F_N,$$

$$F_N \leq G_N,$$

and $\lim_{N \to \infty} F_N = H$.

These results are derived in appendix III. They show that a series of approximations to H can be obtained by considering only the statistical structure of the sequences extending over 1, 2, . . . N symbols. F_N is the better approximation. In fact F_N is the entropy of the Nth order approximation to the source of the type discussed above. If there are no statistical influences extending over more than N symbols, that is if the conditional probability of the next symbol knowing the preceding $(N-1)$ is not changed by a knowledge of any before that, then $F_N = H$. F_N of course is the conditional entropy of the next symbol when the $(N-1)$ preceding ones are known, while G_N is the entropy per symbol of blocks of N symbols.

The ratio of the entropy of a source to the maximum value it could have while still restricted to the same symbols will be called its *relative entropy*. This is the maximum compression possible when we encode into the same alphabet. One minus the relative entropy is the *redundancy*. The redundancy of ordinary English, not considering statistical structure over greater distances than about eight letters is roughly 50%. This means that when we write English half of what we write is determined by the structure of the language and half is chosen freely. The figure 50% was found by several independent methods which all gave results in this neighborhood. One is by calculation of the entropy of the approximations to English. A second method is to delete a certain fraction of the letters from a sample of English text and then let someone attempt to restore them. If they can be restored when 50% are deleted the redundancy must be greater than 50%. A third method depends on certain known results in cryptography.

Two extremes of redundancy in English prose are represented by Basic English and by James Joyce's book "Finigans Wake." The Basic English vocabulary is limited to 850 words and the redundancy is very high.

This is reflected in the expansion that occurs when a passage is translated into Basic English. Joyce on the other hand enlarges the vocabulary and is alleged to achieve a compression of semantic content.

The redundancy of a language is related to the existence of crossword puzzles. If the redundancy is zero any sequence of letters is a reasonable text in the language and any two dimensional array of letters forms a cross-word puzzle. If the redundancy is too high the language imposes too many constraints for large crossword puzzles to be possible. A more detailed analysis shows that if we assume the constraints imposed by the language are of a rather chaotic and random nature, large crossword puzzles are just possible when the redundancy is 50%. If the redundancy is 33%, three dimensional crossword puzzles should be possible, etc.

8. REPRESENTATION OF TILE ENCODING AND DECODING OPERATIONS

We have yet to represent mathematically the operations performed by the transmitter and receiver in encoding and decoding the information. Either of these will be called a discrete transducer. The input to the transducer is a sequence of input symbols and its output a sequence of output symbols. The transducer may have an internal memory so that its output depends not only on the present input symbol but also on the past history. We assume that the internal memory is finite, i.e. there exists a finite number m of possible states of the transducer and that its output is a function of the present state and the present input symbol. The next state will be a second function of these two quantities. Thus a transducer can be described by two functions:

$$y_n = f(x_n, \alpha_n)$$

$$\alpha_{n+1} = g(x_n, \alpha_n)$$

where: x_n is the nth input symbol,

α_n is the state of the transducer when the nth input symbol is introduced,

y_n is the output symbol (or sequence of output symbols) produced when x_n is introduced if the state is α_n.

If the output symbols of one transducer can be identified with the input symbols of a second, they can be connected in tandem and the result is also a transducer. If there exists a second transducer which operates on the output of the first and recovers the original input, the first transducer will be called non-singular and the second will be called its inverse.

Theorem 7: The output of a finite state transducer driven by a finite state statistical source is a finite state statistical source, with entropy (per unit time) less than or equal to that of the input. If the transducer is non-singular they are equal.

Let α represent the state of the source, which produces a sequence of symbols x_i; and let β be the state of the transducer, which produces, in its output, blocks of symbols y_j. The combined system can be represented by the "product state space" of pairs (α, β). Two points in the space, (α_1, β_1) and (α_2, β_2), are connected by a line if α_1 can produce an x which changes β_1 to β_2, and this line is given the probability of that x in this case. The line is labeled with the block of y_j symbols produced by the transducer. The entropy of the output can be calculated as the weighted sum over the states. If we sum first on β each resulting term is less than or equal to the corresponding term for α, hence the entropy is not increased. If the transducer is non-singular let its output be connected to the inverse transducer. If H'_1, H'_2 and H'_3 are the output entropies of the source, the first and second transducers respectively, then $H'_1 \geq H'_2 \geq H'_3 = H'_1$ and therefore $H'_1 = H'_2$.

Suppose we have a system of constraints on possible sequences of the type which can be represented by a linear graph as in Fig. 2. If probabilities $p_{ij}^{(s)}$ were assigned to the various lines connecting state i to state j this would become a source. There is one particular assignment which maximizes the resulting entropy (see Appendix IV).

Theorem 8: Let the system of constraints considered as a channel have a capacity C. If we assign

$$p_{ij}^{(s)} = \frac{B_j}{B_i} C^{-l_{ij}^{(s)}}$$

where $l_{ij}^{(s)}$ is the duration of the sth symbol leading from state i to state j and the B_i satisfy

$$B_i = \sum_{s,j} B_j C^{-l_{ij}^{(s)}}$$

then H is maximized and equal to C.

By proper assignment of the transition probabilities the entropy of symbols on a channel can be maximized at the channel capacity.

9. THE FUNDAMENTAL THEOREM FOR A NOISELESS CHANNEL

We will now justify our interpretation of H as the rate of generating information by proving that H determines the channel capacity required with most efficient coding.

Theorem 9: Let a source have entropy H (bits per symbol) and a channel have a capacity C (bits per second). Then it is possible to encode the output of the source in such a way as to transmit at the average rate $\frac{C}{H} - \varepsilon$ symbols per second over the channel where ε is arbitrarily small. It is not possible to transmit at an average rate greater than $\frac{C}{H}$.

The converse part of the theorem, that $\frac{C}{H}$ cannot be exceeded, may be proved by noting that the entropy of the channel input per second is equal to that of the source, since the transmitter must be non-singular, and also this entropy cannot exceed the channel capacity. Hence $H' \leq C$ and the number of symbols per second = $H'/H \leq C/H$.

The first part of the theorem will be proved in two different ways. The first method is to consider the set of all sequences of N symbols produced by the source. For N large we can divide these into two groups, one containing less than $2^{(h+\eta)N}$ members and the second containing less than 2^{RN} members (where R is the logarithm of the number of different symbols) and having a total probability less than μ. As N increases η and μ approach zero. The number of signals of duration T in the channel is greater than $2^{(c-\theta)T}$ with θ small when T is large. If we choose

$$T = \left(\frac{H}{C} + \lambda\right)N$$

then there will be a sufficient number of sequences of channel symbols for the high probability group when N and T are sufficiently large (however small λ) and also some additional ones. The high probability group is coded in an arbitrary one to one way into this set. The remaining sequences are represented by larger sequences, starting and ending with one of the sequences not used for the high probability group. This special sequence acts as a start and stop signal for a different code. In between a sufficient time is allowed to give enough different sequences for all the low probability messages. This will require

$$T_1 = \left(\frac{R}{C} + \varphi\right)N$$

where φ is small. The mean rate of transmission in message symbols per second will then be greater than

$$\left[(1-\delta)\frac{T}{N} + \delta\frac{T_1}{N}\right]^{-1} = \left[(1-\delta)\left(\frac{H}{C} + \lambda\right) + \left(\delta\frac{R}{C} + \varphi\right)\right]^{-1}$$

As N increases δ, λ and φ approach zero and the rate approaches $\frac{C}{H}$.

Another method of performing this coding and proving the theorem can be described as follows: Arrange the messages of length N in order of decreasing probability and suppose their probabilities are $p_1 \geq p_2 \geq p_3 \ldots \geq p_n$. Let

$$P_s = \sum_1^{s-1} p_i;$$

that is P_s is the cumulative probability up to, but not including p_s. We first encode into a binary system. The binary code for message s is obtained by expanding P_s as a binary number. The expansion is carried out to m_s places, where m_s is the integer satisfying:

$$\log_2 \frac{1}{p_s} \leq m_s < 1 + \log_2 \frac{1}{p_s}$$

Thus the messages of high probability are represented by short codes and those of low probability by long codes. From these inequalities we have

$$\frac{1}{2^{m_s}} \leq p_s < \frac{1}{2^{m_s - 1}}$$

The code for P_s will differ from all succeeding ones in one or more of its m_s places, since all the remaining P_i are at least

$$\frac{1}{2^{m_s}}$$

larger and their binary expansions therefore differ in the first m_s places. Consequently all the codes are dif-

ferent and it is possible to recover the message from its code. If the channel sequences are not already sequences of binary digits, they can be ascribed binary numbers in an arbitrary fashion and the binary code thus translated into signals suitable for the channel.

The average number H' of binary digits used per symbol of original message is easily estimated. We have

$$H' = \frac{1}{N}\Sigma m_s p_s$$

But,

$$\frac{1}{N}\Sigma\left(\log_2 \frac{1}{p_s}\right)p_s \leq \frac{1}{N}\Sigma m_s p_s < \frac{1}{N}\Sigma\left(1 + \log_2 \frac{1}{p_s}\right)p_s$$

and therefore,

$$G_N \leq H' < G_N + \frac{1}{N}$$

As N increases G_N approaches H, the entropy of the source and H' approaches H.

We see from this that the inefficiency in coding, when only a finite delay of N symbols is used, need not be greater than $\frac{1}{N}$ plus the difference between the true entropy H and the entropy G_N calculated for sequences of length N. The per cent excess time needed over the ideal is therefore less than

$$\frac{G_N}{H} + \frac{1}{HN} - 1$$

This method of encoding is substantially the same as one found independently by R. M. Fano.[9] His method is to arrange the messages of length N in order of decreasing probability. Divide this series into two groups of as nearly equal probability as possible. If the message is in the first group its first binary digit will be 0, otherwise 1. The groups are similarly divided into subsets of nearly equal probability and the particular subset determines the second binary digit. This process is continued until each subset contains only one message. It is easily seen that apart from minor differences (generally in the last digit) this amounts to the same thing as the arithmetic process described above.

10. DISCUSSION AND EXAMPLES

In order to obtain the maximum power transfer from a generator to a load a transformer must in general be introduced so that the generator as seen from the load has the load resistance. The situation here is roughly analogous. The transducer which does the encoding should match the source to the channel in a statistical sense. The source as seen from the channel through the transducer should have the same statistical structure as the source which maximizes the entropy in the channel. The content of Theorem 9 is that, although an exact match is not in general possible, we can approximate it as closely as desired. The ratio of the actual rate of transmission to the capacity C may be called the efficiency of the coding system. This is of course equal to the ratio of the actual entropy of the channel symbols to the maximum possible entropy.

In general, ideal or nearly ideal encoding requires a long delay in the transmitter and receiver. In the noiseless case which we have been considering, the main function of this delay is to allow reasonably good matching of probabilities to corresponding lengths of sequences. With a good code the logarithm of the reciprocal probability of a long message must be proportional to the duration of the corresponding signal, in fact

$$\left| \frac{\log p^{-1}}{T} - C \right|$$

must be small for all but a small fraction of the long messages.

If a source can produce only one particular message its entropy is zero, and no channel is required. For example, a computing machine set up to calculate the successive digits of π produces a definite sequence with no chance element. No channel is required to "transmit" this to another point. One could construct a second machine to compute the same sequence at the point. However, this may be impractical. In such a case we can choose to ignore some or all of the statistical knowledge we have of the source. We might consider the digits of it to be a random sequence in that we construct a system capable of sending any sequence of digits. In a similar way we may choose to use some of our statistical knowledge of English in constructing a code, but not all of it. In such a case we consider the source with the maximum entropy subject to the sta-

tistical conditions we wish to retain. The entropy of this source determines the channel capacity which is necessary and sufficient. In the π example the only information retained is that all the digits are chosen from the set 0, 1, . . ., 9. In the case of English one might wish to use the statistical saving possible due to letter frequencies, but nothing else. The maximum entropy source is then the first approximation to English and its entropy determines the required channel capacity.

As a simple example of some of these results consider a source which produces a sequence of letters chosen from among A, B, C, D with probabilities 1/2, 1/4, 1/8, 1/8, successive symbols being chosen independently. We have

$$H = -(1/2 \log 1/2 + 1/4 \log 1/4 + 2/8 \log 1/8) =$$
$$7/4 \text{ bits per symbol.}$$

Thus we can approximate a coding system to encode messages from this source into binary digits with an average of a binary digit per symbol. In this case we can actually achieve the limiting value by the following code (obtained by the method of the second proof of Theorem 9):

A	0
B	10
C	110
D	111

The average number of binary digits used in encoding a sequence of N symbols will be

$$N(1/2 \times 1 + 1/4 \times 2 + 2/8 \times 3) = 7/4 N$$

It is easily seen that the binary digits 0, 1 have probabilities 1/2, 1/2 so the H for the coded sequences is one bit per symbol. Since, on the average, we have 7/4 binary symbols per original letter, the entropies on a time basis are the same. The maximum possible entropy for the original set is $\log 4 = 2$, occurring when A, B, C, D have probabilities 1/4, 1/4, 1/4, 1/4. Hence the relative entropy is 7/8. We can translate the binary sequences into the original set of symbols on a two-to-one basis by the following table:

00	A'
01	B'
01	C'
11	D'

This double process then encodes the original message into the same symbols but with an average compression ratio 7/8.

As a second example consider a source which produces a sequence of A's and B's with probability p for A and q for B. If $p << q$ we have

$$H = -\log p^p (1-p)^{(1-p)}$$
$$= -p \log p (1-p)^{(1-p)/p}$$
$$\doteq p \log \frac{e}{p}$$

In such a case one can construct a fairly good coding of the message on a 0, 1 channel by sending a special sequence, say 0000, for the infrequent symbol A and then a sequence indicating the *number* of B's following it. This could be indicated by the binary representation with all numbers containing the special sequence deleted. All numbers up to 16 are represented as usual; 16 is represented by the next binary number after 16 which does not contain four zeros, namely 17 = 10001, etc.

It can be shown that as $p \rightarrow 0$ the coding approaches ideal provided the length of the special sequence is properly adjusted. . . .

• • •

1.   Nyquist, H., "Certain Factors Affecting Telegraph Speed," *Bell* System *Technical Journal,* April 1924, p. 324; "Certain Topics in Telegraph Transmission Theory," *A. I. E. E. Trans.*, v. 47, April 1928, p. 617.

2.   Hartley, R. V. L., "Transmission of Information," *Bell System Technical Journal,* July 1928, p. 535.

3.   See, for example, S. Chandrasekhar, "Stochastic Problems in Physics and Astronomy," *Reviews of Modern Physics,* v. 15, *No.* 1, January 1943, p. 1.

4.   Kendall and Smith, "Tables of Random Sampling Numbers," Cambridge, 1939.

5.   Letter, digram and trigram frequencies are given in "Secret and Urgent" by Fletcher Pratt, Blue Ribbon Books 1939. Word frequencies are tabulated in "Relative Frequency of English Speech Sounds," G. Dewey, Harvard University Press, 1923.

6.   For a detailed treatment see M. Frechet, "Methods des fonctions arbitraires. Theorie des énénements enchainé dans Ie cas d'un nombre fini d'états possibles." Paris, Gauthier-Villars, 1938.

7.   These are restatements in terms of the graph of conditions given in Frechet.

8.   See, for example, R. C. Tolman, "Principles of Statistical Mechanics," Oxford, Clarendon, 1938.

9.   Technical Report No. 65, The Research Laboratory of Electronics, M. I. T.

12.3

Error Detecting and Error Correcting Codes

R. W. Hamming

From *Bell System Technical Journal* 29 (1950): 147–60.

INTRODUCTORY NOTE TO READING 12.3

Hamming was the first coding theorist to attract widespread interest in his work. He received his Ph.D. in mathematics from the University of Illinois in 1942, and after a stint at Los Alamos, where his job was to keep the Manhattan Project's IBM relay computers functioning, he went to work at Bell Telephone Laboratories, joining the recently hired Claude Shannon in the mathematics department (some of Hamming's early coding work is cited in Shannon's *A Mathematical Theory of Communication* [Reading 12.2]). In 1947, frustrated when a failure in one of Bell Lab's relay computers had spoiled a run of data, Hamming began developing the first error-correction codes (now known as Hamming codes), which enabled computers to find and correct single errors in a stretch of data, as well as to discover double errors. Error correction has since developed into a scientific discipline used in cellular phone transmission, downloadable software or music, or compact disks or DVDs. [JMN]

TEXT OF READING 12.3

1. Introduction

The author was led to the study given in this paper from a consideration of large scale computing machines in which a large number of operations must be performed without a single error in the end result. This problem of "doing things right" on a large scale is not essentially new; in a telephone central office, for example, a very large number of operations are performed while the errors leading to wrong numbers are kept well under control, though they have not been completely eliminated. This has been achieved, in part, through the use of self-checking circuits. The occasional failure that escapes routine checking is still detected by the customer and will, if it persists, result in customer complaint, while if it is transient it will produce only occasional wrong numbers. At the same time the rest of the central office functions satisfactorily. In a digital computer, on the other hand, a single failure usually means the complete failure, in the sense that if it is detected no more computing can be done until the failure is located and corrected, while if it escapes detection then it invalidates all subsequent operations of the machine. Put in other words, in a telephone central office there are a number of parallel paths which are more or less independent of each other; in a digital machine there is usually a single long path which passes through the same piece of equipment many, many times before the answer is obtained.

In transmitting information from one place to another digital machines use codes which are simply sets of symbols to which meanings or values are attached. Examples of codes which were designed to detect isolated errors are numerous; among them are the highly developed 2 out of 5 codes used extensively in common control switching systems and in the Bell Relay Computers,[1] the 3 out of 7 code used for radio telegraphy,[2] and the word count sent at the end of telegrams.

In some situations self checking is not enough. For example, in the Model 5 Relay Computers built by Bell Telephone Laboratories for the Aberdeen Proving Grounds, observations in the early period indicated about two or three relay failures per day in the 8900 relays of the two computers, representing about one failure per two to three million relay operations. The self-checking feature meant that these failures did not introduce undetected errors. Since the machines were run on an unattended basis over nights and weekends, however, the errors meant that frequently the computations came to a halt although often the machines took up new problems. The present trend is toward electronic speeds in digital computers where the basic elements are somewhat more reliable per operation than relays. However, the incidence of isolated failures, even when detected, may seriously interfere with the normal use of such machines. Thus it appears desirable to examine the next step beyond error detection, namely error correction.

We shall assume that the transmitting equipment handles information in the binary form of a sequence of 0's and 1's. This assumption is made both for mathematical convenience and because the binary system is the natural form for representing the open and closed relays, flip-flop circuits, dots and dashes, and perforated tapes that are used in many forms of communication. Thus each code symbol will be represented by a sequence of 0's and 1's.

The codes used in this paper are called *systematic* codes. Systematic codes may be defined[3] as codes in which each code symbol has exactly n binary digits, where m digits are associated with the information while the other $k = n - m$ digits are used for error detection and correction. This produces a *redundancy* R defined as the ratio of the number of binary digits used to the minimum number necessary to convey the same information, that is,

$$R = n/m.$$

This serves to measure the efficiency of the code as far as the transmission of information is concerned, and is the only aspect of the problem discussed in any detail here. The redundancy may be said to lower the effective channel capacity for sending information.

The need for error correction having assumed importance only recently, very little is known about the economics of the matter. It is clear that in using such codes there will be extra equipment for encoding and correcting errors as well as the lowered effective channel capacity referred to above. Because of these considerations applications of these codes may be expected to occur first only under extreme conditions. Some typical situations seem to be:

a. unattended operation over long periods of time with the minimum of standby equipment.

b. extremely large and tightly interrelated systems where a single failure incapacitates the entire installation.

c. signaling in the presence of noise where it is either impossible or uneconomical to reduce the effect of the noise on the signal.

These situations are occurring more and more often. The first two are particularly true of large scale digital computing machines, while the third occurs, among other places, in "jamming" situations.

The principles for designing error detecting and correcting codes in the cases most likely to be applied first are given in this paper. Circuits for implementing these principles may be designed by the application of well-known techniques, but the problem is not discussed here. Part I of the paper shows how to construct special minimum redundancy codes in the following cases:

a. single error detecting codes

b. single error correcting codes

c. single error correcting plus double error detecting codes.

Part II discusses the general theory of such codes and proves that under the assumptions made the codes of Part I are the "best" possible.

PART I: SPECIAL CODES

2. Single Error Detecting Codes

We may construct a single error detecting code having n binary digits in the following manner: In the first $n - 1$ positions we put $n - 1$ digits of information. In the n-th position we place either 0 or 1, so that the entire n positions have an even number of 1's. This is clearly a single error detecting code since any single error in transmission would leave an odd number of 1's in a code symbol.

The redundancy of these codes is, since $m = n - 1$,

$$R = \frac{n}{n-1} = 1 + \frac{n}{n-1}$$

It might appear that to gain a low redundancy we should let n become very large. However, by increasing n, the probability of at least one error in a symbol increases; and the risk of a double error, which would pass undetected, also increases. For example, if $p \ll 1$ is the probability of any error, then for n so large as $1/p$, the probability of a correct symbol is approximately $1/e = 0.3679\ldots$, while a double error has probability $1/2e = 0.1839\ldots$.

The type of check used above to determine whether or not the symbol has any single error will be used throughout the paper and will be called a *parity check*. The above was an *even* parity check; had we used an odd number of 1's to determine the setting of the check position it would have been an odd parity check. Furthermore, a parity check need not always involve all the positions of the symbol but may be a check over selected positions only.

3. Single Error Correcting Codes

To construct a single error correcting code we first assign m of the n available positions as information positions. We shall regard the m as fixed, but the specific positions are left to a later determination. We next assign the k remaining positions as check positions. The values in these k positions are to be determined in the encoding process by even parity checks over selected information positions.

Let us imagine for the moment that we have received a code symbol, with or without an error. Let us apply the k parity checks, in order, and for each time the parity check assigns the value observed in its check position we write a 0, while for each time the assigned and observed values disagree we write a 1. When written from right to left in a line this sequence of k 0's and 1's (to be distinguished from the values assigned by the parity checks) may be regarded as a binary number and will be called the *checking number*.

We shall require that this checking number give the position of any single error, with the zero value meaning no error in the symbol. Thus the check number must describe $m + k + 1$ different things, so that

$$2^k \geq m + k + 1$$

is a condition on k. Writing $n = m + k$ we find

$$2^m \leq \frac{2^n}{n + 1}$$

Using this inequality we may calculate Table I, which gives the maximum m for a given n, or, what is the same thing, the minimum n for a given m.

We now determine the positions over which each of the various parity checks is to be applied. The checking number is obtained digit by digit, from right to left, by applying the parity checks in order and writing down the corresponding 0 or 1 as the case may be. Since the checking number is to give the position

of any error in a code symbol, any position which has a 1 on the right of its binary representation must cause the first check to fail. Examining the binary form of the various integers we find

1 =	1
3 =	11
5 =	101
7 =	111
9 =	1001

Etc.

have a 1 on the extreme right. Thus the first parity check must use positions

$$1, 3, 5, 7, 9, \ldots$$

In an exactly similar fashion we find that the second parity check must use those positions which have 1's for the second digit from the right of their binary representation,

2 =	10
3 =	11
6 =	110
7 =	111
10 =	1010
11 =	1011

Etc.

the third parity check

4 =	100
5 =	101
6 =	110
7 =	111
12 =	1100
13 =	1101
14 =	1110

Table I

n	m	Corresponding k
1	0	1
2	0	2
3	1	2
4	1	3
5	2	3
6	3	3
7	4	3
8	4	4
9	5	4
10	6	4
11	7	4
12	8	4
13	9	4
14	10	4
15	11	4
16	11	5
	Etc.	

15 =	1111
20 =	10100

Etc.

It remains to decide for each parity check which positions are to contain information and which the check. The choice of the positions 1, 2, 4, 8, for check positions, as given in the following table, has the advantage of making the setting of the check positions independent of each other. All other positions are information positions. Thus we obtain Table II.

Table II

Check Number	Check Positions	Positions Checked
1	1	1, 3, 5, 7, 9, 11, 13, 15, 17, . . .
2	2	2, 3, 6, 7, 10, 11, 14, 15, 18,. . .
3	4	4, 5, 6, 7, 12, 13, 14, 15, 20, . . .
4	8	8, 9, 10, 11, 12, 13, 14, 15, 24, . . .
.	.	.
.	.	.
.	.	.

As an illustration of the above theory we apply it to the case of a seven-position code. From Table I we find for $n = 7$, $m = 4$ and $k = 3$. From Table II we find that the first parity check involves positions 1, 3, 5, 7 and is used to determine the value in the first position; the second parity check, positions 2, 3, 6, 7, and determines the value in the second position; and the third parity check, positions 4, 5, 6, 7, and determines the value in position four. This leaves positions 3, 5, 6, 7 as information positions. The results of writing down all possible binary numbers using positions 3, 5, 6, 7, and then calculating the values in the check positions 1, 2, 4, are shown in Table III.

Thus a seven-position single error correcting code admits of 16 code symbols. There are, of course, $2^7 - 16 = 112$ meaningless symbols. In some applications it

may be desirable to drop the first symbol from the code to avoid the all zero combination as either a code symbol or a code symbol plus a single error, since this might be confused with no message. This would still leave 15 useful code symbols.

Table III

Position							Decimal Value of Symbol
1	2	3	4	5	6	7	
0	0	0	0	0	0	0	0
1	1	0	1	0	0	1	1
0	1	0	1	0	1	0	2
1	0	0	0	0	1	1	3
1	0	0	1	1	0	0	4
0	1	0	0	1	0	1	5
1	1	0	0	1	1	0	6
0	0	0	1	1	1	1	7
1	1	1	0	0	0	0	8
0	0	1	1	0	0	1	9
1	0	1	1	0	1	0	10
0	1	1	0	0	1	1	11
0	1	1	1	1	0	0	12
1	0	1	0	1	0	1	13
0	0	1	0	1	1	0	14
1	1	1	1	1	1	1	15

As an illustration of how this code "works" let us take the symbol 0 1 1 1 1 0 0 corresponding to the decimal value 12 and change the 1 in the fifth position to a 0. We now examine the new symbol

0111000

by the methods of this section to see how the error is located. From Table II the first parity check is over positions 1, 3, 5, 7 and predicts a 1 for the first position while we find a 0 there; hence we write a

1.

The second parity check is over positions 2, 3, 6, 7, and predicts the second position correctly; hence we write a 0 to the left of the 1, obtaining

01.

The third parity check is over positions 4, 5, 6, 7 and predicts wrongly; hence we write a 1 to the left of the 0 1, obtaining

101.

This sequence of 0's and 1's regarded as a binary number is the number 5; hence the error is in the fifth position. The correct symbol is therefore obtained by changing the 0 in the fifth position to a 1.

4. Single Error Correcting Plus Double Error Detecting Codes

To construct a single error correcting plus double error detecting code we begin with a single error correcting code. To this code we add one more position for checking all the previous positions, using an even parity check. To see the operation of this code we have to examine a number of cases:

a. No errors. All parity checks, including the last, are satisfied.

b. Single error. The last parity check fails in all such situations whether the error be in the information, the original check positions, or the last check position. The original checking number gives the position of the error, where now the zero value means the last check position.

c. Two errors. In all such situations the last parity check is satisfied, and the checking number indicates some kind of error.

As an illustration let us construct an eight-position code from the previous seven-position code. To do this we add an eighth position which is chosen so that there are an even number of 1's in the eight positions. Thus we add an eighth column to Table III which has:

Table IV

0
0
1
1
1
1
0
0
1
1
0
0
0
0
1
1

PART II: GENERAL THEORY

5. A Geometrical Model

When examining various problems connected with error detecting and correcting codes it is often convenient to introduce a geometric model. The model used here consists in identifying the various sequences of 0's and 1's which are the symbols of a code with vertices of a unit n-dimensional cube. The code points, labelled $x, y, z,$, form a subset of the set of all vertices of the cube.

Into this space of 2^n points we introduce a *distance,* or, as it is usually called, a *metric, $D(x, y)$.* The definition of the metric is based on the observation that a single error in a code point changes one coordinate, two errors, two coordinates, and in general d errors produce a difference in d coordinates. Thus we define the distance $D(x, y)$ between two points x and y as the number of coordinates for which x and y are different. This is the same as the least number of edges which must be traversed in going from x to y. This distance function satisfies the usual three conditions for a metric, namely,

$D(x, y) = 0$ if and only if $x = y$

$D(x, y) = D(y, x) > 0$ if $x \neq y$

$D(z, y) + D(y, z) \geq D(x, z)$ (triangle inequality).

As an example we note that each of the following code points in the three-dimensional cube is two units away from the others,

0 0 1

0 1 0

1 0 0

1 1 1.

To continue the geometric language, a sphere of radius r about a point x is defined as all points which are at a distance r from the point x. Thus, in the above example, the first three code points are on a sphere of radius 2 about the point $(1, 1, 1)$. In fact, in this example any one code point may be chosen as the center and the other three will lie on the surface of a sphere of radius 2.

If all the code points are at a distance of at least 2 from each other, then it follows that any single error will carry a code point over to a point that is *not* a code point, and hence is a meaningless symbol. This in turn means that any single error is detectable. If the minimum distance between code points is at least three units then any single error will leave the point nearer to the correct code point than to any other code point, and this means that any single error will be correctable. This type of information is summarized in the following table:

Table V

Minimum Distance	Meaning
1	uniqueness
2	single error detection
3	single error correction
4	single error correction plus double error detection
5	double error correction Etc.

Conversely, it is evident that, if we are to effect the detection and correction listed, then all the distances between code points must equal or exceed the minimum distance listed. Thus the problem of finding suitable codes is the same as that of finding subsets of points in the space which maintain at least the minimum distance condition. The special codes in sections 2, 3, and 4 were merely descriptions of how to choose a particular subset of points for minimum distances 2, 3, and 4 respectively.

It should perhaps be noted that, at a given minimum distance, some of the correctability may be exchanged for more detectability. For example, a subset with minimum distance 5 may be used for:

a. double error correction, (with, of course, double error detection).

b. single error correction plus triple error detection.

c. quadruple error detection.

Returning for the moment to the particular codes constructed in Part I we note that any interchanges of positions in a code do not change the code in any essential way. Neither does interchanging the 0's and 1's in any position, a process usually called complementing. This idea is made more precise in the following definition:

Definition. Two codes are said to be *equivalent* to each other if, by a finite number of the following operations, one can be transformed into the other:

a. The interchange of any two positions in the code symbols.

b. The complementing of the values in any position in the code symbols. This is a formal equivalence relation (~) since $A \sim A$; $A \sim B$ implies $B \sim A$; and $A \sim B$, $B \sim C$ implies A ~ C. Thus we can reduce the study of a class of codes to the study of typical members of each equivalence class.

In terms of the geometric model, equivalence transformations amount to rotations and reflections of the unit cube.

6. Single Error Detecting Codes

The problem studied in this section is that of packing the maximum number of points in a unit n-dimensional cube such that no two points are closer than 2 units from each other. We shall show that, as in section 2, 2^{n-1} points can be so packed, and, further, that any such optimal packing is equivalent to that used in section 2.

To prove these statements we first observe that the vertices of the n-dimensional cube are composed of those of two $(n-1)$-dimensional cubes. Let A be the maximum number of points packed in the original cube. Then one of the two $(n-1)$-dimensional cubes has at least $A/2$ points. This cube being again decomposed into two lower dimensional cubes, we find that one of them has at least $A/2^2$ points. Continuing in this way we come to a two-dimensional cube having $A/2^{n-2}$ points. We now observe that a square can have at most two points separated by at least two units; hence the original n-dimensional cube had at most 2^{n-1} points not less than two units apart.

To prove the equivalence of any two optimal packings we note that, if the packing is optimal, then each of the two sub-cubes has half the points. Calling this the first coordinate we see that half the points have a 0 and half have a 1. The next subdivision will again divide these into two equal groups having 0's and 1's respectively. After $(n-1)$ such stages we have, upon re-ordering the assigned values if there be any, exactly

the first $n-1$ positions of the code devised in section 2. To each sequence of the first $n-1$ coordinates there exist $n-1$ other sequences which differ from it by one coordinate. Once we fix the n-th coordinate of some one point, say the origin which has all 0's, then to maintain the known minimum distance of two units between code points the n-th coordinate is uniquely determined for all other code points. Thus the last coordinate is determined within a complementation so that any optimal code is equivalent to that given in section 2.

It is interesting to note that in these two proofs we have used only the assumption that the code symbols are all of length n.

7. Single Error Correcting Codes

It has probably been noted by the reader that, in the particular codes of Part I, a distinction was made between information and check positions, while, in the geometric model, there is no real distinction between the various coordinates. To bring the two treatments more in line with each other we redefine a *systematic* code as a code whose symbol lengths are all equal and

a. The positions checked are independent of the information contained in the symbol.

b. The checks are independent of each other.

c. We use parity checks.

This is equivalent to the earlier definition. To show this we form a matrix whose i-th row has 1's in the positions of the i-th parity check and 0's elsewhere. By assumption 1 the matrix is fixed and does not change from code symbol to code symbol. From 2 the rank of the matrix is k. This in turn means that the system can be solved for k of the positions expressed in terms of the other $n - k$ positions. Assumption 3 indicates that in this solving we use the arithmetic in which $1 + 1 = 0$.

There exist non-systematic codes, but so far none have been found which for a given n and minimum distance d have more code symbols than a systematic code. Section 9 gives an example of a non-systematic code.

Turning to the main problem of this section we find from Table V that a single error correcting code has code points at least three units from each other. Thus each point may be surrounded by a sphere of radius 1 with no two spheres having a point in common. Each sphere has a center point and n points on its surface, a total of $n + 1$ points. Thus the space of 2^n points can have at most:

$$\frac{2^n}{n + 1}$$

spheres. This is exactly the bound we found before in section 3.

While we have shown that the special single error correcting code constructed in section 3 is of minimum redundancy, we cannot show that all optimal codes are equivalent, since the following trivial example shows that this is not so. For $n = 4$ we find from Table I that $m = 1$ and $k = 3$. Thus there are at most two code symbols in a four-position code. The following two optimal codes are clearly not equivalent:

0 0 0 0	and	0 0 0 0
1 1 1 1		0 1 1 1

8. Single Error Correcting Plus Double Error Detecting Codes

In this section we shall prove that the codes constructed in section 4 are of minimum redundancy. We have already shown in section 4 how, for a minimum redundancy code of $n - 1$ dimensions with a minimum distance of 3, we can construct an n dimensional code having the same number of code symbols but with a minimum distance of 4. If this were not of minimum redundancy there would exist a code having more code symbols but with the same n and the same minimum distance 4 between them. Taking this code we remove the last coordinate. This reduces the dimension from n to $n - 1$ and the minimum distance between code symbols by, at most, one unit, while leaving the number of code symbols the same. This contradicts the assumption that the code we began our construction with was of minimum redundancy. Thus the codes of section 4 are of minimum redundancy.

This is a special case of the following general theorem: To any minimum redundancy code of N points in $n - 1$ dimensions and having a minimum distance of $2k - 1$ there corresponds a minimum redundancy code of A points in n dimensions having a minimum distance of $2k$, and conversely. To construct the n dimensional code from the $n - 1$ dimensional code we simply add a single n-th coordinate which is fixed by an even parity check over the n positions. This also increases the minimum distance by 1 for the following reason: Any two points which, in the $n - 1$ dimensional code; were at a distance $2k - 1$ from each other had an odd number of differences between their coordinates. Thus the parity check was set oppositely for the two points, increasing the distance between them to $2k$. The additional coordinate could not decrease any distances, so that all points in the code are now at a minimum distance of $2k$. To go in the reverse direction we simply drop one coordinate from the n dimensional code. This reduces the minimum distance of $2k$ to $2k - 1$ while leaving N the same. It is clear that if one code is of minimum redundancy then the other is, too.

9. Miscellaneous Observations

For the next case, minimum distance of five units, one can surround each code point by a sphere of radius 2. Each sphere will contain

$$1 + C(n, 1) + C(n, 2)$$

points, where $C(n, k)$ is the binomial coefficient, so that an upper bound on the number of code points in a systematic code is

$$\frac{2^n}{1 + C(n, 1) + C(n, 2)} = \frac{2^{n+1}}{n^2 + n + 2} \geq 2^m.$$

This bound is too high. For example, in the case of $n = 7$, we find that $m = 2$ so that there should be a code with four code points. The maximum possible, as can be easily found by trial and error, is two.

In a similar fashion a bound on the number of code points may be found whenever the minimum distance between code points is an odd number. A bound on the even cases can then be found by use of the general theorem of the preceding section. These bounds are, in general, too high, as the above example shows.

If we write the bound on the number of code points in a unit cube of dimension n and with minimum distance d between them as $B(n, d)$, then the information of this type in the present paper may be summarized as follows:

$$B(n, 1) = 2^n$$

$$B(n, 2) = 2^{n-1}$$

$$B(n, 3) = 2^m \leq \frac{2^n}{n+1}$$

$$B(n, 4) = 2^m \leq \frac{2^{n-1}}{n}$$

$$B(n-1, 2k-1) = B(n, 2k)$$

$$B(n, 2k-1) = 2^m \leq \frac{2^n}{1 + C(n, 1) + \ldots + C(n, k-1)}$$

While these bounds have been attained for certain cases, no general methods have yet been found for constructing optimal codes when the minimum distance between code points exceeds four units, nor is it known whether the bound is or is not attainable by systematic codes.

We have dealt mainly with systematic codes. The existence of non-systematic codes is proved by the following example of a single error correcting code with $n = 6$.

$$0\ 0\ 0\ 0\ 0\ 0$$

$$0\ 1\ 0\ 1\ 0\ 1$$

$$1\ 0\ 0\ 1\ 1\ 0$$

$$1\ 1\ 1\ 0\ 0\ 0$$

$$0\ 0\ 1\ 0\ 1\ 1$$

$$1\ 1\ 1\ 1\ 1\ 1.$$

The all 0 symbol indicates that any parity check must be an even one. The all 1 symbol indicates that each parity check must involve an even number of posi-

tions. A direct comparison indicates that since no two columns are the same the even parity checks must involve four or six positions. An examination of the second symbol, which has three 1's in it, indicates that no six-position parity check can exist. Trying now the four-position parity checks we find that

1	2			5	6
	2	3	4	5	

are two independent parity checks and that no third one is independent of these two. Two parity checks can at most locate four positions, and, since there are six positions in the code, these two parity checks are not enough to locate any single error. The code is, however, single error correcting since it satisfies the minimum distance condition of three units.

The only previous work in the field of error correction that has appeared in print, so far as the author is aware, is that of M. J. E. Golay.[4]

• • •

1. Franz Alt, "A Bell Telephone Laboratories' Computing Machine"—I, II. Mathematical Tables and Other Aids to Computation, Vol. 3, pp. 1–13 and 60–84, Jan. and Apr. 1948.

2. S. Sparks, and R. G. Kreer, "Tape Relay System for Radio Telegraph Operation," *R.C.A. Review,* Vol. 8, pp. 393–426, (especially p. 417), 1947.

3. In Section 7 this is shown to be equivalent to a much weaker appearing definition.

4. M. J. E. Golay, Correspondence, Notes on Digital Coding, *Proceedings of the I.R.E.,* Vol. 37, p. 657, June 1949.

13
Origins of the Internet

13.1
As We May Think

Vannevar Bush

From *The Atlantic Monthly* 176 (1945): 101–8.

INTRODUCTORY NOTE TO READING 13.1

Vannevar Bush's article describes his proposed "Memex" system for organizing, storing, retrieving, and linking information. Inspired by microfilm technology—which in 1945 represented the most advanced means of storing large amounts of information—Bush conceived of the Memex as consisting of a desk equipped with projection screens, buttons and levers, a keyboard, and a storage system designed to provide instant access to microfilmed books, periodicals, documents, photographs, etc. The Memex system would allow pieces of data to be linked into permanent "information trails" dictated by the individual user's needs, which could be called up again and modified at any future date. Bush imagined the Memex as mechanical analog of the associative faculty of the human brain that could support and extend the powers of human memory and association.

In his effort to envisage a machine that would serve as an analogy to the human memory, Bush's thoughts paralleled those of John von Neumann, who set out the theory of the stored-program computer at almost exactly the same time. Even though both men were thinking and writing about quite different subjects, each was attempting to imagine mechanical ways of processing information that were analogous to the human brain. Von Neumann attempted to model the stored-program computer after an abstract model of the way the brain's information-processing methods were then theoretically understood. He expressed this attempt in his privately circulated *First Draft of a Report on the EDVAC* (1945), incorporating his own ideas and those of the Moore School group working on EDVAC (Reading 8.1). Unlike von Neumann's seminal report, Bush's general exposition of the Memex concept, written for a non-technical audience and emphasizing the individual relationship between user and machine, had little or no influence when it was originally published. Only after the development of the personal computer and the Internet was Bush's paper resurrected as a remarkably early expression of ideas that were eventually realized in different ways as hyperlinks on the World Wide Web and bookmarks or "favorites" stored in web browsers. [JMN]

TEXT OF READING 13.1

This has not been a scientist's war; it has been a war in which all have had a part. The scientists, burying their old professional competition in the demand of a common cause, have shared greatly and learned much. It has been exhilarating to work in effective partnership. Now, for many, this appears to be approaching an end. What are the scientists to do next?

For the biologists, and particularly for the medical scientists, there can be little indecision, for their war has hardly required them to leave the old paths. Many indeed have been able to carry on their war research in their familiar peacetime laboratories. Their objectives remain much the same.

It is the physicists who have been thrown most violently off stride, who have left academic pursuits for the making of strange destructive gadgets, who have had to devise new methods for their unanticipated assignments. They have done their part on the devices that made it possible to turn back the enemy, have worked in combined effort with the physicists of our allies. They have felt within themselves the stir of achievement. They have been part of a great team. Now, as peace approaches, one asks where they will find objectives worthy of their best.

1

Of what lasting benefit has been man's use of science and of the new instruments which his research brought into existence? First, they have increased his control of his material environment. They have improved his food, his clothing, his shelter; they have increased his security and released him partly from the bondage of bare existence. They have given him increased knowledge of his own biological processes so that he has had a progressive freedom from disease and an increased span of life. They are illuminating the interactions of his physiological and psychological functions, giving the promise of an improved mental health.

Science has provided the swiftest communication between individuals; it has provided a record of ideas and has enabled man to manipulate and to make extracts from that record so that knowledge evolves and endures throughout the life of a race rather than that of an individual.

There is a growing mountain of research. But there is increased evidence that we are being bogged down today as specialization extends. The investigator is staggered by the findings and conclusions of thousands of other workers—conclusions which he cannot find time to grasp, much less to remember, as they appear. Yet specialization becomes increasingly necessary for progress, and the effort to bridge between disciplines is correspondingly superficial.

Professionally our methods of transmitting and reviewing the results of research are generations old and by now are totally inadequate for their purpose. If the aggregate time spent in writing scholarly works and in reading them could be evaluated, the ratio between these amounts of time might well be startling. Those who conscientiously attempt to keep abreast of current thought, even in restricted fields, by close and continuous reading might well shy away from an examination calculated to show how much of the previous month's efforts could be produced on call. Mendel's concept of the laws of genetics was lost to the world for a generation because his publication did not reach the few who were capable of grasping and extending it; and this sort of catastrophe is undoubtedly being repeated all about us, as truly significant attainments become lost in the mass of the inconsequential.

The difficulty seems to be, not so much that we publish unduly in view of the extent and variety of present day interests, but rather that publication has been extended far beyond our present ability to make real use of the record. The summation of human experience is being expanded at a prodigious rate, and the means we use for threading through the consequent maze to the momentarily important item is the same as was used in the days of square-rigged ships.

But there are signs of a change as new and powerful instrumentalities come into use. Photocells capable of seeing things in a physical sense, advanced photography which can record what is seen or even what is not, thermionic tubes capable of controlling potent forces under the guidance of less power than a mosquito uses to vibrate his wings, cathode ray tubes rendering visible an occurrence so brief that by comparison a microsecond is a long time, relay combinations which will carry out involved sequences of movements more reliably than any human operator and thousands of times as fast—there are plenty of mechanical aids with which to effect a transformation in scientific records.

Two centuries ago Leibnitz invented a calculating machine which embodied most of the essential features of recent keyboard devices, but it could not then come into use. The economics of the situation were against it: the labor involved in constructing it, before the days of mass production, exceeded the labor to be saved by its use, since all it could accomplish could be duplicated by sufficient use of pencil and paper. Moreover, it would have been subject to frequent breakdown, so that it could not have been depended upon; for at that time and long after, complexity and unreliability were synonymous.

Babbage, even with remarkably generous support for his time, could not produce his great arithmetical machine. His idea was sound enough, but construction and maintenance costs were then too heavy. Had a Pharaoh been given detailed and explicit designs of an automobile, and had he understood them completely, it would have taxed the resources of his kingdom to have fashioned the thousands of parts for a single car, and that car would have broken down on the first trip to Giza.

Machines with interchangeable parts can now be constructed with great economy of effort. In spite of much complexity, they perform reliably. Witness the humble typewriter, or the movie camera, or the automobile. Electrical contacts have ceased to stick when thoroughly understood. Note the automatic telephone exchange, which has hundreds of thousands of such contacts, and yet is reliable. A spider web of metal, sealed in a thin glass container, a wire heated to brilliant glow, in short, the thermionic tube of radio sets, is made by the hundred million, tossed about in packages, plugged into sockets—and it works! Its gossamer parts, the precise location and alignment involved in its construction, would have occupied a master craftsman of the guild for months; now it is built for thirty cents. The world has arrived at an age of cheap complex devices of great reliability; and something is bound to come of it.

2

A record if it is to be useful to science, must be continuously extended, it must be stored, and above all it must be consulted. Today we make the record conventionally by writing and photography, followed by printing; but we also record on film, on wax disks, and on magnetic wires. Even if utterly new recording procedures do not appear, these present ones are certainly in the process of modification and extension.

Certainly progress in photography is not going to stop. Faster material and lenses, more automatic cameras, finer-grained sensitive compounds to allow an extension of the minicamera idea, are all imminent. Let us project this trend ahead to a logical, if not inevitable, outcome. The camera hound of the future wears on his forehead a lump a little larger than a walnut. It takes pictures 3 millimeters square, later to be projected or enlarged, which after all involves only a factor of 10 beyond present practice. The lens is of universal focus, down to any distance accommodated by the unaided eye, simply because it is of short focal length. There is a built-in photocell on the walnut such as we now have on at least one camera, which automatically adjusts exposure for a wide range of illumination. There is film in the walnut for a hundred exposures, and the spring for operating its shutter and shifting its film is wound once for all when the film clip is inserted. It produces its result in full color. It may well be stereoscopic, and record with two spaced glass eyes, for striking improvements in stereoscopic technique are just around the corner.

The cord which trips its shutter may reach down a man's sleeve within easy reach of his fingers. A quick squeeze, and the picture is taken. On a pair of ordinary glasses is a square of fine lines near the top of one lens, where it is out of the way of ordinary vision. When an object appears in that square, it is lined up for its picture. As the scientist of the future moves about the laboratory or the field, every time he looks at something worthy of the record, he trips the shutter and in it goes, without even an audible click. Is this all fantastic? The only fantastic thing about it is the idea of making as many pictures as would result from its use.

Will there be dry photography? It is already here in two forms. When Brady made his Civil War pictures, the plate had to be wet at the time of exposure. Now it has to be wet during development instead. In the future perhaps it need not be wetted at all. There have long been films impregnated with diazo dyes which form a picture without development, so that it is already there as soon as the camera has been operated. An exposure to ammonia gas destroys the unexposed dye, and the picture can then be taken out into the light and examined. The process is now slow, but someone may speed it up, and it has no grain difficulties such as now keep photographic researchers busy. Often it would be advantageous to be able to snap the camera and to look at the picture immediately.

Another process now in use is also slow, and more or less clumsy. For fifty years impregnated papers have been used which turn dark at every point where an electrical contact touches them, by reason of the chemical change thus produced in an iodine compound included in the paper. They have been used to make records, for a pointer moving across them can leave a trail behind. If the electrical potential on the pointer is varied as it moves, the line becomes light or dark in accordance with the potential.

This scheme is now used in facsimile transmission. The pointer draws a set of closely spaced lines across the paper one after another. As it moves, its potential is varied in accordance with a varying current received over wires from a distant station, where these variations are produced by a photocell which is similarly scanning a picture. At every instant the darkness of the line being drawn is made equal to the darkness of the point on the picture being observed by the photocell. Thus, when the whole picture has been covered, a replica appears at the receiving end.

A scene itself can be just as well looked over line by line by the photocell in this way as can a photograph of the scene. This whole apparatus constitutes a camera, with the added feature, which can be dispensed with if desired, of making its picture at a distance. It is slow, and the picture is poor in detail. Still, it does give another process of dry photography, in which the picture is finished as soon as it is taken.

It would be a brave man who would predict that such a process will always remain clumsy, slow, and faulty in detail. Television equipment today transmits sixteen reasonably good pictures a second, and it involves only two essential differences from the process described above. For one, the record is made by a moving beam of electrons rather than a moving pointer, for the reason that an electron beam can sweep across the picture very rapidly indeed. The other difference involves merely the use of a screen which glows momentarily when the electrons hit, rather than a chemically treated paper or film which is permanently altered. This speed is necessary in television, for motion pictures rather than stills are the object.

Use chemically treated film in place of the glowing screen, allow the apparatus to transmit one picture only rather than a succession, and a rapid camera for dry photography results. The treated film needs to be far faster in action than present examples, but it probably could be. More serious is the objection that this scheme would involve putting the film inside a vacuum chamber, for electron beams behave normally only in such a rarefied environment. This difficulty could be avoided by allowing the electron beam to play on one side of a partition, and by pressing the film against the other side, if this partition were such as to allow the electrons to go through perpendicular to its surface, and to prevent them from spreading out sideways. Such partitions, in crude form, could certainly be constructed, and they will hardly hold up the general development.

Like dry photography, microphotography still has a long way to go. The basic scheme of reducing the size of the record, and examining it by projection rather than directly, has possibilities too great to be ignored. The combination of optical projection and photographic reduction is already producing some results in microfilm for scholarly purposes, and the potentialities are highly suggestive. Today, with microfilm, reductions by a linear factor of 20 can be employed and still produce full clarity when the material is re-enlarged for examination. The limits are set by the graininess of the film, the excellence of the optical system, and the efficiency of the light sources employed. All of these are rapidly improving.

Assume a linear ratio of 100 for future use. Consider film of the same thickness as paper, although thinner film will certainly be usable. Even under these conditions there would be a total factor of 10,000 between the bulk of the ordinary record on books, and its microfilm replica. The *Encyclopaedia Britannica* could be reduced to the volume of a matchbox. A library of a million volumes could be compressed into one end of a desk. If the human race has produced since the invention of movable type a total record, in the form of magazines, newspapers, books, tracts, advertising blurbs, correspondence, having a volume corresponding to a billion books, the whole affair, assembled and compressed, could be lugged off in a moving van. Mere compression, of course, is not enough; one needs not only to make and store a record but also be able to consult it, and this aspect of the matter comes later. Even the modern great library is not generally consulted; it is nibbled at by a few.

Compression is important, however, when it comes to costs. The material for the microfilm *Britannica* would cost a nickel, and it could be mailed anywhere for a cent. What would it cost to print a million copies? To print a sheet of newspaper, in a large edition, costs a small fraction of a cent. The entire material of the *Britannica* in reduced microfilm form would go on a sheet eight and one-half by eleven inches. Once it is available, with the photographic reproduction methods of the future, duplicates in large quantities could probably be turned out for a cent apiece beyond the cost of materials. The preparation of the original copy? That introduces the next aspect of the subject.

3

To make the record, we now push a pencil or tap a typewriter. Then comes the process of digestion and correction, followed by an intricate process of typesetting, printing, and distribution. To consider the first stage of the procedure, will the author of the future cease writing by hand or typewriter and talk directly to the record? He does so indirectly, by talking to a stenographer or a wax cylinder; but the elements are all present if he wishes to have his talk directly produce a typed record. All he needs to do is to take advantage of existing mechanisms and to alter his language.

At a recent World Fair a machine called a Vocoder was shown. A girl stroked its keys and it emitted recognizable speech. No human vocal chords entered into the procedure at any point; the keys simply combined some electrically produced vibrations and passed these on to a loud-speaker. In the Bell Laboratories there is the converse of this machine, called a Vocoder. The loudspeaker is replaced by a microphone, which picks up sound. Speak to it, and the corresponding keys move. This may be one element of the postulated system.

The other element is found in the stenotype, that somewhat disconcerting device encountered usually at public meetings. A girl strokes its keys languidly and looks about the room and sometimes at the speaker with a disquieting gaze. From it emerges a typed strip which records in a phonetically simplified language a record of what the speaker is supposed to have said. Later this strip is retyped into ordinary language, for in its nascent form it is intelligible only to the initiated. Combine these two elements, let the Vocoder run the stenotype, and the result is a machine which types when talked to.

Our present languages are not especially adapted to this sort of mechanization, it is true. It is strange that the inventors of universal languages have not seized upon the idea of producing one which better fitted the technique for transmitting and recording speech. Mechanization may yet force the issue, especially in the scientific field; whereupon scientific jargon would become still less intelligible to the layman.

One can now picture a future investigator in his laboratory. His hands are free, and he is not anchored. As he moves about and observes, he photographs and comments. Time is automatically recorded to tie the two records together. If he goes into the field, he may be connected by radio to his recorder. As he ponders over his notes in the evening, he again talks his comments into the record. His typed record, as well as his photographs, may both be in miniature, so that he projects them for examination.

Much needs to occur, however, between the collection of data and observations, the extraction of parallel material from the existing record, and the final insertion of new material into the general body of the common record. For mature thought there is no mechanical substitute. But creative thought and essentially repetitive thought are very different things. For the latter there are, and may be, powerful mechanical aids.

Adding a column of figures is a repetitive thought process, and it was long ago properly relegated to the machine. True, the machine is sometimes controlled by a keyboard, and thought of a sort enters in reading the figures and poking the corresponding keys, but even this is avoidable. Machines have been made which will read typed figures by photocells and then depress the corresponding keys; these are combinations of photocells for scanning the type, electric circuits for sorting the consequent variations, and relay circuits for interpreting the result into the action of solenoids to pull the keys down.

All this complication is needed because of the clumsy way in which we have learned to write figures. If we recorded them positionally, simply by the configuration of a set of dots on a card, the automatic reading mechanism would become comparatively simple. In fact if the dots are holes, we have the punched-card machine long ago produced by Hollerith for the purposes of the census, and now used throughout business. Some types of complex businesses could hardly operate without these machines.

Adding is only one operation. To perform arithmetical computation involves also subtraction, multiplication, and division, and in addition some method for temporary storage of results, removal from storage for further manipulation, and recording of final results by printing. Machines for these purposes are now of two types: keyboard machines for accounting and the like, manually controlled for the insertion of data, and usually automatically controlled as far as the sequence of operations is concerned; and punched-card machines in which separate operations are usually delegated to a series of machines, and the cards then transferred bodily from one to another. Both forms are very useful; but as far as complex computations are concerned, both are still in embryo.

Rapid electrical counting appeared soon after the physicists found it desirable to count cosmic rays. For their own purposes the physicists promptly constructed thermionic-tube equipment capable of counting electrical impulses at the rate of 100,000 a second. The advanced arithmetical machines of the future will be electrical in nature, and they will perform at 100 times present speeds, or more.

Moreover, they will be far more versatile than present commercial machines, so that they may readily be adapted for a wide variety of operations. They will be controlled by a control card or film, they will select their own data and manipulate it in accordance with the instructions thus inserted, they will perform complex arithmetical computations at exceedingly high speeds, and they will record results in such form as to be readily available for distribution or for later further manipulation. Such machines will have enormous appetites. One of them will take instructions and data from a whole roomful of girls armed with simple key board punches, and will deliver sheets of computed results every few minutes. There will always be plenty of things to compute in the detailed affairs of millions of people doing complicated things.

4

The repetitive processes of thought are not confined however, to matters of arithmetic and statistics. In fact, every time one combines and records facts in accordance with established logical processes, the creative aspect of thinking is concerned only with the selection of the data and the process to be employed and the manipulation thereafter is repetitive in nature and hence a fit matter to be relegated to the machine. Not so much has been done along these lines, beyond the bounds of arithmetic, as might be done, primarily because of the economics of the situation. The needs of business and the extensive market obviously waiting, assured the advent of mass-produced arithmetical machines just as soon as production methods were sufficiently advanced.

With machines for advanced analysis no such situation existed; for there was and is no extensive market; the users of advanced methods of manipulating data are a very small part of the population. There are, however, machines for solving differential equations—and functional and integral equations, for that matter. There are many special machines, such as the harmonic synthesizer which predicts the tides. There will be many more, appearing certainly first in the hands of the scientist and in small numbers.

If scientific reasoning were limited to the logical processes of arithmetic, we should not get far in our understanding of the physical world. One might as well attempt to grasp the game of poker entirely by the use of the mathematics of probability. The abacus, with its beads strung on parallel wires, led the Arabs to positional numeration and the concept of zero many centuries before the rest of the world; and it was a useful tool—so useful that it still exists.

It is a far cry from the abacus to the modern keyboard accounting machine. It will be an equal step to the arithmetical machine of the future. But even this new machine will not take the scientist where he needs to go. Relief must be secured from laborious detailed manipulation of higher mathematics as well, if the users of it are to free their brains for something more than repetitive detailed transformations in accordance with established rules. A mathematician is not a man who can readily manipulate figures; often he cannot. He is not even a man who can readily perform the transformations of equations by the use of calculus. He is primarily an individual who is skilled in the use of symbolic logic on a high plane, and especially he is a man of intuitive judgment in the choice of the manipulative processes he employs.

All else he should be able to turn over to his mechanism, just as confidently as he turns over the propelling of his car to the intricate mechanism under the hood. Only then will mathematics be practically effective in bringing the growing knowledge of atomistics to the useful solution of the advanced problems of chemistry, metallurgy, and biology. For this reason there still come more machines to handle advanced mathematics for the scientist. Some of them will be sufficiently bizarre to suit the most fastidious connoisseur of the present artifacts of civilization.

5

The scientist, however, is not the only person who manipulates data and examines the world about him by the use of logical processes, although he sometimes preserves this appearance by adopting into the fold anyone who becomes logical, much in the manner in which a British labor leader is elevated to knighthood. Whenever logical processes of thought are employed—that is, whenever thought for a time runs along an accepted groove—there is an opportunity for the machine. Formal logic used to be a keen instrument in the hands of the teacher in his trying of students' souls. It is readily possible to construct a machine which will manipulate premises in accordance with formal logic, simply by the clever use of relay circuits. Put a set of premises into such a device and turn the crank, and it will readily pass out conclusion after conclusion, all in accordance with logical law, and with no more slips than would be expected of a keyboard adding machine.

Logic can become enormously difficult, and it would undoubtedly be well to produce more assurance in its use. The machines for higher analysis have usually been equation solvers. Ideas are beginning to appear for equation transformers, which will rearrange the relationship expressed by an equation in accordance with strict and rather advanced logic. Progress is inhibited by the exceedingly crude way in which mathematicians express their relationships. They employ a symbolism which grew like Topsy and has little consistency; a strange fact in that most logical field.

A new symbolism, probably positional, must apparently precede the reduction of mathematical transformations to machine processes. Then, on beyond the strict logic of the mathematician, lies the application of logic in everyday affairs. We may some day click off arguments on a machine with the same assurance that we now enter sales on a cash register. But the machine of logic will not look like a cash register, even of the streamlined model.

So much for the manipulation of ideas and their insertion into the record. Thus far we seem to be worse off than before—for we can enormously extend the record; yet even in its present bulk we can hardly consult it. This is a much larger matter than merely the extraction of data for the purposes of scientific research; it involves the entire process by which man profits by his inheritance of acquired knowledge. The prime action of use is selection, and here we are halting indeed. There may be millions of fine thoughts, and the account of the experience on which they are based, all encased within stone walls of acceptable architectural form; but if the scholar can get at only one a week by diligent search, his syntheses are not likely to keep up with the current scene.

Selection, in this broad sense, is a stone adze in the hands of a cabinetmaker. Yet, in a narrow sense and in other areas, something has already been done mechanically on selection. The personnel officer of a factory drops a stack of a few thousand employee cards into a selecting machine, sets a code in accordance with an established convention, and produces in a short time a list of all employees who live in Trenton and know Spanish. Even such devices are much too slow when it comes, for example, to matching a set of fingerprints with one of five million on file. Selection devices of this sort will soon be speeded up from their present rate of reviewing data at a few hundred a minute. By the use of photocells and microfilm they will survey items at the rate of a thousand a second, and will print out duplicates of those selected.

This process, however, is simple selection: it proceeds by examining in turn every one of a large set of items, and by picking out those which have certain specified characteristics. There is another form of selection best illustrated by the automatic telephone exchange. You dial a number and the machine selects and connects just one of a million possible stations. It does not run over them all. It pays attention only to a class given by a first digit, then only to a subclass of

this given by the second digit, and so on; and thus proceeds rapidly and almost unerringly to the selected station. It requires a few seconds to make the selection, although the process could be speeded up if increased speed were economically warranted. If necessary, it could be made extremely fast by substituting thermionic-tube switching for mechanical switching, so that the full selection could be made in one one-hundredth of a second. No one would wish to spend the money necessary to make this change in the telephone system, but the general idea is applicable elsewhere.

Take the prosaic problem of the great department store. Every time a charge sale is made, there are a number of things to be done. The inventory needs to be revised, the salesman needs to be given credit for the sale, the general accounts need an entry, and, most important, the customer needs to be charged. A central records device has been developed in which much of this work is done conveniently. The salesman places on a stand the customer's identification card, his own card, and the card taken from the article sold—all punched cards. When he pulls a lever, contacts are made through the holes, machinery at a central point makes the necessary computations and entries, and the proper receipt is printed for the salesman to pass to the customer.

But there may be ten thousand charge customers doing business with the store, and before the full operation can be completed someone has to select the right card and insert it at the central office. Now rapid selection can slide just the proper card into position in an instant or two, and return it afterward. Another difficulty occurs, however. Someone must read a total on the card, so that the machine can add its computed item to it. Conceivably the cards might be of the dry photography type I have described. Existing totals could then be read by photocell, and the new total entered by an electron beam.

The cards may be in miniature, so that they occupy little space. They must move quickly. They need not be transferred far, but merely into position so that the photocell and recorder can operate on them. Positional dots can enter the data. At the end of the month a machine can readily be made to read these and to print an ordinary bill. With tube selection, in which no mechanical parts are involved in the switches, little time need be occupied in bringing the correct card into use—a second should suffice for the entire operation. The whole record on the card may be made by magnetic dots on a steel sheet if desired, instead of dots to be observed optically, following the scheme by which Poulsen long ago put speech on a magnetic wire. This method has the advantage of simplicity and ease of erasure. By using photography, however one can arrange to project the record in enlarged form and at a distance by using the process common in television equipment.

One can consider rapid selection of this form, and distant projection for other purposes. To be able to key one sheet of a million before an operator in a second or two, with the possibility of then adding notes thereto, is suggestive in many ways. It might even be of use in libraries, but that is another story. At any rate, there are now some interesting combinations possible. One might, for example, speak to a microphone, in the manner described in connection with the speech controlled typewriter, and thus make his selections. It would certainly beat the usual file clerk.

6

The real heart of the matter of selection, however, goes deeper than a lag in the adoption of mechanisms by libraries, or a lack of development of devices for their use. Our ineptitude in getting at the record is largely caused by the artificiality of systems of indexing. When data of any sort are placed in storage, they are filed alphabetically or numerically, and information is found (when it is) by tracing it down from subclass to subclass. It can be in only one place, unless duplicates are used; one has to have rules as to which path will locate it, and the rules are cumbersome. Having found one item, moreover, one has to emerge from the system and re-enter on a new path.

The human mind does not work that way. It operates by association. With one item in its grasp, it snaps instantly to the next that is suggested by the association of thoughts, in accordance with some intricate web of trails carried by the cells of the brain. It has other characteristics, of course; trails that are not frequently followed are prone to fade, items are not fully permanent, memory is transitory. Yet the speed of action, the intricacy of trails, the detail of mental pictures, is awe-inspiring beyond all else in nature.

Man cannot hope fully to duplicate this mental process artificially, but he certainly ought to be able to learn from it. In minor ways he may even improve, for his records have relative permanency. The first idea, however, to be drawn from the analogy concerns selection. Selection by association, rather than indexing, may yet be mechanized. One cannot hope thus to equal the speed and flexibility with which the mind follows an associative trail, but it should be possible to beat the mind decisively in regard to the permanence and clarity of the items resurrected from storage.

Consider a future device for individual use, which is a sort of mechanized private file and library. It needs a name, and, to coin one at random, "memex" will do. A memex is a device in which an individual stores all his books, records, and communications, and which is mechanized so that it may be consulted with exceeding speed and flexibility. It is an enlarged intimate supplement to his memory.

It consists of a desk, and while it can presumably be operated from a distance, it is primarily the piece of furniture at which he works. On the top are slanting translucent screens, on which material can be projected for convenient reading. There is a keyboard, and sets of buttons and levers. Otherwise it looks like an ordinary desk.

In one end is the stored material. The matter of bulk is well taken care of by improved microfilm. Only a small part of the interior of the memex is devoted to storage, the rest to mechanism. Yet if the user inserted 5000 pages of material a day it would take him hundreds of years to fill the repository, so he can be profligate and enter material freely.

Most of the memex contents are purchased on microfilm ready for insertion. Books of all sorts, pictures, current periodicals, newspapers, are thus obtained and dropped into place. Business correspondence takes the same path. And there is provision for direct entry. On the top of the memex is a transparent platen. On this are placed longhand notes, photographs, memoranda, all sorts of things. When one is in place, the depression of a lever causes it to be photographed onto the next blank space in a section of the memex film, dry photography being employed.

There is, of course, provision for consultation of the record by the usual scheme of indexing. If the user wishes to consult a certain book, he taps its code on the keyboard, and the title page of the book promptly appears before him, projected onto one of his viewing positions. Frequently-used codes are mnemonic, so that he seldom consults his code book; but when he does, a single tap of a key projects it for his use. Moreover, he has supplemental levers. On deflecting one of these levers to the right he runs through the book before him, each page in turn being projected at a speed which just allows a recognizing glance at each. If he deflects it further to the right, he steps through the book 10 pages at a time; still further at 100 pages at a time. Deflection to the left gives him the same control backwards.

A special button transfers him immediately to the first page of the index. Any given book of his library can thus be called up and consulted with far greater facility than if it were taken from a shelf. As he has several projection positions, he can leave one item in position while he calls up another. He can add marginal notes and comments, taking advantage of one possible type of dry photography, and it could even be arranged so that he can do this by a stylus scheme, such as is now employed in the telautograph seen in railroad waiting rooms, just as though he had the physical page before him.

7

All this is conventional, except for the projection forward of present-day mechanisms and gadgetry. It affords an immediate step, however, to associative indexing, the basic idea of which is a provision whereby any item may be caused at will to select immediately and automatically another. This is the essential feature of the memex. The process of tying two items together is the important thing.

When the user is building a trail, he names it, inserts the name in his code book, and taps it out on his keyboard. Before him are the two items to be joined, projected onto adjacent viewing positions. At the bottom of each there are a number of blank code spaces, and a pointer is set to indicate one of these on each item. The user taps a single key, and the items are permanently joined. In each code space appears the code word. Out of view, but also in the code space, is inserted a set of dots for photocell viewing; and on each item these dots by their positions designate the index number of the other item.

Thereafter, at any time, when one of these items is in view, the other can be instantly recalled merely by tapping a button below the corresponding code space. Moreover, when numerous items have been thus joined together to form a trail, they can be reviewed in turn, rapidly or slowly, by deflecting a lever like that used for turning the pages of a book. It is exactly as though the physical items had been gathered together from widely separated sources and bound together to form a new book. It is more than this, for any item can be joined into numerous trails.

The owner of the memex, let us say, is interested in the origin and properties of the bow and arrow. Specifically he is studying why the short Turkish bow was apparently superior to the English long bow in the skirmishes of the Crusades. He has dozens of possibly pertinent books and articles in his memex. First he runs through an encyclopedia, finds an interesting but sketchy article, leaves it projected. Next, in a history, he finds another pertinent item, and ties the two together. Thus he goes, building a trail of many items. Occasionally he inserts a comment of his own, either linking it into the main trail or joining it by a side trail to a particular item. When it becomes evident that the elastic properties of available materials had a great deal to do with the bow, he branches off on a side trail which takes him through textbooks on elasticity and tables of physical constants. He inserts a page of longhand analysis of his own. Thus he builds a trail of his interest through the maze of materials available to him.

And his trails do not fade. Several years later, his talk with a friend turns to the queer ways in which a people resist innovations, even of vital interest. He has an example, in the fact that the outraged Europeans still failed to adopt the Turkish bow. In fact he has a trail on it. A touch brings up the code book. Tapping a few keys projects the head of the trail. A lever runs through it at will, stopping at interesting items, going off on side excursions. It is an interesting trail, pertinent to the discussion. So he sets a reproducer in action, photographs the whole trail out, and passes it to his friend for insertion in his own memex, there to be linked into the more general trail.

8

Wholly new forms of encyclopedias will appear, ready made with a mesh of associative trails running through them, ready to be dropped into the memex and there amplified. The lawyer has at his touch the associated opinions and decisions of his whole experience, and of the experience of friends and authorities. The patent attorney has on call the millions of issued patents, with familiar trails to every point of his client's interest. The physician, puzzled by a patient's reactions, strikes the trail established in studying an earlier similar case, and runs rapidly through analogous case histories, with side references to the classics for the pertinent anatomy and histology. The chemist, struggling with the synthesis of an organic compound, has all the chemical literature before him in his laboratory, with trails following the analogies of compounds, and side trails to their physical and chemical behavior.

The historian, with a vast chronological account of a people, parallels it with a skip trail which stops only on the salient items, and can follow at any time contemporary trails which lead him all over civilization at a particular epoch. There is a new profession of trail blazers, those who find delight in the task of establishing useful trails through the enormous mass of the common record. The inheritance from the master becomes, not only his additions to the world's record, but for his disciples the entire scaffolding by which they were erected.

Thus science may implement the ways in which man produces, stores, and consults the record of the race. It might be striking to outline the instrumentalities of the future more spectacularly, rather than to stick closely to methods and elements now known and undergoing rapid development, as has been done here. Technical difficulties of all sorts have been ignored, certainly, but also ignored are means as yet unknown which may come any day to accelerate technical progress as violently as did the advent of the thermionic tube. In order that the picture may not be too commonplace, by reason of sticking to present-day patterns, it may be well to mention one such possibility, not to prophesy but merely to suggest, for prophecy based on extension of the known has substance, while prophecy founded on the unknown is only a doubly involved guess.

All our steps in creating or absorbing material of the record proceed through one of the senses—the tactile when we touch keys, the oral when we speak or listen, the visual when we read. Is it not possible that some day the path may be established more directly?

We know that when the eye sees, all the consequent information is transmitted to the brain by means of electrical vibrations in the channel of the optic nerve. This is an exact analogy with the electrical vibrations which occur in the cable of a television set: they convey the picture from the photocells which see it to the radio transmitter from which it is broadcast. We know further that if we can approach that cable with the proper instruments, we do not need to touch it; we can pick up those vibrations by electrical induction and thus discover and reproduce the scene which is being transmitted, just as a telephone wire may be tapped for its message.

The impulses which flow in the arm nerves of a typist convey to her fingers the translated information which reaches her eye or ear, in order that the fingers may be caused to strike the proper keys. Might not these currents be intercepted, either in the original form in which information is conveyed to the brain, or in the marvelously metamorphosed form in which they then proceed to the hand?

By bone conduction we already introduce sounds into the nerve channels of the deaf in order that they may hear. Is it not possible that we may learn to introduce them without the present cumbersomeness of first transforming electrical vibrations to mechanical ones, which the human mechanism promptly transforms back to the electrical form? With a couple of electrodes on the skull the encephalograph now produces pen-and-ink traces which bear some relation to the electrical phenomena going on in the brain itself. True, the record is unintelligible, except as it points out certain gross misfunctioning of the cerebral mechanism; but who would now place bounds on where such a thing may lead?

In the outside world, all forms of intelligence whether of sound or sight, have been reduced to the form of varying currents in an electric circuit in order that they may be transmitted. Inside the human frame exactly the same sort of process occurs. Must we always transform to mechanical movements in order to proceed from one electrical phenomenon to another? It is a suggestive thought, but it hardly warrants prediction without losing touch with reality and immediateness.

Presumably man's spirit should be elevated if he can better review his shady past and analyze more completely and objectively his present problems. He has built a civilization so complex that he needs to mechanize his records more fully if he is to push his experiment to its logical conclusion and not merely become bogged down part way there by overtaxing his limited memory. His excursions may be more enjoyable if he can reacquire the privilege of forgetting the manifold things he does not need to have immediately at hand, with some assurance that he can find them again if they prove important.

The applications of science have built man a well-supplied house, and are teaching him to live healthily therein. They have enabled him to throw masses of people against one another with cruel weapons. They may yet allow him truly to encompass the great record and to grow in the wisdom of race experience. He may perish in conflict before he learns to wield that record for his true good. Yet, in the application of science to the needs and desires of man, it would seem to be a singularly unfortunate stage at which to terminate the process, or to lose hope as to the outcome.

13.2

Information Flow in Large Communication Nets

Leonard Kleinrock

Proposal for a Ph.D. thesis, submitted to the Massachusetts Institute of Technology on May 31, 1961.

Len Kleinrock in 1970–72 lecturing on Bayes' Theorem.
(Photograph courtesy of Leonard Kleinrock.)

INTRODUCTORY NOTE TO READING 13.2

As a Ph.D candidate at MIT, Leonard Kleinrock was surrounded by many computers. He realized that sooner or later these computers would need to communicate with one another, and decided to develop the technology to make that occur. Early crude store-and-forward networks already existed but no one had elucidated the principles underlying the need for such structures. At the time the best available technology was the telephone system of circuit switching, which was woefully inadequate and inefficient for data communications that occur in bursts. No one had produced a model for data networks, much less an analysis of how they performed under stochastic loads. Moreover, no optimal design procedures existed for laying out the topology, choosing the channel speeds, and selecting the routing procedure and routes on data networks. Responding to these challenges, Kleinrock developed a technology and a mathematical theory of data communication in three works from 1961–64: his thesis proposal dated May 31, 1961, his Ph.D. thesis dated December, 1962, and a book, *Communication Nets*, published in 1964. The key portions of each of these works are reproduced in this anthology. The first two works are published here for the first time in book form. Among the concepts that Kleinrock established as being key to data networks are the following:

- Demand Access, an example of which is packet switching.

- Large Shared Systems, such as high speed channels, and the trading relations among delay, capacity and load.

- Distributed Control, such as distributed routing algorithms.

Kleinrock's thesis proposal of May 31, 1961, reproduced in its entirety in this anthology, laid out the basic structure and parameters of data networks. It focused on the fact that data traffic occurs in bursts—inherently different from telephone traffic—and that a new networking technology was required for data. Kleinrock identified the key performance measures for data networks, including throughput, response time, buffering, loss, and efficiency. He pointed out that the choice of queuing discipline was important for data network performance and posited that the tools of queuing theory were essential for dealing with data networks. In the forty years since the original thesis proposal, a huge field of analysis and design has grown out of this observation.

Kleinrock identified Jackson's model, gained from a study of waiting lines (reference 20 in Reading 13.2), as a basis for analysis, and pointed out ways that this model had to be modified to deal with data networks. This approach launched its own significant field of investigation. Kleinrock also presented early observational results for data networks, including the observation that large shared systems have an inherent efficiency that is proportional to the size of the system. In this thesis proposal he also proved data network theorems for some special network configurations. He would present the solutions to more general cases in his full doctoral dissertation, portions of which we reproduce as Reading 13.3. [JMN]

TEXT OF READING 13.2

I. STATEMENT OF THE PROBLEM:

The purpose of this thesis is to investigate the problems associated with information flow in large communication nets. These problems appear to have wide application, and yet, little serious research has been conducted in this field. The nets under consideration consist of nodes, connected to each other by links. The nodes receive, sort, store, and transmit messages that enter and leave via the links. The links consist of one-way channels, with fixed capacities. Among the typical systems which fit this description are the Post Office System, telegraph systems, and satellite communication systems.

A number of interesting and important questions can be asked about this system, and it is the purpose of this research to investigate the answers to some of these questions. A partial list of such questions might be as follows:

1. What is the probability density distribution for the total time lapse between the initiation and reception of a message between any two nodes? In particular, what is the expected value of this distribution?

2. Can one discuss the effective channel capacity between any two nodes?

3. Is it possible to predict the transient behavior and recovery time of the net under sudden changes in the traffic statistics?

4. How large should the storage capacity be at each node?

5. In what way does one arrive at a routing doctrine for incoming messages in different nets? In fact, can one state some bounds on the optimum performance of the net, independent of the routing doctrine (under some constraint on the set of allowable doctrines)?

6. Under what conditions does the net jam up, i.e., present an excessive delay in transmitting messages through the net?

The solution to this problem will dictate the extent to which the capacity of each link can be used (i.e., the ratio of rate to channel capacity, which is commonly known as the utilization factor).

7. What are the effects of such things as additional intra-node delays, and priority messages?

One other variable in the system is the amount of information that each node has about the state of the system (i.e., how long the queues are in each other node). It is clear that these are critical questions which need answers, and it is the intent of this research to answer some of them.

In attempting the solution of some of these problems, it may well be that the study of a specific system or application will expose the basis for an understanding of the problem. It is anticipated that such a study, as well as a simulation of the system on a digital computer, will be undertaken in the course of this research.

II. HISTORY OF THE PROBLEM:

The application of Probability Theory to problems of telephone traffic represents the earliest area of investigation related to the present communication network problem. The first work in this direction dates back to 1907 and 1908 when E. Johannsen [1][1, 2] published two essays, the one dealing with delays to incoming calls in a manual telephone exchange, and the other being an investigation as to how often subscribers with one or more lines are reported "busy." It was Dr. Johannsen who encouraged A. K. Erlang to investigate problems of this nature. Erlang, an engineer with the Copenhagen telephone exchange, made a number of major contributions to the theory of telephone traffic, all of which are translated and reported in [1]; his first paper (on the Poissonian distribution of incoming calls) appeared in 1909 and the paper containing the results of his main work was published in 1917 in which he considered the effect of fluctuations of service demands on the utilization of the automatic equipment in the telephone exchange.

A few other workers made some contributions in this direction around this time, and a good account of the existing theories up to 1920 is given by O'Dell [2, 3]; his principal work on grading appeared in 1927. Molina [4, 5] was among the writers of that time, many of whom were concerned mainly with attempts at proving or disproving Erlang's formulas, as well as to modify these formulas.

The theory of stochastic processes was developed after Erlang's work. In fact it was Erlang who first introduced the concept of statistical equilibrium, and called attention to the study of distributions of holding times and of incoming calls. Much of modern queuing theory is devoted to the extension of these basic principles with the help of more recent mathematical tools.

In 1928, T. C. Fry [6] published his book (which has since become a classic text) in which he offered a fine survey of congestion problems. He was the first to unify all previous works up to that time. Another prominent writer of that period was C. Palm [7, 8], who was the first to use generating functions, in studying the formulas of Erlang and O'Dell. His works appeared in 1937–1938. During this time, a large number of specific cases were investigated, using the theories already developed, in particular lost call problems. Both Fry and Palm formulated equations (now recognized as the Birth and Death equations) which provide the foundation for the modern theory of congestion.

In 1939, Feller [9] introduced the concept of the Birth and Death process, and ushered in the modern theory of congestion. His application was in physics and biology, but it was clear that the same process characterized many models useful in telephone traffic problems. Numerous applications of these equations were made by Palm [10] in 1943. In 1948, Jensen (see [1]) also used this process, without mentioning its name, for the elucidation of Erlang's work. Kosten [11], in 1949, studied the probability of loss by means of generalized Birth and Death equations. Waiting line and trunking problems were explained by Feller [12] in his widely used book on probability, making use of the theory of stochastic processes. At around 1935, the problems of waiting lines and trunking problems in telephone systems were taken up more by mathematicians than by telephone engineers.

In 1950, C. E. Shannon [13] considered the problem of storage requirements in telephone exchanges, and concluded that a bound can be placed on the size of such storage, by estimating the amount of information used in making the required connections. In 1951, F. Riordan [14] investigated a new method of approach suitable for general stochastic processes. R. Syski [15], in 1960, published a fine book in which he presented a summary of the theory of congestion and stochastic processes in telephone systems, and also cast some of the more advanced mathematical descriptions in common engineering terms.

In the early 1950's, it became obvious that many of the results obtained in the field of telephony were applicable in much more general situations, and so started investigations into waiting lines of many kinds, which has developed into modern Queuing Theory, itself a branch of Operations Research. A great deal of effort has been spent on single node facilities, i.e., a system in which "customers" enter, join a queue, eventually obtain "service" and upon completion of this service, leave the system. P. M. Morse [16] presents a fine introduction to such facilities in which he defines terms, indicates applications, and outlines some of the analytic aspects of the theory. P. Burke [17], in 1956, showed that for independent inter-arrival times (i.e., Poisson arrival), and exponential distribution of service times, the inter-departure times would also be independent (Poisson). In 1959, F. Foster [18] presented a duality principle in which he shows that reversing the roles of input (arrivals) and output (service completions) for a system will define a dual system very much like the original system. In contrast to the abundant supply of papers on single node facilities, relatively few works have been published on multi-node facilities (which is the area of interest to this thesis). Among those papers which have been presented is one by G. C. Hunt [19] in which he considers sequential arrays of waiting lines. He presents a table which gives the maximum utilization factor (ratio of average arrival rate to maximum service rate) for which steady state probabilities of queue length exist, under various allowable queue lengths between various numbers of sequential service facilities. J. R. Jackson [20], in 1957, published a paper in which he investigated networks of waiting lines. His network consisted of a number of service facilities into which customers entered both from external sources as well as after having completed service in another facility. He proves a theorem which stated roughly, says that a steady state distribution for the system state exists, as long as the effective utilization factor for each facility is less than one, and in fact this distribution takes on a form identical to the solution for the single node case.[3] In 1960, R. Prosser [21] offered an approximate analysis of a random routing procedure in a communication net in which he shows that such procedures are highly inefficient but extremely stable (i.e., they degrade gracefully under partial failure of the network).

The two important characteristics of the communication nets that form the subject of this thesis are (1) the number of nodes in the system is large, and (2) each node is capable of storing messages while they wait for transmission channels to become available. As has been pointed out, Queuing Theory has directed most of its effort so far, toward single node facilities with storage. There has been, in addition, a considerable investigation into multi-node nets, with no storage capabilities, mainly under the title of Linear Programming (which is really a study of linear inequalities and convex sets). This latter research considers, in effect, steady-state flow in large connected nets, and has yielded some interesting results. One problem which has attracted a lot of attention is the shortest route problem (also known as the traveling salesman problem). M. Pollack and W. Wiebenson [22] have presented a review of the many solutions to this problem, among which are Dantzig's Simplex Method, Minty's labeling method, and the Moore-D'Esopo method. W. Sewell [23] has also considered this problem in some greater generality, and, by using the structure of the network and the principle of flow conservation, has extended an algorithm due to Ford and Fulkerson in order to solve a varied group of flow problems in an efficient manner. R. Chien [24] has given a systematic method for the realization of minimum capacity communication nets from their required terminal capacity requirements (again considering only nets with no storage capabilities); a different solution to the same problem has been obtained by Gomory and Hu [25]. In 1956, P. Elias, A. Feinstein, and C. E. Shannon [26] showed that the maximum rate of flow through a network, between any two terminals, is the minimum value among all simple cut-sets. Also, in 1956, Z. Prihar [27] presented an article in which he explored the topological properties of communication nets; for example, he showed matrix methods for finding the number of ways to travel between two nodes in a specific number of steps.

In 1959, P.A.P. Moran [23] wrote a monograph on the theory of storage. The book describes the basic probability problems that arise in the theory of storage, paying particular attention to problems of inventory, queuing, and dam storage. It represents one of the few works pertaining to a system of storage facilities.

The results from Information Theory [29] also have relation to the communication net problem considered here. Most of the work there has dealt with communication between two points, rather than communication within a network. In particular, one of the results says that there is a trade-off between message delay and probability of error in the transmitted message. Thus if delays are of no consequence, transmission with an arbitrarily low probability of error can be achieved. However, it is not obvious as yet, what effect such additional intranode delays would have in a large network of communication centers; it seems that some maximum additional delay exists, and if so, this would restrict the use of coding methods, and perhaps put a non-zero lower bound on the error probability.

III. DISCUSSION OF PROPOSED PROCEDURE

The problems associated with a multi-terminal communication net, as posed in the first section, appear to be too difficult for analysis, in an exact mathematical form. That is to say, the calculation of the joint distribution of traffic flow through a large (or even small) network is extremely difficult. Even for networks in which no feedback is present, the mathematics is unmanageable; and for those with feedback, it seems hopeless to attempt an exact solution. The question, then, is to what degree, and in what fashion can we simplify this problem?

Since it is the complicated interconnections that cause most of the trouble, one would like to isolate each node, and perform an individual analysis on it, under some boundary constraints. The node could than be represented by the results of such an analysis. In particular, it is hoped that the node representation would be sufficiently complete, by the use of perhaps two numbers, these numbers being the mean and variance of the traffic handled by the node. Thus, instead of having to derive the complicated joint distribution of the traffic in the network, one may be able to make a fairly accurate characterization by specifying two (or at most a few) parameters.

This approach is not completely naive and without justification. Consider the linear programming techniques [22–26] mentioned in the second section of this proposal. The problems handled by such techniques have a great deal in common with the communication problem at hand. Their problem is that of solving networks in which the commodity (e.g., water, people, information) *flows steadily*. A typical problem would be that of finding the set of solutions (commonly referred to as feasible solutions) which would support a given traffic flow in a network. A solution would consist of specifying the flow capacity for each link between all pairs of nodes. In general, a large number of solutions exist, and a lot of effort has been spent in minimizing the total capacity used for such a problem. One obvious requirement is that the average traffic entering any node must be less than the total capacity leaving the node. Notice that the important statistic here is the *average traffic flow*, and if the flow is *steady*, than we have a deterministic problem. Now, in what way does this problem differ from the problem considered in this proposal? Clearly, the difference is that we do not have a steady flow of traffic. Rather, our

traffic comes in spurts, according to some probability distribution. Consequently, we must be prepared to waste some of our channel capacity, i.e., the channel will sometimes be idle. A good measure of how nonsteady our traffic is, is the variance of the traffic. That is, for zero variance, we are reduced to the special case above, namely, steady flow. As the variance goes up, we can say less and less about the arrival time, and the traffic becomes considerably more random in time. Thus, it is reasonable to expect that the two important parameters which characterize our traffic are the mean and variance of the flow. Notice that a necessary, but clearly not sufficient condition for a feasible solution to our problem is that the average traffic entering the node must be less than the total capacity of channels leaving the node. In 1951, Kendall [30] showed for a single node with Poisson inter-arrival times (at a rate λ per sec), an infinite allowable queue, and an arbitrary service distribution (with mean $1/\mu$ and variance v), that the expected waiting time in the system, $E(t)$ was

$$E(t) = \left(\frac{1}{\mu}\right) + \frac{\left(\frac{1}{\mu}\right)^2 + v}{2\left[\left(\frac{1}{\lambda}\right) - \left(\frac{1}{\mu}\right)\right]}$$

This clearly shows a linear dependence on the variance.

Reference has already been made to J. R. Jackson [20]. The assumptions that he made in his analysis of networks of waiting lines was that the arriving traffic at each node had a Poisson distribution, that the service time was exponentially distributed, and that infinite queues at each node were allowed. With these assumptions, he was able to derive the distribution of traffic at all the nodes. It is important to analyze his assumptions carefully. The Poisson assumption effectively characterized the traffic with two parameters. This same assumption also effectively decoupled the nodes from each other. His results state that if the mean traffic satisfies the necessary condition stated in the previous paragraph, then the resultant traffic can be characterized by a two parameter description.

The question of queuing discipline is an interesting one, and one which causes some difficulties. That is, the node must decide on a method for choosing some member in the queue to be served next. An interesting simplification to this question, and perhaps a key to the solution of the network problem may be obtained as follows. Consider that class of queue disciplines which require that a channel facility never remain idle, as long as the queue is non-empty (clearly this is a reasonable constraint). Now, adopting a macroscopic viewpoint, (i.e., removing all labels from the members in the queue), what can be said about the mean and variance of the waiting time distribution for this class of queue disciplines? It seems that some reasonably tight bounds might exist for this distribution, independent of the particular discipline used. Perhaps some other restriction on the class of disciplines will be required in order to obtain meaningful results. However, under such a set of restrictions, if we can characterize the queue sufficiently well, we may then be placed in a position to obtain some overall behavior for the network. All of the queuing problems solved to date, have considered a particular queue discipline (the microscopic viewpoint), and so the results have been specialized to an extremely large degree. Adopting the macroscopic viewpoint seems to be a natural step, and it is the intention of this research to investigate this avenue.

There appear to be a number of conflicting interests in a network of this type. The things to be considered are: storage capacity at each node; channel capacity at each node; and message delay. There exists a trading relationship among those quantities, and it is necessary to attach some quantitative measures to this trade. In fact, if one wishes to generalize one step further, one can consider a multi-terminal communication system, in which the signals are perturbed by noise in the system. Information theory tells us how to combat this disturbance, and the solution introduces additional delays in message transmission and reception. What effect these additional delays will have on the system is not clear; in fact it becomes difficult to state just what the overall capacity is for such a situation. Questions such as these are extremely important, and deserve attention.

From the statements in this section, it is clear that an approximate analysis is all that can easily be obtained for the network under consideration. Hopefully, the approximate answers will be reasonably useful. One way to check the utilization of the results is simulation. It is fully expected that, in the course of this research, a simulated net of this type will be programmed on one of the local digital computers. The author has access to the Lincoln Laboratory TX-2 computer, as well as the IBM 709. This simulation study should serve as a useful check on the results and perhaps, will also serve as a guide into the research.

IV. Preliminary Investigation

In this section, certain results will be presented, which have been obtained in the preliminary investigation already undertaken. The proofs of the new theorems will be left for the Appendix.

The point of departure is a theorem due to Jackson [20] which has already been referred to. He considers a situation in which there are M departments, the mth department having the following properties ($m = 1, 2, \ldots, M$):

1. N_m servers

2. Customers from outside the system arrive in a Poisson-type time series at mean rate λ_m (additional customers will arrive from other departments in the system).

3. Service is on a first come, first served basis, with infinite storage available for overflow; the servicing time being exponentially distributed with mean $1/\mu_m$.

4. Once served, a customer goes immediately from department m to department k with probability π_{km}; his total service is completed (and he then leaves the system) with probability $1 - \sum_k \pi_{km}$.

Property 4 is the basis on which Jackson calls this system a network of waiting lines. Defining Γ_m as the average arrival rate of customers at department m from all sources inside and outside the system, Jackson states that

$$\Gamma_m = \lambda_m + \sum_k \pi_{mk} \Gamma_k \qquad (1)$$

Now, defining n_m as the number of customers waiting and in service at department m, and defining the state of the system as the vector $(n_1, n_2, \ldots, n_M)$, he proves the following

THEOREM: Define $P_n^{(m)}$ $(m = 1, 2, \ldots, M, n = 0, 1, 2, \ldots)$, the *Pr* [finding n customers in department m in the steady state], by the following equations (where the $P_0^{(m)}$ are determined by the conditions $\sum_n P_n^{(m)} = 1$:

$$P_n^{(m)} = \begin{cases} P_0^{(m)} \left(\dfrac{\Gamma_m}{N_m \mu_m}\right)^n \dfrac{N_m^{\,n}}{n!} & (n = 0, 1, \ldots, N_m) \\[2em] P_0^{(m)} \left(\dfrac{\Gamma_m}{N_m \mu_m}\right)^n \dfrac{(N_m)^{N_m}}{N_m!} & n \geq N_m \end{cases}$$

$$(2)$$

A steady state distribution of the state of the above described system is given by the products

$$P(n_1, n_2, \ldots, n_M) = P_{n_1}^{(1)} P_{n_2}^{(2)} \ldots P_{n_M}^{(M)}$$

$$(3)$$

provided $\Gamma_m < \mu_m N_m$ for $m = 1, 2, \ldots, M$.

This theorem says, in essence, that at least so far as steady states are concerned, the system with which we are concerned behaves as if its departments were independent elementary systems of the following type (which is the type considered by Erlang): Customers arrive in a Poisson type time series at mean rate λ. They are handled on a first come, first serve basis by a system of N identical servers, the servicing times being exponentially distributed with mean $1/\mu$. The steady state distribution of the number of people, n, waiting and in service has been obtained by Erlang, and is the identical form as in Jackson's theorem above, with $N_m = N$, $\Gamma_m = \lambda$, $\mu_m = \mu$, $P_n^{\,m} = P_n$, and with the condition $\lambda < \mu N$. That is, Jackson's problem reduces to that of Erlang's when $M = 1$. However, for $M = 1$, the network property of the system is destroyed. Jackson's result is very neat, and suggests the possibility of being able to handle large nets of the type of interest to this thesis.

Following, is a statement and discussion of some results obtained for systems similar to those considered by Erlang and Jackson; proofs for the theorems are given in the Appendix.

Consider a pair of nodes in a large communication net. When the first of these nodes transmits a message destined for the other, one can inquire as to what the rest of the net appears like, from the point of view of the transmitting node. In answer to this inquiry, it does not seem unreasonable to consider that the rest of the net offers, to the message, a number N, of "equivalent" alternate paths from the first node to the second; the equivalence being a very gross simplification of the actual situation, which, nevertheless, serves a useful purpose. Thus, the system under consideration reduces itself to that considered by Erlang. Now, for given conditions of average traffic flow and total transmitting capacity between the two nodes, the problem as to the optimum value of N presents itself (optimum here referring to that value of N which minimizes the total time spent in the transmitting node, i.e., time spent waiting for a free transmission channel plus time spent in transmitting the message). Thus, as shown in Figure 1, the system consists of N channels, each of capacity C/N bits per second, with Poisson arrivals of mean rate λ, and with the message lengths distributed exponentially with a mean length $1/\mu$ bits.

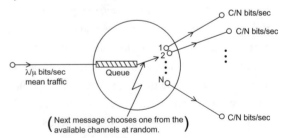

Figure 1: N-channel node considered in Theorem 1.

As is well known, the solution for P_n (defined as the probability of finding n messages in the system in the steady state) is, for $\lambda/\mu C < 1$,

$$P_n = \begin{cases} \dfrac{P_0 \rho^n N^n}{n!} & n \leq N \\[2em] \dfrac{P_0 \rho^n N^N}{n!} & n \geq N \end{cases} \qquad (4)$$

where $\rho = \lambda/\mu C$ is defined as the utilization factor. Note that this is the same solution found by Erlang. From these steady state probabilities, we can easily find $E(t)$, which is the expected value of the time spent in the system, as

$$E(t) = \frac{N}{\mu C} + \frac{P(\geq N)}{\mu C(1 - \rho)} \qquad (5)$$

where

$$P(\geq N) = \frac{P_0(N\rho)^N}{(1 - \rho)N!}$$

and

$$P_0 = \left[\sum_{n=0}^{N-1} \frac{(N\rho)^n}{n!} + \frac{(N\rho)^N}{(1 - \rho)N!} \right]^{-1}$$

We are now ready to state

THEOREM 1: The value of N which minimizes $E(t)$, for all $0 \leq \rho < 1$ is $N = 1$.

Let us look at the expression for $E(t)$ a little closer. Note that the quantity $N/\mu C$ is merely the average time spent in transmitting the message over the channel, once a channel is available. Also, $P(\geq N)$ is the probability that a message is forced to enter the queue. Now, from the independence of the messages, one would expect $E(t)$ to be

$E(t)$ = average time spent in channel + average time spent in queue.

Equation (5) is of the form

$E(t)$ = average time spent in channel + (probability of entering the queue)T

where $T = 1/(1 - \rho)\mu C$.

The physical interpretation of the quantity T is that it is the average time spent in the queue, given that a message will join the queue. The interesting thing here is that the quantity T is independent of N.

Let us now recall one of the basic assumptions of Jackson's theorem, namely, that upon completing ser-

vice in department m, a customer goes immediately to department k with probability π_{km}. If, now, we consider a communication network of nodes and links (channels), it is not at all obvious how we can route massages in the net so as to satisfy this assumption. That is, how can we design a communication network so that an arbitrary message entering node m will, with probability π_{km} be transmitted over that channel which links node m to node k. Clearly, one way to achieve this is to assign each message, as it enters node m, to the channel linking nodes m and k, with probability π_{km}. However, with such a scheme, there would occur situations in which there were messages in the node waiting on a queue at the same time that some of the channels leading out of the node were idle. It seems reasonable, in some cases at least, to prohibit such a condition. Therefore restricting the existence of idle channels if there are any waiting messages, we arrive at the following

THEOREM 2: Given a two channel service facility of total capacity C, Poisson arrivals with mean rate λ, message lengths distributed exponentially with mean length $1/\mu$, and the restriction that no channel be idle if a message is waiting in the queue, then, for an arbitrarily chosen number, $0 \leq \pi_1 \leq 1$ it is *not* possible to find a queue discipline and an assignment of the two channel capacities (the sum being C) such that

Pr (entering message is transmitted on the first channel) $= \pi_1$

for all $0 \leq \rho < 1$ where $\rho = \lambda/\mu C$.

Thus, this theorem shows that one cannot, in general, make an arbitrary assignment of the probability of being transmitted over a particular channel which remains constant for all ρ. However, in the proof of this theorem, it is shown that it is possible to find a queue discipline and a channel capacity assignment such that the deviation of this probability π_1 is rather small over the entire range $0 \leq \rho < 1$.

It is also of interest to note that in the proof of Theorem 2, it is shown that the variation of π_1 is zero over $0 \leq \rho < 1$ for $\pi_1 = 0, 1/2, 1$. In fact this leads to the following

COROLLARY: For the same conditions as Theorem 2, except allowing N channels, and for $\pi_1 = \pi_2 = \ldots = \pi_N = 1/N$, then it is possible to find a queuing discipline and a channel capacity assignment such that

Pr (entering message is transmitted over the ith channel) $= 1/N$ for all $0 \leq \rho < 1$

In proving Theorems 4 and 5, as well as in some other investigations which have been started by the author, the solution to a set of non-linear equations was found to be necessary. As is sometimes possible with such equations, the proper transformation of variables permitted the reduction of these equations to a linear system. This transformation turned out to involve that fundamental quantity ρ, and thus led to

THEOREM 3: Consider an N channel service facility of total capacity C, Poisson arrivals with mean rate λ, message lengths distributed exponentially with mean length $1/\mu$, and an arbitrary queue discipline. Define the utilization factor

$$\rho = \lambda/\mu C$$

Then

$$\rho = 1 - \sum_{n=0}^{\infty} \left(\frac{\overline{C_n}}{C}\right) P_n \qquad (6)$$

where $\overline{C_n}$ = Expected value of the unused capacity given n lines in use and $P_n = Pr$ (finding n messages in the system in the steady state) provided the system reaches a steady state.

Notice that, in Theorem 3, all information regarding the queue discipline is contained and summarized in the quantity $\overline{C_n}$. This theorem corresponds very nicely with one's intuition, as may be seen by rewriting it as

$$\rho = 1 - E \text{ (unused normalized capacity)}$$

where the normalization is with respect to the total capacity C. It is clear that this last equation may, in turn be written as

$$\rho = E \text{ (used normalized capacity)}$$

which says that

$$\lambda/\mu = E \text{ (used capacity)} \qquad (7)$$

Now, since the average number of messages entering per second is λ and their average length is $1/\mu$ bits per message, the quantity λ/μ is clearly the average number of bits per second entering the facility. Recall that the condition for the existence of a steady state for this system is

$$\lambda/\mu C < 1$$

Thus, if we have a steady state solution, we are guaranteed that $\lambda/\mu < C$ (which says that the facility can handle the incoming traffic) and so the expected value of the capacity used by this input rate will merely be λ/μ; this is precisely what equation (7) states.

In even the simplest conceivable communications network, it seems reasonable to require that when a message reaches the node to which it is addressed, it should leave the system i.e., it is delivered. However, in the assumptions considered by Jackson, there is no final address associated with each "message" and so, the correspondence between the problem considered by Jackson, and that of interest to this thesis is not as close as one might hope.

Therefore, let us consider a communication network with $N + 1$ nodes, for which the entering messages have associated with them a final destination (address). Once a message reaches its address, it is dropped from the system immediately. Thus, we are altering the model considered by Jackson only slightly; and in order to keep the rest of the system similar to his, we will consider a completely connected net, with all $\pi_1 = 1/N$ (i.e., upon entering a node, a message will be transmitted over a particular channel with probability $1/N$, unless the node which it just entered is its final destination, in which case the message leaves the system with probability one). Note that the corollary to Theorem 2 allows us to define such π_1. For such a system, it turns out that Jackson's results still apply with some slight modifications, as stated in

THEOREM 4: Consider the completely connected $N + 1$ node system described above. Let each transmission channel leaving node m have capacity C_m/N. Let the incoming messages entering node m from external sources be Poisson at rate λ_m and let the message lengths be exponentially distributed with mean length $1/\mu$. Further, let t_{mj} be the Pr (message entering node m from its external source has, for a final address, node j). Also define $P_n^{(m)}$ as the probability of finding n messages in node m in the steady state. Then

$$P_n^{(m)} \begin{cases} P_0^{(m)}\left(\dfrac{\Gamma_m}{\mu C_m}\right)^n \dfrac{N^n}{n!} & (n = 0, 1, \ldots, N) \\[2em] P_0^{(m)}\left(\dfrac{\Gamma_m}{\mu C_m}\right)^n \dfrac{N^N}{N!} & (n = N, N+1, \ldots) \end{cases} \tag{8}$$

where

$$\Gamma_m = \lambda_m + \sum_{i \neq m} \Gamma_i \frac{\alpha_{im}}{N} \tag{9}$$

and $\alpha_{im} = Pr$ (arbitrary message in node i does not have node m for a final address) provided $\Gamma_m < \mu C_m$ for all $m = 1, 2, \ldots, N+1$.

This theorem is almost identical to Jackson's theorem, as one might expect. Notice that here, the appropriate definition for the utilization factor for node m is $\rho_m = \Gamma_m/\mu C_m$. The definition of Γ_m as given in Eqn. (9) can be shown to agree with the definition for the average arrival rate of messages at node m (analogous to Jackson's definition in Eqn. [1]). The evaluation of α_{im} involves solving a set of simultaneous equations, as does the evaluation of Γ_m. By way of illustration, the solution for Γ_1 and α_{12} in a three node net follows:

$$\Gamma_1 = \frac{2}{3}[2\lambda_1 + \lambda_2 t_{23} + \lambda_3 t_{32}]$$

$$\alpha_{12} = \frac{2}{3}\left[\frac{2\lambda_1 t_{13} + \lambda_2 t_{23}}{\Gamma_1}\right]$$

As already mentioned, P. Burke [17] has shown that in a waiting system with N servers, with Poisson arrivals (mean rate λ) and with exponential holding times (mean holding time for each server = $1/\mu$), the traffic departing from the system is Poisson with mean rate λ, providing the steady state prevails (i.e. pro-

vided $\rho = \lambda/\mu N$ is less than 1). In fact, it is on this basis that Jackson is able to say that his system consists of independent elementary systems; that is, Burke's theorem states that exponential waiting systems (or departments or nodes, as the problem may be defined) always transform Poisson input traffic into Poisson output traffic (with the same mean rates) and thus the departing traffic is not distinguishable from the input traffic. An identical situation exists for the system considered in Theorem 4, and is stated formally in

THEOREM 5: For the system considered in Theorem 4, all traffic flowing within the network is Poisson in nature, and, in particular, the traffic transmitted from node m to any other node in the system in Poisson with mean rate Γ_m/N.

Many of the theorems presented here are fairly specialized to particular conditions on the network topology and on the routing discipline, It is anticipated that a number of them can be extended to less restrictive networks, and such an effort is now being undertaken by the author, since this investigation fits very well with the general aims of the thesis research.

APPENDIX

Proof of Theorems

Before we proceed with the proofs, let us derive a general result for a class of Birth-Death Processes [12]. Let[4]

$P_n(t) = Pr$ [finding n members in system at time t]

$b_n dt = Pr$ [birth of a new member during any interval of length $dt \mid n$ members already in system]

$d_n dt = Pr$ [death of a member during any interval of length dt $\mid n$ members in system]

then, clearly

$$P_0(t + dt) = P_1(t)\,(d_1 dt) + P_0(t)\,(1 - b_0 dt)$$

$$P_n(t + dt) = P_{n+1}(t)\,(d_{n+1}dt) + P_{n-1}(t)\,(b_{n-1}dt) + P_n(t)\,(1 - d_n dt - b_n dt) \qquad n \geq 1$$

From these eqns., we get

$$dP_0(t)/dt = d_1 P_1(t) - b_0 P_0(t) \qquad (A1)$$

$$dP_n(t)/dt = d_{n+1}P_{n+1}(t) + b_{n-1}P_{n-1}(t) - \\ (d_n + b_n)P_n(t) \; n \geq 1 \qquad (A2)$$

Let us now assume the existence of a steady state distribution for $Pn(t)$, that is,

$$\lim_{t \to \infty} P_n(t) = P_n$$

Therefore

$$\lim_{t \to \infty} dP_n(t)/dt = 0$$

and so, we get, for eqns. (A1) and (A2),

$$0 = d_1 P_1 - b_0 P_0$$

$$0 = d_{n+1}P_{n+1} + b_{n-1}P_{n-1} - (d_n + b_n)P_n \qquad n \geq 1$$

The solution to this set of difference equations is

$$P_n = \prod_{i=0}^{n-1} P_0 \left(\frac{b_i}{d_{i+1}} \right) \qquad n \geq 1 \qquad (A3)$$

which may easily be checked.

Theorem 1—proof:
Given

$$E(t) = \frac{N}{\mu C} + \frac{P(\geq N)}{\mu C(1-\rho)}$$

substituting for $P(\geq N)$ and rearranging terms gives us

$$E(t) = \left(\frac{N}{\mu C} \right) \left[1 + \frac{\frac{1}{N(1-\rho)}}{S_N(1-\rho)+1} \right] \qquad (A4)$$

where

$$S_N = \sum_{n=0}^{N-1} (N\rho)^{n-N} \frac{N!}{n!} > 0$$

now

$$S_N = \sum_{n=0}^{N-1} \rho^{n-N} \left[\frac{N}{N} \right] \left[\frac{N-1}{N} \right] \cdots \left[\left(\frac{n+1}{N} \right) \right]$$

therefore

$$S_N \leq \sum_{n=0}^{N-1} \rho^{n-N} = \left(\frac{\rho^{-N}-1}{1-\rho} \right)$$

giving

$$0 < S_N \leq \frac{\rho^{-N}-1}{1-\rho} \qquad (A5)$$

Now, for $N = 1$, eqn. (A4) yields

$$E(t) = \frac{1}{\mu C(1-\rho)} \text{ for } N = 1$$

therefore, it is sufficient to show that

$$E(t) > \frac{1}{\mu C(1-\rho)} \text{ for all } N > 1, 0 \leq \rho < 1$$

using (A5) we get, for (A4)

$$E(t) \geq \left(\frac{N}{\mu C} \right) \left[1 + \frac{\rho^N}{N(1-\rho)} \right]$$

$$E(t) \geq \left[\frac{N(1-\rho)+\rho^N}{\mu C(1-\rho)} \right]$$

Letting $1 - \rho = \alpha$ or $1 - \alpha = \rho$, we see that

$$N(1-\rho) + \rho^N = N\alpha + (1-\alpha)^N \geq N\alpha + 1 - N\alpha = 1$$

thus

$$E(t) \geq \frac{1}{\mu C(1-\rho)}$$

for all N, and in particular, the only case for which the equality holds is $N = 1$. Note that the equality would also hold for $\alpha = 0$ but this implies that $\rho = 1$, which we do not permit. Thus

$$E(t) > \frac{1}{\mu C(1-\rho)} \text{ for } N > 1, 0 \leq \rho < 1$$

which completes the proof.

Theorem 2—proof:
The method of proof will be to show the impossibility of contradicting the theorem.

Suppose $\rho \to 0$. Then P_0 (the probability that in the steady state the system is empty) approaches 1. In such a case, an entering message (which will, with probability arbitrarily close to 1, find an empty system) must be assigned to channel 1 with probability π_1 (and to channel 2 with probability $\pi_2 = 1 - \pi_1$) if one is to have any hope of contradicting the theorem.

Now suppose $\rho \to 1$; then P_0 and P_1 (the probability of one message in the system) both approach 0. Therefore, the channel capacity $C1$ assigned to channel 1 (which implies $C - C_1 = C_2$ for channel 2) must be chosen so that

$\alpha = Pr$ [channel 1 empties before channel 2 |
both channels busy] $= \pi_1$

That is, with probability arbitrarily close to 1, a message entering the node will be forced to join a queue, and so, when it reaches the head of the queue, it will find both channels busy. If this message is to be transmitted over channel 1 with probability π_1, it must be that the channel capacity assignments result in $\alpha = \pi_1$. Note that we have taken advantage of the fact that messages with exponentially distributed lengths exhibit no memory as regards their transmission time. Now,

$$\alpha = \int\limits_{t=0}^{t=\infty} \begin{array}{l} Pr[\text{channel 1 empties in } (t, t+dt) \mid \text{both busy at time 0}] \\ \times Pr[\text{channel 2 is not yet empty by } t \mid \text{both busy at time 0}] \end{array}$$

$$\alpha = \int\limits_0^\infty \mu C_1 e^{-\mu C_1 t} e^{-\mu C_2 t} dt$$

$$\alpha = \frac{\mu C_1}{(\mu C_1 + \mu C_2)} = \frac{C_1}{C}$$

but

$$\alpha = \pi_1$$

therefore

$$C_1 = \pi_1 C$$

and also

$$C_2 = \pi_2 C = (1 - \pi_1)C$$

These two limiting cases for $\rho \to 0$ and $\rho \to 1$ have constrained the construction of our system completely.

Now, let

$r_1 = Pr$ (incoming message is transmitted on channel 1]

$P_n = Pr$ (finding n messages in the system in the steady state]

Then clearly,

$$r_1 = \pi_1 P_0 + q_{21} P_1 + \sum_{n=2}^\infty \pi_1 P_n \qquad (A6)$$

where

$q_{i1} = Pr$ [channel i is busy | only one channel is busy]

that is

$r_1 = E$ [probability of an arbitrary message being transmitted over channel 1]

For q_{21}, we write:

$$q_{21}(t+dt) = \left[\frac{P_0(t)}{P_1(t)}\right](\lambda \pi_2 dt)$$
$$+ \left[\frac{P_2(t)}{P_1(t)}\right](\mu C_1 dt) + q_{21}(t)[1 - \lambda dt - \mu C_2 dt]$$

Assuming a steady state distribution, we get,

$$0 = \left(\frac{P_0}{P_1}\right)\lambda \pi_2 + \left(\frac{P_2}{P_1}\right)\mu C_1 - (\lambda + \mu C_2)q_{21} \qquad (A7)$$

Now, since this system satisfies the hypothesis of the Birth-Death Process considered earlier, we apply Eqn. (A3), with $d_1 = \mu \bar{C}, d_n = \mu C (n \geq 2), b_n = \lambda$, and obtain

$$P_n = \begin{cases} \left(\frac{C}{\bar{C}}\right)\rho^n P_0 & n \geq 1 \\ P_0 & n = 0 \end{cases} \qquad (A8)$$

where

$$\rho = \frac{\lambda}{\mu C}$$

and

$$\overline{C} = E \text{ [capacity in use | one channel is busy]}$$
$$= \mu C_1 q_{11} + \mu C_2 q_{21}$$

Also, recall that $C_1 = \pi_1 C$ and $C_2 = \pi_2 C = (1 - \pi_1)C$. Thus, Eqn. (A7) becomes

$$q_{21} = \left(\frac{\mu \overline{C} \pi_2 + \lambda \pi_1}{\lambda + \mu C \pi_2} \right) \tag{A9}$$

similarly

$$q_{11} = \left(\frac{\mu \overline{C} \pi_1 + \lambda \pi_2}{\lambda + \mu C \pi_1} \right)$$

Now, forming the equation,

$$q_{11} + q_{21} = 1$$

we obtain, after some algebra,

$$\mu \overline{C} = \frac{\mu C (\mu C + 2\lambda)}{2 \mu C + \lambda / \pi_1 \pi_2}$$

$$= \frac{\mu C (1 + 2\rho)}{2 + \rho / \pi_1 \pi_2}$$

We may now write Eqn. (A9) as

$$q_{21} = \frac{\dfrac{\mu C (1 + 2\rho)}{2 + \rho / \pi_1 \pi_2} \pi_2 + \lambda \pi_1}{\lambda + \mu C \pi_2}$$

Simplifying, we get

$$q_{21} = \frac{\pi_1 (\pi_2 + \rho)}{(2 \pi_1 \pi_2 + \rho)} \tag{A10}$$

Returning to Eqn. (A6), we see that the only way in which r_1 can equal π_1 is for $q_{21} = \pi_1$. Eqn. (A10) shows that this is *not* the case, which demonstrates that the theorem cannot be contradicted for an arbitrary π_1, proving the theorem.

However, it can be seen from Eqn. (A10), that $q_{21} = \pi_1$ for $\pi_1 = 0, 1/2, 1$ only. Let us now form r_1 from Eqns. (A6) and (A8):

$$r_1 = P_0 \left[\pi_1 + \left(\frac{\lambda q_{21}}{\mu \overline{C}} \right) + \left(\frac{\pi_1 C}{\overline{C}} \right) \sum_{n=2}^{\infty} \rho^n \right]$$

where P_0 is found from Eqn. (A8) by requiring

$$\sum_{n=0}^{\infty} P_n = 1$$

After substituting and simplifying, we get

$$r_1 = \pi_1 \left[\frac{\pi_1 \rho^2 + (1 - \pi_1^2) \rho + \pi_1 \pi_2}{(1 - 2 \pi_1 \pi_2) \rho^2 + 3 \pi_1 \pi_2 \rho + \pi_1 \pi_2} \right]$$

Figure (A-1) shows a plot of r_1 as a function of ρ, with π_1 as a parameter.

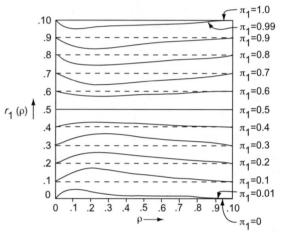

Figure A-1: Variation of r_1 of ρ.

Note that the variation of r_1 is not too great. This illustrates that although Theorem 2 is written as a negative result, its proof demonstrates a positive result, namely, that the variation of r_1 is not excessive. The arrangement which gives this behavior is one in which the channel capacity is divided between the two channels in proportion to the desired probability of using each channel, and for the discipline followed when a message finds both channels empty, one merely chooses channel i with probability π_i.

Corollary to Theorem 2—proof: In proving Theorem 2, it was shown that for $\pi_1 = 1/2$, a suitable system could be found to realize this π_1. This result also follows directly from the complete symmetry of the two channels. Similarly, the proof of this corollary follows trivially from recognizing, once again, the complete symmetry of each of the N channels.

Theorem 3—proof: The system considered in this theorem satisfies the conditions of the Birth-Death Process examined earlier, with

$$b_n = \lambda$$

$$d_n = \mu(C - \overline{C}_n)$$

Thus, by Eqn. (A3), we find

$$P_n = \frac{P_0\left(\frac{\lambda}{\mu}\right)^n}{\left[\prod_{i=1}^{n}(C - \overline{C}_i)\right]} \quad n \geq 1$$

or

$$P_n = \frac{P_0\rho^n}{\left[\prod_{i=1}^{n}(1 - r_i)\right]} \quad n \geq 1 \qquad (A11)$$

where

$$\rho = \frac{\lambda}{\mu C}$$

$$r_i = \frac{\overline{C}_i}{C} \qquad (A12)$$

and $P_n = P_0$ for $n = 0$, by definition.

Let us now solve for P_0:

$$\sum_{n=0}^{\infty} P_n = 1 = P_0\left[1 + \sum_{n=1}^{\infty} R_n\rho^n\right]$$

where

$$R_n = \frac{1}{\prod_{i=1}^{n}(1 - r_i)}$$

Thus

$$P_0 = \frac{1}{\left[1 + \sum_{n=0}^{\infty} R_n\rho^n\right]} \qquad (A13)$$

Now, according to the statement of the theorem, let us form and solve for

$$x = 1 - \sum_{n=0}^{\infty} \left(\frac{\overline{C}_n}{C}\right)P_n$$

Noting that $\overline{C}_0 = C$ by construction, and using Eqns. (A11) – (A13),

$$x = 1 - P_0 - P_0\sum_{n=1}^{\infty} r_n R_n\rho^n$$

$$x = 1 - \frac{1 + \sum_{n=1}^{\infty} r_n R_n\rho^n}{1 + \sum_{n=1}^{\infty} R_n\rho^n}$$

$$x = \frac{1 + \sum_{n=1}^{\infty} R_n\rho^n - 1 - \sum_{n=1}^{\infty} r_n R_n\rho^n}{1 + \sum_{n=1}^{\infty} R_n\rho^n}$$

$$x = \frac{\sum_{n=1}^{\infty} R_{n-1}\rho^n}{1 + \sum_{n=1}^{\infty} R_n\rho^n}$$

$$x = \frac{\rho\sum_{n=1}^{\infty} R_n\rho^n}{1 + \sum_{n=1}^{\infty} R_n\rho^n}$$

It is important to recognize here that R_0 must be defined as

$$R_0 = (1 - r_1)R_1$$

Thus

$R_0 = 1$ (taken now as a definition as well)

and so

$$x = \rho\left(\frac{1 + \sum_{n=0}^{\infty} R_n\rho^n}{1 + \sum_{n=1}^{\infty} R_n\rho^n}\right)$$

or

$$x = \rho$$

which proves the theorem.

Theorem 4—proof: The system considered in this theorem satisfies the conditions of the Birth-Death Process examined earlier. However, we have $N + 1$ nodes, and so we must investigate $N + 1$ probability distributions, $P_n^{(m)}$, where $m = 1, 2, \ldots, N + 1$ and $n = 0, 1, 2, \ldots$. Let the birth and death rates for node m be $b_n^{(m)}$ and $d_n^{(m)}$ respectively. With this notation, we see that

$$b_n^{(m)} = \lambda_m + \sum_{\substack{j = 1 \\ j \neq m}}^{N+1} \left(\frac{\mu C_j}{N}\right) \alpha_{jm} \left[1 - \sum_{i=0}^{N-1} P_i^{(j)}\left(\frac{N-i}{N}\right)\right] \qquad n \geq 0$$

$$d_n^{(m)} = \begin{cases} \dfrac{n(\mu C_m)}{N} & n = 0, 1, \ldots, N \\ \mu C_m & n \geq N \end{cases}$$

An explanation of the $b_n^{(m)}$ is required at this point. λ_m is the input (birth) rate of messages to node m from its external source (by definition). In addition, each of the other N nodes sends messages to node m. Let us consider the jth node's contribution (x_j say) to the input rate of node m ($j \neq m$): Clearly,

$$x_j dt = Pr[Q_1, Q_2, Q_3] = Pr[Q_1 \mid Q_2, Q_3] \, Pr[Q_2, Q_3]$$

where

> Q_1 = event that a message on the channel connecting node j to node m completes its transmission to node m in an arbitrary time interval $(t, t + dt)$
>
> Q_2 = event that an arbitrary message in node j does not have node m for its final address
>
> Q_3 = event that the channel connecting node j to node m is being used

Since Q_2 and Q_3 are independent events, we get

$$x_j dt = Pr[Q_1 \mid Q_2, Q_3] \, Pr[Q_2] \, Pr[Q_3]$$

and for node j,

$$P_r[Q_1 \mid Q_2, Q_3] = P_r[Q_1 \mid Q_3] = \left(\frac{\mu C_j}{N}\right) dt$$

$$P_r[Q_2] = \alpha_{jm}$$

$$P_r[Q_3] = 1 - \sum_{i=0}^{N-1} P_i^{(j)}\frac{(N-i)}{N}$$

The summation on j appearing in the expression for $b_n^{(m)}$ merely adds up the contributions to the input (birth) rate of internally routed messages.

Now, according to the definition of $\overline{C}_n$ in Theorem 3, we can apply the same definition to each of the $N + 1$ nodes in the present theorem. Thus, in this case, we see that

$$\overline{C}_n^{(m)} = \begin{cases} \left[\dfrac{N-n}{N}\right]C & n \leq N \\ 0 & n \geq N \end{cases}$$

and so we recognize, by application of Theorem 3, that

$$1 - \sum_{i=0}^{N-1} P_i^{(j)}\left(\frac{N-i}{N}\right) = \rho_j$$

where, by definition,

$$\rho_j = \frac{\Gamma_j/\mu}{C_j} = \frac{\text{average input rate to node } j}{\text{maximum output rate from node } j}$$

thus

$$b_n^{(m)} = \lambda_m + \sum_{\substack{j = 1 \\ j \neq m}}^{N+1} \frac{\Gamma_j \alpha_{jm}}{N} \qquad \text{all } n \geq 0$$

But, since $b_n^{(m)}$ is independent of n, it obviously satisfies the definition of Γ_m (= average number of messages per second entering node m). Thus

$$b_n^{(m)} = \Gamma_m = \lambda_m + \sum_{\substack{j = 1 \\ j \neq m}}^{N+1} \frac{\Gamma_j \alpha_{jm}}{N}$$

Now, using these birth and death coefficients, we apply eqn. (A3) to get

$$P_n^{(m)} = \begin{cases} P_0^{(m)} \left(\dfrac{\Gamma_m}{\mu C_m} \right)^n \dfrac{N^n}{n!} & (n = 0, 1, \ldots, N) \\[20pt] P_0^{(m)} \left(\dfrac{\Gamma_m}{\mu C_m} \right)^n \dfrac{N^N}{N!} & n \geq 1 \end{cases}$$

In this case, it is clear that the steady state is defined only when

$$\rho_m = \frac{\Gamma_m}{\mu C_m} < 1 \text{ for all } m = 1, 2, \ldots, N + 1$$

This completes the proof of the theorem.

Theorem 5—proof: In order to show that all traffic flowing within the network considered in Theorem 4, is Poisson in nature, it is sufficient to show that

$q(C, t) = Pr$ [a message transmission, in any channel C of the network, is completed in a time interval $(t, t + dt)$, where t is arbitrary] $= k \, dt$

where k is a constant.

Let us show this for an arbitrary channel connecting node j (say) to any other node:

$$q\left(\frac{C_j}{N}, t \right) = P_r[Q_1 | Q_3] P[Q_3]$$

where Q_1 and Q_3 are as defined in the proof of Theorem 4. As shown in the proof of Theorem 4,

$$P_r[Q_1 | Q_3] P[Q_3] = \left(\frac{\mu C_j}{N} \right) \left[1 - \sum_{i=0}^{N-1} P_i^{(j)} \left(\frac{N-i}{N} \right) \right] dt$$

$$= \left(\frac{\mu C_j}{N} \right) \rho_j \, dt$$

and so

$$q\left(\frac{C_j}{N}, t \right) = \left(\frac{\Gamma_j}{N} \right) dt$$

which proves the theorem, and also shows the value of the mean rate for the Poisson traffic to be $\dfrac{\Gamma_j}{N}$.

BIBLIOGRAPHY

1.   Brockmeyer, E. H. L. Halstrom and A. Jensen, The Life and works of A. K. Erlang, Danish Academy of Technical Sciences No.2 (1948)

2.   O'Dell, G. F., Theoretical Principles of the Traffic Capacity of Automatic Switches, P.O.E.E.J. *13*, p. 209 (1920)

3.   O'Dell, G. F., An Outline of the Trunking Aspect of Automatic Telephony, J.I.E.E. *65*, p. 185 (1927)

4.   Molina, E. C., Application of the Theory of Probability to Telephone Trunking Problems, B.S.T.J. *6*, p. 461 (1927)

5.   Molina, E. C., The Theory of Probabilities Applied to Telephone Trunking Problems, B.S.T.J. *1*, p. 69 (1922)

6.   Fry, T. C., Probability and its Engineering Uses, (D. Van Nostrand, 1928)

7.   Palm, C., Inhomogeneous Telephone Traffic in Full-Availability Groups, Ericsson Technics 5, p. 3 (1937)

8.   Palm, C., Analysis of the Erlang Traffic Formulae for Busy-Signal Arrangements, Ericsson Technics, No. 4, p.39 (1938)

9.   Feller, W., Die Grundlagen der Volterraschen Theorie des Kampfes ums Dasein in wahrscheinlichkeitstheoretischer Behandlung, Acta Biotheoretica, 5, p. 11 (1939)

10.   Palm, C., Intensitätsschwankungen im Fernsprechverkehr, Ericsson Technics (Stockholm) No. 44, p. 1 (1943)

11.   Kosten, L. M., J. R. Manning, and F. Garwood, On the Accuracy of Measurements of Probability of Loss in Telephone Systems, J.R.S.S. Ser. B *11*, p.54 (1949)

12. Feller, W., An Introduction to Probability Theory and Its Applications, (John Wiley and Sons, 1950)

13. Shannon, C. E., Memory Requirements in a Telephone Exchange, B.S.T.J. *29*, p. 343 (1950)

14. Riordan, F. W., Telephone Traffic Time Averages, B.S.T.J. *31*, p. 1129 (1951)

15. Syski, R., Introduction to Congestion in Telephone Systems, (Oliver and Boyd, 1960)

16. Morse, P. M., Queues , Inventories, and Maintenance, (John Wiley and Sons, 1958)

17. Burke, P. J., The Output of a Queueing System, Operations Research *4*, p. 699 (1956)

18. Foster, F.G., A Unified Theory for Stock, Storage and Queue Control, Operations Research Quarterly, *10*, p. 121 (1959)

19. Hunt, G. C., Sequential Arrays of Waiting Lines, Operations Research, *4*, p. 674 (1956)

20. Jackson, J. R., Networks of Waiting Lines, Operations Research, *5*, p. 518 (1957)

21. Prosser, R. T., Routing Procedures in Communications Networks, Part 1: Random Procedures, Lincoln Laboratory internal report No. 22G–0041 (1960)

22. Pollack, M., and W. Wiebenson, Solutions of the Shortest Route Problem—A Review, Operations Research, *8*, p. 224 (1960)

23. Jewell, W. S., Optimal Flow Through a Network, M.I.T Sc.D. Thesis (Electrical Engineering Department), (1958)

24. Chien, R. T., Synthesis of a Communication Net, I.B.M. internal report No. E.S–0017 (1960)

25. Gomory, R. E., and T. C. Hu, Multi-Terminal Network Flows, I.B.M. internal report No. RC–318 (1960)

26. Elias, P., A. Feinstein, and C. E. Shannon, A Note on the Maximum Flow through a Network, Transactions I.R.E., *IT*-2, p. 117 (1956)

27. Prihar, Z., Topological Properties of Telecommunication Networks, Proc. I,R.E., *44*, p. 927 (1956)

28. Moran, P. A. P., The Theory of Storage, (London: Methuen and Co. Ltd., New York: John Wiley and Sons, 1959)

29. Shannon, C. E., and W. Weaver, The Mathematical Theory of Communication, (The University of Illinois Press, 1949)

30. Kendall, D. G., Some Problems in the Theory of Queues, J.R.S.S., Ser. B *13*, p. 151 (1951)

• • •

1. Numerals in square brackets refer to the bibliography

2. Reference to Johannsen's work will be found in [1], page 14.

3. Jackson's work is discussed in detail in Section IV.

4. Note that b_n and d_n are assumed to be independent of time.

13.3

Message Delay in Communication Nets with Storage

Leonard Kleinrock

From *Message Delay in Communication Nets with Storage* (Ph.D. thesis, MIT, December 1962), pp. 1–26.

INTRODUCTORY NOTE TO READING 13.3

In his Ph.D. thesis dated December 1962, of which we reproduce Chapter 1, Leonard Kleinrock developed a mathematical theory of data networks, and established principles and results that were critical to the development of the Internet. His work was directly motivated by a desire to study how data networks could be designed, and to uncover the underlying principles of those networks. His method was to approach a problem with the goal of exposing its structure. He found that queuing theory provided many of the essential tools for analyzing and designing these networks. The theory allows the evaluation of throughput, response time, buffering, loss, and efficiency—many of the system level metrics that determine the performance of data networks.

Chapter 1 of Kleinrock's dissertation contains the summary of his mathematical theory of data networks, his tests of the validity of theory by extensive simulation experiments, and his summary of the underlying principles of packet networks. In his mathematical theory Kleinrock developed the basic structure and analytic model for data networks. He solved the model analytically to give an exact result for the mean response time in general data networks and proved more detailed results using his critical Independence Assumption. He produced optimal data network design procedures for laying out the topology, choosing the channel speeds and selecting the routing procedure and routes. (For Kleinrock's thesis proposal of 1961, see Reading 13.2.) [JMN]

TEXT OF READING 13.3

CHAPTER I

Introduction

This thesis is principally concerned with the flow of message traffic in store-and-forward communication nets. Recently, there has been serious interest expressed in this field both for commercial and military application. The object of this work is to provide a basis for understanding and discussing the configuration and operation of a communication net. Such questions as assignment of channel capacity, effect of priority discipline, choice of routing procedure, and design of topological structure are considered in this research.

1.1 Elementary Concepts

In introducing the many concepts associated with communication nets, it is helpful to carry along an example of a specific net; we therefore consider the configuration shown in Fig. 1.1. In this figure, the

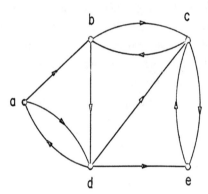

Figure 1.1   Example of a 5 node net.

nodes represent *communication centers,* which ideally might correspond to switching centers in the cities of the United States or in space-borne communication satellites, etc. The ordered connections, or *links,* between the nodes represent one-way *communication channels,* each with their own channel capacity. For our purposes, *messages,* which must pass through the net, consist of the specification of the following quantities: the node of origination; the destination node; the time of arrival to the network; the message length

in bits[1]; and the message priority class. In general, these quantities are specified stochastically according to some probability distribution. As an example, suppose that a message originates at node a in Fig. 1.1 at time $t = 0$, and has for its destination, node e; let its length be 100 bits, and assume that we have no priority structure associated with the messages. Let us follow this test message through the network. Upon entering node a, a decision must be made as to which of the two neighboring nodes, b or d, the message will next be sent. This decision rule is referred to as a *routing procedure*, and is, in general, a function of the current state of the net. Channels leaving and entering a node may be used independently and simultaneously, each one for a different message. Thus, when the test message enters node a, it may find zero, one, or two channels in the process of transmitting other messages. If all channels are busy, then the message joins a queue (waiting line) which is accomplished physically by means of storing the message in a memory. The notion of queues of messages forming at the nodes is a basic characteristic of the communication nets under consideration; we may thus think of the communication net as a network of queues. When the message reaches the front of the queue, the routing procedure then decides which channel the message will be sent over. Let us assume that channel $\overline{ad}$ is chosen. If the capacity of this channel is 2 bits per second, then our message will spend 50 seconds in transmission. Clearly, no other message may use the channel during this time. After the transmission is completed, channel $\overline{ad}$ may then accept a new message from the queue for transmission. Upon reception at node d, the process which took place at node a is essentially repeated, and the message may have to wait on a queue (if all or some of the channels leaving node d are busy). Eventually, however, the message will make its way through the net to its destination at node e. When it arrives at node e, it is considered to be dropped from the net. It is now clear why we refer to these nets as store-and-forward communication nets, viz., in passing through a node, the messages are stored, if necessary, and then forwarded (transmitted) to the next node on the way to their destination The total time that a message spends in the network is referred to as the *message delay*. Further, we introduce the concept of a *traffic matrix* whose *ij* entry describes the average number of messages generated per second which have node *i* as an origin, and node *j* as a destination. The priority classes referred to previously merely dictate the way in which the messages in a queue are ordered (clearly, preferential treatment is given to higher priority messages).

In summary then, we have introduced the following:

1. *nodes*—communication centers which receive, store, and transmit messages.

2. *links*—one-way communication channels.

3. *network*—a finite collection of nodes connected to each other by links.

4. *messages*—specified by their origin, destination, origination time, length, and priority class.

5. *routing procedure*—a decision rule which is exercised when it comes time to route a message from one node to another.

6. *queue*—a waiting line (composed of messages in our case).

7. *queue discipline*—a priority rule which determines a message's relative position in the queue.

8. *message delay*—the total time that a message spends in the net.

9. *traffic matrix*—the *ij* entry in this matrix describes the average number of messages generated per second which have node *i* as an origin and node *j* as a destination.

1.2 The Quantities of Interest

Having introduced the elementary concepts, we now inquire into those quantities which are of interest in our study of communication nets. We consider these quantities from the viewpoint of the user, the opera-

tor, and the designer of the net. Specifically, the user (i.e., the originator and recipient of messages) is concerned with

1. the average message delay

2. the total traffic handling capability of the net.

The operator (i.e., the one who controls the flow of messages through a node) is concerned with

1. the routing procedure

2. the priority discipline

3. the storage capacity at each node.

The designer of the net is interested in

1. the average message delay

2. the total traffic handling capability of the net

3. the routing procedure

4. the priority discipline

5. the storage capacity at each node

6. the channel capacity of each link

7. the topological structure of the net

8. the total cost of the system.

As expected, the designer's interest includes and extends beyond those quantities of interest to the user and operator. We choose, therefore, to investigate all of these quantities, as well as certain trading relations which exist among some of them.

1.3 Description of an Existing Store-and-Forward Communication Net

In this section, we describe an existing store-and-forward communication net. In Sect. 1.4, we then abstract a mathematical model to represent systems of this type for purposes of analysis. We choose for this description, an automatic telegraph switching system (Plan 55A [1][2]) which has been developed by Western Union for the Air Force in order to handle large quantities of military traffic over a world-wide network. The system was recently installed, and consists of ten switching centers (five domestic and five overseas). These switching centers are interconnected over a network of lines or radio channels which comprise the communicating system for automatic relay of telegraph messages. In addition, each of the main switching centers is connected by lines to a set of tributary stations in the region served by that center. Messages originate at the tributary stations, are transmitted to the regional switching center, and then, perhaps to further switching centers, where, finally, they are transmitted to their destination at other tributary stations.

In the switching centers of this system (i.e., Western Union's Plan 55A) messages are received and retransmitted in the form of punched (perforated) paper tape. The message's destination is controlled by routing indicators (normally groups of six letters) recorded on the paper tape as part of the message heading. The switching of messages takes place automatically, except at the points of origin and destination. However, it is possible to convert to manual (push button) switching at each center at any time; this mode of operation is abnormal and is used only in case of failure in the automatic switching devices, or in cases of improper format in the received messages.

Certain measures are included in the operation of the net to protect against errors, excessive delays, and lost messages. Each message is numbered as it is transmitted between centers, and these numbers are checked automatically as the message is received. Messages may be transmitted in code or cipher. If so, then either on-line cryptographic equipment is used, in which case decoding takes place each time a message is received, and encoding takes place each time a message is transmitted. If, on the other hand, the coding is done off-line, then the messages are encoded and decoded only at the points of origination and destina-

tion. In the latter case, care must be taken to avoid the accidental occurrence of the set of characters which signify the end of the message in the encoded message form.

A strict priority or precedence structure is included in the system, and messages are transmitted in this order of precedence. Six priorities are distinguished in the system, and are detected by inspection of two letters, referred to as precedence prosigns, in the message heading.

In each switching center that it passes through, a message is perforated and transmitted twice. The first reperforation takes place as the message is being received into the switching center. The message is then switched and transmitted across office to a transmitting (or sending) line position, where it is reperforated and transmitted again. The perforated paper tape serves as the store or buffer within the switching center.

The format of a message as it passes through a switching center is shown below. The start of message characters *ZCZC* and the sequence numbers from the present and last visited center are followed by the precedence prosign and routing indicators, the text of the message itself, and the end of message characters $\equiv NNNN$. The notation used above is: ↑ figure shift; ↓ letter shift; ≡ line feed; − space; < carriage return. Automatic and manual switching are controlled by certain characters which appear in special places in the message. Both the receiving and transmitting positions within the switching center are designed so as to read the routing indicators and precedence prosigns twice, once in order to set up the appropriate control functions, and once for the purpose of transmission (i.e., transmission either across or out of the office). In cross-office transmission, the cross-office line connections are not established until the entire message has

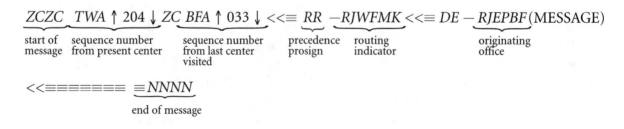

been received into the center (i.e., until the end of message symbols are received); the only exception to this rule comes about when emergency messages are received, in which case the connections are set up immediately.

After establishing the cross-office line, a new sequence number is assigned to the message, and the cross-office transmission commences. This transmission proceeds to perforate a second paper tape across the office, and the transmission ceases upon receipt of the end of message characters, thereby disconnecting the cross-office line. The punched paper tape acts, once again, as the storage facility for the message, and the message awaits its turn (on the tape) until the outgoing transmitter reaches it.

From this sending position, the message is either sent to a tributary (and therefore its destination) or to another switching center; in either case, the message format is similar to that described above. Note that only two sequence numbers are associated with the message at any time as it is relayed through the net; that is, each time a new sequence number is introduced, the least recent number is deleted.

When more than one routing indicator is present in a message heading, it is recognized that this is a multiple address message. These messages are processed in a way such that an individual copy of the message reaches each destination. In this case, the routing indicators are separated so that each copy of the message contains only one routing indicator upon reception at each destination. At a switching center, many of the routing indicators may require the same circuit outlet. This occurs, for example, when more than one routing indicator are for tributaries of the same switching center, or for tributaries of different switching centers which may be reached through the same intermediate center. These messages are sent to the intermediate center only with those routing indicators for which that center is responsible.

The incoming cabinet and the outgoing cabinet are the two principal pieces of equipment in a switching center. These cabinets are linked together by cross-office channels (switching circuits) which carry signals at a rate of 200 words per minute (wpm). In addition,

a director-translator cabinet is required for automatic switching. The director receives information from the paper tape which allows it to control the switching operations pertinent to the message routing. The translator actually carries out these switch settings. In order to reproduce the incoming message, each receiving position is equipped with a printer-perforator. If, in receiving a message, the end of message characters are missing or altered, then two successive start of message signals will be detected; in such a case, an alarm is operated, and the operating attendant is called in. In addition to the printer-perforator, each receiving position also has a loop-gate transmitter which reads characters from the punched tape, and transmits them at 200 wpm across the office to a reperforator at the sending position. In order to carry out the automatic cross-office switching, the receiving position obtains a connection and then transmits the precedence prosign and routing indicator(s) to the director via the loop-gate transmitter. In turn, the director relays the required switching information to the receiving position. The transmitter is now ready to transmit across office. The function of the director-translator cabinet may be taken over by the attendant in the manual operation mode. Electronic pulses on a single conductor are used as transmission signals across office (as opposed to the older torn-tape system which required an attendant to tear the tape off the receiving apparatus, carry this tape across the office, and then insert the tape into an appropriate transmitter).

On the sending side of the office, each sending position is equipped with a multi-magnet reperforator which reproduces messages received over cross-office circuits in the form of punched paper tape once again. The reperforator also receives signals from an automatic message numbering machine. The reperforator is designed to perform certain character checking functions which test the operation of all equipment involved in the cross-office transmission. Failure to check activates an alarm condition which alerts an attendant. All sending positions are equipped with a multicontact transmitter distributor which transmits messages from the paper tape to the channel.

For those inter-center channels which carry heavy traffic loads, several inter-connecting line circuits and sending positions are sometimes required. All sending positions in such a multiple circuit group transmit to identical destinations. Any message for that destination can be switched to any idle circuit within the group.

Messages are received into the center at 60 or 100 wpm; they are then transmitted cross-office at 200 wpm; and finally are retransmitted to outgoing lines at 60 or 100 wpm. Thus, since the cross-office rate is at least twice that of the outgoing lines, a sufficient number of messages can be sent across the office to keep the outgoing lines busy most of the time; consequently, the cross-office transmitters are idle at least half of the time. This being the case, the receiving positions seldom find it necessary to wait for a cross-office connection, and thus no large quantity of backlogged paper tape should form at these positions. In the case of a backlog, the higher cross-office rate should quickly relieve the situation, once a cross-office connection is obtained.

When a receiving position has a message that is to be switched to an outgoing circuit which is busy, the message must wait until a circuit to the desired destination becomes available; if the wait is excessive, or if the message is of extremely high priority, then an alarm is operated which calls an attendant to the position to take suitable action.

In addition to the equipment already described, there is normally provided at each switching center, a traffic control center which simplifies traffic handling and performs certain supervisory functions.[3] In general, this additional equipment includes a connection indicator board, a traffic routing board, a close-out indicator board, and receiving and sending printer sets. The connection indicator board provides visual means for determining which sending and receiving positions are connected over cross-office lines at any time. Such information is useful for maintenance purposes, as well as for certain operating conditions; for example, the supervisor can follow a high priority message through the center with the aid of this board, and thus attend to any excessive delays encountered by

such a message. The traffic routing board is used for making temporary changes in the routing of messages by means of patching cords which are plugged into the jacks in the routing board. The close-out indicator board provides visual signals for indicating which sending positions are either closed out on the cross-office side, or have their transmitters stopped for any reason.

This completes our description of one existing store-and-forward communication net. Although it does not include in its description all current procedures or equipment, this system does exemplify many message switching nets.

1.4 Assumptions

The description in Sect. 1.3 provides us with an existing store-and-forward communication net from which we may abstract a meaningful, idealized mathematical model. The motivation for using an idealized model is simply that of mathematical ease and tractability; at the same time, however, we must insure that the idealizations introduced lead to a model which retains the essential characteristics of the real system. Specifically, we choose the *average message delay* as our measure of network performance. Accordingly, we desire that our model, although idealized, exposes the fundamental behavior of the average message delay in store-and-forward nets.

Consider the elementary concepts presented in Sect. 1.1. We offer this description as a starting point for our model, and now proceed to apply certain assumptions to this description. Specifically, the nodes in this description refer to the switching centers, and we consider that the tributary (or originating) stations are part of the switching center itself. We assume first, that all channels are noiseless, and that all communication centers (nodes) and channels are not subject to damage or destruction (the reliability question). This assumption implies that there are no theoretical or practical problems in transmitting over the channel at a data rate equal to the channel capacity. That is, we may assume that the messages have been encoded into a binary alphabet so that each binary digit corresponds to one bit of data to be transmitted. The encoding required to reduce errors in a noisy channel would introduce additional intra-node delays to the message; we do not consider this case. Furthermore, we assume that cross-office delays are negligible compared to the channel transmission time (a reasonable assumption based upon information on existing and proposed systems).

The study is restricted to data or message traffic, as distinct from telephone or direct wire traffic which has not been considered. We assume that each message has a single destination (as opposed to an all-points message, for example) and that each message must reach that destination before leaving the network (i.e., no defections); this involves the additional assumption of an unlimited storage capacity at each node to supply a "waiting room" for those messages in the queue.

In transmitting between two nodes, a message is considered to be received at the second node only after it is fully received. The consequence of this assumption is that messages may not be retransmitted out of a node at the same time that they are being received into the node. Clearly, this represents, at worst, a slightly conservative assumption as regards the message delay in a node. Moreover, many store-and-forward nets do indeed operate in just this manner because of the difference in channel capacity between incoming and cross-office channels.

The origination times and lengths of the population of messages which will flow through the net cannot be predicted beforehand with complete accuracy. We may, however, describe these random variables statistically by means of their probability density functions. Specifically, we assume that the origination times and lengths of messages are chosen individually and collectively at random; this, of course, implies that the inter-arrival time between messages is exponentially distributed (i.e., Poisson), as is the message length itself. Furthermore, we assume stationarity of these stochastic processes that feed the net.

We have introduced a number of assumptions in arriving at a model for a store-and-forward communication net. We summarize these below:

1. noiseless channels and perfectly reliable nodes and channels

2. negligible cross-office delays

3. restriction to message traffic

4. single destination for each message, and no defections

5. infinite storage capacity at each node

6. full reception of message before retransmission

7. Poisson arrival statistics

8. exponentially distributed message lengths

9. stationarity of the stochastic processes (7 and 8, above).

Whereas assumptions 1–6 do not correspond exactly to the true situation in any real net, they do describe idealizations which are reasonable and close to reality.

Assumptions 7–9 are of a somewhat different nature. In particular, they assign specific distributions to message arrival times and lengths. There is available no quantitative data from which to determine the actual form of these distributions. However, certain data obtained by Molina for telephone traffic corresponds very well to these same assumptions. Moreover, these distributions avoid considerable mathematical complication, and, at the same time, correspond to reasonable (and perhaps conservative) assumptions.

It is appropriate to mention here that many of the results presented in this work include the additional assumption of a *constant* total channel capacity assigned to the net (i.e., the sum of the capacities of all channels in the net is held fixed).

Finally, we note that one additional assumption is required before we arrive at a mathematically tractable model; we delay discussion of this final assumption until Chap. III.

In summary, we state again, that the worth of this model lies mainly in its retention of the essential character of the message delay in a real store-and-forward communication net.

1.5 Notation and Definitions

As a matter of convenience, we define and list below, some of the important quantities and symbols.

γ_{jk}	= the average number of messages entering the network per second, with origin j and destination k.
λ_i	= the average number of messages entering the ith channel per second.
$1/\mu_{jk}$	the average message length, in bits, for messages which have origin j and destination k.
C_i	= the channel capacity of the ith channel.
γ	= the total arrival rate of messages from external sources (see below).
λ	= the total arrival rate of messages to channels within the net (see below).
$\bar{n}$	= the average path length for messages (see below).
$1/\mu$	= the average message length from all sources (see below).
C	= the sum of all channel capacities in the net (see below).
ρ	= the network load; namely, the ratio of the average arrival rate of bits into the net from external sources to the total capacity of the net (see below).
Z_{jk}	= the average message delay for messages with origin j and destination k.
T_i	= the average delay to a message in passing through channel i (this includes both the time on queue and the time in transmission).
T	= the average time that messages spend in the network (see below). This quantity is taken as the measure of performance of a net.
τ	= the traffic matrix, whose entries are γ_{jk}.

We collect below certain relations among the definitions above. Some of these relations are by definition, and others may be obtained by simple manipulation.

$\bar{n}$	$= \dfrac{\lambda}{\gamma}$
$1/\mu$	$= \displaystyle\sum_{j,k} \dfrac{\gamma_{j,k}}{\gamma} \dfrac{1}{\mu_{j,k}}$
ρ	$= \dfrac{\gamma}{\mu C}$
C	$= \displaystyle\sum_i C_i$
γ	$= \displaystyle\sum_{j,k} \gamma_{j,k}$
λ	$= \displaystyle\sum_i \lambda_i$
T	$= \displaystyle\sum_{j,k} \dfrac{\gamma_{j,k}}{\gamma} Z_{j,k} = \sum_i \dfrac{\lambda_i}{\gamma} T_i$

1.6 Summary of Results

1.6.1 Analytic Results

The model chosen is described in Sects. 1.1 and 1.4. This model leads to a rather complex mathematical structure. We have, therefore, found it necessary to modify the original model with the introduction of the Independence Assumption. This assumption is carefully discussed in Chap. III; in essence, it assumes that new lengths are chosen for messages (from an exponential distribution) each time they enter a node. As shown in Chap. III, the new model results in a mathematical description which accurately describes the behavior of the message delay in the original model. As a consequence of the Independence Assumption, and of Theorem A. 1 (due to Burke), we may analyze each node separately in calculating message delay. We then find ourselves in a position to make some positive statements regarding the quantities of interest as described in Sect. 1.2.

The results obtained from this research for the model described above (including the Independence Assumption) will now be summarized. In considering a single node within the net, one finds that there is a large body of knowledge (namely, classical queuing theory) which deals with such problems. Appendix A describes some of the well-known results from that theory. Chapter IV describes several new results for single node systems. Specifically, if one considers the problem of determining the number, N, of output channels from a single node in order to minimize the time that a message spends in the node (queueing time plus transmission time), subject to the constraint that each channel is assigned a capacity equal to C/N, one then finds (Theorem 4.2) that $N = 1$ is the optimum solution. Further, a new interpretation for the utilization factor[4] for a single node with multiple output channels is obtained. The obvious trading relations between message delay, channel capacity, and total traffic handled are also developed.

At this point, a result is obtained which has great bearing on the general network problem. The result gives the assignment of channel capacity to a net consisting of N independent nodes (each with a single output channel, see Fig. 4.4) which minimizes the message delay averaged over the set of N nodes, subject to the constraint that the sum of the assigned capacity is constant. Specifically, if λ_i is the average (Poisson) arrival rate of messages to the ith node, and $1/\mu$ is the average length of these messages (exponentially distributed), then the optimum assignment, C_i, of the channel capacity to the ith node is

$$C_i = \frac{\lambda_i}{\mu_i} + \left[C - \sum_{i=1}^{N} \frac{\lambda_i}{\mu_i} \right] \frac{\sqrt{\frac{\lambda_i}{\mu_i}}}{\sum_{j=1}^{N} \sqrt{\frac{\lambda_j}{\mu_j}}} \qquad (1.1)$$

where C is the fixed total capacity. The function[5] which this minimizes is

$$T = \sum_{i=1}^{N} \frac{\lambda_i}{\lambda} T_i = \frac{\left(\sum_{i=1}^{N} \sqrt{\frac{\lambda_i}{\lambda \mu_i}} \right)^2}{C(1-\rho)} \qquad (1.2)$$

Here, T_i is the average message delay in the ith node, and T is the message delay appropriately averaged over the index i. Theorem 4.4 considers minimizing T (as expressed in Eq. 1.2 above) with respect to the λ_i (assuming $\mu_i = \mu$ for all i), holding λ constant, and subject to the additional constraints that $\lambda_i \geq k_i$ (where we take $k_1 \geq k_2 \ldots \geq k_N$ with no loss of generality). The set of numbers k_i represent lower bounds on the traffic flow through each channel, and correspond

to one form of physical limitation that may exist. The distribution of λ_i which minimizes T is

$$\lambda_i = \begin{cases} \lambda - \sum_{j=2}^{N} k_j & i = 1 \\ k_i & i > 1 \end{cases} \qquad (1.3)$$

For all $k_i = 0$, all traffic is assigned to (any) one of the channels, and by Eq. 1.1 this channel is allotted the total capacity C. In any case, we observe that this solution displays an attempt to cluster the traffic as much as possible. In fact, the results expressed by Theorem 4.2 and by the trading relations of Sect. 4.3 also indicate the desirability of clustering traffic (and therefore the channel capacity as well) in order to minimize message delay.

If we now consider the general case of an interconnected net (as, for example, in Fig. 1.1), with N channels indexed by the subscript i, subject to a fixed routing procedure[6], then we find that Eq. 1.1 continues to describe the optimum channel capacity assignment. The interpretation of λ_i is still the average arrival rate of messages to the ith channel; for this case, we take $\mu_i = \mu$ for all i. Furthermore, the average message delay, T, under this optimum assignment, becomes

$$T = \frac{\bar{n} \left(\sum_{i=1}^{N} \sqrt{\frac{\lambda_i}{\lambda}} \right)^2}{\mu C (1 - \bar{n} \rho)} \qquad (1.4)$$

where $\bar{n}$ is the average path length for messages in the net. The significance of this equation is discussed below in conjunction with the summary of the simulation experiments.

Constraining the sum of the assigned capacities to be constant implies a special form of system cost. In particular, the implication is that the system cost is represented strictly by the total channel capacity C. A more general cost function may be considered by assigning a function d_i, which represents the cost (in dollars, say) of supplying one unit of capacity to the ith channel[7]; thus, $d_i C_i$ represents the total cost of assigning the capacity C_i to the ith channel. The optimal channel capacity assignment, namely, that assignment which minimizes T at a fixed cost

$$D = \sum_{i=1}^{N} d_i C_i$$

has also been derived and is presented in Theorem 4.6. The average message delay, T, which exists for this assignment is also described in Theorem 4.6. Equations 1.1 and 1.2 are seen to be the special case of this theorem in which $d_i = 1$ for all i.

Chapter V explores the manner in which message delay is affected when one imposes a priority structure on the set of messages. Generally, one breaks the message set into P separate groups, the pth group ($p = 1, 2, \ldots, P$) being given preferential treatment over the $p - 1^{st}$ group, etc. A newly derived result for a delay dependent priority system is described, in which a message's priority is increased, from zero, linearly with time in proportion to a rate assigned to the message's priority group. The usefulness of this priority structure is that it provides a number of degrees of freedom with which to manipulate the relative waiting times for each priority group.

An interesting new law of conservation is also proven which constrains the allowed variation in the average waiting times for any one of a wide class of priority structures. Specifically, if we denote by W_p the average time that a message from the pth priority group spends in the queue, then the conservation law states that

$$\sum_{p=1}^{p} \left(\frac{\lambda_p}{\mu_p}\right) W_p = \text{constant with respect to variation of the priority structure}$$

where λ_p and $1/\mu_p$ are, respectively, the average arrival rate and average message length for messages from the pth priority group. The analytic expression for this constant is evaluated in Chap. V. As a result of this law, a number of general statements can be made regarding the average waiting times for any priority structure which falls in this class.[8] A priority structure which results in a system of time-shared service is also investigated. This system presents shorter waiting times for "short" messages and longer waiting times for "long" messages; interestingly enough, the critical message length which distinguishes "short" from "long" turns out to be the average message length for the case of geometrically distributed message lengths.

Random routing procedures for some specialized nets yield to mathematical analysis, and are discussed in Chap. VI. Specifically, a random routing procedure is a routing procedure in which the choice for the next node to be visited is made according to some probability distribution over the set of neighboring nodes. The first result obtained therein is the expected number of steps that a message must take (in a net which carries no other traffic) before arriving at its destination for that class of random routing procedures in which the node to node transitions are describable by circulant[9] transition matrices. This result exposes the increased number of steps that a message must take in a net with random routing. The next quantity of interest is the expected time that a message spends in the net. The solution for this is presented in Theorem 6.3 (which, once again, makes use of the Independence Assumption). A quantitative comparison is made for identical nets between random and fixed routing procedures, demonstrating the superiority of the latter as regards message delay.

The last phase of the research describes the results of a large scale digital simulation of store-and-forward communication nets. The simulation program (written for Lincoln Laboratory's TX-2 computer) is described in Appendix E. Extensive use was made of the simulator in confirming and extending many of the results of this research. For example, it provided a powerful tool for testing the accuracy and suitability of the Independence Assumption. Furthermore, networks of identical topological structure to those described in Chap. VI (Random Routing Procedures) were simulated with fixed routing procedures, and, as predicted, the comparative results indicate that random routing procedures are costly in terms of total traffic handled and message delay. A priority discipline was imposed on the message traffic in some of the runs, and these results indicate that the conservation law of Chap. V holds for nets as well as for a single node.

1.6.2 Experimental Results

With the background of theoretical results obtained in the material described above, a careful experimental investigation was carried out (using the network simulation program) for the purpose of examining the variation of average message delay for different channel capacity assignments, routing procedures, and topologies. These results are presented in Chap. VII.[10] Specifically, it was found that the channel capacity assignment expressed in Eq. 1.1 (to be referred to as the square root channel capacity assignment) was superior to all other assignments tested, not only for fixed routing procedures (as predicted), but also for a class of alternate routing procedures. Further, it was observed that with the square root capacity assignment, fixed routing was always superior to alternate routing for the same traffic and the same net. This result is not surprising when one recognizes that alternate routing procedures are designed to disperse the traffic whenever and wherever it is reasonable to do so.[11] This is in direct opposition to the result expressed by Eq. 1.3 in which it is clear that clustered traffic is to be preferred. However, the simulation results exposed the ability of alternate routing procedures to adapt the traffic flow so as to fit the network topology; specifically, it was observed that under a poor channel capacity assignment (in violation of Eq. 1.1), the performance of alternate routing was superior to fixed routing. This adaptive behavior of alternate routing procedures has considerable significance in the realistic design and operation of a communication net. Specifically, it is generally true that the actual traffic matrix is not known precisely at the time the network is being designed. Indeed, even if the traffic matrix were known, it is probable that the entries, γ_{jk}, in this matrix would be time-varying (i.e., different traffic loads exist at different hours of the day, different days of the week, different seasons of the year, etc.). In the face of either this uncertainty or variation, or both, it becomes impossible to calculate the optimum channel capacity assignment from Eq. 1.1 since the numbers λ_i (which are calculable from the γ_{jk} under a fixed routing procedure) are in doubt. One

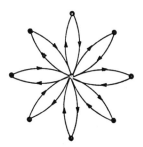

Figure 1.2   The star net configuration

solution to this problem is to use some form of alternate routing which will then adapt the actual traffic flow to the network. Note, however, that a price must be paid for such flexibility, since fixed routing with the square root capacity assignment is itself superior to alternate routing (assuming we have known time-invariant γ_{jk}).

The desirability of a clustered traffic pattern led to consideration of a special topology, namely, the star net, as shown in Fig. 1.2. This net has the property that as much traffic as possible is grouped into each channel; the physical constraint here is that the set of origins and destinations (i.e. , the traffic matrix) is specified independent of the network design, and, so, one is forced to have at least one channel leading to and from each node in the net. The star net yields exactly one channel leading in and out of each node (except, of course, for the central node). The effect of the distribution of traffic (λ_i) and the average path length ($\bar{n}$) on the average message delay in a net with a fixed routing procedure may be seen in Eq. 1.4. In particular, we note that increased clustering of traffic reduces the expression

$$\sum_{i=1}^{N} \sqrt{\frac{\lambda_i}{\lambda}},$$

e.g., see Eq. 1.3. Furthermore, we note that T grows without bound as $\rho \to \frac{1}{\bar{n}}$; recall that $\rho = \gamma/\mu C$ is the ratio of average arrival rate of bits into the net from external sources to the total capacity of the net. Clearly, a minimum value of $\bar{n}$ is desired. However, it is obvious that the adjustment of λ_i alters the value of $\bar{n}$. In particular, for the star net (which has a maximally clustered traffic pattern) we observe that

$1 < \bar{n} < 2$. If we require a reduced $\bar{n}$, we must add channels to the star net, thus destroying some of the clustering of traffic. In the limit as $\bar{n} \rightarrow 1$, we arrive at the fully connected net which has the smallest possible $\bar{n}$, but also the most dispersed traffic pattern. The trade-off between $\bar{n}$ and traffic clustering depends heavily upon ρ. In particular, we find that at low network load, nets similar to the topology of the star net are optimum; as the network load increases, we obtain the optimum topology by reducing $\bar{n}$ (by adding additional channels); and, finally, as $\rho \rightarrow 1$, we require $\bar{n} = 1$ which results in the fully connected net. In all cases, we use the square root channel capacity assignment with a fixed routing procedure.

A number of interesting results obtained with the help of simulation experiments have been described. These results pertain to the behavior of the average message delay (taken as the measure of performance of the net) as the following three design parameters are varied; channel capacity assignment; routing procedure; and topological structure. Specifically, the problem solved is the minimization of the average message delay at a fixed cost (i.e., at fixed total channel capacity). We now summarize the results of Chap. VII.

1. The square root channel capacity assignment as described in Eq. 1.1 results in superior performance as compared to a number of other channel capacity assignments.

2. The performance of a straightforward fixed routing procedure, with a square root capacity assignment, surpasses that of a simple alternate routing procedure.

3. The alternate routing procedure adapts the internal traffic flow to suit the capacity assignment (i.e., the bulk of the message traffic is routed to the high capacity channels). This effect is especially noticeable and important in the case of a poor capacity assignment which may come about due to uncertainty or variation in the applied message traffic.

4. A high degree of non-uniformity in the traffic matrix results in improved performance for the case of a square root channel capacity assignment (due to a more clustered traffic pattern).

5. The quantities essential to the determination of the average message delay are the average path length and the degree to which the traffic flow is clustered. The trade-off between these two quantities allows one to determine the sequence of optimal network topologies which ranges from the star net at small values of network load to the fully connected net as the network load approaches unity.

• • •

1. In transmitting messages, we are concerned with the data rate of transmission which is not necessarily the information rate in the information theoretic sense.

2. Numerals in square brackets refer to the bibliography.

3. This equipment is not required, but is often helpful, and aids in the smooth operation of the switching center.

4. The utilization factor is merely the ratio of average arrival rate of bits into the node to the total transmission rate of bits out of the node.

5. Note that the double subscript, jk, in γ_{jk} may in this case (see Fig. 4.4) be replaced by a single subscript, i; thus, according to Sect. 1.5, $\lambda_i = \gamma_i$ in this special case, and also $\lambda = \gamma$.

6. By a fixed routing procedure, we mean that given a message's origin and destination, there exists a unique path through the net which this message must follow. If more than one path is allowed, we speak of this as an alternate routing procedure.

7. For example, d_i may be taken to be proportional to the length of the ith channel.

8. See Chap. V for an exact description of the class.

9. A circulant matrix is one in which each row of

that matrix is a unit rotation of the row above it (see Eq. 6.2).

10. The simulation experiments described in this chapter were performed *without* the use of the Independence Assumption.

11. In addition, alternate routing procedures, in general, result in an increased average path length ($\bar{n}$)

Waiting Times for Certain Queue Disciplines

Leonard Kleinrock

Extract from Chapter 5 of *Communication Nets: Stochastic Message Flow and Delay* (New York: McGraw-Hill, 1964).

INTRODUCTORY NOTE TO READING 13.4

In these selections from *Communication Nets*, Leonard Kleinrock provided the first description and analysis of the basic algorithm for chopping messages into smaller pieces, later to be known as packets. He derived an exact expression for the mean response time of a packetized message. With this result, he showed that network response time can be improved with packetization, since response time was affected by the length of the message unit and this gave the benefit of preventing long messages from delaying the transmission of short messages. At the time most communications experts in the telephone industry claimed that packet switching was not possible. Kleinrock first published this description and analysis in April 1962.[1] He also presented the same material in his 1962 Ph.D. dissertation. We have extracted relevant sections of the book *Communication Nets* for this anthology. In his work, Kleinrock explicitly stated that he was interested in multi-node facilities as opposed to single node facilities, and that a model of a single-node and its behavior was the building block by which he could compose multi-node networks. [JMN]

---

1   Leonard Kleinrock, Information Flow in Large Communication Nets, *RLE Quarterly* (April, 1962).

TEXT OF READING 13.4

We now explore the manner in which message delay is affected when one introduces a priority structure (or queue discipline) into the set of messages in a single-node facility with a single transmission (or service) channel. In this chapter we shall present some newly derived results for certain queue disciplines; some previously published results are also included for completeness.

In communication nets such as we are considering, messages are forced to form a queue while awaiting passage through a transmission facility, and often a priority discipline describes the queue structure. The rule for choosing which message to transmit next is frequently based on a priority system similar to those studied in this chapter. Generally, one breaks the message set into P separate groups, the pth group ($p = 2, 3, \ldots, P$) being given preferential treatment over the $(p - 1)$st group, etc. Introducing a priority structure into the message set influences the expected value of the time that each priority group spends in the queue. It is this statistic which is of interest to us and which will be solved for. An understanding of the effects of a priority discipline at the single-node level is necessary before one can make any intelligent statements about the multinode case. . . .

A system with a time-shared service facility is also investigated. This system results in shorter waiting times for "short" messages and longer waiting times for "long" messages; interestingly enough, the critical message length which distinguishes short from long turns out to be the average message length for the case of geometrically distributed lengths. . . .

In the application of interest, wherein messages are passing through a transmission facility, the average processing time (time spent in the transmission channel) is $1/\mu_p C$, where, once again, C is the capacity of the channel in bits/sec, and where $1/\mu_p$ is the average message length in bits. However, for the purposes of this chapter, it is convenient to suppress the parameter C, and so we assume that $C = 1$ throughout (with no loss of generality). If one wishes to reintroduce it, one need merely multiply every μ_p by C. . . .

Since we assume that each message has a fixed servicing time (chosen from some exponential distribution) associated with it, we must further assume that when a preempted message reenters the service facility, its servicing is started at the point at which it was interrupted when preemption occurred (this is referred to as *pre-emptive resume*). . . .

In this section we present results for a simple "round-robin" time-shared service facility and compare these results with a straightforward first-come first-served discipline. The round-robin discipline shares the desirable features of a first-come first-served principle and those of a discipline which services short messages first. Such a scheme is a likely candidate for the discipline of a large time-shared computational facility.

Let time be quantized into segments, each Q seconds in length. At the end of each time interval, a new message arrives in the system with probability λQ (result of a Bernoulli trial); thus, the average number of arrivals per second is λ. The service time of a newly arriving message is chosen independently from a geometric distribution such that, for $\sigma < 1$,

$$s_n = (1 - \sigma)\sigma^{n-1} \qquad n = 1, 2, 3, \ldots \qquad (5.22)$$

where s_n is the probability that a message's service time is exactly n time units long (i.e., that its service time is nQ seconds).

The procedure for servicing is as follows: A newly arriving message joins the end of the queue and waits in line in a first-come first-served fashion until it finally arrives at the service facility. The server picks the next message in the queue and performs one unit of service upon it (i.e., services this message for exactly Q seconds). At the end of this time interval, the message leaves the system if its service (transmission) is finished; if not, it joins the end of the queue with its service partially completed, as shown in Fig. 5.6.

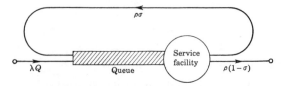

Fig. 5.6. *Round-robin time-shared service system.*

Obviously, a message whose length is n time units long will be forced to join the queue n times in all before its service is completed. . . .

. . . by introducing the round-robin system analyzed in this study, one manipulates the relative waiting time for different messages (while maintaining a constant W) and thus imposes a time-sharing system which gives preferential treatment to short messages.

13·5
The Computer as a Communication Device

J. C. R. Licklider and Robert W. Taylor

From *Science and Technology* 76 (1968).

INTRODUCTORY NOTE TO READING 13.6

In this paper Licklider (see also Readings 10.5 and 10.6) and Robert W. Taylor, who was at the time Director of the Informational Processing Technology Office (IPTA) of ARPA, describe the features of the future ARPANET. This was a speculative paper reflecting the authors' imagination of what people would eventually be able to do with such a network. Nearly fifty years later, it is fascinating to compare their vision with current realities. [JMN]

TEXT OF READING 13.5

In a few years, men will be able to communicate more effectively through a machine than face to face.

That is a rather startling thing to say, but it is our conclusion. As if in confirmation of it, we participated a few weeks ago in a technical meeting held through a computer. In two days, the group accomplished with the aid of a computer what normally might have taken a week.

We shall talk more about the mechanics of the meeting later; it is sufficient to note here that we were all in the same room. But for all the communicating we did directly across that room, we could have been thousands of miles apart and communicated just as effectively—as people—over the distance.

Our emphasis on people is deliberate. A communications engineer thinks of communicating as transferring information from one point to another in codes and signals.

But to communicate is more than to send and to receive. Do two tape recorders communicate when they play to each other and record from each other? Not really—not in our sense. We believe that communicators have to do something nontrivial with the information they send and receive. And we believe that we are entering a technological age in which we will be able to interact with the richness of living information—not merely in the passive way that we have become accustomed to using books and libraries, but as active participants in an ongoing process, bringing something to it through our interaction with it, and not simply receiving something from it by our connection to it.

To the people who telephone an airline flight operations information service, the tape recorder that answers seems more than a passive depository. It is an often-updated model of a changing situation—a synthesis of information collected, analyzed, evaluated, and assembled to represent a situation or process in an organized way.

Still there is not much direct interaction with the airline information service; the tape recording is not changed by the customer's call. We want to emphasize something beyond its one-way transfer: the increasing significance of the jointly constructive, the mutually reinforcing aspect of communication—the part that transcends "now we both know a fact that only one of us knew before." When minds interact, new ideas emerge. We want to talk about the creative aspect of communication.

Creative, interactive communication requires a plastic or moldable medium that can be modeled, a dynamic medium in which premises will flow into consequences, and above all a common medium that can be contributed to and experimented with by all.

Such a medium is at hand—the programmed digital computer. Its presence can change the nature and value of communication even more profoundly than did the printing press and the picture tube, for, as we shall show, a well-programmed computer can provide direct access both to informational resources and to the *processes* for making use of the resources,

COMMUNICATION: A COMPARISON OF MODELS

To understand how and why the computer can have such an effect on communication, we must examine the idea of modeling-in a computer and with the aid of a computer. For modeling, we believe, is basic and central to communication. Any communication between people about the same thing is a common revelatory experience about informational models of that thing. Each model is a conceptual structure of abstractions formulated initially in the mind of one of the persons who would communicate, and if the concepts in the mind of one would-be communicator are very different from those in the mind of another, there is no common model and no communication.

By far the most numerous, most sophisticated, and most important models are those that reside in men's minds, In richness, plasticity, facility, and economy, the mental model has no peer, but, in other respects, it has shortcomings. It will not stand still for careful study. It cannot be made to repeat a run. No one knows just how it works. It serves its owner's hopes more faithfully than it serves reason. It has access only to the information stored in one man's head. It can be observed and manipulated only by one person.

Society rightly distrusts the modeling done by a single mind. Society demands consensus, agreement, at least majority. Fundamentally, this amounts to the requirement that individual models be compared and brought into some degree of accord. The requirement is for communication, which we now define concisely as "cooperative modeling"—cooperation in the construction, maintenance, and use of a model.

How can we be sure that we are modeling cooperatively, that we are communicating, unless we can compare models?

When people communicate face to face, they externalize their models so they can be sure they are talking about the same thing. Even such a simple externalized model as a flow diagram or an outline—because it can be seen by all the communicators—serves as a focus for discussion. It changes the nature of communication: When communicators have no such common framework, they merely make speeches *at* each other; but when they have a manipulable model before them, they utter a few words, point, sketch, nod, or object.

The dynamics of such communication are so model-centered as to suggest an important conclusion: Perhaps the reason present-day two-way telecommunication falls so far short of face-to-face communication is simply that it fails to provide facilities for externalizing models. Is it really seeing the expression in the other's eye that makes the face-to-face conference so much more productive than the telephone conference call, or is it being able to create and modify external models?

THE PROJECT MEETING AS A MODEL

In a technical project meeting, one can see going on, in fairly clear relief, the modeling process that we contend constitutes communication. Nearly every reader can recall a meeting held during the formulative phase of a project. Each member of the project brings to such a meeting a somewhat different mental model of the common undertaking—its purposes, its goals, its plans, its progress, and its status. Each of these models interrelates the past, present, and future states of affairs of (1) himself; (2) the group he represents; (3) his boss; (4) the project.

Many of the primary data the participants bring to the meeting are in undigested and uncorrelated form. To each participant, his own collections of data are interesting and important in and of themselves. And they are more than files of facts and recurring reports. They are strongly influenced by insight, subjective feelings, and educated guesses. Thus, each individual's data are reflected in his mental model. Getting his colleagues to incorporate his data into their models is the essence of the communications task.

Suppose you could see the models in the minds of two would-be communicators at this meeting. You could tell, by observing their models, whether or not communication was taking place. If, at the outset, their two models were similar in structure but different simply in the values of certain parameters, then communication would cause convergence toward a common pattern. That is the easiest and most frequent kind of communication.

When mental models are dissimilar, the achievement of communication might be signaled by changes in the structure of one of the models, or both of them.

If the two mental models were structurally dissimilar, then the achievement of communication would be signaled by structural changes in one of the models or in both of them. We might conclude that one of the communicating parties was having insights or trying out new hypotheses in order to begin to understand the other—or that both were restructuring their mental models to achieve commonality.

The meeting of many interacting minds is a more complicated process. Suggestions and recommendations may be elicited from all sides. The interplay may produce, not just a solution to a problem, but a new set of rules for solving problems. That, of course, is the essence of creative interaction. The process of maintaining a current model has within it a set of changing or changeable rules for the processing and disposition of information.

The project meeting we have just described is representative of a broad class of human endeavor which may be described as creative informational activity. Let us differentiate this from another class which we will call informational housekeeping. The latter is what computers today are used for in the main; they process payroll checks, keep track of bank balances, calculate orbits of space vehicles, control repetitive machine processes, and maintain varieties of debit and credit lists. Mostly they have *not* been used to make coherent pictures of not well understood situations.

We referred earlier to a meeting in which the participants interacted with each other through a computer. That meeting was organized by Doug Engelbart of Stanford Research Institute and was actually a progress-review conference for a specific project. The subject under discussion was rich in detail and broad enough in scope that no one of the attendees, not even the host, could know all the information pertaining to this particular project.

FACE TO FACE THROUGH A COMPUTER

Tables were arranged to form a square work area with five on a side. The center of the area contained six television monitors which displayed the alphanumeric output of a computer located elsewhere in the building but remotely controlled from a keyboard and a set of electronic pointer controllers called "mice." Any participant in the meeting could move a nearby mouse, and thus control the movements of a tracking pointer on the TV screen for all other participants to see.

Each person working on the project had prepared a topical outline of his particular presentation for the meeting, and his outline appeared on the screens as he talked—providing a broad view of his own model. Many of the outline statements contained the names of particular reference files which the speaker could recall from the computer to appear in detail on the screens, for, from the beginning of the project, its par-

ticipants had put their work into the computer system's files.

So the meeting began much like any other meeting in the sense that there was an overall list of agenda and that each speaker had brought with him (figuratively in his briefcase but really within the computer) the material he would be talking about.

The computer system was a significant aid in exploring the depth and breadth of the material. More detailed information could be displayed when facts had to be pinpointed; more global information could be displayed to answer questions of relevance and interrelationship. A future version of this system will make it possible for each participant, on his own TV screen, to thumb through the speaker's files as the speaker talks—and thus check out incidental questions without interrupting the presentation for substantiation.

At a project meeting held through a computer, you can thumb through the speaker's primary data without interrupting him to substantiate or explain.

A communication system should make a positive contribution to the discovery and arousal of interests.

Obviously, collections of primary data can get too large to digest. There comes a time when the complexity of a communications process exceeds the available resources and the capability to cope with it; and at that point one has to simplify and draw conclusions.

It is frightening to realize how early and drastically one does simplify, how prematurely one does conclude, even when the stakes are high and when the transmission facilities and information resources are extraordinary. Deep modeling to communicate—to understand—requires a huge investment. Perhaps even governments cannot afford it yet.

But someday governments may not be able *not* to afford it. For, while we have been talking about the communication process as a cooperative modeling effort in a mutual environment, there is also an aspect of communication with or about an uncooperative opponent. As nearly as we can judge from reports of recent international crises, out of the hundreds of alternatives that confronted the decision makers at each decision point or ply in the "game," on the average only a few, and never more than a few dozen could be considered, and only a few branches of the game could be explored deeper than two or three such plies before action had to be taken. Each side was busy trying to model what the other side might be up to—but modeling takes time, and the pressure of events forces simplification even when it is dangerous.

Whether we attempt to communicate across a division of interests, or whether we engage in a cooperative effort, it is clear that we need to be able to model faster and to greater depth. The importance of improving decision-making processes—not only in government, but throughout business and the professions—is so great as to warrant every effort.

THE COMPUTER—SWITCH OR INTERACTOR?

As we see it, group decision-making is simply the active, executive, effect-producing aspect of the kind of communication we are discussing. We have commented that one must oversimplify. We have tried to say why one must oversimplify. But we should not oversimplify the main point of this article. We can say with genuine and strong conviction that a particular form of digital computer organization, with its pro-

grams and its data, constitutes the dynamic, moldable medium that can revolutionize the art of modeling and that in so doing can improve the effectiveness of communication among people so much as perhaps to revolutionize that also.

But we must associate with that statement at once the qualification that the computer alone can make no contribution that will help us, and that the computer with the programs and the data that it has today can do little more than suggest a direction and provide a few germinal examples. Emphatically we do *not* say: "Buy a computer and your communication problems will be solved."

What we do say is that we, together with many colleagues who have had the experience of working online and interactively with computers, have already sensed more responsiveness and facilitation and "power" than we had hoped for, considering the inappropriateness of present machines and the primitiveness of their software. Many of us are therefore confident (some of us to the point of religious zeal) that truly significant achievements, which will markedly improve our effectiveness in communication, now are on the horizon.

Many communications engineers, too, are presently excited about the application of digital computers to communication. However, the function they want computers to implement is the switching function. Computers will either switch the communication lines, connecting them together in required configurations, or switch (the technical term is "store and forward") messages.

The switching function is important but it is not the one we have in mind when we say that the computer can revolutionize communication. We are stressing the modeling function, not the switching function. Until now, the communications engineer has not felt it within his province to facilitate the modeling function, to make an interactive, cooperative modeling facility. Information transmission and information processing have always been carried out separately and have become separately institutionalized. There are strong intellectual and social benefits to be realized by the melding of these two technologies. There are also, however, powerful legal and administrative obstacles in the way of any such melding.

DISTRIBUTED INTELLECTUAL RESOURCES

We have seen the beginnings of communication through a computer—communication among people at consoles located in the same room or on the same university campus or even at distantly separated laboratories of the same research and development organization. This kind of communication—through a single multiaccess computer with the aid of telephone lines—is beginning to foster cooperation and promote coherence more effectively than do present arrangements for sharing computer programs by exchanging magnetic tapes by messenger or mail. Computer programs are very important because they transcend mere "data"—they include procedures and processes for structuring and manipulating data. These are the main resources we can now concentrate and share with the aid of the tools and techniques of computers and communication, but they are only a part of the whole that we can learn to concentrate and share. The whole includes raw data, digested data, data about the location of data—and documents —and most especially models.

To appreciate the importance the new computer-aided communication can have, one must consider the dynamics of "critical mass," as it applies to cooperation in creative endeavor. Take any problem worthy of the name, and you find only a few people who can contribute effectively to its solution. Those people must be brought into close intellectual partnership so that their ideas can come into contact with one another. But bring these people together physically in one place to form a team, and you have trouble, for the most creative people are often not the best team players, and there are not enough top positions in a single organization to keep them all happy. Let them go their separate ways, and each creates his own empire, large or small, and devotes more time to the role of emperor than to the role of problem solver. The principals still get together at meetings. They still visit one another. But the time scale of their communica-

tion stretches out, and the correlations among mental models degenerate between meetings so that it may take a year to do a week's communicating. There has to be some way of facilitating communication among people without bringing them together in one place.

A single multiaccess computer would fill the bill if expense were no object, but there is no way, with a single computer and individual communication lines to several geographically separated consoles, to avoid paying an unwarrantedly large bill for transmission. Part of the economic difficulty lies in our present communications system. When a computer is used interactively from a typewriter console, the signals transmitted between the console and the computer are intermittent and not very frequent. They do not require continuous access to a telephone channel; a good part of the time they do not even require the full information rate of such a channel. The difficulty is that the common carriers do not provide the kind of service one would like to have—a service that would let one have ad lib access to a channel for short intervals and not be charged when one is not using the channel.

It seems likely that a store-and-forward (i.e., store-for-just-a-moment-and-forward-right-away) message service would be best for this purpose, whereas the common carriers offer, instead, service that sets up a channel for one's individual use for a period not shorter than one minute.

The problem is further complicated because interaction with a computer via a fast and flexible graphic display, which is for most purposes far superior to interaction through a slow-printing typewriter, requires markedly higher information rates. Not necessarily more information, but the same amount in faster bursts—more difficult to handle efficiently with the conventional common-carrier facilities.

It is perhaps not surprising that there are incompatibilities between the requirements of computer systems and the services supplied by the common carriers, for most of the common-carrier services were developed in support of voice rather than digital communication. Nevertheless, the incompatibilities are frustrating. It appears that the best and quickest way to overcome them—and to move forward the development of interactive *communities* of geographically separated people—is to set up an experimental network of multiaccess computers. Computers would concentrate and interleave the concurrent, intermittent messages of many users and their programs so as to utilize wide-band transmission channels continuously and efficiently, with marked reduction in overall cost.

COMPUTER AND INFORMATION NETWORKS

The concept of computers connected to computers is not new. Computer manufacturers have successfully installed and maintained interconnected computers for some years now. But the computers in most instances are from families of machines compatible in both software and hardware, and they are in the same location. More important, the interconnected computers are not interactive, general-purpose, multiaccess machines of the type described by David [1] and Licklider [2]. Although more interactive multiaccess computer systems are being delivered now, and although more groups plan to be using these systems within the next year, there are at present perhaps only as few as half a dozen interactive multiaccess computer *communities*.

These communities are socio-technical pioneers, in several ways out ahead of the rest of the computer world: What makes them so? First, some of their members are computer scientists and engineers who understand the concept of man-computer interaction and the technology of interactive multiaccess systems. Second, others of their members are creative people in other fields and disciplines who recognize the usefulness and who sense the impact of interactive multiaccess computing upon their work. Third, the communities have large multiaccess computers and have learned to use them. And, fourth, their efforts are regenerative.

In the half-dozen communities, the computer systems research and development and the development of substantive applications mutually support each other. They are producing large and growing resources of programs, data, and knowhow. But we have seen only the beginning. There is much more programming and data collection—and much more learning how to cooperate—to be done before the full potential of the concept can be realized.

Obviously, multiaccess systems must be developed interactively. The systems being built must remain flexible and open-ended throughout the process of development, which is evolutionary.

Such systems cannot be developed in small ways on small machines. They require large, multiaccess computers, which are necessarily complex. Indeed, the sonic barrier in the development of such systems is complexity.

These new computer systems we are describing differ from other computer systems advertised with the same labels: interactive, time-sharing, multiaccess. They differ by having a greater degree of open-endedness, by rendering more services, and above all by providing facilities that foster a working sense of community among their users. The commercially available time-sharing services do not yet offer the power and flexibility of soft ware resources—the "general purposeness"—of the interactive multiaccess systems of the System Development Corporation in Santa Monica, the University of California at Berkeley, Massachusetts Institute of Technology in Cambridge and Lexington, Mass.—which have been collectively serving about a thousand people for several years.

The thousand people include many of the leaders of the ongoing revolution in the computer world. For over a year they have been preparing for the transition to a radically new organization of hardware and software, designed to support many more simultaneous users than the current systems, and to offer them—through new languages, new file-handling systems, and new graphic displays—the fast, smooth interaction required for truly effective man-computer partnership.

Experience has shown the importance of making the response time short and the conversation free and easy. We think those attributes will be almost as important for a network of computers as for a single computer.

Today the on-line communities are separated from one another functionally as well as geographically. Each member can look only to the processing, storage and software capability of the facility upon which his community is centered. But now the move is on to interconnect the separate communities and thereby transform them into, let us call it, a supercommunity. The hope is that interconnection will make available to all the members of all the communities the programs and data resources of the entire supercommunity. First, let us indicate how these communities can be interconnected; then we shall describe one hypothetical person's interaction with this network, of interconnected computers.

MESSAGE PROCESSING

The hardware of a multiaccess computer system includes one or more central processors, several kinds of memory—core, disks, drums, and tapes—and many consoles for the simultaneous on-line users. Different users can work simultaneously on diverse tasks. The software of such a system includes supervisory programs (which control the whole operation), system programs for interpretation of the user's commands, the handling of his files, and graphical or alphanumeric display of information to him (which permit people not skilled in the machine's language to use the system effectively), and programs and data created by the users themselves. The collection of people, hardware, and software—the multiaccess computer together with its local community of users—will become a node in a geographically distributed computer network. Let us assume for a moment that such a network has been formed.

For each node there is a small, general-purpose computer which we shall call a "message processor." The message processors of all the nodes are interconnected to form a fast store-and-forward network. The large multi-access computer at each node is connected directly to the message processor there. Through the network of message processors, therefore, all the large computers can communicate with one another. And through them, all the members of the supercommunity can communicate—with other people, with pro-

grams, with data, or with selected combinations of those resources. The message processors, being all alike, introduce an element of uniformity into an otherwise grossly nonuniform situation, for they facilitate both hardware and software compatibility among diverse and poorly compatible computers. The links among the message processors are transmission and high-speed *digital* switching facilities provided by common carrier. This allows the linking of the message processors to be reconfigured in response to demand.

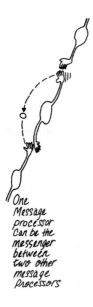

One Message processor can be the messenger between two other message processors

A given pair of nodes may exchange several independent messages for simultaneous users with different interests.

one point or another along the way. In short, the message processors function in the system as traffic directors, controllers, and correctors.

Today, programs created at one installation on a given manufacturer's computer are generally not of much value to users of a different manufacturer's computer at another installation. After learning (with difficulty) of a distant program's existence, one has to get it, understand it, and recode it for his own computer. The cost is comparable to the cost of preparing a new program from scratch, which is, in fact, what most programmers usually do. On a national scale, the annual cost is enormous. Within a network of interactive, multiaccess computer systems, on the other hand, a person at one node will have access to programs running at other nodes, even though those programs were written in different languages for different computers.

The feasibility of using programs at remote locations has been shown by the successful linking of the AN/FSQ-32 computer at Systems Development Corporation in Santa Monica, Calif., with the TX-2 computer across the continent at the Lincoln Laboratory in Lexington, Mass. A person at a TX-2 graphic console can make use of a unique list-processing program at SDC, which would be prohibitively expensive to translate for use on the TX-2. A network of 14 such diverse computers, all of which will be capable of sharing one another's resources, is now being planned by the Defense Department's Advanced Research Projects Agency, and its contractors.

The system's way of managing data is crucial to the user who works in interaction with many other people. It should put generally useful data, if not subject to control of access, into public files. Each user, however, should have complete control over his personal files. He should define and distribute the "keys" to each such file, exercising his option to exclude all others from any kind of access to it; or to permit anyone to "read" but not modify or execute it; or to permit selected individuals or groups to execute but not read it; and so on—with as much detailed specification or as much aggregation as he likes. The system should provide for group and organizational files within its overall information base.

A message can be thought of as a short sequence of "bits" flowing through the network from one multiaccess computer to another. It consists of two types of information: control and data. Control information guides the transmission of data from source to destination. In present transmission systems, errors are too frequent for many computer applications. However, through the use of error detection and correction or retransmission procedures in the message processors, messages can be delivered to their destinations intact even though many of their "bits" were mutilated at

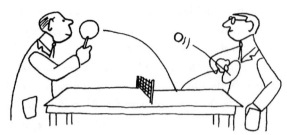

Interactive communication consists of short spurts of dialog . . . .

. . . filibustering destroys communication.

At least one of the new multiaccess systems will exhibit such features. In several of the research centers we have mentioned, security and privacy of information are subjects of active concern; they are beginning to get the attention they deserve.

In a multiaccess system, the number of consoles permitted to use the computer simultaneously depends upon the load placed on the computer by the users' jobs, and may be varied automatically as the load changes. Large general-purpose multiaccess systems operating today can typically support 20 to 30 simultaneous users. Some of these users may work with low-level "assembly" languages while others use higher-level "compiler" or "interpreter" languages. Concurrently, others may use data management and graphical systems. And so on.

But back to our hypothetical user. He seats himself at his console, which may be a terminal keyboard plus a relatively slow printer, a sophisticated graphical console, or any one of several intermediate devices. He dials his local computer and "logs in" by presenting his name, problem number, and password to the monitor program. He calls for either a public program, one of his own programs, or a colleague's program that he

has permission to use. The monitor links him to it, and he then communicates with that program. When the user (or the program) needs service from a program at another node in the network, he (or it) requests the service by specifying the location of the appropriate computer and the identity of the program required. If necessary, he uses computerized directories to determine those data. The request is translated by one or more of the message processors into the precise language required by the remote computer's monitor. Now the user (or his local program) and the remote program can interchange information. When the information transfer is complete, the user (or his local program) dismisses the remote computer, again with the aid of the message processors. In a commercial system, the remote processor would at this point record cost information for use in billing.

WHO CAN AFFORD IT?

The mention of billing brings up an important matter. Computers and long distance calls have "expensive" images. One of the standard reactions to the idea of "on-line communities" is: "It sounds great, but who can afford it?" In considering that question, let us do a little arithmetic. The main elements of the cost of computer-facilitated communication, over and above the salaries of the communicators, are the cost of the consoles, processing, storage, transmission, and supporting software. In each category, there is a wide range of possible costs, depending in part upon the sophistication of the equipment, programs, or services employed and in part upon whether they are custom-made or mass-produced.

Making rough estimates of the hourly component costs per user, we arrived at the following: $1 for a console, $5 for one man's share of the services of a processor, 70 cents for storage, $3 for transmission via line leased from a common carrier, and $1 for software support—a total cost of just less than $11 per communicator hour.

The only obviously untenable assumption underlying that result, we believe, is the assumption that one's console and the personal files would be used 160 hours per month. All the other items are assumed to be shared with others, and experience indicates that time-sharing leads on the average to somewhat greater utilization than the 160 hours per month that we assumed. Note, however, that the console and the personal files are items used also in individual problem solving and decision making. Surely those activities, taken together with communication, would occupy at least 25% of the working hours of the on-line executive, scientist or engineer. If we cut the duty factor of the console and files to one quarter of 160 hours per month, the estimated total cost comes to $16 per hour.

Let us assume that our $16/hr interactive computer link is set up between Boston, Mass., and Washington, D.C. Is $16/hr affordable? Compare it first with the cost of ordinary telephone communication: Even if you take advantage of the lower charge per minute for long calls, it is less than the daytime direct-dial station-to-station toll. Compare it with the cost of travel: If one flies from Boston to Washington in the morning and back in the evening, he can have eight working hours in the capital city in return for about $64 in air and taxi fares plus the spending of four of his early morning and evening hours en route. If those four hours are worth $16 each, then the bill for the eight hours in Washington is $128—again $16 per hour. Or look at it still another way: If computer-aided communication doubled the effectiveness of a man paid $16 per hour then, according to our estimate, it would be worth what it cost if it could be bought right now. Thus we have some basis for arguing that computer-aided communication is economically feasible. But we must admit that the figure of $16 per hour sounds high, and we do not want to let our discussion depend upon it.

Fortunately, we do not have to, for the system we envision cannot be bought at this moment. The time scale provides a basis for genuine optimism about the cost picture. It will take two years, at least, to bring the first interactive computer networks up to a significant level of experimental activity. Operational systems might reach critical size in as little as six years if everyone got onto the bandwagon, but there is little point in making cost estimates for a nearer date. So let us take six years as the target.

In the computer field, the cost of a unit of processing and the cost of a unit of storage have been dropping for two decades at the rate of 50% or more every two years. In six years, there is time for at least three such drops, which cut a dollar down to 12 1/2 cents. Three halvings would take the cost of processing, now $5 per hour on our assumptions, down to less than 65 cents per hour.

Such advances in capability, accompanied by reduction in cost, lead us to expect that computer facilitation will be affordable before many people are ready to take advantage of it. The only areas that cause us concern are consoles and transmission.

In the console field, there is plenty of competition; many firms have entered the console sweepstakes, and more are entering every month. Lack of competition is not the problem. The problem is the problem of the chicken and the egg—in the factory and in the market. If a few companies would take the plunge into mass manufacture, then the cost of a satisfactory console would drop enough to open up a mass market. If large on-line communities were already in being, their mass market would attract mass manufacture. But at present there is neither mass manufacture nor a mass market, and consequently there is no low-cost console suitable for interactive on-line communication.

In the field of transmission, the difficulty may be lack of competition. At any rate, the cost of transmission is not falling nearly as fast as the cost of processing and storage. Nor is it falling nearly as fast as we think it should fall. Even the advent of satellites has affected the cost picture by less than a factor of two. That fact does not cause immediate distress because (unless the distance is very great) transmission cost is not now the dominant cost. But, at the rate things are going, in six years it will be the dominant cost. That prospect concerns us greatly and is the strongest damper to our hopes for near-term realization of operationally significant interactive networks and significant on-line communities.

ON-LINE INTERACTIVE COMMUNITIES

But let us be optimistic. What will on-line interactive communities be like? In most fields they will consist of geographically separated members, sometimes grouped in small clusters and sometimes working individually. They will be communities not of common location, but of *common interest*. In each field, the overall community of interest will be large enough to support a comprehensive system of field-oriented programs and data.

In each geographical sector, the total number of users—summed over all the fields of interest—will be large enough to support extensive general-purpose information processing and storage facilities. All of these will be interconnected by telecommunications channels. The whole will constitute a labile network of networks—ever-changing in both content and configuration.

What will go on inside? Eventually, every informational transaction of sufficient consequence to warrant the cost. Each secretary's typewriter, each data-gathering instrument, conceivably each dictation microphone, will feed into the network.

You will not send a letter or a telegram; you will simply identify the people whose files should be linked to yours and the parts to which they should be linked—and perhaps specify a coefficient of urgency. You will seldom make a telephone call; you will ask the network to link your consoles together,

You will seldom make a purely business trip, because linking consoles will be so much more efficient. When you do visit another person with the object of intellectual communication, you and he will sit at a two-place console and interact as much through it as face to face. If our extrapolation from Doug Engelbart's meeting proves correct, you will spend much more time in computer-facilitated teleconferences and much less en route to meetings.

A very important part of each man's interaction with his on-line community will be mediated by his OLIVER. The acronym OLIVER honors Oliver Selfridge, originator of the concept. An OLIVER is, or will be when there is one, an "on-line interactive vicarious expediter and responder," a complex of computer programs and data that resides within the network and acts on behalf of its principal, taking care of many minor matters that do not require his personal atten-

tion and buffering him from the demanding world. "You are describing a secretary," you will say. But no! Secretaries will have OLIVERS.

At your command, your OLIVER will take notes (or refrain from taking notes) on what you do, what you read, what you buy and where you buy it. It will know who your friends are, your mere acquaintances. It will know your value structure, who is prestigious in your eyes, for whom you will do what with what priority, and who can have access to which of your personal files. It will know your organization's rules pertaining to proprietary information and the government's rules relating to security classification.

Your computer will know who is prestigious in your eyes and buffer you from a demanding world.

Some parts of your OLIVER program will be common with parts of other people's OLIVERS; other parts will be custom-made for you, or by you, or will have developed idiosyncrasies through "learning" based on its experience in your service.

Available within the network will be functions and services to which you subscribe on a regular basis and others that you call for when you need them. In the former group will be investment guidance, tax counseling, selective dissemination of information in your field of specialization, announcement of cultural, sport, and entertainment events that fit your interests, etc. In the latter group will be dictionaries, encyclopedias, indexes, catalogues, editing programs, teaching programs, testing programs, programming systems, data bases, and—most important—communication, display, and modeling programs.

All these will be—at some late date in the history of networking—systematized and coherent; you will be able to get along in one basic language up to the point at which you choose a specialized language for its power or terseness.

When people do their informational work "at the console" and "through the network," telecommunication will be as natural an extension of individual work as face-to-face communication is now. The impact of that fact, and of the marked facilitation of the communicative process, will be very great—both on the individual and on society.

First, life will be happier for the on-line individual because the people with whom one interacts most strongly will be selected more by commonality of interests and goals than by accidents of proximity. Second, communication will be more effective and productive, and therefore more enjoyable. Third, much communication and interaction will be with programs and programmed models, which will be (a) highly responsive, (b) supplementary to one's own capabilities, rather than competitive, and (c) capable of representing progressively more complex ideas without necessarily displaying all the levels of their structure at the same time-and which will therefore be both challenging and rewarding. And, fourth, there will be plenty of opportunity for everyone (who can afford a console) to find his calling, for the whole world of information, with all its fields and disciplines, will be open to him—with programs ready to guide him or to help him explore.

For the society, the impact will be good or bad, depending mainly on the question: Will "to be on line" be a privilege or a right? If only a favored segment of the population gets a chance to enjoy the advantage of "intelligence amplification," the network may exaggerate the discontinuity in the spectrum of intellectual opportunity.

On the other hand, if the network idea should prove to do for education what a few have envisioned in hope, if not in concrete detailed plan, and if all minds should prove to be responsive, surely the boon to humankind would be beyond measure.

Unemployment would disappear from the face of the earth forever, for consider the magnitude of the task of adapting the network's software to all the new generations of computer, coming closer and closer upon the heels of their predecessors until the entire population of the world is caught up in an infinite crescendo of on-line interactive debugging.

ACKNOWLEDGEMENTS

Evan Herbert edited the article and acted as intermediary during its writing between Licklider in Boston and Taylor in Washington. Roland B. Wilson drew the cartoons to accompany the original article.

REFERENCES

1. Edward E. David, Jr., "Sharing a Computer," *International Science and Technology,* June, 1966.

2.   J. C. R. Licklider, "Man-Computer Partnership," *International Science and Technology,* May, 1965.

13.6

Multiple Computer Networks and Intercomputer Communication

Lawrence G. Roberts

From *Proceedings of the First ACM Symposium on Operating System Principles* (1967): 3.1–3.6.

INTRODUCTORY NOTE TO READING 13.6

At a meeting with J. C. R. Licklider in November 1964, Lawrence G. Roberts took on the project of creating the ARPANET. Upon Licklider's resignation as director of ARPA IPTO (Advanced Research Projects Agency Information Processing Technology Office) in February 1965, Ivan Sutherland accepted the position. As second ARPA IPTO director Sutherland awarded the contract for the first network experiment to Roberts. In October 1965 Roberts did the first actual network experiment, tying MIT Lincoln Labs' TX-2 computer to System Development Corporations' SDC Q32. This was the first time that that two computers talked to one another, and the first time that packet switching was used to communicate between computers using the technology developed by Leonard Kleinrock (Readings 13.2, 13.3, 13.4). One year later, Roberts reported on his networking research at MIT in a paper written with Thomas Marill entitled "Towards a Network of Time-Shared Computers." In August 1966 Robert Taylor became the third ARPA IPTO Director and hired Roberts. Appointed ARPA IPTO Chief Scientist in December 1966, Roberts began the design of the ARPANET. In his proposal to Congress, Roberts indicated that the ARPANET would explore computer resource sharing and packet switched communications to ensure reliability. In June 1967 Roberts published his first paper on the design of the ARPANET. That is the paper that we reproduce in this anthology [JMN].

TEXT OF READING 13.6

There are many reasons for establishing a network which allows many computers to communicate with each other to interchange and execute programs or data. The definition of a network within this paper will always be that of a network between computers, not including the network of typewriter consoles surrounding each computer. Attempts at computer networks have been made in the past; however, the usual motivation has been either load sharing or interpersonal message handling. Three other more important reasons for computer networks exist, at least with respect to scientific computer applications. Definitions of these reasons for a computer network follow.

Load Sharing: Both the program and data are transmitted to a remote computer to equalize the load between the two facilities. This type of operation requires identical computers or languages. When a given machine is loaded, consideration can be given to processing the program on another machine. Many determinations must be made before an alternate machine is used (is there an alternate machine for which appropriate software exists, is that alternate machine in a condition to handle the program, will more time and dollars be spent on transmission than if the user waits until the original machine is available, etc.). Such determinations are very difficult and the gain only moderate, hence load sharing is not a major consideration here. However, it is felt that some load equalization will occur in any computer network.

Message Service: In addition to computational network activities, a network can be used to handle interpersonal message transmissions. This type of service can also be used for educational services and conference activities. However, it is not an important motivation for a network of scientific computers.

Data Sharing: The program is sent to a remote computer where a large data base exists. This type of operation will be particularly useful where data files are too large to be duplicated economically. Frequently geographically disbursed individuals need to access a common data base. Access to this data base may be required simply to make an inquiry or may involve executing a complex program using the data base. Use of a single data bank will save hardware required to store the information and will eliminate the need for maintaining multiple files. The term "single data bank" does not necessarily mean the storing of only one copy of each basic data file. This type of use is particularly important to the military for command and control, information retrieval, logistics and war gaming applications. In these cases, one command would send a program to be executed at another center where the data base existed.

Program Sharing: Data is sent to a program located at a remote computer and the answer is returned. Software of particular efficiency or capability exists on certain machines. For example, if machine Y has a good LIST processor, it may be more efficient for users whose local machine is X to use Y for LIST processing jobs. Even if a LIST processor exists for X, the time to execute the program on Y may be sufficiently less than the time to execute on X that the total time (and/or cost, including transmission) may be less. The use of specialized programs at remote facilities makes possible large gains in performance. Perhaps even more important is the potential saving in reprogramming effort.

Remote Service: Just a query need be sent if both the program and the data exist at a remote location. This will probably be the most common mode of operation until communication costs come down. There will be a tendency for other cases to migrate toward this type of operation. For example, in a graphics application, the program would be available or created on the remote computer and it would generate the data structure in its own computer. It would modify and update the data structure from network commands transmitting back display changes. This category includes most of the advantages of program and data sharing but requires less information to be transmitted between the computers.

The advantages which can be obtained when computers are interconnected in a network such that remote running of programs is possible, include advantages due to specialized hardware and software at particular nodes as well as increased scientific communication.

864   Chapter 13: Origins of the Internet

SPECIALIZED HARDWARE

It is felt that new machine configurations can provide improvement factors of from 10 to 100 in the problem area for which they were designed. In some cases very large core and disk will substantially improve performance on existing machines. In other cases the improvements will be brought about by introduction of new systems such as ILLIAC IV[1] and macromodular machines.[2] A network is needed to make full use of machines with specialized efficiency and with a network the development of such computers will be enhanced.

SPECIALIZED SYSTEMS SOFTWARE

Handling jobs of widely varying sizes, particularly when initiated from many locations, presents an extremely difficult scheduling problem for any single machine. A large machine serving a number of smaller machines may provide significant improvements in efficiency by alleviating the scheduling problem. Small time sharing computers may be found to be efficiently utilized when employed as communication equipment for relaying user requests to some larger remote machine on which substantive work is done. What is envisioned is a system in which the local machine serves some limited needs of the user while substantial requirements are satisfied by a remote computer particularly well adapted to handling the problem.

SCIENTIFIC COMMUNICATION

Once it is practical to utilize programs at remote locations, programmers will consider investigating what exists elsewhere. The savings possible from non-duplication of effort are enormous. A network would foster the "community" use of computers. Cooperative programming would be stimulated, and in particular fields or disciplines it will be possible to achieve a "critical mass" of talent by allowing geographically separated people to work effectively in interaction with a system.

APPROACH

Basic Operation. The minimum requirement a system must meet to be eligible for membership in the network is a time-sharing monitor which allows user programs to communicate with at least two terminals. If this requirement is uniformly met, the network can be implemented without major change to the monitor at any installation, by the simple expedient of letting each computer in the network look conceptually upon all the others as though they were its own remote user terminals.

Figuratively speaking, we may think of the computer-to-computer link in such a network as being the result of removing a user terminal from its cable on computer A, removing a user terminal from its cable on computer B, and splicing the two computer cable ends together. Such a network might operate as follows: (See Figure 1). The user dials up his home com-

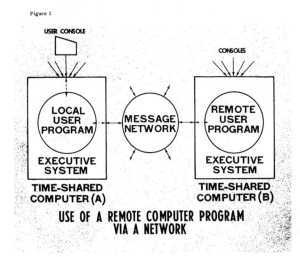

Figure 1

USE OF A REMOTE COMPUTER PROGRAM VIA A NETWORK

puter, CA, from a console. He logs in normally by transmitting characters from his console to the monitor. He sets up a user program and this program, through the second channel, calls the remote computer, logs in, sets up the desired user program on the remote computer, submits parameter data to it and receives the results. Note that neither system was required to behave in an unusual fashion. The monitors did what they always do. The only requirement, as stated earlier, was that the user program be allowed to communicate with two terminals, its own user terminal and the remote computer. Most present-day monitors provide for such a capability.

A computer-computer network link as described above was established in 1966 experimentally between

MIT Lincoln Lab's TX-2 computer and System Development Corporation's Q-32.[3] Both nodes are general purpose, time-shared computers. This link allows programs on either computer to utilize programs such as compilers and graphics systems which exist only at the other node. The basic motivation was to test an initial network protocol, determine how well automatic dial up communications service worked, and determine the extend of the time-sharing monitor changes necessary. This has been done and the link is now utilized by users to increase their capability, thus providing more evaluation data.

Interface Message Processor. One way to make the implementation of a network between a set of time-shared computers more straightforward and unified is to build a message switching network with digital interfaces at each node.

This would imply that a small computer, an interface message processor (IMP), would be located with each main computer to handle a communications interface. It would perform the functions of dial up, error checking, retransmission, routing and verification. Thus the set of IMP's, plus the telephone lines and data sets would constitute a message switching network (See Figure 2).

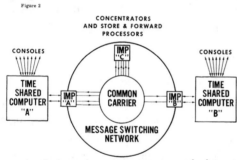

Figure 2

USE OF INTERFACE MESSAGE PROCESSORS (IMP) FOR ROUTING AND CHECKING INTER COMPUTER COMMUNICATION

The major advantage of this plan is that a unified, straightforward design of the network can be made and implemented without undue consideration of the main computer's buffer space, interpret speed and other machine requirements. The interface to each computer would be a much simpler digital connection with an additional flexibility provided by programming the IMP. The network section of the IMP's program would be completely standard and provide

guaranteed buffer space and uniform characteristics, thus the entire planning job is substantially simplified. The data sets and transmission lines utilized between the IMP's would most likely be standardized upon, but as changes occurred in the communication tariffs or data rates, it would be more straightforward just to modify the program for the IMP's rather than twenty different computers. As soon as the need became apparent, additional small computers could be located at strategic connection points within the network to concentrate messages over cross-country lines. Finally, the modifications required to currently operating systems would be substantially less utilizing these small computers since there would be no requirement to find buffer spaces, hold messages for retransmission, verify reception of messages and dial up telephone lines.

ARPA NET

ARPA supports a number of computer research groups throughout the country most of which have their own time-shared computer facility. These researchers have agreed to accept a single network protocol so that they may all participate in an experimental network. The communication protocol is currently being developed. It will conform to ASCII conventions as a basic format and include provisions for specifying the origin, destination, routing, block size, and sum check of a message. Messages will be character strings or binary blocks but the communication protocol does not specify the internal form of such blocks. It is expected that these conventions will be distributed in final form during September 1967.

Figure 3 shows a tentative layout of the network

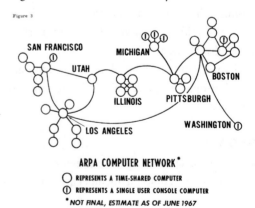

Figure 3

ARPA COMPUTER NETWORK*

○ REPRESENTS A TIME-SHARED COMPUTER
① REPRESENTS A SINGLE USER CONSOLE COMPUTER
* NOT FINAL, ESTIMATE AS OF JUNE 1967

nodes and communication paths. However, since most of the communications will be dial-up, the paths are just hypothetical. It is hoped that concentration and store and forward capability will be available through the use of Interface Message Processors. The development of the IMP's and the use of them at each node will allow store and forward operation as well as speeding the realization of a unified network.

There are 35 computers shown in Figure 3 at 16 locations, there being several computers at most locations. A rough estimate would place the number of consoles attached to the 35 computers by the end of 1967 at 1500 and the number of displays at 150. Assuming four characters per second for typewriters and 20 characters per second for scopes, the total I/O rate to the computers is 9000 char/sec. Estimating that 10% of this I/O communication rate will be forwarded to another computer in the network leads us to an average transmission rate of 60 char/sec per location. Thus, given console type activity on the network (messages of from 10 to 1000 characters) the normal 2000 bits/second type communication should be sufficient at first.

COMMUNICATION NEEDS

The common carriers currently provide 2 or 4 wire, 2 kc lines between two points either dialed or leased, as well as higher band width leased lines and lower band width teletype service. Considering the 2 kc offering, since it is the best dial up service, the use of 2 wire service appears to be very inefficient for the type of traffic predicted for the network. In the Lincoln-SDC experimental link the average message length appears to be 20 characters. Each message must be acknowledged so that the originator may retransmit or free the buffer. Thus the line must be reversed so often that the reversal time will effectively half the transmission rate. Therefore, full duplex, four-wire service is more economic and simpler to use.

Current automatic dialing equipment requires about 20 seconds to obtain a connection and a similar time to disconnect. Thus, the response time is much too long assuming a call is made only after a message arrives and that the line is disconnected if no other messages arrive soon. It has proven necessary to hold a line which is being used intermittently to obtain the one-tenth to one second response time required for interactive work. This is very wasteful of the line and unless faster dial up times become available, message switching and concentration will be very important to network participants.

BIBLIOGRAPHY

1. Slotnick, D. L., "Achieving Large Computing Capabilities through an Array Computer," presented at SJCC (April 1967).

2. Clark, W. A., "Macromodular Computer Systems," *Proc. SJCC* (April 1967).

3. Marill, T. and Roberts, L. G., "Toward a Cooperative Network of Time-Shared Computers," *Proc. FJCC* (1966).

UCLA to be First Station in Nationwide Computer Network

Leonard Kleinrock

Press release dated July 3, 1969.

INTRODUCTORY NOTE TO READING 13.7

This press release dated July 3, 1969 predates the founding of ARPANET. On September 2, 1969 Leonard Kleinrock led a team of engineers in establishing the first network connection between a network switch then known as an Interface Message Processor, and a time-shared host computer, the SDS Sigma 7 mentioned in the press release. One month later the second node was added to ARPANET at Stanford Research Institute, and on October 29 the first host-to-host message was sent from UCLA. According to Kleinrock, "All we wanted to do was to login from our host computer at UCLA to the SRI host computer. We needed to transmit the letters 'log' to SRI, at which point the SRI host would add the letters 'in' to complete the word 'login'." Along with the data connection the researchers set up a telephone connection so that the programmers at each end could talk to each other and report what was appearing at their terminals. The UCLA team began by sending the "L," and asked, "Did you get the l?" The reply from SRI was "Yes." Then they sent the "o" and asked, "Did you get the o?" Again the reply was "Yes." Then just as they were attempting to send the letter "g" the host computer at Stanford crashed. As a result, Kleinrock said, "history now records how clever we were to send such a prophetic first message, namely 'Lo'." [JMN]

TEXT OF READING 13.7

UCLA will become the first station in a nationwide computer network which, for the first time, will link together computers of different makes and using different machine languages into one time-sharing system.

Creation of the network represents a major forward step in computer technology and may serve as the forerunner of large computer networks of the future.

The ambitious project is supported by the Defense Department's Advanced Research Project Agency (ARPA), which has pioneered many advances in computer research, technology and applications during the past decade. The network project was proposed and is headed by ARPA's Dr. Lawrence G. Roberts.

The system will, in effect, pool the computer power, programs and specialized know-how of about 15 computer research centers, stretching from UCLA to M.I.T. Other California network stations (or nodes) will be located at the Rand Corp. and System Development Corp., both of Santa Monica; the Santa Barbara and Berkeley campuses of the University of California; Stanford University and the Stanford Research Institute.

The first stage of the network will go into operation this fall as a subnet joining UCLA, Stanford Research Institute, UC Santa Barbara, and the University of Utah. The entire network is expected to be operational in late 1970.

Engineering professor Leonard Kleinrock, who heads the UCLA project, describes how the network might handle a sample problem:

Programmers at Computer A have a blurred photo which they want to bring into focus. Their program transmits the photo to Computer B, which specializes in computer graphics, and instructs B's program to remove the blur and enhance the contrast. If B requires specialized computational assistance, it may call on Computer C for help.

The processed work is shuttled back and forth until B is satisfied with the photo, and then sends it back to Computer A. The messages, ranging across the country, can flash between computers in a matter of seconds, Dr. Kleinrock says.

UCLA's part of the project will involve about 20 people, including some 15 graduate students. The group will play a key role as the official network measurement center, analyzing computer interaction and network behavior, comparing performance against anticipated results, and keeping a continuous check on the network's effectiveness. For this job, UCLA will use a highly specialized computer, the Sigma 7, developed by Scientific Data Systems of Los Angeles.

Each computer in the network will be equipped with its own interface message processor (IMP) which will double as a sort of translator among the Babel of computer languages and as a message handler and router.

Computer networks are not an entirely new concept, notes Dr. Kleinrock. The SAGE radar defense system of the Fifties was one of the first, followed by the airlines' SABRE reservation system. At the present time, the nation's electronically switched telephone system is the world's largest computer network.

However, all three are highly specialized and single-purpose systems, in contrast to the planned ARPA system which will link a wide assortment of different computers for a wide range of unclassified research functions.

"As of now, computer networks are still in their infancy," says Dr. Kleinrock. "But as they grow up and become more sophisticated, we will probably see the spread of 'computer utilities', which, like present electric and telephone utilities, will service individual homes and offices across the country."

A Protocol for Packet Network Intercommunication

Vinton G. Cerf and Robert E. Kahn

INTRODUCTORY NOTE TO READING 13.8

In the early 1970s ARPANET, and other data networks that were beginning to be constructed around the world, were hampered by the fact that each operated according to different hardware and software protocols, thus making it impossible for them to communicate with one another. ARPANET was using the Network Control Protocol or NCP. This problem was solved by Cerf and Kahn's invention of the Transmission Control Protocol (TCP) cross-network protocol that allowed the creation of an international network of computer networks; i.e., the Internet (a term the authors invented around 1973 as an abbreviation for "inter-networking of networks." The authors laid out the architecture of such a network in this paper:

> It describes gateways, which sit between networks to send and receive "datagrams." Datagrams, similar to envelopes, enclose messages and display destination addresses that are recognized by gateways. Datagrams can carry packets of various sizes. The messages within datagrams are called transmission control protocol (TCP) messages. TCP is the standard program, shared by each network, for loading and unloading datagrams; it is the only element of the international network that must be uniform among the small networks, and it is the crucial element that makes global networking possible.[1]

In 1978 TCP was split into TCP and IP for Internet Protocol. In 1982 the Defense Communications Agency DCA and ARPA established the Transmission Control Protocol (TCP) and Internet Protocol (IP), as the protocol suite, commonly known as TCP/IP, for ARPANET. This led to one of the first definitions of an "internet" as a connected set of networks, specifically those using TCP/IP, and the "Internet" as connected TCP/IP internets. On January 1, 1983 ARPANET required that all connected machines use TCP/IP. On this date TCP/IP became the core Internet protocol and replaced NCP entirely. [JMN]

---

1 Moschovitis, Christos. J. P. *et al., History of the Internet. A Chronology, 1843 to the Present* (Santa Barbara, Calif.: ABC-Clio, 1999), 82.

TEXT OF READING 13.8

Abstract—A protocol that supports the sharing of resources that exist in different packet switching networks is presented. The protocol provides for variation in individual network packet sizes, transmission failures, sequencing, flow control, end-to-end error checking, and the creation and destruction of logical process-to-process connections. Some implementation issues are considered, and problems such as internetwork routing, accounting, and timeouts are exposed.

INTRODUCTION

In the last few years considerable effort has been expended on the design and implementation of packet switching networks [1]–[7],[14],[17]. A principal reason for developing such networks has been to facilitate the sharing of computer resources. A packet communication network includes a transportation mechanism for delivering data between computers or between computers and terminals. To make the data meaningful, computer and terminals share a common protocol (i.e., a set of agreed upon conventions). Several protocols have already been developed for this purpose [8]–[12],[16]. However, these protocols have addressed only the problem of communication on the same network. In this paper we present a protocol design and philosophy that supports the sharing of resources that exist in different packet switching networks.

After a brief introduction to internetwork protocol issues, we describe the function of a GATEWAY as an interface between networks and discuss its role in the protocol. We then consider the various details of the protocol, including addressing, formatting, buffering, sequencing, flow control, error control, and so forth. We close with a description of an interprocess communication mechanism and show how it can be supported by the internetwork protocol.

Even though many different and complex problems must be solved in the design of an individual packet switching network, these problems are manifestly compounded when dissimilar networks are interconnected. Issues arise which may have no direct counterpart in an individual network and which strongly influence the way in which internetwork communication can take place.

A typical packet switching network is composed of a set of computer resources called HOSTS, a set of one or more *packet switches,* and a collection of communication media that interconnect the packet switches. Within each HOST, we assume that there exist *processes* which must communicate with processes in their own or other HOSTS. Any current definition of a process will be adequate for our purposes [13]. These processes are generally the ultimate source and destination of data in the network. Typically, within an individual network, there exists a protocol for communication between any source and destination process. Only the source and destination processes require knowledge of this convention for communication to take place. Processes in two distinct networks would ordinarily use different protocols for this purpose. The ensemble of packet switches and communication media is called the *packet switching subnet.* Fig. 1 illustrates these ideas.

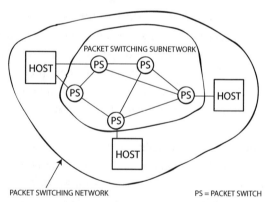

In a typical packet switching subnet, data of a fixed maximum size are accepted from a source HOST, together with a formatted destination address which is used to route the data in a store and forward fashion. The transmit time for this data is usually dependent upon internal network parameters such as communication media data rates, buffering and signaling strategies, routing, propagation delays, etc. In addition, some mechanism is generally present for error handling and determination of status of the networks components.

Individual packet switching networks may differ in their implementations as follows.

1. Each network may have distinct ways of addressing the receiver, thus requiring that a uniform addressing scheme be created which can be understood by each individual network.

2. Each network may accept data of different maximum size, thus requiring networks to deal in units of the smallest maximum size (which may be impractically small) or requiring procedures which allow data crossing a network boundary to be reformatted into smaller pieces.

3. The success or failure of a transmission and its performance in each network is governed by different time delays in accepting, delivering, and transporting the data. This requires careful development of internetwork timing procedures to insure that data can be successfully delivered through the various networks.

4. Within each network, communication may be disrupted due to unrecoverable mutation of the data or missing data. End-to-end restoration procedures are desirable to allow complete recovery from these conditions.

1. Status information, routing, fault detection, and isolation are typically different in each network. thus, to obtain verification of certain conditions, such as an inaccessible or dead destination, various kinds of coordination must be invoked between the communicating networks.

It would be extremely convenient if all the differences between networks could be economically resolved by suitable interfacing at the network boundaries. For many of the differences, this objective can be achieved. However, both economic and technical considerations lead us to prefer that the interface be as simple and reliable as possible and deal primarily with passing data between networks that use different packet switching strategies.

The question now arises as to whether the interface ought to account for differences in HOST or process level protocols by transforming the source conventions into the corresponding destination conventions. We obviously want to allow conversion between packet switching strategies at the interface, to permit interconnection of existing and planned networks. However, the complexity and dissimilarity of the HOST or process level protocols makes it desirable to avoid having to transform between them at the interface, even if this transformation were always possible. Rather, compatible HOST and process level protocols must be developed to achieve effective internetwork resource sharing. The unacceptable alternative is for every HOST or process to implement every protocol (a potentially unbounded number) that may be needed to communicate with other networks. We therefore assume that a common protocol is to be used between HOST'S or processes in different networks and that the interface between networks should take as small a role as possible in this protocol.

To allow networks under different ownership to interconnect, some accounting will undoubtedly be needed for traffic that passes across the interface. In its simplest terms, this involves an accounting of packets handled by each net for which charges are passed from net to net until the buck finally stops at the user or his representative. Furthermore, the interconnection must preserve intact the internal operation of each individual network. This is easily achieved if two networks interconnect as if each were a HOST to the other network, but without utilizing or indeed incorporating any elaborate HOST protocol transformations.

It is thus apparent that the interface between networks must play a central role in the development of any network interconnection strategy. We give a special name to this interface that performs these functions and call it a GATEWAY.

THE GATEWAY NOTION

In Fig. 2 we illustrate three individual networks labelled *A, B,* and *C* which are joined by GATEWAYS *M* and *N*. GATEWAY *M* interfaces network *A* with network *B*, and GATEWAY *N* interfaces network *B* to network *C*. We assume that an individual network may have more than one GATEWAY (e.g., network *B)* and that there may be more than one GATEWAY path to use in going between a pair of networks. The responsibility for properly routing data resides in the GATEWAY.

In practice, a GATEWAY between two networks may be composed of two halves, each associated with its own network. It is possible to implement each half of a GATEWAY so it need only embed internetwork packets in local packet format or extract them. We propose that the GATEWAY handle internetwork packets in a standard format, but we are not proposing any particular transmission procedure between GATEWAY halves.

Let us now trace the flow of data through the interconnected networks. We assume a packet of data from process *X* enters network *A* destined for process *Y* in network *C.* The address of *Y* is initially specified by process *X* and the address of GATEWAY *M* is derived from the address of process *Y.* We make no attempt to specify whether the choice of GATEWAY is made by process *X,* its HOST, or one of the packet switches in network *A.* The packet traverses network *A* until it reaches GATEWAY *M.* At the GATEWAY, the packet is reformatted to meet the requirements of network *B,*

account is taken of this unit of flow between *A* and *B,* and the GATEWAY delivers the packet to network *B.* Again the derivation of the next GATEWAY address is accomplished based on the address of the destination *Y.* In this case, GATEWAY *N* is the next one. The packet traverses network *B* until it finally reaches GATEWAY *N* where it is formatted to meet the requirements of network *C.* Account is again taken of this unit of flow between networks *B* and *C.* Upon entering network *C,* the packet is routed to the HOST in which process *Y* resides and there it is delivered to its ultimate destination.

Since the GATEWAY must understand the address of the source and destination HOSTS, this information must be available in a standard format in every packet which arrives at the GATEWAY. This information is contained in an *internetwork header* prefixed to the packet by the source HOST. The packet format, including the internetwork header, is illustrated in Fig. 3. The source and destination entries uniformly and uniquely identify the address of every HOST in the composite network. Addressing is a subject of considerable complexity which is discussed in greater detail in the next section. The next two entries in the header provide a sequence number and a byte count that may be used to properly sequence the packets upon delivery to the destination and may also enable the GATEWAYS to detect fault conditions affecting the packet. The flag field is used to convey specific control information and is discussed in the section on retransmission and duplicate detection later. The remainder of

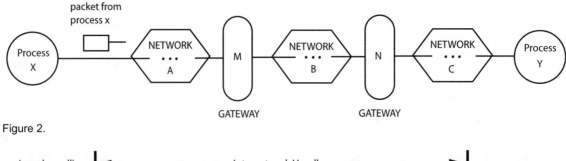

Figure 2.

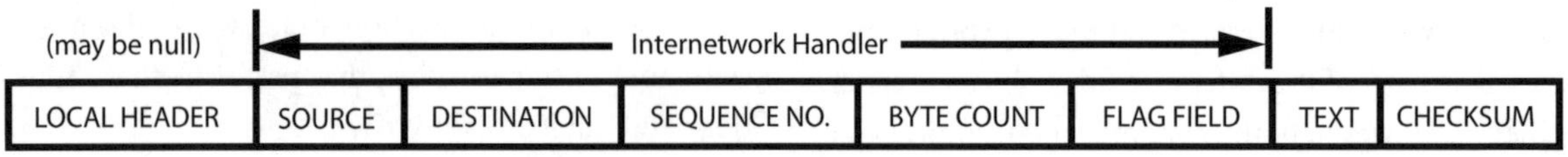

Figure 3.

the packet consists of text for delivery to the destination and a trailing check sum used for end-to-end software verification. The GATEWAY does *not* modify the text and merely forwards the check sum along without computing or recomputing it.

Each network may need to augment the packet format before it can pass through the individual network. We have indicated a *local header* in the figure which is prefixed to the beginning of the packet. This local header is introduced merely to illustrate the concept of embedding an internetwork packet in the format of the individual network through which the packet must pass. It will obviously vary in its exact form from network to network and may even be unnecessary in some cases. Although not explicitly indicated in the figure, it is also possible that a local trailer may be appended to the end of the packet.

Unless all transmitted packets are legislatively restricted to be small enough to be accepted by every individual network, the GATEWAY may be forced to split a packet into two or more smaller packets. This action is called fragmentation and must be done in such a way that the destination is able to piece together the fragmented packet. It is clear that the internetwork header format imposes a minimum packet size which all networks must carry (obviously all networks will want to carry packets larger than this minimum). We believe the long range growth and development of internetwork communication would be seriously inhibited by specifying how much larger than the minimum a packet size can be, for the following reasons.

1. If a maximum permitted packet size is specified then it becomes impossible to completely isolate the internal packet size parameters of one network from the internal packet size parameters of all other networks.

2. It would be very difficult to increase the maximum permitted packet size in response to new technology (e.g. large memory systems, higher data rate communication facilities, etc.) since this would require the agreement and then

implementation by all participating networks.

3. Associative addressing and packet encryption may require the size of a particular packet to expand during transit for incorporation of new information.

Provision for fragmentation (regardless of where it is performed) permits packet size variations to be handled on an individual network basis without global administration and also permits HOSTS and processes to be insulated from changes in the packet sizes permitted in any networks through which their data must pass.

If fragmentation must be done, it appears best to do it upon entering the next network at the GATEWAY since only this GATEWAY (and not the other networks) must be aware of the internal packet size parameters which made the fragmentation necessary.

If a GATEWAY fragments an incoming packet into two or more packets, they must eventually be passed along to the destination HOST as fragments or reassembled for the HOST. It is conceivable that one might desire the GATEWAY to perform the reassembly to simplify the task of the destination HOST (or process) and/or to take advantage of the larger packet size. We take the position that GATEWAY should not perform this function since GATEWAY reassembly can lead to serious buffering problems, potential deadlocks, the necessity for all fragments of a packet to pass through the same GATEWAY, and increased delay in transmission. Furthermore, it is not sufficient for the GATEWAY to provide this function since the final GATEWAY may also have to fragment a packet for transmission. Thus the destination HOST must be prepared to do this task.

Let us now turn briefly to the somewhat unusual accounting effect which arises when a packet may be fragmented by one or more GATEWAY. We assume, for simplicity, that each network initially charges a fixed rate per packet transmitted, regardless of distance, and if one network can handle a larger packet size than another, it charges a proportionally larger price per packet. We also assume that a subsequent increase in any network's packet size does not result in additional cost per packet to its users. The charge to a user thus remains basically constant through any net which must fragment a packet. The unusual effect occurs when a packet is fragmented into smaller packets which must individually pass through a subsequent network with a larger packet size than the original unfragmented packet. We expect that most networks will naturally select packet sizes close to one another, but in any case, an increase in packet size in one net, even when it causes fragmentation, will not increase the cost of transmission and may actually decrease it. In the event that any other packet charging policies (than the one we suggest) are adopted, differences in cost can be used as an economic lever toward optimization of individual network performance.

PROCESS LEVEL COMMUNICATION

We suppose that processes wish to communicate in full duplex with their correspondents using unbounded but finite length messages. A single character might constitute the text of a message from a process to a terminal or vice versa. An entire page of characters might constitute the text of a message from a file to a process. A data stream (e.g. a continuously generated bit string) can be represented as a sequence of finite length messages.

Within a HOST we assume that existence of a transmission control program (TCP) which handles the transmission and acceptance of messages on behalf of the processes it serves. The TCP is in turn served by one or more packet switches connected to the HOST in which the TCP resides. Processes that want to communicate present messages to the TCP for transmission, and TCP's deliver incoming messages to the appropriate destination processes. We allow the TCP to break up messages into segments because the destination may restrict the amount of data that may arrive, because the local network may limit the maximum transmission size, or because the TCP may need to share its resources among many processes concurrently. Furthermore, we constrain the length of a segment to an integral number of 8-bit bytes. This uniformity is most helpful in simplifying the software

needed with HOST machines of different natural word lengths. Provision at the process level can be made for padding a message that is not an integral number of bytes and for identifying which of the arriving bytes of text contain information of interest to the receiving process.

Multiplexing and demultiplexing of segments among processes are fundamental tasks of the TCP. On transmission, a TCP must multiplex together segments from different source processes and produce internetwork packets for delivery to one of its serving packet switches. On reception, a TCP will accept a sequence of packets from its serving packet switch(es). From this sequence of arriving packets (generally from different HOSTS), the TCP must be able to reconstruct and deliver messages to the proper destination processes.

We assume that every segment is augmented with additional information that allows transmitting and receiving TCP's to identify destination and source processes, respectively. At this point, we must face a major issue. How should the source TCP format segments destined for the same destination TCP? We consider two cases.

Case 1): If we take the position that segment boundaries are immaterial and that a byte stream can be formed of segments destined for the same TCP, then we may gain improved transmission efficiency and resource sharing by arbitrarily parceling the stream into packets, permitting many segments to share a single internetwork packet header. However, this position results in the need to reconstruct exactly, and in order, the stream of text bytes produced by the source TCP. At the destination, this stream must first be parsed into segments and these in turn must be used to reconstruct messages for delivery to the appropriate processes.

There are fundamental problems associated with this strategy due to the possible arrival of packets out of order at the destination. The most critical problem appears to be the amount of interference that processes sharing the same TCP-TCP byte stream may cause among themselves. This is especially so at the receiving end. First, the TCP may be put to some trouble to parse the stream back into segments and then distribute them to buffers where messages are reassembled. If it is not readily apparent that all of a segment has arrived (remember, it may come as several packets), the receiving TCP may have to suspend parsing temporarily until more packets have arrived. Second, if a packet is missing, it may not be clear whether succeeding segments, even if they are identifiable, can be passed on to the receiving process, unless the TCP has knowledge of some process level sequencing scheme. Such knowledge would permit the TCP to decide whether a succeeding segment could be delivered to its waiting process. Finding the beginning of a segment when there are gaps in the byte stream may also be hard.

Case 2): Alternatively, we might take the position that the destination TCP should be able to determine, upon its arrival and without additional information, for which process or processes a received packet is intended, and if so, whether it should be delivered then.

If the TCP is to determine for which process an arriving packet is intended, every packet must contain a *process header* (distinct from the internetwork header) that completely identifies the destination process. For simplicity, we assume that each packet contains text from a single process which is destined for a single process. Thus each packet need contain only one process header. To decide whether the arriving data is deliverable to the destination process, the TCP must be able to determine whether the data is in the proper sequence (we can make provision for the destination process to instruct its TCP to ignore sequencing, but this is considered a special case). With the assumption that each arriving packet contains a process header, the necessary sequencing and destination process identification is immediately available to the destination TCP.

Both Cases 1) and 2) provide for the demultiplexing and delivery of segments to destination processes, but only Case 2) does so without the introduction of potential interprocess interference. Furthermore, Case 1) introduces extra machinery to handle flow control on a HOST-to-HOST basis, since there must also be

some provision for process level control, and this machinery is little used since the probability is small that within a given HOST, two processes will be coincidentally scheduled to send messages to the same destination HOST. For this reason, we select the method of Case 2) as a part of the *internetwork transmission protocol.*

ADDRESS FORMATS

The selection of address formats is a problem between networks because the local network addresses of TCP's may vary substantially in format and size. A uniform internetwork TCP address space, understood by each GATEWAY and TCP, is essential to routing and delivery of internetwork packets.

Similar troubles are encountered when we deal with process addressing and, more generally, port addressing. We introduce the notion of *ports* in order to permit a process to distinguish between multiple message streams. The port is simply a designator of one such message stream associated with a process. The means for identifying a port are generally different in different operating systems, and therefore, to obtain uniform addressing, a standard port address format is also required. A port address designates a full duplex message stream.

TCP ADDRESSING

TCP addressing is intimately bound up in routing issues, since a HOST or GATEWAY must choose a suitable destination HOST or GATEWAY for an outgoing internetwork packet. Let us postulate the following address format for the TCP address (Fig. 4).

8	16
NETWORK	TCP IDENTIFIER

The choice for network identification (8 bits) allows up to 256 distinct networks. This size seems sufficient for the foreseeable future. Similarly, the TCP identifier field permits up to 65 536 distinct TCP's to be addressed, which seems more than sufficient for any given network.

As each packet passes through a GATEWAY, the GATEWAY observes the destination network ID to determine how to route the packet. If the destination network is connected to the GATEWAY, the lower 16 bits of the TCP address are used to produce a local TCP address in the destination network. If the destination network is not connected to the GATEWAY, the upper 8 bits are used to select a subsequent GATEWAY. We make no effort to specify how each individual network shall associate the internetwork TCP identifier with its local TCP address. We also do not rule out the possibility that the local network understands the internetwork addressing scheme and thus alleviates the GATEWAY of the routing responsibility.

PORT ADDRESSING

A receiving TCP is faced with the task of demultiplexing the stream of internetwork packets it receives and reconstructing the original messages for each destination process. Each operating system has its own internal means of identifying processes and ports. We assume that 16 bits are sufficient to serve as internetwork port identifiers. A sending process need not know how the destination port identification will be used. The destination TCP will be able to parse this number appropriately to find the proper buffer into which it will place arriving packets. We permit a large port number field to support processes which want to distinguish between many different message streams concurrently. In reality, we do not care how the 16 bits are sliced up by the TCP's involved.

Even though the transmitted port name field is large, it is still a compact external name for the internal representation of the port. The use of short names for port identifiers is often desirable to reduce transmission overhead and possibly reduce packet processing time at the destination TCP. Assigning short names to each port, however, requires an initial negotiation between source and destination to agree on a suitable short name assignment, the subsequent maintenance of conversion tables at both the source and the destination, and a final transaction to release the short name. For dynamic assignment of port names, this negotiation is generally necessary in any case.

SEGMENT AND PACKET FORMATS

As shown in Fig. 5, messages are broken by the TCP into segments whose format is shown in more detail in Fig. 6. The field lengths illustrated are merely suggestive. The first two fields (source port and destination port in the figure) have already been discussed in the preceding section on addressing. The uses of the third and fourth fields (window and acknowledgement in the figure) will be discussed later in the section on retransmission and duplicate detection.

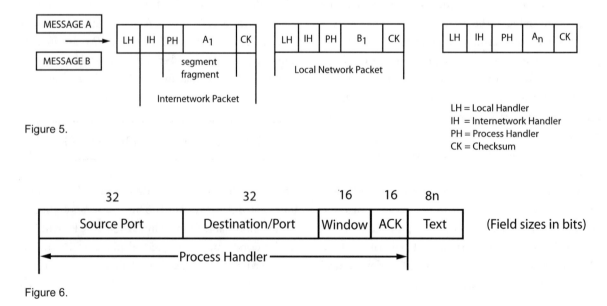

Figure 5.

LH = Local Handler
IH = Internetwork Handler
PH = Process Handler
CK = Checksum

Figure 6.

We recall from Fig. 3 that an internetwork header contains both a sequence number and a byte count, as well as a flag field and a check sum. The uses of these fields are explained in the following section.

REASSEMBLY AND SEQUENCING

The reconstruction of a message at the receiving TCP clearly requires[1] that each internetwork packet carry a sequence number which is unique to its particular destination port message stream. The sequence numbers must be monotonic increasing (or decreasing) since they are used to reorder and reassemble arriving packets into a message. If the space of sequence numbers were infinite, we could simply assign the next one to each new packet. Clearly, this space cannot be infinite, and we will consider what problems a finite sequence number space will cause when we discuss retransmission and duplicate detection in the next section. We propose the following scheme for performing the sequencing of packets and hence the reconstruction of messages by the destination TCP.

A pair of ports will exchange one or more messages over a period of time. We could view the sequence of messages produced by one port as if it were embedded in an infinitely long stream of bytes. Each byte of the message has a unique sequence number which we take to be its byte location relative to the beginning of the stream. When a segment is extracted from the message by the source TCP and formatted for internetwork transmission, the relative location of the first byte of segment text is used as the sequence number for the packet. The byte count field in the internetwork header accounts for all the text in the segment (but does not include the check-sum bytes or the bytes in either internetwork or process header). We emphasize that the sequence number associated with a given packet is unique only to the pair of ports that are communicating (see Fig. 7). Arriving packets are examined to determine for which port they are intended.

The sequence numbers on each arriving packet are then used to determine the relative location of the packet text in the messages under reconstruction. We note that this allows the exact position of the data in the reconstructed message to be determined even when pieces are still missing.

Every segment produced by a source TCP is packaged in a single internetwork packet and a check sum is computed over the text and process header associated with the segment.

The splitting of messages into segments by the TCP and the potential splitting of segments into smaller pieces by GATEWAY creates the necessity for indicating to the destination TCP when the end of a segment (ES) has arrived and when the end of a message (EM) has arrived. The flag field of the internetwork header is used for this purpose (see Fig. 8).

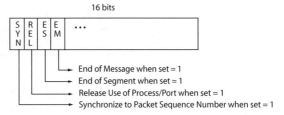

Figure 8.

The ES flag is set by the source TCP each time it prepares a segment for transmission. If it should happen that the message is completely contained in the segment, then the EM flag would also be set. The EM flag is also set on the last segment of a message, if the message could not be contained in one segment. These two flags are used by the destination TCP, respectively, to discover the presence of a check sum for a given segment and to discover that a complete message has arrived.

The ES and EM flags in the internetwork header are known to the GATEWAY and are of special importance when packets must be split apart from propagation through the next local network. We illustrate their use with an example in Fig. 9.

The original message A in Fig. 9 is shown split into two segments A_1 and A_2 and formatted by the TCP into a pair of internetwork packets. Packets A_1 and A_2 have their ES bits set, and A_2 has its EM bit set as well.

0	1	2	...	k	...	
First Message				Second Message		Third Message
Segment	Segment	Segment	Segment	...	
		[SEQ = k]				

Figure 7.

When packet A_1 passes through the GATEWAY, it is split into two pieces: packet A_{11} for which neither EM nor ES bits are set, and packet A_{12} whose ES bit is set. Similarly, packet A_2 is split such that the first piece, packet A_{21}, has neither bit set, but packet A_{22} has both bits set. The sequence number field (SEQ) and the byte count field (CT) of each packet is modified by the GATEWAY to properly identify the text bytes of each packet. The GATEWAY need only examine the internetwork header to do fragmentation.

The destination TCP, upon reassembling segment A_1, will detect the ES flag and will verify the check sum it knows is contained in packet A_{12}. Upon receipt of packet A_{22}, assuming all other packets have arrived, the destination TCP detects that it has reassembled a complete message and can now advise the destination process of its receipt.

RETRANSMISSION AND DUPLICATED DETECTION

No transmission can be 100 percent reliable. We propose a timeout and positive acknowledgement mechanism which will allow TCP's to recover from packet losses from one HOST to another. A TCP transmits packets and waits for replies (acknowledgements) that are carried in the reverse packet stream. If no acknowledgement for a particular packet is received, the TCP will retransmit. It is our expectation that the HOST level retransmission mechanism, which is described in the following paragraphs, will not be

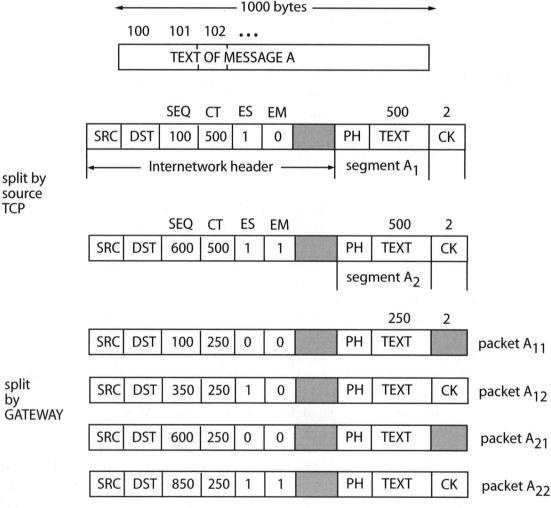

Figure 9.

called upon very often in practice. Evidence already exists[2] that individual networks can be effectively constructed without this feature. However, the inclusion of a HOST retransmission capability makes it possible to recover from occasional network problems and allows a wide range of HOST protocol strategies to be incorporated. We envision it will occasionally be invoked to allow HOST accommodation to infrequent overdemands for limited buffer resources, and otherwise not used much.

Any retransmission policy requires some means by which the receiver can detect duplicate arrivals. Even if an infinite number of distinct packet sequence numbers were available, the receiver would still have the problem of knowing how long to remember previously received packets in order to detect duplicates. Matters are complicated by the fact that only a finite number of distinct sequence numbers are in fact available, and if they are reused, the receiver must be able to distinguish between new transmissions and retransmissions.

A *window* strategy, similar to that used by the French CYCLADES system (voie virtuelle transmission mode [8]) and the ARPANET very distant HOST connection [18]), is proposed here (see Fig. 10).

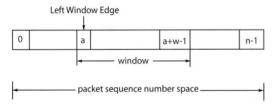

Figure 10.

Suppose that the sequence number field in the internetwork header permits sequence numbers to range from 0 to $n - 1$. We assume that the sender will not transmit more than w bytes without receiving an acknowledgment. The w bytes serve as the window (see Fig. 11). Clearly, w must be less than n. The rules for sender and receiver are as follows.

Sender: Let L be the sequence number associated with the left window edge.

1. The sender transmits bytes from segments whose text lies between L and up to $L + w - 1$.

2. On timeout (duration unspecified), the sender retransmits unacknowledged bytes.

3. On receipt of acknowledgment consisting of the receiver's current left window edge, the sender's left window edge is advanced over the acknowledged bytes (advancing the right window edge implicitly).

Receiver:

1. Arriving packets whose sequence numbers coincide with the receiver's current left window edge are acknowledged by sending to the source the next sequence number expected. This effectively acknowledges bytes in between. The left window edge is advanced to the next sequence number expected.

2. Packets arriving with a sequence number to the left of the window edge (or, in fact, outside of the window) are discarded, and the current left window edge is returned as acknowledgement.

3. Packets whose sequence numbers lie within the receiver's window but do not coincide with the receiver's left window edge are optionally kept or discarded, but are now acknowledged. This is the case when packets arrive out of order.

We make some observations on this strategy. First, all computations with sequence numbers and window edges must be made modulo n (*e.g.,* byte 0 follows byte $n - 1$). Second, w must be less than $n/2^3$; otherwise a retransmission may appear to the receiver to be a new transmission in the case that the receiver can either save or discard arriving packets whose sequence numbers do not coincide with the receiver's left window. Thus, in the simplest implementation, the receiver need not buffer more than one packet per message stream if space is critical. Fourth, multiple packets can be acknowledged simultaneously. Fifth, the receiver is able to deliver messages to processes in their proper order as a natural result of the reassembly mechanism. Sixth, when duplicates are detected, the acknowledgment method used naturally works to resynchronize sender and receiver. Furthermore, if the receiver accepts packets whose sequence numbers lie within the current window but which are not coincident with the left window edge, an acknowledgment consisting of the current left window edge would act as a stimulus to cause retransmission of the unacknowledged bytes. Finally, we mention an overlap problem which results from retransmission, packet splitting, and alternate routing of packets through different GATEWAYS.

A 600-byte packet might pass through one GATEWAY and be broken into two 300-byte packets. On retransmission, the same packet might be broken into three 200-byte packets going through a different HOST. Since each byte has a sequence number, there is no confusion at the receiving TCP. We leave for later the issue of initially synchronizing the sender and receiver left window edges and the window size.

FLOW CONTROL

Every segment that arrives at the destination TCP is ultimately acknowledged by returning the sequence number of the next segment which must be passed to the process (it may not yet have arrived).

Earlier we described the use of a sequence number space and window to aid in duplicate detection. Acknowledgments are carried in the process header (see Fig. 6) and along with them there is provision for a "suggested window" which the receiver can use to control the flow of data from the sender. This is intended to be the main component of the process flow control mechanism. The receiver is free to vary the window size according to any algorithm it desires so long as the window size never exceeds half the sequence number space.[3]

This flow control mechanism is exceedingly powerful and flexible and does not suffer from synchronization troubles that may be encountered by incremental buffer allocation schemes [9], [10]. However, it relies heavily on an effective retransmission strategy. The receiver can reduce the window even while packets are en route from the sender whose window is presently larger. The net effect of this reduction will be that the receiver may discard incoming packets (they may be outside the window) and reiterate the current window size along with a current window edge as acknowledgment. By the same token, the sender can, upon occasion, choose to send more than a window's worth of data on the possibility that the receiver will expand the window to accept it (of course, the sender must not send more than half the sequence number space at any time). Normally, we would expect the sender to abide by the window limitation. Expansion of the window by the receiver merely allows more data to be accepted. For the receiving HOST with a small amount of buffer space, a strategy of discarding all packets whose sequence numbers do not coincide with the current left edge of the window is probably necessary, but it will incur the expense of extra delay and overhead for retransmission.

TCP INPUT/OUTPUT HANDLING

The TCP has a component which handles input/output (I/O) to and from the network.[4] When a packet has arrived, it validates the addresses and places the packet on a queue. A pool of buffers can be set up to handle arrivals, and if all available buffers are used up, succeeding arrivals can be discarded since unacknowledged packets will be retransmitted.

On output, a smaller amount of buffering is needed, since process buffers can hold the data to be transmitted. Perhaps double buffering will be adequate. We make no attempt to specify how the buffering should be done, except to require that it be able to service the network with as little overhead as possible. Packet sized buffers, one or more ring buffers, or any other combination are possible candidates.

When a packet arrives at the destination TCP, it is placed on a queue which the TCP services frequently. For example, the TCP could be interrupted when a queue placement occurs. The TCP then attempts to place the packet text into the proper place in the appropriate process receive buffer. If the packet terminates a segment, then it can be checksummed and acknowledged. Placement may fail for several reasons.

1. The destination process may not be prepared to receive from the stated source, or the destination port ID may not exist.

2. There may be insufficient buffer space for the text.

3. The beginning sequence number of the text may not coincide with the next sequence number to be delivered to the process (e.g., the packet has arrived out of order).

In the first case, the TCP should simply discard the packet (thus far, no provision has been made for error acknowledgments). In the second and third cases, the packet sequence number can be inspected to determine whether the packet text lies within the legitimate window for reception. If it does, the TCP may optionally keep the packet queued for later processing. If not, the TCP can discard the packet. In either case the TCP can optionally acknowledge with the current left window edge.

It may happen that the process receive buffer is not present in the active memory of the HOST, but is stored on secondary storage. If this is the case, the TCP can prompt the scheduler to bring in the appropriate buffer and the packet can be queued for later processing.

If there are no more input buffers available to the TCP for temporary queuing of incoming packets, and if the TCP cannot quickly use the arriving data (e.g., a TCP to TCP message), then the packet is discarded. Assuming a sensibly functioning system, no other processes than the one for which the packet was intended should be affected by this discarding. If the delayed processing queue grows excessively long, any packets in it can be safely discarded since none of them have yet been acknowledged. Congestion at the TCP level is flexibly handled owing to the robust retransmission and duplicate detection strategy.

TCP/PROCESS COMMUNICATION

In order to send a message, a process sets up its text in a buffer region in its own address space, inserts the requisite control information (described in the follow-

ing list) in a transmit control block (TCB) and passes control to the TCP. The exact form of a TCB is not specified here, but it might take the form of a passed pointer, a pseudointerrupt, or various other forms. To receive a message in its address space, a process sets up a receive buffer, inserts the requisite control information in a receive control block (RCB) and again passes control to the TCP.

In some simple systems, the buffer space may in fact be provided by the TCP. For simplicity we assume that a ring buffer is used by each process, but other structures (e.g., buffer chaining) are not ruled out.

A possible format for the TCB is shown in Fig. 11.

1	Source Address	
2	Destination Address	
3	Next Packet Seq.	
4	Current Buffer Size	
5	Next Write Posistion	
6	Next Read Position	
7	End Read Position	
8	No. Retrans.	Max. Retrans.
9	Timeout	Flags
10	Curr. Ack	Window

Figure 11.

The TCB contains information necessary to allow the TCP to extract and send the process data. Some of the information might be implicitly known, but we are not concerned with that level of detail. The various fields in the TCB are described as follows.

1. *Source Address:* This is the full net/HOST/TCP/port number to be used for the next packet the TCP will transmit from this port.

2. *Current Buffer Size:* This is the present size of the process transmit buffer.

3. *Next Write Position:* This is the address of the next position in the buffer at which the process can place new data for transmission.

4. *Next Read Position:* This is the address at which the TCP should begin reading to build the next segment for output.

5. *End Read Position:* This is the address at which the TCP should halt transmission. Initially 6) and 7) bound the message which the process wishes to transmit.

6. *Number of Retransmissions/Maximum Retransmissions:* These fields enable the TCP to keep track of the number of times it has retransmitted the data and could be omitted if the TCP is not to give up.

7. *Timeout/Flags:* The timeout field specifies the delay after which unacknowledged data should be retransmitted. The flag field is used for semaphores and other TCP/process synchronization status reporting, etc.

8. *Current Acknowledgment/Window:* The current acknowledgment field identifies the first byte of data still unacknowledged by the destination TCP.

The read and write positions move circularly around the transmit buffer, with the write position always to the left (module the buffer size) of the read position.

The next packet sequence number should be constrained to be less than or equal to the sum of the current acknowledgment and the window fields. In any event, the next sequence number should not exceed the sum of the current acknowledgment and half of the maximum possible sequence number (to avoid confusing the receiver's duplicate detection algorithm). A possible buffer layout is shown in Fig. 12.

The RCB is substantially the same, except that the end read field is replaced by a partial segment checksum register which permits the receiving TCP to compute and remember partial check sums in the event that a segment arrives in several packets. When the final packet of the segment arrives, the TCP can verify the check sum and if successful, acknowledge the segment.

CONNECTION AND ASSOCIATIONS

Much of the thinking about process-to-process communication in packet switched networks has been influenced by the ubiquitous telephone system. The HOST-HOST protocol for the ARPANET deals explicitly with the opening and closing of simplex connections between processes [9], [10]. Evidence has been presented that message-based "connection-free" protocols can be constructed [12], and this leads us to carefully examine the notion of a connection.

The term *connection* has a wide variety of meanings. It can refer to a physical or logical path between two entities, it can refer to the flow over the path, it

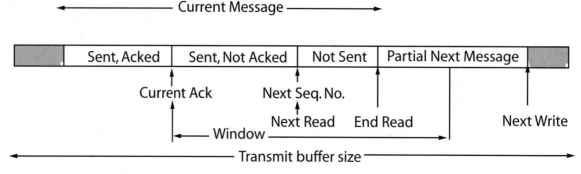

Figure 12.

can inferentially refer to an action associated with the setting up of a path, or it can refer to an association between two or more entities, with or without regard to any path between them. In this paper, we do not explicitly reject the term connection, since it is in such widespread use, and does connote a meaningful relation, but consider it exclusively in the sense of an association between two or more entities without regard to a path. To be more precise about our intent, we shall define the relationship between two or more ports that are in communication, or are prepared to communicate to be an *association*. Ports that are associated with each other are called *associates*.

It is clear that for any communication to take place between two processes, one must be able to address the other. The two important cases here are that the destination port may have a global and unchanging address or that it may be globally unique but dynamically reassigned. While in either case the sender may have to learn the destination address, given the destination name, only in the second instance is there a requirement for learning the address from the destination (or its representative) each time an association is desired. Only after the source has learned how to address the destination can an association be said to have occurred. But this is not yet sufficient. If ordering of delivered messages is also desired, both TCP's must maintain sufficient information to allow proper sequencing. When this information is also present at both ends, then an association is said to have occurred.

Note that we have not said anything about a path, nor anything which implies that either end be aware of the condition of the other. Only when both partners are prepared to communicate with each other has an association occurred, and it is possible that neither partner may be able to verify that an association exists until some data flows between them.

CONNECTION-FREE PROTOCOLS WITH ASSOCIATIONS

In the ARPANET, the interface message processors (IMP's) do not have to open and close connections from source to destination. The reason for this is that connections are, in effect, always open, since the address of every source and destination is never[5] reassigned. When the name and the place are static and unchanging, it is only necessary to label a packet with source and destination to transmit it through the network. In our parlance, every source and destination forms an association.

In the case of processes, however, we find that port addresses are continually being used and reused. Some ever present processes could be assigned fixed addresses which do not change (e.g., the logger process). If we supposed, however, that every TCP had an infinite supply of port addresses so that no old address would ever be reused, then any dynamically created port would be assigned the next unused address. In such an environment, there could never be any confusion by source and destination TCP as to the intended recipient or implied source of each message, and all ports would be associates.

Unfortunately, TCP's (or more properly, operating systems) tend not to have an infinite supply of internal port addresses. These internal addresses are reassigned after the demise of each port. Walden [12] suggests that a set of unique uniform external port addresses could be supplied by a central registry. A newly created port could apply to the central registry for an address which the central registry would guarantee to be unused by any HOST system in the network. Each TCP could maintain tables matching external names with internal ones, and use the external ones for communication with other processes. This idea violates the premise that interprocess communication should not require centralized control. One would have to extend the central registry service to include all HOST'S in all the interconnected networks to apply this idea to our situation, and we therefore do not attempt to adopt it.

Let us consider the situation from the standpoint of the TCP. In order to send or receive data for a given port, the TCP needs to set up a TCB and RCB and initialize the window size and left window edge for both. On the receive side, this task might even be delayed until the first packet destined for a given port arrives. By convention, the first packet should be marked so that the receiver will synchronize to the received sequence number.

On the send side, the first request to transmit could cause a TCB to be set up with some initial sequence number (say, zero) and an assumed window size. The receiving TCP can reject the packet if it wishes and notify the sending TCP of the correct window size via the acknowledgment mechanism, but only if either

1. we insist that the first packet be a complete segment;

2. an acknowledgment can be sent for the first packet (even if not a segment, as long as the acknowledgment specifies the next sequence number such that the source also understands that no bytes have been accepted).

It is apparent, therefore, that the synchronizing of window size and left window edge can be accomplished without what would ordinarily be called a connection setup.

The first packet referencing a newly created RCB sent from one associate to another can be marked with a bit which requests that the receiver synchronize his left window edge with the sequence number of the arriving packet (see SYN bit in Fig. 8). The TCP can examine the source and destination port addresses in the packet and in the RCB to decide whether to accept or ignore the request.

Provision should be made for a destination process to specify that it is willing to LISTEN to a specific port or "any" port. This last idea permits processes such as the logger process to accept data arriving from unspecified sources. This is purely a HOST matter, however.

The initial packet may contain data which can be stored or discarded by the destination, depending on the availability of destination buffer space at the time. In the other direction, acknowledgment is returned for receipt of data which also specifies the receiver's window size.

If the receiving TCP should want to reject the synchronization request, it merely transmits an acknowledgment carrying a release (REL) bit (see Fig. 8)

indicating that the destination port address is unknown or inaccessible. The sending HOST waits for the acknowledgment (after accepting or rejecting the synchronization request) before sending the next message or segment. This rejection is quite different from a negative data acknowledgment. We do not have explicit negative acknowledgments. If no acknowledgment is returned, the sending HOST may retransmit without introducing confusion if, for example, the left window edge is not changed on the retransmission.

Because messages may be broken up into many packets for transmission or during transmission, it will be necessary to ignore the REL flag except in the case that the EM flag is also set. This could be accomplished either by the TCP or by the GATEWAY which could reset the flag on all but the packet containing the set EM flag (see Fig. 9).

At the end of an association, the TCP sends a packet with ES, EM, and REL flags set. The packet sequence number scheme will alert the receiving TCP if there are still outstanding packets in transit which have not yet arrived, so a premature dissociation cannot occur.

To assure that both TCP's are aware that the association has ended, we insist that the receiving TCP respond to the REL by sending a REL acknowledgment of its own.

Suppose now that a process sends a single message to an associate including a REL along with the data. Assuming an RCB has been prepared for the receiving TCP to accept the data, the TCP will accumulate the incoming packets until the one marked ES, EM, REL arrives, at which point a REL is returned to the sender. The association is thereby terminated and the appropriate TCB and RCB are destroyed. If the first packet of a message contains a SYN request bit and the last packet contains ES, EM and REL bits, then data will flow "one message at a time." This mode is very similar to the scheme described by Walden [12], since each succeeding message can only be accepted at the receiver after a new LISTEN (like Walden's RECEIVE) command is issued by the receiving process to its serving TCP. Note that only if the acknowledgment is received by the sender can the association be terminated properly. It has been pointed out[6] that the receiver may erroneously accept duplicate transmissions if the sender does not receive the acknowledgment. This may happen if the sender transmits a duplicate message with the SYN and REL bits set and the destination has already destroyed any record of the previous transmission. One way of preventing this problem is to destroy the record of the association at the destination only after some known and suitably chosen timeout. However, this implies that a new association with the same source and destination port identifiers could not be established until this timeout had expired. This problem can occur even with sequences of messages whose SYN and REL bits are separated into different internetwork packets. We recognize that this problem must be solved, but do not go into further detail here.

Alternatively, both processes can send one message, causing the respective TCP's to allocate RCB/TCB pairs at both ends which rendezvous with the exchanged data and then disappear. If the overhead of creating and destroying RCB's and TCB's is small, such a protocol might be adequate for most low-bandwidth uses. This idea might also form the basis for a relatively secure transmission system. If the communicating processes agree to change their external port addresses in some way known only to each other (i.e., pseudorandom), then each message will appear to the outside world as if it is part of a different association message stream. Even if the data is intercepted by a third party, he will have no way of knowing that the data should in fact be considered part of a sequence of messages.

We have described the way in which processes develop associations with each other, thereby becoming associates for possible exchange of data. These associations need not involve the transmission of data prior to their formation and indeed two associates need not be able to determine that they are associates until they attempt to communicate.

CONCLUSIONS

We have discussed some fundamental issues related to the interconnection of packet switching networks. In particular, we have described a simple but very powerful and flexible protocol which provides for variation in individual network packet sizes, transmission failures, sequencing, flow control, and the creation and destruction of process-to-process associations. We have considered some of the implementation issues that arise and found that the proposed protocol is implementable by HOST'S of widely varying capacity.

The next important step is to produce a detailed specification of the protocol so that some initial experiments with it can be performed. These experiments are needed to determine some of the operational parameters (e.g., how often and how far out of order do packets actually arrive; what sort of delay is there between segment acknowledgments; what should retransmission timeouts be?) of the proposed protocol.

ACKNOWLEDGMENTS

The authors wish to thank a number of colleagues for helpful comments during early discussions of international network protocols, especially R. Metcalfe, R. Scantlebury, D. Walden, and H. Zimmerman; D. Davies and L. Pouzin who constructively commented on the fragmentation and accounting issues; and S. Crocker who commented on the creation and destruction of associations.

REFERENCES

1. L. Roberts and B. Wessler, "Computer network development to achieve resource sharing," in 1970 *Spring Joint Computer Conf., AFIPS Conf. Proc.,* vol. 36. Montvale, N. J.: AFIPS Press, 1970, pp. 543–549.

2. Bolt, Beranek, and Newman, "Specification for the interconnection of a host and an IMP," Bolt Beranek and Newman, Inc., Cambridge, Mass., BBN Rep. 1822 (revised), Apr. 1973.

3. L. Pouzin, "Presentation and major design aspects of the CYCLADES com-

puter network," in *Proc. 3rd Data Communications Symp.*, 1973.

4. F. R. E. Dell, "Features of a proposed synchronous data network," in *Proc. 2nd Symp. Problems in the Optimization of Data Communications Systems,* 1971, pp. 50–57.

5. R. A. Scantlebury and P. T. Wilkinson, "The design of a switching system to allow remote access to computer services by other computers and terminal devices," in *Proc. 2nd Symp. Problems in the Optimization of Data Communications Systems,* 1971, pp. 160–167.

6. D. L. A. Barber, "The European computer network project," in *Computer Communications: Impacts and Implications,* S. Winkler, Ed. Washington , D.C., 1972, pp. 192–200.

7. R. Despres, "A packet switching network with graceful saturated operation," in *Computer Communications: Impacts and Implications,* S. Winkler, Ed. Washington, D.C., 1972, pp. 345–351.

8. R. E. Kahn and W. R. Crowther, "Flow control in a resource-shaping computer network," *IEEE Trans. Commun.,* vol. COM-20, pp. 539–546, June 1972.

9. J. F. Chambon, M. Elie, J. Le Bihan, G. LeLann, and H. Zimmerman, "Functional specification of transmission station in the CYCLADES network. ST-ST protocol" (in French), I.R.I.A. Tech. Rep. SCH502.3, May 1973.

10. S. Carr, S. Crocker, and V. Cerf, "HOST-HOST Communication Protocol In the ARPA Network," in *Spring Joint Computer Conf., AFIPS Conf. Proc.,* vol. 36. Montvale, N.J.: AFIPS Press, 1970, pp. 589–597.

11. A. McKenzie, "HOST/HOST protocol for the ARPA network," in *Current Network Protocols,* Network Information Cen., Menlo Park, Calif., NIC 8246, Jan. 1972.

12. L. Pouzin, "Address format in Mitranet," NIC 14497, INWG 20, Jan. 1973.

13. D. Walden, "A system for interprocess communication in a resource sharing computer network," *Commun. Ass. Comput. Mach.,* vol. 15, pp. 221–230, Apr. 1972.

14. B. Lampson, "A scheduling philosophy for multiprocessing system," *Commun. Ass. Comput. Mach.,* vol. 11, pp. 347-360, May 1968.

15. F. E. Heart, R. E. Kahn, S. Ornstein, W. Crowther, and D. Walden, "The interface message processor for the ARPA computer network," in *Proc. Spring Joint Computer Conf., AFIPS Conf. Proc.,* vol. 36. Montvale, N.J.: AFIPS Press, 1970, pp. 551–567.

16. N. G. Anslow and J. Hanscoff, "Implementation of international data exchange networks," in *Computer Communications: Impacts and Implications,* S. Winkler, Ed. Washington, D. C., 1972, pp. 181–184.

17. A. McKenzie, "HOST/HOST protocol design considerations," INWG Note 16, NIC 13879, Jan. 1973.

18. R. E. Kahn, "Resource-sharing computer communication networks", *Proc. IEEE,* vol. 60, pp. 1397-1407, Nov. 1972.

• • •

1. In the case of encrypted packets, a preliminary stage of reassembly may be required prior to decryption.

2. The ARPANET is one such example.

3. Actually $n/2$ is merely a convenient number to use; it is only required that a retransmission not appear to be a new transmission.

4. This component can serve to handle other protocols whose associated control programs are designated by internetwork destination address.

5. Unless the IMP is physically moved to another site, or the HOST is connected to a different IMP.

6. S. Crocker of APRA/IPT.

14

For Further Reading

Aspray, William. The Scientific Conceptualization of Information: A Survey. *Annals of the History of Computing* 7 (1985): 117–40.

Campbell-Kelly, Martin and Aspray, William. *Computer. A History of the Information Machine*, New York: Basic Books, 1996.

Campbell-Kelly, Martin; Croaken, Mary; Flood, Raymond; and Robson, Eleanor (eds.). *The History of Mathematical Tables: From Sumer to Spreadsheets*. Oxford: Oxford University Press, 2003.

Carter, John and Muir, Percy H. *Printing and the Mind of Man. The Impact of Print on Five Centuries of Western Civilization*. London: Cassell and Company, New York: Holt, Rinehart and Winston, 1967. An expansion of a catalogue of an exhibition of influential books that took place at the British Museum in July 1963. The original exhibition catalogue also described important landmarks in the history of printing technology. The exhibition catalogue was issued under the title *Printing and the Mind of Man. Catalogue of a Display of Printing Mechanisms and Printed Materials Arranged to Illustrate the History of Western Civilization and the Means of the Multiplication of Literary Texts since the XV Century* (London: F.W. Bridges, 1963).

Ceruzzi, Paul E. *A History of Modern Computing*. Cambridge: MIT Press, 1998.

Clair, Colin. *A Chronology of Printing*. New York: Frederick A. Praeger, 1969.

Clark, E. F. *George Parker Bidder, The Calculating Boy*. With an Appreciation of his Calculating Ability by Joyce Linfoot. Bedford, England: KSL Publications, 1983.

Davis, Martin. *The Universal Computer. The Road from Leibniz to Turing*, New York, W. W. Norton, 2000.

Eames, Charles and Ray (Office of). *A Computer Perspective*. Cambridge, MA: Harvard University Press, 1973.

Febvre, Lucien and Martin, Henri-Jean. *The Coming of the Book. The Impact of Printing 1450-1800*. Translated by David Gerard. Edited by Geoffrey Nowell-Smith and David Wootton, 1976.

Feigenbaum, Edward A. and Feldman, Julian, editors. *Computers and Thought*. New York: McGraw-Hill, 1963.

Finkelstein, David and Alistair McCleery (eds.). *The Book History Reader*. London and New York: Routledge, 2002.

Gillmor, Dan. *We the Media. Grassroots Journalism for the People, by the People*. Sebastapol, CA: O'Reilly Media, 2004.

Goldstine, Herman. *The Computer from Pascal to von Neumann*, Princeton: Princeton University Press, 1972.

Hodges, Andrew. *Alan Turing: The Enigma*, New York: Simon and Schuster, 1983.

Holtzmann, Gerard J. and Pehrson, Björn. *The Early History of Data Networks*, Los Alamitos, CA: IEEE Computer Society Press, 1995.

Hook, Diana H. and Norman, Jeremy M. *Origins of Cyberspace. A Library on the History of Computing, Networking, and Telecommunications.* Novato, CA: historyofscience.com, 2002.

Huurdeman, Anton A. *The Worldwide History of Telecommunications.* New York: Wiley-Interscience, 2003.

Hyman, Anthony. *Charles Babbage: Pioneer of the Computer.* Princeton: Princeton University Press, 1982.

Kidwell, Peggy A. and Ceruzzi, Paul E. *Landmarks in Digital Computing.* Washington, D. C.: Smithsonian Institution Press, 1994.

Kurzweil, Raymond. *The Age of Intelligent Machines.* Cambridge, MA: MIT Press, 1990.

Kurzweil, Raymond. *The Age of Spiritual Machines. When Computers Exceed Human Intelligence.* New York: Viking, 1999.

Lee, J. A. N. *Computer Pioneers.* Los Alamitos, CA: IEEE Computer Society Press, 1995.

Leiner, Barry M., Cerf, Vinton G., et al. The Past and Future History of the Internet. *Communications of the ACM* 40 (1997): 102–8.

Martin, Henri-Jean. *The History and Power of Writing.* Translated by Lydia G. Cochrane. Chicago: University of Chicago Press, 1994. See especially Chapter 5: The Arrival of Print.

McCartney, Scott. *ENIAC: The Triumphs and Tragedies of the World's First Computer.* New York: Walker and Company, 1999.

McKitterick, David. *Print, Manuscript and the Search for Order 1450–1830.* Cambridge: Cambridge University Press, 2003.

Morrison, Philip and Morrison, Emily (eds.). *Charles Babbage and his Calculating Engines. Selected Writings by Charles Babbage and Others.* New York: Dover Publications, 1961.

Moxon, Joseph. *Mechanick Exercises on the Whole Art of Printing* (1683-4). Edited by Herbert Davis and Harry Carter. Second Edition. London: Oxford University Press, 1962

Pratt, Vernon. *Thinking Machines: The Evolution of Artificial Intelligence.* Oxford: Basil Blackwell, 1987.

Randell, Brian (ed.). *The Origins of Digital Computers: Selected Papers.* Third Edition. New York: Springer Verlag, 1982.

Rheingold, Howard. *Tools for Thought. The History and Future of Mind-Expanding Technology.* Cambridge, Mass.: MIT Press, 2000.

Rojas, Raúl and Hashagen, Ulf (eds.). *The First Computers: History and Architectures.* Cambridge, MA: MIT Press, 2000.

Shiers, George, assisted by May Shiers. *Early Television: A Bibliographic Guide to 1940.* New York: Garland Publishing, 1997.

Standage, Tom. *The Victorian Internet. The Remarkable Story of the Telegraph and the Nineteenth Century's On-Line Pioneers.* New York: Walker and Company, 1998.

Swade, Doron. *The Cogwheel Brain: Charles Babbage and the Quest to Build the First Computer.* London: Little, Brown, 2000.

Twyman, Michael. *Printing 1770–1970. An Illustrated History of its Development and Uses in England.* London: The British Library, 1998.

Von Neumann, John. *Papers of John von Neumann on Computing and Computer Theory.* Ed. W. Aspray and A. Burks. Cambridge: MIT Press; Los Angeles: Tomash Publishers, 1987.

Waldrop, M. Mitchell. *The Dream Machine. J.C.R. Licklider and the Revolution that Made Computing Personal.* New York: Viking, 2001.

Williams, Michael R. *A History of Computing Technology.* Second ed. Englewood Cliffs, N.J.: Prentice-Hall, 1997.

Wooley, Benjamin. *The Bride of Science. Romance, Reason and Byron's Daughter.* London: Macmillan, 1997.

Index of Names

Miller, George A. 717
Minsky, Marvin 41, 56, 697, 709,
    710, 711, 717, 720, 726, 735
Mitchell, F. D. 116
Mittring, Gert 49
Molina, E. C. 816, 837
Mondeux, Henri 116, 117, 118,
    119
Monge, Gaspard 177
Moniz, Egas 658
Monroe, Charles 192
Moore, E. F. 712, 718
Moore, Gordon E. 55, 451
Moran, P. A. P. 817
More, Trenchard 717
Morgenstern, Oskar 683
Morse, P. M. 816
Morse, Samuel F. B. 3, 51, 52, 181,
    182, 192
Mossotti, O. F. 289, 290, 291
Moxon, Joseph 30, 35
Mozart, W. A. 734
Müller 562
Müller, G. E. 116, 117, 119, 120
Murray, Erskine 213

N

Namias, Jerome 472
Nancy, Viscountess Astor 223
Napier, John 50, 115
Nash, John 717
Needham, Paul 26
Newell, Allen 615, 619, 681, 709,
    717, 720, 733, 743
Newman, Max 301
Newton, Sir Isaac 138, 728
Nordbye, Judge 458
North, J. D. 614
Nyquist, Harry 40, 302, 772

O

O'Dell, G. F. 816

Oettinger, A. E. 704
Ogden, C. K. 567
Onesti, Calzecchi 203
Orwell, George 31

P

Pace, Frank, Jr. 742
Page, C. G. 194, 195
Palm, C. 816
Pannartz, Arnold 28
Pascal, Blaise 137, 232, 545
Pavlov, I. P. 737
Payne, L. C. 727, 729
Pender, Harold 472
Pepinsky, R. 579
Perutz, Max 576
Phillipson, Mrs. 223
Picasso, Pablo 670
Piccolomini, Enea Silvio 26, 27
Pitts, Walter 53, 302, 319, 320,
    329, 330, 335, 566, 710
Plana, G. A. A. 289, 292, 293
Plantamour, Émile 289
Poe, Edgar Allan 682
Poggendorff, J. C. 194
Poincaré, Henri 615
Pole, W. 107
Poletayev, I. A. 737
Pollack, M. 817
Pomerene, James H. 389
Pontavice de Heussey, Comte du
    212
Pontecoulant, comte de. *See* Le
    Dulcet, Philippe Gustave,
    comte de Pontecoulant.
Poulsen, Valdemar 809
Pouzin, L. 887
Preece 205, 208, 215
Priestley, Joseph 659
Prihar, Z. 817
Pring, R. W. 169
Proctor 118

Prony, Gaspard de 130, 131, 232
Prosser, R. 817
Pylyshyn, Zenon W. 48

R

Randell, Brian 48
Rashevsky, Nicholas 710
Razran, Gregory 741
Regiomontanus 653
Reichelderfer, Cmdr. 471, 472
Reichenbach, Hans 563
Reid, Sir James 210
Reifler, Erwin 563
Reis, Philip 193, 194
Rheingold, Howard 319
Richards, I. A. 567
Richens, Dr. 564
Righi, A. 201
Riordan, F. 816
Roberts, Lawrence G. 4, 6, 40, 41,
    57, 863, 870
Robinson, Abraham 717
Rochester, Nathaniel 56, 423, 709,
    710, 711, 717
Rodiginus, Coelius 653
Rogers, Hartley, Jr. 717
Rogers, Samuel 283
Romme 178
Roosevelt, Franklin D. 302
Rose, Kenneth 476
Rosen, J. F. 472
Rosenblith, Walter 718
Rosser, J. B. 670
Rothstein, Jerome 718
Routledge, R. 173
Roy 176
Rückle 116, 117, 118, 120
Russell, Bertrand 319, 324, 709

S

Samuel, Arthur L. 720
Savell, R. E. 620

Wiener, Norbert 39, 40, 41, 309,
310, 313, 319, 320, 563, 564,
566, 651, 657, 658, 659, 663,
733, 736, 737
Wilkes, Maurice V. 46, 49, 54, 55,
56, 107, 397, 417, 439, 493,
529, 545, 580
Williams, Frederic C. 418, 651,
657
Williams, Michael R. 516
Wilson, Roland B. 861
Winsor, Paul 477
Wizel 117
Wobensmith 470
Woolley, Benjamin 231
Worcester, Marquis of 177
Wright brothers 734, 742
Wright, E. M. 683
Wundt, Wilhelm 634

Y
Young, J. Z. 651, 655, 656

Z
Zeldner, Max 565
Zimmerman, H. 887
Zuse, Konrad 48